CRITICAL SURVEY OF MYSTERY AND DETECTIVE FICTION

CRITICAL SURVEY OF MYSTERY AND DETECTIVE FICTION

Revised Edition

Volume 1

Anthony Abbott – L. P. Davies

Editor, Revised Edition
Carl Rollyson
Baruch College, City University of New York

Editor, First Edition
Frank N. Magill

SALEM PRESS, INC.
Pasadena, California   Hackensack, New Jersey

Editor in Chief: Dawn P. Dawson

Editorial Director: Christina J. Moose   *Research Assistant:* Keli Trousdale
Developmental Editor: R. Kent Rasmussen   *Acquisitions Editor:* Mark Rehn
Project Editor: Rowena Wildin Dehanke   *Photo Editor:* Cynthia Breslin Beres
Editorial Assistant: Dana Garey   *Production Editor:* Joyce I. Buchea
Research Supervisor: Jeffry Jensen   *Design and Graphics:* James Hutson

Cover image: Richard R. Epperly, *Mammoth Detective*, February, 1945

Some of the essays in this work, which have been updated, originally appeared in the following Salem Press sets: *Critical Survey of Mystery and Detective Fiction* (1988, edited by Frank N. Magill) and *One Hundred Masters of Mystery and Detective Fiction* (2001, edited by Fiona Kelleghan). New material has been added.

∞ The paper used in these volumes conforms to the American National Standard for Permanence of Paper for Printed Library Materials, Z39.48-1992(R1997).

Library of Congress Cataloging-in-Publication Data

Critical survey of mystery and detective fiction. — Rev. ed. / editor, Carl Rollyson.
    p. cm.
    ISBN 978-1-58765-397-1 (set : alk. paper) — ISBN 978-1-58765-398-8 (vol. 1 : alk. paper) —
ISBN 978-1-58765-399-5 (vol. 2 : alk. paper) — ISBN 978-1-58765-400-8 (vol. 3 : alk. paper) —
ISBN 978-1-58765-401-5 (vol. 4 : alk. paper) — ISBN 978-1-58765-402-2 (vol. 5 : alk. paper)
    1. Detective and mystery stories—History and criticism. 2. Detective and mystery stories—Bio-bibliography.
3. Detective and mystery stories—Stories, plots, etc. I. Rollyson, Carl E. (Carl Edmund)

PN3448.D4C75 2008
809.3'872—dc22
                                                                                    2007040208

First Printing
PRINTED IN THE UNITED STATES OF AMERICA

PUBLISHER'S NOTE

Continuing the Salem Press tradition of the Critical Survey series, *Critical Survey of Mystery and Detective Fiction, Revised Edition* provides detailed analyses of the lives and writings of major contributors to the fascinating literary subgenre of mystery and detective fiction. This greatly expanded five-volume set is the first full revision of a work that originally appeared in 1988. Published in four smaller, unillustrated volumes, the original *Critical Survey of Mystery and Detective Fiction* contained 275 articles about individual authors of mystery and detective fiction and a glossary of terms. This new edition updates or replaces all the original articles and adds entirely new articles on 118 more authors, raising the total to 393 articles, an increase of 43 percent. The original glossary has been expanded and divided into two parts. Moreover, this new edition adds 37 entirely new overview essays and 5 new appendixes, raising to 7 the total number of items in the Resources section of volume 5.

To such well-known mystery writers as Raymond Chandler, Agatha Christie, Sir Arthur Conan Doyle, Erle Stanley Gardner, Dashiell Hammett, Edgar Allan Poe, and Dorothy L. Sayers, this revised edition adds such venerable writers' names as Louisa May Alcott, Edward Stratemeyer, and Margaret Truman. Most of the new author articles, however, are on popular contemporary writers, such as Mary Higgins Clark, Patricia Cornwell, John Dunning, John Grisham, Thomas Harris, Carolyn Hart, Rolando Hinojosa, Scott Turow, and Stuart Woods. A particularly noteworthy addition is J. K. Rowling, the author of the sensationally popular Harry Potter series, whose seventh and final volume was published in 2007.

Mystery and detective fiction is essentially a British and American creation that has long been dominated by British, American, and European writers. One of the most exciting developments in the field, therefore, has been the growing number of new writers of various ethnicities and nationalities. In selecting authors to add to *Critical Survey of Mystery and Detective Fiction*, a particular effort was made to achieve greater ethnic and international diversity. Among the added authors are the African American writers Eleanor Taylor Bland, Walter Mosley, and Barbara Neely and the Chicano writer Rolando Hinojosa. Authors added from other Western Hemispheric countries include the Mexican writer Paco Ignacio Taibo II, Brazilian Luiz Alfredo Garcia-Roza, and three Canadians: William Deverell, David Morrell, and Peter Robinson. New Asian authors include China's Qiu Xiaolong and five writers from Japan: Natsuo Kirino, Seichō Matsumoto, Shizuko Natsuki, Akimitsu Takagi, and Miyuki Miyabe. Africa is represented by the South African author Gillian Slovo; Zimbabwe-born Alexander McCall Smith, who writes about a woman detective in Botswana; and Elspeth Huxley, who set several traditional murder mysteries in fictional East African countries.

Geographically, the largest number of writers are from North America, with 204 from the United States, 10 from Canada, and 1 from Mexico. The next largest group of writers are associated with the British Isles: 149 from England, 12 from Scotland, 8 from Ireland, 5 from Wales, and 1 from Northern Ireland. The rest of Europe is represented by 12 writers from France, 3 from Switzerland, 3 from the Netherlands, 3 from Russia, 2 from Spain, 2 from Sweden, 2 from Germany, and 1 each from Austria, Belgium, Italy, and Georgia. One writer is from Israel. Africa is represented by 4 writers from South Africa, 1 from Zimbabwe, and 1 from Zambia. Asian writers include 5 from Japan, 1 from China, and 1 from India. South America is represented by 2 writers from Argentina and 1 from Brazil. Three Australians are joined by 1 New Zealander.

With the addition of more than three dozen overview essays and new appendixes, *Critical Survey of Mystery and Detective Fiction* now joins Salem's family of fully revised and expanded Critical Surveys of poetry, drama, short fiction, and long fiction. Some authors covered here are also covered in one or more of the other sets, but it should be understood that articles in each set are unique. For example, the article on Mark Twain in *Critical Survey of Long Fiction* focuses on his novels, that in *Critical Survey of Short Fiction* focuses on his short stories and sketches, and the one in the present set focuses on his mystery and detective writings—which are considerably more extensive than many people may realize. Readers will find little overlap in the text of these three articles.

The need for a new edition of *Critical Survey of Mystery and Detective Fiction* is evident in the growing recognition of the genre's importance in modern literature and in the increased attention the genre is receiving in classrooms. The gap between what is perceived as mainstream fiction and mystery genre fiction has narrowed, and mystery fiction is now seen as something far more than mere entertainment, as it often offers special insights into human nature and institutions. Indeed, the syllabus of one college course states that mystery fiction "explores how human consciousness makes sense out of what might otherwise be viewed as random experience and meaningless violence." This, incidentally, is a theme that is discussed at length in many of the overview essays in volume 5.

Another aspect of mystery fiction's receiving increased recognition is what it reveals about different social classes, societies, cultures, and, indeed, entire nations. Mystery fiction probes deeply into the inner workings of every level of society and exposes the strengths and weaknesses of economic, political, and legal institutions. During the days of South Africa's racially oppressive apartheid system, it was often said that one of the best ways to understand the complex problems of that country was to read the mysteries of James McClure, a South African mystery writer whose novels probed deeply into both black and white communities and vividly revealed human dimensions of the day-to-day effects of racial segregation. Similar observations might be made about the mystery and detective fiction of other countries, such as Japan, which is richly represented in *Critical Survey of Mystery and Detective Fiction.*

There was a time when mystery and detective fiction seemed virtually synonymous with the classic "whodunits," in which murders are committed, and then both detectives and readers settle down to sort out clues until the guilty parties are identified and order is restored. The fictional investigators may range from hard-boiled police detectives and private investigators, such as Dashiell Hammett's Sam Spade, to brilliantly intuitive amateurs, such as Agatha Christie's Miss Jane Marple. Such stories are still written, but the modern mystery genre encompasses a vast variety of subgenres that are known by such terms as comic capers, courtroom dramas, cozies, historical mysteries, inverted mysteries (which reveal the culprits immediately), police procedurals, psychological mysteries, and thrillers of various stripes. These subgenres and others are all well represented here, and *Critical Survey of Mystery and Detective Fiction* casts its net even wider to take in authors of espionage and horror stories.

Judging by the distribution of names in volume 5's Categorized Index of Authors, the most popular subgenre among writers in this set is that of the amateur sleuth, represented by 139 writers. That category is closely followed by the rapidly expanding subgenre of police procedurals, with 135 writers, and by thrillers, with 120 writers. The other subgenres in order of representation are private investigator, 92; psychological, 86; hard-boiled, 67; cozies, 65; espionage, 54; inverted, 53; historical, 51; master sleuth, 19; comedy caper, 17; horror, 14; courtroom dramas, 9; and metaphysical and metafictional parodies, 7.

OVERVIEWS

In addition to this edition's large expansion of articles on individual authors, the other major change in this revised edition is the inclusion of 37 completely original overview essays, most of which are as long as 6,000 words. These essays explore the history and nature of the mystery and detective genre and examine the fiction of ethnic writers and writers from other parts of the world. The overviews begin with "Past and Present Mystery and Detective Fiction," a section containing essays on the roots of the genre, the so-called Golden Age of mystery fiction, innovations in the field, literary aspects of mystery fiction, connections between so-called mainstream fiction and the mystery genre, and pulp magazine fiction.

Another group of essays, "Mystery Fiction Around the World," explores mystery fiction in Africa, Asia, Britain, France, Latin America, and the United States as well as mysteries set in exotic locations. The section labeled "Mystery Fiction Subgenres" explores 14 different varieties of mystery fiction, including academic mysteries, cozies, ethnic American mysteries, feminist and lesbian mysteries, forensic mysteries, historical mysteries, horror stories, juvenile and young-adult mysteries, parodies, police procedurals, science fiction and mystery blends, spy novels, thrillers, and true-crime stories. "The Detectives" section contains essays on amateur sleuths, armchair detectives, hard-boiled detectives, and women detectives as well as Sherlock Holmes pastiches. A final group of essays, in "Other Media," examine nonliterary adaptations and other writing genres, such as films, drama, radio dramas, television series, and graphic mystery novels.

RESOURCES AND INDEXES

Critical Survey of Mystery and Detective Fiction, Revised Edition adds 5 new appendixes and greatly expands and divides the original edition's glossary into "Genre Terms and Techniques" and "Crime Fiction Jargon." Added appendixes in the "Resources" section include an annotated bibliography of general works, a guide to Web and electronic resources, lists of major writing awards, a detailed time line of highlights in the history of crime and detective fiction, and a chronological listing of authors. Indexes in this set are geographical and categorized indexes of writers covered in author articles, an index of the principal series characters, and a general subject index.

ORGANIZATION AND FORMAT

As with Salem's other Critical Survey sets, *Critical Survey of Mystery and Detective Fiction* is designed to meet the needs of secondary school and college undergraduate students. Articles on authors are arranged alphabetically, by the names or pen names under which the authors publish their mystery fiction. In some cases, these names differ from those by which the authors are best known. An example is "Edgar Box," the pen name that Gore Vidal used to write several mystery novels.

Each author article is formatted identically, opening with ready-reference data on the author's name, pseudonyms, birth and death dates and places, and types of plots. Because of the large numbers of books that many mystery writers publish, *Critical Survey of Mystery and Detective Fiction* differs slightly from other Critical Survey sets in listing each author's principal works at the *end* of the article, instead of at the beginning. Articles on authors of series fiction—such as Christie's Hercule Poirot stories and John Ball's Virgil Tibbs series—complete the top matter by listing the authors' principal series and offering brief descriptions of the principal series characters.

The main text of all author articles begins with a paragraph or two headed "Contribution" that sums up the author's place in the mystery and detective fiction genre and discusses what sets the author apart from others in the field. This section is followed by one headed "Biography," which provides a brief summary of the author's life, paying particular attention to events relating to the author's mystery and detective fiction.

The heart of every author article is the long "Analysis" section. It begins with an overview of the author's writing that discusses themes, motifs, and writing style. This section is further broken down into subheaded sections on individual works—usually novels—or groups of works. With an average of three subsections per article, *Critical Survey of Mystery and Detective Fiction* contains focused discussions on more than 1,300 individual works.

Immediately following the byline of each article's contributor are lists of the author's principal works, arranged by genres, beginning with principal works of mystery and detective fiction. Individual titles are arranged chronologically and subdivided by series, as appropriate. Finally, each article ends with an annotated bibliography listing works on the author and on the subgenres in which the author writes.

ACKNOWLEDGMENTS

Salem Press would like to thank the many academicians and area experts who contributed to both the original editions and this revised edition. The names and affiliations of all contributors are listed in the first volume of this set. This edition also owes much to its editor, Carl Rollyson, Baruch College, City University of New York.

CONTRIBUTORS

Randy L. Abbott
University of Evansville

Michael Adams
Graduate Center, City University of New York

Patrick Adcock
Henderson State University

Linda K. Adkins
University of Northern Iowa

Stanley Archer
Texas A&M University

Amy J. Arnold
Texas A&M University

Dorothy B. Aspinwall
University of Hawaii at Manoa

Bryan Aubrey
Fairfield, Iowa

Max L. Autrey
Drake University

Philip Bader
Chiang Mai, Thailand

Ehrhard Bahr
University of California, Los Angeles

James Baird
University of North Texas

David Barratt
Farnsfield, England

Thomas F. Barry
University of Southern California

Thomas Beebee
Pennsylvania State University at University Park

Samuel I. Bellman
California State Polytechnic University, Pomona

Taryn Benbow-Pfalzgraf
Wheaton, Illinois

Richard P. Benton
Trinity College, Connecticut

Robert L. Berner
University of Wisconsin at Oshkosh

Cynthia A. Bily
Adrian College

Beatrice Christiana Birchak
University of Houston at Downtown

Margaret Boe Birns
New York University

Nicholas Birns
The New School

Franz G. Blaha
University of Nebraska, Lincoln

Harriet Blodgett
Stanford University

Pegge A. Bochynski
Salem State College

Rochelle Bogartz
Independent Scholar

Bernadette Lynn Bosky
Yonkers, New York

Zohara Boyd
Appalachian State University

William Boyle
Brooklyn, New York

H. Eric Branscomb
Salem State College

Philip M. Brantingham
Loyola University, Chicago

Francis J. Bremer
Millersville University of Pennsylvania

Marie J. K. Brenner
Bethel College

Jean R. Brink
Henry E. Huntington Library

J. R. Broadus
University of North Carolina at Chapel Hill

William S. Brockington, Jr.
University of South Carolina at Aiken

William S. Brooks
University of Bath

James S. Brown
Bloomsburg University

Bill Brubaker
Florida State University

Stefan Buchenberger
Nara Women's University

Roland E. Bush
California State University, Long Beach

Rebecca R. Butler
Dalton Junior College

Susan Butterworth
Salem State College

Edmund J. Campion
University of Tennessee, Knoxville

Hal Charles
Eastern Kentucky University

John J. Conlon
University of Massachusetts at Boston

Deborah Core
Eastern Kentucky University

J. Randolph Cox
Saint Olaf College

Stephen J. Curry
Slippery Rock University of Pennsylvania

Laura Dabundo
Kennesaw College

Dale Davis
Northwest Mississippi Junior College

Rowena Wildin Dehanke
Altadena, California

Bill Delaney
San Diego, California

Paul Dellinger
Wytheville, Virginia

Thomas Derdak
University of Chicago

Joseph Dewey
University of Pittsburgh at Johnstown

M. Casey Diana
University of Illinois, Urbana-Champaign

Jill Dolan
University of Wisconsin at Madison

Krystan V. Douglas
University of New Mexico

Thomas Du Bose
Louisiana State University, Shreveport

Michael Dunne
Middle Tennessee State University

K. Edgington
Towson University

Jeanne B. Elliott
San Jose State University

Robert P. Ellis
Worcester State College

Thomas L. Erskine
Salisbury University

Paul F. Erwin
University of Cincinnati

Jack Ewing
Boise, Idaho

Thomas H. Falk
Michigan State University

James Feast
New York University

Thomas R. Feller
Nashville, Tennessee

Rebecca Hendrick Flannagan
Francis Marion University

Seymour L. Flaxman
City College, City University of New York

Ann D. Garbett
Averett University

C. A. Gardner
Newport News, Virginia

Helen S. Garson
George Mason University

Jill B. Gidmark
University of Minnesota, Twin Cities Campus

Richard E. Givan
Eastern Kentucky University

Sheldon Goldfarb
University of British Columbia

David Gordon
Bowling Green State University

Charles A. Gramlich
Xavier University of Louisiana

Douglas G. Greene
Old Dominion University

Jasmine Hall
Boston College

Steve Hecox
Averett University

Peter B. Heller
Manhattan College

Terry Heller
Coe College

Ginia Henderson
Seattle, Washington

Carlanna L. Hendrick
Governor's School for Science and Mathematics

Diane Andrews Henningfeld
Adrian College

William H. Holland, Jr.
Middle Tennessee State University

Anna R. Holloway
Fort Valley State College

Glenn Hopp
Howard Payne University

Pierre L. Horn
Wright State University

Barbara Horwitz
Long Island University, C. W. Post Campus

E. D. Huntley
Appalachian State University

Mary G. Hurd
East Tennessee State University

Barbara L. Hussey
Eastern Kentucky University

Mary Anne Hutchinson
Utica College of Syracuse University

Jacquelyn Jackson
Middle Tennessee State University

Shakuntala Jayaswal
University of New Haven

Chandice M. Johnson, Jr.
North Dakota State University

JoAnne C. Juett
University of Georgia

Wendi Arant Kaspar
Texas A&M University

Cynthia Lee Katona
Ohlone College

Ravinder Kaur
University of Georgia

Richard Keenan
University of Maryland, Eastern Shore

Fiona Kelleghan
University of Miami

Richard Kelly
University of Tennessee, Knoxville

Sue Laslie Kimball
Methodist College

Wm. Laird Kleine-Ahlbrandt
Purdue University, West Lafayette

James Kline
Santa Barbara, California

Steven C. Klipstein
Suffolk County Community College, Selden Campus

Grove Koger
Boise State University

Henry Kratz
University of Tennessee, Knoxville

Kathryn Kulpa
University of Rhode Island

Rebecca Kuzins
Pasadena, California

Paula Lannert
Austin, Texas

Marilynn M. Larew
University of Maryland, Baltimore County

Michael J. Larsen
Saint Mary's University

Eugene S. Larson
Los Angeles Pierce College

William E. Laskowski
Jamestown College

Leon Lewis
Appalachian State University

Elizabeth Johnston Lipscomb
Randolph-Macon Woman's College

James L. Livingston
Northern Michigan University

Janet Alice Long
Acton, California

Janet E. Lorenz
Los Angeles, California

Michael Loudon
Eastern Illinois University

R. C. Lutz
Madison Advisors

Janet McCann
Texas A&M University

Robert McColley
University of Illinois at Urbana-Champaign

Alice MacDonald
University of Akron

Andrew F. Macdonald
Loyola University, New Orleans

Gina Macdonald
Nicholls State University

Kathryne S. McDorman
Texas Christian University

Grace McEntee
Appalachian State University

Frederick Rankin MacFadden, Jr.
Coppin State College

S. Thomas Mack
University of South Carolina, Aiken

Louis K. MacKendrick
University of Windsor

Victoria E. McLure
Texas Tech University

David W. Madden
California State University, Sacramento

Paul Madden
Hardin-Simmons University

Lois A. Marchino
University of Texas, El Paso

Thomas Matchie
North Dakota State University

Charles E. May
California State University, Long Beach

Laurence W. Mazzeno
Alvernia College

Cecile Mazzucco-Than
Port Jefferson, New York

Patrick Meanor
State University of New York College at Oneonta

Julia M. Meyers
Duquesne University

Edmund Miller
Long Island University, C. W. Post Campus

Mary-Emily Miller
Salem State College

Timothy C. Miller
Millersville University

Sally Mitchell
Temple University

Christian H. Moe
Southern Illinois University, Carbondale

Albert J. Montesi
Saint Louis University

Robert A. Morace
Daemon College

Bernard E. Morris
Modesto, California

Charmaine Allmon Mosby
Western Kentucky University

Marie Murphy
Loyola College

William Nelles
University of Massachusetts, Dartmouth

John Nizalowski
Mesa State College

Holly L. Norton
University of Northwestern Ohio

Kathleen O'Mara
State University of New York College at Oneonta

Janet T. Palmer
North Carolina State University

Robert J. Paradowski
Rochester Institute of Technology

David B. Parsell
Furman University

Judith A. Parsons
Sul Ross State University

David Peck
Laguna Beach, California

Joseph R. Peden
Bernard M. Baruch College, City University of New York

William E. Pemberton
University of Wisconsin at La Crosse

Melissa M. Pennell
University of Lowell

Michael Pettengell
Bowling Green State University

H. Alan Pickrell
Emory & Henry College

Susan L. Piepke
Bridgewater College

Ernest Pinson
Union University

Troy Place
Western Michigan University

Bonnie C. Plummer
Eastern Kentucky University

Clifton W. Potter, Jr.
Lynchburg College

Victoria Price
Lamar University

Maureen J. Puffer-Rothenberg
Valdosta State University

Charles Pullen
Queen's University, Ontario, Canada

B. J. Rahn
Hunter College, City University of New York

Catherine Rambo
Redmond, Washington

Thomas Rankin
Concord, California

R. Kent Rasmussen
Thousand Oaks, California

Abe C. Ravitz
California State University, Dominguez Hills

John D. Raymer
Indiana Vocational Technical College—Northcentral

Jessica Reisman
Miami, Florida

Rosemary M. Canfield Reisman
Charleston Southern University

Betty Richardson
Southern Illinois University, Edwardsville

Edward J. Rielly
Saint Joseph's College of Maine

Dorothy Dodge Robbins
Louisiana Tech University

Vicki K. Robinson
A&T College at Farmingdale, State University of New York

Carl Rollyson
Baruch College, City University of New York

Paul Rosefeldt
Our Lady of Holy Cross College

Jane Rosenbaum
Rider College

Joseph Rosenblum
University of North Carolina, Greensboro

Dale H. Ross
Iowa State University

Mickey Rubenstien
Pasadena, Maryland

Kathy Rugoff
University of North Carolina at Wilmington

J. Edmund Rush
Boise, Idaho

Marilyn Rye
Rutgers University, New Brunswick

Richard Sax
Lake Erie College

Elizabeth D. Schafer
Loachapoka, Alabama

William J. Scheick
University of Texas, Austin

Per Schelde
York College, City University of New York

Casey Schmitt
Herts, United Kingdom

James Scruton
Bethel College

John C. Sherwood
University of Oregon

Paul Siegrist
Fort Hays State University

Thomas J. Sienkewicz
Monmouth College

Charles L. P. Silet
Iowa State University

David C. Smith
University of Maine at Orono

Johanna M. Smith
University of Texas at Arlington

Roger Smith
Portland, Oregon

Ira Smolensky
Monmouth College

Marjorie Smolensky
Augustant College, Illinois

Brian Stableford
Reading, England

Jill Stapleton-Bergeron
University of Tennessee

Gerald H. Strauss
Bloomsburg University

Paul Stuewe
Green Mountain College

Michael Stuprich
Ithaca College

David Sundstrand
Citrus College

Charlene E. Suscavage
University of Southern Maine

Roy Arthur Swanson
University of Wisconsin at Milwaukee

Jack E. Trotter
Trident College

Eileen Tess Tyler
United States Naval Academy

Anne R. Vizzier
University of Arkansas, Fayetteville

Paul R. Waibel
Trinity College, Illinois

Ronald G. Walker
Western Illinois University

Shawncey Webb
Taylor University

Lana A. Whited
Ferrum College

James S. Whitlark
Texas Tech University

John Wilson
Wheaton, Illinois

Malcolm Winton
Royal College of Art

Stephen Wood
Truett McConnell College

Scott Wright
University of St. Thomas

Scott D. Yarbrough
Charleston Southern University

Clifton K. Yearley
State University of New York at Buffalo

Gay Pitman Zieger
Santa Fe Community College

CONTENTS

VOLUME 1

EDITOR'S INTRODUCTION

Since the late 1960's, mystery and detective fiction has become an integral part of the school curriculum and is no longer regarded as mere entertainment or as an inferior branch of literature. Now, a writer such as Raymond Chandler, who wrote scripts for Hollywood and stories for pulp magazines of the 1930's and 1940's, has become required reading in high school and college courses. In a University of New Hampshire graduate course, "Form and Theory of Fiction," Chandler is included alongside celebrated mainstream authors such as Gabriel Garcia Marquez and Cormac McCarthy. The New Hampshire course explores Chandler's use of dialogue, structure, characterization, metaphor, and narrative and is implicitly suggesting that his methods stand up to the most rigorous analysis. Other mystery and detective writers, such as James M. Cain, Horace McCoy, and Cornell Woolrich, whose novels were originally published in cheap paperback editions and were adapted for Hollywood films, have now been canonized in such prestigious publications as Library of America editions.

What accounts for this upgrading of a genre that once was considered merely formulaic, too predictable and stereotypical to rise to the heights of great literature? Major critics in the 1930's and 1940's, such as Edmund Wilson, scorned the "whodunit," the cozy mystery, the thriller, the police procedural—in short, all the variations of a modus operandi that always led to the solving of crimes and melodramatic conflicts between good and evil. Such genre fiction was simplistic and did not deserve the critic's measured attention, Wilson argued.

In part, even the best mystery and detective fiction was devalued precisely because it was popular, and critics associated the greatest literature with a smaller elite or coterie of sophisticated readers. The modernist credo of critics demanded literature that was difficult and required skill in decoding. Works such as James Joyce's novel *Ulysses* (1922) were the epitome of what serious readers should expect from great literature. Even a writer such as the nineteenth century English novelist Charles Dickens, now considered one of

the great writers in the Western canon, was not considered worthy of what influential critic F. R. Leavis deemed "The Great Tradition."

Despite all this, college and high school courses today include mystery and detective fiction in their units on "critical thinking." The Yale-New Haven Teacher's Institute, for example, offers a course titled "Detective Fiction: Focus on Critical Thinking" that aims to sharpen students' ability to interpret evidence and even to come to terms with the phenomena of their daily lives. At its heart, detective fiction is about problem solving, the course syllabus notes. Consequently, the genre can be used across the curriculum in the humanities and sciences—indeed in any course in which word problems must be solved. A detailed lesson plan on the institute's Web site, which also includes a bibliography and references to journal articles about the value of teaching detective fiction, demonstrates just how significant a role the genre has come to play in pedagogy.

Similarly, libraries have disseminated on the Web reading lists and articles about collection management, sorting through the immense variety and quality of mystery and detective fiction. A library literature program at a high school in Pasadena, California, includes a monthly genre discussion group that focuses on mystery and suspense. Home schooling Web sites recommend mystery and detective fiction as an accessible way of teaching reading skills. Rutgers University, in its reading recommendations for senior year high school electives, includes mystery and detective fiction as part of a well-balanced curriculum.

The fact that inclusion of mystery and detective fiction in school curricula was a rarity before the 1960's is due to a different attitude toward the role and subject matter of education. At that time, the classics were taught. Before the twentieth century, the classics meant Greek and Roman literature. English and American literature, let alone the literature of other cultures, did not become a widespread part of the American college curriculum before the early twentieth century. The New England poet Henry Wadsworth

Longfellow was considered a daring innovator when he introduced the study of comparative literature (literature in translation) into the Harvard curriculum during the mid-nineteenth century.

The rediscovery of the writings of the nineteenth century writer Herman Melville during the 1920's spurred academics to begin to study contemporary writers such as Ernest Hemingway, F. Scott Fitzgerald, and William Faulkner—all of whom grew up reading Melville as a recent discovery, incorporating elements of his style into their work. Critics such as Edmund Wilson and Lionel Trilling who wrote for mass circulation magazines as well as literary journals began to integrate contemporary literature into their notions of what it meant for an educated person to be well read. However, Wilson and other influential critics still drew a line between what they considered merely popular contemporary literature and contemporary writers who might deserve to be regarded as competing, so to speak, with the classical writers of European literature.

During the first half of the twentieth century, the academic consensus was that mystery or genre fiction writers were not worthy of inclusion in college and high school courses. Challenging that consensus, Leslie Fiedler, Ray Browne, and other academics began to suggest that literature—even great literature—was more diverse and with deeper roots in popular culture than educators had previously acknowledged. Rather than continuing to replicate ever more abstruse articles about works such as Melville's *Moby Dick* (1851), Browne and others argued that scholars and teachers should expose their students to why popular writers—some of whom were fine stylists—should be studied as closely as the already canonized writers. Browne's creation of the Popular Culture Association suddenly opened up new fields of study for academics, whose articles and books launched systematic studies of writers such as Dashiell Hammett and Eric Ambler, the role of film noir in literature, and elements of mystery and detective fiction that were the underpinnings of many classical works of literature.

To some extent, the distinctions between genre and mainstream fiction that Edmund Wilson, Dwight Macdonald, F. R. Leavis, and other critics found were never as deep as they thought. Faulkner, for example, devoted considerable time to reading Rex Stout and Georges Simenon. Indeed, a published inventory of his library included many of their paperback novels. Moreover, Faulkner's own novel *Absalom, Absalom!* (1936) is structured rather like the gothic thriller/detective novels that he enjoyed reading. The correspondence of other mainstream writers—Rebecca West, for example—reveals a high degree of respect for the so-called pulp writers such as James M. Cain. That Faulkner attempted to write his own series of detective stories, collected in *Knight's Gambit* (1949), with decidedly poor results suggests that the rather sneering attitude certain critics adopted toward genre fiction was unmerited. Faulkner's detective, lawyer Gavin Stevens, is a poor substitute for Hercule Poirot and the cozy mysteries Agatha Christie published with such aplomb. The capacity to write great crime fiction, in other words, requires a certain sort of genius that not all writers—even great mainstream ones—can demonstrate.

As the University of New Hampshire course in the theory and form of fiction suggests, the handling of dialogue and narrative, for instance, can be as impressive in mystery and detective fiction as in any other kind of literature. With the appearance of literary criticism such as John Cawelti's *Adventure, Mystery and Romance: Formula Stories as Art and Popular Culture* (1976), rigid distinctions between high and low, or popular and elite literature, became less meaningful. The range of literary works that academics saw fit to analyze expanded, and opportunities for the inclusion of mystery and detective fiction into school curricula grew.

At the same time, however, mystery and detective fiction has sometimes deserved the critical pastings it has received. Too often, its genre heroes—even in such classics as the Sherlock Holmes series—never change or develop as characters. A character such as Holmes has his eccentricities, to be sure, and his creator, Arthur Conan Doyle, was adept at introducing new aspects of his character. However, the point of the series was that Holmes could never really change and could *always* be relied upon to solve the crime. Considering that the Holmes stories were formula fiction at its best, think of all the imitators that inevitably exhibit less skill than their progenitor.

Perhaps the main reason school curricula now include units on mystery and detective fiction is that the genre itself has matured, as critic and crime novelist Patrick Anderson argues in *The Triumph of the Thriller: How Crooks, Cops, and Cannibals Captured Popular Fiction* (2007). The present, fully revised, and expanded edition of *Critical Survey of Mystery and Detective Fiction* not only acknowledges the new and accomplished writers of this genre, it also explores how the genre itself has changed and grown, especially in terms of characterization and complex narratives.

A series character such as Michael Connelly's Harry Bosch, for example, not only develops and changes from one novel to the next, he suffers the toll that years of involvement in brutal crimes exact on his psyche. Similarly, John Lescroart's defense attorney/detective Dismas Hardy suffers breakdowns and relies on a more experienced attorney to help him win some of his cases. These fallible and vulnerable characters are a far cry from an earlier generation of superhero sleuths who somehow managed repeatedly to tangle with the criminal world without ever becoming corrupted themselves. Compare Scott Turow's legal thrillers with those of Erle Stanley Gardner and the growing sophistication of genre fiction is apparent. Turow's books are studies of the legal system itself, not merely pretexts for writing another whodunit, despite the fact that Gardner's narrative skill remains a touchstone for serious writers such as Turow who are committed to help readers make sense of legal procedures.

Perhaps even more significantly, this new edition of *Critical Survey of Mystery and Detective Fiction* takes into account the ways in which world literature has contributed to the genre of mystery and detective fiction with essays on writers from Asia, Africa, and Latin America. At the same time, American writers such as Charles McCarry and Barry Eisler have explored settings on several continents. Eisler's series character, John Rain, is part Japanese and part Anglo-American. Many other authors covered in these volumes write about African American, Native American, Hispanic, and woman detectives in a wide variety of cultural settings that have transformed mystery and detective fiction into a far less provincial and "cozy" genre.

The overview essays—a major new addition to *Critical Survey of Mystery and Detective Fiction*—acknowledge the explosive developments occurring in world literature that are now being incorporated into school curricula. These overviews cover subjects such as African mystery fiction, Asian mystery fiction, ethnic American mystery fiction, forensic mystery fiction, feminist and lesbian mystery fiction, innovations in the genre, Latin American mystery fiction, pastiches of Sherlock Holmes, and parodies. Topics such as these demonstrate just how much has changed in the mystery and detective field since the first edition of *Critical Survey of Mystery and Detective Fiction*.

The other change in school curricula that this new edition addresses is the role of other media in shaping mystery and detective fiction. With the advent of video tapes and DVDs, the classroom has been extended to include a much broader sense of what literature itself means. Included in the overview sections are essays on topics such as film, graphic mystery novels, radio drama, stage plays, and television series.

As a research tool, this new edition provides students with a great array of sources for further study—not only up-to-date bibliographies for individual authors but also for the overview essays, which are complemented by a separate section of appendixes that contains a general bibliography, a guide to Web resources, a time line of crime and detective fiction, two glossaries, and a chronological list of writers. Finally, a complex set of indexes encourage students to cross-reference writers and types of mystery and detective fiction, so that they will be able to identify writers from specific regions and others who focus on the same subjects.

With the expansion of *Critical Survey of Mystery and Detective Fiction*, a new generation of crime writers comes to the fore, including figures such as Nevada Barr, Lee Child, Michael Connelly, Patricia Cornwell, Colin Dexter, Barry Eisler, Antonia Fraser, Alan Furst, Sue Grafton, Thomas Harris, John Lescroart, David Morell, George Pelecanos, Ian Rankin,

J. K. Rowling, Scott Turow, and Ann Waldron. The range of their work and worldwide audience and their presence in school curricula make these volumes an especially useful guide to developments in contemporary literature.

Despite the significant changes in mystery and detective fiction, the genre itself endures because of certain underlying continuities. Ann Waldron is an example of an author who reinvigorates the genre's old conventions in new settings. She grew up reading the cozy mysteries of Agatha Christie, obviously enjoying the adventures of an amateur sleuth such as Miss Jane Marple and the comfortable English village settings that are disturbed by the sudden eruption of a murder. That world is gone, even though readers can indulge their nostalgia by continuing to enjoy Christie's splendid narratives. Waldron updates Christie by choosing as her primary setting a college town, Princeton, New Jersey, which is still sufficiently small and inbred to provide a cast of eccentric characters who know and suspect one another. By renewing Christie's well-worn formula, Waldron creates witty mysteries featuring an amateur woman sleuth, McLeod Dulany. However, Dulany—unlike Marple—is a modern woman, a journalist and teacher of writing at Princeton University. Dulany is also a southerner whose sharp perceptions of northerners adds another dimension to the culture described in Waldron's Princeton murder series. Moreover, Princeton University as a institutional structure becomes an integral part of the mysteries, so that Waldron is also treading on the familiar ground of the academic mystery subgenre but refreshing it by making her detective an outsider (Dulany is on a leave of absence from her Tallahassee newspaper) who is keen to observe the infighting that occurs in an Ivy League hothouse. Another Waldron mystery, set in a Princeton seminary, fosters a sense of claustrophobia, of seething resentments and conflicts, that are essential to well-wrought mystery.

At the heart of much mystery and detective fiction—no matter the period in which it is written or set—is corruption, a canker spreading through individuals, families, and institutions. Dashiell Hammett and Raymond Chandler perfected this aspect of the genre, and filmmakers such as Howard Hawks, in *The Big Sleep* (1946), and Roman Polanski, in *Chinatown* (1974), have brought the same sensibility to the screen, exposing the incestuous conflicts that are at the core of many family disturbances and the greedy manipulation of public resources. In Barry Eisler's thrillers, John Rain is hired by governments to make assassinations look like natural deaths. While Rain makes no excuses for his horrible line of work—indeed his honesty and torment fully engage the reader's empathy (a rather shocking fact in itself)—Eisler's novels are clearly targeted at the national security states that employ extralegal means of accomplishing policy goals while pretending that are conducting wars against terror. Thus it is not surprising to learn that Eisler, a former Central Intelligence Agency operative, is opposed the U.S. invasion of Iraq and that his view of world politics pervades the plots of his novels.

Contemporary mystery and detective fiction is also distinguished by a cross-fertilization of elements that earlier novelists tended to separate into different series. For example, John Lescroart's Dismas Hardy/Abe Glitsky series combines the police procedural with the legal thriller. At its best, this series features the clash between Hardy's view that police methods must never subvert the legal process and Glitsky's conviction that lawyers often obfuscate the nature of crime, not only making his job harder but also leaving society unprotected and justice denied. A similar tension occurs in several television dramas—most notably in *Law and Order*, in which the structure of a typical episode splits its attention between the detectives who investigate crimes and apprehend criminals and the district attorneys and defense lawyers who cut deals and dilute the punishment of crimes. This series, nevertheless, makes a strong case for the legal justice system, admitting its flaws but also showing why issues of crime and punishment are not, and probably can never be, as simple as catching, convicting, and sentencing perpetrators. Crime and punishment becomes not merely a moral imperative but a political process full of plea-bargaining and other compromises.

Like modern prose fiction, television has become much more sophisticated and complex in its treatment of crime and punishment. Whereas an earlier generation of television shows featured straight-shooting, honest cops such as Jack Webb's Joe Friday in *Dragnet*, or tough-guy cops such as Telly Savalas's Theo Kojak, and Raymond Burr as the shrewd Perry Mason whose defense work exposes police incompetence, the focus has now shifted to legal processes—as in *Law and Order: Special Victims Unit* and the various *CSI* series. Rather than concentrating on super cops and detectives, the scenarios of broadcast networks and cable programs now focus on teams of specialists and forensic scientists. These televised dramas also share screen time with nonfiction documentaries on HBO, A&E, and other cable networks that dramatize subjects such as autopsies and DNA analyses. Figures such as medical examiners have become both television stars and series characters in novels. The probity and steadiness of author Patricia Cornwell's Kay Scarpetta is a throwback to the old-fashioned heroine/detective. In contrast, Helen Mirren's Chief Inspector Jane Tennison in the *Prime Suspect* television series is battling not only the sexism and corruption of her own department but also her own demons.

In this complex history of continuity and change, what never flags—what never can be removed from the genre—is the *pursuit* of crime, whether it is Patricia Highsmith's Mr. Ripley, who gets away with murder, or Sherlock Holmes, who always gets his man. If mystery and detective fiction is incorporated into school curricula it is because of the realization that what was once considered simply entertainment or leisure reading speaks to a deep core of curiosity about human motivations, about the rights and wrongs of human behavior, and about those characters who simply cannot content themselves with the status quo and must intervene in history—sometimes for better but often for worse. How to come to terms with such a world is the overriding theme of mystery and detective fiction in all of its permutations.

Carl Rollyson
Baruch College, City University of New York

COMPLETE LIST OF CONTENTS

VOLUME 1

VOLUME 2

VOLUME 3

VOLUME 4

VOLUME 5

AUTHORS

A

ANTHONY ABBOT
Charles Fulton Oursler

Born: Baltimore, Maryland; January 22, 1893
Died: New York, New York; May 24, 1952
Also wrote as Fulton Oursler
Types of plot: Master sleuth; police procedural

PRINCIPAL SERIES CHARACTERS

THATCHER COLT is a New York City police commissioner (in one book, however, he has retired into private crime-prevention work). Tall, dapper, and poised, Colt is a genius at orchestration of police resources and technology and at the exposure of fraud. He is married to the beautiful Florence Dunbar.

ANTHONY "TONY" ABBOT, a former newspaperman, is secretary to Thatcher Colt during and after his term as commissioner. As the man who most frequently shares Colt's confidences, he takes notes on Colt's cases and narrates the memoirs to promote public belief in the police. He is married to the lively Betty.

MERLE K. DOUGHERTY, New York's district attorney, is often at odds with Colt yet must grudgingly acknowledge his indispensable contributions to the work of the police department.

CONTRIBUTION

Anthony Abbot's contribution to the mystery and detective genre is found in his eight novels chronicling the feats of Thatcher Colt, the reserved but unswerving commissioner of the New York City Police Department. Abbot, as he himself noted, was "one of the first apologists for the police in detective fiction"; as such, he anticipated the development of the police procedural. At a time when most fictional police officers were portrayed as incompetent, dishonest, or, at best, solid but unimaginative, Abbot created a police officer-hero of formidable intelligence. For the most part, however, Abbot was a derivative writer. Popular in their day, the Thatcher Colt novels are now chiefly of historical interest. They are a virtual compendium of the motifs that dominated the American mystery novel in the 1920's and 1930's.

BIOGRAPHY

Anthony Abbot was a pen name of Charles Fulton Oursler, who published many books, both fictional and nonfictional, under the name Fulton Oursler. He was born on January 22, 1893, in Baltimore. Abbot's two sisters died in early childhood. His father worked seven days a week, having supervisory responsibility on a streetcar line; when Abbot was in his teens, however, his father was fired from two jobs, so that the family's economic position became unstable. As a small child, Abbot was taken by his mother to first-class stage plays in Baltimore; these outings were made possible by the theaters' donation of tickets to Abbot's father, whose streetcar schedules accommodated their patrons. During his youth, Abbot read widely and learned to perform magic tricks. His family considered college unaffordable, so he quit school at fifteen and found work as office boy in a law office; he also began to give magic shows at night. While still in his teens, Abbot became a reporter for the Baltimore *American*, thus taking the first step toward fulfilling the vow he had made three years before, near the grave of Edgar Allan Poe, that he would be a writer.

In 1910, Abbot married Rose Keller Karger; eventually, a son and a daughter were born to them. As a journalist, Abbot met local and national politicians and celebrities such as Sarah Bernhardt. He had been told, however, that the only place to pursue his career was New York City, so in 1918 he obtained work there with *Music Trades*, a weekly. This was also the year he sold his first short story, "The Sign of the Seven Shots."

A turning point in Abbot's life was the inception of his work for Bernarr Macfadden, creator and publisher of *Physical Culture*, *True Story*, *True Detective*, and other magazines. Abbot was soon put in charge of Macfadden's editorial enterprises. (Later, he served as an editor for *Reader's Digest*.) During this time, Abbot wrote fiction, went to Hollywood to do scriptwriting, and met many of the famous people who circulated through New York. In 1924, he had met and fallen in love with writer Grace Perkins, which led him to be one of the first Americans to resort to a Mexican divorce as well as a Mexican marriage. When Rose finally granted the divorce, stipulating an alimony settlement, Abbot and Perkins were able to be married in the United States. Abbot had a daughter and a son from this marriage.

Abbot's first novel written using his pseudonym was *About the Murder of Geraldine Foster* (1930; also known as *The Murder of Geraldine Foster*), featuring Thatcher Colt. Encouraged by its success—the novel appeared on the best-seller list, a rarity for a mystery at the time—he produced a series of Colt novels in rapid succession while continuing to publish widely as Fulton Oursler. His best-known work, written as Oursler, was the enormously successful inspirational book *The Greatest Story Ever Told: A Tale of the Greatest Life Ever Lived* (1949), based on his radio series of the same title. (Though skeptical of spiritualism and actively involved in unmasking spiritualist frauds, Abbot had a lifelong interest in religion and in unexplained psychic phenomena; ultimately, he converted to Roman Catholicism.) He died of a heart attack on May 24, 1952.

ANALYSIS

In discussions of popular fiction, critics often use the term "formulaic." Rarely, however, could that term be so literally applied to a body of fiction as it could to the mystery novel of the 1920's and 1930's. During this period, countless writers, attracted by the growing popularity of the genre, approached the task of mys-

tery writing rather as if they were baking a cake: Simply follow the recipe and success will be guaranteed.

THATCHER COLT SERIES

It was in this fashion that Anthony Abbot's Thatcher Colt series was conceived. As a hero, Thatcher Colt has much in common with Sherlock Holmes and other prototypical fictional detectives. Colt's lean, aristocratic features and unflappable manner set him apart from the ordinary run of men. Like Holmes, he is an expert in the science of criminology, while his passion for scientific gadgetry places him in the tradition of a popular American detective of the era, Craig Kennedy. Like Holmes, he frequently keeps his deductions to himself, leaving his subordinates (and the reader) to wait for his explanation of what he has seen that they missed. Colt's Watson, the recorder of his exploits, is his secretary, Anthony "Tony" Abbot. Thus, "Anthony Abbot" is at once the narrator of the Thatcher Colt books and their (ostensible) author—just as "Ellery Queen" (who debuted in 1929, a year before Colt) is at once narrator, protagonist, and author of the Ellery Queen books. The same device had long been used in the Nick Carter series.

Why bother with this transparent stratagem? In Abbot's case, the answer lies in the didactic intent of the Thatcher Colt series—a peculiarly American earnestness. For all of his resemblance to Holmes, Colt is not an amateur sleuth: He is a police officer. While providing the entertainment that was the primary goal of the series, Abbot wanted to send his readers a message regarding the importance of respect for law and order and for professional guardians of the peace. Instead of portraying the police as bumbling oafs or corrupt timeservers, as many mystery writers of the period did, Abbot depicted them (especially as exemplified by Colt) as dedicated and efficient public servants, masters of the new science of crime fighting. The device of Abbot as author/narrator was intended to give the books a pseudodocumentary flavor, reinforcing the authority of their message.

Indeed, Abbot prided himself on the authenticity of the series. In his autobiography, *Behold This Dreamer!* (written as Oursler; 1924), Abbot emphasized this point:

To get my facts right, I dawdled around the old Headquarters Building in Center Street and got my facts straight from the source; and for a fee, the secretary of the police commissioner read the scripts and checked every detail. The books were meticulously accurate.

A reader in the 1980's, faced with the patently melodramatic quality of the Thatcher Colt books, might well receive Abbot's claim with incredulity. These books, meticulously accurate? Certainly it is a long distance from the romanticized adventures of Thatcher Colt (who, despite his professional status, is very much the master sleuth) to the gritty realism of the modern police procedural (where teamwork takes precedence over individual heroics). Nevertheless, with his attention to the actual details of police work, Abbot was preparing the way for that popular subgenre.

Anna R. Holloway

PRINCIPAL MYSTERY AND DETECTIVE FICTION

THATCHER COLT SERIES: *About the Murder of Geraldine Foster*, 1930 (also known as *The Murder of Geraldine Foster*); *About the Murder of the Clergyman's Mistress*, 1931 (also known as *The Crime of the Century* and *Murder of the Clergyman's Mistress*); *About the Murder of the Night Club Lady*, 1931 (also known as *The Murder of the Night Club Lady* and *The Night Club Lady*); *About the Murder of the Circus Queen*, 1932 (also known as *The Murder of the Circus Queen*); *About the Murder of a Startled Lady*, 1935 (also known as *The Murder of a Startled Lady*); *Dark Masquerade*, 1936; *About the Murder of a Man Afraid of Women*, 1937 (also known as *The Murder of a Man Afraid of Women*); *The Creeps*, 1939 (also known as *Murder at Buzzards Bay*); *The Shudders*, 1943 (also known as *Deadly Secret*)

NONSERIES NOVEL: *The President's Mystery Story*, 1935 (as Fulton Oursler; with others)

OTHER SHORT FICTION: *The Wager, and The House at Fernwood*, 1946 (as Fulton Oursler); *These Are Strange Tales*, 1948

OTHER MAJOR WORKS

NOVELS (AS FULTON OURSLER): *Behold This Dreamer!*, 1924; *Sandalwood*, 1925; *Stepchild of the Moon*, 1926; *Poor Little Fool*, 1928; *The World's Delight*, 1929; *The Great Jasper*, 1930; *Joshua Todd*, 1935; *A String of Blue Beads*, 1956

PLAYS (AS FULTON OURSLER): *Sandalwood*, pr. 1926 (with Owen Davis); *Behold This Dreamer*, pr. 1927 (with Aubrey Kennedy); *The Spider*, pr. 1927 (revised 1928; with Lowell Brentano); *All the King's Men*, pr. 1929; *The Walking Gentlemen*, pr. 1942 (with Grace Perkins Oursler); *The Bridge*, pr. 1946

CHILDREN'S LITERATURE (AS FULTON OURSLER): *A Child's Life of Jesus*, 1951

NONFICTION (AS FULTON OURSLER): *The Happy Grotto: A Journalist's Account of Lourdes*, 1913; *The True Story of Bernarr Macfadden*, 1929; *The Flower of the Gods*, 1936 (with Achmed Abdullah); *A Skeptic in the Holy Land*, 1936; *The Shadow of the Master*, 1940 (with ʿAbd Allah Ahmad); *Three Things We Can Believe In*, 1942; *The Precious Secret*, 1947; *Father Flanagan of Boys Town*, 1949 (with Will Oursler); *The Greatest Story Ever Told: A Tale of the Greatest Life Ever Lived*, 1949; *Modern Parables*, 1950; *Why I Know There Is a God*, 1950; *The Greatest Book Ever Written: Old Testament Story*, 1951; *The Reader's Digest Murder Case: A Tragedy in Parole*, 1952; *The Greatest Faith Ever Known*, 1953 (with April Oursler Armstrong); *Lights Along the Shore*, 1954; *Behold This Dreamer!*, 1964

TRANSLATION (AS FULTON OURSLER): *Illustrated Magic*, 1931 (by Ottokar F)

BIBLIOGRAPHY

Breen, Jon L. "About the Murders of Anthony Abbot." *The Armchair Detective* 3 (October, 1969): 1-5. Discussion of Abbot's work by a fellow mystery writer and critic who later won the 2000 Agatha Award for best criticism of mystery and detective fiction.

Haycraft, Howard. *Murder for Pleasure: The Life and Times of the Detective Story.* New York: Carroll & Graf, 1984. History of detective fiction that includes a lengthy "who's who in detection" appendix.

Herbert, Rosemary, ed. *The Oxford Companion to Crime and Mystery Writing.* New York: Oxford University Press, 1999. Encyclopedia-style reference work on detective fiction includes several references to Abbot in relevant entries. Bibliographic references and index.

Scaggs, John. *Crime Fiction*. New York: Routledge, 2005. Contains a chapter on police procedurals that helps place Abbot among his fellow writers.

Steinbrunner, Chris, and Otto Penzler, eds. *Encyclopedia of Mystery and Detection*. New York: McGraw-Hill, 1976. Still the classic source on mystery and detective fiction. A good work for contextualizing Abbot's work thematically, but it lacks bibliographic resources.

CLEVE F. ADAMS

Born: Chicago, Illinois; 1895
Died: Glendale, California; December 28, 1949
Also wrote as Franklin Charles; John Spain
Types of plot: Private investigator; hard-boiled

PRINCIPAL SERIES

Rex McBride, 1940-1955
William Rye, 1942-1950
John J. Shannon, 1942-1950

PRINCIPAL SERIES CHARACTERS

REX MCBRIDE, a freewheeling, wisecracking private investigator and specialist in insurance cases, is tough, with a widely publicized reputation for shady behavior. About thirty-two years old and unmarried, he lives by a simple guiding principle: to fight as dirty as the other guy does.

WILLIAM RYE, a troubleshooter who prefers to be called a confidential agent, is employed by a Los Angeles oil magnate and political boss. In his thirties, Rye is a tough, ruthlessly efficient, no-nonsense individual.

JOHN J. SHANNON, a private investigator and formerly a detective lieutenant on the Los Angeles police force, is tough, temperamental, but at times compassionate. He is unmarried, young, and handsome. He also has a penchant for obscenities.

CONTRIBUTION

Cleve F. Adams was one of few pulp writers to make the successful transition to hardcover publication. Although he is an underrated author, eclipsed by his contemporary, Raymond Chandler, Adams

brought a new dimension to the genre. Chandler's image of the private investigator as knight-errant is inverted by Adams into the image of private investigator as antihero. Working in the hard-boiled tradition of Chandler and Dashiell Hammett, Adams has been acclaimed as "one of the best of the tough detective story writers of the middle and late thirties." His private-investigator novels have been described as unique, having captured "the gray and gritty feel of the time as powerfully as Chandler" and having created an enduring image of the private detective. Adams regarded motive and characterization as the essential elements of mystery and detective fiction. His fast-paced novels present convincing, credible characters and capture the political violence and corruption of the 1930's.

BIOGRAPHY

Cleve Franklin Adams was born in 1895 in Chicago, where he spent his childhood and his youth. In 1919, at the age of twenty-four, Adams moved to California and worked at a variety of jobs, including soda jerk, window trimmer, interior decorator, copper miner, screenwriter, life insurance executive, and detective.

Adams began producing hard-boiled mystery fiction around 1934, writing almost exclusively for pulp magazines such as *Detective Fiction Weekly*, *Double Detective Tales*, *Argosy*, and *Black Mask*. Between 1936 and 1942, he published fifty short mystery stories.

In 1940, Adams published his first detective thriller, *Sabotage*, followed by a second novel, *And Sudden Death*, that same year. In the next eight years, he published thirteen more novels, one of which, *No Wings on a Cop* (1950), was expanded by Robert Leslie Bellem, and another, *Shady Lady* (1955), was completed after his death by Harry Whittington. He also worked as a film director and screenwriter; cofounded, along with W. T. Ballard, the Fictioneers, a group of local Los Angeles writers (including Raymond Chandler); and worked with the Authors League of America. On December 28, 1949, he died of a heart attack at his home in Glendale, California.

ANALYSIS

Cleve Franklin Adams contributed hard-boiled mystery fiction to pulp magazines in the mid-1930's, eventually publishing his first story, "Vision of Violet," in the February, 1936, issue of *Clues: A Journal of Detection*. In the summer of 1940, he was employed by Ken White, editor of *Black Mask*, to "inject new life and vigor into the magazine and to reestablish the magazine's tougher, hard-edged image." This period of apprenticeship allowed him to create several hard-boiled detective heroes, gradually bringing into existence the private eye who would be given the name Rex McBride.

AND SUDDEN DEATH AND SABOTAGE

Adams's first two novels, *Sabotage* and *And Sudden Death*, were published in 1940. With these novels featuring private investigator Rex McBride, Adams created a new, intriguing variation on the detective hero. Instead of a Philip Marlowe or a Sam Spade with whom the reader can empathize, the reader is presented with the antithesis of these characters—Rex McBride, the private investigator as antihero or chauvinist pig: Crude, coarse, and cynical, yet sentimental, he is deficient in morals and enigmatic in nature. McBride "has a capacity for long, brooding silences, sudden ribald laughter, mad fury, and aloof arrogance." No one—clients, police, criminals, or female friends—understands him. McBride, however, get results. Adams, who sees motivation as the crucial element in the mystery and detective genre, notes the impulse that drives him: "his singleness of purpose . . . He has been hired to do a job and he is going to do it. Come hell or high water he's going to do it."

As Adams acknowledges, this conception of the detective hero is an inversion of the hero legend. Unlike Chandler's Marlowe, McBride is not a knightly hero and does not attempt to redeem the corrupt. He is an ordinary man. Although cast in the hard-boiled mold, McBride is a complex individual. His personal involvement with a case may be prompted by the need for justice or simply the need for money. He is emotional and impulsive. By turns he is arrogant, caring, coldhearted, generous, moody, sentimental, and ruthless. Yet it is his changeable nature that makes him human and believable.

Other characters in the novels are also realistically drawn, from clients to villains. As one critic says, Adams "showed a genius for juggling diverse groups of shady characters, each with his or her own greedy objective."

Careful plotting is not a primary characteristic of Adams's fiction. He prefers instead to let situations accumulate until the hero finds himself in a jam. As he views it, the detective who is logically motivated will create suspense; his desire to win will make him a menace to opposing forces. Thus, the other central elements of mystery fiction, suspense and plot, naturally derive from motivation:

> As I see it, suspense is built on MENACE. This urgency both for and against, does not only apply to a detective-mystery story. What matter if it be only a golf tournament. Our hero wants to win, doesn't he? And our villain, or villainess, simply isn't going to stand for his winning . . . He wants to win, too. He wants to win, even if he has to resort to unsportsmanlike shenanigans, by golly. So is he a menace? You bet your sweet life he is. And does the *struggle* between the two opposing forces create SUSPENSE? Well, if the writer has done his job, it should.

Adams's handling of plot and his mode of pacing are typically hard-boiled. His stories are complicated, involving the standard cast of gangsters, treacherous women, unsympathetic police officers, corrupt politicians, and professional criminals. Violent action is generously provided, and crimes are so extravagant and so inextricably tangled together that Adams's protagonist is often faced with almost impossible tasks. McBride's success in getting results stems from his knowledge of the streets and his ability to move freely among its elements.

UP JUMPED THE DEVIL

The enigmatic nature of McBride and the fast-paced action of his violent world are best exemplified in *Up Jumped the Devil* (1943). The first two paragraphs reveal Adams's view of realistic characters and logical airtight motives:

> McBride paused just inside his door and regarded the dead man with some astonishment, for while this was not the first dead man he had ever seen it was certainly the first time he had found one sitting in his own room. Presently it occurred to him that it was not his own room, and he turned, opening the door a trifle wider, and compared the number on the door panel with that on the key he still had in his hand. No, he decided, the mistake was the dead man's, not his.

Further, McBride discovers that his suitcase, a well-traveled but expensive Gladstone that is his pride and joy, has been defaced. The novel thus begins superbly with a dramatic encounter that gets the story moving. Instantly, McBride has a personal stake in the situation. The language is simple, with highly active verbs that create excitement. In addition, the sharpness of McBride's wit and his changing emotions are understandable and logical, revealing Adams's theory that plausibility stems directly from the writer's urge to have characters act like people.

From this point in the novel, Adams creates a breathless pace; suspense mounts from page to page. McBride is faced not only with the major problem of discovering who murdered the man and put him in his room but also with a series of complicated situations and murders. Hired to follow the Chandlers and recover the jewels paid for by his insurance company after they were lost, he must solve each minor situation before he can find the solution to the first murder. He encounters treacherous women, is threatened and deceived by clients and criminals, and is beaten and kicked unconscious.

This piling of incident on incident reveals Adams's weakness with plot. Yet, McBride's character is heightened and motivation is sustained throughout the novel. Although there are several plot threads that must be resolved, the diverse ingredients are blended together well. In the end, McBride is faced with the painful revelation that a woman in whom he is interested has masterminded the jewel theft and has been conspiring with the president of the company in the various sabotage efforts.

Adams's best novels, *Sabotage, Decoy, Up Jumped the Devil*, and *Shady Lady*, are similar in their cynical view of American politics, the variety of their skillfully drawn characters, and the sharp wit of their protagonist, McBride. The diverse elements of Southern California society are excellently drawn. They are novels that should be given serious attention for their contribution to the private-eye genre.

Jacquelyn Jackson

PRINCIPAL MYSTERY AND DETECTIVE FICTION

REX MCBRIDE SERIES: *Sabotage*, 1940 (also known as *Death Before Breakfast* and *Death at the Dam*); *And Sudden Death*, 1940; *Decoy*, 1941; *Up Jumped the Devil*, 1943 (also known as *Murder All Over*); *The Crooking Finger*, 1944; *Shady Lady*, 1955 (with Harry Whittington)

WILLIAM RYE SERIES: *Dig Me a Grave*, 1942 (as Spain); *Death Is Like That*, 1943 (as Spain); *The Evil Star*, 1944 (as Spain)

JOHN J. SHANNON SERIES: *The Private Eye*, 1942; *No Wings on a Cop*, 1950 (with Robert Leslie Bellem)

NONSERIES NOVELS: *The Black Door*, 1941; *The Vice Czar Murders*, 1941 (as Charles; with Robert Leslie Bellem); *What Price Murder*, 1942; *Contraband*, 1950 (also known as *Borderline Cases*)

BIBLIOGRAPHY

Baker, Robert A., and Michael T. Nieztzel. *Private Eyes: 101 Knights—A Survey of American Detective Fiction, 1922-1984*. Bowling Green, Ohio: Bowling Green State University Popular Press, 1985. Discusses the distinctively American aspects of Adams's work. Indexes.

Geherin, David. *The American Private Eye: The Image in Fiction*. New York: F. Ungar, 1985. Examines fictional American private detectives in relation to their British precursors and counterparts. Sheds light on Adams's work. Bibliography and index.

Moore, Lewis D. *Cracking the Hard-Boiled Detective: A Critical History from the 1920s to the Present.*

Jefferson, N.C.: McFarland, 2006. A study of the hard-boiled subgenre from Raymond Chandler to Sue Grafton; provides a framework for understanding Adams.

Nevins, Francis M., Jr. "The World of Cleve F. Adams." *The Armchair Detective* 8 (1974/1975): 195-201. Discusses the rules and conventions unique to Adams's fiction and the character types that inhabit it.

Scaggs, John. *Crime Fiction*. New York: Routledge, 2005. Contains an essay on hard-boiled fiction as well as a section on the Golden Age of mystery; provides a background against which to place Adams.

BORIS AKUNIN
Grigory Shalvovich Chkhartishvili

Born: Tbilisi, Georgian Soviet Socialist Republic, Soviet Union (now in Georgia); May 20, 1956

Also wrote as Grigory Shalvovich Chkhartishvili

Types of plot: Historical; police procedural; amateur sleuth

PRINCIPAL SERIES

Erast Fandorin, 1997-
Nicholas Fandorin, 2000-
Sister Pelagia, 2000-

PRINCIPAL SERIES CHARACTERS

ERAST PETROVICH FANDORIN is a slender, dark-haired member of the Moscow police force in nineteenth century Russia. His piercing blue eyes and a pencil mustache make him quite good-looking. He is also adept in the martial arts, learned from his Japanese manservant, Masa, a samurai whose life he once saved. Through innate luck and a keen intellect, he is able to solve the most challenging mysteries, yet he shows no sign of arrogance. The death of his young wife gave Fandorin an air of sadness that women find attractive.

NICHOLAS FANDORIN, the grandson of Erast Fandorin, lives in Russia during the presidency of Boris Yeltsin. By profession, Nicholas is a historian, but unlike his grandfather, he is more literary and historical sleuth than detective. His story alternates with chapters about Russian historical figures. Nicholas is an unusually tall person, suggesting that he looks down on other people, both literally and figuratively.

SISTER PELAGIA is a novice nun and an undercover detective. Youthful, freckled, and deceptively innocent-looking, she is in fact far too lively, inquisitive, and outspoken to be a nun. Ostensibly a teacher in a diocesan girls' school, she is the power behind Bishop Metrofani, renowned for his solutions to the most baffling mysteries. Pelagia, a lover of masquerade, sometimes poses as her charming, stylish, and fictitious sister, Polina Andreevna Lisitsina, though she worries about the sin of exposing herself to worldly temptation in this disguise.

CONTRIBUTION

Boris Akunin, whose books have sold more than 15 million copies, is unique among Russian-language mystery authors because of his appeal to a mass readership, both in Russia, where he has lived since 1958, and overseas. Observers have attributed this success to the emergence of a large Russian middle class, eager for good books, following the demise of the communist regime. Akunin guessed, correctly, that the transition would create a demand for a genre that had not existed in the Soviet Union—a middle ground between high literature and whodunit fiction. His chief series character, Erast Petrovich Fandorin, is athletic and elegant like James Bond and cerebral like Sherlock Holmes, with additional overtones of Leo Tolstoy's Stepan Arkadyich Oblonsky in *Anna Karenina* (1875-1877; English translation, 1886). The nineteenth century Fandorin arouses nostalgia for the late czarist era, doomed though that period was.

Keenly sensitive to the concerns of the reading public, Akunin has declared his goal to be to entertain and enlighten the middle-class professionals emerging in twenty-first century Russia. The stylistic clarity and multilayered organization of Akunin's novels have raised the tone of popular Russian literature. His new literature serves as a model for what he perceives to be the new Russian character. As he sees it, the emerging Russian middle class has an abundance of energy and goodwill but needs guideposts of all sorts—literary and aesthetic, moral and ethical—as well as the quality entertainment that was denied its members in the Soviet era. These are the contributions Akunin has sought to make—thus far with enormous success—through his writing.

BIOGRAPHY

Boris Akunin was born Grigory Shalvovich Chkhartishvili on May 20, 1956, in Tbilisi, in the Soviet republic of Georgia. His father served in an all-Georgian army artillery unit; his mother taught Russian literature and language. Around Akunin's second birthday, his family moved to Moscow, where he has continued to make his home. Growing up, he immersed himself in the literary works that were to influence him most as an adult. These included the works of Russians Leo Tolstoy, Fyodor Dostoevski, and Anton Chekhov as well as those of Alexandre Dumas, *père*, Robert Louis Stevenson, and Mark Twain. He was also captivated by Kabuki theater and became interested in all aspects of Japanese culture.

In the 1970's, after high school, Akunin enrolled in Moscow State University, majoring in Asian and African studies; he also studied for a time in Germany and Japan. After earning a degree, he worked for several Moscow publishing houses, where he translated scientific literature and later Japanese- and English-language fiction. He realized that emulating the styles of works he translated—including those of Yukio Mishima, Malcolm Bradbury, Kobo Abe, and Peter Ustinov—was excellent preparation for his own writing. Until 2000, he also worked as deputy editor-in-chief of *Inostrannaia literatura*, a foreign literature journal.

In the late 1990's, Akunin felt challenged to write "literary" thrillers when his wife, Erika—a closet fan

of pulp fiction—complained of the trashy fiction that then prevailed. He observed that she covered mystery novels in brown wrapping paper when riding the subway, and he resolved to create fiction that she and others would not feel embarrassed to be seen reading. Initially, however, Akunin was not sure that he wanted to write a whodunit himself, so he attempted to sell his plot ideas to other writers. However, there were no takers, so he took on the task of creating a new middle-ground genre.

Akunin decided to take a pen name—partly because his surname, Chkhartishvili, was difficult even for Russians to pronounce, but also because the playfulness of a nom de plume appealed to him. Some critics speculate that the pseudonym Boris Akunin, or B. Akunin, was meant to suggest the last name of the nineteenth century Russian radical Mikhail Bakunin. Bakunin is generally considered a bourgeois revolutionary, and Akunin has said he is writing for middle-class professionals, who are to be considered Russia's twenty-first century revolutionaries. However, his knowledge of Japanese might have caused him to select the name Akunin, which in Japanese roughly means "evildoer," and Akunin has pointed out that the villain is a highly important figure in detective stories.

Akunin created a series of very successful novels featuring Erast Fandorin, beginning with *Azazel'* (1998, 2000; *The Winter Queen*, 2003). Several of these novels have been translated into English. He also wrote a series on Erast Fandorin's grandson, Nicholas, and one on Sister Pelagia, an amateur sleuth. He also published a nonfictional work on the philosophical implications of suicide, *Pisatel' i samoubiistvo* (1999; the writer and suicide). It includes biographical information on 350 writers who committed suicide, from all countries and all eras.

ANALYSIS

The setting for Boris Akunin's Erast Fandorin novels is a transitional world, that of Russia in the late nineteenth century, some two decades before the Russian Revolution. Akunin's readers also are in transition, moving away from the Soviet era. For years, the Soviet government discouraged people from reading detective fiction, a genre it considered decadent. Even after the end of the communist regime, many citizens, including Akunin's wife, were still influenced by the Soviet assessment. Akunin set for himself the goal of introducing middle-class readers to a new type of story midway between the great literature of Tolstoy and Dostoevski and the pulp fiction that many Russians read in secret. Russians can now read to be entertained rather than fed the party line, and perhaps more important, Akunin's readers can find a link to the national past that the Soviets maligned.

Akunin wanted the Fandorin series to portray a wide range of character types and historical settings. The cast of characters includes actual historical figures as well as fictional creations closely modeled on real-life people. Fandorin's physical description is reportedly based on a portrait of a relative of Peter Ilich Tchaikovsky's patroness that Akunin purchased cheaply in a Moscow flea market. The settings for the novels include the Russo-Turkish War, the coronation of Czar Nicholas II, and Paris in the 1870's. However, these stories cannot claim total historical accuracy, for Akunin makes his readers feel at home by filling gaps in historical knowledge with his imagination. Above all, inspired by the great authors of the nineteenth century, these stories capture the ambiance of those magnificent and strange times.

Akunin seeks to orient his readers in a culture dating before the Soviet era; however, the settings are also a commentary on twenty-first century Russia. For example, in *Smert' Akhilesa* (2000; *The Death of Achilles*, 2006), he describes the graft and bribery that surround the building of the cathedral of Christ the Savior in the nineteenth century. According to Akunin, the same type of graft and bribery are occurring as that cathedral is being restored in the twenty-first century. Perhaps Akunin intends to erect one of his moral guideposts here, to indicate the possibility of something better than these practices.

Akunin envisioned the Fandorin series as covering all varieties of mystery fiction; each novel was to exemplify a particular subgenre. Each novel has a subtitle indicating which subgenre it represents, such as conspiracy, espionage, or hired killer. Despite Akunin's serious purpose, his narratives display a kind of amusing self-consciousness, as did those of his

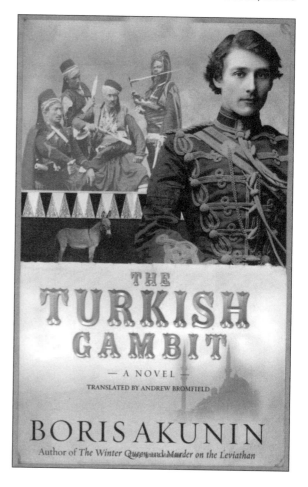

nineteenth century models. For example, his chapters bear subtitles such as "In Which an Account Is Rendered of a Certain Cynical Escapade," and he refers to Fandorin as "our hero." Although he places high value on a coherent plot, he maintains that on some level he writes only for himself, using symbolism and humor that no one else can understand but that please him enormously.

THE WINTER QUEEN

The Winter Queen, the first of the Erast Fandorin series, subtitled "Conspiracy Novel," opens in 1876. Erast Fandorin, twenty years old, has just lost both parents. He joins the Moscow police force, where his first assignment is to look into a student's very public suicide. A second student is murdered, and Fandorin himself narrowly escapes death. The murder investigation leads him to an association governing orphaned boys' schools, to which both students have left generous bequests. This association, led by an English noblewoman, is conspiring to rule the entire world. When Fandorin confronts the Englishwoman, she appears to commit suicide by exploding a bomb. Fandorin has all her coconspirators arrested. Later, another bomb kills the young woman Fandorin has just married, and the story ends with Fandorin walking the streets in shock.

THE TURKISH GAMBIT

Turetski gambit (1998; *The Turkish Gambit*, 2004), set in 1877 during the Russo-Turkish war, is subtitled "Espionage Detective." The secret orders in a telegram from the Russian high command are inexplicably changed, causing the Russian army to waste its effort and the Turks to gain unexpected advantage. A Russian officer is wrongly accused of the crime of tampering with the orders, but Fandorin's remarkable sleuthing unmasks the real culprit, a Turkish secret agent posing as a French journalist. This novel is notable for the number of historical characters and actual events portrayed.

MURDER ON THE LEVIATHAN

Leviafan (1998; *Murder on the Leviathan*, 2004), subtitled "Hermetic Detective" and the third in the Fandorin series, emulates the style of Agatha Christie, with a glamorous setting; extraordinary, secretive characters; and a bizarre murder at the outset. In Paris of 1878, ten people—Lord Littleby, his children, and his servants—are murdered. French detective Gustave Gauche misguidedly follows a clue to the *Leviathan*, a passenger ship on which Fandorin happens to be traveling, headed for a diplomatic assignment in Japan. The aptly named Gauche points the finger at a succession of eccentric but harmless passengers, until Fandorin explodes the Frenchman's theory of the case and solves it himself.

THE DEATH OF ACHILLES

The fourth novel in the Fandorin series, *The Death of Achilles*, is subtitled "Detective of the Hired Killer." Akunin tells this story through the point of view of two characters: Fandorin and his opponent, Achimas. When the two narratives arrive at the same point in time, they merge to reveal the solution.

Fandorin has returned home from a diplomatic assignment in Japan, bringing his Japanese manservant, Masa, whose life he has saved. In Moscow, General Sobolev (called the "Russian Achilles") is found dead of an apparent heart attack; however, Fandorin suspects his longtime friend may have been murdered. He learns that Sobolev was indeed the victim of an ingenious hired killer: Achimas, the same man who killed Fandorin's wife in *The Winter Queen*. Fandorin kills Achimas in a final confrontation.

Despite the enormous destruction and pain he has caused, Achimas is no stereotyped villain. As portrayed by Akunin, Achimas was orphaned as a child in an environment that constantly threatened his survival. In adulthood, he decides that the only way to ensure his survival is to become a paid assassin. Through this portrayal, Akunin was able not only to create a compelling character for his readers but also, as an author, to explore the inner world of a compassionless hired killer.

Thomas Rankin

PRINCIPAL MYSTERY AND DETECTIVE FICTION

ERAST FANDORIN SERIES: *Azazel'*, 1998, 2000 (*The Winter Queen*, 2003); *Turetski gambit*, 1998 (*The Turkish Gambit*, 2004); *Leviafan*, 1998 (*Murder on the Leviathan*, 2004); *Osobye porucheniya*, 1999 (*Special Assignments: The Further Adventures of Erast Fandorin*, 2007); *Statski sovetnik*, 1999; *Koronatsiia; Ili, Poslednii iz romanov*, 2000; *Smert' Akhilesa*, 2000 (*The Death of Achilles*, 2006); *Liubovnitsa smerti*, 2001; *Liubovnik smert*, 2001; *Almaznaia kolesnitsa*, 2003; *Nefritovie chetki*, 2007

NICHOLAS FANDORIN SERIES: *Altyn-tolobas*, 2000; *Vneklassnoe chtenie*, 2002; *F.M.*, 2006

SISTER PELAGIA SERIES: *Pelagiia i belyi bul'dog*, 2000 (*Pelagia and the White Bulldog*, 2006); *Pelagiia i chernyi monakh*, 2001 (*Pelagia and the Black Monk*, 2007); *Pelagiia i krasni petukh*, 2003

OTHER MAJOR WORKS

NOVEL: *Detskaia kniga*, 2005

SHORT FICTION: *Skazki dlia idiotov*, 2000

NONFICTION (AS CHKHARTISHVILI): *Pisatel' i samoubiistvo*, 1999

BIBLIOGRAPHY

Akunin, Boris. "The Bookish Detective." *The Bookseller* 5110 (January 9, 2004): 32. Interview in which Akunin discusses his reasons for using his novels to create "a kind of encyclopedia of different subgenres of the crime novel" and the love of the grand nineteenth century literary style that led him to set his Erast Fandorin tales in that period.

Babich, Dmitry. "The Return of Patriotism?" *Russia Profile* 2, no. 6 (July, 2005): 34-35. Examines the dilemma of secret agents who, like Erast Fandorin, strive to serve their countries while avoiding complicity with unprincipled government officials.

Baraban, Elena V. "A Country Resembling Russia: The Use of History in Boris Akunin's Detective Novels." *Slavic and East European Journal* 48, no. 3 (Fall, 2004): 396-420. Describes Akunin's historical mysteries as a phenomenon of the search for a Russian national identity.

Finn, Peter. "A Case of Crime and Reward: Mystery Writer a Star in Russia." *Washington Post*, April 23, 2006, p. A15. Explains Akunin's success as a balance between authorial professionalism and a lighthearted approach to his subject.

Khagi, Sofya. "Boris Akunin and Retro Mode in Contemporary Russian Culture." *Toronto Slavic Quarterly* 18 (Fall, 2006). Analyzes Akunin's work in the light of worldwide literary nostalgia, on which cultural studies have become increasingly focused. Considers the Nicholas Fandorin character's postmodernist perspective as a foil to that of historical Russian figures.

Klioutchkine, Konstantine. "Boris Akunin." In *Dictionary of Literary Biography: Russian Writers Since 1980*. Boulder, Colo.: Gale Group, 2004. Provides biographical information and a critical survey of Akunin's work to 2004. Describes how Akunin's establishment of a middle ground between highbrow literature and pulp fiction led to his own success and to new opportunities for other Russian-language authors.

Parthé, Kathleen. *Russia's Dangerous Texts: Politics Between the Lines*. New Haven, Conn.: Yale University Press, 2005. This book by a professor of Russian analyzes the historical influence of Russian literature in shaping national identity and explores post-Soviet changes in Russian literary tradition including the discouragement of "junk reading."

LOUISA MAY ALCOTT

Born: Germantown, Pennsylvania; November 29, 1832

Died: Boston, Massachusetts; March 6, 1888

Also wrote as A. M. Barnard

Types of plot: Psychological; thriller

CONTRIBUTION

Although Louisa May Alcott is best known for her classic and most financially successful novel, *Little Women* (1868), as well as other juvenile literature, she found her greatest enjoyment in writing thrillers that allowed her to push the narrow boundaries that were set for her as a Victorian woman. In works such as *A Long Fatal Love Chase* (written 1866; published 1995) and *A Modern Mephistopheles* (1877), she showed the darker side of human nature, depicting female heroines who either succumbed to the pressures of propriety, conforming to the angelic ideal of womanhood, or triumphed over adversity, using society's expectations of them to outwit their adversaries and escape confinement.

Alcott's work also included nonfictional pieces, such as the popular *Hospital Sketches* (1863), based on her stint as a nurse during the American Civil War, and "How I Went Out to Service," based on her work experiences outside writing. Alcott's novel *Work: A Study of Experience* (1873) was also based on her experiences in low-paying, less-than-satisfying jobs before she was able to not only earn a living but also support her immediate family with the money she

Louisa May Alcott.

spirit to be broken. Like the beloved character Jo in *Little Women*, Alcott actively participated in drama and literature, writing plays and a newspaper based on the childhood capers of her and her three sisters. Although her family was often on the brink of poverty, partly because of her father's novel teaching methods and frequent moves, the family's friendship with Ralph Waldo Emerson, Henry David Thoreau, and Nathaniel Hawthorne, prominent Transcendentalists and Concord residents, contributed to the creative and intellectual richness of the young woman's life. The Alcotts were also active in the abolitionist and suffrage movements. They even made their home a stop on the Underground Railroad and harbored fugitive slaves. Later in life Louisa May Alcott would be the first woman in Concord who registered to vote.

The stress of destitution and the devastating effect it had on the Alcotts after a failed attempt at communal living on a farm her father called Fruitlands made Louisa all the more determined to be successful and support her family, preferably achieving wealth and fame. Her initial plan was to become a great actress. As a teenager she wrote, costumed, directed, and starred in plays. Playwriting led to poetry and then her first novel, *The Inheritance*, written circa 1850 but undiscovered and unpublished until 1997. By her late teens, Alcott had worked a number of low-wage jobs, including governess, teacher, seamstress, laundress, and live-in household servant. More pragmatic than her idealistic father, Alcott was determined to turn her stories into money and learned to be a savvy marketer of her work to various publications.

When her book *Flower Fables* (1854) received reviews approving it as worthwhile literature for young people, Alcott was encouraged to continue writing and published *Hospital Sketches*. When she contracted typhoid fever and pneumonia during her service as a nurse, she was sent home with not only her memories of the soldiers for whom she had cared but also a case of mercury poisoning, a result of the treatment she had received, which would compromise her health for the rest of her life.

These publications were followed by the thrillers that Alcott truly enjoyed writing but were published anonymously or under the pseudonym A. M. Barnard

made from writing. Like the heroines of her novels, Alcott was torn between what was considered a respectable lifestyle and her desire to rebel against it. Although *Little Women*, *Little Men* (1871), and other popular, morally oriented works allowed her to achieve economic independence and some pleasure in providing for her family, it was the thrillers that she wrote before her commercial success that allowed her to at least vicariously experience the freedom her heroines did.

BIOGRAPHY

Louisa May Alcott was born in Germantown, Pennsylvania, on November 29, 1832, to Amos Bronson Alcott and Abigail May Alcott, but she spent most of her life in Massachusetts, mainly Concord and Boston. Considered spirited and willful, she did not fit the image of the ideal, docile child of which her Transcendentalist father approved, but she did not allow her and were not considered as respectable or as economically feasible as her literature written for juveniles. She described her juvenile literature as "moral pap for the young" and grew to resent the intrusions on her privacy that her literary fame engendered. However, she knew that it was the best way to provide economic security for her family, and her fame did allow her to meet such literary luminaries as Charles Dickens and Walt Whitman. Alcott provided not only economic security but also emotional stability for her family. When her sister Anna's husband died, leaving her two children fatherless, Louisa provided for them, and when her sister May died in childbirth, Louisa adopted her niece Lulu. Alcott was also the primary means of support for her mother, who suffered from depression and dementia in her later years, and her father, who grew increasingly dependent on her as he aged. Being single, without children, and financially secure throughout her adult life allowed Alcott to travel widely and live well, but the dependence of others on her and her determination to provide for them significantly curtailed her freedom and caused her a great deal of stress.

By the time of her death from spinal meningitis on March 6, 1888, just a few days after her father died, Alcott's book sales had reached the one million mark, and she had earned approximately two hundred thousand dollars, considered a fortune at the time, for her fiction. She had indeed achieved wealth and fame as a writer.

ANALYSIS

Louisa May Alcott wrote most of her thrillers, or what she called her "blood and thunder" stories and novels, from 1863 to 1868, starting with her story "Pauline's Passion and Punishment," which won a prize. Published anonymously or under a pseudonym, these tales often focused on heroines who defied traditional ideals of Victorian womanhood. Attaching her name to them might have tarnished Alcott's reputation, tainting the image readers later had of the morally impeccable author of *Little Women*.

Similar to Alcott's thrillers, her realistic novel *Moods* (1864) portrayed a lack of opportunities for women to develop their full potential, a recurrent theme throughout her work. Rather than writing serials, however, Alcott presented readers with a new cast of characters for each piece she wrote. Two of her most striking characters, Rosamond Vivian in *A Long Fatal Love Chase*, rejected for publication in 1866 as "too sensational" but rediscovered and published in 1995, and Jean Muir in the novella "Behind a Mask: Or, A Woman's Power," elude the attempts of others to pigeonhole them into certain roles (devoted wife for Rosamond and guileless governess for Jean). It is their successful escapes that thrill the reader. These methods of escape are both geographical and psychological, as the heroines leave the homes with which they are familiar to enter new territory and create new lives for themselves, eluding capture or discovery of identity as they travel and renegotiate their roles.

In another major thriller, *A Modern Mephistopheles*, Alcott departed from her defiant heroines to portray the ideal Victorian woman in Gladys Canaris, the young and naïve devoted wife of a man who is doomed by the total devotion he has pledged to his diabolically manipulative employer in return for attaching his own name to his employer's writing to achieve literary fame. Gladys is a foil to Alcott's other heroines who are determined to be independent despite the attempts of others to control them.

Alcott's sensational stories and novels are characterized by confinement and the attempt to break free from it. Male characters such as Philip Tempest in *A Long Fatal Love Chase* and Jasper Helwyze in *A Modern Mephistopheles* attempt to control the heroines through seduction and threats. Jean Muir emerges victorious, securing wealth and position through marriage, as she has sought to do, but Rosamond is defeated and conquered after a long journey and a case of mistaken identity. Whether they emerge triumphant or defeated, Alcott's heroines reflect the challenges women faced and the obstacles they encountered.

"BEHIND A MASK"

"Behind a Mask" is considered one of Alcott's most shocking thrillers for its portrayal of Jean Muir, a divorced former actress who becomes a governess to accomplish her goal of achieving financial security through marriage to an aristocrat. "Behind a Mask" is the kind of "blood and thunder" tale that Alcott truly enjoyed writing. Because of its sensational nature, it was published under the pseudonym of A. M. Barnard. Just as Jean conceals her true identity to deceive her employers, the Coventrys, Alcott concealed her identity to avoid readers' possible prejudice and judgment of her other works based on this subversive novella.

As the story begins, the wealthy Coventrys are discussing the impending arrival of the new governess, Jean Muir. Their conversation shows the preconceived notions they have of poor but educated unmarried women, who have few job options outside being a governess. When Jean arrives, she is shown playing the role of governess, meekly speaking to the Coventrys with her eyes downcast. Later, when she is alone in her bedroom, the reader sees her with her hair down (literally), and she is described as having features that belong to a woman older than she has presented herself, more cynical and tired than the strict but spirited governess that the Coventrys expected.

As the story progresses, Jean is shown endearing the family to her with her down-to-earth but clever and witty ways. Although the women in the family are suspicious of her motives, the men are won over; two of them even fall in love with her. Rejecting the younger, more impetuous Coventry for the older, titled one, Jean skillfully manipulates Sir John, who is already in love with her, to marry her before the other Coventrys, who have discovered that she is a divorced former actress, can protest, thus securing her position as a member of the landed aristocracy.

In its depiction of a woman who knows what she wants and how to get it, and who will stop at nothing to accomplish her goal, regardless of proprieties, "Behind a Mask" was shocking for its time and surprises readers even now with its unapologetically manipulative heroine and what appears to be Alcott's refusal to judge her as she emerges triumphant.

A LONG FATAL LOVE CHASE

Confinement versus freedom is a recurrent theme in Alcott's thrillers, and in *A Long Fatal Love Chase*, that theme is personified in the character of Rosamond Vivian. Living on a remote island under the custody of her grandfather, a recluse who barely tolerates her out of a sense of obligation, Rosamond longs for adventure. When the aptly named Philip Tempest, an acquaintance of her grandfather, arrives on the scene, she is captured by his charm, good looks, and stories about his adventures. When he challenges her to go away with him on his boat and travel to distant lands without the security net of marriage, she balks, but when he tricks her into boarding his boat and sails away with her, she adjusts to the idea and becomes less concerned about the lack of propriety.

When Rosamond discovers that Philip is already married and that his assistant on the boat is actually his son, she flees and encounters a series of characters who aid and abet her as she eludes the vengeful Philip, who shows up when he is least expected, startling readers and Rosamond, who must continually think of ways to conceal her identity and escape to the next refuge. She must also resist believing his promises that he will divorce his wife so that they can live as happily as they did before his deception was discovered.

The tragedy of the story lies in the mistaken identity that leads to Rosamond's death. When she finally reaches her grandfather's home, having come full circle in this adventure, she and her companion, a monk who has helped her and come to love her, are on separate boats, and Philip mistakes Rosamond's boat for that of her companion, crashing into it and causing Rosamond to drown. Like other Alcott heroines, Rosamond does get what she wants, namely peace and refuge from Philip, but at the cost of her life. In this manner Alcott showed the lengths to which women had to go to escape the confinements of society, only to have their lives end in tragedy.

Holly L. Norton

PRINCIPAL MYSTERY AND DETECTIVE FICTION

NOVELS: *A Modern Mephistopheles*, 1877; *A Long Fatal Love Chase*, 1995 (written 1866)

SHORT FICTION: *A Double Life: Newly Discovered Thrillers of Louisa May Alcott*, 1988; *Freaks of Genius: Unknown Thrillers of Louisa May Alcott*, 1991; *Louisa May Alcott Unmasked: Collected Thrillers*, 1995

OTHER MAJOR WORKS

NOVELS: *Moods*, 1864; *Little Women, Part 2*, 1869 (also known as *Good Wives*, 1953); *Work: A Study of Experience*, 1873; *Diana and Persis*, 1879;

Jack and Jill, 1880; *Jo's Boys, and How They Turned Out*, 1886; *The Inheritance*, 1997 (written c. 1850)

SHORT FICTION: *On Picket Duty, and Other Tales*, 1864; *Morning Glories, and Other Stories*, 1867; *Aunt Jo's Scrap-Bag*, 1872-1882 (6 volumes); *Silver Pichers: And Independence, a Centennial Love Story*, 1876; *Spinning-Wheel Stories*, 1884; *A Garland for Girls*, 1887; *Lulu's Library*, 1895; *Alternative Alcott*, 1988; *Louisa May Alcott: Selected Fiction*, 1990; *From Jo March's Attic: Stories of Intrigue and Suspense*, 1993; *The Early Stories of Louisa May Alcott, 1852-1860*, 2000

PLAYS: *Comic Tragedies Written by "Jo" and "Meg" and Acted by the "Little Women,"* 1893

POETRY: *The Poems of Louisa May Alcott*, 2000

CHILDREN'S LITERATURE: *Flower Fables*, 1854; *Little Women*, 1868; *An Old-Fashioned Girl*, 1870; *Little Men*, 1871; *Eight Cousins*, 1875; *Rose in Bloom*, 1876; *Under the Lilacs*, 1878

NONFICTION: *Hospital Sketches*, 1863; *Life, Letters, and Journals*, 1889 (edited by Ednah D. Cheney); *The Journals of Louisa May Alcott*, 1989; *The Sketches of Louisa May Alcott*, 2001

BIBLIOGRAPHY

Eiselein, Gregory, and Anne K. Phillips, eds. *The Louisa May Alcott Encyclopedia*. Westport, Conn.: Greenwood Press, 2001. Comprehensive collection of information on Alcott, including a chronology; alphabetical entries of words, phrases, and names relating to her life and work; a bibliography of Alcott's writings; a bibliography of critical writings on Alcott; an index; and a list of contributors.

Keyser, Elizabeth Lennox. *Whispers in the Dark: The Fiction of Louisa May Alcott*. Knoxville: University of Tennessee Press, 1995. An examination of the genres in which Alcott wrote, including thrillers, and the ways in which they represent the conventions of Victorian womanhood as well as Alcott's more progressive portrayals of women desiring equality; includes a list of works cited and index.

Shealy, Daniel, ed. *Alcott in Her Own Time: A Biographical Chronicle of Her Life, Drawn from Recollections, Interviews, and Memoirs by Family, Friends, and Associates*. Iowa City: University of Iowa Press, 2005. Collection of writings from the 1840's to 1960 from those who met or were influenced by Alcott and her writings; includes photos of the Alcott family and illustrations from her books.

Stern, Madeleine B. *Louisa May Alcott: A Biography*. Rev. ed. New York: Random House, 1996. Authoritative and descriptive account of Alcott's life and work; includes an Alcott bibliography, notes on sources, and index.

_____. *Louisa May Alcott: From Blood and Thunder to Hearth and Home*. Boston: Northeastern University Press, 1998. Collection of essays tracing Alcott's development and her versatility in moving between domestic and sensational fiction to make a career for herself as a writer. Indexed.

THOMAS BAILEY ALDRICH

Born: Portsmouth, New Hampshire; November 11, 1836
Died: Boston, Massachusetts; March 19, 1907
Type of plot: Police procedural

CONTRIBUTION

Thomas Bailey Aldrich, popular poet and essayist and editor for nine years of *The Atlantic Monthly* (1881-1890), contributed three prose volumes of major interest to readers of detective and mystery fiction: *Out of His Head: A Romance* (1862), *Marjorie Daw and Other People* (1873), and *The Stillwater Tragedy* (1880). An astute literary critic and a diligent student of Edgar Allan Poe, Aldrich was attracted to a detective fiction cloaked most often in moods of the fantastic or the supernatural. A prolific poet in the Romantic style, Aldrich inclined in his fiction to the melodramatic and fanciful, and although he sometimes endeavored to portray local-color backgrounds and to sketch realistic social conditions, his Brahmin aloofness and reserved, patrician attitudes often rendered such efforts artificial and unconvincing. Comparable to the creative strategies of Poe, Aldrich's forays into areas of mystery were generally more successful than his occasional excursions into realism, although in *The Stillwater Tragedy* he employed the conventions of the detective novel to mix the gothic with the realistic. Tone and atmosphere were Aldrich's prime concerns, and his stories and novels with themes of detection and mystery, though few in number, hold a significant place in the evolution of the genre.

BIOGRAPHY

Thomas Bailey Aldrich, whose ancestry went back to the Massachusetts Bay Colony, spent his childhood in Portsmouth, New York City, and New Orleans Many of his experiences of that time were later described in his autobiographical novel, *The Story of a Bad Boy* (1869), a classic tale of an American youth. His education included informal study under the watchful eye of his maternal grandfather Thomas Darling Bailey, whose motley collection of romance novels afforded the bookish youngster an escape into enchanted realms. His formal study was with the revered disciplinarian Samuel De Merritt, a rigid grammarian who helped young Aldrich develop his skill in composition. Aldrich was briefly employed in his uncle's successful counting house, but at the age of nineteen the aspiring author published a volume of poems and accepted a job as a junior literary editor, thus embarking on a lifelong career in letters. Before he was thirty, Aldrich had moved to Boston to edit *Every Saturday*, a post he held until 1874.

Quickly recognized as a poet whose work embodied the genteel tradition, Aldrich became associated with Edmund Clarence Stedman, Richard Henry Stoddard, and Bayard Taylor, writers who were also identified with this popular style that dominated American poetry of the post-Civil War era. His reputation as a leading figure on the literary scene was established emphatically by the early 1870's, when, in addition to his acclaimed verse, his celebration of boyhood touched the hearts of readers of all ages and his tale "Marjorie Daw" captured international audiences. Aldrich married Lilian Woodman in 1865, and in 1868 she gave birth to twin sons.

From 1881 to 1890, Aldrich served as editor of *The Atlantic Monthly*, where he proved himself to be a sharp critic of poetry and a fastidious purist in legislating language principles for his prose authors. He retired to devote his time to writing and traveling. By the advent of the twentieth century, however, Aldrich began to recognize that his philosophy of composition was rapidly going out of fashion; the realism that was anathema to him for its "commonplace, polemic, scientific air" had taken root. He maintained scant interest in those who would "strip illusion of her veil" and "vivisect the nightingale." When the National Academy of Arts and Letters was founded in 1904, however, Aldrich was among the first named to membership. After a brief illness, he died in March, 1907, calmly whispering, "I am going to sleep; put out the lights."

ANALYSIS

Thomas Bailey Aldrich was a true product of the Romantic movement in American letters of the nineteenth century, attracted to the fanciful, the sophisticated, and the exotic. Although life around him was increasingly oriented toward the practical and the materialistic, his major focus, even in tales of mystery, was on the imaginatively created world of shadows and suggestion. His most famous story, "Marjorie Daw," concerns a nonexistent main character who lives entirely in the sensibility of the key correspondent. Heralded abroad and widely anthologized, the story reveals Aldrich's keen sense of popular taste, an awareness that he assiduously cultivated in his job as a magazine editor.

OUT OF HIS HEAD

The gothic world of mystery and detective fiction was thus tailor-made for Aldrich's literary proclivities. *Out of His Head* mirrors the arabesque and the bizarre, the chilling and the gruesome. A series of sketches and reveries, the work purports to be edited by Aldrich from the papers of Paul Lynde, a highly articulate but unfortunate gentleman whose "hereditary peculiarity" necessitates his placement in an asylum. There he composes reminiscences of an adventurous life filled with lost love, misery, illness, disease, and death. Lynde resembles many of Poe's morbid heroes, and his Moon Apparatus, an infernal machine with which he tinkers from time to time, reveals the profundity of his imagination. Most interesting in this work are chapters 10 through 14, which form a complete detective story. The narrative focuses on the discovery of a dead body in a sealed chamber. Depositions reveal the impossibility of suicide, and the authorities are naturally puzzled. Lynde, with his acutely penetrating powers of observation, discerns the murderer but reveals his discovery only to the murderer himself, who, Lynde hopes, will be forever driven by his dark conscience. Lynde himself confesses to the crime simply to experience a new and different ecstasy—that of an innocent man hanged.

Although this ultimate experience is denied him, Lynde's literary ruminations—composed by a person "out of his head" and ranging from witchcraft to a fatal, masked incident at the New Orleans Mardi Gras—establish the editor Aldrich as a master of mood and of what Poe called ratiocination.

Thomas Bailey Aldrich. (Library of Congress)

MARJORIE DAW AND OTHER PEOPLE

The literary specter of Poe hangs heavily over two particular tales in Aldrich's *Marjorie Daw and Other People*, especially in the psychological portraits of the protagonists and the nightmarish scenarios involved. "A Struggle for Life" employs a device frequently used by Poe, that of live burial. The narrator is locked in a tomb with the dead body of his beloved; his terror, plan to escape, and strategy to remain alive are memorably evoked. The atmosphere of the macabre also works well in "The Chevalier de Resseguier," a tale whose tonality resembles that of Poe's famous poem "The Raven." Aldrich describes a dialogue between a bibliophile and a skull he had purchased in a bookstore specializing in works devoted to mesmerism, spiritualism, and other psychic and occult phenomena. In detailing the strange impressions of déjà vu and the melancholy fantasy, Aldrich reveals an adroit mastery of the gothic literary aesthetic, while in sustaining the intensity of the disturbed narrator's emotional state throughout the story, Aldrich demonstrates an understanding of Poe's dictum of the "totality of effect."

THE STILLWATER TRAGEDY

The Stillwater Tragedy was both Aldrich's final novel and his only full-length mystery and detective work. It was carefully planned to examine the dark side of life, for Aldrich had come to believe that readers were paying more attention to somber tones in literature than to graceful, pleasant ones. Aiming at a large readership, this proponent of the genteel tradition now steered his literary strategy toward what for him was the unfamiliar environment of realism by combining a murder tale—then popular in the dime novels of the era—with a contemporary tale of the collision of capital and labor in a small New England industrial town.

Aldrich, disturbed at what he perceived to be foreign ideologies infiltrating and corrupting the American sociopolitical system, spoke strongly against unrestricted immigration. In a poem called "Unguarded Gates," in which he asked, "O Liberty," is it "well to leave the gates unguarded?" he warns, be careful "lest from thy brow the clustered stars be torn/ And trampled in the dust." Stillwater, the locale of the murder in The Stillwater Tragedy, is a community whose American laboring class has been exposed to socialistic doctrines by an influx of European immigrants. Another foreign element has come to the village as well—murder.

The murder victim, whose death is scarcely mourned, is Lemuel Shakford, a litigious miser, a capitalist with many enemies from all classes of society. Shakford's murder is set against the background of a destructive general strike. The volatile mixture of people and events is then compounded by the arrival in Stillwater of Edward Taggett, a big-city sleuth with a considerable reputation.

The appearance of the detective enables Aldrich to expand on the range of Dickensian characters in his cast, for Taggett pops up at various places in the community—socializing at the local tavern, working for a time in disguise as a laborer, and even living in the home of the murder victim. The town's scandalmongers, crime theorists, and general gossips are portrayed by Aldrich as a Greek chorus commenting on the action and suggesting further areas to explore in arriving at a solution. The solemn trance in which Stillwater seems to be suspended—the eerily gabled

murder house and the dreary phantasm of the strange detective at work by lamplight in the silent village—is brilliantly realized. With the settlement of the general strike comes the clever unraveling of the solution, but Taggett needs the help and ingenuity of the dead man's cousin to put things in order and return peace of mind to the troubled people of Stillwater.

Historically important for his work in the mystery and detective genre, Aldrich, in depicting methodical, unorthodox detectives at work, brought to the pages of American literature early prototypes of a character type that was to become a staple of subsequent writers. Aldrich's pronounced ability to create a landscape of mystery and sustain a mood of pervasive suspicion is similarly noteworthy. Finally, in *The Stillwater Tragedy* he fused the style of the genteel romantic purveying the incense "of Arabia and the farther east" with that of the sharp-eyed recorder of a small-town crisis.

Abe C. Ravitz

PRINCIPAL MYSTERY AND DETECTIVE FICTION

NOVEL: *The Stillwater Tragedy*, 1880
SHORT FICTION: *Out of His Head: A Romance*, 1862; *Marjorie Daw and Other People*, 1873

OTHER MAJOR WORKS

NOVELS: *The Story of a Bad Boy*, 1869 (illustrated by Harold M. Brett); *Prudence Palfrey*, 1874; *The Queen of Sheba*, 1877; *The Second Son*, 1888 (with Margaret Oliphant)

SHORT FICTION: *Two Bites at a Cherry, with Other Tales*, 1893; *A Sea Turn and Other Matters*, 1902

POETRY: *The Bells: A Collection of Chimes*, 1855; *The Ballad of Babie Bell, and Other Poems*, 1859; *Cloth of Gold, and Other Poems*, 1874; *Flower and Thorn: Later Poems*, 1877; *Mercedes and Later Lyrics*, 1884; *Wyndham Towers*, 1890; *Judith and Holofernes*, 1896; *Unguarded Gates, and Other Poems*, 1895; *The Poems of Thomas Bailey Aldrich: The Revised and Complete Household Edition*, 1897

NONFICTION: *From Ponkapog to Pesth*, 1883; *An Old Town by the Sea*, 1893; *Ponkapog Papers*, 1903

BIBLIOGRAPHY

Aldrich, Mrs. Thomas Bailey. *Crowding Memories.* Boston: Houghton Mifflin, 1920. Written after Aldrich's death, this biography by his wife presents a noncritical view of the author. The text's greatest value is its anecdotal stories about Aldrich and illustrations of the author, his residences, and his friends.

Bellman, Samuel I. "Riding on Wishes: Ritual Make-Believe Patterns in Three Nineteenth-Century American Authors—Aldrich, Hale, Bunner." In *Ritual in the United States: Acts and Representations.* Tampa, Fla.: American Studies Press, 1985. Discusses Aldrich's creation of an imaginary individual in three stories, "A Struggle for Life," "Marjorie Daw," and "Miss Mehetabel's Son." Argues that "things are not what they seem" is the principle of these three stories, which are presented ritualistically in the form of a hoax or tall tale intended to trap the unwary.

Canby, Henry Seidel. *The Short Story in English.* New York: Henry Holt, 1909. Canby discusses Aldrich, Frank R. Stockton, and H. C. Brunner as the masters of the type of short story of the "absurd situation" and incongruity. Calls Aldrich a stylist who infused his personality into tales of trivia and made them delightful.

Cowie, Alexander. *The Rise of the American Novel.* New York: American Book Company, 1951. Cowie discusses Aldrich's novels, commenting on his narrative style. Calls Aldrich a vital writer whose contribution to American literature can be measured in terms of authenticity.

Davidson, Cathy N. *Revolution and the Word: The Rise of the Novel in America.* New York: Oxford University Press, 2004. Comprehensive history of American fiction, including a chapter on nineteenth century Gothic fiction and individualism. Extremely useful for contextualizing Aldrich's work. Bibliographic references and index.

Greenslet, Ferris. *The Life of Thomas Bailey Aldrich.* 1908. Reprint. Port Washington, N.Y.: Kennikat, 1965. A comprehensive biography of Aldrich. Several chapters detail his youth and apprenticeship, with significant attention given to Aldrich's editorship of *The Atlantic Monthly* during the 1880's and to his novels and poetry. An excellent bibliography and illustrations are included.

Knight, Stephen Thomas. *Crime Fiction, 1800-2000: Detection, Death, Diversity.* New York: Palgrave Macmillan, 2004. Study of two hundred years of crime fiction, comparing the nineteenth and twentieth century practitioners of the genre. Sheds light on Aldrich's work.

O'Brien, Edward J. *The Advance of the American Short Story.* New York: Dodd, Mead, 1931. The originator of *The Best American Short Stories* series discusses Aldrich's responsibility for the vogue of the surprise-ending story in the early twentieth century. Says that although "Marjorie Daw" is flawless, many of Aldrich's stories are "pure sleight of hand."

Pattee, Fred Lewis. *The Development of the American Short Story: An Historical Survey.* New York: Harper and Brothers, 1923. In this important early history of the American short story, Pattee summarizes Aldrich's career and discusses the importance of "Marjorie Daw" in establishing an influential short-story type. Says that the story stood for art that is artless, that it has a Daudet-like grace and brilliance with the air of careless improvisation.

Samuels, Charles E. *Thomas Bailey Aldrich.* New York: Twayne, 1965. A general introduction to Aldrich's life and art; includes a chapter on his short stories and sketches; describes "Marjorie Daw" as a masterpiece of compression that won an instant international reputation for Aldrich. Discusses Aldrich's stories of the fanciful gothic and his taste for the macabre.

GRANT ALLEN
Charles Grant Blairfindie Allen

Born: Kingston, Ontario, Canada; February 24, 1848
Died: Hindhead, Surrey, England; October 28, 1899
Also wrote as Cecil Power; Oliver Pratt Rayner; Martin Leach Warborough; J. Arbuthnot Wilson
Types of plot: Amateur sleuth; inverted

CONTRIBUTION

Grant Allen wrote what he himself acknowledged to be potboilers. Most of his works appeared in serial form in popular magazines such as the *Cornhill* and the *Strand*; they were later republished in collections that revolved around a central character. Of these collections, the most famous is *An African Millionaire* (1897). Its central character, Colonel Clay, has been called "the first great thief of short mystery fiction." Besides being the first English writer of "crook fiction," a type of inverted crime story, Allen may have been the first writer to make use of female sleuths: Miss Cayley, in *Miss Cayley's Adventures* (1899), and Hilda Wade, in the novel named for her (1900).

BIOGRAPHY

Grant Allen was born Charles Grant Blairfindie Allen on February 24, 1848, in Kingston, Canada. He was the second and only surviving son of Joseph Antisell Allen, a minister of the Irish church, and Charlotte Ann Grant, daughter of the fifth baron de Longuiel, a French title recognized in Canada. He was first educated by his father, then by a Yale tutor when the family moved to Connecticut. Later, he was sent to private school in Dieppe, France, at the Collège Impériale. From there, he went on to the King Edwards School, Birmingham, and then to Oxford University, where he received a first-class degree in classical moderations in 1871. While at Oxford, Allen married, but his wife became ill soon after their marriage and died within two years.

In 1873, Allen was appointed professor of mental and moral philosophy at the first university for blacks established in Jamaica. Just before leaving for this post, he married Ellen Jerrad, who accompanied him there. As a teaching position, this appointment was a failure. Most of the students were not literate; they were hardly prepared for a study of "mental and moral philosophy." Allen used his extra time there, however, to formulate his evolutionary system of philosophy.

In 1876, the school collapsed, following the death of its founder, and Allen returned to England. On his return, he supported himself and his family by writing. At first he wrote only scientific essays, but later he began adapting his scientific ideas to a fiction format. His first novel, *Philistia*, was published in 1884. He would go on to write more than thirty works of fiction, including detective novels: *An African Millionaire*, published in 1897; *Miss Cayley's Adventures*, published in 1899; and *Hilda Wade*, published in 1900.

In 1892, Allen had acquired a famous neighbor, Arthur Conan Doyle. Although he and Doyle held diametrically opposed political, social, and religious views, they became good friends. In 1899, Allen, realizing that he was dying, asked Doyle to complete the last two chapters of *Hilda Wade*. Doyle followed through on his promise to do so, though he admitted that he was never happy with the result. Allen died on October 28, 1899, of liver disease. He was survived by his wife and a son.

ANALYSIS

Grant Allen would be surprised, at the very least, to find that he is best remembered as a writer of popular fiction. Allen considered himself a naturalist and a philosopher, a disciple of Herbert Spencer, T. H. Huxley, and Charles Darwin. He began writing short stories as a way to illustrate scientific points. His first published work of fiction, "Our Scientific Observations on a Ghost," for example, was not a ghost story but a tale that showed how people could be led to believe in ghosts. Allen described the further circumstances that led to his becoming a writer of fiction in the preface to *Twelve Tales, with a Headpiece, a Tailpiece, and an Intermezzo, Being Select Stories* (1899).

James Payn, on assuming the editorship of the *Cornhill* magazine, returned one of Allen's scientific articles and at the same time wrote to "J. Arbuthnot Wilson" (one of Allen's pseudonyms) to request more short stories. After this, Allen said he was well "on the downward path which leads to fiction."

One can still see in Allen's fiction the influence of his scientific interests, his evolutionary philosophy, and his antiauthoritarian politics. In fact, he turned some of his later fiction into a forum for his views on society. He was most infamous in his lifetime for the novel *The Woman Who Did* (1895), which presents the radical view that marriage is an unnecessary institution.

Allen's political leanings are evident in his assignment of guilt and innocence. He criticizes the police for seeing only the crime and not the context that may have caused it; in one episode of *Hilda Wade*, for example, a murderer is presented as morally innocent because his wife's personality drove him to murder. On the whole, Allen does not hold the police force or professional detectives in high regard. In fact, in one short story, "The Great Ruby Robbery," as well as one episode of *An African Millionaire*, it is the detective who is the criminal. The worst offenders, for Allen, are members of the upper class, regardless of whether they have broken the law. This view is very clearly expressed in *An African Millionaire*, in which crimes committed by a confidence man against a businessman are presented as morally justifiable.

Allen thought of himself as a supporter of women's rights, though his view that a husband should be excused of the murder of a nagging wife hardly strikes one as liberated. He did believe, however, that women should hold positions in the workforce equal to those of men, and that the English system of chaperoning women was merely another form of imprisonment. These views on women come across most forcefully in his portrayal of strong female characters, especially Miss Cayley of *Miss Cayley's Adventures* and the title character of *Hilda Wade*. Both these heroines could be said to be competing with Sherlock Holmes, as they are probably among the first female detectives to appear in print.

MISS CAYLEY'S ADVENTURES

Of the two works, *Miss Cayley's Adventures* is much more enjoyable and much more consistent in tone. Miss Cayley sets off at the beginning of the novel with twopence to her name, determined to travel around the world and have adventures. She is not disappointed. Among her many exploits are rescuing an Englishwoman from an Arabian harem, shooting tigers in India, and saving her lover from a mountain cliff in Switzerland. The stories never pretend to be grounded in reality, but rather have the spirit of rip-roaring yarns. Miss Cayley is a bold, spontaneous, never-say-die heroine. About to leave England in search of her first adventure, she describes her modus operandi to her more conservative friend Elsie:

I shall stroll out this morning . . . and embrace the first stray enterprise that offers. Our Bagdad teems with enchanted carpets. Let one but float my way, and hi! presto! I seize it. I go where glory or a modest competence waits me. I snatch at the first offer, the first hint of an opening.

Artist Gordon Browne's depiction of Lois Cayley for an 1898 story in The Strand Magazine.

Very soon into her adventures, Miss Cayley meets an extremely wealthy young man, Harold Tillington. Miss Cayley refuses to marry Harold, though, because he is so much richer than she; she vows to marry him only when he is penniless and forlorn. The detective plot serves mostly to bring those circumstances about. Toward the end of the novel, Harold is wrongfully accused of fraud by his cousin, a reprehensible member of the aristocracy. Just before he is led away to prison, Miss Cayley marries him and then proceeds to prove his innocence.

HILDA WADE

Hilda Wade is more centrally concerned with crime and detection. Hilda Wade is on a quest to clear her father of the accusation of murder by proving that the real criminal is a renowned doctor, Sebastian. Hilda Wade is presented as a female version of Sherlock Holmes. She has astonishing powers of intuition that match his powers of deduction. She also has a chronicler and admirer, Dr. Cumberledge, to match Holmes's Watson. When they first meet, she astonishes Cumberledge by seeming to know everything about him.

> The occasion for my astonishment was the fact that when I handed her my card, "Dr. Hubert Ford Cumberledge, St. Nathaniel's Hospital," she had glanced at it for a second and exclaimed, without sensible pause or break, "Oh, then, of course, you're half Welsh, as I am. . . ." "Well, m'yes; I am half Welsh," I replied. . . . "But why *then* and *of course*? I fail to perceive your train of reasoning. . . ." "Fancy asking a woman to give you 'the train of reasoning' for her intuitions! . . . Shall I explain my trick, like the conjurers?"

The reference to "conjurers" is reminiscent of Watson exclaiming over Holmes's deductive powers. Doyle had an even more direct influence on the collection, as he wrote the last two episodes following Allen's death.

Hilda Wade is marred, however, by Allen's heavy reliance on the belief that personality was evidenced by physical traits and genetically determined. The novel is also inconsistent in tone. The opening chapters take a somewhat grim and realistic approach, which seems fitting for an account of Hilda's dogged pursuit of her father's betrayer. Toward the middle of the novel, though, the reader is thrust into a fantastic series of episodes that take Hilda Wade and Dr. Sebastian from South Africa through Tibet. In the final chapters, Sebastian confesses, after having been twice saved by Hilda: first from a dangerous fever in Tibet and then by being pulled from the wreckage of the ship that had been taking them back to England. The novel has none of the light humor that makes both *Miss Cayley's Adventures* and *An African Millionaire* so enjoyable.

AN AFRICAN MILLIONAIRE

An African Millionaire is the book for which Allen is probably best remembered, at least among followers of detective fiction. It has been called the first of the field of "crook fiction," in which the hero is not the detective but his nemesis. Readers are probably more familiar with E. W. Hornung's Raffles, but Allen's Colonel Clay preceded Raffles by three years.

An African Millionaire first appeared in twelve successive issues of the *Strand* magazine, starting in June, 1896. The most notable feature of this series is that each story chronicles robberies committed by the same thief, Colonel Clay, against the same victim, the African millionaire of the title, Sir Charles Vandrift. In each case, Colonel Clay plays on a greedy, self-serving instinct in Sir Charles to line his own pockets. In one episode, for example, the colonel, disguised as a timid parson, agrees to sell Sir Charles some paste-diamond jewelry for two thousand pounds. (The parson will not part with them for less because they belonged to his dear mother.) Sir Charles, however, has realized that they are not paste, but real diamonds and worth much more than two thousand pounds. He complacently believes that he has made a great profit off the parson—until he discovers that he has bought his own stolen diamonds.

Allen portrays Colonel Clay as a sort of modern-day Robin Hood: a confidence man who robs the unethical businessman. Allen's own view of businessmen and landowners is more explicitly stated in his science fiction novel *The British Barbarians: A Hill-Top Novel* (1895). In that novel, a traveler from a utopian future asserts that private ownership is a barbaric institution. In *An African Millionaire*, Colonel Clay echoes this view when he explains his motivation for preying on Sir Charles:

Great fleas have little fleas upon their backs to bite 'em, /And these again have lesser fleas, and so *ad infinitum*!

Well that's just how I view myself. *You* are a capitalist and a millionaire. In *your* large way you prey upon society. . . . In *my* smaller way, again, *I* relieve you in turn of a portion of the plunder.

In general, Allen's critique of the businessman and the Victorian aristocracy is expressed less clumsily in this series of adventures than in the more didactic *The British Barbarians*. In fact, the African Millionaire stories are much more interesting and enjoyable as satires on the British upper class than as whodunits (or perhaps in this case, "how-to-do-its"). In one story, for example, Sir Charles is gulled into buying a castle because he and his wife want to acquire aristocratic roots:

Nice antique hall; suits of ancestral armour, trophies of Tyrolese hunters, coats of arms of ancient counts—the very thing to take Amelia's aristocratic and romantic fancy. The whole to be sold exactly as it stood; ancestors to be included at a valuation.

The note of sarcasm here belongs to the narrator, Sir Charles's brother-in-law, Seymour Wentworth. Seymour is also on Sir Charles's payroll as his secretary, and is therefore on Sir Charles's side rather than Colonel Clay's. Nevertheless, Allen uses him quite successfully as a source of sarcastic asides. By putting the sarcastic voice within the ranks of the wealthy, Allen gives his criticisms more validity.

Aside from the satiric tone, the stories are notable for their various twists on the straightforward confidence-man plot that is established in the first two stories. One such twist occurs in "The Episode of the Arrest of the Colonel," in which Sir Charles hires a private detective from an agency to protect him from Colonel Clay. The private detective, however, proves to be Colonel Clay himself, who thus once again triumphs over the hapless Sir Charles. The superhuman skills that Colonel Clay seems to possess and the sheer audacity required to continue to hunt the same victim make him a highly entertaining figure. To say that Colonel Clay is a master of disguise is an understatement. As Seymour proclaims, he is "polymorphic, like the element carbon." (This is also another jab at Sir Charles, who deals

Grant Allen's Colonel Clay in the June, 1896, issue of The Strand Magazine.

in polymorphic carbon—that is, diamonds.) Besides Clay's appearances as the timid parson and the streetwise private detective, he becomes a Byronic Mexican mind reader, an old German scientist, a Scottish diamond merchant, and a Tyrolese count. The reader, like the much-put-upon Sir Charles, begins to suspect anyone in the stories of being Colonel Clay: "Perhaps we were beginning to suspect him everywhere."

Although for the most part very playful and even nonsensical in mood, the stories also impart a sense of paranoia, of beginning to suspect everyone, everywhere, of being the enemy. Indeed, Colonel Clay begins to resemble a fairly harmless version of Professor Moriarty. These stories seem to point, in a small way, toward a growing feeling at the end of the nineteenth century that the world was a large and unsafe place—a feeling that would reach its fullest expression in the American hard-boiled detective story. When everyone you meet is a stranger, who can you trust?

On the whole, though, Allen's stories have not been greatly influential because they are not widely read. Because they are potboilers, they have all but disappeared from library shelves. In the case of *Hilda Wade*, this disappearance can perhaps be left unmourned, for it has all the worst aspects of the potboiler in being melodramatic, sentimental, and inconsistent in tone. *Miss Cayley's Adventures* and *An African Millionaire*, however, are well worth reviving. In both of these works Allen showed himself to be a good storyteller, a writer of rousing and humorous tales of adventure.

Jasmine Hall

PRINCIPAL MYSTERY AND DETECTIVE FICTION

NOVELS: *Kalee's Shrine*, 1886 (with May Cotes; also known as *The Indian Mystery: Or, Kalee's Shrine*); *For Maimie's Sake: A Tale of Love and Dynamite*, 1886; *A Terrible Inheritance*, 1887; *This Mortal Coil*, 1888; *The Devil's Die*, 1888; *The Jaws of Death*, 1889; *Recalled to Life*, 1891; *What's Bred in the Bone*, 1891; *The Scallywag*, 1893; *Under Sealed Orders*, 1894; *A Splendid Sin*, 1896; *Hilda Wade*, 1900 (with Arthur Conan Doyle)

SHORT FICTION: *Strange Stories*, 1884; *The Beckoning Hand, and Other Stories*, 1887; *Ivan Greet's Masterpiece*, 1893; *A Bride from the Desert*, 1896; *An African Millionaire*, 1897; *Twelve Tales, with a Headpiece, a Tailpiece, and an Intermezzo, Being Select Stories*, 1899; *Miss Cayley's Adventures*, 1899; *Sir Theodore's Guest, and Other Stories*, 1902

OTHER MAJOR WORKS

NOVELS: *Philistia*, 1884; *Babylon*, 1885; *In All Shades*, 1886; *The Sole Trustee*, 1886; *The White Man's Foot*, 1888; *A Living Apparatus*, 1889; *Dr. Palliser's Patient*, 1889; *The Tents of Shem*, 1889; *The Great Taboo*, 1890; *Dumaresq's Daughter*, 1891; *The Duchess of Powysland*, 1891; *Blood Royal*, 1892; *An Army Doctor's Romance*, 1893; *At Market Value*, 1894; *The British Barbarians: A Hill-Top Novel*, 1895; *The Woman Who Did*, 1895; *The Type-Writer Girl*, 1897; *Linnet*, 1898; *The Incidental Bishop*, 1898; *Rosalba: The Story of Her Development*, 1899

SHORT FICTION: *The General's Will, and Other Stories*, 1892; *Desire of the Eyes, and Other Stories*, 1895; *Moorland Idylls*, 1896

POETRY: *The Lower Slopes: Reminiscences of Excursions Round the Base of the Hellicon*, 1894

CHILDREN'S LITERATURE: *Tom, Unlimited: A Story for Children*, 1897

NONFICTION: 1877-1890 • *Physiological Aesthetics*, 1877; *The Colour-Sense: Its Origin and Development—An Essay in Comparative Psychology*, 1879; *Anglo-Saxon Britain*, 1881; *The Evolutionist at Large*, 1881 (revised 1884); *Vignettes from Nature*, 1881; *The Colours of Flowers, as Illustrated in the British Flora*, 1882; *Colin Clout's Calendar: The Record of a Summer, April-October*, 1883; *Flowers and Their Pedigrees*, 1883; *Nature Studies*, 1883 (with others); *Biographies of Working Men*, 1884; *Charles Darwin*, 1885; *Common Sense Science*, 1887; *A Half-Century of Science*, 1888 (with T. H. Huxley); *Force and Energy: A Theory of Dynamics*, 1888; *Falling in Love, with Other Essays on More Exact Branches of Science*, 1889; *Individualism and Socialism*, 1889

1891-1900 • *Science in Arcady*, 1892; *The Tidal Thames*, 1892; *Post-Prandial Philosophy*, 1894; *In Memoriam George Paul Macdonell*, 1895; *The Story of the Plants*, 1895 (also known as *The Plants*); *Cities of Belgium*, 1897 (also known as *Belgium: Its Cities*); *Florence*, 1897 (revised 1906); *Paris*, 1897 (revised 1906); *The Evolution of the Idea of God: An Inquiry into the Origins of Religions*, 1897; *Flashlights on Nature*, 1898; *Venice*, 1898; *The European Tour: A Handbook for Americans and Colonists*, 1899; *Plain Words on the Woman Question*, 1900; *The New Hedonism*, 1900

1901-1909 • *County and Town in England, Together with Some Annals of Churnside*, 1901; *In Nature's Workshop*, 1901; *Evolution in Italian Art*, 1908; *The Hand of God, and Other Posthumous Essays*, 1909

EDITED TEXTS: *The Miscellaneous and Posthumous Works of H. T. Buckle*, 1885; *The Natural History of Selborne*, 1900 (by Gilbert White)

TRANSLATION: *The Attis of Caius Valerius Catullus*, 1892

BIBLIOGRAPHY

Donaldson, Norman. Introduction to *An African Millionaire: Episodes in the Life of the Illustrious Col-*

onel Clay. New York: Dover, 1980. Donaldson describes Clay as the first important rogue character in the short-story crime genre.

Greenslade, William, and Terence Rodgers, eds. *Grant Allen: Literature and Cultural Politics at the Fin de Siècle*. Burlington, Vt.: Ashgate, 2005. Collection of scholarly essays detailing Allen's relationship to fin-de-siècle British culture.

Morton, Peter. *The Busiest Man in England: Grant Allen and the Writing Trade, 1875-1900*. New York: Palgrave Macmillan, 2005. The first critical biography of Allen in a century, this book attempts to solve the mystery of why Allen, a member of a wealthy family, was dependent on his writing to support himself. Discusses not only Allen's life but also freelance authorship and journalism in Victorian England. Bibliographic references and index.

_____, comp. *Grant Allen, 1848-1899: A Bibliography*. St. Lucia: University of Queensland, 2002. This comprehensive bibliography is indispensable for serious students of Allen.

Roth, Marty. *Foul and Fair Play: Reading Genre in Classic Detective Fiction*. Athens: University of Georgia Press, 1995. A post-structural analysis of the conventions of mystery and detective fiction. Examines 138 short stories and works from the 1840's to the 1960's. Briefly mentions Allen and helps place him in context.

Schantz, Tom, and Enid Schantz. "Editors' Note." In *The Reluctant Hangman, and Other Stories of Crime*. Boulder, Colo.: Aspen Press, 1973. Useful commentary on the three stories contained in this special, limited edition that includes the original illustrations from the *Strand* magazine.

MARGERY ALLINGHAM

Born: London, England; May 20, 1904
Died: Colchester, Essex, England; June 30, 1966
Types of plot: Amateur sleuth; espionage; police procedural; thriller; cozy

PRINCIPAL SERIES

Albert Campion, 1929-1969

PRINCIPAL SERIES CHARACTERS

ALBERT CAMPION, an aristocrat, Cambridge University graduate, and amateur sleuth, begins the series as a flippant young man, but as the series progresses, he matures, marries Lady Amanda Fitton, and becomes a father. Thin, pale, well bred, and well tailored, he is the kind of man whom no one clearly remembers. Campion's seeming vacuity masks his brilliant powers of observation and deduction. A considerate and honorable person, he is often referred to as like an uncle in whom everyone confides. Although his full name is never disclosed, Allingham indicates that Campion is the younger son of a duke.

AMANDA FITTON, later Lady Amanda Fitton, eventually becomes Campion's wife. Amanda is first introduced in *Sweet Danger* (1933) as a teenage girl with mechanical aptitude. When she reappears several years later, Campion and the cheerful, daring young woman first pretend to be engaged. As their relationship develops, they proceed to a legitimate engagement and finally to marriage. When Albert returns from the war at the end of *Coroner's Pidgin* (1945), Amanda introduces him to her wartime achievement, their three-year-old son Rupert, who continues to appear in later books and at the end of the series is a graduate student at Harvard University. Amanda becomes an aircraft designer, and even after marriage she continues to rise in her firm, finally becoming a company director.

MAGERSFONTEIN LUGG, Campion's valet, is a former convicted cat burglar whose skills and contacts are now used for legal purposes. A bona fide snob, Lugg tries unsuccessfully to keep Campion out of criminal investigations and up to the level of his ducal forebears.

CONTRIBUTION

Along with Ngaio Marsh, Nicholas Blake, and Michael Innes, Margery Allingham was one of those writers of the 1930's who created detectives who were fallible human beings, not omniscient logicians in the Sherlock Holmes tradition. Her mild-mannered, seemingly foolish aristocrat, Albert Campion, can miss clues or become emotionally entangled with unavailable or unsuitable women. Yet, though his judgment may err, his instincts demonstrate the best qualities of his class. Although Allingham is noted for her careful craftsmanship, for her light-hearted comedy, for her psychological validity, and for such innovations as the gang leader with an inherited position and the inclusion of male homosexuals among her characters, she is most often remembered for her realistic, often-satirical depiction of English society and for the haunting vision of evil that dominates her later novels.

BIOGRAPHY

Margery Louise Allingham was born on May 20, 1904, the daughter of Herbert John Allingham, an editor and journalist, and Emily Jane Hughes, her father's first cousin, who also became a journalist. By the time of her birth, the family lived in Essex, where every weekend they entertained a number of other journalists. Although the young Allingham had two siblings, she spent many of her childhood hours alone, often writing. At seven, Allingham published a story in the *Christian Globe*, a publication of which her grandfather was editor. That year she went away to the first of two boarding schools; she left the second, the Perse School for Girls in Cambridge, when she was fifteen.

Finally, Allingham enrolled in the Regent Street Polytechnic in London as a drama student, but her first novel, *Blackkerchief Dick: A Tale of Mersea Island* (1923), an adventure story set in Essex, had already been accepted for publication, and when her friend Philip "Pip" Youngman Carter convinced her that her talents were more suited to writing than to acting, she left school to work on another novel. In 1927 she married Youngman Carter, who had become a successful commercial artist.

With the publication of her first mystery novel, *The White Cottage Mystery*, in 1928, Allingham settled into her career. In *The Crime at Black Dudley* (1929), she introduced Albert Campion, the amateur detective who was to appear in all the mystery novels that followed.

In 1929, Allingham and her husband moved to Essex; in 1934, they purchased their own home, D'Arcy House, expecting to live and work quietly in the little village of Tolleshunt D'Arcy. World War II soon broke out, however, and with Essex an obvious invasion target, Allingham became active in civil defense, while her husband joined the army. Her autobiographical book *The Oaken Heart* (1941) describes the fear and the resolution of Britons such as herself during the first months of the war. In 1944, Allingham returned to her mysteries. She and her husband made periodic visits to their flat in London but lived in D'Arcy House for the rest of their lives. Between 1929, when she wrote the

In Margery Allingham's tenth Albert Campion novel, her amateur sleuth investigates the murder of an old school bully named "Pig" Peters. (Courtesy, Random House)

first Campion mystery, and her early death of cancer on June 30, 1966, Allingham worked steadily, averaging almost a volume a year, primarily novels but also novellas and collections of short stories. Before her husband's death in 1970, he completed *Cargo of Eagles* (1968) and wrote two additional Campion novels.

ANALYSIS

After her pedestrian story of police investigation, *The White Cottage Mystery*, which she later removed from her list of works, Margery Allingham hit on a character who would dominate her novels and the imaginations of her readers for half a century. He was Albert Campion, the pale, scholarly, seemingly ineffectual aristocrat whom she introduced in *The Crime at Black Dudley*. As Allingham herself commented, the changes in Campion's character that were evident over the years reflected changes in the author herself, as she matured and as she was molded by the dramatic events of the times through which she lived.

When Allingham began to write her novels in the 1920's, like many of her generation she had become disillusioned. Unable to perceive meaning in life, she decided to produce a kind of novel that did not demand underlying commitment from the writer or deep thought from the reader, a mystery story dedicated to amusement, written about a witty, bright group of upper-class people who passed their time with wordplay and pranks—and occasionally with murder. In Allingham's first novels, Albert Campion is somewhat like P. G. Wodehouse's Bertie Wooster, pursuing one girl or another while he attempts to outwit an opponent. The fact that Campion's opponent is a murderer is not particularly significant; he is an intellectual antagonist, not a representative of evil. Furthermore, most of the action itself is comic.

LOOK TO THE LADY

In *Look to the Lady* (1931), for example, a formidable country matron abandons her tweeds and pearls for the garb of a mystical priestess, presiding over the rites of the Gyrth Chalice. In her costume, she is hilarious, a target of satire; when she is found dead in the woods, she is of far less interest, and the solution of her murder is primarily an exercise of wit, rather than the pursuit of justice.

DEATH OF A GHOST

With *Death of a Ghost*, in 1934, Allingham's books become less lighthearted but more interesting. Her prose is less mannered and more elegant, her plots less dependent on action and more dependent on complex characterization, her situations and her settings chosen less for their comic potentiality and more for their satiric possibilities. *Death of a Ghost* is the first book in which Allingham examines her society, the first of several in which the world of her characters is an integral part of the plot. Before the murder takes place in *Death of a Ghost*, Allingham must create the world of art, complete with poseurs and hangers-on, just as later she will write of the world of publishing in *Flowers for the Judge* (1936), that of the theater in *Dancers in Mourning* (1937), and finally that of high fashion in *The Fashion in Shrouds* (1938).

Just as Allingham becomes more serious, so does Albert Campion, who abandons even the pretext of idiocy, becoming simply a self-effacing person whose modesty attracts confidences and whose kindness produces trust. In *Sweet Danger* he meets the seventeen-year-old mechanical genius Amanda Fitton. After she reappears in *The Fashion in Shrouds*, Campion's destiny is more and more linked to that of Amanda. If she is good, anyone who threatens her must be evil. Thus, through love Campion becomes committed, and through the change in Campion his creator reflects the change in her own attitude.

TRAITOR'S PURSE

With the rise of Adolf Hitler, it had become obvious that laughter alone was not a sufficient purpose for life. Even the more thoughtful social satire of Allingham's last several books before *Death of a Ghost* was inadequate in the face of brutality and barbarism. Only courage and resolution would defeat such unmistakable evil, and those were the qualities that Allingham dramatized in her nonfictional book about her own coastal Essex village in the early days of the war; those were also the qualities that Albert Campion exhibited in the wartime espionage story *Traitor's Purse* (1941). In that thriller, the forces of evil are dark, not laughable, and the traitorous megalomaniac who is willing to destroy Great Britain to seize power over it is too vicious, too threatening, to evoke satire. Like his country, Albert Campion must stand alone against the odds; with symbolic appropriateness, he has just awakened into bewilderment, aware only that civilization is doomed unless he can defeat its enemies before time runs out.

With *Traitor's Purse*, Allingham abandoned the mystery form until the war was nearly won and she could bring Campion home in *Coroner's Pidgin*. Although for the time being evil had been outwitted and outgunned, Allingham comments that she could never again ignore its existence. The theme of her later novels is the conflict between good and evil. Such works as *The Tiger in the Smoke* (1952) and *Hide My Eyes* (1958) are not based on the usual whodunit formula; early in those books, the criminal is identified, and the problem is not who he is but how he can be caught and punished.

From his first appearance, Campion has worn a mask. In the early, lighthearted comic works, his mask of mindlessness concealed his powers of deduction; in the satirical novels, his mask of detachment enabled him to observe without being observed; in the later works, as a trusted agent of his government, Campion must carefully conceal what he knows behind whatever mask is necessary in the conflict with evil. Clearly the change in Campion was more than mere maturation. As Allingham's own vision of life changed, her view of the mystery story changed, and her detective Campion became a champion in the struggle against evil.

THE CHINA GOVERNESS

The qualities of Allingham's later works are best illustrated in *The China Governess* (1962). The first words of the novel are uttered by a police officer: "It was called the wickedest street in London." Thus, the conflict of good and evil, which is to constitute the action of the book, is introduced. Although the Turk Street Mile has been replaced by a huge housing project, the history of that street will threaten the happiness and the life of Timothy Kinnit. Kinnit, who has recently become engaged, wishes to know his real origins. He was a child of the war, a man who had appeared as a baby among a group of evacuees from Turk Street and was casually adopted by the kindly Eustace Kinnit.

As the novel progresses, past history becomes part of the present. It is in the new apartment house on the site of old Turk Street that a brutal act takes place, the killing of a decent old woman. Yet evil is not confined to Turk Street. During the war, it had followed the evacuees to the Kinnit house in Suffolk, where an East End girl callously abandoned the baby she had picked up so that she might be evacuated from London, a baby whose papers she later used to obtain money under false pretenses. The highly respectable Kinnit family has also not been immune from evil.

In the nineteenth century, a governess in the Kinnit family supposedly committed a famous murder and later killed herself. For one hundred years, the family has kept the secret that is exposed in *The China Governess*: that the murder was actually committed by a young Kinnit girl. At the end of the book, another murderess is unmasked, ironically another governess who is masquerading as a wealthy Kinnit relative and who is finally discovered when she attempts to murder Basil Toberman, a socially acceptable young man who has spitefully plotted to destroy Timothy Kinnit. Thus a typical Allingham plot emphasizes the pervasiveness of evil, which reaches from the past into the present and which is not limited to the criminal classes or to the slums of London but instead reaches into town houses and country estates, pervading every level of society.

The China Governess also illustrates Allingham's effective descriptions. For example, when the malicious Basil Toberman appears, he is "a blue-chinned man in the thirties with wet eyes and a very full, dark-red mouth which suggested somehow that he was on the verge of tears." Thus Allingham suggests the quality of bitter and unjustifiable self-pity that drives Toberman to evil. Later, an intruder who emerges from the slums is described in terms that suggest his similarly evil nature: "He was tall and phenomenally slender but bent now like a foetus . . . He appeared deeply and evenly dirty, his entire surface covered with that dull iridescence which old black cloth lying about in city gutters alone appears to achieve."

Allingham's mastery of style is also evident in her descriptions of setting. For example, on the first page of *The China Governess*, she writes with her usual originality of "The great fleece which is London, clotted and matted and black with time and smoke." Thus metaphor and rhythm sustain the atmosphere of the novel. Similarly, when the heroine is approaching Timothy's supposedly safe country home, the coming danger is suggested by Allingham's description of "a pair of neglected iron gates leading into a park so thickly wooded with enormous elms as to be completely dark although their leaves were scarcely a green mist amid the massive branches."

If evil were limited to the London slums, perhaps it could have been controlled by the police, admirably represented by the massive, intelligent Superintendent Charles Luke. When it draws in the mysterious past and penetrates the upper levels of society, however, Luke welcomes the aid of Albert Campion, who can move easily among people like the Kinnits. In the scene in which Campion is introduced, Allingham establishes his usefulness. Quietly, casually, Campion draws Toberman into an unintentional revelation of character. Because the heroine, who is eavesdropping, has already heard of Campion's sensitivity and reliability, she is ready to turn to him for the help that he gives her, and although he is not omniscient, he sustains her, calms her excitable fiancé, and brilliantly exposes the forces of evil.

Because Allingham builds her scenes carefully, realistically describing each setting and gradually probing every major character, the novels of her maturity proceed at a leisurely pace, which may annoy readers who prefer the action of other mysteries. Allingham is not a superficial writer. Instead, because of her descriptive skill, her satiric gifts, her psychological insight, and her profound dominant theme, she is a memorable one.

Rosemary M. Canfield Reisman
Updated by Fiona Kelleghan

PRINCIPAL MYSTERY AND DETECTIVE FICTION

ALBERT CAMPION SERIES: *The Crime at Black Dudley*, 1929 (also known as *The Black Dudley Murder*); *Mystery Mile*, 1930 (revised 1968); *Look to the Lady*, 1931 (also known as *The Gyrth Chalice Mystery*); *Police at the Funeral*, 1931; *Sweet Danger*, 1933 (also known as *Kingdom of Death* and *The Fear Sign*); *Death of a Ghost*, 1934; *Flowers for the Judge*, 1936

(also known as *Legacy in Blood*); *Dancers in Mourning*, 1937 (also known as *Who Killed Chloe?*); *Mr. Campion, Criminologist*, 1937; *The Case of the Late Pig*, 1937; *The Fashion in Shrouds*, 1938 (revised 1965); *Mr. Campion and Others*, 1939 (revised 1950); *Traitor's Purse*, 1941 (also known as *The Sabotage Murder Mystery*); *Coroner's Pidgin*, 1945 (also known as *Pearls Before Swine*); *The Case Book of Mr. Campion*, 1947; *More Work for the Undertaker*, 1949 (revised 1964); *The Tiger in the Smoke*, 1952; *The Beckoning Lady*, 1955 (also known as *The Estate of the Beckoning Lady*); *Hide My Eyes*, 1958 (also known as *Tether's End* and *Ten Were Missing*); *Three Cases for Mr. Campion*, 1961; *The China Governess*, 1962; *The Mind Readers*, 1965; *Cargo of Eagles*, 1968 (with Youngman Carter); *The Allingham Case-Book*, 1969

NONSERIES NOVELS: *The White Cottage Mystery*, 1928 (revised 1975); *Six Against the Yard*, 1936 (with others); *Black Plumes*, 1940; *Take Two at Bedtime*, 1950 (also known as *Deadly Duo*)

OTHER SHORT FICTION: *Wanted: Someone Innocent*, 1946; *No Love Lost*, 1954

OTHER MAJOR WORKS

NOVELS: *Blackkerchief Dick: A Tale of Mersea Island*, 1923; *Dance of the Years*, 1943 (also known as *The Gallantrys*)

PLAYS: *Dido and Aneas*, pr. 1922; *Water in a Sieve*, pb. 1925

NONFICTION: *The Oaken Heart*, 1941

BIBLIOGRAPHY

Gaskill, Rex W. "Margery Allingham." In *And Then There Were Nine . . . More Women of Mystery*, edited by Jane S. Bakerman. Bowling Green, Ohio: Bowling Green State University Popular Press, 1985. Examines Allingham's place in the canon of female mystery writers. Bibliographic references.

Krutch, Joseph Wood. "Only a Detective Story." In *The Art of the Mystery Story: A Collection of Critical Essays*, edited by Howard Haycraft. Reprint. New York: Carroll and Graf, 1992. Entry discussing Allingham's works in a widely cited and reprinted collection of essays. Bibliographic references and index.

Malmgren, Carl D. *Anatomy of Murder: Mystery, Detective, and Crime Fiction.* Bowling Green, Ohio: Bowling Green State University Popular Press, 2001. Discusses Allingham's *The Tiger in the Smoke.* Bibliographic references and index.

Martin, Richard. *Ink in Her Blood: The Life and Crime Fiction of Margery Allingham.* Ann Arbor, Mich.: UMI Research Press, 1988. Study alternates between biographical chapters and chapters of criticism analyzing the works Allingham produced during the period of her life chronicled in the previous chapter. Bibliography and index.

Pike, B. A. *Campion's Career: A Study of the Novels of Margery Allingham.* Bowling Green, Ohio: Bowling Green State University Popular Press, 1987. Focuses on the representation of Albert Campion and his relationship to other fictional sleuths.

Reynolds, Moira Davison. *Women Authors of Detective Series: Twenty-one American and British Authors, 1900-2000.* Jefferson, N.C.: McFarland, 2001. Examines the life and work of major female mystery writers, including Allingham.

Rowland, Susan. *From Agatha Christie to Ruth Rendell: British Women Writers in Detective and Crime Fiction.* New York: Palgrave, 2001. Allingham is the third of the three major figures discussed in this study, as her novels are compared with those of Christie and Rendell. Bibliographic references and index.

Thorogood, Julia. *Margery Allingham: A Biography.* London: Heinemann, 1991. Discusses the lives of both Allingham and her fictional creation, Campion. Bibliographic references and index.

ERIC AMBLER

Born: London, England; June 28, 1909
Died: London, England; October 22, 1998
Type of plot: Espionage

CONTRIBUTION

Eric Ambler has been called the virtual inventor of the modern espionage novel, and though this is an oversimplification, it suggests his importance in the development of the genre. When he began to write spy novels, the genre was largely disreputable. Most of its practitioners were defenders of the British social and political establishment and right wing in political philosophy. Their heroes were usually supermen graced with incredible physical powers and a passionate devotion to the British Empire, and their villains were often satanic in their conspiracies to achieve world mastery. None of the protagonists in Ambler's eighteen novels is a spy by profession; the protagonists are recognizably ordinary, and Ambler's realistic plots were based on what was actually occurring in the world of international politics. In addition, because he was a craftsman, writing slowly and revising frequently, he succeeded in making the espionage genre a legitimate artistic medium.

Many of Ambler's works have been honored. For example, *Passage of Arms* (1959) earned the Crime Writers' Association's Crossed Red Herrings Award; *The Levanter* (1972) also won the Gold Dagger; and *The Light of Day* (1962) was awarded the 1964 Edgar for best novel by the Mystery Writers of America. In 1975 Ambler was named a Grand Master by the Mystery Writers of America and in 1986 he was awarded the Crime Writers' Association's Cartier Diamond Dagger for lifetime achievement. In 1987, his autobiography *Here Lies: An Autobiography* (1985) received an Edgar Award for best critical/biographical work.

BIOGRAPHY

Eric Clifford Ambler was born in London on June 28, 1909, the son of Alfred Percy Ambler and Amy Madeline Ambler, part-time vaudevillians. He attended Colfe's Grammar School and in 1926 was awarded an engineering scholarship to London University, though he spent much of his time during the two years he was there reading in the British Museum, attending law-court sessions, and seeing films and plays. In 1928 he abandoned his education to become a technical trainee with the Edison Swan Electric Company, and in 1931 he entered the firm's publicity department as an advertising copywriter. A year later, he set himself up as a theatrical press agent, but in 1934 he returned to advertising, working with a large London firm.

Throughout this period, Ambler was attempting to find himself as a writer. In 1930 he teamed up with a comedian, with whom he wrote songs and performed in suburban London theaters. In 1931 he attempted to write a novel about his father. Later, he wrote unsuccessful one-act plays. In the early 1930's he traveled considerably in the Mediterranean, where he encountered Italian fascism, and in the Balkans and the Middle East, where the approach of war seemed obvious to him.

In 1936 Ambler published his first novel of intrigue, *The Dark Frontier*, quit his job, and went to Paris, where he could live cheaply and devote all of his time to writing. He became a script consultant for Hungarian film director/producer Alexander Korda in 1938 and published six novels before World War II.

Ambler joined the Royal Artillery as a private in 1940 but was assigned in 1942 to the British army's combat photography unit. He served in Italy and was appointed assistant director of army cinematography in the British War Office. By the end of the war, he was a lieutenant colonel and had been awarded an American Bronze Star. His wartime experience led to a highly successful career as a screenwriter. He would spend eleven years in Hollywood before moving to Switzerland in 1968. Meanwhile, he resumed novel writing with *Judgment on Deltchev* (1951), the first of his postwar novels. In 1981 he was named an officer of the order of the British Empire. He died in London in 1998.

ANALYSIS

At the beginning of his career, Eric Ambler knew that his strengths were not in the construction of the ingenious plots required in detective fiction. As he was seeking to establish himself as a writer of popular fiction, his only course was the espionage thriller; its popularity in Great Britain was the result of public interest in the secret events of World War I and apprehension about Bolshevism. These concerns were enhanced by the most popular authors in the field—John Buchan, whose Richard Hannay was definitely an establishment figure, and Sapper (the pen name of H. Cyril McNeile), whose Bulldog Drummond stories were reactionary, if not downright fascist, in tone.

Ambler found neither these writers' heroes nor their villains believable, and he viewed their plots, based on conspiracies against civilization, as merely absurd. Having seen fascism in his travels in Italy, he was radically if vaguely socialist in his own political attitudes, and his study of psychology had made it impossible for him to believe that realistically portrayed characters could be either purely good or purely evil.

Ambler decided, therefore, to attempt to write novels that would be realistic in their characters and depictions of modern social and political realities; he also would substitute his own socialist bias for the conservatism—or worse—of the genre's previous practitioners.

THE DARK FRONTIER

His first novel, *The Dark Frontier*, was intended, at least in part, as a parody of the novels of Sapper and Buchan. As such, it may be considered Ambler's declaration of literary independence, and its premises are appropriately absurd. A mild-mannered physicist who has been reading a thriller suffers a concussion in an automobile accident and regains consciousness believing that he is the superhero about whom he has been reading. Nevertheless, the novel also reveals startling prescience in its depiction of his hero's antagonists—a team of scientists in a fictitious Balkan country who develop an atomic bomb with which they intend to blackmail the world. Ambler's technical training had made him realize that such a weapon was inevitable, and though he made the process simpler than it later proved to be, his subject was clearly more significant than his readers could realize.

Though Ambler sought consciously in his first works to turn the espionage genre upside down, he was quite willing to employ many of the elements used by his popular predecessors. Like Buchan's Richard Hannay, his early protagonists were often men trapped by circumstances but willing to enter into the "game" of spying with enthusiasm and determination. In his next three novels, *Background to Danger* (1937), *Epitaph for a Spy* (1938), and *Cause for Alarm* (1938), he set his plots in motion by the device Buchan employed in *The Thirty-nine Steps* (1915). His naïve hero blunders into an international conspiracy, finds himself wanted by the police, and is able to clear himself only by helping to unmask the villains.

What makes these novels different, however, is Ambler's left-wing bias. The villains are fascist agents, working on behalf of international capitalism, and in *Background to Danger* and *Cause for Alarm* the hero is aided by two very attractive Soviet agents. In fact, these two novels must be considered Ambler's contribution to the cause of the popular front; indeed, one of the Soviet agents defends the purge trials of

1936 and makes a plea for an Anglo-Soviet alliance against fascism.

JOURNEY INTO FEAR

Ambler's most significant prewar novels, however, are *A Coffin for Dimitrios* (1939) and *Journey into Fear* (1940). The latter is very much a product of the "phony war" of the winter of 1939-1940, when a certain measure of civilized behavior still prevailed and the struggle against fascism could still be understood in personal terms. The ship on which the innocent hero sails from Istanbul to Genoa is a microcosm of a Europe whose commitment to total war is as yet only tentative. Ambler perfectly captures this ambiguous moment, and Graham, his English hero, is, in a sense, an almost allegorical representation of Great Britain itself, seeking to discover allies in an increasingly hostile world.

A COFFIN FOR DIMITRIOS

A Coffin for Dimitrios is Ambler's most important prewar work, a novel that overturns the conventions of the espionage thriller while simultaneously adopting and satirizing the conventions of the detective story. His protagonist, Charles Latimer, is an English writer of conventional detective stories. In Istanbul, he meets one of his fans, a colonel of the Turkish police, who gives him a foolish plot ("The butler did it") and tells him about Dimitrios Mackropoulos, whose body has washed ashore on the Bosporus.

A murderer, thief, drug trafficker, and white slaver, Dimitrios fascinates Latimer, who sets out on an "experiment in detection" to discover what forces created him. Latimer discovers, as he follows the track of Dimitrios's criminal past through Europe, that Dimitrios is still alive, a highly placed international financier who is still capable of promoting his fortunes by murder. As Latimer comes to realize, Dimitrios is an inevitable product of Europe between the wars; good and evil mean nothing more than good business and bad business. Nevertheless, when Dimitrios has finally been killed, Latimer returns to England to write yet another detective story set in an English country house, even though the premises of his story—that crime does not pay and that justice always triumphs—have been disproved by Dimitrios.

SCREENWRITING AND A HIATUS

Ambler's career as a novelist was interrupted by World War II and by a highly successful career as a screenwriter. Among the many screenplays he wrote are *The Cruel Sea* (1953), which won him an Oscar nomination; *A Night to Remember* (1958), adapted from Walter Lord's 1956 book about the sinking of the *Titanic*; and *Mutiny on the Bounty* (1962). Several of his own novels were adapted into films, as well. *Journey into Fear* was filmed in 1942, directed by and starring Orson Welles, and was re-adapted in 1974. *Epitaph for a Spy* 1938 was adapted to film in 1943 as *Hotel Reserve*, starring James Mason, and *Background to Danger* (1943) starred George Raft, Sydney Greenstreet, and Peter Lorre. *The Mask of Dimitrios*, starring Sydney Greenstreet and Peter Lorre, was filmed in 1944, and *The Light of Day* was adapted as *Topkapi* in 1964.

When Ambler resumed writing novels after an eleven-year hiatus, the world had changed radically. In a sense, the world of the 1930's, though confusing to Ambler's protagonists, was morally simple: Fascism was an easily discerned enemy. By the early 1950's, however, the atomic spies, the revelations of Igor Gouzenko, the Philby conspiracy, and the ambiguities and confusions of the Cold War made the espionage novel, in Ambler's view, a much different phenomenon. For the most part, therefore, his later novels have nothing to do with the conflict between East and West and are usually set on the periphery of the Cold War—in the Balkans, the Middle East, the East Indies, Africa, or Central America. Furthermore, the narrative methods in the later works are more complex, frequently with no single narrative voice, and the tone is sometimes cynical.

JUDGMENT ON DELTCHEV

In 1950 Ambler began collaborating with Charles Rodda (under the pseudonym Eliot Reed) on five novels, but his own novels earned more attention. *Judgment on Deltchev*, his first solo postwar novel, was inspired by the trial of Nickola Petkov, who had been charged with a conspiracy to overthrow the Bulgarian government. Ambler set the novel in an unidentified Balkan country; the novel has little to do with the larger concerns of the Cold War, although its political background is clearly presented as a conflict between "progressives" and reactionaries and Deltchev is accused of attempting to betray his country to "the Anglo-Americans."

The book was the result of Ambler's effort to find a new medium for the espionage novel, and it went further than any of his prewar novels in developing the premises of *Journey into Fear*. There his protagonist's problem was how to discover among a ship's passengers someone he could trust; in *Judgment on Deltchev*, the plot to assassinate the prime minister is peeled away, layer by layer, as Ambler's narrator, an English journalist, attempts to find out what really happened, again and again discovering the "truth," only to see it dissolve as yet another "truth" replaces it.

THE SCHIRMER INHERITANCE AND STATE OF SIEGE

Ambler's next two novels, which continued to exploit his interest in plots that are not what they seem, are of considerable interest, despite flawed endings. *The Schirmer Inheritance* (1953), about an American lawyer's search for a German soldier who is hiding in Greece, where he fought for the Greek communists after the war, is flawed by an unexplained change of heart by the young woman who accompanies the lawyer as his interpreter; she is manhandled by the German and yet suddenly and without explanation falls in love with him. In *State of Siege* (1956), set in a fictitious country in the East Indies, Ambler develops an apparently real love between his narrator, an English engineer, and a Eurasian girl and then permits him to abandon her when he finally is able to escape from the country.

After this shaky interlude, however, Ambler produced a series of novels that thoroughly explored the possibilities of the novel of intrigue and provided a variety of models for future practitioners.

THE LIGHT OF DAY AND DIRTY STORY

Ambler's usual hero is an average, reasonable person, but in *The Light of Day* and *Dirty Story* (1967), he makes a radical turn. Arthur Abdel Simpson, his Anglo-Egyptian narrator, is an opportunist with few real opportunities. In *The Light of Day*, Simpson, who works as a guide in Athens to pursue his career as a minor thief and pimp, is caught rifling a client's luggage and is blackmailed into cooperating with him. Later, when arms are found behind a door panel of the car he agrees to drive across the Turkish border, the Turkish police force him to cooperate with them. Simpson's neutral position, in between two forces that in his view are equally exploitative and threatening, would seem to be Ambler's comment on the modern dilemma.

In this novel and in *Dirty Story*, in which Simpson is entangled first in the production of pornographic films and then in the politics of Central Africa but survives to become a trader in phony passports, the narrator may be odious, but he is also better than those who manipulate him. The narrator's strategy—to tell people what they want to hear, to play opponents against one another, to survive as best he can—is, Ambler seems to suggest, the same, in a sense, as everyone has been using since 1945.

THE INTERCOM CONSPIRACY

This vision informs *The Intercom Conspiracy* (1969), probably Ambler's most distinguished postwar novel. It is based on an idea that appears frequently in Cold War espionage fiction—that the innocent bystander will find little to choose between the intelligence services of the two sides—while avoiding the mere paranoia that usually characterizes developments of this theme. It deals with the elderly, disillusioned heads of the intelligence services of two smaller North Atlantic Treaty Organization countries; they purchase a weekly newsletter, then feed its editor classified information that is so menacing in nature that the major intelligence agencies must pay for its silence. With this work, Ambler seemed to make the ultimate statement on espionage—as an activity that finally feeds on itself.

THE SIEGE OF THE VILLA LIPP

Ambler's other postwar works continued to exploit the themes he had already developed, but one of them, *The Siege of the Villa Lipp* (1977), is a remarkable experiment, the story of an international banker who launders illegally acquired funds for a variety of criminals. Here Ambler translates the tactics of modern intelligence agencies into the terms of modern business practices, in a sense returning to the premises from which he worked in his earliest fiction. His descriptions of the way banking laws and methods can be manipulated are so complex, however, that the novel too

often reads like an abstract exercise in economics.

All Ambler's novels develop what he has called his primary theme: "Loss of innocence. It's the only theme I've ever written." This seems to suggest his view of the plight of humanity in its confusing predicament during the period that has seen the rise and fall of fascism, the unresolved conflicts of the Cold War, and the increasing difficulty of the individual to retain integrity before the constant growth of the state. The methods that he has employed in the development of this vision, his great narrative skill, his lean and lucid prose, and his determination to anchor the espionage genre firmly within the conventions of modern literary realism, make his achievement the first truly significant body of work in the field of espionage fiction.

Robert L. Berner

PRINCIPAL MYSTERY AND DETECTIVE FICTION

NOVELS: *The Dark Frontier*, 1936 (revised 1990); *Background to Danger*, 1937 (also known as *Uncommon Danger*); *Cause for Alarm*, 1938; *Epitaph for a Spy*, 1938; *A Coffin for Dimitrios*, 1939 (also known as *The Mask of Dimitrios*); *Journey into Fear*, 1940; *Judgment on Deltchev*, 1951; *The Schirmer Inheritance*, 1953; *State of Siege*, 1956 (also known as *The Night-Comers*); *Passage of Arms*, 1959; *The Light of Day*, 1962; *A Kind of Anger*, 1964; *Dirty Story*, 1967; *The Intercom Conspiracy*, 1969; *The Levanter*, 1972; *Doctor Frigo*, 1974; *The Siege of the Villa Lipp*, 1977 (also known as *Send Me No More Roses*); *The Care of Time*, 1981

OTHER MAJOR WORKS

SHORT FICTION: *Waiting for Orders*, 1991 (expanded as *The Story So Far: Memories and Other Fictions*, 1993)

SCREENPLAYS: *The Way Ahead*, 1944 (with Peter Ustinov); *United States*, 1945; *The October Man*, 1947; *The Passionate Friends: One Woman's Story*, 1949; *Highly Dangerous*, 1950; *Gigolo and Gigolette*, 1951; *The Magic Box*, 1951; *The Card*, 1952; *Rough Shoot*, 1953; *The Cruel Sea*, 1953; *Lease of Life*, 1954; *The Purple Plain*, 1954; *Yangtse Incident*, 1957; *A Night to Remember*, 1958; *The Wreck of the Mary Deare*, 1960; *Mutiny on the Bounty*, 1962; *Love Hate Love*, 1970

NONFICTION: *The Ability to Kill, and Other Pieces*, 1963 (essays); *Here Lies: An Autobiography*, 1985

EDITED TEXT: *To Catch a Spy: An Anthology of Favourite Spy Stories*, 1964

BIBLIOGRAPHY

Ambrosetti, Ronald J. *Eric Ambler*. New York: Twayne, 1994. A standard biography examining Ambler's life and works.

Cawelti, John G., and Bruce A. Rosenberg. *The Spy Story*. Chicago: University of Chicago Press, 1987. A useful genre study that provides background for understanding Ambler.

Eames, Hugh. *Sleuths, Inc.: Studies of Problem Solvers—Doyle, Simenon, Hammett, Ambler, Chandler*. Philadelphia: J. B. Lippincott, 1978. Discusses Ambler's distinctive approach to his genre and his relationship to other notable mystery writers.

Hitz, Frederick P. *The Great Game: The Myth and Reality of Espionage*. New York: Alfred A. Knopf, 2004. Hitz, the former inspector general of the Central Intelligence Agency, compares famous fictional spies and spy stories—including those of Ambler—to real espionage agents and case studies to demonstrate that truth is stranger than fiction.

Horsley, Lee. *The Noir Thriller*. New York: Palgrave, 2001. Focused genre study places Ambler in relation to his fellow practitioners of the noir thriller. Covers four of Ambler's novels produced between 1936 and 1940.

Lewis, Peter. *Eric Ambler*. New York: Continuum, 1990. The first full-length study of Ambler.

Wolfe, Peter. *Alarms and Epitaphs: The Art of Eric Ambler*. Bowling Green, Ohio: Bowling Green State University Popular Press, 1993. A very good, full-length critical study.

CHARLOTTE ARMSTRONG

Born: Vulcan, Michigan; May 2, 1905
Died: Glendale, California; July 18, 1969
Also wrote as Jo Valentine
Types of plot: Thriller; psychological; amateur sleuth; cozy

PRINCIPAL SERIES

MacDougal Duff, 1942-1945

PRINCIPAL SERIES CHARACTER

MacDougal Duff is a retired history teacher who has become an amateur detective. He is Scottish, unmarried, and middle-aged, with the reputation of "being able to see through a stone wall," although his main instrument for finding solutions is common sense.

CONTRIBUTION

The majority of Charlotte Armstrong's suspense works detail the perilous voyage of an innocent person who, often by chance, is drawn into an underground world of intrigue and terror. Her stories revolve around whether something will be found or found out before a time limit is reached. Interest is centered on whether something will be done in time rather than on how a problem will be solved. In an innovative manner, she generally traces the progress of both the heroes and the villains as they work to obtain the same goal. Thematically, her fiction brings up a debate between a hard-boiled postwar cynicism and a sentimental idealism; it chronicles the mental distress of a major character who has to forge his own philosophy based on a synthesis of these two attitudes. Her prose also represents a synthesis of these strands, and though generally terse and tense, it is relieved with touches of humor.

Armstrong blends elements from Cornell Woolrich, in the way she reveals a violent underside to the everyday world, and Shirley Jackson, in the way she carefully constructs a dark atmosphere and in her expert character portraiture. Her strong female characters prefigure the independent female characters who were to emerge more fully later in the century, and her frequent use of occult themes anticipated the penchant for the supernatural in popular fiction that was to emerge in the 1970's.

BIOGRAPHY

Charlotte Armstrong was born on May 2, 1905, in Vulcan, Michigan, to Frank Hall Armstrong and Clara Pascoe Armstrong. Her mother was Cornish. Her father was of Yankee stock, an engineer at an iron mine. In her autobiographical novel *The Trouble in Thor* (1953), the character based on her father, the engineer Henry Duncane, is a kind of amateur detective. In exploring a problem in the mine, Duncane

> never seemed to fumble. If he did not at once perceive the source of trouble and its remedy, he at once began to look for it. And Duncane's groping was so full of purpose; he hunted for cause with such order and clarity, that he was totally reassuring.

Armstrong attended high school in her hometown and went on to the University of Wisconsin, completing her bachelor of arts degree at Barnard College in 1925. She became a career woman in New York City. Her first job was selling classified advertisements over the telephone at *The New York Times*. She also worked as a fashion reporter and a secretary in an accounting firm. On January 21, 1928, she married Jack Lewi, an advertising man.

Armstrong retired to private life and eventually to the rearing of three children, managing to write in her spare moments. She began with poems and then moved to plays. Her tragedy, *The Happiest Days* (pr. 1939), and her comedy, *Ring Around Elizabeth* (pr. 1941), were both produced on Broadway. Neither did well at the box office, but while the second was in rehearsal, she sold her first mystery, *Lay on, Mac Duff!* (1942).

This and her next two novels were of the amateur investigator type and were moderately well received, but she seemed to find her métier with *The Unsuspected* (1946), which was a work of suspense. This work was filmed in 1947, and she relocated to Holly-

wood with her family from New Rochelle, New York, to supervise the screenplay.

The family remained in California, living in Glendale, and Armstrong continued writing. Her novel *Mischief* (1950) was adapted for film as *Don't Bother to Knock* (1952). In 1957, she received the Mystery Writers of America's Edgar Allan Poe Award for her novel *A Dram of Poison* (1956). Armstrong died after an illness on July 18, 1969, at Memorial Hospital in Glendale, California.

ANALYSIS

Marilyn Monroe brutally strikes her uncle from behind with an ashtray. A dead look is in her eyes. This is one nightmarish scene from the film *Don't Bother to Knock*. Charlotte Armstrong's works were particularly suitable for film treatment because of her tight plotting, her skill at cutting back and forth between the actions of different characters as the work builds toward a climax, and her use of visually striking images. Furthermore, her themes were those that were found in film noir of the 1940's and 1950's. She often described how an innocent character was drawn into a web of intrigue and murder, or she described the machinations of a manipulative, controlling, and murdering father figure.

To illustrate how easily an average person could be led astray, Armstrong often opened with some trivial event that became the first in a series of events that led inexorably into a troubling underworld. Even in her early, amateur detective works—*Lay on, Mac Duff!*, *The Case of the Weird Sisters* (1943), and *The Innocent Flower* (1945)—she had the sleuth, MacDougal Duff, become accidentally involved in the crime he would have to solve. Yet these novels, which make up the MacDougal Duff series, were not characteristic of her mature work, in which she focused on how an average person had to call up his own resources to escape or solve a crime.

THE WITCH'S HOUSE

Typical of these works in which the opening emphasized the way an average citizen can be caught in an undertow is *The Witch's House* (1963). Professor O'Shea is leaving his office and notices a colleague slipping something into his pocket. It looks like a stolen microscope part. Unable to question or even stop the observed professor in a mob of passing students, O'Shea ends up chasing him in his automobile. The chase leads him into a plot involving blackmail, incest, and murder.

A DRAM OF POISON

Another, even more original strategy Armstrong used to ground a suspense plot might be called the nonopening. *A Dram of Poison* uses this technique. The novel describes the bachelor life of Professor Gibson, chronicles his courtship and marriage to Rosemary James, and finally tells of his disillusionment with his wife. More than half of the novel has passed before the suspense plot proper—in which a disguised bottle of poison is mislaid—begins. All the materials and human predispositions that will lead to a harrowing tale of suspense are rooted in a simple, undramatic tale of a May-December romance.

Armstrong noted that she was not interested in puzzling her readers with a mystery, but in creating suspense. She distinguished between the genres by bringing up the hackneyed scene of a heroine tied to the railroad tracks. According to Armstrong, "If we were to come upon the scene *after* the train has been by, we will be involved in a whodunit." If the work is suspense, the girl has not yet been run over: "It has not happened yet. We, as readers, don't want to see it happen. We fear that it may."

In *The Witch's House*, for example, O'Shea is badly hurt and taken in and concealed by a senile old woman. All the necessary clues are plain to the reader, but the question remains: Will he be located by the people who are searching for him before he dies of his wounds? It is the pressure of time, then, that turns the screws of suspense. Armstrong pointed out that an "ordeal is converted to suspense with the addition of a time limit."

THE DREAM WALKER

Not only did Armstrong give her heroes a small and rapidly dwindling amount of time to achieve their object, but she gave equal time to the villains as well. In keeping with her ideas about the transparency of suspense, Armstrong did not hide the villains' attempts to carry out their plots; she made them an integral part of the story line. In *The Dream Walker* (1955), for example, much of the suspense and fasci-

nation of the tale arise from watching how the mastermind of a plot to discredit an elder statesman works to cover his own tracks and tries to outguess both those battling him and his own henchmen. It is not only the observation of the heroes' reactions, but also the back-and-forth reactions of each side in a deadly game that create an engrossing text.

In Armstrong's novels, tremendous stress is placed on the Everyman who is put in a desperate situation. Not only is the protagonist faced with a crime, but also he or she is often forced to look at the world in a new way. The result is a synthesis of realism and idealism, with those starting too far in either direction learning to be either more caring or less sentimentally dependent.

MISCHIEF

Jed Towers in *Mischief* begins as a cynic. He is introduced while in the act of breaking up with his girlfriend because she wanted to show charity to a panhandler. By the end of the novel, he has grown enough to return to the hotel room where he had left an innocent child with an unbalanced babysitter, telling himself, "Mind your own business. Take care of yourself, because you can be damn sure nobody else will." Knowing his involvement may hurt his career, he nevertheless discards his unconcerned worldview and acts like a man.

THE UNSUSPECTED

In *The Unsuspected*, Mathilda Frazier must make a change in the opposite direction. Her overly trusting, blind dependence on her guardian has to be abandoned, and she must face the evil in the world. In an ending in which Armstrong matches psychological change to symbolic image, Mathilda rejects her mentor by diving into a pit of garbage to rescue someone whom the mentor has trapped there. (This ending is in opposition to that of *Mischief*, where Jed must run upstairs to save the menaced child.)

CHARACTERIZATION

Armstrong's concern with characters who grow is clear. She has said, "The most fascinating characters are those who change under the pressure of happenings." Her fiction centers on such characters and involves finely shaded character drawings. Her picture of Professor Gibson in *A Dram of Poison* is a masterly example. With consummate delicacy, she details Gibson's gradual disillusionment with his wife and himself, spurred by the acerbic comments of his sister.

Armstrong is equally adept at portraying women. She often developed heroines who were strong, outspoken, and forthright. Anabel O'Shea, who appears in *The Witch's House*, is a model of this type. When her husband disappears, she assesses the lackadaisical, or at least bored, attitude of the police, who view the missing person as a straying husband, and determines that she must find him on her own. She proves herself wily, resourceful, and persevering in the search; dogged in following leads; and undaunted by the interfering do-gooders or villains who appear in her path. Anabel O'Shea is an example of the independent female character whom Armstrong was already developing in the 1940's (in *The Unsuspected*'s Aunt Jane, for example). She created a pattern for the type of self-assured woman that would play a large part in popular literature of the 1960's and 1970's.

It might be added that one of Anabel O'Shea's most charming characteristics is her ability to see some humor in her situation, and it is one of Armstrong's trademarks to inject comedy into even her most unsettling works. In *The Witch's House*, comic relief is provided by the characters of Parsons and Vee Adams. Both humorously romanticize and misinterpret the disappearances. Parsons, the university gossip, ascribes the whole situation to a Russian plot, while Vee, the daughter of one of the missing men, depicts herself as a tragic heroine, dreaming of graveyards and headstones. These characters' comic misapprehensions introduce a strain of comedy into the generally distressing story.

This novel also brings up another major Armstrong theme, that of the fallen or partially fallen father figure. Vee Adams's father, in this novel, though a respected academic, has been secretly corrupted and betrayed by his young wife. More characteristically, Armstrong's plots involve a paternal character who has fallen one degree and may fall further.

THE GIFT SHOP

In *The Gift Shop* (1967), the father's earlier peccadillo may bring down his son, a state governor. The father, Paul Fairchild, had a brief liaison that produced a

daughter who is now to be kidnapped to force the father's eldest son, the governor, to pardon the murderer, Kurtz. Further extending the thematic richness of this story, Armstrong has Kurtz's daughter be the one trying to kidnap Fairchild's little girl, so that the plot breaks down into a battle between a daughter and a son—Fairchild's youngest son tries to find and protect the missing girl—to preserve their fathers' tarnished reputations.

It might be said that many of Armstrong's concerns and stylistic decisions emerge from the chastened worldview that arose in the United States during and after World War II. The involvement of the United States in this war ended a period of isolation and, more important, involved the common people in the armed forces and on the home front in a common struggle. It was a war that called on everyone. These historical conditions must have played a part in Armstrong's deep interest in how an ordinary person reacts when plunged into unusual and trying situations. Furthermore, the returning veterans brought back with them a serious, realistic, unsentimental attitude toward the world and world politics. Such an attitude is visible in Armstrong's disdain for corny emotionalism and her unflinchingly honest appraisal of authority figures. Her works lack the squeamishness associated with many earlier female writers and employ sparing but open, dispassionate descriptions of physical violence and torture.

Paradoxically, it is also these attitudes that shape Armstrong's outlook on the occult. Armstrong constantly uses supernatural components in her writings, thus becoming one of the first to use in suspense works an element that would become prominent in American popular writing in the 1970's; still, as may be guessed, she brings in this element only to debunk it. *The Dream Walker*, for example, concerns the small-time actress Cora Steffani, who begins to achieve notoriety by her supernatural excursions. She falls asleep for a few minutes and awakens to recall vividly a meeting with a famous person in another part of the country. It is learned that at exactly the same time in that other part of the country Cora, or a woman closely resembling her, has met the famous person under the same circumstances of which Cora has dreamed. Clearly, there are actually two women, and they are involved in an ingenious, subterranean subterfuge, but all the trappings of a supernatural story are present.

REALISM

Finally, it should be pointed out that Armstrong's style embodies the same stance of detached but caring realism that her best characters are led to adopt. Chiefly concerned with human psychology, she spends little space on the description of setting or milieu but concentrates on conversation, action, and character portrayal. She is always precise and concise, writing simple, unadorned sentences that prove perfect at conveying her no-nonsense point of view. Take this thumbnail sketch from *The Dream Walker*, which describes how a rich, idle young man has been led into bad company:

> So there he was. Shut out. With the income, to be sure, but understanding nothing about its sources. Raymond's education, I can guess, was the most superficial gloss. He seemed to have nothing to do but spend money he never made.
>
> He got to spending his money in a strange place.

In this passage Armstrong conveys a complex mixture of psychological and social circumstances in the humblest language and caps and condenses the whole downward progress of Raymond with her final, evocative, but still simple sentence. Each word is chosen with thoughtfulness and with the construction of the entire text in mind.

LEMON IN THE BASKET

Although she seldom departed from this reserved style, at climactic points in her story she could use simple but effective strategies to convey the excitement of the moment. In *Lemon in the Basket* (1967), the heroine is running up the stairs to save the little Arabian prince just as the assassin is about to enter his room. Armstrong builds to the moment of truth with a series of disconnected clauses:

> As Inga went into the boy's bathroom to fetch him a glass of water . . .
>
> As the door to that east guest room, that had been standing on a slant, began to swing inward, opening . . .
>
> As the boy sat absolutely still, staring into the eyes of the sudden man . . .

By the lightning-like juxtaposition of several simultaneous scenes, she is able to create a harrowing moment without departing from her use of simple, undramatic description.

After all, it is a world of suspense and terror, the one of which Charlotte Armstrong wrote and in which she lived during the long aftermath of World War II. Not only was she brilliant at creating stories that registered some of the angst of this situation but also, in the philosophies her major characters developed, she offered a coherent way of facing this unfriendly world.

James Feast

PRINCIPAL MYSTERY AND DETECTIVE FICTION

MACDOUGAL DUFF SERIES: *Lay on, Mac Duff!*, 1942; *The Case of the Weird Sisters*, 1943; *The Innocent Flower*, 1945 (also known as *Death Filled the Glass*)

NONSERIES NOVELS: 1946-1960 • *The Unsuspected*, 1946; *The Chocolate Cobweb*, 1948; *Mischief*, 1950; *The Black-Eyed Stranger*, 1951; *Catch-as-Catch-Can*, 1952 (also known as *Walk Out on Death*); *The Trouble in Thor*, 1953 (also known as *And Sometimes Death*); *The Better to Eat You*, 1954 (also known as *Murder's Nest*); *The Dream Walker*, 1955 (also known as *Alibi for Murder*); *A Dram of Poison*, 1956; *The Seventeen Widows of Sans Souci*, 1959

1961-1970 • *Something Blue*, 1962; *Then Came Two Women*, 1962; *A Little Less than Kind*, 1963; *The Mark of the Hand*, 1963; *The One-Faced Girl*, 1963; *The Witch's House*, 1963; *Who's Been Sitting in My Chair?*, 1963; *The Turret Room*, 1965; *Dream of Fair Woman*, 1966; *Lemon in the Basket*, 1967; *The Gift Shop*, 1967; *The Balloon Man*, 1968; *Seven Seats to the Moon*, 1969; *The Protégé*, 1970

OTHER SHORT FICTION: *The Albatross*, 1957; *Duo*, 1959; *I See You*, 1966

OTHER MAJOR WORKS

PLAYS: *The Happiest Days*, pr. 1939; *Ring Around Elizabeth*, pr. 1941

SCREENPLAYS: *The Unsuspected*, 1946; *Don't Bother to Knock*, 1952

BIBLIOGRAPHY

Cromie, Alice. Preface to *The Charlotte Armstrong Reader*. New York: Coward-McCann, 1970. Overview of Armstrong's most important and distinctive work.

Dellacava, Frances A. *Sleuths in Skirts: Analysis and Bibliography of Serialized Female Sleuths*. New York: Routledge, 2002. Good for contextualizing Armstrong's gothic mysteries. Bibliographic references and index.

Klein, Kathleen Gregory, ed. *Great Women Mystery Writers: Classic to Contemporary*. Westport, Conn.: Greenwood Press, 1994. Contains an essay on Armstrong detailing her life and works.

Knight, Stephen Thomas. *Crime Fiction, 1800-2000: Detection, Death, Diversity*. New York: Palgrave Macmillan, 2004. Broad overview of the important trends and developments in two centuries of detective fiction. Places Armstrong in her greater historical context.

The New Yorker. Review of *The Case of the Weird Sisters*. 18 (January 30, 1943): 64. Brief but useful review of one of Armstrong's most famous works, the second in her MacDougal Duff series.

MICHAEL AVALLONE

Born: New York, New York; October 27, 1924
Died: Los Angeles, California; February 26, 1999
Also wrote as Michele Alden; James Blaine; Nick Carter; Troy Conway; Priscilla Dalton; Mark Dane; Jean-Anne de Pre; Fred Frazer; Dora Highland; Amanda Jean Jarrett; Stuart Jason; Steve Michaels; Memo Morgan; Dorothea Nile; Edwina Noone; Vance Stanton; Sidney Stuart; Max Walker; Lee Davis Willoughby
Types of plot: Private investigator; historical; thriller; espionage

PRINCIPAL SERIES

Ed Noon, 1953-1993
Nick Carter, 1964
April Dancer, 1966
Coxeman, 1968-1971
Craghold, 1971-1975
Satan Sleuth, 1974-1975
Butcher, 1979-1982

PRINCIPAL SERIES CHARACTER

ED NOON is a private investigator portrayed in more than thirty novels. He is a swashbuckling detective-for-hire who risks life and limb in the course of solving crimes. Fluent in street talk, he seasons his conversation with quotes and quips of baseball and motion-picture immortals, and he is not averse to using wisecracks to fluster cops or suspected criminals.

CONTRIBUTION

Michael Avallone produced more than 150 novels and a host of short stories within the first three decades of his writing career. Many of his works were published as drugstore-rack flashy-cover paperbacks with provocative titles such as *Never Love a Call Girl* (1962), *Sex Kitten* (1962), and *And Sex Walked In* (1963). His best work, however, is crime fiction. Although he wrote many volumes under pseudonyms and many of them are gothics, it was his famous Ed Noon series of crime novels that captured fans of mystery fiction. He brought stories of crime detection down to the level of high school dropouts, with fast-moving plots, lusty women, and fistfights. Where Agatha Christie might carefully plant clues to the murder of a single country gentleman or woman, Avallone spiced up his chapters with murders, suicides, and gun battles that left a slew of corpses to be accounted for. Smarter than the cops he often works with, Ed Noon solves his jigsaw puzzle at the end of each novel in a flurry of heart-stopping action.

BIOGRAPHY

Michael Angelo Avallone, Jr., was born in New York on October 27, 1924. He attended Theodore

Roosevelt High School in the Bronx. Like millions of his generation, he went into military service in World War II; he served in the United States Army from 1943 to 1946 and was discharged with the rank of sergeant. On his return from military service, he became a stationery salesperson, a position he held for nine years (1946-1955). He was married to Lucille Asero in 1949 and they had one son. In 1960, he was married to Fran Weinstein and they had one daughter and one son.

An avid motion-picture fan in his youth, Avallone toyed with writing his own scripts. He entered the literary world in 1953 with the publication by Holt, Rinehart of his first detective novel, *The Tall Delores*. During the next five years, while writing his first ten Ed Noon books, he served as an editor for Republic Features in New York (1956-1958) and for Cape Magazines, New York (1958-1960).

During the 1960's, when the United States was torn asunder by the rise of the Civil Rights movement, the war on poverty, the hippie counterculture, and the anti-Vietnam War crusade, Avallone churned out nearly fifty books under the pseudonyms Nick Carter, Sidney Stuart, Priscilla Dalton, Edwina Noone, Dorothea Nile, and Troy Conway. In the early 1970's, he wrote under the names Jean-Anne de Pre and Vance Stanton. Under his own name he produced another twenty-seven books by 1978. Many were novelizations of popular screenplays; others were gothics. His works, many of them marketed as slick-cover drugstore paperbacks, sold well enough to provide Avallone with a comfortable income. He eventually moved to East Brunswick, New Jersey.

Often the subject of controversy among authors and critics of crime fiction, Avallone enjoyed the role his books provided him. He shared the secrets of his success in writing and publishing crime novels in "How I Sold a Series of Paperback Mystery Novels" (published in 1971 in *Writer's Digest*), which focuses on his Ed Noon series. He served as chairman of the television committee (1958-1960) and the film committee (1965-1970) of the Mystery Writers of America. Frequently he appeared before school audiences in New York and New Jersey schools. He fired off a series of pointed articles critical of other scholars and

young critics in the mystery-fiction field. By 1980, he was to enjoy a series of sympathetic articles by his peers about his contributions to the field of crime fiction. He died in Los Angeles in 1999.

ANALYSIS

Often grouped with contemporaries such as Mickey Spillane, Davis Dresser, and Henry Kane, Michael Avallone found himself writing in a similar vein and for a very similar audience. Challenging situations, introduced in Avallone's first series of private-eye novels, are resolved by a rough-and-tumble six-foot character named Ed Noon, who dominated a slew of books issued between 1953 and 1993.

THE TALL DELORES

Private investigator Noon is a city slicker whose street talk is filled with wisecracks that defuse or create explosive situations while shielding a mind clever enough to unravel tangled affairs. In Avallone's first novel, *The Tall Delores*, Noon introduces himself and his style:

> Great business, this private-peeper racket. You get paid to look through keyholes, mess up fresh playboys for old guys who wanted to scare them off their child brides, find missing persons who usually preferred to stay lost, and get your own face pushed in once in awhile. For a fee, of course.
>
> I'm buck-hungry like the rest of my fellow Americans. And not crazy about taxes either. So money dominated all the time I had. My time was anybody's who could pay for it.
>
> And now the Tall Delores wanted me to find Harry (also Tall) Hunter for her for the fifth part of a grand. Well, it was worth it. I'd done things for a part of a grand before that weren't so grand.

For some forty years this American detective hero was to roam the streets, exuding his love for films, baseball, and beautiful women, while trying to keep the world straight for middle-class America. "With this recipe Avallone has inadvertently created a private Nooniverse," writes critic Francis M. Nevins, Jr. Other critics were appalled by Avallone's atrocious misuse of language, plots that lacked substance, and freakish scenes. Yet Noon carved a place for himself in mystery fiction, and if literary giants and academics

scorned his technique, it did not bother his fans (or Avallone's publishers).

Apparently, some confusion exists over which book was actually Avallone's first Ed Noon book. Many lists cite *The Spitting Image* (1953) as the first; in *The Spitting Image*, however, Noon is hired because he had solved the case of *The Tall Delores*. The Library of Congress card catalog numbers confirm that *The Tall Delores* preceded *The Spitting Image*.

AVALLONE'S NOONIVERSE

Avallone matched the prolific production and copied a bit of the creative style of England's famous Edgar Wallace in the three decades of his mystery and fiction writing. As the postwar world unfolded, Avallone's works reflected the American cultural trends toward realism and away from modesty and the growing concern

about crime and juvenile delinquency. His graphic descriptions of nudity preceded the appearance of *Playboy*'s playmates in the raw; his hard-knuckled physical violence came before *West Side Story* (1957) carried that mode to the stage and screen. Avallone's Nooniverse and Mickey Spillane's characters opened the way for James Bond and his more sophisticated European settings. College students quoted lines from Avallone and Spillane as they toiled over William Shakespeare and John Milton. The age of the paperback began just as Avallone began publication; ironically, his first three Noon books had first editions in hardcover (his third was titled *Dead Game*, 1954).

Avallone joined other Eisenhower-era writers in indulging in a new frankness about sex. This openness is reflected in Ed Noon titles issued in the 1950's and 1960's: *The Case of the Bouncing Betty* (1957), *The Case of the Violent Virgin* (1957), *Lust Is No Lady* (1964), and *The February Doll Murders* (1966).

Perhaps the most mind-boggling of Ed Noon's escapades occurs in *Shoot It Again, Sam* (1972), in which the private eye, accompanying a corpse sitting up in a casket being sent back East, is captured by foreign agents and brainwashed into believing that he is the real Sam Spade. In his spy novels written under the pseudonym Nick Carter—*The China Doll, Run, Spy, Run*, and *Saigon* (all published in 1964)—the plots take even stranger twists.

OTHER SERIES

The scope of Avallone's crime novels was ever-widening as he interspersed his writing of the Noon series with numerous other series produced under pen names such as Nick Carter, Sidney Stuart, Priscilla Dalton, Edwina Noone, Dorothea Nile, Troy Conway, Jean-Anne de Pre, Vance Stanton, and Stuart Jason. The books written under women's names are gothics. Four volumes of short stories were collected and published: *Tales of the Frightened* (1963), *Edwina Noone's Gothic Sampler* (1966), *Where Monsters Walk* (1978), and *Five Minute Mysteries* (1978). In addition, after 1960 he published more than fifty other novels, many of which were novelizations of screenplays (as were many of his crime novels).

In Avallone's good-guy, bad-guy world, specific cultural icons are repeatedly celebrated. His novels are liberally sprinkled, for example, with references to baseball teams and outstanding players of his generation. One of the most fascinating aspects of Avallone's crime novels is the way in which they reflect his love for motion pictures. A fan of films produced in the 1930's and 1940's, he filled his plots and dialogues with allusions to Hollywood masterpieces. Whereas Edgar Wallace moved from crime fiction to theater and film writing in his career, Avallone adapted screenplays to crime novels; both writers profited by such shifts.

In sum, it can be said that Avallone's novels reflect the passions and prejudices of middle America in the mid-twentieth century. Of his favorite protagonist Avallone said, "I might as well be keeping a diary when I write the Ed Noon books." Thoughtful readers experience these books as uncensored, often garbled, yet strangely compelling flights of heroic fantasy.

Paul F. Erwin

PRINCIPAL MYSTERY AND DETECTIVE FICTION

ED NOON SERIES: 1953-1960 • *The Tall Delores*, 1953; *The Spitting Image*, 1953; *Dead Game*, 1954; *Violence in Velvet*, 1956; *The Case of the Bouncing Betty*, 1957; *The Case of the Violent Virgin*, 1957; *The Crazy Mixed-Up Corpse*, 1957; *The Voodoo Murders*, 1957; *Meanwhile Back at the Morgue*, 1960

1961-1970 • *The Alarming Clock*, 1961; *The Bedroom Bolero*, 1963 (also known as *The Bolero Murders*); *The Living Bomb*, 1963; *There Is Something About a Dame*, 1963; *Lust Is No Lady*, 1964 (also known as *The Brutal Kook*); *The Fat Death*, 1966; *The February Doll Murders*, 1966; *Assassins Don't Die in Bed*, 1968; *The Horrible Man*, 1968; *The Doomsday Bag*, 1969 (also known as *Killer's Highway*); *The Flower-Covered Corpse*, 1969

1971-1978 • *Death Dives Deep*, 1971; *Little Miss Murder*, 1971 (also known as *The Ultimate Client*); *London, Bloody London*, 1972 (also known as *Ed Noon in London*); *Shoot It Again, Sam*, 1972 (also known as *The Moving Graveyard*); *The Girl in the Cockpit*, 1972; *Kill Her—You'll Like It!*, 1973; *Killer on the Keys*, 1973; *The Hot Body*, 1973; *The X-Rated Corpse*, 1973; *The Big Stiffs*, 1977; *Dark on Monday*, 1978

NICK CARTER SERIES (AS CARTER): *Run, Spy,*

Run, 1964 (with Valerie Moolman); *Saigon*, 1964 (with Valerie Moolman); *The China Doll*, 1964 (with Valerie Moolman)

APRIL DANCER SERIES: *The Birds of a Feather Affair*, 1966; *The Blazing Affair*, 1966

COXEMAN SERIES (AS CONWAY): *Come One, Come All*, 1968; *The Man-Eater*, 1968; *A Good Peace*, 1969; *Had Any Lately?*, 1969; *I'd Rather Fight than Swish*, 1969; *The Big Broad Jump*, 1969; *The Blow-Your-Mind Job*, 1970; *The Cunning Linguist*, 1970; *A Stiff Proposition*, 1971; *All Screwed Up*, 1971; *The Penetrator*, 1971

CRAGHOLD SERIES (AS NOONE): *The Craghold Legacy*, 1971; *The Craghold Creatures*, 1972; *The Craghold Curse*, 1972; *The Craghold Crypt*, 1973

SATAN SLEUTH SERIES: *Fallen Angel*, 1974; *The Werewolf Walks Tonight*, 1974; *Devil, Devil*, 1975

BUTCHER SERIES (AS JASON): *Slaughter in September*, 1979; *The Judas Judge*, 1979; *Coffin Corner, U.S.A.*, 1980; *Death in Yellow*, 1980; *Kill Them Silently*, 1980; *Go Die in Afghanistan*, 1981; *The Hoodoo Horror*, 1981; *Gotham Gore*, 1982; *The Man from White Hat*, 1982

NONSERIES NOVELS: 1963-1970 • *Shock Corridor*, 1963; *The Doctor's Wife*, 1963; *The Main Attraction*, 1963 (as Michael); *Felicia*, 1964 (as Dane); *The Night Walker*, 1964 (as Stuart); *90 Gramercy Park*, 1965 (as Dalton); *Corridor of Whispers*, 1965 (as Noone); *Dark Cypress*, 1965 (as Noone); *Heirloom of Tragedy*, 1965 (as Noone); *The Darkening Willows*, 1965 (as Dalton); *The Man from U.N.C.L.E.: The Thousand Coffins Affair*, 1965; *The Silent, Silken Shadows*, 1965 (as Dalton); *Young Dillinger*, 1965 (as Stuart); *Daughter of Darkness*, 1966 (as Noone); *Kaleidoscope*, 1966; *Madame X*, 1966; *Mistress of Farrondale*, 1966 (as Nile); *Terror at Deepcliff*, 1966 (as Nile); *The Evil Men Do*, 1966 (as Nile); *The Second Secret*, 1966 (as Dalton); *The Victorian Crown*, 1966 (as Noone); *The Felony Squad*, 1967; *The Man from AVON*, 1967; *Hawaii Five-O*, 1968; *Mannix*, 1968; *My Secret Life with Older Women*, 1968 (as Blaine); *Seacliffe*, 1968 (as Noone); *The Coffin Things*, 1968; *The Incident*, 1968; *The Vampire Cameo*, 1968 (as Nile); *Hawaii Five-O: Terror in the Sun*, 1969; *Missing!*, 1969; *The Killing Star*, 1969;

A Bullet for Pretty Boy, 1970; *One More Time*, 1970; *The Cloisonné Vase*, 1970 (as Noone)

1971-1982 • *A Sound of Dying Roses*, 1971 (as de Pre); *Keith Partridge, Master Spy*, 1971; *The Night Before Chaos*, 1971; *The Third Woman*, 1971 (as de Pre); *When Were You Born?*, 1971; *Aquarius, My Evil*, 1972 (as de Pre); *Die, Jessica, Die*, 1972 (as de Pre); *The Fat and Skinny Murder Mystery*, 1972; *The Walking Fingers*, 1972; *Who's That Laughing in the Grave?*, 1972; *153 Oakland Street*, 1973 (as Highland); *The Beast with Red Hands*, 1973 (as Stuart); *The Third Shadow*, 1973 (as Nile); *Warlock's Woman*, 1973 (as de Pre); *Death Is a Dark Man*, 1974 (as Highland); *Only One More Miracle*, 1975; *Charlie Chan and the Curse of the Dragon Queen*, 1981; *The Cannonball Run*, 1981; *Friday the Thirteenth Part Three*, 1982; *The Scarborough Warning*, n.d.

OTHER SHORT FICTION: *Tales of the Frightened*, 1963; *Edwina Noone's Gothic Sampler*, 1966 (as Noone); *Five Minute Mysteries*, 1978; *Where Monsters Walk*, 1978

OTHER MAJOR WORKS

NOVELS: 1960-1970 • *All the Way*, 1960; *Stag Stripper*, 1961; *The Little Black Book*, 1961; *Women in Prison*, 1961; *Flight Hostess Rogers*, 1962; *Never Love a Call Girl*, 1962; *Sex Kitten*, 1962; *Sinners in White*, 1962; *The Platinum Trap*, 1962; *And Sex Walked In*, 1963; *Lust at Leisure*, 1963; *Station Six—Sahara*, 1964; *Krakatoa, East of Java*, 1969; *Beneath the Planet of the Apes*, 1970; *Hornets' Nest*, 1970; *Keith, the Hero*, 1970; *The Doctors*, 1970; *The Haunted Hall*, 1970; *The Last Escape*, 1970; *The Partridge Family*, 1970

1971-1983 • *Love Comes to Keith Partridge*, 1973; *The Girls in Television*, 1974; *Carquake*, 1977; *CB Logbook of the White Knight*, 1977; *Name That Movie*, 1978; *Son of Name That Movie*, 1978; *The Gunfighters*, 1981 (as Willoughby); *A Woman Called Golda*, 1982; *Red Roses Forever*, 1983 (as Jarrett)

BIBLIOGRAPHY

Adrian, Kelly. "Mike Avallone: One of the Un-Angry Young Men." *The Mystery Readers/Lovers Newsletter* 1 (June, 1968): 3-5. Brief profile of the author and his work, focused on his calm and professional demeanor.

Benvenuti, Stefano, and Gianni Rizzoni. *The Whodunit: An Informal History of Detective Fiction*. Translated by Anthony Eyre. New York: Macmillan, 1980. Originally published in Italian, this study of the genre places Avallone's work in its historical context.

Haycraft, Howard, ed. *The Art of the Mystery Story: A Collection of Critical Essays*. Reprint. New York: Carroll & Graf, 1983. Massive compendium of essays exploring all aspects of the mystery writer's craft. Provides context for understanding Avallone's work.

Mertz, Stephen. "Rapping with Mike: A Michael Avallone Appreciation, Interview, and Checklist," in *The Not So Private Eye* 8 (1980): 2-9. Discussion of Avallone's contributions to detective fiction followed by an interview with the author and a bibliography of his works.

Pepper, Andrew. *The Contemporary American Crime Novel: Race, Ethnicity, Gender, Class*. Edinburgh: Edinburgh University Press, 2000. Overview of twentieth century American crime fiction focusing on the representation of social identity and its importance to the development of the genre. Sheds light on Avallone's novels. Bibliographic references and index.

B

MARIAN BABSON
Ruth Stenstreem

Born: Salem, Massachusetts; December 15, 1929
Types of plot: Cozy; amateur sleuth; psychological; thriller

PRINCIPAL SERIES

Douglas Perkins and Gerry Tate, 1971-
Trixie and Evangeline, 1986-

PRINCIPAL SERIES CHARACTERS

DOUGLAS PERKINS and GERRY TATE are partners of the London public relations firm Perkins and Tate. They get involved in solving murders through their publicity work. Not a cat lover, Perkins ends up doing publicity for a cat show and becomes a cat owner himself.

TRIXIE DOLAN and EVANGELINE SINCLAIR are two former stars of the silver screen who find their acting talents are no longer in demand. They stumble into murders that must be investigated.

CONTRIBUTION

Marian Babson displays in her crime novels a debt to Agatha Christie and other writers from the period known as the Golden Age of mysteries. However, the world envisioned by Babson is an irrational one, far from the orderly, hierarchical world of the English tea cozies. Her characters, children among them, tend to be lonely, alienated individuals striving for order in a chaotic world. Animals, particularly cats, contribute to the dynamics of Babson's mysteries, often revealing submerged personality traits of their owners. Skilled in character analysis, Babson delves into the minds of outwardly normal people, questioning the very meaning of normality. She has more interest in exploring the psychological effects of suspicion on characters than in focusing on murder itself or subsequent justice.

Seldom do detectives—professional or amateur—unravel the mystery; rather, the culprits continue their lives of violence, ultimately bringing about discovery through their own actions. Babson experiments with a variety of narrative techniques and professional settings. Her first-person narrators, who hold few illusions about life, usually appear more concerned with the terror of the suspected threat than with the crime itself.

Although reviewers in the United States and in Babson's adopted England have generally paid little attention to her work, she has managed to carve out a niche for herself. Her quirky characters, experiments in narrative style, and humorous, if sometimes implausible, plots have earned Babson a dedicated following on both sides of the Atlantic. Her ten years as head of the Crime Writers' Association (1976-1986) also endeared her to her colleagues. In 2004, Malice Domestic gave Babson its Agatha Award for lifetime achievement for her contributions to mystery and detective fiction.

BIOGRAPHY

Born in New England on December 15, 1929, Marian Babson moved to London in 1960 and continues to make her home there, with periodic visits to the United States. Details of her private life remain scant. She worked briefly on the campaign of a Boston politician, where she learned the basics of public relations. Her experiences lent to the creation of her first series hero, Douglas Perkins, a publicist-turned-detective. Later, she worked as a secretary on temporary stints for a variety of employers, including a pop singer, a psychiatrist, a safe maker, and a solicitor. In 1976, she became secretary of the Crime Writers' Association, a post she held until 1986.

Babson has said that her writing mysteries evolved from her fondness for reading them. Between 1971 and 1987, she wrote more than twenty mysteries. In one interview, she named straight suspense and crime mixed with comedy as her two favorite genres, yet she does not limit her work to them, saying, "I don't think writers ought to be too predictable." Her versatility is evidenced by her work for various magazines, including *Woman's Realm* and *Woman's Own*.

ANALYSIS

In Marian Babson's work, murder usually does not initiate the mystery. Instead, the characters, including the children, attempt to regain some order as they suffer from unexpected and unprovoked disruptions to their lives. In *A Trail of Ashes* (1984; also known as *Whiskers and Smoke*), Rosemary empathizes with the young as they learn that "life was not the way it was presented on the television screen. When people were cruelly wounded, they did not leap up with a merry laugh after the commercial—they lay there and bled." Characters in Babson's mysteries do bleed, if only metaphorically, and they continue to struggle with loneliness.

A TRAIL OF ASHES

Babson frequently provides pets as companions for her disaffected characters. Errol, a Maine coon cat featured in *A Trail of Ashes*, offers little consolation for the Blakes when they first arrive. He typifies an aggressive, undisciplined society that prides itself on independence. Rosemary explains, "The brute was twice the size of our lovely Esmond; a burly, thick-necked, square-headed animal, given an unexpectedly rakish look by the fact that the tip of one ear had evidently been chewed off in some private dispute of long ago." Ultimately, assertive Errol and the Blakes establish a rapport, a tribute to newfound friendships.

PORTRAYAL OF CHILDREN

Babson's sensitive portrayal of children in crime novels was displayed early in her career. Typically, these children struggle with unsettling disruption in their lives: parental abuse, neglect, or death. In *Unfair Exchange* (1974), nine-year-old Fanny displays an obnoxious attitude that proves to be a reaction to the neglect by her vivacious yet thoughtless mother, Caro-

line. Babson captures the dichotomy of Fanny's character by showing the child seeking comfort by clutching a huge stuffed giraffe she has named for a sports car, Alfa-Romeo. Twinkle, the child star in *Murder, Murder, Little Star* (1977), appears as arrogant and rude as Fanny. Twinkle's ineffectual mother accompanies her on the set but offers no real support. Narrator Frances Armitage, hired as Twinkle's chaperone, recognizes the loneliness of the child and her career concerns. Thought to be ten but really a teenager, Twinkle fears the loss of good parts. Once her life is no longer in jeopardy, Twinkle seems destined for a role suggested by Frances: Lady Jane Grey, the child bride and queen.

The inhabitants of Babson's world are invariably victims of loneliness and emotional deprivation. Though her stories are not unleavened by wit, the worlds she creates leave her readers with the sense that events are random after all, and that little is worthy of trust.

PERKINS AND TATE SERIES

Cover-Up Story (1971), Babson's first crime novel, relays the exploits of series character Douglas Perkins of the public relations firm Perkins and Tate. Perkins finds himself embroiled in a mystery while representing an American country music troupe led by the tyrannical Black Bart. When one of the performers is injured under suspicious circumstances, Perkins and his partner Gerry Tate must find the murderer while trying to maintain peace among the rest of the troupe's unusual members. In *Murder on Show* (1972; also known as *Murder at the Cat Show*), death calls on Perkins again—this time at a cat show he and partner Tate have been hired to publicize. When a gold cat statue goes missing and the show organizer turns up dead, Perkins must unravel the mystery, while trying to maintain his studied ambivalence toward an endearing kitten clamoring for his attention. In *Tourists Are for Trapping* (1989), Perkins and Tate investigate the death of an elderly member of an American tourist group, and *In the Teeth of Adversity* (1990), they help a dentist to the stars deal with the bad press surrounding the death of a top model in his office.

Although the Perkins series novels have been praised for their plotting and characterization, some critics describe them as apprentice novels, in which Babson was able to hone her narrative and comedic style in addition to developing several of her recurrent themes and plot devices such as the centrality of feline characters, quirky plot scenarios, and the way her protagonists stumble unintentionally on mysterious and deadly events.

THE LORD MAYOR OF DEATH

The Lord Mayor of Death (1977) involves Kitty, a five-year-old who is easier to like than Babson's other child characters, Fanny and Twinkle, but no less lonely. Irishman Michael Carney lures Kitty into accompanying him to ceremonial festivities. The red lunch box he gives her contains a bomb with which he plans to kill the lord mayor of London and nearby celebrants.

A victim of child abuse, Michael loathes children, a fact that emerges as his thoughts are presented. Nevertheless, he must cater to Kitty's whims to accomplish his plan. Increasingly aware of children's unpredictability, Carney has to placate the fretful Kitty. Fearfully, he remembers, "When kids had tantrums, they threw things." By presenting the lunch box to Clover the Clown to boost his spirits, Kitty unknowingly thwarts Carney's plans. The tension in the novel arises from the juxtaposition of innocent children with a murderous villain.

THE TWELVE DEATHS OF CHRISTMAS

The Twelve Deaths of Christmas (1979), set in a London rooming house, demonstrates Babson's narrative skill in presenting multiple murders. An omniscient narrator alternates with the crazed, unknown murderer in giving accounts of the seemingly random murders and the subsequent fear they instill. Adroit placing of red herrings enables the murderer's identity to remain a secret until the end. The reader, however, traces a tortuous descent through layers of madness as the murderer wrestles with a sense of alienation, painful headaches, and incomprehension of events.

The murderer, finally diagnosed as suffering from a brain tumor, uses free association in selecting unconventional instruments of death. For example, when walking in Queen Mary's Rose Garden on the sixth day of Christmas, the murderer notices a metal pull ring torn from a can and recalls a metal loop with a blade, a device used in a post office for opening pack-

ages. This thought is followed by feelings of irritation toward a youthful mugger, lying in a drunken stupor while his blaring transistor radio shatters the peace of the garden. "I remember something else, too," the murderer muses. "Blood makes a excellent fertilizer for roses." Increasingly, he becomes paranoid but remains superficially normal, smiling and waving to neighbors but thinking, "I hate them all." Vivid description reinforces the disquieting atmosphere in the rooming house. The table set for the Christmas feast holds, among other things, "skeletal stalks of celery" and a carving knife "nearly as long and sharp as a sword."

DANGEROUS TO KNOW

Babson's *Dangerous to Know* (1980) is notable for some of her most effective imagery. Certainly, Tom Paige, the newsman narrator, could be expected to manipulate words skillfully. Working the graveyard shift, when wire services around the world shut down for the night, Tom expresses his disillusionment with the modern world. Describing teleprinters, he remarks, "They're the mechanical Recording Angels of the twentieth century. Everything spread out before your eyes and everything given the same value."

Later, he decries the superficiality of newspapers and their reading audience: "Life in a newspaper office is full of loose ends." He despairs of the possibility of writing for an educated reading public, eager to resolve substantive issues. His already jaundiced attitude toward humankind becomes even more cynical when he learns that his trusted coworkers share the guilt for recent crimes, including murder. The conclusion of the mystery offers little consolation to the reader who anticipates the reestablishment of order.

THE CRUISE OF A DEATHTIME

With *The Cruise of a Deathtime* (1983), Babson returns to multiple murders and an Agatha Christie-like resolution. This work won the first Poisoned Chalice Award, which recognizes works for the large number of bizarre murders they incorporate. The murders and the suspects are confined to the *Empress Josephine*, a cruise ship headed for Nhumbala, ten days' trip from Miami. Among the victims are five film viewers "*skewered* to their seats—rights through the back of their chairs!" An extortion note threatens additional

murders each day of the cruise. The resolution of the mystery is reminiscent of Christie's *Ten Little Niggers* (1939; also known as *And Then There Were None*).

As Babson isolates her characters on the cruise ship, she explores people's insensitivity to one another. The novel begins with an introduction to Mortie Ordway and Hallie Ordway, television quiz show contestants who "had triumphed, winning not only the Loot of a Lifetime, but climaxing it by winning the Cruise of a Lifetime, as well." Their making fools of themselves on the show had entertained innumerable viewers, who never considered the emotional cost to the Ordways, called "Oddways" by the offensive quizmaster. Their villainy is shown to be in part a response to their having become objects of derision. Before shooting her pearl-handled revolver, passenger Mrs. Anson-Pryce recognizes the complicity of society in criminal activities: "Truly, we manufacture our own monsters."

WEEKEND FOR MURDER

Weekend for Murder (1985; also known as *Murder on a Mystery Tour*) also evokes memories of Golden Age predecessors, set as it is in secluded Chortlesby Manor. Woven throughout the novel are allusions to famous authors and their works; for example, the manor's cat is named Roger Ackroyd and two of the characters are Sir Cedric Strangeways and Lieutenant Algernon Moriarty. The culprit, a disaffected literary critic, draws on pre-1940 mysteries as he plots his crime. A playful tone pervades the book.

THE CAT WHO WASN'T A DOG

In *The Cat Who Wasn't a Dog* (2003; also known as *Not Quite a Geisha*), the sixth installment in the Trixie Dolan and Evangeline Sinclair series, Babson's grand dames of the stage find themselves embroiled in a new mystery when fellow actress Dame Cecile Savoy and another actress friend discover Savoy's beloved Pekinese dead. Mystery soon engulfs the aging actresses when they become implicated in the death of a taxidermist with whom Savoy has consulted for the preservation of her precious Pekinese and in the disappearance of a housekeeper.

As in most of her works, Babson's plot involves a savvy and exotic cat—this time, a Japanese bobtail named Cho Cho San, who knows more than she is telling about the murders. Babson makes no secret of the murderer's identity, but the sniping between the four actresses and their desperate efforts to disentangle themselves from suspicion of murder provides ample entertainment.

ONLY THE CAT

Only the Cat (2007; also known as *Only the Cat Knows*) breaks little new ground, but Babson delivers another quirky mystery that requires subtle feline skills to unravel. Everett Oversall, a wealthy and reclusive tycoon, employs a stable of beautiful women at his remote castle. When one of them, Vanessa, goes into a coma after a fall, her twin brother Vance decides to unravel the mystery.

Experienced as a female impersonator, Vance goes undercover as his sister to unravel the mystery behind her accident. In typical fashion, Vanessa's cat Gloriana is the only trustworthy figure involved in the mystery and ultimately proves invaluable to his investigation.

Babson's characters lack the depth of previous books, but she depicts Vance's increasingly desperate attempts to maintain his female persona to excellent comedic effect.

Beatrice Christiana Birchak
Updated by Philip Bader

PRINCIPAL MYSTERY AND DETECTIVE FICTION

PERKINS AND TATE SERIES: *Cover-Up Story*, 1971; *Murder on Show*, 1972 (also known as *Murder at the Cat Show*); *Tourists Are for Trapping*, 1989; *In the Teeth of Adversity*, 1990

TRIXIE AND EVANGELINE SERIES: *Reel Murder*, 1986; *Encore Murder*, 1989; *Shadows in Their Blood*, 1991; *Even Yuppies Die*, 1993; *Break a Leg, Darlings*, 1995; *The Cat Who Wasn't a Dog*, 2003 (also known as *Not Quite a Geisha*)

NONSERIES NOVELS: 1973-1980 • *Pretty Lady*, 1973; *The Stalking Lamb*, 1974; *Unfair Exchange*, 1974; *Murder Sails at Midnight*, 1975; *There Must Be Some Mistake*, 1975; *Untimely Guest*, 1976; *Murder, Murder, Little Star*, 1977; *The Lord Mayor of Death*, 1977; *Tightrope for Three*, 1978; *So Soon Done For*, 1979; *The Twelve Deaths of Christmas*, 1979; *Dangerous to Know*, 1980; *Queue Here for Murder*, 1980 (also known as *Line Up for Murder*)

1981-1990 • *Bejewelled Death*, 1981; *Death Beside the Seaside*, 1982 (also known as *Death Beside the Sea*); *Death Warmed Up*, 1982; *A Fool for Murder*, 1983; *The Cruise of a Deathtime*, 1983; *A Trail of Ashes*, 1984 (also known as *Whiskers and Smoke*); *Death Swap*, 1984 (also known as *Paws for Alarm*); *Weekend for Murder*, 1985 (also known as *Murder on a Mystery Tour*); *Death in Fashion*, 1985; *Fatal Fortune*, 1987; *Guilty Party*, 1988

1991-2007 • *The Diamond Cat*, 1994; *Canapés for the Kitties*, 1997 (also known as *Miss Petunia's Last Case*); *The Company of Cats*, 1999 (also known as *The Multiple Cat*); *To Catch a Cat*, 2000 (also known

as *A Tealeaf in the Mouse*); *The Cat Next Door*, 2001 (also known as *Deadly Deceit*); *Please Do Feed the Cat*, 2004 (also known as *Retreat from Murder*); *Only the Cat*, 2007 (also known as *Only the Cat Knows*)

BIBLIOGRAPHY

Cooper, Ilene. Review of *The Cat Next Door*, by Marian Babson. *Booklist* 98, no. 15 (April 1, 2002): 1308. In this work, Tikki the cat helps solve a murder of a family member in the garden. Reviewer notes that there are too many characters but that many will still enjoy the novel.

_____. Review of *The Cat Who Wasn't a Dog*, by Marian Babson. *Booklist* 100, no. 1 (September 1, 2003): 67. Reviewer finds the novel centering on Trixie and Evangeline to be entertaining. Notes the presence of a cat and recipes, two features of Babson's works.

Kirkus Reviews. Review of *Only the Cat*, by Marian Babson. 75, no. 7 (April 1, 2007): 308. The reviewer finds this novel about a female impersonator investigating his twin's death to be improbable but enjoyable and suspenseful.

Klein, Kathleen Gregory, ed. *Great Women Mystery Writers: Classic to Contemporary*. Westport, Conn.: Greenwood Press, 1994. Contains a biocritical essay on Babson looking at her works and life.

Priestman, Martin, ed. *The Cambridge Companion to Crime Fiction*. New York: Cambridge University Press, 2003. Contains chapters on postwar British crime fiction, women detectives, and the Golden Age, which provide background from which to evaluate Babson's style.

Zaleski, Jeff. Review of *To Catch a Cat*, by Marian Babson. *Publishers Weekly* 247, no. 47 (November 20, 2000): 50. In this suspenseful psychological thriller, an eleven-year-old boy witnesses a murder while stealing a cat. Reviewer praises Babson's mastery of suspense.

DESMOND BAGLEY

Born: Kendal, Cumbria, England; October 29, 1923
Died: Southampton, England; April 12, 1983
Types of plot: Amateur sleuth; espionage

CONTRIBUTION

Desmond Bagley wrote fourteen novels. His work has often been recommended to the young adult reader as well as to the adult fan of suspense and adventure fiction. His typical main character is an intelligent man who thinks of himself as an ordinary working-man. The protagonist is able to use his wits as well as his special hobbyist or professional expertise to solve mysteries or, more likely, to escape danger. The settings include countries or environments—South Africa, the Yucatán, Greenland, Iran—that are foreign to most English readers' experience. Suspense, special knowledge, and setting all contribute to the reader's sense of discovery and enjoyment. Bagley puts himself in the camp of John le Carré, considering espionage more evil than necessary, rather than in the camp of Ian Fleming, whose hero cannot lose or be representative of anything less than the right. Bagley did not become as famous as did le Carré or Robert Ludlum in espionage or as Dick Francis has become in tales of the amateur sleuth. It may be that Bagley's novels lack the signature touches, the disenchanted George Smiley, the ultracomplex plots, the horse-racing connection, which have made the reputations of these authors. Nevertheless, Bagley's novels are worth discovering. His main characters have integrity, and they are driven to solve their various problems in ways that engage the reader.

BIOGRAPHY

Desmond Bagley was born Simon Bagley in Kendal, in the county of Westmorland, 260 miles north of London. His parents ran a theatrical boardinghouse, where, as a small child, he met Basil Rathbone, who was playing Shakespearean roles with Sir Frank Benson's touring company at the time. Bagley attended schools in Bolton and Blackpool, but he did not follow in the public school tradition. The spirit of Bagley's characters is discernible in his own act of quitting school at the age of fourteen to take on his first job, as a printer's devil. He subsequently worked in a factory making plastic electrical fittings and, when World War II broke out, in an aircraft factory, making parts for planes.

In 1947, Bagley traveled to South Africa. He is said to have departed from Blackpool during a blizzard, to have gone three thousand miles across the Sahara Desert guided by star and compass, and to have traveled across Nigeria, then west to Kampala, Uganda, where he contracted malaria. Next he traveled down the African continent, working in asbestos and gold mines, until he reached Natal Province, South Africa. There, he wrote feature stories for the press and pieces for radio, worked as a nightclub photographer, and began to indulge his hobbies of sailing and motorboating. Bagley became a freelance journalist in 1957, and he later became a script writer for a South African subsidiary of Twentieth Century Fox. He married Joan Margaret Brown in 1960.

Bagley lived his later years on the English Channel island of Guernsey. In 1983, he suddenly became ill and was taken to the Southampton General Hospital, where he died on April 12.

ANALYSIS

Desmond Bagley's early novels offer the kind of suspense that is created when a workingman fights against the odds. The first two published, *The Golden Keel* (1963) and *High Citadel* (1965), offer pure adventure, and most of the villains are purely bad.

The thoughts of Bagley's characters are portrayed through a first-person narrative or are implied through a third-person point of view. Despite the ordinariness of their voices, Bagley's characters can be found exploring existential questions in the mode of John le Carré's writing. Bagley's protagonists search for their identities, having lost wives, brothers, memories, names, jobs, or faces (by plastic surgery).

Bagley customarily began writing with the first chapter and "a group of people in an interesting situation and environment." He knew "roughly" how he wanted the book to end. Then, "the characters and environment interact (I regard the place as another character in the book) and the plot grows organically like a tree." The result is that Bagley's main characters, such as Jaggard in *The Enemy*, undergo an experience that parallels life and adds to the reader's store of experience accordingly.

THE GOLDEN KEEL

The Golden Keel takes place in an environment with which the author is familiar (South Africa), and it has a main character, Peter Halloran, who bears a resemblance to the author, having worked in an aircraft factory during World War II, emigrated to South Africa with no ready job or capital, and spent time with boats. Bagley's characters are in some ways rough, and they are ready to risk an adventure. Halloran, for example, has just lost his wife. He has strong survival instincts, but he now has less to lose. The language of this book is sometimes awkwardly plain—at the beginning, for example, and during romantic scenes. Bagley is a good storyteller, however, and the fun and excitement of the book prevail. It is a story of man against the sea as well as of man against man.

HIGH CITADEL

The setting of *High Citadel* includes snow-covered mountains complete with avalanches and blizzards. The major character, O'Hara, an alcoholic pilot about to lose his last job, has a reason for his character flaws: He was tortured as a Korean War prisoner. His ordeal in the story is brought on by the actions of South American communist terrorists, and it allows him to purge himself of the effects of his war experience. This book, while concentrating on O'Hara, is narrated in the third person so that Bagley can enter the minds of other characters fighting the terrorists. The narrator moves back and forth across a mountain pass, between characters, so that the readers may view the battle lines of the high citadel. Discovering whether the stranded victims of the plane crash will survive an attack makes an exciting reading experience.

These and the other amateur-sleuth adventure books also contain fascinating specialized information about such things as geology, archaeology, rain forests, and mountain climbing. Bagley said that he researched ex-

tensively throughout his career as a novelist. He acquired information about avalanches for *The Snow Tiger* (1974), for example, during a period of twelve years, in remote places such as the Antarctic and the South Pole and by talking to snow and ice scientists. He said that he took photographs but no notes, that he had a retentive memory, "a mind like flypaper."

THE SPOILERS

Even in the early books, however, Bagley goes beyond interesting facts and mere suspense to touch on concerns with political intrigue. In *The Spoilers* (1969), the characters are amateur agents rather than amateur sleuths. The assembled team is made up of the protagonist, who is a doctor, and one idealist, one con man, two mercenaries, one torpedo specialist, and one fast-talking journalist. Their mission is to make an assault on the drug trade in the Middle East and includes a strange and secret underground bombing in Iran.

In his later novels, Bagley continued to deliver intense stories of one person's mind, creating sophisticated plots using a storehouse of tricks and motifs, such as handlers and operatives, special techniques for following a subject, and ghastly, customized ammunition—all available to the authentic spy. Bagley did not, apparently, consider himself a writer in a certain genre of fiction. He claimed to be mystified by his reputation as a writer of crime and suspense: "My books are not specifically about crime although some people think they are." He admitted to fitting under the umbrella of suspense. "Yet," he went on to say, "all novels must have suspense or they are nothing."

LANDSLIDE AND THE FREEDOM TRAP

Bagley should also be remembered for his interest in the question of identity. This can be seen as early as *Landslide* (1967). The book is a good adventure story: A geologist is hunted by and exposes murderers, and he alerts the area to a geological fault that will jeopardize lives. Yet paralleling the physical threats involved in the adventure story are the psychological dangers for the protagonist, Robert Boyd. This man was burned so severely in an accident that he could not be identified with certainty. He might have been one of two different people, one antisocial, one not, before he suffered amnesia and had plastic surgery, which gave him a completely new face. He fears that he may have an evil side that will return if his memory comes back. Boyd earns love and respect without solving the mystery of his identity.

In *The Vivero Letter* (1968), the protagonist reacts against the overheard words of a thoughtless girl. She calls him a gray little man, and in reaction he is emboldened to launch an expedition into the steamy jungles of the Yucatán. In *The Tightrope Men* (1973), an innocent civilian has been given plastic surgery while he is unconscious, and he wakes up looking like a certain Finnish scientist sought by the Russians. In *The Freedom Trap* (1971; revised as *The Mackintosh Man*, 1973), appearance fools the reader. The protagonist appears to be an incarcerated criminal and speaks as such in his own voice, but he proves to be a government agent whom no one left alive in the government knows to be an agent.

THE ENEMY

In *The Enemy* (1977), Bagley brings together a down-to-earth male protagonist, high suspense, specialized information, political issues, and espionage. This novel serves as a good example of Bagley's mature voice and of his having achieved control of the ingredients of his art. Unlike his early female characters, Penelope Ashton in *The Enemy* is drawn with enough subtlety to avoid false notes, sufficiently engaged in the action to engage the reader's sympathy, and as technically proficient and resourceful as Malcom Jaggard, the protagonist. The maturity and authority of Jaggard are evident in his voice, and as the book is told in first person, Jaggard's voice is the dominant element of Bagley's style.

Jaggard characterizes himself early in the book as someone who tries to make no false claims. (By the end of the book, it will have become clear how difficult, though important, it is to do so.) When he talks about his growing acquaintance with Penelope Ashton, modesty, self-mockery, and an intentional restraint characterize his voice and style: "And, as they say, one thing led to another and soon I was squiring her around regularly. . . . We could have been a couple of Americans doing the tourist bit." "Squiring her around" and "the tourist bit" are ordinary clichés that show the character's intentional avoidance of elitism.

Bagley leads his readers to the experiences of secondary characters through the narrator's viewpoint. Jaggard is conscientiously tentative about describing what may be in someone else's mind. Sometimes he retreats to being sure only about his own thoughts: "After six weeks of this I think we both thought that things were becoming pretty serious. I, at least, took it seriously enough to go to Cambridge to see my father."

Bagley's style also includes humor. A situation in a Swedish town in *The Enemy* is described as

> becoming positively ridiculous; two of Cutler's men were idling away their time in antique shops ready for the emergence of Ashton [Penny's father] and Benson and unaware that they were being watched by a couple of Russians who, in their turn, were not aware of being under the surveillance of the department. It could have been a Peter Sellers comedy.

Later, Jaggard says, "I followed behind, passing Ashton who was already carrying a tail like a comet."

The fun is only a backdrop, however, to the serious themes of the novel. Jaggard's authority is demonstrated when Jaggard says, "You won't get me back in the department. I'm tired of lies and evasions; I'm tired of self-interest masquerading as patriotism. It came to me when Cregar [a dishonest, power-hungry member of the House of Lords] called me an honest man. . . . How could an honest man do what I did to Ashton?" (Jaggard refrained from telling Ashton the truth because of the agency's orders. Ignorance of the truth led to Ashton's death.)

Bagley is a writer who follows rules of decency, and thus he is often recommended to young adult readers. Jaggard does what most young adults would like to do, telling his employers repeatedly to "stuff it." In *The Enemy*, Bagley continues to offer both young and old readers the catharsis of suspense. There are searches for a man who assaulted Penny's sister with battery acid and exciting searches for Penny's father and his valet (which entail a look into the past, from which it is determined that Penny's father, Ashton, was a brilliant physicist and Russian defector). There are searches for Ashton's cleverly hidden research and a desperate search for Penny herself when she disappears from sight.

A catharsis of a new kind is provided, however—a purging that depends on admitting that the good man is not always rescued alive, that the good elements in government do not necessarily emerge victorious, that even the hero does not always get to live happily ever after. As Jaggard says at the beginning of the last chapter, "this is not a fairy tale." In this chapter, it is learned that he is terminally ill.

As in the previous novels, *The Enemy* shows evidence of research having been done in specialized areas—this time computer programs, model railroads, and genetic engineering. The railroad-schedule microprocessors are discovered to be a disguised computer, fascinatingly described, for storage of Ashton's theoretical genetic research. There is much information about *Escherichia coli*, a species of intestinal bacteria, about mutations of it caused by the splicing of DNA strings, and about dangers to the human race if this sort of engineering is not controlled.

Espionage and intrigue in *The Enemy* are not gratuitous. Competing power-hungry departments within the British government exemplify the human faults of pride, covetousness, and consequent deceit. The one supervisor Jaggard has believed to be true finally equivocates and is prepared to make deals in the end, while Jaggard himself has betrayed Ashton.

At the time Bagley wrote *High Citadel*, he seemed to have thought that political decisions could be made sharply and with clarity. The North Koreans were evil, there were evil effects from their torturing of O'Hara, and the enemy in the South American setting of that novel is also evil. The main character, O'Hara, must learn to conquer his psychological problems, and this action constitutes a vague subplot. There is nothing vague about who the villains are, however, and only the female characters in the novel and a college professor have any qualms about using a range of weapons, ending with bombing, to hurt and kill the communists. By 1977, Bagley was less definite. In his books of that time, the main character's fellow spy is more likely than not to be a double agent, and the people supposedly on the same side at home may not be helping. *The Enemy* begins with these quotations: "We have met the enemy, and he is ours," from Oliver Hazard Perry, heroic American commodore; "We have met the enemy, and he is us," from Walt Kelly, subversive sociological cartoonist.

Anna R. Holloway

PRINCIPAL MYSTERY AND DETECTIVE FICTION

NOVELS: *The Golden Keel*, 1963; *High Citadel*, 1965; *Wyatt's Hurricane*, 1966; *Landslide*, 1967; *The Vivero Letter*, 1968; *The Spoilers*, 1969; *Running Blind*, 1970; *The Freedom Trap*, 1971 (revised as *The Mackintosh Man*, 1973); *The Tightrope Men*, 1973; *The Snow Tiger*, 1974; *The Enemy*, 1977; *Flyaway*, 1978; *Bahama Crisis*, 1980; *The Legacy*, 1982; *Windfall*, 1982; *Night of Error*, 1984; *Juggernaut*, 1985

BIBLIOGRAPHY

Bagley, Desmond. "A Word with Desmond Bagley." Interview by Deryk Harvey. *The Armchair Detective* 7 (August, 1974): 258-260. A revealing interview that details Bagley's approach to writing and his appraisal of the state of the mystery genre in the mid- to late twentieth century.

_____. Interview. *The Mystery FANcier* 7 (March/April, 1983): 13-18. Bagley discusses his work and his writing process.

Keating, H. R. F., ed. *Whodunit? A Guide to Crime, Suspense, and Spy Fiction.* New York: Van Nostrand Reinhold, 1982. Reader's guide to various crime genres focused especially on the representation of criminals. Index. Provides context for understanding Bagley's work.

Priestman, Martin, ed. *The Cambridge Companion to Crime Fiction.* New York: Cambridge University Press, 2003. Critical study consisting of fifteen overview essays devoted to specific genres or periods within crime fiction. Contains a chapter on spy fiction as well as one on thrillers that will shed light on Bagley's works. Bibliographic references and index.

Roth, Marty. *Foul and Fair Play: Reading Genre in Classic Detective Fiction.* Athens: University of Georgia Press, 1995. A post-structural analysis of the conventions of mystery and detective fiction. Examines 138 short stories and works from the 1840's to the 1960's. Contains some mention of Bagley and places his work in context.

Winn, Dilys, ed. *Murder Ink: The Mystery Reader's Companion.* New York: Workman, 1977. Overview of the mystery genre, its conventions, and its practitioners. Helps readers understand Bagley's place in the genre.

H. C. BAILEY

Born: London, England; February 1, 1878
Died: Llanfairfechen, North Wales; March 24, 1961
Type of plot: Private investigator

PRINCIPAL SERIES

Reggie Fortune, 1920-1948
Joshua Clunk, 1930-1950

PRINCIPAL SERIES CHARACTERS

REGGIE FORTUNE studied medicine to become a family practitioner but instead becomes fully employed by Scotland Yard as a medical expert in cases of murder. Married to Joan Amber early in the series, the cherubic Fortune prefers a quiet country life in the company of flowers, his Persian cat, and good food. An unsolved crime, however, awakens limitless zeal and a surprising ruthlessness.

JOSHUA CLUNK, the surviving partner of Clunk and Clunk, is the solicitor of choice among London's lower-class criminals. Chanting bits of hymns and gushing piety, old Josh is suspected by all of hypocrisy and double-dealing. He deploys a staff of talented and attractive investigators, usually to expose large-scale and dangerous criminals.

CONTRIBUTION

Short stories about Reggie Fortune, first collected as *Call Mr. Fortune* in 1920, won an immediate following both in Great Britain and in the United States. Ingenious in plot, full of arresting characterization, and equally satisfying as detective puzzles or as moral fables, these stories established H. C. Bailey as a master of his art and Fortune as one of the world's great fictional detectives. In 1930 the series of novels featuring Joshua Clunk began. These works had elaborate plots; to Bailey's great skill in narration were added extended development of character, a variety of narrative voices and points of view, and a special concern for youths, especially the poor and the victimized. In 1934, Fortune also began appearing in novels; he appeared solely in novels after 1940.

Involved in police procedures, and normally on excellent terms with the Criminal Investigation Department, Fortune must nevertheless be considered a private investigator because of his independent judgments and actions, especially when he finds the police futile or mistaken. Drawling, purring Reggie and crooning, gushing Joshua are exactly alike in the intelligence with which they perceive and the energy with which they attack the wicked. Both will deceive the police and execute their own justice if by doing so they can protect the innocent or prevent a clever criminal from escaping.

BIOGRAPHY

H. C. Bailey was born Henry Christopher Bailey in London on February 1, 1878, and he lived most of his life there. After preparing at the City of London School, he studied at Corpus Christi College, Oxford University, and was graduated with honors in classics in 1901. From 1901 to 1946, he worked for London's *Daily Telegraph*, advancing from drama critic to war correspondent and finally to editorial writer.

Bailey wrote his first novel while still an undergraduate. With only slight variation, he managed to publish a substantial historical novel each year, 1901 through 1928; by that time, he had also, with a coauthor, written a play based on one of his novels, written a history of the Franco-Prussian War, and written what became the first four collections of Reggie Fortune stories. The thirtieth and last historical novel, *Mr. Cardonnel*, appeared in 1931. Unlike his detective stories, Bailey's historical novels vary enormously in scene and characters. *The Roman Eagles* (1928), a history for children, is set in ancient Britain at the time of Julius Caesar's invasion. *Mr. Cardonnel* begins in 1658, the last year of Oliver Cromwell's reign. *The God of Clay* (1908) is about the young Napoleon Bonaparte. Other tales have medieval settings, take place during the revolt of the Netherlands against Spain, or carry the reader to nineteenth century Italy. Apart from being good yarns, these works represent much knowledge and sympathy, and all were completed while Bailey worked at the *Daily Telegraph*.

In 1908 Bailey married Lydia Haden Janet Guest. They had two daughters and lived in a London suburb. Bailey wrote as if he enjoyed writing; his books were largely created between dinner and bedtime. His other hobbies were walking and gardening, both of which

receive attention in his novels. Bailey was a founding member of the Detection Club, founded around 1930. E. C. Bentley, author of *Trent's Last Case* (1913), was another member, as well as being Bailey's colleague at the *Daily Telegraph*. G. K. Chesterton, whose Father Brown has much in common with Fortune and Clunk, was "Ruler" of the club until his death in 1936. Hugh Walpole, Agatha Christie, and Dorothy L. Sayers were among the other members.

Bailey was short and lean, with ample black hair, a black mustache, and thick eyeglasses. He concentrated his imaginative and creative life in his work, and was a retiring and respectable citizen. In many of his novels he created settings where mountains meet the sea: He and his wife retired to such a place, in North Wales. He died in 1961.

ANALYSIS

The critics who argue that H. C. Bailey's detective fiction is dated, dull, and full of class prejudice are mistaken. Though only nineteen years younger than Arthur Conan Doyle, Bailey was distinctly a man of the twentieth century. His plots exhibit a perceptive candor about sexual motives and human aberrations. There is none of the snobbery that holds that ancestry, education, or profession guarantee superiority. There is also no "land of hope and glory" patriotism. If liberal churchmen and civil servants are often narrow-minded and self-important in Bailey's work, so too are retired army officers and landed gentlemen. Fortune avoids the pomp and ceremony of upper-class institutions whenever he can; he is kind to his brother-in-law the bishop, but he is not impressed by him. Fortune favors his eating clubs, not on the basis of their membership but for the quality of their muffins. Mr. Clunk is of humble origins and chiefly serves the poor; Bailey intends that the reader think Clunk a humbug for his pious cant, his Gospel Hall work, and his profitable investments, but case after case finds him lavish in good works. Clunk is the nemesis of pretentious charitable institutions that exploit the poor and helpless.

HONOUR AMONG THIEVES

Bailey has a rare gift for portraying sympathetically the poor and neglected of society. "The Brown Paper" (in *Mr. Fortune Here*, 1940) explores the friendship of two working-class Londoners: Ann Stubbs, an orphan in her early teens, and Jim Hay, a robust deliveryman a few years older. *Honour Among Thieves* (1947) shows, among many other things, the growth of trust and affection between Alf Buck, who has fled his criminal past to work a truck farm, and Louisa Connell, who has escaped from reform school. There is the further fine touch of showing this relationship develop through the eyes of Alf's younger brother, who resents Lou as a ruinous intrusion and fails to understand his brother's growing interest in her. Clunk, without their knowledge, protects all of them both from Alf and Lou's past criminal associates and from the police.

THE VERON MYSTERY

Yet Bailey does not represent moral character as depending on social class; if spoiled and selfish types are often found among the prosperous and secure, he is merely holding a mirror to reality. Some of his middle- and upper-class characters are honest, reliable, and generous in spirit; some of his working-class types are villains to the core. He will sometimes show diabolical cooperation between servants and masters; in *The Veron Mystery* (1939), a shrewd old serving woman first tries to protect her dying master, then speeds him to his grave in an effort to protect his estranged but worthy son.

Bailey's stories and novels offer a rich variety of women. They come from all classes and backgrounds and range from stammering infants to wise ancients. There are dedicated, efficient professionals—such as Dr. Isabel Cope in *The Life Sentence* (1946)—candid college students, spunky teenagers, philosophical single women, and devoted wives and mothers. A single short story from 1939 presents the Honorable Victoria Pumphrey, a charming and masterful detective whom the reader unfortunately sees only in her first case. This Bailey rarity, "A Matter of Speculation," may be found in *Ellery Queen's Anthology*, issue 15, 1968. Yet without wickedness and murder there would be no detective stories, and Bailey's women, though usually interesting, are sometimes murderous. Indeed, his female criminals are alarming in their resourcefulness and numbing in their malice and villainy. If demonstrating that the female is deadlier than the male is misogynistic, Bailey stands convicted.

THE BISHOP'S CRIME

Children figure in many of the stories and novels, tiresomely so according to detractors. Imperiled children often contribute to the suspense and anxiety induced by Bailey's plots; the author's ability to represent the minds of small children is extraordinary. They are far from alike; in *The Bishop's Crime* (1940), the reader first meets Bishop Rankin's daughter Peggy Rankin, ten years old, outside after dark to steal plums. When Fortune finally wins the trust of this high-spirited girl, she contributes to the solution of the mystery.

Apart from the series heroes themselves, Bailey has one large group of characters who, taken altogether, may be too good to be true. Many of his stories have love stories as subordinate plots; in these, there are a number of young men whose devotion to their ladies is chivalric, unconditional, and selfless.

REGGIE FORTUNE

The character of Reggie Fortune changes hardly at all through a very long series of stories and novels, though in the latter tales Fortune does remark about his advancing years and reflect on cases of earlier days. Plump, baby-faced, and blond, Fortune prefers lying down to sitting, and sitting to walking. A gourmet with a large appetite, he avoids distilled liquor altogether, but enjoys table wines. He prefers the quiet country life to the bustle of the city. Whenever possible he will sleep late and start his day with a long soak in the tub. He enjoys his pipe and cigars in moderation. He protests when called to cases but, once engaged, proves capable of rapid sprints, long hikes, and furious—everyone except Fortune would say recklessly dangerous—driving. Fortune was dropping his final *g*'s before Lord Peter Wimsey came on the scene, and he was dropping many parts of speech as well. His manner of speaking is usually brief, like old-fashioned telegrams, interspersed with quaint expressions such as "Oh my hat!" and "My only Aunt!"

Joan Amber, Fortune's wife, rarely plays a large role in his adventures, but she appears often enough to have a distinct style and character. Joan is far happier in society than Fortune, but, lovely as she is, she goes out to enjoy people rather than to be admired. She sometimes prods her husband to get him started on a case, but she never interferes once he has started. Un-

Medical expert Reggie Fortune assists Scotland Yard in this illustration from H. C. Bailey's 1923 short story "The President of San Jacinto."

doubtedly devoted, Joan nevertheless sustains a line of teasing banter that might well irritate a man less pleased with himself than Fortune. Elise, the cook of the household, is always offstage; the reader knows her by the exotic feasts she prepares for the Fortunes. Sam, the chauffeur, on the other hand, is considerably more than a servant; when the police are unable or unwilling to help, Fortune often calls on Sam to do some discreet investigating. Sam has sharp eyes and a clever mind. He is also tough and reliable in the tight spots.

All discussions of Fortune must take up the debate over whether he is an intuitive detective, operating with a sort of sixth sense for crime, or an innocent. Reggie Fortune describes himself as a simple, natural man: His talent for finding clues and drawing far-reaching inferences from them may indeed illustrate how an unfettered human intelligence can work unaffected by prejudice and preconceived theory. He does not, in fact, recognize killers as such on first meeting them, but he can usually tell if pain or torment are present; on the other hand, he invariably recognizes goodness when he meets it. All readers would agree that he is a fine judge of character; devoted fans might add that that is a function of his good heart as well as his learning and experience. A typical case for Reggie Fortune is one in which the police are either baffled or have accepted a simple explanation that fails to take everything into account. The detective's zeal comes both from a need to right wrongs and from a vast array of exact knowledge that permits him to see what conscientious police officers often miss. Along the way he displays a commanding knowledge of physiology, the effects of various wounds and poisons, and the healing arts. Yet some of his cases are solved by his command of ancient languages and literatures and an understanding of history. Bailey's achievement in his portrayal of Fortune is of the same order as Rex Stout's with Nero Wolfe: Both writers have created credible geniuses.

Though he is based in London, most of Fortune's cases take him to provincial towns and villages, where the police are often honest and sometimes intelligent but rarely both. If the detective inspectors on the scene are rarely crooked, they are quite often obstructive, so that Fortune must overcome their obstacles as well as those created by criminals. The turning point in many of his cases comes when he has finally persuaded the Honorable Sidney Lomas to send in Superintendent Bell and Inspector Underwood of the Central Intelligence Division.

JOSHUA CLUNK

Joshua Clunk, whose cases often take him to the provinces as well, must labor even harder to engage the attention of the police or to prevent them from charging the innocent while the guilty go free. Well along in years, sallow of complexion, preening his gray whiskers, with prominent eyes and false teeth, Clunk rivals Erle Stanley Gardner's Bertha Cool as the most immediately unattractive crime fighter in detective fiction. His comfortable suburban home resembles Fortune's in having a large garden and an atmosphere of serenity, but the overall tone could hardly be more different. One sees even less of Mrs. Clunk than of Mrs. Fortune. She is, nevertheless, the perfect mate for the old puritan, sharing his pleasure and activity in the Gospel Hall he founded and in which he preaches. The couple call each other "Dearie," and Mrs. Clunk never questions her husband concerning his curious activities. Sunday at the Clunks is given to attending divine services (three of them) with large meals and cozy naps. Clunk will not work or even drive his automobile on a Sunday, unless, as he puts it, the Lord's work demands an exception: Then he hails a taxi and pursues his case with typical energy.

Gushing exaggerated praise and compliments on staff and police alike, squeaking when alarmed, pattering in and out of rooms on his short legs, interlarding his animated talk with verses of hymns, and chewing or sucking candy, the energetic Clunk somehow stirs and guides staff and police to discover criminals and liberate the innocent. One can sometimes get through an entire adventure without Clunk's appearing in court, but the reader finds him in this setting often enough to know that he is quick-witted, knowledgeable, and persuasive. Indeed, some of the best scenes in the series take place in courtrooms. For sheer genius in seeing the significance of things and reasoning inferentially, Clunk is at least the equal of Fortune and may be (partly as a result of Bailey's own ironic camouflage) the most underrated of the great fictional detectives.

It is a device of this series that Clunk should be out of the action much more than he is in it. Most often the reader sees the plots unfolding with no detective present—Bailey always uses third-person, omniscient narrative—or, once the initially unrelated episodes begin to form a pattern, one or another of Clunk's assistants is followed through his laborious investigations. His assistants often question Clunk's directions—and even his motives. The assistants—usually Victor Hopley, Jock Scott, or Miss John—are notable for their sensible decency and good taste, yet the reader is never in doubt that the cases are Clunk's, and however much his assistants grumble or question, they continue working for the old hypocrite.

Clearly Fortune and Clunk have much in common— and so do the elaborate stories in which they operate.

Scenery plays a considerable role in the tales; indeed, Fortune himself maintains that the rivalry between the fertile lowlands and the chalky hills was at the basis of the crimes in the adventure consequently called *Black Land, White Land* (1937). Certainly the landscape plays a large role in *The Veron Mystery*. One of the leading characteristics of a Fortune or Clunk plot is that the detectives can solve the crime at hand only by solving a much older one, left unsolved by the authorities of its day, or worse, mistakenly solved by convicting and punishing someone who was really innocent. That is another leading characteristic of both series: Bailey's villains are not content to murder out of malice or greed; they delight in finding innocent victims and framing them. Fortune and Clunk are therefore frequently engaged in reevaluating a case that well-meaning police have accepted from the hands of clever criminals.

Most controversial among the traits these detectives share is their willingness to arrange and even execute justice on their own account: A favorite device is to so apply pressure on partners in crime that they turn on one another, usually with lethal violence. Yet saving the cost of a trial is by no means the main goal: Bailey's heroes are usually acting to protect the injured innocent or the honestly redeemed. Their means are often disturbing—one winces when Clunk or Fortune quietly suppresses evidence or rearranges it; their ends, on the other hand—the restoration of wholesome, useful life—are admirable.

It has already been suggested that the quality of the Fortune stories, followed by the Clunk and Fortune novels, remained consistently high. Over the course of Fortune's and Clunk's literary lives, however, some social change is evident. The earliest Fortune stories sometimes reflect the exuberance that affected the arts in the 1920's. Nevertheless, the tone reached by the mid-1920's remained fairly uniform until World War II, when Reggie Fortune gave up much of the luxury that had attended his life at home. This austerity lasted to the end of the series; plush living had hardly returned to Great Britain by 1948. During the war against Adolf Hitler, Fortune and Clunk sometimes challenged German spies; international intrigue had not been a feature of the series before that point. With their restrained and serious atmosphere, the wartime novels are, perhaps, the most consistently good; at least they feature new levels of complexity in plot and new depths of villainy among the wicked. Bailey's last four novels have all his trademark characteristics but an even leaner style. He was always terse, but here there is more reliance on dialogue, both to advance the stories and to define character, and a minimum of description.

As a storyteller, Bailey displays wisdom, learning, and skill in entertaining combination. His stories and novels occur in particular times and places, but they illustrate values of valor, innocence, and truth, in conflict with hate, greed, and cruelty. Arranged in challenging puzzles full of colorful characters artfully drawn, his novels are classics.

Robert McColley

PRINCIPAL MYSTERY AND DETECTIVE FICTION

REGGIE FORTUNE SERIES: *Call Mr. Fortune,* 1920; *Mr. Fortune's Practice,* 1923; *Mr. Fortune's Trials,* 1925; *Mr. Fortune, Please,* 1927; *Mr. Fortune Speaking,* 1929; *Mr. Fortune Explains,* 1930; *Case for Mr. Fortune,* 1932; *Mr. Fortune Wonders,* 1933; *Shadow on the Wall,* 1934; *Mr. Fortune Objects,* 1935; *A Clue for Mr. Fortune,* 1936; *Black Land, White Land,* 1937; *This Is Mr. Fortune,* 1938; *The Great Game,* 1939; *Mr. Fortune Here,* 1940; *The Bishop's Crime,* 1940; *Meet Mr. Fortune,* 1942; *No Murder,* 1942 (also known as *The Apprehensive Dog*); *Mr. Fortune Finds a Pig,* 1943; *The Cat's Whisker,* 1944 (also known as *Dead Man's Effects*); *The Life Sentence,* 1946; *Saving a Rope,* 1948

JOSHUA CLUNK SERIES: *Garstons,* 1930 (also known as *The Garston Murder Case*); *The Red Castle,* 1932; *The Sullen Sky Mystery,* 1935; *Clunk's Claimant,* 1937 (also known as *The Twittering Bird Mystery*); *The Veron Mystery,* 1939 (also known as *Mr. Clunk's Text*); *The Little Captain,* 1941 (also known as *Orphan Ann*); *Dead Man's Shoes,* 1942 (also known as *Nobody's Vineyard*); *Slippery Ann,* 1944 (also known as *The Queen of Spades*); *The Wrong Man,* 1945; *Honour Among Thieves,* 1947; *Shrouded Death,* 1950

NONSERIES NOVEL: *The Man in the Cape,* 1933

OTHER MAJOR WORKS

NOVELS: 1901-1910 • *My Lady of Orange,* 1901; *Karl of Erbach,* 1902; *The Master of Gray,* 1903; *Rimingtons,* 1904; *Beaujeu,* 1905; *Under Castle Walls,* 1906 (also known as *Springtime*); *Raoul, Gentleman of Fortune,* 1907 (also known as *A Gentleman of Fortune*); *Colonel Stow,* 1908 (also known as *Colonel Greatheart*); *The God of Clay,* 1908; *Storm and Treasure,* 1910

1911-1920 • *The Lonely Queen,* 1911; *The Suburban,* 1912; *The Sea Captain,* 1913; *The Gentleman Adventurer,* 1914; *The Highwayman,* 1915; *The Gamesters,* 1916; *The Young Lovers,* 1917; *The Pillar of Fire,* 1918; *Barry Leroy,* 1919; *His Serene Highness,* 1920

1921-1940 • *The Fool,* 1921; *The Plot,* 1922; *The Rebel,* 1923; *Knight at Arms,* 1924; *The Golden Fleece,* 1925; *The Merchant Prince,* 1926; *Bonaventure,* 1927; *Judy Bovenden,* 1928; *Mr. Cardonnel,* 1931; *The Bottle Party,* 1940

PLAY: *The White Hawk,* pr., pb. 1909 (with David Kimball; dramatization of Bailey's novel *Beaujeu*)

CHILDREN'S LITERATURE: *The Roman Eagles,* 1928

NONFICTION: *Forty Years After: The Story of the Franco-German War, 1870,* 1914

BIBLIOGRAPHY

Priestman, Martin. *The Cambridge Companion to Crime Fiction.* New York: Cambridge University Press, 2003. Contains a chapter on the Golden Age of mystery writing as well as one on the private eye, which provide a perspective on Bailey's work.

Purcell, Mark. "The Reggie Fortune Short Stories: An Appreciation and Partial Bibliography." *The Mystery Readers/Lovers Newsletter* 5, no. 4 (1972): 1-3. Lists Purcell's favorites among the Reggie Fortune stories with an explanation of what makes the listed stories noteworthy.

Rzepka, Charles J. *Detective Fiction.* Malden, Mass.: Polity, 2005. Overview of detective fiction written in English focuses on the relationship between literary representations of private detectives and the cultures that produce those representations. Provides context for understanding Bailey's work.

Sarjeant, William A. S. "'The Devil Is with Power': Joshua Clunk and the Fight for Right." *The Armchair Detective* 17, no. 3 (1984): 270-279. Looks at one of Bailey's famous characters and examines his function.

_____. "In Defense of Mr. Fortune." *The Armchair Detective* 14, no. 4 (1981): 302-312. Focuses on one of Bailey's most famous characters and delves into his function both within the writer's works and within the larger world of detective fiction.

JOHN BALL

Born: Schenectady, New York; July 8, 1911
Died: Encino, California; October 15, 1988
Type of plot: Police procedural

PRINCIPAL SERIES

Virgil Tibbs, 1965-1986
Chief Jack Tallon, 1977-1984

PRINCIPAL SERIES CHARACTERS

VIRGIL TIBBS is a black detective officer on the Pasadena, California, police force. Unmarried, he is described as about thirty years old in the first novel and remains in his thirties throughout the series. Cool, competent, self-possessed, and systematic, Tibbs has risen above his deprived boyhood in the segregated South of the 1940's, yet in his job he must repeatedly confront the effects of discrimination and hatred.

JACK TALLON, a thirty-four-year-old sergeant on the Pasadena police force, leaves the stress and strain of urban violence and major crime to become chief of police in the small town of Whitewater, Washington. There he discovers a need for police professionalism equal to that of the big city: Even in small towns, fighting crime calls for a particular kind of character, teamwork, and integrity.

CONTRIBUTION

John Ball's mystery novels document his status as a pioneering master of the police procedural genre. These finely crafted, intricately plotted works focus directly on the minutiae of criminal investigation, emphasizing both the efficiency of plodding routine and the necessity of dovetailing teamwork in solving and preventing crime. He concentrated on different aspects of these tasks in his two series. Virgil Tibbs works primarily on his own, meticulously piecing details together until the entire complicated picture emerges. Jack Tallon, on the other hand, is—as chief of police—the consummate organizer and team player; his solutions to problems arise from organized group efforts. Taken together, the two series (along with Ball's nonseries mysteries) develop what might be called a systems approach to crime and detection. This focus on teamwork and on following established procedures was Ball's trademark.

BIOGRAPHY

John Dudley Ball, Jr., was born in Schenectady, New York, on July 8, 1911, to John Dudley, Sr., a research scientist, and Alena L. Wiles Ball. He attended Carroll College in Waukesha, Wisconsin, earning his bachelor's degree in 1934. After becoming a commercial pilot for Pan American World Airways, he joined the United States Army Air Transport Command at the outbreak of World War II, serving as a flight instructor and a member of a flight crew until 1946. Following his service, Ball pursued a career as a music critic and annotator, first as a writer of liner notes for Columbia Masterworks Records (1946-1949) and music editor for the *Brooklyn Eagle* (1946-1950) and then as a columnist for the *New York World-Telegram*. Ball also worked as a music commentator for WOL, a radio station in Washington, D.C. During this time he published his first books, on the record industry and early recordings of classical music. Later, Ball worked in advertising and for various public relations enterprises.

In 1958, he joined the Institute of the Aerospace Sciences (IAS) as public relations director, a post he held until 1961, when IAS was absorbed by the larger American Rocket Society. At that point Ball joined DMS News Service, a publishing company in Beverly Hills, where he was employed as editor in chief until 1963. He served as writer, chairman, and editor in chief for the University of California Mystery Library Program. During the mid-1970's Ball also became a sworn deputy sheriff in Los Angeles County and a volunteer associate of the City of Pasadena Police Department.

The year 1958 marked Ball's return to book publication. Since then he wrote or edited more than thirty books, including fourteen mystery novels, winning the Edgar Allan Poe Award (1966) and the Crime Writers' Association's Gold Dagger Award (1966), both for *In the Heat of the Night* (1965). In addition, Ball wrote some four hundred articles on aviation, music, astronomy, and travel. He died October 15, 1988, in Encino, California.

ANALYSIS

John Ball's first mystery in the Virgil Tibbs series, *In the Heat of the Night*, both catapulted him to popular and critical acclaim and established the central themes of his work. Virgil Tibbs was an instant hit. Appearing as he did at the height of the agitation for civil rights of the mid-1960's, he incarnated many of the qualities that the public wished to attribute to members of the recently insurgent African Americans. Tibbs is simultaneously proud and circumspect, sensitive to the outrages of prejudice yet aware that public attitudes cannot be forced, only quietly persuaded. Tibbs is a vector in the campaign for universal human tolerance; he forces a recognition of his humanity through his superior achievements.

IN THE HEAT OF THE NIGHT

In the Heat of the Night remains Ball's most popular and most widely acclaimed book, though it certainly is not his best. It captured and holds the popular imagination more for its setting and its central character than for its style or the quality of the plot. The novel opens in the middle of a heat wave in Wells, a small town in the still-segregated North Carolina of the early 1960's. The town stagnates in poverty. To improve economic conditions, a local civic organization is sponsoring a musical

festival, headed by the great conductor Mantoli. In the small hours of one sweltering morning, Mantoli is found murdered. The local good-old-boy police chief, hired more for availability than skill, lurches into action. Sent to the train station to check for suspects, a deputy spots a likely one: a thirty-year-old black, alone and flashing a suspicious amount of money. The case is apparently already solved.

When the chief interrogates him, however, the man—Virgil Tibbs—states that he has earned that money working as a police officer in Pasadena, California; that unlike anyone on the Wells police force he has experience in homicide work; and that the chief has already made mistakes that could make solving the crime impossible. The chief is dumbfounded. Bad enough to lose a prime suspect, but far worse to have that suspect—a black man—humiliate him in the process. To save face, he resolves to get rid of this rival, but the case has such heavy political and economic implications that he finds himself forced to ask Tibbs to stay on as an officially requisitioned consultant. Meanwhile, tensions rise as the heat continues to bake the town. Economic survival depends on solving the crime and salvaging the festival, tarnished by the murder and shorn of a big-name conductor and impresario. Further, Tibbs threatens the social and racial equilibrium of the segregated town: His position gives him authority over white people accustomed to unanimous consent about keeping blacks in their place.

Throughout this potentially explosive situation, Tibbs keeps his composure, complacently tolerating even the casual insults that segregation imposes on him. He too, however, suffers in the heat: After all, to escape this kind of situation, he had gone to California, where a man could expect to be judged by the quality of his work rather than the color of his skin. Still, he remains professional, methodically proceeding with his investigation and providing lessons in tolerance along the way. Tibbs's professionalism shows most in his method and attention to detail; in instance after instance, he sees what others overlook, and he is constantly aware of the figure in the pattern he is attempting to reveal. In the process he is able to keep the chief from jeopardizing his own career by arresting the wrong man. Significantly, the climax of the novel occurs when Tibbs deliberately breaches the decorum of segregation by demanding service at a whites-only diner; thus, he is able to demonstrate that bigotry is the real culprit in the case. The novel ends with the chief's acknowledging that Tibbs is a man; the chief leaves him to await his train on a whites-only bench, though he refrains from shaking hands with Tibbs.

The book is cinematic, as novels of setting and character often are, and its screen adaptation was a phenomenal success. Released in 1967, the film won five Academy Awards, including Best Picture and Best Actor (Sidney Poitier). Still, although this acclaim had much to do with the book's popularity, the film fails to capture the essence of the novel. The book's distinction is founded on its depiction of police procedure, its patient analysis of routinely acquired details of fact, and its theme of transracial tolerance—that is, the acknowledgment of our common humanity as the only means of achieving harmonious social order. Before this novel appeared, few American crime

writers had centered on painstaking, depersonalized methodology as a basis for their fiction; in other traditions, only Margery Allingham, E. C. Bentley, Michael Innes, and Ngaio Marsh had treated it extensively, and they either emphasize the eccentricity of their police detectives or place them in quite exceptional situations. As a precedent, the enormously successful television series *Dragnet* (1951-1959, 1967-1970) must be acknowledged, though even there, attention to eccentricity predominates. Virgil Tibbs reverses this. His ethnicity creates expectations of eccentricity, but Tibbs is the essence of impersonal normality, of basic humanity. His behavior is that of the superior culture: He "outwhites" the whites. His is the dispassionate soul, the cool intellect struggling to understand, and in the process transcending, prejudged boundaries. His is the colorless, raceless future of humanity, achieved through exercise of compassion and reason. In this respect he is a remote descendant of the character of Jim in Mark Twain's *The Adventures of Huckleberry Finn* (1884).

THE EYES OF BUDDHA

Some of the later Virgil Tibbs books realize these themes more successfully. All of them, to be sure, lack the steaminess of setting, the readily identifiable tension, the overt racial confrontation of *In the Heat of the Night*. Further, because they advance the same themes, they remain less innovative. Even so, the best of them, *The Eyes of Buddha* (1976) and *Then Came Violence* (1980), raise Virgil Tibbs to greater definition. Racial confrontation is absent from these novels; in fact, in both novels Tibbs is isolated, shown as an exceptional individual working on his own. In *The Eyes of Buddha*, Tibbs is given temporary leave from his official duties to pursue a private case of an heiress who had vanished from a beauty pageant. His investigation winds a tangled path to eventual success in Katmandu, where he is given the opportunity to confront an alien culture and where his discoveries also lead to solution of an apparently unrelated case back in Pasadena.

THEN CAME VIOLENCE

In *Then Came Violence*, Tibbs is forced to lead a dual life: While ostensibly continuing to carry out his normal police work, he is also detailed to the State Department of the United States to provide cover for the exiled family of a progressive democratic African chief of state under attack by insurrectionist forces. The wife of the president proves to be a female African counterpart of Tibbs himself. Poised, articulate, the product of a composite culture, she is willing—like her husband—to put her life on the line to realize her vision of a better society. Clearly, this vision corresponds to the object of Tibbs's vocation as a police officer. His goal is not merely to solve crimes, still less to capture or punish criminals, but also to create an atmosphere in which peace and justice can flourish. The dual role imposed on Tibbs here nearly undoes him. Not only is he on duty all the time, denied the repose and relaxation necessary to function efficiently, but also he finds himself falling in love with the woman he has sworn to protect and keep inviolate. In the end, Tibbs does solve a tricky armed robbery case and a convoluted vigilante operation, but he loses the woman and family he has come to love—they escape to a more secure refuge in Switzerland when it is found that the husband-father may still be alive. Tibbs, though personally devastated, accepts this situation philosophically, as does she: It is part of the price the gifted must pay to secure some semblance of order in society.

This pattern of the exceptional idealistic loner required by circumstance to subordinate himself to higher purposes would be overbearing if attention were not continually directed toward established methodology and teamwork. What emerges is an interlocking set of paradoxes in the novelistic world of Ball. For example, Tibbs is the only man in Southern California qualified to serve as consort to the wife of a deposed African leader, but at every opportunity, Ball shows him to be dependent on the joint efforts of the police force, every member of which possesses unique qualifications. More than once Tibbs's Japanese American partner, Bob Nakamura, is referred to as a genius in his own right, and every police team is a composite of professional specialists. Similarly, Tibbs often arrives at his solutions by the most startling leaps of intuition, yet these revelations hinge on disparate details assembled by plodding routine. Again, everyone seems well disposed and perfectly attuned to the other members of his team.

In such a world it is sometimes difficult to imagine where any impetus to crime could originate. On occasion this lends an air of unreality to the proceedings, and the characters begin to look like mannequins going through mechanical motions. Ball has sometimes been faulted for the stiffness of his dialogue, but when his world works, as it does in the best of this series, these objections become irrelevant, blotted out by the consistency of vision. In Ball's world, the world of Virgil Tibbs, evil exists, but it can be countered by the goodwill of talented men working together with singleness of purpose.

POLICE CHIEF

These themes carry over into the Chief Jack Tallon series. On its face the fictional premise for this series seems completely different. In *Police Chief* (1977), Jack Tallon begins as a police sergeant in Pasadena. After putting in overtime on an emergency hostage situation in which one police officer is killed and a bus accident in which six die, he looks up from the bodies to see his terror-stricken wife in the crowd of onlookers; at that moment he remembers that this evening was to have been their wedding anniversary celebration.

Recognizing that the constant mayhem and crises of major urban police work are taking their toll on his private life, he applies for the position of chief of police in Whitewater, eastern Washington, population ten thousand. On arrival, he discovers a calmer environment but a small staff of largely unqualified personnel. He accepts the challenge of developing a professional team out of this collection of people and soon learns that violence and personal strain are not confined to the big city. A series of brutal rapes occurs, accompanied by a malicious underground campaign that holds the new chief himself, the intruder into this cozy world, responsible.

Dismayed by this lack of trust, Tallon nevertheless devotes himself completely to this problem, recruiting help from the community to augment his limited force. He initiates a training program for the staff, emphasizing the necessity of detail work and routine. Soon his efforts begin to show results. By piecing together isolated clues, he is able to break a drug ring at the local college. Tallon's force gains confidence and pride with increasing competence, and the community's good-will mounts. Aware of the enhanced character of his people, Tallon resists pressure to call in the heavy guns of the local sheriff. Finally he is able to put into action a plan to trap the rapist—one that is, ironically, almost ruined by the interference of a well-meaning citizen newly motivated by pride in his community. The rapist is revealed to be a native of the town, the assistant to the editor of the local newspaper. Peace returns to the community, but only at the expense of the revelation that the seeds of violence are everywhere, that no place is safe, and that everyone is responsible for combating the evil that constantly reappears.

These themes weave through the Tallon series as well as the Tibbs series, as do certain insistent motifs. One is the image of a young woman who has chosen to escape from a situation of luxury or celebrity by retreating into a religious community, sometimes turning her back on her family. Another is the necessity of tolerance, of recognizing a common humanity, especially with apparently unorthodox groups. Often this appears in inverted form, as when Ball connects violence or crime with the mindless malice implicit in prejudice, whether racial, social, sexual, or religious. Connected with this theme is a sympathetic treatment of Asian religions and cultures and of syncretistic religious movements.

Yet dominating these motifs, and to a certain extent absorbing them, are the dual touchstones of personal pride and integrity. Ball's central characters believe in themselves but nevertheless strive to improve. Although confident in their own abilities, they know that unaided they can do little; so they give themselves to others unreservedly, becoming consummate team players and tireless workers and in the process instilling pride and competence in other members of the team. This approach to character seems somehow Asian; Ball's characters possess the discipline, the selflessness, and the concentration of the Asian warrior. Aware of the smallness of their share in the divine plan, they remain equally aware of the uniqueness and the necessity of their contribution to the welfare of the whole.

James L. Livingston

PRINCIPAL MYSTERY AND DETECTIVE FICTION

VIRGIL TIBBS SERIES: *In the Heat of the Night*, 1965; *The Cool Cottontail*, 1966; *Johnny Get Your Gun*, 1969 (revised as *Death for a Playmate*, 1972); *Five Pieces of Jade*, 1972; *The Eyes of Buddha*, 1976; *Then Came Violence*, 1980; *Singapore*, 1986

CHIEF JACK TALLON SERIES: *Police Chief*, 1977; *Trouble for Tallon*, 1981; *Chief Tallon and the S.O.R.*, 1984

NONSERIES NOVELS: *The First Team*, 1971; *Mark One: The Dummy*, 1974; *The Killing in the Market*, 1978 (with Bevan Smith); *The Murder Children*, 1979

OTHER SHORT FICTION: *The Upright Corpse*, 1979

OTHER MAJOR WORKS

NOVELS: *Rescue Mission*, 1966; *Miss 1000 Spring Blossoms*, 1968; *Last Plane Out*, 1970; *The Fourteenth Point*, 1973; *The Winds of Mitamura*, 1975; *Phase Three Alert*, 1977

CHILDREN'S LITERATURE: *Operation Springboard*, 1958; *Spacemaster I*, 1960; *Judo Boy*, 1964; *Arctic Showdown*, 1966

NONFICTION: *Records for Pleasure*, 1947; *The Phonograph Record Industry*, 1947; *Edwards: U.S. Air Force Flight Test Center*, 1962; *Dragon Hotel*, 1968; *Ananda: Where Yoga Lives*, 1982; *We Live in New Zealand*, 1984

EDITED TEXTS: *The Mystery Story*, 1976; *Cop Cade*, 1978

BIBLIOGRAPHY

Ball, John. "Virgil Tibbs." In *The Great Detectives*, edited by Otto Penzler. Boston: Little, Brown, 1978. Argues for the place of Detective Tibbs in the pantheon of great literary detectives.

"John Ball: Seventy-seven, Writer Noted for Virgil Tibbs." *Los Angeles Times*, October 18, 1988, p. 26. Describes his life and career and notes the genesis of the character Tibbs.

Panek, LeRoy Lad. *An Introduction to the Detective Story*. Bowling Green, Ohio: Bowling Green State University Popular Press, 1987. Introductory overview of detective fiction by a major, prolific scholar of the genre. Provides context for understanding Ball.

Pepper, Andrew. *The Contemporary American Crime Novel: Race, Ethnicity, Gender, Class.* Edinburgh: Edinburgh University Press, 2000. Examination of the representation and importance of various categories of identity in mainstream American crime fiction, including black detectives such as Tibbs.

Reddy, Maureen T. *Traces, Codes, and Clues: Reading Race in Crime Fiction.* New Brunswick, N.J.: Rutgers University Press, 2003. Comparative analysis of race in both American and British crime fiction. Sheds light on African American detectives, including Tibbs. Bibliographic references and index.

Walsh, Louise D. "Collector Tracks Down Fiction's Black Sleuths." *The Washington Post*, September 8, 1988, p. J01. In this article about a Washington, D.C., area collector of fiction featuring black detectives, the effect of the Tibbs character is discussed.

Winks, Robin W. *Modus Operandi: An Excursion into Detective Fiction.* Boston: D. R. Godine, 1982. Brief but suggestive history and critique of the detective genre. Helps place Ball's writing in the greater context.

HONORÉ DE BALZAC
Honoré Balzac

Born: Tours, France; May 20, 1799
Died: Paris, France; August 18, 1850
Types of plot: Espionage; police procedural; psychological; thriller; inverted

CONTRIBUTION

Honoré de Balzac wrote his fictional works as the self-appointed secretary of French society. It was natural, therefore, that he should consider the police (both political and judicial), this newest and most efficient branch of modern, autocratic governments. He was in fact one of the earliest writers of French fiction to recognize the police as society's best defender against subversives and criminals.

Like members of other powerful and arbitrary organizations, Balzac's police officers were shown to be relentless in their missions and cruel in their vengeance. Thus, he was less interested in police work as such than in the psychological study of police officers of genius—not only for their Machiavellian cynicism and superior understanding of people but also for their quest to dominate and rule the world. Such theories of vast conspiratorial associations and of intellectual power influenced later novelists, including Fyodor Dostoevski, Maurice Leblanc, Pierre Souvestre, Marcel Allain, and Ian Fleming, among others.

BIOGRAPHY

The eldest of four children, Honoré de Balzac was born as Honoré Balzac on May 20, 1799, in Tours, France, where his father was a high government official. His mother inculcated in young Honoré a taste for the occult and for Swedenborgian metaphysics. After his early studies, distinguished only by the breadth of his reading, Balzac attended law school while auditing classes at the Sorbonne.

Although Balzac was graduated in 1819, he rejected a legal career and decided instead to write plays. His first work, a verse tragedy about Oliver Cromwell, was judged a failure by friends and family. Undaunted by their verdict, however, Balzac began writing penny dreadfuls and gothic thrillers under various pseudonyms. Furthermore, he expected to become rich by establishing a publishing company, a printing office, and a type foundry; all three, in turn, went bankrupt and saddled him with insurmountable debts.

Not until 1829 did Balzac—using his real name—enjoy a modest success, with the publication of *Les Chouans* (1829; *The Chouans*, 1890). Driven as much by a need for money as by his desire to re-create the world, between 1829 and 1848 this new Prometheus wrote some one hundred titles that make up his monumental *La Comédie humaine* (*The Comedy of Human Life*, 1885-1893, 1896; best known as *The Human*

Honoré de Balzac. (Library of Congress)

Comedy, 1895-1896, 1911). He also published several literary magazines, short on subscribers but long on brilliant analysis, as shown by his study of Stendhal in the September 25, 1840, issue of *Revue parisienne*. In addition, Balzac's plays were usually well received by both critics and the public, as were the essays, newspaper pieces, and *Les Contes drolatiques* (1832-1837; *Droll Stories*, 1874, 1891).

In November of 1832, Balzac received a fan letter from the Ukraine signed "L'Étrangère." Thus began his life's greatest love affair, with the cultivated Countess Éveline Hanska. Besides pursuing a voluminous correspondence, the lovers met as often as opportunity and money allowed. Nevertheless, after her husband died in 1841, she continued to evade the marriage proposals of a financially strapped and increasingly ill Balzac (he suffered from cardiac hypertrophy), until March 14, 1850, when she finally married him. After the couple returned to Paris on May 21, Balzac's condition quickly worsened. He died soon after, on August 18, 1850.

ANALYSIS

Honoré de Balzac first practiced his craft by imitating, often slavishly, the sensational romances of Ann Radcliffe, Charles Robert Maturin, and Matthew Gregory Lewis, with their fantasies of the grotesque and the horrible. Balzac also learned that fiendish wickedness and sadistic sensuality can heighten the pleasure of a thrill-seeking public. Although he never officially acknowledged his early efforts, he incorporated many of their lessons in his later works, especially in the tales of the supernatural and criminal.

THE HUMAN COMEDY

Balzac's magnum opus, *The Human Comedy*, is a vast and detailed panorama of French society of the first half of the nineteenth century. In fact, Oscar Wilde has remarked, "The nineteenth century, as we know it, is largely an invention of Balzac." In nearly one hundred novels and stories evolve some two thousand fictional characters, who appear in various milieus, types, and professions, from Paris to the provinces, from old maids to poor relations, from lawyers to police officers and gangsters.

THE CHOUANS

Corentin is rightly the most famous of Balzac's police officers. He enters the scene in *The Chouans*, the first book to which Balzac signed his name, adding the self-ennobling particle *de*. Set in Brittany in 1799, the novel is a mixture of sentimental love story and political police intrigue. The obvious villain of the piece is Corentin, the spiritual, if not natural, son of Joseph Fouché, Napoleon Bonaparte's minister of police. In spite of his youth (he was born around 1777), Corentin already possesses all the qualities required of a great secret agent, because he has learned from his mentor and chief how to tack and bend with the wind. Everything about him is wily, feline, mysterious: His green eyes announce "malice and deceit," he has an "insinuating dexterity of address," he seeks to obtain respect, and he seems to say, "Let us divide the spoil!"

Always willing to suspect evil motives in human behavior and too clever to hold to only one position, Corentin already embodies Balzac's concept of the superior being, although in elementary form. To succeed, Corentin rejects no methods; he knows well how to use circumstances to his own ends. Furthermore, morality always changes and may not even exist, according to this modern Machiavellian, who is unconcerned with praise or blame: "As to betraying France, we who are superior to any scruples on that score can leave them to fools. . . . My patron Fouché is deep . . . enough, [and] he has always played a double game." To this conception of life can be added a natural bent for everything that touches police work. The idea, so dear to Balzac, that "there are vocations one must obey" is a kind of professional determinism that forces one to turn to what is already possible within him and to act and think accordingly.

Although not a series character in the accepted sense, Corentin does reappear in several other novels, particularly in *Une Ténébreuse Affaire* (1841; *The Gondreville Mystery*, 1891), in which he again acts in several covert operations, this time to protect various cabinet members unwisely involved in an attempted coup against Napoleon Bonaparte, and in *Splendeurs et misères des courtisanes* (1838-1847, 1869; *The Splendors and Miseries of Courtesans*, 1895). In *The Splendors and Miseries of Courtesans*, he plays the role of a private detective and works more to keep in practice than out of financial need.

THE GONDREVILLE MYSTERY

The Gondreville Mystery offers an excellent example of a ruthless police force, temporarily foiled perhaps but mercilessly victorious in the end. The novel also reveals that the political police are so unprincipled that they doctor the evidence and manipulate the facts to frame the innocent and thereby hide their own crimes. If, in the process, their victims are executed or imprisoned, it only serves to reinforce the notion of a powerful police, made all the more so when self-interest or wounded pride is at stake:

In this horrible affair passion, too, was involved, the passion of the principal agent [Corentin], a man still living, one of those first-rate underlings who can never be replaced, and [who] has made a certain reputation for himself by his remarkable exploits.

HISTORY OF THE THIRTEEN

Balzac's own worldview is made evident in the laying out of the ministerial plot and its subsequent cover-up. Indeed, the author of *Histoire des treize* (1834-

1835; *History of the Thirteen*, 1885-1886) loves to invent secret societies, either benevolent or nefarious, as a means of increasing the individual's power or, more likely, that of the government, which he calls "a permanent conspiracy." Because the political police are given a virtual carte blanche in the defense of the government and the ruling class, they are quick to take advantage of their status; they act arbitrarily and with impunity, often outside the law, thereby becoming so powerful that Balzac thought of them as a state within the state.

THE SPLENDORS AND MISERIES OF COURTESANS

Corentin is ably assisted by Contenson, a virtuoso of disguise, and by Peyrade, a crafty former nobleman with a perfect knowledge of aristocratic manners and language. Twenty years after their success in *The Gondreville Mystery*, all three are reunited in *The Splendors and Miseries of Courtesans*. Following a series of fantastic adventures replete with poisoned cherries, hidden passageways, rapes, and kidnappings—in short, all the melodramatic devices of Balzac's apprenticeship— they are ultimately instrumental in thwarting the villain's machinations.

Quite different from the political police are the judicial police, for their primary function is to prevent crimes and arrest criminals. Both because of the niceties required by law and because of their official and overt role, they are depicted in Balzac's novels as less sinister and frightening. Thus, their reputation is reduced, especially because even the well-known Sûreté seldom seems to succeed in apprehending thieves and murderers.

It is not that these police officers have more scruples, but that they lack the immense powers of action at Corentin's disposal. Unlike their political counterparts, they rely mostly on *agents provocateurs* and on denunciations from citizens who, attracted by financial rewards or driven by passion, often aid in the capture of criminals. For example, it is thanks to Mlle Michonneau that Bibi-Lupin can arrest Vautrin, a convict escaped from the hulks of Toulon and hiding at Mme Vauquer's boardinghouse.

In addition to differences in their functions and methods, the judicial police attract a very particular type of individual: Many officers are either ne'er-do-wells or come from the ranks of supposedly reformed criminals. Whereas political agents show intelligence, perspicacity, and perverse cunning, those of the official forces are generally mediocre and easily duped, this despite the popular saw that it takes a thief to catch a thief. Among these latter, though clearly superior, is Bibi-Lupin. An interesting character, being himself a former convict, Bibi-Lupin organized and has headed the Brigade de Sûreté since 1820.

DADDY GORIOT

Bibi-Lupin first appears in *Le Père Goriot* (1834-1835; *Daddy Goriot*, 1860; also known as *Père Goriot*). In it, on the arrest of his former chainmate, he hopes that Vautrin will attempt to escape, which would furnish him with the legal pretext to kill his archenemy. This clever trick might well have worked if only Vautrin were not Vautrin and had not suddenly sensed the trap. In *The Splendors and Miseries of Courtesans*, the Sûreté chief will again be ordered to fight against Vautrin, who this time is disguised as Abbé Carlos Herrera as his part in an elaborate but foiled swindle. (This is the same case on which Corentin and his associates are working.)

Bibi-Lupin does in fact recognize Vautrin's voice and a scar on his left arm, yet he cannot prove beyond a doubt that Herrera and Vautrin are indeed one and the same. Yet because of his experience with prisons, their special slang and mores, acquired during his own stays at Nantes and Toulon, Bibi-Lupin counts on the possibility that several inmates may unwittingly betray their leader. His strategy does not lack shrewdness, although it fails because the accused has immediately resumed his ascendance over his fellow gang-members. In a last attempt to unmask the false abbot, the police chief tries to make him betray himself by putting him in a cell with one of his former protégés.

Once more, Vautrin sees through Bibi-Lupin's ruse; he speaks only in Italian with his friend—to the indescribable rage of the spy who watches them, does not understand a word, and does not know what to do. Balzac creates a universe that is forbidden to the uninitiated, one in which the superior man frustrates his enemies' schemes and achieves his ends thanks to a secret language, a code, a magic formula, a system that remains impenetrable to all outsiders.

This duel between two mortal rivals can only end in the defeat of Bibi-Lupin, who is obviously outclassed by Vautrin. Tricks that would have succeeded with lesser people do not work with such a formidable adversary. Furthermore, accused by his superiors not only of having stolen from arrested suspects but also, and especially, "of moving and acting as if you alone were law and police in one," Bibi-Lupin realizes only too late his danger. Later, he can but watch as his former prison companion becomes his deputy and then replaces him six months later. That Vautrin, like any good and honest bourgeois, should retire after some fifteen years of police service filled with daring exploits—during which time he acted as Providence incarnate toward those his unorthodox methods had saved from ruin or scandal—is ironic, considering his view of the world.

Vautrin is the master criminal of *The Human Comedy*. Like all fictional criminals of genius, he wants much more than the vain satisfactions that money brings. He seeks above all to dominate, not to reform, a society that he despises and whose hypocritical middle-class morality he scorns. "Principles don't exist, only events. Laws don't exist, only circumstances," he explains to an all-too-attentive Eugène de Rastignac in *Père Goriot*. Such lucidity and cynicism, combined with an inflexible will, have led this satanic "poem from hell" to consider crime the supreme revolt against an intrinsically unjust world—a revolt further intensified by his homosexuality.

In the end, however, Vautrin goes over to the other side and becomes head of the Sûreté, just as his model, François-Eugène Vidocq, had done. Vidocq, whose memoirs had been published in 1828-1829, was a good friend of Balzac and often told him of his police adventures or his prison escapes, as numerous as they were extraordinary. Besides Vidocq, Vautrin is said to resemble other historical figures such as Yemelyan Pugachev and Louis-Pierre Louvel, a result of Balzac's technique of using historical originals, which he reinterprets, recreates, and ultimately transforms.

Vautrin does not believe that there are insurmountable barriers between the police and the underworld, and it does not disturb him to "supply the hulks with lodgers instead of lodging there," as long as he can command: "Instead of being the boss of the hulks, I shall be the Figaro of the law. . . . The profession a man follows in the eyes of the world is a mere sham; the reality is in the idea!"

In Balzac's opinion, police work does not consist of tracking down clues, questioning suspects, and solving crimes, but rather of arresting subversives, real or imagined, solely out of political necessity. Although he admires the nobility and courage of those who resist and finds his political operatives and their methods odious, Balzac recognizes that, regardless of the number of innocent men and women crushed in their path, they must all play their essential part in the eternal struggle between Order and Chaos.

Pierre L. Horn

PRINCIPAL MYSTERY AND DETECTIVE FICTION
NOVELS (ALL PART OF THE HUMAN COMEDY):
Les Chouans, 1829 (*The Chouans*); *Histoire des treize*, 1834-1835 (*History of the Thirteen*, 1885-1886; also known as *The Thirteen*; includes *Ferragus, chef des dévorants*, 1834 [*Ferragus, Chief of the Devorants*; also known as *The Mystery of the Rue Solymane*]; *La Duchesse de Langeais*, 1834 [*The Duchesse de Langeais*]; and *La Fille aus yeux d'or*, 1834-1835 [*The Girl with the Golden Eyes*]); *Le Père Goriot*, 1834-1835 (*Daddy Goriot*, 1860; also known as *Père Goriot*); *Splendeurs et misères des courtisanes*, 1838-1847, 1869 (*The Splendors and Miseries of Courtesans*, 1895; includes *Comment aiment les filles*, 1838, 1844 [*The Way That Girls Love*]; *À combien l'amour revient aux vieillards*, 1844 [*How Much Love Costs Old Men*]; *Où mènent les mauvais chemins*, 1846 [*The End of Bad Roads*]; and *La Dernière Incarnation de Vautrin*, 1847 [*The Last Incarnation of Vautrin*]); *Une Ténébreuse Affaire*, 1842 (*The Gondreville Mystery*, 1891)

OTHER MAJOR WORKS
NOVELS: *La Comédie humaine*, 1829-1848 (17 volumes; *The Comedy of Human Life*, 1885-1893, 1896 [40 volumes]; also known as *The Human Comedy*, 1895-1896, 1911 [53 volumes]; includes all titles listed in this section); *Physiologie du mariage*, 1829 (*The Physiology of Marriage*); *Gobseck*, 1830 (En-

glish translation); *La Maison du chat-qui-pelote*, 1830, 1869 (*At the Sign of the Cat and Racket*); *La Peau de chagrin*, 1831 (*The Wild Ass's Skin*; also known as *The Fatal Skin*); *Le Chef-d'œuvre inconnu*, 1831 (*The Unknown Masterpiece*); *Sarrasine*, 1831 (English translation); *La Femme de trente ans*, 1832-1842 (includes *Premières fautes*, 1832, 1842; *Souffrances inconnues*, 1834-1835; *À trente ans*, 1832, 1842; *Le Doigt de Dieu*, 1832, 1834-1835, 1842; *Les Deux Rencontres*, 1832, 1834-1835, 1842; and *La Vieillesse d'une mère coupable*, 1832, 1842); *Le Curé de Tours*, 1832 (*The Vicar of Tours*); *Louis Lambert*, 1832 (English translation); *Maître Cornélius*, 1832 (English translation); *Eugénie Grandet*, 1833 (English translation, 1859); *La Recherche de l'absolu*, 1834 (*Balthazar: Or, Science and Love*, 1859; also known as *The Quest of the Absolute*); *Melmoth réconcilié*, 1835 (*Melmoth Converted*); *Le Lys dans la vallée*, 1836 (*The Lily in the Valley*); *Histoire de la grandeur et de la décadence de César Birotteau*, 1837 (*History of the Grandeur and Downfall of César Birotteau*, 1860; also known as *The Rise and Fall of César Birotteau*); *Illusions perdues*, 1837-1843 (*Lost Illusions*); *Pierrette*, 1840 (English translation); *Le Curé de village*, 1841 (*The Country Parson*); *Mémoires de deux jeunes mariées*, 1842 (*The Two Young Brides*); *Ursule Mirouët*, 1842 (English translation); *La Cousine Bette*, 1846 (*Cousin Bette*); *Le Cousin Pons*, 1847 (*Cousin Pons*, 1880)

SHORT FICTION: *Les Contes drolatiques*, 1832-1837 (*Droll Stories*, 1874, 1891)

PLAYS: *Cromwell*, wr. 1819-1820, pb. 1925; *Vautrin*, pr., pb. 1840 (English translation, 1901); *La Marâtre*, pr., pb. 1848 (*The Stepmother*, 1901, 1958); *Le Faiseur*, pr. 1849 (also known as *Mercadet*; English translation, 1901); *The Dramatic Works*, pb. 1901 (2 volumes; includes *Vautrin*, *The Stepmother*, *Mercadet*, *Quinola's Resources*, and *Pamela Giraud*)

NONFICTION: *Correspondance*, 1819-1850, 1876 (*The Correspondence*, 1878); *Lettres à l'étrangère*, 1899-1950; *Letters to Madame Hanska*, 1900 (translation of volume 1 of *Lettres à l'étrangère*)

BIBLIOGRAPHY

Bell, David F. *Real Time: Accelerating Narrative from Balzac to Zola*. Urbana: University of Illinois Press,

2004. Examines the representation of time and its relationship to narrative—always a key issue in mystery fiction and in literature involving revelation or suspense. Compares Balzac to Stendhal, Alexander Dumas, *père*, and Émile Zola. Bibliographic references and index.

Bloom, Harold, ed. *Honoré de Balzac*. Philadelphia: Chelsea House, 2003. Collection of critical essays on Balzac by leading scholars. Includes discussions of the structure of the author's realism and his representation of a fictional universe. Bibliographic references and index.

Festa-McCormick, Diana. *Honoré de Balzac*. Boston: Twayne, 1979. An excellent introduction to the works of Balzac. Festa-McCormick describes with much subtlety Balzac's evolution as a novelist, and she makes insightful comments on his representation of women. This book contains a very well annotated bibliography.

Kanes, Martin, ed. *Critical Essays on Honoré de Balzac*. Boston: G. K. Hall, 1990. Divided into sections on literary vignettes and essays (1837-1949) and critical essays (subsections covering periods from 1850 to 1990). Includes a detailed introduction, a bibliography, and an index.

Robb, Graham. *Balzac: A Life*. New York: W. W. Norton, 1994. A detailed biographical account of the life and work of Balzac. Focuses on his philosophic perspectives as well as his fiction; speculates on the psychological motivation underlying his work.

Thomas, Gwen. "The Case of the Missing Detective: Balzac's *Une Ténébreuse Affaire*." *French Studies* 48 (July, 1994): 285-298. Discusses how Balzac anticipates a number of detective story conventions. Argues that Balzac retains gaps and indeterminacies in his work and that his final revelation is a literary device rather than a logical conclusion.

Zweig, Stefan. *Balzac*. Edited by Richard Friedenthal. Translated by William Rose and Dorothy Rose. New York: Viking Press, 1946. Although slightly dated, this fascinating book reads almost like a novel about his life.

ROBERT BARNARD

Born: Burnham-on-Crouch, Essex, England; November 23, 1936
Also wrote as Bernard Bastable
Types of plot: Cozy; historical

PRINCIPAL SERIES

Superintendent Perry Trethowan, 1981-
Chief Inspector Charlie Peace, 1989-

PRINCIPAL SERIES CHARACTERS

SUPERINTENDENT PERCIVAL "PERRY" TRETHOWAN, a Scotland Yard detective, is ostracized by his aristocratic family of zany eccentrics. Originally assigned to the vice squad, he first appears on an assignment to investigate the spectacular death of his own father. All the Trethowan mysteries are written in the first person; readers are informed that he is a large man, but rather than being self-revealing, Perry is the consummate observer.

CHIEF INSPECTOR CHARLIE PEACE first appears in a Trethowan mystery, *Bodies* (1986), as a black gym employee. He returns as a series character, a newly hired police officer in *Death and the Chaste Apprentice* (1989). Subsequently transferred to Yorkshire, he quietly fields and ignores racial slurs. Ever laconic and sardonic, he efficiently solves mysteries with humor, sometimes teaming with the older, widowed detective Mike Oddie.

CONTRIBUTION

A literary critic and academic scholar, Robert Barnard is recognized as one of the leading practitioners of the pure detective story. As a mystery writer, he works within the classic tradition and is often said to have inherited Agatha Christie's mantle, for like her, he writes of murder among everyday people and often uses conventional plotting devices. His works, however, unlike Christie's, are often humorous and filled with social satire. Barnard's novels follow the customary plot progression from buildup, to crime, to investigation by police, to solution; however, Barnard experiments, sometimes using a first-person narrator or offering several narrators' points of view. His settings are not the street corner, the gang, the brothel, or even the police station. Rather, he centers his novels at opera houses, local pubs, writers' conventions, English villages, universities, parishes, and theaters.

Barnard has been well received in Great Britain, although he acknowledges that it was his American audience that enabled him to leave his professorship in Norway in 1983 to return to England and become a full-time writer. Barnard suggests that fellow mystery writers remember their purpose, noting, "I write only to entertain." Also, he advises them to cherish the conventions, and, in general, to seek not to spoil the recipe of this popular genre.

BIOGRAPHY

Robert Barnard was born on November 23, 1936, in Burnham-on-Crouch, Essex, England. His father was a farm laborer turned writer who wrote what Barnard calls "very sub-Barbara Cartland" romance stories for weekly magazines. At Balliol College, Oxford, Barnard initially read history but soon changed to English. He received his bachelor's degree with honors in 1959, worked in the Fabian Society bookstore, and then took a post as lecturer at the University of New England in New South Wales, Australia, in 1961.

During Barnard's five years in Australia, he met and married Mary Louise Tabor, and read deeply in the Victorian period, specializing in Charles Dickens, the Brontës, and Elizabeth Gaskell. He began to write for academic journals, then attempted a comic novel, but the plot never developed. He next wrote a crime novel concerning Nazi looting, using standard detective-fiction structure. It was rejected by publishers, but a Collins editor encouraged him to send another

manuscript. Collins then published his first mystery, *Death of an Old Goat* (1974). This first mystery, set in Australia, reflects his distaste for teaching there and especially for the snobbish British visiting professors with its numerous satirical portraits. In the novel, bumbling police Inspector Royale investigates the murder of visiting professor Bellville-Smith.

Barnard's wife wished to move to Europe, so in 1966, he accepted a position at the University of Bergen, Norway. He lectured while he studied for his doctorate, graduating in 1971 after writing his dissertation on imagery and theme in the novels of Dickens. In 1976, he accepted a position at the University of Tromsø in Tromsø, Norway, the northernmost university in the world, three degrees north of the Arctic Circle. He came to love Norway, its beauty, its friendliness, and its peace. He set two of his mysteries there, *Death in a Cold Climate* (1980) and *Death in Purple Prose* (1987).

In 1983, Barnard resigned his teaching position in Norway and returned to England to settle in Leeds, having been abroad for twenty-two years. His sense of objectivity as a "returning exile" enabled him to see England through clear and freshly critical eyes. He enjoyed teaching and felt he had done a good job but now intended to take advantage of his growing market to support himself by his writing. Shortly after settling in Leeds, he noted that the very generous reviews in the United States helped to sell his works there and enabled him to live off his earnings.

In addition to his mystery novels and his short stories for mystery magazines, Barnard wrote the first book-length critical study of Agatha Christie, *A Talent to Deceive: An Appreciation of Agatha Christie* (1980), which contains a bibliography and short-story index compiled by Louise Barnard. He has also written extensively on Charlotte Brontë and serves as chair of the Brontë Society.

In 2003, Barnard received the Crime Writers' Association's Cartier Diamond Dagger Award for lifetime achievement in crime writing. He has been nominated numerous times for the Edgar Award and has won the Nero Wolfe Award for *A Scandal in Belgravia* (1991). In 1988, he won the Anthony Award for best short story for "Breakfast Television" in 1988, the

Agatha Award for best short story for "More Final than Divorce" in 1988, and the Macavity Award for best short story for "The Woman in the Wardrobe."

ANALYSIS

Robert Barnard, like Agatha Christie, locates his mysteries, for the most part, in cozy, comfortable settings. They do not occur in alleys, in exotic dens, or crime-ridden slums but rather in respectable locations: gossipy English villages, clerical convocations, academic halls, conventions of specialists, arts festivals, and theaters. His first mystery is set in Australia and two later ones take place in Norway, reflecting the author's travels. However, his main focus, even when living elsewhere, is England with its prep schools, Anglican parishes, by-elections, and its minor royalty. For Barnard's readers, this is part of his appeal: tea cozies, lawn fêtes, rectors, and constables.

Barnard's plots are conventionally crafted. They usually involve a closed circle of suspects, among whom various relationships and secrets are exposed, all following the commission of the murder. He admires Christie's careful approach to plotting, citing her as a genius in the "double-bluff" method and its skillful use of red herrings. However, perhaps, like those of Charles Dickens whom he also admires, his plots are not his major strength. They are sometimes contrived and improbable, or they rely too heavily on withholding vital clues or on providing unforeseen twists at the end. Barnard told an interviewer that his stories are not totally preplanned. He begins with a good idea of the murder, victim, motive, and murderer. Then, however, he often generates the story as he writes, for he thinks with his pen in hand—unlike Christie, who had every detail worked out in advance.

Plots in Barnard's works are often, as in Dickens, secondary; however, both authors pour compensatory energy into the creation of characters, many of whom are originals and quite memorable. Barnard asserts he is "always pinching things" from Dickens, and they are both certainly masters at vividly depicting lower-class characters. For example, Jack Phelan in *A City of Strangers* (1990) is described as "wearing a vest that displayed brawny and tattooed arms gone nastily to flesh, and a prominent beer gut. His trousers were

filthy, and he sat on a crate in a garden littered with the dismembered remains of cars." Barnard also provides an amusing variety of clerical types, a wicked caricature of an American scholar, gay models and body builders, an aging actress, and even an obscure member of the royal household.

The names of Barnard's characters are inventive and also reminiscent of those of Dickens: Marius Fleetwood is a ladies' man, though readers are told he began as a grocer improbably named Bert Winterbottom. Barnard says he has to guard against becoming too Dickensian and resorting too easily to caricature, for his strength is to write more realistically and display an acute eye for sharply drawn social and domestic detail, as in *Mother's Boys* (1981). His characters are powerfully delineated and easily recognizable; for example, with Declan O'Hearn, in *The Corpse at the Haworth Tandoori* (1998), Barnard creates a new human being, so unusual and recognizable that readers would know him if he walked into a room. In *Out of the Blackout* (1984), he experiments with a new realism and an unusual piece of detection in which the central character, taken as a five-year-old child from London during the Blitz, is searching for his real identity.

Realism is evident in Barnard's depiction of the sometimes self-referential world of writing and publishing. He explores authors of all kinds: writers of mysteries, romances, biographies, and memoirs. He deftly provides a sharply drawn social milieu of the subculture of male models; he gives memorable depictions of the realities of divorce and is especially good at depicting the dysfunctional family.

Barnard experimented under the pseudonym Bernard Barnstable with four realistic historical novels. *To Die Like a Gentleman* (1993) is set in Victorian England, with the period style well achieved through letters and diary accounts, allowing for multiple viewpoints. Two other historical novels feature Wolfgang Amadeus Mozart as a narrator-detective and allow Barnard to display his knowledge of music and to make satirical comments on eighteenth century English society. *A Mansion and Its Murder* (1998) concerns a late nineteenth century banker and captures the fin de siècle culture in England.

Barnard is capable of creating memorable short works as well. Most of the sixteen short stories collected in *Death of a Salesperson* (1989) are ironic crime narratives in the style of the *Alfred Hitchcock Presents* (1955-1962) television show. His topics in this collection, as in his longer detective fiction, include satires on the art world, academia's foibles, and the stately home tradition. Like Roald Dahl's stories, those of Barnard are based on a winning combination of humor and shock.

In commenting on his series characters, Barnard notes that he does not overuse them, for they tend to dictate the tone of the book, and he prefers to vary the tone. Also, he insists that the crime novel is not deep nor psychological in focus, but formulaic, populist, and designed to entertain. To interest his audience, he updates the well-worn English scene with academics who leave their wives for graduate students, with the nastier sides of divorce, and with some ambiguous twists on sexual orientation. Overall, in his plotting, Barnard is never obsessed by evil; rather, he is much more interested in meanness and in human failings, especially in the lack of self-knowledge.

Although Barnard's plots are pleasingly realized and his characters are memorable, his style is often his most powerful feature. Unlike Christie, he writes with humor, both gentle and light and also biting and satirical. He has an ear for dialogue—always observing and listening and recording, determined that his dialogue be as lively as possible. In general, his ability to write in ways that shock, entertain, delight, and surprise gives testimony to the variety and power of his style.

DEATH IN A COLD CLIMATE

Death in a Cold Climate is set in Tromsø, Norway, where Bernard taught for several years. It conveys a strong sense of how somber and depressing a Scandinavian winter can be and provides an understanding of a foreign culture that is essential to the plot. The murder victim is an outsider, a young Englishman. Symbolically, the story opens at the darkest time of the year, and the competent Norwegian police inspector Fagermo takes until the spring return of the sun to solve the murder. Barnard provides humorous remarks on Norwegian foods and Scandinavian pretense as well as a moving picture of the Korvold family.

SHEER TORTURE

Sheer Torture (1981) introduces Barnard's Detective Perry Trethowan, his first recurring detective figure, and one who narrates his own story. For fourteen years, Perry has been happily disowned by his loony, aristocratic family and is married to Jan, who is working on a degree in Arabic. Perry's superior orders him to investigate the bizarre death of his father, who, wearing spangled tights, has been murdered in a medieval torture machine called a strappado. Perry is more embarrassed than grieved by the event but manages to solve the kinky murder. Some critics call this novel a cross between the novels of the British writers Roald Dahl and Ngaio Marsh.

POLITICAL SUICIDE

In *Political Suicide* (1986), Barnard displays his withering views of the British electoral process and gives himself wide scope to satirize the political machinations of the Tories, the Social Democrats, and the Labour Party. There are also fringe parties galore: the John Lennon Lives Party, the Bring Back Hanging Party, and the Richard III Was Innocent Party. Some critics have compared his election passages to those of Dickens in *Pickwick Papers* (1836-1837). A Tory member of Parliament has been found drowned in the Thames. The three candidates vying to fill his vacant position in Bootham, Yorkshire, provide Barnard with many opportunities for scathing satire, for they are all among the suspects interviewed by Superintendent Sutcliffe, who takes until the final pages to reveal the motive, means, and opportunity of the murderer.

DEATH IN PURPLE PROSE

Death in Purple Prose, a Perry Trethowan series novel that depicts literary groups, finds the detective again involved with his loony, aristocratic family. Perry accompanies his sister Cristobel to a convention of the World Association of Romantic Novelists (WARN), held in Bergen, Norway. Here Bernard draws lightly on his own father's profession as a romance writer as well as on his years spent in Norway. He satirizes the romance-novel industry, and when a famous writer is murdered, secrets are revealed. Malevolent rivals for the title of conference queen range from the sensibly attired Mary Sweeny with her hard, glinting eye to the coy and sugary Amanda Fairchild.

THE MISTRESS OF ALDERLEY

In *The Mistress of Alderley* (2002), a Detective Sergeant Charlie Peace mystery, the murdered man is an aging lothario, Marius Fleetwood, who, although he still lives with his wife, claims multiple past and current mistresses. His current official mistress, the retired actress Caroline Fawley, thinks he is hers, exclusively. However, when Fleetwood is murdered, Peace finds, among other things, that the dead man had also been trysting with Caroline's daughter, an oversexed opera star. Satire is aimed at the local clergy, at techno-kids, and at a fussy dower-house gentleman and his rough sister. The whole nasty mess is cleared up when the murderer is discovered at the very end to be the daughter's jealous lover. English slang abounds ("swish," "breakfast fry-up," "Guy Fawkes") as well as allusions to famous people in the news such as Hillary Clinton and Guy Ritchie.

Marie J. K. Brenner

PRINCIPAL MYSTERY AND DETECTIVE FICTION

SUPERINTENDENT PERRY TRETHOWAN SERIES: *Sheer Torture*, 1981 (also known as *Death by Sheer Torture*); *Death and the Princess*, 1982; *The Missing Brontë*, 1983 (also known as *The Case of the Missing Brontë*); *Bodies*, 1986; *Death in Purple Prose*, 1987 (also known as *The Cherry Blossom Corpse*)

INSPECTOR CHARLIE PEACE SERIES: *Death and the Chaste Apprentice*, 1989; *A Fatal Attachment*, 1992; *A Hovering of Vultures*, 1993; *The Bad Samaritan*, 1995; *No Place of Safety*, 1997; *The Corpse at the Haworth Tandoori*, 1998; *Unholy Dying*, 2001; *The Bones in the Attic*, 2001; *The Mistress of Alderley*, 2002; *The Graveyard Position*, 2004; *A Fall from Grace*, 2007

NONSERIES NOVELS: *Death of an Old Goat*, 1974; *A Little Local Murder*, 1976; *Death on the High C's*, 1977; *Blood Brotherhood*, 1977; *Unruly Son*, 1978 (also known as *Death of a Mystery Writer*); *Posthumous Papers*, 1979 (also known as *Death of a Literary Widow*); *Death in a Cold Climate*, 1980; *Mother's Boys*, 1981 (also known as *Death of a Perfect Mother*); *Little Victims*, 1983 (also known as *School for Murder*); *Corpse in a Gilded Cage*, 1984; *Out of the Blackout*, 1984; *The Disposal of the Living*, 1985

(also known as *Fête Fatale*); *Political Suicide*, 1986; *The Skeleton in the Grass*, 1987; *At Death's Door*, 1988; *A City of Strangers*, 1990; *A Scandal in Belgravia*, 1991; *The Masters of the House*, 1994; *Touched by the Dead*, 1999 (also known as *A Murder in Mayfair*); *A Cry from the Dark*, 2003; *Dying Flames*, 2005

NONSERIES NOVELS (AS BASTABLE): *To Die Like a Gentleman*, 1993; *Dead, Mr. Mozart*, 1995; *Too Many Notes, Mr. Mozart*, 1995; *A Mansion and Its Murder*, 1998

OTHER MAJOR WORKS

SHORT FICTION: *Death of a Salesperson*, 1989; *The Habit of Widowhood and Other Murderous Proclivities*, 1996

NONFICTION: *Imagery and Themes in the Novels of Dickens*, 1974; *A Talent to Deceive: An Appreciation of Agatha Christie*, 1980; *A Short History of English Literature*, 1984 (also known as *A History of English Literature*, 1994); *Emily Brontë*, 2000; *Brontë Encyclopedia*, 2007

BIBLIOGRAPHY

Barnard, Robert. "Growing Up to Crime." In *Colloquium on Crime*, edited by Robin W. Winks. New York: Scribner, 1986. Bernard discusses his creative process, focusing on improvisation and on the use of caricature, humor, and, suspense; also discusses mystery novels as a genre.

_____. *A Talent to Deceive: An Appreciation of Agatha Christie*. Rev. ed. New York: Mysterious Press, 1987. Barnard's work on the author whom he most admired sheds light on his understanding of the classical detective novel and how he interpreted it in his own works.

_____. "Why oh Why? Motivation in the Crime Novel." *Writer* 108, no. 8 (August, 1995): 3. Barnard talks about writing mysteries, particularly cozies, and creating plausible motives for crimes.

Breen, Jon L. "Robert Barnard." In *Mystery and Suspense Writers: The Literature of Crime, Detection, and Espionage*, edited by Robin W. Winks. New York: Scribner, 1998. Provides biographical details, an analysis of Barnard's critical writings, and a look at the historical novels and short stories.

Ford, Susan Allen. "Stately Homes of England: Robert Barnard's Country House Mysteries." *Clues* 23, no. 4 (Summer, 2005): 3-14. Ford analyzes Barnard's use of the traditional detective novel form used in the Golden Age of mysteries. Compares his work to that of Agatha Christie and Ngaio Marsh.

Herbert, Rosemary. "Robert Barnard." In *The Fatal Art of Entertainment: Interviews with Mystery Writers*. New York: Hall, 1994. Updates a 1985 interview, covering Barnard's use of personal experience in his fiction, his favorite writers, and his attitudes toward literary allusion and the populist entertainment aspects of the mystery genre.

NEVADA BARR

Born: Yerington, Nevada; March 1, 1952
Types of plot: Amateur sleuth; police procedural; hard-boiled

PRINCIPAL SERIES
Anna Pigeon, 1993-

PRINCIPAL SERIES CHARACTER
ANNA PIGEON works for the National Park Service as a law enforcement agent in numerous parks. Small and middle-aged, Anna often finds herself fighting discrimination against women and championing ecological concerns even as she deciphers the clues to a variety of murders in a range of scenic locations.

CONTRIBUTION
Nevada Barr provides a unique perspective within the canon of mystery and detective fiction written by women. By making her detective park ranger Anna Pigeon, Barr can traverse diverse terrain rather successfully. As a woman in a mostly male world, Anna can explore and indict the National Park Service's often patriarchal rules and policies. In addition, because of the nature of National Park Service appointments, Anna can describe and delight in natural habitats across the United States without this movement from place to place becoming arbitrary or forced. Thus, Barr's novels offer readers impressions of some of the most interesting natural habitats in the United States. Though Anna's approach to crime seems a bit amateurish because the National Park Service does not expect its employees to have to deal with crimes, her or-

ganized and analytic nature makes her a natural investigator. Barr's detective novels not only contain crime and detection but also comment on ecological concerns in a variety of picturesque natural habitats and inequality in the workplace, even as her works maintain a humanistic interest in the narrator and her concerns.

BIOGRAPHY
Nevada Barr was born in Yerington, Nevada, on March 1, 1952, to Dave Barr and Mary Barr, both pilots; her sister Molly also became a pilot. Though born in her namesake state, Nevada spent her early years in Susanville, California, at a small mountain airport where her parents worked. She received a bachelor's degree in speech and drama from California Polytechnic State University in San Luis Obispo in 1974 and a master of fine arts in acting from the University of California, Irvine. After graduate school, Barr gravitated toward New York City, where she spent five years serving as a member of the Classic Stage Company and performing in several off-Broadway productions. Later, she moved to Minneapolis and spent several years in the theater there. She also worked in advertising in a variety of capacities, appearing in commercials and industrial films. Her career in writing began in 1978, though her first published novel, *Bittersweet*, a historical Western novel about two women, was published in 1984.

Because of her first husband's interest in conservation and wildlife, Barr began working as a seasonal employee for the National Park Service in 1989. These seasonal jobs allowed her to work in the parks during the summer months while pursuing her acting and writing during the rest of the year. Her first appointment was at Isle Royale National Park in Michigan in 1989, her second at Guadalupe National Park in Texas in 1990, and her third, for two seasons in 1991-1992, at Mesa Verde National Park in Colorado. To gain full-time status within the National Park Service, Nevada transferred to Natchez Trace National Park in 1993, where she worked for two year before leaving the park service to work full-time on her writing.

In 1993 Barr published her first mystery novel, *Track of the Cat*, set in Guadalupe National Park, where she had previously worked. This novel won the 1994 Agatha Award for best first novel and the 1994 Anthony Award for best novel. Subsequent novels also have garnered a number of nominations and awards. *Firestorm* (1996) was nominated for the Anthony Award for best novel and was awarded France's Prix du Roman d'Aventure. *Blind Descent* (1998) was nominated for both an Anthony Award and a Macavity Award. *Deep South* (2000) also received an Anthony Award nomination. Barr and her second husband, former National Park Service ranger Richard Jones, live in New Orleans, Louisiana.

ANALYSIS

Nevada Barr's mystery series featuring National Park Service ranger Anna Pigeon is unusual among series featuring a female sleuth in that the novels do not fit neatly into any one genre of mystery and detective fiction. On one hand, Anna is certainly a kind of private investigator, hard-boiled in her self-imposed isolation from others as well as independent, for the most part, from family and romantic liaisons that limit her ability to move from park to park without consequence. Though she maintains connections with her psychologist sister Molly, her sister lives in New York City while Anna traipses from park to park across the United States. Indeed, the nature of the park service, as outlined in Barr's *Track of the Cat*, suggests that most park workers do not stay in one park indefinitely so as not to become too invested in one area. Though Anna goes to New York when Molly becomes gravely ill in the seventh novel in the series, *Liberty Falling* (1999), neither Molly's illness in this novel nor Anna's

marriage to local sheriff and minister Paul Davidson in *Hard Truth* (2005) limit Anna's involvement in solving crimes nor the necessary traveling. Even when Anna falls in love—twice during the series, first with Federal Bureau of Investigation (FBI) agent Frederick Stanton, who will eventually pair with her sister Molly, and second with Davidson—she resists putting herself in any emotionally needy situation. Furthermore, with Anna's general cynicism, she can maintain a level of objectivity that serves her well when investigating crimes. Like her hard-boiled predecessors, Anna regularly gets shot, beat up, pushed down mountains, and kidnapped without deterring her from resuming the investigation the next day.

Although she has the personality and many other qualities of a hard-boiled private investigator, Anna's job actually involves her in quasi-police work. Though she often has to concede to local police authorities or FBI operatives while investigating a case, her position in the park allows her to carry weapons and enforce the laws of the parks. In this regard, Barr's novels suggest the police procedural. Anna must follow the protocol of her job regarding the gathering of evidence and the interrogation of suspects. Though her authority is sometimes undermined by those higher in command in the park service, Anna, unlike private investigators, is a central character at a crime scene.

Despite her tough demeanor and her savvy police skills, Anna Pigeon often approaches crime as would an amateur sleuth. Although no one pays her to discover the truth behind a crime, Anna goes beyond her park ranger responsibilities to solve mysteries. These explorations manage to put her into extraordinarily dangerous situations without much forethought or management on her part. For example, she might be taking a walk late at night when she discovers a clue that might lead to a killer. Instead of calling for backup or pursuing the lead in the morning, Anna might walk into a trap. Furthermore, she often seems ill-equipped to handle these emergencies even though she inevitably triumphs by the end of the novel.

Barr's use of national parks as settings for her works allows a level of integrity often missing from series that involve an amateur detective. Though private investigators and police officers might have a never-ending caseload that could be the basis for multiple novels, park rangers typically do not see crime on such a scale. The very nature of the itinerant park ranger, however, allows Barr to transport Anna Pigeon to a variety of new settings with new possibilities for crimes. Because the crimes occur at different parks, Anna's repeated investigation of so much murderous activity does not strain credulity.

The national park settings also add a further dimension to Barr's tightly woven, often psychological mysteries. Anna Pigeon revels in the unique surroundingsof each park at which she works. Whether she is exploring the lush, humid swamps of lower Mississippi or the deep, icy waters of Lake Superior in Michigan, Anna describes, experiences, and appreciates the places where she works. Barr's descriptions of park ranger work—both its tedium and its surprises—connect with these natural surroundings to create an engulfing perception of place and an admiration for each park. Place is so critical to the plot of the novels that Barr typically provides a map of the park area in question in each book. Within each park, Anna must learn new skills such as fire suppression, caving techniques, and even waitressing in order to survive. Thus, Barr's novels become windows into multiple environments but from a distinctive, insider perspective.

Thematically, Barr's mysteries often revolve around ecological concerns. Frequently, murders occur because people get greedy and infringe on park land to make money or curry favor. For example, in *Blind Descent*, a caver dies because she realizes an oil company has drilled into a federally owned cave, and in *Deep South*, a young girl is murdered because she stumbles on a Civil War reenactor's nefarious scheme to make money. Though the crimes in these novels sometimes seem unrelated to the environment of the park, inevitably the plot will unfold to show how the murder or murders often directly involve an infringement on park lands.

In addition to expressing environmental concerns, Barr's novels also often have a decidedly feminist agenda. Anna Pigeon must dodge male insults and insinuations as she moves her way up the National Park Service's bureaucratic ladder. Especially after she achieves leadership roles, Anna undergoes intense scru-

tiny by the men who must serve beneath her. Barr's presentation of Anna as a strong-willed but politic member of a labyrinthine political network showcases the inherent biases of the organization even as it shows Anna's ability to play by the rules. Despite efforts from others to keep her from her job, Anna believes in the sanctity of the park, the importance of due process, and the integrity of personal experience. Barr's novels enhance female-centered justice, even as they extol the virtues of natural habitats and a kind of vigilante honesty. Anna might take matters into her own hands, but she does not shirk from the consequences of those actions.

TRACK OF THE CAT

Track of the Cat, which introduces Anna Pigeon, incorporates many of the themes of subsequent novels

NEW YORK TIMES BESTSELLING AUTHOR
of *Flashback*

NEVADA BARR

TRACK OF THE CAT

The First Anna Pigeon Novel

in the series. Anna, an emotionally isolated woman in a mostly male environment, must deal with patronizing bureaucrats with gender biases and capitalistic agendas. Furthermore, the alluring descriptions of landscape and the flora and fauna of Guadalupe National Park give the text an open quality that invites readers to share in the exploration of the terrain as well as the exploration of the murder. Other elements of the novel make it unusual for the genre. *Track of the Cat* showcases Barr's interest in gender roles and the environment. During the course of the novel, Anna questions her sexuality when she becomes enchanted by a lesbian worker at the park. She also fights her first battle against a mostly male and capitalist enemy in favor of an environmental concern, in this case, the preservation of the innocent mountain lion who is falsely accused of committing the murder that precipitates the initial investigation. Anna's vigilance in protecting a park's habitat becomes a reoccurring theme in later novels.

BLIND DESCENT

Blind Descent, like Barr's earlier *Firestorm*, accentuates her interest in the locked-room mystery. The setting for this novel is the uninhabited, largely fictionalized Lechuguilla Cave, located adjacent to Carlsbad Caverns in New Mexico, an extreme area that only a few people ever explore. The who, how, and why of this mystery are all intertwined and enigmatic. Barr augments the narrowly defined plot with two related elements. First, the author enhances this mystery with the particulars of rock climbing, rappelling, spelunking, and cave investigation. The crime situation requires the investigator to understand the mechanics of these activities, as well as the ecological issues at stake when investigating pristine wilderness, whether it be above or, as in this case, below ground. Second, Barr focuses on Anna's near paralyzing claustrophobia when faced with the challenge and necessity of underground exploration, further defining Anna's character even as this fear also assists in provoking a similar fear in the reader. Barr uses the restrictions of the cave to highlight the internal restrictions of the characters, thus creating a cleaner narrative structure on which to resolve the complexities of the mystery.

DEEP SOUTH

Set against the backdrop of the Natchez Trace Parkway National Park in Mississippi, *Deep South* marks a transformation in Barr's depiction of Anna Pigeon. Though Anna had been depicted as a nomadic and independent character in the first seven novels of the series, Barr shows Anna taking on more traditional roles, particularly in her relationships with characters, and more important, with place. Though in all of the Pigeon books Barr depicts place with keen detail, as she moves into the South, the detail becomes less objectively observed and more intimately involved. When the reader learns that Anna has taken a permanent position at the Natchez Trace Parkway National Park, the concept of "permanent" sets the tone for the rest of the novel. The relationships Anna forms seem more important because of their potential engagement in her future, though Anna maintains a level of wariness about the idea of settling down. A second novel about Natchez Trace Parkway, *Hunting Season* (2002), allowed her to investigate this territory again as it deepened characterization and the sense of place.

Rebecca Hendrick Flannagan

PRINCIPAL MYSTERY AND DETECTIVE FICTION

ANNA PIGEON SERIES: *Track of the Cat*, 1993; *A Superior Death*, 1994; *Ill Wind*, 1995 (also known as *Mountain of Bones*); *Firestorm*, 1996; *Endangered Species*, 1997; *Blind Descent*, 1998; *Liberty Falling*, 1999; *Deep South*, 2000; *Blood Lure*, 2001; *Hunting Season*, 2002; *Flashback*, 2003; *High Country*, 2004; *Hard Truth*, 2005

OTHER MAJOR WORKS

NOVELS: *Bittersweet*, 1984; *Naked Came the Phoenix*, 2001 (with others)

NONFICTION: *Seeking Enlightenment Hat by Hat: A Skeptic Path to Religion*, 2003

EDITED TEXTS: *Nevada Barr Presents Malice Domestic Ten: An Anthology of Original Traditional Mystery Stories*, 2001; *Deadly Housewives*, 2006

BIBLIOGRAPHY

Barr, Nevada. Web Site of Nevada Barr. http://www .nevadabarr.com. This Web site is maintained by

Nevada's sister Molly Barr and contains up-to-date information on Barr's books. The site also hosts a gallery of the two sisters' art, as well as photos of Nevada when she worked for the National Park Service. Though not necessarily a scholarly source, the personal elements of this site make it worthwhile when studying Nevada Barr.

Cava, Francis. *Sleuths in Skirts: A Bibliography and Analysis of Serialized Female Sleuths.* New York: Routledge, 2002. This book contains a compendium of information about female sleuths, including brief descriptions of heroines. The extended bibliography of detectives and works includes Nevada Barr's Anna Pigeon. Index.

Line, Less. "Guadalupe Gumshoe." *Audubon* 105 (September, 2003): 22-23. Line's profile accentuates Barr's interest in natural habitats and provides an overview of her work as a mystery novelist whose protagonist operates as a National Park Service ranger. This article also provides interesting statistics about national park violence and staffing as it relates to events within Barr's novels.

Nolan, Tom. "For a Clue, Look Up." *The Wall Street Journal*, July 11, 2003, p. W19. This profile of Barr focuses primarily on her writing style and her success with mysteries. Also includes information

relative to her nonfictional work, *Seeking Enlightenment Hat by Hat.*

Rancourt, Linda. "Murder She Writes." *National Parks Magazine* 69 (September/October, 1995): 30-35. This article in a National Park Service journal appeared early in Barr's career, highlighting the importance of her National Park Service work in her writing. Drawing on workers' comments from the various parks mentioned in Barr's first three novels, as well as Barr's comments on her own work, Rancourt shows how Barr combines her job of National Park ranger with that of mystery novelist.

Reynolds, Moira Davison, ed. *Women Authors of Detective Series: Twenty-One American and British Authors, 1900-2000.* Jefferson, N.C.: McFarland, 2001. Describes Barr's work as well as that of twenty other female authors of detective fiction in the twentieth century.

Shindler, Dorman T. "Taking on History's Mysteries." Review of *Flashback*, by Nevada Barr. *Publishers Weekly* 250, no. 4 (January 27, 2003): 230. Ostensibly a review of Barr's *Flashback*, this interview also addresses her use of history in both her mysteries and her historical Western, *Bittersweet.*

ROBERT BARR

Born: Glasgow, Scotland; September 16, 1850
Died: Woldingham, Surrey, England; October 21, 1912
Also wrote as Luke Sharp
Type of plot: Private investigator

PRINCIPAL SERIES

Eugène Valmont, 1904-1906

PRINCIPAL SERIES CHARACTER

EUGÈNE VALMONT is a private investigator in London, formerly chief detective to the French govern-

ment, of indeterminate age, perhaps in his mid-forties, and unmarried. He is arrogant, self-celebrating, and procedurally impeccable; his admirably incisive deductions frequently mistake appearance for fact in Barr's knowing parody of the genre.

CONTRIBUTION

In the character of Eugène Valmont, Robert Barr capitalized on the popularity of detective fiction and gentlemanly sleuths, whose antecedents were Arthur Conan Doyle's Sherlock Holmes and Edgar Allan Poe's C. Auguste Dupin. His perspective, however, was distinctly ironic: Valmont's investigations, when not completely trivial, are often failures. Barr satirized the school of literary masterminds through a firm control of the devices of the form. He was a master of burlesque narrative, in which a final reversal of the situation in point turns the suspicious events into innocent practices. Banal solutions put the supposed complications into a nonsinister perspective, offering comic resolutions within the normal complexities and deceptions of "serious" detective fiction. Barr's consulting detective, who is anything but self-effacing, has been suggested as a model for Agatha Christie's Hercule Poirot, first envisioned in 1916, and there are appreciable likenesses of character. Valmont's continuing appearances in anthologies testify to the success of Barr's inspired and offbeat creation.

BIOGRAPHY

Robert Barr was born in Glasgow, Scotland, on September 16, 1850, the eldest of eight children of Robert Barr, a carpenter, and his wife, Jane Barr. The family moved to Wallacetown, Ontario, in 1854, and thereafter to Windsor. After teaching provisionally at rural posts in Kent County, Barr entered the Toronto Normal School in 1873 (a period satirized in his novel *The Measure of the Rule*, 1907), earning a third-class teaching certificate. He taught in Wallacetown and Walkerville and became principal of the Windsor Central School.

By this time, Barr was an intermittent contributor of comic pieces to the Bothwell *Advance* and the Toronto satirical magazine *Grip*. The Detroit Free Press accepted his mock-heroic account of an 1875 voyage around Lake Erie's south shore; in 1876, he joined the paper's staff, working first as a reporter, later as a columnist, and finally as its exchange editor.

In 1881, Barr established the British edition of the newspaper in London; he contributed interviews, obituaries, character sketches, anecdotes, facetious travel notes, and columns. By the 1890's, journalism had become a lucrative career for him. In 1892, he and humorist Jerome K. Jerome founded *The Idler*, a glossy, lavishly illustrated monthly magazine that enjoyed immediate success and that featured an impressive list of contributors. Barr coedited *The Idler* through 1895

and again from 1902 until it ceased publication in 1911. His first collection of stories appeared in 1883, his first novel in 1894. Fluent in profanity, he was a sociable raconteur, a constant smoker, and a vigorous clubman.

Barr built his own home, Hillhead, in Woldingham, Surrey, where he was an invaluable and solicitous friend to his neighbor Stephen Crane, and also associated with other literary figures of the day. His hobbies included cycling, golf, photography, and travel—to Algeria, Germany, Switzerland, Scotland, Italy, the United States, and Canada. In 1900, he was awarded an honorary master of arts by the University of Michigan. Barr died at Woldingham on October 21, 1912, survived by a son, a daughter, and a grandchild.

ANALYSIS

Robert Barr's principal talent lay in the cleverness and ingenuity of his plots, particularly in his ability to devise ironic twists to otherwise straightforward situations. He had no particular command of naturalistic detail; his locations remain almost completely functional. His narrative language is formally correct and elegantly characterless. None of his characters is realized with any physical or psychological depth; they remain lightly sketched and one-dimensional, excelling only in badinage and facetious dialogue. He wrote with a facility that came from his journalistic background, addressing the voracious popular market for superficial fiction. Until he created Eugène Valmont, his inventiveness and wit existed almost completely at the level of romantic froth.

"THE GREAT PEGRAM MYSTERY"

A number of detective and mystery stories and novels preceded Barr's success with *The Triumphs of Eugène Valmont* (1906). "The Great Pegram Mystery" (originally published in *The Idler* of 1892 as "Detective Stories Gone Wrong—The Adventures of Sherlaw Kombs") was a distinct departure from his usual short-story practice. Not unlike the Holmesian prototype, Sherlaw Kombs plays the violin, scorns Scotland Yard, anticipates a visitor before his arrival and skillfully deduces his occupation and mission, uses a magnifying glass at the scene of the apparent crime, makes calculations to the inch, and meticulously unravels the sequence of events *ex post facto*. Kombs insists on dealing only with facts, and, within the boundaries of circumstantial evidence, his reconstruction is faultless. His aide, Whatson, the narrator, is an exclamatory naïve admirer and straight man, of no assistance whatever.

One would hope that Barr's friend Doyle greeted this inspired silliness with magnanimity, for Kombs mistakes for suicide a case of robbery and murder that occurred, as a devastating touch, nowhere near the location of the body in a train compartment. The pastiche is of a high order. It is augmented by Kombs's precise and completely self-assured investigation, and by his wonderfully tongue-in-cheek justification of his conclusions (the "motive"):

> Nothing is more calculated to prepare the mind for self-destruction than the prospect of a night ride on the Scotch Express, and the view from the windows of the train as it passes through the northern part of London is particularly conducive to thoughts of annihilation.

This story was included in Ellery Queen's anthology *The Misadventures of Sherlock Holmes* (1944).

FROM WHOSE BOURNE?

The novella *From Whose Bourne?* (1893) further anticipated Barr's attention to detective fiction. In it, a ghost assists in clearing his wife, who is wrongfully suspected of having poisoned him at a dinner party. The French spirit-detective Lecocq, a precursor of Eugène Valmont, possesses all the formality, pride, and obtuseness of Sherlaw Kombs: He seems adept only at collating the obvious facts in their logical order, an exercise that he considers child's play. Though the story is protracted and unfocused in development—the ostensible impulse behind the two prime suspects is purely romantic—it does demonstrate Barr's fondness for the unusual solution (here, an inadvertently switched drug) beyond the obligatory complications at the level of the apparently guilty parties.

REVENGE!

The mystery stories collected in *Revenge!* (1896) are considerably more satisfactory. Ranging over a variety of international locales, the majority of the tales conclude with the discomfiture or death of the antagonists by such devices as dynamite, naphtha, billiards,

revolvers, an avalanche, and the stock exchange. "An Alpine Divorce," for example, develops the situation of a couple who hate each other. The wife commits suicide by flinging herself off a cliff in Switzerland, having first framed her husband in public for her prospective murder. In "Which Was the Murderer?" a woman must smother her wounded and possibly dying husband with a pillow to ensure that his assailant does not escape the charge of murder.

These stories are confined by rapid development, minimal attention to physical environment, a more or less genteel level of society, virtually interchangeable characters at best distinguished by their sex or position, and a formal, literate, but featureless style. Nevertheless, they often prove Barr's considerable powers of invention and show how masterfully he could work within the limits of the popular short-story format.

THE TRIUMPHS OF EUGÈNE VALMONT

The Triumphs of Eugène Valmont was for Barr a triumph of complementary character and style: Valmont's singular nature is, effectively, often the principal content of his cases. He is the only individual with any real depth in these stories. The collection, in which Barr rose well above his journalistic competence, represents his single sustained foray into the genre of detective fiction.

Though he is consistently opinionated, autocratic, and self-satisfied during his investigations, Eugène Valmont possesses an undeniable charm; his quirks and fixations make him entirely distinctive. His appeal is only augmented by his preening. Sublimely convinced of his own superiority and thoroughness, he prides himself on his urbanity of manner, though he is galled by having been mocked in the French press. His deductions are incisive and eminently plausible, even when radically misdirected. At times, however, he relies on intuition, rather than on proof or evidence. He has monumental vanity, Gallic vivacity, and an unshakable dedication. He is also much interested in the financial rewards accruing from private practice.

It is Valmont's character that sustains these stories: His sometimes intelligent obtuseness, his blindness to the obvious, and his unceasing identification of criminal activity are delightful. He is prone to discover suspicious circumstances and complications where none exist. He has a "fixed rule never to believe that I am at the bottom of any case until I have come on something suspicious," and his conclusions often supplant normal human insight or consideration of alternative truths. Valmont can coolly explain or rationalize any discrepancy between his projections and the reality of a sequence of events.

Though Valmont prides himself on his calmness and imperturbability, the nature of the English disturbs him. He is infinitely condescending toward British police methods, against which he rails constantly, bemusedly, and patronizingly. He believes that the concept of innocence until guilt is proved is ridiculous, as he explains what to him are his justifiable violations of due process in the face of English conservative thought. Throughout his questionable triumphs, the inexplicability of the nation's mentality is a repeated target in crafty asides: "It is little wonder the English possess no drama, for they show scant appreciation of the sensational moments in life; they are not quickly alive to the lights and shadows of events."

For Valmont, the English personality is epitomized in the stolid Spenser Hale of Scotland Yard, who is often the butt of his barbs. It is Hale who Valmont blames for his own inflation of elementary cases: "Sometimes the utter simplicity of the puzzles which trouble him leads me into an intricate involution entirely unnecessary in the circumstances." Conversely, even though he harps repeatedly on his dismissal by the French government, managing to glorify himself in the process, Valmont celebrates the people and culture of France at every opportunity:

> It is my determination yet to write a book on the comparative characteristics of the two people. I hold a theory that the English people are utterly incomprehensible to the rest of humanity, and this will be duly set out in my forthcoming volume.

Valmont's diction is almost completely formal and grammatically elegant, though he lapses occasionally into supposedly French inversions and amusing turns of English idiom. While Valmont is deflecting anarchist activities in Paris, he is complimented on his verbal facility:

Monsieur Valmont, you have stated the case with that clear comprehensiveness pertaining to a nation which understands the meaning of words, and the correct adjustment of them; that felicity of language which has given France the first place in the literature of nations.

"THE MYSTERY OF THE FIVE HUNDRED DIAMONDS"

In "The Mystery of the Five Hundred Diamonds," the first sequence of connected stories in *The Triumphs of Eugène Valmont*, Valmont must guarantee the safe transport out of France to the purchaser of an ill-starred necklace consigned to public auction. He assumes that fraud is inevitable and that the successful bidder is a hitherto unknown prince of criminals, and thus he gives chase. The detailed and protracted pursuit on foot, by coach, and by boat, complicated by such red herrings as miscues, disguises, transfer of the goods, and an American detective, is excitingly and effectively rendered. Here the point is the elaboration of Valmont's method and resources rather than his initial error of identification and creation of a task that did not require his talent for complication.

"THE ABSENT-MINDED COTERIE"

The essence of Valmont is evident in "The Absent-Minded Coterie," a sequence of four chapters that has enjoyed an enduring anthology life. *Ellery Queen's Mystery Magazine* of March, 1950, celebrated the adventure in "A Poll of Twelve on the Best Dozen Detective Stories," along with works of such writers as G. K. Chesterton, Dorothy L. Sayers, Edgar Allan Poe, Arthur Conan Doyle, and Aldous Huxley. In the story, Scotland Yard's presumption of an illegal coining establishment and recruitment of Valmont leads to an apparent confidence scheme run by a curiosity-shop owner who, in an amusing irrelevancy, also writes Christian Science pamphlets under a pseudonym. Absentminded buyers of goods are thought to lose track of their debts over the course of the collection of weekly installments. Valmont bristles with suspicion, but he has no hard evidence of wrongdoing. With an uncharacteristic sneering heavy-handedness, he accuses one of the merchant's canvassers of merely playing the innocent. Throughout, the modest operative metaphor of a London fog is appropriate to the supposed victims of the alleged scheme and even more to Valmont himself, who is undeniably clever but wrong, misled by his earnest determination to uncover deceit. He is left unrepentant but nonplussed by the canvasser's explanation of his and his employer's quite legitimate and well-intentioned enterprise. Here, as elsewhere, Barr does not dwell on Valmont's reaction to the facts; the story ends with the revelation, not with discomfiture, self-recrimination, or rationalization.

Valmont's "triumphs," whether real, petty, or nonexistent, are more a vindication of his personality than practical and satisfactory demonstrations of his self-proclaimed genius as a detective. With this satiric version of the master sleuth, Barr made a distinctive contribution to the growing pantheon of literary investigators, before wit and insight were joined to physical derring-do in the later, more forceful forms of the genre.

Louis K. MacKendrick

PRINCIPAL MYSTERY AND DETECTIVE FICTION

EUGÈNE VALMONT SERIES: *The Triumphs of Eugène Valmont*, 1906

NONSERIES NOVELS: *The Face and the Mask*, 1894; *A Woman Intervenes: Or, The Mistress of the Mine*, 1896; *The Mutable Many*, 1896; *Jennie Baxter, Journalist*, 1899; *A Prince of Good Fellows*, 1902; *Over the Border*, 1903; *A Chicago Princess*, 1904; *A Rock in the Baltic*, 1906; *The Watermead Affair*, 1906; *The Girl in the Case*, 1910; *Lady Eleanor, Lawbreaker*, 1911

OTHER SHORT FICTION: *From Whose Bourne?*, 1893; *Revenge!*, 1896; *The Strong Arm*, 1899; *The Woman Wins*, 1904; *Tales of Two Continents*, 1920; *The Adventures of Sherlaw Kombs*, 1979

OTHER MAJOR WORKS

NOVELS: *In the Midst of Alarms*, 1894; *One Day's Courtship, and The Heralds of Fame*, 1896; *Tekla*, 1898 (also known as *The Countess Tekla*); *The Victors*, 1901; *The O'Ruddy*, 1903 (with Stephen Crane); *The Lady Electra*, 1904; *The Speculations of John Steele*, 1905; *The Tempestuous Petticoat*, 1905; *The Measure of the Rule*, 1907; *Young Lord Stranleigh*,

1908; *Cardillac*, 1909; *Stranleigh's Million*, 1909; *The Sword Maker*, 1910; *Lord Stranleigh, Philanthropist*, 1911; *The Palace of Logs*, 1912; *A Woman in a Thousand*, 1913; *Lord Stranleigh Abroad*, 1913; *My Enemy Jones: An Extravaganza*, 1913 (also known as *Unsentimental Journey*)

SHORT FICTION: *Strange Happenings*, 1883; *In a Steamer Chair, and Other Shipboard Stories*, 1892; *The Helping Hand, and Other Stories*, 1920

PLAYS: *An Evening's Romance*, pr. 1901 (with Cosmo Hamilton); *The Conspiracy*, pr. 1907; *Lady Eleanor, Lawbreaker*, pr. 1912; *The Hanging Outlook*, pr. 1912 (with J. S. Judd)

NONFICTION: *The Unchanging East*, 1900; *I Travel the Road*, 1945

BIBLIOGRAPHY

Barzun, Jacques, and Wendell Hertig Taylor. *A Catalogue of Crime*. Rev. ed. New York: Harper & Row, 1989. Massive, nearly one-thousand-page critical bibliography of mystery, detective, and spy stories. Provides context for understanding Barr. Includes an index.

Kestner, Joseph A. *The Edwardian Detective, 1901-1915*. Brookfield, Vt.: Ashgate, 2000. Discusses Barr's literary production within the context of the detective fiction being written in England in the first decade and a half of the twentieth century.

Klinck, Carl F., ed. *Literary History of Canada*. Vol 1. 2d ed. Buffalo, N.Y.: University of Toronto Press, 1976. Detailed four-volume history of Canadian literature and literary culture is a good source for understanding Barr's background. Bibliographies and indexes.

MacGillivray, S. R. "Robert Barr." In *The Oxford Companion to Canadian Literature*, edited by Eugene Benson and William Toye. 2d ed. New York: Oxford University Press, 1997. Examines Barr's place, and the place of detective fiction as such, within the body of Canadian literature.

Parr, John. "The Measure of Robert Barr." *Journal of Canadian Fiction* 3, no. 2 (1974): 21-31. Evaluates Barr as a Canadian author and a contributor to a properly Canadian literary culture.

FRANCIS BEEDING
John Leslie Palmer and Hilary Aidan St. George Saunders

JOHN LESLIE PALMER
Born: Oxford, England; September 4, 1885
Died: Hampstead, England; August 5, 1944
Also wrote as Christopher Haddon; David Pilgrim
   (with Hilary Aidan St. George Saunders)

HILARY AIDAN ST. GEORGE SAUNDERS
Born: Clifton, England; January 14, 1898
Died: Naussau, the Bahamas; December 16, 1951
Also wrote as Barum Browne (with Geoffrey
   Dennis); Cornelius Cofyn (with John de Vere
   Loder); David Pilgrim (with John Leslie Palmer)
Types of plot: Espionage; police procedural; psycho-
   logical

PRINCIPAL SERIES
Colonel Alastair Granby, 1928-1946

PRINCIPAL SERIES CHARACTER
COLONEL ALASTAIR GRANBY (later a general),
D.S.O., of the British Intelligence Service. In *Take It
Crooked* (1932), he marries Julia Hazelrig. A man of
short stature with twinkling eyes, he quotes William
Shakespeare and enjoys good food and drink. He
eventually becomes head of the British Secret Service.

CONTRIBUTION
The pseudonymous collaboration as Francis
Beeding of John Leslie Palmer and Hilary Aidan St.
George Saunders began in the 1920's, when both
served in the League of Nations Permanent Secretariat. Living and working in Geneva, both were no doubt
keenly aware of the European nations' fears and frustrations, which persisted after the signing of the Treaty
of Versailles. There was a degree of paranoia, demonstrated in part by the dread that Germany, bitter and
burdened by war reparations, was secretly rearming. It
is not surprising that, set against a background of rumors, one in which espionage was sure to be a part of
any covert rearmament effort, espionage stories would
become increasingly evident in the popular literature.

The partnership of Palmer and Saunders produced a
series of entertaining espionage novels that, because
of their quality, appealed to the sophisticated reader of
the day. No less appealing was the other fiction produced by the two. Writing is supposed to be a lonely
business, and successful literary collaborations are
few, but that of Palmer and Saunders lasted for more
than twenty years, during which, as Francis Beeding,
they produced more than thirty popular novels.

BIOGRAPHY
John Leslie Palmer was born on September 4,
1885. He was educated at Balliol College, Oxford,
where he was the Brackenbury scholar. Palmer married Mildred Hodson Woodfield in 1911, and the
union produced a son and a daughter. Palmer was
drama critic and assistant editor of *The Saturday Review of Literature* in London from 1910 until 1915, after which he was drama critic of London's *Evening
Standard* until 1919. During the same period, he
served in the British War Trade Intelligence Department. Palmer was a member of the British delegation
to the Paris Peace Conference, and from 1920 to 1939,
he was on the staff of the League of Nations Permanent Secretariat in Geneva. He produced several novels, one play, and numerous nonfictional works, most
concerning the theater, including a study of the life
and works of Molière, and a two-volume work titled
Political [Comic] Characters of Shakespeare (1945-
1946). Palmer died on August 5, 1944.

Hilary Aidan St. George Saunders, born January
14, 1898, was, like his collaborator, a graduate of Oxford's Balliol College. After the death of his first wife,
Helen Foley, in 1917, he married Joan Bedford. During World War I, Saunders served in the Welch Guards
and was awarded the Military Cross. He worked on the
staff of the League of Nations Permanent Secretariat
from 1920 to 1937 and was with the British Air Ministry during World War II. He was librarian of the British House of Commons from 1946 to 1950. Both
anonymously and under his own name, Saunders pro-

duced a number of works concerned with military operations. Saunders died December 16, 1951.

ANALYSIS

For their literary quality alone, the espionage novels of Francis Beeding are notable for their period. Where others might have written for those who sought fast-paced thrills and chilling descriptions of death and torture, Beeding's style appealed to the reader requiring softer, more cultured entertainment. His style would satisfy those who enjoyed characterizations of ordinary people of wit and charm with tastes for good food and wine, fashion, travel, and the arts. Stories by Beeding also show an understanding of the reader who requires a semblance of plausibility in character and plot but who is able to recognize absurdity and accept it willingly when it makes for an entertaining read.

THE THREE FISHERS

In Beeding's espionage novels, characters sometimes display a type of humor not unlike that of Ian Fleming's James Bond, whose spying for the British came later. In *The Three Fishers* (1931), the young Ronald Briercliffe, on a secret mission to Paris on behalf of British intelligence, is taken prisoner by Francis Wyndham, whose intention is to make a fortune for himself by creating an international panic during which military conflict would resume between France and Germany. For the term of his imprisonment, Briercliffe is confined to a small, narrow room in the attic of Wyndham's Paris home. Shortly, and by clever means, Briercliffe manages to escape, but within a very few hours, he is recaptured and returned to Wyndham, having in the meantime narrowly escaped both being buried alive and being disfigured with acid. Exhausted, he is delivered to the same small room, where he flings himself on the bed and whispers, "Home again."

Traveled readers might be gratified by the sense of authenticity Beeding gives by furnishing detailed descriptions of movement within the cities where activity in his espionage novels takes place. The following passage is from *The Three Fishers*, the setting for which is Paris:

> "Gare de Lyon," said Wyndham, "and drive as fast as you can."

The driver let in his clutch and they ran swiftly down the Quai Henri Quatre. They made the Gare de Lyon in less than three minutes. Wyndham paid off his man, entered the departure side of the great station, crossed to the arrival side and chartered another taxi.

> "The Port de Vincennes," he said, "and go slowly. I want to buy a hat."

Wyndham bought his hat in the Boulevard Diderot and then in front of a café in the Place de la Nation he paid the man off, saying that he had changed his mind and would go no farther.

THE HIDDEN KINGDOM

For the armchair traveler, Thomas Preston, the principal figure in *The Hidden Kingdom* (1927), generously gives to the reader a sense of place and a heightened anticipation of the action to come in his description of a scene in Barcelona:

> We were standing in the Plaza del Rey, on the site of the old Roman forum. It was approached on three sides by narrow streets, but on the north side it was unbroken. The sun was behind me, shining full upon a mediæval tower that rose above a line of small houses. Under the tower was a glint of splendour, where the rays of the sun caught the brass and lit the brilliant uniforms of the band. . . . But it was the houses themselves, their windows full of people in a hundred attitudes of attention, which gave to the scene its peculiar atmosphere. They were the houses of small folk who had come and gone about their business in the town for centuries, and who still in this little square . . . crowded out the past and filled one with a sense of the happy continuity of life.

The above are but two among dozens of examples in each of the novels which furnish something special in the way of scene development. The action in Beeding's novels takes place in Austria, England, Germany, Italy, Morocco, and Switzerland, as well as France and Spain, and architecture and customs are richly described—bonuses not found in all espionage novels of the period.

PRETTY SINISTER

Among other treats offered Beeding's readers are the passages describing his characters' brief moments of dining, not one of which fails to mention the selection of wine or wines, as may be seen in *Pretty Sinister* (1929):

"Yes, old boy, not at all bad, but I think they have rather overdone the mushrooms."

Granby surveyed his sole with appreciation.

"I like this place," said Merril.

"I'm glad you're glad," returned Granby, looking with a twinkle at his companion, who was a little flushed.

Beside them a Romanée Conti, lying in its wicker basket, gleamed through the dust and cobwebs of twenty years.

"A thought old for Burgundy, if you follow the modern fashion, but 1908 was a wonderful year," murmured his host. "I suggest that a little later on we just wet the nose in Perrier Jouet '17. That will go down rather well with the *pêches flambées*."

Beeding's are among the best examples of popular espionage fiction written between the two world wars. The purposes and objectives of the League of Nations for a time provided underlying ideas for Beeding's novels, and for the student of history, that is perhaps what sets Beeding apart. Not only would such themes have given the modern reader a sense of involvement in current events, but they give later readers a special perspective on the period as well.

Several characters in the novels are employed by the league, and Geneva is often the setting. The league's covenant against the private manufacture of arms and its promise to prevent such manufacture is used in *The Seven Sleepers* (1925) and in *The Four Armourers* (1930). *The Six Proud Walkers* (1928), *The Five Flamboys* (1929), *The Three Fishers*, and *The One Sane Man* (1934) each have a villainous character whose goal is to gain wealth or position via the destruction of the peace pledged and supported by the League of Nations.

THE NINE WAXED FACES

Eventually, Beeding began using world events as background for his espionage novels. *The Nine Waxed Faces* (1936) is set against the Nazi takeover of Austria, and the characters Hagen and Caferelli are names used to represent Adolf Hitler and Benito Mussolini. The Spanish Civil War is the subject of *Hell Let Loose* (1937), and the Nazi invasion of Czechoslovakia is covered in *The Ten Holy Terrors* (1939). Although Beeding's heroes exhibit some of the typical prejudices of the period and they are not above a show of nationalism, awareness and concern is reflected, on the part of the author, for the grave political events of two decades.

THE HOUSE OF DR. EDWARDES

Beeding succeeds in providing color, adventure, and amusement in his espionage novels. For the remainder of his work, however, Beeding seems to have had a different plan. *Death Walks in Eastrepps* (1931) is a departure for him, as he delves into psychology for a look at a killer who is motivated by the injustice done to his dead mother. *The House of Dr. Edwardes* (1927; also known as *Spellbound*) is an earlier attempt at a psychological study. The villain is a madman who mentally enslaves the inmates of an exclusive Swiss mental hospital, requiring them to perform satanic rituals. It was this novel that provided material for a film

Director Alfred Hitchcock adapted Beeding's novel The House of Dr. Edwardes *to the screen as the classic suspense film* Spellbound.

made by Alfred Hitchcock, taking its title from the American edition of the novel: *Spellbound*.

Paula Lannert

PRINCIPAL MYSTERY AND DETECTIVE FICTION

COLONEL ALASTAIR GRANBY SERIES: *The Six Proud Walkers*, 1928; *Pretty Sinister*, 1929; *The Five Flamboys*, 1929; *The Four Armourers*, 1930; *The League of Discontent*, 1930; *Take It Crooked*, 1932; *The Two Undertakers*, 1933; *The One Sane Man*, 1934; *The Eight Crooked Trenches*, 1936 (also known as *Coffin for One*); *The Nine Waxed Faces*, 1936; *Hell Let Loose*, 1937; *The Black Arrows*, 1938; *The Ten Holy Terrors*, 1939; *Eleven Were Brave*, 1940; *Not a Bad Show*, 1940 (also known as *The Secret Weapon*); *The Twelve Disguises*, 1942; *There Are Thirteen*, 1946

PROFESSOR KREUTZEMARK SERIES: *The Seven Sleepers*, 1925; *The Hidden Kingdom*, 1927

INSPECTOR GEORGE MARTIN SERIES: *The Norwich Victims*, 1935; *No Fury*, 1936 (also known as *Murdered: One by One*); *He Could Not Have Slipped*, 1939

NONSERIES NOVELS: *The Little White Hag*, 1926; *The House of Dr. Edwardes*, 1927 (also known as *Spellbound*); *The Devil and X.Y.Z.*, 1931 (by Saunders as Barum Browne); *Death Walks in Eastrepps*, 1931; *The Three Fishers*, 1931; *Murder Intended*, 1932; *The Emerald Clasp*, 1933; *Mr. Bobadil*, 1934 (also known as *The Street of the Serpents*); *Death in Four Letters*, 1935; *The Death-Riders*, 1935 (by Saunders as Cornelius Cofyn); *The Erring Under-Secretary*, 1937; *The Big Fish*, 1938 (also known as *Heads Off at Midnight*); *Under the Long Barrow*, 1939 (by Palmer as Christopher Haddon; also known as *The Man in the Purple Gown*); *Mandragora*, 1940 (by Palmer as Christopher Haddon; also known as *The Man with Two Names*); *The Sleeping Bacchus*, 1951 (by Saunders)

OTHER MAJOR WORKS

NOVELS: *So Great a Man*, 1937 (as Pilgrim); *No Common Glory*, 1941 (as Pilgrim); *The Great Design*, 1944 (as Pilgrim); *The Emperor's Servant*, 1946 (as Pilgrim)

OTHER MAJOR WORKS (BY PALMER)

NOVELS: *Peter Paragon: A Tale of Youth*, 1915; *The King's Men*, 1916; *The Happy Fool*, 1922; *Looking After Joan*, 1923; *Jennifer*, 1926; *Timothy*, 1931

PLAY: *Over the Hills*, pr. 1912, pb. 1914

NONFICTION: *The Censor and the Theatres*, 1912; *The Comedy of Manners*, 1913; *The Future of the Theatre*, 1913; *Comedy*, 1914; *Bernard Shaw: An Epitaph*, 1915 (also known as *George Bernard Shaw, Harlequin or Patriot?*); *Rudyard Kipling*, 1915; *Studies in the Contemporary Theatre*, 1927; *Molière: His Life and Works*, 1930; *Ben Jonson*, 1934; *The Hesperides: A Looking-Glass Fugue*, 1936; *Political [Comic] Characters of Shakespeare*, 1945-1946 (2 volumes)

OTHER MAJOR WORKS (BY SAUNDERS)

NONFICTION: *Bomber Command: The Air Ministry's Account of Bomber Command's Offensive Against the Axis*, 1941; *The Battle of Britain, August-October, 1940: An Air Ministry Record*, 1941; *Combined Operations, 1940-1942*, 1943 (by Saunders; also known as *Combined Operations: The Official Story of the Commandos*); *Return at Dawn: The Official Story of the New Zealand Bomber Squadron of the R.A.F.*, 1943; *Per Ardua: The Rise of British Air Power, 1911-1939*, 1944; *Pioneers! O Pioneers!*, 1944; *Ford at War*, 1946; *The Left Hand Shakes: The Boy Scout Movement During the War*, 1948; *Valiant Voyaging: A Short History of the British India Steam Navigation Company in the Second World War*, 1948; *The Green Beret: The Story of the Commandos, 1940-1945*, 1949; *The Middlesex Hospital, 1745-1948*, 1949; *The Red Cross and the White: A Short History of the Joint War Organization of the British Red Cross Society and the Order of St. John of Jerusalem*, 1949; *The Red Beret: The Story of the Parachute Regiment at War*, 1951; *Westminster Hall*, 1951; *Royal Air Force, 1939-1945*, 1954 (with Denis Richards; 3 volumes)

BIBLIOGRAPHY

Hanson, Gillian Mary. *City and Shore: The Function of Setting in the British Mystery.* Jefferson, N.C.: McFarland, 2004. Analyzes Beeding's use of setting in *Death Walks in Eastrepps*. Bibliographic references and index.

Kaplan, E. Ann. *Trauma Culture: The Politics of Terror and Loss in Media and Literature*. New Brunswick, N.J.: Rutgers University Press, 2005. Includes a chapter on trauma in Alfred Hitchcock's *Spellbound*, an adaptation of Beeding's *The House of Dr. Edwardes*.

Panek, LeRoy Lad. *An Introduction to the Detective Story*. Bowling Green, Ohio: Bowling Green University Popular Press, 1987. This work tracing the history of the detective story contains a chapter on the Golden Age mystery and mentions Beeding.

_____. *The Special Branch: The British Spy Novel, 1890-1980*. Bowling Green, Ohio: Bowling Green University Popular Press, 1981. Scholarly study of British espionage thrillers geared toward the nonscholar and written by a major critic in the academic study of mystery and detective fiction. Provides perspective on Beeding's work.

Turnbull, Malcolm J. *Victims or Villains: Jewish Images in Classical English Detective Fiction*. Bowling Green, Ohio: Bowling Green University Popular Press, 1998. Contains a discussion of Beeding's *The Five Flamboys* in the chapter on the Golden Age portrayal of Jews in English mysteries.

JOSEPHINE BELL
Doris Bell Collier

Born: Manchester, Lancashire, England; December 8, 1897
Died: Place unknown; April 24, 1987
Types of plot: Amateur sleuth; psychological; police procedural; thriller; cozy

PRINCIPAL SERIES

David Wintringham and Steven Mitchell, 1937-1958
Claude Warrington-Reeve and Steven Mitchell, 1959-1963
Henry Frost, 1964-1966
Amy Tupper, 1979-1980

PRINCIPAL SERIES CHARACTERS

DR. DAVID WINTRINGHAM is a gifted amateur sleuth whose professional training provides him with skills that enable him to solve crimes. A family man, he possesses keen powers of observation, intense curiosity, dogged determination, courage, and strong moral principles.

INSPECTOR STEVEN MITCHELL of Scotland Yard, who advances to chief superintendent, is a model of the hardworking but uninspired police officer. Ordinary in every sense, he is pleasant but nondescript in appearance and is endowed with average intelligence and homely virtues. His kindness and patience during interviews build trust and often elicit valuable information. His painstaking attention to routine police investigation also contributes to his success.

CLAUDE WARRINGTON-REEVE, a kind but arrogant London barrister who works with Chief Superintendent Mitchell on three cases, is an altogether more flamboyant figure and is cast in the mold of the eccentric master sleuth of Golden Age detective fiction. He drives a fast black Jaguar and in one book dramatically fells a culprit on the golf course with a long drive.

DR. HENRY FROST, a retired general practitioner who appears in two novels, exhibits many of the same character traits as David Wintringham: strength of will, keen observation, a talent for logical deduction, tenacity, and a fundamental moral sense. He is skilled at finding and interpreting physical evidence at the scene of the crime and then building a chain of evidence to reach a solution to the problem.

MISS AMY TUPPER, featured in two novels, is an energetic, inquisitive, indomitable elderly single woman who spurs police investigation into crimes by asking questions that they cannot ignore. She is motivated by sympathy for crime victims and by a desire for justice.

CONTRIBUTION

Since the 1920's, respectable, middle-class English-women have been committing murder on paper to the delight of millions of readers. They constitute a recognized group, if not a formal school, of skilled practitioners of the genre. Although Josephine Bell did not begin publishing detective stories until late in the Golden Age of crime fiction between the two world wars, she was definitely of the same historical and literary generation as Agatha Christie, Dorothy L. Sayers, Ngaio Marsh, and Margery Allingham. She was "among the most reliable of those intelligent, unsensational women writers who have created a peculiarly English corner in this kind of fiction," and she deserves to be remembered along with those other great writers of the period for the excellence of her craftsmanship. Her novels are notable for the imaginative patterning of their puzzles, realistic portrayal of people from various walks of life, skillful rendering of place, deft evocation of atmosphere, interesting subject matter, and gentle, ironic humor.

Bell's career as a crime writer reflected the historical and literary development of the genre over a period of nearly fifty years. She demonstrated considerable talent in a variety of crime fiction. During the heyday of the classic detective novel, she mastered its conventions and wrote whodunits. After World War II, as the genre evolved to include more types of crime novels, Bell exhibited both flexibility and versatility by extending her canon to include the gothic novel, the police procedural, and the thriller.

BIOGRAPHY

Josephine Bell was born Doris Bell Collier, the second of three children of Maud Tessimond Windsor and Joseph Edward Collier, a surgeon in Manchester. Doris was very fond of her father, who died of cancer when she was seven years old. Her mother was married a second time to Jean Estradier, a French teacher, and had one child by him, a girl named Alice. Young Doris did not get on well with her stepfather, so she was happy to leave for boarding school when she was twelve. She attended the Godolphin School, Salisbury, where she met Dorothy L. Sayers. In Doris's first year, Sayers was already a senior.

On leaving school in 1916, Doris applied to study medicine at Newnham College, Cambridge University. At college, she took a keen interest in rowing and stroked in the very first Newnham eight. When she went to University College Hospital to do her clinical training, no accommodation for female medical students existed, so she had to sleep in a side ward. At University College Hospital she met Norman Dyer Ball, a fellow student, and was married to him in 1923; four children were eventually born to them.

Doris and her husband went into general practice together in Greenwich in 1927. In 1936, Norman was killed in an automobile accident. After her husband's death, Doris moved her small family to Guildford in Surrey, where she started a general practice of her own. At the same time, to supplement her income, she decided to become a professional writer. *Murder in Hospital*, already complete when her husband died, was published in 1937; she produced one or two novels a year for the next half century. She was a founding member of the Crime Writers' Association. After retiring from medical practice in 1954, she devoted herself to writing, sailing, theatergoing, and community involvement. She died in 1987.

ANALYSIS

Josephine Bell was not a literary innovator, nor was she an abject conformist. She did not introduce new devices or make significant changes in existing conventions of the genre. Instead, she was scrupulous in observing the traditions of the classic detective story—except for the treatment of her detective hero: She rejected the idea of the eccentric master sleuth in favor of more realistic characterization. In fact, she surpassed many of the Golden Age writers in realistic presentation of both principal and secondary characters. Furthermore, unlike many of her contemporaries, who did not change with the times, after World War II Bell introduced greater range and depth of psychological development in her characters and even portrayed individuals with personality disorders. She strove continually to create lifelike characters and often drew on her wide experience of human nature in representing humankind's foibles, follies, and vices.

Bell's career as a professional crime writer spanned

fifty years. For the first twenty years, she wrote a series of books featuring a detective team composed of a gifted amateur, Dr. David Wintringham, and a Scotland Yard professional, Inspector Steven Mitchell. They worked together on eight cases—approximately half of the tales—and Wintringham appeared alone in seven other mysteries. Mitchell functioned on his own in only one story; Bell subsequently paired him with a more flamboyant amateur partner, Claude Warrington-Reeve, in three other whodunits. Bell followed the Golden Age tradition in favoring the gifted amateur over the more pedestrian police officer but departed from it by failing to endow her medical amateur with an eccentric personality. Wintringham's character is consistently realistic and undramatic. Although Mitchell is more than simply a Watson-type foil, he is always secondary to the more compelling figures of Wintringham and Warrington-Reeve.

DR. DAVID WINTRINGHAM

Although Dr. David Wintringham is the main character, no information concerning his physical appearance or social background is given. His personality is revealed through his thoughts, conversation, and behavior. Some critics have suggested that Bell's reputation suffered because she failed to create a great detective, that Wintringham's personality was not vivid enough to draw a large following. There may be some truth in this charge. Post-World War II writers who created ordinary, unsensational sleuths developed the personalities and personal lives of their characters more fully. Without peculiar mannerisms, idiosyncratic habits, and extravagant gestures to rivet attention, a character must be developed more fully to compensate for the loss of drama.

Wintringham's professional training provides him with skills that enable him to be a good detective. He possesses keen powers of observation, intense curiosity, dogged determination, and a strong commitment to truth and justice. Bell frequently draws parallels between doctoring and detecting—that is, between scientific investigation and police investigation.

> "That's right." The Inspector smiled approvingly.
> "You're getting more thorough. Not so much of the
> I've-had-an-inspiration about you this time, is there?"

> "You forget that I am doing research of a kind," answered David. "It is a very sobering experience."
> "Really? I always understood it was packed full of thrills."
> "Not a bit of it. You ought to know better. Your own work is research; it is also popularly regarded as exciting. Is it packed full of thrills?"
> "I should say not."
> "There you are."
> For a few minutes the two men reflected on their drab existence.

INSPECTOR STEVEN MITCHELL

More is revealed about Mitchell through direct description. In *Murder in Hospital*, he is presented as looking homely in the typical mackintosh and bowler hat of the Central Intelligence Division detective. He is further characterized in *Death on the Borough Council* (1937) as "a medium-sized man with an ordinary pleasant-featured face." His family background is described in the first novel, which also includes an account of his motives for joining the police force.

> Inspector Mitchell came of a respectable middle-class family who had always lived in one or other of the South London suburbs, moving about for no apparent reason from one small and genteel villa to another. His father's work in a city office tethered them within reasonable distance of it, but like so many suburban families they seemed unable to settle anywhere permanently. This fact and his varied schooling produced in young Mitchell a restlessness that was not really fundamental to his character, but made him refuse the chance of a job in the office where his father worked to seek the excitement he supposed inseparable from life in the police force.
>
> That he had been wrong in this supposition he never really noticed. The routine work and discipline were entirely to his liking. He settled down well and worked hard. He had good average brains and infinite patience, while his kind manner towards witnesses had often elicited facts that would have been withheld from more brilliant officers.

Neither character changes much, although Bell makes an effort to represent realistically the passing of time. Over the course of the first five novels, Wintringham's personal life progresses at a normal rate. In the novel, he is engaged to be married to Jill; in the second, they have been married and are expecting their first child; in the third, their son, Nicky, is a toddler; and in the fifth, the family has grown by the addition of a daughter, Susan. In addition, Mitchell's success is charted as he advances through the ranks of the police hierarchy from inspector to chief superintendent.

The pattern of the relationship between Wintringham and Mitchell as well as of the deductive method is set in the first few books. A crime occurs within Wintringham's domain or purview; Mitchell is assigned to the case as the investigating officer from Scotland Yard; Wintringham offers to help unofficially because of inside knowledge or connections; Mitchell rejects Wintringham's help at first, but then welcomes it when Wintringham turns up valuable information. "'It's against all the rules,' grumbled Mitchell. 'But I'd rather, by a long chalk, have you working where I can see you, than behind my back.'" Wintringham frequently provides some vital medical evidence that leads to the solution of the crime, while Mitchell works quietly in the background, interviewing suspects and collecting facts by routine police methods. Eventually, they pool the results of their labors and find the solution by means of logical deduction. Confrontation and apprehension of the culprit follow.

THE UPFOLD WITCH AND DEATH ON THE RESERVE

In the early 1960's, Bell introduced a second amateur medical sleuth in the character of Henry Frost, a retired general practitioner who appears in two novels, *The Upfold Witch* (1964) and *Death on the Reserve* (1966). Frost exhibits many of the same personality traits as Wintringham: a strong will, an eye for detail, a developed logical sense, and moral fiber. In some ways he might be seen as a more mature version of Wintringham.

AMY TUPPER

The only other character in Bell's later fiction to stage a comeback was Miss Amy Tupper, who made her debut in *Wolf! Wolf!* (1979) and played a part in *A Question of Inheritance* (1980). She is an inquisitive elderly single woman who spurs official investigation of crimes by asking questions that had not occurred to the police. Her private inquiries turn up important information that helps solve the mystery.

Bell follows the formula of classic detective fiction introduced by Edgar Allan Poe in the mid-nineteenth century. This formula is natural for her and for her sleuth, because the deductive method follows the steps of the empirical scientific method: observation, interviewing, research, formulating a hypothesis, testing the hypothesis, and presentation of results. These steps are repeated until all relevant facts are accounted for and all questions are answered.

PUZZLE NOVELS

In the manner of the works of Freeman Wills Crofts and R. Austin Freeman, Bell's detective novels often focus more on the problem or puzzle than on the personality of the sleuth. She was attracted to detective fiction for the same reasons she enjoyed medicine—because she liked to solve problems. Bell sets the puzzle and then teases out the solution. Emphasis is placed on the steps leading to identification of the villain. Through skillful manipulation of the omniscient narrative viewpoint, she introduces seemingly unrelated characters, events, and facts; then she painstakingly reveals how the discrete pieces of the puzzle come together to form a fascinating pattern. That is, the detective uncovers facts that he eventually assembles into an intricate but coherent pattern, much as the doctor does in medical research.

In novels of this sort—for example, *The Port of London Murders* (1938)—as in those with an inverted structure, Bell was less concerned to disguise the identity of the criminal than to disclose the complexity of the crime and the ingenuity of its solution. Still, despite her focus on how the investigators solve the puzzle rather than on who committed the crime, she cleverly masks the identity of the culprit, who often is the least likely suspect. Good examples of this technique occur in *Death on the Borough Council*, *Death at Half-Term* (1939), *Easy Prey* (1959), *The Upfold Witch*, and *Death of a Con Man* (1968).

MURDER IN HOSPITAL

Bell's plotting can sometimes be faulted for too much reliance on coincidence, both in gathering evidence and in solving the puzzle. For example, in *Murder in Hospital* Wintringham just happens to pass through a certain hospital ward when the doctor in charge is about to inoculate a child with antidiphtheria serum without asking if she had received a previous injection. Patients sensitized by prior injections require smaller doses and could be killed by the amount administered initially. In a blinding flash of insight, Wintringham realizes how several unexplained deaths have been caused and by whom. Similar coincidences occur often enough in other novels to strain credibility.

VILLAINS AND VICTIMS

Different types of villains march through the pages of Bell's novels. Some are people dominated by greed, such as Gordon Longford in *The Port of London Murders*, Cyril Dewhurst in *Death at Half-Term*, Stephen Coke in *Easy Prey*, and Roy Waters in *Death of a Con Man*. A few, such as Edgar Trouncey in *Death on the Reserve* and John Wainwright in *The Upfold Witch*, are motivated by a combination of sexual desire and greed. Some are neurotic individuals who are driven by fanatic obsessions—for example, the mad scientist in *Murder in Hospital*, the rabbit keeper in *Death on the Borough Council*, and the religious megalomaniac in *The Innocent* (1982). Others are criminally insane—for example, the paranoid schizophrenic Simon Fawcett in *The Hunter and the Trapped* (1963). Whoever they are and whatever their crimes, however, they are provided with a quick exit at the end of the story, often in the form of a suicidal attempt to avoid being taken into custody.

In her early novels, Bell also follows the Golden Age protocol regarding victims. They are either unattractive persons for whom the reader could never grieve or too underdeveloped as characters to be missed. Victims are usually hapless individuals who are destroyed by chance, those who threaten the security of the villain, or people whose deaths would lead to profit for the killer.

Bell has employed a variety of closed communities as settings; she sometimes limits the setting in terms of place or in terms of social group. Murders occur in areas such as a hospital, a library, a public school, a nature reserve, an archaeological dig, and the ever-popular country village. In two novels, Bell also limits suspects within the community of a religious sect. Whatever the scene of the crime, she provides excellent local color, evoking in the reader a sense of each place's mood and atmosphere.

LATER WORKS

Beginning in the 1950's, Bell began to try her hand at a variety of other types of crime fiction. She drew on the gothic tradition in *To Let, Furnished* (1952) and again in *New People at the Hollies* (1961). She went to great lengths to acquire knowledge of forensics and police procedures so that she could get the details right. Of all her books, *Bones in the Barrow* (1953) is most often cited for careful attention to police routine. During the 1970's and 1980's, she wrote several romantic thrillers, including *Death of a Poison-Tongue* (1972) and *A Pigeon Among the Cats* (1974). In these novels, a young heroine finds herself in a dangerous situation involving murder and is finally rescued through a combination of her own efforts and outside assistance. In the latter works, Bell uses the genre to discuss and expose important social problems such as the danger of superstition, the inadequacy of social services, unethical recruitment practices of coercive religious sects, and drug addiction. A retrospective view of Bell's career discloses both an ability to adjust to changing styles in the genre and an ability to write in a variety of mystery modes. Her work very much reflects the development of the genre over fifty years, the evolution of the detective story to the crime novel, the whodunit to the "whydunit."

B. J. Rahn

PRINCIPAL MYSTERY AND DETECTIVE FICTION

DAVID WINTRINGHAM AND STEVEN MITCHELL SERIES: *Murder in Hospital*, 1937; *Death on the Borough Council*, 1937; *Fall over Cliff*, 1938; *The Port of London Murders*, 1938; *Death at Half-Term*, 1939 (also known as *Curtain Call for a Corpse*); *From Natural Causes*, 1939; *All Is Vanity*, 1940; *Trouble at Wrekin Farm*, 1942; *Death at the Medical Board*, 1944; *Death in Clairvoyance*, 1949; *The Summer School Mystery*, 1950; *Bones in the Barrow*, 1953; *Fires at Fairlawn*, 1954; *Death in Retirement*, 1956; *The China Roundabout*, 1956 (also known as *Murder on the Merry-Go-Round*); *The Seeing Eye*, 1958

CLAUDE WARRINGTON-REEVE AND STEVEN MITCHELL SERIES: *Easy Prey*, 1959; *A Well-Known Face*, 1960; *A Flat Tyre in Fulham*, 1963 (also known as *Fiasco in Fulham* and *Room for a Body*)

HENRY FROST SERIES: *The Upfold Witch*, 1964; *Death on the Reserve*, 1966

AMY TUPPER SERIES: *Wolf! Wolf!*, 1979; *A Question of Inheritance*, 1980

NONSERIES NOVELS: *The Backing Winds*, 1951; *To Let, Furnished*, 1952 (also known as *Stranger on a Cliff*); *Double Doom*, 1957; *The House Above the River*, 1959; *New People at the Hollies*, 1961; *Adventure with Crime*, 1962; *The Hunter and the Trapped*, 1963; *The Alien*, 1964; *No Escape*, 1965; *The Catalyst*, 1966; *Death of a Con Man*, 1968; *The Fennister Affair*, 1969; *The Wilberforce Legacy*, 1969; *A Hydra with Six Heads*, 1970; *A Hole in the Ground*, 1971; *Death of a Poison-Tongue*, 1972; *A Pigeon Among the Cats*, 1974; *Victim*, 1975; *The Trouble in Hunter Ward*, 1976; *Such a Nice Client*, 1977 (also known as *A Stroke of Death*); *A Swan-Song Betrayed*, 1978 (also known as *Treachery in Type*); *A Deadly Place to Live*, 1982; *The Innocent*, 1982

OTHER MAJOR WORKS

NOVELS: *The Bottom of the Well*, 1940; *Martin Croft*, 1941; *Alvina Foster*, 1943; *Compassionate Adventure*, 1946; *Total War at Haverington*, 1947; *Wonderful Mrs. Marriot*, 1948; *The Whirlpool*, 1949; *Cage-Birds*, 1953; *Two Ways to Love*, 1954; *Hell's Pavement*, 1955; *The Convalescent*, 1960; *Safety First*, 1962; *The Alien*, 1964; *Tudor Pilgrimage*, 1967; *Jacobean Adventure*, 1969; *Over the Seas*, 1970; *The Dark and the Light*, 1971; *To Serve a Queen*, 1972; *In the King's Absence*, 1973; *A Question of Loyalties*, 1974

NONFICTION: *Crime in Our Time*, 1962

BIBLIOGRAPHY

Brean, Herbert. Preface to *Crimes Across the Sea: The Nineteenth Annual Anthology of the Mystery Writers of America*, edited by John Creasey. New York: Harper & Row, 1964. Preface to an anthology that includes Bell's work, discusses her in relation to such other contributors as Ellery Queen and Julian Symons.

Dubose, Martha Hailey, with Margaret Caldwell Thomas. *Women of Mystery: The Lives and Works of Notable Women Crime Novelists*. New York: St. Martin's Minotaur, 2000. The focus of this study is on Bell's contemporaries rather than on her, but it mentions her in passing and provides an important study of the milieu in which she wrote.

Hanson, Gillian Mary. *City and Shore: The Function of Setting in the British Mystery*. Jefferson, N.C.: McFarland, 2004. Analyzes Bell's use of setting in *The Port of London Murders*. Bibliographic references and index.

White, Terry, ed. *Justice Denoted: The Legal Thriller in American, British, and Continental Courtroom Literature*. Westport, Conn.: Praeger, 2003. This bibliography covers legal thrillers from early to later writers. Contains a brief biography of Bell.

ARNOLD BENNETT

Born: Shelton, near Hanley, England; May 27, 1867
Died: London, England; March 27, 1931
Types of plot: Amateur sleuth; thriller

PRINCIPAL SERIES

Five Towns, 1902-1916

CONTRIBUTION

Arnold Bennett was, above all, a professional writer. He wrote numerous novels, plays, short stories, and books of commentary; he also wrote one of the most influential columns on the book world during his lifetime. This column, entitled "Books and Persons," appeared in *The New Age* from 1908 to 1911 under the pseudonym Jacob Tonson and under his own name in *The London Standard* from 1926 to 1931. His criticism and analysis of the detective novel at the end of the 1920's was significant in shaping the genre. His use of detailed description and his depictions of middle- and lower-class life provide his readers with insight into how others live and think.

BIOGRAPHY

Arnold Bennett was born Enoch Arnold Bennett in the Potteries, a section of England that was to provide many of the scenes for his writing. He worked at a variety of jobs and eventually became editor in the 1890's of *Woman*, a magazine produced for middle-class English women. He began to write reviews and short stories both for this journal and other, similar publications. Eventually, his success led to a novel and a full-time writing career. He formed a close relationship with James B. Pinker, one of the most significant early literary agents. From 1900 until his death, Bennett was one of the leading figures in the English literary world and, along with H. G. Wells and John Galsworthy, can be considered to be a founder of the Edwardian school of realistic fiction. His novels of the Five Towns area in England—including *Anna of the Five Towns* (1902), *The Grim Smile of the Five Towns* (1907), *The Old Wives' Tale* (1908), *Clayhanger* (1910), *Hilda Lessways* (1911), and *These Twain* (1915)—are especially

noteworthy. Many of his other novels, in particular *The Grand Babylon Hotel* (1902) and *Riceyman Steps* (1923), are still widely read. During World War I, Bennett wrote on wartime life and worked as a publicist for the English government.

Bennett was married to a French poet, Marguerite Soulié. Later, the couple separated, and Bennett was married to Dorothy Cheston. This union resulted in one daughter, Virginia. Bennett traveled widely throughout Europe and the Mediterranean, often using his yacht for lengthy excursions. In addition, he lived for long periods of time in Paris. Wherever he went, he observed carefully, noting his observations in his jour-

Arnold Bennett.

nal. He used this material, especially the more mundane aspects, in his work. Bennett suffered from a severe stammer, and many believe that this disability aided his writing—only through writing could he communicate in a straightforward, efficient manner.

Bennett was a successful playwright, and his work appeared on London West End stages for more than twenty years. His friendships with other writers such as Eden Phillpotts, H. G. Wells, and John Galsworthy were instrumental in helping him write fiction; this group fought very strongly against censorship and insisted on describing life as it really happened. Bennett was the epitome of the professional writer, working each day to schedule, meeting his deadlines with ease, offering his help and commentary to other writers, and even providing funds for those whom he thought needed his assistance. (Among the latter were D. H. Lawrence and James Joyce.) Bennett's use of detective story conventions was simply an example of his professionalism, as he believed that good, careful, competent writers should make use of whatever methods and techniques moved their stories along. Bennett continued to write until the end of his life. He died of typhoid fever early in 1931.

ANALYSIS

Arnold Bennett began his career working as an editor, a position that allowed him to read many raw manuscripts. Among these were several detective stories. As he began to prepare for his life as a professional author, he read widely in the mystery and detective genre and was especially influenced by the work of Émile Gaboriau. As Bennett began his own work, he employed aspects of detection in his novels, as in *The Grand Babylon Hotel*, which features corpses, and the detection mysteries posed by corpses, within a general description of life in a luxurious resort hotel. Bennett was also interested enough in detection to work for several months with his close friend H. G. Wells on the writing of a play called "The Crime." The play was never produced because it was to open with a corpse on the stage, something thought by producers to bring bad luck. The text of the play is no longer extant.

THE LOOT OF CITIES

In 1903, Bennett began a series of short-fiction pieces for *The Windsor Magazine*. The six interconnected stories were published in 1904 as the novel *The Loot of Cities*, and the book was republished in the United States in 1972 as a volume designed for collectors of little-known detective fiction. In the book, a detective, Cecil Thorold, also a millionaire, is out for a good time. He eventually falls in love with one of the other characters after traveling to Brussels, Switzerland, and the Mediterranean. The book, although not one of Bennett's best, illustrates his style and his method of description.

HUGO

Bennett's next venture into these themes was the novel *Hugo* (1906), which is little known. The work is modeled to some degree on the style of Gaboriau and uses coincidence, as well as Bennett's sense of mood and life in foreign areas, to drive the plot. Bennett tends to contrast life in cities and towns in his writing, and, although it is traditional for the city to be denigrated in these comparisons, Bennett is more interested in comparing life in the city and the country objectively. Decisions that his characters make are often ironic ones, molded by the nature of their environments and their early lives.

THE CITY OF PLEASURE

Bennett's novel *The City of Pleasure* (1907) is an effort to contrast two persons who operate a giant amusement park in London. The story actually centers on crime, suspense, danger, burglary, and missing funds, concluding with a love-story ending. Although the book is not an example of typical detective fiction, it depends on the conventions of that genre. Police seldom appear in Bennett's work; the detection and punishment of crimes occur primarily through coincidence.

LATER WORKS AND SHORT STORIES

Bennett continued to use the elements of detective fiction in some of his later novels, especially *The Price of Love* (1914) and *The Strange Vanguard* (1928). The first of these features the mystery of a missing sum of money and the impact of the missing funds on the lives and loves of his characters, especially as suspicion falls on one or another of them. The second is a light piece of fiction, but a kidnapping and considerable intrigue put it into the category of detective fiction.

Bennett wrote with a facile pen and could produce materials for publication in very short order, without much need for correction. He had a great sense of style, and although his short stories are not well known, they read quickly, have an air of truth about them (even after many years), and hold the modern reader's interest. Several of them that appeared in magazines are straight detective fiction, with the best of these being "Murder," which appeared in *Liberty* on October 1, 1927, and was collected in *The Night Visitor* (1931). The short story is worth remembering, as it pokes fun at methods of detection, particularly those of the police and fictional characters similar to Sherlock Holmes. It was Bennett's way of making light of the lesser aspects of detective-fiction writing.

On the basis of this work one might misjudge Bennett as a dabbler in detective fiction. Yet Bennett's

comments on writing and writers were extremely important in his own time and have been collected in *Arnold Bennett: The Evening Standard Years, "Books and Persons," 1926-1931* (1974). Several of the pieces included in this volume, essays on style, were important in developing the methodology of John Dickson Carr and other mystery writers of the late 1920's and 1930's. The young detective story writer can still profit by reading Bennett's remarks on style, character, plot, and, above all, the need to rid one's work of clichés. Bennett believed that the detective story could be as respectable as a classic novel, and he encouraged novice detective-fiction writers whenever he could. His essays on the genre constitute a veritable self-help guide.

Bennett may not be remembered for his own detective fiction, although his work in that area is admirable. His real contribution was his willingness to treat detective fiction seriously, criticize it within the bounds of general fiction, and offer his advice to those essaying work in the genre—and for this Bennett should be recognized.

David C. Smith

PRINCIPAL MYSTERY AND DETECTIVE FICTION

FIVE TOWNS SERIES: *Anna of the Five Towns*, 1902; *Leonora*, 1903; *Tales of the Five Towns*, 1905; *Whom God Hath Joined*, 1906; *The Grim Smile of the Five Towns*, 1907; *The Old Wives' Tale*, 1908; *Clayhanger*, 1910; *Helen with the High Hand*, 1910; *The Card*, 1911 (also known as *Denry the Audacious*); *Hilda Lessways*, 1911; *The Matador of the Five Towns*, 1912; *The Regent*, 1913 (also known as *The Old Adam*); *The Price of Love*, 1914; *These Twain*, 1915; *The Lion's Share*, 1916

NONSERIES NOVELS: *The Grand Babylon Hotel*, 1902 (also known as *T. Racksole and Daughter*); *Hugo*, 1906; *The City of Pleasure*, 1907; *The Strange Vanguard*, 1928 (also known as *The Vanguard*, 1927)

OTHER SHORT FICTION: *The Loot of Cities*, 1905; *The Night Visitor*, 1931

OTHER MAJOR WORKS

NOVELS: *A Man from the North*, 1898; *The Gates of Wrath*, 1903; *A Great Man*, 1904; *Teresa of Watling Street*, 1904; *Sacred and Profane Love*, 1905 (also known as *The Book of Carlotta*); *The Sinews of War*, 1906 (with Eden Phillpotts; also known as *Doubloons*); *The Ghost*, 1907; *Buried Alive*, 1908; *The Statue*, 1908 (with Phillpotts); *The Glimpse*, 1909; *The Pretty Lady*, 1918; *The Roll-Call*, 1918; *Lilian*, 1922; *Mr. Prohack*, 1922; *Riceyman Steps*, 1923; *Elsie and the Child*, 1924; *Lord Raingo*, 1926; *Accident*, 1928; *Piccadilly*, 1929; *Imperial Palace*, 1930; *Venus Rising from the Sea*, 1931

Short fiction: *The Woman Who Stole Everything*, 1927

Plays: *Polite Farces for the Drawing-Room*, pb. 1899; *Cupid and Commonsense*, pr. 1908; *What the Public Wants*, pr., pb. 1909; *The Honeymoon: A Comedy in Three Acts*, pr., pb. 1911; *Milestones: A Play in Three Acts*, pr., pb. 1912 (with Edward Knoblock); *The Great Adventure: A Play of Fancy in Four Acts*, pr. 1912; *The Title*, pr., pb. 1918; *Judith*, pr., pb. 1919; *Sacred and Profane Love*, pr., pb. 1919; *Body and Soul*, pr., pb. 1922; *The Love Match*, pr., pb. 1922; *Don Juan de Marana*, pb. 1923; *London Life*, pr., pb. 1924 (with Knoblock); *Flora*, pr. 1927; *Mr. Prohack*, pr., pb. 1927 (with Knoblock); *The Return Journey*, pr. 1928

Nonfiction: *Journalism for Women*, 1898; *Fame and Fiction*, 1901; *How to Become an Author*, 1903; *The Truth About an Author*, 1903; *Things That Interested Me*, 1906; *Things Which Have Interested Me*, 1907, 1908; *Literary Taste*, 1909; *Those United States*, 1912 (also known as *Your United States*); *Paris Nights*, 1913; *From the Log of the Velsa*, 1914; *The Author's Craft*, 1914; *Over There*, 1915; *Books and Persons: Being Comments on a Past Epoch, 1908-1911*, 1917; *Things That Have Interested Me*, 1921, 1923, 1926; *Selected Essays*, 1926; *Mediterranean Scenes*, 1928; *The Savour of Life*, 1928; *The Journals of Arnold Bennett*, 1929, 1930, 1932-1933; *Arnold Bennett: The Evening Standard Years, "Books and Persons," 1926-1931*, 1974

Bibliography

Anderson, Linda R. *Bennett, Wells, and Conrad: Narrative in Transition*. New York: St. Martin's Press, 1988. A focused introduction to Bennett's fiction as well as that of H. G. Wells and Joseph Conrad.

Broomfield, Olga R. R. *Arnold Bennett*. Boston: Twayne, 1984. Criticism and interpretation from Twayne's English Authors series. Includes a bibliography and an index.

Drabble, Margaret. *Arnold Bennett*. Reprint. Boston: G. K. Hall, 1986. Drawing from Bennett's *Journals* and letters, this biography focuses on Bennett's background, childhood, and environment, which it ties to his literary works. Profusely illustrated, containing an excellent index and a bibliography of Bennett's work.

Kestner, Joseph A. *The Edwardian Detective, 1901-1915*. Brookfield, Vt.: Ashgate, 2000. Study of the brief but distinctive Edwardian period in detective fiction. Discusses Bennett's detective fiction and relates it to the author's fiction in general, as well as to the detective stories of his fellow Edwardians.

Roby, Kinley. *A Writer at War: Arnold Bennett, 1914-1918*. Baton Rouge: Louisiana State University Press, 1972. Although primarily biographical, this book also offers valuable insights into Bennett's work during and after World War I. Contains works cited and an excellent index.

Squillace, Robert. "Arnold Bennett's Other Selves." In *Marketing the Author: Authorial Personae, Narrative Selves, and Self-Fashioning, 1880-1930*, edited by Marysa Demoor. New York: Palgrave Macmillan, 2004. Discusses the different personae assumed by Bennett to market his various works. Useful for understanding the relationship between Bennett's detective fiction and his other work.

_____. *Modernism, Modernity, and Arnold Bennett*. Lewisburg, Pa.: Bucknell University Press, 1997. Squillace argues that Bennett saw more clearly than his contemporary novelists the emergence of the modern era, which transformed a male-dominated society to one open to all people regardless of class or gender. Very detailed notes and a bibliography acknowledge the work of the best scholars.

Wright, Walter F. *Arnold Bennett: Romantic Realist*. Lincoln: University of Nebraska Press, 1971. Sees Bennett as vacillating between the two extremes of Romanticism and realism and describes his novels as mildly experimental.

E. C. BENTLEY

Born: London, England; July 10, 1875
Died: London, England; March 30, 1956
Also wrote as E. Clerihew
Types of plot: Amateur sleuth; cozy

PRINCIPAL SERIES

Philip Trent, 1913-1938

PRINCIPAL SERIES CHARACTER

PHILIP TRENT, in his thirties, became famous for publicly solving crimes in the columns of *The Record*. A successful painter, he is by no means arty, and despite a love of poetry, he has the enviable knack of getting along with all sorts of people. He is the ideal young Englishman of his day.

CONTRIBUTION

In crime fiction, vivid, enduring character, not to be confused with caricature, is rare, as it is often cramped by the machinery of the plot. Also, to the practiced reader, mystery often becomes anything but insoluble. In Philip Trent, however, E. C. Bentley created a memorable companion, and in *Trent's Last Case* (1913, revised 1929), the first book in which Trent appeared, he devised a plot of successive thrilling denouements and an ending quite impossible to foresee. The book was written to divert the course of English detective fiction, and in this, as well as in sales and reviews, it was an outstanding success.

Sherlock Holmes, an important figure of Bentley's youth, so dominated the field that his inventor, Arthur Conan Doyle, was called on to solve real crimes. Bentley challenged Doyle's icy, introverted, infallible hero with a good-humored, susceptible extrovert who caught the public mood and became as much a model for less original writers as Sherlock Holmes had been. The shift in the heroic notion from the disdainful self-sufficiency of Holmes to the sociable misapprehensions of Trent prefigures the change in sensibility accelerated by World War I, in which old certainties as well as young men died.

BIOGRAPHY

It would be hard to invent a background more representative than Edmund Clerihew Bentley's of the English Edwardian governing class. His father was an official in the Lord Chancellor's department, the equivalent of a ministry of justice. He was educated at a private London boys' school, St. Paul's, and at nineteen, he won a history scholarship to Merton College, in Oxford. He made friends at school with G. K. Chesterton, who remained his closest friend for life, and at Oxford University with John Buchan and Hilaire Belloc. All would become famous writers.

At Oxford, Bentley became president of the Oxford Union, a skeleton key to success in many careers, and experienced the "shame and disappointment" of a second-class degree. Down from Oxford and studying law in London, he published light verse and reviews in magazines. In 1901, he married Violet Alice Mary Boileau, the daughter of General Neil Edmonstone Boileau of the Bengal Staff Corps. Bentley was called to the bar the following year but did not remain in the legal profession, having, in the words of a friend, all the qualifications of a barrister except the legal mind. He went instead into journalism, a profession he loved and in which he found considerable success.

For ten years, Bentley worked for the *Daily News*, becoming deputy editor. In 1912, he joined the *Daily Telegraph* as an editorialist. In 1913, he published *Trent's Last Case*. It was an immediate, and, for its author, an unexpected success. Strangely, nothing was heard of its hero, Philip Trent, for another twenty-three years.

Although *Trent's Last Case* was repeatedly reprinted, translated, and filmed, Bentley went on writing editorials for the *Daily Telegraph*, and it was not until two years after his retirement from journalism in 1934 that there appeared *Trent's Own Case*, written with H. Warner Allen. A book of short stories, *Trent Intervenes*, followed in 1938, and *Those Days: An Autobiography* appeared in 1940. *Elephant's Work*, a mystery without Trent, which John Buchan had advised him to write as early as 1916, appeared in 1950.

In 1939, with younger journalists being called to arms, Bentley returned to the *Daily Telegraph* as chief literary critic; he stayed until 1947. After the death of his wife in 1949, he gave up their home in London and lived out the rest of his life in a London hotel. Of their two sons, one became an engineer, and the other, Nicolas, became a distinguished illustrator and the author of several thrillers.

ANALYSIS

Trent's Last Case stands in the flagstoned hall of English crime fiction like a tall clock ticking in the silence, always chiming perfect time. From the well-bred simplicity of that famous, often-adapted title to the startling last sequence, everything is unexpected, delightful, and fresh. The ingenious plot twists through the book like a clear stream, never flooding, never drying up, but always glinting somewhere in the sunlight and leading on into mysterious depths.

In this landscape, the characters move clearly and memorably, casting real, rippling shadows and at times, as in real life, disappearing for a moment from view. It is a consciously moral vision, as the opening sentence proclaims: "Between what matters and what seems to matter, how should the world we know judge wisely?" The morality, although not quite orthodox, is the morality of a decent man to whom life presents no alternative to decency. It is a morality that the hero and his creator share.

Trent's Last Case is the work of a man who thought, as many have thought, that he could write a better detective story than those he had read. Having satisfied himself and others on this point, he did not write another crime novel until after he had retired from what he always regarded as his real work, newspaper journalism.

A better background for an English detective-fiction writer than E. C. Bentley's is difficult to imagine. His father was involved with crime and its punishment through his work as an official in the Lord Chancellor's department; Bentley's own classical education, followed by three years studying history at Oxford, insisted on the importance of clear, grammatical speech and orderly ideas; in his period in chambers when qualifying as a barrister, he came into contact with the ponderous engines of judgment and witnessed the difficulties to be encountered encompassing the subtle complexities of truth; and finally, he had acquired the habit of summoning words to order in his capacity as a daily journalist.

To the happy accident of birth among the English governing class in its most glorious years, nature added a playfulness with words—a talent that brought a new noun into the English language. Bentley was sixteen and attending a science class at St. Paul's when four lines drifted into his head:

> Sir Humphrey Davy
> Abominated gravy.
> He lived in the odium
> Of having discovered Sodium.

The form amused him and his friends, and he carried on writing in it, eventually for *Punch*, and published a collection in 1905. This collection, entitled *Biography for Beginners*, was Bentley's first book; it was brought out under the name of E. Clerihew. For a time, clerihews rivaled limericks in popularity, and something of their spirit and cadence survives in the light verse of Ogden Nash and Don Marquis. Some of this playfulness shows through in Trent's conversation; although Bentley hopes in vain that the reader will believe that Trent's "eyes narrowed" as he spotted a clue and that "both men sat with wrinkled brows," the style is generally nimble and urbane and does not impede the action.

The language runs aground only when confronted by American speech. These are the words in which the closest lieutenant of one of the most powerful men on earth addresses an English gentleman and a high-ranking Scotland Yard detective: "I go right by that joint. Say, cap, are you coming my way too?" Bentley edited and wrote introductions to several volumes of short stories by Damon Runyon, whose work he enjoyed all of his life, and it is likely that his American idiom derives from this source.

TRENT'S LAST CASE

Bentley, in 1911, left the deputy editorship of the *Daily News*, which he had joined because it was "bitterly opposed to the South African war. I believed earnestly in liberty and equality. I still do." He became an

Philip Trent in a 1938 issue of The Strand Magazine.

editorial writer for the *Daily Telegraph*, which gave him more time for himself. *Trent's Last Case* came out two years later. It redefined the standards by which this kind of fiction is judged.

In *Trent's Last Case*, an American of vast wealth living in England is murdered. He has acquired his fortune by the unscrupulous but not unusual strategy of manipulating markets and intimidating those who bar his way. Yet it cannot be the wealth that Bentley condemns but the corruption of those who spend their lives in the pursuit of it, since hereditary landowners in Great Britain possessed wealth of a far more enduring and substantial sort. Bentley saw the new breed of American tycoon as insatiable, callous, and criminal—the murder was thought at first to be the work of underworld connections. Where F. Scott Fitzgerald saw Jay Gatsby, his rich bootlegger, as a figure of romance, even a kind of apotheosis of the American Dream, Bentley saw Sigsbee Manderson as the quintessence of evil.

The implicit belief that a gentlemanly and conviv-ial existence is a mirror of the moral life, if not indeed the moral life itself, and that evildoing leads to madness, or is indeed madness itself, gives the book a moral certitude that crime writers in more fragmented times have found hard to match. Yet certitude can still be found in British life, at least that part of it sustained by an expensive education and inherited wealth. The rich conventionally bring with them an agreeable social style; the nouveau riche do not. A society based on acquired wealth, such as American society, could make a hero out of Gatsby; a society based on inherited wealth made a villain out of Manderson.

Trent epitomizes the difference between English and American fictional detectives. The English detective, coming from the high table of society (Trent, Lord Peter Wimsey), is far more clever than the mainly working-class police. The reader is unlikely to quibble. In the United States, the best crime fiction has been written around the type of private eye who seldom knows where the next client is coming from (Dashiell Hammett, Raymond Chandler, Ross Macdonald) or around hard-pressed cops doing their all-too-fallible best (Ed McBain). In a republic, the best fictional detectives come from the people; in a kingdom, they come from privilege. Trent's tangible presence derives from his background and his circumstances being so close to those of his creator.

Sigsbee Manderson's passing is regretted only by those who stood to lose money by it. One of those who did not was his wife. Nevertheless, Mabel Manderson is the antithesis of all the double-crossing dames brought to a peak of perfection if not credibility by Hammett and Chandler and subsequently parodied in the espionage stories of the Cold War.

Goodness, as John Milton and others have found, is harder to embody than evil. Mabel Manderson in less talented hands would have become a stock character, but in Bentley's, she is the ideal woman, fair and caring and moral. In turning her back on a vast fortune for love, she follows her heart as blithely as Trent, by his chivalrous behavior toward her, follows the public-school ethic of his day, an ethic that a year later would accompany the doomed young officer conscripts into the trenches and later still the young fighter pilots into the Battle of Britain.

The popular appeal of crime writing relies on the author's ability to make the reader care about what happens next. Bentley achieves this by careful plotting and by making people and events interesting in themselves. Bentley's engineering was always too solid to need passages of violent action or Chandler's remedy for an ailing plot—having somebody come through the door with a gun. Bentley in any case did not believe in gore: "My outlook was established by the great Victorians, who passed on to me the ideas of the Greeks about essential values, namely, physical health, freedom of mind, care for the truth, justice, and beauty."

Bentley was nevertheless a product of his background in attitude to servants. A manservant must instantly recognize a gentleman and address him with a subtly different deference from that with which he would address a detective. Manderson's manservant passes this test, calling Trent "Sir" and the detective merely "Mr. Murch." It at once becomes clear that this is not to be a case in which the butler did it.

Yet Mr. Manderson's maid, French in the fashion of the time and consequently lacking in reserve, is severely rebuked: "A star upon your birthday burned, whose fierce, severe, red, pulseless planet never yearned in heaven, Celestine. Mademoiselle, I am busy. Bonjour." This reprimand strangely mixes misogyny, class contempt, and xenophobia. To an Englishwoman of equal social standing, however, Trent behaves with unexceptional gallantry. With Mrs. Manderson, he is the unworthy knight, she the princess in the tower. Indeed, Mrs. Manderson emerges as the central, and finest, character in the book. Whereas in the Hammett-Chandler school women are conventionally untrustworthy to the degree that they are desirable, Mabel Manderson is as idealized as any fine lady in troubadour verse. That she symbolizes the importance of family life becomes even more clear later in *Trent's Own Case*.

An attempt, as Bentley put it, at "a new kind of detective story," *Trent's Last Case* was an immediate success and its reputation and sales in many languages continue to grow. The *Dictionary of National Biography* called it "the best detective novel of the century." *The New York Times* described the novel as "one of the few classics of crime fiction." John Carter, one of the

founding editors of *Time* magazine, said it was "the father of the contemporary detective novel" and marked "the beginning of the naturalistic era." The critic Frank Swinnerton viewed it as "the finest long detective story ever written." Finally, continuous praise has been heaped on it by other writers of crime: "An acknowledged masterpiece," Dorothy L. Sayers; "One of the three best detective stories ever written," Agatha Christie; "The finest detective story of modern times," G. K. Chesterton; "The best detective story we have ever read," G. D. H. Cole and Margaret Cole; "A masterpiece," Edgar Wallace.

Nothing else Bentley wrote had such success, including his autobiography. Detective stories are a reaffirmation of the medieval morality plays, in which evil is always vanquished and good always triumphant. To these reassuring fables, Bentley brought a new complexity, a humbling of the overweening intellect, and a glorification of the modesty of the heart. The occasional shortcomings in sympathy derive from his milieu, which exerted such an influence over his vision; the completely original mixture of ingenuity and good humor has never been matched and is all Bentley's own.

Malcolm Winton

PRINCIPAL MYSTERY AND DETECTIVE FICTION
PHILIP TRENT SERIES: *Trent's Last Case*, 1913 (revised 1929; also known as *The Woman in Black*); *Trent's Own Case*, 1936 (with H. Warner Allen); *Trent Intervenes*, 1938

NONSERIES NOVEL: *Elephant's Work*, 1950 (also known as *The Chill*)

OTHER MAJOR WORKS
POETRY: *Biography for Beginners*, 1905 (as Clerihew); *More Biography*, 1929; *Baseless Biography*, 1939; *Clerihews Complete*, 1951 (also known as *The Complete Clerihews*); *The First Clerihews*, 1982 (with G. K. Chesterton and others)

NONFICTION: *Peace Year in the City, 1918-1919: An Account of the Outstanding Events in the City of London During the Peace Year*, 1920; *Those Days: An Autobiography*, 1940; *Far Horizon: A Biography of Hester Dowden, Medium and Psychic Investigator*, 1951

Edited texts: *More than Somewhat*, 1937 (by Damon Runyon); *Damon Runyon Presents Furthermore*, 1938; *The Best of Runyon*, 1938; *The Second Century of Detective Stories*, 1938

Bibliography

Chesterton, G. K. *Autobiography*. 1936. Reprint. London: Hutchinson, 1969. Novelist Chesterton details his relationship to Bentley and the mutual influence of the two writers.

_____. *Come to Think of It: A Book of Essays*. London: Methuen, 1930. Includes Chesterton's thoughts on the work of his friend and colleague.

Haycraft, Howard. *Murder for Pleasure: The Life and Times of the Detective Story*. 1941. Reprint. New York: Carroll and Graf, 1984. Organizes the history of detective fiction into a "biography" and situates Bentley's works in relation to others in the narrative.

Kestner, Joseph A. *The Edwardian Detective, 1901-1915*. Brookfield, Vt.: Ashgate, 2000. Discusses the brief but distinctive Edwardian period in detective fiction. Compares Bentley to such other Edwardians as Chesterton and John Buchan.

Panek, LeRoy. "E. C. Bentley." In *Watteau's Shepherds: The Detective Novel in Britain, 1914-1940*. Bowling Green, Ohio: Bowling Green University Popular Press, 1979. Compares Bentley to his contemporaries and details his contribution to and reception by British culture.

Roth, Marty. *Foul and Fair Play: Reading Genre in Classic Detective Fiction*. Athens: University of Georgia Press, 1995. A post-structural analysis of the conventions of mystery and detective fiction. Examines 138 short stories and works from the 1840's to the 1960's. Sheds light on Bentley's work.

ANTHONY BERKELEY
Anthony Berkeley Cox

Born: Watford, Hertfordshire, England; July 5, 1893
Died: London, England; March 9, 1971
Also wrote as A. B. Cox; Francis Iles; A. Monmouth Platts
Types of plot: Amateur sleuth; inverted; psychological; thriller

Principal series
Roger Sheringham, 1925-1945
Ambrose Chitterwick, 1929-1937

Principal series characters

Roger Sheringham, an amateur sleuth and mystery aficionado, was created initially to parody an unpleasant acquaintance of the author. Anthony Berkeley's readers, however, warmed to him, and he reappeared in other novels, with his offensiveness—an all-knowing insouciance—much subdued and rendered more genial, but retaining his urbanity and sophistication.

Ambrose Chitterwick, an unlikely, mild-mannered detective, negates all popular images of the sleuth but nevertheless solves baffling crimes.

Contribution

Anthony Berkeley achieved fame during one of the periods in which mystery writing was ascendant. In the 1920's, he was frequently linked with Agatha Christie, Dorothy L. Sayers, and S. S. Van Dine as one of the four giants in the field. Indeed, John Dickson Carr, himself a giant, called Berkeley's *The Poisoned Chocolates Case* (1929) one of the best detective stories ever written. Nevertheless, Berkeley parted company with them, particularly with Christie—even though she did prove to be, if not the most durable, certainly the most enduring of the quartet—as he moved from the mystery as intellectual conundrum toward an exploration of the limits within which the genre could sustain psychology and suspense. One can almost imagine Berkeley wondering: "What if the reader knew from the first paragraph who the murderer was? How would one generate suspense?" Thereon, he pioneered the inverted mystery, told from the criminal's point of view or, in a further twist, from the perspective of the victim.

Berkeley was more than equal to the challenges that he drew from the genre, and his work has been justly celebrated for its perspicuity. His characters are rich and deeply realized as he pursues the implications of the murderous motive on their psyches. Although his plots are sometimes contrived (plot machinations are not his principal focus), his stories are shot through with elegance, intelligence, and grace.

One last contribution that Berkeley tendered was to the performing arts. One of his Francis Iles novels—*Malice Aforethought: The Story of a Commonplace Crime* (1931)—was adapted for television in Great Britain in 1979, while another one, *Before the Fact* (1932), was adapted by Alfred Hitchcock into his 1941 classic film *Suspicion* with Cary Grant and Joan Fontaine, and *Trial and Error* (1937) was directed by Vincent Sherman and scripted by Barry Trivers as *Flight from Destiny* (1941). Hitchcock, at least via his screenwriter, betrayed the novelist's conception of a fit resolution to the thriller; Hitchcock evidently believed that he knew the marketplace better than did the original artist.

BIOGRAPHY

Anthony Berkeley was born Anthony Berkeley Cox in Watford, Herfordshire, England, and his given names would later become indelibly linked with those of the top British mystery authors of the Golden Age. As a child, he attended a day school in Watford and at Sherborne College, Wessex. He later studied at University College, Oxford, where he earned a degree in classics. After World War I started in 1914, he enlisted in the British Army and eventually attained the rank of lieutenant. However, he became a victim of gas warfare on a French battlefield and left the army with permanently damaged health.

In 1917 Berkeley married Margaret Fearnley Farrar. That marriage ended in 1931 and was followed a year later by Berkeley's marriage to a woman variously identified as Helen Macgregor or Helen Peters. This marriage lasted little more than a decade. Meanwhile, Berkeley worked at several occupations, including real estate. He was a director of a company called Publicity Services and one of two officers of another firm called A. B. Cox, Ltd.

Berkeley's writing and journalistic career as Anthony Berkeley and Francis Iles lasted several decades. He began by contributing witty sketches to *Punch*, the English humor magazine, but soon discovered that writing detective fiction was more remunerative. The year 1925 was a boom time for Berkeley. That year he published the classic short story "The Avenging Chance" and (as A. B. Cox) the comic opera *Brenda Entertains*, the novel *The Family Witch: An Essay in Absurdity*, and the collection *Jugged Journalism*. He carefully guarded his privacy from within the precincts of the fashionable London area known as St. John's Wood.

As Anthony Berkeley, he founded the Detection Club in 1928. A London organization, the club brought together top British crime writers dedicated to the care and preservation of the classic detective story. The very existence of the organization attested to the popularity of mystery and detective writing in the 1920's. In 1929 Berkeley published his masterpiece, *The Poisoned Chocolates Case*, in which members of the club appeared as thinly disguised fictional characters.

Berkeley had a considerable effect on the way that the Detection Club was chartered; while the oath that candidates for membership had to swear reflects Berkeley's own wit—it parodies the Oath of Confirmation of the Church of England—it also works to confirm on the practitioners of mystery writing the status and standards of a serious and well-regarded profession, if not an art. Berkeley collaborated with other club members on several round-robin tales and anthologies: *Behind the Screen* (serialized in *The Listener*, 1930), *The Scoop* (serialized in *The Listener*, 1931; reprinted as *The Scoop, and, Behind the Screen*, 1983), *The Floating Admiral* (1931; reprinted in 1980); *Ask a Policeman* (1933, reprinted 1987), *Six Against the Yard: In Which Margery Allingham, An-*

thony Berkeley, Freeman Wills Crofts, Father Ronald Knox, Dorothy L. Sayers, Russell Thorndike Commit the Crime of Murder Which Ex-Superintendent Cornish, C.I.D., Is Called upon to Solve (1936; also known as *Six Against Scotland Yard*), *The Anatomy of Murder* (1936), and *More Anatomy of Murder* (1936).

Although Berkeley published his last novel in 1939, he continued reviewing mysteries for the rest of his life. As Francis Iles, he wrote for the *London Daily Telegraph* in the 1930's, for *John O'London's Weekly* in 1938, for the *London Sunday Times* after World War II, and for the *Manchester Guardian* from the mid-1950's to 1970. He also wrote articles dedicated to his fascination with crime, such as his 1937 essay "Was Crippen a Murderer?"

Interestingly, although Berkeley sought to prevent the public from intruding on his personal affairs, he was not insensitive to professional obligations. Like Charles Dickens and Arthur Conan Doyle before him, he recognized public demands, affably molding his detective, in this case Roger Sheringham, into a more likable and engaging creature when it became apparent that that was what the public desired. This is one of many parallels between serial publication as practiced by Dickens and the series of novels that many detective writers published. Anthony Cox died in 1971, his privacy inviolate and the immortality of Anthony Berkeley assured.

ANALYSIS

The classic English murder mystery enjoyed a golden age in the 1920's. Whether the mystery's triumph resulted from the confidence that followed the postwar boom or from a prescient awareness that this era of prosperity would soon come to an end, the public imagination was captured by erudite, self-sufficient, all-knowing, and in some instances debonair detectives— the likes of Lord Peter Wimsey, Hercule Poirot, and Philo Vance. The reading public was entranced by someone who had all the answers, someone for whom the grimmest, grimiest, and most gruesome aspects of life—murder most foul—could be tidied up, dusted off, and safely divested of their most dire threats so that life could continue peaceful, placid, and prosperous.

Roger Sheringham gets into a jam in "The Avenging Chance."

"THE AVENGING CHANCE"

Anthony Berkeley entered the increasingly fertile field of mysteries, becoming a major figure with the 1925 publication of the often-reprinted short story "The Avenging Chance," which featured detective Roger Sheringham, on whom his author bestowed the worst of all possible characteristics of insufferable amateur sleuths. A British World War I veteran who has become successful at writing crime novels, Sheringham is vain, sneering, and in all ways offensive. The story was, in fact, conceived as a parody, as the following passage illustrates:

Roger Sheringham was inclined to think afterwards that the Poisoned Chocolates Case, as the papers called it, was perhaps the most perfectly planned murder he had ever encountered. The motive was so obvious, when you knew where to look for it—but you didn't know; the method was so significant when you had grasped its real essentials—but you didn't grasp them; the traces were so thinly covered, when you had realised what was covering them—but you didn't realise. But for a piece of the merest bad luck, which the murderer could not possibly have foreseen, the crime must have been added to the classical list of great mysteries.

However, the story proved sufficiently popular to inspire its as yet unnamed author to expand it into a novel, which is now considered to be one of Berkeley's four classics, *The Poisoned Chocolates Case*. His other important novels are *Malice Aforethought, Before the Fact*, and *Trial and Error*. He actually wrote many others, now considered forgettable, having in fact been forgotten and fallen out of print.

THE POISONED CHOCOLATES CASE

The Poisoned Chocolates Case is clever and interesting: Its premise is based on the detective club Berkeley founded. A private, nonprofessional organization of crime fanciers reviews a case that has, in true English mystery fashion, stumped Scotland Yard. Six members will successively present their solutions to the mysterious death of a wealthy young woman, who, it seems, has eaten poisoned chocolates evidently intended for someone else. The reader is presented with a series of possible scenarios (some members suggest more than one), each one more compelling than the last. Thus Berkeley exhausts all the possible suspects, not excepting the present company of putative investigators. Berkeley even goes so far as to present a table of likely motives, real-life parallel cases, and alleged killers, reminiscent of the techniques of Edgar Allan Poe, who based the fictional artifice of "The Mystery of Marie Rogêt" on a genuine, unsolved mystery. (Berkeley does this as well in his 1926 *The Wychford Poisoning Case*.)

Like that of Poe, Berkeley's method is logical, or ratiocinative, as the chroniclers of C. Auguste Dupin or Sherlock Holmes might aver. Thus, *The Poisoned Chocolates Case* is remarkable less for its action and adventure—there are no mean streets or brawls here—than for its calm, clear rationale. This is murder most civilized, gleaming only momentarily in the twilight of the British Empire. It is, moreover, murder, in this pretelevision era, by talking heads. Thus, the author

must find a way other than plot convolutions to generate interest, to say nothing of suspense, since he is, in effect, retelling his story five times.

Yet Berkeley creates a crescendo of climaxes and revelations of solutions, with Roger Sheringham, the detective presumptive, assigned by the luck of the draw the fourth presentation. He is twice trumped by superior solutions, for the last, and most perfect answer, belongs to the slightest and most insignificant of the club's communicants, Ambrose Chitterwick. Roger is rendered beside himself by this untoward and alien chain of events, and the conventions of the genre are no less disturbed. This final solution cannot be proved, however, so that at the end the reader is left baffled by the ironies and multiplicities of the mystery's solution, not unlike the messy and disheveled patterns of life itself.

TRIAL AND ERROR

Also published under the name Anthony Berkeley was *Trial and Error*, which posits a mild-mannered, unprepossessing protagonist, Mr. Todhunter. Already under a death sentence imposed by an incurable illness, Mr. Todhunter, like the last and best ratiocinator in *The Poisoned Chocolates Case*, is most improbable in his role: He has decided that the way to achieve meaning in life is to kill someone evil. Thus, the reader is presented with a would-be murderer in search of a crime. The murder, then, within the structure of the text, is a pivotal climax rather than the more usual starting point for the principal plot developments. *Trial and Error* is one of Berkeley's first exercises with the inverted mystery; it enabled him to experiment with the form, expand and extend it, at the same time indulging his instincts for parody of the methods, and particularly the characters, of mysteries.

Berkeley's method is to sacrifice convention and routine for the sake of characterization. How will these people react when the terms of their worlds, the conditions under which they have become accustomed to acting, are suddenly shifted? What will Mr. Todhunter be like as a murderer, for example? These are the concerns of the author. Berkeley believes that the unexpected is not a device that results from the complexities and permutations of plot, but is the effect of upending the story from the very beginning. He is not finished with poor Mr. Todhunter's inversion, for *Trial and Error* proceeds to tax its antihero with the challenge of seeing someone else wrongly convicted for Todhunter's crime. With Berkeley's knowledge of the law securely grounding the story, Mr. Todhunter must therefore, honorably if not entirely happily, undertake to secure a legal death sentence for himself. There is yet another, final turn to the screw of this most ironic plot before Berkeley releases it.

MALICE AFORETHOUGHT AND BEFORE THE FACT

Under the nom de plume Francis Iles, Berkeley wrote *Malice Aforethought, Before the Fact*, and *As for the Woman* (1939)—the last a little-known, generally unavailable, and not highly regarded endeavor. The first two, however, are gems. Here is even more experimentation and novelty within the scope of the novel. *Malice Aforethought* centers on the revenge of a henpecked husband, another of Berkeley's Milquetoasts, who, when finally and unmercifully provoked, is shown to be the equal of any murderer. Yet he, like Berkeley's earlier protagonists, must suffer unforeseen consequences for his presumption: his arrest and trial for a murder of which he is innocent, following his successful evasion of the charge of which he is guilty, uxoricide.

Malice Aforethought famously announces at the outset that the murder of a wife will be its object: "It was not until several weeks after he had decided to murder his wife that Dr. Bickleigh took any active steps in the matter. Murder is a serious business." The story then proceeds to scrutinize the effect on this downtrodden character of such a motive and such a circumstance. Thus, character is again the chief interest. Similarly, in *Before the Fact*, it is fairly clear that the plain, drab heiress will be killed in some fashion by her impecunious, improvident, and irresponsible husband. As with *Trial and Error*, greater attention is devoted to the anticipation of the murder than to its outcome. In *Before the Fact*, the author clearly knows the extent to which the heroine's love for her beleaguering spouse will allow her to forgive and excuse his errancy. Played against this knowledge is the extent to which the husband is capable of evil. One might hazard the observation that the book becomes a prophetic

textbook on abuse—in this example, mental and psychological—to which a wife can be subjected, with little hope of recourse.

The imbalances and tensions within the married estate obviously intrigue Berkeley. Both of the major Iles novels follow the trajectory of domestic tragedies. In contrast, *The Poisoned Chocolates Case* remains speculative, remote, apart from the actual—virtually everything in it is related at second or third hand. Similarly, Mr. Todhunter is an uninformed and incurious old bachelor, also abstracted from life, until his self-propelled change. Berkeley's range is wide.

Uniting these four books, besides their intriguing switches and switchbacks, are Berkeley's grace and ironic wit. His section of the Detection Club round-robin *Ask a Policeman* (1933) delightfully spoofs Dorothy L. Sayers's Lord Peter Wimsey. "The Policeman Only Taps Once" (1936), likewise, parodies James M. Cain's *The Postman Always Rings Twice*. His novels are urbane, well-paced, well-crafted specimens of the interlude between a passing postwar age and an advancing prewar time. They depict the upper-middle and lower-upper classes attempting to deal with a slice of life's particular but unexpected savagery and ironic, unyielding justice. In each case, characters willingly open Pandora's box, whereupon they discover that they have invited doom by venturing beyond their stations. What they find is in fact a kind of looking-glass world, one similar to what they know, which is now forever elusive, but horrifyingly inverted and contradictory.

Within the civilized and graceful casing that his language and structure create—which duplicates the lives these characters have been leading up to the point at which the novels open—Berkeley's characters encounter a heart of darkness, a void at the center of their lives. It was probably there all along, but only now have they had to confront it. Berkeley exposes through ironic detective fiction the same world that T. S. Eliot was revealing in poetry in the 1920's: a world of hollow, sere, and meaningless lives, where existence is a shadow and the only reality is death. What more fitting insight might a student of murder suggest?

Laura Dabundo
Updated by Fiona Kelleghan

PRINCIPAL MYSTERY AND DETECTIVE FICTION

ROGER SHERINGHAM SERIES: *The Layton Court Mystery*, 1925; *The Wychford Poisoning Case*, 1926; *Roger Sheringham and the Vane Mystery*, 1927 (also known as *The Mystery at Lover's Cave*); *The Silk Stocking Murders*, 1928; *The Second Shot*, 1930; *Top Storey Murder*, 1931 (also known as *Top Story Murder*); *Murder in the Basement*, 1932; *Jumping Jenny*, 1933 (also known as *Dead Mrs. Stratton*); *Panic Party*, 1934 (also known as *Mr. Pidgeon's Island*); *The Roger Sheringham Stories*, 1994; *The Avenging Chance, and Other Mysteries from Roger Sheringham's Casebook*, 2004

AMBROSE CHITTERWICK SERIES: *The Piccadilly Murder*, 1929; *The Poisoned Chocolates Case*, 1929; *Trial and Error*, 1937

NONSERIES NOVELS: *The Family Witch*, 1925 (as Cox); *The Professor on Paws*, 1926 (as Cox); *The Wintringham Mystery*, 1926 (as Cox; revised as *Cicely Disappears*, 1927); *Cicely Disappears*, 1927 (as Platts); *Mr. Priestley's Problem*, 1927 (as Cox; also known as *The Amateur Crime*, 1928); *Malice Aforethought: The Story of a Commonplace Crime*, 1931 (as Iles); *The Floating Admiral*, 1931 (with others); *Before the Fact*, 1932 (as Iles); *Ask a Policeman*, 1933 (with Milward Kennedy and others); *Not to Be Taken*, 1938 (also known as *A Puzzle in Poison*); *As for the Woman*, 1939 (as Iles); *Death in the House*, 1939

OTHER MAJOR WORKS

SHORT FICTION: *Brenda Entertains*, 1925 (as A. B. Cox); *Jugged Journalism*, 1925 (as Cox)

PLAYS: *Mr. Priestley's Adventure*, pr. 1928 (adaptation of his novel; also known as *Mr. Priestley's Night Out* and *Mr. Priestley's Problem*)

NONFICTION: *O England!*, 1934 (as Cox); *The Anatomy of Murder*, 1936 (with Helen Simpson and others)

BIBLIOGRAPHY

"Anthony Berkeley Cox." In *Twelve Englishmen of Mystery*, edited by Earl Bargannier. Bowling Green, Ohio: Bowling Green University Popular Press, 1984. Discusses Berkeley as a distinctively English writer and analyzes the relationship of British culture to his work.

Haycraft, Howard. *Murder for Pleasure: The Life and Times of the Detective Story*. 1941. Reprint. New York: Carroll and Graf, 1984. Organizes the history of detective fiction into a "biography," and situates Berkeley's works in relation to others in the narrative.

_____, ed. *The Art of the Mystery Story: A Collection of Critical Essays*. Rev. ed. New York: Biblio and Tannen, 1976. Includes a critique of Berkeley's detective fiction.

Johns, Ayresome. *The Anthony Berkeley Cox Files*. London: Ferret Fantasy, 1993. Bibliography of works by and about the author.

Malmgren, Carl D. *Anatomy of Murder: Mystery, Detective, and Crime Fiction*. Bowling Green, Ohio: Bowling Green State University Popular Press, 2001. Discusses Berkeley alongside such disparate fellow authors as Fyodor Dostoevski, Edgar Allan Poe, and Dorothy L. Sayers. Details his contribution to the genre.

Roth, Marty. *Foul and Fair Play: Reading Genre in Classic Detective Fiction*. Athens: University of Georgia Press, 1995. A post-structural analysis of the conventions of mystery and detective fiction. Examines 138 short stories and works from the 1840's to the 1960's. Helps place Berkeley among his fellow writers.

Symons, Julian. *Bloody Murder: From the Detective Story to the Crime Novel—A History*. Rev. ed. New York: Viking, 1985. Critical study by Symons, a fellow mystery writer, that includes consideration of Berkeley's contributions to crime fiction.

Turnbull, Malcolm J. *Elusion Aforethought: The Life and Writing of Anthony Berkeley Cox*. Bowling Green, Ohio: Bowling Green State University Popular Press, 1996. Combined biography and critical study, situating Berkeley's works alongside relevant episodes in his life.

AMBROSE BIERCE

Born: Horse Cave Creek, Ohio; June 24, 1842
Died: Mexico(?); January, 1914(?)
Types of plot: Horror; psychological; metaphysical and metafictional parody

CONTRIBUTION

Ambrose Bierce has been labeled a misanthrope or pessimist, and his short stories dealing with murder have been misunderstood as the work of a man who, obsessed with the idea of death, showed himself incapable of compassion. A less moralistic and biographical reevaluation of the work of Bierce, however, discovers his intellectual fascination with the effect of the supernatural on the human imagination. Further, his morally outrageous murder stories, collected by the author under the title of "The Parenticide Club" in *The Collected Works of Ambrose Bierce* (1909-1912), are tall tales, which are certainly not to be taken at face value. Their black humor, combined with the cool understatement of the voice of their criminal or psychopathic narrators, serves to reflect a society gone to seed and to poke fun at the murderous state of American life in the West during the Gilded Age.

BIOGRAPHY

The tenth of seventeen children, Ambrose Gwinnett Bierce was born on June 24, 1842, on a small farm in Horse Cave Creek in southeastern Ohio. To escape life on the frontier (his family soon pushed farther west to Indiana), the boy began to devour every scrap of literature he could obtain on the homestead of his parents. After an uneventful youth, Bierce saw a chance for adventure at the outbreak of the Civil War. He enlisted with the Ninth Indiana Infantry shortly before his twentieth birthday, on April 19, 1861. Serving the Union until the end of the war, Bierce earned a reputation for courage on some of the major battlefields of the Western theater and participated in General William Tecumseh Sherman's devastating drive through the Carolinas.

After the war, Bierce settled in San Francisco, taught himself writing, and began work as an editor

with a regular gossip column in the city's *News Letter.* On Christmas Day, 1871, he married well-to-do Mollie Day. Bierce's in-laws made it possible for the young couple to leave for England, where Bierce wrote for magazines and saw the publication of his first three books, all under the pen name of Dod Grile. Mollie's return to the United States and the birth of their third child there forced Bierce to return in 1875. The next years saw the death of his parents and an abortive attempt to become the manager of a mining company in the Dakota Territory. Back in San Francisco, Bierce began writing a regular column for William Randolph Hearst's *San Francisco Examiner* in 1887. Bierce separated from Mollie in 1888, and in 1891 his son Day was killed in a duel. During this period Bierce composed some of his best-known short stories, gruesome tales of war alternating with macabre mysteries and ghost stories. These were published in the *San Francisco Examiner*'s famously lurid Sunday supplement, to which Guy de Maupassant and Sir Arthur Conan Doyle also contributed. Bierce published *Tales of Soldiers and Civilians* (1891) and *Can Such Things Be?* (1893). These two collections of short stories brought him literary acclaim and lasting recognition; it is in these volumes that his murder and horror fiction is to be found.

Bierce continued to work as a journalist of some standing for Hearst's papers, but his later fiction fell in both quality and popularity. His pithy humor column, *The Devil's Dictionary,* was collected and published in 1906 as *The Cynic's Word Book* (an unfortunate retitling that was probably at least partly responsible for the book's lackluster reception). Bierce devoted most of his last years, from 1909 to 1912, to the collation and editing of his collected works, a mammoth task that to critics smacked of unwarranted pride and that failed to sell.

Depressed and in poor health, Bierce informed his family and friends that he would travel to wartorn Mexico to report on the revolution. His last letter dates from December 26, 1913, reportedly sent from Chihuahua, though this letter does not survive except as a

Ambrose Bierce. (Library of Congress)

copy transcribed by its receiver. Of his death nothing is known. None of the many American diplomats or journalists in Mexico at that time recorded seeing Bierce, though queries about his whereabouts were made. His mysterious disappearance made him the enduring literary and popular icon that his last attempts at publication had not. Rumors of Bierce's presence at Pancho Villa's camp or his death at this or that battle gave rise to a romantic figure that Carlos Fuentes appropriated for his novel *Gringo Viejo* (1985; *The Old Gringo*, 1985). Bierce is also reimagined as an investigative journalist/amateur detective by Oakley Hall in a series that began in 1998 with *Ambrose Bierce and the Queen of Spades.*

ANALYSIS

Ambrose Bierce was not a writer of detective fiction by intent, and he did not write mysteries in the modern sense of the word. The common denominator of his short stories is that they all deal with death— death caused by war, humans, or the supernatural. The presentation of death, however, often follows the methods one would expect in detective fiction, a genre nascent in the days of Bierce. There is the attempt to discover the cause of death through rational cogitation, and perhaps the most important figure in the aftermath of the death is that of the coroner. Although a minor character, Bierce's coroner succeeds in reinstating order and reining in the chaos that has crept into the narrative through what has often been a true tour de force of the imagination. Certainty is reestablished but at a price: Somebody is irrefutably dead.

"THE HAUNTED VALLEY"

Bierce's first short story, "The Haunted Valley" (it first appeared in *Overland Monthly*, 1871, and was revised for *Can Such Things Be?*), anticipated the themes and devices of much of his later work. As in most of his stories, the setting is Bierce's contemporary American West, a land and a people he knew exceptionally well and to which he brought his own particular brand of the gothic. In exchange, he received initiation to the tall tale, a form that thrived at the campfires of the pioneers, and a subgenre that Bierce would cultivate to perfection. At the core of "The Haunted Valley" is the mystery surrounding the death of the "Chinaman" and the role of his white employer-tormentor, a roguish innkeeper. The narrator, a nameless traveler, discovers the enigma surrounding the fate of the two. Yet, typical for Bierce, this knowledge cannot serve to bring forth temporal punishment of the villain. An all-white jury has acquitted the innkeeper in a fashion typical of the corruptness of the courts of Bierce's fiction and his contemporary surroundings.

Retribution is meted out in a careful and deliberate manner, however, and the denouement of his earliest story proves exemplary of the way in which, in Bierce's work, victims entangle themselves in webs of their own making. Here, the innkeeper insists on the almost abnormal power with which looks are charged. Sensing his master's special susceptibility to the supernatural, his hired hand tricks him into believing that he sees the Asian's eye. The villain is so shocked that he dies, and a certain black sense of retribution prevails, made absolute by the fact that the trickster goes mad as a result of his action.

"A Watcher by the Dead"

The use of the supernatural is a hallmark of Bierce's fiction; unfortunately, he has been mistaken for a writer who relies on sheer horror to enhance otherwise undistinguished writing. Therefore it is important to see that often the horror of Bierce's stories, which inevitably end in one or more violent deaths, comes from within the human mind rather than from any outside source. As such, Bierce's mystery stories explore the realm and the abyss of the human imagination and its susceptibility to primal beliefs. Any rejection of this aspect of the human condition will lead to the destruction of doubters, whose pride or simple insistence on their powers of reason will be shattered after they have met one of Bierce's fiendish tempters.

"A Watcher by the Dead" (in *Tales of Soldiers and Civilians*) is a great illumination of that. Here, a doctor declares categorically:

> The superstitious awe with which the living regard the dead . . . is hereditary and incurable. One needs no more be ashamed of it than of the fact that he inherits, for example, an incapacity for mathematics, or a tendency to lie.

Thus, decades before Carl Jung and Northrop Frye, the question of humanity's collective memory is raised. Bierce's stay in Great Britain may have acquainted him with the ideas of English agnostics who tried to replace the Christian demand to do good with the discovery of a tribal memory, that part of people that may guide them to learn from the past and be morally better than the ape of Darwinian theory. Nevertheless, the doctor's provocative and condescending words are challenged by a cocksure stranger, Jarette. The two agree on an experiment in which Jarette will stay alone in a barred room for a night with what he thinks is a corpse. Soon, Jarette feels terror, and the friend who has been playing dead cannot help but "come alive," killing the other as he does so. Unfortunately, the doors remain locked, and the accomplice, now indeed alone with a corpse, goes mad; the disaster is complete with the ruin of the doctor's career.

"The Death of Halpin Frayser"

The idea of human susceptibility to the supernatural, although always with a new turn of the plot, is indeed the basis of many of Bierce's mysteries. He plotted his fiction around the exploration of all imaginable variants on this theme; intellectually, Bierce's short stories have something of the mathematical precision of Johann Sebastian Bach's fugues. Far from making his writing repetitive or formulaic, however, Bierce's central idea is always developed one step further, reexamined or turned on its head to reveal a new insight. In "The Death of Halpin Frayser" (in *Tales of Soldiers and Civilians*), the joke is partially on the reader, who is set up by a quote from an "ancient" text that warns about the evil that comes from the soulless bodies of former loved ones. Next, there is Halpin, falling in a strange forest and dreaming that his mother strangles him. His corpse is found by a detective and a deputy. In the story's final twist, it turns out that Halpin has not been killed by himself in a panicked frenzy but by the murderer of his mother while he was dreaming of his death.

"Stanley Fleming's Hallucination"

Most of Bierce's later stories incorporate the supernatural. "Stanley Fleming's Hallucination" (in *Can Such Things Be?*) is carefully constructed to mirror the previous stories. Here, the protagonist hallucinates being attacked by a large dog in his bedroom; a consulting physician reads a book on wraiths and lemurs downstairs while his patient dies. Incredibly, Bierce's story insists:

> When the man was dead an examination disclosed the unmistakable marks of an animal's fangs deeply sunken into the jugular vein.
>
> But there was no animal.

The thinner the borderline between self-induced terror of the supernatural and the "real" appearance of the unreal, the more haunting Bierce's work becomes. Stories such as "The Thing at Nolan" and "The Difficulty of Crossing a Field" (in *Can Such Things Be?*) have become classics of the uncanny; the unnatural appearances and disappearances that they recount strike one because of their seemingly mundane setting. It takes a developed craft to transform the vanishing of a farmer while crossing "a closed-cropped pasture of some ten acres, level and without a tree, rock, or any natural or artificial object on its surface" into a chilling story.

"THE PARENTICIDE CLUB"

There is another, more roguish side to Bierce, a side that has for decades disturbed righteous critics who have failed truly to read his tall tales, casting them aside as morally indigestible morsels from the table of a great cynic, major misanthrope, and minor writer. "An Imperfect Conflagration," one of the four short stories that form "The Parenticide Club" centers on the diligently plotted and violent demise of the parents of a prodigal narrator, who relates his story with grand understatement, keeping his ironic detachment to the point of sardonic indifference while relating the equally grand account of his and his parents' misdoings. The opening of "An Imperfect Conflagration" shows how effectively the voice of the narrator lures the reader into an obviously amusing but seemingly amoral story:

> Early one June morning in 1872 I murdered my father—an act which made a deep impression on me at the time. This was before my marriage.

Reading about his later marriage, one is immediately confronted with the double denial of a "correct" response to the patricide—everlasting shock on the part of the murderer is replaced by a "deep" but clearly temporary "impression," and the sense of appropriate temporal punishment by society is thwarted by the knowledge that the groom-to-be has obviously been spared the rope, firing squad, or at least lengthy incarceration.

In another fiendish turn, the narrative often prevents the reader from feeling any sympathy for the victims and instead induces clandestine siding with the perpetrator of the crime. Father and son are professional burglars, and the dishonesty of the father while dividing the spoils of their nighttime exploits causes the son to "remov[e] the old man from his vale of tears."

In "Oil of Dog," Bierce's darkest tale among the four stories, the reader is matter-of-factly introduced to a family straight out of hell: " . . . my father being a manufacturer of dog-oil and my mother having a small studio in the shadow of the village church, where she disposed of unwelcome babes." Thus, the context is set for a narrative that concludes with father and mother killing each other in a fierce fight over who is to melt down the other for sale as "canine" oil. Critics who recoil from such unadulterated and unmitigated horror have regularly failed to see the real thrust of Bierce's narratives.

In his "Negligible Tales" (in *Can Such Things Be?*), Bierce excels at poking fun at the evil realities of his world. By enlarging them to truly absurd proportions, he avoids the sour tone of the disgruntled moralist and assumes the role of the old fiend to bring home his point.

It is important to see that the parenticides in these tall tales are essentially motivated by commercial reasons: The burglar son does not want to be cheated out of his spoils by his father, whom he kills (prudently taking out a life insurance policy on him before disclosing the body). "Oil of Dog" has at its center a thriving commercial enterprise that, by selling its quack cure to an eager community, prospers from the bodies of unwanted ones until greed takes over the proprietors and they begin to melt down less easily missed people. Shut down, the business runs its logical course toward self-consumption—a powerful comment by Bierce on the true nature of the age of the robber barons, mining magnates, and real-estate czars of the American West of his times.

Bierce's dark mysteries and cynically embellished tall tales continue to provide enjoyable reading not only because they say so much about his era, when a deep interest in the supernatural accompanied progress in the hard sciences and when the ideal of the self-reliant, hardworking yeoman farmer was shown to be the fool's choice by the ever-increasing success of people devoted to the ruthless amassing of money, but also because his work can be savored on a purely artistic level. His short stories are diamonds of the genre: Their style is direct, precise, crafty, and to the point, and their plots twist and turn in ever-unpredictable directions toward the certain end—death.

R. C. Lutz
Updated by Janet Alice Long

PRINCIPAL MYSTERY AND DETECTIVE FICTION

SHORT FICTION: *Cobwebs: Being the Fables of Zambri the Parse*, 1884; *Tales of Soldiers and Civilians*, 1891 (also known as *In the Midst of Life*, 1898); *Can Such Things Be?*, 1893; *Fantastic Fables*, 1899; *My Favourite Murder*, 1916; *Ghost and Horror Stories of Ambrose Bierce*, 1964; *The Collected Fables of Ambrose Bierce*, 2000 (S. T. Joshi, editor)

OTHER MAJOR WORKS

POETRY: *Vision of Doom*, 1890; *Black Beetles in Amber*, 1892; *How Blind Is He?*, 1896; *Shapes of Clay*, 1903; *Poems of Ambrose Bierce*, 1995

NONFICTION: *Nuggets and Dust Panned in California*, 1873; *The Fiend's Delight*, 1873; *Cobwebs from an Empty Skull*, 1874; *The Dance of Death*, 1877; *The Dance of Life: An Answer to the Dance of Death*, 1877 (with Mrs. J. Milton Bowers); *The Cynic's Word Book*, 1906 (better known as *The Devil's Dictionary*); *The Shadow on the Dial, and Other Essays*, 1909; *Write It Right: A Little Blacklist of Literary Faults*, 1909; *The Letters of Ambrose Bierce*, 1922; *Twenty-one Letters of Ambrose Bierce*, 1922; *Selections from Prattle*, 1936; *Ambrose Bierce on Richard Realf by Wm. McDevitt*, 1948; *A Sole Survivor: Bits of Autobiography*, 1998 (S. T. Joshi and David E. Schultz, editors); *The Fall of the Republic, and Other Political Satires*, 2000 (Joshi and Schultz, editors)

TRANSLATION: *The Monk and the Hangman's Daughter*, 1892 (with Gustav Adolph Danziger; of Richard Voss's novel)

MISCELLANEOUS: *The Collected Works of Ambrose Bierce*, 1909-1912; *Shadows of Blue and Gray: The Civil War Writings of Ambrose Bierce*, 2002 (Brian M. Thomsen, editor)

BIBLIOGRAPHY

Berkove, Lawrence. *Presciption for Adversity: The Moral Art of Ambrose Bierce*. Columbus: Ohio State University Press, 2002. Iconoclastic study that revises the traditional view of Bierce as a cynic.

Bierce, Ambrose. *A Much Misunderstood Man: Selected Letters of Ambrose Bierce*. Edited by S. T. Joshi and David E. Schutz. Columbus: Ohio State University Press, 2003. A collection of the author's correspondence calculated to nourish a more sympathetic portrait than is usually presented of Bierce.

_____. *Phantoms of a Blood-Stained Period: The Complete Civil War Writings of Ambrose Bierce*. Edited by Russell Duncan and David J. Klooster. Amherst: University of Massachusetts, 2002. This volume collects all of Bierce's Civil War writings and places each piece in the historical context of the war. The lengthy introduction describes Bierces's battlefield experiences and discusses their effect on the psyche and literary expression of the writer.

Butterfield, Herbie. "'Our Bedfellow Death': The Short Stories of Ambrose Bierce." In *The Nineteenth Century American Short Story*, edited by A. Robert Lee. Totowa, N.J.: Barnes and Noble, 1985. A brief, general introduction to the themes and techniques of some of Bierce's most representative short stories.

Conlogue, William. "A Haunting Memory: Ambrose Bierce and the Ravine of the Dead." *Studies in Short Fiction* 28 (Winter, 1991): 21-29. Discusses Bierce's symbolic use of the topographical feature of the ravine as a major symbol of death in five stories, including "Killed at Resaca," "Coulter's Notch," and "The Coup de Grace." Shows how the ravine symbolizes the grave, the underworld, and lost love for Bierce, all derived from his Civil War memories and the death of his first love.

Davidson, Cathy N. *The Experimental Fictions of Ambrose Bierce: Structuring the Ineffable*. Lincoln: University of Nebraska Press, 1984. Discusses how Bierce intentionally blurs distinctions between such categories as knowledge, emotion, language, and behavior. Examines how Bierce blurs distinctions between external reality and imaginative reality in many of his most important short stories.

Hoppenstand, Gary. "Ambrose Bierce and the Transformation of the Gothic Tale in the Nineteenth-Century American Periodical." In *Periodical Literature in Nineteenth-Century America*, edited by Kenneth M. Price and Susan Belasco Smith. Charlottesville: University Press of Virginia, 1995. Examines Bierce's relationship to the San Francisco periodicals, focusing on the influence he had in bringing the gothic tale into the twentieth century; discusses themes and conventions in "The Damned Thing" and "Moxon's Master."

Morris, Roy, Jr. *Ambrose Bierce: Alone in Bad Company.* New York: Crown, 1996. A compelling biography that reviews Bierce's literary career alongside the writer's life. Morris argues that Bierce's

cynicism was both real and deeply rooted, a lasting depression left over from Bierce's Civil War experiences and built on by personal tragedy and disappointment. Bierce's mysterious disappearance, according to Morris, was a cleverly made ruse to cover his own suicide—an attempt to make the end of his already peculiar life an enduring work of gothic fiction.

EARL DERR BIGGERS

Born: Warren, Ohio; August 26, 1884
Died: Pasadena, California; April 5, 1933
Types of plot: Police procedural; master sleuth

PRINCIPAL SERIES

Charlie Chan, 1925-1932

PRINCIPAL SERIES CHARACTER

CHARLIE CHAN is a middle-aged Chinese detective on the police force in Honolulu, Hawaii. Short and stout, but agile, he advances from sergeant to inspector in the course of the series. He solves his cases through patience, attention to detail, and character analysis.

CONTRIBUTION

In Charlie Chan, Earl Derr Biggers created one of the most famous fictional detectives of all time. The amusing Chinese detective with the flowery, aphoristic language became widely known not only through the six novels in which he is featured but also through the many films in which he appeared. There were in fact more than thirty Charlie Chan films made from 1926 to 1952, not to mention some forty television episodes in 1957, a television feature in 1971, and a television cartoon series in 1972. In addition, in the 1930's and 1940's, there were radio plays and comic strips based on Biggers's character. A paperback novel, *Charlie Chan Returns*, by Dennis Lynds, appeared in 1974. Chan has become an American literary folk hero to rank with Tom Sawyer and Tarzan of the Apes, and

he has inspired the creation of numerous other "cross-cultural" detectives.

BIOGRAPHY

Earl Derr Biggers was born in Warren, Ohio, on August 26, 1884, to Robert J. Biggers and Emma Derr Biggers. He attended Harvard University, where he earned his bachelor's degree in 1907. He worked as a columnist and drama critic for the Boston *Traveler* from 1908 to 1912, when he was discharged for writing overly critical reviews. His first play, *If You're Only Human*, was produced in 1912 but was not well received. That same year, he married Eleanor Ladd, with whom he remained married until he died. The couple had one child, Robert Ladd Biggers, born in 1915. His first novel, *Seven Keys to Baldpate* (1913), a kind of farcical mystery-melodrama, was exceedingly popular, and in the same year a play by George M. Cohan based on the novel enjoyed even greater success; over the years, it inspired five different film versions.

In the next eleven years, Biggers was quite prolific. Aside from a number of short stories for such magazines as *The Saturday Evening Post*, he wrote two short novels, *Love Insurance* (1914) and *The Agony Column* (1916), frothy romantic mysteries, and several plays, which enjoyed only moderate success. None of his plays was published.

In 1925 Biggers came into his own with the publication of the first Charlie Chan novel, *The House*

Without a Key, first serialized, like all the other Chan novels, in *The Saturday Evening Post*. With the exception of one short novel, *Fifty Candles* (1926), after 1925 Biggers devoted himself exclusively to Chan, producing five more novels about him. Biggers died of a heart attack in Pasadena, California, on April 5, 1933. A volume of his short stories, *Earl Derr Biggers Tells Ten Stories* (1933), appeared posthumously.

ANALYSIS

When Earl Derr Biggers wrote his first Charlie Chan novel, he had already been practicing his craft for a number of years. He had developed a smooth and readable colloquial style in the four novels and numerous short stories he had already published. In the several plays he had written or collaborated on, he had developed a knack for writing dialogue. Thus, he was at the peak of his literary powers in 1925, when Chan first burst into print in the pages of *The Saturday Evening Post*. All of his preceding novels had some characteristics of the mystery in them, but they would best be described as romantic melodramas rather than crime novels.

The Chan novels, particularly the earlier ones, are invested with the spirit of high romance and appeal to the natural human desire to escape the humdrum of everyday existence. Thus Biggers chooses exotic and picturesque settings for them: a Honolulu of narrow streets and dark alleys, of small cottages clinging to the slopes of Punchbowl Hill, and a Waikiki that in the 1920's was still dominated by Diamond Head, not by high-rise hotels. He makes abundant use of moonlight on the surf, of palm trees swaying in the breeze, and of aromatic blooms scenting the subtropical evening. The streets are peopled with "quaint" Asians and the occasional native Hawaiian; the hotel lobbies house the white flotsam and jetsam of the South Seas in tired linens.

The reader is introduced to the speech of the Hawaiian residents, peppered with Hawaiian words such as *aloha*, *pau*, and *malihini*. Then, a part of this romantic picture, and at the same time contrasting with it, there is the rotund and humdrum figure of the small Chinese detective. In three of the novels Chan is on the mainland, seen against the fog swirling around a pent-

house in San Francisco, in the infinite expanse of the California desert, and on the snow-clad banks of Lake Tahoe.

There is also a strong element of nostalgia in Biggers's works. One is reminded, for example, of the good old days of the Hawaiian monarchy, when Kalakaua reigned from the throne room of Iolani Palace. Also, in San Francisco the loss of certain infamous saloons of the old Tenderloin is deplored, and in the desert the reader encounters the last vestiges of the once-prosperous mining boom in a down-at-heel cow town and an abandoned mine. Biggers delights in contrasting the wonders of nature with those of modern civilization, such as the radio and the long-distance telephone.

Parallel to the mystery plot, each novel features a love story between two of the central characters. The young man involved often feels the spirit of adventure in conflict with his prosaic way of life. This conflict is embodied in the person of John Quincy Winterslip of *The House Without a Key*, a blue-blooded Boston businessman who succumbs to the spell of the tropics and to the charms of an impoverished girl who resides in Waikiki. It is also present in Bob Eden of *The Chinese Parrot* (1926), the wastrel son of a rich jeweler who finds that there are attractions to be found in the desert and in connubial bliss that are not present in the bistros of San Francisco.

The heroines of these romances are usually proud and independent liberated women, concerned about their careers: Paula Wendell, of *The Chinese Parrot*, searches the desert for sites for motion pictures, while June Morrow, of *Behind That Curtain* (1928), is an assistant district attorney in San Francisco. They are torn between their careers and marriage and deplore the traditional feminine weaknesses. "I don't belong to a fainting generation," says Pamela Potter in *Charlie Chan Carries On* (1930), "I'm no weakling." Leslie Beaton of *Keeper of the Keys* (1932) had "cared for a spineless, artistic brother; she had learned, meanwhile, to take care of herself." Chan makes no secret of his belief that a woman's place is in the home. In fact, although he seems to admire all these liberated women, at one point he remarks, "Women were not invented for heavy thinking." Still, as the reader learns in *Char-*

lie Chan Carries On, he sends his daughter Rose to college on the mainland.

THE HOUSE WITHOUT A KEY

The first two novels are narrated mainly from the perspective of the other characters, rather than from that of Charlie Chan. That enables the author to present him as a quaint and unusual person. When he first comes on the scene in *The House Without a Key*, Biggers provides a full description: "He was very fat indeed, yet he walked with the light dainty step of a woman. His cheeks were as chubby as a baby's, his skin ivory tinted, his black hair close-cropped, his amber eyes slanting." When Minerva Winterslip, a Bostonian single woman, first sets eyes on him, she gasps because he is a detective. In popular American literature of the 1920's, Chinese were depicted in the main either as cooks and laundrymen or sinister characters lurking in opium dens. Biggers consciously chose a Chinese detective for the novelty of it, perhaps inspired by his reading about a real-life Chinese detective in Honolulu, Chang Apana (Chang Ah Ping).

There is more than a little fun poked at Chan in the early novels. His girth is frequently mentioned. He is self-deprecatory and polite to others almost to the point of obsequiousness. He speaks in a bizarre mixture of flowery and broken English, leaving out articles and confusing singulars and plurals. The very first words he speaks in the series are odd: "No knife are present in neighborhood of crime." Chan confuses prefixes, as in "unprobable," "unconvenience," "insanitary," and "undubitably," one of his favorite words, and is guilty of other linguistic transgressions. He

Swedish actor Warner Oland (right) played Earl Derr Biggers's Chinese American sleuth Charlie Chan in sixteen films during the 1930's. (Museum of Modern Art, Film Stills Archive)

spouts what are intended to be ancient Chinese maxims and aphorisms at every turn, sometimes quoting Confucius: "Death is the black camel that kneels unbid at every gate," "It is always darkest underneath the lamp," and "In time the grass becomes milk." He is often underestimated, even scorned, by the whites with whom he comes into contact—Captain Flannery of the San Francisco police in *Behind That Curtain* is particularly unkind.

In spite of the amusement with which Biggers writes of him, Chan emerges as an admirable, sympathetic figure. He is kind, loyal, persistent, and tenacious. His Asian inscrutability is misleading, as his "bright black eyes" miss nothing. In spite of his rotundity, he is light on his feet and can sometimes act with remarkable agility. He is a keen student of human behavior—he has little use for scientific methods of detection, believing that the most effective way of determining guilt is through the observation of the suspects. "Chinese are psychic people," Chan is fond of saying, and he frequently has hunches that stand him in good stead. He possesses great patience, a virtue with which he believes his race is more richly endowed than other races.

Chan was born in China, "in thatched hut by side of muddy river," and at the beginning of the series has lived in Hawaii for twenty-five years. He resides on Punchbowl Hill with his wife, whom he met on Waikiki Beach, and children. Chan has nine children at the beginning of the series (eleven by the end). In his early years in Hawaii, Chan worked as a houseboy for a rich family. In *The Chinese Parrot*, when he masquerades as a cook, he has a chance to practice his cooking, although he believes that kitchen work is now beneath his dignity. He also masters an outrageous pidgin English, although it hurts his pride when he must affect it.

In the course of the series, Chan increases in dignity. He advances from sergeant to inspector, and his exploits become widely known. His English retains its quaint vocabulary but loses much of its earlier pidgin quality, except for the occasional omission of an article. Although the earlier works are told mainly from the perspective of the other characters, in the later ones the story is often told from the perspective of Chan

himself. One reads what he sees and what passes through his mind. If this diminishes somewhat the quality of the superhuman, it makes him more human, so that instead of viewing him with a combination of awe and amusement, one can more readily identify with him.

It is instructive to compare two scenes that take place in Chan's bungalow on Punchbowl Hill. In *The House Without a Key* he greets a visitor dressed in

> a long loose robe of dark purple silk, which fitted closely at the neck and had wide sleeves. Beneath it showed wide trousers of the same material, and on his feet were shoes of silk, with thick felt soles. He was all Oriental now, suave and ingratiating but remote, and for the first time John Quincy was really conscious of the great gulf across which he and Chan shook hands.

THE BLACK CAMEL

In an amusing chapter in *The Black Camel* (1929), the reader encounters Chan at breakfast. Here one finds that Henry Chan, his eldest son, is a man of the world, or at least is making his way in the field of business, and speaks in a slangy manner that causes Chan to wince. His two older daughters are more interested in the illusions of Hollywood than in anything else. They constitute a typical American family, in spite of their Asian origins. The reader also finds that Chan's wife speaks the kind of pidgin that Chan so much decries in others and that he felt humiliated to have to affect when he was playing the part of the cook Ah Kim in *The Chinese Parrot*.

THE CHINESE PARROT AND BEHIND THAT CURTAIN

There is some continuity in the novels apart from the character of Chan himself and a certain logic to justify Chan's forays to the mainland, where Biggers probably thought he would have more scope for his talents than in the sleepy town of Honolulu in the 1920's. In *The Chinese Parrot*, he travels to San Francisco to deliver an expensive necklace for an old friend who had employed him in his youth. He also travels to the desert as part of this same commission. In *Behind That Curtain*, Chan becomes embroiled in another mystery while waiting for the ship to take him home from the one he has just solved. At this time he meets Inspector Duff of Scotland Yard, whom he later meets in Honolulu, where Duff has gone to ferret out the perpetrator of a murder that has been committed in London. When Duff is wounded, Chan goes to San Francisco to catch the culprit. While in San Francisco he is hired by someone who has read in the papers of his exploits to go to Lake Tahoe to unravel a mystery for him.

Biggers's mysteries tend to have the same romantic nature as his settings. They tend to involve relationships from the past, long-festering enmities or complicated plans for revenge or extortion. While they are never so fantastic as to be completely unbelievable, they are not realistic either. Biggers employs coincidence and such melodramatic devices as false identities, impersonations, and chance encounters.

In the spirit of the classical mystery of the 1920's, Biggers more or less plays fair with his readers, allowing them to see clues that Chan alone has the perspicacity to interpret correctly. In the classical tradition, Chan reveals the killer in the final pages of the work. Biggers is good at building suspense, often by placing the life of one of the sympathetic characters in jeopardy. The mysteries are generally such that the reader has a strong idea as to the identity of the murderer long before the denouement, even if he cannot put his finger on the pertinent clue, and much of the suspense comes from waiting for the narrator to confirm a suspicion.

In a sense, the mysteries are secondary. They serve as a kind of backdrop for the romantic setting, the love affair that unfolds as the mystery is solved, and, above all, for the personality of Chan. It must be admitted that Chan's status as a folk hero depends more on the cinema image projected by Warner Oland and Sidney Toler, and such catchphrases as "number one son" and "Correction, please," than on the character portrayed in Biggers's books. Still, the series has a lasting charm derived from the peculiar combination of mystery, romance, and gentle humor that Biggers achieved—and of the nostalgia they evoke for the Waikiki Beach and the Honolulu of the 1920's.

Henry Kratz

PRINCIPAL MYSTERY AND DETECTIVE FICTION

CHARLIE CHAN SERIES: *The House Without a Key*, 1925; *The Chinese Parrot*, 1926; *Behind That Curtain*, 1928; *The Black Camel*, 1929; *Charlie Chan Carries On*, 1930; *Keeper of the Keys*, 1932

NONSERIES NOVELS: *Seven Keys to Baldpate*, 1913; *Love Insurance*, 1914; *Inside the Lines*, 1915 (with Robert Welles Ritchie; novelization of Biggers's play); *The Agony Column*, 1916 (also known as *Second Floor Mystery*); *Fifty Candles*, 1926

OTHER SHORT FICTION: *Earl Derr Biggers Tells Ten Stories*, 1933

OTHER MAJOR WORKS

PLAYS: *If You're Only Human*, pr. 1912; *Inside the Lines*, pr. 1915; *A Cure for Incurables*, pr. 1918 (with Lawrence Whitman); *See-Saw*, pr. 1919; *Three's a Crowd*, pr. 1919 (with Christopher Morley); *The Ruling Passion*, pb. 1924

BIBLIOGRAPHY

Breen, Jon L. "Charlie Chan: The Man Behind the Curtain." *Views and Reviews* 6, no. 1 (Fall, 1974): 29-35. Discusses the fictional detective's mystique and explains his reliance on that mystique to solve crimes.

_____. "Murder Number One: Earl Derr Biggers." *The New Republic* 177 (July 30, 1977): 38-39. Review of Biggers's contributions to detective fiction.

Haycraft, Howard. *Murder for Pleasure: The Life and Times of the Detective Story.* 1941. Reprint. New York: Carroll and Graf, 1984. Organizes the history of detective fiction into a "biography," and situates Biggers's works in relation to others in the narrative.

Penzler, Otto. *Earl Derr Biggers' Charlie Chan.* New York: Mysterious Bookshop, 1999. Detailed study of Biggers's most famous creation.

_____. *The Private Lives of Private Eyes, Spies, Crime Fighters, and Other Good Guys.* New York: Grosset and Dunlap, 1977. Examines the representation of the domestic space and experience of crime-fiction protagonists, comparing their private lives to the lives of those whose privacy they routinely violate in their investigations.

Roth, Marty. *Foul and Fair Play: Reading Genre in Classic Detective Fiction.* Athens: University of Georgia Press, 1995. A post-structural analysis of the conventions of mystery and detective fiction. Examines 138 short stories and works from the 1840's to the 1960's. Helps place Biggers within the context of the genre.

Schrader, Richard J., ed. *The Hoosier House: Bobbs-Merrill and Its Predecessors, 1850-1985—A Documentary Volume.* Detroit: Gale, 2004. History of Biggers's publisher; details Biggers's career with Bobbs-Merrill, as well as the careers of such other authors as Ayn Rand, C. S. Forester, and L. Frank Baum. Bibliographic references and index.

NICHOLAS BLAKE
C. Day Lewis

Born: Ballintubbert, Ireland; April 27, 1904
Died: Hadley Wood, Hertfordshire, England; May 22, 1972
Also wrote as C. Day Lewis
Types of plot: Amateur sleuth; inverted; psychological; thriller; cozy

PRINCIPAL SERIES
Nigel Strangeways, 1935-1966

PRINCIPAL SERIES CHARACTER

NIGEL STRANGEWAYS, an amateur sleuth, is sometimes found writing scholarly treatises on esoteric topics before he is interrupted by a case. A tall, lean man with blue eyes and unkempt blond hair, he woos and marries a world-famous explorer, Georgia Cavendish. After her heroic death in World War II, he takes up with Clare Massinger, a sculptor, even though she refuses to marry him. Strangeways enjoys unraveling a mystery, although he sometimes finds himself respecting, even admiring, some of the murderers he uncovers.

CONTRIBUTION

The word often and accurately used in descriptions of Nicholas Blake's twenty mystery novels is "literate." He started writing mysteries in the period known as the Golden Age of the form in Great Britain, a period with such thoughtful and articulate practitioners as Michael Innes, Dorothy L. Sayers, Ngaio Marsh, and Margery Allingham. Blake excelled in his dual role as poet and mystery writer, producing, in the esti-mation of some critics, better mysteries than poems. His poetic talents undoubtedly influenced his novels, whether detective stories, thrillers, or crime novels. In the quantity and quality of literary allusion, in the diversity of characterization and physical description, and in the overt use of his own personal experience, Blake was of the class of writers who raised the standards of mystery fiction.

BIOGRAPHY

Nicholas Blake was born Cecil Day-Lewis in Ballintubbert, Ireland, on April 27, 1904, the only son of the Reverend F. C. Day-Lewis and Kathleen Blake Squires. After the death of his mother in 1908, his aunt helped to rear him, following his father, an Irish Protestant clergyman, as he moved from one London parish to another. Blake attended Sherborne School and Wadham College, Oxford University, where he received a master's degree.

He taught at various schools from 1927 until 1935, running into trouble with school administrators because of his leftist political views. He married Constance Mary King, the daughter of one of his former teachers, in 1928, and the couple had two sons. Desperately in need of more money, Blake, who had read many mysteries himself, wrote and published his first one, *A Question of Proof*, in 1935. He was a member of the Communist Party in Great Britain from 1935 to 1938, and though he never resigned from it, his political views changed, particularly after the Spanish Civil War. He worked for the Ministry of Information during World War II and was made a commander of the Order of the British Empire in 1950.

Blake divorced his first wife in 1951 and the same year married Jill Balcon, with whom he had a son and a daughter. His professional reputation remained high: He held the position of professor of poetry at Oxford University (1951-1956) and director of the publishing firm Chatto and Windus (1954-1972). He was the Charles Eliot Norton professor of poetry at Harvard University (1964-1965), and finally, poet laureate of England, from 1968 until his death in 1972.

ANALYSIS

Summarizing his views on why authors write mystery fiction, Nicholas Blake said frankly—in the essay "The Detective Story: Why?"—that money was certainly a major motive for most. His first mystery novel, *A Question of Proof*, Earl F. Bargainnier reports, was written because Blake could think of no other honest way to come up with one hundred pounds to pay for a leaking roof.

Like the many academics of his day and those who have followed him, however, Blake's own pleasure as a reader of mysteries contributed to his pleasure in writing them. In the same essay, he also noted that every drug addict wants to introduce other people to the habit, a habit that allows a tamed, civilized, "a-moral" society to revel in the pleasures of imaginary murder. It is a pleasure possibly of great significance to anthropologists of the future, Blake predicted; in the twenty-first century, the detective novel would be studied as the folk myth of the twentieth century, the rise of crime fiction coinciding with the decline of religion. Without the outlet for the sense of guilt provided by religion, Blake proposed, individuals turn to the detective novel, with its highly formalized ritual, as a means of purging their guilt. That is why the criminal, the high priest of the ritual, and the detective, the higher power who destroys the criminal, appeal equally to readers; they represent the light and dark sides of human nature. Blake draws the parallel between the denouement of a detective novel and the Christian concept of the Day of Judgment, when the problem is triumphantly resolved and the innocent suspects are separated from the guilty.

NIGEL STRANGEWAYS

The solemnity of such views underlying the addictive attraction of mystery fiction is counterbalanced in Blake's novels by what Julian Symons called their "bubbling high spirits" and the author's evident pleasure in "playing with detection." That quality of glee comes through in the range of the twenty novels Blake wrote, which sometimes delightfully echo other great amateur detectives and novels, reassuring readers that they are in the company of a fellow addict. There is, for example, a hint of Sayers's Lord Peter Wimsey in Blake's Nigel Strangeways. A tall, lean man with sandy-colored hair that habitually falls over his forehead, guileless pale-blue eyes, and an abstracted look, Strangeways, like Wimsey, has that deceptive innocence and gently comic air that often lead suspects to confide in him. Similarly, though Strangeways is paid for his work, his preoccupation between cases appears to be that of the gifted dilettante. Strangeways meets his first wife on a case; a world-famous explorer, Georgia Cavendish, is, like Sayers's Harriet Vane, an independent woman with a well-established career before marriage to the great amateur detective.

Other striking variations on the standard mystery include the first-person criminal in *The Beast Must Die* (1938), recalling Agatha Christie's *The Murder of Roger Ackroyd* (1926), and the academic murder mystery construct of *The Morning After Death* (1966). Blake's *A Penknife in My Heart* (1958) seems, on the surface, so similar to Patricia Highsmith's *Strangers on a Train* (1950) that Blake inserted a note to say that it was only after his book had gone to press that he discovered the amazing coincidence, as he had not read her book or seen the film.

Such similarities merely highlight the elements shared by the body of mystery fiction produced during what is referred to as the Golden Age of the genre in the 1920's, 1930's, and 1940's in Great Britain. As readers became more sophisticated and demanding, and as more writers entered the field, the quality of writing was raised. Blake was one of a handful of dons who took up the challenge of satisfying the exacting standards of this popular form, which required adherence to a formula as well as something fresh and challenging.

Blake's analysis of this demand was that it required the juxtaposition of fantasy with reality that defines detective fiction and that there were two ways to achieve this juxtaposition: to put unreal characters into realistic situations or to put real characters into unreal or at least improbable situations. The second was the more prevalent, certainly in Blake's fiction. It became a standard feature, according to LeRoy Lad Panek, for the great detective to be depicted as a sophisticated and cultured human being who might occasionally flounder and make a mistake.

To accommodate as well the period's passion for puzzles, Panek reports, the Golden Age novel often contains maps, time tables, cautionary and informative footnotes, and other devices designed to engage the reader's intellect in the story; these details make the great detective more realistic, ostensibly a person whose thinking process the reader can follow. Blake's Strangeways often makes lists of motives and suspects or of questions about a case, thus neatly playing fair with readers by providing them with a full range of possibilities while simultaneously confusing them so thoroughly that the narrative interest is maintained because they still need Strangeways to pick among the plausible alternatives.

Though Blake's Strangeways follows the tradition of the great detective—the intelligent, perceptive, and immensely likable amateur sleuth—the author's complex other life brought a distinctive note to this Golden Age tradition. Not only an active and highly respected poet, Blake was also a leftist; he considered himself a revolutionary. Bargainnier suggests that in the battle between the poetic and political impulses within Blake, the poet won. Indeed, though he never formally gave up his membership in the Communist Party, Blake ceased to be involved actively. Yet the conflict between the contemplative and active life appears, as Bargainnier points out, in the recurring theme of schizophrenia in the mystery novels; in more than one novel, a character will wonder if he unknowingly committed a crime because there is another, hidden side to his nature.

Blake's leftist leanings also appear in his attitude toward the detective novel. In the essay referred to above, Blake writes that there is a class bias in crime fiction; the detective novel, with the hero almost al-

ways on the side of law and order, appeals almost exclusively to the upper and professional classes, who have a stake in maintaining a stable society. The lower-middle and working classes read thrillers, where the criminal of the thriller is often its hero and nearly always a romantic figure, a descendant of the Robin Hood myth.

One way in which Blake bridged this gap he perceived between the classes in their choice of reading matter was probably also a result of his mind-set as a poet, a mind-set that more than any other genre calls for John Keats's "negative capability," that ability to subdue one's own personality and give onself up to another's. Consequently, Blake's novels evince an unusual sympathy, even admiration, for the criminal. Enumerating the fates of the murderers in Blake's novels, Bargainnier notes that more than half of the criminals commit suicide or are killed by others—that is, removed from the scene before they can face the established judicial system.

Following the conventions of the detective novel, the plot in a Blake novel unfolds over a relatively short period of time and the cast of characters is confined. What characterizes Blake, however, is his long view of the genesis of a crime. In novel after novel, Strangeways will learn information about characters, buried for twenty or thirty years, that serves as clues to the present situation. Thus, in *Thou Shell of Death* (1936), Strangeways finds the key to the death of a national air hero by investigating a mysterious incident in his past when he was an obscure handyman in Ireland; in *End of Chapter* (1957), he tracks down the cause of an intensely intimate rivalry between his co-workers to their roles in a tragic case of doomed romance; in *The Corpse in the Snowman* (1941), he picks up hints of the tragedy that changed a high-spirited young girl into a reckless drug addict.

The emphasis on the past is apparent in another feature of Blake's works. Bargainnier points out that an unusually large number of children and teenagers appear in the novels. Sometimes the youths are directly involved in the crime, such as the little boy whose death in a hit-and-run incident in *The Beast Must Die* precipitates the story or the children whose lives become the battleground for control in *The*

Corpse in the Snowman; the fate of a beloved child long dead motivates the run of malice and murder in *End of Chapter*. In *The Widow's Cruise* (1959), *The Morning After Death*, and *Head of a Traveler* (1949), the conditioning of childhood experiences and tendencies becomes, similarly, important to analyzing the behavior of the adults in the present.

Golden Age fiction was characterized by its highly literate quality. Panek notes that the detective novelists, appealing to their well-educated readers, had characters who cited "[Charles] Dickens by the cartload and [William] Shakespeare by the ton." A certain amount of banter about writers and writing and a self-referential quality was common. Here again, the well-read poet C. Day Lewis permeates the writing of Blake the mystery novelist. Julian Symons remarks that Blake

> brought to the Golden Age detective story a distinctly literary tone, and also in his early books a Left Wing political attitude. Both of these things were unusual at the time. I can remember still the shock I felt when on the first page of Blake's first book, *A Question of Proof*, T. S. Eliot's name was mentioned. (I should be prepared to offer odds that there are less than a dozen crime stories written during the decades between the wars in which the name of any modern poet appears.)

It is not only that literary allusions abound in Blake's writing but also, more important, that an intimate knowledge of literature assumes a major role in the solution of some of the mysteries. Toward the end of *Thou Shell of Death*, for example, Strangeways berates himself for not immediately recognizing the significance of the victim's quoting a line from a Jacobean play. The poet's propensity for metaphor, to yoke unlike things together, leads Strangeways, in *The Widow's Cruise*, to link the nervous behavior of swans, which he had observed months before, to the strange behavior of two sisters he encounters on a cruise.

HEAD OF A TRAVELER

Though *The Private Wound* (1968), his last novel, is the most autobiographical of Blake's works, it is in *Head of a Traveler* (the title itself is a line from A. E. Housman's parody of a Greek tragedy) that the influence of the poet on the novelist becomes central. The novel begins with Strangeways's journal, as he jots

down his impressions of a visit to the estate of a distinguished English poet, Robert Seaton. Strangeways notices the "cataleptic trance of white and yellow roses" and is himself entranced by the house:

> It was like getting out into a dream. Walking past the front of the house, glancing in at the drawing-room windows, one might have expected to see a group of brocaded figures arrested in courtiers' attitudes around a Sleeping Beauty, the stems of roses twining through their ceremonious fingers.

In this novel, as in so many of Blake's novels, Strangeways's early perceptions are prescient. The dreamlike, fairy-tale atmosphere of a Sleeping Beauty he picks up from the house does indeed prove to account for much inexplicable behavior on the part of both the poet, who has been pretending to be busy with a long poem, and of his wife, whose two main loves in life are the house, which once belonged to her family, and her husband's work, which she and the rest of the family protect with an awe that makes it impossible for Seaton to write. For Strangeways, the house is animated:

> The fairy-tale house, so unreal when first he had seen it, was still less real to-day; then it had been the fabulous exuberance of its roses, the trance of high summer; now it was as if *Plash Meadow*, having drunk too deep of horrors, suffered from a blighting hangover.

He realizes that the poet's work is at the "very roots of the case." A crucially suggestive clue for him is the sense that only since the murder of his brother has Seaton finally written a great poetic sequence. By not only piecing together his observations but also, more important, trusting his instinctive understanding of a poet's life and personality, Strangeways does, finally, deconstruct the false suicide note to clear the poet of murder and find the truth. The image of catalepsy from the first page is repeated:

> Robert jumped at the opportunity to leave Plash Meadow, to break the cataleptic trance it had thrown upon his Muse, to return to the conditions under which—however grim they had been—he had in the past produced poetry. To kill Oswald would be to destroy his last chance of freeing the creator in himself.

This novel, which ends with Strangeways unable to decide whether he should report the true murderer, displays all the distinctive qualities of Blake's detective fiction: It is sophisticated, lyrical, psychologically acute, and, withal, high-spirited. His novels were the result of the needs of the poet fulfilled by the talents of the mystery writer.

Shakuntala Jayaswal

PRINCIPAL MYSTERY AND DETECTIVE FICTION

NIGEL STRANGEWAYS SERIES: *A Question of Proof*, 1935; *Thou Shell of Death*, 1936 (also known as *Shell of Death*); *There's Trouble Brewing*, 1937; *The Beast Must Die*, 1938; *The Smiler with the Knife*, 1939; *Malice in Wonderland*, 1940 (also known as *The Summer Camp Mystery* and *Malice with Murder*); *The Corpse in the Snowman*, 1941 (also known as *The Case of the Abominable Snowman*); *Minute for Murder*, 1947; *Head of a Traveler*, 1949; *The Dreadful Hollow*, 1953; *The Whisper in the Gloom*, 1954 (also known as *Catch and Kill*); *End of Chapter*, 1957; *The Widow's Cruise*, 1959; *The Worm of Death*, 1961; *The Sad Variety*, 1964; *The Morning After Death*, 1966

NONSERIES NOVELS: *A Tangled Web*, 1956 (also known as *Death and Daisy Bland*); *A Penknife in My Heart*, 1958; *The Deadly Joker*, 1963; *The Private Wound*, 1968

OTHER MAJOR WORKS

NOVELS: *The Friendly Tree*, 1936; *Starting Point*, 1937; *Child of Misfortune*, 1939

PLAY: *Noah and the Waters*, pb. 1936

POETRY: 1925-1940 • *Beechen Vigil, and Other Poems*, 1925; *Country Comets*, 1928; *Transitional Poem*, 1929; *From Feathers to Iron*, 1931; *The Magnetic Mountain*, 1933; *A Time to Dance, and Other Poems*, 1935; *Collected Poems, 1929-1933*, 1935; *Overtures to Death, and Other Poems*, 1938; *Poems in Wartime*, 1940; *Selected Poems*, 1940

1941-1960 • *Word over All*, 1943; *Short Is the Time: Poems, 1936-1943*, 1945; *Collected Poems, 1929-1936*, 1948; *Poems, 1943-1947*, 1948; *Selected Poems*, 1951 (revised 1957, 1969, 1974); *An Italian Visit*, 1953; *Collected Poems*, 1954; *Pegasus, and*

Other Poems, 1957; *The Newborn: D.M.B., 29th April 1957*, 1957

1961-1992 • *The Gate, and Other Poems*, 1962; *Requiem for the Living*, 1964; *A Marriage Song for Albert and Barbara*, 1965; *The Room, and Other Poems*, 1965; *Selected Poems*, 1967; *The Abbey That Refused to Die: A Poem*, 1967; *The Whispering Roots*, 1970; *The Poems, 1925-1972*, 1977 (Ian Parsons, editor); *The Complete Poems of C. Day Lewis*, 1992

CHILDREN'S LITERATURE: *The Otterbury Incident*, 1948

NONFICTION: *A Hope for Poetry*, 1934; *Revolution in Writing*, 1935; *The Colloquial Element in English Poetry*, 1947; *The Poetic Image*, 1947; *The Poet's Task*, 1951; *The Poet's Way of Knowledge*, 1957; *The Buried Day*, 1960; *The Lyric Impulse*, 1965; *A Need for Poetry?*, 1968

EDITED TEXT: *The Collected Poems of Wilfred Owen*, 1963

TRANSLATIONS: *The Georgics of Virgil*, 1940; *The Graveyard by the Sea*, 1946 (Paul Valéry); *The Aeneid of Virgil*, 1952; *The Eclogues of Virgil*, 1963

BIBLIOGRAPHY

Bayley, John. *The Power of Delight: A Lifetime in Literature—Essays, 1962-2002*. New York: W. W. Norton, 2005. The collected essays of this major critic feature one on Blake (C. Day Lewis) and his use of pastiche, both in poetry and in fiction. Index.

Day-Lewis, Sean. *Day-Lewis: An English Literary Life*. London: Weidenfeld & Nicolson, 1980. The first son of Blake wrote this year-by-year biography of his father within a decade of his father's death. Family members and friends contributed material to an objective but intimate portrait of the poet. Both the poetry publications and the crime novels under the name Nicholas Blake are discussed.

Gindin, James. "C. Day Lewis: Moral Doubling in Nicholas Blake's Detective Fiction of the 1930's." In *Recharting the Thirties*, edited by Patrick J. Quinn. Cranbury, N.J.: Associated University Presses, 1996. Discusses the moral elements of Blake's fiction that place it distinctively within the Great Britain of the 1930's. Bibliographic references and index.

Malmgren, Carl D. *Anatomy of Murder: Mystery, Detective, and Crime Fiction*. Bowling Green, Ohio: Bowling Green State University Popular Press, 2001. Discusses Blake's *Head of a Traveler* and *A Penknife in My Heart*. Bibliographic references and index.

"Nicholas Blake." In *Modern Mystery Writers*, edited by Harold Bloom. New York: Chelsea House, 1995. Critical, scholarly examination of Blake's work and its place in the mystery-fiction canon. Bibliographic references.

Roth, Marty. *Foul and Fair Play: Reading Genre in Classic Detective Fiction*. Athens: University of Georgia Press, 1995. A post-structural analysis of the conventions of mystery and detective fiction. Examines 138 short stories and works from the 1840's to the 1960's. Helps place Blake within the context of the genre.

Smith, Elton Edward. *The Angry Young Men of the Thirties*. Carbondale: Southern Illinois University Press, 1975. In his first chapter, "C. Day-Lewis: The Iron Lyricist," Smith outlines the dilemma of British poets in the 1930's, a decade of worldwide economic collapse. This study of poetry is thus useful for contextualizing the poet's detective fiction as well.

ELEANOR TAYLOR BLAND

Born: Boston, Massachusetts; December 31, 1944
Type of plot: Police procedural

PRINCIPAL SERIES

Detective Marti MacAlister, 1992-

PRINCIPAL SERIES CHARACTERS

MARTI MACALISTER is an African American homicide detective in her forties with ten years' experience with the Chicago Police Department. After the mysterious suicide of her husband, an undercover narcotics detective, she joins the police force in Lincoln Prairie, a suburb sixty miles north, as a way to help her and her two children handle their grief. Meticulous, organized, patient, Detective MacAlister is a model of tenacity, investigative perseverance, and compassionate police work.

MATTHEW "VIK" JESSENOVIK, MacAlister's partner and the son of a police officer, is a gruff veteran of the Lincoln Prairie detective force. Despite his deep-seated reservations about women detectives, which derive from his Old World Catholic assumptions as a second-generation Pole, he ultimately complements his partner and ably assists in the demands of investigatory police work.

CONTRIBUTION

Eleanor Taylor Bland's highly successful Marti MacAlister series reflects the standard elements of the police procedural: the faith in tireless investigation and the momentum toward resolution via insight, rather than intuition, and the reaching of an inevitable conclusion based on common sense and legwork. However, Bland's character, Marti MacAlister, broke new ground as an African American woman. Because the series has a modern time frame, MacAlister faces only subtle discrimination and the occasional off-putting remark, and her commitment to police work ensures her the respect of her colleagues. Given the two partners' diverse backgrounds, the series affirms the viability of multiculturalism in the workplace. A strong feminist role model, MacAlister has come to terms with the death of a husband, the responsibilities of two children, and ultimately the complex emotional experience of a remarriage and stepchildren.

What further distinguishes the MacAlister series is its commitment to pressing social issues and its unflagging sympathy for those who are voiceless victims of social and economic distress—abused women and children, the homeless, the mentally ill, alcoholics, drug addicts, the unemployed, and the elderly.

BIOGRAPHY

Eleanor Taylor Bland was nearly fifty before she published her first novel. Born Eleanor Taylor in Boston on New Year's Eve, 1944, into lower-middle-class circumstances, Bland learned from her cab-driver father and her stay-at-home mother the virtue of stoic patience, the importance of love, a lifelong respect for family, and the importance of a Christian-centered morality. Bland married a sailor when she was only fourteen. When his tour of duty ended, they were stationed in Illinois along Lake Michigan, and they decided to stay. During the mid-1970's, Bland was diagnosed with cancer. Doctors initially gave her little chance of survival, and she endured a rigorous regimen to combat the disease, an experience that encouraged her to return to school. Although she loved reading and considered English, Bland completed a bachelor's degree in accounting at Southern Illinois University in 1981 and, after relocating to Waukegan, enjoyed a successful career (1981-1999) as a cost accountant for Abbott Laboratories, the pharmaceutical and health care giant.

In the early 1990's, Bland, divorced and helping to raise an infant grandson while working full-time, began to read mysteries in her spare time. She was intrigued by police procedurals, finding in their meticulous investigative protocols a parallel to the accounting field. It occurred to her to try writing a procedural centered on the kind of character she knew best: a single African American working mom living in the suburbs north of Chicago, who loves her family and sympathizes with the underdog. Because her background was not in police work, she thoroughly researched the manuscript, learning the methodologies of detective work to give her manuscript a gritty verisimilitude.

Dead Time, Bland's first Marti MacAlister mystery, was published in 1992 and found a wide and generous response among both genre fans and critics. Bland captured both the unglamorous detail work of police investigation—the low-octane thrill of assembling evidence, weighing testimony, and ultimately piecing together a reliable reading of a crime—while stage managing suspense with satisfying twists. In the following years, Bland published MacAlister titles with admirable regularity, despite a recurrence of health problems in 1999.

Although Bland completed a handful of short stories and edited a groundbreaking anthology of mystery stories written by African Americans, her commitment remained to the series and to the evolution of the Marti MacAlister character both professionally and personally. MacAlister continued her stellar success as a homicide detective, turning down offers for advancement to lieutenant to stay on the street, and her children matured into responsible young adults. MacAlister herself came to terms first with her husband's death and then with the challenge of remarriage with a paramedic named Ben Walker. In the later titles in the series, Bland began to explore age and illness (both Jessenovik's wife and Ben have faced medical crises). Bland relished her rapport with her readers and became noted for frequenting conventions, book signings, and online discussion groups.

ANALYSIS

Eleanor Taylor Bland's Marti MacAlister lacks the eccentric idiosyncrasies that often distinguish procedural protagonists. She never swears or makes wisecracks, and she respects authority (except a particularly ambitious female lieutenant who has emerged in the later titles in the series as something of a nemesis). She attends to paperwork diligently and seldom resorts to violent engagement, strong-armed interrogations, High Noon dramatics, shootouts, or police work that bends the rules to effect a high-stakes arrest. She never drinks (save her addiction to coffee), and she lacks cinematic sexiness (she is, by her own admission, overweight, an imposing five feet, ten inches, and one hundred sixty pounds). Her off-duty life is far from exciting; she is happiest on those rare evenings when she can enjoy a Whoopi Goldberg video marathon with her children and then make love with her husband. The MacAlister series lacks the full-throttle feel of other modern procedurals: Its protagonist simply builds a case, does the job, and when there is a preponderance of evidence, brings in the perpetrator, police work that seldom dazzles but always succeeds.

The series centers on the psychology of investigation: the piecing together of forensic evidence and witness testimonies, the grueling eighteen-hour days, and the ultimate moment of insight (often presaged by one of MacAlister's high-stress headaches and her inevitable turn to acetaminophen). As procedurals, each volume focuses on a single investigation, although other cases, frequently cold cases, become entangled. Given Bland's omniscient narration and the shifts from MacAlister to the victims and at times to the killers, readers often know the killer's identity and can therefore follow the twists of police investigations.

While maintaining the genre's intricate methodologies, the MacAlister series has created a central character who generates reader sympathy, unusual in the genre (conventionally, readers either admire the central character's acumen or envy his or her cool). Bland counterpoints the mayhem of MacAlister's investigations with the ordinary life she maintains as a working mother. She shows MacAlister encouraging her kids to stay committed to school, while she adjusts to being a young widow and enters into a romance with Ben Walker. Bland anatomizes with candor and delicacy the dynamics of grief (Ben's wife had been killed by a drunk driver) even as it gives way to new love. MacAlister enjoys a close relationship with her mother and her daughter, each generation offering moral insight to the next. Although her relationship with her son is more problematic (she is painfully aware of his need for a male role model), she maintains a generous communication with him. In addition, MacAlister maintains friendships with a variety of recurring characters, which underscores her sympathetic heart and the value she invests in friendship.

Although as procedurals, the novels in the series regularly center on murders among the privileged or those motivated by greed, career ambitions, and a desire to better their social position, each volume constructs a case that also involves Bland's sympathy for the victims. Her victims exist on the margins of urban society and are the collateral damage of overworked government agencies: street people, dropouts, prostitutes, AIDS patients, battered wives, the mentally handicapped, addicts, and most of all, children. (Bland herself became a recognized community activist in the Waukegan area.) That MacAlister frequently relies on the help and testimony of those who are often ignored by other investigators gives those typically rendered voiceless a compelling narrative presence and gives

the series its compassionate awareness that the forgotten deserve attention, respect, and assistance. Without abandoning the intricate twists of the procedural to indulge in obvious polemics, Bland fashions such misfits into vivid characters who come across with verisimilitude and poignancy.

DEAD TIME

The initial murder victim in the first Marti MacAlister procedural, *Dead Time*, is one of society's throwaways, a Jane Doe schizophrenic choked to death in a flophouse. MacAlister, new to the Lincoln Prairie force, listens to the junkies and winos, whose testimony the first-response officers simply ignore. Still haunted by the shooting death of her husband a year and half earlier, MacAlister quickly becomes enmeshed in a gruesome series of stranglings, the explanation of which leads her and her partner back fifteen

"ONE OF TODAY'S MOST TALENTED MYSTERY WRITERS." —*Booklist*

DEAD TIME

THE FIRST MARTI MACALISTER MYSTERY

ELEANOR TAYLOR BLAND
Acclaimed author of *Whispers in the Dark*

years to the death of a singer apparently accidentally electrocuted on a naval base while preparing to entertain troops headed to Vietnam.

With meticulous care, MacAlister and Jessenovik unearth a jewelry smuggling and fencing operation under the direction of a ruthless special operations officer, who used the chaotic final years of the Vietnam War as a cover for his wrongdoing. Although Bland deftly handles the intricate details of the investigation, what distinguishes this novel is the group of five homeless kids whom MacAlister befriends. The children are squatting illegally in the flophouse the night of the murder and their testimony is crucial, which puts them in danger from the special operations officer. MacAlister goes beyond merely keeping them safe so that they can help piece together the case, making them her special project, which gives the narrative a compassionate feel, appropriate to a mystery set at Christmas time.

DONE WRONG

In *Done Wrong* (1995), the fourth installment in the series, Marti MacAlister emerges into her strength not merely by dint of her unraveling a most intricate case involving police cover-ups and drug trafficking but also because she is compelled to confront her dark suspicions surrounding the apparent suicide of her husband, Johnny, found shot through the head by his own gun during a drug bust in a Chicago cemetery three years earlier. When an undercover narcotics officer, Johnny's former partner, apparently commits suicide by jumping from the second floor of a Chicago parking garage, MacAlister cannot accept the medical examiner's ruling. On her own time, she returns to Chicago with Jessenovik and begins the difficult work of focusing her acumen on her husband's undercover world.

MacAlister upends an entrenched departmental administration intent on burying the circumstances of Johnny's death: Johnny knew that a careless police officer had killed a child in a earlier drug bust in which a considerable sum of money had disappeared, and MacAlister begins to glimpse the depth of cooperation between corrupt city detectives and the street kings of the drug empire. However, she comes ultimately to the peace that she has sought—the knowledge that her husband had not committed suicide but rather had

most likely died as part of a departmental vendetta. *Done Wrong* is compelling for its shadowy uncertainties, typical of procedurals that involve undercover work with its inevitable moral ambiguities as police officers become part of the criminal world. What sustains this novel, however, is MacAlister's emotional growth as she makes her peace with the past: She revisits the neighborhood where she grew up, now a drug war zone, and reestablishes ties with Johnny's friends. She also confronts her present (she and her daughter have a frank discussion about birth control) and plans at last for a future that can include Ben Walker.

WINDY CITY DYING

The tenth novel in the series, *Windy City Dying* (2002), is distinguished by Bland's decision to hand over part of the narrative center to the psychology of a deranged serial killer—a university-educated African American who has been released after serving fifteen years for killing a coworker at a prestigious financial firm when evidence of his bookkeeping irregularities surfaced. The released felon begins to exact vengeance on those he sees as responsible for his ruin, not by killing them but rather killing their loved ones to make them suffer more keenly. Because MacAlister's first husband was the arresting officer, MacAlister herself is on the killer's list but has been saved for last as her death would provide the most obvious link to the killer's case. Given the numerous (and brutal) killings and the shifting point of view and the shattering of linear narration, the novel reveals a new confidence in Bland as writer. Bland manipulates suspense by counterpointing MacAlister's gradual realization of the ties between the multiplying murders with her own peril as the killer stalks her and Ben, whom MacAlister has just married.

Investigating the emerging pattern brings MacAlister once again to confront the ghost of her first husband; his coded notebooks help her break the case. What further distinguishes this novel is the eventual showdown in a hospital stairwell when MacAlister confronts the killer, dressed as a woman. She draws her weapon and kills the psychopath, a singular moment in the MacAlister series. The novel is of interest to series aficionados because, as part of the investigation, MacAlister revisits the five street children who appeared in the first volume (one of the children is initially accused in the first killing). She is saddened to find that since that Christmas five years earlier, the foster care system and street life have driven the children toward alcohol and violence and have robbed them of their self-esteem and any sense of a future. In contrast, MacAlister's own daughter faces a difficult decision of whether to devote herself after high school to the longshot possibility of Olympic success in volleyball. The young woman forsakes the opportunity for athletic stardom to make her commitment to her family, part of the series' larger theme of the powerful counterforce of love in a dangerous and chaotic world.

Joseph Dewey

PRINCIPAL MYSTERY AND DETECTIVE FICTION

MARTI MACALISTER SERIES: *Dead Time*, 1992; *Slow Burn*, 1993; *Gone Quiet*, 1994; *Done Wrong*, 1995; *Keep Still*, 1996; *See No Evil*, 1998; *Tell No Tales*, 1999; *Scream in Silence*, 2000; *Whispers in the Dark*, 2001; *Windy City Dying*, 2002; *Fatal Remains*, 2003; *A Dark and Deadly Deception*, 2005; *Suddenly a Stranger*, 2007; *A Cold and Silent Dying*, 2004, *A Dark and Deadly Deception*, 2005

OTHER MAJOR WORKS

EDITED TEXT: *Shades of Black: Crime and Mystery Stories by African-American Authors*, 2004

BIBLIOGRAPHY

Fabre, Michel, and Robert E. Skinner. *Conversations with Chester Himes*. Jackson: University of Mississippi Press, 1995. Invigorating conversations with the African American procedurals writer whose influence Bland acknowledges. Provides cultural context for understanding the African American approach to procedurals, specifically how black detectives helped counter stereotypes.

Klein, Kathleen Gregory, ed. *Diversity and Detective Fiction*. Bowling Green, Ohio: Bowling Green State University Popular Press, 1999. Although geared for narrative theorists and targeted to teachers interested in using procedurals, the collection provides a context to appreciate Marti MacAlister as a landmark contribution to a genre that, because of its urban roots, readily lent itself to diversity.

_____. *The Woman Detective: Gender and Genre*. Champaign: University of Illinois Press, 1995. Surveys more than sixty female detectives and private eyes with specific interest in a feminist reading that sees these groundbreaking fictional characters as social and cultural templates.

Panek, LeRoy Lad. *The American Police Novel*. Jefferson, N.C.: McFarland, 2003. A sweeping survey that traces the genre in post-World War II America and catalogs the genre's plot devices, character types, symbols, and themes. Challenges the perception of the genre as male dominated by tracing its inclusion of gender, race, sexual orientation, and age diversity.

Vicarel, Jo Ann. *A Reader's Guide to the Police Procedural*. Boston: G. K. Hall, 1999. Indispensable reference, a thorough explication of the genre that includes themes and narrative elements as well as major writers and their works. Helpful in distinguishing the genre from the more familiar (and flashier) private investigator genre.

ROBERT BLOCH

Born: Chicago, Illinois; April 5, 1917
Died: Los Angeles, California; September 23, 1994
Also wrote as Tarleton Fiske; Will Folke; Nathan
    Hindin; E. K. Jarvis; Wilson Kane; John
    Sheldon; Collier Young
Type of plot: Psychological

CONTRIBUTION

Robert Bloch wrote many crime novels as well as science-fiction novels, screenplays, radio and television plays, and hundreds of short stories. Working in the tradition of H. P. Lovecraft, Bloch portrayed characters who are plagued by their psychological imbalances. In addition, he gave new life to the surprise ending. Often readers are shocked or even appalled at the ending with which they are confronted. Unlike many writers in the genre, Bloch did not always let those who are right succeed or even live. In fact, many times those who are good are the ones who die.

The characters Bloch employed are quite ordinary. They are hotel owners, nuns, psychiatrists, and secretaries. The use of seemingly normal people as inhabitants of a less than normal world is part of what made Bloch one of the masters of the psychological novel. His novels do not have vampires jumping out of coffins; instead, they have hotel owners coming out of offices and asking if there is anything you need.

BIOGRAPHY

Robert Albert Bloch was born on April 5, 1917, in Chicago. He attended public schools in Milwaukee, Wisconsin. During his early years in school, Bloch was pushed ahead from the second grade to the fifth grade. By the time he was in sixth grade, the other children were at least two years older than he. Although Bloch was more interested in history, literature, and art than were most children his age, he was not an outsider and was, in fact, the leader in many of the games in the neighborhood.

At the age of nine, Bloch attended a first-release screening of the 1925 silent classic *Phantom of the Opera*, starring Lon Chaney. He was at once converted to

the genres of horror and suspense. In the 1930's, he began reading the horror stories of H. P. Lovecraft. When he was fifteen, he wrote to Lovecraft asking for a list of the latter's published works. After an exchange of letters, Lovecraft encouraged Bloch to try writing fiction. By the time he was seventeen, Bloch had sold his first story to *Weird Tales* magazine. As a tribute to his mentor, Bloch wished to include Lovecraft in a short story titled "The Shambler from the Stars." Lovecraft authorized Bloch to "portray, murder, annihilate, disintegrate, transfigure, metamorphose or otherwise manhandle the undersigned." Lovecraft later reciprocated by featuring a writer named Robert Blake in his short story "The Haunter of the Dark."

Bloch worked as a copywriter for the Gustav Marx advertising agency in Milwaukee, Wisconsin, from 1942 to 1953. Copywriting did not get in the way of creative writing, however. Besides a short stint as a stand-up comic—Bloch was often in much demand as a toastmaster at conventions because of his wit—he wrote scripts for thirty-nine episodes of the 1944 radio horror show *Stay Tuned for Terror*, based on his own stories. After leaving advertising, he turned to freelance writing full-time. Bloch was married twice, first to Marion Holcombe, with whom he had a daughter, Sally Francy. In 1964 he married Eleanor Alexander.

In 1959 Bloch received the Hugo Award at the World Science Fiction Convention for his short story "The Hellbound Train." The following year he received the Screen Guild Award and the Ann Radcliffe Award for literature. He served as the president of Mystery Writers of America (1970-1971). *The Skull* received the Trieste Film Festival Award in 1965. He received the Los Angeles Science Fiction Society Award in 1974 and the Comicon Inkpot Award in 1975. The World Fantasy Convention presented him with its Life Achievement Award in 1975. He also received the Cannes Fantasy Film Festival First Prize for *Asylum*.

Bloch earned several Bram Stoker Awards, granted by the Horror Writers Association, for his autobiography, *Once Around the Bloch: An Unauthorized Autobiography* (1993) in 1994, for his fiction collection

The Early Fears (1994) in 1995, for his novelette "The Scent of Vinegar" in 1995, and for lifetime achievement in 1990. At the 1991 World Horror Convention he was proclaimed a Grand Master of the field. Likewise, the World Science Fiction Association presented Bloch with a Hugo Special Award for "50 Years as an SF Professional" in 1984. Bloch died of esophageal cancer in 1994.

ANALYSIS

Robert Bloch began his writing career at the age of seventeen when he sold his first short story to *Weird Tales* magazine. His early crime novels *The Scarf* (1947) and *The Kidnapper* (1954) reflect his fascination with psychology and psychopathic behavior. Bloch was quite prolific and published *Spiderweb* and *The Will to Kill*, in addition to *The Kidnapper*, in 1954. He later revised *The Scarf* to tighten the ending and eliminate any sympathy the reader might have felt for the main character, a psychopathic killer. Although Bloch's efforts at the early stages of his professional career cannot be called uninteresting, they are flawed by a certain amount of overwriting that serves to dilute the full impact of the situation at hand.

PSYCHO

In 1959, Bloch published *Psycho*, the compelling tale of Norman Bates, the owner of the Bates Motel. In his novel, Bloch brings together all the terrifying elements that have been present in his earlier works. Bates, like many of Bloch's past and future characters, is an apparently normal human being. The citizens of Fairvale think he is a little odd, but they attribute this to the fact that he found the bodies of his mother and "Uncle" Joe after they died from strychnine poisoning.

Psycho has become the model for psychological fiction. The character of Norman has also become a model because he appears to be so normal. In fact, until near the end of the novel, the reader does not know that Mrs. Bates is not, in fact, alive. The part of Norman's personality that is still a small boy holds conversations with Mrs. Bates that are so realistic that the reader is completely unaware of the split in Norman's personality. The horror the reader feels when the truth is discovered causes the reader to rethink all previous events in the novel.

One of the most successful scenes in *Psycho* occurs when the detective Milton Arbogast goes to the house to speak with Mrs. Bates. Norman attempts to persuade his "mother" not to see the detective. Bloch writes:

> "Mother, please, *listen* to me!"
>
> But she didn't listen, she was in the bathroom, she was getting dressed, she was putting on make-up, she was getting ready. *Getting ready.*
>
> And all at once she came gliding out, wearing the nice dress with the ruffles. Her face was freshly powdered and rouged, she was pretty as a picture, and she smiled as she started down the stairs.
>
> Before she was halfway down, the knocking came.
>
> It was happening, Mr. Arbogast was here; he wanted to call out and warn him, but something was stuck in his throat. He could only listen as Mother cried gaily, "I'm coming! I'm coming! Just a moment, now!"
>
> And it *was* just a moment.
>
> Mother opened the door and Mr. Arbogast walked in. He looked at her and then he opened his mouth to say something. As he did so he raised his head, and that was all Mother had been waiting for. Her arm went out and something bright and glittering flashed back and forth, back and forth—
>
> It hurt Norman's eyes and he didn't want to look. He didn't have to look, either, because he already knew.
>
> Mother had found his razor . . .

The reader can clearly see from the above passage how convinced Norman is that his mother is indeed alive. It is also evident how skilled Bloch is at convincing his reader that a particular character is at least reasonably sane.

PSYCHO II

A similar situation occurs in *Psycho II* (1982), in which Norman Bates escapes from the state mental hospital. Dr. Adam Claiborne, certain that Norman is alive, even after the van in which he escaped has been found burned, goes to California to attempt to find Norman. By all accounts, Norman is still alive and leaving evidence to support this theory. In fact, Claiborne claims to see Norman in a grocery store. The reader is, however, shocked to learn at the end of the novel that Norman did indeed die in the van fire and that the killer is Dr. Claiborne himself. Again, the reader must rethink the events preceding the startling disclosure.

In none of his novels does Bloch rely on physical descriptions of characters to convey his messages. For example, the reader knows relatively little about Norman Bates. He wears glasses, is overweight, and has a mother fixation, among other psychological problems. By the end of the novel, the reader is well aware of Norman's mental state. Before that, the reader, like the citizens of Fairvale, sees him as a little odd, even more so after the murder of Mary Crane, but the reader has no clue as to the extent of his problems until the end of the novel. This is what makes Norman, as well as the rest of the mentally unstable inhabitants of Bloch's world, so frightening. Bloch gives the reader a vague physical picture of many of his characters so that the reader is left to fill in the details that make these characters turn into the reader's next-door neighbors. Bloch's antagonists could be anyone. They appear normal or near normal on the outside; it is what is inside them that makes them so dangerous.

In spite of Bloch's talent, his novels are predictable. After one has read several, one can almost always guess the ending. Although the reader is not always correct, he or she is normally quite close to discovering who the criminal is. The problem with predictability in works such as Bloch's is that the impact of the surprise ending, to which he gave new life, is diminished when the reader had been reading several of his books in quick succession.

Since the publication of *Psycho*, Bloch wrote a number of novels and short stories, as well as scripts for such series as *Alfred Hitchcock Presents* and *Thriller*. He also wrote science-fiction novels and short stories. Although Bloch became better-known after the release of the film *Psycho* by Alfred Hitchcock, it cannot be said that this novel is the "only"

Tony Perkins (left) played Norman Bates in the 1960 film adaptation of Robert Bloch's novel Psycho. *Janet Leigh (right) played the woman who makes the mistake of stopping for the night at the Bates Motel.* (Museum of Modern Art, Film Stills Archive)

good novel Bloch wrote. His style tightened following his first publications, and *Psycho* marked his development from a merely good novelist to one who achieved a lasting place in the genre.

NIGHT-WORLD

Although Bloch wrote in the style of H. P. Lovecraft, his novels cannot be said to imitate those of Lovecraft. Lovecraft is known for gruesome tales guaranteed to keep the reader awake until the wee hours of the morning if the reader is silly enough to read them in an empty house. Bloch's novels tend more toward the suspenseful aspects of Lovecraft without many of the gory details. Lovecraft gives the reader detailed accounts of the horrible ends of his characters. In *Night-World* (1972), Bloch simply tells the reader that a character has been decapitated and that his head has rolled halfway down an airport runway. The nonchalant way in which Bloch makes this pronouncement has more impact on the reader than any number of bloody descriptions.

Bloch terrified the audience by writing about criminals who seem to be normal people. These are the people one sees every day. The crimes that these supposedly normal people commit and the gruesome ends to which they come have also become quite normal.

Bloch's reaction to the atrocities of society was to make them seem normal, thereby shocking the reader into seeing that the acts and ends are not normal, but rather abnormal and more shocking and devastating than people realize.

Victoria E. McLure
Updated by Fiona Kelleghan

PRINCIPAL MYSTERY AND DETECTIVE FICTION

NOVELS: *The Scarf*, 1947 (also known as *The Scarf of Passion*); *Spiderweb*, 1954; *The Kidnapper*, 1954; *The Will to Kill*, 1954; *Shooting Star*, 1958; *Psycho*, 1959; *The Dead Beat*, 1960; *Firebug*, 1961; *Terror*, 1962; *The Couch*, 1962; *The Star Stalker*, 1968; *The Todd Dossier*, 1969; *Night-World*, 1972; *American Gothic*, 1974; *There Is a Serpent in Eden*, 1979 (also known as *The Cunning Serpent*); *Psycho II*, 1982; *Night of the Ripper*, 1984; *Robert Bloch's Unholy Trinity*, 1986; *The Kidnapper*, 1988; *Lori*, 1989; *Screams: Three Novels of Suspense*, 1989; *Psycho House*, 1990; *The Jekyll Legacy*, 1991 (with Andre Norton)

SHORT FICTION: 1945-1970 • *The Opener of the Way*, 1945; *Terror in the Night, and Other Stories*, 1958; *Pleasant Dreams—Nightmares*, 1960 (also known as *Nightmares*); *Blood Runs Cold*, 1961; *Atoms and Evil*, 1962; *More Nightmares*, 1962; *Yours Truly, Jack the Ripper: Tales of Horror*, 1962 (also known as *The House of the Hatchet, and Other Tales of Horror*); *Bogey Men*, 1963; *Horror-7*, 1963; *Tales in a Jugular Vein*, 1965; *The Skull of the Marquis de Sade, and Other Stories*, 1965; *Chamber of Horrors*, 1966; *The Living Demons*, 1967; *This Crowded Earth, and Ladies' Day*, 1968

1971-1990 • *Fear Today—Gone Tomorrow*, 1971; *Cold Chills*, 1977; *The King of Terrors*, 1977; *Out of the Mouths of Graves*, 1979; *Such Stuff as Screams Are Made Of*, 1979; *Unholy Trinity*, 1986; *Final Reckonings: The Selected Stories of Robert Bloch, Vol. 1*, 1987 (also known as *The Complete Stories of Robert Bloch*); *Bitter Ends: The Selected Stories of Robert Bloch, Vol. 2*, 1987 (also known as *The Complete Stories of Robert Bloch*); *Last Rites: The Selected Stories of Robert Bloch, Vol. 3*, 1987 (also known as *The Complete Stories of Robert Bloch*); *Lost in Time and Space with Lefty Feep*, 1987 (with John Stanley);

Midnight Pleasures, 1987; *Fear and Trembling*, 1989

1991-2000 • *The Early Fears*, 1994; *Robert Bloch: Appreciations of the Master*, 1995 (with Richard Matheson and Ricia Mainhardt); *The Vampire Stories of Robert Bloch*, 1996; *Flowers from the Moon and Other Lunacies*, 1998; *The Devil with You! The Lost Bloch, Volume I*, 1999 (with David J. Schow); *Hell on Earth: The Lost Bloch, Volume II*, 2000 (with Schow)

OTHER MAJOR WORKS

NOVELS: *It's All in Your Mind*, 1971; *Sneak Preview*, 1971; *Reunion with Tomorrow*, 1978; *Strange Eons*, 1979

SHORT FICTION: *Sea-Kissed*, 1945; *Bloch and Bradbury*, 1969 (with Ray Bradbury; also known as *Fever Dream, and Other Fantasies*); *Dragons and Nightmares*, 1969; *The Best of Robert Bloch*, 1977; *Mysteries of the Worm*, 1979; *The Fear Planet and Other Unusual Destinations*, 2005 (Stefan R. Dziemianowicz, editor)

RADIO PLAYS: *Stay Tuned for Terror*, 1944-1945 (series)

SCREENPLAYS: *The Cabinet of Caligari*, 1962; *The Couch*, 1962 (with Owen Crump and Blake Edwards); *Strait-Jacket*, 1964; *The Night Walker*, 1964; *The Psychopath*, 1966; *The Deadly Bees*, 1967 (with Anthony Marriott); *Torture Garden*, 1967; *The House That Dripped Blood*, 1970; *Asylum*, 1972; *The Amazing Captain Nemo*, 1979

TELEPLAYS: *Alfred Hitchcock Presents* television series, 1955-1961 ("The Cuckoo Clock," "The Greatest Monster of Them All," "A Change of Heart," "The Landlady," "The Sorcerer's Apprentice," "The Gloating Place," "Bad Actor," and "The Big Kick"); *Thriller* series, 1960-1961 ("The Cheaters," "The Devil's Ticket," "A Good Imagination," "The Grim Reaper," "The Weird Tailor," "Waxworks," "Till Death Do Us Part," and "Man of Mystery"); *Star Trek* series, 1966-1967 ("Wolf in the Fold," "What Are Little Girls Made Of?" and "Catspaw")

NONFICTION: *The Eighth Stage of Fandom: Selections from Twenty-five Years of Fan Writing*, 1962 (Earl Kemp, editor); *The Laughter of the Ghoul: What Every Young Ghoul Should Know*, 1977; *Out of My Head*, 1986; *H. P. Lovecraft: Letters to Robert*

Bloch, 1993 (David E. Schultz and S. T. Joshi, editors); *Once Around the Bloch: An Unauthorized Autobiography*, 1993

EDITED TEXTS: *The Best of Fredric Brown*, 1977; *Psycho-paths*, 1991; *Monsters in Our Midst*, 1993; *Lovecraft's Legacy*, 1996 (with Robert Weinberg and Martin H. Greenberg); *Robert Bloch's Psychos*, 1997

BIBLIOGRAPHY

Bloch, Robert. "The Movie People." In *Roger Ebert's Book of Film*, edited by Roger Ebert. New York: W. W. Norton, 1997. Bloch's firsthand account of the Hollywood studio system and his observations on the nature of the industry. Bibliographic references.

_____. *Once Around the Bloch: An Unauthorized Autobiography*. New York: Tor, 1995. Originally written the year before he died, this autobiography of Bloch was republished posthumously.

_____. *The Robert Bloch Companion: Collected Interviews, 1969-1986*. San Bernardino, Calif.: Borgo Press, 1990. Collection of several key interviews given by Bloch about his life and work over a seventeen-year period.

Bloom, Clive, ed. *Gothic Horror: A Reader's Guide from Poe to King and Beyond*. New York: St. Martin's Press, 1998. Includes an essay by Bloch about horror writers, as well as meditations on the genre by many other famous authors. Bibliographic references.

Haining, Peter. *The Classic Era of American Pulp Magazines*. Chicago: Chicago Review Press, 2000. Looks at Bloch's contribution to the pulps and the relationship of pulp fiction to its more respectable literary cousins.

Horsley, Lee. *The Noir Thriller*. New York: Palgrave, 2001. A scholarly, theoretically informed study of the thriller genre, including Bloch's contribution to that genre. Bibliographic references and index.

Lovecraft, H. P. *Selected Letters V, 1934-1937*. Edited by August Derleth and James Turner. Sauk City, Wis.: Arkham House, 1976. Includes letters exchanged between the teenage Bloch and the great American master of horror.

Matheson, Richard, and Ricia Mainhardt, eds. *Robert Bloch: Appreciations of the Master*. New York: Tor, 1995. Includes fiction by Bloch, as well as tributes to him by other authors who have been influenced by him.

LAWRENCE BLOCK

Born: Buffalo, New York; June 24, 1938
Also wrote as William Ard; Jill Emerson; Chip Harrison; Paul Kavanagh; Sheldon Lord; Andrew Shaw
Types of plot: Inverted; private investigator; comedy caper

PRINCIPAL SERIES

Evan Tanner, 1966-
Chip Harrison, 1970-
Matthew Scudder, 1976-
Bernie Rhodenbarr, 1977-
Martin Ehrengraf, 1983-
J. P. Keller, 1994-

PRINCIPAL SERIES CHARACTERS

EVAN TANNER is an agent working for an unnamed, secret government agency, who cannot sleep because of a shrapnel wound to the brain. When not working, he spends his spare time joining various oddball political movements.

CHIP HARRISON is a private investigator and assistant to Leo Haig, an overweight private detective who raises tropical fish and patterns his life after Nero Wolfe. Acting as Haig's Archie Goodwin in his two mystery adventures, he is full of humorous references to various mystery writers and their characters as well as to his own sexual exploits.

MATTHEW SCUDDER is a private investigator and an alcoholic former police officer who works without a license. Guilt-ridden because he accidentally killed a young girl in a shootout, he drowns his despair with alcohol and occasionally accepts a case to pay the rent.

BERNIE RHODENBARR is a burglar and amateur sleuth who steals for a price. In his amusing capers, Bernie, who derives an emotional thrill from thievery, usually winds up in trouble when dead bodies appear in places he illegally enters. He then must play detective to clear himself.

MARTIN EHRENGRAF is a dapper little criminal-defense attorney who believes that all his clients are innocent. To prove it, he is willing to use every trick in the lawyer's black bag and will even kill to win his cases.

J. P. KELLER is an appealing, conscientious hired assassin who is a thorough professional, cool but always on the lookout for a girlfriend. For a killer, he is an occasionally whimsical man prone to loneliness and self-doubt, the sort who worries about what kind of present to give the woman who walks his dog.

CONTRIBUTION

Lawrence Block is a storyteller who experiments with several genres, including espionage, detective, and comedy caper fiction. Regardless of the genre, he delivers a protagonist with whom his readers can empathize, identify, and even secretly wish to accompany on the different adventures. Block's tone ranges from the serious and downbeat in the Matt Scudder novels to the lighthearted and comical found in the works featuring Bernie Rhodenbarr and Chip Harrison. His characters are outsiders to conventional society, and Block captures their true essence through their first-person vernaculars. Furthermore, his vivid and realistic descriptions of the deadbeats, the bag ladies, the pimps, the police officers—both good and bad—and those hoping for something better portray New York City as a place devoid of glitter and elegance. Writer Stephen King has called Block the only "writer of mystery and detective fiction who comes close to replacing the irreplaceable John D. MacDonald."

Several of Block's novels were (rather poorly) adapted to film. These include *Nightmare Honeymoon* (1973), the 1983 Shamus Award-winning *Eight Million Ways to Die* (1986), and *The Burglar in the Closet* (as *Burglar*, 1987, starring Whoopi Goldberg).

BIOGRAPHY

Lawrence Block was born on June 24, 1938, in Buffalo, New York. He attended Antioch College in Yellow Springs, Ohio, from 1955 to 1959. In 1957, he became an editor for the Scott Meredith literary agency but left one year later to pursue a professional writing career. In 1960 he married Loretta Ann Kallett, with whom he had three daughters. In 1973 he and his wife were divorced. Ten years later he married Lynne Wood. Fond of travel, they visited eighty-seven countries by the end of the twentieth century.

Block's first books were soft-core sex novels (for which he used the pseudonyms Andrew Shaw, Jill Emerson, and—as did Donald E. Westlake—Sheldon Lord), which were released in paperback. In fact, for many years his novels were published as paperback originals. He is a multiple winner of nearly every major mystery award for his writing. He won Edgar Awards for his short stories "Keller on the Spot," "Keller's Therapy," and "By Dawn's Early Light," and his novel *A Dance at the Slaughterhouse* (1991). He received a Nero Wolfe Award for *The Burglar Who Liked to Quote Kipling* (1979), a Shamus Award for *Eight Million Ways to Die* (1982), a Maltese Falcon Award for *When the Sacred Ginmill Closes* (1986), and an Anthony Award for *Master's Choice, Volume II*. He has served as a member of the board of directors of the Mystery Writers of America, which honored him with the title of Grand Master in 1994, and as president of the Private Eye Writers of America. In 1964 he became associate editor of the *Whitman Numismatic Journal*, a position that reflects his interest in and knowledge of coins. For many years he was a contributing editor for *Writer's Digest*, for which he wrote a monthly column on fiction writing. His seminar for writers, "Write for Your Life," saw great success.

ANALYSIS

Lawrence Block is one of the most versatile talents in the mystery field. His desire to entertain his readers is evident in the many categories of mystery fiction that he has mastered. With each subgenre, Block utilizes a fresh approach to the protagonists, the plots, and the tone and avoids relying on established formulas.

With Evan Tanner, introduced in *The Thief Who Couldn't Sleep* (1966), Block created an agent who, faced with the prospect of rotting away in a foreign jail, reluctantly accepts his new career. While most private detectives are former police officers, thus having the proper knowledge and experience for their new professions, Chip Harrison's previous employment in a bordello offered no formal training for working for Leo Haig. Bernie Rhodenbarr, the polished and sophisticated amateur sleuth, is actually a burglar for hire. With the character of Matthew Scudder, Block destroys the cliché of the hard-drinking private detective by making Scudder an alcoholic who wrestles with the demons of his past.

Block is a master at creating the right tone for each series of mysteries. The Tanner novels are laced with wisecracks and screwball characters. The Rhodenbarr novels not only are full of lighthearted comedy but also contain fascinating burglar lore such as how to deal with locks, alarms, and watchdogs. With his two Chip Harrison mysteries, *Make Out with Murder* (1974) and *The Topless Tulip Caper* (1975), Block's sense of humor is fully developed. (Two earlier Chip Harrison novels are actually erotica rather than mysteries.) The nineteen-year-old private eye's adventures with Haig are full of mystery in-jokes and puns. In the short story "Death of the Mallory Queen," Chip and Haig encounter a suspect named Lotte Benzler, which is clearly a play on the name Otto Penzler, the well-known mystery bookstore owner, authority, and critic.

Chip's tales parody the tough, hard-boiled detective stories, but they are also Block's tribute to Rex Stout's Nero Wolfe-Archie Goodwin legacy. In sharp contrast, though, are the novels featuring Matt Scudder. The stark, unsentimental prose lends these books a serious, somber tone, as glib dialogue and flowery metaphors would only ruin the effect for which Block strives: to allow his readers to enter the mind of a man who is haunted by his guilt.

What Block's characters have most in common is that they are outsiders to the world in which they live. Walking the thin line between law and lawlessness, these men disregard the conforming demands of a complacent society. Bernie Rhodenbarr, for example, as a thief and an amateur sleuth, is a descendant of the outlaw of the Wild West or the gangster of the Roaring Twenties, both elevated to the status of folk heroes by the early dime novels and pulps. Bernie is able to beat the system and get away with it. When someone needs something stolen, Bernie is more than happy to oblige—for a price. His profession satisfies a secret desire that must be common to many readers, that of wanting something more exciting than the usual nine-to-five routine. Bernie is not, however, a completely amoral character. There are times when he does feel some guilt for his stealing, but as he says, "I'm a thief and I have to steal. I just plain love it."

THE BURGLAR IN THE CLOSET

Bernie's illegal excursions into other people's homes, however, often lead him into trouble. In *The Burglar in the Closet* (1978), before he can finish robbing the apartment that belongs to his dentist's former wife, the woman comes home with a new lover. Trapped in her bedroom closet, Bernie must wait during their lovemaking and hope they fall asleep so that he can safely escape. The woman is later murdered, and Bernie must discover who killed her to keep himself from being accused of the crime. As amateur sleuth, Bernie holds the advantage of not belonging to an official police force and is therefore not hampered by rules and procedures. With Bernie, Block adds a new twist on the role of the detective. Instead of being on a quest for justice or trying to make sense of the crimes of others, Bernie is motivated by more self-centered feelings. Like Philip Marlowe, Lew Archer, and a host of other detectives, Bernie is an outsider to the world through which he must travel on his investigation, but he is motivated by his need to save his own neck.

THE SINS OF THE FATHERS

Perhaps the most complex and believable of Block's series characters is Matthew Scudder, the alcoholic private detective who is introduced in *The Sins of the Fathers* (1976). Scudder is a former police officer who abandoned his roles as law enforcement officer, husband, and father after an incident that shattered his world. While in a bar one night after work, he witnessed two punks rob and kill the bartender. Scudder followed the two and shot them both, killing one and wounding the other. One of Scudder's bullets, however, ricocheted and hit a seven-year-old girl named Estrellita Rivera, killing her instantly. Although Scudder was cleared of any blame in the tragic shooting and was even honored by the police department for his actions in apprehending the bartender's killers, he could not clear his own conscience. After resigning from the force and leaving his wife and two sons, Scudder moved into a hotel on Fifty-seventh Street in Manhattan to face his guilt in lonely isolation.

A STAB IN THE DARK

Scudder's alcoholism is a central theme throughout each novel, and if the books are read in sequence, the alcoholism increasingly dominates Scudder's life. He suffers blackouts more frequently, and twice he is told to stop his drinking if he wants to live. As the alcoholism becomes worse, so does Scudder's isolation from those for whom he cares. In *A Stab in the Dark* (1981), a female friend, a sculptress and fellow alcoholic, tries to make Scudder confront his drinking, but he denies having a problem and says that a group such as Alcoholics Anonymous would not work for him. By the end of the book, the woman refuses to see Scudder any longer, as she herself has decided to seek help.

EIGHT MILLION WAYS TO DIE

Eight Million Ways to Die, published in 1982, is the turning point in the Scudder series. It is a superior novel for its social relevance and psychological insights into the mind of an alcoholic. In this book, Scudder has made the first steps toward confronting his alcoholism by attending regular meetings of Alcoholics Anonymous. He is hired by a prostitute, Kim Dakkinen, who wants to leave her pimp to start a new life. Afraid that the pimp, Chance, will talk her out of her plans or hurt her, Kim wants Scudder to act as a go-between with Chance. When Kim is murdered a few days later, Scudder suspects Chance, who had earlier agreed to Kim's freedom. Chance, however, asserts his innocence and hires Scudder to find Kim's murderer. Thus, Scudder's quest to solve the murder holds the chance for him to quit drinking. "Searching for Kim's killer was something I could do instead of drinking. For a while."

In this novel, Scudder's isolation is more complete. Because of his worsening alcoholism, he has been barred from buying any alcohol at Armstrong's and

becomes an outcast among the drinkers who have been a major part of his life for many years. Each day without a drink is a minor victory, but his mind is obsessed with the need for a drink. Scudder has also begun going to daily meetings of Alcoholics Anonymous. Usually he sits off to the side or in the back, listening with cynical disdain to the statements of the many problem drinkers. To him, their saccharine-sweet tales of hope sound absurd in contrast to the brutal fate suffered by Kim. Not only is Scudder an outsider to his fellow drinkers, but also he is an outsider to those hoping for a life free of alcohol. He can admit to himself that he has a problem but is unable to do so in public. He needs the help the support group can give, but he wants to tackle the problem alone. This conflict between appearance and reality recurs throughout the novel. Scudder appears to be handling his period of drying out, but in reality he is afraid to leave the bottle behind and fearful of the future.

With Chance, Block has created a man who longs for power and who must lead a double life to maintain it. He lives in a quiet neighborhood, pretending to be the faithful manservant of a nonexistent, wealthy retired doctor, so as not to arouse suspicion from his neighbors. He appears to care for his prostitutes, support them financially, and encourage them to follow their dreams. In reality, though, Chance demands complete loyalty from his girls. He uses them for his own financial gain and need for power. Coming from a middle-class background, he studied art history in college. When his father died, however, he left school, enlisted in the military, and was sent to Vietnam. When he returned, he became a pimp and created a new identity, that of Chance. In the end, however, he is left with nothing. Because of Kim's murder and another girl's suicide, the rest of his prostitutes leave him.

The world that Block depicts in *Eight Million Ways to Die* is precariously balanced on the edge between appearance and reality, hope and despair, life and death. Although Chance's prostitutes appreciate his care and protection, they want something better for their lives. One dreams of being an actress, another, of being a poet. There is hope that they will leave their present professions and pursue these dreams, but underneath there is the impression that they will never do so.

Another perspective is furnished by the stories of hope told by the members of Alcoholics Anonymous. Each alcoholic who publicly admits his problem tells of a past life full of despair. These stories are contrasted with the tales of modern urban horror that Scudder reads in the newspapers. In one case, Scudder hears about an elderly woman who was killed when her friend found an abandoned television and brought it to her house; when he turned on the television, it exploded. A bomb had been rigged inside, probably as part of a mob execution attempt that failed when the target grew suspicious and discarded the television.

These tragically absurd tales of people who die sudden, violent deaths serve as proof of life's fragile nature. The ways that people die are just as numerous as the body counts. As a police officer tells Scudder, "You know what you got in this city? . . . You got eight million ways to die." The prospect of death scares Scudder. In the end, he realizes the seriousness of his alcohol addiction and his desperate need for help, even if it comes only one day at a time. As the novel closes, he is finally able to say, "My name is Matt, . . . and I'm an alcoholic." With the Scudder novels, Block has achieved a "kind of poetry of despair." Scudder is a man who loses a part of himself but takes the first steps in building a new life.

J. P. KELLER SERIES

Stories about a wistful hit man named J. P. Keller began appearing in *Playboy* magazine in the 1990's. Often anthologized, many of these stories were arranged into episodic novels. Keller got a dog in his second story, "Keller's Therapy," and soon had a dog walker to care for the dog while he was on assignment. The charm of the Keller stories is the lonely, bachelor existence of an ordinary, likable man who kills people for a living.

SMALL TOWN

Block, a native New Yorker, responded to the terrorist attacks of September 11, 2001, with the novel *Small Town* (2003). Told from the points of view of several characters, this novel explores the catalytic effects of the attack, including serial murder on a small scale. Many critics consider *Small Town*, which finely balances suspense, psychological insight, and comic

timing, while hearkening back to Block's early soft-porn days, to be his finest novel.

Dale Davis
Updated by Fiona Kelleghan and Janet Alice Long

PRINCIPAL MYSTERY AND DETECTIVE FICTION

EVAN TANNER SERIES: *The Thief Who Couldn't Sleep*, 1966; *The Cancelled Czech*, 1966; *Tanner's Twelve Swingers*, 1967; *Two for Tanner*, 1967 (also known as *The Scoreless Thai*); *Here Comes a Hero*, 1968; *Tanner's Tiger*, 1968; *Me Tanner, You Jane*, 1970; *Tanner on Ice*, 1998

CHIP HARRISON SERIES (AS HARRISON): *No Score*, 1970; *Chip Harrison Scores Again*, 1971; *Make Out with Murder*, 1974 (also known as *The Five Little Rich Girls*); *The Topless Tulip Caper*, 1975; *Introducing Chip Harrison*, 1984 (includes *No Score* and *Chip Harrison Scores Again*); *A/K/A Chip Harrison*, 1984 (includes *Make Out with Murder* and *The Topless Tulip Caper*)

MATTHEW SCUDDER SERIES: *The Sins of the Fathers*, 1976; *In the Midst of Death*, 1976; *Time to Murder and Create*, 1977; *A Stab in the Dark*, 1981; *Eight Million Ways to Die*, 1982; *When the Sacred Ginmill Closes*, 1986; *Out on the Cutting Edge*, 1989; *A Ticket to the Boneyard*, 1990; *A Dance at the Slaughterhouse*, 1991; *Down on the Killing Floor*, 1991; *A Walk Among the Tombstones*, 1992; *The Devil Knows You're Dead*, 1993; *A Long Line of Dead Men*, 1994; *Even the Wicked*, 1996; *Everybody Dies*, 1998; *Hope to Die*, 2001; *All the Flowers Are Dying*, 2005

BERNIE RHODENBARR SERIES: *Burglars Can't Be Choosers*, 1977; *The Burglar in the Closet*, 1978; *The Burglar Who Liked to Quote Kipling*, 1979; *The Burglar Who Studied Spinoza*, 1980; *The Burglar Who Painted Like Mondrian*, 1983; *The Burglar Who Traded Ted Williams*, 1994; *The Burglar Who Thought He Was Bogart*, 1995; *The Burglar in the Library*, 1997; *The Burglar in the Rye*, 1999; *The Burglar on the Prowl*, 2004

MARTIN EHRENGRAF SERIES: *Ehrengraf for the Defense*, 1994

J. P. KELLER SERIES: *Hit Man*, 1998; *Keller's Greatest Hits: Adventures in the Murder Trade*, 1998; *Hit List*, 2000; *Keller's Adjustment* (a novella;

in *Transgressions*, 2005); *Hit Parade*, 2006

NONSERIES NOVELS: *Babe in the Woods*, 1960 (as Ard); *Markham: The Case of the Pornographic Photos*, 1961 (also known as *You Could Call It Murder*); *Death Pulls a Double Cross*, 1961 (also known as *Coward's Kiss*); *Mona*, 1961 (also known as *Sweet Slow Death* and *Grifter's Game*); *Cinderella Sims*, 1961 (also known as *Twenty-Dollar Lust*; as Shaw); *Lucky at Cards*, 1964 (as Lord); *The Girl with the Long Green Heart*, 1965; *Deadly Honeymoon*, 1967; *After the First Death*, 1969; *The Specialists*, 1969; *Such Men Are Dangerous: A Novel of Violence*, 1969 (as Kavanagh); *The Triumph of Evil*, 1971 (as Kavanagh); *Not Comin' Home to You*, 1974 (as Kavanagh); *Ariel*, 1980; *Code of Arms*, 1981 (with Harold King); *Into the Night*, 1987 (a manuscript by Cornell Woolrich, completed by Block); *Random Walk: A Novel for a New Age*, 1988; *Small Town*, 2003

SHORT FICTION: *Sometimes They Bite*, 1983; *Like a Lamb to the Slaughter*, 1984; *Some Days You Get the Bear*, 1993; *One Night Stands*, 1998; *The Collected Mystery Stories*, 1999; *The Lost Cases of Ed London*, 2001 (includes *The Naked and the Deadly*, *Twin Call Girls*, and *Stag Party Girl*); *Enough Rope: Collected Stories*, 2002

OTHER MAJOR WORKS

NOVEL: *Ronald Rabbit Is a Dirty Old Man*, 1971

NONFICTION: *Writing the Novel: From Plot to Print*, 1979; *Telling Lies for Fun and Profit*, 1981; *Write for Your Life: The Book About the Seminar*, 1986; *Spider, Spin Me a Web: Lawrence Block on Writing*, 1988; *Lawrence Block: Bibliography 1958-1993*, 1993 (with others); *After Hours: Conversations with Lawrence Block*, 1995 (with Ernie Bulow)

SCREENPLAY: *The Funhouse*, 1981

EDITED TEXTS: *Death Cruise: Crime Stories on the Open Seas*, 1999; *Master's Choice*, 1999; *Master's Choice, Volume II*, 2000; *Opening Shots*, 2000; *Manhattan Noir*, 2006

BIBLIOGRAPHY

Block, Lawrence. Lawrence Block. http://www .LawrenceBlock.com. The author's own Web site offers updates on Block's new and upcoming titles. Block comments on many of his own works and provides much information on his career. Includes informative links to Web interviews.

Block, Lawrence, and Ernie Bulow. *After Hours: Conversations with Lawrence Block*. Albuquerque: University of New Mexico Press, 1995. An interview with the grand master by a scholar and critic of the mystery genre. This work is full of historical insights into the pulp industry and the methods of one of the leading mystery writers of the twentieth century.

Block, Lawrence, and Tom Callahan. "Lawrence Block, Master of Mystery." *Writer* 116, no. 7 (July, 2003): 22. This lengthy and interesting interview with Block coincided with the release of *Small Town*. Block discusses his writing methods and, in particular, beginning a half-finished novel set in Manhattan from scratch after the destruction of the World Trade Center.

King, Stephen. "No Cats: An Appreciation of Lawrence Block and Matt Scudder." In *The Sins of the Fathers*, by Lawrence Block. Arlington Heights, Ill.: Dark Harvest, 1992. This long and admiring critical essay by the best-selling horror novelist serves as the introduction to the hardcover reissue of the first Matt Scudder mystery.

Priestman, Martin. *The Cambridge Companion to Crime Fiction*. New York: Cambridge University Press, 2003. An excellent, all-around trove of information for the reader. Priestman discusses hit men, including Keller, who frequently lead rather ordinary lives outside their profession, and contrasts them with the more literary assassins who possess a psychologically explicated criminal brain.

PIERRE BOILEAU and THOMAS NARCEJAC

PIERRE BOILEAU
Born: Paris, France; April 28, 1906
Died: Beaulieu-sur-Mer, France; January 16, 1989

THOMAS NARCEJAC
Born: Roche-sur-Mer, France; July 3, 1908
Died: Nice, France; June 9, 1998
Types of plot: Psychological; inverted

CONTRIBUTION

It is no exaggeration to state that through the efforts of crime writer Pierre Boileau and his collaborator, Thomas Narcejac, a new type of thriller was created. Together, under the pseudonym Boileau-Narcejac, they wrote studies in abnormal psychology rooted in the philosophical outlook of existentialism current in the Paris of the immediate pre- and post-World War II period. Film directors such as Alfred Hitchcock brought Boileau's and Narcejac's treatments of human duplicity and gullibility to a wider audience than that previously enjoyed by most thrillers.

Their tales are puzzles of intricate design that require the reader's close attention. Each novel contains at least one startling development; some contain several. Many of the stories deal with people worn out by their mundane existence and who grasp at perceived opportunities to find some meaning in their lives. Their gullibility is matched by the amorality and artfulness of more vital characters, who trick them into doing things they had never considered doing.

BIOGRAPHY

Born on April 28, 1906, in the Monmartre section of Paris to a shipping-firm manager and a housewife, Pierre Boileau was an accounting student for a time, studying at a Parisian school of commerce, although he became increasingly unhappy with his father's choice of careers for him. Before he became a writer, he first learned a considerable amount about other people from his work as an architect, a writer of advertising copy, a textile worker, and a restaurant waiter. Writing when he could find time, Boileau eventually

wrote several early novels, the third of which, *Le Repos de Bacchus*, won the 1938 Prix du Roman d'Aventures.

Because he was thought to be an opponent of Nazism, Boileau was made a political prisoner in 1939, just after the German invasion of France. Fortunately for him and for literature, Boileau was not executed or jailed but rather was forced to serve in the French Welfare Department, visiting various penal institutions to talk to inmates. In these institutions, he learned much about crime and the criminal's way of looking at life; this information would aid him immensely in his creation of crime fiction. After 1942, the year he was freed from his internment, Boileau began to turn to active mystery writing, publishing several well-regarded works.

Thomas Narcejac was born as Pierre Ayraud in 1908 to "a family with a well-established sea-going tradition." He attended school in Poitiers and later received a degree in philosophy from the Faculté des Lettres in Paris. As a result of a childhood accident that had half-blinded him, he could not follow his family's seafaring tradition; instead, he decided to teach. Becoming interested in the techniques of detective fiction, he began to write, often throwing the results, he states, "into the waste-paper basket as fast as I produced them." Some survived, however, and in 1948 he too received the Prix du Roman d'Aventures. All of his literary ventures were written under the pen name Thomas Narcejac because he wished to keep his professional life distinct from his literary one.

The two writers' destinies joined when Boileau noticed in a bookstore window a work written by Narcejac, a book that offered both a striking critique of modern detective novels and solutions to their problems. Thus inspired, Boileau wrote frequently to Narcejac about transforming the mystery genre; this correspondence led eventually to their forming a partnership in June of 1948. They pledged to put their theories to work in a collaborative novel. Written in 1952, *Celle qui n'était plus* (*The Woman Who Was No More*, 1954) was published by the house of Demoël, then had the good fortune to be adapted by director Henri-Georges Clouzot into *Les Diaboliques* (1955; *Diabolique*, 1955). Another collaboration resulted in *D'entre les morts* (1954; *The Living and the Dead*, 1956), which, when filmed by Hitchcock, became the widely acclaimed thriller *Vertigo* (1958). Boileau died in 1989 and Narcejac in 1998.

ANALYSIS

The novels of Pierre Boileau and Thomas Narcejac deal with the subject of appearances. Their main characters discover the validity of the old saying, "Things are not as they appear." Frequently, their tales of suspense and intrigue proceed in a murky, unreal atmosphere characterized by heavy fog or creeping darkness at twilight. Characters deceived in one way or another by people whom they have trusted stumble alone through the half-lit scene symbolizing moral ambiguity and their lack of vision. Here, in this foggy place, people listen only to inner, selfish directives, abandoning both reason and decency in the process.

Generally these characters are weak individuals who lead aimless, unhappy lives, starved of meaning and romantic fulfillment. Their lives bear a notable resemblance to the empty, absurd lives led in the existentialist novels of Jean-Paul Sartre and Albert Camus. Puppets of fate, these characters lack inner direction, and lacking direction, they frantically grasp at straws, looking for some form of secular salvation. Love often is the most appealing form of salvation they seek: they believe that it will carry them to a place far from their boring lives.

Boileau and Narcejac offer painful portraits of normal individuals who become studies in abnormal psychology. Obsessed with an idea or a particular person, these characters gradually create a realm all their own. These private worlds would not be destructive, were it not that they lead to danger and difficulties as well as, on occasion, death.

THE WOMAN WHO WAS NO MORE

Their fantasies become the stuff of murder mysteries because their obsessions are not self-generated but rather have been created for them by others who can profit from them. In *The Woman Who Was No More*, for example, a character named Fernand Ravinel is

monstrously tricked by his mistress, Lucienne, and his wife, Mireille, into killing himself and leaving Mireille a large amount of insurance money. Typically, the tale begins in a literal fog, this one having drifted into a French city from the sea. Accompanied by the ominous sound of a ship's foghorn, Ravinel begins the most fateful day of his miserable life. The ship carries Mireille, whom he has promised to help murder.

The fog without is emblematic both of confusion within Ravinel's mind and of the creeping evil enveloping his soul. Given a sampler of his thoughts, the reader immediately realizes that Ravinel is a weak, selfish egotist with no redeeming qualities. Only an ordinary traveling salesman, he somehow manages to see himself as a man wronged by a wife who cannot comprehend his greatness.

Tension builds as Ravinel talks to Lucienne about the coming murder; they will commit it together to receive money from the insurance policy Mireille recently took out when Ravinel bought his policy. Lucienne, being the stronger and more intelligent of the two, takes the lead and forces Ravinel to stick with his assigned role. Nevertheless, he cannot stop thinking about the woman whom he is about to kill and about some of the things she has done for him.

The two killers administer a sedative to the unsuspecting Mireille and then drown her in a bathtub. Initially, Ravinel denies to himself that he has done anything wrong; he numbly helps Lucienne get rid of the corpse, but he cannot stop his memories of his wife.

Brilliantly, Boileau and Narcejac allow scenes from Ravinel's past life to rise ghostlike from deep inside Ravinel's unconscious mind; her image begins to haunt him, giving him no peace. Almost as quickly as Ravinel finds a way to justify the crime, another vision of Mireille floods his imagination, driving him toward a nervous breakdown. The existentialist Ravinel is not troubled by fears of having offended God; rather, he has to admit to himself that life seems unrewarding and unpleasant. Nevertheless, he cannot place the blame on himself, where it really belongs. There is no self-recognition in his disordered mind, only self-pity and fear. The more he thinks, the more frightened he becomes of being discovered and seen as a common murderer.

He creates elaborate rationalizations. He blames Mireille and Lucienne, not himself, for any lack of ardor in their relations. The murder, he postulates, happened only because of his wife's inability to appreciate her husband. The boredom that weighs heavily on him is the fault of the dull people around him and of the dull place where he lives. In short, there is no chance of his accepting any measure of responsibility for his actions. Little by little, the reader comes to realize the unlikeliness of a bright woman such as Mireille ever being attracted to Ravinel.

Later, a complication arises: Ravinel cannot locate the body, which he had dumped in a millpond. His concern turns to panic when Mireille fails to float to the surface. It is as if she has come back to life, he speculates, although he quickly dismisses the thought. Yet, despite Ravinel's best efforts, the notion that his wife is alive keeps resurfacing. Finally, it becomes not only possible but also likely that she lives. What is left of his composure is destroyed by an actual sighting of the supposedly dead Mireille. Though he could not see her clearly, he knows that it was her.

The reader wonders about what is happening: Is Ravinel hallucinating, is the fog creating a specter out of nothing, or is Mireille risen from the dead and walking the earth? At this point, the novel seems to be nothing more than a routine "haunting" with a ghost taking vengeance on the living. Yet Boileau and Narcejac have created something far more complex.

When a mentally retarded girl, Henrietta, informs Ravinel that she just saw someone who looks like Mireille, his mental anguish becomes acute. The last turn of the screw happens when he receives a letter having Mireille's signature at the bottom that states, in her characteristically breezy way, that she loves him.

In a spectacular finale, Ravinel, delirious from terror and guilt, receives another note from his "dead" wife indicating that she will see him that night at their home. At this point, neither Ravinel nor the reader knows what will happen. As the light fades with the dusk, so does Ravinel's courage. Waiting breathlessly inside the house, Ravinel at last hears footsteps approaching his room—the familiar footsteps of his wife. Mad with horror and in need of release from his crippling guilt, Ravinel does the only thing possible: He kills himself.

Boileau and Narcejac do not end the book there, though it would be a conventionally satisfying way to end a horror or mystery novel. The last scene is reserved for the arisen Mireille, who only pretended to be murdered, and Lucienne, her friend and (it is implied) lover. Mireille congratulates Lucienne on a job well done. They believe that they have performed a service to society, ridding it of a boring, unpleasant man.

THE LIVING AND THE DEAD

The startling turnabout displayed in *The Woman Who Was No More* is also used to good effect elsewhere in the Boileau-Narcejac canon. Fog, depravity, duplicity, and amoral drift are once again present in their masterpiece, *The Living and the Dead*. The main character is an ordinary man, Flavières, who is recruited by his supposed friend Gévigne to follow Gévigne's wife to see why she acts so strangely. By

Set primarily in San Francisco, Alfred Hitchcock's 1958 film
Vertigo *was adapted from* The Living and the Dead.

agreeing to shadow the beautiful Madeleine, Flavières unwittingly becomes a victim of a terrible plot to murder the real Madeleine. Flattered by the attentions of his old friend, he decides to follow her throughout Paris if necessary to determine the cause of the alleged madness.

On the surface, Madeleine appears to be exactly what Gévigne says she has been: an erratic, unpredictable woman of strange moods. Flavières becomes fully convinced of her mental instability when he sees her jump into the Seine River in an apparent suicide attempt. She is saved by him from drowning and yet is not happy about being rescued.

As in their other novels, Boileau and Narcejac demonstrate the deceptiveness of appearances, especially when they are orchestrated by cynical and amoral people. As in *The Woman Who Was No More*, Madeleine reappears, after falling from a church tower onto a stone pavement. Flavières, witness to the final act of Madeleine's madness, tries to forget her and get on with his life. Yet he is constantly reminded of her, and finds that he cannot forget her. Years after her fatal plunge, Flavières sees her again in a crowded theater, then in other places, until he becomes certain that it is she. Madeleine—or rather the woman who once pretended to be her—has forgotten all about him; she fails to recognize him at first when he introduces himself. Caught and unhappy about being recognized, Madeleine first tries to lie her way out of her predicament, claiming that he is imagining things. When the lies fail to work, she confesses that she is Madeleine but will tell him nothing else.

Finally, she blurts out that she is not really Madeleine but instead is Renée Sourange. She had been recruited by Gévigne to impersonate his wife, a woman without mental problems of any kind, to convince a third party that Madeleine had committed suicide. Actually, she had been pushed from the belfry by her husband. Flavières's report of the "suicide" added authenticity to the story given to the police by Gévigne.

In a second twist, when Renée tells the enraged and disappointed Flavières the rest of the story, he strangles her. His rage is kindled not only by the fact that he was taken for a fool but also by the fact that the truth has destroyed his vision of a woman too good for this world.

In a third twist at the end of the novel, Flavières, being escorted in handcuffs, asks the officers if he can kiss Renée's dead body. With tears in his eyes, he does so, leaving an ambiguous message: Did he love Renée just as he had loved Madeleine, or did he still see her as Madeleine? Perhaps that gesture of farewell was also a gesture of forgiveness.

Two of the best collaborators in the mystery and detective genre, Boileau and Narcejac, with their highly ambiguous endings, twists and turns of plot, and extraordinary insights into the psyches of both victim and villain, established themselves as craftsmen of the highest order.

John D. Raymer

PRINCIPAL MYSTERY AND DETECTIVE FICTION

NOVELS: 1930-1950 • *André Brunel, policier*, 1934 (by Boileau); *La Pierre qui tremble*, 1934 (by Boileau); *La Promenade de minuit*, 1934 (by Boileau); *Le Repos de Bacchus*, 1938 (by Boileau); *La Police est dans l'escalier*, 1947 (by Narcejac); *La Mort est du voyage*, 1948 (by Narcejac); *Le Mauvais Cheval*, 1950 (by Narcejac)

1951-1960 • *Celle qui n'était plus*, 1952 (*The Woman Who Was No More*, 1954); *Les Visages de l'ombre*, 1953 (*Faces in the Dark*, 1954); *D'entre les morts*, 1954 (*The Living and the Dead*, 1956); *Les Louves*, 1955 (*The Prisoner*, 1957); *Au bois dormant*, 1956 (*Sleeping Beauty*, 1959); *Le Mauvais Œil*, 1956 (*The Evil Eye*, 1959); *Les Magiciennes*, 1957; *À cœur perdu*, 1959 (*Heart to Heart*, 1959); *L'Ingénieur qui aimait trop les chiffres*, 1959 (*The Tube*, 1960)

1961-1970 • *Maléfices*, 1961 (*Spells of Evil*, 1961); *Les Victims*, 1964 (*Who Was Clare Jallu?*, 1965); *Et mon tout est un homme*, 1965 (*Choice Cuts*, 1966); *La Mort a dit, peut-être*, 1967; *Delirium*, 1969; *Les Veufs*, 1970; *Maldonne*, 1970

1971-1981• *La Vie en miettes*, 1972; *Opération primevère*, 1973; *Frère Judas*, 1974; *La Tenaille*, 1975; *Le Second Visage d'Arsène Lupin*, 1975; *La Lèpre*, 1976; *L'Âge bête*, 1978; *Carte vermeille*, 1979; *Le Serment d'Arsène Lupin*, 1979; *Terminus*, 1980; *Box Office*, 1981

SHORT FICTION: *Usurpation d'identité*, 1959 (by Narcejac)

OTHER MAJOR WORKS

NONFICTION: *Esthétique du roman policier*, 1947 (by Narcejac); *La Fin d'un bluff: Essai sur le roman policier noir américain*, 1949 (by Narcejac); *Le Cas "Simenon,"* 1950 (*The Art of Simenon*, 1952; by Narcejac); *Le Roman policier*, 1964; *Tandem: Ou, Trente-cinq ans de suspense*, 1986

BIBLIOGRAPHY

Indick, William. *Psycho Thrillers: Cinematic Explorations of the Mysteries of the Mind*. Jefferson, N.C.: McFarland, 2006. Detailed analysis of the psychological thriller in film, which was directly influenced by Boileau and Narcejac's literary inventions. Bibliography, filmography, and index.

Sayers, Dorothy L. *Les Origines du Roman Policier: A Wartime Wireless Talk to the French*. Translated by Suzanne Bray. Hurstpierpoint, West Sussex, England: Dorothy L. Sayers Society, 2003. Address to the French by the famous English mystery author, discussing the history of French detective fiction and its relation to the English version of the genre. Sheds light on Boileau and Narcejac's work.

Schwartz, Ronald. *Noir, Now and Then: Film Noir Originals and Remakes, 1944-1999*. Westport, Conn.: Greenwood Press, 2001. This study of film noir and later remakes includes analysis of two adaptations of *The Living and the Dead* and four adaptation of *The Woman Who Was No More*.

Wakeman, John, ed. "Pierre Boileau" and "Thomas Narcejac." In *World Authors, 1950-1970*. New York: Wilson, 1975. Each author receives an entry in this massive list of the writers of the world and their accomplishments.

JORGE LUIS BORGES

Born: Buenos Aires, Argentina; August 24, 1899
Died: Geneva, Switzerland; June 14, 1986
Also wrote as H. Bustos Domecq; B. Suárez Lynch
Type of plot: Metaphysical and metafictional parody

CONTRIBUTION

Jorge Luis Borges's primary contribution to the detective genre is his recognition and exploitation of the fact that the genre is the quintessential model for pattern and plot in fiction. An admirer of the stories of Edgar Allan Poe since childhood, Borges saw that Poe's development of the detective story was closely related to his theories of the highly patterned short-story genre in general; he also knew very early in his career that G. K. Chesterton's Father Brown detective stories were built on the paradoxical union of a highly rational plot with a mystic undercurrent.

Although few of Borges's short fictions are detective stories in the conventional sense, many of them make specific reference to the genre and use detective-story conventions to focus on the nature of reality as a highly patterned fictional construct. Borges was influential in showing that detective fiction is more fundamental, more complex, and thus more worthy of serious notice than critics in the past had thought it to be.

BIOGRAPHY

Jorge Luis Borges was born on August 24, 1899, in Buenos Aires, Argentina, the son of Jorge Guillermo Borges, a lawyer and psychology teacher, and Leonor Acevedo de Borges, a descendant of old Argentine and Uruguayan stock. A precocious child who spent much of his childhood indoors, Borges later said that his discovery of his father's library was the chief event in his life; he began writing at the age of six, imitating classical Spanish authors such as Miguel de Cervantes.

Attending school in Switzerland during World War I, Borges read, and was strongly influenced by, the French Symbolist poets and such English prose writers as Robert Louis Stevenson, G. K. Chesterton, and Thomas Carlyle. After the war, Borges spent two years in Spain, where he became the disciple of Rafael Casinos Assens, leader of the Ultraist movement in poetry, and where he began writing poetry himself.

Jorge Luis Borges. (© Washington Post; reprinted by permission of the District of Columbia Public Library)

In 1935, Borges's first book of stories, *Historia universal de la infamia* (*A Universal History of Infamy*, 1972), appeared. He wrote his most important stories, published in 1941 under the title *El jardín de senderos que se bifurcan* (the garden of forking paths), while recovering from blood poisoning four years later. Another collection of stories, *Ficciones, 1935-1944* (English translation, 1962) was published in 1944 and promptly awarded a prize by the Argentine Society of Writers. After he criticized the regime of dictator Juan Perón, however, Borges was "promoted" from his librarian's job to that of inspector of poultry and rabbits, a position from which he promptly resigned. When the military government took over from Perón, Borges was appointed head of the National Library; in 1956, he was awarded the National Prize in Literature. Because of increasing blindness he was forced to stop reading and writing in the late 1950's; his mother became his secretary, however, and he continued to work by dictation.

In 1961, Borges was awarded a major European prize with Samuel Beckett, an event that launched his international reputation and that led to his being invited to lecture in the United States. The following year, translations of his books began to appear and he received several honorary doctorates and literary prizes from universities and professional societies. He died in Geneva, Switzerland, on June 14, 1986, after a long and distinguished career.

ANALYSIS

Jorge Luis Borges was undoubtedly the most "literary" of all practitioners of the detective story; in fact, he stated that he found within himself no other passion and almost no other exercise than literature. His interest in detective fiction stemmed from early encounters with the stories of Edgar Allan Poe, whom he called the originator of the detective story, and G. K. Chesterton, whose combination of mysticism and ratiocination he admired most.

Borges repeatedly acknowledged his debt to the detective-story genre. What he admired most about the form is that whereas much modern literature is full of incoherence and opinion, the detective story represents order and what he called "the obligation to invent." Indeed, the intrinsic relationship between the detective story and Borges's fiction centers on the related issues of order, pattern, and plot, qualities that to him are most pronounced in short fiction. Borges rejected both the naïve realism and the discursive psychologizing of the novel, preferring instead the aesthetic tightness and consequent fantastic irrealism of the short story.

In one of his most famous statements on detective fiction, "Chesterton and the Labyrinths of the Detective Story," Borges notes that whereas the detective novel borders on the character or psychological study, the detective story is an exercise in formal patterning and should abide by the following rules: The number of characters should be minimal; the resolution should tie up all loose ends; the emphasis should be on the "how" rather than the "who"; and the mystery should be so constructed that it is fit for only one solution, a solution at which the reader should marvel.

"THE APPROACH TO ALMOTÁSIM"

Borges's fascination with the possibilities of the detective story as a model for his fiction actually began with an experiment, with the 1936 essay "El acercamiento a Almotásim" ("The Approach to Almotásim"). The work is presented as a Borges review of a detective novel titled "The Approach to Almotásim," written by a Bombay lawyer named Mir Bahadur Ali. Although Bahadur is fictitious and the novel is nonexistent, Borges summarizes its plot—his own fiction within this fictional review—and characterizes the novel as a union of rational detective fiction and Persian mysticism—a combination similar to that which Borges perceived in the works of Chesterton.

The plot of the fictional novel involves a nameless Bombay law student who kills, or thinks he kills, a Hindu in a street battle between Hindus and Muslims and who proceeds to flee the police—a flight that later turns into a pursuit of a man pure of soul. The novel ends just as the student finds this man, whose name is Almotásim. What most interests Borges the reviewer in the story is Almotásim as an image of the incarnation of the spiritual within the physical—a concept central to the stories of Chesterton. The story also introduces Borges's concern with fiction as a metaphor for reality, rather than reality as a basis for fiction.

SIX PROBLEMS FOR DON ISIDRO PARODI

Borges has called one of the chief events of his life his friendship with Adolfo Bioy Casares, with whom he began editing classic detective novels and writing collaboratively in the 1940's. Together they invented a third writer, Honorio Bustos Domecq, the pseudonym for the creator of a fictional detective named Isidro Parodi who is featured in their first collaborative book, *Seis problemas para don Isidro Parodi* (1942; *Six Problems for Don Isidro Parodi*, 1981). Don Parodi, as his name suggests, is a parody of the rational detective; he is the reasoner and practitioner of absolute inaction, an armchair detective who cannot become involved in the events of the solution of a mystery because he is in a prison cell.

"AN EXAMINATION OF THE WORK OF HERBERT QUAIN"

Most of Borges's fictions emphasize, in one way or another, the highly formalized literariness and the mystical undercurrent of the detective story. In "Un examen de la obra de Herbert Quain" ("An Examination of the Work of Herbert Quain"), Borges comments on a detective novel by a fictional author, summarizing the plot in the most conventional fashion. The twist of the story is that the solution proves to be erroneous and leads the reader back to discover another solution, which makes the reader more discerning than the detective.

"IBN HAKKAN AL-BOKHARI, DEAD IN HIS LABYRINTH"

In "Abenjacán the Bojarí, muerto en su laberinto" ("Ibn Hakkan al-Bokhari, Dead in His Labyrinth"), Borges presents a dichotomy, similar to the one Poe developed in "The Purloined Letter," between the poet and the mathematician. Dunraven, a poet, tells the story of al-Bokhari, who killed his cousin Zaid, stole his money, and smashed in his face with a rock. Later, al-Bokhari dreams about the murder; in the dream, Zaid says that he will get his revenge by killing al-Bokhari the same way. Al-Bokhari builds himself a labyrinth in England in which to hide, but he is later found dead, with his face obliterated. Unwin, a mathematician, is unconvinced by the story and unravels the mystery by arguing that it was Zaid who was the culprit—who stole al-Bokhari's money and then fled to England, where he built a maze to lure al-Bokhari there. Such metamorphoses of the identities of the maker of the maze and the one trapped in it are classic rules of the game, says Dunraven, accepted conventions that the reader agrees to follow. Indeed, the poet as the maker of the story and the mathematician as the one who solves its twisted plot represent conventions of united bipolar dualities that Borges uses in other stories.

"THE GARDEN OF FORKING PATHS"

"The Garden of Forking Paths," published in *Ellery Queen's Mystery Magazine* in 1948, is patterned after that variant of the mystery-story genre known as the espionage thriller. The central figure is a Chinese English professor spying for the Germans. In a first-person statement, presumably made after his capture, Dr. Yu Tsun tells of his plan to communicate the secret location of a British artillery site to his German chief before Captain Richard Madden captures him.

The story revolves around two of Borges's favorite

themes—the idea of time and the concept of the labyrinth—which are unified with Yu Tsun's plan when he goes to the home of Stephen Albert, an expert on Chinese culture who happens to have in his possession the dual undertaking of one of Yu Tsun's ancestors, a book and a maze. This undertaking Yu Tsun now discovers to be a single task, for the book itself is a maze, an infinite labyrinth of time. The hero of this labyrinthine work, instead of choosing one alternative from many and thus eliminating the others, as is common in fiction, chooses all of them simultaneously and thus creates forking paths. Borges's story concludes when Yu Tsun kills Stephen Albert just as Richard Madden arrives, knowing that when his chief sees the story in the newspaper he will understand that the secret location of the British artillery is a city named Albert. Having no way to say the secret word, he thus reveals it the way fiction always does: indirectly, through an event.

"DEATH AND THE COMPASS"

Borges's most explicit treatment of the detective story is "La muerte y la brújula" ("Death and the Compass"), in which he inverts several of the conventions Poe invented. First, there is the famous sleuth Lönnrot, created in the mold of Poe's C. Auguste Dupin, who sees himself as a pure thinker. Second, there is the police commissioner Treviranus, who is skeptical of the sleuth's methods. Third, there is the archvillain, Red Scharlach, counterpoised against the detective as his nemesis but also as his alter ego. Finally, there is the mystery itself, a mystery of no common nature.

The story is actually a parody of the detective story as originated by Poe, for its plot, although dependent on the detective's use of pure reason to solve the mystery, actually parodies this use of reason. The events begin with a mysterious murder that the police commissioner considers a simple case of robbery and chance, an explanation that Lönnrot rejects as too simple. Because the case involves a dead rabbi, he prefers a religious explanation, an explanation based on the clue provided by a piece of paper with the words "The first letter of the Name has been spoken" typed on it.

Soon after, two more crimes occur, at the scene of which are references to the second and the final letter of the Name. Lönnrot is so convinced that all three crimes are related that he carefully examines Jewish lore and discovers that the crimes are symmetrical in both time and space, creating at first a triangle but suggesting to him that the mysterious Name is the name of God—JHVH—and that a fourth crime will take place on a certain date at a specific place.

When the detective arrives at the suspected time and place, the usual detective-story conventions are reversed. What Lönnrot finds there is his enemy, Red Scharlach. The explanation for the mystery, usually mouthed by the detective, but here revealed by the criminal, affirms that Treviranus was right about the first crime—it was simple robbery. Once Red Scharlach found out that Lönnrot was on the case, however, he wove a labyrinth to catch him—by committing the second crime himself and by staging the third, knowing that the detective would use the rabbinical explanation of the Tetragrammaton, the name of God, and thus fall in his trap by hypothesizing a fourth crime. The story thus ends not with the capture of the criminal but with the fourth crime—the murder of the detective.

"Death and the Compass" makes use of many of the conventions of the detective story, not the least of which is that the detective is caught by the detective story's most powerful convention—the search for an explanation for a mystery through purely patterned reason. If Lönnrot is caught by being too much Dupin, he is also caught because he has forgotten one of the crucial elements of the Father Brown stories—that, whereas the detective is only the critic who seeks to solve the mystery of the plot, it is the criminal who is the artist, the one who creates a plot. In "Death and the Compass," Lönnrot is caught by purely literary means—ensnared by the criminal artist's plot and his own sophistical reasoning.

Borges is the capstone figure of detective fiction in the twentieth century. Anticipating the concerns of postmodern fiction, Borges realized that reality is not the composite of the simple empirical data that humans experience every day; it is much more subjective, metaphysical, and thus mysterious than that. The detective story reminds the reader, says Borges, that reality is a highly patterned human construct, like fiction itself.

Charles E. May

PRINCIPAL MYSTERY AND DETECTIVE FICTION

SHORT FICTION: *Seis problemas para don Isidro Parodi*, 1942 (as Domecq with Adolfo Bioy Casares; *Six Problems for Don Isidro Parodi*, 1981)

OTHER MAJOR WORKS

NOVEL: *Un modelo para la muerte*, 1946 (as Lynch; with Bioy Casares)

SHORT FICTION: *Historia universal de la infamia*, 1935 (*A Universal History of Infamy*, 1972); *El jardín de senderos que se bifurcan*, 1941; *Ficciones, 1935-1944*, 1944 (English translation, 1962); *Dos fantasías memorables*, 1946 (as Domecq; with Bioy Casares); *El Aleph*, 1949, 1952 (translated in *The Aleph, and Other Stories, 1933-1969*, 1970); *La muerte y la brújula*, 1951; *La hermana de Eloísa*, 1955 (with Luisa Mercedes Levinson); *Cuentos*, 1958; *Crónicas de Bustos Domecq*, 1967 (as Domecq; with Bioy Casares; *Chronicles of Bustos Domecq*, 1976); *El informe de Brodie*, 1970 (*Doctor Brodie's Report*, 1972); *El matrero*, 1970; *El congreso*, 1971 (*The Congress*, 1974); *El libro de arena*, 1975 (*The Book of Sand*, 1977); *Narraciones*, 1980

SCREENPLAYS: *"Los orilleros" y "El paraíso de los creyentes,"* 1955 (with Bioy Casares); *Les Autres*, 1974 (with Bioy Casares and Hugo Santiago)

POETRY: *Fervor de Buenos Aires*, 1923, 1969; *Luna de enfrente*, 1925; *Cuaderno San Martín*, 1929; *Poemas, 1923-1943*, 1943; *Poemas, 1923-1953*, 1954; *Obra poética, 1923-1958*, 1958; *Obra poética, 1923-1964*, 1964; *Seis poemas escandinavos*, 1966; *Siete poemas*, 1967; *El otro, el mismo*, 1969; *Elogio de la sombra*, 1969 (*In Praise of Darkness*, 1974); *El oro de los tigres*, 1972 (translated in *The Gold of Tigers: Selected Later Poems*, 1977); *La rosa profunda*, 1975 (translated in *The Gold of Tigers*); *La moneda de hierro*, 1976; *Historia de la noche*, 1977; *La cifra*, 1981; *Los conjurados*, 1985; *Selected Poems*, 1999

NONFICTION: 1925-1930 • *Inquisiciones*, 1925; *El tamaño de mi esperanza*, 1926; *El idioma de los argentinos*, 1928; *Evaristo Carriego*, 1930 (English translation, 1984); *Figari*, 1930

1931-1950 • *Discusión*, 1932; *Las Kennigar*, 1933; *Historia de la eternidad*, 1936; *Nueva refutación del tiempo*, 1947; *Aspectos de la literatura gauchesca*, 1950

1951-1960 • *Antiguas literaturas germánicas*, 1951 (with Delia Ingenieros; revised as *Literaturas germánicas medievales*, 1966, with Maria Esther Vásquez); *Otras Inquisiciones*, 1952 (*Other Inquisitions*, 1964); *El "Martin Fierro,"* 1953 (with Margarita Guerrero); *Leopoldo Lugones*, 1955 (with Betina Edelberg); *Manual de zoología fantástica*, 1957 (with Guerrero; *The Imaginary Zoo*, 1969; revised as *El libro de los seres imaginarios*, 1967, *The Book of Imaginary Beings*, 1969); *La poesía gauchesca*, 1960

1961-2001 • *Introducción a la literatura norteamericana*, 1967 (with Esther Zemborain de Torres; *An Introduction to American Literature*, 1971); *Prólogos*, 1975; *Cosmogonías*, 1976; *Libro de sueños*, 1976; *Qué es el budismo?*, 1976 (with Alicia Jurado); *Siete noches*, 1980 (*Seven Nights*, 1984); *Nueve ensayos dantescos*, 1982; *The Total Library: Non-fiction, 1922-1986*, 2001 (Eliot Weinberger, editor)

EDITED TEXTS: *Antología clásica de la literatura argentina*, 1937; *Antología de la literatura fantástica*, 1940 (with Bioy Casares and Silvia Ocampo); *Antología poética argentina*, 1941 (with Bioy Casares and Ocampo); *El compadrito: Su destino, sus barrios, su música*, 1945, 1968 (with Silvina Bullrich); *Poesía gauchesca*, 1955 (with Bioy Casares; 2 volumes); *Libro del cielo y del infierno*, 1960, 1975 (with Bioy Casares); *Versos*, 1972 (by Evaristo Carriego); *Antología poética*, 1982 (by Leopoldo Lugones); *Antología poética*, 1982 (by Franciso de Quevedo); *El amigo de la muerte*, 1984 (by Pedro Antonio de Alarcón)

TRANSLATIONS: *Orlando*, 1937 (of Virginia Woolf's novel); *La metamórfosis*, 1938 (of Franz Kafka's novel *Die Verwandlung*); *Un bárbaro en Asia*, 1941 (of Henri Michaux's travel notes); *Bartleby, el escribiente*, 1943 (of Herman Melville's novella *Bartleby the Scrivener*); *Los mejores cuentos policiales*, 1943 (with Bioy Casares; of detective stories by various authors); *Los mejores cuentos policiales, segunda serie*, 1951 (with Bioy Casares; of detective stories by various authors); *Cuentos breves y extraordinarios*, 1955, 1973 (with Bioy Casares; of short stories by various authors; *Extraordinary Tales*, 1973); *Las palmeras salvajes*, 1956 (of William

Faulkner's novel *The Wild Palms*); *Hojas de hierba*, 1969 (of Walt Whitman's *Leaves of Grass*)

MISCELLANEOUS: *Obras completas*, 1953-1967 (10 volumes); *Antología personal*, 1961 (*A Personal Anthology*, 1967); *Labyrinths: Selected Stories, and Other Writings*, 1962, 1964; *Nueva antología personal*, 1968; *Selected Poems, 1923-1967*, 1972 (also includes prose); *Adrogue*, 1977; *Obras completas en colaboración*, 1979 (with others); *Borges: A Reader*, 1981; *Atlas*, 1984 (with María Kodama; English translation, 1985)

BIBLIOGRAPHY

Aizenberg, Edna, ed. *Borges and His Successors*. Columbia: University of Missouri Press, 1990. Collection of essays by various critics on Borges's relationship to such writers as Italo Calvino and Umberto Eco, his influence on such writers as Peter Carey and Salvador Elizondo, and his similarity to such thinkers as Michel Foucault, Paul de Man, and Jacques Derrida.

Bell-Villada, Gene H. *Borges and His Fiction: A Guide to His Mind and Art*. Chapel Hill: University of North Carolina Press, 1981. An excellent introduction to Borges and his works for North American readers. Provides detailed commentary concerning Borges's background, his many stories, and his career, all the while downplaying the Argentine writer's role as a philosopher and intellectual and emphasizing his role as a storyteller. A superb study.

Frisch, Mark F. *You Might Be Able to Get There from Here: Reconsidering Borges and the Postmodern*. Madison, N.J.: Fairleigh Dickinson University Press, 2004. Careful study of the meaning of the term "postmodernism" in relation to Borges and his fiction, offering a variety of perspectives on the intersections of postmodernism with Borges and with other cultural elements. Bibliographic references and index.

Irwin, John T. *The Mystery to a Solution: Poe, Borges, and the Analytic Detective Story*. Baltimore: Johns Hopkins University Press, 1994. Reads Borges as an intentional imitator and reinventor of Edgar Allan Poe's style of detective fiction, detailing the

transformations though which Borges put the form.

Kefala, Eleni. *Peripheral (Post) Modernity: The Syncretist Aesthetics of Borges, Piglia, Kalokyris and Kyriakidis*. New York: P. Lang, 2007. Argues that Borges engages in postmodern syncretism, that is, that he mixes aesthetic elements that are normally mutually exclusive in order to question the conventions of the genres—such as detective fiction—within which he chooses to work. Bibliographic references and index.

Nunez-Faraco, Humberto. "In Search of *The Aleph*: Memory, Truth, and Falsehood in Borges's Poetics." *The Modern Language Review* 92 (July, 1997): 613-629. Discusses autobiographical allusions, literary references to Dante, and cultural reality in the story "El Aleph." Argues that Borges's story uses cunning and deception to bring about its psychological and intellectual effect.

Sabajanes, Beatriz Sarlo. *Jorge Luis Borges: A Writer on the Edge*. New York: Verso, 1993. A good introduction to Borges. Includes bibliographical references and an index.

Stabb, Martin S. *Borges Revisited*. Boston: Twayne, 1991. A follow-up to Stabb's *Jorge Luis Borges*, published in 1970. Emphasis is on Borges's post-1970 writings, how the "canonical" (to use Stabb's term) Borges compares to the later Borges, and "a fresh assessment of the Argentine master's position as a major Western literary presence." An excellent study, particularly used in tandem with Stabb's earlier book on Borges.

_____. *Jorge Luis Borges*. New York: Twayne, 1970. An excellent study of Borges intended by its author "to introduce the work of this fascinating and complex writer to North American readers." Includes an opening chapter on Borges's life and career, followed by chapters on the Argentine writer's work in the genres of poetry, essay, and fiction, as well as a concluding chapter entitled "Borges and the Critics."

Williamson, Edwin. *Borges: A Life*. New York: Viking, 2004. Drawing on interviews and extensive research, the most comprehensive and well-reviewed Borges biography.

ANTHONY BOUCHER
William Anthony Parker White

Born: Oakland, California; August 21, 1911
Died: Berkeley, California; April 29, 1968
Also wrote as Theo Durrant; H. H. Holmes;
  Herman Muddgett
Types of plot: Amateur sleuth; private investigator;
  police procedural

PRINCIPAL SERIES
  Fergus O'Breen, 1939-1942
  Sister Ursula, 1940-1942

PRINCIPAL SERIES CHARACTERS
FERGUS O'BREEN is a private investigator, around thirty, with red hair and a fondness for yellow sweaters. He has a sharp, analytical mind and is attracted to young, not-too-bright women. He is a heavy smoker and a recreational drinker.

LIEUTENANT A. JACKSON is with the homicide division of the Los Angeles Police Department (LAPD). He is around thirty, tall, handsome, single, and intelligent, but he always has the help of an amateur sleuth in solving his murder cases.

LIEUTENANT TERENCE MARSHALL is also with the homicide division of the LAPD. Tall, handsome, and happily married, he is a closet intellectual. He can be seen as a married version of Lieutenant Jackson in the Fergus O'Breen series.

SISTER URSULA is of the order of the Sisters of Martha of Bethany. Of indeterminate age, she is compassionate, devout, an amateur sleuth par excellence, and instrumental in the solution of Marshall's cases.

CONTRIBUTION
Anthony Boucher entered the field of mystery and detective fiction in 1937, just as the Golden Age of that genre was drawing to a close. The five novels he published under the Boucher pseudonym and two others under the name H. H. Holmes were typical of one branch of the field at the time: intellectually frothy entertainments offering several hours of pleasant diversion. Boucher's plots were clever murder puzzles that could be solved by a moderately intelligent reader from the abundant clues scattered generously throughout the narrative. The murders were antiseptic affairs usually solved in the end by an engaging deductionist. The characters (or suspects) were often intriguing but always only superficially developed. The settings were potentially interesting but somehow unconvincing. Boucher was, however, one of the first writers to bring a high degree of erudition and literary craftsmanship to the field of popular mystery and detective fiction.

Boucher was much more important to the field as a critic and as an editor than as a writer. As a mystery and detective critic with columns in the *San Francisco Chronicle*, *The New York Times Book Review*, *Ellery Queen's Mystery Magazine*, and the *New York Herald Tribune Book Review*, Boucher showed that he could recognize talented writers and important trends in the field. As an editor, he had a penchant for extracting the best from the contributors to the journals and anthologies that he oversaw.

Boucher's greatest contributions to the mystery and detective field, however, did not come through his novels or short stories. After a successful but exhausting stint as a plot developer for radio scripts for shows featuring Sherlock Holmes and Gregory Hood, Boucher began editing and writing book reviews in the fields of both science fiction and mystery and detective fiction. As an editor, he excelled, creating *The Magazine of Fantasy and Science Fiction* and turning it into one of the first literate journals in that field. He brought the same skills to *True Crime Detective*, which he edited from 1952 to 1953. He encouraged many young talents in both the genres of science fiction and mystery and detective fiction, including Richard Matheson, Gore Vidal, and Philip José Farmer.

The Mystery Writers of America recognized Boucher three times as the top critic of mystery and detective crime fiction. As a critic and an editor, he was gentle, humorous, and always compassionate, and he was usually able to provoke the best efforts of those whose work he assessed. In no small way, he contributed through his criticism and editing to the emergence in the 1950's of a real literature of mystery and detective fiction.

BIOGRAPHY

Anthony Boucher was born William Anthony Parker White on August 21, 1911, in Oakland, California. He was the only child of James Taylor White and Mary Ellen (née Parker) White, both physicians and both descended from pioneers of the California/Oregon region. His maternal grandfather was a lawyer and a superior court judge, and his paternal grandfather was a captain in the United States Navy. Despite being an invalid during most of his teenage years, Boucher was graduated from Pasadena High School in 1928 and from Pasadena Junior College in 1930. From 1930 to 1932, he attended the University of Southern California (USC), majoring in German. He spent most of his time outside classes at USC in acting, writing, and directing for little theater. Boucher was graduated from USC in 1932 with a bachelor of arts and an undergraduate record sufficient for election to Phi Beta Kappa and the offer of a graduate scholarship from the University of California at Berkeley. He received his master of arts degree from that institution in 1934 on acceptance of his thesis, "The Duality of Impressionism in Recent German Drama."

The academic life apparently having lost its appeal for Boucher after he received the master of arts degree (he had planned to be a teacher of languages), he embarked on an unsuccessful career as a playwright. When his plays failed to sell, he tried his hand at mystery writing and sold his first novel to Simon and Schuster in 1936 (it was published the following year). He adopted the pseudonym "Boucher" (rhymes with "voucher") to keep his crime-fiction career separate from his still-hoped-for career as a playwright. During the next six years, Simon and Schuster published four more of Boucher's murder mysteries. During the same period, Duell, Sloan and Pearce published two of his novels under the pen name of H. H. Holmes.

During this phase of his career, Boucher married Phyllis Mary Price, a librarian, in 1928. They had two children, Lawrence Taylor White and James Marsden White. By 1942, Boucher's interests had shifted from the writing of mystery fiction to editing and science fiction. During the remainder of his career, Boucher edited several periodicals in both the mystery and science-fiction fields, including *True Crime Detective* (1952-1953) and *The Magazine of Fantasy and Science Fiction* (1949-1958). He also edited many anthologies in both fields, wrote radio scripts for mystery shows, and had several book review columns. His reviews of mystery and detective books won for him the Mystery Writers of America's Edgar Allan Poe Award for best mystery criticism in 1946, 1950, and 1953. Boucher died in his home in Berkeley, California, on April 29, 1968.

ANALYSIS

Anthony Boucher began writing mystery and detective fiction as a way to support himself while he pursued a never-realized career as a playwright. All five novels published under the Boucher pseudonym and those published as H. H. Holmes between 1937 and 1942 are well-constructed murder-detection puzzles featuring a deductionist hero or heroine and often a locked-room theme. The characters in his novels are not well developed, are almost exclusively Caucasian with bourgeois attitudes and goals, and are always secondary to the puzzle and its solution. Only rarely do the novels mention the social and political issues of the period during which they were written, and they offer no particular insights into the several potentially interesting subcultures in which they are set. In short, the Boucher-Holmes novels are examples of much of the Golden Age mystery and detective literature, in which the crime and its solution through logical deduction are paramount.

Taken collectively, the Boucher-Holmes novels are the epitome of one branch of Golden Age mystery and detective fiction. They are amusing escapist works of no particular literary merit. Boucher, an only child from a comfortable middle-class background, did not have the worldly experience of a Dashiell Hammett. Thus, his characters were portrayed in a narrow world in which ugliness, if it existed at all, derived from character flaws, not from social realities. He did not possess the poetic insight into the human condition of a Ross Macdonald or a Raymond Chandler, so his characters lack depth, and the situations that he created for them are generally unconvincing.

Boucher was much more successful in his short stories, in which characterization is less important than in novels. Nick Noble, an alcoholic ex-cop who was featured in "Black Murder," "Crime Must Have a Stop," and "The Girl Who Married a Monster," is a much more engaging character than any of those appearing in Boucher's longer works. Fergus O'Breen and Sister Ursula are also more believable when they appear in short stories. *Ellery Queen's Mystery Magazine, Playboy*, and *Esquire* are only a few of the many journals that published Boucher's short stories.

THE CASE OF THE SEVEN OF CALVARY

In many ways Boucher's first novel set the pattern for those that followed. Set on the Berkeley campus of the University of California, *The Case of the Seven of Calvary* (1937) introduces several promising characters whose personalities prove to be disappointingly bland. The novel demonstrates Boucher's acquaintance with literature in four languages, with ancient heresies combated by the Roman Catholic Church, and his intimate knowledge of several forms of tobacco usage. Virtually nothing comes through, however, concerning academic life at Berkeley in the 1930's or the mechanics of the little-theater movement, in which most of the characters in the novel are involved and with which the author had considerable experience. Still, the novel is well plotted, the deductionist (a professor of Sanskrit) sufficiently Sherlockian, and the clues abundant enough to make the puzzle enjoyable.

THE CASE OF THE BAKER STREET IRREGULARS

Boucher was heavily influenced by Arthur Conan Doyle and fascinated by Sherlock Holmes, as demonstrated in all of his novels, but particularly in the third, *The Case of the Baker Street Irregulars* (1940). Again, Boucher introduces a cast of initially fascinating but ultimately flaccid characters, most of them members of an informal Holmes fan club (a real organization of which Boucher was a member). Again the plot is clever, this time revolving around various Doyle accounts of the adventures of the sage of Baker Street.

The hoped-for insights into the subculture in which the novel is set—in this case, the film industry in Hollywood—are again absent. Boucher does have his characters make several innocuous political observations, vaguely New Dealish and more or less antifascist, but one of the primary characters, a Nazi spy, comes off as a misguided idealist and a basically nice fellow. The deductionist in the novel is an Los Angeles Police Department (LAPD) homicide lieutenant who appears in several of Boucher's novels, A. Jackson (his first name is never given).

THE CASE OF THE SOLID KEY

In his other appearances in Boucher's novels (*The Case of the Crumpled Knave*, 1939; *The Case of the Solid Key*, 1941; and *The Case of the Seven Sneezes*, 1942), Jackson has considerable help in solving his cases from Fergus O'Breen, a redheaded, yellow-sweater-wearing private detective. Despite the sweater and the hair, O'Breen is surely one of the most colorless private eyes in all of mystery fiction, his blandness exceeded only by that of A. Jackson. In *The Case of the Solid Key*, considered by his fans to be Boucher's best, O'Breen and Jackson deduce the perpetrator of an ingenious locked-room murder from among some potentially exciting but typically undeveloped characters, including a Charles Lindbergh-like idealist and a voluptuous film star (Rita La Marr, no less) who remains incognito during most of the novel. Once again, Boucher sets the action of the novel against a backdrop of the little-theater movement, the actual workings of which are largely unexplored in the novel. *The Case of the Solid Key* also includes some unconvincing dialogue concerning politics and social issues, with Boucher's own New Deal convictions emerging victorious over the selfish, big-business attitudes of a spoiled rich girl who always gets her comeuppance (a stereotype that appears in several of Boucher's stories).

ROCKET TO THE MORGUE

Boucher created a potentially more engaging but characteristically incomplete deductionist, Sister Ursula, in two novels published under the pseudonym H. H. Holmes. Sister Ursula, a nun of the order of the Sisters of Martha of Bethany, helps Lieutenant Terence Marshall of the LAPD homicide division solve murders in *Nine Times Nine* (1940) and *Rocket to the Morgue* (1942). The characters in the latter novel are drawn in part from the science-fiction writers' community in the Los Angeles of the early 1940's and are thinly disguised fictionalizations of such science-fiction luminaries as John W. Campbell, Robert Heinlein, and L. Ron Hubbard. The plot revolves around another locked room and is amusingly complicated and pleasantly diverting. The novel contains the obligatory spoiled rich girl, several conversations mildly critical of the socioeconomic status quo, and several comments mildly lamenting the imminent outbreak of war.

Paul Madden

Updated by Fiona Kelleghan

PRINCIPAL MYSTERY AND DETECTIVE FICTION

FERGUS O'BREEN SERIES: *The Case of the Seven of Calvary*, 1937; *The Case of the Crumpled Knave*, 1939; *The Case of the Baker Street Irregulars*, 1940 (also known as *Blood on Baker Street*); *The Case of the Solid Key*, 1941; *The Case of the Seven Sneezes*, 1942

SISTER URSULA SERIES (AS HOLMES): *Nine Times Nine*, 1940; *Rocket to the Morgue*, 1942

NONSERIES NOVEL (AS DURRANT, WITH OTHERS): *The Marble Forest*, 1951 (also known as *The Big Fear*)

OTHER SHORT FICTION: *Exeunt Murderers: The Best Mystery Stories of Anthony Boucher*, 1983

OTHER MAJOR WORKS

SHORT FICTION: *Far and Away: Eleven Fantasy and Science-Fiction Stories*, 1955; *The Compleat Werewolf, and Other Tales of Fantasy and Science Fiction*, 1969; *The Compleat Boucher: The Complete Short Science Fiction and Fantasy of Anthony Boucher*, 1999

NONFICTION: *Ellery Queen: A Double Profile*, 1951; *Multiplying Villainies: Selected Mystery Criticism, 1942-1968*, 1973; *Sincerely, Tony/Faithfully, Vincent: The Correspondence of Anthony Boucher and Vincent Starrett*, 1975 (with Vincent Starrett)

EDITED TEXTS: *The Pocket Book of True Crime Stories*, 1943; *Great American Detective Stories*, 1945; *Four and Twenty Bloodhounds: Short Stories*

Plus Biographies of Fictional Detectives—Amateur and Professional, Public and Private—Created by Members of Mystery Writers of America, 1950; *The Best from Fantasy and Science Fiction*, 1952-1959; *A Treasury of Great Science Fiction*, 1959; *Best Detective Stories of the Year: Sixteenth Annual Collection*, 1961; *The Quality of Murder: Three Hundred Years of True Crime*, 1962 (compiled by members of the Mystery Writers of America); *The Quintessence of Queen: Best Prize Stories from Twelve Years of Ellery Queen's Mystery Magazine*, 1962 (also known as *A Magnum of Mysteries*); *Best Detective Stories of the Year*, 1963-1965

BIBLIOGRAPHY

Nevins, Francis M., Jr. "Introduction: The World of Anthony Boucher." In *Exeunt Murderers: The Best Mystery Stories of Anthony Boucher*, edited by Francis M. Nevins, Jr., and Martin H. Greenberg. Carbondale: Southern Illinois University Press, 1983. Discusses the rules and conventions unique to Boucher's fiction and the character types that inhabit it.

Roth, Marty. *Foul and Fair Play: Reading Genre in Classic Detective Fiction*. Athens: University of Georgia Press, 1995. A post-structural analysis of the conventions of mystery and detective fiction. Examines 138 short stories and works from the 1840's to the 1960's. Provides perspective to Boucher's work.

Sallis, James. "The Compleat Boucher." *Fantasy and Science Fiction* (April, 2000): 36-41. Review of a 1999 collection of Boucher's complete science-fiction and fantasy works, appraising the author's career and the importance of the collection.

Spencer, David G. "The Case of the Man Who Could Do Everything." *Rhodomagnetic Digest* 2 (September, 1950): 7-10. An examination of the works of Boucher that focuses on his Fergus O'Breen series.

White, Phyllis, and Lawrence White. *Boucher: A Family Portrait*. Berkeley, Calif.: Berkeley Historical Society, 1985. Biographical study of Boucher and his family, revealing the influences of his upbringing on his work.

EDGAR BOX
Gore Vidal

Born: West Point, New York; October 3, 1925
Also wrote as Gore Vidal
Type of plot: Amateur sleuth

PRINCIPAL SERIES

Peter Cutler Sargeant II, 1952-1954

PRINCIPAL SERIES CHARACTER

PETER CUTLER SARGEANT II, a public relations agent and amateur sleuth. A young Harvard graduate with a background in journalism, he is a tough, unsentimental professional who gets involved in solving murder cases only when his curiosity is piqued and his own safety is at stake.

CONTRIBUTION

Gore Vidal is a historical and social novelist. His three detective novels, *Death in the Fifth Position* (1952), *Death Before Bedtime* (1953), and *Death Likes It Hot* (1954), published under the pseudonym Edgar Box, were written early in his career and are not considered to be among his best work. Nevertheless, all three detective novels demonstrate his skill at social criticism and solid command of the murder mystery genre. Although not exactly a classic example of the hard-boiled detective, Peter Cutler Sargeant II is an objective, shrewd observer of humanity. Like other rationalistic detectives, he pays close attention not only to material evidence but also to human motivations. He likes to proceed by a process of elimination, examining the most obvious suspects before realizing that the case is far more complex than he had initially imagined. As is so often true in murder mysteries, Sargeant has a mind that is much more supple than that of the police officers and other fatuous characters who try to outwit him in his cases.

BIOGRAPHY

Gore Vidal (Edgar Box) was born Eugene Luther Vidal to Eugene Vidal and Nina Gore Vidal on October 3, 1925, at the United States Military Academy in West Point, New York. Shortly thereafter, his family moved to Washington, D.C.—the setting of much of Vidal's fiction—and lived with his maternal grandfather, Senator Thomas Pryor Gore of Oklahoma. Vidal's parents were divorced when he was ten. His mother married Hugh D. Auchincloss, and Vidal lived at the Auchincloss estate in Virginia while attending St. Alban's School in Washington.

By the time Vidal was graduated from Phillips Exeter Academy in 1940, he had toured England and the United States and renamed himself Gore Vidal. He joined the army in 1943, studied engineering at the Virginia Military Institute for one term, and was appointed to the rank of maritime warrant officer on October 24, 1944. *Williwaw*, his novel about his war experiences, was published in 1946.

After the war, Vidal traveled widely in Europe,

Gore Vidal in 1948. (Library of Congress/ Carl Van Vechten Collection)

Central America, and the United States, making his living writing and lecturing. After completing his modestly successful detective series in 1954 as Edgar Box, he abandoned that name and became a highly successful television writer for two years, authoring such scripts as *Barn Burning* (televised August 17, 1954) and *The Turn of the Screw* (televised February 13, 1955). By 1956, he was also writing film scripts for Metro-Goldwyn-Mayer. His stage play, *Visit to a Small Planet: A Comedy Akin to a Vaudeville*, published in 1956, ran for 338 performances on Broadway in 1957. Even more successful was his play *The Best Man: A Play About Politics*, which ran for 520 performances in 1960.

A political commentator, drama critic for *The Reporter*, candidate for Congress (in 1960) and for the Senate (in 1982), Vidal has been a prolific writer and a provocative public personality. His best-known and most highly acclaimed novels are *Julian* (1964), *Myra Breckinridge* (1968), *Burr* (1973), and *Lincoln* (1984). He has achieved even greater reputation as an essayist. His principal collection of nonfictional prose is *Homage to Daniel Shays: Collected Essays, 1952-1972* (1972).

ANALYSIS

Gore Vidal has admitted that he did not set out to write mystery novels to make a new contribution to the genre. He was a professional writer in need of an income. Just as he later turned to television and film writing for money, so detective novels represented an opportunity for him to support himself. Because he is an accomplished writer, however, Vidal's three mystery novels as Edgar Box are not negligible achievements. They are distinguished by a strong sense of plot and a complicated array of interesting suspects. When he knows the milieu of his characters particularly well—as in the Long Island setting of *Death Likes It Hot*—he achieves a fascinating blend of social criticism and detection.

There are certain aspects of Vidal's detective, Peter Cutler Sargeant II, that must be tolerated if his investigations are to be appreciated. Sargeant is a well-built male with a considerable appetite for young women. Although his romances figure significantly in all three

novels, they are treated in a somewhat perfunctory fashion—as though Vidal feels obligated to give Sargeant a love interest but cannot summon much enthusiasm for the task. By modern standards, Sargeant would be considered something of a sexist—although his male chauvinism is not much different from the superior attitude he takes toward most human beings, who seem to him fatuous, manipulative, and sometimes downright silly. To a certain extent, he simply shares the characteristics of many fictional detectives, whose line of work encourages suspicion of motivations and professions of sincerity.

In none of the three novels is Sargeant hired as a detective. On the contrary, he is engaged by the head of a ballet company, a politician running for president, and an ambitious society matron to handle their public relations. It is only after a murder is committed that his curiosity is aroused. Usually, his employer enlists his aid in getting out of a jam occasioned by a murder and all the bad publicity such a crime entails. Even then, Sargeant reluctantly seeks out the murderer only after his own life is endangered. This would seem to be an effective novelistic stratagem because it enables Sargeant to remain objective (he has not been looking for work as a detective) but involved (he may be the next victim). The problem is that Vidal uses the same stratagem in each novel, so that as a series, his novels fail to sustain themselves; they seem too gimmicky. It is too much to suppose that a public relations man would become involved in so many murder cases.

Like many fictional detectives, Sargeant often discovers the identity of the murderer before he has evidence to present to the police. It is the chain of circumstances that he analyzes, the relationships he has had with the suspects, the stories they have told him, and some word or occurrence that suddenly provides the spark for his intuitive solution to a case. This reading of human nature, of clues that do not really exist except in the mind of the intellectually superior detective, distinguishes Sargeant from the plodding, unimaginative police detectives who are his adversaries.

Vidal is successful in creating empathy for Sargeant by having his detective freely admit his ignorance. Sargeant makes many mistakes. Often he takes leaps in the dark, asserting that he has information when he has none at all. A considerable amount of bluff goes into Sargeant's interrogation of suspects. What finally makes him successful, however, is his willingness to wrestle with his own lack of evidence.

DEATH IN THE FIFTH POSITION

A typical example of Sargeant's self-questioning can be found in *Death in the Fifth Position*. A ballerina has fallen to her death during a performance. Someone has cut the cord that suspended her high above the stage. At first, her drug addict husband is suspected. Then he dies in his apartment—perhaps as a suicide but possibly as a victim of the real murderer. Sargeant has to recalculate a list of suspects. He sits worriedly at his employer's desk for "several minutes." Then "idly, with a pencil stub," he writes the names of everyone in the company who could have committed the crime. He puts the name of his girlfriend, Jane, a dancer in the company who has received better roles since the death of the ballerina, at the bottom of the list and draws a box around it, as if to protect her. On the next page he writes "Why?" and "How?" Then he answers a series of questions about motive with what he knows about each of the suspects. He is able to cross his girlfriend off the list because she was not next in line to succeed the dead ballerina. The only lingering doubt about her is whether she might have had some other private motive—there has been talk that the dead ballerina was in love with Jane.

Thus, Sargeant moves slowly, almost excluding suspects but never entirely ruling anyone out, so that the mystery deepens. Eventually, the possible murderers are eliminated and Sargeant fastens onto the most probable guilty party. He ultimately solves his case by creating a situation in which he knows enough to trap the criminal into a confession or into behavior that reveals his or her guilt. In *Death in the Fifth Position*, his working out of the solution on paper is like the blocking out of a play; that is, Sargeant is a superb director of his actors, but he cannot completely envision the perpetrator of the murder until he gets the characters to move in certain directions.

Death in the Fifth Position is actually the weakest of the three novels, for Vidal's command of the milieu of a dance company seems weak. It is not unusual to stock a detective novel with stereotypical characters, but *Death in the Fifth Position* seems particularly unimaginative in this respect. The Russian ballerina, Eglanova, for example, speaks in exactly the kind of bad Russian accent found in Hollywood B films, and Louis, the aggressively gay dancer who pursues Sargeant, is such a caricature that his behavior is not so much humorous as it is tiresome.

DEATH BEFORE BEDTIME

Vidal is on sounder ground with *Death Before Bedtime*, which is set in the political atmosphere of Washington, D.C. This is familiar territory for a novelist who creates interesting, devious characters: a political wife who might be hardened and cynical enough to have murdered her unfaithful husband, a senator aspiring to the presidency; the senator's promiscuous daughter, whose careless love life is somehow connected to his death; the senator's devious assistant, who is intimately tied to shady business dealings that may have led him to murder his boss; and a prominent businessman from the senator's home state who is rumored to have faced ruin when he failed to get the politician's support for an important government contract. The intricate cast of suspects and colorful personalities makes *Death Before Bedtime* a stimulating novel of mystery, intrigue, romance, and politics.

DEATH LIKES IT HOT

Even better and by far the most amusing novel in the series is *Death Likes It Hot*, set during a summer on Long Island at the mansion of an ambitious society matron, Mrs. Veering, who has hired Sargeant to manage publicity for a huge party she has planned for the fall. Here Sargeant's personality and his feel for society are wonderfully congruent. Although he is in the business of inflating people's reputations, Sargeant loves to poke holes in their pretensions, as in his description of the Ladyrock Yacht Club on Easthampton:

> Members of the Club are well-to-do (but not wealthy), socially accepted (but not quite "prominent"), of good middle-class American stock (proud of their ancient lineage that goes back usually to some eighteenth century farmer).

It is almost possible to imagine Sargeant making these parenthetical remarks out of the side of his mouth. Vidal's economical style—putting in a few sentences what this society thinks of itself, the words it uses for itself, and how little there is to justify its claims—is at its best in this novel.

One of the finest characters in the Sargeant series is Brexton, a well-known but enigmatic artist suspected of arranging his wealthy wife's drowning. His behavior is not at all predictable, and his character is not summarized in the clichés that mar Vidal's other mysteries. Perhaps this is the reason that Sargeant finds him such a sympathetic character. Brexton is shrewd and knows even better than Sargeant that people should not be taken at their word. A sample of the dialogue between these two characters—at a point when Mrs. Veering (also a suspect) has had what purports to be a heart attack—reveals the shrewd, understated interplay between detective and suspect. Notice how Brexton answers Sargeant's questions by saying as little as possible:

"Has Mrs. Veering had heart attacks before? Like this?"

"Yes. This is the third one I know of. She just turns blue and they give her some medicine; then she's perfectly all right in a matter of minutes."

"Minutes? But she seemed really knocked out. The doctor said she'll have to stay in bed a day or two."

Brexton smiled. "Greaves *said* the doctor said she'd have to stay in bed."

This sank in, bit by bit. "Then she . . . well, she's all right now?"

"I shouldn't be surprised."

The reason dialogue like this is especially effective is that it shows Sargeant learning his job, taking his cues from a very sophisticated but guarded informant. Brexton will not make Sargeant's job easy for him, but he is perfectly willing to prevent him from being misled.

Death Likes It Hot was about as far as Vidal could take his Sargeant series. With this last novel, he was able to rectify some of the series' faults by putting his detective in an environment that could be much more carefully described and was more functional in terms of a mystery story plot. In other words, as Sargeant becomes knowledgeable about this particular society, he is better able to detect the murderer. This is not really

the case in the other two novels. Almost nothing significant is learned about the ballet world in *Death in the Fifth Position*, and the world of politics figures importantly only in the first part of *Death Before Bedtime*, which really turns on the demented personality of one of the characters. It is difficult to see how Vidal could have continued the series without making it ridiculous. How could Sargeant have continued to become involved in murder cases without becoming a professional detective? If Vidal had turned him into a professional detective, Sargeant's distinctive qualities—his aloofness from matters of crime until his personal safety is at stake, his reluctance to solve a murder case until circumstances force him to act—would have been destroyed. *Death Likes It Hot* fulfills the modest strengths of the Sargeant series; Vidal was wise not to continue writing in the mystery genre after this triumph.

Carl Rollyson

PRINCIPAL MYSTERY AND DETECTIVE FICTION

PETER CUTLER SARGEANT II SERIES: *Death in the Fifth Position*, 1952; *Death Before Bedtime*, 1953; *Death Likes It Hot*, 1954

OTHER MAJOR WORKS

NOVELS (AS VIDAL): 1946-1950 • *Williwaw*, 1946; *In a Yellow Wood*, 1947; *The City and the Pillar*, 1948 (revised 1965); *The Season of Comfort*, 1949; *A Search for the King: A Twelfth Century Legend*, 1950; *Dark Green, Bright Red*, 1950

1951-1970 • *The Judgment of Paris*, 1952 (revised 1965); *Messiah*, 1954 (revised 1965); *Julian*, 1964; *Washington, D.C.*, 1967; *Myra Breckinridge*, 1968; *Two Sisters: A Memoir in the Form of a Novel*, 1970

1971-2000 • *Burr*, 1973; *Myron*, 1974; *1876*, 1976; *Kalki*, 1978; *Creation*, 1981; *Duluth*, 1983; *Lincoln*, 1984; *Empire*, 1987; *Hollywood: A Novel of America in the 1920's*, 1990; *Live from Golgotha*, 1992; *The Smithsonian Institution*, 1998; *The Golden Age*, 2000

SHORT FICTION (AS VIDAL): *A Thirsty Evil: Seven Short Stories*, 1956; *Clouds and Eclipses: The Collected Short Stories*, 2006

PLAYS (AS VIDAL): *Visit to a Small Planet: A*

Comedy Akin to a Vaudeville, pb., 1956; pr. 1957; *The Best Man: A Play About Politics*, pr., pb. 1960; *Romulus: A New Comedy*, pr., pb. 1962; *An Evening with Richard Nixon*, pr. 1972

SCREENPLAYS (AS VIDAL): *The Catered Affair*, 1956; *Suddenly, Last Summer*, 1959 (with Tennessee Williams); *The Best Man*, 1964 (adaptation of his play); *Last of the Mobile Hot-Shots*, 1969; *Caligula*, 1977

TELEPLAYS (AS VIDAL): *Visit to a Small Planet, and Other Television Plays*, 1956; *Dress Gray*, 1986

NONFICTION (AS VIDAL): *Rocking the Boat*, 1962; *Reflections upon a Sinking Ship*, 1969; *Homage to Daniel Shays: Collected Essays, 1952-1972*, 1972; *Matters of Fact and of Fiction: Essays, 1973-1976*, 1977; *The Second American Revolution, and Other Essays, 1976-1982*, 1982; *At Home: Essays, 1982-1988*, 1988; *Screening History*, 1992; *The Decline and Fall of the American Empire*, 1992; *United States: Essays, 1952-1992*, 1993; *Palimpsest: A Memoir*, 1995; *Virgin Islands, A Dependency of United States: Essays, 1992-1997*, 1997; *Gore Vidal, Sexually Speaking: Collected Sex Writings*, 1999; *The Last Empire: Essays, 1992-2000*, 2000; *Dreaming War: Blood for Oil and the Cheney-Bush Junta*, 2002; *Perpetual War for Perpetual Peace: How We Got to Be So Hated*, 2002; *Imperial America*, 2004; *Point to Point Navigation: A Memoir, 1964-2006*, 2006

MISCELLANEOUS (AS VIDAL): *The Essential Gore Vidal*, 1999 (Fred Kaplan, editor); *Inventing a Nation: Washington, Adams, Jefferson*, 2003; *Conversations with Gore Vidal*, 2005 (Richard Peabody and Lucinda Ebersole, editors)

BIBLIOGRAPHY

Altman, Dennis. *Gore Vidal's America*. Malden, Mass.: Polity, 2005. Comprehensive look at every aspect of Vidal's life that includes a chapter on his career as a writer, including the works written as Edgar Box. Bibliographic references and indexes.

Baker, Susan, and Curtis S. Gibson. *Gore Vidal: A Critical Companion*. Westport, Conn.: Greenwood Press, 1997. A helpful book of criticism and interpretation of Vidal's work. Includes bibliographical references and index.

Dick, Bernard F. *The Apostate Angel: A Critical Study of Gore Vidal*. New York: Random House, 1974. An entertaining and perceptive study, based on interviews with Vidal and on use of his papers at the University of Wisconsin at Madison. Dick focuses on Vidal's work rather than on his biography. The book contains footnotes and a bibliography.

Harris, Stephen. *The Fiction of Gore Vidal and E. L. Doctorow: Writing the Historical Self*. New York: P. Lang, 2002. Discusses Vidal's strong identification with history as reflected in his writing.

Kaplan, Fred. *Gore Vidal: A Biography*. New York: Doubleday, 1999. A comprehensive biography of the novelist, playwright, scriptwriter, essayist, and political activist who helped shape American letters during the second half of the twentieth century.

Kiernan, Robert F. *Gore Vidal*. New York: Frederick Ungar, 1982. This study of Vidal's major writings tries to assess his place in American literature and gives astute descriptions of the Vidalian style and manner. The book, which uses Vidal's manuscript collection, contains a brief note and bibliography section.

Parini, Jay, ed. *Gore Vidal: Writer Against the Grain*. New York: Columbia University Press, 1992. Vidal's distaste for much of the academic study of modern fiction has been mirrored in a lack of academic study of his work. Jay Parini sought to redress the balance by compiling this work, which deals with both Vidal's fiction and nonfiction.

Stanton, Robert J., and Gore Vidal, eds. *Views from a Window: Conversations with Gore Vidal*. Secaucus, N.J.: Lyle Stuart, 1980. A compilation of interviews excerpted and arranged along themes. Vidal comments on his and other authors' works, on sexuality, and on politics. Vidal edited the manuscript and made corrections, with changes noted in the text.

Vidal, Gore. *Point to Point Navigation: A Memoir*. New York: Doubleday, 2006. Covers the years 1964 to 2006, detailing Vidal's experiences and his reflections on writing (his own and others'), as well as culture generally.

M. E. BRADDON
Mary Elizabeth Braddon Maxwell

Born: London, England; October 4, 1835
Died: Richmond, England; February 4, 1915
Also wrote as Aunt Belinda; Lady Caroline
    Lascelles; Babington White
Types of plot: Psychological; thriller

CONTRIBUTION

In the 1860's, crime literature was scorned by critics as the entertainment of subliterates. Only a few writers—primarily, Edgar Allan Poe, Wilkie Collins, Charles Dickens, and Edward Bulwer-Lytton—had developed the crime novel into a literary form for the middle and upper classes. To their efforts, M. E. Braddon added profoundly realistic psychological development of characters, especially female characters. She was among the first, also, to use the crime novel as a vehicle for radical social commentary, particularly concerning the condition of women and the moral corruption of the middle classes. In addition, Braddon polished the technique, made famous by Wilkie Collins in *The Woman in White* (1860), of allowing a step-by-step revelation of a case, so that the reader learns of evidence along with the detective. Her wit, too, was unusual in her age. Braddon's novels are also noteworthy for the camera-like accuracy with which she depicted an astonishing variety of settings; to the horror of her contemporary critics, she could describe the drinking and gambling places of men as vividly as the claustrophobic atmosphere of a rural village or the glittering decorations of a wealthy woman's private rooms.

BIOGRAPHY

Mary Elizabeth Braddon was the daughter of Henry Braddon, a solicitor, and his Irish wife, Fanny White Braddon. Henry Braddon was financially irresponsible and an unfaithful husband. He was separated from his wife while Mary Elizabeth Braddon was still a child. A sister, Margaret, eleven years older than Mary, married an Italian and settled in Naples. A brother, Edward, six years older, moved to India and

then to Tasmania, eventually becoming prime minister there.

Mary Elizabeth Braddon was educated by her mother, who encouraged her reading and writing, except when finances allowed a governess or a school. At the age of nineteen, Braddon determined to support them both by going on the stage, in defiance of all that was then considered proper. Despite protests from relatives, she acted for several years under the name Mary Seyton.

In 1860, Braddon met the Irish publisher John Maxwell. They lived together. Marriage was impossible because Maxwell was already married; his wife was in a Dublin mental asylum. Maxwell and Braddon were to have six children, five of whom survived childhood, before they could marry in 1874, on the death of his wife. The scandal was considerable. Despite this, Braddon made a home for Maxwell's five children, their own children, and her mother. The warmth of that home is described by a son, William B. Maxwell, in *Time Gathered* (1938).

Braddon's prolific career began in earnest as an attempt to support Maxwell's publishing ventures. *Lady Audley's Secret* (1862) brought her immediate fame, and she became permanently typed as a sensation novelist (although she tended to turn away from crime in many of her later works). By the late 1860's, Maxwell and Braddon were financially established. They eventually owned much property and traveled on the Continent; they moved in a circle that included distinguished figures from the worlds of theater, art, literature, politics, and even society, despite their scandals. Braddon continued writing until her death, her last novel, *Mary*, being posthumously published in 1916.

ANALYSIS

Sensation novels were a scandal of the 1860's. The term, poorly defined then, as now, was used to condemn fiction by such writers as Nathaniel Hawthorne, Charles Dickens, Wilkie Collins, and Charles Reade, as well as that by M. E. Braddon and many lesser figures. Condemnation focused on the novelists' preoccupation with crimes, mostly murder, arson, and bigamy. Much of the criticism was thinly concealed class snobbery: Sensation novels spread the values of the working class, not of the governing classes. They were not genteel. In these novels, crime was not confined to the poor. In the stately homes of England, the novels suggested, there was considerable crime, but these criminals, unlike the poor, were often protected by their wealth and power. Then, too, sensation novelists often presented psychologically motivated, even sympathetic, people as criminals; their criminals were not stereotypical representatives of evil that had been found in the earlier gothic, romantic, and Newgate fiction from which these novels sprang. Also, critics perceptively observed, and objected to, female characters who successfully defied Victorian proprieties and challenged masculine authority.

By these criteria, Braddon was the most sensational of them all, and her reputation, too, was tainted by the scandals of her personal life. *Lady Audley's Secret* was notorious. It was also widely read. It appeared in October, 1862; by the end of that year, eight editions had been printed. Braddon knew exactly what she was doing. In *The Doctor's Wife* (1864), she created the figure of sensation novelist Sigismund Smith, who satirizes himself and his author with his methodical analysis of the number of corpses needed to satisfy public taste. Yet there is more than cold calculation in Braddon's work.

In his definitive and excellent *Sensational Victorian: The Life and Times of Mary Elizabeth Braddon* (1979), Robert Lee Wolff notes the social satire underlying Braddon's work. He observes her critiques of Victorian class structure, and he proves her to be politically radical, although not revolutionary, showing that, in her later works, she revealed her radicalism quite openly. Yet this radicalism would have been obvious from the first to sophisticated female readers of her day. In *Lady Audley's Secret*, for example, the dramatic tension does not evolve from the war of good against evil. To satisfy Victorian prudery, Braddon told that story, making sure that the forces of goodness are finally triumphant, but she fashioned the narrative in such a way that the sophisticated reader is virtually forced to identify with the forces of evil, as personified by Lady Audley. Lady Audley loses, but dramatic tension arises because the reader hopes that she will not. Similarly, in *Aurora Floyd* (1863), the reader is made to sympathize with a bigamist who foreshadows that in Thomas Hardy's *Tess of the D'Urbervilles* (1891): Both authors insist that their criminal heroines are actually pure women. In *The Captain of the Vulture* (1862), there are two heroines, both bigamists. *Birds of Prey* (1867) and *Charlotte's Inheritance* (1868) function a bit differently; both are direct attacks on the morality of the middle class. In these novels, too, with one exception, the strongest characters are the women.

LADY AUDLEY'S SECRET

In *Lady Audley's Secret*, the opponents are Lady Audley, the former Lucy Maldon, and her detective stepnephew, Robert Audley, who remorselessly secures the evidence that will ruin her. Robert Audley is motivated by his belief that his is the hand of God and by his somewhat erratic loyalty to one of Lady Audley's husbands, George Talboys. Much more space, however, is given to the justification of Lady Audley. Born into poverty, she is the daughter of an insane mother and an alcoholic father; her childhood is punctuated by nightmares in which her mother attempts to kill her. She knows that her beauty is her only asset, and she resolves to make a successful marriage. She believes that she has done so when she marries George Talboys, but his father disapproves, and the young couple is allowed to wallow in squalor. The girl complains; thereafter, the conventional reader is free to believe that she, as a nagging wife, deserves whatever happens to her. The worldly reader, however, will react differently when Talboys abandons his wife and infant son, leaving only a note to say that he will return when he has made his fortune. He does not communicate again in the years that follow. Lucy must support herself, her son, and her father. She does so, changing her name and taking employment as a governess. When she is courted by the wealthy Sir Michael Audley, she convinces herself that, long abandoned, she is free to marry. As Audley's wife, she is an idealized lady of the manor, joyously improving conditions on his estate and alleviating the poverty that she herself has found so painful. She makes her husband's life a paradise.

All that is ruined when Talboys reappears and doggedly locates Lucy. She pushes him down a well. Although the conventional reader will see this as a coldblooded murder, the worldlier woman will view it as somewhat justified, if a bit excessive. Robert Audley determines to catch her. She tries to kill him also but merely murders a lout who has blackmailed her. She is forced into a confession, after which she is institutionalized in a bleak Belgian madhouse in which she dies. Robert Audley now has the satisfaction of knowing that he has ruined her life and broken his uncle's heart. Pleased with his work, he ends the story in an aura of prudish self-righteousness. Conventional virtue has won, but Braddon's attitude toward that virtue is clearly one of disdain.

AURORA FLOYD

Aurora Floyd is similarly subversive. At the time, Victorian critics were outraged when Aurora strikes a servant for beating her dog, but Braddon was clearly on the side of Aurora; the servant who attacks the dog also proves capable of murder. Worse than this unmannerly behavior, however, is the fact that Aurora is a bigamist. The victim of great wealth, she has run away from school to marry her father's handsome, but worthless, groom. Believing that husband dead, she accepts a proposal from proud, aristocratic Talbot Bulstrode, but he breaks the engagement when she will not explain the mystery of her past. According to the mores of the day, Bulstrode is right; according to the author, he is quite wrong. Braddon has Bulstrode admit this when he sees Aurora prove herself an excellent wife to his friend, John Mellish.

Through repeated references, Braddon makes it clear that *Aurora Floyd* was her retelling of William Shakespeare's *Othello* (1604). Othello, she implied, was not a true hero: Mellish is. Generous and in no way authoritarian, he supports his wife regardless of her past, remarries her when her first husband has reappeared and been murdered, and stands by her, with only one lapse of faith, when Aurora is suspected of that murder; he is, in short, capable not only of trusting his wife's innocence but also of sympathetically comprehending her guilt. Consequently, Aurora and Mellish live happily at the end of the novel, as Othello and his more innocent Desdemona did not.

BIRDS OF PREY AND CHARLOTTE'S INHERITANCE

Ostensibly, *Birds of Prey* and *Charlotte's Inheritance* retell the story of William Palmer, who was tried for murder in 1856. Like Palmer, Braddon's villainous Philip Sheldon is a surgeon who murders a friend to conceal financial difficulties and who then attempts to murder female relatives (Palmer successfully, Sheldon not) for their insurance money.

Yet there are hints throughout that Braddon was also telling Dickens how he should have written "Hunted Down" and Bulwer-Lytton, whom she admired, how he should have written *Lucretia* (1846), both fictional retellings of the similarly motivated true crimes of Thomas Griffiths Wainewright. Both the Dickens and Bulwer-Lytton works are weakened by their melodramatic villains, mere stick figures exemplifying evil. In contrast, Braddon directly and uncompromisingly confronted the immorality of middle-class greed. Sheldon represents that class, and he is, in fact, associated with other such professionals—an attorney and a physician—who condone his original murder rather than risk financial ruin by reporting it. On the other hand, the four men who act as detectives in the two novels are, with one exception (a French gentleman), the underdog outcasts of this society. One is a French mountebank suggestive of the later Hercule Poirot. Another is an unsuccessful confidence man. The third is the equally unsuccessful apprentice of the confidence man, turned successful journalist. It is significant, however, that all these men are helpless to rescue Sheldon's stepdaughter, whom he is slowly poisoning. Only when the women of the novels band together, mistress and servant alike, can the girl be saved.

THE CAPTAIN OF THE VULTURE

Braddon also wrote historical crime novels, as, for example, *The Captain of the Vulture*, set in the eighteenth century. In this novel, she presents two sympathetic female bigamists. The stronger of the two is Sally Pecker, mistress of the village inn. Sally has been educated by life. Her first husband abandoned her after mistreating her, and he maliciously carried off her much-loved infant son. She has found rest in the village of the story and married the kindly innkeeper. Sally befriends Millicent Duke, the novel's young heroine, who is the victim of her wealth, her isolation in a rural village, her reading of the romantic novels favored by Victorian moralists, and her decadent father and brother. The latter marry her off to George Duke, apparently a sea captain but actually associated with pirates and slavers. He disappears, and after many years, Millicent marries the love of her girlhood. Her first husband reappears and is murdered; Millicent is arrested and tried for the crime. With Sally's help, Millicent has transcended her earlier weakness, and, in a courtroom scene that anticipates the later courtroom dramas of Erle Stanley Gardner, she denounces the true culprit. There are detectives in the story, but they are well intentioned bunglers, who succeed only in arresting Millicent. The other males are weak or they are criminal, although extenuating circumstances surround one such character. Sally Pecker's son reappears, and not surprisingly, in view of his environment, he is a criminal. Yet he is allowed a tranquil death in his mother's arms, for he is clearly one of society's victims.

These novels exemplify the techniques of Braddon's crime fiction and explain why her novels were notorious in their age. Still, while she upset the conventional, she attracted an admiring audience, which included Alfred, Lord Tennyson, William Ewart Gladstone, William Makepeace Thackeray, Charles Dickens, Edward Bulwer-Lytton, Charles Reade, Robert Louis Stevenson, George Moore, Sir James Barrie, and Henry James, among others. Their admiration was well directed. Braddon wrote prolifically and unevenly, but, at her best, she rivals any crime novelist of her age and ranks among the best of mainstream novelists.

Unfortunately, modern critics and scholars have tended to accept the verdict of scandalized Victorian moralists. From her death in 1915 to the mid-twentieth century, she was almost completely ignored. The result is that, until publication of Wolff's *Sensational Victorian*, even the facts of Braddon's life, such as her date of birth, were incorrectly stated in standard reference sources when they were given at all.

Betty Richardson

PRINCIPAL MYSTERY AND DETECTIVE FICTION

VALENTINE HAWKEHURST SERIES: *Birds of Prey*, 1867; *Charlotte's Inheritance*, 1868

DETECTIVE FAUNCE SERIES: *Rough Justice*, 1889; *His Darling Sin*, 1899

NONSERIES NOVELS: 1860-1870 • *Three Times Dead: Or, The Secret of the Heath*, 1860 (revised as *The Trail of the Serpent*, 1861); *The Black Band: Or, The Mysteries of Midnight*, 1861-1862 (also known as *What Is This Mystery?*); *Lady Audley's Secret*, 1862; *The Captain of the Vulture*, 1862 (also known as *Darrell Markham: Or, The Captain of the Vulture*); *The Lady Lisle*, 1862; *Aurora Floyd*, 1863; *Eleanor's Victory*, 1863; *John Marchmont's Legacy*, 1863; *The Outcast: Or, The Brand of Society*, 1863-1864 (also known as *Henry Dunbar: The Story of an Outcast*); *The Doctor's Wife*, 1864; *The Lawyer's Secret*, 1864; *Only a Clod*, 1865; *Sir Jasper's Tenant*, 1865; *Diavola: Or, The Woman's Battle*, 1866-1867 (also known as *Run to Earth* and *Nobody's Daughter: Or, The Ballad-Singer of Wapping*); *Rupert Godwin*, 1867; *The White Phantom*, 1868; *Oscar Bertrand: Or, The Idiot of the Mountain*, 1869; *The Factory Girl: Or, All Is Not Gold That Glitters*, 1869; *The Octoroon: Or, The Lily of Louisiana*, 1869

1871-1880 • *Robert Ainsleigh*, 1872 (also known as *Bound to John Company: Or, The Adventures of Misadventures of Robert Ainsleigh*); *To the Bitter End*, 1872; *Lucius Davoren: Or, Publicans and Sinners*, 1873 (also known as *Publicans and Sinners*); *Lost for Love*, 1874; *Taken at the Flood*, 1874; *A Strange World*, 1875; *Hostages to Fortune*, 1875; *Dead Men's Shoes*, 1876; *An Open Verdict*, 1878; *Leighton Grange: Or, Who Killed Edith Woodville*, 1878? (also known as *The Mystery of Leighton Grange*); *Just As I Am*, 1880; *The Story of Barbara, Her Splendid Misery and Her Gilded Cage*, 1880 (also known as *Her Splendid Misery*)

1881-1890 • *Le Pasteur de Marston*, 1881; *The Fatal Marriage: Or, The Shadow in the Corner*, 1885; *Wyllard's Weird*, 1885; *One Thing Needful, and Cut By the County*, 1886 (also known as *Penalty of Fate: Or, The One Thing Needful*); *Like and Unlike*, 1887; *The Fatal Three*, 1888; *The Day Will Come*, 1889

1891-1910 • *The Venetians*, 1892; *Thou Art the*

Man, 1894; *Sons of Fire*, 1895; *London Pride: Or, When the World Was Younger*, 1896 (also known as *When the World Was Younger*); *Her Convict*, 1907; *During Her Majesty's Pleasure*, 1908; *Beyond These Voices*, 1910

OTHER MAJOR WORKS

NOVELS: 1866-1880 • *The Lady's Mile*, 1866; *Circe: Or, Three Acts in the Life of an Artist*, 1867; *Dead Sea Fruit*, 1868; *The Blue Band: Or, The Story of a Woman's Vengeance*, 1869?; *Fenton's Quest*, 1871; *The Lovels of Arden*, 1871; *Strangers and Pilgrims*, 1873; *Joshua Haggard's Daughter*, 1876; *George Caulfield's Journey*, 1879; *The Cloven Foot*, 1879; *Vixen*, 1879

1881-1890 • *Asphodel*, 1881; *His Secret*, 1881; *Wages of Sin*, 1881; *Flower and Weed*, 1882; *Mount Royal*, 1882; *Married in Haste*, 1883; *Phantom Fortune*, 1883; *The Golden Calf*, 1883; *Under the Red Flag*, 1883; *Ishmael*, 1884 (also known as *The Ishmaelite*); *Only a Woman*, 1885; *Mohawks*, 1886; *The Little Woman in Black*, 1886; *Whose Was the Hand?*, 1889; *One Life, One Love*, 1890

1891-1900 • *Gerard: Or, The World, the Flesh, and the Devil*, 1891 (also known as *The World, the Flesh, and the Devil*); *All Along the River*, 1893; *Under Love's Rule*, 1897; *In High Places*, 1898; *The Infidel*, 1900

1901-1916 • *The Conflict*, 1903; *A Lost Eden*, 1904; *The Rose of Life*, 1905; *The White House*, 1906; *Dead Love Has Chains*, 1907; *Our Adversary*, 1909; *The Green Curtain*, 1911; *Miranda*, 1913; *Mary*, 1916

SHORT FICTION: *Ralph the Bailiff, and Other Tales*, 1862 (also known as *Dudley Carleon*); *The Summer Tourist: A Book for Long and Short Journeys*, 1871; *Milly Darrell, and Other Tales*, 1873 (also known as *Meeting Her Fate*); *My Sister's Confession, and Other Stories*, 1876; *In Great Waters*, 1877; *Weavers and Weft, and Other Tales*, 1877; *Shadow in the Corner*, 1879 (also known as *Figure in the Corner, and Other Stories*); *Great Journey, and Other Stories*, 1882

PLAY: *The Missing Witness*, pb. 1880

POETRY: *Garibaldi, and Other Poems*, 1861

CHILDREN'S LITERATURE: *Aladdin: Or, The Wonderful Lamp*, 1880; *The Good Hermione*, 1886 (as Aunt Belinda); *The Christmas Hirelings*, 1894

MISCELLANEOUS: *Flower and Weed, and Other Tales*, 1884; *Under the Red Flag, and Other Tales*, 1886; *All Along the River*, 1894

BIBLIOGRAPHY

Bedell, Jeanne F. "Amateur and Professional Detectives in the Fiction of Mary Elizabeth Braddon." *Clues: A Journal of Detection* 4, no. 1 (Spring/Summer, 1983): 19-34. Comparison of two types of detectives in Braddon's tales raises issues about the public and private spheres and professionalism in Victorian England.

Carnell, Jennifer. *The Literary Lives of Mary Elizabeth Braddon: A Study of Her Life and Work.* Hastings, East Sussex, England: Sensation Press, 2000. Voluminous, definitive study of Braddon's life and writing.

Klein, Kathleen Gregory, ed. *Great Women Mystery Writers: Classic to Contemporary.* Westport, Conn.: Greenwood Press, 1994. Contains a biocritical essay examining aspects of the life and work of Braddon.

Peterson, Audrey. *Victorian Masters of Mystery: From Wilkie Collins to Conan Doyle.* New York: F. Ungar, 1984. Discussion of Victorian culture and its relation to the invention of the mystery genre that helps readers evaluate Braddon.

Showalter, Elaine. *A Literature of Their Own: British Women Novelists from Brontë to Lessing.* Rev. ed. Princeton, N.J.: Princeton University Press, 1999. Seminal feminist text on the history of the British novel that helps readers place Braddon in the literary world.

Tromp, Marlene, Pamela K. Gilbert, and Aeron Haynie, eds. *Beyond Sensation: Mary Elizabeth Braddon in Context.* Albany: State University of New York Press, 2000. Compilation of cultural studies essays that analyze the place both of Braddon and of sensation in Victorian culture.

Wolff, Robert Lee. *Sensational Victorian: The Life and Fiction of Mary Elizabeth Braddon.* New York: Garland, 1979. Biography of Braddon combined with analysis of her work and its contribution to sensational fiction.

ERNEST BRAMAH
Ernest Bramah Smith

Born: Manchester, Lancashire, England; March 20, 1868

Died: Somerset, England; June 27, 1942

Type of plot: Amateur sleuth

PRINCIPAL SERIES

Max Carrados, 1914-1934

PRINCIPAL SERIES CHARACTERS

MAX CARRADOS, a wealthy bachelor and amateur detective, around thirty-five, is totally blind. His blindness has led him to develop other senses, and he is able to read newspaper headlines by running his sensitive fingers over them, to monitor scents and sounds undetectable by others, and even to sense subtle changes in temperature.

LOUIS CARLYLE, a private-inquiry agent and disbarred solicitor, who calls for Carrados's aid when he is stumped or when he has a client who cannot afford to pay. Very intelligent and capable, he requires assistance only on truly baffling cases.

PARKINSON is servant and eyes to Carrados. Extraordinarily observant, he is able to remember every detail of his surroundings, even to the size of a glove lying on a table four weeks before. He is the ideal detective's assistant, asking no questions, following orders to the letter, revealing nothing.

CONTRIBUTION

In Max Carrados, Ernest Bramah created the first blind fictional detective, ushering in a host of blind, paralyzed, overweight, and otherwise disabled sleuths. Unlike many of those who followed him, however, Carrados is not truly disabled by his physical limitations. Because he has developed his other senses so acutely, his lack of sight is no real hindrance to him, and he gently mocks his sighted colleagues who are so often misled by what they see. Carrados's blindness opens up new avenues to the writer. Because Carrados cannot see, Bramah is forced to come up with different ways by which evidence is gathered and examined, giving a fresh angle to conventional material.

Nevertheless, Bramah's detective is not defined solely in terms of his blindness. A very kind man, he has a remarkable wit, demonstrated most memorably in his exchanges with Louis Carlyle, and a rigorous sense of justice, which at one point compels him to urge a murderer to commit suicide. Modern readers of Bramah may not find much that is new in terms of plot, but they will find much to appreciate in the strong characterizations and humor of the stories.

BIOGRAPHY

Very little is known about Ernest Bramah's life, and it was his lifelong wish that it be so. Throughout his professional life, he demonstrated a remarkable skill at avoiding personal interviews, preferring to keep his private life private. His publisher was compelled in a 1923 introduction to assert that, in fact, Ernest Bramah was a real person and not a pseudonym for another author.

He was born Ernest Bramah Smith in Manchester, England, and most sources give the date as either 1868 or 1869. From his autobiographical first book, *English Farming and Why I Turned It Up* (1894), it can be learned that he dropped out of high school to try his hand at farming. It was not a success. Bramah subsequently turned to journalism and became a correspondent for a small newspaper. Later, in London, he became secretary to the publisher Jerome K. Jerome and eventually joined the editorial staff of Jerome's periodical, *To-day*. Bramah left *To-day* to become editor of a new trade magazine for clergymen, *The Minister*, and stayed there until the magazine folded.

It was at this point that he became a full-time writer for magazines, creating the Max Carrados and Kai Lung stories that were later published in book-length collections. Bramah's first book of detective fiction, *Max Carrados*, was published in 1914, when he was in his mid-forties; his only Max Carrados novel, *The Bravo of London* (1934), appeared when he was in his mid-sixties.

In addition to his writing, Bramah had a great interest in numismatics (an interest shared with Max Carrados), and he is the author of a nonfictional book on British coins, *A Guide to the Varieties and Rarity of English Regal Copper Coins: Charles II-Victoria, 1671-1860* (1929).

Bramah's Kai Lung stories, and some of his popular articles, deal so convincingly with Asian geography and culture that it has often been speculated that he lived for a time in Asia. That may in fact be true, but there is no evidence to support it. A small and thin man, Bramah lived as a recluse in his later life. He died in Somerset on June 27, 1942.

ANALYSIS

In Ernest Bramah's Max Carrados stories, the reader finds the best of two worlds: The stories contain many of the conventional crimes and criminals that are greeted as old friends by those who have read widely in mystery and detective fiction, yet they center on a detective who is utterly new and who insistently provides a fresh view of the conventional material.

MAX CARRADOS

Max Carrados was blinded as an adult, when a twig hit his eyes during a riding accident. The injury left him sightless, but the appearance of his eyes is unchanged. In his introduction to *The Eyes of Max Carrados* (1923), Bramah explains that

> so far from that crippling his interests in life or his energies, it has merely impelled him to develop those senses which in most of us lie half dormant and practically unused. Thus you will understand that while he may be at a disadvantage when you are at an advantage, he is at an advantage when you are at a disadvantage.

Carrados, understandably, prefers to work when he is at an advantage; thus he conducts many of his investigations at night, and he manages to hold a roomful of villains at bay simply by extinguishing the lights. Even in a well-lit room, however, Carrados is able to perform remarkable feats: He is able to read newspaper headlines, playing cards, and photographic negatives by running his extremely sensitive fingers over them; by knowing what to look for and guessing where to search, he can locate a single petal on the

The kidnapping of Max Carrados in a 1926 issue of Pearson's Magazine.

ground or a few strands of hair caught in a bramble; he can recognize the voice or pattern of footsteps of a person he has not encountered in several years; and he is able, by identifying the odor of the adhesive, to determine that a man is wearing a false mustache.

Though Carrados's achievements may seem to readers incredible and superhuman, Bramah went to some pains in his introduction to *The Eyes of Max Carrados* to establish that, historically, blind people have indeed accomplished much, and Carrados is only one example of the tremendous capabilities of the blind. "Although for convenience the qualities of more than one blind prototype may have been collected within a single frame," each of the things that Carrados can do is certainly possible. "Carrados's opening exploit, that of accurately deciding an antique coin to be a forgery, by the sense of touch, is far from being unprecedented."

Carrados is not above feigning helplessness when it will help him obtain information. When it suits him, he can be remarkably clumsy, knocking over a framed picture (and stealing the piece of glass with the finger-print on it), accidentally opening the door to a dark-room (to confront the suspect within), or bumping into furniture (so he can whisper to the accomplice who reaches out to help him). These accidents are typically followed by Carrados's humble apology—"'sorry', he shrugs, 'but I am blind.'"

With one exception, the rather unsuccessful novel *The Bravo of London*, Max Carrados solves his mysteries within the span of the short story. Yet even within this genre Bramah manages to establish characters that live and breathe and intrigue the reader. Bramah's recurring characters—Carrados, Louis Carlyle, Parkinson, Inspector Beedle—are so engaging in part because they are revealed to be flawed. Witty, kindly, and generous as Carrados is, he also has a cold streak and is not immune to vanity. Previous to his reunion with Carrados, Carlyle has been disbarred because of an indiscretion (although not a crime), and he does not take cases from clients who cannot pay. In only a few sentences, Bramah presents a succinct and rather appealing suggestion of Inspector Beedle's character:

> the inspector nodded and contributed a weighty mono-syllable of sympathetic agreement. The most prosaic of men in the pursuit of his ordinary duties, it nevertheless subtly appealed to some half-dormant streak of vanity to have his profession taken romantically when there was no serious work on hand.

Bramah's crime fighters are believable, likable characters, not overly virtuous supermen.

This passage also shows something of Bramah's own style. The sentences are economical and carry a constant faint touch of irony. "This is how people are," Bramah seems to say, "and is it not amusing?" The teasing is always gentle, always affectionate—Bramah enjoys his characters, finds pleasure in the silliness of social climbing and the vagaries of human relationships, and laughs at human weakness rather than denying it.

As in this passage, with its reference to the inspector's "weighty monosyllable," most of the action in the stories is revealed through dialogue. Although the narrator is a third-person omniscient one, little is revealed

that is not spoken aloud by one character to another. The reader may know that Carrados intends to conduct a search but will not learn what is found until Carrados tells someone else. Carrados likes to work alone, and not even the reader is allowed into his confidence until he is ready to reveal all. Even when the detective expresses dissatisfaction with himself, he does so by muttering to himself; the reader is permitted to over-hear the muttering but not to enter into Carrados's mind. Does he ever feel fear in a dangerous spot or have fits of self-pity about his blindness? The reader never knows any more than the other characters in the stories know.

Certainly one of Carrados's most attractive characteristics is his ironic wit. Exchanges between Carrados and Carlyle are filled with sarcasm and affectionate teasing, but the blind man is at his best when sparring with criminals:

> "If you happen to come through this alive and are interested you might ask Zinghi to show you a target of mine that he keeps. Seven shots at twenty yards, the target indicated by four watches, none of them so loud as the one [your friend is] wearing. . . ."
>
> "I wear no watch," muttered Dompierre, expressing his thought aloud.
>
> "No, Monsieur Dompierre, but you wear a heart, and that not on your sleeve," said Carrados. "Just now it is quite as loud as Mr. Montmorency's watch. It is more central too—I shall not have to allow any margin. . . ."
>
> "Monsieur," declared Dompierre earnestly. . . . "Take care: killing is a dangerous game."
>
> "For you—not for me," was the bland rejoinder. "If you kill me you will be hanged for it. If I kill you I shall be honourably acquitted. You can imagine the scene—the sympathetic court—the recital of your villainies—the story of my indignities. Then with stumbling feet and groping hands the helpless blind man is led forward to give evidence. Sensation!"

BRAMAH'S CRIMINALS

If Max Carrados and his friends are made to resemble flesh-and-blood men, the same cannot be said for Bramah's criminals. Even in Bramah's time, his evil-doers would have been familiar to anyone widely read in mystery fiction: They are mysterious strangers from

India, Christian Scientists, philandering husbands, mad scientists, and Jews, and they are usually painted rather flatly. As a group, they are unusually crafty and intelligent, but they are not—with a few exceptions—complex characters whom one could perhaps forgive or grudgingly admire. One exception to this rule is the professional thief, often with an international reputation, who has lived by his wits for years and is a proper intellectual match for Carrados. Still, even these characters begin to be recognizable as a type, the "internationally renowned criminal," and are indistinguishable one from another.

Another exception to the flatly evil villain sometimes turns out not to be a villain at all, but a misunderstood hero. Once Carrados, in the midst of obtaining definitive evidence against the "villain," comes to understand the man's true nature (and in Bramah's stories, criminal masterminds are always male), he uses his wits to ensure that the crime-that-is-not-a-crime is carried through successfully, even while the police (whom he had called when he had arrest in mind) are on their way. It is in these stories that readers encounter another fascinating aspect of Carrados's personality, and one of Bramah's own fascinations with the business of solving crimes.

CRIME IS NOT A GAME

The truth is, Bramah appears to believe, that solving a crime is not always as rewarding as one would suppose. Often, Carrados finds himself on the trail of someone whom he would rather not catch; he finds it distasteful at times to ruin careers or marriages or to waste the taxpayers' money on preserving justice for evil men. At these times, he wishes that he had not become involved in the case. In fact, in many ways he is never truly involved, at least not emotionally. He is interested in solving the puzzle, not in bringing criminals to trial, and he prefers to let the police take over as soon as he can present the evidence to them. In the scenes in which Carrados agonizes over the consequences of his decision to take on a case, Bramah develops one of his recurring themes—the idea that crime is not simply a puzzle or a game, but something that really occurs, and with genuine human consequences. The theme is presented gently and in no way detracts from one's pleasure in reading the stories;

Bramah is writing mystery fiction, not tracts. Nevertheless, he wants his readers to leave his stories with a better understanding of the capabilities of the blind and the realities of a crime-ridden world.

If Bramah's plots have one shortcoming, it is one that modern readers will find more annoying than did his contemporaries. In some tales, the mystery is solved more through divine intervention than through the ingenuity of the detective. In one case, for example, a pair of enormously clever thieves who have made a reputation on two continents escape with a large fortune. As they are almost away, with virtually no chance of being caught, they are suddenly confronted with the notion of God's goodness and their own sinfulness. They repent and bring the money back. Though writers as great as William Shakespeare have found it necessary to include coincidence in their plots because coincidence is, in fact, a part of life, mystery stories that are resolved in this way tend to be rather unsatisfying.

The most satisfying resolutions are Carrados's alone, and the special twist that clicks everything into place usually occurs offstage, in Carrados's mind or in the course of one of his secret investigations. These are not mysteries that readers could solve if only they were clever enough—unless they happened to be experts on Greek tetradrachms (like Bramah and Carrados) or on local British history. The fun is in watching how Carrados does it, not in trying to beat him to the solution.

At his best, though, Bramah is a master of the short story in which everything fits, nothing is wasted, evil men get their due, and damsels in distress are rescued—all in a highly entertaining fashion.

Cynthia A. Bily

PRINCIPAL MYSTERY AND DETECTIVE FICTION

MAX CARRADOS SERIES: *Max Carrados*, 1914; *The Eyes of Max Carrados*, 1923; *The Specimen Case*, 1924; *Max Carrados Mysteries*, 1927; *The Bravo of London*, 1934

OTHER MAJOR WORKS

NOVELS: *The Mirror of Kung Ho*, 1905; *What Might Have Been*, 1907 (also known as *The Secret of* the League); *A Little Flutter*, 1930; *The Moon of Much Gladness*, 1932 (also known as *The Return of Kai Lung*)

SHORT FICTION: *The Wallet of Kai Lung*, 1900; *Kai Lung's Golden Hours*, 1922; *Kai Lung Unrolls His Mat*, 1928; *Kai Lung Beneath the Mulberry-Tree*, 1940; *Kai Lung: Six Uncollected Stories from "Punch,"* 1974

NONFICTION: *English Farming and Why I Turned It Up*, 1894; *A Guide to the Varieties and Rarity of English Regal Copper Coins: Charles II-Victoria, 1671-1860*, 1929

BIBLIOGRAPHY

Bleiler, E. F. Introduction to *Best Max Carrados Detective Stories*, by Ernest Bramah. New York: Dover, 1972. Surveys Bramah's Max Carrados series and discusses the features that make its best entries stand out.

Kestner, Joseph A. *The Edwardian Detective, 1901-1915.* Brookfield, Vt.: Ashgate, 2000. Reads Bramah as emerging from and, to some extent, continuing the Edwardian tradition in detective fiction.

Penzler, Otto. "Collecting Mystery Fiction: Max Carrados." *The Armchair Detective* 16 (1983): 122-124. The editor of *The Armchair Detective* discusses the Max Carrados series and its worthiness to be considered for addition to one's personal collection.

White, William. "Ernest Bramah: A First Checklist." *Bulletin of Bibliography* 20, no. 6 (1958): 127-131. A bibliography of Bramah's earlier work.

_____. "Ernest Bramah in Anthologies, 1914-1972." *The Armchair Detective* 10 (1977): 30-32. A bibliography that lists Bramah's shorter works that have appeared in anthologies.

_____. "Ernest Bramah in Periodicals, 1890-1972." *Bulletin of Bibliography* 32 (January/March, 1975): 33-34, 44. A listing of Bramah's works that appeared in periodicals over his career.

CHRISTIANNA BRAND
Mary Christianna Milne

Born: Malaya; December 17, 1907
Died: Place unknown; March 11, 1988
Also wrote as Mary Ann Ashe; Annabel Jones; Mary Roland; China Thompson
Types of plot: Master sleuth; cozy

PRINCIPAL SERIES
Inspector Cockrill, 1942-1955

PRINCIPAL SERIES CHARACTER

INSPECTOR COCKRILL is in the Sherlock Holmes tradition of detectives who have almost supernatural powers but who disclose little about their methods of reasoning until the case is over. The elderly Cockrill's outward manner is crusty, but he is kind and has a paternal affection for young women. A perceptive judge of character, he sympathizes with human weakness, though he is indefatigable in his search for truth.

CONTRIBUTION

Christianna Brand may be considered a pioneer of the medical thriller, as her highly honored 1944 novel *Green for Danger* preceded by decades the popular works of Patricia Cornwell and Robin Cook. Indeed, H. R. F. Keating called it the finest novel of the Golden Age of mystery fiction. Her detective fiction illustrates the dictum of Georg Wilhelm Friedrich Hegel that a change in quantity may become transformed into a change in quality. The standard British mystery emphasized complex plotting in which the reader was challenged to decipher the clues to the perpetrator of the crime.

Brand's works took the emphasis on surprise to new heights: Sometimes the key to the story emerged only with the novel's last line. Few readers proved able to match wits with her Inspector Cockrill, and if he was not present, she had other ways to fool the audience. On one occasion, she "gave away" the story by a subtle clue in the first paragraph. Also, many of her books show an irrepressible humor that she carried to much further lengths than most of her contemporaries.

BIOGRAPHY

Christianna Brand was born Mary Christianna Milne in Malaya in December, 1907, and grew up there and in India. She was sent to England to attend a Franciscan convent school in Somerset, an area of England known for its beauty. Her happiness at school received a rude upset when her father lost all of his money; she had to begin earning her own living at the age of seventeen.

Brand went through a rapid succession of ill-paid jobs, mostly in sales, but also in modeling, professional ballroom dancing, receptionist and secretarial work, shop assistant work, interior design, and governess work. At one point, she opened a club for working girls in a slum section of London. Her financial prospects took a turn for the better when she met and fell in love with a young surgeon, Roland Lewis. She married him in 1939 and became Mary Christianna Lewis in her personal life.

Before her marriage, Brand had already begun to write. Her decision to try detective stories had behind it no previous experience in fiction writing. (It is said that she wrote her first book, *Death in High Heels*, 1941, while working as a salesgirl, as a way to fantasize about killing a coworker.) She nevertheless was soon a success, and her second novel won a prize of one thousand dollars offered by Dodd, Mead and Company for its prestigious Red Badge series. Her early success proved to be no fluke; by the time of the publication of *Green for Danger* (1944), she had come to be generally regarded as one of the most important mystery writers of her time.

Brand once more did the unexpected by ceasing to write mystery novels according to her hitherto successful recipe. Instead, she turned to short stories. After the appearance of *Starrbelow* (1958), she did not write another mystery novel for ten years. Her writing career, however, was by no means over. She had in the meantime tried her hand at several other varieties of fiction, including historical romances and screenplays.

Although she never achieved the renown for these that her mysteries had brought her, her Nurse Matilda series of novels for children gained wide popularity. She returned to the ranks of mystery novelists in the late 1960's. She died in on March 11, 1988, in the arms of her husband of fifty years, Roland Lewis.

ANALYSIS

An author who, like Christianna Brand, has achieved a reputation for the ability to surprise her readers faces a difficult task. Her readers, once forewarned, will be expecting deception and hence will be on their guard. Nevertheless, Brand managed to pull off one surprise after another in each of her most famous mysteries. In her stress on bafflement, she was hardly original, but the seemingly impossible culprits she produced made her achievement in this area virtually unequaled.

There is much more to Brand than surprise. There is almost always in her work a romance, an idealistic love affair whose sexual elements are minimal. In her work, heroines at once fall in love with the man whom they will eventually marry, although only after overcoming numerous obstacles. Remarkably, in Brand's novels this approach to romance is carried to such lengths that it does not seem at all cloying or stereotypical. Rather, it is yet another manifestation of her unusually pronounced sense of humor.

Brand, whatever one may think of her, is certainly no unalloyed optimist. Often, her characters must realize a bitter truth about close friends. In *Green for Danger*, for example, the overriding ambition of many of the nurses makes them petty and nasty. In Brand's view of things, even "ordinary" people may harbor serious failings. Her murderers are not obvious villains but characters undistinguishable from anyone else in the novel, until their bitter secret is exposed.

Here, the element of romance often reappears, although this time more somberly. The murderer's secret usually involves either a disgruntled lover or someone whose ambition consumes all ordinary restraint. The motives of ambition and unrequited love, like the heroine's experience of falling in love, operate in an absolute fashion. Idealism and an awareness of evil thus work to balance each other, making Brand's stories less unrealistic than a first encounter with one of her romantic heroines would lead one to suspect. All of this, further, is overlaid with a veneer of humor, making up in high spirits for what it lacks in sophistication.

GREEN FOR DANGER

As just presented, the characteristics of Brand's novels hardly seem a program for success. She managed, however, to put all the diverse pieces together in an effective way, as a closer look at *Green for Danger* illustrates. In this work, sometimes regarded as her best, a patient in a military hospital for bombing victims dies on the operating table. At first, his death hardly attracts notice, being regarded as an accident (by some mischance, the man's anesthetic had been contaminated). It soon develops, however, that more than accident is involved. Testimony of several student nurses who were present at the scene shows indisputably that foul play has occurred. The murderer can only have been one of the seven people present in the operating room theater, but not even the ingenious probing of Inspector Cockrill suffices to reveal the culprit. Still, the inspector is far from giving up.

Cockrill devises a characteristically subtle plan to trap the murderer into attempting another killing during surgery. His plan almost backfires, as the culprit possesses an ingenuity that, however twisted by malign ambition, almost matches that of Cockrill himself.

When the method of the murderer at last is revealed, even the experienced mystery reader will be forced to gasp in astonishment. Although dominant in *Green for Danger*, this element of surprise does not stand alone. A young nurse who has aroused suspicion is the person responsible for bringing Cockrill into the case. She is in love with a young doctor; although her romantic feelings do not receive detailed attention, they are unmistakably present. Although the reader will hardly take this nurse seriously as a suspect, since otherwise the romance would face utter ruin, this fact provides little or no aid in stealing a march on Cockrill.

Romance and murder are a familiar combination; to join humor with them is not so common. Brand does so by means of amusing descriptions of the petty rivalries and disputes among the nurses and other members of the hospital staff. The points that induce them to quarrel generally are quite minor: For example, someone has taken over another's locker space, or wishes to listen to a radio program that another dislikes. These irritations soon flare up into severe disputes, which, however humorously depicted, serve to remind the reader of Brand's belief that murderous rage lies close at hand to more everyday feelings.

Brand's contention was based on personal experience. Before her marriage, she felt an enormous dislike for one of her fellow workers. This animosity, she conjectured, was of the sort that might easily lead to murder. It was this experience that colored her development of the motivation of her murderers and added a starkly realistic touch to her romantic and humorous tendencies.

LONDON PARTICULAR

For a lesser author, the old combination of traits Brand's novel presented might seem difficult to repeat—but not for Brand. In *London Particular* (1952; also known as *Fog of Doubt*), she again startles the reader. This time she does so by withholding until the last line of the book the method of the murderer in gaining access to a house he seemingly had no opportunity to reach. After one has read this last line, one realizes that Brand had in fact given away the essential clue to the case in the book's first paragraph. So subtly presented is the vital fact, however, that almost every reader will pass it by without a second glance.

In this book, Brand's strong interest in romance comes to the fore. The characters' various romantic attachments receive detailed attention; the many rivalries and jealousies present among the main characters serve to distract the reader from solving the case. Again characteristically for Brand, true love eventually triumphs, and the culprit is the victim of an uncontrollable and unrequited passion for another of the principal characters.

TOUR DE FORCE

Green for Danger stresses surprise, *London Particular*, romance. A third novel, *Tour de Force* (1955), emphasizes the final element in Brand's tripartite formula: humor. The story is set on an imaginary island in the Mediterranean, near a resort where a number of English tourists have gone for vacation. Among them is the now-retired Cockrill, as well as his sister, Henrietta. A murder quickly arouses the local gendarmerie to feverish but ineffective activity. Their burlesque of genuine detection, consisting of an attempt to pin the blame on one tourist after another until each possibility is disproved, does not even exempt Cockrill. His efforts to solve the case are foiled at every turn by police bumbling.

Firmly behind the police is the local despot, who threatens the tourists with dire penalties unless he at once receives a confession. The dungeon on the island is evidently of medieval vintage, and the petty satrap whose word is law on the island regards this prison as a major attraction of his regime.

Here, for once, surprise, though certainly present, does not have its customary spectacular character. Instead, the reader receives a series of lesser shocks, as one person after another seems without a doubt to be guilty, only to be replaced by yet another certain criminal. Cockrill eventually discloses the truth with his usual panache.

BUFFET FOR UNWELCOME GUESTS

Brand's short stories further developed some of the techniques of her novels. In several stories in the collection *Buffet for Unwelcome Guests: The Best Short Mysteries of Christianna Brand* (1983), Inspector Cockrill figures in inverted plots. Here the reader knows the identity of the criminal, and the interest lies in following the efforts of the detective to discover him. This technique poses a severe test to a writer such as Brand who values suspense. Can there be surprises in a story in which the identity of the criminal is given to the reader at the outset? Brand believed that there could, and one can see from the popularity of her stories that many readers agreed with her. One of these, "The Hornets' Nest," won first prize in a contest sponsored by *Ellery Queen's Mystery Magazine.*

Brand's style does not have the innovative qualities of her plots. It is, however, a serviceable instrument, both clear and vigorous. She tends to emphasize, more than most detective story authors, long descriptive passages of scenery. In her depiction of the imaginary island in *Tour de Force*, she captures with great skill the atmosphere of several Mediterranean islands favored by British tourists. A reason for the popularity

of *Green for Danger* lies in its stylistically apt portrayal of the loneliness of women whose husbands and boyfriends had gone to fight in World War II. Here she once more relied on personal experience, for her own husband was away on military service for much of the war.

Another feature of Brand's style was characteristic of the writers of her generation, though not of younger authors. In writing of love, she had no interest in depicting sexual encounters in detail, or even in acknowledging their existence. Sex, along with obscene language, is absent from her books; these could only interfere with the unreal but captivating atmosphere she endeavored to portray.

THE HONEY HARLOT

To this generalization there is, however, a significant exception. *The Honey Harlot* (1978) is a novel of sexual obsession; here, the approach to love differs quite sharply from that of her more famous mysteries. Her characteristic work does not lie in this direction, and this novel was not followed by one of similar type.

To sum up, Brand carried some of the elements of the classic British detective story—in particular surprise, romance, and humor—to extremes. In doing so, she established a secure place for herself as an important contributor to the mystery field.

David Gordon
Updated by Fiona Kelleghan

PRINCIPAL MYSTERY AND DETECTIVE FICTION

INSPECTOR COCKRILL SERIES: *Heads You Lose*, 1941; *Green for Danger*, 1944; *The Crooked Wreath*, 1946 (also known as *Suddenly at His Residence*); *Death of Jezebel*, 1948; *London Particular*, 1952 (also known as *Fog of Doubt*); *Tour de Force*, 1955; *The Three-Cornered Halo*, 1957; *The Spotted Cat, and Other Mysteries: The Casebook of Inspector Cockrill*, 2001

INSPECTOR CHARLESWORTH SERIES: *Death in High Heels*, 1941; *The Rose in Darkness*, 1979

INSPECTOR CHUCKY SERIES: *Cat and Mouse*, 1950; *A Ring of Roses*, 1977

NONSERIES NOVELS: *Starrbelow*, 1958 (as Thompson); *Court of Foxes*, 1969; *Alas, for Her That Met Me!*, 1976 (as Ashe); *The Honey Harlot*, 1978; *The Brides of*

Aberdar, 1982; *Crime on the Coast, and No Flowers by Request*, 1984 (with others)

SHORT FICTION: *What Dread Hands?*, 1968; *Brand X*, 1974; *Buffet for Unwelcome Guests: The Best Short Mysteries of Christianna Brand*, 1983 (Francis M. Nevins, Jr., and Martin H. Greenberg, editors)

OTHER MAJOR WORKS

NOVELS: *The Single Pilgrim*, 1946 (as Roland); *The Radiant Dove*, 1974 (as Jones)

SCREENPLAYS: *Death in High Heels*, 1947; *The Mark of Cain*, 1948 (with W. P. Lipscomb and Francis Cowdry); *Secret People*, 1952 (with others)

CHILDREN'S LITERATURE: *Danger Unlimited*, 1948 (also known as *Welcome to Danger*); *Nurse Matilda*, 1964; *Nurse Matilda Goes to Town*, 1967; *Nurse Matilda Goes to Hospital*, 1974

NONFICTION: *Heaven Knows Who*, 1960

EDITED TEXTS: *Naughty Children: An Anthology*, 1962

BIBLIOGRAPHY

Barnard, Robert. "The Slightly Mad, Mad World of Christianna Brand." *The Armchair Detective* 19, no. 3 (Summer, 1986): 238-243. Discusses the off-kilter nature of Brand's stories and characters and their importance to her overall work.

Brand, Christianna. "Inspector Cockrill." In *The Great Detectives*, edited by Otto Penzler. Boston: Little, Brown, 1978. Brand's own description of her most famous and successful character.

Briney, Robert E. "The World of Christianna Brand." In *Buffet for Unwelcome Guests: The Best Short Mysteries of Christianna Brand*, edited by Francis M. Nevins, Jr., and Martin H. Greenberg. Carbondale: Southern Illinois University Press, 1983. An examination of the internal logic and character of the world generated by Brand's fiction, as well as the relationship between that world and the mysteries, detectives, and murderers that inhabit it.

Klein, Kathleen Gregory, ed. *Great Women Mystery Writers: Classic to Contemporary*. Westport, Conn.: Greenwood Press, 1994. Contains an essay that examines the life and writings of Brand.

Malmgren, Carl D. *Anatomy of Murder: Mystery, Detective, and Crime Fiction*. Bowling Green, Ohio: Bowling Green State University Popular Press, 2001. Discusses Brand's *London Particular*. Bibliographic references and index.

Penzler, Otto. "In Memoriam, 1907-1988." *The Armchair Detective* 21, no. 3 (Summer, 1998): 228-230. An obituary and appreciation of Brand, detailing her place in the history of British detective fiction.

_____. "The Works of Christianna Brand." In *Green for Danger*. Topanga, Calif.: Boulevard, 1978. An overview of the author's work, provided as a foreword to an edition of her most famous and most popular detective novel.

Rowland, Susan. *From Agatha Christie to Ruth Rendell: British Women Writers in Detective and Crime Fiction*. New York: Palgrave, 2001. Discusses several of Brand's colleagues. A good source on the conventions of the genre and the context of Brand's contributions to it. Bibliographic references and index.

Symons, Julian, ed. *The Hundred Best Crime Stories*. London: The Sunday Times, 1959. Places Brand as the author of one of the hundred best crime stories of all time.

LILIAN JACKSON BRAUN

Born: Chicopee Falls, Massachusetts; June 20, 1913
Also wrote as Ward Jackson
Types of plot: Cozy; amateur sleuth

PRINCIPAL SERIES

The Cat Who, 1966-

PRINCIPAL SERIES CHARACTERS

JAMES MACKINTOSH QWILLERAN is a charismatic mustached journalist. A Chicago native, he has worked as a police reporter and foreign correspondent and published a book about crime. After a divorce and alcoholism disrupt his career, he accepts a position as an arts reporter with a midwestern newspaper, initiating his unexpected partnership with a cat in the solution of a murder. After adopting that cat and another, the cosmopolitan Qwilleran pursues journalism while investigating mysterious events in various settings, particularly Moose County, where he moves after he inherits a fortune and becomes a philanthropist. He is affectionate toward his cats and recognizes their special attributes.

KOKO is a male Siamese cat formally named Kao K'o Kung. He befriends Qwilleran, who lives in the building owned by the art critic who is Koko's original master. After the art critic is murdered, Koko becomes Qwilleran's pet and exhibits behavior that helps Qwilleran discover clues that solve mysteries. Koko has sixty whiskers, which Qwilleran believes causes Koko to be more sensitive and intuitive. During Koko's early detecting career, the police chief issued him a press card to honor his contributions.

YUM YUM is a female Siamese cat younger and smaller than Koko. Her original owner, Signe Tait, called her Freya, while Signe's husband George Tait referred to her as Yu, meaning jade, which he collected. After Yum Yum helps Koko and Qwilleran resolve a murder case involving the Taits, Qwilleran provides her a home and new name. Yum Yum often assumes a more passive role than Koko.

CONTRIBUTION

Lilian Jackson Braun popularized animal mysteries in the late twentieth century, effectively creating a subgenre of cat mysteries that inspired other authors to invent their own versions of feline sleuths. Beginning with short stories published during the 1960's in mystery collections, Braun incorporated her artistic and professional experiences and interests in her cat mysteries to create a fictional world that attracted a diverse readership.

Scholars mostly dismissed Braun's mysteries as being unsubstantial and lacking literary merit. Critics gave her writing mixed reviews. While some reviewers demeaned her cat mysteries as cute and contrived, others praised her unique presentation of mystery characterizations and situations. Editor Anthony Boucher included Braun's work in the eighteenth annual edition of his *Best Detective Stories of the Year* (1963).

Despite Braun's early success, publishing three novels in the cat mystery series from 1966 to 1968, she found that publishers preferred hard-boiled novels and did not create any additional books in the series until nearly two decades later in 1986. This time, Braun quickly secured a loyal following that consistently purchased her books, assuring her commercial success. Her books became a literary phenomenon, selling millions of copies in the United States and in foreign editions and appearing on best-seller lists.

The Cat Who Saw Red (1986) was nominated for an Edgar Award by the Mystery Writers of America, and *The Cat Who Played Brahms* (1987) received an Anthony Award nomination. The Winter, 1990, issue of *Mystery Readers Journal*, discussing animal mysteries, recognized Braun's pioneering role in that mystery subgenre.

BIOGRAPHY

Lilian Jackson Braun was born Lilian Jackson on June 20, 1913, at Chicopee Falls, Massachusetts, to Charles Jackson and Clara Ward Jackson. Braun's parents had emigrated from northern England to the United States, where her father made tools for factory machines. During Braun's childhood, several of her father's coworkers boarded in her parents' Springfield, Massachusetts, home. Braun was an only child until she was nine, when her brother, Lloyd, was born, followed by the birth of her sister, Florence.

During the 1920's, the Jackson family moved from Massachusetts to Detroit, Michigan, where Charles Jackson secured employment as a toolmaker with a motor company. Braun later credited her father's inventiveness and her mother's imagination for shaping her storytelling skills. At dinner, Braun and her siblings were expected to provide detailed accounts describing their experiences at school.

As a girl, Braun read Sherlock Holmes mysteries and camped with her Girl Scout troop. A Detroit Tigers fan, she composed funny verses about baseball. When she was fifteen, Braun sold baseball poems, which she referred to as spoems, to the *Detroit News*. Using the pseudonym Ward Jackson, she contributed articles to *The Sporting News* and *Baseball Magazine*. Braun also wrote for her high school's newspaper and literary magazine.

When Braun was sixteen years old, she graduated from high school. Although she wanted to earn a college degree to teach school, she instead sought employment to assist her family during the Depression. During baseball season, Braun wrote poems for the *Detroit News*. In 1929, Braun began writing advertising copy as a freelance employee for the Crowley Knower Company's store. In 1930 the Ernst Kern Company hired her to work full-time creating advertisements, then had her direct public relations. She worked for that company for the next eighteen years.

Around 1943, Lilian Jackson married Paul Braun, an accountant. In 1948 she accepted an editorial position at the *Detroit Free Press*. Braun's husband gave her a Siamese kitten for her fortieth birthday. A fan of the W. S. Gilbert and Arthur Sullivan opera *The Mikado* (1885), she named the kitten Koko. Koko's death after a neighbor shoved him out a tenth-floor window was the catalyst for the Cat Who series. Dealing with her grief, Braun wrote the short story, "The Sin of Madame Phloi." *Ellery Queen's Mystery Magazine* published the story in 1962 and requested additional cat mysteries. It was this story that Anthony Boucher se-

lected for inclusion in the eighteenth annual *Best Detective Stories of the Year.*

Braun continued to write, and her short story "Magnificent Shed" was published in the October, 1965, issue of *Journal of the American Institute of Architects*. She won American Institute of Architects writing awards. Then, an E. P. Dutton editor contracted Braun to write cat mystery novels. Braun completed four manuscripts, three of which were published during the mid-1960's before her publisher stated that no market existed for further cat mysteries. Braun's husband died in 1967.

Braun continued writing for the *Detroit Free Press* until her 1978 retirement. The next year, she married actor Earl Bettinger. They resided in Bad Axe, Michigan, and owned a log cabin by Lake Huron. Braun renewed her literary career in the 1980's when a Berkley editor offered her a multibook contract. She added to the Cat Who series at the rate of about a book per year. Braun also wrote a column for the *Lilian Jackson Braun Newsletter* and forewords for Gina Spadafori's and Dr. Paul D. Pion's *Cats for Dummies* (1997) and books discussing the Cat Who novels. She and her husband bought a home in the Blue Ridge Mountains near Tyron, North Carolina, where they became active in the community, supporting the Flat Rock Playhouse and Polk County library. The Tryon Movie Theatre hosted a tribute to Braun in April, 2005.

ANALYSIS

Lilian Jackson Braun creates mysteries that contain elements of classic whodunits accented with modern twists to explore themes of justice, duty, and community. Her depiction of cats who contributed to the discovery of clues and were aware of sinister elements in humans was a unique technique when she began writing cat mysteries in the 1960's. Braun's feline depictions were authentic, never demonstrating unrealistic behaviors or responses. Her feline characters do not talk or exhibit any supernatural means of communicating with humans.

Braun's storytelling relies on an omniscient narrator describing Qwilleran's experiences and revealing details about his cats through the journalist's perspective. Qwilleran interacts with the cats, interpreting their natural curiosity and destructiveness as signals that serve to point out clues he should investigate. His unexpected role as a wealthy man and philanthropist represents the theme of redemption as he generously shares his money with others to improve their lives.

Braun's sense of place contributes to the realism of her books. Appropriating scenes with which she is familiar, she capably creates urban and rural settings for her fictional Down Below and Moose County. She enriches her stories with her knowledge of regional history and traditions that connect generations. Expanding her cast and settings, Braun incorporates sufficient variety to create unique, compelling stories.

By the early twenty-first century, however, many of Braun's novels seemed to consist mostly of a series of scenes lacking a cohesive story. Her writing style was often stiff and did not have the continuity and flow found in her previous stories. Plots often relied on coincidences, and characters were not well developed. Many characters were unlikable and self-indulgent. Although the theme of altruism remained, it lacked the sincerity evidenced in earlier novels. Crimes did not demand the same attention and pursuit of justice as they had in Braun's early mysteries. Sometimes Qwilleran never elaborated how he came to a solution, and murderers often were dealt with by an accidental death or by the suspect leaving Moose County. Characters did not respond realistically to major losses. Braun's excessive use of exclamation points seemed contradictory to her characters' limited enthusiasm.

THE CAT WHO COULD READ BACKWARDS

In the first book of her series, *The Cat Who Could Read Backwards* (1966), Braun introduces her protagonists, James Qwilleran and Koko. Qwilleran's past is referred to as he humbly accepts a position as an arts reporter for the *Daily Fluxion* and reunites with his childhood friend Arch Riker, who becomes an integral character in the series. Although he lacks artistic experience, Qwilleran eagerly approaches his assignments, intending to prove he is a capable reporter despite his previous failures as a husband and an alcoholic. As he interacts with colleagues and artists, he learns that the newspaper's art critic, George Bonifield Mountclemens III, is a reclusive individual who writes acerbic reviews.

After accepting an invitation to dine with Mount-

clemens, Qwilleran leases an apartment in the critic's building and soon begins to perform errands for Mountclemens, including tending his Siamese cat. Qwilleran interviews artists and attends art events, becoming familiar with the local artistic community. He becomes involved in the aftermath of several murders, including that of Mountclemens. Qwilleran and Mountclemens's cat, which Qwilleran renames Koko, establish a bond. Qwilleran becomes aware of suspicious places and objects because of Koko's inquisitiveness, and that awareness helps him identify the murderer and motive.

Qwilleran's determination to start his life anew and his self-discipline embody the themes of possibility and opportunity that Braun creates in her early Cat Who books.

THE CAT WHO SAW RED

Braun retained her distinctive style when she resumed her series with *The Cat Who Saw Red* in 1986, nearly two decades after she first published a Cat Who novel. Her protagonist Qwilleran still works for the *Daily Fluxion*, but he is now a food critic and no longer covers art. He and the cats live at the Maus Haus surrounded by an eclectic group of neighbors. His devotion to Koko and Yum Yum has intensified and he is more perceptive of their helpful behavior.

Koko types significant combinations of letters and numbers on Qwilleran's typewriter, scratches a victim's notebook, and paws at pictures with Yum Yum. A red book agitates Koko, and he and Yum Yum create a yarn trap that snares a killer. Braun's sophisticated style and complex plotting enable the cats' unusual behavior to seem plausible to readers and perhaps intentional, done in the aim of helping Qwilleran secure justice for their friend's murder.

THE CAT WHO PLAYED POST OFFICE

After receiving an inheritance from Fanny Klingenschoen in *The Cat Who Played Brahms*, Qwilleran contemplates whether he should accept the stipulations that are part of receiving that fortune. To receive the fortune, Qwilleran must live in the Klingenshoen mansion in Pickax for five years. In *The Cat Who Played Post Office* (1987), he decides to move to Pickax. Braun eases Qwilleran's transition to unfamiliar territory by transferring to Pickax the character of Iris Cobb, who had been his landlady when he lived in

Junktown in *The Cat Who Turned On and Off* (1968).

Qwilleran wins new friends because of his pleasing personality and generosity, creating the Klingenschoen Foundation to improve his adopted community. He involves himself in local activities and investigates why a maid vanished from the mansion. Koko plays notes on the piano, locates a diary, and knocks out an intruder with a vase. Qwilleran learns how Pickax's past influences its present, reinforcing his resolve to stay. He eventually establishes a home in an apple barn in *The Cat Who Knew a Cardinal* (1991) and secures the Klingenschoen estate in *The Cat Who Moved a Mountain* (1992). Qwilleran accelerates his altruism and observes his cats to aid investigations of mysterious events, which are commonplace in Moose County.

THE CAT WHO HAD SIXTY WHISKERS

Although *The Cat Who Had Sixty Whiskers* (2007) begins with Qwilleran boasting that Koko has sixty whiskers, enhancing his intuitiveness, both cats, mostly interested in food, seem more passive regarding mysteries. When librarian Polly Duncan, Qwilleran's romantic interest, travels to Paris, Qwilleran becomes lonely. He pursues several column ideas for his Qwill Pen column in *The Moose County Something*, but none of the subjects sustains his interest, and he relies on readers' contributions to fill his space. Qwilleran's moodiness becomes tedious.

Qwilleran meets an eccentric piano tuner whose fiancée dies after having an allergic reaction to a bee sting. When Qwilleran realizes who purposefully hid the dead woman's bee kit, he does not seek that person's arrest. He socializes with neighbors at his condominium, meeting an attorney named Barbara Honiger, who has moved into Polly's vacated apartment.

Qwilleran uncharacteristically mentions his dislike for visitors who want to view the apple barn. When he hears that the apple barn has been destroyed, he displays a moodiness and cavalier attitude that are frustrating to readers as is his sudden courtship of Barbara. Much of this novel, like several others preceding it, including *The Cat Who Dropped a Bombshell* (2006), seem inconsistent with the themes of friendship, commitment, and acceptance that are the essence of the Cat Who series.

Elizabeth D. Schafer

PRINCIPAL MYSTERY AND DETECTIVE FICTION

THE CAT WHO SERIES: 1966-1990 • *The Cat Who Could Read Backwards*, 1966; *The Cat Who Ate Danish Modern*, 1967; *The Cat Who Turned On and Off*, 1968; *The Cat Who Saw Red*, 1986; *The Cat Who Played Brahms*, 1987; *The Cat Who Played Post Office*, 1987; *The Cat Who Knew Shakespeare*, 1988; *The Cat Who Sniffed Glue*, 1988; *The Cat Who Went Underground*, 1989; *The Cat Who Talked to Ghosts*, 1990; *The Cat Who Lived High*, 1990

1991-2007 • *The Cat Who Knew a Cardinal*, 1991; *The Cat Who Moved a Mountain*, 1992; *The Cat Who Wasn't There*, 1992; *The Cat Who Went into the Closet*, 1993; *The Cat Who Came to Breakfast*, 1994; *The Cat Who Blew the Whistle*, 1995; *The Cat Who Said Cheese*, 1996; *The Cat Who Tailed a Thief*, 1997; *The Cat Who Sang for the Birds*, 1998; *The Cat Who Saw Stars*, 1998; *The Cat Who Robbed a Bank*, 1999; *The Cat Who Smelled a Rat*, 2001; *The Cat Who Went Up the Creek*, 2002; *The Cat Who Brought Down the House*, 2003; *The Cat Who Talked Turkey*, 2004; *The Cat Who Went Bananas*, 2004; *The Cat Who Dropped a Bombshell*, 2006; *The Cat Who Had Sixty Whiskers*, 2007

OTHER MAJOR WORKS

SHORT FICTION: *The Cat Who Had Fourteen Tales*, 1988; *Short and Tall Tales: Moose County Legends Collected by James Mackintosh Qwilleran*, 2002; *The Private Life of the Cat Who . . . Tales of Koko and Yum Yum from the Journal of James Mackintosh Qwilleran*, 2003

BIBLIOGRAPHY

Christensen, Wendy. "Life with Lilian Jackson Braun." *Cat Fancy* 37, no. 11 (November, 1994): 40-43. Braun provides details about cats she has owned and her writing process.

Dubose, Martha Hailey, with Margaret Caldwell Thomas. *Women of Mystery: The Lives and Works of Notable Women Crime Novelists.* New York: St. Martin's Minotaur, 2000. Contains an essay on Braun that describes how the death of her cat Koko motivated her to write and how her books's popularity goes beyond cat lovers.

Feaster, Sharon A. *The Cat Who . . . Companion*. New York: Berkley Publishing Group, 1998. Comprehensive guide includes synopses, lists of characters and places, and trivia for Cat Who books. Also contains maps and an interview with Braun.

Headrick, Robert J., Jr. *The Cat Who Quiz Book*. New York: Berkley Publishing Group, 2003. Braun wrote the foreword for this compendium of questions and answers about characters, places, plots, clues, and quotations in the Cat Who series. Lists foreign edition titles.

Johnson, Maria C. "Imaginary Felines Keep Their Paws on Lilian Jackson Braun." *Greensboro (N.C.) News and Record*, May 26, 1991, p. F1. Detailed feature article written by a reporter near Braun's North Carolina home includes personal information not in other sources.

Kaufman, Joanne. "The Cat Woman Who Writes Mysteries." *The Wall Street Journal*, March 15, 2006, p. D16. Examines criticism of Braun's writing and its reception within the mystery genre.

Nelson, Catherine A. "The Lady Who . . ." *The Armchair Detective* 24, no. 4 (Fall, 1991): 388-394, 396-398. An interview with Braun, who discusses her writing successes and aspects of her life before the Cat Who series. Includes photographs of Braun, her cats, and office.

JON L. BREEN

Born: Montgomery, Alabama; November 8, 1943

Types of plot: Comedy caper; master sleuth; amateur sleuth

PRINCIPAL SERIES

Ed Gorgon, 1971-
Jerry Brogan, 1983-
Rachel Hennings, 1984-
Sherlock Holmes, 1987-
Sebastian Grady, 1994-

PRINCIPAL SERIES CHARACTERS

ED GORGON is a baseball umpire with a flair for solving major league puzzlers.

JERRY BROGAN is a hefty racetrack announcer who uses imaginative methods to both squeeze into his announcer's booth and to unravel criminal schemes.

RACHEL HENNINGS is the owner of a haunted bookstore in California who moves among the dead, the undead, and the not-dead-at-all.

SHERLOCK HOLMES is the iconic supersleuth created by Sir Arthur Conan Doyle.

SEBASTIAN GRADY is a Hollywood detective whose sidekick is a cat.

CONTRIBUTION

Jon L. Breen's contribution to mystery and detective fiction has been twofold. He is first a scholar who has performed invaluable service to those interested in the genre, compiling carefully annotated bibliographies. He is also a recognized reviewer and critic, having written reviews for a number of periodicals, including *Ellery Queen's Mystery Magazine*, *The Armchair Detective*, and *The American Standard*. Acknowledged as a critic, he has received the Mystery Writers of America's Edgar Allan Poe Award in 1982, 1985, and 1991. He was also the winner of the Agatha Award for critics in 2000. With his wife, Rita A. Breen, he coedited an anthology of eleven novelettes selected from the *American Magazine*.

Breen has also contributed to mystery literature by producing many short stories and novels. In these he has explored parody and pastiche, combined his interest in sports with his love of books, and demonstrated his knowledge of the classic mystery story. His novels have been well received and favorably reviewed in the United States and in Great Britain.

BIOGRAPHY

Jon Linn Breen was born on November 8, 1943, to Frank William Breen and Margaret Wolfe Breen. His parents' professions may have influenced his own choice of profession and his love of scholarship: His father was a librarian and his mother a teacher. Breen's college years were spent in California, where he received a bachelor's degree from Pepperdine College (now University) in 1965. He then attended the University of Southern California, where in 1966 he completed an master's degree in library science, a profession he would never completely abandon. During these years he was also a sports broadcaster for a radio station in Los Angeles. An interest in sports continues to be one of Breen's major avocations and has influenced his writing.

After serving in the military from 1967 to 1969, including a year in Vietnam, Breen returned to library work. He served at several educational institutions in California before becoming the head reference librarian at California State College (now University), Dominguez Hills, a position he held until 1975. He then took a position as the reference and collections development librarian at Rio Hondo Community College at Whittier, California. In 1970, he married Rita Gunson, a teacher, of Yorkshire, England. She has coedited with her husband a volume of novelettes.

Breen's first short story appeared in *Ellery Queen's Mystery Magazine* in 1966, when he was twenty-three years old. That first effort was followed by more short stories, reviews, reference works, critical biographies, essays, and three respected novels. By his own admission, Breen followed the ambitious goal of becoming what he calls an "all-rounder," in the tradition of writers Anthony Boucher, Julian Symons, and H. R. F. Keating. The goal has motivated him to achieve success in diverse areas of research and literature within the mystery and detective genre.

ANALYSIS

In the course of an interview, Jon L. Breen once evaluated the major strengths of his novels as their humor and their appealing characters. Breen's humor owes much to his forays into parody and pastiche. In *Hair of the Sleuthhound: Parodies of Mystery Fiction*

(1982), Breen, in his preface to the volume, tries to distinguish between the two; either because of his careful scholarship, characteristic of his work, or the honesty of his approach to writing, an equally important characteristic, he does not manage to provide a clear distinction; the two forms are intertwined and difficult to separate. Furthermore, the most successful parodies, Breen maintains, are those done in affection and with respect, without hostility. That attitude is obvious in Breen's work. The authors whom he parodies have accepted his work as flattering and have noted its humor. While Breen's parody may be the sincerest form of flattery, it can also be an important form of criticism—and therein, perhaps, lies its key distinction from pastiche.

Breen's humor is close to that defined as the ready perceiving of the comic or the ludicrous, effectively expressed. It is marked also by warmth, tolerance, and a sympathetic understanding of the human condition. Gentle as this humor may be, Breen is capable of creating hilarious scenes. *Listen for the Click* (1983) can be regarded as a spoof of the classic amateur-sleuth plot. The final scene is a parody of the typical gathering of suspects during which the culprit is unmasked. A situation that in less practiced hands might be both tiresome and trite, under Breen's control leads to a satisfactory resolution of the mystery and a genuinely comic scene.

THE GATHERING PLACE

Breen is also capable of handling subtler humor adroitly. In scenes with less action and more dialogue, his touch is equally deft. Neither labored nor forced, his lines are witty, suited to his characters, and well paced. When Rachel Hennings, protagonist of *The Gathering Place* (1984), inherits her uncle's secondhand bookstore in Los Angeles, she interrupts her college career in Arizona to manage the shop, which is a literary landmark. In the past a favorite haunt of literary figures and their friends, it has a charming ambience and appeals to her tastes and interests. While at college, she has been pursued by an amorous if tense young faculty member. Resigned to her leaving Arizona, the young professor calls his brother in Los Angeles, who is the book editor for a local newspaper, asking that he assist Rachel in getting settled. Rachel and the editor are attracted to each other, but he considers her his brother's girl. Their conversation in which Rachel tries to express her feelings is characterized by Breen's control of scene and dialogue. The tone is light; there is no weighty introspection or serious self-analysis. In this author's work, only the less sympathetic characters take themselves very seriously.

Rachel is an independent young woman, determined to succeed in her bookshop. Confronted by a motley lot of representatives of the world of the best seller, as well as the friendly ghosts she senses in her uncle's shop, she proves equal to the challenges presented to her. As in the case of other Breen characters, she is attractive and has a winning personality.

TRIPLE CROWN AND LISTEN FOR THE CLICK

As Breen suggests, his characters are one of his strengths. They are varied and attractive. Jerry Brogan, the protagonist of both *Triple Crown* (1985) and *Listen for the Click*, is an overweight racetrack announcer. He is bright and decent, a former public relations man who has found satisfaction and pleasure in his small and narrow announcer's booth, although his weight calls for imaginative methods of entering that cramped space. Devoted to his aunt and dedicated to doing a good job calling the races but somewhat uncertain about his relationship with his girlfriend, Brogan is eminently likable. He is not cast in the traditional hero mold, nor is he an antihero, but rather a figure with whom it is very easy to identify.

Brogan's aunt, Olivia Barchester, a charming eccentric given to avid reading of mystery and detective fiction and owning a certain talent for investigation and deduction, is not only a friendly parody of famous sleuths who have gone before her but also a carefully drawn and attractive figure in her own right.

The ability to depict memorable characters and the penchant for humor in his novels may be exemplified best by Breen's minor characters, Stan Digby and Gaston Miles in *Listen for the Click*. Respectively a would-be mystery writer and a seedy con artist, combining their talents to take the apparently artless Olivia Barchester for her fortune, the two contribute much to the success of the novel.

KILL THE UMPIRE

One of Breen's best known characters, Ed Gorgon, gives the author opportunity to set his classical-style mysteries in the unlikely world of major league baseball. Gorgon is an umpire. In 2003, Breen collected sixteen Gorgon stories in *Kill the Umpire*. Always the critic, Breen accompanied his stories with commentary dealing with the development and growing sophistication of his storytelling and Gorgon's aging over thirty years of making calls between murders.

EYE OF GOD

In 2006, *Eye of God* was released to mixed reviews. Breen foresaw controversy but was intrigued by the idea of homicidal criminality existing at the heart of American televangelism. The religious conversion of one of the main characters at the outset of the novel and the uncritical exploration of the inner sanctum of the Religious Right made many readers uncomfortable. Some fans, however, found the novel interesting and original.

PLOT AND STYLE

In a discussion of his work, Breen has said that he finds the plot to be the most difficult part of the undertaking. Breen is on record as an admirer of some of the most complex plots of mystery and detective fiction, and it is not surprising that craftsmanship in this area is of major importance to him. His story lines are strong and his powers of construction formidable. Reviewers are not critical of his plots, with the exception of *The Gathering Place*, in which, according to one critic, Breen pushes the reader's credulity too far. Rachel becomes involved in a psychic experience in her shop when she becomes a "medium" for long-dead writers who use her to expose a ghostwriting scandal. She also discovers that she can sign authentic signatures of these same beneficent spirits in an automatic writing session when the pen moves unbidden by her hand, creating a cache of signed editions coveted by collectors. Even an act of final retribution implies that these ghosts are determined to punish the guilty and protect the innocent. It is not surprising that some critics insist that Breen has strained the fabric of his story, or that the premise on which the tale hangs is too bizarre to be acceptable. A critic for *The New York Times*, however, believes that the author never intended his readers to take the premise seriously, and as in his other novels, it is the entertainment that Breen affords that is important.

Breen's attention to detail, which enhances the authenticity of his scenes and adds to the completeness of his descriptions, is also noteworthy, especially in a genre where attention to detail is an important factor. His timing and placement of clues and his avoidance of the loose ends that can distract and frustrate the reader account for much of the popularity of his novels. The foregoing comments should not, however, suggest that realism in the literary sense is the first goal of the author. His is not the tough or hard-boiled approach to crime and mystery fiction. There is no gratuitous violence or lurid description of corpses, though murders are committed and acts of violence do occur. Sex is neither exploited nor ignored; it plays a part in the lives of Breen's characters and in his plots but never dominates the action. Nor is Breen's treatment of women exploitative. Women are presented quite naturally as equally intelligent and capable as their male counterparts. On the other hand, the author does not pander to the female audience by exaggeration. Balance is another of the author's unheralded achievements.

Breen's style, which has been described as "breezy" by more than one critic, is extremely readable. No doubt the author, who is also an able craftsman, would be dismayed that a novel could be devoured so quickly, given the time it must take to achieve the flow of plot and words. His prose is economical and clear. His dialogue, especially in the more humorous scenes, is well conceived. The pages are not burdened with complex sentences or banalities.

SCHOLARSHIP

Breen's lengthy love affair with mystery and detective fiction—he began reading and collecting at the age of twelve—seems to give him a unique place among authors of this genre. Few can claim his knowledge of the history of the movement or exhibit such intimate understanding of the contributions of individual authors of the past. As a result, he is as important for his scholarly work as he is for his fiction. For example, *Novel Verdicts: A Guide to Courtroom Fiction* (1985), a critical bibliography of courtroom fiction, while not claiming to be comprehensive, is a very complete and detailed guide. A set of guidelines influencing the choice of entries is clearly stated. Each book included has a lengthy courtroom scene or focuses on a trial.

Entries are restricted to cases in American or British courts or cases in parts of the world that use English in their legal systems. All entries carry annotations outlining plot and action, and a critique of the accuracy of legal knowledge.

Breen's thorough knowledge of the mystery genre, as critic and scholar, parodist and practitioner, makes him a unique figure among mystery writers, particularly interesting to the mystery buff for his mastery of the difficult parody form as well as for his similarity to other masters of the genre. Above all, Breen's novels are sheer fun, promising to delight readers with their well-crafted plots, judiciously drawn characters, wealth of realistic detail, and fine timing.

Anne R. Vizzier
Updated by Janet Alice Long

PRINCIPAL MYSTERY AND DETECTIVE FICTION

ED GORGON SERIES: *Kill the Umpire*, 2003

JERRY BROGAN SERIES: *Listen for the Click*, 1983 (also known as *Vicar's Roses*); *Triple Crown*, 1985; *Loose Lips*, 1990; *Hot Air*, 1991

RACHEL HENNINGS SERIES: *The Gathering Place*, 1984; *Touch of the Past*, 1988

NONSERIES NOVELS: *Eye of God*, 2006

SHORT FICTION: *Hair of the Sleuthhound: Parodies of Mystery Fiction*, 1982; *The Drowning Icecube, and Other Stories*, 1999

OTHER MAJOR WORKS

NONFICTION: *A Little Fleshed Up Around the Crook of the Elbow: A Selected Bibliography of Some Literary Parodies*, 1970; *The Girl in the Pictorial Wrapper*, 1972; *What About Murder? A Guide to Books About Mystery and Detective Fiction*, 1981; *Novel Verdicts: A Guide to Courtroom Fiction*, 1985

EDITED TEXTS: *American Murders*, 1986 (with Rita A. Breen); *Sleuths of the Century*, 2000 (with Edward Gorman); *Synod of Sleuths: Essays on Judeo-Christian Detective Fiction*, 1990 (with Martin H. Greenberg)

BIBLIOGRAPHY

Bottum, Joseph. "*Kill the Umpire*: The Calls of Ed Gorgon." Review of *Kill the Umpire*, by Jon L.

Breen. *The Weekly Standard* 9, no. 30 (April 12-April 19, 2004): 47. This favorable review notes that the Ed Gorgon sports-themed stories in this collection span more than thirty years and that Breen writes reviews for the publication.

Breen, Jon L. Interview in *Ellery Queen's Mystery Magazine.* June, 1979, pp. 57-58. Breen's critical reviews appeared in Ellery Queen for years. This is an interesting turn-of-the-tables.

_____. *Novel Verdicts: A Guide to Courtroom Fiction.* 2d ed. Lanham, Md.: Scarecrow Press, 1999. A revised bibliography that contains more than eight hundred entries of books dealing with courtroom dramas published by 1997.

_____. *What About Murder? A Guide to Books About Mystery and Detective Fiction.* 2d ed. Metuchen, N.J.: Scarecrow Press, 1993. A bibliography of more than two hundred murder novels published through 1981 with annotations by Breen. Provides insights into Breen's view of mysteries.

Callendar, Newgate. Review of *The Gathering*, by Jon L. Breen. *The New York Times*, May 20, 1984, p. A39. Reviewer notes that the premise of the book is not believable but states that Breen did not intend to make his readers believers but to entertain them.

Watt, Peter Ridgway, and Joseph Green. *The Alternative Sherlock Holmes: Pastiches, Parodies, and Copies.* Burlington, Vt.: Ashgate, 2003. A book that must have been written with Breen in mind. This large volume explores the fiction directly inspired by Holmes and Watson.

SIMON BRETT

Born: Worcester Park, Surrey, England, October 28, 1945

Types of plot: Amateur sleuth; cozy

PRINCIPAL SERIES

Charles Paris, 1975-
Mrs. Pargeter, 1986-
Fethering, 2000-

PRINCIPAL SERIES CHARACTERS

CHARLES PARIS is a broken-down, alcoholic actor with a libertine nature. Forty-seven years old, he has been divorced for fifteen years in the first novel. He gets along well with his former wife, who runs a school for girls. He sometimes takes temporary jobs such as painting houses or helps out his friends. Trying to liven up his routine life, he pursues meaningless sexual encounters and amateur detective work.

MRS. MELITA PARGETER is the attractive widow of a master criminal, who had serious links to the underworld but never got her involved in any nefarious ac-tivities. When he died, he left her wealthy and also left her his address book. Her husband's associates have all gone straight, but they provide a wealth of resources that enable the widow to make copies of jewelry and find vehicles. Mrs. Pargeter lives in an upscale subdivision. The novels' action tends to happen during the daytime, while the neighborhood husbands are off to work, so it is their wives who experience the uncertainties of living near a sleuth.

CAROLE SEDDON is a prim and proper resident of Fethering, a self-contained retirement community on the southern coast of England. Divorced shortly after retiring from her career in government service, she is trying to live a quiet life when she is forced to investigate a death on the beach.

JUDE is the bohemian neighbor of Carole Seddon, in Fethering, who becomes involved in her neighbor's investigation. She uses only one name, has a colorful past, and earns her living from aromatherapy and alternative medicine. Jude is the liberal, emotional side of this pair.

CONTRIBUTION

Simon Brett is a versatile writer, equally at home with mystery, children's literature, radio, television, and theatrical drama. For his first mystery series character, Brett looked to the middle-aged actors with whom he worked. They fascinated him, in part because he found them to be so obsessed with themselves. "Somebody defined an actor as someone whose eyes glaze over when the conversation moves away from him," he said. He created Charles Paris as an amalgam of many of the actors he has known. Brett described Charles to an interviewer: "If anyone starts attacking the theater, he will leap to the defense, but he does have this kind of detachment so that he can sit on the sidelines and . . . see the share of idiocy and greed and all the worst human values."

Brett is a past chairman of the Crime Writers' Association (1986-1987). In 2000, he became president of the prestigious Detection Club. He received nominations for Edgar Awards in 1984 for his "Big Boy, Little Boy," *A Shock to the System* (1984) in 1986, and "Ways to Kill a Cat" in 1998.

BIOGRAPHY

Born in a southern suburb of London shortly after the end of World War II, Simon Anthony Lee Brett is the son of John Brett, a surveyor, and Margaret Lee, a schoolteacher. His secondary education was at Dulwich College, where he won a scholarship to Wadham College, Oxford, to study history. He graduated with first class honors, but only after serving as president of the University Dramatic Society and as director of the Oxford Late-Night Revue on the Fringe at the Edinburgh Festival. He married Lucy Victoria McLaren in 1971, and they subsequently raised two sons and a daughter.

In 1968, Brett became a radio producer for the British Broadcasting Corporation (BBC). He also began writing plays. His first production, *Mrs. Gladys Moxon*, debuted in London in 1970. His next play, *Did You Sleep Well?* was staged the following year and another, *Third Person*, in 1972. His interest in plays gave way to radio and television scripts, earning him the 1973 Writers Guild of Great Britain Award for the best radio feature script, and then he decided to branch out

into novels. While with the BBC, he produced the first episode of *The Hitchhiker's Guide to the Galaxy* (1978), a radio series.

The BBC assigned Brett to produce a series of adaptations of Dorothy L. Sayers's Lord Peter Wimsey mysteries. Brett says he worked closely with the writer who was adapting the books into scripts and his experience "sort of demystified the genre." This association with the Wimsey project showed him that a good mystery is series of dialogues, with the sleuth interviewing various characters: "If you can actually make the dialogue interesting, there is usually one fact that has to emerge from these encounters; . . . the top wasn't on the bottle of whiskey . . . and you can make an interesting scene around that." Although he was not sure of his ability to create the puzzle plots typical of mysteries, he knew that he could write dialogue and decided to write a mystery.

Brett published his first mystery, *Cast, in Order of Disappearance*, the start of the Charles Paris series, in 1975. In 1986, after eleven years of producing a Charles Paris novel annually, Brett created a new series featuring Mrs. Pargeter. In 2000, he started a third, featuring two women in the coastal town of Fethering.

ANALYSIS

Simon Brett likes to weave irony and humor into his stories, commenting obliquely on the aspects of British society in which each of his series is set. In the Charles Paris novels, he looks at the egomaniacs of the theater, the young performers who are clawing their way up and the older performers who are easing their way down. With Mrs. Pargeter, the aging but sexually attractive widow gives readers a look at a variety of underworld characters, whom she calls on to help her with certain investigative tasks, both savory and unsavory. In the Fethering series, he puts together a middle-aged, conservative and quiet divorced woman who has been forced into retiring from the Home Office and a jarring neighbor with a wild and loose, outgoing personality; here, there is less commentary on a facet of society than more of a contrast between two opposites.

In stories outside these series, Brett features weaker characters who react to life's problems by turning to crime. The most popular of these was *A Shock to the System*, in which oil-company executive Graham Marshall's career is threatened, and he resorts to murder. This 1984 novel was made into a 1990 film starting Michael Caine.

Brett's mysteries have been categorized as "British cozies," which leaves the author "amazed and amused," although he acknowledges that he and other British writers have not produced much fiction in the hard-boiled genre, although British readers do enjoy this genre. Brett has said that he writes about amateur sleuths rather than police detectives because the novels about the latter are essentially just puzzles, where all that matters is identifying the murderer. He thinks that the detectives in these works have become interchangeable characters and that nearly no good puzzles are left. With an amateur sleuth, he finds more leeway to describe some part of the world in the background, such as the milieu of theater productions, horse racing, or the wine trade.

DEAD GIVEAWAY

In the eleventh Charles Paris novel, *Dead Giveaway* (1985), Charles is invited to be a contestant on the pilot of a television game show similar to *What's My Line?* (1950-1967), where panelists guess who he is and what he does. The faded actor is resigned to the realization that this is a challenge because few people would recognize him. As the big wheel is spun at the climax of the show, the sleazy, skirt-chasing host falls dead, poisoned by cyanide in his gin. The host had upset many people, providing many suspects for his murder. One of them, who had worked on a show about poisons and had handled the host's glass, enlists Charles's aid. Charles knows something about the timing of the poisoning, because he himself was secretly sipping the gin earlier. As usual, the novel features a healthy dollop of irony and wit.

A NICE CLASS OF CORPSE

Mrs. Pargeter has been compared to Agatha Christie's Miss Marple, but Brett described her as "not quite so accepting as Miss Marple. She has her own standards and she does not like pretension. She's very happy to put people down." Her elegance is tempered with flashiness.

In *A Nice Class of Corpse* (1986), the first work in the series, Brett mixes Mrs. Pargeter's systematic method of detection with entries in a criminal's diary. Several deaths have been attributed to accidents that happen only to the elderly, but Mrs. Pargeter suspects murder, and the diary confirms her belief for the reader. She finds fake jewels in a safe, catches a thieving employee of the Devereux seaside hotel, and uncovers the diary's writer.

THE BODY ON THE BEACH

The Fethering series begins in *The Body on the Beach* (2000) with the growing friendship of two opposites, forcibly retired civil servant Carole Seddon and flamboyant flower child Jude. Carole finds a body on the beach, his throat slashed, but when she returns with the police, the body is gone and they write her off as hysterical. It does not help that she has washed her dog and her kitchen floor before calling them. The next day, a dead teenager washes up on the beach, and

DEAD GIVEAWAY

"The portrait of backstairs TV antics is wickedly accurate."
—*The Times*

Simon Brett

the grieving mother wants it kept quiet. Jude and Carole question local residents and discover tensions among regular patrons of the local pub.

Here again, Brett's strength is the depth of his characterizations, although it seems a bit over the top for him to withhold any details of Jude's prior life or even her last name. The matching of opposite personalities works well, however, and both make a good contrast to Mrs. Pargeter.

J. Edmund Rush

PRINCIPAL MYSTERY AND DETECTIVE FICTION

CHARLES PARIS SERIES: *Cast, in Order of Disappearance*, 1975; *So Much Blood*, 1976; *Star Trap*, 1977; *An Amateur Corpse*, 1978; *A Comedian Dies*, 1979; *The Dead Side of the Mike*, 1980; *Situation Tragedy*, 1981; *Murder Unprompted*, 1982; *Murder in the Title*, 1983; *Not Dead, Only Resting*, 1984; *Dead Giveaway*, 1985; *What Bloody Man Is That?*, 1987; *A Series of Murders*, 1989; *Corporate Bodies*, 1991; *A Reconstructed Corpse*, 1993; *Sicken and So Die*, 1995; *Dead Room Farce*, 1997

MRS. PARGETER SERIES: *A Nice Class of Corpse*, 1986; *Mrs, Presumed Dead*, 1988; *Mrs. Pargeter's Package*, 1990; *Mrs. Pargeter's Pound of Flesh*, 1992; *Mrs. Pargeter's Plot*, 1996; *Mrs. Pargeter's Point of Honour*, 1998

FETHERING SERIES: *The Body on the Beach*, 2000; *Death on the Downs*, 2001; *The Torso in the Town*, 2002; *Murder in the Museum*, 2003; *The Hanging in the Hotel*, 2004; *The Witness at the Wedding*, 2005; *The Stabbing in the Stables*, 2006; *Death Under the Dryer*, 2007

NONSERIES NOVELS: *A Shock to the System*, 1984; *Dead Romantic*, 1985; *The Christmas Crimes at Puzzel Manor*, 1991; *Singled Out*, 1995

SHORT FICTION: *Tickled to Death, and Other Stories of Crime and Suspense*, 1985 (also known as A Box of Tricks: Short Stories)

OTHER MAJOR WORKS

NOVELS: *After Henry*, 1988; *The Booker Book*, 1989; *The Penultimate Chance Saloon*, 2006

PLAYS: *Mrs. Gladys Moxon*, pr. 1970; *Did You Sleep Well?*, pr. 1971; *Third Person*, pr. 1972; *Drake's Dream*, pr. 1977 (with Lynne Riley and Richard Riley); *Murder in Play*, pb. 1994; *Mr. Quigley's Revenge*, pb. 1995; *Silhouette*, pr. 1998; *The Tale of Little Red Riding Hood*, pb. 1998; *Sleeping Beauty*, pb. 1999; *Putting the Kettle on*, pb. 2002; *A Bad Dream*, pb. 2005

RADIO PLAYS: *Semi-circles*, 1982; *Gothic Romances*, 1982; *A Matter of Life and Death*, 1982; *Cast, in Order of Disappearance*, 1984

TELEPLAYS: *A Promising Death*, 1983; *The Crime of the Dancing Duchess*, 1983

CHILDREN'S LITERATURE: *Molesworth Rites Again*, 1983; *The Three Detectives and the Missing Superstar*, 1986; *How to Stay Topp*, 1987; *The Three Detectives and the Knight in Armor*, 1987; *How to Be a Little Sod*, 1989; *Look Who's Walking: Further Diaries of a Little Sod*, 1994; *Not Another Little Sod*, 1997

NONFICTION: *Frank Muir Goes Into —*, 1978 (with Frank Muir); *The Second Frank Muir Goes Into —*, 1979 (with Muir); *The Third Frank Muir Goes Into —*, 1980 (with Muir); *Frank Muir on Children*, 1980; *The Fourth Frank Muir Goes Into —*, 1981 (with Muir); *The Child Owner's Handbook*, 1983; *Bad Form: Or, How Not to Get Invited Back*, 1984; *People-Spotting: The Human Species Laid Bare*, 1985; *The Wastepaper Basket Archive*, 1986; *Hypochondriac's Dictionary of Ill Health*, 1994 (with Sarah Brewer); *Crime Writers and Other Animals*, 1998; *Baby Tips for Grandparents*, 2006

EDITED TEXTS: *The Faber Book of Useful Verse*, 1981; *Frank Muir Presents the Book of Comedy Sketches*, 1982 (with Muir); *Take a Spare Truss: Tips for Nineteenth Century Travellers*, 1983; *The Faber Book of Parodies*, 1984; *The Faber Book of Diaries*, 1987; *The Detection Collection*, 2006

BIBLIOGRAPHY

Cannon, Peter. Review of *A Hanging in the Hotel*, by Simon Brett. *Publishers Weekly* 251, no. 29 (July 19, 2004): 198. A favorable review of a Fethering series novel that finds Jude investigating the death of an inductee in a men's club.

Fletcher, Connie. Review of *Murder in the Museum*, by Simon Brett. *Booklist* 99, no. 17 (May 1, 2003):

1536. Review of this installment in the Fethering series praises the combination of social satire and traditional cozy.

Priestman, Martin. *The Cambridge Companion to Crime Fiction.* New York: Cambridge University Press, 2003. Chapters on the Golden Age of detective fiction and postwar British crime fiction provide background on Brett's works.

Swaim, Don. Simon Brett Interview with Don Swaim. http://wiredforbooks.org/simonbrett/ 1986 and 1989. Raw interviews for Don Swaim's two-minute CBS radio series, *Book Beat.* The 1986 interview is more than thirty-nine minutes long and discusses *Dead Giveaway* and Charles Paris, plus differences between British and American mystery writing, radio and television. The 1989 interview is more than fifteen minutes long and discusses both Paris and Mrs. Pargeter.

FREDRIC BROWN

Born: Cincinnati, Ohio; October 29, 1906
Died: Tucson, Arizona; March 11, 1972
Types of plot: Private investigator; hard-boiled

PRINCIPAL SERIES

Ed and Am Hunter, 1947-1963

PRINCIPAL SERIES CHARACTERS

ED and AMBROSE "AM" HUNTER are nephew and uncle, private detectives based in Chicago. Ed is the young nephew, very idealistic; Am is a retired circus performer, a more mature, seasoned individual. Thus, the two men combine naïveté and idealism with experience and sobriety, making a balanced team when dealing with sordid street life.

CONTRIBUTION

Fredric Brown's contribution to the detective novel lies in his inventive plots and his realistic portrayals of life at the bottom. In *The Screaming Mimi* (1949), he draws a grim picture, at the novel's beginning, of an alcoholic reporter on a binge—a veritable slice of life. A specialist in the trick ending and the clever title, Brown was not much of a stylist and showed in many ways his early training in the pulp-magazine field. He liked the hard-boiled style but preferred to avoid strict adherence to its conventions. In the mid-1950's and later, when he tailored his fiction to the new men's magazines such as *Playboy* and *Dude*, Brown's style became more polished and sophisticated.

Brown's detective and mystery fiction was professional and clever. His characters borrowed much from the *Black Mask* school of writing (he contributed one story to the magazine). Unfortunately, few of his characters are memorable; most are one-dimensional. His main contribution to the field lies in his original plots and ingenious endings.

BIOGRAPHY

Fredric Brown (all of his life he fought against being called "Frederick") was born in Cincinnati, Ohio, on October 29, 1906. As a teenager, he lost his parents in consecutive years, 1920 and 1921, and was forced to work at odd jobs to support himself. During the 1920's, he attended Hanover College in Hanover, Indiana, as well as Cincinnati University. He married in 1929 and moved to Milwaukee, where he worked as a proofreader for several publishers until he finally settled down at the *Milwaukee Journal.* There he remained until 1947, when he moved to New York, having been offered a position as an editor for a chain of pulp magazines.

It was in 1938 that Brown sold his first story, "The Moon for a Nickel," which appeared in *Street and Smith's Detective Story Magazine.* From that time on, Brown sold regularly to the pulps, writing in a variety of genres, from *Dime Mystery* to *Planet Stories* to *Weird Tales*. He built a considerable following among pulp readers.

Brown's first popular success came with the publication of his first novel, *The Fabulous Clipjoint* (1947), which introduced the nephew-and-uncle team of Ed and Am Hunter. The novel won the Edgar Allan Poe Award of the Mystery Writers of America in 1948. Brown's literary fortunes improved, and he moved to New York to take up a major editorial position; moreover, he divorced his first wife, Helen.

A succession of popular crime novels followed, beginning with *The Dead Ringer* in 1948 and *The Screaming Mimi* in 1949. In that latter year Brown met Elizabeth Charlier, married her, and moved to Taos, New Mexico. The chain of pulps had folded, but Brown, fortuitously, had found a new career as a popular crime novelist. As television became a greater power in the entertainment field, Brown also found many of his stories being purchased for adaptation to television.

Brown's health had never been good, and it was not helped by his sporadic heavy drinking. Respiratory problems also developed, and in 1954 Brown and his wife, Elizabeth, moved to Tucson, Arizona, for his health. Although he had been writing for such high-paying magazines as *Playboy* and *Dude*, Brown was no longer able to keep up the pace. His last novel, *Mrs. Murphy's Underpants*, published in 1963, was not up to his usual mark. A few more stories appeared under his name, but his full-time writing days were past. He died of emphysema in Tucson on March 11, 1972, at the age of sixty-five.

ANALYSIS

Fredric Brown's early writing for the pulps was formative for his style, which was never very polished. Accustomed to tailoring his stories to the standard pulp stereotypes, he was able to distinguish himself mainly by devising unusual plot twists or endings. His story titles also show an inventive air: "A Little White Lye," "Murder While You Wait," "The Dancing Sandwiches." Once, in need of a clever title, he bought one from a fellow writer for ten dollars: "I Love You Cruelly." Although his prose was never outstanding,

Brown did attract a large following who appreciated the tough-guy type of story and the realism of Brown's settings (often in Chicago).

THE FABULOUS CLIPJOINT

Many of his early stories are forgettable, but with *The Fabulous Clipjoint* Brown managed to create a fascinatingly complex plot, amid the background of a sleazy carnival. His detective team, Ed and Am Hunter, is different and appealing. Oddly enough, though, the best of Brown's crime novels do not belong to this series: *The Screaming Mimi* and *The Far Cry* (1951). Both novels have unusual characters and focus on a rather seamy milieu. The milieu is well drawn, but modern readers who are not accustomed to the clichés of pulp style may find the one-dimensional nature of many of the characters unappealing. The tough talk is there, but the soul is missing.

Brown himself did not engage in discussions of the theoretical basis of his work or of the detective novel in general; he was a professional author and considered writing a job one did for money. Nevertheless, he did follow the standard pulp guidelines: a catchy opener, unusual characters, a new twist in the plot, and above all, a smash finish. This conventionality probably crippled his development as a stylist—but it did make him attractive to editors. Brown's ingenious twists of plot were just what editors sought to enliven the routine nature of much pulp fiction.

THE SCREAMING MIMI

In *The Screaming Mimi*, one of Brown's best-known crime novels, all of his assets and his debits are visible. It was the only Brown novel to be made into a film (with the same title, in 1958, starring Anita Ekberg and Philip Carey). The setting of the novel is Chicago of the 1940's. The hero is a newspaper reporter who is inclined to go on occasional binges, and the novel opens as the reporter, Sweeney, is just coming out of his latest bender. "Sweeney sat on a park bench, that summer night, next to God. Sweeney rather liked God, although not many people did." Here is a characteristic Brown touch—the clever play with words. "God" happens to be another bum, named Godfrey.

Brown lavishes much care on his descriptions of the Chicago night scene: Bughouse Square, Clark

Street, and North State Street. His accurate portrayal of down-and-outers is a credit to his thorough knowledge of the settings of his novels and his interest in low-life characters.

The mystery centers on a mysterious "Ripper" who has been attacking young women of unsound reputation. Sweeney stumbles onto the scene of an attack; the victim is a nightclub dancer, Yolanda Lang. She manages to survive the assault. Sweeney, stunned by her beauty, decides to swear off drinking for the time being to get to know her and find the Ripper.

There are elements of the novel that remind one of the standard 1940's Hollywood crime film of the order now known as film noir. However, there also are original touches. The hero, Sweeney, is an unsavory character who has just crawled out of the gutter. Another interesting character is Doc Greene, the owner of a nightclub named El Madhouse, where Yolanda does her dancing. Greene pretends to be literary, but makes mistakes when dropping the names of authors and books. In describing Greene's eyes, Brown writes: "Somehow, too, they managed to look both vacant and deadly. They looked like reptile's eyes, magnified a hundredfold, and you expected a nictitating membrane to close upon them." Brown's is a style that mingles old clichés with a turn of the verbal screw.

More sophisticated readers may find this kind of description shopworn. The following could have come from *Dime Detective*:

> Stopped in mid-sentence, she stared at him. She asked, "You aren't another shamus, are you? This place was lousy with 'em. . . ."
>
> Sweeney stuck out a paw and the detective took it, but not enthusiastically.
>
> It wasn't quite believable somehow.

The core of this novel, as with so many novels of the hard-boiled variety, is the wanderings of the hero, the low-life characters, the strange settings, the brushes with the law. In this regard, Brown followed the standard formula, but in choosing as his protagonist an alcoholic newspaper reporter, he applied the twist that makes the story different.

At the end of the story, the murderer proves to be the very Yolanda with whom the hero is in love and

who inspired him to come out of his binge and try to solve the mystery of the Ripper. In the last few paragraphs of the novel, Sweeney, having solved the murder and lost his love, is seen back on the street, sharing a fifth of booze (or two) with Godfrey. "Sweeney shuddered. He pulled two flat pint bottles out of the side pockets of his coat and handed one of them to God. . . ."

This, one might say, is the clever twist. There is no happy ending. Brown was a writer who hated happy endings, even though he was forced on many occasions to write them. In his novels, Brown had enough control over his material that he was able to write the endings he wanted.

There are many admirers of Brown who claim that he wrote his best prose not in the crime-fiction field but in the area of science fiction. He did have a steadfast following in this genre, and many of his science-fiction stories avoid the clichés of pulp fiction. Nevertheless, there are many Brown mystery fans who believe, with critic Bill Pronzini, that "the largest number [of his mystery stories] are tales of merit and high craftsmanship."

Independent judgment, however, must find that Fredric Brown did not blaze many trails as a crime writer, although he certainly provided much entertainment for readers. His talents did not approach the level of a Georges Simenon, a Nicolas Freeling, or a P. D. James. Brown was a competent professional in the realm of pulp fiction, but he is clearly not a candidate for university seminar discussions on the detective novel.

Philip M. Brantingham

PRINCIPAL MYSTERY AND DETECTIVE FICTION

ED AND AM HUNTER SERIES: *The Fabulous Clipjoint*, 1947; *The Dead Ringer*, 1948; *The Bloody Moonlight*, 1949 (also known as *Murder by Moonlight*); *Compliments of a Fiend*, 1950; *Death Has Many Doors*, 1951; *The Late Lamented*, 1959; *Mrs. Murphy's Underpants*, 1963

NONSERIES NOVELS: *Murder Can Be Fun*, 1948 (also known as *A Plot for Murder*); *The Screaming Mimi*, 1949; *Here Comes a Candle*, 1950; *Night of the Jabberwock*, 1950; *The Case of the Dancing*

Sandwiches, 1951; *The Far Cry*, 1951; *The Deep End*, 1952; *We All Killed Grandma*, 1952; *Madball*, 1953; *His Name Was Death*, 1954; *The Wench Is Dead*, 1955; *The Lenient Beast*, 1956; *One for the Road*, 1958; *The Office*, 1958; *Knock Three-One-Two*, 1959; *The Mind Thing*, 1961; *The Murderers*, 1961; *The Five-Day Nightmare*, 1962

SHORT FICTION: *Mostly Murder*, 1953; *Nightmares and Geezenstacks*, 1961; *The Shaggy Dog and Other Murders*, 1963

OTHER MAJOR WORKS

NOVELS: *What Mad Universe*, 1949; *The Lights in the Sky Are Stars*, 1953 (also known as *Project Jupiter*); *Martians, Go Home*, 1955; *Rogue in Space*, 1957

SHORT FICTION: *Space on My Hands*, 1951; *Science-Fiction Carnival*, 1953 (with Mack Reynolds); *Angels and Spaceships*, 1954 (also known as *Star Shine*); *Honeymoon in Hell*, 1958; *Daymares*, 1968; *Paradox Lost and Twelve Other Great Science Fiction Stories*, 1973; *The Best of Fredric Brown*, 1977

CHILDREN'S LITERATURE: *Mitkey Astromouse*, 1971 (illustrated by Heinz Edelmann)

BIBLIOGRAPHY

Baird, Newton. *A Key to Fredric Brown's Wonderland.* Georgetown, Calif.: Talisman Literary Research, 1981. Contains both a critical study and an annotated bibliography of Brown's work.

_____. "Paradox and Plot: The Fiction of Fredric Brown." *The Armchair Detective* 9-11 (June, 1976-January, 1978). Serialized study of the narrative structure of Brown's fiction.

Haining, Peter. *The Classic Era of American Pulp Magazines.* Chicago: Chicago Review Press, 2000. Discusses Brown's work in the pulps and the role of pulp fiction in American culture.

Horsley, Lee. *The Noir Thriller.* New York: Palgrave, 2001. Scholarly, theoretically informed study of the thriller genre. Examine's Brown's *The Fabulous Clipjoint*, *The Screaming Mimi*, and *The Lenient Beast.*

Seabrook, Jack. *Martians and Misplaced Clues: The Life and Work of Fredric Brown.* Bowling Green, Ohio: Bowling Green State University Popular Press, 1993. Detailed critical biography discussing the relationship between Brown's personal experiences and his fiction.

SANDRA BROWN

Born: Waco, Texas; June 12, 1948
Also wrote as Laura Jordan; Rachel Ryan; Erin St. Claire
Types of plot: Thriller; psychological

CONTRIBUTION

After Sandra Brown's suspense thriller *Mirror Image* (1991) made *The New York Times* best-seller list, she became one of America's most prolific and popular authors, with a large and dedicated fan base. She has published more than sixty-five novels, many of them *New York Times* best sellers. Her works have been translated into more than thirty languages, and millions of copies of her novels have been sold in audio formats. Brown began her writing career as a romance novelist, but in the early 1990's, her novels became increasingly more complex and suspense filled as she steadily moved into the mystery, crime, and thriller genres. It was her ability to combine two popular genres—romance and suspense—that not only placed her novels in the popular subgenre known as romantic suspense but also positioned her as one of America's top mystery writers. Brown is highly regarded by fans for her engaging, suspenseful plots, which feature false leads, sinister motives, positioned and highly detailed characters, and unpredictable endings. *The Crush* (2002) became Brown's fiftieth *New York Times* best seller. Her 1992 novel *French Silk* was

Sandra Brown. (AP/Wide World Photos)

made into an American Broadcasting Company (ABC) television film starring Susan Lucci in 1994.

Brown's awards include the American Business Women's Association's Distinguished Circle of Success, the B'nai B'rith's Distinguished Literary Achievement Award, the A. C. Greene Award, and the Romance Writers of America's Lifetime Achievement Award.

BIOGRAPHY

Sandra Brown was born on June 12, 1948, in Waco, Texas, to journalist Jimmie Brown and to counselor Martha Cox. She grew up in Fort Worth, Texas, and attended Texas Christian University before leaving to attend Oklahoma State University and the University of Texas at Arlington, where she majored in English. In 1968, when she was working a summer job

as a dancer at Six Flags Over America, she married Michael Brown.

Before Brown started to write for a living, she worked as the manager of a Merle Norman Cosmetics Studio in Tyler, Texas (1971-1973), as a weather reporter for WFAA-TV in Dallas (1976-1979), as a model for the Dallas Apparel Mart (1976-1987), and as a reporter for the nationally syndicated television show *PM Magazine*, which aired from the 1970's to 1980's. All her life, she had been an avid reader of detective novels, and after losing her job as a weather reporter in 1979, she decided to take a risk and write professionally. She describes that decision as a kind of epiphany and claims that from this point she could clearly see that she was meant to spend the rest of her life as a writer. After reading and studying a variety of romance novels and books on how to write, the burgeoning author placed her typewriter on a card table and began her writing career.

After attending a romance writers' conference, Brown wrote her first romance novel, and her work was first published in 1981. Harlequin Romances failed to purchase her first novel, but Dell Books took a chance on the new writer. Two of her romance novels, *Love's Encore* (1981) and *Love Beyond Reason* (1981), were accepted for publication within thirteen days of each other. During the following ten years, the prolific Brown wrote an average of six romance novels per year using the pseudonyms Erin St. Claire, Laura Jordan, and Rachel Ryan (her children's names). In 1991, when her *Mirror Image* hit *The New York Times* best-seller list, Brown became one of America's best-selling authors. She began to drop the pseudonyms and to use her own name. In addition to writing novels, Brown serves as the chief executive officer of her own multimillion-dollar publishing empire, and in terms of financial earnings, she is ranked with such best-selling authors as Tom Clancy, Stephen King, J. K. Rowling, and Danielle Steel.

Brown and her husband, Michael, a former news anchor and the owner of a video production company, produced an award-winning documentary film, *Dust to Dust* (2002), about asbestos contamination in Libby, Montana.

ANALYSIS

Critics say that more than any other factor, it is Sandra Brown's strong storytelling ability and her ability to combine romance, terror, and suspense that set her apart from other writers. In addition, Brown appeals to both male and female readers, who find themselves constantly changing their minds about the identities of her villains. She manages to keep readers in suspense with her greatly detailed, richly plotted novels. Critics also praise Brown for her ability to weave false leads and highly unpredictable, sinister motives into her intricate plotlines. Although all of Brown's thrillers have been called "vulgar" and "bloodthirsty" by reviewers, who note the "raunchy" sex scenes, Brown's books continue to sell well.

Highly regarded for her novels of romantic suspense, Brown thinks of her books primarily as suspense crime novels that incorporate a spicy love story. Her plots generally follow a predictable outline, with each featuring a fiercely independent female protagonist who encounters an extremely violent situation, usually involving murder, and finds herself in dire need of masculine help. However, differentiating the good guys from the bad guys is never easy in the Brown novel. Brown's plots invariably play out against a backdrop of complex family secrets that are revealed one by one and discovered when least expected.

Brown invariably makes her protagonist a high-powered, successful, career-minded woman, who although highly self-sufficient, finds herself in danger and in need of help. For example, the protagonist of Brown's *Charade* (1994), is a soap-opera star in danger of dying unless she receives a heart transplant. Many of Brown's novels are set in the Deep South, and this setting, complete with swamps, plantations, and creepy Spanish oaks, lends itself well to the menacing atmosphere that surrounds her characters. Brown's *Mirror Image*, *Breath of Scandal* (1991), and *French Silk* are all set in the hot and sultry city of New Orleans, an atmosphere that has appeal for readers desiring to escape their own prosaic lives and enter into a dangerous fantasy world of sex and high intrigue. In addition, Brown's suspense novels incorporate a large number of highly complex characters, who are one by one drawn against their wishes into a dark unfolding plot. The characters, and Brown's readers, remain completely unaware of the hidden family secrets that act as the underpinnings of Brown's plots, and it is the revelation of these secrets that draws the characters into the never-ceasing action. In addition, Brown differs from other writers in that she breaks away from predictable, formulaic happy endings and oftentimes opts for dark endings.

CHARADE

In *Charade*, if soap-opera star Cat Delany does not receive a heart transplant, she will die. After the operation, Cat, who is simply happy to be alive, is stalked by a killer who seeks revenge on her because she is the recipient of his former lover's heart. Suddenly, Cat's world closes in on her, and she finds she can trust no one, not even the new love in her life, the crime writer Alex Pierce, who might be her stalker. This is another fast-paced Brown book that maintains suspense by hiding the identity of the killer. It also contains Brown's formulaic independent female heroine who finds herself in a vulnerable situation at the hands of a handsome predator.

FRENCH SILK

French Silk, a romantic suspense novels, is set in one of Brown's Deep South locales, New Orleans. After evangelist Jackson Wilde is murdered, District Attorney Robert Cassidy finds himself with a long list of suspects. Wilde's young wife, Ariel, who has been having an affair with her husband's son, tops the list. However, the search for the killer soon zooms in on Claire Laurent, who owns the French Silk mail-order lingerie company, a target of Wilde's antipornography campaign. As the weather in the city heats up, more problems develop for District Attorney Cassidy, who finds himself falling in love with the suspect, who has been lying to him in an effort to protect her mentally deficient mother at whose hands she suffered as a child. Although Laurent is attracted to Cassidy, her abusive childhood causes her to remain terrified of commitment, so she keeps him at a distance. Once again, *French Silk* contains Brown's trademark independent female protagonist in need of male protection in addition to her penchant for dark family secrets.

CHILL FACTOR

Chill Factor (2005), unlike many of Brown's thrillers, is set in winter in a small North Carolina town where yet another independent woman finds herself in dire need of rescuing after she is trapped in a mountain cabin with a man who might possibly be a killer. After the loss of their three-year-old daughter, Lilly and Dutch Burton decide divorce might be the solution to their ongoing problems. When Lilly's car skids off a mountain road shortly after she leaves the Burtons' cabin barely ahead of a storm, she hits a handsome hiker named Tierney, and she and the injured man wait out the blizzard in the cabin. Lilly calls her husband, Dutch, but he cannot reach her because of the snow. Later, Dutch finds out that Tierny is a serial killer who has recently killed five women. Here, as in her other novels, Brown casts the killer as a writer.

RICOCHET

Set in the Deep South, *Ricochet* (2006) is filled with Brown's nonstop suspense, steamy settings, and sex scenes. From the minute Georgia detective Duncan Hatcher sees the shy, refined, and lovely Elise Laird at a police awards banquet, he cannot help but fall in love with her. However, she is off limits because she is married to a local judge, who constantly ruins Hatcher's chances of bringing the region's drug lord to justice. After Elise, a former topless dancer, shoots a burglar in self-defense, Hatcher is called to her fabulous home, where she confides in him that her husband, with the aid of the drug lord, set her up to be the victim of the intruder. Hatcher attempts to downplay his increasing feelings for her, and Elise soon vanishes, but not before another body turns up.

BREATH OF SCANDAL

The Deep South, in this case South Carolina, is the setting for Brown's popular *Breath of Scandal* (1991). Jade Sperry, another of Brown's strong female protagonists in need of male help, is bent on avenging the pain and suffering inflicted on her by three classmates who raped her while she was in high school. The rape caused her boyfriend to commit suicide, and she found herself pregnant as a result of the attack. Another of Brown's highly intelligent protagonists, Jade worked her way through college as a single mother and became successful despite the scandal and the trauma.

However, she is unable to achieve a lasting, fulfilling relationship with a man until Dillon Burke, the handsome contractor she puts in charge of a construction project, comes into her life.

EXCLUSIVE

Like many of Brown's other books, political thriller *Exclusive* (1996) is full of family secrets that create nonstop suspense. Reporter Barrie Travis is granted an exclusive interview with the First Lady of the United States after the death of her baby, seemingly from sudden infant death syndrome (SIDS). However, Barrie discovers that the baby might have been the victim of murder and that a former presidential adviser—who is possibly the First Lady's lover—might be involved in the death. All this, however, is just the beginning of the unveiling of the First Family's dark secrets.

M. Casey Diana

PRINCIPAL MYSTERY AND DETECTIVE FICTION

NOVELS: *Mirror Image*, 1991; *French Silk*, 1992; *Where There's Smoke*, 1993; *Charade*, 1994; *The Witness*, 1995; *Exclusive*, 1996; *Fat Tuesday*, 1997; *Unspeakable*, 1998; *The Alibi*, 1999; *Standoff*, 2000; *The Switch*, 2000; *Envy*, 2001; *The Crush*, 2002; *Hello, Darkness*, 2003; *White Hot*, 2004; *Chill Factor*, 2005; *Ricochet*, 2006; *Play Dirty*, 2007

OTHER MAJOR WORKS

NOVELS: 1981-1985 • *Love Beyond Reason*, 1981 (as Ryan); *Love's Encore*, 1981 (as Ryan); *Hidden Fires*, 1982 (as Jordan); *The Silken Web*, 1982 (as Jordan); *Not Even for Love*, 1982 (as St. Claire); *Eloquent Silence*, 1982 (as Ryan); *A Treasure Worth Seeking*, 1982 (as Ryan); *Breakfast in Bed*, 1983; *Relentless Desire*, 1983; *Tempest in Eden*, 1983; *Temptation's Kiss*, 1983; *Tomorrow's Promise*, 1983; *Prime Time*, 1983 (as Ryan); *A Kiss Remembered*, 1983 (as St. Claire); *A Secret Splendor*, 1983 (as St. Claire); *Seduction by Design*, 1983 (as St. Claire); *Bittersweet Rain*, 1984 (as St. Claire); *Words of Silk*, 1984 (as St. Claire); *In a Class by Itself*, 1984; *Send No Flowers*, 1984; *Sunset Embrace*, 1984; *Riley in the Morning*, 1985; *Thursday's Child*, 1985; *Another Dawn*, 1985; *Led Astray*, 1985 (as St. Claire); *A Sweet Anger*, 1985 (as St. Claire); *Tiger Prince*, 1985 (as St. Claire)

1986-1990 • *Above and Beyond*, 1986 (as St. Claire); *Honor Bound*, 1986 (as St. Claire); *Twenty-Two Indigo Place*, 1986; *The Rana Look*, 1986; *Demon Rumm*, 1987; *Fanta C*, 1987; *Sunny Chandler's Return*, 1987; *The Devil's Own*, 1987 (as St. Claire); *Two Alone*, 1987 (as St. Claire); *Adam's Fall*, 1988; *Hawk O'Toole's Hostage*, 1988; *Slow Heat in Heaven*, 1988; *Tidings of Great Joy*, 1988; *Thrill of Victory*, 1989 (as St. Claire); *Long Time Coming*, 1989; *Temperatures Rising*, 1989; *Best Kept Secrets*, 1989; *A Whole New Light*, 1989; *Texas! Lucky*, 1990; *Texas! Chase*, 1990

1991-2002 • *Breath of Scandal*, 1991; *Another Dawn*, 1991; *Texas! Sage*, 1992; *The Rana Look*, 2002

BIBLIOGRAPHY

Beardon, Michelle. "Sandra Brown: Suburban Mom and Prolific Bestseller." *Publishers Weekly* 242, no. 28 (July 10, 1995): 39. Profile of Brown that looks at her life as well as her financially successful writing career.

Brown, Sandra. "The Risk of Seduction and the Seduction of Risk." In *Dangerous Men and Adventurous Women*, edited by Jayne Ann Krentz. Philadelphia: University of Pennsylvania Press, 1992. Best-selling author Brown discusses the psychology behind the romantic inclinations of her strong, independent female characters and their attraction to good-looking but ultimately dangerous men.

Machan, Dyan. "Romancing the Buck." *Forbes* 159, no. 11 (June, 1997): 44-45. This article examines Sandra Brown's decision to switch from the romance genre to the more substantial and far more profitable mystery, suspense, and thriller genres and the risk involved in this decision.

Rapp, Adrian, Lynda Dodgen, and Anne K. Kaler. "A Romance Writer Gets Away with Murder." *Clues: A Journal of Detection* 21 (Spring/Summer, 2000): 17-21. Scholarly article that details how Brown integrated her talent for writing successful romances into the thriller, suspense, and mystery genres, a move that catapulted her into mainstream fiction as a best-selling author.

Raskin, Barbara. "Moguls in Pumps." *The New York Times Book Review*, May 31, 1992, p. 739. Compares Brown's best-selling *French Silk* with Ivana Trump's *For Love Alone* (1992) and Judith Krantz's *Scruples Two* (1992) to illustrate the rags-to-riches or poor-girl-makes-good theme employed in each novel.

Rice, Melinda. "How to Become a Best-Seller." *D Magazine—Dallas/Fort Worth* 27, no. 6 (June 1, 2000): 80. A profile of the author that concentrates on how she went from being a romance writer to a writer of suspense and mystery and how she manages the business end of her work.

LEO BRUCE
Rupert Croft-Cooke

Born: Edenbridge, Kent, England; June 20, 1903
Died: Bournemouth, England; June 10, 1979
Types of plot: Private investigator; amateur sleuth; cozy

PRINCIPAL SERIES
Sergeant William Beef, 1936-1952
Carolus Deene, 1955-1974

PRINCIPAL SERIES CHARACTERS

SERGEANT WILLIAM BEEF, a village police officer turned private investigator, is married to a quiet countrywoman who thinks the world of her husband. Large, red-faced, plodding, and enamored of pubs (he loves beer, whiskey, and dart games), Beef is a remarkably astute detective whose methods, while slow, are amazingly thorough. Beef is somewhat peeved that he is not as famous as Hercule Poirot or Albert Campion, despite the almost constant presence of his biographer, Lionel Townsend; on more than one occasion, Beef complains that Townsend's books imply that luck rather than skill is the secret to Beef's successes.

LIONEL TOWNSEND is a freelance writer and Sergeant Beef's biographer and companion in detection. Constantly irritated by Beef's methodical nature and endless dart playing, the university-educated Townsend makes it clear that he would much prefer to chronicle the exploits of a more glamorous detective, someone such as Lord Peter Wimsey, for example. When faced with another of Beef's pub stops, Townsend sourly compares his own experiences with those of Dr. Watson. A bachelor, Townsend keeps a flat in the genteel vicinity of the Marble Arch and thinks disparaging thoughts about Beef's "drab little house . . . as near Baker Street as he had been able to manage."

CAROLUS DEENE, a senior history master at the Queen's School, Newminster, is an amateur sleuth during school holidays and weekends. Forty years old and widowed, he is an "uncomfortably rich man," who lives for his two consuming interests, teaching history and investigating crime. Working almost exclusively from interviews with those involved, Deene formulates "the kind of wild hypothetical imaginary stuff which might easily turn out to hold the seeds of truth." In fact, he is as famous for his wild theorizing as for his ability to solve the puzzles of crime. He makes it clear that he is motivated both by an intellectual curiosity and by a desire to find out the truth.

HUGH GORRINGER, the headmaster of the Queen's School, is possessed of a huge pair of hairy ears. Torn between an obsession with protecting the school from adverse publicity and an overwhelming curiosity about Deene's adventures, Gorringer initially disapproves of Deene's involvement in detection but almost always manages to find an excuse to be present at the events providing a solution to the crime.

RUPERT PRIGGLEY is a precocious Queen's School student who frequently invites himself to accompany Deene. In the Deene series, Priggley provides most of the commentary on and criticism of the detective genre.

MRS. STICK, Deene's highly respectable housekeeper, disapproves of his hobby of investigating crime and threatens to give notice if he does not stop. Insistent on calling things by their proper names, Mrs. Stick can be counted on to mispronounce the French names of the dishes she serves to Deene.

CONTRIBUTION

Leo Bruce's Sergeant William Beef and Carolus Deene novels have been praised as "superb examples of classic British mystery," his plots have been described as "brilliantly ingenious," and Bruce himself has been called "a master of the genre." Yet, if his fame rests on his skill with the classic form, his chief importance to the history of the genre lies in his perfection of the immensely entertaining and parodic self-conscious detective novel, a subgenre that questions and revises, edits and inverts, occasionally criticizes and lampoons—all with a wry ironic tone—the conventions of the traditional whodunit. In the Sergeant Beef novels, certainly, and to a slightly lesser extent in the Carolus Deene series, the principal characters seem not only aware of their fictional existence but also inclined to use that recognition to remark on their counterparts in other detective stories, on the plots devised by other crime writers, and on the genre as a whole. For the well-read connoisseur of detective fiction, this artifice, which would be a disaster from the pen of a less gifted writer, invests Bruce's fiction with a double significance: The novels are intricate puzzles that tantalize and fascinate and most of all entertain, and they are also theoretical works in that they provide analytical commentary on the literary form they represent. Thus, Bruce manages, in this most popular of fiction genres, to obey that age-old dictum that literature must both delight and instruct.

BIOGRAPHY

Leo Bruce was born Rupert Croft-Cooke on June 20, 1903, in Edenbridge, Kent, England, the son of Hubert Bruce Cooke and Lucy Taylor Cooke. Little information—beyond the standard sketchy biographical data—is available on Bruce's life. He was educated at Tonbridge School, Kent, and Wellington College (now Wrekin College); from 1923 to 1926, he attended the University of Buenos Aires, where he founded and edited a weekly magazine, *La Estrella*.

Bruce's career seems primarily to have involved either writing or the military, both in England and abroad. The exceptions were two years (1929-1931) spent as an antiquarian bookseller, and one year's experience as a lecturer at the English Institute Montana in Zugerberg, Switzerland. Beginning with a stint in the British Army Intelligence Corps in 1940, Bruce went on to serve in the 1942 Madagascar offensive (for which he was awarded the British Empire Medal) and as commander of the Third Gurkha Rifles in 1943. Continuing his service on the Indian subcontinent from 1944 to 1946, Bruce was a field security officer in the Poona and Delhi districts and an intelligence school instructor in Karachi, West Pakistan. He returned to England to work as the book critic for *The Sketch* before deciding to concentrate on his freelance writing career.

Earlier, during the 1930's, Bruce had spent several years as a writer; during that decade, he wrote plays, some twenty books, one collection of short fiction, and translations of Spanish works. After his years in the military, he produced several autobiographical volumes, biographies of a wide variety of figures (including a controversial life of Lord Alfred Douglas), at least three books on cookery, some poetry, and even one foray into literary criticism—a commentary on several Victorian writers. All along, Bruce was writing the detective novels that would earn for him acclaim as "a major British detective story writer of salient merit."

Bruce's first detective novel, *Case for Three Detectives* (1936), was also the first book for which he employed the pseudonym Leo Bruce, under which all of his detective novels would be published. In this book, Bruce introduced the plebeian Sergeant Beef, whose exploits he recounted until 1952, when Bruce inexplicably abandoned Beef after eight novels. The wealthy, university-educated Carolus Deene first appeared in *At Death's Door* in 1955. Bruce wrote only a few more books after he abandoned the detective novel in 1974. He died on June 10, 1979.

ANALYSIS

On the surface, the Sergeant Beef novels and the Carolus Deene novels appear to be quite dissimilar.

The Beef chronicles have an engaging middle-class ponderousness that is wholly in keeping with Sergeant Beef's person and behavior, while the Deene stories sparkle with wit and iridescent one-liners. Aside from his shadow, Lionel Townsend, Sergeant Beef has only a small cast of supporting players—his nearly invisible wife and Chief Inspector Stute of the Special Branch—onstage with him; Carolus Deene must constantly deal with a crowd of regulars—Hugh Gorringer and his wife, Mrs. Stick and her laconic husband, the sometimes annoying but always bright Rupert Priggley, and Deene's friend John Moore of the Criminal Investigation Department—who are so brilliantly realized as characters that they add life and entertainment to the novels without detracting from the suspenseful narratives. Beef is decidedly, unabashedly bourgeois with a strong element of the working class; Deene describes himself as "repulsively rich" and lives in a Queen Anne house presided over by an eminently respectable housekeeper who serves him gourmet meals with vintage wine. William Beef investigates crimes because detection is his profession; Deene detects out of a love for puzzles (he is constantly in competition with another schoolmaster for the morning newspaper's crossword) and an obsession with finding the truth. Beef's detractors call him lucky rather than competent; Deene has a reputation for improbable theories that turn out to be accurate.

Superficial differences aside, however, Leo Bruce's two detective series have important characteristics in common. Bruce's novels are conventional stories of the type known variously as traditional British, Golden Age detective story, whodunit, or even puzzle mystery. As examples of a classic form familiar to aficionados of crime and mystery fiction, the Sergeant Beef and Carolus Deene books display Bruce's adept handling of genre conventions: the basically comic universe, the presence of a great detective, locked rooms and perfect alibis, the closed circle of suspects from which the murderer (the crime in question is always murder) is eventually identified, clues—obvious and otherwise—and misdirections, a believable solution that somehow restores order to a society turned topsy-turvy, and the great detective's summing up of the facts of the case. Even Bruce's settings are familiar: little English villages with quaint hyphenated names located on or near bodies of water or distinct geological formations, proper seaside resorts, picturesque cottages and stately country homes, and respectable London suburbs. Although the murders are violent, Bruce rarely if ever provides explicit details of either method or aftermath; his treatment of crime has the delicacy and understatement of the traditional detective novels rather than the gritty realism of the newer, American crime novel. Bruce's characters belong to the world of the Golden Age: His detectives carry no weapons and rely solely on the interview and the reenactment for results; minor characters are succinctly sketched character types—respectable citizens, eccentrics, obsequious tradespeople, loyal or disgruntled domestics, dotty parsons.

CASE FOR THREE DETECTIVES

Another similarity between the two series is the self-mocking tone present in many of the individual books. Bruce excelled at constructing self-parodying detective novels in which some characters display a tendency to remark—often critically—on the conventions of the genre and the expectations of readers long familiar with those conventions. Bruce's first detective novel sets the tone for the rest. In *Case for Three Detectives*, Sergeant Beef solves a murder that completely baffles three eminent sleuths—Lord Simon Plimsoll, Monsieur Amer Picot, and Monsignor Smith—clearly intended as parodies of Wimsey, Poirot, and Father Brown. The Sergeant Beef novels are particularly self-conscious; they are narrated by a writer of detective fiction, more specifically, by the novelist who records and then fictionalizes the adventures of Sergeant Beef. Lionel Townsend, the writer, has very specific—and rather elitist—ideas about the nature of detective fiction, ideas with which Sergeant Beef does not agree, and their frequent arguments turn on such matters as plot development, the detective's personality, the role of a Watson, and the criteria by which readers judge the success or failure of a detective series. Bruce also calls attention to his fiction by alluding to characters who exist only in crime novels or by naming other authors. In one instance, Lionel Townsend's more intelligent brother suggests to Beef that he have Aldous Huxley or E. M. Forster write up his cases.

COMMENTS ON THE GENRE

Bruce continued his oblique commentary on detective fiction in the Carolus Deene series, chiefly in the conversations between Deene and his junior Watson, Rupert Priggley. Armed with the affected cynicism of the adolescent, Priggley frequently makes reference to the clichés of badly written detective fiction. Listening to Deene interview a suspect whose answers are predictable, Priggley blurts, "Oh, God, . . . we'll have an Indian poison unknown to science in a minute." He mocks Deene about asking "some fabulously unexpected question," and complains, "You've no idea how dated you are. All this looking for clues and questioning suspects and being mysterious about your theory till the last minute—it went out ages ago." He then goes on to point out the traits of modern fiction; clearly, none applies to the Deene stories. Rupert Priggley even manages a comparison of the English and American genres:

> If you suppose that at your time of life you can turn yourself into one of these hardboiled, steel-gutted, lynx-eyed American sleuths who carry guns and risk their lives every few pages, you're wildly mistaken. You're English, sir, as English as Sherlock Holmes and Hercule (*Ma foi!*) Poirot.

Bruce clearly has wide knowledge of the conventions of the genre in which he writes, and he has entertainingly taken advantage of his position as a practitioner to comment on the strengths and weaknesses of his chosen form.

DEATH IN ALBERT PARK AND CRACK OF DOOM

Bruce displays a fondness for misdirection caused by the red-herring murder, that is, the murder of an unrelated person—even a stranger—to conceal the circumstances of the planned killing. Mr. Crabbett in *Death in Albert Park* (1964) stabs two other women in addition to his wife so that the killings will look like serial murder in the Jack the Ripper tradition. A retired colonel kills a woman to throw suspicion on her husband for both that murder and the colonel's murder of his own brother in *Crack of Doom* (1963). The plots of *Jack on the Gallows Tree* (1960) and *Die All, Die Merrily* (1961), among others, involve murder committed for the purpose of concealing the identity of a killer. In each case, the choice of an unrelated victim proves a major mistake for the killer; the cover-up murder provides Beef or Deene with the clues essential to the solution of the puzzle.

HUMOR AND MURDER

Murder may be a grim business, but the world of the traditional British detective novel is a comic one, informed largely by human folly and imperfection. In Bruce's fictional world, much of the humor derives from the pretenses of people who try, often unsuccessfully, to adhere to an artificial code of conduct. Bruce's comedy is dark at times, but it provides opportunity for laughter even as it probes the social restrictions and demands that lead the weak to frustration and finally to murder, or into the fantastic delusions of the totally egotistical man who plans a murder simply to know for himself that he has taken a life and gotten away with it. In one case, a ridiculous feud between two devout churchwomen—one a High Church devotee, the other rabidly Low Church—results in death. More often, however, the motive is money—money with which to buy recognition, to ensure social success, to continue in a luxurious lifestyle, to further ambition, or to gain freedom from imagined restrictions. A husband who married his wife for money soon resents his dependence and kills her for his freedom. A man does away with the other heirs to a fortune he wishes to enjoy alone. Another, believing himself to be his aunt's heir, kills her only to discover that she has written him out of her will. What all these killers believe is that somehow money will earn for them the respect of their associates and peers, that money will help make up for their social deficiencies and will confer on them the cachet they so desperately want. The murderers are sometimes pathetically ridiculous in their machinations.

A master at manipulating the English language, Bruce neatly lampoons his characters with his capsule descriptions that home in on their affectations, on their foibles. Mr. Gorringer is introduced as "a large and important-looking man with a pair of huge crimson ears whose hairy cavities were marvellously attuned to passing rumour." A secretary is declared to be as neat as the proverbial new pin: "She looked rather like a new pin, her long, narrow person rising to an inverted flowerpot hat." The faithful Mrs. Stick mangles beyond recognition the French names she insists on using for her culinary efforts; she serves up these delicacies with a bottle of "Shah Toe Ma Gokes." The very proper Miss Tissot arrogantly disapproves of everything about Carolus Deene—and says so quite bluntly—but when he offers to buy an aperitif for her, she orders one before the invitation is completed.

Bruce also clearly enjoys inventing names or juxtaposing names in incongruous contexts, often as a means of gently ridiculing the various public pretenses with which his detectives come in contact. In one novel the available newspapers are listed as *The Daily Horror*, *The Daily Wail*, *The Daily Explosion*, and *The Daily Smirch*. A prominent local is reverently referred to as "Colonel Lyle de Lisle De lisle L'Isle," while a pretentious London club seems to accept only those whose names are hyphenated—thus the manager blithely refers to Cyril Nutt-Campion and Cecil Waveney-Long and Adrian Stokes-Gray, even Ronnie Bright-Wilson, all in the same brief conversation. The names of victims and culprits alike are grin producing, often because they reflect character or profession so well: Hilton Gupp is a fishy sort of man-about-town; Lady Drumbone is a member of Parliament who lectures loud and long on sundry crackpot causes; Cosmo Ducrow is a fabulous rich recluse; Grazia Vaillant lives for her crusade to introduce incense and ornate vestments to her village church, which is decidedly Protestant. Ambitious young police officers have improbable names such as Spender-Hennessy or Galsworthy; lesser characters sport the names Fagg, Chickle, Flipps, or Pinhole. Even pets do not escape Bruce's name game; one dog breeder's menagerie is named after various Marxist heroes.

Although Bruce did not formulate a theoretical statement about the nature and characteristics of the detective novel, as so many of his colleagues have done, his own work exemplifies a coherent and well-articulated approach to the genre as he saw and practiced it. Clearly Bruce was a traditionalist, a creator of classically restrained and very English detective novels. Yet he was also an innovator in that he used the genre to ridicule its own excesses. Bruce's contribution to detective fiction is a fairly substantial body of work that both entertains and edifies, that engages and provokes.

E. D. Huntley

PRINCIPAL MYSTERY AND DETECTIVE FICTION

SERGEANT BEEF SERIES: *Case for Three Detectives*, 1936; *Case Without a Corpse*, 1937; *Case with Four Clowns*, 1939; *Case with No Conclusion*, 1939; *Case with Ropes and Rings*, 1940; *Case for Sergeant Beef*, 1947; *Neck and Neck*, 1951; *Cold Blood*, 1952

CAROLUS DEENE SERIES: *At Death's Door*, 1955; *Death for a Ducat*, 1956; *A Louse for the Hangman*, 1958; *Dead Man's Shoes*, 1958; *Our Jubilee Is Death*, 1959; *Furious Old Women*, 1960; *Jack on the Gallows Tree*, 1960; *A Bone and a Hank of Hair*, 1961; *Die All, Die Merrily*, 1961; *Nothing Like Blood*, 1962; *Crack of Doom*, 1963 (also known as *Such Is Death*); *Death in Albert Park*, 1964; *Death at Hallows End*, 1965; *Death on the Black Sands*, 1966; *Death at St. Asprey's School*, 1967; *Death of a Commuter*, 1967; *Death on Romney Marsh*, 1968; *Death with Blue Ribbon*, 1969; *Death on Allhallowe'en*, 1970; *Death by the Lake*, 1971; *Death in the Middle Watch*, 1974; *Death of a Bovver Boy*, 1974

NONSERIES NOVELS (AS CROFT-COOKE): *Seven Thunders*, 1955; *Thief*, 1960; *Clash by Night*, 1962; *Paper Albatross*, 1965; *Three in a Cell*, 1968; *Nasty Piece of Work*, 1973

OTHER SHORT FICTION: *Pharaoh with His Waggons, and Other Stories*, 1937

OTHER MAJOR WORKS

NOVELS (AS CROFT-COOKE): 1930-1940 • *Give Him the Earth*, 1930; *Troubadour*, 1930; *Cosmopolis*, 1932; *Night Out*, 1932; *Her Mexican Lover*, 1934; *Picaro*, 1934; *Shoulder the Sky*, 1934; *Blind Gunner*, 1935; *Crusade*, 1936; *Kingdom Come*, 1936; *Rule, Britannia*, 1938; *Same Way Home*, 1939; *Glorious*, 1940

1941-1960 • *Ladies Gay*, 1946; *Octopus*, 1946 (also known as *Miss Allick*); *Wilkie*, 1948 (also known as *Another Sun, Another Home*); *The White Mountain*, 1949; *Brass Farthing*, 1950; *Three Names for Nicholas*, 1951; *Nine Days with Edward*, 1952; *Harvest Moon*, 1953; *Fall of Man*, 1955; *Barbary Night*, 1958

1961-1975 • *Wolf from the Door*, 1969; *Exiles*, 1970; *Under the Rose Garden*, 1971; *While the Iron's Hot*, 1971; *Conduct Unbecoming*, 1975

SHORT FICTION (AS CROFT-COOKE): *A Football for the Brigadier, and Other Stories*, 1950

PLAYS (AS CROFT-COOKE): *Banquo's Chair*, pb. 1930; *Deliberate Accident*, pr. 1934; *Tap Three Times*, pb. 1934; *Gala Night at "The Willows,"* pb. 1950

RADIO PLAYS (AS CROFT-COOKE): *You Bet Your Life*, 1938 (with Beverley Nichols); *Peter the Painter*, 1946; *Theft*, 1963

POETRY (AS CROFT-COOKE): *Songs of a Sussex Tramp*, 1922; *Tonbridge School*, 1923; *Songs South of the Line*, 1925; *The Viking*, 1926; *Some Poems*, 1929; *Tales of a Wicked Uncle*, 1963

NONFICTION (AS CROFT-COOKE): 1927-1950 • *How Psychology Can Help*, 1927; *Darts*, 1936; *God in Ruins: A Passing Commentary*, 1936; *The World Is Young*, 1937 (also known as *Escape to the Andes*); *How to Get More out of Life*, 1938; *The Man in Europe Street*, 1938; *The Circus Has No Home*, 1941 (revised 1950); *How to Enjoy Travel Abroad*, 1948; *Rudyard Kipling*, 1948; *The Moon Is My Pocket: Life with the Romanies*, 1948

1951-1960 • *Cities*, 1951 (with Noël Barber); *The Sawdust Ring*, 1951 (with W. S. Meadmore); *Buffalo Bill: The Legend, the Man of Action, the Showman*, 1952 (with W. S. Meadmore); *The Life for Me*, 1952; *The Blood-Red Island*, 1953; *A Few Gypsies*, 1955; *Sherry*, 1955; *The Verdict of You All*, 1955; *The Tangerine House*, 1956; *Port*, 1957; *The Gardens of Camelot*, 1958; *Smiling Damned Villain: The True Story of Paul Axel Lund*, 1959; *The Quest for Quixote*, 1959 (also known as *Through Spain with Don Quixote*); *English Cooking: A New Approach*, 1960; *The Altar in the Loft*, 1960

1961-1970 • *Madeira*, 1961; *The Drums of Morning*, 1961; *The Glittering Pastures*, 1962; *Wine and Other Drinks*, 1962; *Bosie: The Story of Lord Alfred Douglas, His Friends, and His Enemies*, 1963; *Cooking for Pleasure*, 1963; *The Numbers Came*, 1963; *The Last of Spring*, 1964; *The Wintry Sea*, 1964; *The Gorgeous East: One Man's India*, 1965; *The Purple Streak*, 1966; *The Wild Hills*, 1966; *Feasting with Tigers: A New Consideration of Some Late Victorian*

Writers, 1967; *The Happy Highways*, 1967; *The Ghost of June: A Return to England and the West*, 1968; *Exotic Food: Three Hundred of the Most Unusual Dishes in Western Cookery*, 1969

1971-1977 • *The Licentious Soldiery*, 1971; *The Unrecorded Life of Oscar Wilde*, 1972; *The Dogs of Peace*, 1973; *The Caves of Hercules*, 1974; *The Long Way Home*, 1974; *Circus: A World History*, 1976 (with Peter Cotes); *The Green, Green Grass*, 1977

EDITED TEXTS (AS CROFT-COOKE): *Major Road Ahead: A Young Man's Ultimatum*, 1939; *The Circus Book*, 1948

TRANSLATIONS (AS CROFT-COOKE): *Twenty Poems from the Spanish of Becquer*, 1927 (by G. A. Dominguez Becquer); *The Last Days of Madrid: The End of the Second Spanish Republic*, 1939 (by Segismundo Casado)

BIBLIOGRAPHY

Bargainnier, Earl F. "The Self-Conscious Sergeant Beef Novels of Leo Bruce." *The Armchair Detective* 18 (Spring, 1985): 154-159. A brief study of the self-referential and metafictional aspects of Bruce's work.

Barzun, Jacques, and Wendell Hertig Taylor. Introduction to *Furious Old Women*, by Leo Bruce. Overview of Bruce's career that places *Furious Old Women* in the context of his other work, and of the larger genre of which it is a part.

Gohrbandt, Detlev, and Bruno von Lutz, eds. *Seeing and Saying: Self-Referentiality in British and American Literature*. New York: P. Lang, 1998. Study of the sort of self-referential narrative strategies employed by Bruce in his Sergeant Beef series.

Van Dover, J. K. *We Must Have Certainty: Four Essays on the Detective Story*. Selinsgrove, Pa.: Susquehanna University Press, 2005. Traces the evolution, conventions, and ideological investments of detective fiction. Invaluable for understanding the aspects of that fiction on which Bruce's work comments.

KEN BRUEN

Born: Galway, Ireland; 1951
Types of plot: Hard-boiled; police procedural; private investigator

PRINCIPAL SERIES

Detective Sergeant (later Inspector) Brant, 1998-
Jack Taylor, 2001-

PRINCIPAL SERIES CHARACTERS

SERGEANT BRANT is introduced in *A White Arrest* (1998) as a corrupt, brutishly violent London detective who is feared and respected by his peers. An antihero, Brant is a rage-filled, pugnacious bully who maintains a complicated but curiously loyal relationship with the few detectives and police officers whom he respects. He occasionally betrays an interest in Irish culture and is an avid reader of Ed McBain, the American author of police procedurals. He respects strength and sees violence as a necessary tool of law enforcement. He places little trust in the legal system, preferring to mete out justice in an ad hoc fashion.

JACK TAYLOR is a Galway-based former member of the Garda Síochána, the police force of Ireland. Expelled for drinking and substance abuse, he now occupies a gray area between the law and the criminal world and is viewed with distrust by both sides. He works as a private investigator—or a "finder," as he calls himself in *The Guards* (2001), the novel in which he is introduced—in a country where, he says, there are no private investigators because they are viewed as informers or traitors. His circle is a relatively narrow one. He maintains an antagonistic and guilt-ridden relationship with his mother and her priest, as well as a few delicate relationships that could barely be called friendships, apparently based on circumstance and necessity, with his bartender, his landlady, and a former colleague from the Guards.

CONTRIBUTION

With the publication of the first Jack Taylor mystery, *The Guards*, in 2001, Ken Bruen found broad popular and critical acclaim within the mystery and detective genre. The popularity of this novel in Europe and later in the United States prompted the reissue of several of Bruen's earlier works; the first three Sergeant Brant novels—*A White Arrest* (1998), *Taming the Alien* (1999), and *The McDead* (2000)—were collected and reissued in the United States as *The White Trilogy* (2003).

Bruen's novels are significant for their treatment of two popular detective subgenres. As their protagonist's penchant for Ed McBain's novels of the 87th Precinct suggests, the Brant novels are contemporary police procedurals of a particularly dark and gritty nature. The novelty lies in the juxtaposition of the setting (London) and the narrative style, which is heavily influenced by American noir. The Jack Taylor novels are private investigator novels that are also unusual in terms of their setting (Galway), because as the narrator maintains, there are no private investigators in Ireland.

Bruen's stature as a writer of mystery and detective fiction is reflected in the number of awards and recognitions his works have received. *The Guards* was an Edgar Award finalist and Shamus Award winner, and several of his other novels have appeared on annual lists of best novels.

BIOGRAPHY

Ken Bruen was born in 1951 in Galway, Ireland, to a middle-class family. During Bruen's childhood, Galway, on the western coast of Ireland, was a small town in which everybody knew everybody else. It has since become one of Ireland's largest cities, with its share of big-city problems. Raised in a bookless household, Bruen described himself as a quiet boy who stood out in a society in which high value is placed on the art of conversation. His father, an insurance salesman, did

not encourage his reading or his quest for education. Bruen once stated that much of his life was spent trying to earn his father's respect, even though his father was not impressed by the English degrees that he earned. Although his father did not outwardly approve of his writing career, Bruen once found a cache of clippings about his novels among his father's effects, which he interpreted as a posthumous expression of paternal approval for his literary vocation.

After college and graduate school, Bruen spent many years traveling the world and holding a variety of jobs, including teaching positions in Kuwait and Vietnam, a position as a security guard in the World Trade Center, and acting jobs in low-budget films.

In 1978 Bruen accepted a teaching position in Brazil that led to a horrific experience that changed the course of his life. Arrested with four other foreigners in a Rio de Janeiro bar after a brawl, he was held without being charged for the next four months in a Brazilian cell where he experienced physical, psychological, and sexual abuse at the hands of his guards and fellow inmates. He retreated from these horrors into what he has described as a catatonia from which he spent a long time recovering.

On his release, Bruen moved to South London, where he would spend the next several years and where his career as a serious writer began to take shape. He also resumed teaching and met his wife, Philomena. After fifteen years in London, Bruen returned to Galway, where his daughter was born.

Several echoes from significant events in Bruen's life can be found in his novels. The settings of South London and Galway, for example, are the most familiar towns in Bruen's life. Additionally, his daughter was born with Down syndrome, like the character Serena-May, the child of Jack Taylor's friends Jeff and Cathy. His brother and several members of his wife's family struggled with or succumbed to alcoholism, and Bruen once said that a brother-in-law was the model for the character Tommy in *American Skin* (2006).

ANALYSIS

After some early attempts at literary fiction and several well-received London-based crime thrillers including *Rilke on Black* (1996), *The Hackman Blues*

(1997), and *Her Last Call to Louis MacNeice* (1997), Ken Bruen achieved critical and commercial success with the publication of *The Guards*, a Jack Taylor novel, in 2001. Although his career as a novelist did not begin with the Sergeant Brant and Jack Taylor series, they are his most popular novels and among his most effective. In both series, Bruen brings a markedly American style to unusual settings like London and Galway. The literary influences Bruen claims are, with the exception of Samuel Beckett, more American than Irish: Raymond Chandler, David Goodis, James M. Cain, Dashiell Hammett, Elmore Leonard, James Ellroy, Joseph Koenig, George V. Higgins, and James Crumley. Bruen's economy of language makes for a staccato read that effectively mirrors the thought processes of the characters. The plots of the novels advance at a breakneck speed.

THE WHITE TRILOGY

Although Bruen's South London police procedurals have come to be known as the Brant novels, Detective Sergeant Brant shares the stage with several other significant characters, particularly in the first three novels in the series, reissued as *The White Trilogy*, where he has no more than equal billing with his boss, Chief Inspector Roberts. The police procedural often describes the actions of an ensemble rather than an individual. In the first Brant novel, *A White Arrest*, Roberts and Brant are referred to as R&B, rhythm and blues, in what seems like an echo of the team Fire and Ice in *The Black Dahlia* (1987) by James Ellroy, whom Bruen cites as an influence. Also introduced early in the novel is WPC (Woman Police Constable) Falls, who as a black woman is Brant's unlikely protégé. In *A White Arrest*, a serial killer called the Umpire is targeting the English cricket team, and a vigilante group is murdering drug dealers. As is common in the genre of police procedurals, the narrative is presented in the third person by a narrator who, although omniscient, does not divulge much about the inner lives or feelings of the characters—little more, at least, than the characters divulge to one another. Marital infidelity and the death of a dog are handled with dark humor amid allusions to British and American pop culture.

In *Taming the Alien*, the second novel in the trilogy, Brant travels to Ireland and the United States in pursuit of a fugitive with whom he finds a strange affinity, while WPC Falls struggles with an arsonist and the loss of a baby and Chief Inspector Roberts learns that he has skin cancer. *The McDead*, the third novel in the trilogy, pits Brant and Roberts against an Irish gangster over the death of Roberts's estranged brother. As elsewhere in the world of Bruen's London novels, revenge is presented as the best resolution available to the characters. The characterization is accomplished almost entirely through dialogue, with only limited commentary from the narrator, most of it darkly humorous.

LATER BRANT NOVELS

The line that separates the police from the criminals in the Brant novels is hard to identify; it has more to do with point of view than with the intrinsic qualities of any of the police officers who are recurrent characters. *Blitz* (2002) opens with Brant assaulting and destroying the reputation of the police psychiatrist who is supposed to be evaluating him, framing one his workplace enemies in the process. WPC Falls develops an unlikely relationship with a young, racist member of the British National Party, and Roberts tries to come to terms with the death of his wife. In the midst of the hunt for a serial killer who is targeting police officers, the various characters, all damaged in one way or another, support each other in small ways, almost as if by accident. The unlikely partnership between Brant and Porter Nash, an openly gay detective, is particularly interesting; Brant is violently unstable, but he is not a bigot.

Vixen (2003) pits the detectives against a female serial killer and further personal complications, and *Calibre* (2006) features a serial killer who targets rude people. In *Ammunition* (2007), Brant is shot by a crazed gunman while in a pub.

As is often the case with mystery and detective series, the Brant novels can be read out of order with only minimal difficulties; while there is continuity between them in terms of character development, each story is more or less discrete.

THE JACK TAYLOR NOVELS

The Jack Taylor novels, in contrast to the Brant novels, are much more closely related. The juxtaposition of these Galway novels with the Brant novels reveals the range of Bruen's talents; these first-person narratives are introspective and almost confessional

(though in an unsentimental way), while the Brant novels are not. If the characters in the Brant novels feel guilt or remorse, it is not foregrounded in the narrative. In general, the reader sees only as much of the characters as their peers would see. Jack Taylor, in contrast, is painfully aware of his sins and failures, though he often seems unable to rectify them. Character development, at least with regard to the protagonist, is much more detailed and explicit. Taylor's narration features lists, revealing the fragile discipline with which he hangs on to what is left of his life. It is also significant that Taylor is a voracious reader; his narration is full of literary allusions.

The first novel in the series, *The Guards*, shows Taylor wallowing in drunken self-pity, bitter over his dismissal from the police force, until he agrees to help a woman find out what has happened to her daughter. He is aided by his friend Sutton. In this novel the reader is introduced to Cathy, a young English former junkie who tries to pass as Irish, and Jeff, the bartender she eventually marries. These tenuous connections form Taylor's extended family. The novel ends on a dark note that refuses to glorify the loner lifestyle that generations of detective novelists have depicted as romantic.

In *The Killing of the Tinkers* (2002), Taylor has returned to Galway after a year hiding out in London only to be commissioned to investigate the murder of young "travellers," a nomadic group originating in Ireland and found in the United Kingdom and the United States. The novel is also particularly interesting because it features a crossover between the Jack Taylor series and the Brant novels in the person of Keegan, a British police officer with a predilection for the novels of Ed McBain.

In *The Magdalen Martyrs* (2003), Taylor is in worse health and spirits than ever and assists a mysterious character by locating a person formerly associated with the Magdalen laundries, prisonlike facilities created by the Roman Catholic Church to house prostitutes, unwed mothers, and other women deemed to be in trouble.

The Dramatist (2004) opens with a reformed Jack Taylor who no longer drinks or uses cocaine. His former dealer, now in jail in Dublin, enjoins him to investigate his sister's death, which has been incorrectly ruled an accident. Taylor's literary training serves him well as he works to solve a case that the police do not even acknowledge as a murder.

In *Priest* (2006), Taylor has just returned to Galway after a stay in a mental institution, suffering from guilt at having perhaps caused the death of a child. He is called to investigate the murder of a pedophile priest, whose decapitated body has been found in the confessional.

Like the best novels in any genre, Bruen's detective novels ultimately defy being pigeonholed in a particular category; they are detective fiction, certainly, but they are so stylish and concise that they reward literary analysis. With many mysteries, the compulsion to read is abrogated by the solution to the puzzle or the mystery itself; however, Bruen's novels, like the best novels in any genre, are worth rereading.

James S. Brown

PRINCIPAL MYSTERY AND DETECTIVE FICTION

SERGEANT BRANT SERIES: *A White Arrest*, 1998 (also known as *The White Trilogy, Book 1*); *Taming the Alien*, 1999 (also known as *The White Trilogy, Book 2*); *The McDead*, 2000 (also known as *The White Trilogy, Book 3*); *Blitz*, 2002 (also known as *Blitz: Or, Brant Hits the Blues*); *Vixen*, 2003; *Calibre*, 2006; *Ammunition*, 2007

JACK TAYLOR SERIES: *The Guards*, 2001; *The Killing of the Tinkers*, 2002; *The Magdalen Martyrs*, 2003; *The Dramatist*, 2004; *Priest*, 2006

SHORT FICTION: *Funeral: Tales of Irish Morbidities*, 1992; *Shades of Grace*, 1993; *Martyrs*, 1994; *Sherry, and Other Stories*, 1994; *Time of Serena-May and Upon the Third Cross*, 1995 (also known as *Time of Serena-May and Upon the Third Cross: A Collection of Short Stories*)

OTHER MAJOR WORKS

NOVELS: *Rilke on Black*, 1996; *The Hackman Blues*, 1997; *Her Last Call to Louis MacNeice*, 1997; *London Boulevard*, 2001; *Dispatching Baudelaire*, 2004; *American Skin*, 2006; *Bust*, 2006 (with Jason Starr)

EDITED TEXTS:

Dublin Noir: The Celtic Tiger Versus the Ugly American, 2006

BIBLIOGRAPHY

Anderson, Patrick. *The Triumph of the Thriller: How Cops, Crooks, and Cannibals Captured Popular Fiction*. New York: Random House, 2007. Contains a section on *The Guards* and *Calibre*, praising the humor.

Breen, Jon L. "The Police Procedural." In *Mystery and Suspense Writers: The Literature of Crime, Detection, and Espionage, I-II*, edited by Robin W. Winks and Maureen Corrigan. New York: Scribner's, 1998. An article on the police procedural subgenre by the novelist and critic Jon L. Breen.

Bruen, Ken. The Website of Ken Bruen. http://www .kenbruen.com. The author's Web site includes synopses of his novels and a discussion board.

MacDonald, Craig. *Art in the Blood: Crime Novelists Discuss Their Craft*. A collection of interviews with contemporary crime novelists that features a substantial interview with Bruen.

Murphy, Paula. "'Murderous Mayhem': Ken Bruen and the New Ireland." *Clues: A Journal of Detection* 24, no. 2 (Winter, 2006): 3-16. An exploration of how Bruen's Jack Taylor series addresses the preoccupations of postmillennial Ireland.

Swierczynski, Duane. "Through the Looking Glass: A Conversation with Ken Bruen." *Mystery Scene* 88 (Winter, 2005): 36-37. An interview with the author about his life and work.

JOHN BUCHAN
Lord Tweedsmuir

Born: Perth, Scotland; August 26, 1875
Died: Montreal, Quebec, Canada; February 11, 1940
Types of plot: Espionage; thriller

PRINCIPAL SERIES

Richard Hannay, 1915-1936
Sir Edward Leithen, 1916-1941
Dickson Mc'Cunn, 1922-1935

PRINCIPAL SERIES CHARACTERS

RICHARD HANNAY is a mining engineer from South Africa. His virtues are tenacity, loyalty, kindness, and a belief in "playing the game." A self-made man, he is respected as a natural leader by all who know him.

SIR EDWARD LEITHEN is a great English jurist who frequently finds himself in adventures. Although he is always willing to accept challenges, he is less keen than Hannay to seek out adventure and danger.

DICKSON MC'CUNN, a retired Scottish grocer, is a simple man with a Scottish burr who recruits a group of ragamuffins from the slums to aid him in his adventures. More so than Hannay or Leithen, Mc'Cunn is the common man thrust into uncommon experiences. He succeeds by sheer pluck and common sense, his own and that of the boys he informally adopts.

CONTRIBUTION

John Buchan is best known for *The Thirty-nine Steps* (1915), an espionage tale that succeeds through the author's trademarks: splendid writing, a truly heroic hero, and a sense of mission. Buchan eschews intricate plotting and realistic details of the spy or detective's world; his heroes are ordinary people who find themselves in extraordinary situations. Buchan's classic tales are closer to the adventure stories of writers such as H. Rider Haggard or P. C. Wren than to true detective or espionage fiction. Like Graham Greene, who cites him as an influence, Buchan writes "entertainments" with a moral purpose; less ambiguous than Greene, Buchan offers the readers versions of John Bunyan's *The Pilgrim's Progress from This World to That Which Is to Come* (1678), with the moral testing framed as espionage adventures.

BIOGRAPHY

Born in 1875, John Buchan was the eldest son of a Scots clergyman. His childhood was formed by the Border country landscape, wide reading, and religion; these influences also shaped his later life. He won a scholarship to Glasgow University, where he was soon recognized as a leader and a fine writer. Continuing his studies at Oxford University, he supported himself with journalism. With writing as his vocation, Buchan devised an exhaustive plan that included writing fiction, journalism, and histories in addition to pursuing his Oxford degree.

After completing his studies, Buchan accepted a government position in South Africa, an opportunity that allowed him to fulfill his desire for exotic travel. Though he did not lack the prejudices of his era, Africa became a beloved place to Buchan and was the setting of several of his fictions, including *Prester John* (1910). On returning to England, Buchan contin-

ued a double career as a barrister and as an editor for *The Spectator*, a leading periodical. His marriage in 1907 caused him to work even harder to ensure adequate finances for his wife and for his mother, sisters, and brothers.

Buchan served as a staff officer during World War I, as high commissioner of the Scottish Presbyterian Church, and as a member of Parliament. He completed his career of public service as governor general of Canada. By this time, he had received a peerage: He was now Lord Tweedsmuir. His varied responsibilities allowed him to travel extensively, and he was fascinated by the more distant explorations of others. As he grew older, though, his Scottish and Canadian homes and his family claimed a larger share of his attention.

The record of Buchan's public achievement shows a full life in itself, but throughout his public life he was always writing. His work includes histories, biographies, travel books, and especially fiction. A number of hours each day were set aside for writing. Buchan

John Buchan. (Library of Congress)

depended on the extra income from his popular novels, and he disciplined himself to write steadily, regardless of distractions. He continued to write and work even when his health declined. When he died suddenly of a stroke in 1940, he left behind nearly seventy published books.

ANALYSIS

John Buchan was already known as a political figure, biographer, and historian when he published his first "shocker," as he called it, *The Thirty-nine Steps*, in 1915. It is not surprising, then, that he chose to have the tale appear anonymously in its serial form in *Blackwoods* magazine. Extravagant praise from friends and the general public, however, caused him to claim the work when it later appeared in book form.

THE THIRTY-NINE STEPS

The Thirty-nine Steps was not truly a sudden departure for Buchan. Perhaps the recognition the book received helped him to realize the extent to which this shocker formed a part of much of his earlier work; he had planned it with the same care accorded to all of his writings. In 1914, he told his wife that his reading of detective stories had made him want to try his hand at the genre: "I should like to write a story of this sort and take real pains with it. Most detective story-writers don't take half enough trouble with their characters, and no one cares what becomes of either corpse or murderer."

An illness that prevented Buchan's enlistment in the early days of the war allowed him to act on this interest, and *The Thirty-nine Steps* came into being. The popularity of the book with soldiers in the trenches convinced the ever-Calvinist Buchan that producing such entertainments was congruent with duty. The book's popularity was not limited to soldiers or to wartime, however, and its hero, Richard Hannay, quickly made a home in the imagination of readers everywhere.

An energetic, resourceful South African of Scots descent, Hannay has come to London to see the old country. He finds himself immensely bored until one evening, when a stranger named Scudder appears and confides to Hannay some information regarding national security. The stranger is soon murdered, and Hannay, accused of the killing, must run from the police and decipher Scudder's enigmatic codebook, all the while avoiding Scudder's killers and the police. Hannay soon realizes that Scudder's secret concerns a German invasion, which now only he can prevent.

Some critics have observed that various plot elements make this tale go beyond the "borders of the possible," which Buchan declared he had tried to avoid. In spite of negative criticism, *The Thirty-nine Steps* won immediate popularity and remains a durable, beloved work of fiction. Its popularity stems from several sources, not the least of which is the nature of its hero. Hannay, as the reader first sees him, is a modest man of no particular attainments. Only as he masters crisis after crisis does the reader discover his virtues.

In a later book, Hannay says that his son possesses traits he values most: He is "truthful and plucky and kindly." Hannay himself has these characteristics, along with cleverness and experience as an engineer and South African trekker. His innate virtues, in addition to his background, make him a preeminently solid individual, one whom Britons, in the dark days of 1915, took to heart. Hannay's prewar victory over the Germans seemed prophetic.

Part of Hannay's appeal in *The Thirty-nine Steps* is outside the character himself, created by his role as an innocent bystander thrust into the heart of a mystery. It was perhaps this aspect of the novel that appealed to Alfred Hitchcock, whose 1935 film of the novel is often ranked with his greatest works. One of Hitchcock's favorite devices is the reaction of the innocent man or woman accused of murder, a premise he used in films such as *North by Northwest* (1959) and *Saboteur* (1942), among others. Yet little of Buchan's hero survives in Hitchcock's treatment: The great director's Hannay is a smooth, articulate ladies' man, and Scudder is transformed into a female spy.

Women are completely absent from Buchan's novel. In Hannay's next adventure, *Greenmantle* (1916), a woman is admitted to the cast of characters, but only as an archvillainess. In the third volume of the series, *Mr. Standfast* (1919), a heroine, Mary Lamingham, finally appears. She is repeatedly described as looking like a small child or "an athletic boy," and she is also a spy—in fact, she is Hannay's superior. (Hannay's successes in forestalling the German invasion have resulted in his becoming an occasional British agent.) *The Three Hostages* (1924) finds them married, but Mary is not oppressed by domestic life. She disguises herself and takes an active role in solving the kidnapping that actuates that novel.

Buchan allows Hannay to change through the years in his experiences, if not in his character. In *The Thirty-nine Steps*, he is alone in his adventures, his only comradeship found in his memory of South African friends and in his loyalty to the dead Scudder. As his history continues, he acquires not only a wife and son but also a circle of friends who share his further wartime espionage activities. Peter Pienaar, an older Boer trekker, joins the war effort, aiding Hannay with his fatherly advice. John Blenkiron, a rather comical American industrialist, is enlisted in *Greenmantle* and *Mr. Standfast* to help befuddle the Germans. One of Buchan's favorite devices is the "hide in plain sight" idea, which Blenkiron practices. He moves among the Germans freely, trusting that they will not recognize him as a pro-British agent.

THE THREE HOSTAGES AND THE ISLAND OF SHEEP

Hannay's espionage exploits cause him to be made a general before the end of the war. He then becomes a country gentleman. In *The Three Hostages* and *The Island of Sheep* (1936; also known as *The Man from the Norlands*), Buchan uses Hannay's transformation from a rootless, homeless man to a contented husband and father to show another of his favorite themes—that peace must be constantly earned. An appeal from a desperate father causes Hannay to risk everything to help free a child from kidnappers in *The Three Hostages*. In *The Island of Sheep*, a plea from the son of an old friend makes Hannay and some middle-aged friends confront themselves: "I'm too old, . . . and too slack," Hannay says when first approached. Nevertheless, he and his allies rally to defend their friend's son from vicious blackmailers in this tale, which is pure adventure with little mystery involved. *The Island of Sheep* is the least successful of the Hannay novels, which seem to work more dynamically when Hannay is offered challenges to his ingenuity. In *The Island of Sheep*, only his willingness to undergo hardship and danger is tested.

Another weakening element of this last Hannay novel is the lack of powerful adversaries. At one point, one of Hannay's companions characterizes the leader of the blackmailers, an old spy, D'Ingraville, as the devil incarnate, but the label is not validated by what the reader sees of D'Ingraville; it is instead a false attempt to heighten a rather dreary plot. Such is not the case in *The Thirty-nine Steps*, however, in which the reader is wholly convinced of the consummate evil of Ivery; he is the man with the hooded eyes, a master of disguise who finally meets his death in *Mr. Standfast*.

In *The Thirty-nine Steps*, Ivery is described as "more than a spy; in his foul way he had been a patriot." By the time Buchan wrote *Mr. Standfast*, however, he was thoroughly sick of the destruction and waste of the war. Ivery then becomes not simply a powerful adversary but the devil that creates war itself. Sentencing him to a death in the trenches, Hannay says, "It's his sort that made the war. . . . It's his sort that's responsible for all the clotted beastliness." Ivery's seductive interest in the virginal Mary not only intensifies the plot but also symbolizes the constant war of good against evil.

GOOD AND EVIL AND A MISSION

This basic conflict of good and evil animates the first three Hannay novels, which are clearly of the espionage genre. For Buchan, espionage was an appropriate metaphor for the eternal conflict. The author's Calvinistic background had taught him to see life in terms of this struggle and to revere hard work, toughness, and vigilance as tools on the side of good.

A major literary and moral influence on Buchan's life was *The Pilgrim's Progress from This World to That Which Is to Come*, the seventeenth century classic of devotional literature that crystallized Buchan's own vision of life as a struggle for a divine purpose. Thus, his heroes always define themselves as being "under orders" or "on a job" from which nothing can deter them. This attitude is a secular equivalent of a search for salvation. Hannay, Mc'Cunn, and Leithen are all single-minded in their devotion to any responsibility they are given, and such responsibility helps give meaning to their lives. In *Sick Heart River* (1941; also known as *Mountain Meadow*), for example, when Leithen is told by his doctors that he is dying, he wishes only to be given a "job," some task or mission to make his remaining months useful. Because Buchan's heroes represent pure good opposed to evil, their missions are elevated to the status of quests.

A journey with a significant landscape is always featured. Buchan loved the outdoors and conveyed in his fiction the close attention he paid to various locales. In *The Thirty-nine Steps*, London is the equivalent of Bunyan's Slough of Despond from which Hannay must escape. In addition, the spy's quest always ends in some powerfully drawn location, which is then purged of the adversary's ill influence and restored to its natural beauty. Buchan's tendency to use landscape in this symbolic fashion sometimes overrules his good fictional sense, however, as in *The Island of Sheep*, when Hannay and a few allies leave Scotland to confront the blackmailers on the lonely island home of the victim.

The sense of mission that sends Hannay to the Norlands is also found in a second Buchan hero, Dickson Mc'Cunn. One of Buchan's gifts was to create varied central characters, and Mc'Cunn could hardly be more different from Hannay, though they share similar values. A retired grocer, Mc'Cunn enjoys the pleasures of a simple life with his wife, believing somewhat wistfully that the romance of life has eluded him. Then he discovers a plot to depose the monarch of Evallonia, a mythical East European kingdom. Once involved, he carries out his duties with the good common sense that distinguishes him.

THE HOUSE OF THE FOUR WINDS

Unlike Hannay, Mc'Cunn is not physically strong or especially inventive, but he prides himself on being able to think through problems and foresee how people are likely to behave. In the course of his adventures—which always seem to surprise him—Mc'Cunn informally adopts a gang of street urchins, the Gorbals Die-Hards. As the Mc'Cunn series continues, the boys grow up to be successful young men. One of them, Jaikie, a student at Cambridge University, becomes the central character of *The House of the Four Winds* (1935). Jaikie discovers new trouble in Evallonia and calls on Mc'Cunn for help; Mc'Cunn leaves his salmon fishing and goes to Evallonia disguised as a grand duke returning from exile. After a brief military en-

counter, the trouble is forestalled, and Mc'Cunn returns happily to Scotland.

A third Buchan hero is Sir Edward Leithen. According to Buchan's wife, it is he who most resembles Buchan himself and speaks in his voice. Leithen lacks the simplicity of Mc'Cunn and the colorful background of Hannay. He is a distinguished jurist and member of Parliament, a man noted for his learning, hard work, and generosity. The tone of Leithen's tales is generally more detached and contemplative than that of Hannay's (both heroes narrate their adventures). This method has the effect of making Leithen into a character like Joseph Conrad's Marlow, who has been called Conrad's "moral detective."

JOHN MACNAB

Oddly enough, Leithen is at the center of *John Macnab* (1925), one of Buchan's lightest tales. Leithen and a few friends, discontent with their staid lives, decide to challenge some distant landlords by poaching on their grounds. Their adventures nearly get them shot, but Leithen and his friends are refreshed by the activity; they have now earned their comfort by risking it.

SICK HEART RIVER

Buchan's last novel, *Sick Heart River*, features Leithen, now old and dying. He does not bemoan his fate, however, but wishes only for some quest on which to expend his last months. He wants to be "under orders" as he was in the war. When he hears of a man lost in the Canadian wilderness, he believes that it is his duty to risk what is left of his life to try to rescue the man. His only right, he believes, is the right to choose to do his duty.

Though *Sick Heart River* has some characteristics of a mystery, it is really an adventure story and is more of a morality play than either mystery or adventure. Thus, it forms an appropriate end to Buchan's career as a novelist. For Buchan, the greatest mystery is the secret of human nature and human destiny. That mystery is solved by strength of character, through the working out of one's own destiny. Buchan's commitment to these great questions, carried through by his superbly vigorous writing, guarantees that his fiction will long be enjoyed.

Deborah Core

PRINCIPAL MYSTERY AND DETECTIVE FICTION

RICHARD HANNAY SERIES: *The Thirty-nine Steps*, 1915; *Greenmantle*, 1916; *Mr. Standfast*, 1919; *The Three Hostages*, 1924; *The Island of Sheep*, 1936 (also known as *The Man from the Norlands*)

SIR EDWARD LEITHEN SERIES: *The Power-House*, 1916; *John Macnab*, 1925; *The Dancing Floor*, 1926; *Sick Heart River*, 1941 (also known as *Mountain Meadow*)

DICKSON MC'CUNN SERIES: *Huntingtower*, 1922; *Castle Gay*, 1930; *The House of the Four Winds*, 1935

NONSERIES NOVELS: *The Courts of the Morning*, 1929; *A Prince of the Captivity*, 1933

OTHER SHORT FICTION: *The Watcher by the Threshold, and Other Tales*, 1902 (revised 1918); *The Moon Endureth: Tales and Fancies*, 1912; *The Runagates Club*, 1928; *The Gap in the Curtain*, 1932; *The Best Short Stories of John Buchan*, 1980

OTHER MAJOR WORKS

NOVELS: *Sir Quixote of the Moors, Being Some Account of an Episode in the Life of the Sieur de Rohaine*, 1895; *John Burnet of Barns*, 1898; *A Lost Lady of Old Years*, 1899; *The Half-Hearted*, 1900; *Prester John*, 1910 (also known as *The Great Diamond Pipe*); *Salute to Adventurers*, 1915; *The Path of the King*, 1921; *Midwinter: Certain Travellers in Old England*, 1923; *Witch Wood*, 1927; *The Blanket of the Dark*, 1931; *The Free Fishers*, 1934

SHORT FICTION: *Grey Weather: Moorland Tales of My Own People*, 1899; *Ordeal by Marriage*, 1915

POETRY: *The Pilgrim Fathers: The Newdigate Prize Poem 1898*, 1898; *Poems, Scots and English*, 1917 (revised 1936)

CHILDREN'S LITERATURE: *Sir Walter Raleigh*, 1911; *The Magic Walking-Stick*, 1932; *The Long Traverse*, 1941 (also known as *Lake of Gold*)

NONFICTION: 1896-1910 • *Scholar Gipsies*, 1896; *Sir Walter Raleigh*, 1897; *Brasenose College*, 1898; *The African Colony: Studies in the Reconstruction*, 1903; *The Law Relating to the Taxation of Foreign Income*, 1905; *A Lodge in the Wilderness*, 1906; *Some Eighteenth Century Byways, and Other Essays*, 1908

1911-1920 • *What the Home Rule Bill Means*, 1912; *Andrew Jameson, Lord Ardwall*, 1913; *The Marquis of Montrose*, 1913; *Britain's War by Land*, 1915; *Nelson's History of the War*, 1915-1919 (24 volumes); *The Achievements of France*, 1915; *The Battle of Jutland*, 1916; *The Battle of Somme, First Phase*, 1916; *The Future of the War*, 1916; *The Purpose of the War*, 1916; *The Battle of Somme, Second Phase*, 1917; *The Battle-Honours of Scotland, 1914-1918*, 1919; *The Island of Sheep*, 1919 (with Susan Buchan); *Francis and Riversdale Grenfell: A Memoir*, 1920; *The History of South African Forces in France*, 1920

1921-1930 • *Miscellanies, Literary and Historical*, 1921 (2 volumes); *A Book of Escapes and Hurried Journeys*, 1922; *Days to Remember: The British Empire in the Great War*, 1923 (with Henry Newbolt); *The Last Secrets: The Final Mysteries of Exploration*, 1923; *The Memory of Sir Walter Scott*, 1923; *Lord Minto: A Memoir*, 1924; *Some Notes on Sir Walter Scott*, 1924; *The History of the Royal Scots Fusiliers, 1678-1918*, 1925; *The Man and the Book: Sir Walter Scott*, 1925; *Two Ordeals of Democracy*, 1925; *Homilies and Recreations*, 1926; *The Fifteenth Scottish Division, 1914-1919*, 1926 (with John Stewart); *To the Electors of the Scottish Universities*, 1927; *Montrose*, 1928; *The Cause and the Causal in History*, 1929; *What the Union of the Churches Means to Scotland*, 1929; *Lord Rosebery, 1847-1930*, 1930; *Montrose and Leadership*, 1930; *The Kirk in Scotland, 1560-1929*, 1930 (with George Adam Smith); *The Revision of Dogmas*, 1930

1931-1947 • *The Novel and the Fairy Tale*, 1931; *Julius Caesar*, 1932; *Sir Walter Scott*, 1932; *Andrew Lang and the Border*, 1933; *The Margins of Life*, 1933; *The Massacre of Glencoe*, 1933; *Gordon at Khartoum*, 1934; *Oliver Cromwell*, 1934; *The Principles of Social Service*, 1934; *The Scottish Church and the Empire*, 1934; *The University, the Library, and the Common Weal*, 1934; *The King's Grace, 1910-1935*, 1935 (also known as *The People's King: George V*); *The Western Mind, an Address*, 1935; *A University's Bequest to Youth, an Address*, 1936; *Augustus*, 1937; *Presbyterianism: Yesterday, Today, and Tomorrow*, 1938; *The Interpreter's House*, 1938; *Canadian Occasions: Addresses by Lord Tweedsmuir*, 1940; *Com-*

ments and Characters, 1940 (W. Forbes Gray, editor); *Memory Hold-the-Door*, 1940 (also known as *Pilgrim's Way: An Essay in Recollection*); *The Clearing House: A Survey of One Man's Mind*, 1946 (Lady Tweedsmuir, editor); *Life's Adventure: Extracts from the Works of John Buchan*, 1947

EDITED TEXTS: *Essays and Apothegms of Francis Lord Bacon*, 1894; *Musa Piscatrix*, 1896; *The Compleat Angler: Or, The Contemplative Man's Recreation*, 1901; *The Long Road to Victory*, 1920; *Great Hours in Sport*, 1921; *A History of English Literature*, 1923; *The Nations of Today: A New History of the World*, 1923-1924; *The Northern Muse*, 1924; *Modern Short Stories*, 1926; *South Africa*, 1928; *The Teaching of History*, 1928-1930 (11 volumes); *The Poetry of Neil Munro*, 1931

BIBLIOGRAPHY

Buchan, Anna. *Unforgettable, Unforgotten*. London: Hodder and Stoughton, 1945. A personal look at Buchan's life by one of his sisters. Indexed and illustrated, it is especially good for his early life.

Buchan, William. *John Buchan: A Memoir*. Toronto: Griffen House, 1982. Written by his son, this very readable biography humanizes Buchan by concentrating on his personal, rather than public, life. Based on William's childhood memories, as well as his own expertise as a novelist, poet, and literary critic. Bibliography and index.

Butts, Dennis. "The Hunter and the Hunted: The Suspense Novels of John Buchan." In *Spy Thrillers: From Buchan to le Carré*, edited by Clive Bloom. New York: St. Martin's Press, 1990. Places Buchan at the beginning of the generic lineage that concludes with John le Carré's realist Cold War espionage narratives.

Cawelti, John G., and Bruce A. Rosenberg. *The Spy Story*. Chicago: University of Chicago Press, 1987. Cawelti's essay, "The Joys of Buchaneering," argues that Buchan's Richard Hannay stories are the crucial link between the spy adventures and the espionage novels of the twentieth century. Buchan developed a formula that was adopted and given various twists by successive authors. Includes an excellent bibliography and appendixes.

Daniell, David. *The Interpreter's House: A Critical Assessment of John Buchan*. London: Nelson, 1975. Concentrates on the tension between Calvinism and Platonism in Buchan's life, identified as the key to appreciating and understanding Buchan and his works. Scholarly and very thorough, the book refutes many of the common myths about Buchan.

Green, Martin. *A Biography of John Buchan and His Sister Anna: The Personal Background of Their Literary Work*. Lewiston, N.Y.: Edwin Mellen Press, 1990. A useful study of how literary talent is developed. This is a strictly chronological approach, except for the first chapter, "Heroic and Non-Heroic Values." Includes notes and bibliography.

Hitz, Frederick P. *The Great Game: The Myth and Reality of Espionage*. New York: Alfred A. Knopf, 2004. Hitz, the former inspector general of the Central Intelligence Agency, compares fictional spies in the work of Buchan and others to actual intelligence agents. His purpose is to demonstrate that truth is stranger than fiction.

Kruse, Juanita. *John Buchan and the Idea of Empire: Popular Literature and Political Ideology*. Lewiston, N.Y.: Edwin Mellen Press, 1989. Explores the role of colonialism and imperialism in Buchan's literary works.

Lownie, Andrew. *John Buchan: The Presbyterian Cavalier*. Rev. ed. Boston: D. R. Godine, 2003. As the subtitle indicates, Lownie is concerned with developing the Scottish roots of Buchan's writing. This very helpful biography includes a chronology, family tree, notes, and bibliography.

Smith, Janet Adam. *John Buchan and His World*. New York: Charles Scribner's Sons, 1979. Only 128 pages, this is an updated version of an earlier biography. Makes use of new materials provided by Buchan's family and publisher. Illustrated and well written, the biography concentrates on Buchan's life as both a writer and a public servant.

WILLIAM F. BUCKLEY, JR.

Born: New York, New York; November 24, 1925
Types of plot: Espionage; thriller

PRINCIPAL SERIES

Blackford Oakes, 1976-

PRINCIPAL SERIES CHARACTER

BLACKFORD OAKES, according to many critics, is an idealized version of his author: good-looking and well dressed, a Cold War Central Intelligence Agency operative with an offhand, almost drowsy manner of delivering his opinions that belies his strong inner convictions. Thoroughly at home with his identity as an American, he is determined to defend the American way at any cost. Still, the amiable and compassionate personality of Oakes has led some of Buckley's detractors to say that Oakes is not like Buckley at all.

CONTRIBUTION

In an effort to achieve what William F. Buckley, Jr., has called ideological egalitarianism, many authors of Cold War espionage thrillers have portrayed both Western and communist spies as equally amoral or equally heroic. In such portrayals, there is little to recommend either side. Buckley, a staunch traditionalist, views this moral relativism as an evil that prevents individuals from coming down squarely on the side of what is right and that does injustice to the American ideals of liberty that he has spent a lifetime defending. His contribution to the genre of espionage has been to create a world of clearly defined moral alternatives, accepting and even welcoming the likelihood that opposing values will polarize those who adopt them. This perspective on moral and political values makes Buckley's fiction an extension of his work as a conservative political philosopher.

Buckley's craftsmanlike thrillers present antagonists who, for the most part, are not simply caricatures of evil but fully realized individuals, intelligent and credible, with traits the reader can respect and admire. Indeed, one can feel compassion for certain of these characters, even though they are always on the wrong side while the Americans are always on the right side.

BIOGRAPHY

William F. Buckley, Jr., was born William Francis Buckley, the sixth of ten children in New York City on November 24, 1925, to William Frank Buckley, Sr., a Texas attorney, and Aloise Steiner Buckley. At the age of five, the young Buckley decided to change his middle name to Frank so that his entire name would be identical to his father's. The senior Buckley was a formative influence on his son, imparting to all of his children not only a resolute traditionalism but also the rebellious spirit of a conservative who had fallen from power. That spirit was aroused in the senior Buckley during the Mexican Revolution (1910-1921), when insurgents took control of that nation, seized the Buckley family petroleum assets, and destroyed the family's influence. From then on, the father never missed an opportunity to inspire hatred of revolution in his children.

The family had other assets, however, principally in Venezuela, where William, Jr., spent most of his first year. Between the ages of four and eight, he lived with his family in Europe. Although the theme of conservatives who are outside the power structure would surface in many ways throughout Buckley's writings, his overseas experiences tended to mitigate the influence of his father's isolationism.

Another early trait of Buckley was his defiant stance toward the administrators and faculties of the schools he attended. At the age of thirteen, while enrolled in Saint John's Beaumont School in England, he heard of the Munich Agreement, whereby British prime minister Neville Chamberlain conceded Czechoslovakia to Nazi Germany. In protest, Buckley hung an American flag over his bed—a gesture defiant of the administration but not in keeping with his father's isolationism. Later, as a Yale undergraduate, Buckley proposed a speech attacking the liberalism of the university faculty. Furious that the administration would not allow the speech, he afterward developed the same ideas into his first book, *God and Man at Yale: The Superstitions of "Academic Freedom"* (1951), which immediately put him in the national limelight.

Buckley graduated from Yale in 1950, and in July

William F. Buckley, Jr., in 1965, when he was running for mayor of New York City.
(AP/Wide World Photos)

saw as the plight of conservatives who lacked power. Buckley was convinced that a nationwide publication, well financed and edited, could increase public awareness of the conservative philosophy and give the conservaties an equal voice in the debate over political and social issues. Moreover, he was one of the few who had a strong sense of the direction such a publication should take.

From the beginning, *The National Review* exhibited the trademark Buckley wit and sarcasm that set it off from other staunchly conservative publications, which tended to get mired in a solemn, moralizing tone. However, no one could mistake the seriousness of Buckley's total dedication to changing the status quo. Initially, without questioning specific tenets of belief, *The National Review* seemed to support just about any political conservative. Within a few years, however, Buckley and his publication became instrumental in sharpening the definition of conservatism in the United States—distancing it, for example, from both isolationism and anti-Semitism, which before his time had been identified with conservatism in the public mind.

Buckley achieved significant influence, which for many years was associated primarily with *The National Review*, and the publication achieved the political results he had envisioned for it. In time, he found additional avenues of expression. His Blackford Oakes novels of espionage, begun in the 1970's, were one such avenue.

of that year he married Patricia Austin Taylor, from Vancouver, British Columbia. The couple's son, Christopher Taylor Buckley, was born in 1952. In 1951, Buckley was offered employment by the Central Intelligence Agency (CIA); he and Patricia were stationed in Mexico City. Concurrently, he worked as an editor for *The American Mercury*—the publication made famous in the 1920's by H. L. Mencken—but resigned after a year when the editors refused to publish an article he had written. The experience left him feeling that the United States needed a new conservative periodical.

In 1955, he founded such a publication, *The National Review*, with financial backing from his father and other prominent conservatives. Some backers had initially expressed skepticism, not about the validity of the cause but about the public reception of the conservative message. Although a Republican, Dwight D. Eisenhower, was president during this period, Buckley and others felt that the moderate Eisenhower did not truly represent the conservative philosophy. This, too, contributed to Buckley's preoccupation with what he

ANALYSIS

William F. Buckley, Jr., had been publishing books for twenty-five years by the time he came to write the Blackford Oakes novels. The story goes that he told his book editor he wanted to write something like a "Forsyth novel." The editor thought Buckley planned a story akin to John Galsworthy's *Forsyte Saga* (1922), perhaps featuring Buckley's colorful family. Buckley, however, was thinking of Frederick Forsyth's *The Day of the Jackal* (1971), about a hired killer who agrees to assassinate French president Charles de Gaulle.

The book that Buckley produced—the first in the Blackford Oakes series—was *Saving the Queen* (1976), based in part on his own brief experience with the CIA in the early 1950's during the Cold War period. The prevailing belief, articulated by novelists such as Graham Greene and John le Carré, was that espionage involved no morally worthy goals but was simply a sordid game or at best a means of livelihood. Buckley was disgusted with books and films that portrayed the CIA as morally reprehensible, with plots that suggested (as he described it with characteristic sarcasm) that "the evil spirit behind the killing . . . was the President of the United States or, to be really dramatic and reach all the way up, maybe even Ralph Nader." So he "took a deep breath and further resolved that the good guys would be—the Americans."

In Blackford Oakes, Buckley's spy novels present what the author calls "the distinctively American male": a hero who is intelligent but not pedantic, compassionate but not soft, a believer but not naïve, and a patriot but not a flag-waver. Blackford Oakes has much in common with his author as he is politically conservative but still very much the rebel. Buckley envisioned Oakes as a independent-minded American; he draws him as addressing his superiors with mutinous drollery and appreciating life's luxuries but expressing his satisfaction in an artless Yankee manner. In *High Jinx* (1986), Buckley describes Oakes thus: "At twenty-eight he wasn't yet willing to defer any presumptive physical preeminence in any group." Fictional he may be, but Oakes is his own man and not his creator's puppet.

The American virtues embodied by Oakes appear seriously threatened by the Soviets in the Cold War milieu of the 1950's and 1960's. The Soviets invaded Hungary to put down a popular uprising; Fidel Castro came to power—and later set up a missile base—in Cuba, ninety miles from Florida; and the Soviet Union launched a satellite well ahead of the United States. Oakes and his agency are engaged in a serious struggle

to defend the tradition of freedom at all costs. As Buckley intended—and as might be expected from an author with his intense patriotism—the heroes and villains are in fact easily distinguishable.

SEE YOU LATER, ALLIGATOR

Buckley's creed may be obvious, but he acknowledges and examines the complexity of the moral issues involved. For, despite the nobility of the cause, his hero Oakes is compelled to admit that both sides in the Cold War lie, cheat, and steal. An individual of Buckley's intelligence could do no less in his writing, nor could any less be expected in a well-crafted, credible work of fiction. Moreover, Buckley portrays the opposition in a curiously human, even compassionate, light. In *See You Later, Alligator* (1985), about Cuba during the missile crisis of 1962, Buckley portrays the Marxist Che Guevara as a humanitarian figure deserving of admiration and sympathy, and Fidel Castro is a fully realized character.

See You Later, Alligator finds President John F. Kennedy sending Oakes to Cuba in 1961. The assignment is to find out if Guevara, an official in Castro's government, is serious about a proposal he has made to reduce the antagonism between Washington, D.C., and Havana. Meanwhile, contrary to this proposal, Castro has become convinced he must arm Cuba with nuclear missiles to keep the Americans from invading. Despite obstacles, Oakes learns about the missiles and alerts the CIA to the threat. This novel incorporates a trademark Buckley device: the "behind-the-scenes" explanation of real historical events, an explanation that can be neither proved nor disproved.

A VERY PRIVATE PLOT

In 1995, Senator Hugh Blanton summons Blackford Oakes, now retired, to testify before Congress about a bygone CIA operation that reportedly almost triggered a nuclear war. Although Oakes refuses to divulge the details, the reader is given the "inside" story in *A Very Private Plot* (1994): that ten years earlier Oakes had encountered a moral dilemma when a group of young Russians conspired to murder Soviet premier Mikhail Gorbachev. When Oakes informed then-president Ronald Reagan, they were both uncertain whether to warn the adversary, Gorbachev, or withhold the warning to protect Oakes's key information source. *A Very Private Plot* illustrates Buckley's skill in engrossing the reader in stories about historical events whose outcome is already common knowledge. Buckley's real target in the novel is Blanton's attempt to pass what is nearly an ex post facto law against espionage.

LAST CALL FOR BLACKFORD OAKES

Last Call for Blackford Oakes (2005), a kind of sequel to *A Very Private Plot*, is set in 1987, when Oakes is sixty-one years old. The story follows him to Moscow, this time with clear orders from President Reagan to uncover and foil a plot against the life of Gorbachev. The story mixes real with imaginary events as Buckley presents cameos of Garry Trudeau, Gore Vidal, Norman Mailer, and Graham Greene. Meanwhile, this latest rumor of an assassination plot proves false. Instead, Oakes has an intense confrontation with Kim Philby, a real-life double agent who in 1963 defected from the free world to the Soviet Union, and the action shifts to a dreadful psychological battle between spies who have almost run their race.

SPYTIME

Not a part of the Blackford Oakes series, *Spytime: The Undoing of James Jesus Angleton* (2000) relates both actual and fictitious events in the life of James Jesus Angleton (1917-1987), a historic figure who was associate deputy director of operations for counterintelligence in the CIA. The book explores the intellectual thrill of espionage: Like a brilliant chess player, Angleton displayed an uncanny intuition regarding adversaries' motives. However, the overzealous Angleton eventually was fired and blamed, fairly or unfairly, for the CIA's moral and ethical failures. Some critics complained that, as portrayed by Buckley, Angleton is not a fully realized character.

Thomas Rankin

PRINCIPAL MYSTERY AND DETECTIVE FICTION

BLACKFORD OAKES SERIES: *Saving the Queen*, 1976; *Stained Glass*, 1978; *Who's on First*, 1980; *Marco Polo, if You Can*, 1982; *The Story of Henri Tod*, 1984; *See You Later, Alligator*, 1985; *High Jinx*, 1986; *Mongoose, RIP*, 1987; *Tucker's Last Stand*, 1990; *A Very Private Plot*, 1994; *The Blackford Oakes Reader*, 1994; *Last Call for Blackford Oakes*, 2005

NONSERIES NOVELS: *The Temptation of Wilfred Malachey*, 1985; *Brothers No More*, 1995; *The Redhunter: A Novel Based on the Life of Senator Joe McCarthy*, 1999; *Spytime: The Undoing of James Jesus Angleton*, 2000; *Elvis in the Morning*, 2001; *Nuremberg: The Reckoning*, 2002; *Getting It Right*, 2003

OTHER MAJOR WORKS

NONFICTION: 1951-1970 • *God and Man at Yale: The Superstitions of "Academic Freedom,"* 1951; *McCarthy and His Enemies: The Record and Its Meaning*, 1954 (with L. Brent Bozell); *Up from Liberalism*, 1959; *Rumbles Left and Right: A Book About Troublesome People and Ideas*, 1963; *The Unmaking of a Mayor*, 1966; *The Jeweler's Eye: A Book of Irresistible Political Reflections*, 1968; *Quotations from Chairman Bill: The Best of William F. Buckley, Jr.*, 1970; *The Governor Listeth: A Book of Inspired Political Revelations*, 1970

1971-1980 • *Cruising Speed: A Documentary*, 1971; *Inveighing We Will Go*, 1972; *Four Reforms: A Guide for the Seventies*, 1973; *United Nations Journal: A Delegate's Odyssey*, 1974; *Execution Eve, and Other Contemporary Ballads*, 1975; *Airborne: A Sentimental Journey*, 1976; *A Hymnal: The Controversial Arts*, 1978

1981-1990 • *Atlantic High: A Celebration*, 1982; *Overdrive: A Personal Documentary*, 1983; *Right Reason*, 1985; *Racing Through Paradise: A Pacific Passage*, 1987; *On the Firing Line: The Public Life of Our Public Figures*, 1989; *Gratitude: Reflections on What We Owe to Our Country*, 1990

1991-2007 • *Windfall: End of the Affair*, 1992; *In Search of Anti-Semitism*, 1992; *Happy Days Were Here Again: Reflections of a Libertarian Journalist*, 1993; *Buckley: The Right Word*, 1996; *Nearer, My God: An Autobiography of Faith*, 1997; *Let Us Talk of Many Things: The Collected Speeches of William F. Buckley, Jr.*, 2000; *The Fall of the Berlin Wall*, 2004; *Miles Gone By: A Literary Autobiography*, 2004; *Cancel Your Own Goddam Subscription: Notes and Asides from the National Review*, 2007

EDITED TEXTS: *Did You Ever See a Dream Walking? Conservative Thought in the Twentieth Century*, 1987; *Keeping the Tablets: Modern American Conservative Thought*, 1988

BIBLIOGRAPHY

Bridges, Linda, and John R. Coyne, Jr. *Strictly Right: William F. Buckley Jr. and the American Conservative Movement*. Hoboken, N.J.: Wiley, 2007. Long-time employees of *The National Review* wrote this biography of Buckley that focuses on the magazine and its influence on conservatives.

Buckley, William F., Jr. *Let Us Talk of Many Things: The Collected Speeches of William F. Buckley, Jr.* Roseville, Calif.: Forum, 2000. Includes the text of a speech delivered October 2, 1984, about the origin of the Blackford Oakes series.

_____. *Miles Gone By: A Literary Autobiography.* Washington, D.C.: Regnery, 2004. Includes reminiscences about the origin of the Blackford Oakes series and individual titles.

Judis, John. *William F. Buckley, Jr.: Patron Saint of the Conservatives*. New York: Simon & Schuster, 1988. Briefly describes the background of *Saving the Queen* and the physical appearance of Blackford Oakes, and comments on Buckley's evenhandedness in portraying adversaries.

Rubins, Josh. "Blackford Oakes, One Stand-Up Guy." Review of *A Very Private Plot*, by William F. Buckley, Jr. *The New York Times*, February 6, 1994. Examines Buckley's playful style and the challenge ofportraying historical events whose outcome is widely known.

JOHN BURDETT

Born: North London, England; July 24, 1951
Types of plot: Police procedural; thriller; courtroom drama

PRINCIPAL SERIES
Sonchai Jitpleecheep, 2003-

PRINCIPAL SERIES CHARACTERS

SONCHAI JITPLEECHEEP is biracial, born during the Vietnam War, the prodof a Thai prostitute and one of her customers, an American soldier on furlough in Bangkok. In his early thirties, he has straw-colored hair, a sharp nose, and is taller than the average Thai. A devout Buddhist—a believer in karma, meditation, reincarnation, and living in poverty—who is fluent in Thai, French, English, and American slang and speaks a smattering of other languages, Sonchai is a detective with the Bangkok police department. He works out of District 8, an area crammed with bars and sex clubs catering to both domestic visitors and an incredible variety of *farang* (foreign) tourists.

NONG JITPLEECHEEP is Sonchai's mother, once a beautiful young woman in great demand for her services as a prostitute. During her heyday, Nong traveled, accompanied by her beloved son, to live with foreign lovers in France, Germany, the United States, and elsewhere, and she also speaks several languages. Now approaching fifty years of age, retired, and living in a small Thai village, Nong keeps current with modern technology via computer and cell phone and is up on the latest jargon. Contemptuous of the repressed Western attitude toward sex, so different from Thai openness and acceptance of sex as a natural part of life, she enters into partnership with Colonel Vikorn in the operation of a brothel specifically for aging Westerners, called the Old Man's Club.

COLONEL VIKORN, a short, squat man in his sixties, is the police chief of District 8 and Sonchai's boss. Like his counterparts from Bangkok's other districts, he has grown wealthy and powerful by taking advantage of his position to become involved in a variety of questionable activities—the import and export of drugs, transactions in stolen works of art, and rake-offs from the sex trade—in a city where such what Westerners would view as corruption is a normal, everyday part of doing business.

CONTRIBUTION

John Burdett has given the mystery world a unique detective working in a fresh literary setting. After demonstrating his talents for characterization, sharp dialogue, complex plotting, dark wit, and keen observation in writing his debut work, the courtroom drama-thriller *A Personal History of Thirst* (1996), he exploited an event of worldwide proportions for his second novel. *The Last Six Million Seconds* (1997) is centered on what was the impending transfer of power in Hong Kong from British to Chinese hands. As he had practiced law in Hong Kong for twelve years leading up to the takeover, his choice of subject matter was no surprise. However, although Southeast Asia, a vibrant, booming corner of the world, fascinated Burdett, Hong Kong was a creative dead end because the local film industry, led by the likes of John Woo and Jackie Chan, had already made the sights and sounds of the city familiar to an international audience. So Burdett, after traveling widely in search of the perfect setting, selected a lesser known though equally exotic and colorful setting for his next novels, moving the action a thousand miles south and west to the virgin territory—in the literary sense—of Bangkok. It was a wise choice as he was already acquainted with Bangkok from frequent recreational trips. Once the location was settled, Burdett immersed himself in the culture, history, and geography of his adopted country.

Burdett's firsthand research and his personal experiences in dealing professionally with ethnically diverse individuals involved in a wide spectrum of criminal behavior show to good advantage in his Sonchai novels. He skillfully engages all of the readers' senses in describing the intricacies and attitudes of Bangkok society, much of which revolves around the world's most active and open sex trade. He brings to life intriguing characters who are engaged directly or peripherally with the sex industry. His hero, an observant, introspective hard-boiled detective slightly softened with the pacifist tenets of Buddhism and susceptible to all the temptations that surround him, is likable despite his many faults. All these qualities have brought Burdett a warm reception from readers and critics alike, though acceptance of the Sonchai novels in the United States has been slower than in other parts of the world.

BIOGRAPHY

John Burnett was born on July 24, 1951, in north London, the son of police officer Frank Burdett and seamstress Eva Burdett. Interested in writing from his early teens, Burdett later turned to law as a means of earning a living.

He attended the University of Warwick, where he was particularly interested in the work of D. H. Lawrence and Graham Greene, and graduated in 1973. He afterward earned a degree at the College of Law and qualified as a barrister, in which capacity he worked for a time in London, practicing family law, before being sent to the British colonies as a government attorney. Burdett practiced for ten years in the criminal courts of Hong Kong, then went into private practice, eventually becoming a partner in the prestigious law firm of Johnson, Stokes, and Master. Burdett married Laura Liguori in 1995, and the couple produced one daughter before divorcing.

While still employed as a lawyer, Burdett used his spare time to write his first novel, *A Personal History of Thirst*, a London-based love triangle between ambitious working-class lawyer James Knight, a man named Oliver Thirst whom Knight successfully defended on a charge of theft, and Daisy Smith, a woman who was romantically involved with both men and is accused of killing Thirst. Burdett's second novel, *The Last Six Million Seconds*, was a thriller set in Hong Kong just before the Chinese takeover, in which half-Irish, half-Chinese detective Chan Siukai investigates a series of gruesome murders—the first salvo in a power struggle among various diverse factions including British diplomats, American mobsters, Chinese communists, and others to control Hong Kong after the transition of governments.

Although neither novel performed particularly well critically or commercially (though both were later adapted as audio recordings and have been optioned for film), Burdett resigned from the law firm to travel the world in search of an intriguing—and underused—setting in which to base a series of mystery novels. After rejecting Morocco as a possible venue for his stories, Burdett selected Bangkok (which Thais call Krung Thep, the "city of angels"), where he had often vacationed while practicing law in Hong Kong.

For research purposes, he traveled to a monastery for a two-week meditation course on Theravada Buddhism—the form practiced in Southeast Asia—and spent many hours in the city's red-light district absorbing the atmosphere and befriending bar girls.

Burdett's first novel set in Thailand, *Bangkok Eight*, appeared in 2003. The first of a series featuring detective Sonchai Jitpleecheep—a unique character who is equal parts hard-boiled, hip, and Buddhist—the novel was critically acclaimed for its original sleuth; its intriguing secondary characters; its detailed descriptions that give the flavor of an exotic, chaotic city unfamiliar to many readers; and for its incorporation of Asian culture and philosophy. The series continued with the publication of *Bangkok Tattoo* (2005) and *Bangkok Haunts* (2007).

ANALYSIS

The groundwork for John Burdett's critically acclaimed Sonchai Jitpleecheep mystery novels was laid in his second book, *The Last Six Million Seconds*. Like much of his later work, that novel is set in an exotic environment (Hong Kong), which allows for extensive sensual description. It deals with factual issues endemic to the region (the struggle for power among various factions in a time and place of political upheaval). It also features a detective of mixed blood (the half-Irish, half-Chinese protagonist, Inspector "Charlie" Chan Siukai) who brings a unique perspective to his investigation as he covers his culturally diverse territory.

Burdett has carried the strengths of *The Last Six Million Seconds* to his Sonchai novels, enhancing and deepening them. The first of the series, *Bangkok Eight*, is almost a sensory overload, a welter of pungent smells, strange sounds, foreign tastes, tactile textures as different as stone and silk, and sights captured as crisp as black-and-white snapshots, all of which contribute in capturing the atmosphere and frenetic pace of the Thai capital. Bangkok, though as bustling a metropolis as Hong Kong, has the sex industry at its heart and soul. This business, though presented openly and without shame throughout the red-light district twenty-four hours a day, seven days a week to an eager international customer base, the trade has dark and devious underpinnings. Associated with the sex industry is a full range of criminal behavior: brisk drug deal-ings, fierce battles over territory, sexual assaults, and perversions that are beyond the realm of social acceptance. Much of this criminal behavior leads to violence, resulting in deaths, which, if they occur in his district, Number 8, come to the attention of detective Sonchai, who works under the auspices of his commander, Colonel Vikorn.

A unique creation, Sonchai is a walking dichotomy. A Vietnam War-era product of the union between an anonymous American soldier and a young Thai prostitute, Sonchai embodies both Western brashness and Eastern circumspection. He has features that are a blend of Caucasian and Thai, and speaks both English and Thai fluently, so he is simultaneously a native and an outcast. He is equally attracted to and repelled by women. He lives in simplicity and poverty, though he sometimes has access to large sums of money. His noir outlook is darkness with light around the edges, thanks to Sonchai's devotion to Buddhism; though he may be forced to resort to physical violence, inwardly he is in contemplation. He is a relatively incorruptible upholder of the law, yet he expediently violates certain provisions when necessary: to maintain alertness Sonchai occasionally ingests *yaa baa*, a drug that is a combination of methamphetamine and fertilizer; to relax he smokes *ganja* and sometimes drinks to excess; he accepts bribes; and he seeks personal vengeance. He is by turns respectful of and contemptuous toward his superior, Vikorn, who has become wealthy and powerful through his long-term and unabashed commitment to corruption. Vikorn, recognizing Sonchai's talent for deduction, allows the detective considerable leeway in conducting investigations, only stepping in when the sleuth infringes on the colonel's under-the-table income or when dignitaries are involved, where diplomacy and an administrator's capacity to negotiate would be useful.

Sonchai and Vikorn are both well drawn, as are all characters, who speak in realistic and distinctive voices, because of Burdett's ear for the rhythm and cadence of speech. *Bangkok Eight* has a wide, diverse cast. Several Americans are slyly portrayed: the United States Embassy attaché Jack Nape (perhaps a pun on "jackanapes"?), his assistant Ted Rosen, and Federal Bureau of Investigation (FBI) agent, Kimberly Jones, who is attracted to but flummoxed by Sonchai's contradictory disposition. Another influential, wealthy American, gem dealer and closet pervert Sylvester Warren, is seen as haughty and condescending. Elijah Bradley, the older brother of the American soldier whose death at the beginning of the novel precipitates the rest of the plot, is down to earth. A German former lover of Sonchai's mother—whom Sonchai compassionately assists by smuggling money to him—Fritz von Staffen loses his racial superiority and his thick head of hair while serving a long sentence in a primitive Thai prison for drug smuggling. A central character is Fatima, a beautiful half-black, half-Thai woman who started life as a boy but underwent complete gender reassignment to please a lover, unaware that she was being reshaped to match a particular vision in the mind of a murderer.

Later entries in the series also touch on the sex trade. *Bangkok Tattoo* is precipitated by the mutilation murder of a Central Intelligence Agency (CIA) operative, suspected to be the work of a beautiful bar girl. Complications naturally ensue with appearances by American agents, officers of the Thai army, religious fundamentalists, Japanese gangsters, and tattoo artists. Likewise, *Bangkok Haunts* begins with a video depicting the ultimate perversion, eroticism that results in murder.

The voice of the Sonchai series is as distinctive as the setting and is the thread that binds the many seemingly unrelated pieces of the central puzzle together. Told in first-person present tense from Sonchai's viewpoint as a half-caste Buddhist, the narrative incorporates elements of seemingly fatalistic Eastern philosophy, hard-boiled sensibilities, modern realities, and cross-cultural beliefs and attitudes. The stories themselves are complex though rewarding, tales of revenge, corruption, greed, and lust, in an unfamiliar environment where the Western temperament does not apply and the standard conventions of mystery, deduction, and a tidy, full resolution are constantly shattered.

BANGKOK EIGHT

A fascinating, if challenging, novel, *Bangkok Eight* opens with a bang. Detective Sonchai Jitpleecheep and his partner—and soul brother in the Buddhist sense—Pichai Apiradee, are under orders from their commander, Colonel Vikorn, They are following William Bradley, a very large African American soldier em-

ployed at the United States Embassy and suspected of being a major drug merchant, as he drives around the sprawling city in a Mercedes-Benz. The two police officers lose the soldier in the crush of traffic but, acting on a tip, locate the car under a bridge, where its door handles have been blocked with pieces of steel. When Sonchai and Pichai approach, a gigantic, drug-addled python is in the process of trying to swallow the American. The police officers unblock the doors, releasing an avalanche of drugged cobras, one of which bites Pichai in the eye, killing him as dead as the American.

The initial incident propels Sonchai, an intriguing, one-of-a-kind character, into a tangled investigation that involves many different parties—local authorities, the CIA, the FBI, drug dealers, merchants in stolen artwork, individuals engaged in some of the more bizarre aspects of the indigenous sex trade, and border tribesmen—in a case wherein various threads violently intersect.

BANGKOK HAUNTS

The third in the series, *Bangkok Haunts* drags Detective Sonchai Jitpleecheep—now living with a former prostitute pregnant with their child—into a case that begins with an anonymously received snuff film, in which Damrong, a woman the police officer knows, cares for, and erotically dreams about, has allegedly been killed. In the course of his investigation, Sonchai involves young, attractive FBI agent Kimberly Jones, and the sexual tension between the two increases as they join forces in following a twisting path toward the heart of the crime in pursuit of the perpetrator. *Bangkok Haunts* was critically well received for its tangled plot, authentic dialogue, well-rounded characters, fascinating setting, and multifaceted exploration of culture and crime.

Jack Ewing

PRINCIPAL MYSTERY AND DETECTIVE FICTION

SONCHAI JITPLEECHEEP SERIES: *Bangkok Eight*, 2003; *Bangkok Tattoo*, 2005; *Bangkok Haunts*, 2007

NONSERIES NOVELS: *A Personal History of Thirst*, 1996; *The Last Six Million Seconds*, 1997

BIBLIOGRAPHY

Anderson, Patrick. *The Triumph of the Thriller: How Cops, Crooks, and Cannibals Captured Popular*

Fiction. New York: Random House, 2007. Contains a brief biography of Burdett along with analysis of *Bangkok Eight* and *Bangkok Tattoo*.

Dunn, Adam. "Crime and Cops, Thai-Style." Review of *Bangkok Eight*, by John Burdett. *Publishers Weekly* 250, no. 19 (May 12, 2003): 41-42. A starred review of *Bangkok Eight*, termed part thriller, part mystery, and part exploration of Thai attitudes toward sex, plus a brief interview with Burdett, who notes difficulties in interesting American audiences in non-American topics. Though praising the author's fresh approach to noir themes, the structure, and the depth of the novel, the review mildly criticizes the anticlimactic final chapter.

Grossman, Lev. "If You Read Only One Mystery Novel This Summer . . . Oh, Who Are We Trying to Kid? There's No Way We Could Choose Just One: Here Are Six of the Season's Twistiest, Tautest, Most Tantalizing Tales of Sleuthery." Review of *Bangkok Eight*, by John Burdett. *Time*, August 11, 2003, 58-60. This highly favorable review cites the exotic feel and flavor of the novel, which is featured alongside new works by Walter Mosley, Mark Haddon, and others.

Hepner, Will. Review of *The Last Six Million Seconds*, by John Burdett. *Library Journal* 122, no. 2 (February 1, 1997): 104. The reviewer praises the novel for its protagonist, Hong Kong Royal Police chief "Charlie" Chan, who employs forensics and bureaucratic maneuvering to untangle a triple murder. The reviewer also notes the good characterizations, excellent use of the details of locale, and the complex plot.

Nathan, Paul. "Rights: Road from Hong Kong." *Publishers Weekly* 243, no. 7 (April 22, 1996): 24. A brief history of how Burdett's *A Personal History of Thirst* was brought from manuscript to print; includes details of film rights for the author's first two novels.

Publishers Weekly. Review of *A Personal History of Thirst*, by John Burdett. 242, no. 51 (December 18, 1995): 41. A favorable review that calls attention to the novel's underlying theme: the highlighting of ironies in the British class system. The reviewer notes the novel's three-part structure and terms it a "sharp-eyed morality tale."

Wright, David. Review of *Bangkok Eight*, by John Burdett. *Library Journal* 128, no. 10 (June 1, 2003): 163. A highly favorable review that pays particular tribute to the author's highly original sleuth; the consistent pace of a plot that encompasses psychological, cultural, metaphysical and mysterious conundrums; and the evocative, exotic portrayal of the Thai capital.

JAMES LEE BURKE

Born: Houston, Texas; December 5, 1936
Types of plot: Hard-boiled; thriller

PRINCIPAL SERIES
Dave Robicheaux, 1987-
Billy Bob Holland, 1997-

PRINCIPAL SERIES CHARACTERS
DAVE ROBICHEAUX is a police detective and recovering alcoholic working in and around his hometown, the south Louisiana city of New Iberia. Somewhat cynical and disillusioned with the justice system, Robicheaux is a quiet man whose lifelong dream is to raise a family. He finds himself constantly thrown into a world populated by criminals and psychopaths, where he must use violent means to protect those he loves and restore a sense of order.

BILLY BOB HOLLAND is a former Texas Ranger who has gone to law school and works as a defense attorney. Like Robicheaux, however, trouble seems to seek him out, and often he ends up resorting to violence to bring evil people to justice.

CONTRIBUTION

Within a decade after publishing his first mystery novel, James Lee Burke established his reputation as one of America's premier practitioners of the genre. What sets him apart from others writing in a form that frequently emphasizes complex plotting at the expense of characterization and thematic development is his ability to incorporate elements of serious, mainstream fiction into his work. Burke explores important social, moral, and even philosophical themes while still incorporating the requisite elements of suspense and action expected in the kind of hard-boiled detective fiction that is his trademark.

Perhaps because Burke began his career writing other forms of fiction, he pays less attention to the kind of careful plotting found in the work of other mystery writers, and his heroes are thoughtful, introspective, and literate men. Through them Burke explores questions about human relationships—love, family, estrangement, alienation, and social responsibility—and about environmental issues such as the despoiling of the land by exploitative businesses. He also uses his novels to examine the role of corrupt, lax, or simply inefficient governmental officials in promoting or allowing the kinds of evil that pose real dangers to civil society.

BIOGRAPHY

James Lee Burke was born on December 5, 1936, in Houston, Texas. His mother was a Texan and his father a native of New Iberia, Louisiana, who worked for the oil and gas industry in the region. Early in his life Burke determined to become a writer. After completing high school, he enrolled at Southwestern Louisiana Institute (now the University of Louisiana at Lafayette) but did not graduate. Later he enrolled at the University of Missouri, earn-

ing a bachelor's degree in 1959 and a master's degree the following year.

Burke's first published works are what could be considered mainstream fiction. Modest success came relatively early. *Half of Paradise* (1965), a novel he completed when he was only twenty-three, was published to critical acclaim in 1965, and his next work, *To the Bright and Shining Sun* (1970), received a similar reception when it appeared in 1970. However, his third novel, *Lay Down My Sword and Shield* (1971), did not fare as well; critics panned it, and for fifteen years after it appeared in 1971, Burke did not sell another novel to a major publisher. To support himself, he worked at a variety of jobs, including social worker, oil-lease negotiator, newspaper reporter, and college English instructor. During the 1970's he fought alcoholism, finally achieving sobriety with the help of a twelve-step program in 1977.

After the publication of his third novel, he continued to write and submit his work for publication but without

James Lee Burke. (Tomm Furch/Courtesy, Hyperion Books)

success. More than a hundred publishers rejected *The Lost Get-Back Boogie* (1986), the story of a Louisiana convict transplanted to Montana. Finally, Burke revised and shortened the novel before offering it to Louisiana State University Press, which had published a collection of his short stories in 1985. The novel appeared in 1986 and was nominated for the Pulitzer Prize.

Burke became a mystery writer almost by accident. In 1984, challenged by a friend, he tried his hand at a mystery novel. The result was *The Neon Rain*, a work set in New Orleans and introducing Detective Dave Robicheaux. Published in 1987, the novel immediately established Burke as a new voice in the genre. The Robicheaux novels began to appear at the rate of one each year, and the third in the series, *Black Cherry Blues* (1989), earned the 1989 Edgar Award for the year's best novel from the Mystery Writers of America.

By 1990 Burke's growing popularity brought sufficient financial security that he was finally able to devote full time to writing. He began dividing his time between homes in Montana and south Louisiana, the locales in which much of his fiction is set. The series of Robicheaux novels was interrupted in 1997 when Burke brought out *Cimarron Rose* (1997), the first of a new series of mysteries featuring Billy Bob Holland, a Texan whose fictionalized family history is modeled on Burke's mother's family. The work earned him his second Edgar Award, making Burke one of the few writers to receive multiple honors from the Mystery Writers Association. Additional novels featuring Robicheaux and Holland followed regularly, although Burke took time away from mystery fiction in 2001 to complete *White Doves at Morning* (2002), a historical novel set during the Civil War.

ANALYSIS

The designation of James Lee Burke as a member of the hard-boiled school of mystery and detective fiction is fully justified. His novels are dark and often cynical, filled with raw and earthy language spoken by characters from the lowest strata of society. Exceptionally adept at creating atmosphere in his work, Burke writes vividly about the places where the action of his novels occurs. Sometimes these settings mirror the mayhem and chaos being acted out by his charac-

ters; more often, however, the idyllic backdrops of the south Louisiana bayou country or the mountains and plains of Montana form a sharp contrast to the violence being perpetrated in them—and to them.

Burke's characters, good as well as bad, are prone to resort to violence to achieve their ends. His protagonists do not hesitate to mete out their own form of justice when they perceive that the legal system may not deliver the verdict they believe to be right. At the same time, they are not one-dimensional but rather more like the heroes of existential writers Albert Camus or Jean-Paul Sartre than those of Mickey Spillane or Raymond Chandler. Robicheaux and the cast of characters in the novels in which he is featured are reminiscent of characters created by southern writers such as William Faulkner and Flannery O'Connor. There are echoes of southern gothic reminiscent of Faulkner's *Sanctuary* (1931) and *Requiem for a Nun* (1951) throughout the Robicheaux series. In Burke's fiction, as in Flannery O'Connor's most celebrated novel, a truly good man—or woman—is sometimes very hard to find.

Burke's novels exude a great sense of irony as well. Both his major protagonists are men who emerge from violent pasts. Robicheaux is a Vietnam veteran who witnessed the horrors of war firsthand and suffers from alcoholism all his life. Holland, a former Texas Ranger, lives with the guilt of knowing he accidentally killed his partner during a drug raid. Both want to settle down to family life and escape the dangerous world in which they have been immersed. Robicheaux marries four times and even adopts a young Central American girl in his vain attempt to achieve some measure of normalcy in his life. Both Robicheaux and Holland have deep roots in the places in which they live, and environmental issues become a major theme in a number of the books.

What Burke demonstrates through all of his novels is that, no matter how hard these men try, they can never be at peace; they think too much and care too much about their families, their heritage, and their environment to let evil forces run unchecked. That is the central thematic issue running through the individual stories that make up the canon of one of America's great voices in mystery and detective fiction.

THE NEON RAIN

In *The Neon Rain*, the first of the Dave Robicheaux novels, Burke establishes a complex personal history for his protagonist while taking readers on an exciting and dangerous journey through the New Orleans underworld. Robicheaux's crusade to identify and apprehend the murderer of a young prostitute leads him into a web of sinister activity that eventually ends with his discovering a plot to smuggle arms to Nicaraguan rebels. His personal life is constantly in danger, and although he is thwarted in his investigation on more than one occasion, he manages to escape death and identify not only the prostitute's murderer but also the head of the smuggling ring, a retired Army general bent on preventing Nicaragua from falling to the communists as Vietnam had.

Robicheaux receives help in his investigation from his partner, Detective Cletus Purcel, whose moral code is considerably more lax and whose personal life is in even greater disarray than Robicheaux's. The two have a relationship that Burke has described as akin to that of Don Quixote and Sancho Panza; their friendship allows them to forgive each other's failings no matter how egregious. Robicheaux also receives help of another kind from Annie Ballard, a social worker who recognizes in him an essential goodness that lies beneath the violent streak he exhibits when his life, or the lives of those he loves, is in danger. Both characters figure prominently in later novels in the Robicheaux series.

BLACK CHERRY BLUES

The third novel in the Robicheaux series, *Black Cherry Blues*, takes Robicheaux to Montana, another locale that Burke knows intimately. Following the suspected murderers of men involved in what he thinks may be a shady oil-lease deal, Robicheaux discovers that the trail leads to Sally Dio, a Mafia don for whom Clete Purcel is now working as a security guard. Robicheaux discovers that Dio is engaged in land speculation that involves swindling Native Americans out of the oil rights on tribal lands. Once again, Robicheaux's life is threatened, but Purcel comes to his aid; between them they do considerable damage to those Robicheaux suspects of trying to hurt him and of threatening his adopted daughter Alafair, who has accompanied him to Montana.

As *Black Cherry Blues* demonstrates, Burke's Robicheaux becomes more thoughtful and self-reflective in each succeeding novel of the series. The protagonist is now a widower, the death of his wife, Annie, having been chronicled in *Heaven's Prisoners* (1988), the second novel in the series. While Robicheaux tracks down murderers, he must fulfill the duties of a single parent, caring for the daughter he and Annie had adopted. These added complications make Robicheaux seem more like an Everyman, the character Burke has identified as his detective's literary prototype and forebear.

CIMARRON ROSE

Cimarron Rose, the first of the novels featuring Billy Bob Holland, revolves around attempts by the former Texas Ranger turned defense attorney to clear his illegitimate son, Lucas Smothers, of the murder of a young girl. Holland's investigation takes him into the world of the rich East Enders of Deaf Smith, Texas. One of his principal suspects is a young man from the East End who suffers from fetal alcohol syndrome, another a psychopathic drifter who seems to know quite a bit about Holland's past. Holland also stumbles into the midst of a federal investigation of drug operations and ends up falling in love with the agent working undercover in the local sheriff's office. Federal investigators are being aided by a Mexican drug agent who Holland recognizes as a former drug runner whom he had wounded years earlier in the attack during which Holland accidentally shot his partner, L. Q. Navarro. The complicated plot is resolved when Lucas is acquitted and Holland is able to identify the girl's killer.

In *Cimarron Rose*, Burke offers some serious reflections on the way the past influences the present. The action is interrupted regularly when Holland reads the diary of his great-grandfather, an outlaw turned preacher, a technique that allows Burke to suggest historical parallels between Holland and his ancestors. Burke also incorporates dream sequences in which Holland talks with his dead partner; the conversations function much like interior monologues, revealing not only what Holland must do to save Lucas but also how he must exorcise the demons from his past that give rise to his own violent tendencies.

PEGASUS DESCENDING

In *Pegasus Descending* (2006), nearly two decades after making his first appearance in *The Neon Rain*, an older, wiser, and even more philosophic Dave Robicheaux is again working full-time as a detective in the Iberia Parish Sheriff's Office. When circumstances surrounding the apparent suicide of a college girl seem suspicious to him, he launches an investigation that brings him face-to-face with gangsters attempting to take over casino gambling operations in southern Louisiana. As Robicheaux gets closer to the truth, people begin to get hurt or die; Robicheaux must rely again on his friend Cletus Purcel to help identify the killers and foil his enemies' plans. In the process he is able to settle an old score by bringing to justice the man responsible for the murder of a friend slain twenty years earlier, when the alcoholic Robicheaux had been too drunk to prevent the killing.

In *Pegasus Descending*, Burke continues his exploration of themes that have interested him since the publication of his first Robicheaux novel: the plight of the people of south Louisiana trying to preserve their culture against the growing encroachment of outsiders; the exploitation of the working classes by those with money, power, or influence, and by corrupt government officials; and the duty of good people to stand up to injustice even if it means putting themselves in harm's way. Unlike many other writers of mystery and detective fiction, however, Burke brings a level of realism to his characters reminiscent of that found in mainstream fiction. The most notable example of this quality in *Pegasus Descending* is Burke's focus on the fact that his detective is aging. At the same time Robicheaux deals ruthlessly with those who perpetrate violence, he becomes even more cognizant of his own mortality and of the preciousness of the life he enjoys in the region of America where he was born and lives.

Laurence W. Mazzeno

PRINCIPAL MYSTERY AND DETECTIVE FICTION

DAVE ROBICHEAUX SERIES: *The Neon Rain*, 1987; *Heaven's Prisoners*, 1988; *Black Cherry Blues*, 1989; *A Morning for Flamingos*, 1990; *A Stained White Radiance*, 1992; *In the Electric Mist with Confederate Dead*, 1993; *Dixie City Jam*, 1994; *Burning Angel*, 1995; *Cadillac Jukebox*, 1996; *Sunset Limited*, 1998; *Purple Cane Road*, 2000; *Jolie Blon's Bounce*, 2002; *Last Car to Elysian Fields*, 2003; *Crusader's Cross*, 2005; *Pegasus Descending*, 2006; *The Tin Roof Blowdown*, 2007

BILLY BOB HOLLAND SERIES: *Cimarron Rose*, 1997; *Heartwood*, 1999; *Bitterroot*, 2001; *In the Moon of Red Ponies*, 2004

OTHER MAJOR WORKS

NOVELS: *Half of Paradise*, 1965; *To the Bright and Shining Sun*, 1970; *Lay Down My Sword and Shield*, 1971; *Two for Texas*, 1982 (also known as *Sabine Spring*); *The Lost Get-Back Boogie*, 1986; *Present for Santa*, 1989; *Spy Story*, 1990; *Texas City, 1947*, 1992; *White Doves at Morning*, 2002

SHORT FICTION: *The Convict, and Other Stories*, 1985

NONFICTION: *Ohio's Heritage*, 1989

BIBLIOGRAPHY

Anderson, Patrick. *The Triumph of the Thriller: How Cops, Crooks, and Cannibals Captured Popular Fiction.* New York: Random House, 2007. Contains an analysis of Burke's *Crusader's Cross* and some biographical information.

Bogue, Barbara. *James Lee Burke and the Soul of Dave Robicheaux: A Critical Study of the Crime Fiction Series.* Jefferson, N.C.: McFarland, 2006. Provides a sketch of autobiographical elements in the Robicheaux novels; addresses topics such as the role of women, the search for the father, alcoholism, the impact of war and its stresses, the justice system, and the presence of the supernatural in the novels.

Coale, Samuel. *The Mystery of Mysteries: Cultural Differences and Designs.* Bowling Green, Ohio: Bowling Green State University Popular Press, 2000. A chapter on Burke's fiction outlines principal themes and characterization in the Robicheaux novels and links Burke with other southern writers. Also includes an interview with Burke.

Pepper, Andrew. *The Contemporary American Crime Novel: Race, Ethnicity, Gender, Class.* Edinburgh, Scotland: Edinburgh University Press, 2000. Discusses Burke's novels as examples of the race, gender, and class conflicts that plague American society; extensive character analysis of Burke's detective Dave Robicheaux.

Schwartz, Richard B. *Nice and Noir: Contemporary*

American Crime Fiction. Columbia: University of Missouri Press, 2002. Discusses Burke's success as a regional novelist and as a master of creating setting and atmosphere; comments on his concerns for issues of family and heritage.

W. J. BURLEY
William John Burley

Born: Falmouth, Cornwall, England; August 1, 1914
Died: Holywell, Cornwall, England; November 15, 2002
Types of plot: Police procedural; cozy

PRINCIPAL SERIES
Wycliffe, 1970-2002

PRINCIPAL SERIES CHARACTERS

CHARLES WYCLIFFE is detective chief superintendent in the English West Country. Small of stature and cerebral—he gives the impression of being a monk rather than a police officer—he is interested in human behavior and motivation. His wife, Helen, and their children provide an occasional domestic backdrop that adds some dimension to his character. Wycliffe's professional colleagues change as they are promoted and transferred during the course of the series.

CHIEF INSPECTOR JAMES GILL, tough and cynical, is Wycliffe's chief aide in the early novels.

JOHN SCALES rises from being the squad's detective sergeant responsible for photography to being the most imaginative of Wycliffe's inspectors.

SERGEANT KERSEY works well with Wycliffe on a local case and eventually becomes a detective inspector.

DETECTIVE SERGEANT LUCY LANE becomes the first female member of the squad in *Wycliffe and the Four Jacks* (1985).

DR. FRANKS, the pathologist, with his passions for fast cars and young women, is a friend and colleague throughout the series.

HUGH BELLINGS, deputy chief constable, is a polit-

ically oriented administrator with whom Wycliffe is often at odds.

CONTRIBUTION

When W. J. Burley's Detective Superintendent Wycliffe reflects on how the study of the human species is far more engaging than the study of animals, he speaks for the author as well. Before Burley turned to writing mysteries past the age of fifty, he was a professionally trained zoologist. His novels are studies of human psychology and sociology, particularly of the inhabitants of small towns. Wycliffe is an engaging but not fully developed character who acts as the means through which readers encounters a range of interesting personalities and situations. The strength of the novels is in the local color Burley evokes and in his strong characterizations of the people Wycliffe observes. Though Burley—long a member but not a participant in the Crime Writers' Association—won no major awards for his writing, he was honored in a more tangible way by having his Wycliffe series dramatized on television. The popular broadcasts (more numerous than his books) not only provided considerable wherewithal to the author but also introduced his work to a large audience.

BIOGRAPHY

William John Burley was born in Falmouth, Cornwall, England, on August 1, 1914, the sixth child and first son in his family. His parents—William John Rule Burley and Annie Curnow Burley—were both natives of the West Country, and Burley's Cornish roots are at least five generations deep.

Trained as an engineer at Truro Central Technical Schools (1926-1930) and on scholarship at the Institution of Gas Engineers (1931), Burley rose to become manager of various gas undertakings in the southwest of England (including Truro Gas Company, 1938; Okehampton Gas Company, 1940; Crewkerne Gas and Coke Company, 1944; and Camborne Gas Company, 1946). Burley married school secretary Muriel Wolsey in 1938, and the couple produced two sons, Alan John and Nigel Philip. Because Burley was in an occupation judged vital to the United Kingdom during World War II, he was not inducted into the military but instead served as a sergeant in the Home Guard.

Burley in 1946 began attending natural history classes and became fascinated with local insect life. In 1950 he abandoned his career in energy—and lost his pension—to study zoology on a state scholarship at Balliol College, Oxford. After he graduated with an honors degree in zoology in 1953, Burley went into teaching. He was head of the biology department at Richmond and East Sheen Country Grammar School for boys (1953-1955) before he became the head of the biology department and sixth-form tutor at Newquay Grammar School in Cornwall. Burley settled in Newquay with his wife and two children and remained at the school until his formal retirement.

Burley wrote his first novel, *A Taste of Power*, set in a school and featuring amateur detective Henry Pym, in 1966 and followed it with *Three-Toed Pussy* (1968), which introduced his best-known character, Superintendent Charles Wycliffe. After one more Pym novel, *Death in Willow Pattern* (1969), Burley returned to the Wycliffe series with *To Kill a Cat* (1970) and, except for occasional excursions outside the series, concentrated primarily on Wycliffe for the rest of his career.

Burley retired from teaching in 1974 to devote himself full time to writing. His background in the biological sciences and his interest in organic and social evolution show themselves in his various novels, especially in a nonseries work, *The Sixth Day* (1978). A science-fiction adventure, *The Sixth Day* concerns various groups of twentieth century men who are carried into the future by alien life-forms who have colonized the then-desolated Earth and who expose the humans to different life-forms and systems of social integration.

Throughout Burley's writing career, however, it was the Wycliffe novels that occupied most of the author's time and captured the bulk of reader attention. Burley's status was given a tremendous boost in 1993 when a pilot featuring the fictional police officer, "Wycliffe and the Cycle of Death," with actor Jack Shepherd in the title role, was broadcast in the United Kingdom. The following year, six Wycliffe episodes based on the books were broadcast, and through 1998 more than thirty-five episodes aired, giving Burley— then past his eightieth year—a level of financial comfort that he had not previously enjoyed. Despite his late success, Burley continued to write and produced four additional Wycliffe titles despite failing eyesight. He was working on a twenty-third novel in the series, *Wycliffe's Last Lap*, and had a twenty-fourth planned (*Wycliffe and the Dream Castle*) when he died in November, 2002.

ANALYSIS

W. J. Burley's mystery novels are rich in setting and character. The Wycliffe series is set in the West Country of Cornwall and Devon, an area Burley knew well and skillfully described. As head of the regional Criminal Investigation Division, Charles Wycliffe roams the area. Some of the murders he solves are close to his home base of Plymouth; others may occur in coastal resorts, on an island, in a hilly tin-mining region, or elsewhere in the Cornish countryside. Burley conveys a sense not only of the area's natural beauty and the character of its communities but also of the personalities of its people.

Wycliffe, the son of a Herfordshire tenant farmer, started his career in the police force as a beat officer at the age of nineteen. He made a name for himself as a detective in a Midland town and rose to the rank of detective chief superintendent, which he holds when the series begins. He met his wife, Helen, early in his career. The Wycliffes have twin children, and their relationship with them grows, as do their children, in the course of the series. The twins, David and Ruth, complete postgraduate studies and advance to careers of their own. Professional success enables the Wycliffes to buy the Watch House, a seaside home with a garden and a view of the estuary. Wycliffe's Nonconformist upbringing and socialist views make him a bit uneasy about these outward signs of success, but Helen helps him learn to indulge himself and tries to develop his cultural instincts. Wycliffe, however, finds it hard to change his nature. He remains at heart a moralist who will mortify himself through self-denial when faced with a difficult decision. His socialism occasionally shows in his antipathy to prosperous businessmen.

Wycliffe is attracted to his job because it gives him an opportunity to interact with people. In almost all the novels, Wycliffe compares himself to a scientific observer of animal species.

> Some men watched animals, building little hides to spy on badgers, birds or deer, but Wycliffe could not understand them. From a window on to a street, from a seat in a pub or a park, or strolling round a fairground, it was possible to observe a far more varied species, more complex, more intelligent, more perceptive and vastly richer in the pattern of their emotional response.

In many ways, Wycliffe's task is more difficult than that of an animal expert, for "he worked with human beings, on whom all studies had to be done in the wild."

Wycliffe gains an understanding of his own identity by seeing in others the same intimate thoughts and desires that he himself harbors. The same drive leads him to read autobiographies and diaries and to immerse himself in all aspects of a victim's life and surroundings when he is conducting an investigation. Interrogations are handled like conversations as he probes to learn more about the people involved in a case. As he absorbs data from his observations and from the reports of his team, Wycliffe withdraws into himself, becoming taciturn and irritable.

> In the course of an investigation, after a seemingly endless series of interrogations, interviews and reports, when his ideas were confused and contradictory, his mind would suddenly clear and the salient facts stand out in sharp relief as though a lens had suddenly brought them into proper focus. At this stage he would not necessarily distinguish any pattern in the facts but he would, from then on, be able to classify and relate them so that a pattern would eventually emerge.

Wycliffe does not conform to the police force's ideal for conducting an investigation; he does too much of the investigative work himself and spends too little time coordinating tasks and organizing paperwork. Burley does, however, give some insight into the actual procedures of police work that occur around Wycliffe. He also gives the reader a view of the everyday tasks and office politics that consume much of Wycliffe's time, regardless of whether there is an investigation in progress.

The focus of these novels, however, is not on Wycliffe but on the people involved in a murder—the victims, their families and friends, the suspects, and the criminals. In some of the novels, Wycliffe is a latecomer to the action, the story having been well advanced before the police become involved. Burley delves into violence that erupts from a variety of sources: from the consequences of a smoldering and overprotective love (*To Kill a Cat* and *Death in a Salubrious Place*, 1973); from an illegitimate birth long kept secret (*Guilt Edged*, 1971; *Wycliffe and the Beales*, 1983; and *Wycliffe and the Quiet Virgin*, 1986); from greed and business deceit (*Wycliffe in Paul's Court*, 1980); from an attempt to prevent the revelation of a long-standing art fraud (*Wycliffe and the Winsor Blue*, 1987); from drug dealing and blackmail (*Death in Stanley Street*, 1974); from a desire for revenge for wrongful conviction in a murder case (*Wycliffe and the Pea-Green Boat*, 1975); from the trauma suffered by a victim and her family in a case of vicious schoolgirl hazing (*Wycliffe and the Schoolgirls*, 1976); from fear of disinheritance (*Wycliffe and the Scapegoat*, 1978); from the consequences of an unsolved robbery and murder committed years before (*Wycliffe and the Four Jacks*); and from the desire of a suicide's friends to punish the man who had pushed him to despair (*Wycliffe's Wild Goose Chase*, 1982). Although the motives are varied, there is one thing these violent acts share: deep roots. Long-hidden secrets become known, long-nursed grievances explode, and long-festering relationships finally produce violence.

Crime involves Wycliffe with all elements of society, from an old Catholic country family to antiquarian book dealers, from a former convict managing a seedy seaside boardinghouse to a member of Parliament, from a leading author of popular yet critically acclaimed books to a widowed lighthouse keeper, and from a terminally ill rock star to the manager of a tourist caravan park. Burley is interested in the entire range of people who inhabit and visit his West Country, and he succeeds in making them come alive. As their lives and dreams are exposed, the reader, like Wycliffe, gains greater insight into the human condition.

WYCLIFFE AND THE TANGLED WEB

Set in a fictionalized version of the tiny Cornish seaside village of Mevagissey, *Wycliffe and the Tangled Web* (1988) unfolds at a leisurely pace. The story revolves around seventeen-year-old Hilda Clemo, a pretty, bright, if odd, girl whose visit to the local doctor propels the plot into motion. Soon after meeting with her boyfriend, Ralph Martin, Hilda vanishes, and when no trace of her is found for two days, Wycliffe and his team of investigators—Kersey, Scales, Lane, and others—is called in. During their weeklong enquiry, Wycliffe and his minions scour the surrounding area and question a variety of individuals as they methodically draw ever closer to the solution of what happened, when it happened, and who is responsible. They discover suspects in the disappearance—the boyfriend, the smarmy husband of Hilda's sister, the half-wit son of a relative living nearby—one after another before Hilda's body shows up in a quarry pond several days after police divers had already searched it. Possible motives for her murder change over time: originally, it was thought that the reason for her death was her pregnancy—Hilda had told several people she was going to have a baby—until an autopsy reveals that she was not pregnant. A connection to a missing, valuable Pissaro painting is revealed, pointing the finger of guilt at several possible candidates, before the real and uncomplicated cause of death comes to light: a simple impulsive reaction to Hilda's cruelty in telling the hurtful lie about her pregnancy to the wrong person.

Wycliffe and the Tangled Web illuminates the particular strengths of the series: Burley's ability to capture the atmosphere of small-town Cornwall; his skill in drawing believable, unique characters and the relationships between them; and his keen ear in reproduc-

ing dialogue. Mostly, Burley aptly demonstrates that the solutions to crimes in police procedurals lie not in the talents of a single law enforcer—Wycliffe, while efficient at using his resources and effective at orchestrating the investigation, is a plodder rather than someone capable of making brilliant leaps of deduction—but in the cumulative effect of an experienced team working together toward a common goal.

WYCLIFFE AND THE GUILD OF NINE

Burley's last completed installment in the Wycliffe series, *Wycliffe and the Guild of Nine* (2000) reintroduces characters from an earlier entry, *Wycliffe and the Quiet Virgin*. Set ten years later, the book opens with Wycliffe brooding over the fact that his new commanding officer is a woman and contemplating the recent death of Francine, a young woman who figured prominently in *Wycliffe and the Quiet Virgin*. The murder happens on the moors, where an astrologically influenced man named Archer and his pragmatic wife, Lina, have set up an artist's colony called the Guild of Nine. Francine, who had intended to invest in the colony, is found dead, asphyxiated because a gas heater has been deliberately sabotaged. Called into the case, Wycliffe discovers that several colonists have secrets that would make them reluctant to have police involvement. Complications arise, suspects multiply, and possibilities abound when two additional murders are perpetrated after Wycliffe's arrival. *Wycliffe and the Guild of Nine*, with Burley's trademark well-rounded characters and evocative setting, is a fitting conclusion to the popular Wycliffe series.

Francis J. Bremer
Updated by Jack Ewing

PRINCIPAL MYSTERY AND DETECTIVE FICTION

HENRY PYM SERIES: *A Taste of Power*, 1966; *Death in Willow Pattern*, 1969

CHARLES WYCLIFFE SERIES: *Three-Toed Pussy*, 1968; *To Kill a Cat*, 1970; *Guilt Edged*, 1971; *Death in a Salubrious Place*, 1973; *Death in Stanley Street*, 1974; *Wycliffe and the Pea-Green Boat*, 1975; *Wycliffe and the Schoolgirls*, 1976; *The Schoolmaster*, 1977; *Wycliffe and the Scapegoat*, 1978; *Wycliffe in Paul's Court*, 1980; *Wycliffe's Wild Goose Chase*, 1982; *Wycliffe and the Beales*, 1983; *Wycliffe and the*

Four Jacks, 1985; *Wycliffe and the Quiet Virgin*, 1986; *Wycliffe and the Winsor Blue*, 1987; *Wycliffe and the Tangled Web*, 1988; *Wycliffe and the Cycle of Death*, 1990; *Wycliffe and the Dead Flautist*, 1991; *Wycliffe and the Last Rites*, 1992; *Wycliffe and the Dunes Mystery*, 1993; *Wycliffe and the House of Fear*, 1995; *Wycliffe and the Redhead*, 1997; *Wycliffe and the Guild of Nine*, 2000

NONSERIES NOVELS: *The Sixth Day*, 1978; *Charles and Elizabeth*, 1979; *The House of Care*, 1981

NONFICTION: *Centenary History of the City of Truro*, 1977

BIBLIOGRAPHY

Berlins, Marcel. *The Times*, April 18, 1998, p. 3. This discussion about the state of the crime novel notes the trend toward ultrarealism, and the financial success of authors whose works are successfully portrayed on television, including Burley.

Burley, W. J. WJBurley.com: Celebrating a Unique Author. http://wjburley.com. Web site devoted to Burley. Contains a biography, information about his novels, the television series, and how he wrote novels.

Crossley, Jack. "A Policeman's Unhappy Lot." *The Times*, July 30, 1994. Brief profile of Burley looks at his motivation for writing and his love of Cornwall.

Fletcher, Connie. "Mysteries." Review of *Wycliffe and the Pea-Green Boat*, by W. J. Burley. *Booklist* 72, no. 8 (December 15, 1975): 551. This is a favorable review, which cites the skill of the author in using the past to explain present circumstances.

Hanson, Gillian Mary. *City and Shore: The Function of Setting in the British Mystery*. Jefferson, N.C.: McFarland, 2004. Looks at many major British novelists and their works in which setting was important. Sheds light on how Burley's fellow writers used setting, which was important to Burley.

Hubin, Allen J. "Criminals at Large." *Death in Willow Pattern*, by W. J. Burley. *The New York Times*, April 19, 1970, p. 37. Contains a favorable review in which Burley's lesser known protagonist Dr. Henry Pym, zoologist and sleuth, is invited to examine a wealthy nobleman's valuable family library during Christmas holiday and incidentally to investigate charges that the nobleman has been writing a series of poison-pen letters.

Pronzini, Bill, and Marcia Muller, eds. *1001 Midnights: The Aficionado's Guide to Mystery and Detective Fiction*. New York: Arbor House, 1986. Contains a brief analysis of Burley's *Wycliffe and the Scapegoat* by Pronzini and Newell Dunlap, which—through praising the colorful setting (an ancient All Hallow's Eve ritual in a small English town that involves a wheel of fire), and the well-drawn characters—pans the author's lack of flair and the book's pedestrian solution.

Publishers Weekly. Review of *Wycliffe and the Quiet Virgin*, by W. J. Burley. 230, no. 14 (October 3, 1986): 98. Contains an unfavorable review. Praises the author's occasional evocative descriptions of the Cornish country but criticizes the novel's formulaic plot, somewhat plodding style, and its easily solved puzzle.

W. R. BURNETT

Born: Springfield, Ohio; November 25, 1899
Died: Santa Monica, California; April 25, 1982
Also wrote as John Monahan; James Updyke
Types of plot: Inverted; hard-boiled; police procedural

CONTRIBUTION

W. R. Burnett was a prolific novelist and screenwriter. His most popular and enduring work was in the area of crime fiction, a subgroup within the mystery and detective genre. Burnett helped to shape and refine the conventions of the hard-boiled crime novel—a type of fiction that seems particularly suited to dramatizing the garish and violent urban world of the twentieth century. His novels and films are rich with underworld characters, scenes, and dialogue that would become the stock-in-trade of other writers; in the popular imagination, his work was a revelation of how mobsters and modern outlaws thought, acted, and spoke in the urban jungle.

Burnett knew gangsters, did extensive research on some of them, and made a close study of crime's causes and effects. He sought in his works to present the criminal outlook and criminal activity in a direct and dramatic fashion, without explicit authorial comment or judgment. He believed that crime is an inevitable part of society, given human frailties and desires, and that it must be seen in its own terms to be understood. This belief explains the shock caused by many of his novels on first publication and his occasional difficulties with film censors. Burnett's crime stories, then, are characterized by a sense of objectivity, authenticity, and revelation. They realistically convey the glittery surface and shadowy depths of American society.

BIOGRAPHY

William Riley Burnett was born in Springfield, Ohio, on November 25, 1899, of old American stock. He attended grammar schools in Springfield and Dayton, high school in Columbus, and preparatory school in Germantown, Ohio. He was an adequate student and an avid athlete. In 1919, he enrolled in the college of journalism at Ohio State University but stayed for only one semester. In 1920, he married Marjorie Louise Bartow; they were divorced in the early 1940's. In 1943, he married Whitney Forbes Johnstone; they had two sons.

From 1920 to 1927, Burnett worked in an office as a statistician for the Bureau of Labor Statistics; he hated office work but hung on while he tried tirelessly, but fruitlessly, to establish himself as a writer. Frustrated with his situation, he left Ohio for Chicago in 1927, taking a job as a night clerk in a seedy hotel. Bootlegging, prostitution, violence, and corruption were rampant at the time. Rival gangs indiscriminately carried out their territorial wars with tommy guns and explosives. Al Capone was king. The impact on Burnett's imagination was profound. Gradually, he came to know and understand the city and found in it the material and outlook he needed to become a successful writer.

Little Caesar (1929), Burnett's first published novel, quickly became a best seller. The film rights were purchased by Warner Bros., and the film version, which appeared in 1931, was a sensational success. In 1930, Burnett went west to California and worked as a screenwriter to subsidize his literary endeavors. He remained in California for the rest of his life.

Burnett had a long, productive, and financially rewarding career in films. He worked with some of Hollywood's best writers, directors, and actors. He also wrote scripts for a number of popular television series in the 1950's and 1960's. Nevertheless, he was first and foremost a writer of fiction, producing more than thirty novels and several shorter works during a career that spanned five decades.

Burnett wrote many novels outside the mystery and detective genre, stories dealing with a wide variety of subjects—boxing, dog racing, political campaigns, fascism in the 1930's, eighteenth century Ireland, the modern West Indies, the American frontier, and others. His strength, however, was as a writer of crime fiction; on this his reputation rests securely. In 1980, he was honored by the Mystery Writers of America with the Grand Masters Award. He died in California on April 25, 1982.

ANALYSIS

In the introduction to the 1958 American reprint of *Little Caesar*, W. R. Burnett describes the elements out of which he created this career-launching novel. He recalls his arrival in Chicago and describes how the noise, pace, color, violence, and moral anarchy of the city shocked and stimulated him. He went everywhere, taking notes and absorbing the urban atmosphere that he would later use as a background. A scholarly work on a particular Chicago gang (not Capone's) gave him a basic plotline, the idea of chronicling the rise and fall of an ambitious mobster. From a hoodlum acquaintance, he derived a point of view from which to narrate the story—not the morally outraged view of law-abiding society, as was usually the case in crime stories of the time, but rather the hard-boiled, utterly pragmatic view of the criminal.

These were the essential ingredients on which Burnett's genius acted as a catalyst. These ingredients can be found in all of his crime fiction: the menacing atmosphere of the modern city, where human predators and prey enact an age-old drama; the extensive knowledge of the underworld and its denizens; the grandiose plans undone by a quirk of fate; the detached tone that suggests a full acceptance of human vice and frailty without overlooking instances of moral struggle and resistance; the sense that criminals are not grotesques or monsters but human beings who respond to the demands of their environment with ruthless practicality; and the colloquial style. Some of the novels focus on the career of a single criminal, while others are more comprehensive in their treatment of crime and society.

LITTLE CAESAR

Little Caesar is the story of Cesare "Rico" Bandello, a "gutter Macbeth" as Burnett once referred to him in an interview. Rico comes to Chicago, joins one of the bigger gangs involved in the various lucrative criminal enterprises of the period, and eventually takes over as leader by means of his single-minded ferocity and cleverness. Everything Rico does is directed toward the aggrandizement of his power, influence, and prestige. He has few diversions, distractions, or vices—even the usual ones of mobsters. As he goes from success to success over the bodies of those who get in his way, he aspires to ever-greater glory, until fate intervenes, sending him away from Chicago and into hiding, where eventually he stops a police officer's bullet.

Rico is a simple but understandable individual: ambitious, austere, deadly. To some degree, the exigencies and opportunities of jazz-age Chicago made such men inevitable, as Burnett clearly suggests in the book. Rico's story is presented dramatically, in vivid scenes filled with crisp dialogue and the argot of mean streets; this mode of presentation conveys a powerful sense of immediacy, authenticity, and topicality. Just as powerful is the archetypal quality of Burnett's portrait of Rico, who emerges as the epitome of the underworld overachiever. This combination of the topical and the archetypal was extremely potent; it accounts for the fact that *Little Caesar* greatly

Edward G. Robinson (right) played the title role in the 1931 film adaptation of W. R. Burnett's first novel, Little Caesar. *(Museum of Modern Art, Film Stills Archive)*

influenced subsequent portrayals of gangsters in the United States.

ORGANIZED CRIME

Burnett was interested not only in the character and exploits of individuals who chose a life of crime but also in criminal organizations that increasingly were seen to corrupt the American political and legal establishments, especially after the end of World War II. The most extended exploration of this subject is found in his trilogy comprising *The Asphalt Jungle* (1949), *Little Men, Big World* (1951), and *Vanity Row* (1952). These novels dramatize gangland operations and the progressive corruption of a city political administration.

It is important to note that the Kefauver Senate hearings on organized crime in the early 1950's, which were omnipresent in newspapers, magazines, and on television, made these stories seem particularly timely and authentic. Burnett, however, did not claim to have inside knowledge about a vast, highly organized and hierarchical crime network controlled by the Mafia and linked to Sicily. His underworld is more broadly based and is peopled by many ethnic types as well as by native Americans. In other words, Burnett recognized that crime is rooted in human nature and aspirations and that it should not be attributed—as it often was in the wake of the hearings—to ethnic aberration or foreign conspiracy. The epigraph, taken from the writing of William James, that prefaces *The Asphalt Jungle* makes this point about human nature: "MAN, biologically considered . . . is the most formidable of all beasts of prey, and, indeed, the only one that preys systematically on its own species."

THE ASPHALT JUNGLE

The setting of *The Asphalt Jungle* as well as *Little Men, Big World* and *Vanity Row* is a midsized, midwestern city that is physically and morally disintegrating. In *The Asphalt Jungle*, a new police commissioner is appointed to brighten the tarnished image of the city police force to improve the current administration's chances for reelection. The move is completely cynical on the part of the administration brass, yet the new commissioner does his best against strong resistance and bureaucratic inertia. Paralleling the commissioner's agonizingly difficult cleanup campaign is the planning and execution of a million-dollar jewelry heist by a team of criminal specialists, who are backed financially by a prominent and influential lawyer. The narrative movement between police activity and criminal activity serves to heighten suspense and to comment on the difficulty of any concerted human effort in an entropic universe.

In *The Asphalt Jungle*, there is a genuine, if somewhat ineffectual attempt to deal with serious crime and official corruption within the city. The moral landscape may contain large areas of gray; there may be disturbing parallels and connections between police and criminal organizations. By and large, however, one can tell the guardians from the predators.

LITTLE MEN, BIG WORLD

In *Little Men, Big World*, there are several key political people involved with local crime figures, and a symbiotic relationship of some sort between political machines and organized crime seems inevitable. Thus, at the end of the story, a corrupt judge explains to a friend that in politics, "*success* breeds corruption." One needs money to get and keep power. When legitimate sources of revenue are exhausted, it is natural to look to those who need protection to stay in business—gambling-house proprietors, bookies, panderers, and the like. In this novel, the city has reached what Burnett calls a state of imbalance. Not only is official corruption extensive and debilitating, but its exposure occurs purely by chance as well. Any housecleaning that results is superficial.

VANITY ROW

In *Vanity Row*, the political machine is so riddled with corruption that the highest people in the administration are themselves directly involved with criminal activity—illegal wiretaps, conspiracy, perjury, frameups—as they attempt by any means to retain power in a morally chaotic environment. When the story opens, a top administration official is found murdered. He was the mediator between the administration and the Chicago syndicate in a dispute over the cost of allowing local distribution of the wire service, a service that was necessary to the illegal offtrack betting industry.

The mayor and his associates assume that their friend was killed by the Mob as a warning to lower the price. In response, they order their "special investigator" in the police force to muddy the waters and make sure that the connection between the dead man, themselves, and the syndicate is not discovered by the police. Burnett implies that there is nothing to keep the predators in check. The only hope for the city is that eventually the administration will succumb to its own nihilistic, anarchic impulses and make way for a reform group so the cycle can begin anew.

In each of these novels, the story is timely, the presentation is objective or dramatic, the language is colloquial, and the tempo is fast paced. In them, Burnett moved beyond a concern with individual criminals to explore the world of criminal organizations and corrupt political administrations.

GOODBYE, CHICAGO

In his last published novel, *Goodbye, Chicago: 1928, End of an Era* (1981), Burnett deals with the imminent collapse, through internal rot, of an entire society. The novel focuses on the Capone syndicate, the archetypal American crime organization, and on a small group of dedicated Chicago police officers attempting to deal with crime and corruption on an almost apocalyptic scale.

The story begins with a woman's body being fished from the river by crew members on a city fireboat. As in Charles Dickens's *Our Mutual Friend* (1864-1866), which opens with the discovery of a body floating in the Thames, the investigation of this death reveals a web of corruption connecting all levels of society and both sides of the law. Of all Burnett's novels, this one best shows the devastating effects of the interaction and interdependency of American legal and criminal organizations in the twentieth century.

The story is not divided into chapters or parts; instead, it unfolds in brief scenes whose juxtaposition is by turns ironic, suspenseful, comic, or grotesque. This cinematic technique of quick crosscutting seems particularly appropriate to a story revealing strange and unexpected connections among people and dramatizing their frantic, self-destructive activity in the final months before the onset of the Great Depression.

HIGH SIERRA

In his crime fiction, Burnett wrote about a gritty underworld that he knew well, a world of professional thieves, killers, thugs, mugs, con men, crime czars, and corrupt officials. Thus, his crime stories remain convincing even decades after their publication. If Burnett were merely convincing, however, his books would have little more than historical interest. He is also a skilled novelist. There is, as film director John Huston once remarked, a powerful sense of inevitability about Burnett's stories. Character, situation, and destiny are thoroughly intertwined and appropriate. Consider for example, the fate of Roy Earle, the protagonist of *High Sierra* (1940).

Roy Earle, a proud and solitary figure, is a legendary gunman and former member of the Dillinger gang of bank robbers. At the beginning of the story, he is released from prison and drives west through the American desert toward what he hopes will be an oasis—an exclusive California hotel with a fortune in money and jewels protected by a temptingly vulnerable security system. The robbery itself is well planned and executed. Nevertheless, as always with Burnett's fiction, things go awry, and the promise of wealth proves maddeningly illusory. Finally, in another wasteland—which ironically completes the deadly circle begun in the opening sequence—Roy makes a defiant and heroic last stand among the cold, high peaks of the Sierras. Thus, characterization, imagery, and structure are remarkably integrated in this Depression-era story of a futile quest for fulfillment in a hostile environment.

POWERFUL SCENES AND CHARACTERS

Burnett's novels are packed with powerful scenes and tableaux of underworld activity and characters that became part of the iconography of crime writing: the would-be informant gunned down on church steps; funerals of dead mobsters who are "sent off" with floral and verbal tributes from their killers; the ambitious mobster making an unrefusable offer to a "business" rival; the ingenious sting operation; the caper executed with clockwork precision; the car-bomb assassination; and many more. Many of the images one associates with crime fiction and film have their first or most memorable expression in Burnett's works.

The novels contain a gallery of memorable characters; even minor characters are sketched with a Dickensian eye for the idiosyncratic and incongruous. The following, for example, is the introduction to police investigator Emmett Lackey, a minor figure in *Vanity Row*:

Lackey was a huge man of about forty. He was not only excessively tall, six five or more, but also very wide and bulky, weighing just under three hundred pounds. And yet, in spite of his size, there was nothing formidable about him. He looked soft, slack, and weak. Small, evasive blue eyes peered out nervously at the world from behind oldfashioned, gold-rimmed glasses. His complexion was very fair, pink and white, and had an almost babyish look to it. His manner was conciliatory in the extreme and he always seemed to be trying to appease somebody. . . .

But behind Lackey's weak smiles were strong emotions.

The brief sketch captures a recurring theme in all Burnett's crime stories—the use of masks to hide a vulnerable or corrupt reality. Many of Burnett's characters are obsessively secretive, especially the more powerful ones, who are happy to work in the background and manipulate those onstage, who take greater risks for far less gain.

Burnett has a wonderful ear for dialogue and authentic American speech, which partly explains the fact that so many of his novels were successfully adapted to film. For example, two crime reporters are talking about a voluptuous murder suspect in *Vanity Row*: According to the first, "That picture . . . It didn't do her justice." The second responds, "A picture? How could it? . . . It would take a relief map." The brassy, earthy language his characters use always seems natural to their personality, place, and calling.

Burnett's crime novels are believable, energetic, and literate. As some dramatists of William Shakespeare's time used the melodramatic conventions of the revenge play to explore the spiritual dislocations of their age, so Burnett used the conventions of crime fiction to explore dark undercurrents—urban decay, the symbiosis between criminal and legal institutions, the prevalence of masks in a hypocritical society, the elusiveness of truth and success in a mysterious world. In other words, there is a considerable amount of substance in Burnett's fiction, which explains their translation into more than twelve languages and constant reprintings. They are important and enduring portraits of life and death in the urban jungle.

Michael J. Larsen

PRINCIPAL MYSTERY AND DETECTIVE FICTION

NOVELS: *Little Caesar*, 1929; *The Silver Eagle*, 1931; *Dark Hazard*, 1933; *Six Days' Grace*, 1937; *High Sierra*, 1940; *The Quick Brown Fox*, 1942; *Nobody Lives Forever*, 1943; *Tomorrow's Another Day*, 1945; *Romelle*, 1946; *The Asphalt Jungle*, 1949; *Little Men, Big World*, 1951; *Vanity Row*, 1952; *Big Stan*, 1953 (as Monahan); *Underdog*, 1957; *Round the Clock at Volari's*, 1961; *The Cool Man*, 1968; *Goodbye, Chicago: 1928, End of an Era*, 1981

OTHER MAJOR WORKS

NOVELS: *Iron Man*, 1930; *Saint Johnson*, 1930; *The Giant Swing*, 1932; *Goodbye to the Past: Scenes from the Life of William Meadows*, 1934; *The Goodhues of Sinking Creek*, 1934; *King Cole*, 1936; *The Dark Command: A Kansas Iliad*, 1938; *Stretch Dawson*, 1950; *Adobe Walls*, 1953; *Captain Lightfoot*, 1954; *It's Always Four O'Clock*, 1956 (as Updyke); *Pale Moon*, 1956; *Bitter Ground*, 1958; *Mi Amigo*, 1959; *Conant*, 1961; *Sergeants Three*, 1962; *The Goldseekers*, 1962; *The Widow Barony*, 1962; *The Abilene Samson*, 1963; *The Winning of Mickey Free*, 1965

SCREENPLAYS: 1931-1950 • *The Finger Points*, 1931 (with John Monk Saunders); *The Beast of the City*, 1932; *Some Blondes Are Dangerous*, 1937 (with Lester Cole); *King of the Underworld*, 1938 (with George Bricker and Vincent Sherman); *High Sierra*, 1941 (with John Huston); *The Get-Away*, 1941 (with Wells Root and J. Walter Ruben); *This Gun for Hire*, 1941 (with Albert Maltz); *Wake Island*, 1942 (with Frank Butler); *Action in the North Atlantic*, 1943 (with others); *Background to Danger*, 1943; *Crash Dive*, 1943 (with Jo Swerling); *San Antonio*, 1945 (with Alan LeMay); *Nobody Lives Forever*, 1946; *Belle Starr's Daughter*, 1948; *Yellow Sky*, 1949 (with Lamar Trotti)

1951-1963 • *The Iron Man*, 1951 (with George Zuckerman and Borden Chase); *The Racket*, 1951 (with William Wister Haines); *Vendetta*, 1951 (with Peter O'Crotty); *Dangerous Mission*, 1954 (with others); *Captain Lightfoot*, 1955 (with Oscar Brodney); *I Died a Thousand Times*, 1955; *Illegal*, 1955 (with James R. Webb and Frank Collins); *Accused of Murder*, 1957 (with Robert Creighton Williams); *Septem-*

ber Storm, 1961 (with Steve Fisher); *Sergeants Three*, 1962; *The Great Escape*, 1963 (with James Clavell)

TELEPLAY: *Debt of Honor*, c. 1960

NONFICTION: *The Roar of the Crowd*, 1965

BIBLIOGRAPHY

Faragoh, Francis Edward. *Little Caesar: Screenplay.* Special ed. Eye, Suffolk, England: ScreenPress Books, 2001. Special, updated edition of the screenplay adaptation of Burnett's novel that brought him lasting fame.

Horsley, Lee. *The Noir Thriller.* New York: Palgrave, 2001. Scholarly treatise on the thriller genre discussing five of Burnett's novels, from *Little Caesar* to *Underdog.* Bibliography and index.

Madden, David, ed. *Tough Guy Writers of the Thirties.* Carbondale: Southern Illinois University Press, 1979. Collection of scholarly essays about the hard-boiled subgenre and its practitioners; provides insight into Burnett's works.

Mate, Ken, and Pat McGilligan. "Burnett: An Interview." *Film Comment* 19 (January/February, 1983): 59-68. Interview with Burnett focusing on his many years in Hollywood and his experiences with the studios over four decades.

Moore, Lewis D. *Cracking the Hard-Boiled Detective: A Critical History from the 1920's to the Present.* Jefferson, N.C.: McFarland, 2006. Places Burnett's work in the context of the other writers of hard-boiled detective fiction and helps chart the changes in his work over time as a function of the changes in the wider subgenre.

Seldes, Gilbert. Foreword to *Little Caesar.* New York: Dial Press, 1958. Foreword to Burnett's first detective novel by the editor of *The Dial*, discussing Burnett and his work's importance to the genre.

REX BURNS

Born: San Diego, California; June 13, 1935

Also wrote as Tom Sehler

Types of plot: Police procedural; private investigator

PRINCIPAL SERIES

Gabe Wager, 1975-

Devlin Kirk, 1987-

PRINCIPAL SERIES CHARACTER

GABE WAGER is a detective sergeant on the Denver police force, assigned initially to Organized Crime (narcotics) and subsequently to Homicide. A "coyote" of mixed Hispanic-Anglo background, Wager is personally reserved, dedicated to his work, essentially isolated, and driven by his own demanding standards of honesty and duty.

CONTRIBUTION

Winner of the 1975 Mystery Writers of America Edgar Award for best first novel, The Alvarez Journal (1975) established Rex Burns as a realistic writer with a spare and honest style. Without relying on violent action or bizarre characters, Burns shaped the police procedural into a novel that presents a convincing portrait of a man at work in a job that is both consuming and tedious. The realities of police work mean that building a case that will hold up in court may well be more difficult than discovering the identity of a criminal. The books featuring detective Gabriel Villanueva "Gabe" Wager, which Burns describes as "chapters" in a larger work, are noteworthy for the author's skill in using indirection and accretion to reveal the depths of a character who is reserved, self-contained, and virtually inflexible. His Colorado settings expose a working-class Rocky Mountain West that tourists never see. In addition to the Edgar Award, Burns has been a three-time recipient of the Top Hand Award from the Colorado League of Authors.

BIOGRAPHY

Rex Raoul Stephen Sehler Burns was born in San Diego, California, on June 13, 1935. His father, who dreamed of retiring from the navy to edit a local newspaper, was killed during World War II. Burns was graduated from Stanford University in 1958 and then did a tour of active duty with the United States Marine Corps Reserves, during which he served as regimental legal officer and reached the rank of captain. In 1959, he married Emily Sweitzer; the couple had three sons.

In 1961, Burns began graduate work at the University of Minnesota. He earned an master of arts degree in 1963 and a doctorate in American studies in 1965. His doctoral research took an interdisciplinary approach to American culture in the first half of the nineteenth century. Examining the "gospel of success" by looking at popular reading, children's literature, labor periodicals, and the works of Nathaniel Hawthorne, his dissertation became the basis of a scholarly book published in 1976 as *Success in America: The Yeoman Dream and the Industrial Revolution*. From 1965 to 1968, Burns was an assistant professor and director of freshman English at Central Missouri State College. In 1968, he moved to the University of Colorado at Denver, where he was active in the faculty assembly and chairman of the University Senate (1974-1975). He was promoted to associate and then full professor. He spent time as a Fulbright lecturer in Greece (1969-1970) and in Argentina (1977).

Beginning in 1971, in addition to teaching and scholarly writing, Burns began serving as a consultant to the Denver District Attorney's office. The first of his detective novels was published in 1975. He remained a full-time professor; the popularity of late afternoon and evening classes for the students of an urban public university, who are often working adults, allowed him to spend mornings writing and to produce a book every year or two.

Burns has published numerous reviews of mystery fiction and maintained a regular review column for the *Rocky Mountain News*. A contributor to *Scribner's Mystery and Suspense Writers*, he also serves as an adviser to the *Oxford Companion to Mystery*. In 2001, he signed on with the Starz Encore Mystery Channel as host of a recurring segment called *Anatomy of a Mys-*

tery—brief studies of elements found in mystery writing, with examples of popular films that employ those elements. He retired from teaching at the University of Colorado but still serves as professor emeritus in English.

ANALYSIS

In "The Mirrored Badge" in *Colloquium on Crime: Eleven Renowned Mystery Writers Discuss Their Work* (1986), Rex Burns describes the police procedural as a "novel of manners" and asserts that he was drawn to the form because he disliked the "false portrayals of cops and robbers which, especially in the mass media, can be perilous to viewers who accept them as real." He also addresses the relationship between detective fiction and questions of psychological and moral importance. Although the genre requires a strict form, he writes, "crime is chaotic, an eruption into the ordered, public surface of our lives from some dark reservoir below—an intrusion, that is, of life's formlessness." The detective writer is thus faced with the problem of exploring the irrational: While "the detective wants only to solve the crime, the writer is faced with the need to explain it." That attempt, Burns suggests, "can lead the mystery writer to the limits of explaining the possibly inexplicable."

Burns's style is generally spare yet sharp. In an article for *The Writer* in March, 1984, he used the term "imagistic compression" to identify his technique of description: "to determine, usually in revision, what precise image, in the fewest words, will blossom in the reader's mind and make a setting visible to his imagination." He also seeks descriptive techniques that contribute to the development of the action. As the people at the Mormon ranch in *The Avenging Angel* (1983) prepare for attack, the smoke rising from the house's chimney "stood like a ghostly flagpole against the sky." The flagpole simile, as Burns points out, not only sharpens the scene but also captures the "paradox of a domestic fire on a quiet evening and the smoke as a beacon for the invaders." His dialogue is, in similar fashion, low-key yet distinctive. In particular, he uses the jargon of various occupations and the grammar and rhythms that betray education and social class to identify characters through their speech.

Burns uses a variety of physical and cultural settings to avoid the predictability of the police procedural, which, like actual detective work, tends to fall into repetitive patterns. He makes Gabe Wager a workaholic loner who goes undercover, pursues investigations on his own time, takes on detached assignments, and reluctantly agrees to use some of his accumulated vacation time when it dawns on him that he can go fishing in a locale that seems to have something to do with a questionable death. Thus, Burns can give Wager some of the range and independence of a private eye while letting him have access to the resources found only in a major law enforcement agency and subjecting him to the legal constraints of actual police work.

GABE WAGER

The character of Gabe Wager is a central attraction of Burns's writing. In his scholarly book on nineteenth century American culture, Burns identified two opposing traditions of success: the materialistic American Dream of the self-made individual rising from rags to riches and the competing ideal of competence, independence, and morality embodied in the image of the yeoman who possessed "wealth somewhat beyond [his] basic needs, freedom from economic or statutory subservience, and the respect of the society for fruitful, honest industry." To an extent, Gabe Wager is a twentieth century version of the sturdy yeoman: a working man who preserves his capacity for independent action by refusing either to join the union or to accept blindly the policies and politics of his superiors. The virtue of his independence is an extraordinarily strong sense of duty; the danger is in the inflexibility of his self-imposed moral code; and the price is loneliness.

Burns sees Wager's "hard struggle for self-definition in a world that has its labels all ready to apply" as giving him "a rigidity that is both strength and weakness." Wager is not wholly at home in either Chicano or Anglo culture. During his childhood in a barrio in Denver, relatives disapproved of his mother for having married an outsider.

Wager joined the Marines at sixteen and served for eight years in a period that stretched from the Korean Demilitarized Zone to Vietnam's Landing Zone Delta,

and as a consequence missed the normal experiences of the teen and early adult years, a time when most men learn something about women. There is a broken marriage in his background and a relationship with fellow police officer Jo Fabrizio that is constantly endangered by his emotional distance and stubborn pride.

Although the books use a third-person restricted viewpoint—everything is seen as if it had passed through Wager's consciousness—Wager is as reticent in his inner life as he is in his dealings with other people. Burns skillfully uses minimal outcroppings of introspection to humanize the humorless, self-sufficient workaholic.

Both the narrative voice and Wager's personal awareness, for example, undercut his apparent self-certainty in a spare passage such as this from *The Avenging Angel*: "What the hell, you didn't have to like your partner; all you had to do was work with him. Wager could tell himself that, and he could almost believe it."

THE ALVAREZ JOURNAL

Burns's first novel, *The Alvarez Journal*, established his dedication to the concrete reality of police work: No shot is fired, and the protagonist spends most of the book sitting in a car on surveillance. In the series that built on that beginning, Burns merged the structure and realism of the police procedural with the traditional American figure of an isolated hero who acts as a force for moral restitution.

Burns's "novel of manners" depicts the characteristic methods, mores, and folkways of various specialized subcultures, including that of the working police officer. In many police procedural series, the unit or squad serves as a substitute for the secure world of an idealized family, with unchanging characters cast in continuing roles and predictable relationships. Although the Gabe Wager books do contain some recurring characters in addition to the protagonist, they also portray the shifting nature of twentieth century police work: departmental administrators come and go, technologies and legal constraints change, and new social stresses arise. In addition, relationships among partners alter as their personal lives and their attitudes are shaped by experiences on or off the job.

To mirror the texture and actuality of the exterior world, Burns ties many of Wager's cases to other fairly closed subcultures. The world of rodeo in *Ground Money* (1986), of nude dancers in *Strip Search* (1984), of fundamentalist Mormonism in *The Avenging Angel*, of small-time modeling agencies in *Speak for the Dead* (1978) are given verisimilitude through concrete details. Only after the detective acquires insider knowledge and comes to appreciate the subculture's characteristic values and mental habits can he understand the patterns and motives that point to a solution.

THE AVENGING ANGEL

The techniques, characterization, and moral focus of the Gabe Wager novels are evident in *The Avenging Angel*. The novel opens with police routine, as Wager and his partner examine the body of a person found shot dead on a roadside. While the photographers, forensic teams, and uniformed patrol units do their jobs, Wager "let his mind play over the scene again, trying to see it from the angle of the victim. Then from that of the killer." The detective uses his imagination to visualize the scene and grope for the essence of its details, while the novelist economically uses the detective's visualization to create mood and atmosphere:

> The rigor told Wager that the man was probably shot right here. Probably the killer or killers walked the victim straight down the embankment and stood just there while he turned to face them. Wind. Almost always a night wind out here on the prairie east of Denver and its bright glow. Maybe a step or two closer for a good shot. . . . Perhaps the victim's arms were already held out—don't shoot me, I don't have anything; perhaps they flew up as the bullet hit his chest like a baseball bat and knocked him flat and numb with shock and dead before he hit the ground. . . . Then he—or they—went through the pockets very quickly, not needing a light because of the sky glow of Denver. . . . Then that note, which was to tell someone why the man was shot, if not who pulled the trigger. Wager guessed that the note had been folded and resting in the killer's pocket, ready for use. Folded precisely into a rectangle whose edges were flush all around. When you're in the dark, and in a hurry, and you've just killed a man, you don't take time to align the edges of a folded slip of paper. That's something you do when you're carefully planning ahead.

The folded slip of paper is a photocopied drawing of an angel holding a sword. When a second such drawing turns up on a corpse in Pueblo and a third on a body in remote Grant County on the western slope, Wager is sent to look for connections. He discovers a rugged, thinly populated region of benchland and desert that retains a small-town openness and a frontier tolerance for individual differences—including the presence of unreconstructed Mormon polygamists. Because of his own nonjudgmental attitude, Wager is able to gain insight into the religious and political schisms among the Mormon groups and link the drawing to the nineteenth century religious vigilantes known as "avenging angels."

The information leads him—back in Denver—to a house full of massacred women and children; he returns to Grant County to join with the sheriff's office and one of the Mormon tribes to trap the murdering fanatics. The plan is endangered, however, by leaks from within; Wager realizes only at the last moment that two of the murders had been committed not for religious reasons but by a deputy sheriff who thereby secured water rights to develop land that he owned. Wager's solo expedition to a distant part of the state and the isolation of the physical setting and the society reinforce the essential isolation of his own character, and the knowledge that some law officers are corrupted by greed demonstrates the necessity for Wager's independence and self-reliance.

A passage in *The Avenging Angel* defines Gabe Wager's attitude toward crime:

> A cop accepted the importance of the rules that tried to order the randomness of life and death, and his job was to go after those who did not accept the rules. Usually they were merely the careless ones; on rare occasions they were the ones who were neither careless nor blind to the rules, but who knew them and chose to stay outside them. . . . They reasoned what they did and they struck like feeding sharks at those penned in by the rules; they were the ones who crossed the line between order and chaos, and who brought to their victims not only a fear of death but a terror of the soul.

In this passage, Burns presents his own intellectual analysis of the source of evil in plain language suited to a working detective. The police officer, further-more, deals with people and the immediate conse-quences that harm individual victims; the morality that matters, in that context, is sometimes not contained in legal and social policies. In *The Alvarez Journal*, a criminal is caught but the crime continues; in *Angle of Attack* (1979), Wager drops information that motivates the mob to eliminate a criminal against whom the po-lice are unable to build a case. He measures himself by his own scrupulous concept of duty: "He knew when he did a good job or a poor one; nobody else's blame, nobody else's satisfaction really counted." The inside leaks and the existence of law enforcement officers who use their position for private ends justify Wager's self-sufficiency and the necessity of creating his own standard of ethics.

THE KILLING ZONE

In *The Killing Zone* (1988), the murder victim is a black politician, and the book's sophisticated explora-tion of urban political and racial relations is as inter-esting as the solution to the crime. Equally impressive is the sensitive portrayal of the people whose lives are shaped by their role in a particular social context. Most realistic novelists presumably make characters con-vincing by learning to put themselves inside other people and to see the world through their eyes. Burns creates a detective who uses the same method to un-derstand both criminals and victims.

The Gabe Wager series established Burns as a writer of detective novels with believable characters solidly embedded in a realistic social milieu. *Suicide Season* (1987) introduced the more upscale, glitzy, high-tech side of Denver life with private investigator Devlin Kirk, Stanford graduate, law school dropout, and former Secret Service agent who is a partner with former police detective Homer Bunchcroft in a firm that specializes in company security and executive protection. Although the Kirk series provided Burns with a new focus, he continues to write Gabe Wager novels. He has written that the Gabe Wager novels are single chapters in "a larger work that has its own archi-tecture."

Sally Mitchell
Updated by Philip Bader

PRINCIPAL MYSTERY AND DETECTIVE FICTION

GABE WAGER SERIES: *The Alvarez Journal*, 1975; *The Farnsworth Score*, 1977; *Speak for the Dead*, 1978; *Angle of Attack*, 1979; *The Avenging An-gel*, 1983; *Strip Search*, 1984; *Ground Money*, 1986; *The Killing Zone*, 1988; *Endangered Species*, 1993; *Blood Line*, 1995; *The Leaning Land*, 1997

DEVLIN KIRK SERIES: *Suicide Season*, 1987; *Parts Unknown*, 1990; *Body Guard*, 1991

OTHER MAJOR WORKS

NOVELS: *When Reason Sleeps*, 1991 (as Sehler)

NONFICTION: *Success in America: The Yeoman Dream and the Industrial Revolution*, 1976

EDITED TEXT: *Crime Classics: The Mystery Story from Poe to the Present*, 1990 (with Mary Rose Sullivan)

BIBLIOGRAPHY

Burns, Rex. "Characterization." *The Writer* 101, no. 5 (May, 1988): 11-14. Burns discusses how he devel-oped his two main characters, Gabe Wager and Devlin Kirk. He notes the importance of a balance between consistency and change when creating a character for a series.

_____. Rex Burns. http://www.rexburns.com. Burns's official Web site offers news of upcoming publica-tions, descriptions of published works, and a biog-raphy.

Kelleher, Harry. "In the Dry, Dusty Distance, Gabe Wager Rides Again." Review of *The Leaning Land*, by Rex Burns. *Denver Post*, October 19, 1997, p. E05. Reviewer finds the novel, centering on four deaths on the Ute reservation, satisfying as a mys-tery but says it lacks emotional impact, partly be-cause Gabe Wager is a remote character and the setting is sparsely populated areas of western Colo-rado.

Library Journal. Review of *The Avenging Angel*, by Rex Burns. 108, no. 3 (February 1, 1983): 223. Re-viewer praises the novel's literary quality, depth of character, and its descriptions of the Colorado set-ting.

_____. Review of *Suicide Season*, by Rex Burns. 110, no. 12 (June 1, 1987): 131. In this Devlin Kirk novel, he investigates the suicide of the primary suspect in a corporate espionage case. The reviewer found the novel to be an "engrossing mystery."

Priestman, Martin, ed. *The Cambridge Companion to Crime Fiction*. New York: Cambridge University Press, 2003. Priestman covers crime fiction from the eighteenth century to the present and includes analyses of thrillers and spy fiction, the Victorian era, female and African American detectives, and postmodern uses of the detective genre.

Winks, Robin, ed. *Colloquium on Crime: Eleven Renowned Mystery Writers Discuss Their Work*. New York: Scribner, 1986. Contains an essay by Burns that describes his view of the police procedural and mystery writing.

C

JAMES M. CAIN

Born: Annapolis, Maryland; July 1, 1892
Died: Hyattsville, Maryland; October 27, 1977
Types of plot: Hard-boiled; inverted

CONTRIBUTION

James M. Cain is best remembered as the tough-guy writer (a label he eschewed) who created *The Postman Always Rings Twice* (1934) and *Double Indemnity* (1936). Both books have enjoyed as much popularity as their film versions. Though Cain gained some fame as a Hollywood scriptwriter, he did not write the screen adaptations of either *The Postman Always Rings Twice* or *Double Indemnity*, which attained the status of classic films noirs. Cain had a significant impact on French writers, notably Albert Camus, who nevertheless denied the influence as forthrightly as Cain had done with that of Ernest Hemingway. In the Europe and United States of the 1930's, years in which laconic, unsentimental, hard-boiled fiction found ready readership, Cain contributed mightily to this style of writing. That his work is still popular in the twenty-first century is testament to his gift for spare prose and his insight into the darkness of the human soul.

Cain's narrative style entails a simple story, usually a "love rack" triangle of one woman and two men, presented at a very swift pace. His economy of expression was greater than that of any of the other tough-guy writers. Cain's characters and situations were consistent with no sociological or philosophical theme, although many were illustrative of the inevitability of human unhappiness and the destructiveness of the dream or wish come true. It was this structural and narrative purity, devoid of sentimentality and sustained by the perspective of the antiheroic wrongdoer, that won for Cain an enthusiastic readership in France, including the admiration of Albert Camus, and a secure place in the history of American literature.

BIOGRAPHY

James Mallahan Cain, born in Annapolis, Maryland, on July 1, 1892, was the first of the five children of James William Cain and Rose Mallahan Cain. His father was an academician, a professor at St. John's College in Annapolis, and later, in Chesterton, Maryland, president of Washington College, from which James M. Cain was graduated in 1910 and where he later, from 1914 through 1917, taught English and mathematics and completed work on his master's degree in dramatic arts. His early ambition to become a professional singer had been abandoned before his graduate work and teaching at Washington College, but his love of music never diminished. Throughout his life, Cain retained his ambition to become a successful playwright despite his repeated failures in dramaturgy and his own ultimate realization of the misdirection of this ambition.

Cain's career in writing began with newspaper work, first with the *Baltimore American* in 1918 and then with the *Baltimore Sun*. He edited the *Lorraine Cross*, his infantry-company newspaper, during his service with the Seventy-ninth Infantry Division in France. He returned from World War I to resume work on the *Baltimore Sun*, and in 1920 he married Mary Rebecca Clough, the first of his four wives. Cain's articles on the William Blizzard treason trial in 1922 were published by *The Atlantic Monthly* and *The Nation*. He then became a feature writer and columnist for the *Baltimore Sun*. His inability to complete a novel set in the mining area of West Virginia, the site of the Blizzard trial, preceded and apparently brought about his departure from the *Baltimore Sun*; he then began teaching English and journalism at St. John's College.

H. L. Mencken furthered Cain's career by publishing his article "The Labor Leader" in *The American*

James M. Cain. (AP/Wide World Photos)

Cain published his first book, *Our Government*, a series of satirical dramatic dialogues, in 1930. He achieved national recognition with his first short story, "Pastorale," published two years earlier, and his first novel, *The Postman Always Rings Twice*, published four years later. When the *New York World* changed ownership in 1931, Cain became managing editor of *The New Yorker* magazine but left that position in favor of Hollywood, where he worked irregularly from 1931 to 1947 as a scriptwriter for various studios. He continued to write novels and short stories and to see much of his fiction adapted to the screen by other scriptwriters. His attempt during this period to establish the American Authors' Authority, a guild protective of authors' rights, failed under considerable opposition.

Cain moved to Hyattsville, Maryland, in 1948. It was there that he and his fourth wife spent the remainder of their lives. After his wife died, Cain, having made the move with the intent to create high literature, continued to write, but with barely nominal success, until his death, at the age of eighty-five, on October 27, 1977.

ANALYSIS

Despite midcareer pretensions to high literature, James M. Cain wrote, admittedly, for two reasons: for money and because he was a writer. He had no lasting illusions about great literary art and had only contempt for critics who sought intellectual constructs in works of literature and who, for their own convenience, lumped writers into schools. Cain opposed and resisted the notion of the tough-guy school, and yet he developed a first-person style of narration that, in its cynical and incisive presentation of facts, merits the appellation "tough" or "hard-boiled." Critic David Madden calls him "the twenty-minute egg of the hard-boiled writers."

This style proved profitable, and Cain, in his own hard-boiled way, believed that "good work is usually profitable and bad work is not." In the case of his fiction, this proved to be true. His work was profitable and remained in print during and after his lifetime. Good or bad, fiction is what Cain wanted most to write; he is quoted in an interview as saying, "You hire

Mercury magazine (which had just been founded) and by putting him in touch with Walter Lippmann, who provided him with an editorial-writing position on the *New York World*. In 1925 his publication of a much-praised dialogue in *The American Mercury* fed Cain's ambition to write plays. His first effort, *Crashing the Gate*, produced in the following year, proved to be a failure. His two attempts, in 1936 and 1953, to adapt *The Postman Always Rings Twice* to the stage also failed—along with *7-11* (1938) and an unproduced play titled "The Guest in Room 701," completed in 1955.

Cain's marriage to Mary Clough was dissolved in 1927, after which he married Elina Sjöstad Tyszecha, a Finnish woman with two children. The marriage ended in divorce in 1942. Cain was subsequently married to Aileen Pringle and, after his third divorce, Florence Macbeth. He had no children with any of his wives.

out to do other kinds of writing that leaves you more and more frustrated, until one day you burst out, say to hell with it all and go sit down somewhere and write the thing you truly want to write."

Yet it seems that it was not the mystery story in which Cain was most interested, despite his recognition in this genre by the Mystery Writers of America (which gave him its Grand Masters Award in 1970), but something like the novelistic equivalent of Greek tragedy. His frustration at his failure in dramaturgy was profound; it makes sense that his novels, like classical Greek tragic drama, demonstrate the essential unhappiness of life, the devastation borne by the hubris manifest in the lust and greed that lead to murder, and the human desires that predispose people to incest, homosexuality, or pedophilia. Cain's fictional personae are always minimal, as they are in Greek tragedy, and his descriptions of his characters are as spare in detail as a delineative tragic mask.

"PASTORALE"

"Pastorale," Cain's first published short story, contains the standard constituents of almost all of his fiction: a selfishly determined goal, excessive and ill-considered actions in pursuit of that goal, and the inability of the pursuer to abide the self into which the successful actions have transformed the pursuer. A yokel narrator relates that Burbie and Lida, who want to be together, plot to kill Lida's husband, a man much older than she. Burbie enlists Hutch, a vicious opportunist, with the false bait of a money cache. Burbie, lusting after Lida, and Hutch, greedy for money, kill the old man.

Hutch, who learns that the money cache was a mere twenty-three dollars but not that it had been scraped together by Burbie and Lida, decapitates the corpse, intending to make a gift of the head to Lida. The intent is frustrated when Hutch drowns, and after Hutch's body and the husband's remains are discovered, it is assumed that Hutch was the sole killer. Burbie, although free to possess Lida, confesses everything and awaits hanging as the story ends. The story is abetted by Cain's standard elements of sex and violence.

THE POSTMAN ALWAYS RINGS TWICE

In 1934, Cain published his first novel, *The Postman Always Rings Twice*, which proved to be his mas-

terpiece. In the story, a man and a woman, consumed by lust for each other and by monetary greed, successfully conspire to kill the woman's husband, again a man older than she but with a going business that will ensure the solvency of the conspirators. The incapacity of the principals to accommodate themselves to the fulfillment of their dream leads to the death of the woman and, as the novel closes, the imminent execution of the man.

The opening line of *The Postman Always Rings Twice* ("They threw me off the hay truck about noon") came to be acclaimed as a striking example of the concise, attention-getting narrative hook. Cain's use of "they" is existentialist in its positing of the Other against the Individual. Jean-Paul Sartre's story "Le Mur" ("The Wall") begins in the same way: "They threw us into a big, white room. . . ." The last chapter of *The Postman Always Rings Twice*, like its first paragraph, makes much use of the pronoun "they," culminating with "Here they come," in reference to those who will take the narrator to his execution. This classical balance of beginning and ending in the same context is characteristic of Cain's work.

DOUBLE INDEMNITY

Double Indemnity, Cain's masterly companion to *The Postman Always Rings Twice*, appeared first in serial installments during 1936 and was published again, in 1943, along with "Career in C Major" and "The Embezzler." *Double Indemnity* presents a typical Cain plot: A man and a woman conspire to murder the woman's husband so that they can satisfy their lust for each other and profit from the husband's insurance. Their success is a prelude to their suicide pact.

Cain's literary reputation rests chiefly on these two works. Ross Macdonald called them "a pair of native American masterpieces, back to back." Cain looked on both works as romantic love stories rather than murder mysteries; nevertheless, they belong more to the category of the thriller than to any other. In their brevity, their classical balance, and their exposition of the essential unhappiness of human existence, they evince tragedy. Cain did not see himself as a tragedian; he insisted that he "had never theorized much about tragedy, Greek or otherwise" and yet at the same time admitted that tragedy as a "force of circumstances

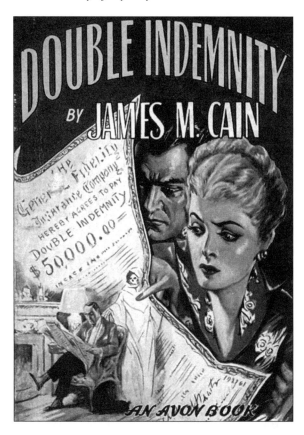

driving the protagonist to the *commission of a dreadful act*" (his father's definition) applied to most of his writings, "even my lighter things."

SERENADE

The two novels that followed the back-to-back masterpieces were longer works, marked by the readability, but not the golden conciseness, of their predecessors. *Serenade* (1937) is the story of a singer whose homosexuality has resulted in the loss of his singing voice, which is restored through his consummated love for a Mexican prostitute. The triangle in this novel is once more a woman and two men, the difference being that the woman kills the man's homosexual lover. The man joins his beloved in her flight from the law until she is discovered and killed. The discovery owes to the man's betrayal of their identities by failing to suppress his distinctive singing voice at a critical time. Cain's knowledge of music underscores *Serenade*, just as it gives form to "Career in C Major" and *Mildred Pierce* (1941).

MILDRED PIERCE

Mildred Pierce is the story of a coloratura soprano's amorality as much as it is the story of the titular character and her sublimated incestuous desire for the soprano who is her daughter. There is sex and violence in the novel but no murder, no mystery, and no suspense. The novel opens and closes with Mildred Pierce married to a steady yet unsuccessful man who needs to be mothered. Mildred does not mother him, and the two are divorced, the man finding his mother figure in a heavy-breasted woman and Mildred disguising her desire for her daughter as maternal solicitude. Mildred achieves wealth and success as a restaurateur, and her daughter wins renown as a singer. Mildred's world collapses as her daughter, incapable of affection and wickedly selfish, betrays and abandons her. Mildred, reconciled with her husband, whose mother figure has returned to her husband, finally finds solace in mothering him.

LOVE'S LOVELY COUNTERFEIT

Mildred Pierce is written in the third person, a style of narration that is not typical of Cain, who employed it in only a few of his many novels. It was followed by another third-person novel, *Love's Lovely Counterfeit* (1942), a gangster-thriller and a patent tough-guy novel, peopled with hoods (with names such as Lefty, Bugs, and Goose), corrupt police, and crime lords. The novel displays Cain's storytelling at its best and is perhaps his most underrated work.

PAST ALL DISHONOR AND MIGNON

Always conscientious about research for his novels, Cain, in his bid to become a serious writer, tended in novels such as *Past All Dishonor* (1946) and *Mignon* (1962) to subordinate his swift mode of narration to masses of researched details. Both of these novels are set in the 1860's, both are embellished with a wealth of technical details that are historically accurate, and both have a hard-boiled narrator who, with a basic nobility that gets warped by lust and greed, is hardly distinguishable from his twentieth century counterparts in Cain's other fiction. Like *The Postman Always Rings Twice, Past All Dishonor* ends with the narrator's saying "Here they come" as the nemeses for his crimes close in on him. Like *Mignon*, in which the narrator's loss of his beloved will be lamented with "there was my love, my life, my beautiful little Mignon, shooting by in the muddy water," *Past All Dishonor* has the narrator bemoan his loss with "my wife, my love, my life, was sinking in the snow."

There is a discernible sameness to Cain's fiction. He tends to make his leading male characters handsome blue-eyed blonds, he makes grammatically correct but excessive use of the word "presently," his first-person narrators all sound alike, and his inclination is manifestly toward the unhappy ending (although several of his novels end happily). One upbeat novel is *The Moth* (1948), in which the leading male character loves a twelve-year-old girl. Again, almost all Cain's fiction, with the prominent exception of *Mildred Pierce*, is a variation on his first two works of fiction.

SINFUL WOMAN AND JEALOUS WOMAN

The two novels by Cain that indisputably can be called murder mysteries are *Sinful Woman* (1947) and *Jealous Woman* (1950). Both novels focus on the solving of a murder, both have happy endings, and both are rated among Cain's worst performances. Cain himself wrote them off as bad jobs. *Sinful Woman*, like *Mildred Pierce*, *Love's Lovely Counterfeit*, and another, *The Magician's Wife* (1965), is written in third-person narration, which Cain comes close to mastering only in *Love's Lovely Counterfeit*.

THE BUTTERFLY

The Butterfly (1947), a story of a man with an incestuous bent for a young woman whom he mistakenly assumes to be his daughter, is perhaps the last of Cain's best work; it includes the now-famous preface in which he disavows any literary debt to Hemingway while affirming his admiration of Hemingway's work. Most of Cain's post-1947 novels were critical and commercial disappointments. In addition to those already mentioned, these include *The Root of His Evil* (1951, first written in 1938), *Galatea* (1953), *The Rainbow's End* (1975), and *The Institute* (1976)—none of which is prime Cain, although *Galatea* and *The Rainbow's End* flash with his narrative brilliance.

CLOUD NINE

Cloud Nine, written by Cain when he was seventy-five, was edited by his biographer, Roy Hoopes, and published posthumously in 1984. It contains the usual sex and violence, including rape and murder. Its narra-

tor, however, is not antiheroic but a highly principled thirty-year-old man only mildly touched by greed who marries a sexy and very intelligent sixteen-year-old girl. His half brother is an evil degenerate whose villainy is unrelieved by any modicum of goodness. The narrator's dream comes true, and the story has a happy ending. The septuagenarian Cain was more than temporally remote from the hard-boiled Cain of the 1930's, who would have made the villain the narrator and given the story a tragic cast.

Roy Arthur Swanson
Updated by Fiona Kelleghan and
Taryn Benbow-Pfalzgraf

PRINCIPAL MYSTERY AND DETECTIVE FICTION

NOVELS: *The Postman Always Rings Twice*, 1934; *Serenade*, 1937; *Mildred Pierce*, 1941; *Love's Lovely Counterfeit*, 1942; *Past All Dishonor*, 1946; *The Butterfly*, 1947; *Sinful Woman*, 1947; *The Moth*, 1948; *Jealous Woman*, 1950; *The Root of His Evil*, 1951 (also known as *Shameless*, 1979); *Galatea*, 1953; *Mignon*, 1963; *The Magician's Wife*, 1965; *Rainbow's End*, 1975; *The Institute*, 1976; *Cloud Nine*, 1984

SHORT FICTION: *Double Indemnity*, 1936; *The Embezzler*, 1940; *Career in C Major and Other Stories*, 1943; *Three of a Kind: Career in C Major, The Embezzler, Double Indemnity*, 1943; *The Baby in the Icebox, and Other Short Fiction*, 1981 (posthumous, Roy Hoopes, editor); *Career in C Major, and Other Fiction*, 1986 (Roy Hoopes, editor)

OTHER MAJOR WORKS

NOVEL: *The Enchanted Isle*, 1985

PLAYS: *Crashing the Gates*, pr. 1926; *Theological Interlude*, pb. 1928 (dialogue); *Trial by Jury*, pb. 1928 (dialogue); *Citizenship*, pb. 1929 (dialogue); *Will of the People*, pb. 1929 (dialogue); *The Governor*, pb. 1930; *Don't Monkey with Uncle Sam*, pb. 1933 (dialogue); *The Postman Always Rings Twice*, pr. 1936 (adaptation of his novel); *7-11*, pr. 1938

SCREENPLAYS: *Algiers*, 1938; *Stand up and Fight*, 1938; *Gypsy Wildcat*, 1944

NONFICTION: *Our Government*, 1930; *Sixty Years of Journalism*, 1986 (Hoopes, editor)

MISCELLANEOUS: *The James M. Cain Cookbook:*

Guide to Home Singing, Physical Fitness, and Animals (Especially Cats), 1988 (essays and stories; edited by Roy Hoopes and Lynne Barrett)

BIBLIOGRAPHY

Fine, Richard. *James M. Cain and the American Authors' Authority.* Austin: University of Texas Press, 1992. A solid study of Cain's attempt to create an American Authors' Authority in the mid-1940's. The AAA would have been a national writers' organization with wide-ranging powers to protect its members' property rights. Fine argues that the failure of the AAA contributed to the economic marginalization of American writers.

Haining, Peter. *The Classic Era of American Pulp Magazines.* Chicago: Chicago Review Press, 2000. Discusses Cain's career as a pulp author, the role of pulp magazines in American culture, and Cain's contribution to the form. Index.

Hoopes, Roy. *Cain.* New York; Holt, Rinehart and Winston, 1982. This comprehensive biography of Cain is divided into four chronological parts. Covers his years in Maryland and France, New York, Hollywood, and Hyattsville. Includes an afterword on Cain as newspaperman. Supplemented by extensive sources and notes, a list of Cain's publications, a filmography, and an index.

Horsley, Lee. *The Noir Thriller.* New York: Palgrave, 2001. A scholarly, theoretically informed study of the thriller genre and its embrace of the dark thematic material that lent itself to adaptation into film noir. Cain is prominently featured. Bibliographic references and index.

Madden, David. *Cain's Craft.* Metuchen, N.J.: Scarecrow Press, 1985. A collection of essays exploring Cain's literary techniques by one of his earliest academic champions. Madden compares some of Cain's works to novels by other writers and addresses the ways his books have been adapted to the screen.

_____. *James M. Cain.* New York: Twayne, 1970. An excellent introductory volume that accepts Cain's varied reputation as an excellent, a trashy, an important, and an always popular writer. Approaches every major aspect of his work on several levels, including his life in relation to his writing, analysis of his characters, and his technical expertise. Complemented by notes, a bibliography of primary and secondary sources, and an index.

Marling, William. *The American Roman Noir: Hammett, Cain, and Chandler.* Athens: University of Georgia Press, 1995. An intriguing exercise in literary criticism that links the hard-boiled writing of Cain, Dashiell Hammett, and Raymond Chandler to contemporary economic and technological changes. Marling sees them as pioneers of an aesthetic for the postindustrial age.

Nyman, Jopi. *Hard-Boiled Fiction and Dark Romanticism.* New York: Peter Lang, 1998. Examines the fiction of Cain, Dashiell Hammett, Ernest Hemingway, and Horace McCoy.

Shaw, Patrick W. *The Modern American Novel of Violence.* Troy, N.Y.: Whitston, 2000. Discusses the representation of violence in *The Postman Always Rings Twice.* Bibliographic references.

Skenazy, Paul. *James M. Cain.* New York: Continuum, 1989. A comprehensive study of Cain's work. Skenazy is more critical of his subject's writing than is Madden but acknowledges Cain's importance and his continuing capacity to attract readers.

STEPHEN J. CANNELL

Born: Los Angeles, California; February 5, 1941
Types of plot: Private investigator; hard-boiled; police procedural

PRINCIPAL SERIES

Shane Scully, 2001-

PRINCIPAL SERIES CHARACTER

SHANE SCULLY, a tough-talking Los Angeles Police Department sergeant, investigates such criminal activities as police corruption, murder, and bribery. His investigations take him into the worlds of rap music, drug smuggling, money laundering, and political intrigue on the national and local levels. In his relentless pursuit of truth and justice, he faces off with members of organized crime and corrupt police and politicians. As the series develops, so does his relationship with Alexa, a police officer whom he eventually marries. Scully's tough ways are softened by his having a loving relationship with Alexa and a son, Chooch, whose mother was a prostitute and who, like Alexa, plays a part in some of Scully's investigations, turning crime fighting into a family enterprise.

CONTRIBUTION

Writing first for television, Stephen J. Cannell created a new kind of detective, one who is flawed, flouts authority, and is comfortable being nonviolent and slightly odd. This kind of protagonist is more human than heroic but manages to defeat evildoers nevertheless. Though somewhat of a loner, the detective has loyal friends who often provide aid and comic relief. The unusual and unexpected attracted Cannell from the beginning of his writing career. His main characters do not hesitate to break the law or use violence in the name of justice. After writing more than fifteen hundred television dramas, Cannell turned to writing novels with the same energy, commitment, and imagination that made his television scripts successful. The broader canvas of the novel enabled him to develop more complicated plots, to create more complex interaction among a larger group of characters, and to ex-

pand the main character's background and relationships.

The premise of many of Cannell's plots is violent conflict perpetrated by a menagerie of evil characters in gritty locations, earning him the nickname the "Merchant of Mayhem" and the reputation of a writer who features "bullets and babes." Some critics, perhaps doubting that a writer as prolific and successful as Cannell could be very good, have called his characters cartoonlike and shallow and his plots too action-oriented and too violent. However, the popularity of his television shows and novels and the longevity of his success are proof that he knows what makes writing good entertainment and how to provide it.

BIOGRAPHY

Stephen Joseph Cannell was born in Los Angeles on February 5, 1941, and grew up in nearby Pasadena, where he eventually settled with his wife, Marcia. Cannell's father, Joseph, was very successful in the interior decorating business and instilled in his son a strong work ethic and a good business sense. Stephen's mother, Carolyn Baker Cannell, was active in business as well, serving on the boards of several corporations.

Cannell's learning disability, dyslexia, caused him to repeat the first and fourth grades in school, and he eventually had to attend a remedial school. He excelled in sports, however, and was popular, always part of the in crowd. He attended the University of Oregon, where a creative writing professor encouraged him to write. After graduation in 1964, he returned to Los Angeles and married Marcia C. Finch, with whom he fathered two sons and two daughters; one of his sons died at the age of fifteen. Cannell began working for his father and writing after work each day and on the weekends. After five years, he finally sold a television script, an episode of *It Takes a Thief* (1968-1970), and followed that success with scripts for *Mission: Impossible* (1988-1990) and *Ironside* (1967-1975). He was hired as story editor and head writer on *Adam-12* (1968-1975), then worked as executive producer for

Roy Huggins, who became his mentor. Cannell quickly expanded his activities while continuing to write scripts. He both produced and coproduced many shows, creating and cocreating more than forty series. He also directed in television and did some acting.

After eight successful years as a prolific scriptwriter and producer and inspired by the business principles of his father, Cannell formed his own studio in 1979, starting with four employees and eventually reaching two thousand. Within twelve years, his was the third largest studio in Hollywood television, averaging at least five shows on television every year. As his company grew, Cannell diversified his efforts, producing films, commercials, and other television fare. He formed the Cannell Studios in 1986 and moved his company to Canada to reduce production costs.

Along the way, Cannell won many awards, including the Mystery Writers Award in 1975; an Emmy Award in 1978 for outstanding drama series, for *The Rockford Files* (1974-1980); a Saturn Award for lifetime career achievement in 2005; and in 2006, both the Brandon Tartikoff Legacy Award and the Paddy Chayefsky Laurel Award for television writing achievement.

In 1995, having had his fill of television, Cannell sold his production company and turned to writing novels. His first novel, *The Plan*, was published in 1995, and he published many additional series and nonseries novels, many of them best sellers. His lifelong struggle with dyslexia, which was not diagnosed until he was thirty-five years old, fueled his struggle to succeed and led to his serving as the national chairperson for the Orton Dyslexia Society and promoting awareness and understanding of the affliction in public speeches.

Stephen J. Cannell. (Courtesy, Allen & Unwin)

ANALYSIS

Stephen J. Cannell, an exceptionally fast writer with a fertile imagination, demonstrated an uncanny ear for the rhythms and vocabulary of streetwise characters and a talent for humor and for plot-driven drama. He once said that he developed his fictional heroes from the point of view of their attitudes, which he believed, along with their flaws, made them believable and interesting. His fiction reflects these gifts in ample supply: It is fast-paced, full of conflict, often violent, and peopled by oddball characters. He once said that he was more interested in a character's flaws than in his virtues; to Cannell, the flaws become virtues, making the character easily identifiable, interesting, and often likable.

In his novels, Cannell brought with him the same taste for action, complex plotting, finely etched quirky characters, and edgy, well-tuned dialogue that marked his television scripts. His first full-length novel, *The Plan*, builds on Cannell's formulaic plot and character development. The action covers territory from Los Angeles to New York to the Caribbean; the main character, Ryan Bolt, is an unlikely hero. He is a television producer who faces a mighty crime organization in a high-stakes attempt to put its man in the White House; along the way, Bolt falls in love with a woman who happens to be the bad guy's sister. The novel became a best seller and encouraged Cannell to continue in this genre, producing novels in quick succession, with many of them achieving best-seller status. All of them display the Cannell gift for fast action, surprising turns in the action, engaging characters, and snappy dialogue, a combination that rivets the thrill-seeking reader with its suspenseful outcomes.

An essential element in Cannell's fiction is its focus on contemporary issues and subjects that have made the news or have captured the attention of readers of the news and audiences of films and television. *Final Victim* (1997) deals with computer hacking, criminal profiling, and a maniacal serial killer who carves up his victims with a scalpel. One of Cannell's gifts is to repeat himself without becoming predictable or stale, and he does so by making his people believable and interesting and by continuing to surprise the reader even when it all seems familiar.

The hero of *Final Victim*, John Lockwood, has, like Jim Rockford, a problem with guns: Lockwood has never hit anyone at whom he has shot. Lockwood is another unlikely hero, a customs agent who is at odds with his superiors, resents authority, and generally does what he wants in order to catch the criminal. Some of the novel's entertainment comes from Cannell's playful names, Haze Richards, for example, as the presidential candidate; Beano X. Bates as a con man; a prosecutor nicknamed Tricky Vicky; women named Lucinda, Malavida, and Miss Laura Luna; and a long list of other names that seem oddly appropriate yet humorously inappropriate.

Some critics have bemoaned the amount of violence in Cannell's writing and the focus on misfits and on the seamier aspects of human behavior. Cannell was accused of taking part in the perceived trend of "dumbing down" television, but he did not let such criticism change the way he wrote or what he wrote. He has said that he writes for the fun of it, not for the money or for the awards, though his shows have made him very rich and earned many awards. He wants to entertain, and he sees entertainment as a blend of humor, unusual situations, and characters with interesting flaws and odd habits. He believes that fiction must move along—hence his emphasis on action; he believes that characters should be interesting and realistic—hence the flawed antiheroes and host of quirky minor characters.

THE TIN COLLECTORS

This first novel in the Shane Scully series, *The Tin Collectors* (2001), contains an element that appears in most of Cannell's fiction: a wrongly accused protagonist who strives to clear himself of criminal charges. His (sometimes her) journey to redemption is dangerous, violent, and bloody. He champions the underdog, despises pretense and sham, doubts authority, saves good people whenever he can, and mourns their death when he cannot. He values the qualities that make the world a better place, including truth, honesty, justice, and love. At the end of the action, evil is exposed, and he is shown to be not only innocent but also capable of deep feelings and love.

The first three novels in the Shane Scully series are narrated in the third person, then Cannell shifts to first-person narrative in the next three, bringing the main character closer to the reader, who sees the action through Scully's eyes and follows the main character's thinking more closely.

In the first novel of the series, Shane Scully, a Los Angeles police sergeant, shoots a fellow police officer and is accused of murder. In his quest to prove his innocence, he is befriended by Alexa Hamilton, a sergeant in Internal Affairs. She and Scully follow a trail of corruption from Los Angeles to Miami, where they survive a shootout at the Biscayne Bay estate of singer Elton John. Back at Lake Arrowhead, they rescue two kidnap victims—one of them turns out to be

Scully's son—and survive a shootout in which they both are wounded while killing half a dozen bad guys. A motorboat chase ends with Scully on fire and an attack from a helicopter, which Alexa shoots out of the air. Ultimately they uncover a conspiracy that involves the Long Beach City Council, the mayor of Los Angeles, the chief of police, a powerful land developer, and dozens of police officers. Scully takes his son to live with him, and Alexa and he declare a mutual attraction that promises a long future together.

THE DEVIL'S WORKSHOP

In *The Devil's Workshop* (1999), Cannell chose a female protagonist, Stacy Richardson, to fight a conspiracy of scientists who plan to use genetic engineering to rid the world of certain ethnic groups. Like her male counterparts in Cannell's other novels, she is ordinary—she is a doctoral candidate married to the chairman of the department of microbiology at the University of Southern California. Events, including the death of her husband, turn her into a supersleuth and indomitable action hero bent on finding her husband's killers. Before the evil plot of the scientists is exposed and another threat to the world is thwarted, white supremacists become involved, along with a pair of wild hobos, a Hollywood producer, and a hero of Desert Storm; into the mix Cannell adds a train chase across the country and through hobo jungles that ends up in Washington, D.C. He creates a kaleidoscope of characters, events, names, and places that has become characteristic of his fiction as a whole. The technique is predictable but what emerges from it is consistently suspenseful, surprising, and pleasing to his readers.

HOLLYWOOD TOUGH

In 2001, Cannell returned to the Los Angeles police force for his main character, Shane Scully, perhaps wanting to stay close to his hometown. In the third novel in the Shane Scully series, *Hollywood Tough* (2003), Scully takes the reader into the seamy, crime-ridden streets of Los Angeles, and the plot mingles Mafia types, homegrown "gangstas," a likable confidence man, Hollywood stars, and a variety of other very dissimilar types. In addition to displaying an intimate knowledge of the film industry and its denizens, Cannell gives full display to his well-honed skill in capturing the nuances of different accents and voices. Readers have found that Cannell's version of Brooklynese rings true, and he successfully captures the speech of Hispanics, African Americans, the film-industry people, and women.

RUNAWAY HEART

Six months after *Hollywood Tough*, Cannell published his ninth novel, *Runaway Heart* (2003), whose protagonist is a former partner of Shane Scully. Jack Wirta was shot in the spine while on duty as a Los Angeles police officer and is now a private investigator addicted to painkillers. Crusading attorney Herman Strockmire calls on Wirta to help him find the killer of his assistant, who had hacked into the files of a firm doing genetic research for the United States government. In the hunt, Strockmire, his beautiful daughter Susan, and Wirta discover a sinister government plot to replace human soldiers with genetically engineered animals. A mutual attraction between Susan and Wirta develops while the pair, along with Strockmire, battle the forces of evil in an effort to save the world. In Cannell's fictional laboratory, love thrives and evil is destroyed.

Cannell's greatest skill is his ability to create plots full of surprising twists, exciting action, and realistic dialogue. He is superb at creating characters, the odd ones more prevalent than the ordinary ones; and he is a master at building suspense as the plot unfolds in a seemingly endless stream. His plots have a familiar shape: At the outset, the protagonist's fortunes are at a low ebb, but they rise steadily, thanks to his toughness, his intelligence, and his moral goodness, along with a little help from his friends, and a loving companion. For Cannell, ridding the world of evildoers is a holy quest of purification, not only of the world but also of his heroes. He never loses sight of the action, however, and the perils that his hero faces. The Cannell equation is simple and foolproof: Greater dangers bring greater excitement, and if the evil is great, so much greater will be the victory when it is achieved.

Bernard E. Morris

PRINCIPAL MYSTERY AND DETECTIVE FICTION

SHANE SCULLY SERIES: *The Tin Collectors*, 2001; *The Viking Funeral*, 2002; *Hollywood Tough*, 2003; *Vertical Coffin*, 2004; *Cold Hit*, 2005; *White Sister*, 2006

NONSERIES NOVELS: *The Plan*, 1996; *Final Victim*, 1997; *King Con*, 1997; *Riding the Snake*, 1998; *The Devil's Workshop*, 1999; *Runaway Heart*, 2003; *No Chance* (with Janet Evanovich), 2007

OTHER MAJOR WORKS

SCREENPLAYS: *The Gypsy Warriors*, 1978; *Dead Above Ground*, 2002

TELEPLAYS: *Columbo: Double Exposure*, 1973; *Scott Free*, 1976; *Richie Brockelman: The Missing Twenty-Four Hours*, 1976; *The November Plan*, 1976; *The Jordan Chance*, 1978; *Dr. Scorpion*, 1978; *The Gypsy Warriors*, 1978; *The Chinese Typewriter*, 1979; *Stone*, 1979; *The Night Rider*, 1979; *Nightside*, 1980; *Brothers-in-Law*, 1985; *Thunderboat*, 1989; *The Great Pretender*, 1991; *Greyhounds*, 1994; *The Rockford Files: A Blessing in Disguise*, 1995; *The Rockford Files: Godfather Knows Best*, 1996; *The Rockford Files: Friends and Foul Play*, 1996; *Hunter: Return to Justice*, 2002; *Hunter: Back in Force*, 2003; *It Waits*, 2005; *The Tooth Fairy*, 2006

BIBLIOGRAPHY

Cannell, Stephen J. "Archive of American Television Interview with Stephen J. Cannell." Interview by Stephen J. Abramson. http://video.google.com. Academy of Television Arts & Sciences Foundation, 2004. A nine-part, four-and-a-half-hour series of videotaped interviews covering Cannell's life and career from his childhood to June, 2004; includes Cannell's comments on the art of fiction writing.

Edelstein, Robert. "Stephen J. Cannell." *Broadcasting and Cable* 137, no. 3 (January 15, 2003): A8. A profile of Cannell that concentrates on his career in television although it discusses his move to writing. Praises his ability to create memorable and unusual characters and to write rapidly and well.

Keller, Julia. "A Novel Idea: Former Television Giant Stephen Cannell Chooses Writing Books over Hollywood." *Knight Ridder Tribune News Services*, September 28, 2005, p. 1. This profile of Cannell done on his release of *Cold Hit* (2005) examines his decision to turn to novel writing not for the money but for his love of writing. He speaks of his dyslexia and a college professor who motivated him.

Marc, David, and Robert J. Thompson. *Prime Time, Prime Movers: From "I Love Lucy" to "L.A. Law"—America's Greatest TV Shows and the People Who Created Them.* Syracuse, N.Y.: Syracuse University Press, 1995. Discusses television comedy shows and dramas and the people who made them; includes a chapter on Roy Huggins, who was Cannell's mentor, and Cannell himself. Although it focuses on Cannell as a television writer, it sheds light on his work as a novelist.

Pickett, Debra. "Sunday Lunch with . . . Stephen J. Cannell." *Chicago Sun-Times*, September 17, 2006, p. A20. Profile and interview with Cannell looks at his success and his values, which he says were influenced by his being born into wealth, the death of his fifteen-year-old son, his dyslexia, and his father's death.

Thompson, Robert J. *Adventures on Prime Time: The Television Programs of Stephen J. Cannell.* New York: Praeger, 1990. Sees Cannell as the epitome of the television "auteur" and surveys his television career and his works up to the success of *Wiseguy* (1987-1990). Helps readers understand Cannell's background.

HARRY CARMICHAEL
Leopold Horace Ognall

Born: Montreal, Quebec, Canada; June 20, 1908
Died: Leeds, England; April 12, 1979
Also wrote as Hartley Howard
Types of plot: Amateur sleuth; thriller; espionage

PRINCIPAL SERIES

    Glenn Bowman, 1951-1979
    Piper and Quinn, 1952-1978
    Philip Scott, 1964-1967

PRINCIPAL SERIES CHARACTERS

GLENN BOWMAN is the English equivalent of the American hard-boiled detective. The Bowman thrillers involve violence, sex, and intricate plotting.

JOHN PIPER is an insurance assessor, QUINN a crime reporter; their professions personally involve them in the crimes they investigate. Piper is the major or sole investigator in more of the novels, though Quinn dominates some of the books, especially those published in the 1970's. Generally, the two work together, the cynical humorist Quinn contrasting with the outwardly stable and competent Piper.

PHILIP SCOTT is a fringe member of a British espionage group. The two Scott books involve the same sort of intricate plotting, sex, and violence found in the Bowman series.

CONTRIBUTION

Harry Carmichael's thirty-odd novels featuring John Piper and his friend Quinn have been consistently underrated, although several authorities have pointed to the excellence of the series. Most impressive is the atmosphere of the books, seedy and grim though not depressing or despairing. Piper mourns his late wife, Ann, but he remarries in the course of the series; his essential aloneness and that of his generally hungover friend Quinn, who never marries, function as the psychological reality in which sordid criminal greed occurs. The plots are all puzzle mysteries, although the crimes are not of the impossible variety and the clues are all given fairly. In these and other re-

spects, the series maintains its quality from beginning to end.

BIOGRAPHY

Harry Carmichael was born Leopold Horace Ognall in Montreal, Canada, on June 20, 1908. Educated in Scotland, he worked in his father's business and then for various newspapers as reporter and editor, an important source of authoritativeness for his mysteries featuring the reporter Quinn. He also spent four years as an efficiency expert—the British say "engineer"—for the government; most of his life, however, was spent as a full-time freelance writer. Carmichael loved writing and said that he could not imagine a better way to live. Married in 1932, he had three children, two sons and one daughter, by his wife, Cecelia. One of his books, *Department K* (1964), was made into a film, *Assignment K* (1968), featuring Michael Redgrave. Carmichael continued to write up to his death on April 12, 1979, in Leeds.

ANALYSIS

The more than three dozen novels by Harry Carmichael featuring the insurance assessor John Piper and the reporter Quinn (his first name is not used) are most significant for plots that generally keep the basic events hidden from the reader, who is misled (along with the police) by the wiles of the criminals.

MURDER BY PROXY

The characteristic elements of a Carmichael plot appear in one of the best of the series, *Murder by Proxy* (1967), in which Piper meets his second wife, Jane Heywood, and falls in love at first sight. In this novel, Richard Armstrong, sentenced to jail for over a year for fraud involving the theft of more than twenty-five thousand pounds, escapes from the police surveillance initiated after he has served his sentence. The novel deals extensively with Armstrong until near the end, when he dies in a fire, but the main criminal is his partner, who has coerced Armstrong's wife into framing Armstrong. This plot has the wife and partner arranging an insurance fraud with Armstrong as the goat. The reader is brilliantly misdirected; even the money Armstrong is convicted of taking has never been taken.

Aspects of this plot are typical of the series. Armstrong is the victim and is eventually murdered, but he deludes himself (and the reader) that he is cheating, indeed ruining his partner. This complicity of the victim, who is at least as criminal or morally corrupt as the murderer, is Carmichael's favorite pattern. It occurs in *False Evidence* (1976), with the self-righteous and vicious reaction of Dr. Ainsworth to his wife's seducer, as well as in *Stranglehold* (1959), in which the victim has been plotting to kill the murderer. Again and again, the reader is misled. In *Death Counts Three* (1954), a mystery solved by Piper without Quinn, Walter Parr, who presumably runs off with his employer's money, has been murdered and buried by his employer. Such ironic reversals keep the mysteries sufficiently involved so that the murderer's identity is well hidden—even in the novels of the 1970's, books in which Carmichael limits the field of suspects.

This reversal of the "truth" of the action is central to the mystery and detective genre, as the title of a work of criticism on mystery stories indicates: *What Will Have Happened: A Philosophical and Technical Essay on Mystery Stories* (1977), by Robert Champigny, analyzes what many critics have noted about such stories. Once the mystery is solved, past actions must be reinterpreted, sometimes necessitating long explanations by the detective, as in the Dr. Thorndyke series by R. Austin Freeman, where the concluding explanations are long and technical. The Carmichael stories, however, emphasize the "false" plot to an extraordinary degree, while arranging the endings in a way that makes long explanations unnecessary. The earlier stories often include a final meeting between criminal and detective in which the truth is revealed. Thus in the Piper story *Justice Enough* (1956), the truth comes out in the concluding visit by Piper to the hospital room of Mrs. Eastwood, who with her lover had planned the murder of her husband. As she had been almost killed herself in the disposal of the body, she appears to be a victim, not the instigator of the crime. The chapter gives a detailed explanation, although the dramatic nature of the scene makes it effective enough.

NAKED TO THE GRAVE

More typical of Carmichael's endings, especially in the later stories, is the lack of virtually any explanation, the story being laid out so clearly that the reader can apprehend the real situation. For example, *Naked to the Grave* (1972) has an entirely simple crime: A gardener, hearing of a woman's gambling winnings, kills her for them and later kills a gossip who knows too much. This simple tale is covered by a complex story of marital infidelity and greed that has nothing to do with the crime. The final confrontation between Piper and Quinn—this case is more Piper's—and the murderer is brief and sordidly pathetic. No explanation beyond a few simple facts is needed.

This superiority in constructing the mystery plot is combined with strong psychological portraits of Quinn and Piper, the police, and the suspects. In his famous preface to *The Second Shot* (1930), Anthony Berkeley predicted that psychological clues would become more important than clues of motive and opportunity. Although the Carmichael stories do deal with motive and opportunity, they all emphasize character psychology. All the major actors are analyzed in detail, not the least being Piper and Quinn themselves as a contrasting pair, though not in the Holmes-Watson mold. Each does appear alone, Quinn in a couple of stories, Piper in five. A good example of Quinn working by himself is *Requiem for Charles* (1960), a barroom mystery with a bartender as murderer and with the amusing Detective-Superintendent Mullett, who has a penchant for quoting William Shakespeare and William Congreve. The works in which Piper is featured tend to have strong thriller elements, as in the intricately plotted *Justice Enough*, which has Piper traveling around England and Spain, frequently encountering physical danger. In fact, recurrent physical involvement or danger is standard in the series, emphasized most strongly in the novels of the 1950's and 1960's. In *Stranglehold*, Quinn is in an automobile accident and is suspected of slaying his driver. The same book has Piper almost murdered in a car attack. In *Vendetta* (1963), mainly Piper's case, Piper saves Quinn from a fiery death. In *Put Out That Star* (1957), one of the few stories to show Quinn on the verge of marriage, Quinn and Piper save each other's lives.

Despite the physicality of some of the cases, however, the novels depend on thought and character. Piper is the dignified member of the pair. His first wife, Ann, died in an automobile accident while Piper was driving. His sad, guilty memory of her, the experience of his life without her, are brought up throughout the series, even after his second marriage. This successful, competent, action-oriented man of the world, handsome, well built, beautifully dressed, is always alone, plagued by his thoughts and feelings. Quinn, with his mocking, alcoholic, smoke-fogged view of the world, with his slight build and careless dress, suffers too. Yet Quinn has his strengths, and his writings on crime command the respect even of the police.

Although they differ so much, Quinn and Piper work in basically the same way. They interview suspects and then think again and again about what they have been told. This reporting of the sleuths' thoughts is characteristic of the stories. Seemingly innocent conversations are remembered, repeated, analyzed, until they are reinterpreted. In *Death Counts Three*, a scream at the beginning is repeated through the book in Piper's thoughts until it is tied in with a dying scream from the murderer, with whom Piper has fallen in love. In *Put Out That Star*, a few drops of blood on a suitcase are mulled over frequently, and in Naked to the Grave, Piper keeps rehearsing the sounds of a husband opening a door, about to find his murdered wife. These repeated analyses of one event or clue, almost cinematographic, recall Agatha Christie's repeated use of a scene in some of her later books. As with Christie, understanding the scene leads to the solving of the puzzle, though the scene in *Naked to the Grave* does not: It functions, instead, as a red herring.

OF UNSOUND MIND AND TOO LATE FOR TEARS

The motives in the series are generally simple: sex and money. Rarely are more exotic motives found, though *Of Unsound Mind* (1962) has Piper and Quinn analyzing a series of seven apparently unconnected deaths, all labeled suicides by the coroner. This novel begins with Quinn, like Mr. Pinkerton in David Frome's *Mr. Pinkerton Goes to Scotland Yard* (1934), betting that Scotland Yard never hears of many murders. Like Mr. Pinkerton, Quinn goes investigating and proves his point. Most of the tales, however, involve simple plots based on love triangles and financial greed. *Too Late for Tears* (1973) is based on a husband avenging a wife who had been seduced years before. The murderer is far more sympathetic than the victim; indeed, the second murder in this story seems to have little purpose except to give an adequate reason to have the murderer caught and sentenced without offending the readers' sense of justice, a criticism that could be made also of *The Motive* (1974) and *False Evidence*.

The Piper and Quinn series is one of the best in detective fiction for plot and character. The atmosphere may seem grim to many, although the sordidness is not necessarily depressing. Indeed, much in the series is lightened by a comic spirit, especially Quinn's exchanges with his solicitous landlady, Mrs. Buchanan, a woman with a thick Scottish accent that Quinn mimics with absurd effects, and Quinn's frequent bar and hangover scenes. The police, too, are sometimes comic; most often mentioned is Inspector—later Superintendent—Hoyle of Scotland Yard, sarcastic toward but trusting of Piper and Quinn. In fact, Carmichael created a succession of well-realized police personalities of various pleasant and unpleasant types, from the literary Superintendent Mullett to Inspector Byram, who suspects Quinn of murder in *Remote Control* (1970). The police, though portrayed as "straight" characters, nevertheless tend to add to the comic effects of the stories and so lighten Carmichael's cynical depictions of betrayal and greed.

Stephen J. Curry

PRINCIPAL MYSTERY AND DETECTIVE FICTION

GLENN BOWMAN SERIES (AS HOWARD): 1951-1960 • *The Last Appointment*, 1951; *The Last Deception*, 1951; *Death of Cecilia*, 1952; *The Last Vanity*, 1952; *Bowman Strikes Again*, 1953; *The Other Side of the Door*, 1953; *Bowman at a Venture*, 1954; *Bowman on Broadway*, 1954; *No Target for Bowman*, 1955; *Sleep for the Wicked*, 1955; *A Hearse for Cinderella*, 1956; *The Bowman Touch*, 1956; *Key to the Morgue*, 1957; *The Long Night*, 1957; *Sleep, My Pretty One*, 1958; *The Big Snatch*, 1958; *Deadline*, 1959; *The Armitage Secret*, 1959; *Extortion*, 1960; *Fall Guy*, 1960

1961-1970 • *I'm No Hero*, 1961; *Time Bomb*, 1961; *Count Down*, 1962; *Portrait of a Beautiful Harlot*, 1966; *Routine Investigation*, 1967; *The Secret of Simon Cornell*, 1969; *Cry on My Shoulder*, 1970; *Room Thirty-seven*, 1970

1971-1979 • *Million Dollar Snapshot*, 1971; *Murder One*, 1971; *Epitaph for Joanna*, 1972; *Nice Day for a Funeral*, 1972; *Highway to Murder*, 1973; *Dead Drunk*, 1974; *Treble Cross*, 1975; *Payoff*, 1976; *One-Way Ticket*, 1978; *The Sealed Envelope*, 1979

PIPER AND QUINN SERIES: 1952-1960 • *Death Leaves a Diary*, 1952; *The Vanishing Track*, 1952; *Deadly Night-Cap*, 1953; *School for Murder*, 1953; *Death Counts Three*, 1954 (also known as *The Screaming Rabbit*); *Why Kill Johnny?*, 1954; *Money for Murder*, 1955; *Noose for a Lady*, 1955; *Justice Enough*, 1956; *The Dead of the Night*, 1956; *Emergency Exit*, 1957; *Put Out That Star*, 1957 (also known as *Into Thin Air*); *. . . Or Be He Dead*, 1958; *James Knowland, Deceased*, 1958; *Stranglehold*, 1959 (also known as *Marked Man*); *The Seeds of Hate*, 1959; *Requiem for Charles*, 1960 (also known as *The Late Unlamented*)

1961-1970 • *Alibi*, 1961; *Of Unsound Mind*, 1962; *The Link*, 1962; *Vendetta*, 1963; *Flashback*, 1964; *Safe Secret*, 1964; *Post Mortem*, 1965; *Suicide Clause*, 1966; *Murder by Proxy*, 1967; *A Slightly Bitter Taste*, 1968; *Death Trap*, 1970; *Remote Control*, 1970

1971-1978 • *Most Deadly Hate*, 1971; *The Quiet Woman*, 1971; *Naked to the Grave*, 1972; *Candles for the Dead*, 1973; *Too Late for Tears*, 1973; *The Motive*, 1974; *False Evidence*, 1976; *A Grave for Two*, 1977; *Life Cycle*, 1978

PHILIP SCOTT SERIES (AS HOWARD): *Department K*, 1964 (also known as *Assignment K*); *The Eye of the Hurricane*, 1968

NONSERIES NOVELS: *A Question of Time*, 1958; *Confession*, 1961; *Double Finesse*, 1962 (as Howard); *The Stretton Case*, 1963 (as Howard); *Out of the Fire*, 1965 (as Howard); *Counterfeit*, 1966 (as Howard); *The Condemned*, 1967

BIBLIOGRAPHY

Callendar, Newgate. Review of *Remote Control*, by Harry Carmichael. *The New York Times Book Review* 76 (April 11, 1971): 18. Callendar's review emphasizes the work's place within British and American detective fiction.

Chernaik, Warren. "Mean Streets and English Gardens." In *The Art of Detective Fiction*, edited by Warren Chernaik, Martin Swales, and Robert Vilain. New York: St. Martin's Press, 2000. Chernaik's contrast of America's mean streets and genteel English gardens helps contextualize the distinctive nature of Carmichael's seedy English settings.

Moore, Lewis D. *Cracking the Hard-Boiled Detective: A Critical History from the 1920's to the Present.* Jefferson, N.C.: McFarland, 2006. Detailed study of both the American and the British versions of the hard-boiled detective. Bibliographic references and index. Provides context for understanding Carmichael's work.

Scaggs, John. *Crime Fiction.* New York: Routledge, 2005. Contains an essay on hard-boiled fiction that sheds light on Carmichael's novels.

JOHN DICKSON CARR

Born: Uniontown, Pennsylvania; November 30, 1906
Died: Greenville, South Carolina; February 27, 1977
Also wrote as Carr Dickson; Carter Dickson; Roger Fairbairn
Types of plot: Amateur sleuth; historical; cozy

PRINCIPAL SERIES

Henri Bencolin, 1930-1938
Dr. Gideon Fell, 1933-1967
Sir Henry Merrivale, 1934-1953
History of London Police, 1957-1961
New Orleans, 1968-1971

PRINCIPAL SERIES CHARACTERS

HENRI BENCOLIN, *juge d'instruction* of Paris, is a slender, elegantly dressed aristocrat, with a face that reminds suspects of Mephistopheles. There is an undercurrent of cruelty in Bencolin's makeup, and he frequently treats suspects with contempt. His interest in crime is solely in the puzzle.

JEFF MARLE, a young American living in Paris, whose father knew Bencolin in college, recounts the cases. Marle also narrates *Poison in Jest* (1932), in which Bencolin does not appear.

DR. GIDEON FELL is the opposite of Bencolin. He weighs nearly three hundred pounds and reminds suspects not of Satan but of Father Christmas. A historian, he has a wool-gathering mind and is interested in many types of obscure knowledge. He is warmhearted and genial and solves crimes to help those entangled in suspicion.

CHIEF INSPECTOR DAVID HADLEY of Scotland Yard, one of the more intelligent police officers in fiction, often works with Fell but who does not always follow Fell's leaps of imagination.

SIR HENRY MERRIVALE, a qualified barrister and physician, has a childish temper and a scowling appearance, as though he has smelled a bad egg. Like Fell, however, he is interested in helping those caught up in "the blinkin' awful cussedness of things in general."

INSPECTOR HUMPHREY MASTERS, who brushes his grizzled hair to hide his bald spot, works with Sir Henry but complains that he is always involved in cases that are seemingly impossible.

CONTRIBUTION

John Dickson Carr insisted that fair-play clueing is a necessary part of good detective fiction. Each of his books and short stories was constructed as a challenge to the reader, with all clues given to the reader at the same time as the detective. Within this framework, however, Carr was an innovator, combining mystery and detection with true-crime reconstruction, slapstick comedy, historical novels, and fantasy. Carr is best known, however, for his mastery of the locked-room murder and related forms of miracle crimes. In his books, victims are found within hermetically sealed rooms which were—so it seems—impossible for the murderers to enter or leave. Murders are also committed in buildings surrounded by unmarked snow or sand, and people do things such as enter a guarded room or dive into a swimming pool and completely vanish. Thus Carr's stories are constructed around two puzzles for the detective (and the reader) to solve— whodunit and "howdunit."

BIOGRAPHY

John Dickson Carr was born on November 30, 1906, in Uniontown, Pennsylvania, the son of Julia Carr and Wooda Nicolas Carr. His father, a lawyer and politician, served in Congress from 1913 to 1915. After four years at the Hill School in Pottstown, Pennsylvania, John Carr attended Haverford College and became editor of the student literary magazine, *The Haverfordian*. In 1928, he went to France to study at the Sorbonne, but he preferred writing and completed his first books, a historical novel that he destroyed, and *Grand Guignol*, a Bencolin novella that was soon published in *The Haverfordian*. Expanded, it became *It Walks by Night*, published by Harper and Brothers in 1930.

In 1932, Carr married an Englishwoman, Clarice

John Dickson Carr. (Library of Congress)

Cleaves, moved to Great Britain, and for about a decade wrote an average of four novels a year. To handle his prolific output, he began to write books under the nonsecret pseudonym of Carter Dickson. In 1939, Carr found another outlet for his work—the radio. He wrote scripts for the British Broadcasting Corporation (BBC), and after the United States government ordered him home in 1941 to register for military service, he wrote radio dramas for the Columbia Broadcasting System (CBS) program *Suspense*. Ironically, the government then sent him back to Great Britain, and for the rest of the war he was on the staff of the BBC, writing propaganda pieces and mystery dramas. After the war, Carr worked with Arthur Conan Doyle's estate to produce the first authorized biography of Sherlock Holmes's creator.

A lifelong conservative, Carr disliked the postwar Labour government, and in 1948 he moved to Mamaroneck, New York. In 1951, the Tories won the election, and Carr returned to Great Britain. Except for some time spent in Tangiers working with Adrian Doyle on a series of pastiches of Sherlock Holmes,

Carr alternated between Great Britain and Mamaroneck for the next thirteen years before moving to Greenville, South Carolina. Suffering from increasing illness, Carr ceased writing novels after 1972, but he contributed a review column to *Ellery Queen's Mystery Magazine* and was recognized as a Grand Master by the Mystery Writers of America in 1963. He died on February 27, 1977, in Greenville.

ANALYSIS

John Dickson Carr occupies an important place in the history of detective fiction, primarily because of his plot dexterity and his sense of atmosphere. No other author juggled clues, motives, and suspects with more agility, and none rang more changes on the theme of murder-in-a-locked-room and made it part of a feeling of neogothic terror.

IT WALKS BY NIGHT

His first novel, *It Walks by Night*, featuring Henri Bencolin, begins with a long statement about "a misshapen beast with blood-bedabbled claws" that prowls about Paris by night. The crime—beheading in a room all of whose entrances are watched—seems to have been committed by supernatural means. At the conclusion, however, Bencolin demonstrates that all that was necessary was a human murderer with human methods—and much clever misdirection by the author. *It Walks by Night* is a well-constructed book, but the atmosphere in it and in the next three Bencolin novels is synthetic. The mystery writer Joseph Hansen much later called *It Walks by Night* "all fustian and murk," an overstatement but accurate in that the mood sometimes gets in the way of the story.

FROM BENCOLIN TO FELL AND MERRIVALE

Except for a reappearance in 1937 in *The Four False Weapons*, which lacks the oppressive mood of the earlier books, Bencolin disappeared from Carr's books, and Carr turned to two new detectives, Dr. Gideon Fell in 1933 and Sir Henry Merrivale in 1934 (books about the latter were published under the pseudonym Carter Dickson). On the publication of the second Fell book, *The Mad Hatter Mystery* (1933), Dorothy L. Sayers wrote a review indicating that Carr had learned how to present mood and place: "He can create atmosphere with an adjective, and make a picture from a wet iron railing, a dusty table, a gas-lamp blurred by fog. He can alarm with an allusion or delight with a rollicking absurdity—in short, he can write . . . in the sense that every sentence gives a thrill of positive pleasure."

FAIR-PLAY TRICKS

Carr's books and short stories were strongly influenced by the writings of G. K. Chesterton, creator of Father Brown. He based the character and appearance of Fell on Chesterton, and like Chesterton, he loved the crazy-quilt patterns created by the incongruous. Carr wrote novels involved with such things as a street that no one can find, a bishop sliding down a banister, clock parts found in a victim's pocket, and unused weapons scattered about the scene of the crime. Also like Chesterton, Carr was uninterested in physical clues. There is no dashing about with a magnifying glass—Fell and Merrivale are too large to bend over a clue in Holmesian fashion—or the fine analysis of fingerprints, bullets, and bloodstains. Instead, the detective solves the crime by investigating less material indicators, clues based on gesture and mood, of things said and things left unsaid, which lead to understanding the pattern of the crime.

Carr's lack of interest in material clues was matched by his lack of interest in genuine police investigation. Many of the fair-play novelists of the Golden Age (the 1920's and the 1930's) allow the reader to follow the investigation of the detective, whether he is a gifted amateur such as Lord Peter Wimsey or a police detective such as Inspector French. In Carr's first book, the reader does follow the Sûreté's investigations, but two of Bencolin's later cases are placed outside France so that the detective will not have access to police laboratories. By the 1940's, Carr rarely emphasized detection per se in his books. The viewpoint character does not often participate with the amateur detective or the police in their investigations; he is instead overwhelmed by the mystery and the danger that the crime seems to pose to himself or to someone he loves.

Carr's emphasis was always fundamentally on the fair-play solution, not on detection. In his essay "The Grandest Game in the World," he defined the detective story not as a tale of investigation but as

a conflict between criminal and detective in which the criminal, by means of some ingenious device—alibi, novel murder method, or what you like—remains unconvicted or even unsuspected until the detective reveals his identity by means of evidence that has also been conveyed to the reader.

In some of Carr's later novels, especially *In Spite of Thunder* (1960) and *The Witch of the Low-Tide: An Edwardian Melodrama* (1961), the detective knows whodunit long before the conclusion of the story, but he does not reveal what is happening, for he is playing a cat-and-mouse game with the murderer. The reader, consequently, is trying to discover not only the solution to the crime but also why the detective is acting and speaking in a cryptic manner.

SIR HENRY MERRIVALE SERIES

The emphasis on fair-play trickery helps to understand the structure of the Sir Henry Merrivale novels. The first Merrivale novel, *The Plague Court Murders* (1934), is almost as atmospheric as the early Bencolin stories, as Carr makes the reader believe that a seventeenth century hangman's assistant has returned from the dead to commit murder. As the series developed, however, Carr increasingly made H. M. (as his friends call him) a comic character. Merrivale refers to members of the government as "Horseface," "Old Boko," and "Squiffy," and he addresses a jury as "my fatheads." His cases begin with Merrivale dictating scurrilous memoirs, learning how to play golf, taking singing lessons, chasing a runaway suitcase, or, in a memorable short story, stepping on a banana peel and falling flat on his behind. Carr always had a fondness for the Marx Brothers and other slapstick comedians, but his main reason for using comedy in his Merrivale novels is that "once we think an author is only skylarking, a whole bandwagon of clues can go past unnoticed."

The clues, whether interpreted by Bencolin, Fell, or Merrivale, usually lead to the solution of a locked-room murder or a seemingly impossible disappearance or some other variety of miracle crime. The locked-room murder has a long history, going back even before Edgar Allan Poe used it in the first detective story, "The Murders in the Rue Morgue." Before Carr, Chesterton was the greatest exponent of the miracle problem, writing more than twenty-five stories about impossible disappearances, murders seemingly caused by winged daggers, and the like. Carr came to love tricks and impossibilities by reading Chesterton, and he invented about one hundred methods for explaining the apparently impossible. In *The Three Coffins* (1935), Carr interrupts the story to allow Fell to deliver a locked-room lecture, discussing all the methods previously used to get a murderer into and out of a room whose doors and windows are securely locked.

Carr often ties the impossible crime to the past. From early books such as *The Red Widow Murders* (1935) to late ones including *Deadly Hall* (1971), Carr has ancient crimes repeated in the present. Carr was a historian manqué; he believed that "to write good history is the noblest work of man," and he saw in houses and artifacts and old families a continuation of the past in the present. This love of history adds texture to his novels. His books make heavy use of such props as old castles, ancient watches, cavalier's cups, occult cards, and Napoleonic snuffboxes. In addition, the concept that the past influences the present suggests that a malevolent influence is creating the impossible crimes, and this in turn allows Carr to hint at the supernatural.

Most of Carr's mystery-writing contemporaries were content to have the crime disturb the social order, and at the conclusion to have faith in the rightness of society restored by the apprehension and punishment of the criminal. Carr, however, had the crime shake one's faith in a rational universe. By quoting from seemingly ancient manuscripts and legends about witches and vampires, Carr implies that only someone in league with Satan could have committed the crime. Except for one book (*The Burning Court*, 1937) and a few short stories ("New Murders for Old," "The Door to Doom," and "The Man Who Was Dead"), however, Carr's solutions never use the supernatural. Even when he retold Poe's story "The Tell-Tale Heart" as a radio play, he found a solution to the beating of the heart that involved neither the supernatural nor the guilty conscience of the protagonist. If the comparison is not pushed too far, Carr's detectives act as exorcists. Bencolin, Fell, and Merrivale arrive on the scene and banish the demons as they show that the apparently impossible actually has a rational explanation.

Carr's interest in history was connected with the fact that he was never comfortable in his own age. A friend from his college days described Carr as a neo-romantic, and his writings in *The Haverfordian* show a strong interest in historical romance. At the same time, he wrote an adventure story that combined elements from E. Phillips Oppenheim and the Ruritanian-Graustarkian novels of Anthony Hope and George Barr McCutcheon. Carr believed that the world should be a place where high adventure is possible. One of the characters in an early Carr novel, *The Bowstring Murders* (1933), hopes to find adventures in "the grand manner," with Oppenheimian heroines sneaking into his railway carriage and whispering cryptic passwords. Many of Carr's novels written during the 1930's feature young men who travel to France or England to escape from the brash, materialistic world of America. Shortly after he moved to England, he wrote:

> There is something spectral about the deep and drowsy beauty of the English countryside; in the lush dark grass, the evergreens, the grey church-spire and the meandering white road. To an American, who remembers his own brisk concrete highways clogged with red filling-stations and the fumes of traffic, it is particularly pleasant. . . . The English earth seems (incredibly) even older than its ivy-bearded towers. The bells at twilight seem to be bells across the centuries; there is a great stillness, through which ghosts step, and Robin Hood has not strayed from it even yet.

In 1934, Carr published *Devil Kinsmere* under the pseudonym of Roger Fairbairn. Although the book has some mystery in it, it is primarily a historical adventure story set in the reign of Charles II. Two years later, Carr wrote *The Murder of Sir Edmund Godfrey* (1936), which treats a genuine murder of 1678 as a fair-play detective story, complete with clues, suspects, and a totally unsuspected murderer. Neither of these books sold well, and for some years Carr did not attempt historical reconstruction except in some radio scripts he wrote for the BBC in London and for CBS in New York. Notable among these is a six-part Regency drama, "Speak of the Devil," about the ghostly manifestations of a woman who had been hanged for murder. As in his novels, Carr produced a rational explanation for the supernatural.

Following the conclusion of World War II, however, two things encouraged Carr to try his hand at historical detective novels. First, the election of a Labour government in Great Britain, and the continued rationing increased Carr's dislike of the twentieth century. Second, the success of his *The Life of Sir Arthur Conan Doyle* (1949) gave him what is now called "name recognition" to the extent that he believed that he could take a chance with a new type of novel.

THE DEVIL IN VELVET

Carr's gamble paid off, for *The Bride of Newgate*, a Regency novel published in 1950, sold very well, and its successor, *The Devil in Velvet* (1951), did even better. In the latter, Carr stretched the genre of the classic detective story to its limits, for it involved elements of fantasy. The hero, a middle-aged college professor of the twentieth century, longs to return to Restoration England, so he sells his soul to Satan and occupies the body of a dissolute cavalier. His goal is to prevent a murder and, when he fails to do so, to solve it. Though the solution is well clued, it breaks several rules of the fair-play detective story. The book was in large part wish-fulfillment for Carr, however, who, like the hero, wanted to escape his own era. In two later novels, *Fire, Burn!* (1957) and *Fear Is the Same* (1956), time travel also connects the twentieth century to ages that Carr preferred.

Between 1950 and 1972, Carr concentrated on detective novels in a period setting, with an occasional Fell novel tossed in. Six of his historical novels fit into two series, one about the history of Scotland Yard, the other about New Orleans at various times. His final novels, especially *Deadly Hall* and *The Hungry Goblin: A Victorian Detective Novel* (1972), show a decline in readability, probably a result of Carr's increasing ill health. They lack the enthusiasm of his previous books, and the characters make set speeches rather than doing anything. Even his final books are cleverly plotted, however, with new locked-room and impossible-crime methods. At his death in 1977, with almost eighty books to his credit, he had shown that with ingenuity and atmosphere, the fair-play detective story was one of the most entertaining forms of popular literature.

Douglas G. Greene

PRINCIPAL MYSTERY AND DETECTIVE FICTION

HENRI BENCOLIN SERIES: *It Walks by Night*, 1930; *The Lost Gallows*, 1931; *Castle Skull*, 1931; *The Corpse in the Waxworks*, 1932 (also known as *The Waxworks Murder*); *The Four False Weapons*, 1937; *The Door to Doom, and Other Detections*, 1980

GIDEON FELL SERIES: *Hag's Nook*, 1933; *The Mad Hatter Mystery*, 1933; *The Eight of Swords*, 1934; *The Blind Barber*, 1934; *Death-Watch*, 1935; *The Three Coffins*, 1935 (also known as *The Hollow Man*); *The Arabian Nights Murder*, 1936; *To Wake the Dead*, 1938; *The Crooked Hinge*, 1938; *The Problem of the Green Capsule*, 1939 (also known as *The Black Spectacles*); *The Problem of the Wire Cage*, 1939; *The Man Who Could Not Shudder*, 1940; *The Case of the Constant Suicides*, 1941; *Death Turns the Tables*, 1941 (also known as *The Seat of the Scornful*); *Till Death Do Us Part*, 1944; *He Who Whispers*, 1946; *The Sleeping Sphinx*, 1947; *Dr. Fell, Detective, and Other Stories*, 1947; *Below Suspicion*, 1949; *The Third Bullet, and Other Stories*, 1954; *The Dead Man's Knock*, 1958; *In Spite of Thunder*, 1960; *The House at Satan's Elbow*, 1965; *Panic in Box C*, 1966; *Dark of the Moon*, 1967; *The Dead Sleep Lightly*, 1983

SIR HENRY MERRIVALE SERIES (AS CARTER DICKSON): *The Plague Court Murders*, 1934; *The White Priory Murders*, 1934; *The Red Widow Murders*, 1935; *The Unicorn Murders*, 1935; *The Magic-lantern Murders*, 1936 (also known as *The Punch and Judy Murders*); *The Peacock Feather Murders*, 1937 (also known as *The Ten Teacups*); *The Judas Window*, 1938 (also known as *The Crossbow Murder*); *Death in Five Boxes*, 1938; *The Reader Is Warned*, 1939; *And So to Murder*, 1940; *Nine—and Death Makes Ten*, 1940 (also known as *Murder in the Submarine Zone* and *Murder in the Atlantic*); *Seeing Is Believing*, 1941 (also known as *Cross of Murder*); *The Gilded Man*, 1942 (also known as *Death and the Gilded Man*); *She Died a Lady*, 1943; *He Wouldn't Kill Patience*, 1944; *The Curse of the Bronze Lamp*, 1945 (also known as *Lord of the Sorcerers*); *My Late Wives*, 1946; *The Skeleton in the Clock*, 1948; *A Graveyard to Let*, 1949; *Night at the Mocking Widow*, 1950; *Behind the Crimson Blind*, 1952; *The Cavalier's Cup*, 1953; *The Men Who Explained Miracles*, 1963

HISTORY OF LONDON POLICE SERIES: *Fire, Burn!*, 1957; *Scandal at High Chimneys: A Victorian Melodrama*, 1959; *The Witch of the Low-Tide: An Edwardian Melodrama*, 1961

NEW ORLEANS SERIES: *Papa Là-Bas*, 1968; *The Ghosts' High Noon*, 1969; *Deadly Hall*, 1971

NONSERIES NOVELS: *Poison in Jest*, 1932; *The Bowstring Murders*, 1933 (first edition as Carr Dickson and subsequent editions as Carter Dickson); *Devil Kinsmere*, 1934 (as Fairbairn; revised as *Most Secret*, 1964); *The Burning Court*, 1937; *The Third Bullet*, 1937 (as Carter Dickson); *Fatal Descent*, 1939 (with John Rhode, pseudonym of Cecil John Charles Street, and as Carter Dickson; also known as *Drop to His Death*); *The Emperor's Snuff-Box*, 1942; *The Bride of Newgate*, 1950; *The Devil in Velvet*, 1951; *The Nine Wrong Answers*, 1952; *Captain Cut-Throat*, 1955; *Patrick Butler for the Defence*, 1956; *Fear Is the Same*, 1956; *The Demoniacs*, 1962; *The Hungry Goblin: A Victorian Detective Novel*, 1972; *Crime on the Coast*, 1984 (with others)

OTHER SHORT FICTION: *The Department of Queer Complaints*, 1940 (as Carter Dickson; also known as *Scotland Yard: Department of Queer Complaints*); *The Exploits of Sherlock Holmes*, 1954 (with Adrian Conan Doyle)

OTHER MAJOR WORKS

NOVELS: *Grand Guignol*, 1929

RADIO PLAYS: *The Bride Vanishes*, 1942; *The Devil in the Summerhouse*, 1942; *Will You Make a Bet with Death?*, 1942; *Cabin B-13*, 1943; *The Hangman Won't Wait*, 1943; *The Phantom Archer*, 1943; *Most Secret*, 1964

NONFICTION: *The Murder of Sir Edmund Godfrey*, 1936; *The Life of Sir Arthur Conan Doyle*, 1949; *The Grandest Game in the World: A Brilliant Critique*, 1963

EDITED TEXTS: *Maiden Murders*, 1952; *Great Stories*, 1959 (by Arthur Conan Doyle)

BIBLIOGRAPHY

Amis, Kingsley. "Unreal Detectives." In *What Became of Jane Austen? and Other Questions*. New York: Harcourt Brace Jovanovich, 1970. An appreciation of Carr (among others) by one of Britain's leading postwar writers. To Amis, Dr. Fell is one of only three worthy successors to Sherlock Holmes, and Carr's best novels are "minor masterpieces."

Greene, Douglas C. *John Dickson Carr: The Man Who Explained Miracles*. New York: Otto Penzler Books, 1995. Indispensable biography and full-length study of Carr's works, with an exhaustive bibliography. Greene's main thesis is that Carr's explanations of seemingly miraculous events reveal a fundamental belief in the rationality of the universe.

_____. "A Mastery of Miracles: G. K. Chesterton and John Dickson Carr." *Chesterton Review* 10 (August, 1984): 307-315. This article pays homage to Carr's work particularly as it relates to that of G. K. Chesterton. Greene concentrates on Carr's short fiction but includes some biographical information too. Notes on sources are given at the end of the article.

Joshi, S. T. *John Dickson Carr: A Critical Study*. Bowling Green, Ohio: Bowling Green State University Popular Press, 1990. Joshi's study complements that of Douglas C. Greene. Joshi finds Carr's thematic interest to be ethical: Carr's explanations show the pervasiveness of human evil. Valuable chapters on Carr's philosophy and theories of detective writing.

Malmgren, Carl D. *Anatomy of Murder: Mystery, Detective, and Crime Fiction*. Bowling Green, Ohio: Bowling Green States University Popular Press, 2001. Includes readings of four of Carr's novels. Bibliographic references and index.

Panek, LeRoy. *An Introduction to the Detective Story*. Bowling Green, Ohio: Bowling Green State University Popular Press, 1987. References to Carr's work—in particular, his short fiction—are scattered throughout this text. Good for setting Carr in the context of his time. An index and a list of reference works are given at the end, and a separate list of history and criticism texts is also included.

_____. "John Dickson Carr." In *Watteau's Shepherds: The Detective Novel in Britain, 1914-1940*. Bowling Green, Ohio: Bowling Green University Popular Press, 1979. Despite Carr's nationality, he is considered one of the finest British mystery writers. In his text, Panek devotes a detailed chapter to Carr, covering Carr's most famous detectives and works, including both long and short fiction. An appendix outlines the structure of the detective story. Supplemented by a chronology of Carr's works, notes on the Carr chapter, and an index.

Taylor, Robert Lewis. "Two Authors in an Attic, Part I." *The New Yorker* 27 (September 8, 1951): 39-44, 46, 48.

_____. "Two Authors in an Attic, Part II." *The New Yorker* 27 (September 15, 1951): 36-40, 42, 46, 48, 51. This pair of articles is extremely useful for detailed biographical information, as well as for Carr's own thoughts on his writing. Carr discusses with Taylor which writers influenced him most and goes into detail about his political and philosophical views. Invaluable for getting a personal look at Carr, despite its lack of references.

NICK CARTER

AUTHORS

NICK CARTER (DIME NOVELS AND PULPS)

? Andrews; A. L. Armagnac; ? Babcock; ? Ball; William Perry Brown (1847-1923); George Waldo Browne (1851-1930); Frederick Russell Burton (1861-1909); O. P. Caylor; Stephen Chalmers (1880-1935); Weldon J. Cobb; William Wallace Cook (1867-1933); John Russell Coryell (1851-1924); Frederick William Davis (1858-1933); William J. de Grouchy; E. C. Derby; Frederic M. Van Rensselaer Dey (1861-1922); ? Ferguson; Graham E. Forbes; W. Bert Foster (1869-1929); Thomas W. Hanshew (1857-1914); Charles Witherle Hooke (1861-1929); ? Howard; W. C. Hudson (1843-1915); George C. Jenks (1850-1929); W. L. or Joseph Larned; ? Lincoln; Charles Agnew MacLean (1880-1928); ? Makee; St. George Rathborne (1854-1938); ? Rich; ? Russell; Eugene T. Sawyer (1846-1924); Vincent E. Scott; Samuel C. Spalding; ? Splint; Edward Stratemeyer (1862-1930); Alfred B. Tozer; ? Tyson; R. F. Walsh; Charles Westbrook; ? Willard; Richard Wormser.

NICK CARTER (KILLMASTER)

Frank Adduci, Jr.; Jerry Ahern (1946-   ); Bruce Algozin; Michael Avallone (1924-1999); W. T. Ballard (1903-1980); Jim Bowser; Nicholas Browne; Jack Canon; Bruce Cassiday (1920-2005); Ansel Chapin; Robert Colby; DeWitt S. Copp; Bill Crider (1941-   ); Jack Davis; Ron Felber; James Fritzhand; Joseph L. Gilmore (1929-   ); Marilyn Granbeck (1927-   ); David Hagberg (1942-   );

Ralph Hayes (1927-   ); Al Hine (1915-1974); Richard Hubbard (d. c. 1974); H. Edward Hunsburger; Michael Jahn (1943-   ); Bob Latona; Leon Lazarus (1920-   ); Lew Louderback (1930-   ); Dennis Lynds (1924-2005); Douglas Marland; Arnold Marmor; Jon Messmann; Valerie Moolman; Homer Morris; Craig Nova; William C. Odell; Forrest V. Perrin; Larry Powell; Daniel C. Prince; Robert J. Randisi (1951-   ); Henry Rasof; Dan Reardon; William L. Rohde; Joseph Rosenberger; Steve Simmons; Martin Cruz Smith (1942-   ); George Snyder; Robert Derek Steeley; John Stevenson; Linda Stewart; Manning Lee Stokes; Bob Stokesberry; Dee Stuart; Dwight Vreeland Swain (1915-1992); Lawrence Van Gelder; Robert E. Vardeman (1947-   ); Jeffrey M. Wallmann (1941-   ); George Warren; Saul Wernick (1921-   ); Lionel White (1905-1985); Stephen Williamson.

Types of plot: Private investigator; hard-boiled; espionage

PRINCIPAL SERIES

Nick Carter (dime novels and pulps), 1886-1949
Nick Carter/Killmaster, 1964-1990

PRINCIPAL SERIES CHARACTER

NICK CARTER, as portrayed in the dime novels and pulp magazines of the late nineteenth and early twentieth centuries, is a private investigator of uncommon ability. Short (about five feet, four inches) and preter-

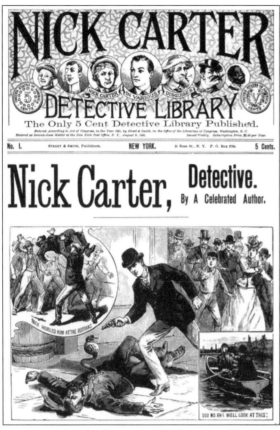

Cover of the first issue of the Nick Carter Detective Library, *which chronicled Nick Carter's adventures from 1891 until 1915.*

the title "The Old Detective's Pupil; Or, The Mysterious Crime of Madison Square," Nick Carter's career has spanned more than a century. In origin, Carter exemplified the American individualist with the superior intellect of a Sherlock Holmes. From the self-confident youngster to the mature head of his own detective agency, from the hard-boiled crime fighter to the oversexed spy, Nick Carter has changed with his times. No other character offers such an encompassing reflection of the beliefs and motives of the American public.

BIOGRAPHY

Nick Carter was delivered into this world by the hands of John Russell Coryell in 1886. Street and Smith published Coryell's first three installments of Nick Carter, and at a luncheon not long after, Carter's fate as a serial character was sealed. Ormond G. Smith, president of the Street and Smith firm, decided to award Frederic M. Van Rensselaer Dey the opportunity of continuing the Carter saga. Dey accepted in 1891 and for the next seventeen years produced a 25,000-word story a week for a new weekly to be called the *Nick Carter Detective Library*, beginning with *Nick Carter, Detective* (1891). After the first twenty installments of the *Nick Carter Library* had appeared, Carter was reinstated in the *New York Weekly*, which was primarily a family-oriented publication.

The publications containing Carter material changed names frequently. In 1897, the *Nick Carter Library* became the *Nick Carter Weekly* and then the *New Nick Carter Weekly*, and then again the *New Nick Carter Library*. Finally, in 1912 the title changed to *Nick Carter Stories*. Old installments began appearing under new titles, a fact that has created headaches for those wishing to compile bibliographies of Nick Carter material. In 1897, Street and Smith had begun the Magnet Library—a kind of grandfather to the modern paperback—and used Carter stories along with those featuring other detectives, including reprints of Sherlock Holmes tales.

The majority of these books were signed by "Nicholas Carter," and some stories that had featured Nick Carter, detective, in earlier publications were changed to incorporate other detective protagonists. The series

naturally strong, he is a master of disguise. He gradually took on more hard-boiled characteristics, in keeping with literary fashion. After a hiatus in the 1950's, Carter reappeared in the 1960's with a new identity: master spy. In this second incarnation he is sophisticated, possessed of enormous sexual magnetism, and like the first Nick Carter, physically powerful.

CONTRIBUTION

On the title page of many Street and Smith dime novels, Nick Carter is dubbed "the greatest sleuth of all time." The resourceful personage of Nick Carter, a "house name" used by three different publishers, has certainly outlasted most of his competition; appearing in more detective fiction than any other character in American literature, Nick Carter seems as ageless as the sturdiest of monuments. Beginning with the September 18, 1886, issue of the *New York Weekly*, under was replaced in 1933 by the *Nick Carter Magazine*. *Nick Carter Stories* was given a pulp format and in 1915 became the influential semimonthly *Detective Story Magazine*, edited by "Nicholas Carter" (actually Frank E. Blackwell). The first issue contains work by a variety of writers including Nathan Day and Ross Beeckman, as well as one Nick Carter reprint.

The *Nick Carter Magazine* (later called *Nick Carter Detective Magazine*) lasted only forty issues; it published many novelettes by "Harrison Keith," a character created by "Nicholas Carter" in the Magnet Library series. Immediately following, a Nick Carter story appeared in *The Shadow Magazine*; its author, Bruce Ellit, received a rare byline. Ellit would later write scripts for a number of Nick Carter comic strips, which became a regular feature of *Shadow Comics* until 1949.

With the advent of radio, the ever-adaptable Nick Carter left the failing pulps and recaptured public interest, beginning in 1943, with the weekly radio series *The Return of Nick Carter*. The early action-packed scripts were edited by Walter B. Gibson and remained true to the concept of the Street and Smith character. The radio series, soon called *Nick Carter, Master Detective*, starred Lon Clark and ran until 1955.

The film industry, too, made use of this popular character. As early as 1908, Victor Jasset produced *Nick Carter*, which was followed by *The New Exploits of Nick Carter* (1909), *Nick Carter vs. Pauline Broquet* (1911), and *Zigomar vs. Nick Carter* (1912). Several other films featuring Nick Carter were made before Metro-Goldwyn-Mayer produced *Nick Carter, Master Detective* (1939), starring Walter Pidgeon. This was followed by *Phantom Raiders* and *Sky Murder*, both from 1940. In 1946 a fifteen-chapter serial titled *Chick Carter, Detective* was produced starring Nick's son (based on the radio series), but in them Nick is neither shown nor mentioned. After two French productions in the 1960's, Carter surfaced on American television in *The Adventures of Nick Carter*, a series pilot set in early twentieth century New York City and starring Robert Conrad.

In 1964, another phase of Nick Carter's life began. Lyle Kenyon Engel, originator of the packaged books concept, began working with Walter B. Gibson on reissuing old Shadow material, and Engel decided to ob-

tain the rights to Nick Carter from Condé Nast, which had inherited the hibernating character from Street and Smith. Carter was resurrected as America's special agent with a license to kill. Nick was now a suave lady-killer who worked for the top-secret espionage agency AXE. This agency, the name of which is taken from the phrase "Give 'em the axe," is called on whenever world freedom is threatened. Carter, sometimes referred to as "Killmaster" or "N-3" (also "N3"), is no longer an independent detective but works for a supervisor, Mr. Hawks, who operates out of the agency's Washington, D.C., cover—the Amalgamated News and Wire Services. Carter's constant companions are a Luger named Wilhelmina, a stiletto called Hugo, and Pierre, a nerve-gas bomb. This is the Nick Carter who emerges from the first Killmaster novel, *Run, Spy, Run* (1964). More than 250 books were published in the

Among the many magazines bearing the "Nick Carter" brand name was Nick Carter Detective Magazine, *which appeared under that title only in 1936.* (Courtesy, Condé Nast Publications)

Killmaster series between 1964 and 1990. The last Nick Carter book was *Dragon Slay* (1990).

ANALYSIS

Nicknamed "the Little Giant" within the pages of Street and Smith's dime novels, Nick Carter was approximately five feet, four inches in height and astoundingly muscular. Robert Sampson quotes an early description of Carter that enumerates his talents: "He can lift a horse with ease, and that, too, while a heavy man is seated in the saddle. Remember that he can place four packs of playing cards together, and tear them in halves between his thumb and fingers." Carter was schooled in the art of detection by his father, Sim Carter; he mastered enough knowledge to assist him through several lifetimes. He soon gets the opportunity to use these skills, as his father is murdered in his first case.

More than any other detective, the early Nick Carter depends on changing his identity to solve the crime. These adventures, in which few actually see the real face of Nick, are overflowing with delightful Carter-made characters such as "Old Thunderbolt," the country detective, and Joshua Juniper, the "archetypical hayseed." These disguises enable Carter to combat several archfiends. The most famous of these is Dr. Quartz, who first appeared in a trilogy of adventures with Nick Carter in 1891. Having preceded Professor Moriarty by two years, Quartz can be considered the first recurring villain in detective fiction. Although Quartz is supposedly killed, he returns as "Doctor Quartz II" in 1905 with little explanation.

Quartz typifies much of what would be later mimicked in Hollywood and on the paperback stands. He practices East Indian magic and is accompanied by exotic characters such as the Woman Wizard, Zanoni, and Dr. Crystal. In one episode, Quartz brainwashes Carter into believing that he is an English lord named Algernon Travers. Zanoni, commissioned to pass herself off as his wife, falls in love with him and spoils Quartz's plans. She saves Nick's life, and the detective's three companions, Chick, Patsy, and Ten-Ichi, arrive just in time. The body of Quartz is sewed inside a hammock and dropped into the depths of the sea.

After the disguises ceased to appear, Carter as a character proved himself to be adaptable. He had already broken new ground in popular fiction by being the first author/hero in the majority of his adventures, a trend that would be followed in the Ellery Queen series. As the installments increased (the number of titles concerning Nick Carter in the dime novels alone exceeds twelve hundred) and the dime novel gave way to the pulp era, Carter took on more hard-boiled characteristics. Although his stay in the pulps was fairly short-lived, his character mirrored that of other detectives. Though as a character he had matured, Carter was embarking on adventures that were even more farfetched than before.

DANGER KEY

In 1964, in the wake of James Bond, Carter was resurrected as one who could fight better, love longer, swim farther, drive faster, and utilize more gadgets than any other superspy. The ethics of the old Nick Carter melted away like ice in straight whiskey. In books such as *Danger Key* (1966), Carter fights dangerously clever Nazis and sadistic Asians while enjoying an array of bikinied nymphets. Through yoga he is able to perform impossible feats (he is repeatedly trapped underwater, miles from the nearest air tank). In the atomic age, those who differ from the American Caucasian are portrayed as a dangerous threat to world peace and indeed to survival itself.

THE VENGEANCE GAME

With the advent of the Rambo films in the early 1980's, Carter's image changed yet again, although more subtly. His adventures were frequently set within the context of then-current events; he battled Tehran terrorists, for example, and *The Vengeance Game* (1985) is a retelling of the marine bombing in Beirut. As Nick Carter changed, his popularity prompted many spin-offs, most of which were short-lived. Carter undoubtedly reflects the ideology of his times, though there are certain constants (each adventure since 1964 is dedicated to the "men of the Secret Services of the United States of America"). For more than one hundred years, Nick Carter has pledged himself to uphold American morality against all foes and fears, both foreign and domestic.

Michael Pettengell

PRINCIPAL MYSTERY AND DETECTIVE FICTION

NICK CARTER (DIME NOVELS AND PULPS) SE-RIES: 1886-1887 • *The Old Detective's Pupil*, 1886; *One Against Twenty-One*, 1886; *A Wall Street Haul*, 1886; *The American Marquee*, 1887

1887-1917, A-C • *The Amazonian Queen; The Automobile Fiend; A Bad Man from Montana; A Bad Man from Nome; Bare-Faced Jimmy, Gentleman Burglar; A Beautiful Anarchist; The Brotherhood of Free Russia; By Command of the Czar; The Chemical Clue; The Conquest of a Kingdom; The Conspiracy of a Nation; The Countess Zita's Defense; The Crime Behind the Throne; The Crimson Clue; The Cross of Daggers*

1887-1917, D-F • *The Dead Man in the Car; A Dead Man's Hand; The Devil Worshippers; The Diplomatic Spy; Doctor Quartz Again; Doctor Quartz's Last Play; Doctor Quartz, the Second; Doctor Quartz, the Second, at Bay; An Emperor at Bay; The Empire of Goddess; Eulalia, the Bandit Queen; The Face at the Window; Facing an Unseen Terror; The Famous Case of Doctor Quartz; The Fate of Doctor Quartz; A Fight for Millions; Four Scraps of Paper*

1887-1917, G-L • *The Gentleman Crook's Last Act; The Ghost of Bare-Faced Jimmy; The Gold Mine; The Great Hotel Murders; The Great Spy System; The Haunted Circus; Her Shrewd Double; Holding Up a Nation; Ida, the Woman Detective; Idayah, the Woman of Mystery; The Index of Seven Stars; The International Conspiracy; Ismalla, the Chieftain; The Jiu-Jitsu Puzzle; Kairo, the Strong; Kid Curry's Last Stand; The Klondike Bank Puzzle; The Last of Mustushimi; The Last of the Outlaws; The Last of the Seven; A Life at Stake; The Little Giant's Double; Looted in Transit*

1887-1917, M • *The Madness of Morgan; Maguay, the Mexican; The Making of a King; The Man from Arizona; The Man from Nevada; The Man from Nowhere; The Master Crook's Match; The Master Rogue's Alibi; The Midnight Visitor; Migno Duprez, the Female Spy; Miguel, the Avenger; A Million Dollar Hold-Up; Murder for Revenge; A Mystery from the Klondike; A Mystery in India Ink; The Mystery Man of 7-Up Ranch; The Mystery of the Mikado*

1887-1917, N • *Nick Carter After Bob Dalton* (also known as *Nick Carter a Prisoner*); *Nick Carter Among the Bad Men; Nick Carter and the Circus Crooks* (also known as *Fighting the Circus Crooks*); *Nick Carter and the Convict Gang; Nick Carter and the Guilty Governor; Nick Carter and the Hangman's Noose; Nick Carter and the Nihilists; Nick Carter at the Track; Nick Carter in Harness Again; Nick Carter's Master Struggle; Nick Carter's Midnight Visitor; Nick Carter's Strange Power; Nick Carter's Submarine Clue; The Nihilists' Second Move*

1887-1917, O-P • *Old Broadbrim in a Deep Case Sea Struggle; Old Broadbrim Leagued with Nick Carter; Old Broadbrim's Clew from the Dead; The Passage of the Night Local; Patsy's Vacation Problem; Pedro, the Dog Detective; A Plot for a Crown; The Plot of the Stantons; Plotters Against a Nation; A Plot Within a Palace; The Princess' Last Effort; The Prison Cipher; The Prison Demon; A Pupil of Doctor Quartz*

1887-1917, Q-S • *The Queen of the Seven; The Red Button; Return from the Dead; The Secret Agent; The Secret of the Mine; Secrets of a Haunted House; The Seven-Headed Monster; The Skidoo of the K.U. and T.; A Strange Bargain*

1887-1917, T-V • *Ten-Ichi, the Wonderful; The Thirteen's Oath of Vengeance; Three Thousand Miles of Freight; The Tiger Tamer; A Tragedy of the Bowery; Trailing a Secret Thread; The Two Chittendens; The Veiled Princess*

1887-1917, W-Z • *A White House Mystery; A Woman to the Rescue; The Woman Wizard's Hate; Zanoni the Terrible; Zanoni the Transfigured; Zanoni, the Woman Wizard*

1888-1897 • *The Crime of a Countess*, 1888; *Fighting Against Millions*, 1888; *The Great Enigma*, 1888; *The Piano Box Mystery*, 1888; *A Stolen Identity*, 1888; *A Titled Counterfeiter*, 1888; *A Woman's Hand*, 1888; *Nick Carter, Detective*, 1891; *An Australian Klondyke*, 1897; *Caught in the Toils*, 1897; *The Gambler's Syndicate*, 1897; *A Klondike Claim*, 1897; *The Mysterious Mail Robbery*, 1897; *Playing a Bold Game*, 1897; *Tracked Across the Atlantic*, 1897

1898 • *The Accidental Password; Among the Counterfeiters; Among the Nihilists; At Odds with Scotland Yard*, 1898; *At Thompson's Ranch; A Chance Discovery; Check No. 777; A Deposit Fault Puzzle; The Double *Shuffle Club; Evidence by Telephone; A Fair Criminal; Found on the Beach; The Man from India; A Millionaire Partner*

1899 • *The Adventures of Harrison Keith, Detective; A Bite of an Apple, and Other Stories; The Clever Celestial; The Crescent Brotherhood; A Dead Man's Grip; The Detective's Pretty Neighbor, and Other Stories; The Diamond Mine Case; Gideon Drexel's Millions, and Other Stories; The Great Money Order Swindle; A Herald Personal, and Other Stories; The Man Who Vanished; Nick Carter and the Green Goods Men; Nick Carter's Clever Protégé; The Puzzle of Five Pistols, and Other Stories; Sealed Orders; The Sign of Crossed Knives; The Stolen Race Horse; The Stolen Pay Train, and Other Stories; The Twelve Tin Boxes; The Twelve Wise Men; Two Plus Two; The Van Alstine Case; Wanted by Two Clients*

1900 • *After the Bachelor Dinner; Brought to Bay; Convicted by a Camera; The Crime of the French Cafe, and Other Stories; Crossed Wires; The Elevated Railroad Mystery, and Other Stories; A Frame Work of Fate; A Game of Craft; Held for Trial; Lady Velvet; The Man Who Stole Millions; Nick Carter Down East; Nick Carter's Clever Ruse; Nick Carter's Girl Detective; Nick Carter's Retainer; Nick Carter's Star Pupils; A Princess of Crime; The Silent Passenger; A Victim of Circumstances*

1901 • *The Blow of a Hammer, and Other Stories; A Bogus Clew; The Bottle with the Black Label; Desperate Chance; The Dumb Witness, and Other Stories; In Letters of Fire; The Man at the Window; The Man from London; The Man of Mystery; Millions at Stake, and Other Stories; The Missing Cotton King; The Mysterious Highwayman; The Murray Hill Mystery; The Price of a Secret; A Prince of a Secret; A Prince of Rogues; The Queen of Knaves, and Other Stories; A Scrap of Black Lace; The Seal of Silence; The Steel Casket, and Other Stories; The Testimony of a Mouse; A Triple Crime*

1902 • *At the Knife's Point; Behind a Mask; The Claws of the Tiger; A Deal in Diamonds; A Double-Handed Game; A False Combination; Hounded to Death; Man Against Man; The Man and His Price; A Move in the Dark; Nick Carter's Death Warrant; Played to a Finish; A Race for Ten Thousand; The Red*

Signal; Run to Earth; A Stroke of Policy; A Syndicate of Rascals; The Tell-Tale Photographs; The Toss of a Coin; A Trusted Rogue; Two Villains in One; The Vial of Death; Wearing the Web

1903 • *The Barrel Mystery; A Blackmailer's Bluff; A Blood-Red Badge; A Blow for Vengeance; A Bonded Villain; The Cashiers' Secret; The Chair of Evidence; A Checkmated Scoundrel; Circumstantial Evidence; The Cloak of Guilt; The Council of Death; The Crown Diamond; The Fatal Prescription; A Great Conspiracy; The Guilty Governor; Heard in the Dark; The Hole in the Vault; A Masterpiece of Crime; A Mysterious Game; Paid with Death; Photographer's Evidence; A Race Track Gamble; A Ring of Dust; The Seal of Death; A Sharper's Downfall; The Twin Mystery; Under False Colors*

1904 • *Against Desperate Odds; Ahead of the Game; Beyond Pursuit; a Broken Trail; A Bundle of Clews; The Cab Driver's Secret; The Certified Check; The Criminal Link; Dazaar, the Arch Fiend; A Dead Witness; A Detective's Theory; Driven from Cover; Following a Chance Clew; The "Hot Air" Clew; In the Gloom of Night; An Ingenious Stratagem; The Master Villain; A Missing Man; A Mysterious Diagram; Playing a Lone Hand; The Queen of Diamonds; The Ruby Pin; A Scientific Forger; The Secret Panel; The Terrible Threat; The Toss of the Penny; Under a Black Veil; With Links of Steel; The Wizards of the Cue*

1905 • *Accident or Murder?; A Baffled Oath; The Bloodstone Terror; The Boulevard Mutes; A Cigarette Clew; The Crime of the Camera; The Diamond Trail; Down and Out; The Four-Fingered Glove; The Key Ring Clew; The Living Mask; The Marked Hand; A Mysterious Graft; Nick Carter's Double Catch; Playing for a Fortune; The Plot That Failed; The Pretty Stenographer Mystery; The Price of Treachery; A Royal Thief; A Tangled Case; The Terrible Thirteen; Trapped in His Own Net; A Triple Identity; The Victim of Deceit; A Villainous Scheme*

1906 • *Baffled, but Not Beaten; Behind a Throne; The Broadway Cross; Captain Sparkle, Private; A Case Without a Clue; The Death Circle; Dr. Quartz, Magician; Dr. Quartz's Quick Move; From a Prison Cell; In the Lap of Danger; The "Limited" Hold-Up; The Lure of Gold; The Man Who Was Cursed; Marked for Death*; *Nick Carter's Fall*; *Nick Carter's Master-piece*; *Out of Death's Shadow*; *A Plot Within a Plot*; *The Sign of the Dagger*; *Through the Cellar Wall*; *Trapped by a Woman*; *The Unaccountable Crook*; *Under the Tiger's Claws*; *A Voice from the Past*

1907 • *An Amazing Scoundrel*; *The Bank Draft Puzzle*; *A Bargain in Crime*; *The Brotherhood of Death*; *The Chain of Clues*; *Chase in the Dark*; *A Cry for Help*; *The Dead Stranger*; *The Demon's Eye*; *The Demons of the Night*; *Done in the Dark*; *The Dynamite Trap*; *A Fight for a Throne*; *A Finger Against Suspicion*; *A Game of Plots*; *Harrison Keith, Sleuth*; *Harrison Keith's Big Stakes*; *Harrison Keith's Chance Clue*; *Harrison Keith's Danger*; *Harrison Keith's Dilemma*; *Harrison Keith's Greatest Task*; *Harrison Keith's Oath*; *Harrison Keith's Struggle*; *Harrison Keith's Triumph*; *Harrison Keith's Warning*; *The Human Fiend*; *A Legacy of Hate*; *The Man of Iron*; *The Man Without a Conscience*; *Nick Carter's Chinese Puzzle*; *Nick Carter's Close Call*; *The Red League*; *The Silent Guardian*; *The Woman of Evil*; *The Woman of Steel*; *The Worst Case on Record*

1908 • *The Artful Schemer*; *The Crime and the Motive*; *The Doctor's Stratagem*; *The False Claimant*; *A Fight with a Fiend*; *From Peril to Peril*; *A Game Well Played*; *A Girl in the Case*; *The Hand That Won*; *Hand to Hand*; *Harrison Keith's Chance Shot*; *Harrison Keith's Crooked Trail*; *Harrison Keith's Diamond Case*; *Harrison Keith's Double Mystery*; *Harrison Keith's Dragnet*; *Harrison Keith's Fight for Life*; *Harrison Keith's Mystic Letter*; *Harrison Keith's Queer Clue*; *Harrison Keith's Strange Summons*; *Harrison Keith's Tact*; *Harrison Keith's Time Lock Case*; *Harrison Keith's Weird Partner*; *Harrison Keith's Wireless Message*; *A Hunter of Men*; *In Death's Grip*; *Into Nick Carter's Web*; *Nabob and Knave*; *Nick Carter's Cipher*; *Nick Carter's Promise*; *A Plunge into Crime*; *The Prince of Liars*; *A Ring of Rascals*; *The Silent Partner*; *The Snare and the Game*; *A Strike for Freedom*; *Tangled Thread*; *A Trap of Tangled Wire*; *When the Trap Was Sprung*; *Without a Clue*

1909 • *At Mystery's Threshold*; *A Blindfold Mystery*; *Death at the Feast*; *A Disciple of Satan*; *A Double Plot*; *Harrison Keith and the Phantom Heiress*; *Harrison Keith at Bay*; *Harrison Keith, Magician*;

Harrison Keith's Abduction Tangle; *Harrison Keith's Battle of Nerve*; *Harrison Keith's Cameo Case*; *Harrison Keith's Close Quarters*; *Harrison Keith's Death Compact*; *Harrison Keith's Double Cross*; *Harrison Keith's Dual Role*; *Harrison Keith's Green Diamond*; *Harrison Keith's Haunted Client*; *Harrison Keith's Lucky Strike*; *Harrison Keith's Mummy Mystery*; *Harrison Keith's Padlock Mystery*; *Harrison Keith's River Front Ruse*; *Harrison Keith's Sparkling Trail*; *Harrison Keith's Triple Tragedy*; *In Search of Himself*; *A Man to Be Feared*; *A Master of Deviltry*; *Nick Carter's Swim to Victory*; *Out of Crime's Depths*; *A Plaything of Fate*; *A Plot Uncovered*; *Reaping the Whirlwind*; *Saved by a Ruse*; *The Temple of Vice*; *When the Wicked Prosper*; *A Woman at Bay*

1910 • *Behind Closed Doors*; *Behind the Black Mask*; *A Carnival of Crime*; *The Crystal Mystery*; *The Disappearing Princess*; *The Doom of the Reds*; *The Great Diamond Syndicate*; *Harrison Keith—Star Reporter*; *Harrison Keith's Cyclone Clue*; *Harrison Keith's Death Watch*; *Harrison Keith's Labyrinth*; *Harrison Keith's Perilous Contract*; *Harrison Keith's Poison Problem*; *Harrison Keith's River Mystery*; *Harrison Keith's Studio Crime*; *Harrison Keith's Wager*; *The King's Prisoner*; *The Last Move in the Game*; *The Lost Chittendens*; *A Nation's Peril*; *Nick Carter's Auto Trail*; *Nick Carter's Convict Client*; *Nick Carter's Persistence*; *Nick Carter's Wildest Chase*; *One Step Too Far*; *The Rajah's Ruby*; *The Scourge of the Wizard*; *Talika, the Geisha Girl*; *The Trail of the Catspaw*

1911 • *At Face Value*; *Broken on Crime's Wheel*; *A Call on the Phone*; *Chase for Millions*; *Comrades of the Right Hand*; *The Confidence King*; *The Devil's Son*; *An Elusive Knave*; *A Face in the Shadow*; *A Fatal Margin*; *A Fatal Falsehood*; *For a Madman's Millions*; *The Four Hoodoo Charms*; *The Gift of the Gods*; *The Handcuff Wizard*; *The House of Doom*; *The House of the Yellow Door*; *The Jeweled Mummy*; *King of the Underworld*; *The Lady of Shadow*; *A Live Wire Clew*; *Madam "Q"*; *The Man in the Auto*; *A Masterly Trick*; *A Master of Skill*; *The Mystery Castle*; *Nick Carter's Close Finish*; *Nick Carter's Intuition*; *Nick Carter's Roundup*; *Pauline—A Mystery*; *A Plot for an Empire*; *The Quest of the "Lost Hope"*; *A Question of Time*;

The Room of Mirrors; The Second Mr. Carstairs; The Senator's Plot; Shown on the Screen; The Streaked Peril; A Submarine Trail; The Triple Knock; The Vanishing Emerald; A War of Brains; The Way of the Wicked; A Weak-Kneed Rogue; When a Man Yields; When Necessity Drives; The Whirling Death

1912 • *Bandits of the Air; The Buried Secret; By an Unseen Hand; A Call in the Night; The Case of the Two Doctors; Clew by Clew; The Connecting Link; The Crime of a Century; The Crimson Flash; The Dead Man's Accomplice; The Deadly Scarab; A Double Mystery; The Fatal Hour; The House of Whisper; In Queer Quarters; In the Face of Evidence; In the Nick of Time; The Man with a Crutch; The Man with a Double; A Master Criminal; A Mill in Diamonds; The Missing Deputy Chief; The Mysterious Cavern; Nick Carter and the Gold Thieves; Nick Carter's Chance Clue; Nick Carter's Counterplot; Nick Carter's Egyptian Clew; Nick Carter's Last Card; Nick Carter's Menace; Nick Carter's Subtle Foe; On a Crimson Trail; Out for Vengeance; The Path of the Spendthrift; A Place for Millions; A Plot for a Warship; The Red Triangle; The Rogue's Reach; The Seven Schemers; The Silver Hair Clue; A Stolen Name; Tangled in Crime; The Taxicab Riddle; Tooth and Nail; The Trail of the Yoshiga; A Triple Knavery; A Vain Sacrifice; The Vampire's Trail; The Vanishing Heiress; When Jealousy Spurs; The Woman in Black; A Woman of Mystery; Written in Blood*

1913 • *The Angel of Death; The Babbington Case; Brought to the Mark; Caught in a Whirlwind; The Clutch of Dread; Cornered at Last; The Day of Reckoning; Diamond Cut Diamond; Doomed to Failure; A Double Identity; Driven to Desperation; A Duel of Brains; The Finish of a Rascal; For the Sake of Revenge; The Heart of the Underworld; The House Across the Street; In Suspicion's Shadow; In the Shadow of Fear; The International Crook League; Knots in the Noose; The Kregoff Necklace; The Man Who Fainted; A Maze of Motives; The Midnight Message; A Millionaire's Mania; The Mills of the Law; A Moving Picture Mystery; Nick and the Red Button; Nick Carter's New Assistant; Nick Carter's Treasure Chest Case; On the Eve of Triumph; Plea for Justice; Points to Crime; The Poisons of Exili; The Purple*

Spot; Repaid in Like Coin; A Riddle of Identities; A Rogue of Quality; The Sign of the Coin; The Spider's Parlor; The Sting of the Adder; The Sway of Sin; The Thief in the Night; A Tower of Strength; Toying with Fate; The Turn of a Card; The Unfinished Letter; Weighed in the Balance; When a Rogue's in Power; When All Is Staked; When Clues Are Hidden; While the Fetters Were Forged; Whom the Gods Would Destroy

1914 • *After the Verdict; Birds of Prey; A Blind Man's Daughter; Bolts from Blue Skies; The Bullion Mystery; Called to Account; Crime in Paradise; The Crook's Blind; The Deeper Game; Dodging the Law; The Door of Doubt; A Fight for Right; The Fixed Alibi; The Gloved Hand; The Grafters; A Heritage of Trouble; In the Toils of Fear; Instinct at Fault; The Just and the Unjust; The Keeper of the Black Hounds; Knaves in High Places; The Last Call; The Man of Riddles; The Man Who Changed Faces; The Man Who Paid; The Microbe of Crime; A Miscarriage of Justice; Not on the Records; On the Ragged Edge; One Object in Life; Out with the Tide; A Perilous Parole; A Rascal of Quality; The Red God of Tragedy; A Rogue Worth Trapping; A Rope of Slender Threads; The Sandal Wood Slipper; The Skyline Message; The Slave of Crime; Spoilers and the Spoils; The Spoils of Chance; A Struggle with Destiny; A Tangled Skein; The Thief Who Was Robbed; The Trail of the Fingerprints; Unseen Foes; The Wages of Rascality; Wanted: A Clew; When Destruction Threatens; With Shackles of Fires; The Wolf Within*

1915 • *As a Crook Sows; The Danger of Folly; The Gargoni Girdle; The Girl Prisoner; Held in Suspense; In Record Time; Just One Slip; The Middle Link; A New Serpent in Eden; On a Million-Dollar Trail; The $100,000 Kiss; One Ship Wreck Too Many; Rascals and Co.; Satan's Apt Pupil; Scourged by Fear; The Soul Destroyers; A Test of Courage; To the Ends of the Earth; Too Late to Talk; A Weird Treasure; When Brave Men Tremble; When Honors Pall; Where Peril Beckons; The Yellow Brand*

1916 • *Broken Bars; The Burden of Proof; The Case of Many Clues; A Clue from the Unknown; The Conspiracy of Rumors; The Evil Formula; From Clue to Clue; The Great Opium Case; In the Grip of Fate;*

The Magic Necklace; *The Man of Many Faces*; *The Man Without a Will*; *A Mixed-Up Mess*; *Over the Edge of the World*; *The Red Plague*; *Round the World for a Quarter*; *Scoundrel Rampant*; *The Sealed Door*; *The Stolen Brain*; *The Trail of the Human Tiger*; *Twelve in a Grave*; *When Rogues Conspire*

1917 • *The Adder's Brood*; *For a Pawned Crown*; *Found in the Jungle*; *The Hate That Kills*; *The Man They Held Back*; *The Needy Nine*; *Outlaws of the Blue*; *Paying the Price*; *The Sultan's Pearls*; *Won by Magic*

1918 • *The Amphi-Theatre Plot*; *Blood Will Tell*; *Clew Against Clew*; *The Crook's Double*; *The Crossed Needles*; *Death in Life*; *A Network of Crime*; *Snarled Identities*; *The Yellow Label*; *A Battle for the Right*; *A Broken Bond*; *Hidden Foes*; *Partners in Peril*; *The Sea Fox*; *A Threefold Disappearance*

1920-1927 • *The Secret of the Marble Mantle*, 1920; *A Spinner of Death*, 1920; *Wildfire*, 1920; *Doctor Quartz Returns*, 1926; *Nick Carter Corners Doctor Quartz*, 1926; *Nick Carter and the Black Cat*, 1927; *Nick Carter and the Shadow Woman*, 1927; *Nick Carter Dies*, 1927; *Nick Carter's Danger Trail*, 1927; *Death Has Green Eyes*, n.d.; *Crooks' Empire*, n.d. (also known as *Empire of Crime*); *Bid for a Railroad*, n.d. (also known as *Murder Unlimited*); *Death on Park Avenue*, n.d. (also known as *Park Avenue Murder!*); *Murder on Skull Island*, n.d. (also known as *Rendezvous with a Dead Man*); *Power*, n.d. (also known as *The Yellow Disc Murder*).

NICK CARTER/KILLMASTER SERIES: 1964-1967 • *Run, Spy, Run*, 1964; *Checkmate in Rio*, 1964; *The China Doll*, 1964; *Fraulein Spy*, 1964; *Safari for Spies*, 1964; *A Bullet for Fidel*, 1965; *The Eyes of the Tiger*, 1965; *Istanbul*, 1965; *The Thirteenth Spy*, 1965; *Danger Key*, 1966; *Dragon Flame*, 1966; *Hanoi*, 1966; *The Mind Poisoners*, 1966; *Operation Starvation*, 1966; *Spy Castle*, 1966; *The Terrible Ones*, 1966; *Web of Spies*, 1966; *Assignment: Israel*, 1967; *The Chinese Paymaster*, 1967; *The Devil's Cockpit*, 1967; *Double Identity*, 1967 (also known as *Strike of the Hawk*); *The Filthy Five*, 1967; *The Golden Serpent*, 1967; *A Korean Tiger*, 1967; *Mission to Venice*, 1967; *The Red Guard*, 1967; *Seven Against Greece*, 1967; *The Weapon of Night*, 1967

1968-1970 • *Amsterdam*, 1968; *The Bright Blue Death*, 1968; *Fourteen Seconds to Hell*, 1968; *Hood of Death*, 1968; *The Judas Spy*, 1968; *Macao*, 1968; *Operation: Moon Rocket*, 1968; *Temple of Fear*, 1968; *The Amazon*, 1969; *Berlin*, 1969; *Carnival for Killing*, 1969; *The Casbah Killers*, 1969; *The Cobra Kill*, 1969; *The Defector*, 1969; *The Doomsday Formula*, 1969; *The Human Time Bomb*, 1969; *The Living Death*, 1969; *Operation Che Guevara*, 1969; *Operation Snake*, 1969; *Peking and The Tulip Affair*, 1969; *The Sea Trap*, 1969; *The Red Rays*, 1969; *Rhodesia*, 1969; *The Arab Plague*, 1970; *The Black Death*, 1970; *Cambodia*, 1970; *The Death Strain*, 1970; *The Executioners*, 1970; *Jewel of Doom*, 1970; *The Mind Killers*, 1970; *Moscow*, 1970; *The Red Rebellion*, 1970; *Time Clock of Death*, 1970

1971-1973 • *Ice Bomb Zero*, 1971; *The Mark of Cosa Nostra*, 1971; *Assault on England*, 1972; *The Cairo Mafia*, 1972; *The Inca Death Squad*, 1972; *The Omega Terror*, 1972; *Agent Counter-Agent*, 1973; *Assassination Brigade*, 1973; *Butcher of Belgrade*, 1973; *The Code*, 1973; *Code Name: Werewolf*, *The Death's-Head Conspiracy*, 1973; *The Devil's Dozen*, 1973; *Hour of the Wolf*, 1973; *The Kremlin File*, 1973; *The Liquidator*, 1973; *Night of the Avenger*, 1973; *Our Agent in Rome Is Missing . . .* , 1973; *The Peking Dossier*, 1973; *The Spanish Connection*, 1973

1974-1977 • *Assassin: Code Name Vulture*, 1974; *The Aztec Avenger*, 1974; *Beirut Incident*, 1974; *Death of the Falcon*, 1974; *Ice Trap Terror*, 1974; *The Man Who Sold Death*, 1974; *Massacre in Milan*, 1974; *The N3 Conspiracy*, 1974; *Sign of the Cobra*, 1974; *Vatican Vendetta*, 1974; *Counterfeit Agent*, 1975; *Dr. Death*, 1975; *The Jerusalem File*, 1975; *The Katmandu Contract*, 1975; *Six Bloody Summer Days*, 1975; *The Ultimate Code*, 1975; *The Z Document*, 1975; *Assignment: Intercept*, 1976; *Death Message: Oil 74-2*, 1976; *The Fanatics of Al Asad*, 1976; *The Gallagher Plot*, 1976; *The Green Wolf Connection*, 1976; *A High Yield in Death*, 1976; *The List*, 1976; *The Nichovev Plot*, 1976; *The Sign of the Prayer Shawl*, 1976; *The Snake Flag Conspiracy*, 1976; *Triple Cross*, 1976; *The Vulcan Disaster*, 1976; *Plot for the Fourth Reich*, 1977

1978-1980 • *Deadly Doubles*, 1978; *The Ebony*

Cross, 1978; *The Pamplona Affair*, 1978; *Race of Death*, 1978; *Revenge of the Generals*, 1978; *Trouble in Paradise*, 1978; *Under the Wall*, 1978; *The Asian Mantrap*, 1979; *The Doomsday Spore*, 1979; *Hawaii*, 1979; *The Jamaican Exchange*, 1979; *The Nowhere Weapon*, 1979; *The Pemex Chart*, 1979; *The Redolmo Affair*, 1979; *Reich Four*, 1979; *The Satan Trap*, 1979; *Thunderstrike in Syria*, 1979; *Tropical Deathpact*, 1979; *And Next the King*, 1980; *Day of the Dingo*, 1980; *Death Mission: Havana*, 1980; *Eighth Card Stud*, 1980; *Suicide Seat*, 1980; *Tarantula Strike*, 1980; *Ten Times Dynamite*, 1980; *Turkish Bloodbath*, 1980; *War from the Clouds*, 1980

1981-1983 • *Cauldron of Hell*, 1981; *The Coyote Connection*, 1981; *The Dubrovnik Massacre*, 1981; *The Golden Bull*, 1981; *The Ouster Conspiracy*, 1981; *The Parisian Affair*, 1981; *Pleasure Island*, 1981; *The Q-Man*, 1981; *Society of Nine*, 1981; *The Solar Menace*, 1981; *The Strontium Code*, 1981; *Appointment in Haiphong*, 1982; *Chessmaster*, 1982; *The Christmas Kill*, 1982; *The Damocles Threat*, 1982; *Deathlight*, 1982; *The Death Star Affair*, 1982; *The Dominican Affair*, 1982; *Dr. DNA*, 1982; *Earth Shaker*, 1982; *The Hunter*, 1982; *The Israeli Connection*, 1982; *The Last Samurai*, 1982; *The Mendoza Manuscript*, 1982; *Norwegian Typhoon*, 1982; *Operation: McMurdo Sound*, *The Puppet Master*, 1982; *Retreat for Death*, 1982; *The Treason Game*, 1982

1984-1986 • *Death Hand Play*, 1984; *The Kremlin Kill*, 1984; *The Mayan Connection*, 1984; *Night of the Warheads*, 1984; *San Juan Inferno*, 1984; *Zero Hour Strike Force*, 1984; *Blood of the Scimitar*, 1985; *Blood Raid*, 1985; *The Execution Exchange*, 1985; *Last Flight to Moscow*, 1985; *Macao Massacre*, 1985; *The Normandy Code*, 1985; *Pursuit of the Eagle*, 1985; *The Tarlov Cipher*, 1985; *The Vengeance Game*, 1985; *White Death*, 1985; *The Berlin Target*, 1986; *Blood Ultimatum*, 1986; *The Cyclops Conspiracy*, 1986; *The Killing Ground*, 1986; *Mercenary Mountain*, 1986; *Operation Petrograd*, 1986; *Slaughter Day*, 1986; *Tunnel for Traitors*, 1986

1987-1990 • *Crossfire Red*, 1987; *Death Squad*, 1987; *East of Hell*, 1987; *Killing Games*, 1987; *Terms of Vengeance*, 1987; *Pressure Point*, 1987; *Night of the Condor*, 1987; *The Poseidon Target*, 1987; *Target*

Red Star, 1987; *The Terror Code*, 1987; *Terror Times Two*, 1987; *The Andropov File*, 1988; *Dragonfire*, 1988; *Bloodtrail to Mecca*, 1988; *Deathstrike*, 1988; *Lethal Prey*, 1988; *Spykiller*, 1988; *Bolivan Heat*, 1988; *The Rangoon Man*, 1988; *Code Name Cobra*, 1988; *Afghan Intercept*, 1988; *Countdown to Armageddon*, 1988; *Black Sea Bloodbath*, 1988; *The Deadly Diva*, 1989; *Invitation to Death*, 1989; *Day of the Assassin*, 1989; *The Korean Kill*, 1989; *Middle East Massacre*, 1989; *Sanction to Slaughter*, 1989; *Holiday in Hell*, 1989; *Law of the Lion*, 1989; *Hong Kong Hit*, 1989; *Deep Sea Death*, 1989; *Arms of Vengeance*, 1989; *Hell-Bound Express*, 1989; *Isle of Blood*, 1989; *Singapore Sling*, 1990; *Ruby Red Death*, 1990; *Arctic Abduction*, 1990; *Dragon Slay*, 1990

BIBLIOGRAPHY

Cook, Michael L., ed. *Monthly Murders: A Checklist and Chronological Listing of Fiction in the Digest Size Monthly Magazines in the United States and England*. Westport, Conn.: Greenwood Press, 1982. Useful for keeping track of Carter's various appearances in periodical publications.

Cox, J. Randolph. *The Dime Novel Companion: A Source Book*. Westport, Conn.: Greenwood Press, 2000. Contains an informative introduction to the dime novel publishing world from which Carter sprang, as well as discussion of Street & Smith.

_____. "More Mystery for a Dime: Street & Smith and the First Pulp Detective Magazine." *Clues: A Journal of Detection* 2 (Fall/Winter, 1981): 52-59. Examination of the role of Carter's publishers—and of the character himself—in the success and popularity of pulp fiction.

Fujiwara, Chris. *Jacques Tourneur: The Cinema of Nightfall*. Jefferson, N.C.: McFarland, 1998. Includes analysis of Tourneur's two Nick Carter films, *Nick Carter, Master Detective* (1939) and *Phantom Raiders* (1940). Bibliographic references and index.

Murray, Will. "The Saga of Nick Carter, Killmaster." *The Armchair Detective* 15 (Fall, 1982): 316-329. Informative discussion of Nick Carter's superspy phase, in which the character was modified to capitalize on the popularity of James Bond.

"The Nick Carter Stories." In *Mystery and Suspense*

Writers: The Literature of Crime, Detection, and Espionage, edited by Robin W. Winks and Maureen Corrigan. New York: Scribner's Sons, 1998. Comparison of Carter to other famous detectives and of his creators to other mystery and espionage writers.

Reynolds, Quentin. *The Fiction Factory: Or, From Pulp Row to Quality Street*. New York: Random House, 1955. Meticulous history of the Street & Smith publishing house, the publishers of the early dime novels featuring Nick Carter.

Sampson, Robert. *Glory Figures*. Vol. 1 in *Yesterday's Faces: A Study of Series Characters in the Early Pulp Magazines*. Bowling Green, Ohio: Bowling Green State University Popular Press, 1983. Compares Carter to other popular pulp heroes, such as Doc Savage and the Shadow.

Srebnick, Amy Gilman, and René Lévy, eds. *Crime and Culture: An Historical Perspective*. Burlington, Vt.: Ashgate, 2005. Study focused largely on the evolution of crime literature around the start of the twentieth century. Concludes with a discussion of Nick Carter. Bibliographic references and index.

VERA CASPARY

Born: Chicago, Illinois; November 13, 1899
Died: New York, New York; June 13, 1987
Type of plot: Thriller

CONTRIBUTION

Vera Caspary's tales of life in large American cities and their suburbs are among the most evocative in the annals of mystery writing. Many of her works, however, have suffered the fate of less powerfully written works by lesser writers because they are out of print and hard to find even on library shelves. Without overtly judging the mores of her twentieth century America, Caspary nevertheless depicts a society of aloof, self-absorbed, and predatory loners and their unrealistic, selfless victims. Dreamers and romantics have little chance of seeing their dreams come true, and too many times they open themselves up to friendship or love, only to be hurt or killed by those whom they trusted.

Caspary's characters each have individual voices and distinct, original, and often unforgettable personalities. The majority of her characters are developed as three-dimensional rather than as the often disposable, one-dimensional characters of much mystery fiction. Neither her main characters nor her richly constructed settings are easily passed over en route to the conclusion of her stories, for she spends time and effort making certain that they are as real as possible. Caspary writes not only to entertain but also to say something important about the kind of people and places she knows best.

BIOGRAPHY

Vera Caspary was born in Chicago on November 13, 1904, and spent most of her early years in that city. After graduation from the Chicago public schools, she took a variety of jobs, all of which helped her amass the experiences that she would later draw on in her books. She wrote copy at an advertising agency, worked as a stenographer, directed a correspondence academy, and served as an editor of the magazine *Dance* for two years before turning to freelance writing. Before becoming a mystery writer, however, she wrote novels of a highly romantic coloration between the years 1929 and 1932; in the mid-1930's, she began writing screenplays for Hollywood producers, an activity she continued until well into the 1960's.

In 1943, Caspary published what would become her most successful and most remembered mystery novel, *Laura*, which also became a well-received Broadway play and a film directed by Otto Preminger in 1944. In 1949, she married I. G. Goldsmith. Success with *Laura* led to the production of fourteen other mysteries, the most noted artistically having been

Evvie (1960). Caspary received the Screen Writers Guild Award for her screenplays in 1950. She died on June 13, 1987, in New York.

ANALYSIS

Vera Caspary's mystery tales often feature women as central characters. With their obscure or provincial backgrounds, they are often career women who have come to the big city for a climb up the corporate ladder or opportunists looking for a rich Mr. Right. Sometimes they are suburbanites unhappy with their situations.

In terms of technique, Caspary uses the devices of the red herring, multiple viewpoint, and double ending to great effect. In *Laura*, for example, just as the circumstantial case against Shelby Carpenter, Laura's suitor, becomes strong, the focus shifts to Laura herself, and the circumstantial evidence against her seems to make her, rather than Shelby, the true murderer of her young friend. The reader is allowed to discover that the murdered girl, Diane Redfern, and Shelby had had an affair that might have led to an even deeper romantic entanglement if it had been allowed to continue. Yet, in the background, out of sight and mind for a good portion of the novel, Waldo Lydecker, the murderer, congratulates himself on escaping detection. Only after it is apparent that Waldo had not only a motive (jealousy) but also a weapon like that which had killed Diane (a cane with a hidden shotgun), does he become the chief suspect.

Caspary's skill at creating double endings and writing from various perspectives makes her writing of exceptional interest. The tale of *Laura*, for example, is told from several angles: first from the perspective of Waldo Lydecker (an appropriately subtle and self-serving report on a murder by a man who committed it); then, when Waldo stops writing, the story is picked up by a more disinterested party—Mark McPherson, the Scottish-born police detective. Straightforward and austerely written, McPherson's commentary is completely different in word choice and tone from Waldo's effete, precious, and self-serving version of things. Last comes Laura's own account of what transpired, which is, again, much different from what was said before. She is transfixed by the evil she witnesses,

and her commentary is full of concern and awe.

Caspary handles double endings, like multiple viewpoints, with great skill. At the end of *Evvie*, the advertising agency head, Carl Busch, a headstrong, vain, and at times violent man, is arrested for Evvie's murder, thus providing a seeming end to the novel, appropriate and commonsensical. Yet the novel has not run its course. Before it can end, there is a surprise waiting for readers: It was not the ad man who killed Evvie (nor was it the sinister gangster Silent Lucas described pages earlier); rather, it was the mentally retarded handyman.

In another example, *The Man Who Loved His Wife*, it is reasonable and even probable for the reader to assume that Elaine Strode was framed by her husband and her stepson and his wife because her husband created a diary that, on his death, would brand Elaine not only as an adulteress but as a murderer as well. There would appear to be no truth to his accusations, and his growing hatred of her seems to be the work of an unhinged mind. Toward the novel's end, when it is determined by the police detectives that Fletcher Strode was strangled when a dry cleaning bag was placed over the airhole in his neck from which he breathed, readers are led to think that the son and his wife had something to do with it. They would, after all, have a strong motive (insurance money) and the ability to conceive of the plan.

Nevertheless, with a characteristically wry twist, Caspary allows the novel to end with Elaine's confessing to the murder. The author has a laugh at the readers' expense, for anyone who truly followed the evidence in the case would know that it must have been Elaine who killed Fletcher. Yet, because readers like Elaine, they tend to overlook the evidence and vote with their hearts, not their minds. The facts are that Elaine, bored and restless, did have a brief affair, did get tired of seeing her husband lying inert in bed, did resent his bullying, and therefore solved all her problems by killing him.

Caspary's murderers, seldom obvious killers, range from the unusual and absurd to everyday people encountered on any street of any city. They have little in common with one another except a need to exert power. Some are genuine monsters; others are merely pawns of their own inner demons. Products of the heterogenous, violent American cities and suburbs, they carry out the inner directives that others also receive but on which they fail to act. Just as interesting as Caspary's murderers are her victims. Sometimes readers know much about the victim before his or her death; other times, reader only learn about him or her through the reminiscences of others. In *Evvie*, for example, victim Evelyn Ashton, though she is dead from the outset of the novel, is resurrected for readers by the narrator Louise Goodman. The book becomes not only a murder mystery but also a celebration of the life of a career woman who loved much and died a sordid death.

Social commentary is an important part of Caspary's stories. Implicit in her work is the idea that Americans have created a dangerous society, a cultural split between the haves and have-nots, where the rich ignore the poor and flaunt their wealth and the poor, for their part, envy and hate the rich. Such a society always has violence below the surface, ready to erupt. The immorality of such a society is not so much a result of the breakdown of morals among bohemians but among those of the mainstream who set society's tone. In this period of human conflict, the moral calluses people have developed keep them from developing appropriate responses to the needs of others. Locked in selfishness and motivated by greed, Caspary's world is one in which human life is cheap. With her implicit critique of American mores, Caspary is more than a pedestrian mystery writer. She is a wonderfully accurate portrayer of young, romantic people living in an indifferent milieu that, by necessity, must destroy romance.

LAURA

Laura is set in New York City's well-heeled Lower East Side. Laura Hunt, the protagonist, is a lovely although spoiled young woman to whom men are easily drawn. Charming, intelligent, and upwardly mobile, she is emblematic of all Caspary's female protagonists. Despite the fact that Laura is resourceful, she is neither as self-sufficient nor as knowing as she believes herself to be. To her horror, she discovers early in the story that trusting, resourceful women can be the targets of murderers.

When it is made apparent that a female friend was murdered by mistake and that the real victim was to

The 1944 film adaptation of Vera Caspary's novel Laura *is now considered a classic of film noir.*

have been Laura herself, she becomes both disillusioned with human nature and extremely frightened. For perhaps the first time in her life, Laura finds that despite her beauty, wit, education, and money, life is no more secure for her than it is for a prostitute on the street. When detective Mark McPherson appears to ask her questions about her friend's death, she opens herself up to him, only to discover her vulnerability once more. She finds that she is a murder suspect, but she hopes that McPherson can shield her from harm.

Her self-perceived ability to evaluate the character of others is also severely undermined when she is told that the murderer must certainly be someone who knows her well. Finding no one close to her who fits that description, Laura is clearly baffled for the first time in her life. She not only learns to distrust people but also discovers that distrusting others is the basis of modern urban life.

EVVIE

More hedonistic but no less vulnerable than Laura Hunt, Evelyn Ashton—better known as Evvie—of the novel *Evvie* seems only to discover her worth through the men she loves, most of whom are of the fly-by-night variety. Idealistic and sensitive like Laura, Evvie wants to ease the painful existence of the less fortunate people she encounters in Chicago's streets, believing that by opening herself to them she will not be harmed. This dangerously cavalier attitude leads to her death when she allows a mentally retarded man whom she barely knows into her apartment, and he proceeds to bludgeon her to death with a candlestick in a fit of sexually induced frustration. Evvie's destruction can be seen as confirming the belief of conservative American society about the fate of young women who come to large cities and lead a single lifestyle there.

Unintentionally, perhaps, Caspary may be exhibiting this mainstream outlook that posits the idea that cities are evil and that single women ought to get married and live in the safer suburbs. Independence and rebelliousness will lead only to destruction. Evvie, wanting to lead a bohemian life, allows urban violence into her life and dies because of it. By so doing, she serves as a convenient scapegoat for her suburban sisters, who enjoy hearing tales of big-city adventurers without exposing themselves to big-city dangers.

THE MAN WHO LOVED HIS WIFE

Like Laura and Evvie, Elaine Strode of *The Man Who Loved His Wife* (1966) is a remarkable and resourceful woman of many talents who is victimized by a man. Yet, unlike them, she is also capable of being a victimizer and murderer. Caspary here seems to have altered her view of women's potential for violence. It would be hard to imagine the women in her stories about the 1920's, 1930's, and 1950's as anything but kind and considerate. Elaine, on the other hand, though as remarkable a woman as Laura or Evvie, is much tougher than either. Victimized to a limited extent by her domineering husband, Fletcher, Elaine takes charge of their lives after he loses his booming voice to cancer of the larynx. Unable to force his wife to do his bidding, he has to resort to manipulation based on her alleged sympathy for his plight.

Elaine, later found to be guilty of Fletcher's murder by strangulation, is overall an appealing character—strong beautiful, intelligent, well-read, and resourceful, a good match for a successful, egotistical husband. Like other Caspary women, however, she is not content to remain a housebound American wife. For her, marriage has become hell. Distraught because of both her loss of physical contact with Fletcher and his increasingly paranoid delusions about her secret affairs, Elaine decides to change what she can change, despite the fact that these alterations can be ushered in only by murder.

Because she is highly sexed, Elaine resembles other Caspary characters whose physical needs often get them into trouble. By being overtly sexual, Elaine breaks a long-standing American taboo, a holdover from Victorian days, against women being sexually adventurous (even though men can be as venturesome as they wish).

One theme that emerges in Caspary's crime novels is a sense that conformity brings rewards to those who choose it over bohemianism and that those few who do rebel will often pay a fearsome price for their defiance of custom. Caspary's female characters are free spirits who choose to follow any force that dominates them, whether it be the pursuit of money, of fame, or of love. Male characters are magnetically drawn to these women and encourage them to be unconventional, yet they also try to take advantage of them.

This is not to imply that Caspary's Evvie, Laura, or other female characters are always admirable, for there is a certain lassitude to their personalities, a kind of amoral drift as a result of lack of concern for the effects of their actions, that makes them flawed characters. One of the author's gifts is that she, unlike many crime-novel writers, is able to render rounded portraits of these women and the men who surround them. That they sometimes act in contradictory or paradoxical ways is an indication that Caspary has created flesh-and-blood characters rather than one-dimensional cutouts.

John D. Raymer
Updated by Fiona Kelleghan

PRINCIPAL MYSTERY AND DETECTIVE FICTION

NOVELS: *Laura*, 1943; *Bedelia*, 1945; *Stranger than Truth*, 1946; *The Murder in the Stork Club*, 1946 (also known as *The Lady in Mink*); *The Weeping and the Laughter*, 1950 (also known as *Death Wish*); *Thelma*, 1952; *False Face*, 1954; *The Husband*, 1957; *Evvie*, 1960; *A Chosen Sparrow*, 1964; *The Man Who Loved His Wife*, 1966; *The Rosecrest Cell*, 1967; *Final Portrait*, 1971; *Ruth*, 1972; *Elizabeth X*, 1978 (also known as *The Secret of Elizabeth*); *The Secrets of Grown-Ups*, 1979

OTHER MAJOR WORKS

NOVELS: *Ladies and Gents*, 1929; *The White Girl*, 1929; *Blind Mice*, 1930 (with Winifred Lenihan); *Music in the Street*, 1930; *Thicker than Water*, 1932; *Wedding in Paris*, 1956; *The Dreamers*, 1975

PLAYS: *Geraniums in My Window*, pb. 1934 (with Samuel Ornitz); *Laura*, pr. 1947 (with George Sklar); *Wedding in Paris: A Romantic Musical Play*, pb. 1956

SCREENPLAYS: *I'll Love You Always*, 1935; *Easy Living*, 1937 (with Preston Sturges); *Scandal Street*, 1938 (with Bertram Millhauser and Eddie Welch); *Service Deluxe*, 1938 (with others); *Sing, Dance, Plenty Hot*, 1940 (with others); *Lady from Louisiana*, 1941 (with others); *Lady Bodyguard*, 1942 (with Edmund L. Hartmann and Art Arthur); *Bedelia*, 1946 (with others); *Claudia and David*, 1946 (with Rose Franken and William Brown Meloney); *Out of the Blue*, 1947 (with Walter Bullock and Edward Eliscu); *A Letter to Three Wives*, 1949 (with Joseph L. Mankiewicz); *Three Husbands*, 1950 (with Eliscu); *I Can Get It for You Wholesale*, 1951 (with Abraham Polonsky); *The Blue Gardenia*, 1953 (with Charles Hoffman); *Give a Girl a Break*, 1954 (with Albert Hackett and Frances Goodrich); *Les Girls*, 1957 (with John Patrick)

BIBLIOGRAPHY

Bakerman, Jane S. "Vera Caspary's Fascinating Females: Laura, Evvie, and Bedelia." *Clues: A Journal of Detection* 1, no. 1 (Spring, 1980): 46-52. This comparison of Caspary's most famous and striking female characters reveals the mechanics of the author's representation of gender.

Carlin, Lianne. Review of *Laura*, by Vera Caspary. *The Mystery Lovers/Readers Newsletter* 3, no. 3 (February, 1970): 31. A review geared toward avid fans of the genre.

Caspary, Vera. *The Secrets of Grown-Ups*. New York: McGraw-Hill, 1979. The author's autobiography; essential reading for those who seek her own opinions on her life and work.

Giffuni, Cathe. "A Bibliography of Vera Caspary." *Clues* 16, no. 2 (Fall/Winter, 1995): 67-74. Useful checklist of Caspary's works.

Huang, Jim, ed. *They Died in Vain: Overlooked, Underappreciated, and Forgotten Mystery Novels*. Carmel, Ind.: Crum Creek Press, 2002. Caspary's *Laura* is a surprising entry in this book about underappreciated works of detective fiction.

Klein, Kathleen Gregory, ed. *Great Women Mystery Writers: Classic to Contemporary*. Westport, Conn.: Greenwood Press, 1994. Contains an essay on the life and work of Caspary.

McNamara, Eugene. *"Laura" as Novel, Film, and Myth*. Lewiston, N.Y.: Edwin Mellen Press, 1992. Compares the novel and the film as texts, as well as discussing popular perceptions of each.

Malmgren, Carl D. *Anatomy of Murder: Mystery, Detective, and Crime Fiction*. Bowling Green, Ohio: Bowling Green State University Popular Press, 2001. Includes discussion of *Laura*. Bibliographic references and index.

Penzler, Otto, ed. *The Great Detectives*. Boston: Little, Brown, 1978. Argues for including Caspary's Detective Mark McPherson among the mystery genre's "great detectives."

SARAH CAUDWELL
Sarah Caudwell Cockburn

Born: Cheltenham, Gloucestershire, England; May 27, 1939
Died: London, England; January 28, 2000
Types of plot: Cozy; comedy caper

PRINCIPAL SERIES
Hilary Tamar, 1981-2000

PRINCIPAL SERIES CHARACTER
HILARY TAMAR, middle-aged and of indeterminate gender, is a professor of medieval legal history at Oxford who keeps closely in touch with a group of barristers that contains several former students: Michael Cantrip, Desmond Ragwort, Selena Jardine, and Julia Larwood. The four young barristers, who share business quarters at 62 New Square in London, help Tamar solve cases, serving as auxiliary detectives by doing supplemental legwork to find evidence. They often are more involved in the thick of the action than the more intellectual Tamar, making the professor somewhat of a classic armchair detective. Although Tamar often relies on these reports from the field in making assessments of evidence and pursuing trails of inquiry, the professor nevertheless wields considerable intellectual authority and is charismatic in a cerebral way. Because the professor's gender is not revealed, Tamar is often referred to as simply Professor Tamar, the academic rank providing an ascribed identity in place of the unspecified gender.

CONTRIBUTION
Although the heyday of the lighthearted, cerebral mystery is often seen as the 1920's and 1930's, Sarah Caudwell reanimated this subgenre for the modern era. Her work's playfulness and zany high spirits, its acute observation of human foibles, and its intellectual trenchancy give it a distinct tone treasured by many readers. Although critics have sometimes found Caudwell overly derivative of Golden Age mystery novelists such as Dorothy L. Sayers and Michael Innes, her mystery plots depend far less on puzzles and more on a law-

yerlike detection of a loophole that her detective often perceives just in time to apprehend the criminal. In another departure from Golden Age mysteries, Caudwell took the puzzle story and plunged it into the milieu of supersonic airlines, the European Union, faxes, and feminism; she showed readers that the traditional detective story is not just an anachronism but, in the right hands, can be a vital contemporary form.

Caudwell also contributed much more rigor to a traditional aspect of the murder mystery: inheritance law and the intricacies of who gets the money after a person unexpectedly expires. As a tax lawyer, Caudwell was aware of loopholes and eccentricities in the British tax code that would supply a motive for murder when none was readily apparent. Caudwell's legal knowledge permeates the entire series and provides a realism that contributes to her novels' characteristic flavor.

Above all, however, Caudwell is best known for introducing a detective with no definite gender; this intriguing aspect allows Caudwell to move beyond the narrative of mystery into the mystery of the identity of the person who solves them.

BIOGRAPHY
Sarah Caudwell Cockburn (pronounced COH-burn), who published her mysteries as Sarah Caudwell, was born to a family of prominent left-wing intellectuals in 1930's England. Her father, Claud Cockburn, was an influential radical journalist, a well-known sympathizer with the policies of the Soviet Union, and a highly regarded novelist. He was connected by marriage or friendship with such well-known British intellectuals as Evelyn Waugh, Malcolm Muggeridge, and Graham Greene. He married Jean Ross, his second wife, and the couple had Sarah before divorcing. He then, in 1940, married Patricia Arbuthnot Byron, with whom he had three sons, Patrick, Alexander, and Andrew. All three of Sarah Caudwell's half siblings became successful, at times controversial, political journalists. Sarah's work, on the

other hand, was cheerfully free of any political relevance.

Caudwell graduated from the University of Aberdeen in northeast Scotland with a baccalaureate degree in classics, then studied law at St. Anne's College, Oxford, at the time a women's college. Infuriated by the men-only policy of the Oxford Union, the university's famous debating society, Caudwell attempted to enter the premises of the union wearing male clothing as a protest. She qualified to practice as a barrister—a lawyer specializing in advocacy at trials before the Chancery Bar, which, in Caudwell's lifetime, dealt mainly with issues of estates and trusts. She practiced there for the better part of a decade, then was hired by Lloyd's of London, an insurance company, as a tax-law specialist. Caudwell, unlike her series protagonist, was never a professor of law, nor was legal history a particular speciality of hers. Her knowledge of inheritance and tax law, however, did play a major role in the narrative construction of the Hilary Tamar mysteries.

Though Caudwell's plots and characters might seem quintessentially English, her books were well received in the United States, appreciated not only by Anglophiles but also by practicing attorneys. Their covers were frequently illustrated by Edward Gorey, the best-known American artist associated with illustrating mystery fiction.

Caudwell lived for much of her life with her mother, Jean Ross, and her mother's sister in the southwest London suburb of Barnes. She never married and no romantic attachments are a matter of public record. She died of esophageal cancer shortly before what would have been her sixty-first birthday. Caudwell was a frequent pipe smoker; her half brother Alexander attributed her relatively early death from cancer to this habit.

Caudwell was an inveterate theatergoer, and her play, *The Madman's Advocate,* was staged in Nottinghamshire, England, in 1994, and in New York in 1995; the play, however, has never been published, nor did it receive any additional stagings in the author's lifetime.

ANALYSIS

Although the unspecified gender of Professor Hilary Tamar should not overshadow the wit and intellec-

tual cogency of Sarah Caudwell's detective novels, it is certainly the feature of her work that has garnered the most attention. This is, perhaps, because it lays bare crucial if often suppressed issues in the detective genre. Does the detective need a gender? In the traditional detective story, the detective is gendered but often sexless. Agatha Christie's Hercule Poirot is obviously a man, and he often encourages young couples to marry and presides over marriages but is never personally involved in any union; that he has no perceptible love life is generally of little interest to his fans. He is free to remain the "mind" of the novel. If Hilary Tamar is, as some readers suspect, in fact, a woman, it is possible that Tamar is Caudwell's way of indicating that male detectives such as Poirot appear to be professionally unconstrained by their gender identity and are free to work as almost disembodied intellects. Caudwell, who had criticized Christopher Isherwood's partial portrait of her mother, Jean Ross, as the madcap flapper Sally Bowles in his Berlin stories, was aware of the potential narrative traps and scripts associated with women that would limit her protagonist's personal identity.

Hilary Tamar was the first detective to be without a specified gender; this innovation was heightened by Tamar's narration of the the four books in the series. Previous writers had featured female detectives with deliberately androgynous names and characters, such as American writer Marvin Kaye's Hilary Quayle in the 1970's, but Tamar was the first to be utterly genderless. Whereas the male hard-boiled writers of the 1930's gave their detectives aggressively masculine personae in contradistinction to the traditional detective's identity as genderless thinking machine, Caudwell emancipated her character entirely from characteristics determined by gender.

As with many names used for both men and women, the name Hilary was originally a largely male name; however, by the 1970's it had become more frequently used as a name for women. Caudwell deliberately gave her protagonist an ambisexual name to direct readers playfully at an enigma whose permanent shrouding is not simply a gimmick but a conceptual question that keeps readers alert and guessing throughout the series. Intriguingly, however, Tamar is clearly a woman's name, borne by two female characters in the Bible; it is also the name of a well-known river in the English shire of Cornwall.

The society Caudwell portrays might seem parochial, cloistered, and elitist at times, and some of its preoccupations might seem fey, but it is also of considerable appeal because its blend of intellect, camaraderie, and humane values represents the best of British civilization. What makes characters commendable in Caudwell's universe is their charm, compassion, and curiosity, rather than blood descent or even meritocracy in the conventional sense. Jokes, conversation, and irreverence are the unifying chords of the ensemble of spirited young friends. The group also accepts one another's frailties and their more than occasional bouts of foolishness. Though unlike Tamar, all the young colleagues are depicted as sexually active, none have settled down permanently with a partner, contributing to the series' celebration of a time of seemingly permanent and endless youth and freedom.

Caudwell was never a writer who relentlessly churned out a book every year or two. This made her oeuvre resemble that of a literary writer, one who does not feel the pressure to produce work at regular intervals. In addition, she did not use her detective as merely a superficial unifier of a disparate chain of plots. Each of the four Hilary Tamar mysteries feature situations appropriate for her detective, and all are steeped in a particular mood and milieu that demonstrate something about Tamar. As Caudwell's career progressed, her books lengthened and often contained more digressions and subplots. Readers who had been attracted by the firm, hard prose of *Thus Was Adonis Murdered* (1981) sometimes found this more leisured pace disconcerting, but the longer format was another factor that brought Caudwell's mysteries closer to the mainstream novel.

Thus Was Adonis Murdered

In *Thus Was Adonis Murdered*, Julia Larwood, one of the young barristers who work with Hilary Tamar, goes to Venice and is smitten by a young man. After Larwood manages to cajole the man into bed, however, she is shocked when he dies during their sexual encounter. She quickly realizes she is being framed for his death. Larwood's cohorts, including Tamar, even-

tually come to her assistance, but this is delayed because of the narrative device of the story, an epistolary tale in which Julia's letters home deliver each new installment of her unlikely ordeal. While the hapless Julia lends her predicament a farcical aspect, a subtheme of the book is cultural encounters between England and Italy. Readers learn much about various Venetian traditions, some of which turn out to be key to the plot.

The Shortest Way to Hades

In *The Shortest Way to Hades* (1985), Deirdre Galloway is the sole member of a large family who will not assent to a conspiracy designed to evade taxation due on a family trust that benefits another Galloway, Camilla. This determination, prompted by greed and not integrity, costs her her life. All the other Galloways are suspects, but only Tamar's specialized knowledge will aid her former pupils, who are handling the affair for the trust, in getting to the bottom of the puzzle. Greek islands in the Aegean Sea play the crosscultural role assumed by Venice in the previous novel and provide both the venue of the denouement and its conceptual rationale.

The Sirens Sang of Murder

In *The Sirens Sang of Murder* (1989), telexes sent by Michael Cantrip, the lone Cambridge graduate among the coven of Tamar's Oxford-educated barristers, play the role that Julia's letters from Italy assumed in Caudwell's first volume. Cantrip careens around the Channel Islands, a notorious tax haven, as well as the French mainland, trying to ferret out the truth of the affairs of the Daffodil Settlement, a dispiritedly complicated trust in which the fortunes of many individuals are tangled. Cantrip, being a man, is more likely to engage in physical action than his female counterparts, but this does not mean that he is in any way proficient at it. Indeed, he falls victim to a number of humiliations, some of them traps set by his enemies, some products only of his own foolishness. A secondary plot is provided by Cantrip's ridiculous attempt to collaborate with Julia Larwood on a steamy romance novel, which ends up being not nearly as exciting as the real-life plot in which Cantrip finds himself enmeshed.

THE SYBIL IN HER GRAVE

Fortune-telling and insider stock trading are usually seen as being in disparate worlds, but Caudwell's last novel, *The Sybil in Her Grave* (2000), brings the two together. Julia Larwood's Aunt Regina, who lives in the southeast English county of Sussex, has cultivated the friendship of local fortune-teller Isabella del Camino, a flamboyant newcomer much resented by the established community. Aunt Regina has had good news lately, as an investment made by herself and some friends has given her a tidy profit. However, one of Julia's barrister colleagues, Selena Jardine, in the course of investigating the affairs of a rich banker, discovers that Aunt Regina's profits may well have come from illegal insider trading. Could Isabella have been, in two senses of the word, the medium for this information? As is usual in Caudwell's novels, there is a European side to the action—this time in France, which further complicates a particularly intricate and tangled plot.

Nicholas Birns

PRINCIPAL MYSTERY AND DETECTIVE FICTION

HILARY TAMAR SERIES: *Thus Was Adonis Murdered*, 1981; *The Shortest Way to Hades*, 1985; *The Sirens Sang of Murder*, 1989; *The Sibyl in Her Grave*, 2000

NONSERIES NOVELS: *The Perfect Murder: Five Great Mystery Writers Create the Perfect Crime*, 1991 (with others)

PLAY: *The Madman's Advocate*, pr. 1994

BIBLIOGRAPHY

Dubose, Martha Hailey, with Margaret Caldwell Thomas. *Women of Mystery: The Lives and Works of Notable Women Crime Novelists*. New York: St. Martin's Minotaur, 2000. Contains a brief entry on her life and works.

Dyer, Lucinda. "Is She or Isn't He?" *Publishers Weekly* 248, no. 15 (April 9, 2001): 38. A capsule summary of the questions surrounding Hilary Tamar's gender identity.

Edwards, Martin. "Sarah Caudwell: A Most Ingenious Legal Mind." *Mystery Scene* 87 (2004): 50-51. Informal, enthusiastic appreciation of Caudwell's mysteries and the contributions the author's legal background made to them.

Flanders, Laura. "Crossing the Bar." *Women's Review of Books* 17, no. 7 (April, 2000): 5-6. Caudwell's niece, a prominent American radio personality, gives a personal tribute to her aunt that also contains some trenchant reflections on her work.

Kendrick, Walter. "Fiction in Review." *Yale Review* 81, no. 4 (October, 1993): 131-133. Kendrick, the late scholar and regular reviewer for *The Village Voice*, contends that the nongendered narrator of Jeannette Winterson's *Written on the Body* takes Caudwell's Hilary Tamar as a significant precedent.

King, Nina. "Wit and Polish." *Washington Post Book World*, July 23, 2000, p. X04. The well-known

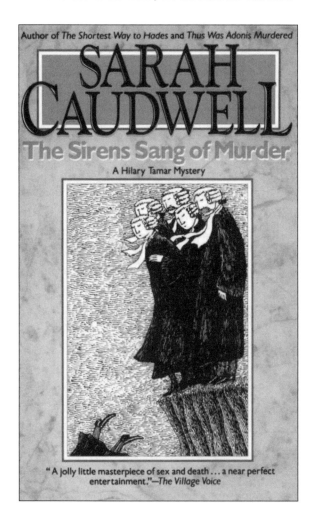

Author of *The Shortest Way to Hades* and *Thus Was Adonis Murdered*

SARAH CAUDWELL
The Sirens Sang of Murder
A Hilary Tamar Mystery

"A jolly little masterpiece of sex and death ... a near perfect entertainment."—*The Village Voice* book critic commends Caudwell's last novel in the course of an obituary tribute and identifies what American readers valued in Caudwell's fiction.

Klein, Kathleen Gregory, ed. *Great Women Mystery Writers: Classic to Contemporary.* Westport, Conn.: Greenwood Press, 1994. Contains a biocritical essay about Caudwell.

May, Radhika. "Murder Most Oxford." *Contemporary Review* 277, no. 1617 (October, 2000): 232-239. In

a survey of detective fiction set in Oxford from the era of Dorothy L. Sayers to the year 2000, May spotlights Caudwell's contribution.

Russell, Sharon A. "Gender and Voice in the Novels of Sarah Caudwell." In *Women Times Three: Writers, Detectives, Readers*, edited by Kathleen Gregory Klein. Bowling Green, Ohio: Bowling Green Univeristy Popular Press, 1995. By far the most academic and theoretical treatment of Caudwell.

JOHN NEWTON CHANCE

Born: London, England; 1911
Died: Cornwall, England; August 3, 1983
Also wrote as John Drummond; John Lymington; David C. Newton
Types of plot: Private investigator; thriller

PRINCIPAL SERIES

Sexton Blake, 1944-1955

PRINCIPAL SERIES CHARACTER

SEXTON BLAKE is the hero of numerous dime novels. With a residence on Baker Street, a faithful assistant, and a motherly landlady, he would seem to be a clone of Sherlock Holmes. Yet Blake is less intellectual and more spontaneous. His cases offer the reader action and adventure in the style of the Nick Carter novels.

CONTRIBUTION

A prolific author of popular fiction, John Newton Chance wrote in several genres—including science fiction and juvenile fiction. Writing under his own name, he produced close to one hundred thrillers, among the best being *The Screaming Fog* (1944), *The Eye in Darkness* (1946), and *The Killing Experiment* (1969). Recurring characters in these novels are Superintendent "Smutty" Black, Jonathan Blake, David Chance, Mr. DeHavilland, and John Marsh. Working in the same literary tradition, that of the crime thriller, Chance wrote the Sexton Blake series under the name of John Drum-

mond. This series consists of some two dozen mysteries that were to constitute Chance's most sustained literary effort. Using the pseudonym of John Lymington, Chance became an outstanding writer of science fiction with such works as *The Night Spiders* (1964), *Froomb!* (1964), and *Ten Million Years to Friday* (1967). His international reputation seems to rest primarily on these works.

Throughout his narratives, Chance evidences fine talent in handling setting, especially the creation of atmosphere. He populates his settings with some vivid and memorable characters; they are usually purposely overdrawn, frequently grotesque, and always entertaining. His characters have been compared to those of Charles Dickens and even Geoffrey Chaucer. Further, Chance had a highly developed sense of timing—so crucial to both thrillers and detective fiction—and a deft touch in the handling of individual scenes in his novels.

BIOGRAPHY

John Newton Chance was born in London in 1911, the son of Robert Newton Chance, a comic-strip editor. In addition to his private educational training, he attended secondary school in London and Streatham Hill College. He was married to Shirley Savill, with whom he later collaborated on at least one book, and they had three sons.

Chance began his literary career in 1931 with a story written for the British Broadcasting Corporation.

Later, writing for the *Sunday Graphic*, he produced "Murder Mosaics," a series of mystery dramas that, taken together, constituted a serial murder novel. After the publication of *Murder in Oils* in 1935, he became well known as an author of popular fiction and remained so throughout much of the twentieth century. His best works were produced from the 1930's to the 1950's; the later books, often categorized as potboilers, did not maintain the same high standards. Even for his fine early works, Chance did not receive the critical recognition he deserved, and his fame remains largely restricted to England.

During World War II, Chance flew with the Royal Air Force; he was invalided out of the service in 1944. His wartime experiences, as well as his literary ones, are chronicled in his autobiographical work *Yellow Belly* (1959). Chance died in Cornwall, England, on August 3, 1983.

ANALYSIS

Unlike most writers of thrillers and detective fiction, John Newton Chance does not demonstrate strength in the plotting of his works. Yet he largely offsets this weakness by creating a memorable atmosphere and by drawing vivid characters. Chance consistently makes use of a gothic setting—usually a mansion, castle, or palace that is deteriorating. Typically, these structures have many rooms and are filled with strange chambers, secret passages, and underground labyrinths. Trapdoors, sliding panels, shadowy hallways, and heavy gothic furnishings are the rule.

The Screaming Fog offers an excellent example of Chance's gothic setting. From a distance, the village where the action takes place looks like some dream castle. It sits on a hill and is enveloped in mist, the roofs of the houses shining with a golden transparency. A closer look reveals the small English town to be shrouded in the "devilish breath of the smuggler's marsh." It was once a haven for smugglers, and all inns and barns are connected by passages and wells to a system of catacombs beneath the town. Also, the town is spiritually isolated, and the citizenry has consciously tried to maintain this isolation. Bordering the old walled town is the mud of the marshes that sucks victims down into its heaving bosom. The local inn, called the Leather Pot, a focal point in the story, is filled with menacing shadows and is backed up against the city wall; beyond that wall is a sheer drop to the marshes below. In *The Screaming Fog*, Chance rejects the sleepy country village and manor house settings so common to British mystery novels. Instead, he uses strange settings pregnant with evil, hostility, and fear.

Using such settings to encourage his reader to suspend disbelief, Chance proceeds to offer fittingly bizarre and grotesque scenes: a skeleton wears a wristwatch, a lifelike dummy's head falls off and rolls across the floor, and a skeleton wearing a suit, shirt, and tie is found in a cupboard.

Chance's skill in characterization is on the same advanced level as his handling of setting. With the exception of Sexton Blake, he avoids centering his novels on one series character; instead, he repeatedly brings several performers back on his literary stage, gaining continuity but not limiting himself to one personality. As one would expect, those recurring characters are the protagonists of the works: Superintendent "Smutty" Black, the chief of police who looks like a deformed dwarf, and Mr. DeHavilland, a Rabelaisian character who upstages all others. Both first appear in Chance's second novel, *Wheels in the Forest* (1935), and they reappear each time the author returns to the setting of the little forest village of Wey. David Chance, who is not given a first name until his third role, in *The Eye in Darkness*, is a former actor and a former thief now turned champion of justice and law. Chance, along with his fiancée, Sally Wilding, a beautiful journalist, first appears in *The Screaming Fog*. Also prominent in the novels is Jonathan Blake, who enters in *The Affair at Dead End* (1966). The blind menace named Rolf and his Circe-like wife, Evelyn, who also first appear in *The Screaming Fog*, are so delightfully villainous that they are brought back for repeat performances.

Chance's many outstanding creations bear resemblance to those of Charles Dickens; they would not seem out of place on a Chaucerian pilgrimage and could grace the pages of François Rabelais. Chance draws his characters with a few broad strokes. His villains are especially grotesque; they include freaks, recluses, madmen, tyrants, and Satan figures. Although these supervillains consistently lose the battle between good and evil, they usually steal the attention and often the hearts of the readers.

Chance's handling of his characters often reflects the influence of drama and the stage. His characters are overdrawn, often deformed, and their actions are bold and exaggerated. Chance likes a filled stage and constantly rushes his characters on and off the boards; he shifts scenes skillfully, engrossing the reader. (Illustrating these dramatic touches is the delightful series of comic encounters at the inn in *The Red Knight*, 1945.) Chance typically populates his fiction with a supporting cast of stock characters: scheming maids, suspicious family retainers, absentminded divines, shrewish wives, aspiring lovers beset by obstacles, and bumbling, good-natured gentry. One of the continuing characters in the novels, the former actor David Chance, is periodically forced into the role of private investigator. Also, the narratives often include dramatic performances; for example, in both *The Screaming Fog* and *The Red Knight* the action moves to its climax in a public performance scene.

Chance often falters in the plotting of his novels—although the basic conception behind the plot frequently displays a fine imagination. The problem usually arises in his efforts to sustain the action and development and to resolve the problems and conflicts in the narratives. Although his earlier works are considered far superior to his later ones, even Chance's novels of the 1930's and 1940's suffered from weak plots. For example, the plot in *The Screaming Fog* is exaggerated to the point of self-parody. Two young journalists have stumbled on an odd village where the leading townspeople, including the mayor and the chief of police, are plotting to take over the whole of England. This coterie of human freaks have stationed key men in every important town in England, and they have planted time bombs in strategic locations all over the country. The explosions are to occur at one o'clock in the morning; chaos will reign, and the leading townspeople will take control. The character Chance and Sally Wilding must uncover the plot and thwart it, thereby saving England. It is not surprising when Chance solves the problem, saves the country—and finds love. The archvillains, Rolf and Evelyn, survive

to oppose Chance again in *The Red Knight* (the sequel, which suffers from an even more mundane plot). In Chance's novels the motivation is often unclear, the crime is frequently only incidental, and the lines of development are vague.

THE EYE IN DARKNESS

Although his thrillers are flawed, Chance proved quite skillful at writing detective fiction. Bridging the gap between the two forms, the character Chance moves from a supporting role in *The Screaming Fog* and *The Red Knight* to the lead role in *The Eye in Darkness*, a somewhat standard whodunit—but a very good one. Lacking the grotesque elements, the humor, and many of the gothic gimmicks of the earlier works, *The Eye in Darkness* concentrates on a most worthy criminal, a cleverly conceived crime, and brilliant sleuthing. Paul Marlowe, an aging magician and delightful villain who arouses fear and hate while still eliciting the reader's sympathy, is the evil patriarch of Deadwater Park, where the tale is set. Devilish in appearance, action, and speech, he engineers an intricate and engaging plot that rivals those of the best of literary criminals. Having gathered his relatives together, he explains to them one evening that he is a dying man and is leaving a large sum of money to each. Yet all will be disinherited if he, Marlowe, is still alive the next morning. It would seem he has arranged for his own murder that night; he calls the situation an "experiment with human nature." Murder in *The Eye in Darkness* is to be a family affair.

The first victim is Mr. Raymond, the family solicitor, who is strangled in the library. The suspects are Laura Mallison, who is compared to a bejeweled Persian cat, and her husband, Joe, who has the appearance of a small lizard; Ann Marlowe, a golden-haired beauty, and her young lover, Tony Marston, a somewhat sullen but handsome knight; Betty Mears, the maid, who may be Marlowe's illegitimate daughter; and Barribal, the enigmatic family retainer. When the first two of these suspects also fall victim to the murderer, the solution should be made much more simple, but instead the situation becomes even more confused.

David Chance is forced to assume the role of detective. Trying to reach his wife, who is giving birth, he is thwarted by a snowstorm and seeks shelter at Deadwater Park. There he learns of the three murders, and an attack is made on his own life. For self-preservation, if nothing else, he must discover the murderer. Assisting him is Dr. Hay, an unflappable old physician. Chance's investigation uncovers insidious hate and madness within the family. In addition, this detective novel offers a cast of characters isolated by the storm, a locked-room murder, blackmail, and many red herrings.

Unlike most of Chance's novels, *The Eye in Darkness* is well plotted. Telescoping the action into one night, the author creates and maintains fine suspense. The solution is a surprise, and the revelation scene is skillfully handled. The explanation is interspersed with action, creating an excitement often missing in other detective fiction. Whereas other Chance plots, especially in the thrillers, falter as the novel progresses, here the action is effectively sustained.

In Chance's fiction, individual scenes often display flashes of outstanding narrative skill. For example, the opening scene of each novel is usually one of well-calculated action meant to ensnare the reader: These include the garroting of a man in *The Red Knight*, the frenzied attempt to reach a pregnant woman in *The Eye in Darkness*, and the mysterious meeting of the cast at the Grindell house in *Spy on a Spider* (1987). Other noteworthy scenes include one at the inn in *The Red Knight* where there is great movement, turmoil, and confusion, and, in the same novel, the description of the epic battle and the resulting pandemonium.

THE SCREAMING FOG AND THE RED KNIGHT

Proving to be Chance's most effective narrative device, the flight-and-pursuit motif creates much drama in his fiction, and chase scenes are carefully inserted to heighten the action at key stages. Many of them are found in the early thrillers—for example, the flight of Sally and Chance through the underground passages and later over the rooftops as they are pursued by a bevy of freakish killers. Other chases involve an automobile; these include Colonel Handy's reckless drive across the marshes in *The Screaming Fog*, and, in *The Red Knight*, Chance's hectic ride through countryside and villages in an effort to beat Sally's taxi to the train station. In these scenes, a fine sense of recklessness is evident. Chance seems to have relished such overstated dramatic scenes.

Contributing to the sense of action in the novels is Chance's very effective use of counterpointing. He is able to sustain several exciting scenes until they merge. An example from *The Screaming Fog* is the segment balancing corresponding scenes by shifting from the villains who are planning Chance's downfall to Sally as she is attacked by Carne in the cellar to Chance sleeping in his chair at the inn. A similar example from *The Red Knight* features skillful movement back and forth from the scene where two of Rolf's men try to kidnap Sally to a parallel scene where three other of Rolf's men encounter Chance and DeHavilland on the lawn and face a strong counterattack. Finally, an even more effective use of this counterpointing is found in the inferior *Spy on a Spider*, where the scene shifts back and forth among the three settings for the novel: the house in the Lake District, the castle on Spider Island (three scenes on three floors there), and the old steamer lying off the coast. These separate scenes are handled simultaneously and are clearly shown to affect one another.

Complementing the setting as well as the action in the novels are vivid imagery, melodrama, and comic devices and situations. The latter are especially effective; throughout Chance's thrillers, one finds humor and comic relief. As Chance the character undergoes a series of hair-raising experiences, he is clearly having a good time despite the ever-present danger. Accompanied by his golden spaniel, he can laugh at horrible situations. The humor invested in both the characters and the actions is primarily Rabelaisian. For example, Bushy Bruin's lecture on the belly as the inspiration for and foundation of the arts is a prize comic mini-dissertation. Humor especially abounds in the several novels featuring Mr. DeHavilland.

ROMANCE

A secondary but significant element in Chance's narratives is romance, an area in which he lacked assurance. Often noted in various novels is the love between Chance and Sally Wilding, for example, but this is never effectively demonstrated. In *The Eye in Darkness*, the narrator even states that he is "no good" at sentimental scenes and then proceeds to demonstrate this fact in his handling of both romantic and familial love. Much later, in *Spy on a Spider*, Chance made an effort to convey the emotion of love in his fiction; yet the depiction of romance and passion did not come easily to him. Instead, he excelled at depicting the harsher emotions—primarily hate, envy, greed, and fear.

Chance's novels are clearly not intellectual; at their best, they offer an escape from the ordinary and a playful sense of humor. Although his plots tend to be imitative (they borrow from sources ranging from William Shakespeare's plays to Lewis Carroll's *Alice in Wonderland*), his skill in writing individual scenes, his creation of a distinctive atmosphere, and his development of memorable characters guarantee a place for Chance in the history of the mystery and detective genre.

Max L. Autrey

PRINCIPAL MYSTERY AND DETECTIVE FICTION

SEXTON BLAKE SERIES (AS DRUMMOND): *The Essex Road Crime*, 1944; *The Manor House Menace*, 1944; *The Painted Dagger*, 1944; *The Riddle of the Leather Bottle*, 1944; *The Tragic Case of the Station Master's Legacy*, 1944; *At Sixty Miles an Hour*, 1945; *The House on the Hill*, 1945; *The Riddle of the Mummy Case*, 1945; *The Mystery of the Deserted Camp*, 1948; *The Town of Shadows*, 1948; *The Case of the "Dead" Spy*, 1949; *The Riddle of the Receiver's Hoard*, 1949; *The Secret of the Living Skeleton*, 1949; *The South Coast Mystery*, 1949; *The Case of L. A. C. Dickson*, 1950; *The House in the Woods*, 1950; *The Mystery of the Haunted Square*, 1950; *Hated by All!*, 1951; *The Case of the Man with No Name*, 1951; *The Mystery of the Sabotaged Jet*, 1951; *The Secret of the Sixty Steps*, 1951; *The House on the River*, 1952; *The Mystery of the Five Guilty Men*, 1954; *The Case of the Two-Faced Swindler*, 1955; *The Teddy-Boy Mystery*, 1955

NONSERIES NOVELS: 1935-1940 • *Murder in Oils*, 1935; *Wheels in the Forest*, 1935; *The Devil Drives*, 1936; *Maiden Possessed*, 1937; *Rhapsody in Fear*, 1937; *Death of an Innocent*, 1938; *The Devil in Greenlands*, 1939; *The Ghost of Truth*, 1939

1941-1950 • *The Screaming Fog*, 1944 (also known as *Death Stalks the Cobbled Square*); *The Red Knight*, 1945; *The Eye in Darkness*, 1946; *The Knight and the Castle*, 1946; *The Black Highway*, 1947; *Co-ven Gibbet*, 1948; *The Brandy Pole*, 1949; *The Night of the Full Moon*, 1950

1951-1960 • *Aunt Miranda's Murder*, 1951; *The Man in My Shoes*, 1952; *The Twopenny Box*, 1952; *The Jason Affair*, 1953 (also known as *Up to Her Neck*); *The Randy Inheritance*, 1953; *Jason and the Sleep Game*, 1954; *The Jason Murders*, 1954; *Jason Goes West*, 1955; *A Shadow Called Janet*, 1956; *The Last Seven Hours*, 1956; *Dead Man's Knock*, 1957; *The Little Crime*, 1957; *Affair with a Rich Girl*, 1958; *The Man with Three Witches*, 1958; *The Fatal Fascination*, 1959; *The Man with No Face*, 1959; *Alarm at Black Brake*, 1960; *Lady in a Frame*, 1960

1961-1965 • *Import of Evil*, 1961; *The Night of the Settlement*, 1961; *Triangle of Fear*, 1962; *Anger at World's End*, 1963; *The Forest Affair*, 1963; *The Man Behind Me*, 1963; *Commission for Disaster*, 1964; *Death Under Desolate*, 1964

1966-1970 • *Stormlight*, 1966; *The Affair at Dead End*, 1966; *The Double Death*, 1966; *The Case of the Death Computer*, 1967; *The Case of the Fear Makers*, 1967; *The Death Women*, 1967; *The Hurricane Drift*, 1967; *The Mask of Pursuit*, 1967; *The Thug Executive*, 1967; *Dead Man's Shoes*, 1968; *Death of the Wild Bird*, 1968; *Fate of the Lying Jade*, 1968; *Mantrap*, 1968; *The Halloween Murders*, 1968; *The Rogue Aunt*, 1968; *Involvement in Austria*, 1969; *The Abel Coincidence*, 1969; *The Ice Maidens*, 1969; *The Killer Reaction*, 1969; *The Killing Experiment*, 1969; *A Ring of Liars*, 1970; *The Mirror Train*, 1970; *The Mists of Treason*, 1970; *Three Masks of Death*, 1970

1971-1975 • *A Wreath of Bones*, 1971; *The Cat Watchers*, 1971; *The Faces of a Bad Girl*, 1971; *A Bad Dream of Death*, 1972; *Last Train to Limbo*, 1972; *The Dead Tale-Tellers*, 1972; *The Man with Two Heads*, 1972; *The Farm Villains*, 1973; *The Grab Operators*, 1973; *The Love-Hate Relationship*, 1973; *The Canterbury Kilgrims*, 1974; *The Girl in the Crime Belt*, 1974; *The Shadow of the Killer*, 1974; *The Starfish Affair*, 1974; *Hill Fog*, 1975; *The Devil's Edge*, 1975; *The Monstrous Regiment*, 1975

1976-1980 • *A Fall-Out of Thieves*, 1976; *Return to Death Valley*, 1976; *The Frightened Fisherman*, 1976; *The Laxham Haunting*, 1976; *The Murder Makers*, 1976; *Motive for a Kill*, 1977; *The House of the Dead*

Ones, 1977; *End of an Iron Man*, 1978; *The Ducrow Folly*, 1978; *A Drop of Hot Gold*, 1979; *The Guilty Witness*, 1979; *Thieves' Kitchen*, 1979; *A Place Called Skull*, 1980; *The Black Widow*, 1980; *The Death Watch Ladies*, 1980; *The Mayhem Madchen*, 1980

1981-1987 • *The Death Importer*, 1981; *The Mystery of Edna Favell*, 1981; *Madman's Will*, 1982; *The Hunting of Mr. Exe*, 1982; *The Shadow in Pursuit*, 1982; *Terror Train*, 1983; *The Death Chemist*, 1983; *The Traditional Murders*, 1983; *Looking for Samson*, 1984; *Nobody's Supposed to Murder the Butler*, 1984; *The Bad Circle*, 1985; *Time Bomb*, 1985; *Spy on a Spider*, 1987

OTHER MAJOR WORKS

NOVELS (AS LYMINGTON): *Night of the Big Heat*, 1960; *The Giant Stumbles*, 1960; *The Grey Ones*, 1960; *The Coming of the Strangers*, 1961; *A Sword Above the Night*, 1962; *The Screaming Face*, 1963; *The Sleep Eaters*, 1963; *Froomb!*, 1964; *The Green Drift*, 1965; *The Star Witches*, 1965; *Ten Million Years to Friday*, 1967; *Give Daddy the Knife, Darling*, 1969; *The Nowhere Place*, 1969; *The Year Dot*, 1972; *The Hole in the World*, 1974; *A Spider in the Bath*, 1975; *Starseed on Gye Moor*, 1977; *The Grey Ones, A Sword Above the Night*, 1978; *The Waking of the Stone*, 1978; *A Caller from Overspace*, 1979; *Voyage of the Eighth Mind*, 1980; *The Power Ball*, 1981; *The Terror Vision*, 1982; *The Vale of the Sad Banana*, 1984

SHORT FICTION: *The Night Spiders*, 1964

CHILDREN'S LITERATURE: *The Black Ghost*, 1947; *The Dangerous Road*, 1948 (as Newton); *Bunst and the Brown Voice*, 1950-1953; *The Jennifer Jigsaw*, 1951

NONFICTION: *Yellow Belly*, 1959; *The Crimes at Rillington Place: A Novelist's Reconstruction*, 1961

BIBLIOGRAPHY

Anderson, Patrick. *The Triumph of the Thriller: How Cops, Crooks, and Cannibals Captured Popular Fiction*. New York: Random House, 2007. Comprehensive history of the American thriller provides the tool to understand Chance's accomplishments and contributions to the genre's English version.

Horsley, Lee. *Twentieth-Century Crime Fiction*. New York: Oxford University Press, 2005. Very useful overview of the history and parameters of the crime-fiction genre; helps place Chance's work within that genre.

The Times Literary Supplement. Review of *The Red Knight*, by John Newton Chance. June 16, 1945, p. 296. Review of the book featuring the characters Chance and Sally reveals what his contemporaries thought of Chance.

The Times Literary Supplement. Review of *The Screaming Fog*, by John Newton Chance. September 9, 1944, p. 437. Review of another Chance and Sally adventure provides an idea of Chance's reception in his native England.

RAYMOND CHANDLER

Born: Chicago, Illinois; July 23, 1888
Died: La Jolla, California; March 26, 1959
Types of plot: Private investigator; hard-boiled

PRINCIPAL SERIES
Philip Marlowe, 1939-1958

PRINCIPAL SERIES CHARACTER
PHILIP MARLOWE is a private investigator and was formerly an investigator for the Los Angeles district attorney's office; he has never married. Marlowe is thirty-three years old in *The Big Sleep* (1939), and in the penultimate novel, *The Long Goodbye* (1953), he is forty-two. He is a tough, street-smart man with a staunch, though highly individual, code of ethics. This code not only defines his personal and professional character but also is the source of both his pride and his often-embittered alienation.

CONTRIBUTION
On the basis of only seven novels, two dozen short stories, and a few articles and screenplays, Raymond Chandler firmly established himself in the pantheon of detective-fiction writers. Though he was by no means the first to write in a hard-boiled style, Chandler significantly extended the range and possibilities for the hard-boiled detective novel. Along with Dashiell Hammett, Chandler created some of the finest works in the genre, novels that, many have argued, stand among the most prominent—detective or otherwise—in the twentieth century. Chandler's achievement is largely a result of three features: a unique, compelling protagonist, a rich, individual style, and a keen concern for various social issues. He established the measure by which other hard-boiled fiction would be judged, and numerous other detective novelists, including Mickey Spillane, Ross Macdonald, and Robert B. Parker, have acknowledged a strong indebtedness to Chandler's work.

BIOGRAPHY
Raymond Thornton Chandler was born on July 23, 1888, in Chicago, the only child of Maurice Benjamin Chandler and Florence Dart Thornton. Within a few years, his parents separated, and Maurice Chandler disappeared entirely. In 1896, Florence Chandler brought Raymond to London, where he attended Dulwich College. Chandler was an excellent student, and the experiences of a British public school education shaped his character indelibly. After leaving Dulwich in 1905, Chandler spent a year in France and then Germany; he then returned to England and secured a civil service job, which he left to become a writer. During this period, he wrote for various newspapers and composed some poetry (many of these pieces have been collected in *Chandler Before Marlowe: Raymond Chandler's Early Prose and Poetry*, 1973). In 1912, he returned to the United States and settled in California, but, with the outbreak of World War I, he enlisted in the Canadian army, saw action, was injured, and eventually returned to civilian life and California.

In 1919, after various jobs, Chandler became an executive (eventually a vice president) with the Dabney Oil Syndicate, and after the death of his mother in 1924 he married Cissy Pascal, a woman sixteen years his senior. In 1932, as his drinking increased and his behavior became more erratic, Chandler was fired. In 1933, his first story was published in the pulp magazine *Black Mask*, and he continued writing stories for the next six years, until the publication of *The Big Sleep* in 1939. In 1943, after the publication of three novels and more stories, Chandler went to work for Paramount Studios as a screenwriter, eventually working on the scripts for *Double Indemnity* (1944) and *The Blue Dahlia* (1946), both of which were nominated for Academy Awards and the latter of which earned an Edgar Allan Poe Award from the Mystery Writers of America. With these successes, Chandler commanded increasingly higher salaries, largely unprecedented in their day.

Chandler left Hollywood in 1946 and moved to La Jolla, where he remained for the next ten years. After a long and painful illness, his wife died in 1954. The next year, Chandler drank heavily and attempted suicide, and from 1956 to 1957 he lived alternately in

Raymond Chandler. (Library of Congress)

London and La Jolla. In 1955, he was awarded his second Edgar, for *The Long Goodbye*, and in 1959 he was elected president of the Mystery Writers of America, but within a month, on March 26, 1959, he died of pneumonia.

ANALYSIS

Raymond Chandler began his writing career in London in 1908 as a poet. He would have remained anonymous, however, had he not begun publishing hard-boiled detective stories in *Black Mask* magazine in 1933. He worked slowly, producing twenty-one stories in five years, learning the craft under the tutelage of *Black Mask* editor "Cap" Shaw and attempting to match and even exceed his inspiration, Dashiell Hammett. With the publication of *The Big Sleep*, his first novel, Chandler not only reached his mature style but also created his most enduring protagonist, Philip Marlowe. In addition, one finds in that novel many of the themes and concerns that became representative of Chandler himself.

PHILIP MARLOWE

In Marlowe, Chandler wanted a new kind of detective hero, not simply a lantern-jawed tough guy with quick fists. Such a hero he found in Arthurian romance—the knight, a man dedicated to causes greater than himself, causes that could restore a world and bestow honor on himself. References and allusions to the world of chivalry are sprinkled liberally throughout the Marlowe novels. (The name Marlowe is itself suggestive of Sir Thomas Malory, author of *Le Morte d'Arthur*, 1485.) In *The Big Sleep*, Marlowe visits the Sternwood mansion at the beginning of the novel and notices a stained-glass panel in which a damsel is threatened by a dragon and a knight is doing battle. Marlowe stares at the scene and concludes, "I stood there and thought that if I lived in the house, I would sooner or later have to climb up there and help him. He didn't seem to be really trying." Later, after foiling a seduction, Marlowe looks down at his chessboard and muses, "Knights had no meaning in this game. It wasn't a game for knights."

In *The High Window* (1942), a character calls Marlowe a "shop-soiled Galahad," and the title of the next novel, *The Lady in the Lake* (1943), is an ironic reference to the supernatural character in Arthurian legends who provides Excalibur but who also makes difficult demands. At one point in that novel, Marlowe refers to life as "the long grim fight," which for a knight would be exactly the case. In *The Long Goodbye*, Marlowe becomes involved in Terry Lennox's fate simply by accident but mainly because Lennox appears vulnerable. As Marlowe explains late in the novel to another character, "I'm a romantic. . . . I hear voices crying in the night and I go see what's the matter."

In keeping with his knightly attitudes, Marlowe practices sexual abstinence despite countless seduction attempts. In every novel, women are attracted to Marlowe and he to them. He continually deflects their advances, however, and dedicates himself to the rigors of the case. Chandler wrote about the necessity of keeping a detective's interest solely on the case, but he tired of what he saw as the inhuman quality of such a man in such a business. Thus, in *The Long Goodbye*, Marlowe sleeps with Linda Loring, though he refuses to run away with her to Paris. In *Playback* (1958), he sleeps with two women, but the novel ends with his sending Linda Loring money to return to California. In "The Poodle Springs Story," a fragment of what was to be the next Marlowe novel, Chandler marries Marlowe to Loring and has them living, uneasily, in wealthy Palm Springs (here, Poodle Springs).

Marlowe also is scrupulously honest in his financial dealings, taking only as much money as he has earned and often returning fees he thinks are excessive or compromising. In case after case, Marlowe simply refuses money; as he explains in *The Big Sleep*, "You can't make much money at this trade, if you're honest." In *Farewell, My Lovely* (1940), Marlowe persists in his investigation even after he has been warned by the police, simply because he accepted a fee and failed to protect his client adequately. As he explains at one point in *The Long Goodbye*,

> I've got a five-thousand-dollar bill in my safe but I'll never spend a nickel of it. Because there was something wrong with the way I got it. I played with it a little at first and I still get it out once in a while and look at it. But that's all—not a dime of spending money.

It follows then that Marlowe's first allegiance is to the case or client; "The client comes first, unless he's crooked. Even then all I do is hand the job back to him and keep my mouth shut." Perhaps the most dramatic evidence of this attitude comes in *The Long Goodbye*, when Marlowe remains silent and in jail for three days after being beaten by the police, rather than confirm what they already know. Later in the novel, he gives an official Photostat of a death confession, knowing that he may be beaten or killed by any number of outraged parties, because he wants to clear the name of his dead client-friend, Terry Lennox.

Often these clients become friends. In the case of Terry Lennox, however, a short but intense friendship is ultimately betrayed when the supposedly dead Lennox appears at the end of the novel and exhibits little appreciation for the difficulties through which he has put Marlowe. In *Farewell, My Lovely*, Marlowe establishes a brief friendship with Red Norgaard, a former police officer who helps Marlowe get aboard a gambling ship. The most long-standing friendship, though, is with Bernie Ohls, the chief investigator with the Los Angeles district attorney's office. Marlowe and Ohls were once partners, and though the relationship is strained since Marlowe's dismissal, Ohls frequently bails Marlowe out of trouble or smooths over matters with the authorities to allow the private eye to continue his investigation.

Another important aspect of Marlowe's code involves his uneasy attitude toward the law. Marlowe is clearly outraged by the exploitation around him, as criminal bosses, small-time hoods, and corrupt police allow crime to flourish. Marlowe is committed to a better world, a world that certainly does not exist in his Los Angeles, or anywhere else for that matter. As Marlowe disgustedly explains to Terry Lennox,

> You had nice ways and nice qualities, but there was something wrong. You had standards and you lived up to them, but they were personal. They had no relation to any kind of ethics or scruples. . . . You were just as happy with mugs or hoodlums as with honest men . . . You're a moral defeatist.

Such an attitude explains Marlowe's mixed relations with the police. In almost every novel, Chandler portrays fundamentally honest, hard-working police offset by venal, brutal cops, usually from Bay City (Chandler's fictitious locale based on Santa Monica). Consistently, members of the district attorney's office are the best of these figures, men of principle and dedication. A look at *Farewell, My Lovely* provides a representative example of Chandler's treatment of these characters.

FAREWELL, MY LOVELY

Detective-lieutenant Nulty, an eighteen-year veteran, is a tired, resigned hack who dismisses the murder of a black bar-owner as "another shine killing" that will win for him no headlines or picture in the papers. His greatest flaws are his apathy and laziness; he even invites Marlowe into the case so that the private eye can solve matters for him.

Randall of Central Homicide is a lean, crisp, efficient police officer. He repeatedly warns Marlowe to drop the case and remains suspicious of Marlowe's motives. Randall continually and unsuccessfully tries to pry information loose from Marlowe, and their relationship is one of competition and grudging respect.

On the other hand, Blane, of the Bay City force, is a crooked cop who delights in beating Marlowe. Lacking any moral fiber, Blane is content to do the bidding of corrupt mobsters who own the town. His partner, Lieutenant Galbraith, is uneasy about the compromises he has made. At one point, he offers a compelling explanation for his position:

> Cops don't go crooked for money. Not always, not even often. They get caught in the system. They get you where they have you do what is told them or else. . . . A guy can't stay honest if he wants to. . . . That's what's the matter with this country. He gets chiseled out of his pants if he does. You gotta play the game dirty or you don't eat. . . . I think we gotta make this little world all over again.

Marlowe clearly cannot accept such rationalizations and responds: "If Bay City is a sample of how it works, I'll take aspirin."

The important contribution Chandler makes with these figures is to balance the view of the police in detective fiction. The classic formula, established by Edgar Allan Poe and embraced by countless other writers, depicted police as well-intentioned bunglers. In hard-boiled fiction, the police are often brutal competitors with the private eye, but in Chandler's works they are human beings; allowed more of the stage, they often explain themselves and their world. Those who are corrupt are revealed as especially pernicious creatures because they have become part of the major network of crime; they aid and abet corruption rather than uphold their sworn duty to fight it. Too often "law is where you buy it," which explains the need for a man such as Marlowe.

Marlowe has equally ambivalent attitudes about women, and in each novel different types of women are paired off against each other. One critic, Michael Mason, contends that in Chandler's novels the "moral scheme is in truth pathologically harsh on women" and that "[w]arm, erotic feeling and loving contact with a woman are irreconcilable for Marlowe." Although Mason's contentions deserve attention, they overlook the fundamental nature and reasons for Marlowe's dilemma.

In *Farewell, My Lovely*, Marlowe claims that he likes "smooth shiny girls, hardboiled and loaded with sin," and indeed he is more than casually interested in the voluptuous Helen Grayle. Anne Riordan, however, the police officer's daughter and Marlowe's confidante and assistant on the case, also commands much of Marlowe's attention. Marlowe's problem stems from his knightly view—he is continually torn between idealism and reality and cannot find a compromise between the two. One part of Marlowe seeks the ideal, perfect woman, a modern-day Guinevere, and Anne Riordan, with her background, independence, and intelligence, appears to be the perfect woman for Marlowe. Her house is a haven from crime and brutality, and Marlowe instinctively runs there after his incarceration in Dr. Sonderborg's drug clinic. Invited to stay the night, Marlowe refuses, worried that the sordidness of his world will invade the sanctuary of Riordan's life.

Another part of Marlowe is disgusted with women such as Helen Grayle and the dissolute Jesse Florian. They are either unintelligent and ugly or morally depraved, lustful creatures who pose threats to the knight's purity. They are seen as calculating and capable of deflecting the detective's attention and easily destroying him.

Marlowe's problem is clearly that he cannot see women as falling between these extremes. Thus, he is destined to be continually attracted but ultimately disappointed by women, and what makes his condition all the worse is his knowledge of it. Marlowe knows that he expects too much, that his sentiments are extreme and hopelessly sentimental. As Chandler reveals in the novel's last scene, where Marlowe argues with Randall that Helen Grayle may have died to spare her aged husband, "Randall said sharply: 'That's just sentimental.' 'Sure. It sounded like that when I said it. Probably all a mistake anyway.'"

Chandler was also aware of this hopeless position in which Marlowe was cast, and in the last two novels he gave Marlowe lovers to humanize some of these attitudes. True to form, however, Marlowe has difficulties finally committing to any of these women; in *Playback*, he explains his position,

> Wherever I went, whatever I did, this was what I would come back to. A blank wall in a meaningless room in a meaningless house. . . . Nothing was any cure but the hard inner heart that asked for nothing from anyone.

Perhaps Chandler's greatest contribution to the genre, after the figure of Marlowe, is his distinctive style. He relies heavily on highly visual and objective descriptions that place a reader in a definite place at a definite time. Though he often changed the names of buildings and streets, Chandler has amazed readers with the clarity and accuracy of his depictions of Hollywood and Los Angeles of the 1930's and 1940's.

Chandler also devotes considerable attention to dialogue, attempting to render, although in a hyperbolic way, the language of the street, a language in which private eyes and hoodlums would freely converse. Chandler is especially adept at changing the tone, diction, and grammar of different characters to reflect their educational background and social status. The

hallmark of his distinctive style, however, is his use of wildly colorful metaphors and similes, such as his description of Moose Malloy's gaudy outfit in *Farewell, My Lovely*, "Even on Central Avenue, not the quietest dressed street in the world, he looked about as inconspicuous as a tarantula on a slice of angel food."

Marlowe's speech is full of slang, wisecracks, colloquialisms, under- and overstatements, and clichés. The effect of having Marlowe narrate his own adventures is to emphasize the character's interior space—his thoughts and emotions—over a rapidly unfolding series of actions. As Chandler explains in a letter:

> All I wanted to do when I began writing was to play with a fascinating new language, to see what it would do as a means of expression which might remain on the level of unintellectual thinking and yet acquire the power to say things which are usually only said with a literary air.

Chandler's overriding desire, as he reveals in another letter, was "to accept a mediocre form and make something like literature out of it [which] is in itself rather an accomplishment."

In making "something like literature" out of the hard-boiled formula, Chandler consistently relies on literary allusions, setting the detective's hidden frame against the banality of the world he inhabits. (To make these allusions more credible, Chandler establishes in *The Big Sleep* that Marlowe has spent some time in college.) Thus, Marlowe refers to Samuel Pepys's diary in *The High Window* and frequently alludes to William Shakespeare's *Richard III* (c. 1592) in *Farewell, My Lovely*. In fact, Chandler originally wanted to title that novel "The Second Murderer" after one of the characters in *Richard III*, but his editor discouraged the idea.

Chandler also delights in referring to various other detective novels in the course of his narratives. In *Playback*, for example, Marlowe picks up and quickly discards a paperback "about some private eye whose idea of a hot scene was a dead naked woman hanging from the shower rail with the marks of torture on her." The reference is almost certainly to a Mickey Spillane novel. In many of the novels, Marlowe refers derisively to S. S. Van Dine's Philo Vance, expressing Chandler's own distaste for Golden Age detective fiction.

Frequently, Chandler has Marlowe warn a client or a cop that a case cannot be solved through pure deductive reasoning, as a Sherlock Holmes or Hercule Poirot might. As Marlowe reveals in *The Big Sleep*,

> I don't expect to go over ground the police have covered and pick up a broken pen point and build a case from it. If you think there is anybody in the detective business making a living doing that sort of thing, you don't know much about cops.

Readers and critics have frequently lamented Chandler's Byzantine plots that end inconclusively or unconvincingly. Indeed, many of the problems resulted from Chandler's practice of cannibalizing short stories to construct the plots of his novels. In letters, Chandler repeatedly admits his shortcomings with plotting, as he does when remarking: "As a constructionist I have a dreadful fault; I let characters run away with scenes and then refuse to discard the scenes that don't fit. I end up usually with the bed of Procrustes."

These plots within plots that often end enigmatically, however, also reveal Chandler's deep-seated belief that crimes, like life itself, often defy clear, rational explanation. The plot of *Farewell, My Lovely*, which has been criticized for being confused, actually offers an ingenious comment on the irrationality of crime and motive. As he stumbles over crooked cops, crime bosses, quack doctors and spiritualists, gambling ships, and a host of other obstacles, Marlowe is convinced that an intricate conspiracy has been devised to keep him from the truth. As the conclusion reveals, however, many of these events and people operate independently of one another. Rather than inhabiting a perversely ordered world, Marlowe wanders through a maze of coincidence. Instead of the classic detective's immutably rational place, Marlowe lives in an existential universe of frustrated hopes, elliptical resolutions, and vague connections. The fundamental condition of life is alienation—that of the detective and everyone else.

In this way, Chandler infuses his novels with a wide range of social commentary, and when he is not examining the ills of television, gambling, and the malleability of the law, Chandler's favorite subject is California, particularly Los Angeles and Hollywood.

Chandler had a perverse fascination with California; though he claimed he could leave it at any time and never miss it, the fact is that once he settled in California, he never left for any extended period of time.

THE LITTLE SISTER

Over and over again, Marlowe is disgusted with California, which he describes in *The Little Sister* (1949) as "the department-store state. The most of everything and the best of nothing." Without firmly established history and traditions, California and Los Angeles are open to almost any possibility, and those possibilities are usually criminal. For Marlowe, Los Angeles is the modern equivalent of a medieval Lost City:

> Out there in the night of a thousand crimes people were dying, being maimed, cut by flying glass, crushed against steering wheels or under heavy car tyres. People were being beaten, robbed, strangled, raped, and murdered. People were hungry, sick, bored, desperate with loneliness or remorse or fear, angry, cruel, feverish, shaken by sobs. A city no worse than others, a city rich and vigorous and full of pride, a city lost and beaten and full of emptiness.

As bad as it may be, however, Marlowe would never think of leaving.

As *The Little Sister* reveals, Los Angeles, and by extension California, has been permanently shaped by the presence of Hollywood and the films. Events repeatedly seem unreal and illusory, and characters appear to be little more than celluloid projections thrown into the world. Such unreality and insubstantiality breed corruption and exploitation; people accept filth and degradation, and Marlowe finds himself as the lone wanderer trying to dispel the dream.

David W. Madden

PRINCIPAL MYSTERY AND DETECTIVE FICTION

PHILIP MARLOWE SERIES: *The Big Sleep*, 1939; *Farewell, My Lovely*, 1940; *The High Window*, 1942; *The Lady in the Lake*, 1943; *The Little Sister*, 1949; *The Long Goodbye*, 1953; *Playback*, 1958; *The Raymond Chandler Omnibus: Four Famous Classics*, 1967; *The Second Chandler Omnibus*, 1973; *Poodle Springs*, 1989 (incomplete manuscript finished by

Robert B. Parker); *Later Novels and Other Writings*, 1995

OTHER SHORT FICTION: *Five Murderers*, 1944; *Five Sinister Characters*, 1945; *Finger Man, and Other Stories*, 1946; *Red Wind*, 1946; *Spanish Blood*, 1946; *The Simple Art of Murder*, 1950; *Trouble Is My Business*, 1950; *Pick-up on Noon Street*, 1952; *Smart-Aleck Kill*, 1953; *Pearls Are a Nuisance*, 1958; *Killer in the Rain*, 1964 (Philip Durham, editor); *The Smell of Fear*, 1965; *The Midnight Raymond Chandler*, 1971; *The Best of Raymond Chandler*, 1977; *Stories and Early Novels*, 1995

OTHER MAJOR WORKS

PLAYS: *Double Indemnity*, pr. 1946 (with Billy Wilder); *The Blue Dahlia*, pb. 1976; *Playback*, pb. 1985

SCREENPLAYS: *And Now Tomorrow*, 1944 (with Frank Partos); *Double Indemnity*, 1944 (with Wilder); *The Unseen*, 1945 (with Hagar Wilde and Ken England); *The Blue Dahlia*, 1946; *Strangers on a Train*, 1951 (with Czenzi Ormonde and Whitfield Cook)

NONFICTION: *The Blue Dahlia*, 1946 (Matthew J. Bruccoli, editor); *Raymond Chandler Speaking*, 1962 (Dorothy Gardiner and Katherine Sorely Walker, editors); *Chandler Before Marlowe: Raymond Chandler's Early Prose and Poetry*, 1973 (Bruccoli, editor); *The Notebooks of Raymond Chandler and English Summer*, 1976 (Frank MacShane, editor); *Raymond Chandler and James M. Fox: Letters*, 1978; *Selected Letters of Raymond Chandler*, 1981 (MacShane, editor); *The Raymond Chandler Papers: Selected Letters and Non-fiction, 1909-1959*, 2000 (Tom Hiney and MacShane, editors)

BIBLIOGRAPHY

Babener, Liahna K. "Raymond Chandler's City of Lies." In *Los Angeles in Fiction*, edited by David Fine. Albuquerque: University of New Mexico Press, 1984. The chapter on Chandler is a study of the image patterns in his novels. The volume as a whole is an interesting discussion of the importance of a sense of place, especially one as mythologically rich as Los Angeles. Includes notes.

Bruccoli, Matthew J., and Richard Layman. *Hard-boiled Mystery Writers: Raymond Chandler, Dashiell Hammett, Ross Macdonald*. New York: Carroll and Graf, 2002. A handy supplemental reference that includes interviews, letters, and previously published studies. Illustrated.

Chandler, Raymond. *Raymond Chandler Speaking*. Edited by Dorothy Gardiner and Katherine Walker. Berkeley: University of California Press, 1997. Collected interviews given by Chandler about his characters, stories, life, and influences, among other topics. Bibliographic references and index.

Hiney, Tom. *Raymond Chandler: A Biography*. New York: Atlantic Monthly Press, 1997. A brief biography of Chandler that discusses his education in England, his relationship to Los Angeles, and the plots and characters of his most important detective novels and stories.

Knight, Stephen. "'A Hard Cheerfulness': An Introduction to Raymond Chandler." In *American Crime Fiction: Studies in the Genre*, edited by Brian Docherty. New York: St. Martin's Press, 1988. This is a discussion of the values and attitudes that define Philip Marlowe and that make him unusual in the genre of hard-boiled American crime fiction.

Lehman, David. "Hammett and Chandler." In *The Perfect Murder: A Study in Detection*. New York: Free Press, 1989. Chandler is represented in this comprehensive study of detective fiction as one of the authors who brought out the parable at the heart of mystery fiction. A useful volume in its breadth and its unusual appendixes, one a list of further reading, the other, an annotated list of the critic's favorite mysteries. Includes two indexes, one of concepts, and one of names and titles.

Moss, Robert F., ed. *Raymond Chandler: A Literary Reference*. New York: Carroll & Graf, 2003. An extremely useful compilation of primary documents relating to Chandler's life and work. Includes letters, interviews, and other documents produced both by Chandler and by friends and colleagues. Extensive bibliographic resources and index.

Norrman, Ralf. *Wholeness Restored: Love of Symmetry as a Shaping Force in the Writings of Henry James, Kurt Vonnegut, Samuel Butler and Ray-*

mond Chandler. New York: Peter Lang, 1998. Discusses Chandler's *The Long Goodbye.* Examines his use of symmetry in narrative, comparing Chandler's employment of the device to writers of genres other than detective fiction.

Phillips, Gene D. *Creatures of Darkness: Raymond Chandler, Detective Fiction, and Film Noir.* Lexington: University Press of Kentucky, 2000. Though this work focuses largely on Chandler's Hollywood output, it contains some useful information.

Skinner, Robert E. *The Hard-Boiled Explicator: A Guide to the Study of Dashiell Hammett, Raymond Chandler, and Ross Macdonald.* Metuchen, N.J.: Scarecrow Press, 2002. This volume is indispensable for the scholar interested in tracking down unpublished dissertations as well as mainstream criti-

cism. Brief introductions of each author are followed by annotated bibliographies of books, articles, and reviews.

Van Dover, J. K., ed. *The Critical Response to Raymond Chandler.* Westport, Conn.: Greenwood Press, 1995. A collection of essays examining Chandler's literary output. Includes bibliographical references and an index.

Widdicombe, Toby. *A Reader's Guide to Raymond Chandler.* Westport, Conn.: Greenwood Press, 2001. Detailed account of the fictional world created by Chandler, the places it contains, and the people who inhabit it. Also includes a chronology of the author's life and publications and a brief biography linking Chandler's life to the dominant themes in his fiction.

LESLIE CHARTERIS
Leslie Charles Bowyer Yin

Born: Singapore; May 12, 1907
Died: Windsor, England; April 15, 1993
Type of plot: Thriller

PRINCIPAL SERIES

Simon "the Saint" Templar, 1928-1980 (stories by other writers continued, with Charteris's approval)

PRINCIPAL SERIES CHARACTER

SIMON "THE SAINT" TEMPLAR, a modern Robin Hood. Templar changes but does not obviously age. Despite Charteris's incorporation of real-world events as a means of alluding to Templar's increasing years, screen depictions feature a perpetually youthful man. The Saint of the early stories resides in London. He lives the good life, made possible by his earnings as an adventurer. He is witty and debonair but also ruthless. Just before World War II, he moves to the United States, where he becomes a far more serious and solitary figure.

CONTRIBUTION

In Simon Templar, Leslie Charteris fashioned the perfect hero of popular fiction for the twentieth century. Templar, known by his sobriquet, the Saint, possesses all the modern virtues: He is bright and clever, but not intellectual; he is charming and sensitive, but not effete; he is a materialist who relishes good food, good drink, luxurious surroundings, and the company of beautiful women, but he lives by a strict moral code of his own devising.

Templar is "good," as his nickname indicates, but his view of good and evil does not derive from any spiritual or ethical system and has nothing whatever to do with Anglo-Saxon legalisms. Rather, his morality is innate and naturalistic. He is one of the very fittest in an incredibly dangerous world, and he survives with aplomb and élan. Even when he becomes more political (serving as an American agent during World War II), he supports only the causes that square with his own notions of personal freedom. He is always the secular hero of a secular age. As such, he has lived the life of the suave adventurer for more than sixty years, in novels, short stories, comic strips, motion pictures, and television series. Moreover, because Simon Templar is not a family man, James Bond and every Bond manqué may properly be viewed as the illegitimate literary progeny of the Saint.

BIOGRAPHY

Leslie Charteris was born Leslie Charles Bowyer Yin on May 12, 1907, in Singapore, the son of Dr. S. C. Yin, a Chinese surgeon and Englishwoman Florence Bowyer. A slight air of mystery attaches to Charteris's origins. His father was reputed to be a direct descendant of the Yin family who ruled China during the Shang Dynasty (c. 1700-1027 B.C.E.). Charteris recalls that he learned Chinese and Malay from native servants before he could speak English and that his parents took him around the world three times before he was twelve. He valued the education afforded by this cosmopolitan experience far more than his formal education, which he received in England—at Falconbury School, Purley, Surrey (1919-1922) and at Rossall School, Fleetwood, Lancashire (1922-1924). However, he worked eagerly on school magazines, and sold his first short story at the age of seventeen.

After leaving school for a brief stay in Paris in 1924, Charteris was persuaded to enter King's College, Cambridge, in 1925. He stayed for little more than a year, spending his time reading voraciously in the fields of criminology and crime fiction. He left the university to pursue a career as a writer when his first full-length crime novel was accepted. Around this same time, he changed his name by deed poll to Leslie Charteris, though sources differ as to the year. At first, despite the popularity of the Saint, Charteris struggled to support himself, taking odd jobs in England, France, and Malaya un-

til 1935. Syndicated comic strips, such as *Secret Agent X-9* (mid-1930's) and *The Saint* (1945-1955), helped further his career, as did his work as a Hollywood scriptwriter. When his novel *The Saint in New York* (1935) was brought to the screen in 1938, Charteris gained international fame.

Over the next several years, Charteris developed a dashing persona, of which a monocle and a small mustache were manifestations. He married Pauline Schishkin in 1931 and was divorced from her in 1937. His only child, Patricia Ann, was born of this marriage. Charteris first came to the United States in 1932 and went to Hollywood the following year. He eventually returned to England but moved to New York after his divorce. In 1938, he married Barbara Meyer, an American, from whom he was divorced in 1943. That same year, he married Elizabeth Bryant Borst, a singer. He was naturalized an American citizen in 1946. He was divorced again in 1951, and the next year he married Audrey Long, a film actress.

Charteris also worked as a scenarist, columnist, and editor. His avocations—eating, drinking, shoot-

The Saint as he appeared in Popular Detective *magazine in 1938.*

ing, fishing, flying, and yachting—mirror those of his dapper hero. His odd jobs reportedly included working in a tin mine and a rubber plantation, prospecting for gold, hiring on as a seaman on a freighter, fishing for pearls, bartending, working at a wood distillation plant, and becoming a balloon inflator for a fairground sideshow. He took a pilot's license, traveled to Spain, and became a bullfighting aficionado. He invented a universal sign language, which he named Paleneo. He once listed himself as his favorite writer. In 1992, he was awarded the Crime Writers' Association's Cartier Diamond Dagger for lifetime achievement. He died in Windsor, England, in 1993.

ANALYSIS

Leslie Charteris's first novel, *X Esquire*, appeared in 1927 and was quickly followed by *Meet the Tiger* (1928), the first of the series that would make its author famous. It took some time, however, for the Tiger to evolve into the Saint. Charteris required another two years and another three novels to develop this character satisfactorily. When Charteris began writing Saint stories for *The Thriller* in 1930, Simon Templar had finally settled into a personality that would catch the fancy of the reading public.

To begin with, the hero's name was masterfully chosen. Along with other connotations, the name Simon suggests Simon Peter (Saint Peter), foremost among the apostles and an imperfect man of powerful presence. The name Templar reminds the reader of the Knights Templar, twelfth century crusaders who belonged to a select military-religious order. Thriller fiction at the time Charteris began to write was replete with young veterans of World War I who were disillusioned, restless, disdainful of law and social custom, and eager for any adventure that came to hand. Simon Templar was very much a member of this order. Like the Knights Templar and the outlaws of Sherwood Forest, the Saint and his fictional colleagues set out to rout the barbarians and foreigners. The villains of many thrillers of the period were foreigners, Jews, and blacks. Charteris certainly adopted the convention, and for this reason it has been remarked that his early novels sometimes had a racist, fascist cast to them.

"THE MILLION POUND DAY"

In chapter 1 of "The Million Pound Day," the second of three novelettes in *The Holy Terror* (1932), the Saint saves a fleeing man from a black villain, clad only in a loincloth, who is pursuing him along a country lane. The black is perfectly stereotypical. He is a magnificent specimen physically but is savage and brutal. He exudes primeval cruelty, and the Saint "seemed to smell the sickly stench of rotting jungles seeping its fetid breath into the clean cold air of that English dawn." The reader should not, however, make too much of such passages. Racial and ethnic sensibilities have been heightened considerably since 1932, so that the chauvinism and offhand use of racial epithets found in the work of some of the finest writers of Charteris's generation (for example, Evelyn Waugh) are quite jolting to the modern reader.

On the other hand, Charteris himself was something of an outsider in those days. Although he often deferred to the prejudices of his readers, his work contained a consistent undercurrent of mockery. Simon Templar mixes effortlessly with the members of the ruling class, but as often as not, his references to them are contemptuous. Like a Byronic hero, his background is mysterious, romantic, and essentially classless. It is significant that, during a period in which most fictional heroes are members of the officer class with outstanding war records, Simon Templar has no war record.

"THE INLAND REVENUE"

An example of how the Saint—and Charteris—tweak British smugness is found in "The Inland Revenue," the first of the novelettes in *The Holy Terror.* As chapter 2 opens, Simon Templar is reading his mail at the breakfast table. "During a brief spell of virtue some time before," Templar has written a novel, a thriller recounting the adventures of a South American "super-brigand" named Mario. A reader has written an indignant letter, taking issue with Templar's choice of a "lousy Dago" as his hero rather than an Englishman or an American. The letter writer grew so furious during the composition of his screed that he broke off without a closure. His final line reads, "I fancy you yourself must have a fair amount of Dago blood in you." Templar remarks with equanimity that at that point the poor fellow had probably been removed to "some distant asylum."

The earlier Saint stories are marked by such playful scenes. They are also marked by a considerable amount of linguistic playfulness and ingenuity. For example, Charteris often peppers the stories with poetry that is more or less extrinsic to the plot. In chapter 3 of "The Inland Revenue," Templar is composing a poem on the subject of a newspaper proprietor who constantly bemoans the low estate of modern Great Britain. He writes of this antediluvian:

> For him, no Transatlantic flights,
> Ford motor-cars, electric lights,
> Or radios at less than cost
> Could compensate for what he lost
> By chancing to coagulate
> About five hundred years too late.

The Saint's disdain for authority is more pronounced in the early books. He dispenses private justice to enemies with cognomens such as "the Scorpion," and at the same time delights in frustrating and humiliating the minions of law and order. His particular foil is Claud Eustace Teal, a plodding inspector from Scotland Yard. Chief Inspector Teal is a device of the mystery genre with antecedents stretching back at least as far as the unimaginative Inspector Lestrade of the Sherlock Holmes stories.

"THE MELANCHOLY JOURNEY OF MR. TEAL"

There is—on the Saint's part, at least—a grudging affection that characterizes the relationship between Teal and him. "The Melancholy Journey of Mr. Teal" in *The Holy Terror* is, in part, the story of a trap the Saint lays for Inspector Teal. Templar allows Teal temporarily to believe that he has finally got the goods on his nemesis, then Templar springs the trap and so shocks and mortifies the inspector that he appears to age ten years on the spot. The Saint has totally conquered his slow-witted adversary, yet "the fruits of victory were strangely bitter."

THE SAINT EVOLVES

The Saint's romantic interest in the early stories is Patricia Holm. Their relationship is never explored in detail, but it is clearly unconventional. The narrator hints at sexual intimacy by such devices as placing the beautiful Patricia, without explanatory comment, at Templar's breakfast table. Charteris moved to the United States in the late 1930's, and the Saint moved with him. In *The Saint in Miami* (1940), Patricia, Hoppy Iniatz (Templar's muscleman bodyguard), and other series regulars are in the United States as well. They fall away, however, as Simon Templar undergoes two decided changes.

First, the sociable Saint of the stories set in England evolves during the 1940's into a hero more in the American mold. The mystery genre in the United States was dominated at that time by the hard-boiled loner, such as Raymond Chandler's private eye, Philip Marlowe. During the war years, the Saint defends democracy, becoming more of a loner in the process. He never evolves into an American, but he becomes less of an Englishman. Eventually, he becomes a citizen of the world, unencumbered by personal relationships, taking his adventures and his women where he finds them.

Second, the Saint, like so many real people, was changed by his own success. Charteris had collaborated on a screenplay as early as 1933 and, during 1940 and 1941, he worked on three Saint films. He had earlier written a syndicated comic strip entitled *Secret Agent X-9*; he adapted Simon Templar to the medium in *Saint*, a strip that ran from 1945 to 1955. He had edited *Suspense* magazine in the 1940's, and he turned this experience to the Saint's account as well. Charteris was editor of *The Saint Detective Magazine* (later retitled *The Saint Mystery Magazine*) from 1953 to 1967. The wit, the clever use of language, the insouciance of the early stories and novels, however, did not translate well to films, comic strips, or television.

Still, the Saint of the screen remained very British. The first of the films, *The Saint in New York* (not written by Charteris), was produced in 1938, during a period in which a large contingent of British actors had been drawn to Hollywood. Among this group was Louis Hayward, who portrayed the Saint in his first screen appearance. The Saint films were rather short, low-budget pictures, designed for exhibition as part of a twin bill. George Sanders, a leading character actor in major Hollywood productions for more than thirty years, was an early Simon Templar. He was succeeded in the role by his brother, Tom Conway, who resembled him greatly and whose voice was virtually identical to his.

As played by the brothers, the Saint was a sophisticated, well-dressed adventurer with a limpid manner. He spoke in flawless stage English, and his mature looks were emphasized by a pencil-thin mustache. Although Charteris had nothing to do with most of the films, he did collaborate on the screenplays for *The Saint's Double Trouble* (1940), *The Saint's Vacation* (1941), and *The Saint in Palm Springs* (1941). During the 1940's, he sold many Saint stories to American magazines, and he also wrote a radio series, *Sherlock Holmes*. The Saint also appeared in various productions on British, American, and Swiss radio from 1940 to 1951, with a return to British radio in 1995.

Saint films appeared at regular intervals through 1953, when the advent of television moved the popular Simon Templar from the large to the small screen. Several television movies appeared, as well as further feature-length films. During the 1960's, Roger Moore became television's Simon Templar. Moore was a larger, more physically imposing, more masculine Saint than his predecessors. This series was filmed in England, and it established London once again as the Saint's home base. Also back, largely for comic effect, was the stolid Inspector Teal.

In the next decade, Ian Ogilvy played the part and was the most youthful and handsome Saint of them all. His television series *Return of the Saint* took a new look at the classic hero, transforming him from a man outside the law serving his own brand of justice to one who helped the police by solving crimes with his wits rather than through further crime and violence. Initially perturbed by the Saint's increasingly youthful appearance, Charteris remarked,

God knows how we shall reconcile this rejuvenation with the written word, where there is incontrovertible internal evidence that by this time Simon Templar has got to be over seventy. After all, he is clearly recorded as having been over thirty during Prohibition, which senile citizens like me recall as having ended in 1933. Perhaps the only thing is to forget such tiresome details and leave him in the privileged limb of such immortals as Li'l Abner, who has never aged a day.

The Saint novels continued to appear with regularity through 1948, but their energy was largely spent. Simon Templar had become a profitable industry, of which Leslie Charteris was chairman of the board. For the next three decades, except for *Vendetta for the Saint* (1964), very little work of an original nature appeared. Charteris worked at some other projects, including a column for *Gourmet Magazine* (1966-1968). *Arrest the Saint*, an omnibus edition, was published in 1956. *The Saint in Pursuit*, a novelization of the comic strip, appeared in 1970. The remaining output of the period consisted largely of short-story collections. Many of the stories were adapted from the popular television series and were written in collaboration with others. In fact, Charteris often contented himself with polishing and giving final approval to a story written largely by someone else.

In the 1980's, the Saint even wandered over into the science-fiction genre. Not surprisingly, critics judged this work decidedly inferior to the early Saint stories. In fact, Charteris specifically began first collaborating with other writers, and then approving novels and stories written solely by others, as a means of ensuring that the Saint legacy would continue after his death. Other Saint novels and story collections, produced in collaboration with Charteris or alone, have involved such writers as Donne Avenell, Burl Barer, Peter Bloxsom, Jerry Cady, Jeffrey Dell, Terence Feely, Jonathan Hensleigh, Ben Holmes, Donald James, John Kruse, Fleming Lee, D. R. Motton, Michael Pertwee, Christopher Short, Leigh Vance, Graham Weaver, and Norman Worker. In 1997, four years after Charteris's death, the motion picture *The Saint*, starring Val Kilmer as the Saint, was released.

The Saint's golden age was the first decade of his literary existence. The wit and charm of the hero and the prose style with which his stories were told will form the basis for Charteris's literary reputation in the years to come.

Patrick Adcock
Updated by C. A. Gardner

PRINCIPAL MYSTERY AND DETECTIVE FICTION
BILL KENNEDY SERIES: *X Esquire*, 1927; *The White Rider*, 1928

SIMON "THE SAINT" TEMPLAR SERIES: 1928-1930 • *Meet the Tiger*, 1928 (also known as *The Saint Meets the Tiger*); *Enter the Saint*, 1930; *Knight Templar*, 1930 (also known as *The Avenging Saint*); *The Last Hero*, 1930 (also known as *The Saint Closes the Case* and *The Saint and the Last Hero*)

1931-1940 • *Alias the Saint*, 1931; *Featuring the Saint*, 1931; *She Was a Lady*, 1931 (also known as *Angels of Doom* and *The Saint Meets His Match*); *Getaway*, 1932 (also known as *Saint's Getaway*); *The Holy Terror*, 1932 (also known as *The Saint Versus Scotland Yard*); *Once More the Saint*, 1933 (also known as *The Saint and Mr. Teal*, 1933); *The Brighter Buccaneer*, 1933; *Boodle*, 1934 (also known as *The Saint Intervenes*); *The Misfortunes of Mr. Teal*, 1934 (also known as *The Saint in London*); *The Saint Goes On*, 1934; *The Saint in New York*, 1935; *The Saint Overboard*, 1936; *The Ace of Knaves*, 1937 (also known as *The Saint in Action*); *Thieves' Picnic*, 1937 (also known as *The Saint Bids Diamonds*); *Follow the Saint*, 1938; *Prelude for War*, 1938 (also known as *The Saint Plays with Fire*); *The Happy Highwayman*, 1939; *The Saint in Miami*, 1940; *The Saint's Double Trouble*, 1940 (with Ben Holmes)

1941-1950 • *The Saint in Palm Springs*, 1941 (with Jerry Cady); *The Saint's Vacation*, 1941 (with Jeffrey Dell); *The Saint Goes West*, 1942; *The Saint at Large*, 1943; *The Saint Steps In*, 1943; *The Saint on Guard*, 1944; *Lady on a Train*, 1945; *Paging the Saint*, 1945; *The Saint Sees It Through*, 1946; *Call for the Saint*, 1948; *Saint Errant*, 1948

1951-1960 • *The Second Saint Omnibus*, 1951; *The Saint in Europe*, 1953; *The Saint on the Spanish Main*, 1955; *Arrest the Saint*, 1956; *The Saint Around the World*, 1956; *Thanks to the Saint*, 1957; *Concerning the Saint*, 1958; *Señor Saint*, 1958; *The Saint Cleans Up*, 1959; *The Saint to the Rescue*, 1959

1961-1982 • *Trust the Saint*, 1962; *The Saint in the Sun*, 1963; *Vendetta for the Saint*, 1964 (with Harry Harrison); *The Saint in Pursuit*, 1970 (with Fleming Lee); *The Saint and the People Importers*, 1971 (with Lee); *Saints Alive*, 1974; *The Saint's Sporting Chance*, 1980; *The Fantastic Saint*, 1982

NONSERIES NOVELS: *Daredevil*, 1929; *The Bandit*, 1929 (also known as *The Black Cat*)

OTHER MAJOR WORKS

RADIO PLAYS: *Sherlock Holmes* series, c. 1940 (with Denis Green)

SCREENPLAYS: *Midnight Club*, 1933 (with Seton I. Miller); *The Saint's Double Trouble*, 1940 (with Ben Homes); *The Saint in Palm Springs*, 1941 (with Jerry Cady); *The Saint's Vacation*, 1941 (with Jeffrey Dell); *Lady on a Train*, 1945 (with Edmund Beloin and Robert O'Brien); *River Gang*, 1945 (with others); *Two Smart People*, 1946 (with others); *Tarzan and the Huntress*, 1947 (with Jerry Grushkind and Rowland Leigh)

NONFICTION: *Spanish for Fun*, 1964; *Paleneo: A Universal Sign Language*, 1972

EDITED TEXTS: *The Saint's Choice of Humorous Crime*, 1945; *The Saint's Choice of Impossible Crime*, 1945; *The Saint's Choice of Hollywood Crime*, 1946; *The Saint Mystery Library*, 1959-1960; *The Saint Magazine Reader*, 1966 (with Hans Santesson; also known as *The Saint's Choice*)

TRANSLATION: *Juan Belmonte, Killer of Bulls: The Autobiography of a Matador*, 1937 (by Juan Belmonte and Manuel Chaves Nogales)

BIBLIOGRAPHY

Barer, Burl. *The Saint: A Complete History in Print, Radio, Film, and Television of Leslie Charteris' Robin Hood of Modern Crime, Simon Templar, 1928-1992*. Jefferson, N.C.: McFarland, 1993. Comprehensive reference guide to the character's many appearances through 1992.

Blakemore, Helena. "The Novels of Leslie Charteris." In *Twentieth-Century Suspense: The Thriller Comes of Age*, edited by Clive Bloom. New York: St. Martin's Press, 1990. Examines Charteris specifically as a crafter of suspense stories and analyzes the use of suspense in his work.

Greene, Suzanne Ellery. *Books for Pleasure: Popular Fiction, 1914-1945*. Bowling Green, Ohio: Bowling Green State University Popular Press, 1974. This broader study looks at the Saint as a popular character in general, not merely as the protagonist of mystery thrillers.

Lofts, William Oliver Guillemont, and Derek Adley. *The Saint and Leslie Charteris*. Bowling Green,

Ohio: Bowling Green State University Popular Press, 1972. Discussion of the importance and representation of the Saint character geared toward a popular audience.

Mechele, Tony, and Dick Fiddy. *The Saint*. London: Boxtree, 1989. An examination of the many incarnations of the Saint, commenting on performances of actors who have played him, as well as his print incarnations.

O'Neill, Dan. "Time to Remember: The Sign of the Saint Left Huge Mark on the Thriller." *South Wales Echo*, May 13, 2002, p. 16. Article discusses the creation of the Saint and the print, radio, and film versions as well as Charteris's life.

Osgerby, Bill. "'So You're the Famous Simon Templar': The Saint, Masculinity, and Consumption in the Early 1960's." In *Action TV: Tough-Guys, Smooth Operators, and Foxy Chicks*, edited by Bill Osgerby and Anna Gough-Yates. New York: Routledge, 2001. Analysis of the Saint's television incarnation from the point of view of gender studies and cultural studies. Bibliographic references and index.

Simper, Paul. *Saint: Behind the Scenes with Simon Templar*. New York: TV Books, 1997. Short book looking at the making of the television shows featuring Charteris's character.

Trewin, Ion. Introduction to *Enter the Saint*. London: Hodder and Stoughton, 1930. Commentary on the novel and its author by a famous and successful editor and publisher.

JAMES HADLEY CHASE
René Brabazon Raymond

Born: London, England; December 24, 1906
Died: Corseaux-sur-Vevey, Switzerland; February 6, 1985
Also wrote as James L. Docherty; Ambrose Grant; Raymond Marshall
Type of plot: Thriller

PRINCIPAL SERIES

Dave Fenner, 1939-1940
Vic Malloy, 1949-1950
Brick-Top Corrigan, 1950-1951
Steve Harmas, 1952-1963
Don Micklem, 1954-1955
Frank Terrell, 1964-1970
Mark Girland, 1965-1969
Al Barney, 1968-1972
Helga Rolfe, 1971-1977

PRINCIPAL SERIES CHARACTERS

DAVE FENNER, a former reporter who has become a private detective, is a loner, known for surviving innumerable violent, suspenseful situations. He is the main character in Chase's most popular novel, *No Orchids for Miss Blandish* (1939).

BRICK-TOP CORRIGAN is an unscrupulous private detective who leaves his clients without solving any cases, taking half of his fee with him. He worked as a commando before becoming a private eye.

STEVE HARMAS, a chief investigator who solves cleverly plotted insurance frauds. His beautiful wife, Helen, assists in solving these crimes in the art deco world of California in the 1930's.

DON MICKLEM, a millionaire, lives the life of a playboy and becomes involved in international intrigue.

FRANK TERRELL, a private investigator who works in Paradise City, Florida. He operates in a world of false identity, theft, and murder.

MARK GIRLAND, a former agent for the Central Intelligence Agency who lives a carefree and fast life in Paris, where he enjoys pleasures of the moment, particularly those involving beautiful women. Seeking always to earn money with as little effort as possible,

Girland has his adventures when he is hired by the CIA on special assignments in Paris.

AL BARNEY, a dissipated former skin diver, serves as the narrator of two novels set in Paradise City, Florida.

CONTRIBUTION

The canon of James Hadley Chase, comprising more than eighty-five books, has earned for him a reputation as the king of thriller writers in England and on the Continent. In France he is even compared with Fyodor Dostoevski and Louis-Ferdinand Céline. (Such hyperbole, however, must be attributed to the ephemeral popularity of the films based on his novels.) At the other end of the spectrum are those judgments by Julian Symons and George Orwell, who write, respectively, that Chase's work ranges from "shoddy" to "secondhand James M. Cain" and that it is filled with gratuitous sadism, brutality, and corruption, "a daydream appropriate to a totalitarian age."

Chase's own comment that he wrote "for a good read . . . for a wide variety of readers" comes closest to a true analysis of his work. In many ways, his works resemble the James Bond thrillers of Ian Fleming. Yet they are thrillers usually without the plot complexity and climactic endings, the sophistication in the main characters, and the well-chosen detail in description characteristic of Fleming. Chase's work typically involves violence wreaked on the innocent and weak as well as the guilty and strong, frequent though nongraphic sexual encounters, the hyperbolic machismo of the private investigator, and a tone of danger, excitement, and suspense.

BIOGRAPHY

James Hadley Chase was born René Brabazon Raymond on December 24, 1906, in London, England. After completing his education at King's School in Rochester, Kent, he left home and began selling encyclopedias door-to-door. Later he worked as a traveler for the book wholesaler Simpkin, Marshall in London. It was at this time that he wrote his highly successful first novel, *No Orchids for Miss Blandish* (1939; revised, 1961; also known as *The Villain and the Virgin*). The book is said to have sold more than 1 million cop-

ies in five years. It became one of the best-selling mysteries ever written and was made into a film in 1951. Four of Chase's other novels were made into films between 1951 and 1959. Chase later served as a squadron leader in the Royal Air Force and became an editor of the Royal Air Force journal. He married Sylvia Ray, with whom he had one son.

Although Chase set most of his novels in the United States, he made very few visits there, and then only to New Orleans and Florida. He preferred to learn about the United States from encyclopedias, slang dictionaries, and maps. Chase was reticent about his life and career, believing that his readers were uninterested in his personal affairs and asked only that he conscientiously write entertaining novels. If his books were selling well, he did not bother with interviews or the critics' responses. Chase died in Switzerland in 1985.

ANALYSIS

The career of James Hadley Chase began in 1939 with the stunning success of *No Orchids for Miss Blandish*. This success, along with the timeliness of his style and tone, gave impetus to his continued popularity. Critics have had varied responses to *No Orchids for Miss Blandish* and his later works. Many judged his first novel unnecessarily violent, with one reader counting forty-eight acts of aggression, from rape to beatings to murder—approximately one every fourth page. Yet this violence clearly appealed to many readers. Later critics regarded Chase's work as part of the hard-boiled American school initiated by Raymond Chandler and Dashiell Hammett (and continued by Ross Macdonald and John D. MacDonald). Others, seeing more depth in his work, suggest that Chase's novels depict the bleakness of twentieth century America, which must remain unredeemed unless a new social structure is developed. This view, however, is not substantiated by Chase's own comments on his work.

The violence in Chase's novels is in fact far from being gratuitous; it is an essential element of the fantasy world of the hard-boiled thriller. This world is no less stylized than the world of the classic British detective story of Agatha Christie. Although the latter portrays an ordered universe cankered by a single act of murder, Chase's books depict an ordered world held

together by raw power, ceaselessly pummeled by the violence of lesser, opportunistic powers. Succeeding in such a society requires that the protagonist be more intellectually, emotionally, and physically powerful than the villains, while in the classic detective story, the hero need only be intellectually and emotionally stronger. This third, physical element, as in the hands of Chase and other members of the hard-boiled school, is another dimension of the same struggle for ascendency between good and evil.

Along the same lines, critics note that Chase's heroes are often less than upright and trustworthy. Their motivation to fight on the side of good is often nothing more than financial; they are mercenaries in a power-hungry and materialistic world. For example, Mark Girland would never have become a special agent for the Central Intelligence Agency (CIA) if he had not needed the money. Yet this seemingly callous attitude underscores the quality of life in a post-

Darwinian world, where only the fittest survive and where idealism weighs one down, makes one less effective. It must be remembered that in all detective stories, heroes are heroes not because they are ethical but because they are effective and ultimately successful, whether they operate in the locked room or the world at large. Their methods are suited to the environment to ensure victory. Chase's detectives are loners, answerable only to themselves. Their ethical codes fit those of their society only if that society happens to agree with them.

Such traits in Chase's heroes are even more apparent when the books are categorized according to the classic characteristics of the American hard-boiled school. American hard-boiled detective stories are a hybrid of the traditional detective story and the mainstream novel. This hybrid results in less formulaic works. Set in American small towns or in the heated worlds of New York City or Los Angeles instead of London or English villages, these novels also feature more rounded characters. As more and more books in the hard-boiled school were written, however, they developed their own conventions of character: the fighting and lusty loner of a protagonist; his tolerant but admiring superior; the many pretty women who are strongly attracted to him; the fewer beautiful, exotic, mysterious, and dangerous women who are also strongly attracted to him; and the villains, either stupid or brilliant but always viciously brutal. Yet the potential does exist for even more rounded characters.

Although the plots, too, are said to be more plausible than those in the classic detective story, this is not necessarily the case. Extreme numbers of violent acts, a set of four or five murders trailing a detective through an evening's adventure in a single town, can hardly be considered plausible. Chase's plots fit such a mold, realistic because they involve commonplace things and events in the real world, unrealistic because they are based in plots of intrigue, with enormous webs of sinister characters woven together in strange twists and knots. Often involving robbery or the illusion of robbery, the overt greed in Chase's unsavory characters causes multiple murders and cruelty.

In *No Orchids for Miss Blandish*, a small-time gang steals a diamond necklace; *The Things Men Do*

(1953) involves diamond theft from the postal van service; *You've Got It Coming* (1955, revised 1975), is based on the theft of industrial diamonds worth $3 million; *You're Dead Without Money* (1972) shows hero Al Barney working out the events surrounding the theft of a famous stamp collection. Thefts such as these lead to violence that grows in almost geometric progression as the novel develops.

To suggest that Chase's works are scathing social commentaries calling for a new social structure would be inaccurate. Nowhere in the texts are there hints of statements proposing ideological change of any kind. The world, though violent and unpredictable, is drawn as a literary given, a place that is unchanging, not because humans are incapable of improving it but because it sets the tone for the story.

In the end, then, Chase provided the best analysis of Chase: He gave his reader "a good read," but he was not simply portraying the amoral world to which George Orwell alludes. Rather, Chase's heroes entertainingly adapt to whatever environment they enter; their success lies in their recognition that in the mean and dirty world of criminals and evil ideologies, to survive, they themselves must be the meanest and the dirtiest.

YOU HAVE YOURSELF A DEAL

One of Chase's works that exemplifies the conventions he uses is *You Have Yourself a Deal* (1966), a Mark Girland tale set in Paris and the south of France. Girland is asked by the director of the CIA to assist in the safekeeping and debriefing of a beautiful blond amnesia victim who was once the mistress of a fearsome Chinese nuclear scientist. Girland has recently lost five thousand dollars on "three, miserable horses" and is forced to earn what little he can as a street photographer. Therefore, when two CIA strongmen come to ask his assistance, he happily agrees, but not before sending one of them somersaulting down a long flight of stairs to serious injury and punching the other until he falls to his knees gasping. Girland has found the two of them somewhat overbearing and pushy.

Such is the tone of the novel. The blond woman, Erica, is sought by the Russians, who want her information, and by the Chinese, who want her dead.

Girland discovers, however, that she is involved in the theft of a priceless black pearl from China, a common twist in a Chase plot. Also typical is the resolution, which lies in the discovery of look-alike sisters, the more virtuous of whom is killed. Other innocent characters are murdered also: Erica's young and devoted nurse is shot, and the longtime secretary to the CIA chief is thrown to the ground from her upper-story apartment.

The world in which Girland operates is hostile, and it justifies his own violent excesses and other less than noble behavior. As an American in Paris, he is motivated entirely by his own financial gain and the fun of the mission, not at all by ethics or patriotic duty. This is especially true when he learns that Erica will not be a national security bonanza but could be a financial windfall to him, worth some half million dollars if the pearl is recovered and sold. At a lavish romantic dinner paid for by the CIA, Girland offers to leave his mission, go with her, find the pearl, and sell it. "I'm not only an opportunist," he tells her, "I am also an optimist." This is, however, the mind-set he must have to succeed in this world—a world of evil Asians, "with the unmistakeable smell of dirt," and Russian spies, one of whom is "fat and suety-faced" and has never been known "to do anyone a favor."

Clearly Chase fits neatly into the hard-boiled American school of detective fiction, even allowing for his English roots. His books are, indeed, escapist and formulaic, but they are successfully so. Chase's work is of consistent quality and time and again offers the reader the thrills and suspense that are the hallmarks of this mid-twentieth century genre.

Vicki K. Robinson

PRINCIPAL MYSTERY AND DETECTIVE FICTION

DAVE FENNER SERIES: *No Orchids for Miss Blandish*, 1939 (revised 1961; also known as *The Villain and the Virgin*); *Twelve Chinks and a Woman*, 1940 (revised as *Twelve Chinamen and a Woman*, 1950; also known as *The Doll's Bad News*)

VIC MALLOY SERIES: *You're Lonely When You're Dead*, 1949; *Figure It Out for Yourself*, 1950 (also known as *The Marijuana Mob*); *Lay Her Among the Lilies*, 1950 (also known as *Too Dangerous to Be Free*)

BRICK-TOP CORRIGAN SERIES (AS MARSHALL): *Mallory*, 1950; *Why Pick on Me?*, 1951

STEVE HARMAS SERIES: *The Double Shuffle*, 1952; *There's Always a Price Tag*, 1956; *Shock Treatment*, 1959; *Tell It to the Birds*, 1963

DON MICKLEM SERIES (AS MARSHALL): *Mission to Venice*, 1954; *Mission to Siena*, 1955

FRANK TERRELL SERIES: *The Soft Centre*, 1964; *The Way the Cookie Crumbles*, 1965; *Well Now, My Pretty—*, 1967; *There's a Hippie on the Highway*, 1970

MARK GIRLAND SERIES: *This Is for Real*, 1965; *You Have Yourself a Deal*, 1966; *Have This One on Me*, 1967; *Believed Violent*, 1968; *The Whiff of Money*, 1969

AL BARNEY SERIES: *An Ear to the Ground*, 1968; *You're Dead Without Money*, 1972

HELGA ROLFE SERIES: *An Ace up My Sleeve*, 1971; *The Joker in the Pack*, 1975; *I Hold the Four Aces*, 1977

NONSERIES NOVELS: 1939-1950 • *He Won't Need It Now*, 1939 (as Docherty); *The Dead Stay Dumb*, 1939 (also known as *Kiss My Fist!*); *Lady—Here's Your Wreath*, 1940 (as Marshall); *Miss Callaghan Comes to Grief*, 1941; *Just the Way It Is*, 1944 (as Marshall); *Miss Shumway Waves a Wand*, 1944; *Blondes' Requiem*, 1945 (as Marshall); *Eve*, 1945; *I'll Get You for This*, 1946; *Make the Corpse Walk*, 1946 (as Marshall); *More Deadly than the Male*, 1946 (as Grant); *The Flesh of the Orchid*, 1948; *Trusted Like the Fox*, 1948 (as Marshall); *The Paw in the Bottle*, 1949 (as Marshall); *You Never Know with Women*, 1949

1951-1960 • *But a Short Time to Live*, 1951 (as Marshall); *In a Vain Shadow*, 1951 (as Marshall); *Strictly for Cash*, 1951; *The Fast Buck*, 1952; *The Wary Transgressor*, 1952 (as Marshall); *I'll Bury My Dead*, 1953; *The Things Men Do*, 1953 (as Marshall); *This Way for a Shroud*, 1953; *Safer Dead*, 1954 (also known as *Dead Ringer*); *The Sucker Punch*, 1954 (as Marshall); *Tiger by the Tail*, 1954; *Ruthless*, 1955 (as Marshall); *The Pickup*, 1955 (as Marshall); *You've Got It Coming*, 1955 (revised 1975); *You Find Him—I'll Fix Him*, 1956 (as Marshall); *Never Trust a Woman*, 1957 (as Marshall); *The Guilty Are Afraid*, 1957; *Hit and Run*, 1958 (as Marshall); *Not Safe to Be Free*, 1958 (also known as *The Case of the Strangled Starlet*); *The World in My Pocket*, 1959; *Come Easy—Go Easy*, 1960; *What's Better than Money?*, 1960

1961-1970 • *A Lotus for Miss Quon*, 1961; *Just Another Sucker*, 1961; *A Coffin from Hong Kong*, 1962; *I Would Rather Stay Poor*, 1962; *One Bright Summer Morning*, 1963; *Cade*, 1966; *The Vulture Is a Patient Bird*, 1969; *Like a Hole in the Head*, 1970

1971-1980 • *Want to Stay Alive?*, 1971; *Just a Matter of Time*, 1972; *Have a Change of Scene*, 1973; *Knock, Knock! Who's There?*, 1973; *Goldfish Have No Hiding Place*, 1974; *So What Happens to Me?*, 1974; *Three of Spades*, 1974; *Believe This, You'll Believe Anything*, 1975; *Do Me a Favour—Drop Dead*, 1976; *My Laugh Comes Last*, 1977; *Consider Yourself Dead*, 1978; *A Can of Worms*, 1979; *You Must Be Kidding*, 1979; *Try This One for Size*, 1980; *You Can Say That Again*, 1980

1981-1984 • *Hand Me a Fig-Leaf*, 1981; *Have a Nice Night*, 1982; *We'll Share a Double Funeral*, 1982; *Not My Thing*, 1983; *Hit Them Where It Hurts*, 1984

PLAYS: *Get a Load of This*, pr. 1941 (with Arthur Macrea); *No Orchids for Miss Blandish*, pr. 1942 (with Robert Nesbitt; adaptation of his novel of the same name); *Last Page*, 1946

EDITED TEXT: *Slipstream: A Royal Air Force Anthology*, 1946 (with David Langdon)

BIBLIOGRAPHY

Calcutt, Andrew, and Richard Shepard. *Cult Fiction: A Readers' Guide*. Lincolnwood, Ill.: Contemporary Books, 1999. Chase's works and his fans are compared with those of other writers who have acquired a cult following.

Horsley, Lee. *The Noir Thriller*. New York: Palgrave, 2001. This scholarly study of the thriller covers four of Chase's novels, including *No Orchids for Miss Blandish* and *The Wary Transgressor*. Bibliography and index.

Orwell, George. "Raffles and Miss Blandish." In *The Collected Essays, Journalism and Letters of George Orwell*, edited by Sonia Orwell and Ian Angus. London: Secker and Warburg, 1968. Orwell, one of England's most famous authors and essayists, compares Chase's *No Orchids for Miss Blandish* with the Raffles stories of E. W. Hornung.

Smith, Susan Harris. "No Orchids for George Orwell." *The Armchair Detective* 9 (February, 1976): 114-115. A response to Orwell's essay, defending Chase's work from Orwell's critique.

West, W. J. *The Quest for Graham Greene*. New York: St. Martin's Press, 1998. Explores the relationship between Chase and Greene and the influence of the one's works on the other.

G. K. CHESTERTON

Born: London, England; May 29, 1874
Died: Beaconsfield, Buckinghamshire, England; June 14, 1936
Types of plot: Amateur sleuth; cozy

PRINCIPAL SERIES

Father Brown, 1911-1935

PRINCIPAL SERIES CHARACTER

FATHER BROWN, a rather ordinary Roman Catholic priest, is at first sight a humorous figure in a shabby black habit with an umbrella and an armful of brown-paper parcels. Having a realistic view of human nature, he is able to solve crimes by applying common-sense reasoning. As the series progresses, he becomes increasingly concerned not only with solving the crime but also with redeeming the criminal.

CONTRIBUTION

In the Father Brown series, the detective short story came of age. The world portrayed in the stories reflects the real world. The stories are not meant merely to entertain, for example, by presenting an intriguing puzzle that is solved by a computer-like sleuth who possesses and applies a superhuman logic, à la Sherlock Holmes. Instead, Father Brown, by virtue of his role as a parish priest who has heard numerous confessions, has a better-than-average insight into the real state of human nature. Such insight allows the priest-sleuth to identify with the criminal, then to apply sheer commonsense reasoning to uncover the criminal's identity. G. K. Chesterton is interested in exposing and exploring spiritual and moral issues, rather than merely displaying the techniques of crime and detection.

The Father Brown stories, like all Chesterton's fictional works, are a vehicle for presenting his religious worldview to a wider audience. They popularize the serious issues with which Chesterton wrestled in such nonfictional works as *Orthodoxy* (1908) and *The Everlasting Man* (1925).

BIOGRAPHY

Gilbert Keith Chesterton was born on May 29, 1874, in London of middle-class parents. Between 1887 and 1892, he attended St. Paul's School, a private day school for boys. From 1892 to 1895, he studied at the Slade School of Art, a part of the University of London.

Chesterton did not distinguish himself academically, although evidence of his future greatness was present. When only sixteen, he organized a debating club, and in March of 1891 he founded the club's magazine, *The Debater*. His limited talent as an artist bore fruit later in life, when he often illustrated his own books and those of close friends.

Prior to publication of his first two books in 1900, Chesterton contributed verse, book reviews, and essays to various periodicals, including the *Bookman*. He also did editorial work for two publishers between 1895 and 1901.

By the beginning of the twentieth century, Chesterton was widely recognized as a serious journalist. Throughout his life, despite his fame as a novelist, literary critic, poet, biographer, historian, playwright, and even philosopher-theologian, he never described himself as anything other than a journalist.

In 1901, Chesterton married Frances Blogg, the eldest daughter of a London diamond merchant. Shortly thereafter, they moved to Beaconsfield, where they lived until his death on June 14, 1936. Chesterton published his first mystery collection, *The Club of Queer Trades*, in 1905. The first collection of Father Brown detective stories appeared in 1911. He was elected the first president of the Detection Club, an association of mystery writers, at its founding in 1929. The mystery and detective tales were but a small part of an immense and varied literary output. Chesterton published around one hundred books during his lifetime. His autobiography and ten volumes of essays were published posthumously. His journalistic pieces number into the thousands.

Chesterton was a colorful figure. Grossly overweight, he wore a black cape and a wide-brimmed floppy hat; he had a bushy mustache and carried a sword-stick cane. The public remembers him as the lovable and whimsical creator of Father Brown; scholars also remember him as one of the most prolific and influential writers of the twentieth century.

G. K. Chesterton. (Library of Congress)

ANALYSIS

G. K. Chesterton began writing detective fiction in 1905 with a collection of short stories titled *The Club of Queer Trades*. Between 1905 and the appearance of the first collection of Father Brown stories in 1911, Chesterton also published a detective novel, *The Man Who Was Thursday: A Nightmare*, in 1908. There followed, in addition to the Father Brown series, one more detective novel and several additional detective short-story collections. It was the Father Brown stories, however, that became the most popular—though some critics believe them the least important—of Chesterton's works.

Students of Chesterton as an author of detective fiction make several general observations. They note that, like many who took up that genre, Chesterton was influenced by Edgar Allan Poe. It is often said that the plots of many of the Father Brown stories are variations on the plot of Poe's story "The Purloined Letter," in which an essential clue escapes the observer's attention because it fits with its surroundings.

Chesterton was influenced also by Charles Dickens, whom he admired greatly, and about whom he wrote a biography (considered one of his most valuable works of literary criticism). Chesterton learned from Dickens the art of creating an atmosphere and of giving his characters a depth that makes them memorable. In this area Chesterton's achievement rivals that of Arthur Conan Doyle. Sherlock Holmes and Father Brown have outlived their rivals, in part because readers come to know them and their world too well to forget them.

Students of Chesterton agree, however, that there is one area in particular that distinguishes Chesterton's detective fiction from that of Doyle—and that of virtually all other mystery writers before him. This distinctive element accounts for critics' observation that Chesterton lifted the detective story beyond the level of light fiction into the realm of serious literature. Chesterton's hallmark is an ever-present concern with spiritual and moral issues: locating and exploring the guilt that underlies and is responsible for criminal activity. Some critics trace this emphasis on a universe with moral absolutes to Dickens's influence. The fact that it is a common theme throughout all Chesterton's writings, both fiction and nonfiction, however, suggests that, although written to entertain, his detective stories were a means of popularizing ideas he argued on a different level in his more serious, nonfictional works.

FATHER BROWN SERIES

It is easy to see how Chesterton's orthodox Roman Catholic worldview permeates the Father Brown stories. It is evident in his understanding of the nature of criminal activity, as well as in the methodology by which Father Brown solves a mystery, and in his primary purpose for becoming involved in detection.

When the two Father Brown collections published before World War I are compared with those published after the war, a change in emphasis is revealed. In *The Innocence of Father Brown* (1911) and *The Wisdom of Father Brown* (1914), the emphasis is on Father Brown's use of reason informed by faith, along with certain psychological insights gained from his profession, to solve a particular crime. In *The Incredulity of Father Brown* (1926), *The Secret of Father Brown* (1927), and *The Scandal of Father Brown* (1935), the emphasis is on using reason not only to identify the criminal but also to obtain a confession—and with it, the salvation of the criminal's soul.

Chesterton found the inspiration for Father Brown in 1904, when he first met Father John O'Connor, the Roman Catholic parish priest of St. Cuthbert's, Bradford, England. Writer and priest became lifelong friends; it was Father O'Connor who received Chesterton into the Roman Catholic Church on July 30, 1922, and who sang the Requiem Mass for him on June 27, 1936. O'Connor even served as the model for the illustration of Father Brown on the dust jacket of *The Innocence of Father Brown.*

Chesterton was impressed with O'Connor's knowledge of human nature warped by sin. O'Connor had a deep insight into the nature of evil, obtained through the many hours he had spent in the confessional. Chesterton observed that many people consider priests to be somehow divorced from the "real world" and its evil; O'Connor's experience, however, gave evidence that such was not the case. Thus, Chesterton became interested in creating a fictional priest-sleuth, one who outwardly appeared innocent, even naïve, but whose profound understanding of the psychology of evil

would give him a definite edge over the criminal—and over the average detective. Much of the reader's pleasure in the Father Brown stories lies in the ever-present contrast between the priest's appearance of worldly innocence and his astute insight into the workings of men's hearts and minds.

Chesterton's worldview, and therefore Father Brown's, assumes a moral universe of morally responsible people who possess free will. Yet every person's nature has been affected by the presence of sin. There exists within all human beings—including Father Brown—the potential for evil. Committing a crime is an exercise of free will, a matter of choice; the criminal is morally responsible for his or her acts. Chesterton will have nothing to do with the notion that some force outside the individual can compel the person to commit a criminal act. Crime is a matter of choice—and therefore there is the possibility of repentance and redemption for the criminal.

Many writers of detective fiction create an element of surprise by showing the crime to have been committed by one who appears psychologically incapable of it. In Chesterton's stories, by contrast, all the criminals are psychologically capable of their crimes. In fact, Father Brown often eliminates suspects by concluding that they are incapable of the crime being investigated.

It is Father Brown's recognition of the universality of sin that is the key to his method of detection. It is sometimes assumed that since Father Brown is a priest, he must possess supernatural powers, some spiritual or occult source of knowledge that renders him a sort of miracle-working Sherlock Holmes. Nothing could be farther from the truth. Chesterton makes it very clear that Father Brown does not possess any supernatural insight, that he relies on nothing more than the usual five senses. Whatever advantage Father Brown as a priest has over the average person lies in his exceptional moral insight, and that is a by-product of his experience as a parish priest.

"THE GREEN MAN"

Father Brown possesses an unusually keen sense of observation, but, unlike Sherlock Holmes, he does not apply it to the facts discoverable by an oversized magnifying glass. The essential clues, instead, are generally found in individuals' behavior and conversation. In "The Green Man," for example, Father Brown and a lawyer, Mr. Dyke, are interrupted and informed that Admiral Sir Michael Craven drowned on his way home:

> "When did this happen?" asked the priest.
> "Where was he found?" asked the lawyer.

This seemingly innocuous pair of responses provides Father Brown with the clue to the lawyer's identity as the murderer of Admiral Craven. It is not logical for one to ask *where* the body of a seaman returning home from sea was found.

Father Brown's method of detection is aimed at discovering the truth behind the appearance of things. His method rises above the rational methods of the traditional detective. The latter seeks to derive an answer from observation of the facts surrounding a crime. He fails because he cannot "see" the crime. Father Brown's method, on the other hand, succeeds because the priest is able to "create" the crime. He does so by identifying with the criminal so closely that he is able to commit the act himself in his own mind.

"THE SECRET OF FATHER BROWN"

In "The Secret of Father Brown," a fictional prologue to the collection of stories by the same title, Father Brown explains the secret of his method of detection to a dumbfounded listener:

> "The secret is," he said; and then stopped as if unable to go on. Then he began again and said:
> "You see, it was I who killed all those people."
> "What?" repeated the other in a small voice out of a vast silence.
> "You see, I had murdered them all myself," explained Father Brown patiently. "So, of course, I knew how it was done." . . .
> "I had planned out each of the crimes very carefully," went on Father Brown. "I had thought out exactly how a thing like that could be done, and in what style or state of mind a man could really do it. And when I was quite sure that I felt exactly like the murderer myself, of course I knew who he was."

Father Brown's secret lies in his acceptance of the simple truth that all men are capable of doing evil.

Thus, the Father Brown stories and other detective works by Chesterton are never simply clever stories built around a puzzle; they are moral tales with a deep religious meaning. In the stories written after World War I, Chesterton placed greater emphasis on Father Brown's role as a priest—that is, his goal being not simply determining the identity of the criminal but also gaining salvation of the offender's soul. Central to all the stories is Chesterton's belief that although people themselves are incapable of doing anything about the human predicament, God has come to their aid through his son, Jesus Christ, and the Church.

In *Orthodoxy*, Chesterton compares the Church to a kind of divine detective, whose purpose is to bring people to the point where they can acknowledge their crimes (that is, their sins), and then to pardon them. The same idea appears in *Manalive* (1912), a kind of detective story-allegorical comedy, and in *The Everlasting Man*, a response to H. G. Wells's very popular *The Outline of History* (1920). In his *Autobiography*, published posthumously in 1936, Chesterton identifies himself with his fictional creation, Father Brown—a revelation that supports the assertion that the Father Brown stories were meant by their author to do more than merely entertain.

"THE QUEER FEET"

There is much social satire in the Father Brown stories and other of Chesterton's fictional works. In everything that he wrote, Chesterton was an uncompromising champion of the common people. In stories such as "The Queer Feet," for example, he satirizes the false distinctions that the upper classes perpetuate to maintain their privileged position within the status quo. In this particular story, the aristocrats are unable to recognize the thief who moves among them, simply because the waiters, like the "gentlemen," are dressed in black dinner jackets.

The Father Brown stories remain favorites of connoisseurs of mystery and detective fiction, for in their depth of characterization, their ability to convey an atmosphere, and the intellectually challenging ideas that lie just below the surface of the stories, they are without equal. Still, their quality may vary. By the time Chesterton was writing the stories that appear in *The Scandal of Father Brown*, they had become a major means of financial support for *G. K.'s Weekly*. When informed by his secretary that the bank account was getting low, Chesterton would disappear for a few hours, then reappear with a few notes in hand and dictate a new Father Brown story. It was potboiling, but potboiling at its best.

Chesterton inspired a number of authors, among them some of the best mystery writers. The prolific John Dickson Carr was influenced by him, as was Jorge Luis Borges—not a mystery writer strictly speaking, with the exception of a few stories, but one whose work reflects Chesterton's interest in the metaphysics of crime and punishment. Of all the mystery writers who acknowledged their debt to Chesterton, however, perhaps none is better known than Dorothy

An illustration that G. K. Chesterton himself drew for The Club of Queer Trades *in 1905.*

L. Sayers. A great admirer of Chesterton, she knew him personally—and followed in his footsteps as president of the Detection Club.

Paul R. Waibel

PRINCIPAL MYSTERY AND DETECTIVE FICTION

FATHER BROWN SERIES: *The Innocence of Father Brown*, 1911; *The Wisdom of Father Brown*, 1914; *The Incredulity of Father Brown*, 1926; *The Secret of Father Brown*, 1927; *The Scandal of Father Brown*, 1935

NONSERIES NOVELS: *The Man Who Was Thursday: A Nightmare*, 1908; *Manalive*, 1912; *The Floating Admiral*, 1931 (with others)

OTHER SHORT FICTION: *The Club of Queer Trades*, 1905; *The Man Who Knew Too Much, and Other Stories*, 1922; *Tales of the Long Bow*, 1925; *The Moderate Murder and the Honest Quack*, 1929; *The Poet and the Lunatics: Episodes in the Life of Gabriel Gale*, 1929; *Four Faultless Felons*, 1930; *The Ecstatic Thief*, 1930; *The Vampire of the Village*, 1947; *The Paradoxes of Mr. Pond*, 1936

OTHER MAJOR WORKS

NOVELS: *Basil Howe: A Story of Young Love*, wr. 1894, pb. 2001; *The Napoleon of Notting Hill*, 1904; *The Ball and the Cross*, 1909; *The Flying Inn*, 1914; *The Return of Don Quixote*, 1926

SHORT FICTION: *The Tremendous Adventures of Major Brown*, 1903; *The Perishing of the Pendragons*, 1914; *Stories*, 1928; *The Sword of Wood*, 1928

PLAYS: *Magic: A Fantastic Comedy*, pr. 1913; *The Judgment of Dr. Johnson*, pb. 1927; *The Surprise*, pb. 1952

POETRY: *Greybeards at Play: Literature and Art for Old Gentlemen—Rhymes and Sketches*, 1900; *The Wild Knight, and Other Poems*, 1900 (revised 1914); *The Ballad of the White Horse*, 1911; *A Poem*, 1915; *Poems*, 1915; *Wine, Water, and Song*, 1915; *Old King Cole*, 1920; *The Ballad of St. Barbara, and Other Verses*, 1922; *Poems*, 1925; *The Queen of Seven Swords*, 1926; *Gloria in Profundis*, 1927; *Ubi Ecclesia*, 1929; *The Grave of Arthur*, 1930

NONFICTION: 1901-1910 • *The Defendant*, 1901; *Robert Louis Stevenson*, 1902 (with W. Robertson Nicoll); *Thomas Carlyle*, 1902; *Twelve Types*, 1902 (revised as *Varied Types*, 1903, and also known as *Simplicity and Tolstoy*); *Charles Dickens*, 1903 (with F. G. Kitton); *Leo Tolstoy*, 1903 (with G. H. Perris and Edward Garnett); *Robert Browning*, 1903; *Tennyson*, 1903 (with Richard Garnett); *Thackeray*, 1903 (with Lewis Melville); *G. F. Watts*, 1904; *Heretics*, 1905; *Charles Dickens: A Critical Study*, 1906; *All Things Considered*, 1908; *Orthodoxy*, 1908; *George Bernard Shaw*, 1909 (revised edition, 1935); *Tremendous Trifles*, 1909; *Alarms and Discursions*, 1910; *The Ultimate Lie*, 1910; *What's Wrong with the World*, 1910; *William Blake*, 1910

1911-1920 • *A Defence of Nonsense, and Other Essays*, 1911; *Appreciations and Criticisms of the Works of Charles Dickens*, 1911; *The Future of Religion: Mr. G. K. Chesterton's Reply to Mr. Bernard Shaw*, 1911; *A Miscellany of Men*, 1912; *The Conversion of an Anarchist*, 1912; *The Victorian Age in Literature*; *Thoughts from Chesterton*, 1913; *London*, 1914 (with Alvin Langdon Coburn); *Prussian Versus Belgian Culture*, 1914; *The Barbarism of Berlin*, 1914; *Letters to an Old Garibaldian*, 1915; *The Crimes of England*, 1915; *The So-Called Belgian Bargain*, 1915; *A Shilling for My Thoughts*; *Divorce Versus Democracy*, 1916; *Temperance and the Great Alliance*, 1916; *A Short History of England*, 1917; *Lord Kitchener*, 1917; *Utopia of Usurers, and Other*

Essays, 1917; *How to Help Annexation*, 1918; *Charles Dickens Fifty Years After*, 1920; *Irish Impressions*, 1920; *The New Jerusalem*, 1920; *The Superstition of Divorce*, 1920; *The Uses of Diversity*, 1920

1921-1930 • *Eugenics and Other Evils*, 1922; *What I Saw in America*, 1922; *Fancies Versus Fads*, 1923; *St. Francis of Assisi*, 1923; *The End of the Roman Road: A Pageant of Wayfarers*, 1924; *The Superstitions of the Sceptic*, 1924; *The Everlasting Man*, 1925; *William Cobbett*, 1925; *A Gleaming Cohort, Being from the Words of G. K. Chesterton*, 1926; *The Catholic Church and Conversion*, 1926; *The Outline of Sanity*, 1926; *Culture and the Coming Peril*, 1927; *Robert Louis Stevenson*, 1927; *Social Reform Versus Birth Control*, 1927; *Do We Agree? A Debate*, 1928 (with George Bernard Shaw); *Generally Speaking*, 1928 (essays); *G. K. C. as M. C., Being a Collection of Thirty-seven Introductions*, 1929; *The Thing*, 1929; *At the Sign of the World's End*, 1930; *Come to Think of It*, 1930; *The Resurrection of Rome*, 1930; *The Turkey and the Turk*, 1930

1931-1940 • *All Is Grist*, 1931; *Is There a Return to Religion?*, 1931 (with E. Haldeman-Julius); *Chaucer*, 1932; *Christendom in Dublin*, 1932; *Sidelights on New London and Newer York, and Other Essays*, 1932; *All I Survey*, 1933; *G. K. Chesterton*, 1933 (also known as *Running After One's Hat, and Other Whimsies*); *St. Thomas Aquinas*, 1933; *Avowals and Denials*, 1934; *Explaining the English*, 1935; *The Well and the Shallows*, 1935; *As I Was Saying*, 1936; *Autobiography*, 1936; *The Man Who Was Chesterton*, 1937; *The End of the Armistice*, 1940

1941-1971 • *The Common Man*, 1950; *The Glass Walking-Stick, and Other Essays from the "Illustrated London News," 1905-1936*, 1955; *Lunacy and Letters*, 1958; *Where All Roads Lead*, 1961; *The Man Who Was Orthodox: A Selection from the Uncollected Writings of G. K. Chesterton*, 1963; *The Spice of Life, and Other Essays*, 1964; *Chesterton on Shakespeare*, 1971

EDITED TEXTS: *Thackeray*, 1909; *Samuel Johnson*, 1911 (with Alice Meynell); *Essays by Divers Hands*, 1926

MISCELLANEOUS: *Stories, Essays, and Poems*, 1935; *The Coloured Lands*, 1938; *The Collected Works of G. K. Chesterton*, 1986-1999 (35 volumes)

BIBLIOGRAPHY

Accardo, Pasquale J., John Peterson, and Geir Hasnes, eds. *Sherlock Holmes Meets Father Brown*. Shelburne, Ont.: Battered Silicon Dispatch Box, 2000. Collection of criticism and related work that attempts to gain for scholars of Chesterton's Father Brown character the same prestige and critical energy that has been enjoyed for decades by scholars of Sherlock Holmes.

Bloom, Harold, ed. *G. K. Chesterton*. New York: Chelsea House, 2006. Includes two essays on Chesterton and the grotesque, as well as several considering his Catholicism in various contexts. Bibliographic references and index.

Boyd, Ian. *The Novels of G. K. Chesterton: A Study in Art and Propaganda*. New York: Barnes and Noble, 1975. A good study of Chesterton's six major novels, as well as his collections of short stories. Discusses the novels in four periods: early, the eve of World War I, postwar (Distributist), and late.

Buechner, Frederick. *Speak What We Feel (Not What We Ought to Say): Reflections on Literature and Faith*. San Francisco: HarperSanFrancisco, 2001. Discusses Chesterton's novel *The Man Who Was Thursday*.

Chesterton, G. K. *The Autobiography of G. K. Chesterton*. San Francisco: Ignatius Press, 2006. Contains his 1936 autobiography with an introduction by Randall Paine. Describes his identification with his character Father Brown.

Clipper, Lawrence J. *G. K. Chesterton*. New York: Twayne, 1974. In this useful introduction to the works of Chesterton, Clipper does a fine job of describing the recurring themes in Chesterton's fictional and nonfictional writings. He analyzes very well Chesterton's poetry and literary criticism. Contains an excellent annotated bibliography.

Correu, Michael. *Gilbert: The Man Who Was G. K. Chesterton*. New York: Paragon House, 1990. Biography of Chesterton focusing on the more controversial aspects of his personality.

Kestner, Joseph A. *The Edwardian Detective, 1901-1915*. Brookfield, Vt.: Ashgate, 2000. Chesterton is compared to his fellow Edwardians in this tightly focused study of the British detective genre.

Pearce, Joseph. *Wisdom and Innocence: A Life of G. K. Chesterton*. San Francisco: Ignatius Press, 1996. A scholarly and well-written biography of Chesterton. Contains many quotations from his works and good analysis of them, as well as useful data on his family and friends.

Wills, Garry. *Chesterton*. New York: Doubleday, 2001. This biography is a revised edition of *Chesterton: Man and Mask* (1961).

PETER CHEYNEY
Reginald Evelyn Peter Southouse Cheyney

Born: London, England; February 22, 1896
Died: London, England; June 26, 1951
Types of plot: Hard-boiled; espionage

PRINCIPAL SERIES
Alonzo MacTavish, 1943-1946
Lemmy Caution, 1936-1953
Slim Callaghan, 1937-1953
Dark series, 1942-1950

PRINCIPAL SERIES CHARACTERS

ALONZO MACTAVISH, a rogue and a gentleman jewel thief, engages in elaborate ruses.

LEMMY CAUTION, an American G-man, slugs hoodlums, solves murders, and meets up with many dangerous dames. Caution narrates in a rough-and-tumble present tense that contributes to the speed and camp of the novels.

SLIM CALLAGHAN, a virtuoso liar and hard-boiled private eye, is also canny, resourceful, and tough. He chain-smokes Players cigarettes as he sleuths in the dark streets of London. In the second novel, Callaghan Investigations has prospered and relocated from Chancery Lane to Berkeley Square, where Callaghan also keeps an apartment.

EFFIE THOMPSON, Callaghan's secretary, in the first book is called EFFIE PERKINS. Attractive and caustic, Effie barely contains her jealousy and anger over the many beautiful women Callaghan encounters.

DETECTIVE INSPECTOR GRINGALL of New Scotland Yard is Callaghan's rival on the police force. Although often exasperated by Callaghan's withholding of evidence, Gringall nevertheless gradually comes to respect Callaghan's basic integrity and shrewdness.

EVERARD PETER QUAYLE, the spymaster, coolly juggles his operatives so that each knows only as much as is needed for his part in a particular mission.

ERNIE GUELVADA is an agent who likes to perform his jobs with an artistic flair.

SHAUN ALOYSIUS O'MARA is a special operative who is called in whenever a job appears endangered.

CONTRIBUTION

At a time when British crime fiction exerted a strong influence on American writers, Peter Cheyney was the first British author to show that he was influenced by crime fiction in the United States. His novels about tough G-man Lemmy Caution and private eye Slim Callaghan combined fast action with surprises. A popular mystery writer with no literary pretensions, Cheyney sold more than 1.5 million books in 1944 alone. An examination of his popularity shows that he was versatile in the ways he could entertain his large audience. As he progressed, his writing became more subtle, and in his Dark series near the end of his career, Cheyney produced books that vividly conveyed a picture of the divided world of wartime espionage and its cynicism, violence, and double-crosses.

BIOGRAPHY

Peter Cheyney was born Reginald Evelyn Peter Southouse Cheyney on February 22, 1896, in the East End of London. His father helped operate a fish stall at Billingsgate, and his mother ran a corset shop in Whitechapel. Cheyney started writing while still in grammar school, publishing poems and articles in boys' maga-

zines. When his oldest brother found work as a performer in music halls, Cheyney became attracted to vaudeville and the stage. At seventeen, he was reworking comedy skits in knock-about farces and even toured briefly with one company as its stage manager.

World War I interrupted this informal apprenticeship, and Cheyney enlisted in the army, rising to the rank of lieutenant. After the war, he published two volumes of sentimental verse and wrote many songs and hundreds of short stories. In 1919, he married the first of his three wives.

Cheyney's initial attempt at a crime novel, a manuscript intended for the Sexton Blake series, was rejected in 1923. He was also undistinguished in his work as a shopkeeper, bookmaker, radio performer (adopting the first name Peter), politician (supporting Sir Oswald Mosley's British Union of Fascists), and editor.

At the age of forty, Cheyney achieved popularity on his own with his first published novel, *This Man Is Dangerous* (1936), the book that introduced Lemmy Caution. When a reviewer predicted that readers would reject any Cheyney book not about Caution, Cheyney accepted the challenge and wrote *The Urgent Hangman* (1937), the first of many Slim Callaghan novels. Nevertheless, Cheyney considered the espionage novels that he wrote in the 1940's his best work.

One of the most prolific and popular crime writers of his day, Cheyney published at least two books a year, though he was more popular in England and France than in the United States. He died in 1951.

ANALYSIS

Peter Cheyney's most notable literary trait was his ability to surprise his readers with unexpected twists, hidden motives, and double-crosses. This unpredictability marked nearly all Cheyney's highly popular works and can even be traced to the short stories Cheyney wrote during the 1920's. His first recurring character, Alonzo MacTavish, appeared in a series of stories in which Cheyney honed his skills as a creator of surprising plots.

"SOLD!"

MacTavish is a gentleman jewel thief and rogue patterned after E. W. Hornung's amateur cracksman,

A. J. Raffles. The story "Sold!" furnishes a good example of Cheyney's use of surprise. In it, one of MacTavish's gang seemingly sells out his boss by alerting the police to MacTavish's next heist. When arrested with the goods, MacTavish indignantly claims that the stones in his possession are duplicates he purchased elsewhere and that he had arranged to show the fakes to the owner of the genuine jewels that night. He even challenges the police to summon the owner to verify his story; arriving at headquarters later, the owner does so. While this meeting is taking place, however, one of MacTavish's men steals the real jewels from the owner's safe, the creation of the duplicates having been MacTavish's ploy to lure the owner away from his home and supply a solid alibi during the robbery. Both police and reader spot the ruse too late. Even after the reader learns to expect a surprise in a Cheyney story, the author's misdirection usually produces enough twists to outfox any wary reader.

LEMMY CAUTION SERIES

The surprises in the Lemmy Caution books, which Cheyney began in 1936, center primarily on their action and pace, qualities that made the books very popular in England. Cheyney was the first British writer to attempt to copy the idiom of the hard-boiled crime fiction that appeared in pulp magazines such as *Black Mask* and *Dime Detective*. Mixing imitation Yankee slang with the argot of cops and crooks, narrator-hero Lemmy Caution ("let me caution you") pursues both foes and women with unshackled energy: "The big curtain that is swung across the dance floor goes away to one side an' one of the niftiest legged choruses I have ever lamped starts in to work a number that would have woke up a corpse."

G-man Caution was shaped by the popularity of characters such as Carroll John Daly's Race Williams and Robert Leslie Bellem's Dan Turner. Daly and Bellem both published regularly in the pulps; every issue of *Spicy Detective* featured a Dan Turner story. The American gangster film, which also rose to great popularity at this time, supplied another likely influence on the Caution books. Films such as *Little Caesar* (1930), *The Public Enemy* (1931), and the many others ground out by Warner Bros. acquainted the public with Hollywood's version of mobsters. A subplot in-

volving rival Chicago bootleggers in Cheyney's novel *Dark Hero* (1946), for example, broadly parallels Howard Hawks's 1932 film *Scarface*, and references to film stars and filmgoing dot many of Cheyney's books. Also new and popular in the early 1930's were newspaper comic-strip cops such as Chester Gould's *Dick Tracy* (syndicated in 1931), *Dan Dunn, Secret Operative 48* (1933), and Dashiell Hammett's and Alex Raymond's *Secret Agent X-9* (1934). The exaggerated, full-throttle style of the Caution books even reads like a novelized comic strip for adults, as in this example from *Don't Get Me Wrong* (1939):

> Some little curtains at the back part an' out comes Zellara. Here is a dame who has got somethin'. She is a real Mexican. Little, slim an' made like a piece of indiarubber. She has got a swell shape an' a lovely face with a pair of the naughtiest lookin' brown eyes I have ever seen in my life. She sings a song an' goes into a rumba dance. This baby has got what it takes all right.
>
> Me, I have seen dames swing it before but I reckon that if this Zellara hadda been let loose in the Garden of Eden Adam woulda taken a quick run-out powder an' the serpent woulda been found hidin' behind the rose-bushes with his fingers crossed. At the risk of repeatin' myself I will tell you guys that this dame is a one hundred per cent exclusive custom-built 1939 model fitted with all the speed gadgets an' guarantees not to skid goin' round the corners.

When the pulps gave way to paperback originals, detectives such as Race Williams, Dan Turner, Hammett's Continental Op, the Shadow, Doc Savage, and others made room for the likes of Mickey Spillane's Mike Hammer, who in many ways is a more sexual, violent version of Lemmy Caution. The tongue-in-cheek humor of the Caution books turned up later in paperbacks by writers such as Richard S. Prather. A clear echo of the voice of Lemmy Caution can be heard in Prather's private eye Shell Scott: "Man, she had a shape to make corpses kick open caskets—and she was dead set on giving me rigor mortis." Another of Cheyney's literary descendants was Ian Fleming. Before writing *Casino Royale* (1953), the first James Bond novel, Fleming studied Cheyney's work carefully. When a reviewer later referred to Bond as a Lemmy Caution for the higher classes, Fleming was delighted.

SLIM CALLAGHAN SERIES

In his series about hard-boiled British private eye Slim Callaghan, Cheyney maintained his popularity and combined his gift for surprise with writing that was much more understated. This restrained quality largely resulted from the change of setting from the United States (which Cheyney never visited until 1948) in the Caution books to England in the Callaghan novels. The switch from the headlong, first-person narration of Lemmy Caution to third-person narration also gave the Callaghan novels a grittier, more objective tone.

In the third book of the series, *You Can't Keep the Change* (1940), Cheyney introduced Windemere "Windy" Nikolls as Callaghan's assistant (replacing operative Monty Kells, who had been killed in the second novel). In subsequent adventures, Nikolls assumed the role of the wisecracking sidekick who flirts with secretary Effie Thompson, reminisces about his many dames, follows up leads, and generally provides comic relief. Windy is, if anything, aptly named, but the breezy street slang that was the staple of the Caution books is in the Callaghan series mostly confined to Windy. This change of emphasis struck a new balance for Cheyney. Windy, the background operative, is the man of instinct and action—not unlike Lemmy Caution—while the hero, Callaghan, who uses muscle when necessary, primarily thinks his way through a case by winnowing the real clues from the red herrings, untangling motives, and hazarding on some lucky hunches.

Such changes not only produced subtler books but also freed Cheyney to give more personality to his series hero. Callaghan himself is a seedy, hard-bitten, outwardly cynical detective who conceals a soft spot for a pretty face and figure. Cheyney applied his talent for surprise and intricate plotting to Callaghan's character as well. Sometimes surprising the reader by seeming to betray his own client, Callaghan might also plant incriminating evidence to frame another suspect or appear to blackmail someone linked to the case simply to enrich himself. This playing of both ends against the middle shapes the early novels more than the later ones, although most characters throughout the series size up Callaghan as an opportunist.

Callaghan's shady conduct is always explained, however, in the final chapters as simply tactics to gain time or goad the culprit into revealing his guilt. If Callaghan has a code, in fact, it would be to remain faithful to his client. The later, less violent novels even indicate a slight softening of the detective. In the opening chapters of *They Never Say When* (1944), for example, after he has found a client's jeweled coronet and stopped her blackmailer, Callaghan returns her retainer of a thousand pounds because, he says, the jobs were too easy. Cheyney wrote a number of Caution novels and Callaghan novels, and numerous short stories about these characters; this British hard-boiled tradition was later to continue in the works of James Hadley Chase and Carter Brown.

DARK SERIES

If the Callaghan books took the surprises of the MacTavish stories and the action of the Caution novels and added to them a more subdued, Hammett-like writing style, the Dark series of novels that Cheyney wrote in the 1940's was somewhat more ambitious. In these books, Cheyney began to focus more on character and theme. Although various characters recur in many of the novels in this group, the series is distinguished more by its brooding, sinister atmosphere than by any unifying hero. In fact, no single character appears in every book of the series, and some of the novels do not even deal directly with espionage.

For example, in *Dark Hero*, Cheyney presents a character study of a naïve youth who slides into crime and violence. Indirect exposition and a shifting narrative focus supply pieces of this character's personality. The prologue describes the wartime efforts of the hero, Rene Berg, to revenge himself on the subcommandant of his prisoner-of-war camp. Chapter 1 follows Berg after the war as he mysteriously contacts old acquaintances in his effort to hunt down and kill a woman who had also betrayed him. Flashing back to Prohibition Chicago, chapter 2 uncovers the roots of these two betrayals. A young Berg first arrives in the city in this chapter and gradually falls in with bootleggers at the midpoint of the novel. By breaking up the linear exposition of most crime novels and by revealing the effects of Berg's actions before their causes emerge, Cheyney is able to probe Berg's motivations and to highlight his changing emotions more clearly.

Cheyney's fondness for involved plots and double-crosses lent itself perfectly to the shadow world of wartime espionage, where loyalties were suspect and treachery existed everywhere. *Dark Duet* (1942) is a good example of Cheyney's work in espionage fiction. The two protagonists, Michael Kane and Ernie Guelvada, are British agents assigned to kill a female saboteur loose in England. Cheyney's concern with the tensions between love and war both sharpens character and gives greater coherence and suspense to the developing story: Kane has concealed his espionage work from his lover, Valetta Fallon, and constantly warns his partner Guelvada about the perils of emotionalism in their work. It develops that Guelvada's least suspicious approach to the saboteur necessitates an innocent flirtation with her. After her eventual liquidation, Kane and Guelvada seek her paymasters in Lisbon, where Guelvada meets a former lover unknowingly in league with a Nazi agent. Suddenly, the truth of Kane's warnings begins to register on him. In the climax of the novel, the Nazis plan to retaliate against Kane by working through Valetta Fallon back in England. Exploiting her loneliness, they insinuate an agent into her company to kindle a romance and win her confidence. Through him, the Nazis tell Valetta that Kane has betrayed England and is really a secret German spy. Cheyney's surprises in the denouement of *Dark Duet* include Nazis working as false Scotland Yard men to feed Valetta more lies about Kane's wartime activities. Before the tension is resolved, both Kane and Guelvada must face squarely the difficulties of the conflicting pull between the lonely efficiency of the secret agent and his normal desire for company. Each ends the book alone.

Published in the 1940's, the Dark novels appeared at a time when espionage fiction was evolving from the patriotic chivalry and uncomplicated politics of John Buchan's thrillers to the more cynical, morally ambiguous climate of post-1960's spy novels. A breakthrough book that had helped trigger this change was W. Somerset Maugham's *Ashenden: Or, The British Agent* (1928). Eric Ambler's early spy novels (such as *Background to Danger*, 1937, and *Epitaph for a Spy*, 1938) also contributed to this development by emphasizing character, good writing, and a keen polit-ical sense. Ambler published six of these novels before the start of World War II. Cheyney's Dark series played its part as well, and the atmosphere and tone of later books such as *The Secret Ways* (1959) by Alistair MacLean and Donald Hamilton's series of paperbacks about agent Matt Helm recall to some extent the sinister landscape in Cheyney's novels of intrigue. By the time of Len Deighton's *The Ipcress File* (1962) and John le Carré's *The Spy Who Came in from the Cold* (1963), the action thriller of the World War II period had deepened into the more sophisticated and more literary espionage fiction of the Cold War.

Cheyney propounded no theory about crime fiction. He produced his books quickly and maintained a growing popularity in his lifetime. Yet this success was based on great versatility—unexpected twists, lower-keyed writing in the Callaghan novels, and an emphasis on character and theme in the Dark series.

Glenn Hopp

PRINCIPAL MYSTERY AND DETECTIVE FICTION

ALONZO MACTAVISH SERIES: *The Adventures of Alonzo MacTavish*, 1943; *Alonzo MacTavish Again*, 1943; *The Murder of Alonzo*, 1943; *He Walked in Her Sleep, and Other Stories*, 1946 (also known as *MacTavish*)

LEMMY CAUTION SERIES: *This Man Is Dangerous*, 1936; *Dames Don't Care*, 1937; *Poison Ivy*, 1937; *Can Ladies Kill?*, 1938; *Don't Get Me Wrong*, 1939; *You'd Be Surprised*, 1940; *Your Deal, My Lovely*, 1941; *Never a Dull Moment*, 1942; *You Can Always Duck*, 1943; *I'll Say She Does!*, 1945; *G Man at the Yard*, 1946; *Time for Caution*, 1946

SLIM CALLAGHAN SERIES: *The Urgent Hangman*, 1937; *Dangerous Curves*, 1939 (also known as *Callaghan*); *You Can't Keep the Change*, 1940; *It Couldn't Matter Less*, 1941 (also known as *Set-Up for Murder*); *Sorry You've Been Troubled*, 1942 (also known as *Farewell to the Admiral*); *The Unscrupulous Mr. Callaghan*, 1943; *They Never Say When*, 1944; *Uneasy Terms*, 1946; *Vengeance with a Twist, and Other Stories*, 1946; *You Can't Trust Duchesses, and Other Stories*, 1946; *A Tough Spot for Cupid, and Other Stories*, 1952; *Velvet Johnnie, and Other Stories*, 1952; *Calling Mr. Callaghan*, 1953

DARK SERIES: *Dark Duet*, 1942 (also known as *The Counter Spy Murders*); *The Stars Are Dark*, 1943 (also known as *The London Spy Murders*); *Date After Dark, and Other Stories*, 1944; *The Dark Street*, 1944 (also known as *The Dark Street Murders*); *Dark Hero*, 1946; *Dark Interlude*, 1947 (also known as *The Terrible Night*); *Dark Wanton*, 1948; *Dark Bahama*, 1950 (also known as *I'll Bring Her Back*)

NONSERIES NOVELS: *Another Little Drink*, 1940 (also known as *A Trap for Bellamy* and *Premeditated Murder*); *Sinister Errand*, 1945 (also known as *Sinister Murders*); *Dance Without Music*, 1947; *The Curiosity of Etienne MacGregor*, 1947 (also known as *The Sweetheart of the Razors*); *Try Anything Twice*, 1948 (also known as *Undressed to Kill*); *One of Those Things*, 1949 (also known as *Mistress Murder*); *You Can Call It a Day*, 1949 (also known as *The Man Nobody Saw*); *Lady, Behave!*, 1950 (also known as *Lady Beware*); *Ladies Won't Wait*, 1951 (also known as *Cocktails and the Killer*)

OTHER SHORT FICTION: *You Can't Hit a Woman, and Other Stories*, 1937; *Knave Takes Queen*, 1939; *Mr. Caution—Mr. Callaghan*, 1941; *Love with a Gun, and Other Stories*, 1943; *The Man with the Red Beard, and Other Stories*, 1943; *Account Rendered*, 1944; *A Tough Spot for Cupid, and Other Stories*, 1945; *Dance Without Music*, 1945; *Escape for Sandra*, 1945; *Night Club*, 1945 (also known as *Dressed to Kill*); *The Adventures of Julia*, 1945 (also known as *The Killing Game*); *A Spot of Murder, and Other Stories*, 1946; *The Man with Two Wives, and Other Stories*, 1946; *A Matter of Luck, and Other Stories*, 1947; *Lady in Green, and Other Stories*, 1947; *Cocktail for Cupid, and Other Stories*, 1948; *Cocktail Party, and Other Stories*, 1948; *Fast Work, and Other Stories*, 1948; *Information Received, and Other Stories*, 1948; *The Unhappy Lady, and Other Stories*, 1948; *The Lady in Tears, and Other Stories*, 1949; *Velvet Johnnie, and Other Stories*, 1952; *G Man at the Yard: A Lemmy Caution Novel and Three Short Sto-* ries, 1953; *The Mystery Blues, and Other Stories*, 1954 (also known as *Fast Work*)

OTHER MAJOR WORKS

PLAYS: *Three Character Sketches*, pb. 1927

RADIO PLAYS: *Knave Takes Queen*, 1941; *The Callaghan Touch*, 1941; *The Key*, 1941; *Again—Callaghan*, 1942; *The Lady Talks*, 1942; *Concerto for Crooks*, 1943; *Parisian Ghost*, 1943; *The Callaghan Come-Back*, 1943; *The Perfumed Murderer*, 1943; *The Adventures of Julia*, 1945; *Way Out*, 1945; *Duet for Crooks*, 1946; *Pay-Off for Cupid*, 1946

SCREENPLAYS: *Wife of General Ling*, 1937 (with others); *Uneasy Terms*, 1948

POETRY: *Poems of Love and War*, 1916; *To Corona, and Other Poems*, 1917

EDITED TEXT: *Best Stories of the Underworld*, 1942

MISCELLANEOUS: *Making Crime Pay*, 1944; *No Ordinary Cheyney*, 1948

BIBLIOGRAPHY

Harrison, Michael. *Peter Cheyney, Prince of Hokum: A Biography*. London: N. Spearman, 1954. At more than three hundred pages, this is by far the most comprehensive source on Cheyney's life and career.

Horsley, Lee. *The Noir Thriller*. New York: Palgrave, 2001. Scholarly, theoretically informed study of the thriller genre. Includes readings of Cheyney's *Dames Don't Care*, *Can Ladies Kill?*, and *You'd Be Surprised*.

Roth, Marty. *Foul and Fair Play: Reading Genre in Classic Detective Fiction*. Athens: University of Georgia Press, 1995. A post-structuralist analysis of the conventions of mystery and detective fiction. Examines 138 short stories and works from the 1840's to the 1960's. Briefly mentions Cheyney and helps readers place him within the context of the genre.

LEE CHILD
James Grant

Born: Coventry, England; October 29, 1954
Type of plot: Thriller

PRINCIPAL SERIES
Jack Reacher, 1997-

PRINCIPAL SERIES CHARACTER
JACK REACHER is a former military police officer. The second son of a Marine father and a French mother, he was born in Berlin in 1960 and grew up at military bases all over the world. He attended West Point and rose to the rank of major before being let go in 1997 as a result of defense budget cuts. On his return to the United States, Reacher became a wandering loner, a modern knight-errant. Reacher has no set occupation but becomes involved in the problems of others because of chance circumstance or events from his past. He is physically imposing: six feet, five inches tall, and 250 pounds. He is a skilled marksman and a ruthless fighter, and his sense of justice is deep-seated and implacable.

CONTRIBUTION
Lee Child's key decision in creating Jack Reacher was to make him free from any psychological problems; unlike other modern thriller/mystery heroes, Reacher is in no way dysfunctional. In this way, Reacher resembles the character that initially inspired Child when he was thinking about creating a mystery/thriller hero: John D. MacDonald's Travis McGee. Reacher is consciously constructed as an almost mythical hero, whose antecedents stretch back to Homer and beyond. Even though Reacher appeared before the terrorist attacks of September 11, 2001, he is the perfect hero for the post-9/11 world, being smart, capable, ruthless, and always in search of justice, yet able to temper action with mercy when appropriate. Child's audience has grown with each book in the series, and his popularity has been strengthened by the regularity with which each book appears and the works' overall high quality. Child has said that he regards his promise to produce a book a year as an obligation not only to his publishers but also to his fans. The books have been generally well received, and fans of the novels have organized Web sites about Reacher. Child does pay attention to fans' concerns, questions, and suggestions; he informed readers as to how Reacher became the man he is by writing *The Enemy* (2004), which takes place when Reacher was an officer in the military police.

BIOGRAPHY
Lee Child was born James Grant on October 29, 1954, in Coventry, England. As a boy, he enjoyed reading novels by Enid Blyton and the Gimlet series by Captain W. E. Johns. He grew up in Birmingham, won a scholarship to St. Edward's School (the same school that J. R. R. Tolkien attended), and went to college in Sheffield, reading law. He says that his skill in writing came from a physics teacher who valued concision over verbosity. Child spent eighteen years with Granada Television as a television presentation director and later union shop steward, then was let go with other veteran employees as an economizing measure. In search of a new career in his mid-forties, with a wife and daughter, Child gave himself a year to write a novel. After it was published, he moved to New York, his wife's hometown, in 1998. He began producing Reacher novels at the rate of one per year. Although Reacher's character and the plots he is involved in seem ideally suited for cinematic adaptation, plans to film Child's work have not materialized.

Child shares certain qualities with Reacher: for example, both are tall, which led to Reacher's name. Both defended older brothers in playground fights, both can tell the exact time without using a timepiece (a holdover from his television days, says Child), and both are New York Yankee fans. *Killing Floor* (1997) won the Anthony Award and the Barry Award in 1998, and *Die Trying* (1998) won the Thumping Good Read Award from the W. H. Smith Group in 1999. *Tripwire* (1999) won the Washington Irving Award in 1999, and

Lee Child in 2006. (AP/Wide World Photos)

Running Blind (2000) won it the following year. In 2005 Child won the Bob Kellogg Good Citizen Award for Outstanding Contribution to the Internet Writing Community and the Nero Award for *The Enemy*.

ANALYSIS

Lee Child's greatest accomplishment is creating a believable thriller hero for the twenty-first century. Almost all thriller heroes require a certain suspension of disbelief. Ian Fleming's James Bond had the seeds of parody within him from the first novel, an aspect that the films about the character would ultimately reveal. Mitch Rapp, the hero of the political thrillers by Vince Flynn, is almost superhuman in his dispatching of foes. By making Reacher a former military police officer, Child takes advantage of the generally positive image the military enjoys in the United States.

Child gives Reacher the physical tools to accom-

plish his tasks and the knowledge of weaponry so beloved by certain fans of the genre. However, it is the basic premise of Reacher's character—that he learned his skills in the U.S. Army's military police and that his wandering was caused by his upbringing and the manner in which he was let go—that makes his appearance in a different part of the country at the beginning of each novel and his talent in unraveling the mystery and enforcing its solution all the more believable. MacDonald got around this credibility problem by making McGee a salvage expert. Child makes Reacher a sort of knight-errant, who wanders the countryside of his native land and becomes involved with people, sometimes almost against his will.

Child knows that the literary heritage of Jack Reacher begins with the heroes of the classics, then passes through medieval knights to the cowboy heroes of the American West. The tension in the Western hero is between his rugged individualism and the needs of the community; once the latter becomes too dominant, the hero rides off. In Reacher's case, as he readily admits, he always leaves. In some of the novels, Reacher becomes involved in a case through family or quasi-family pressures. His older brother and his fate haunt Reacher, as does the last quest of his military mentor and father figure, Leon Garber. However, often Reacher becomes involved by merely being in what he views as the wrong place at the right time.

During the course of Child's novels, the victims often are forced to grow into more capable, more self-aware characters. They are shaken out of their complacency because their mindless acceptance of a shifty business ethos has put them at the mercy of ruthless predators. A character whom Reacher dismisses as a Yuppie later grows into a character whom Reacher actually likes. If a husband does not develop into a better person, then his wife sometimes does. Even if victims express their independence by threatening Reacher, in one sense, Reacher's task has been accomplished.

Child fuses in Reacher both the intellectual and physical aspects of the hero, unlike MacDonald, who endowed his hero Travis McGee with physical strength and McGee's sidekick, Meyer Meyer, with intellect. However, Child often splits his villains into a team composed of mastermind and superhuman henchman. The superhuman villain is often so imposing that Reacher seems outmatched—but the hero still manages to vanquish his foe. The masterminds are devious, but they are not bent on world domination or even on attacking the United States. Rather, they are motivated by the more commonplace of the seven deadly sins—greed, anger, and lust. They are nonetheless savage in carrying out their plans, and Reacher is equally savage in stopping them and exacting a rough-hewn justice.

Child walks a fine line in depicting both the villains' depravity and Reacher's quest for retribution. The modern thriller writer is always in danger of going over the edge in the depiction of violence: not enough violence, and the novel seems tame; too much, and the reader seems to be wallowing in sadism. Child seems to have a fairly precise knowledge of what is excessive; for example, the villain's torture and execution of two police officers in *Tripwire* is only hinted at by the mention of a scream. Child knows when to use his readers' imagination to fill in what the villain is doing.

Like almost all unattached thriller heroes, Reacher has a romance in every novel. The relationships are all sufficiently motivated so that none seems entirely gratuitous, although Child has been criticized for featuring basically the same woman, the "Reacher woman"—a tall, thin, blond professional in her early thirties—as Reacher's love interest in every novel. Reacher has been hurt in the past, losing someone he cared about to a villain, so he carries a whiff of the Byronic hero about him, but this quality is largely negated by his powerful and strong image.

The basic question about Reacher is the one asked about all heroes: Why is he heroic? Fleming's James Bond is, in the end, fulfilling Admiral Nelson's command that every Englishman do his duty. Child's Reacher, however, is only a few dollars away from vagrancy. Reacher admits that he always wanted to be a police officer, but because he was the son of a military man, he became an officer in the military police. However, now that he has been let go because of a reduction in forces, he values his freedom: He calls his first six months in the United States the happiest period of his life. When pressed by villains who sneer and ask if he is making the world safe for democracy, Reacher answers that he is a "representative" of all victims of the villains and that he "stands up" for those victims. In a candid moment, he admits that his hatred for "the big smug people" overshadows any connection he might feel with the little guys. In giving Reacher this trait, a British author has created a quintessentially American hero.

KILLING FLOOR

Child's first Jack Reacher novel, *Killing Floor*, is a variation of the southern gothic theme in which the lurid underpinnings of a town are hidden beneath a glossy sheen of perfection. Reacher must defeat the source of the "swamp," as he calls Margrave, Georgia, a vicious villain with wolflike teeth and, it is hinted, psychosexual problems. The plot relies on a huge coincidence that connects the villain's schemes with Reacher's family, which Child explains just adequately enough by describing Reacher's love of the blues. The climax is satisfyingly apocalyptic, although Reacher's reasons for abandoning his romantic interest are somewhat perfunctory, relying on readers' familiarity with the necessity for this separation as a genre convention.

Killing Floor demonstrates Child's skill in writing a riveting opening scene and establishing a sense of place. Unlike private investigators who are often tied down to one corner of the country, Reacher is able to roam all over the country and see each place with a fresh eye, as Child does. Also, while the novel is narrated in the first person, it is only one of three Reacher novels written in this point of view. Reacher's voice is generally flat and serviceable, with only a flash of poetic intensity now and then.

TRIPWIRE

In *Tripwire*, Child's third book in the series, Reacher faces a particularly nasty villain, "Hook" Hobey, who does things with his hook that J. M. Barrie's villainous Captain Hook never dreamed of doing. Child shows himself to be a master at describing New York City and the rural environs around West Point, and the villain's lair is not secluded in the countryside but right in the midst of Manhattan, in the ill-fated World Trade Center. Once again Reacher is brought into this situation because of past loyalties, this time to his mentor in the military police, Leon Garber, whose daughter serves as

Reacher's love interest in this novel. At the end of the novel, Reacher has both a girlfriend and a house, but readers know that by the next novel, both ties will have been loosened.

A major stylistic change in *Tripwire* is Child's switch to a third-person point of view, the point of view he uses in the majority of his novels. Child maintains that it affords him more freedom in creating suspense. It also enables him to segment the narrative into smaller, more easily readable chunks and engage in more character investigation—even of the villain. However, it also makes for some awkward narrative moments, such as Reacher's being informed of the revelation that clears up the entire mystery—which is not revealed to the readers. As if to make sure the reader knows that Child realizes he is not playing fair, Reacher asks for this information to be repeated three times, and it is, with the reader remaining uninformed each time. The humor in Child's novels does not extend only to Reacher's wiseacre replies.

PERSUADER

Persuader perhaps is Child's finest Reacher novel, containing a beginning both exciting and mystifying, a double narrative and plot that explains Reacher's involvement in the present case, a thoroughly evil villain and his even more repugnant superhuman henchman, a wicked witch's castle that is almost out of a fairy tale, and a damsel who must be rescued and whose last name, fittingly, is Justice.

William E. Laskowski

PRINCIPAL MYSTERY AND DETECTIVE FICTION

JACK REACHER SERIES: *Killing Floor*, 1997; *Die Trying*, 1998; *Tripwire*, 1999; *Running Blind*, 2000; *Echo Burning*, 2001; *Without Fail*, 2002; *Persuader*, 2003; *The Enemy*, 2004; *One Shot*, 2005; *The Hard Way*, 2006; *Bad Luck and Trouble*, 2007

BIBLIOGRAPHY

Anderson, Patrick. *The Triumph of the Thriller: How Cops, Crooks, and Cannibals Captured Popular Fiction*. New York: Random House, 2007. Contains a short biography of Child along with analysis of *Without Fail* and *One Shot*.

Child, Lee. Interview with Lee Child by David Thomas. *The Sunday Telegraph*, April 1, 2007, p. O16. This interview with Child examines why he writes and includes a discussion of thrillers. Child was asked to write a James Bond novel but refused.

_____. "Lee Child: Late to the Crime Scene." Interview by Dick Donahue. *Publishers Weekly* 251, no. 22 (May 31, 2004): 44-45. A detailed yet concise interview with Child, covering the main facets of his career.

_____. "Lee Child: The Loner They Love." Interview by Benedicte Page. *Bookseller* (March 24, 2006): 20-21. Contains an interview with Child at a tenth anniversary party for his Reacher series.

_____. The Official Site of Lee Child and Jack Reacher. http://www.leechild.com. Child's Web site has valuable links to online interviews and a forum for his fans, also known as Reacher's Creatures.

Maslin, Janet. "Intrepid Hero Coolly Navigates a Grisly World of Hurt." Review of *The Hard Way*, by Lee Child. *The New York Times*, May 11, 2006, p. E11. This review of the tenth Reacher novel, *The Hard Way*, emphasizes Child's skill in plotting and in documenting Reacher's thought process.

Trachtenberg, Jeffrey. "Odd Twist for Hero of Popular Thrillers: Women Like Him, Too." *The Wall Street Journal*, June 10, 2006, p. A1. Shows that women make up a large portion of Child's readers and attributes this popularity to an increasing acceptance by women of violence in the media and a post-9/11 outlook on the world's dangers.

ERSKINE CHILDERS

Born: London, England; June 25, 1870
Died: Dublin, Ireland; November 24, 1922
Types of plot: Espionage; thriller

CONTRIBUTION

Erskine Childers's fame as a mystery novelist rests on a single work of literary genius, *The Riddle of the Sands: A Record of Secret Service Recently Achieved* (1903), which introduced a new literary genre to English literature: the espionage adventure thriller. The only novel Childers ever wrote, it achieved instant acclaim when first published in England and has found admiring readers through many editions published since. It was published first in the United States in 1915 and has continued to be reissued almost every decade since then. John Buchan, writing in 1926, called it "the best story of adventure published in the last quarter of a century." It paved the way for Joseph Conrad's *The Secret Agent* (1907), John Buchan's *The Thirty-nine Steps* (1915), W. Somerset Maugham's *Ashenden: Or, The British Agent* (1928), and many similar espionage adventure thrillers by English novelists such as Graham Greene, Ian Fleming, Len Deighton, and John le Carré.

Childers invented the device of pretending that a manuscript narrating the adventure of two young men sailing a small boat in German coastal waters had come to his attention as an editor. He immediately saw the need to publish it to alert the general public to a situation that endangered the national security. He hoped that the story would cause public opinion to demand prompt changes in British national defense policy. Childers deliberately chose the adventure-story genre as a more effective means to influence public opinion than the more uninspired prose of conventional political policy treatises. This has remained an underlying purpose of many subsequent espionage adventure novelists.

BIOGRAPHY

Erskine Childers was born Robert Erskine Childers in London on June 25, 1870, the second son of Robert Caesar Childers, a distinguished English scholar of East Indian languages, and Anna Mary Barton, daughter of an Irish landed family from Glendalough, County Wicklow, Ireland. The early death of Childers's father resulted in the removal of the family from England to the Barton family's home in Ireland, and it was there that Erskine Childers was reared and ultimately found his nationality. He was educated in a private school in England and at Trinity College, Cambridge University. After receiving his bachelor's degree in 1893, he was appointed a clerk in the House of Commons, serving there from 1895 until he resigned in 1910 to devote his efforts to achieving Home Rule for Ireland.

In 1900, Childers joined a volunteer company and served in action in the war against the Boers in South Africa. The daily letters sent to his sisters and relations, recording his impressions of the war as he was experiencing it, were edited by them and published without his knowledge as a surprise on his return (1900). The success of this volume of correspondence with the public led to Childers's second literary work, a history of the military unit in which he served (1903), and ultimately a volume in the London *Times*'s history of the Boer Wars (1907).

During the long parliamentary recesses, Childers had spent his free time sailing a small thirty-foot yacht in the Baltic and North Seas and the English Channel. He had first learned to love the sea as a boy in Ireland, and he was to use his knowledge of these waters in July, 1914, to smuggle a large shipment of arms and ammunition from a German supply ship off the Belgian coast into the harbor of Howth, north of Dublin, to arm the Irish National Volunteers, a paramilitary organization formed to defend Ireland against the enemies of Home Rule. These arms were later used in the Easter Rebellion of 1916, which proclaimed the founding of the Irish Republic.

Childers's experiences as a yachtsman were put to good use in his first and only effort to write a novel, *The Riddle of the Sands*, published in 1903 and immediately making its author a celebrity. Shortly thereafter, while visiting Boston and his old military company, Childers met and married his American wife, Mary Alden

Osgood, who was his constant companion in war and peace, on sea and land, until his death. She espoused his own enthusiasm for the freedom of Ireland, for republicanism, and for the joys of yachting.

When war between Germany and Great Britain erupted in the late summer of 1914, Childers became a naval intelligence officer with special responsibility for observing the German defenses along the Frisian coast, the scene of his 1903 novel. He learned how to fly aircraft and was among the first to engage in naval air reconnaissance. For his services he received the Distinguished Service Cross and retired with the rank of major in the Royal Air Force. Returning to civilian life in 1919, Childers espoused the cause of the Irish Republic and was a tireless propagandist for the Republican movement in Irish, English, and foreign presses. He was elected to the Irish Republican parliament in 1921 and appointed minister for propaganda. He served as principal secretary to the Irish delegation that negotiated the peace treaty with England in the fall and winter of 1921.

Childers refused, however, to accept the treaty during the ratification debates, clinging steadfastly to the Republican cause along with Eamon de Valera, the Irish president. When the treaty was nevertheless ratified, Childers refused to surrender and joined the dissident members of the Irish Republican Army as it pursued its guerrilla tactics against its former comrades, who now composed the new government of the Irish Free State. He was hunted down by his former colleagues, captured in his own childhood home in the Wicklow hills, and singled out to be executed without trial and before his many friends might intervene. He was shot by a firing squad at Beggar's Bush barracks in Dublin on November 24, 1922. His unswerving loyalty to and services on behalf of the Irish Republic were ultimately honored by the Irish people who elected his son, Erskine Hamilton Childers, fourth president of the Irish Republic in 1973.

ANALYSIS

For readers who are yachtsmen, sailors, or deep-sea fishermen, Erskine Childers's depiction of the joys, hardships, and terrors of the sea and the skills needed to master the oceanic forces in his sole novel,

The Riddle of the Sands, are stunningly vivid, authentic, and insightful. His tale is a classic depiction of the sport of yachting, and the novel continues to find an appreciative audience among its admirers. In an essay on Childers, E. F. Parker noted, "In Ireland he is a legendary hero—one of the founders of the nation—but outside Ireland in the rest of the English speaking world, it is as a yachtsman he is best remembered and as the author of the splendid yachting thriller *The Riddle of the Sands*."

THE RIDDLE OF THE SANDS

Childers's *The Riddle of the Sands* has been considered a masterpiece from three different perspectives. First, it is a remakable piece of political propaganda. Childers explicitly claimed that he had "edited" the manuscript for the general public to alert it to dangers to the English nation's security posed by German naval maneuvers allegedly detected by two English amateur yachtsmen while sailing among the Frisian Islands off the northwestern coast of Imperial Germany. Childers had seen action as an ordinary soldier in the recent Boer Wars and had become very critical of Great Britain's military inadequacies. He had written several historical accounts of the Boer Wars before publishing *The Riddle of the Sands* and subsequently wrote several other military treatises urging specific reforms in British tactics and weaponry.

In the preface to *The Riddle of the Sands*, Childers reported that he opposed "a bald exposition of the essential facts, stripped of their warm human envelope," as proposed by the two young sailor adventurers. He argued that

in such a form the narrative would not carry conviction, and would defeat its own end. The persons and the events were indissolubly connected; to evade, abridge, suppress, would be to convey to the reader the idea of a concocted hoax. Indeed, I took bolder ground still, urging that the story should be made as explicit and circumstantial as possible, frankly and honestly for the purpose of entertaining and so of attracting a wide circle of readers.

Two points may be made about these remarks. First, the novel can be seen as a clever propaganda device to attract public attention to Great Britain's weaknesses in its military defenses. In fact, Childers's novel coincided with a decision by British naval authorities to investigate their North Sea naval defenses and adopt measures that came in good stead during the Great War, which broke out in 1914. (See the epilogue Childers inserted at the end of the story.) Childers's novel proved to be a successful stimulus for public support for national defense policy reforms. Significantly, the book was banned from circulation in Germany. Childers's use of an espionage adventure novel to comment on wider issues of national defense policies has been emulated by many later authors of espionage adventure thrillers.

Second, the novelist achieved a masterful characterization of the two heroes, Carruthers and Davies. The readers' knowledge of these men unfolds gradually and naturally through the action. A steady buildup of mystery is structured on a chronological framework and descriptions of wind and weather reflective of a traditional sea captain's log. Verisimilitude is also heightened by myriad colorful details of personal dress, habits, moods, meals, and the trivia of the tasks of the two sailors. Details of the boat—its sounds and movements—along with the descriptions of the islands, sandbanks, and estuaries where the story unfolds are used to create spellbinding realism for the reader. In his preface, Childers states that he had foreseen and planned this method of exposition as necessary to involve the reader personally in the underlying propagandistic purposes of the novel.

From a third perspective, the novel is a tale of the hero's personal growth to new levels of maturity through exposure to physical and moral challenges unexpectedly confronted. Carruthers, a rather spoiled, bored, and supercilious young man, is suddenly caught up in an adventure that will test his mettle and allow the reader to watch him develop unexpected strengths of a psychological, moral, and intellectual character. His companion Davies is a masterful, self-contained, and skillful yachtsman who is seemingly as mature and psychologically solid as Carruthers is not. Yet Davies also is undergoing the pain of growth through an aborted romance with the only woman in the novel, the daughter of the suspected spy.

Carruthers, out of sheer desperation to escape his previous boredom and not look the fool before his companion, is gradually introduced to the skills and spartan lifestyle of the master yachtsman Davies. He also detects a mystery about Davies and, after some testing of his spirit, is told of a strange event that Davies encountered while sailing along the Frisian Islands off the German coast. Intrigued, and now thoroughly admiring the manliness and virtues of Davies, he joins in a potentially dangerous effort to explore the channels and sandbanks lying between the Frisian Islands and the German coast.

The direct, simple construction of Childers's prose and its ability to create character and atmosphere through vivid and detailed yet economical description probably were the product of his earliest form of writing: the diary-as-letter, which he wrote almost daily during his South African adventure in 1900. That his letters were able to be successfully published without the author's knowledge or redrafting suggests that Childers's literary style was influenced by the directness of the letter form and the inability to adorn the prose, given the unfavorable physical situation in which the fledgling soldier-diarist found himself. The prose has a modern clarity and directness rarely found in late Victorian novels.

It is not surprising that Childers became a successful journalist and newspaper editor during the Irish war for independence. His ability to convey scenes with an economy of words yet richness of detail was already a characteristic of his prose in his great novel published in 1903.

Joseph R. Peden

PRINCIPAL MYSTERY AND DETECTIVE FICTION

NOVEL: *The Riddle of the Sands: A Record of Secret Service Recently Achieved*, 1903

OTHER MAJOR WORKS

NONFICTION: *In the Ranks of the C.I.V.: A Narrative and Diary of Personal Experiences with the C.I.V. Battery (Honourable Artillery Company) in South Africa*, 1900; *The H.A.C. in South Africa: A Record of the Services Rendered in the South African War by Members of the Honourable Artillery Company*, 1903 (with Basil Williams); *The "Times" History of the War in South Africa*, 1907 (volume 5); *War and Arme Blanche*, 1910; *German Influence on British Cavalry*, 1911; *The Framework of Home Rule*, 1911; *The Form and Purpose of the Home Rule*, 1912; *Military Rule in Ireland*, 1920; *Is Ireland a Danger to England?*, 1921; *The Constructive Work of Dail Eireann*, 1921 (with Alfred O'Rahilly); *Clause by Clause: A Comparison Between the "Treaty" and Document No. 2*, 1922; *What the Treaty Means*, 1922; *A Thirst for the Sea: The Sailing Adventures of Erskine Childers*, 1979

EDITED TEXT: *Who Burnt Cork City? A Tale of Arson, Loot, and Murder*, 1921 (with O'Rahilly)

BIBLIOGRAPHY

Boyle, Andrew. *The Riddle of Erskine Childers*. London: Hutchinson, 1977. An early examination of the enigmas at the heart of Childers's life and the difficulty of understanding his motivations.

Cox, Tom. *Damned Englishman: A Study of Erskine Childers*. Hicksville, N.Y.: Exposition, 1975. Focuses on the relationship between Childers's Englishness and his embrace of the Irish Republican Army.

Hitz, Frederick P. *The Great Game: The Myth and Reality of Espionage*. New York: Alfred A. Knopf, 2004. Hitz, the former inspector general of the Central Intelligence Agency, compares fictional spies in the work of Childers and others to actual intelligence agents to demonstrate that truth is stranger than fiction.

Kestner, Joseph A. *The Edwardian Detective, 1901-1915*. Brookfield, Vt.: Ashgate, 2000. Study of the brief but distinctive Edwardian period in detective fiction. Discusses the importance of Childers and the Edwardians in the genesis of modern spy fiction.

Piper, Leonard. *Dangerous Waters: The Life and Death of Erskine Childers*. New York: Palgrave Macmillan, 2003. Biography of Childers, emphasizing the extent to which his life was as full of intrigue, violence, and conspiracy as any of his novels.

Ring, Jim. *Erskine Childers*. London: John Murray, 1997. Looks at Childers's family papers and other sources to document the author's attempts to follow his conscience in political and colonial matters, attempts that would ultimately lead to his execution.

Seed, David. "The Adventure of Spying: Erskine Childers's *The Riddle of the Sands*." In *Spy Thrillers: From Buchan to Le Carré*, edited by Clive Bloom. New York: St. Martin's Press, 1990. A study of Childers's famous novel and its central role in the history of modern realist spy fiction.

AGATHA CHRISTIE
Agatha Mary Clarissa Mallowan

Born: Torquay, Devon, England; September 15, 1890

Died: Wallingford, Oxfordshire, England; January 12, 1976

Also wrote as Mary Westmacott

Types of plot: Amateur sleuth; private investigator; cozy

PRINCIPAL SERIES

Hercule Poirot, 1920-1975
Tommy and Tuppence Beresford, 1922-1973

Superintendent Battle, 1925-1944
Jane Marple, 1930-1976
Ariadne Oliver, 1934-1961

PRINCIPAL SERIES CHARACTERS

HERCULE POIROT, a private detective, after retiring from the Belgian police force in 1904, lives mostly in London. Short, with an egg-shaped head, eyes that turn a deeper shade of green at significant moments, and an elegant military mustache, he wears a striped three-piece suit and patent leather shoes. His foreign accent and uncertain command of English suggest a buffoon (as does his surname: "poireau" in colloquial French means simpleton or fool), but "the little grey cells" are always seeking and finding the truth.

CAPTAIN ARTHUR HASTINGS is Poirot's faithful, though dull-witted, chronicler. Hastings, wounded in World War I, is investigating a case for Lloyd's of London when he meets Poirot. Even after he marries Dulcie Duveen and moves to Argentina, Hastings reappears occasionally to assist in and record his friend's adventures.

LIEUTENANT THOMAS BERESFORD and PRUDENCE COWLEY BERESFORD, better known as Tommy and Tuppence, were childhood friends. Shortly after World War I, in which Tommy was twice wounded, they establish the International Detective Agency. Tommy has the common sense and Tuppence the intuition that make them successful in their cases, which usually involve international intrigue. The couple age realistically; by the time of their last adventure they are both more than seventy years old and living at the Laurels in Hollowquay.

SUPERINTENDENT BATTLE, the father of five children, is a large, muscular man who never displays emotion. Though little given to imagination, he believes that no one is above suspicion.

JANE MARPLE, who first appears as a seventy-four-year-old never-married woman in 1930 and hardly ages thereafter, lives in the village of St. Mary Mead. Tall, thin, with fluffy white hair and china-blue eyes, she is given to gardening, which provides her with an excuse to be outside at convenient moments, and bird-watching, a hobby that requires the use of a pair of binoculars—which she sometimes trains on nonfeathered bipeds. Her intuition is flawless.

ARIADNE OLIVER, an Agatha Christie alter ego who produces a prolific quantity of successful detective novels, is something of a feminist. She is attractive though untidy and is always experimenting with her plentiful gray hair. Despite her vocation, her detecting abilities sometimes falter.

CONTRIBUTION

Through some seventy mystery novels and thrillers as well as 149 short stories and more than a dozen

Agatha Christie. (Library of Congress)

plays, Agatha Christie helped create the form of classic detective fiction, in which a murder is committed and many are suspected. In the end, all but one of the suspects are eliminated, and the criminal dies or is arrested. Working within these conventions, Christie explored their limits through numerous variations to create her intellectual puzzles. Much of the charm of her work derives from its use of the novel-of-manners tradition, as she explores upper-middle-class life in the English village, a milieu that she made peculiarly her own.

Typical of the novel of manners, Christie's works offer little character analysis, detailed description, or philosophy about life; as she herself noted, "Lots of my books *are* what I should describe as 'light-hearted thrillers.'" Simply written, demanding no arcane knowledge, requiring only careful attention to facts, her works repeatedly challenge readers to deduce from the clues they have been given the identity of the culprit before she reveals the always surprising answer.

BIOGRAPHY

Agatha Christie was born Agatha Mary Clarissa Miller just outside Torquay, England, on September 15, 1890, to Frederick Alvah Miller and Clarissa Margaret Beohmer Miller. Because her two older siblings were at school, Agatha spent much time alone, which she passed by inventing characters and adventures for them. She was also often in the company of her two grandmothers (who later served as models for Jane Marple). Though she received no formal education except in music, she read voraciously and showed an early interest in writing, publishing a poem in the local newspaper at the age of eleven.

At eighteen, bored while recovering from influenza, Christie (then Miller) took her mother's suggestion to write a story. Her first attempt, "The House of Beauty," was published in revised form as "The House of Dreams" in the *Sovereign Magazine* in January, 1926, and two other stories from this period later grew into novels. Turning to longer fiction, she sent a manuscript titled "Snow upon the Desert" to Eden Phillpotts, a popular novelist who was a family friend, and he referred her to his agent, Hughes Massie, who would become hers as well.

After her marriage to Archie Christie on Christmas Eve, 1914, she went to work, first as a nurse and then as a pharmacist. The latter post gave her a knowledge of poisons as well as free time to apply that information as she composed *The Mysterious Affair at Styles: A Detective Story* (1920). Rejected by several publishers, the manuscript went to John Lane at the Bodley Head in 1917, where it lay buried for two years. In 1919, the year Christie's daughter, Rosalind, was born, Lane called Christie into his office and told her that he would publish the novel (with some changes), and he signed Christie to a five-book contract. *The Mysterious Affair at Styles* sold a respectable two thousand copies in its first year, but Christie had not yet begun to think of herself as a professional writer, even after *The Man in the Brown Suit* (1924) earned for her enough money to buy a car.

Indeed, Christie did not need to write professionally as long as her husband supported her. In 1926, though, the year of her first major success with *The Murder of Roger Ackroyd*, her life changed: Archie an-

nounced that he wanted a divorce. Coupled with the recent death of her mother, this news overwhelmed Christie, who, suffering from hysterical amnesia, vanished for ten days in December. The resulting publicity boosted sales, a fortunate result as she now depended on her fiction to live.

On an excursion to Iraq in 1929, Christie met Max Mallowan, an archaeologist fifteen years her junior; they were married in Edinburgh on September 11, 1930. For the next decade she would travel between the Middle East and England while producing seventeen novels and six short-story collections. The war years were equally productive, yielding seventeen works of fiction and an autobiography.

In 1947, to help celebrate the birthday of the Queen Mother, Christie created a half-hour radio play, *Three Blind Mice*, which in 1952 opened in London's West End as *The Mousetrap*, a play that was to break all theatrical records. Her novels also fared well. *A Murder Is Announced* (1950) was her first book to sell more than fifty thousand copies in one year, and every book of hers thereafter sold at least as many. Honors, too, flowed in. These included the Grand Master Award from the Mystery Writers of America (1955), the New York Drama Critics Circle Award for best foreign play (1955, for *Witness for the Prosecution*, pr. 1953), commander of the British Empire (1956), an honorary doctorate from the University of Exeter (1961), and dame of the British Empire (1971).

In 1970, at the age of eighty, Christie published her eightieth book. A fall the next year broke her hip, and she never fully recovered. On January 12, 1976, she died at her home in Wallingford, England, and she was buried at St. Mary's Churchyard in nearby Cholsey.

ANALYSIS

By 1980 Agatha Christie's books had sold more than four hundred million copies in 102 countries and 103 languages. Only the Bible and William Shakespeare have sold more, and they have had a few centuries' head start. If all the American editions of *Peril at End House* (1932) were placed end to end, they would reach from Chicago to the moon. *The Mousetrap*, which has earned millions of dollars, has exceeded all previous record runs by several decades, and Christie is the only playwright to have had three plays being performed simultaneously in London's West End while another was being produced on Broadway. To what do her works owe the popularity that has earned for her the title "Queen of Crime"?

The solution to this mystery lies in Christie's combination of originality and convention, a fusion evident already in her first published novel, *The Mysterious Affair at Styles*. The detective she introduces here, Hercule Poirot, resembles not only Sherlock Holmes but also Marie Belloc Lowndes's Hercule Popeau, who had worked for the Sûreté in Paris, and Hercule Flambeau, the creation of G. K. Chesterton. Gaston Leroux's hero of *Le Mystère de la chambre jaune* (1907; *The Mystery of the Yellow Room*, 1908), Joseph Rouletabille, as well as Rouletabille's rival, Frederick Larson, also contributed to Poirot, as did Christie's observations of Belgian refugees in Torquay. Similarly, Captain Arthur Hastings derives from Holmes's chronicler, Dr. Watson: Both have been wounded in war, both are unable to dissemble and hence cannot always be trusted with the truth, both are highly susceptible to female beauty, both see what their more astute friends observe, yet neither can correctly interpret the evidence before him.

However conventional these characters are, though, they emerge as distinct figures. One cannot imagine Sir Arthur Conan Doyle's cerebral detective referring to himself as "Papa" Holmes the way Christie's calls himself "Papa Poirot." To Holmes's intellect Christie has added a heart, one that has been captured by Countess Vera Rossakoff. Poirot refers to her much as Holmes speaks of Irene Adler, but one would not suspect Holmes of harboring any of the matrimonial or sexual interest toward Adler that Poirot seems to have for his "remarkable woman."

The differences between Hastings and Watson are equally noticeable, Christie's narrator being less perceptive and more comic. Watson is not "of an imbecility to make one afraid," nor would Watson propose to a woman he hardly knows. Christie's modifications made Poirot an enduring figure—Nicaragua put him on a postage stamp—but she quickly realized that Hastings lacked substance. He appears in only eight of the thirty-four Poirot novels, and as early as 1926 she

sent him to Argentina, allowing another character to recount *The Murder of Roger Ackroyd*.

THE MYSTERIOUS AFFAIR AT STYLES

Like this detecting duo, the plot of *The Mysterious Affair at Styles* draws on the tradition of detective fiction but bears Christie's individual stamp. There is the murder in the locked room, a device popularized by John Dickson Carr. The wrong man is arrested and tried for the crime. Abiding by the rules of mysteries, Christie sets before the reader all the clues that Poirot discovers, often going so far as to number them. Yet the work exhibits a subtlety and misdirection characteristic of Christie's work. For example, she reproduces a letter that the victim supposedly wrote on the night she was murdered. The reader naturally tries to find some hidden meaning in the words, when in fact the clue lies in the spacing within the date. Early in the book one learns that Evelyn Howard has a low voice and mannish figure; still, when someone impersonates Arthur Inglethorp, the reader assumes that the impostor is a male.

The reader is not likely to make much of the fact that Evelyn Howard's father was a doctor or pay attention when Mary Cavendish says that her mother died of accidental poisoning from a medicine she was taking, even though Mrs. Inglethorp has been using a tonic containing strychnine. When Evelyn Howard finds the brown paper used to wrap a parcel containing a false beard, one assumes that she has fulfilled Poirot's expectations of her abilities. Since Poirot has taken her into his confidence, one hardly suspects that she is involved in the murder. Moreover, she seems too straightforward and blunt, too likable and reliable to be guilty.

Her cousin Arthur Inglethorp, on the other hand, seems too obviously the killer; even the dull-witted Hastings suspects him, and Hastings's suspicion should be enough to exonerate anyone. Inglethorp has an obvious motive—money—and is supposedly having an affair with another woman. Before leaving Styles early in the novel, Evelyn Howard further implicates him by telling Hastings to be especially wary of Mr. Inglethorp. Given all these clues, no one familiar with the conventions of the genre would regard him as the criminal. Any lingering doubt, moreover, seems removed when Poirot remarks that considering Mrs. Inglethorp's kindness to the Belgian refugees, he would not allow her husband, whom she clearly loved, to be arrested now. One presumes that Poirot means that he is now sure that Arthur Inglethorp is innocent, though in fact the detective simply means "now," before the case against Inglethorp is complete.

The Mysterious Affair at Styles tricks the reader not only by making the most likely and least likely suspects both guilty of the crime but also by introducing many false leads. Dr. Bauerstein, a London toxicologist, unexpectedly appears at Styles on the night of the murder and is found very early the next morning walking, fully dressed, in front of the gates to the manor. Why does Lawrence Cavendish, Mrs. Inglethorp's son by her previous marriage, persist in maintaining that death was accidental? Why does Mary Cavendish cry out, when she learns that her mother-in-law has been poisoned, "No, no—not that—not that!" Why does she claim to have heard sounds in Mrs. Inglethorp's room when she could not possibly have heard them? What is one to make of the strychnine in John Cavendish's drawer or of Lawrence Cavendish's fingerprints on another bottle of the poison?

Typical, too, is the focus on the solution rather than the crime. Although Christie presents an account of Mrs. Inglethorp's final convulsions, the details are not gruesome because the description is sanitized. In most of Christie's subsequent works, the murders occur offstage; significantly, the word "murder" itself does not often appear in her titles, particularly not in the titles that she, as opposed to her American publishers, chose. The reader's reaction to her crimes is therefore not "How terrible!" but "Who did it? How? Why?" Like Christie's detectives, the reader embarks on an intellectual quest to solve an intricate puzzle, not an emotional journey of revenge or purgation.

RED HERRINGS AND PLAIN EVIDENCE

Christie often allows the reader to engage in self-deceit. In *The Body in the Library* (1942), the clues are again so plain that one dismisses them as red herrings. In *The Murder at the Vicarage* (1930), the obvious suspects confess quite early, much to Jane Marple's surprise. The reader assumes that she believes that someone else is the actual culprit and so dismisses the

admissions of guilt. Actually, Miss Marple is merely perplexed that two people who worked so hard to create an alibi should give themselves up voluntarily. One would not expect the police officer in *Hercule Poirot's Christmas* (1939) to be the murderer any more than one would suspect Lettitia Blacklock, the apparent target of at least two murder attempts, of being the killer in *A Murder Is Announced*.

In each case, Christie presents the evidence; Dora Bunner, for example, often says "Lotty" instead of "Letty," a clear indication that Lettitia Blacklock is someone else. Yet the reader will dismiss these slips as signs of Dora Bunner's absentmindedness. Christie's most notable adaptations of conventional plotting appear in *The Murder of Roger Ackroyd*, in which the sympathetic narrator—who, like Evelyn Howard, seems to be in league with Poirot—turns out to be the killer, in *Murder on the Orient Express* (1934), in which all the suspects are in fact guilty, and in *Ten Little Niggers* (1939; also known as *And Then There Were None*), where all the suspects are victims.

ORDEAL BY INNOCENCE

At the same time that the crime itself is presented dispassionately, Christie recognizes its effect on the innocent. Cynthia Murdock and Lawrence Cavendish cannot be happy together as long as each secretly suspects the other of Mrs. Inglethorp's murder. The Argyle family (*Ordeal by Innocence*, 1958) is not pleased to learn that John Argyle did not kill his mother, for if John is not guilty, another family member must be, and no one can be trusted until the actual culprit is identified.

Such considerations are about as philosophical as Christie gets, though. For her the story is all; philosophy and psychology never go beyond the obvious. Much of the appeal of Christie's work lies in this very superficiality. Just as one needs no special knowledge of mysterious poisons or English bell-ringing rituals to solve her crimes, so to understand her criminals' motives one need not look beyond greed, hate, or love.

CHARACTERIZATION

Characterization is similarly simple, again not to detract from the story. Mr. Wells, the attorney in *The Mysterious Affair at Styles*, is presented as "a pleasant man of middle-age, with keen eyes, and the typical lawyer's mouth." Lawrence Cavendish looks "about forty, very dark with a melancholy clean-shaven face." Caroline Sheppard, in *The Murder of Roger Ackroyd*, hints that her brother is "weak as water," but one does not otherwise get that impression of him.

Even Christie's most fully realized characters remain in many ways ambiguous. Readers were surprised to learn, for example, that Jane Marple is tall; the fact emerges rather late in the novels about her. So, too, Poirot, though seemingly minutely described, is in some ways enigmatic. There is, for example, the mystery about his age: If he retired from the Belgian police force in 1904, he should be about eighty by the time of Mrs. Inglethorp's death and 130 by the time of his own. His head is egg-shaped, but which way does the egg lie (or stand)? Exactly what are military mustaches? Christie cultivated this ambiguity, objecting to a dust jacket that showed so much as Poirot's striped pants and shoes. She preferred to allow readers to supply the details from their own experience or imagination.

UNIVERSALITY

Even the English village that she made particularly her own milieu for murder is but roughly sketched. Christie can offer detailed floor plans or maps when this information is necessary, but Wychwood (*Murder Is Easy*, 1939) might easily be Jane Marple's St. Mary Mead or Styles St. Mary:

> Wychwood . . . consists mainly of its one principal street. There were shops, small Georgian houses, prim and aristocratic, with whitened steps and polished knockers, there were picturesque cottages with flower gardens. There was an inn, the Bells and Motley, standing a little back from the street. There was a village green and a duck pond, and presiding over them a dignified Georgian house.

This easy transferability of her settings applies even to her most exotic locales; Mesopotamia seems no more foreign than Chipping Cleghorn.

The lack of specific detail has given her works timelessness as well as universality. Speaking of *Death Comes as the End* (1944), set in the Egypt of the Eleventh Dynasty, Christie observed, "People are the same in whatever century they live, or where." In keeping with

the novel-of-manners tradition she does chronicle the life of the period: *A Murder Is Announced* shows how Britishers attempted to cope with post-World War II hardships through barter and the black market, with children who read *The Daily Worker*, with social changes that brought the breakup of the old manors and caused servants to disappear, and with new technology such as central heating. A decade later, St. Mary Mead has a new housing development, and Gossington Hall gets new bathrooms (*The Mirror Crack'd from Side to Side*, 1962). Such changes are, however, superficial. As Christie writes, "The new world was the same as the old. The houses were different, . . . the clothes were different, but the human beings were the same as they had always been."

If live-in maids have vanished, a part-time cleaning person will serve as well to keep a house tidy and a plot complicated. Though the village is no longer the closed world it once was, all the suspects can still fit into the Blacklock drawing room or the dining room of Bertram's Hotel. The real action in Christie's works occurs within the reader's mind while sorting real clues from false, innocent characters from guilty. As long as people enjoy such intellectual games, Christie's books will endure, for, with her masterful talent to deceive, she has created highly absorbing puzzles. She will always be the first lady of crime.

Joseph Rosenblum

PRINCIPAL MYSTERY AND DETECTIVE FICTION

HERCULE POIROT SERIES: 1920-1930 • *The Mysterious Affair at Styles: A Detective Story*, 1920; *The Murder on the Links*, 1923; *Poirot Investigates*, 1924; *The Murder of Roger Ackroyd*, 1926; *The Big Four*, 1927; *The Mystery of the Blue Train*, 1928

1931-1940 • *Peril at End House*, 1932; *Lord Edgware Dies*, 1933 (also known as *Thirteen at Dinner*); *Murder on the Orient Express*, 1934 (also known as *Murder on the Calais Coach*); *Murder in Three Acts*, 1934; *Death in the Clouds*, 1935 (also known as *Death in the Air*); *The A. B. C. Murders: A New Poirot Mystery*, 1936; *Murder in Mesopotamia*, 1936; *Dumb Witness*, 1937 (also known as *Poirot Loses a Client*); *Murder in the Mews, and Other Stories*, 1937 (also known as *Dead Man's Mirror, and Other Stories*);

Death on the Nile, 1937; *Appointment with Death: A Poirot Mystery*, 1938; *Hercule Poirot's Christmas*, 1939 (also known as *Murder for Christmas: A Poirot Story*); *The Regatta Mystery, and Other Stories*, 1939; *One, Two, Buckle My Shoe*, 1940 (also known as *The Patriotic Murders*, 1941); *Sad Cypress*, 1940

1941-1950 • *Evil Under the Sun*, 1941; *Five Little Pigs*, 1942 (also known as *Murder in Retrospect*); *Poirot on Holiday*, 1943; *The Hollow: A Hercule Poirot Mystery*, 1946; *Poirot Knows the Murderer*, 1946; *Poirot Lends a Hand*, 1946; *The Labours of Hercules: Short Stories*, 1947 (also known as *Labors of Hercules: New Adventures in Crime by Hercule Poirot*); *Taken at the Flood*, 1948 (also known as *There Is a Tide . . .*)

1951-1960 • *The Under Dog, and Other Stories*, 1951; *Mrs. McGinty's Dead*, 1952; *After the Funeral*, 1953 (also known as *Funerals Are Fatal*); *Hickory, Dickory, Dock*, 1955 (also known as *Hickory, Dickory, Death*); *Dead Man's Folly*, 1956; *Cat Among the Pigeons*, 1959; *The Adventures of the Christmas Pudding, and Selection of Entrées*, 1960

1961-1975 • *Double Sin, and Other Stories*, 1961; *The Clocks*, 1963; *Third Girl*, 1966; *Hallowe'en Party*, 1969; *Elephants Can Remember*, 1972; *Hercule Poirot's Early Cases*, 1974; *Curtain: Hercule Poirot's Last Case*, 1975

TOMMY AND TUPPENCE BERESFORD SERIES: *The Secret Adversary*, 1922; *Partners in Crime*, 1929; *N or M? The New Mystery*, 1941; *By the Pricking of My Thumb*, 1968; *Postern of Fate*, 1973

SUPERINTENDENT BATTLE SERIES: *The Secret of Chimneys*, 1925; *The Seven Dials Mystery*, 1929; *Murder Is Easy*, 1939 (also known as *Easy to Kill*); *Towards Zero*, 1944

JANE MARPLE SERIES: *The Murder at the Vicarage*, 1930; *The Thirteen Problems*, 1932 (also known as *The Tuesday Club Murders*, 1933); *The Body in the Library*, 1942; *The Moving Finger*, 1942; *A Murder Is Announced*, 1950; *They Do It with Mirrors*, 1952 (also known as *Murder with Mirrors*); *A Pocket Full of Rye*, 1953; *4:50 from Paddington*, 1957 (also known as *What Mrs. McGillicuddy Saw!*); *The Mirror Crack'd from Side to Side*, 1962 (also known as *The Mirror Crack'd*, 1963); *A Caribbean Mystery*, 1964;

At Bertram's Hotel, 1965; *Thirteen Clues for Miss Marple: A Collection of Mystery Stories*, 1965; *Nemesis*, 1971; *Sleeping Murder*, 1976 (posthumous); *Miss Marple's Final Cases*, 1979

ARIADNE OLIVER SERIES: *Parker Pyne Investigates*, 1934 (also known as *Mr. Parker Pyne, Detective*); *Cards on the Table*, 1936; *The Pale Horse*, 1961

NONSERIES NOVELS: *The Man in the Brown Suit*, 1924; *The Sittaford Mystery*, 1931 (also known as *The Murder at Hazelmoor*); *The Floating Admiral*, 1931 (with others); *Why Didn't They Ask Evans?*, 1934 (also known as *Boomerang Clue*, 1935); *Ten Little Niggers*, 1939 (also known as *And Then There Were None*, 1940); *Death Comes in the End*, 1944; *Sparkling Cyanide*, 1945 (also known as *Remembered Death*); *Crooked House*, 1949; *They Came to Baghdad*, 1951; *Destination Unknown*, 1954 (also known as *So Many Steps to Death*, 1955); *Ordeal by Innocence*, 1958; *Endless Night*, 1967; *Passenger to Frankfurt*, 1970; *The Scoop, and Behind the Screen*, 1983 (with others)

OTHER SHORT FICTION: *The Mysterious Mr. Quin*, 1930; *The Hound of Death, and Other Stories*, 1933; *The Listerdale Mystery, and Other Stories*, 1934; *The Mystery of the Baghdad Chest*, 1943; *The Mystery of the Crime in Cabin 66*, 1943; *Problem at Pollensa Bay, and Christmas Adventure*, 1943; *The Veiled Lady, and The Mystery of the Baghdad Chest*, 1944; *Murder Medley*, 1948 (with others); *The Witness for the Prosecution, and Other Stories*, 1948; *The Mousetrap and Other Stories*, 1949 (also known as *Three Blind Mice and Other Stories*); *Star over Bethlehem, and Other Stories*, 1965 (as Mallowan); *The Golden Ball, and Other Stories*, 1971; *The Harlequin Tea Set, and Other Stories*, 1997

OTHER MAJOR WORKS

NOVELS: *Giants' Bread*, 1930 (as Westmacott); *Unfinished Portrait*, 1934 (as Westmacott); *Absent in the Spring*, 1944 (as Westmacott); *The Rose and the Yew Tree*, 1948 (as Westmacott); *Blood Will Tell*, 1951; *A Daughter's a Daughter*, 1952 (as Westmacott); *The Burden*, 1956 (as Westmacott)

PLAYS: *Black Coffee*, pr. 1930; *Ten Little Niggers*, pr. 1943 (also known as *Ten Little Indians*, pr. 1944);

Appointment with Death, pr., pb. 1945; *Murder on the Nile*, pr., pb. 1946; *The Hollow*, pr. 1951; *The Mousetrap*, pr. 1952; *Witness for the Prosecution*, pr. 1953; *Spider's Web*, pr. 1954; *Towards Zero*, pr. 1956 (with Gerald Verner); *Verdict*, pr., pb. 1958; *The Unexpected Guest*, pr., pb. 1958; *Go Back for Murder*, pr., pb. 1960; *Rule of Three: Afternoon at the Seaside, The Patient, The Rats*, pb. 1962; *Afternoon at the Seaside*, pr. 1962; *The Patient*, pr. 1962; *The Rats*, pr. 1962; *Fiddlers Three*, pr. 1971; *Akhnaton*, pb. 1973 (also known as *Akhnaton and Nefertiti*)

POETRY: *The Road of Dreams*, 1925; *Poems*, 1973

CHILDREN'S LITERATURE: *Thirteen for Luck: A Selection of Mystery Stories for Young Readers*, 1961; *Surprize! Surprize! A Collection of Mystery Stories with Unexpected Endings*, 1965

NONFICTION: *Come Tell Me How You Live*, 1946; *An Autobiography*, 1977

BIBLIOGRAPHY

Bargainner, Earl F. *The Gentle Art of Murder.* Bowling Green, Ohio: Bowling Green State University Popular Press, 1980. With an extensive bibliography and two indexes of characters and short-story titles, this book is a boon to those searching for an elusive reference. Bargainner analyzes Christie's works as separate achievements, each a pearl on an exquisite necklace, and he praises her ability to experiment with detective fiction "by employing elements not generally considered compatible with it."

Bayard, Pierre. *Who Killed Roger Ackroyd? The Mystery Behind the Agatha Christie Mystery.* London: Fourth Estate, 2000. Detailed study of Christie's unfinished final project.

Bloom, Harold, ed. *Agatha Christie.* Philadelphia: Chelsea House, 2002. Compilation of essays on Christie's work and its place in the detective genre and in English literature by leading literary and cultural scholars. Bibliographic references and index.

Bunson, Matthew. *The Complete Christie: An Agatha Christie Encyclopaedia.* New York: Pocket Books, 2001. Aims to be the definitive reference work in a relatively crowded field.

Cade, Jared. *Agatha Christie and the Eleven Missing Days.* London: Peter Owen, 1998. Questions Christie's disappearance. Includes bibliographical references, a list of works, and an index.

Christie, Agatha. *An Autobiography.* New York: Dodd, Mead, 1977. Although published the year after her death, this book, which was written over a fifteen-year period, concludes in 1965, when the author was seventy-five years old. While her mysterious disappearance in the 1920's is not explained, probably because of Christie's instincts for privacy, there are interesting details about happier events and comments about the creation of her works that are invaluable.

_____. *Come Tell Me How You Live.* New York: Dodd, Mead, 1946. Published under the name of Agatha Christie Mallowan, a lighthearted book of reminiscences about archaeological experiences with Max Mallowan, her husband, in the Middle East. Reflects the happiness of Christie's second marriage, as well as her own sense of humor.

Fido, Martin. *The World of Agatha Christie: The Facts and Fiction Behind the World's Greatest Crime Writer.* Holbrook, Mass.: Adams Media, 1999. An extremely critical account of Christie and her fiction.

Makinen, Merja. *Agatha Christie: Investigating Femininity.* New York: Palgrave Macmillan, 2006. Study of the representation of gender in Christie's mysteries. Bibliographic references and index.

Osborne, Charles. *The Life and Crimes of Agatha Christie.* London: HarperCollins, 2000. Combined biography and study of Christie's works and their extensive effects on the mystery genre.

Shaw, Marion, and Sabine Vanacker. *Reflecting on Miss Marple.* London: Routledge, 1991. After a brief chronology of Christie's life, Shaw and Vanacker devote four chapters to one of her most memorable detectives, in the course of which they make a case for viewing Miss Marple as a feminist heroine. They do so by reviewing the history of female writers and the Golden Age of detective fiction, as well as the social context of Christie's Miss Marple books. The never-married Miss Marple, they conclude, is able to solve her cases by exploiting prejudice against unmarried older women.

MARY HIGGINS CLARK

Born: Bronx, New York; December 24, 1929
Also wrote as The Adams Round Table (with
   Thomas Chastain)
Types of plot: Amateur sleuth; psychological; cozy;
   thriller

PRINCIPAL SERIES

Alvirah and Willy Mehan, 1987-

PRINCIPAL SERIES CHARACTERS

ALVIRAH AND WILLY MEHAN are a comic working-class pair of amateur detectives who became free
to travel and stumble on mysteries after Alvirah won a
lottery. Alvirah has a nose for trouble, which leads her
to a kidnapping amid a winter's storm, a stolen Christmas tree, an abandoned baby, and a mobster-laden
cruise.

CONTRIBUTION

Mary Higgins Clark, one of the most popular and
prolific modern suspense writers, has been called the
"Queen of Suspense." Her fast-paced, tightly plotted
award-winning best sellers capturing daily terrors
have attracted readers worldwide for more than thirty
years. In the tradition of Pat Flower, Margaret Millar,
and Mignon Eberhardt, authors noted for portraying
vulnerable women facing evil, Clark is at her best
when she is writing about women who rise above personal weaknesses to protect and defend those less capable. Her success lies in part in her ability to understand the worries of wives, mothers, and working
women: their fears for their children, their alienation
from the men in their lives, their personal insecurities,
their vaguely disturbing childhood memories, and
their growing awareness of deception and lies beneath
people's smiles. She connects the intimate and personal with broader public concerns to heighten the
sense of suspense. Clark, who publishes one or two
novels or story collections per year, weaves disparate
plot strands into unexpected wholes, often exploring
the same theme on multiple levels (for example, providing different degrees and types of betrayals or jealousies). Her strength is in creating vivid scenes that
make readers experience apprehension, fear, discovery, and catharsis.

BIOGRAPHY

The daughter of Irish restaurant owner Luke Joseph Higgins and Nora C. (Durkin) Higgins, Mary
Higgins grew up in the Bronx and attended Villa
Maria Academy and Ward Secretarial School. She
wrote her first poem at seven and frightened friends
with scary ghost stories. The sudden deaths of her father and her older brother Joe affected her deeply. At
seventeen she became a Remington Rand advertising
assistant. Creative writing classes at New York University inspired her to join a writing group that became
the Adams Round Table and eventually led to five
short-story collections. While working as a Pan Am
flight attendant (1949-1950), she married long-time
friend and airline executive Warren F. Clark. When her
husband died in 1964, Clark was left with five children
to support. She wrote and produced radio scripts for
Robert G. Jennings (1965-1970) while writing in her
free time. When her first published book, *Aspire to the
Heavens: A Biography of George Washington* (1969),
proved a commercial failure, she turned to the mystery
genre. In 1970 she went to work for Aerial Communi-
cations, where she served ten years as vice president,
partner, and radio programming creative director/pro-
ducer.

Clark's publication of *Where Are the Children?*
(1975) earned more than $100,000 in paperback royal-
ties and marked the beginning of her long, successful
second career as a mystery writer attuned to childhood
fears, mother-child relationships, the traumatic loss of
family members, and the spine-tingling fears of
women alone in the dark. In 1978 she married attorney
Raymond Charles Ploetz and moved to his Minnesota
farm but soon had the marriage annulled. She received
a bachelor's degree in philosophy from Fordham University, graduating summa cum laude in 1979. In 1980
she became chair of the board and creative director of
David J. Clark Enterprises in New York. Not until her

second thriller, *A Stranger Is Watching* (1977), earned a $500,000 advance, more than $1 million in paperback rights, and film rights from Metro-Goldwyn-Mayer did Clark feel she had the financial security she needed to leave Aerial and raise her family in comfort. In 1989 she signed a then-record-breaking $11.4 million contract with Simon & Schuster and in 1992 a $35 million contract.

Clark served as president of the Mystery Writers of America in 1987 and has since served on the board of directors. As chair of the International Crime Writers Congress, she attended a Federal Bureau of Investigation lecture on serial killers using personal ads to entice victims, which became the inspiration for *Loves Music, Loves to Dance* (1991). Her literary interests have led her to join various authors' guilds and academies, including the American Irish Historical Society. In 1996 Clark established the *Mary Higgins Clark Mystery Magazine*, which publishes mystery and suspense stories.

In 1996, she married retired chief executive officer John J. Conheeney, whose name she uses in her private life. Their renovated home in Spring Lake, New Jersey, became the setting of *On the Street Where You Live* (2001). Clark continues to write novels, sometimes with her daughter Carol Higgins Clark, with whom she revived the Alvirah and Willy Mehan series by creating several Christmas-themed novels. Clark contributes regularly to periodicals on a wide variety of topics. More than twelve of her works have been filmed.

With more than fifty million books in print, Clark enjoys best-seller status worldwide. Her many awards include the New Jersey Author Award in 1969 for *Aspire to the Heavens*, the Grand Prix de Littérature Policière in 1980 for *A Stranger Is Waiting*, thirteen honorary doctorates, and the titles of dame of the Order of St. Gregory the Great, dame of Malta, and dame of the Holy Sepulcher of Jerusalem. In 2000 she was named Grand Master by the Mystery Writers of America.

ANALYSIS

Mary Higgins Clark, whose book titles frequently come from those of songs, builds suspense quickly, with action moving forward rapidly as a sympathetic heroine rescues herself (and others) from a deranged

One of the most unusual mystery magazines ever published, the Mary Higgins Clark Mystery Magazine *was an erratically issued, full-size "slick" published by* Family Circle *that lasted only from 1996 to 2001.*

killer. Amid the suspense, Clark often comments on relevant social topics: dishonest fertility specialists (*The Cradle Will Fall*, 1980), greedy health maintenance organizations (HMOs) profiting at the expense of patients (*We'll Meet Again*, 1999), the failures of the federal witness protection program (*Pretend You Don't See Her*, 1995), and financial/pharmaceutical conspiracies (*The Second Time Around*, 2003). In her novels, she typically establishes a chain of responsibility involving blackmail and silence—fear of losing one's job, intimidation, and pride in knowing secrets—that makes more than one individual culpable.

Clark's characters are everyday people trapped in frightening situations amid the commonplace: a newlywed who discovers her husband's terrible secrets, a woman who finds the contractor building her new house is not what he seems, and a grieving stepdaughter who is buried alive. The psychological and philosophical are vital to her creative method. Her heroines may be a photographer and amateur sculptor (*Moonlight Becomes You: A Novel*, 1996), a Manhattan real estate agent (*Pretend You Don't See Her*), the owner of an exclusive boutique (*While My Pretty One Sleeps*, 1989), a radio psychologist investigating disappearances (*You Belong to Me*, 1998), or just ordinary homemakers and mothers, but they all undergo a test of strength and prove extraordinary in their ability to endure and overcome adversity. Often they discover links between their private lives and a murderer, always an unquestionably deranged monster, whose evil lies hidden behind a respectable facade (such as the plastic surgeon who puts the beautiful face of a murder victim on patient after patient). A typical Clark heroine is Celia Foster Nolan (*No Place Like Home*, 2005), who as a child was falsely accused of murdering her parents. Her husband buys her family's house and presents it to her for her birthday, unaware of its special terrors. She becomes haunted by the past, especially when her parents' real killer stalks her and her son. A less common protagonist is the serial killer in *Nighttime Is My Time* (2004), a former geek once tormented by his high school classmates who seeks revenge by targeting members of the popular crowd at his twentieth reunion.

Clark is a master at conveying the back story and relevant facts through dialogue, multiple perspectives, stories within stories, and simultaneous episodes, while maintaining suspense and moving the action forward. Sometimes the suspense comes from uncertainty about the villain's identity or what the known killer will get away with before the heroine realizes the truth; sometimes there is a countdown to disaster; frequently, Clark leads readers' attention one way while she slowly builds a set of clues to implicate a far less obvious character. *Daddy's Little Girl* (2002) and *The Second Time Around* experiment with a first-person narrator.

Clark writes about the psychological (personality disorders in *Loves Music, Loves to Dance*; multiple personalities and childhood sexual abuse in *All Around the Town*, 1992; a stalker's mind-set in *Nighttime Is My Time*), medical science (genetic manipulation and in vitro fertilization in *I'll Be Seeing You*; nursing homes plagued by sudden death in *Moonlight*

Becomes You; plastic surgery in *Let Me Call You Sweetheart*, 1995, and *We'll Meet Again*), and household crime (burglaries in *Stillwatch*, 1984). A political thriller set among the Washington, D.C., elite, *Stillwatch* depicts two strong women, one modeled on Geraldine Ferraro, while *Weep No More, My Lady* (1987), with multiple suspects, is a celebrity mystery set at an exclusive spa. Occasionally, Clark's lifelong interest in the supernatural appears, for example, the ghost of the heroine's murdered mother in *While My Pretty One Sleeps*, the haunted house in *Remember Me* (1994), or the psychic phenomena in *Before I Say Goodbye* (2000), in every other way a political suspense story. The serial killer who stalks young women in a present-day New Jersey resort town (*On the Street Where You Live*) believes himself to be the reincarnation of a killer from the past century and plans over a twelve-day period to commit his historical crimes all over again.

Clark's sources are friends and family, news events, and personal experiences. Her tightly woven plots capture the suspicions that can plague family members facing murder close to home. Her themes include the insidious effects of the past on the present, human frailty (jealousy, greed, arrogance), vulnerability and innocence, the far-ranging effects of violence, abuses of the justice system, the dehumanization of systems supposedly existing for the public weal, the corrupting effect of money and politics, betrayals of trust both personal and professional, and questions of identity.

WHERE ARE THE CHILDREN?

Clark's first suspense novel, *Where Are the Children?*, set in a misty, stormy Cape Cod and inspired by a New York trial of a woman accused of murdering her children, sets the pattern for her future novels in that it features a vulnerable young woman who, in a time of crisis, proves to be a resourceful survivor. Nancy Harmon, although innocent, is freed from certain conviction for gruesomely murdering her two children by a legal technicality. Relocated and remarried but still traumatized seven years later, she is forced to revisit the nightmare when the real killer tries to repeat his crime, abducting and abusing Nancy's two children from her second marriage. Nancy, confused and terrified, must find the truth: A manipulative murderer with a multiple-personality disorder happily drugged his wife, killed his own children, and plans to murder Nancy's children. Despite the complicated back story, the novel spans only one day.

A Stranger Is Watching

In *A Stranger Is Watching*, Clark questions a 1976 Supreme Court ruling permitting the death penalty. She sets her story over a three-day period leading to the eve of the execution of Ronald Thompson, who has been erroneously convicted of murdering Nina Peterson, and sends her heroine journalist Sharon Martin into harm's way in his defense. Sharon has fallen in love with Nina's husband, Steve, who is suffering because of his wife's death and trying to comfort his six-year-old son Neil, who witnessed his mother's murder. The real killer, a psychopath, takes Sharon and Neil hostage and hides them under Grand Central Station, which he intends to blow up. In a countdown to the execution and explosion, Clark intensifies the terror by shifting the point of view among Sharon, Neil, Steve, the killer, and the third-person narrator.

The Cradle Will Fall

The Cradle Will Fall, a medical thriller inspired by the first test-tube baby, occurs over a week and features the recently widowed Katie DeMaio, an ambitious young prosecutor pathologically fearful of hospitals. When Kate is admitted to Westlake Hospital after a minor driving accident, she sees out her hospital window, amid snow and sleet, a familiar figure hiding a woman's body in his car. When she discovers the next day that the woman's death has been declared a suicide, Kate does not believe it, knowing that the dead woman had desperately wanted a child and was six months pregnant. She begins an investigation into the illegal activities of fertility specialists, including insertion of embryos into the wombs of sterile women. The most terrifying event in the novel is when the heroine must undergo surgery in the very hospital where the doctors she is investigating practice.

A Cry in the Night

A Cry in the Night (1982) is a gothic tale set on a remote Minnesota farm and inspired by Daphne du Maurier's *Rebecca* (1938), Robert Bloch's *Psycho* (1959), and Clark's second marriage. This story depends on the gullibility of Jenny MacParland, a divorced mother of two girls, making ends meet in a fashionable Manhattan art gallery. A Minnesota painter, whose portrait of a beautiful woman seems hauntingly familiar, sweeps Jenny off her feet. Her innocent assumption of this Prince Charming's goodness and her desire to please prove dangerous to her personal safety. She finds herself trapped in a horrifying world: An exquisite mansion becomes a prison, her life and those of her children are threatened, and the secrets of her husband's first wife reveal his own dark reality.

Gina Macdonald

PRINCIPAL MYSTERY AND DETECTIVE FICTION

ALVIRAH AND WILLY MEEHAN SERIES: *Weep No More, My Lady*, 1987; *Death on the Cape, and Other Stories*, 1993; *The Lottery Winner: Alvirah and Willy Stories*, 1994; *All Through the Night*, 1998; *Deck the Halls*, 2000 (with Carol Higgins Clark); *The Christmas Thief*, 2004 (with C. H. Clark); *Santa Cruise*, 2006 (with C. H. Clark)

NONSERIES NOVELS: 1975-1990 • *Where Are the Children?*, 1975; *A Stranger Is Watching*, 1977; *The Cradle Will Fall*, 1980; *A Cry in the Night*, 1982; *Stillwatch*, 1984; *While My Pretty One Sleeps*, 1989; *The Anastasia Syndrome, and Other Stories*, 1989

1991-2000 • *Loves Music, Loves to Dance*, 1991; *All Around the Town*, 1992; *I'll Be Seeing You*, 1993; *Remember Me*, 1994; *Silent Night: A Novel*, 1995; *Let Me Call You Sweetheart*, 1995; *Pretend You Don't See Her*, 1995; *Moonlight Becomes You: A Novel*, 1996; *My Gal Sunday*, 1996; *You Belong to Me*, 1998; *We'll Meet Again*, 1999; *Before I Say Goodbye*, 2000

2001-2007 • *He Sees You When You're Sleeping*, 2001 (with C. H. Clark); *On the Street Where You Live*, 2001; *Daddy's Little Girl*, 2002; *The Second Time Around*, 2003; *Nighttime Is My Time*, 2004; *No Place Like Home*, 2005; *Two Little Girls in Blue*, 2006; *I Heard That Song Before*, 2007

OTHER MAJOR WORKS

NOVELS: *Sight Unseen*, 1990; *Angel of Mercy*, 1990; *Starting Over*, 1991; *Count Your Blessings*, 1992; *Cody's Last Stand*, 1992; *Good Morning, Miss Greene*, 1992; *Plumbing for Willy*, 1993 (with C. H.

Clark); *Groom Unknown*, 1994; *Two Hearts, Too Late*, 1994; *Early Harvest*, 1994; *The Plot Thickens*, 2000

CHILDREN'S LITERATURE: *Ghost Ship: A Cape Code Story*, 2007

NONFICTION: *Aspire to the Heavens: A Biography of George Washington*, 1969 (reissued as *Mount Vernon Love Story*, 2002); *Mother* (with Maya Angelou and Amy Tan), 1996; *Kitchen Privileges: A Memoir*, 2001

EDITED TEXTS (AS THE ADAMS ROUND TABLE): *Missing in Manhattan*, 1986; *Justice in Manhattan*, 1995; *Murder in the Family*, 2002

BIBLIOGRAPHY

Clark, Mary Higgins. *Kitchen Privileges: A Memoir.* New York: Simon & Schuster, 2002. The title of this memoir refers to the boardinghouse that Clark's mother ran. The work deals with her childhood influences, her early life, and her first marriage.

De Roche, Linda. *Revisiting Mary Higgins Clark: A Critical Companion*. Westport, Conn.: Greenwood Press, 2003. Updates Peltzer's earlier work with novels published 1996-2002 and provides plots, characters, thematic analysis, and critical readings. Comprehensive bibliography. Film guide. Indexed.

Klein, Kathleen Gregory, ed. *Great Women Mystery Writers: Classic to Contemporary.* Westport, Conn.: Greenwood Press, 1994. Essays on over one hundred women writers, including Clark; a useful overview essay on women mystery writers places Clark in the genre. Indexed.

Macdonald, Gina. "We'll Meet Again." In *Beacham's Encyclopedia of Popular Fiction*. Vol. 14. New York: Gale Press, 2001. Analyzes the social concerns, themes, characters, techniques, literary precedents, and related titles of this novel. The encyclopedia includes analyses of five other Clark novels.

Peltzer, Linda C. *Mary Higgins Clark: A Critical Companion*. Westport, Conn.: Greenwood Press, 1995. Analyzes Clark's early work, suspense conventions, and literary/family influences. Indexed.

ANNA CLARKE

Born: Cape Town, South Africa; April 28, 1919
Died: Brighton, East Sussex, England; November 7, 2004
Types of plot: Amateur sleuth; inverted; psychological

PRINCIPAL SERIES

Paula Glenning, 1985-1996

PRINCIPAL SERIES CHARACTER

PAULA GLENNING is a lecturer in English literature at a London university. Small and fair, she is in her early thirties and divorced when she first appears. She is untidy, sensitive, and cares deeply about people whom she believes are hurt.

CONTRIBUTION

Anna Clarke's novels are primarily psychological studies of what makes seemingly ordinary people commit crimes; as such her works have much in common with those of Ruth Rendell. Unlike Rendell, however, Clarke rarely finds the mystery as intriguing as the mind of the criminal—and the mind of the sleuth. Her plots are nevertheless tightly woven and sometimes surprising in that, for a while, the reader may believe the sleuth to be the potential criminal or the criminal the potential victim. Clarke reveals a world in which psychological horrors lurk behind the commonplace, a world in which the innocent are forced to confront their own darkness and that of others.

Many of Clarke's plots make use of literary references or revolve about the world of literature: Characters may be authors or literary critics. Frequently, the police believe the crime to be an unfortunate accident. They are not, however, "perfect crimes," for always an interested party recognizes the crime and the criminal. What makes Clarke's work particularly interesting and realistic is that the sleuth is no master of detection; rather, one average person (or, more often, two or three people) will arrive at the truth. Her tight plotting and strong character development have earned her a place in the world of mystery fiction.

BIOGRAPHY

Anna Clarke was born on April 28, 1919, in Cape Town, South Africa, the daughter of Fred Clarke and Edith Annie Gillams Clarke. Her parents were both educators, and Clarke grew up with a love for reading. She attended schools in Cape Town and Montreal and attended universities in Toronto and Oxford. Planning a career in mathematics, she studied for and received an external degree in economics from London University in 1945. A severe illness, however, cut short her career plans, and she went to work as a publisher's secretary in London. She was a private secretary for Victor Gollancz from 1947 to 1950, and in 1951 she took a similar job with Eyre and Spottiswoode, where she worked until 1953.

In 1956 Clarke became the administrative secretary for the British Association for American Studies, a post she retained until 1962. Plagued by the lingering effects of her illness, she quit full-time work and eventually returned to university studies, receiving a bachelor's degree from the Open University in 1973 and a master of arts degree from the University of Sussex, Brighton, in 1975.

As an escape from office jobs, which she hated, Clarke turned to writing. Having no success with so-called straight novels, she began writing mysteries. Between 1968 and 1996, she produced twenty-seven novels of mystery and suspense. Clarke died on November 7, 2004, in Brighton, East Sussex.

ANALYSIS

Anna Clarke's mysteries are often not what the average reader of detective fiction expects; in fact, they are frequently not mysteries in any traditional sense but studies in the development of a murderer. A number of elements make Clarke's novels strong and intriguing; the most interesting of these are her use of multiple sleuths, her focus on the psychology of crime, and the literary motif that runs through many of her works. These secure Clarke's place among mystery writers.

Clarke's use of multiple sleuths is the most unusual element of her writing. Although she introduced a series character, Paula Glenning, in *Last Judgement* (1985), in her earlier work she used different characters in each mystery. Her detectives are always amateurs because her interest lies in the human mind rather than in crime and detection. Indeed, unlike the traditional detective story, a Clarke story does not begin with a crime. Either the crime does not occur until the final chapters, or there is no awareness that a crime has occurred.

Perhaps surprisingly, Clarke's approach to characterization does not lead to loose plotting. Indeed, her plots are tightly constructed. Because there is frequently no mystery for the reader to attempt to solve before the detective does, there is no need for red herrings and their attendant problems for a writer who must discreetly insert them. In *Last Judgement*, the plot moves inevitably from opening action to denouement. Although references to James's obsessive desire to possess his grandfather's papers suggest that he is capable of murdering the old man, the focus is always on Mary and her decline into madness. Also, the occasional breaks in action serve only to create suspense. Even in *Plot Counter-Plot* (1974), a complicated story of two authors at personal and professional odds with each other, there are no loose ends.

This care with plotting stems from Clarke's literary interests, which in turn provide a motif for much of her work. In *Last Judgement*, characters include a renowned author, two professors of English literature, and a literary critic. The plot, as character James Goff points out on several occasions, resembles *The Aspern Papers* (1888) by Henry James. At the center of this plot is the struggle for possession of the notebooks, letters, and drafted novels of the great author. Again, in *My Search for Ruth* (1975) it is a literary form that dominates: A young woman writes a chronicle while searching for her true identity. According to the critic

Larry E. Grimes, Ruth chooses "a compulsive, personal, primary encounter with the stuff of literature itself—image, character, plot."

Clarke said of her writing, "As far as I have any conscious feeling about writing novels at all beyond the obsessional story-telling, I am interested in the workings of the human mind and their effects on character and action." This is borne out by all aspects of her work. Her characterization, her nontraditional use of sleuths and of criminal acts, her tightly woven plots, and even the literary motif she adopts so frequently support her interest in the mind. She is the purest of mystery writers, for as Nancy Pick says in *Desire to Kill* (1982), "All human beings are the stuff of which murderers are made." It is this premise that lies at the root of mystery and detective fiction.

LAST JUDGEMENT

In *Last Judgement*, there are crimes against the heart or spirit, but there is no criminal act until the next-to-last chapter. The result is that the story, in part, is about how a number of individuals either come to understand that some violence will occur or remain oblivious to its possibility. For example, a male nurse, Hector Greenaway, sees Mary Morrison, the central character, as a trapped, weak animal that is likely to be dangerous; yet when he voices his concern to Dr. Joan Conway, the doctor sees only a young woman overworked and worried by her frail stepfather's ill health. Hector does not understand how he knows what he does of Mary.

Similarly, Paula Glenning at one point comes to realize that Mary is laughing silently at her. Paula relives the scene:

> She had had an overpowering sense of oppression in that horrible dark, dead room, and had seen Mary as trapped and crushed by it, unable to free herself.
>
> But had Mary really felt like that? . . . It was Paula who had given way to her feelings. Was Mary such a helpless victim? Had she found her own way out?
>
> Perhaps she had made up her mind to murder the old man. Perhaps she had already done so.

It is this sensitivity to atmosphere that marks Clarke's amateur detectives.

Mary Morrison's madness is precipitated by change.

Her stepfather's grandson has begun to spend time with her in the hope of gaining access through her to the private papers of his grandfather, England's greatest novelist. As G. E. Goff's secretary, Mary could perhaps smooth the way for James Goff, long estranged from his grandfather. Suspecting James's motives, but hoping that his true motive is to see her, Mary for the first time believes that love is possible for her, that she has not been entombed by her mother's dying wish that she care for her aged stepfather. Against this is the desire of another man, Richard Grieve, to have the papers, and G. E.'s suspicion that Mary is plotting against him, a suspicion that leads him to reveal brutally the truth to her about her natural father and her beloved mother. This revelation, combined with the pressure of deciding what to do about the papers, drives Mary to madness.

Since her mother's death, Mary has been somewhat unstable and needs someone to talk to. For Mary, it is her dead mother with whom she discusses her problems. This is a natural human action; it is only the extreme to which she takes the action that marks it as madness.

DESIRE TO KILL

Clarke's use of sensitive amateur detectives is most noticeable in *Desire to Kill*. In this work, Nancy Pick and George Cunningham, two residents of a retirement home, discuss the other residents over games of chess. They reach the conclusion, based only on observation, that one of their number, Amy Langford, is quite mad and has systematically set about killing other residents through a series of apparent accidents. At one point, in an attempt to understand what is happening, they voice their vague misgivings:

> "Damn it, there's so little to go on. Just this vague feeling that something is very wrong, some malevolent force at work. The more we talk, the stronger it gets. You, too?"
>
> "Me, too. Look here, if we haven't any facts, let's tackle it from the psychological angle. Let's look for examples of malevolence. Who is there connected with Digby Hall who is actually capable of scheming to make somebody else suffer?"

Here, encapsulated, is the process Clarke's detectives follow.

A key term is "psychological angle." In creating her characters, Clarke concentrates on the thoughts that lie behind actions. In *Desire to Kill* the reader sees the disintegration of Amy Langford, and, as is often the case in Clarke's novels, disruption of a lifestyle causes that disintegration. With her husband's death, Amy has lost the center of her life; her son, unwilling to cater to her, places her in a retirement home. Feeling abandoned and lost, Amy speaks to her reflection in a mirror: "Don't worry, Amy. . . . You've not been completely deserted. I'm going to look after you." This is a very human response, but it marks the beginning of her madness. She continues, "I'm going to make sure that you get your due and that those who won't give it you will suffer for it." This becomes a motif through the book; Amy turns to the comfort of her reflection, her alter ego, whenever she is confused or frightened, and each time she descends more deeply into madness. The last time she looks in the mirror, she sees an image that appears momentarily at peace but becomes frightened almost immediately.

> "I can't help you," she cried aloud. "I don't know what to do. I know you want me to kill Mr. Horder, because he disappointed you so badly. But I don't want to kill him. I want to be his friend. I like him. And he likes me!"

So strong is Clarke's writing that both Amy Langford and Mary Morrison are believable even in extreme madness.

PLOT COUNTER-PLOT

This need to talk without fear of being overheard takes another form in *Plot Counter-Plot*. Mystery novelist Helen Mitchell lets loose her fears and her madness in a novel she is writing, her last novel. She has no life of her own; rather, she knows that her "most successful character creation of all was that of Helen Mitchell." Now her greatest fear is about to come true: "Ever since I began to write it has haunted me, this fear that my imagination could take over my real life and that I could behave like one of the characters in my novels, even to the point of committing murder." Yet Helen, by her own admission, has no real life, and as a character she has no real confidants, so she pours her fears, her madness, and her last acts into a novel.

Clarke's literary connections are most evident in *Plot Counter-Plot*, wherein an author, Helen Mitchell, has an affair with Brent Ashwood, a writer with only one book in him; he attempts to steal her work—a novel based on him—and present it as an autobiographical novel. As the two plot against each other, the literary tangle thickens. Even the overall structure of the book shows an attentiveness to literary form; a prologue and epilogue establish the "real" world of Helen Mitchell and explain her writing of the "novel," which appears between prologue and epilogue. It is this fictional creation that details her life with Brent and carries the plot of the mystery. It is the real world of the epilogue that provides the climax and the final plot twist.

Clarke's concern with literary qualities is reflected in her style. Sentence patterns flow and build to a climax. For example, she begins *Plot Counter-Plot* thus:

> At last I am alone in the room and can take up my pen to start the novel that may be the last one I shall ever write. I must work quickly and lose no time, for I must write in secret and everything I have written must be hidden from human eye. Jane Austen, it is said, slipped her manuscript sheets under the blotter to conceal them from the inquisitive glances of visiting acquaintances. My reason for concealment is more sinister.

Here the long, winding sentences reflect her subject: hidden texts. The punch of the last sentence emphasizes the sinister events to follow.

Another of Clarke's stylistic strengths lies in her descriptive passages. In *Last Judgement*, she details the beginnings of a deadly fire:

> The avalanche on the floor was now well alight, and pieces of burning paper were flying around the room, settling on the curtains, the winged armchair, the upright chairs, and the tables. The desk was already in flames and the carpet smouldering. Nothing, nobody on earth could stop it now. She had fulfilled her destiny. The entire room was ablaze.

The images of the avalanche bring a new understanding of fire to the reader. Though deadly and inescapable, the fire is beautiful in a frightening way.

Krystan V. Douglas
Updated by Philip Bader

PRINCIPAL MYSTERY AND DETECTIVE FICTION

PAULA GLENNING SERIES: *Last Judgement*, 1985; *Cabin 3033*, 1986; *The Mystery Lady*, 1986; *Last Seen in London*, 1987; *Murder in Writing*, 1988; *Whitelands Affair*, 1989; *The Case of the Paranoid Patient*, 1991; *The Case of the Ludicrous Letters*, 1994; *The Case of the Anxious Aunt*, 1996

NONSERIES NOVELS: *The Darkened Room*, 1968; *A Mind to Murder*, 1971; *The End of the Shadow*, 1972; *Plot Counter-Plot*, 1974; *My Search for Ruth*, 1975; *Legacy of Evil*, 1976; *The Deathless and the Dead*, 1976 (also known as *This Downhill Path*); *Letter from the Dead*, 1977; *One of Us Must Die*, 1977; *The Lady in Black*, 1977; *Poison Parsley*, 1979; *The Poisoned Web*, 1979; *Last Voyage*, 1980; *Game, Set, and Danger*, 1981; *Desire to Kill*, 1982; *We the Bereaved*, 1982; *Soon She Must Die*, 1984; *Legacy of Evil*, 1991

TRANSLATION: *Clinical Papers and Essays on Psychoanalysis*, 1955 (by Karl Abraham)

BIBLIOGRAPHY

Adrian, Mike. "Obituary: Anna Clarke, Prolific Author of 'Cosies' and 'Biblio-mysteries.'" *The Independent*, December 28, 2004, p. 33. Obituary of Clarke notes that the author was first published at the age of fifty and wrote prolifically thereafter. Notes her fondness for biblio-mysteries, mysteries involving literature.

Klein, Kathleen Gregory, ed. *Great Women Mystery Writers: Classic to Contemporary.* Westport, Conn.: Greenwood Press, 1994. Contains an essay that discusses the life and writings of Clarke.

Library Journal. Review of *Last Judgement*, by Anna Clarke. 110, no. 2 (February 1, 1985): 115. Reviewer finds the work to be more an atmospheric story than a mystery. Criticizes the work for its melodrama and lack of believability.

Mabe, Chauncey. "A Child's Loss Makes for Superior Thriller." Review of *My Search for Ruth*, by Anna Clarke. *Sun Sentinel*, September 18, 1988, p. 8F. Discusses the work in which Ruth searches for her own identity as she lives with the headmistress of a boarding school, Miss Murray. Reviewer finds the novel psychologically satisfying and believable.

Rye, Marilyn. "Anna Clarke." In *Great Women Mystery Writers*, edited by Kathleen Gregory Klein. Westport, Conn.: Greenwood Press, 1994. Bio-critical study of Clarke's life and writing. Individual entries also include suggestions of writers with similar styles, as well as Internet resources for mystery and crime-fiction enthusiasts.

Vicarel, JoAnn. Review of *The Mystery Lady*, by Anna Clarke. *Library Journal* 111, no. 16 (October 1, 1986): 113. Review of a Paula Henning book in which Henning is to write a biography of romantic novelist Rosie O'Grady. Reviewer criticizes the work for containing too much talk between Henning and James Goff and finds it disappointing overall.

JON CLEARY

Born: Sydney, New South Wales, Australia;
November 22, 1917
Types of plot: Hard-boiled; police procedural

PRINCIPAL SERIES

Scobie Malone, 1966-

PRINCIPAL SERIES CHARACTER

SCOBIE MALONE is a rough-hewn young detective sergeant with Y Division of the police force of Sydney, Australia. Malone is courageous, straightforward, and plainspoken; in short, he possesses those virtues usually associated with the Australian man.

CONTRIBUTION

Jon Cleary is a writer of several genres of fiction, which share a high standard of craftsmanship. Whether adventures, mysteries, or popular novels, Cleary's works feature well-paced narratives, a strong sense of atmosphere, and realistic dialogue. His work reflects an awareness of social problems and his sympathy for suffering, even misguided, humanity. His mystery fiction is marked by such compelling characterizations that it consistently rises above the level of the formulaic.

Cleary began his writing career with a collection of short fiction about his military service in the Middle East during World War II. In 1966, he published the first in a long string of mystery novels featuring Scobie Malone, a rugged but sympathetic Australian detective. Through the voice of his intrepid detective, Cleary has produced a series that reflects the changing focus of mystery and crime narratives over several decades, as well as major social and cultural shifts in Australian society.

In a writing career that has spanned more than five decades, Cleary has produced short and long fiction, plays, radio plays, teleplays, and screenplays, in addition to his substantial contributions in the mystery and detective genre. His works have appeared in numerous foreign language translations. Cleary received the Edgar Allan Poe Award from the Mystery Writers Association for his 1974 novel *Peter's Pence*. Other awards include the Australian Broadcasting Commission prize for radio drama in 1944, the Australian Literary Society's Crouch Medal for the best Australian novel in 1950, and the Australian Crime Writers' Association Lifetime Achievement Award in 1996.

BIOGRAPHY

Jon Stephen Cleary was born on November 22, 1917, in one of the tougher, poorer districts of Sydney, New South Wales, Australia. His father, Matthew Cleary, was a laborer, and his mother, Ida Brown Cleary, a homemaker; after Jon's birth, six more children were eventually born to them. Cleary has written that he has some of his father's working-class temperament and some of his mother's tightfistedness. He attended the Marist Brothers School at Randwick, New South Wales, from 1924 to 1932. He left school at age fifteen and worked at a variety of jobs, including commercial traveler, delivery man, laundry worker, sign painter, bush worker, and commercial artist.

When Cleary entered the army in 1940, he was considering a full-time career in commercial art. He served in the Australian Imperial Forces in the Middle East, New Guinea, and New Britain until 1945 and began to write during this period. By the time of his discharge, he had attained the rank of lieutenant and had sold several stories to American magazines. He had enough money to support himself for two years, during which time he planned to discover whether he could earn his living as a writer. With the exception of his employment as a journalist with the government of Australia News and Information Bureau in London (1948-1949) and in New York (1949-1951), he has worked exclusively as a freelance writer of fiction since 1945.

In 1946, Cleary met Constantine "Joy" Lucas, a resident of Melbourne, Australia, on a ship bound for England. They were married on September 6, two weeks after disembarking, and eventually became the parents of two daughters, Catherine and Jane. Joy died in 2003. Cleary, a practicing Roman Catholic, is essentially apolitical but has stated that he leans slightly to the left. He published a collection of short stories,

These Small Glories, in 1946 and began producing books at the rate of nearly one per year.

Cleary is also a dramatist and scenarist. He lives in New South Wales but travels constantly. Many of his stories are set in remote locales, and he has asserted that he never writes about a region of which he does not possess firsthand knowledge. His writing career has been marked by continued success in several fields of fiction.

ANALYSIS

Jon Cleary has written that the three things he most despises are hypocrisy, bigotry, and jingoism; his sympathies and his antipathies are apparent in his fiction. The reader senses his moral outrage at the unjust treatment of homeless Jews, as portrayed in *The Safe House* (1975). *Justin Bayard* (1955) contains an angry denunciation of absentee landlords in the Australian outback. *The Liberators* (1971) is, in part, a sympathetic study of the plight of the Bolivian Indians, who have long been exploited by the economic, political, and ecclesiastical power structure; in this novel, a young American priest and a United Nations agronomist attempt to help the Indians gain their rights.

Rejecting the label of didactic writer, Cleary admits that he allows himself to express his opinions in his novels from time to time, when to do so will not retard the pace of the narrative. *The Liberators*, considered by many to be one of Cleary's finest novels, succeeds in developing a serious theme without being preachy, while its sociological aspect melds naturally with the exciting and suspenseful plot.

THE SUNDOWNERS

Cleary set out to be a great writer, and he has written a number of serious novels. One of these, *The Sundowners* (1952), has become a minor classic and is by far Cleary's best-known work. It sold more than one million copies and has become assigned reading in many high school and college courses. In 1960, it was successfully adapted as a film (for which Cleary himself wrote the screenplay), featuring Robert Mitchum, Deborah Kerr, and Peter Ustinov. *The Sundowners* recounts a year in the life of Paddy Carmody and his family. Paddy is an itinerant Australian ranch worker, appealing but irresponsible. It is, in part, an initiation

novel—Paddy's son, Sean, attains manhood in the Australian wilderness of the 1920's. The novel is warmly nostalgic yet unsentimental in tone.

THE MOVE TO POPULAR FICTION

Despite the financial and critical success of *The Sundowners*, Cleary had decided by the age of thirty-five that he lacked the mental equipment to achieve greatness. He was aware, however, that he had a fine sense of narrative, an ability to convey atmosphere, and a gift for writing dialogue. He therefore made the conscious decision to give up his dream of writing the great novel and to use his gifts instead to produce the very best popular novels of which he was capable. For several decades, he has been eminently successful in that effort. As a matter of fact, Cleary's talent is so impressive that on occasion critics, in the course of praising his work, have expressed the wish that he would set for himself loftier literary goals. They consider him capable of attaining them. Cleary attempted a large-scale social novel in the manner of John P. Marquand, whom he admires. He worked for more than a year on a long novel dealing with political life in Sydney between 1930 and 1955, but his publisher rejected the manuscript.

Cleary's crime fiction is so varied that it is not easy to classify. Many of his novels hug the generic line between the thriller and the adventure story. Even *The Sundowners*, which is not considered an adventure story, contains quite a bit of adventure. Although Cleary denies that his novels contain messages, they usually have serious and well-developed themes. He enjoys exploring character as it is revealed through conflict in remote and often-forbidding regions of the globe. In *The Pulse of Danger* (1966), he recounts a thrilling chase over the Himalayas. *The Liberators* is set in an isolated Bolivian village, high in the Andes. Cleary's experience as a mountain climber helped him make this story credible.

A thumbnail summary of several other novels will attest the variety of Cleary's subject matter. In *Back of Sunset* (1959), a young Australian doctor gives up his lucrative practice in Sydney and joins a flying service that delivers medical care to isolated regions. *The Green Helmet* (1957) is a tale of automobile racing. *The Long Pursuit* (1967) is an account of a group of refugees making their escape from Singapore in 1942. *Justin Bayard*, set in the outback, has been called an Australian Western. *Vortex* (1977) is the story of man's struggle against nature in rural Missouri, along the so-called Tornado Alley. *The Safe House* takes place in the immediate postwar period; it tells the dual story of displaced Jews attempting to slip past the British into the homeland in Palestine and of defeated Nazis fleeing to sanctuary in South America.

PETER'S PENCE

Cleary won an Edgar Allan Poe Award in 1974 for *Peter's Pence*, published in the same year. Saint Peter is the Peter of the ironic title, and the setting is the Vatican. The reader is reminded that Cleary is a Catholic who has said that his travels through Asia and Africa have persuaded him that Rome is not always right. *Peter's Pence* tells the story of an attempt by an international gang of thieves to loot the Vatican. The gang utilizes the subterranean passages of Saint Peter's Basilica to make off with the church's priceless art treasures.

THE HIGH COMMISSIONER

In 1966, *The High Commissioner*, the first of the Scobie Malone novels, appeared (this was the fourth of Cleary's novels to be adapted as a motion picture). By dint of hard work, Malone has attained the rank of detective sergeant in the Sydney police force. A number of parallels between the young police officer and his creator are rapidly evident to the reader with some knowledge of Cleary's personal history. Malone is the child of an Irish, Roman Catholic, working-class couple, Con and Brigid Malone. He grew up in a terrace house on a narrow street in Erskineville, a tenement district. His parents had wanted him to become a priest, but he became a police officer instead. Scobie felt no particular sense of vocation for police work; it was simply a job. Nevertheless, the work ethic is strong in him, and he takes pride in doing his job well. Scobie is engaged to Lisa Pretorious, a young Dutchwoman whose well-to-do parents live temporarily in Melbourne.

HELGA'S WEB

In *The High Commissioner*, Scobie goes to London on a security detail, and his adventures take place in the British metropolis. In the second novel of the series, *Helga's Web* (1970), he is back in the city of his birth. Sydney, Cleary's lusty and boisterous hometown, is itself a character in this novel. After Helga Brand is found strangled in the Sydney Opera House, Malone follows a trail that leads through all levels of Sydney society. Helga's web is spread from Parliament to show business, from the enclaves of the rich to Sydney's docks. The plot is intriguing, but, as in the other Scobie Malone novels (*Ransom*, 1973, is the third), its greatest strength lies in the characterization. A domestic scene from the early chapters of *Helga's Web* serves as an example.

By way of introducing his fiancé to his parents, Scobie brings Lisa to their small terrace house for dinner. As they eat, they can hear the neighbors fighting just beyond the tissue-thin walls. Con is in an expansive mood, because he has had a peripheral contact with the opera house murder and has gotten his picture in the newspapers. Brigid is ill-concealing her prejudice against a future daughter-in-law who is not Catholic, working-class, or Australian. Nevertheless, Lisa doggedly plies her considerable charm and succeeds in winning over Con completely. The lifelong socialist and rhetorical revolutionary ends by making allowances for the girl's birth and breeding. This scene, though not essential to the movement of the plot, grounds Scobie and those close to him in reality and makes the reader care for them.

RANSOM

In *Ransom*, Malone and Lisa, his wife, are visiting New York City on election eve. Lisa is kidnapped, along with the mayor's wife. The kidnappers demand the release of five anarchists being held in the Tombs. As Malone investigates, learning first the identity and eventually the location of the kidnappers, the reader is treated to a view of New York City through Australian eyes. Cleary's crime fiction, like his general fiction, combines suspenseful plots with solid characterization and a deep sense of humanity.

THE DARK SUMMER CYCLE

Dark Summer (1991) is the first of a cycle of four Scobie Malone mysteries set in Sydney in which Cleary blends mystery with sociology to depict changes in the fabric of life in the Australian capital. The death of a police informant leads Malone to investigate what might prove to be related murders in the

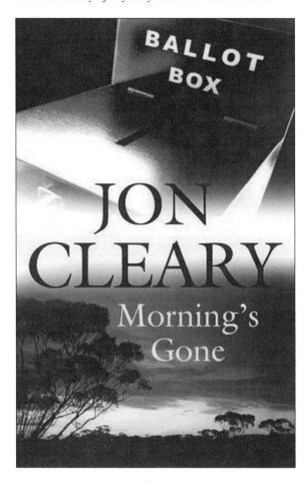

Sydney docklands, a former haunt of his estranged father, and discovers an elaborate drug ring. *Bleak Spring* (1993) follows Malone's search for the killer of Will Rockne, a suburban Sydney lawyer. An intriguing cast of characters include a suspiciously detached widow, a cadre of disreputable bankers, street thugs, a menacing Russian, and the posthumous discovery of $5 million in Rockne's personal safe. In *Autumn Maze* (1994), Malone delves into the complex world of Sydney politics when the son of the police minister son turns up dead. *Winter Chill* (1995), the fourth in the cycle, finds Malone facing a potentially explosive international incident when a prominent American lawyer is found murdered on the Sydney monorail.

MORNING'S GONE

In *Morning's Gone* (2007), Cleary turns to the landscape of politics. His protagonist is Matt Durban,

a seasoned Australian politician who returns to his roots in rural Collamundra to reconnect with his constituency and his family. The strain of political life has begun to erode his marriage and alienate Durban from his family. However, other forces may be at work to cripple his political ambitions when a decades-old murder of a young woman—Durban's former girlfriend—makes fresh headlines. Cleary provides a detailed character study of an ambitious but principled politician and his fiercely independent wife, both of whom have made powerful enemies over the years. *Morning's Gone*, like most of Cleary's best-known works, combines powerful storytelling with a keen interest in the interior lives of his characters.

Patrick Adcock
Updated by Philip Bader

PRINCIPAL MYSTERY AND DETECTIVE FICTION

SCOBIE MALONE SERIES: *The High Commissioner*, 1966; *Helga's Web*, 1970; *Ransom*, 1973; *Now and Then, Amen*, 1988; *Babylon South*, 1989; *Murder Song*, 1990; *Dark Summer*, 1991; *Pride's Harvest*, 1991; *Bleak Spring*, 1993; *Autumn Maze*, 1994; *Winter Chill*, 1995; *Endpeace*, 1996; *A Different Turf*, 1997; *Five Ring Circus*, 1998; *Dilemma*, 1999; *The Bear Pit*, 2000; *Yesterday's Shadow*, 2001; *The Easy Sin*, 2002; *Degrees of Connection*, 2003

NONSERIES NOVELS: *You Can't See Around Corners*, 1947; *The Long Shadow*, 1949; *Just Let Me Be*, 1950; *The Climate of Courage*, 1954 (also known as *Naked in the Night*); *Justin Bayard*, 1955 (also known as *Dust in the Sun*); *A Flight of Chariots*, 1963; *Forests of the Night*, 1963; *The Fall of an Eagle*, 1964; *The Pulse of Danger*, 1966; *The Long Pursuit*, 1967; *Season of Doubt*, 1968; *The Liberators*, 1971 (also known as *Mask of the Andes*); *Peter's Pence*, 1974; *The Safe House*, 1975; *A Sound of Lightning*, 1976; *High Road to China*, 1977; *Vortex*, 1977; *The Beaufort Sisters*, 1979; *A Very Private War*, 1980; *The Golden Sabre*, 1981; *The Faraway Drums*, 1982; *The City of Fading Light*, 1985; *Dragons at the Party*, 1987; *Morning's Gone*, 2007

SHORT FICTION: *These Small Glories*, 1946; *Pillar of Salt*, 1963

OTHER MAJOR WORKS

NOVELS: *The Sundowners*, 1952; *The Green Helmet*, 1957; *Back of Sunset*, 1959; *North from Thursday*, 1960; *The Country of Marriage*, 1962; *Remember Jack Hoxie*, 1969; *The Ninth Marquess*, 1972 (also known as *Man's Estate*); *Spearfield's Daughter*, 1982

PLAY: *Strike Me Lucky*, pr. 1963

RADIO PLAY: *Safe Horizon*, 1944

SCREENPLAYS: *The Siege of Pinchgut*, 1959 (with Harry Watt and Alexander Baron); *The Sundowners*, 1960; *The Green Helmet*, 1961; *Sidecar Racers*, 1975 (also known as *Sidecar Boys*)

TELEPLAY: *Just Let Me Be*, 1957

BIBLIOGRAPHY

Dickinson, Jane. Review of *Dilemma*, by Jon Cleary. *Denver Rocky Mountain News*, June 18, 2000, p. 8E. Favorable review of this Scobie Malone novel about the kidnap and murder of a five-year-old child. Praises Cleary's solid psychological insights and writing.

Kelly, Ed. Review of *Dark Summer*, by Jon Cleary. *Buffalo News*, September 5, 1993, p. Book. Review of this Scobie Malone book calls Cleary a "standout" among contemporary crime-fiction writers. Notes the brisk interactions between Malone and his partner, Russ Clements, and the details about Malone's family. Also identifies a resemblance to J. J. Marric's novels about George Gideon.

Knight, Stephen. *Continent of Mystery: A Thematic History of Australian Crime Fiction*. Vic., Australia: Melbourne University Press, 1997. A chronicle of nearly two centuries of Australian crime fiction that covers hundreds of authors, including Cleary, and evaluates their contributions to the country's unique slant on crime and mystery fiction.

_____. *Crime Fiction, 1800-2000: Detection, Death, Diversity*. New York: Palgrave Macmillan, 2004. Knight provides a useful overview of the crime genre in the last two centuries, with discussions of various authors, works, and influences. Helps place Cleary in the mystery genre.

Pitt, David. Review of *Morning's Gone*, by Jon Cleary. *Booklist* 103, no. 17 (May 1, 2007): 41. Review of this novel about how a politician's past comes to haunt him is called "a revealing character study" about a politician and his wife.

LIZA CODY

Born: London, England; April 11, 1944

Types of plot: Private investigator; amateur sleuth

PRINCIPAL SERIES

Anna Lee, 1980-

Eva Wylie, 1992-

PRINCIPAL SERIES CHARACTERS

ANNA LEE, a former police officer turned private investigator, is employed by Brierly Security in London, where she is the lone female detective in a sea of circling male sleuths. In her quest to solve crimes, Lee is a capable and determined young woman, but she finds herself impeded by workplace and societal gender barriers. Estranged from her family and unable to form long-term attachments to men, Lee finds solace in her friendship with her downstairs neighbors.

BEA and SELWYN, Lee's neighbors, rent the unit below hers. The couple, a long-suffering wife and her poet-husband, act as an emotional counterpoint to the private detective's tough-skinned rational demeanor. Often they elicit Lee's aid and even her sympathies.

MARTIN BRIERLY is Lee's boss, an egoist who second-guesses her competence for the job in spite of her obvious contributions to the firm.

EVA WYLIE supports herself through an assortment of odd jobs, including bouncer, scrapyard security guard, and amateur sleuth. Wylie wrestles professionally under the moniker "the London Lassassin." Although streetwise, Wylie lacks social grace and mental quickness. Not as tough as her large bulk and gruff demeanor suggest, she is emotionally more fragile than Lee.

CONTRIBUTION

Award-winning author Liza Cody is recognized for broadening the scope of the British detective genre. Not content merely with incorporating a modern female detective into the mold, she has created works that complicate what it means to be a detecting woman in a field traditionally reserved for tough male protagonists and spinsterish female amateurs. Identified primarily with her two feminist detective series, featuring Anna Lee and Eva Wylie, Cody also writes short fiction and novels of suspense.

Certain features of Cody's style resemble those of master detective writer Raymond Chandler. Her prose is realistic and sparse, replete with believable and frequently witty dialogue. Like Chandler's characters, Cody's detectives are loners wary of connections with others but in search of them nonetheless. The world they investigate is a dark one, in which human nature is deceptive and the task of piecing together clues labyrinthine.

Cody is notable for her development of original female detectives, both professional and amateur, and for her examination of the intersection of gender, authority, and justice in her works. Like her contemporaries, American authors Sara Paretsky and Sue Grafton, Cody populates her novels with sleuthing women who are tough-minded, physically strong, independent in lifestyle, and otherwise defiant of sexual stereotypes.

BIOGRAPHY

Born Liza Nassim on April 11, 1944, Liza Cody spent her childhood in London. Attracted to the visual and graphic arts, she studied at the London Art School and later at the Royal Academy School of Art, where she excelled at painting and design. Cody's training and abilities led her to a position at Madame Tussauds wax museum in London, where she worked as a studio technician. An interesting milieu for a future writer of crime fiction, Tussauds houses some grim likenesses of notorious London killers, including Jack the Ripper. Cody found additional employment as a graphic designer and painter, but it was not in the art world that she would leave her mark on British popular culture. On the successful publication of her first novel, *Dupe* (1980), Cody focused her energies full time on writing.

Cody would pen additional novels featuring Anna Lee, including *Bad Company* (1982), *Stalker* (1984), *Head Case* (1985), *Under Contract* (1986), and *Backhand* (1991). The popularity of Anna Lee led to a successful British television series based on Cody's novels produced by London Weekend Television (LWT) Productions. Later, Arts & Entertainment (A&E) aired the five episodes on American television. Purportedly Cody's dissatisfaction with the medium's interpretation of her chief character, Anna Lee, led the author to begin a new series with a different female lead, professional wrestler Eva Wylie.

Cody dedicated the 1990's to developing her series of novels featuring Eva Wylie. The appearance of *Bucket Nut* (1992) is a dividing mark in Cody's oeuvre. Instead of featuring an upwardly mobile professional sleuth, like Anna Lee, at the helm of the investigation, the Eva Wylie series focuses on an amateur sleuth from a lower sphere of society, one who circulates among the most desperate of human beings, frequently social outcasts with nothing to lose. *Monkey Wrench* (1994) and *Musclebound* (1997) soon followed. Although her characters and their circumstances were descending, Cody's reputation as a writer was rising into the ranks of Britain's most respected writers of modern detective fiction.

Cody achieved recognition as a writer of short fiction as well. Widely anthologized in mystery and detective collections, she has published independent collections of short stories including *Murder and Company* (1988) and *The Lucky Dip, and Other Stories* (2003). In addition to her ongoing work as an author, she has edited volumes of detective fiction, assisting Michael Lewin with the numerically designated Culprit series. The inaugural volume, *First Culprit: An Annual of Crime Stories* appeared in 1992 to great acclaim.

ANALYSIS

Although Liza Cody's characters cross literary boundaries in terms of gender expectations, scholars are split on their response to the author's female detectives and their placement in the genre. Some critics believe that Cody's women, in addition to defying traditional depictions of female sleuths, break with stereotypes of the literary detective in general, truly transforming the genre. Others insist that Cody's protagonists, Anna Lee and Eva Wylie, are essentially male private eyes in drag. Many critics have noted resemblances between Cody's British Anna Lee and her American counterparts, Sue Grafton's Kinsey Millhone and Sara Paretsky's V. I. Warshawski, primarily their independent natures. Eva Wylie, however, appears to have no equal in the field of feminist detective fiction.

In the Anna Lee series, the title character finds herself not only solving crimes but also battling workplace politics. Lee's boss, Commander Martin Brierly (a thorn in Lee's side), and his office manager, Beryl Doyle (as old-fashioned and traditional as the doily that her name suggests), are committed to upholding the patriarchal hierarchy of their small investigative firm, one that puts Lee on the bottom rung. Her boss assigns her only the most minor of cases, which typically balloon into significant and difficult investigations. Over the years her successes garner Lee a private office and the begrudging respect of her employer. Still, the final novel of the series, *Backhand* (1991), concludes with Lee in a homeless and jobless state, less secure than in her inaugural appearance in *Dupe*.

In many respects, Anna Lee is a woman in a man's world, capable of doing the job but slowed by social roadblocks she must circumvent. As a female detective, Lee breaks new ground in urban, rural, and foreign environs (subsequent novels take her out of London to the English countryside, on tour with a rock star, and across the ocean to Florida), but her progress is impeded by entrenched attitudes of male privilege. In Cody's novels, Lee's grit and intellect are often insufficient tools to forge gender equality where it is not wanted: the male-dominant enclave of a private detective agency. Ironically, Lee's status as a marginalized player at Brierly's allows her to see events with enhanced clarity and to pursue cases with greater freedom. She finds herself on the same fringes of society where the criminals she seeks take refuge. Self-reliant

in the extreme (she has trust issues), alienated from her family (out of touch with her respectable middle-class sisters), and underappreciated by colleagues (who find both her gender and her methods suspect), Lee finds companionship with her neighbors, Bea and Selwyn, and in short-lived sexual encounters with men who come into and go out of her life with increasing frequency.

The Lee series can be read as a fictional chronicle of a working woman's slow but steady progress in the investigative field during the 1980's. In contrast, Cody's 1990's series featuring Eva Wylie (the wily Eve) further disrupts traditions associated with women protagonists in British detective fiction. Anna Lee might be a distant relative of mystery great Agatha Christie's Miss Marple, but Wylie is not even descended from the same family tree. A wrestler by avocation and a part-time security guard by financial necessity, Wylie's forays into detection are the product of dire circumstance, not professional calling. Her moniker on the wrestling circuit is the "London Lassassin," and her bulk, street smarts, and reputation for toughness equip her to navigate, if not negotiate, the murky regions of the city's underside. Like Lee, Wylie is beyond the pale but at a greater distance. By virtue of her gender, class, and occupation (and occasional lack thereof), Wylie is thrice removed from mainstream detective fiction and its traditions.

DUPE

Critics have dubbed Anna Lee Britain's first feminist private eye. Her debut in *Dupe* finds Lee, a former police officer, joining a private detective firm, Brierly Security. Her first case involves the suspicious death of a black sheep socialite, Deirdre Jackson. When the young woman's parents doubt the accidental nature of their daughter's car wreck, Lee investigates, discovering in the process evidence of wrongdoing and a cover-up. Further complicating her investigation are the barriers Lee faces in the workplace. Her patriarchal boss, Martin Brierly, objects to women detectives in general, and Lee in particular. He seems intent on proving her incompetence despite her progress in the investigation.

In 1980 *Dupe* received the British Crime Writers' Association's John Creasey Memorial Award and was nominated for the Edgar Award in the same calendar year. Critics responded positively to the lead character's unique personality, part steely-eyed detective and part sympathetic human being. Anna Lee is a woman who possesses the rational acumen to re-create a crime scene and track events back to the killer. Equally, her ability to sympathize with the victim's family, if not perhaps the deceased (whose disagreeable reputation in life follows her to her grave), spurs Lee's dedication to the case. The heroine's blend of overt intelligence and covert compassion proved so appealing a combination to readers that Cody featured her in five additional novels. Lee even makes cameo appearances in the Eva Wylie novels. Ironically, in these works, Lee, now in charge of her own agency, is perceived by Wylie to be a suspicious outsider. When Lee attempts to hire Wylie on one occasion and thus legitimize the underdog's status, the wrestler rejects her offer.

BUCKET NUT

Approaching the marginalization of women from a different vantage point, *Bucket Nut* (1992) introduces Eva Wylie, professional wrestler and amateur sleuth. Because Wylie is a member of the underclass, her identification is with the criminals and those labeled miscreants by society; law enforcement officials are the "others," those not to be believed. Cody provides sufficient background information on Wylie to explain her deep-rooted suspicion of authority and her solidarity with the downtrodden. Abandoned by her drunken mother, Wylie was reared in a series of abusive foster homes. Trust issues are second nature to the adult Wylie, and her wariness is her amulet against harm in the first installment of the series.

In the process of resolving a case involving extortion, drug running, and a missing person, Wylie commits a few criminal acts herself, including the heist of a vehicle and a wallet. Because her neighborhood is populated by Mafia men, drug dealers, and a jazz club singer with connections to both, Wylie's interactions with ne'er-do-wells are frequent and her avoidance of law enforcement all too necessary. Critics raved about this new female antidetective. Loud, crude, in-your-face Wylie is not necessarily likable, but she is unforgettable. The novel merited the prestigious Crime Writers' Association's Silver Dagger Award for 1992.

LUCKY DIP, AND OTHER STORIES

The seventeen entries in *Lucky Dip, and Other Stories* (2003) feature an assortment of women in dire predicaments, most of whom survive their ordeals and live to tell their tales. Although many of the stories appeared in previous anthologies, two are new to the volume, and two, "Doing It Under the Table" and "Chalk Mother," were originally radio dramas broadcast by the British Broadcasting Corporation. The title story, "Lucky Dip," which received an Anthony for best short story in 1993, features an abandoned urchin navigating life on the backstreets of London. In stark contrast to the title story, the stories "Where's Stacy?" and "A Card or a Kitten" are quirky, lighthearted tales reflective of the arena in which they take place, Florida. Readers who prefer mysteries of a darker nature will be pleased with the remainder of the entries, set in Cody's trademark murky environs of London.

Dorothy Dodge Robbins

PRINCIPAL MYSTERY AND DETECTIVE FICTION

ANNA LEE SERIES: *Dupe*, 1980; *Bad Company*, 1982; *Stalker*, 1984; *Head Case*, 1985; *Under Contract*, 1986; *Backhand*, 1991

EVA WYLIE SERIES: *Bucket Nut*, 1992; *Monkey Wrench*, 1994; *Musclebound*, 1997

NONSERIES NOVELS: *Gimme More*, 2000

SHORT FICTION: *Murder and Company*, 1988 (with others); *Lucky Dip, and other Stories*, 2003

OTHER MAJOR WORKS

NOVELS: *Rift*, 1988

EDITED TEXTS: *First Culprit: An Annual of Crime Stories*, 1992 (with Michael Lewin); *Second Culprit: An Annual of Crime Stories*, 1993 (with Lewin); *Third Culprit: An Annual of Crime Stories*, 1994 (with Lewin)

BIBLIOGRAPHY

Breen, Jon. Review of *The Lucky Dip, and Other Stories*, by Liza Cody. *Ellery Queen's Mystery Magazine* (July, 2004). Breen notes that while most of the stories in this collection involve criminal activity, a few are not traditional representations of the genre.

Hadley, Mary. *British Women Mystery Writers: Six Authors of Detective Fiction with Female Sleuths.* Jefferson, N.C.: McFarland, 2002. Examines the evolution of the female detective in British fiction from the 1960's to the year 2000. One of the featured authors is Cody.

Irons, Glenwood, and Joan Worthing Roberts. "From Spinster to Hipster: The Suitability of Miss Marple and Anna Lee." In *Feminism in Women's Detective Fiction*, edited by Glenwood Irons. Toronto: University of Toronto Press, 1995. Compares Anna Lee to her detective predecessor, Agatha Christie's Miss Marple, acknowledging that Cody has updated the genre by coarsening the image of the female investigator.

Klein, Kathleen Gregory. *The Woman Detective: Gender and Genre.* Urbana: University of Illinois Press, 1988. Views private investigator Anna Lee as less capable than her male complements in the genre. Questions whether Cody has truly liberated the female detective or fallen back on stereotypes.

_____, ed. *Great Women Mystery Writers: Classic to Contemporary.* Westport, Conn.: Greenwood Press, 1994. Contains a biocritical essay on Cody.

Publishers Weekly. Review of *Monkey Wrench*, by Liza Cody. 242, no. 15 (April, 1995): 57. Praises the authenticity of Cody's Eva Wylie and her environs, the seedy London district where wrestlers, drug users, and prostitutes converge.

Zvirin, Stephanie. Review of *Musclebound*, by Liza Cody. *Booklist* 93, no. 22 (August, 1997): 1882. Notes the manner in which the skeptical former wrestler and amateur sleuth, Eva Wylie, departs from Cody's previous heroine, the analytic private investigator Anna Lee.

MARGARET COEL

Born: Denver, Colorado; October 11, 1937
Type of plot: Amateur sleuth

PRINCIPAL SERIES

Vicky Holden and Father John O'Malley, 1995-

PRINCIPAL SERIES CHARACTERS

VICKY HOLDEN is an Arapaho attorney who has returned to the Wind River Reservation area in Wyoming to practice law. She hopes to help her people but faces traditional cultural views that now see her as an outsider because she divorced her husband and studied and lived within the white culture. With her two children, Lucas and Susan, now grown, she tries to make her own way personally and professionally. Her efforts to aid her Arapaho clients, usually individuals with little money or social standing, lead to professional interactions with Father John O'Malley and to a strong romantic interest in him.

FATHER JOHN O'MALLEY, a Jesuit priest and recovering alcoholic, arrives at St. Francis Mission on the Wind River Reservation seeking a refuge where he can carry out his efforts at recovery. Before long, he develops great respect and fondness for the Arapahos, and they in turn come to trust him. He reciprocates Vicky's romantic feelings for him, but they both know that his vow of celibacy and his dedication to his priestly vocation preclude any sort of sexual relationship.

TED GIANELLI is the local Federal Bureau of Investigation agent. A friend of Father John, he shares the priest's love of Italian opera. Much of his time is spent trying to persuade Father John to stay out of harm's way as the priest becomes involved in criminal cases that threaten his life as well as Vicky's.

BEN HOLDEN is Vicky's former husband and the father of her children. Although Ben is well respected by most people who know him, his heavy drinking and physical abuse of Vicky destroyed their marriage. Ben makes occasional appearances in the novels until he is murdered in *The Shadow Dancer* (2002).

ADAM LONE EAGLE is an attorney whose personal and professional relationship with Vicky fluctuates greatly. In *Killing Raven* (2003), he persuades Vicky to take a position at a new casino, inadvertently putting her in a position that could lead to her death. In later novels he becomes Vicky's lover and law partner, although the relationship inevitably seems like something of a consolation prize for Vicky, who cannot have the man whom she most wants.

CONTRIBUTION

Margaret Coel's series about Vicky Holden and Father John O'Malley is among the most culturally rich of several detective series featuring Native American detectives. The series places a high premium on psychological realism, depicting in depth the main characters in their complex mixtures of desires, ambitions, fears, and anxieties. The author to whom Coel is most often compared is Tony Hillerman.

Coel has kept the Holden and O'Malley series flowing smoothly and steadily, producing about a novel per year since 1995 as well as short stories about the characters. The novels have usually been reviewed favorably, with positive comments focusing on Coel's realistic character development and her accurate depictions of Arapaho history and culture. Although not Native American, Coel has engaged in extensive research on Arapaho culture and history for years. She regularly visits the Wind River Reservation and St. Stephen's Mission (the model for the fictional St. Francis Mission).

Coel has made the best-seller lists of such newspapers as *The New York Times*, *Los Angeles Times*, and *Denver Post*. Both *The Spirit Woman* (2000) and *The Shadow Dancer* won the Colorado Book Award, with the former also winning the Willa Cather Award for best novel of the West.

BIOGRAPHY

Margaret Coel was born Margaret Speas on October 11, 1937, in Denver, Colorado, to Samuel F. Speas and Margaret (McCloskey) Speas. She earned a bachelor's degree at Marquette University in Milwaukee, Wisconsin, where she met her future husband, George W. Coel. They married on July 22, 1962, and had three

children, William, Kristin, and Lisa.

Coel began a career as a journalist in 1960, reporting for the *Westminster Journal* in Westminster, Colorado. She worked for the *Boulder Daily Camera* in Boulder as a feature writer from 1972 to 1975. She then continued writing as a freelancer and, over the years, occasionally served as a writing instructor and lecturer at the University of Colorado and other institutions.

Coel's interest in Western history grew out of her family background. A fourth-generation member of a pioneer family, she has given credit to her father, who worked for a railroad, for her early interest in history and Native Americans. Her father's stories about railroading in the West led to a collaborative effort between daughter and father, *Goin' Railroading: A Century on the Colorado High Iron* (1986). Several years earlier, she had published her first book, *Chief Left Hand: Southern Arapaho* (1981), about a chief who was mortally wounded at the Sand Creek massacre in 1864 in Colorado.

Deeply interested in the history of the Native Americans of Colorado, Coel has explained that her special interest in Arapahos derives from her recognition of their history as traders and their profound spirituality. After attending a lecture by novelist Tony Hillerman, famous for his novels dealing with Navajo culture, Coel began considering writing fiction. She spent about four years working on her first novel, *The Eagle Catcher* (1995). Berkley Publishing decided to publish it, but only in paperback. When the book became one of the winners in a contest sponsored by the University Press of Colorado, the university press agreed to release it in hardback. The substantial sales led Berkley to publish each subsequent novel in the series first in hardback and later in paperback.

In 1995, Coel began concentrating on fiction, publishing about a novel per year about Vicky Holden and Father John. She has also started writing a series of short stories about these characters, basing the plots of each story on one of the ten Arapaho commandments, which are similar to, but worded sightly differently from, the standard Judeo-Christian commandments.

The Holden and O'Malley series reflects several aspects of Coel's life. One is Coel's long-term study of Arapaho history and culture, consistently demonstrated in the many aspects of Arapaho culture present in and often at the heart of the narratives. Others include her Catholicism and Irish heritage. A lifelong Catholic, she grew up attending Catholic schools in Denver and joined an Irish-Catholic parish. She was not able to follow several relatives to the Jesuit-run Regis University in Denver (which then admitted only men), so she attended another Jesuit institution, Marquette. However, Regis is the site of an occasional visit from Father John, whose membership in the Jesuits reflects the author's long-term respect for the religious order. Father John's love for opera and his past experience as a history teacher also are reflections of the author's interests.

ANALYSIS

Margaret Coel's stories feature Vicky Holden and Father John O'Malley as amateur sleuths from widely different backgrounds: a divorced Arapaho female attorney and a Boston-Irish Jesuit priest. The pairing, which quickly assumes the level of close friendship and mutual respect and before long tempts both toward a romantic entanglement that they cannot honorably consummate, establishes dual cultural contexts for the stories. Between Vicky and Father John, though, there is no clash of cultures, as Father John, deeply interested in Arapaho history and profoundly respectful of the tribe's culture, quickly achieves status as the "Indian priest."

Although Vicky and Father John do not experience a cultural divide, cultural clashes emerge in other areas of their lives. Vicky, having been immersed for years in a white culture during law school and then at a Denver law firm, and now known to her people as Hi sei ci nihi, or Woman Alone, because of her divorce, is treated as more of an outsider by the Arapahos than is the Boston Jesuit. Vicky's last name, "Holden," represents her attempts to hold on to her cultural heritage despite her lengthy stay outside it. Meanwhile, Father John feels largely separated from his Jesuit community because of his alcoholism and his feeling that his superiors have little confidence in him.

These intercultural and psychological dimensions reflect Coel's belief that the success of a mystery story depends on characters who resonate with readers. Reading Coel's stories is like following two close friends through the ups and downs of their lives and rooting for them to find happiness and to triumph in their risky efforts to bring criminals to justice and exonerate the innocent.

Because neither Vicky nor Father John is a professional detective or private investigator, their forays into criminal investigation grow out of their broader desire to help others, Vicky by assisting her usually poverty-stricken clients and Father John by helping his parishioners. Father John consistently defines parishioners far more broadly than just those who attend Mass at St. Francis, a practice that helps lead to the great trust that the Arapaho community places in him. Similarly, Vicky regularly takes on clients that no one else wants, much to the chagrin of her law partner, Adam Lone Eagle.

The popularity of the series also grows out of the extensive cultural and historical context provided within the stories. History is regularly surfacing in the present, and cultural attitudes ranging from deep respect for elders to a spiritual intermingling of traditional and Christian rituals permeate the novels and short stories. These elements are usually integrated effectively and accurately into the stories, the result of Coel's care in planning her stories and her wide-ranging and ongoing research. In addition to reading extensively about Arapaho history, Coel regularly visits the reservation and consults with both Arapahos and Jesuits to ensure that the stories are respectful of Arapaho ways and realistically depict what an Arapaho woman and a Jesuit priest might credibly do.

In addition, many of the stories involve current issues affecting Native Americans as well as other segments of American society. Land and water rights, alcoholism, drug abuse, building of casinos on reservation land, poverty, efforts to retain one's cultural heritage, ownership of cultural artifacts, and sexual abuse of minors by priests, as well as many other contemporary issues, appear within Coel's stories, further wedding the past to the present.

THE STORY TELLER

One of the most culturally rich novels in the series, *The Story Teller* (1998), finds Vicky and Father John trying to solve the murder of a graduate student, Todd

Harris. Harris was planning to manage a new Arapaho museum on the grounds of St. Francis Mission after he completed his graduate work, but while doing research for his thesis, he discovered an extremely valuable ledger.

The novel draws heavily on Coel's earlier research into the Sand Creek massacre for the book *Chief Left Hand*. It also reflects the growing interest in Native American cultural and funerary objects and the application of the Native American Graves Protection and Repatriation Act. The ledger, a book designed for recording expenditures and revenue and used to draw pictures depicting important events, is the catalyst for the mystery.

This ledger, which contains information about the Sand Creek massacre, would prove that Arapahos as

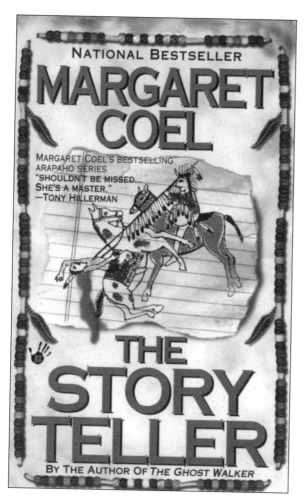

well as Cheyennes died during the attack, a fact now widely accepted but earlier in dispute. The book is of enormous financial value, which provides the primary reason for the theft and murders that ensue.

WIFE OF MOON

Wife of Moon (2004) fuses past and present through a pair of crimes related to photographs. The museum at St. Francis Mission is displaying photographs by the famous photographer Edward S. Curtis. A descendant of the tribal chief in one of the photographs is murdered, and the library curator is missing.

The novel conveys the ongoing romantic tension between Father John and Vicky, who attempt to restrain their love for each other by remaining apart, but who are brought together by the murder and Vicky's defense of a husband accused of murdering his wife. At the same time, Adam Lone Eagle expresses increased romantic interest in Vicky while pushing for them to become law partners. Again Coel synthesizes the main characters' interrelationships, mysteries that must be solved, and the merging of past and present.

THE DROWNING MAN

The Drowning Man (2006) moves Vicky and Father John further along their life paths and seemingly farther apart. Vicky is established in both a romantic relationship and a professional partnership with Adam Lone Eagle. Neither arrangement, though, is going particularly well. Father John is worried that his years at St. Francis Mission may be coming to an end, as he finally has an assistant, Father Ian McCauley, who is both competent and seemingly content to be at the mission, making him a viable possibility as a replacement.

The mystery turns on a large petroglyph called the Drowning Man that is cut out of a cliff and stolen. At the same time, Vicky is called on to reopen the case of Travis Birdsong, who is serving time for manslaughter. He is believed to have killed his partner after they stole a similar petroglyph seven years earlier. Vicky believes that Travis is innocent of manslaughter, even if he was involved in the theft, and, much against the wishes of both her partner and the Arapaho elders, agrees to help him. The two petroglyph thefts turn out to be related, and Vicky's actions put her life in serious jeopardy, which means that Father John also faces great danger in coming to her aid.

The stealing of the petroglyph in Coel's novel reflects the real-life need to protect Native American artifacts from theft by unscrupulous collectors. The novel also touches on the issue of Native American land rights and the sex abuse scandal that has rocked the Catholic Church. Complicating Father John's attempts to reach out to Arapaho youth on the reservation is his discovery that the elderly priest who has come to the reservation, supposedly to live out his final days, is guilty of having molested juveniles. As in the previous novels, Coel manages to bring the past vividly into the present and confront the challenge of maintaining past traditions while addressing current problems.

Edward J. Rielly

PRINCIPAL MYSTERY AND DETECTIVE FICTION

VICKY HOLDEN AND FATHER JOHN O'MALLEY SERIES: *The Eagle Catcher*, 1995; *The Ghost Walker*, 1996; *The Dream Stalker*, 1997; *The Story Teller*, 1998; *The Lost Bird*, 1999; *The Spirit Woman*, 2000; *The Thunder Keeper*, 2001; *The Shadow Dancer*, 2002; *Killing Raven*, 2003; *Wife of Moon*, 2004; *Eye of the Wolf*, 2005; *The Drowning Ma*n, 2006; *The Girl with Braided Hair*, 2007

TEN COMMANDMENT SERIES: *Dead End*, 1997; *Hole in the Wall*, 1998; *Honor*, 1999; *Stolen Smoke*, 2000; *My Last Goodbye*, 2002; *Bad Heart*, 2004; *Day of Rest*, 2005; *Nobody's Going to Cry*, 2006

OTHER MAJOR WORKS

NOVELS: *The Sunken Sailor*, 2004 (with others)

NONFICTION: *Chief Left Hand: Southern Arapaho*, 1981; *The Next 100 Years: A Report*, 1983; *The Tivoli: Bavaria in the Rockies*, 1985 (with Jane Barker and Karen Gilleland); *Goin' Railroading: A Century on the Colorado High Iron*, 1986 (with Sam Speas; revised as *Goin' Railroading: Two Generations of Colorado Stories*, 1991); *A New Westminister*, 1987; *Four Hundred Fifty Best Sales Letters for Every Selling Situation*, 1991 (with Gilleland); *The Pride of Our People: The Colorado State Capitol*, 1992

BIBLIOGRAPHY

Browne, Ray B. *Murder on the Reservation: American Indian Crime Fiction*. Madison: University of Wisconsin Press/Popular Press, 2004. Includes discussions of Coel under a variety of headings, most usefully in the sections "The Making of the Author" and "Cultural Background." Indexed.

Coel, Margaret. Margaret Coel. http://www.margaret coel.com. Author's Web site includes substantial information about the author and her books, interviews and articles, and links to other sites, including one for the Wind River Reservation.

Donaldson, John K. "Native American Sleuths: Following in the Footsteps of the Indian Guides." In *Telling the Stories: Essays on American Indian Literatures and Cultures*, edited by Elizabeth Hoffman Nelson and Malcolm A. Nelson. New York: Peter Lang, 2001. Discusses only books in which the central character is a Native American and therefore does not discuss Coel's novels, despite Vicky Holden sharing sleuthing duties with Father John O'Malley, but provides good information on the subgenre of Native American detective fiction. Indexed.

"Margaret Coel: Love of History Leads to Mysteries." *Wyoming Library Roundup* 48, no. 4 (Fall, 2006): 5-7. Discusses the biographical factors that led Coel to begin writing about Arapahos.

Trenholm, Virginia Cole. *The Arapahoes, Our People*. 1970. Reprint. Norman: University of Oklahoma Press, 1986. Traces Arapaho history from prehistoric times to the late twentieth century with considerable attention to the Arapaho way of life. Illustrations, maps, indexed.

OCTAVUS ROY COHEN

Born: Charleston, South Carolina; June 26, 1891
Died: Los Angeles, California; January 6, 1959
Types of plot: Private investigator; amateur sleuth; police procedural

PRINCIPAL SERIES

David Carroll, 1919-1922
Jim Hanvey, 1923-1934
Max Gold, 1945-1947
Marty Walsh, 1948-1950

PRINCIPAL SERIES CHARACTERS

DAVID CARROLL, the slender, boyish, blue-eyed star detective of Berkeley City, is a nationally famous private investigator. He respects the methodical procedures of his police counterparts and sometime allies, but his own gifts lie in the use of psychology and intuition.

JIM HANVEY, a large, somewhat pear-shaped man with disturbing fishlike eyes, is deliberate of movement, though not as slow-witted as he appears. A large gold toothpick, which was given to him by one of his favorite criminals, hangs on a gold chain from his vest; when not otherwise occupied—with food, observation, or "figgering"—he constantly plays with it.

MAX GOLD is a black-eyed, black-haired detective with the New York City Police Department's homicide squad. Laconic, yet unfailingly polite, he methodically eliminates false leads, refusing to jump to conclusions, although he usually does not arrive at the solution solely through his own efforts.

MARTY WALSH, of the Los Angeles Police Department, looks more like a real estate salesperson than a police detective. He is "short and slender and neat," but his keen eyes belie his innocuous appearance.

CONTRIBUTION

Although he was more famous for his southern black dialect fiction of the 1920's and early 1930's, which he considered neither biased nor derogatory, Octavus Roy Cohen also created a memorable detective. *Jim Hanvey, Detective* (1923), the collection of short fiction that first recounted the adventures of the big, slow-moving, cigar-smoking sleuth, was considered by Ellery Queen to be "a book of historical value with a high quality of literary style." Two of the short stories, "Common Stock" and "Pink Bait," were later chosen by Eugene Thwing as part of his anthology of mystery fiction, *The World's Best One Hundred Detective Stories* (1929). In addition, Cohen's work represented one of the early, minor crossovers to the more realistic detective fiction of Dashiell Hammett and Raymond Chandler.

BIOGRAPHY

Born and reared in Charleston, South Carolina, Octavus Roy Cohen attended Porter Military Academy, from which he was graduated in 1908. After receiving his bachelor of science degree from Clemson College in 1911, Cohen worked first as a civil engineer, then as a journalist, before he passed the bar in 1913. Two years later, he decided to become a writer full time. In October of 1914, he was married to Inez Lopez; they had one son, named for his father. In 1935, the family moved to New York, where Cohen continued his writing career; later, they moved to Los Angeles.

Cohen's first book, *The Other Woman* (1917; with J. U. Giesy), marked the beginning of his prolific literary career. According to *The New York Times*, at the time of his death he had written at least 250 short stories and contributed fiction to *The Saturday Evening Post* and *Collier's* magazine as well as producing "more than sixty books [and] five plays." In addition, he had written for the highly popular *Amos 'n' Andy* radio show from 1945 to 1946. One of his plays, *Come Seven* (pr. 1920), which was adapted from his novel of the same name, had a run of more than seventy performances on Broadway. Cohen died of a stroke at the age of sixty-seven in Los Angeles.

ANALYSIS

Critics have received Octavus Roy Cohen's detective fiction with mixed emotions. Anthony Boucher considered Cohen, in his early phase, one of the precursors of "the tough, realistic school"; others have been less sure of his contribution.

The uncertainty stems in part from the fact that Cohen was not an innovator. Rather, he was a skilled recreator of an established formula who used some interesting variations that seem to prefigure other later techniques. His best-known creation, Jim Hanvey, remained squarely within the tradition of what Julian Symons calls the detective as "Plain Man." Unlike the detectives modeled on Sherlock Holmes, the Plain Man had no superhuman powers of ratiocination; nor did he share the Holmesian detective's lack of "emotional attachments and . . . interest in everyday life." Hanvey is a clever and resourceful man, but his investigative ability—like that of Sam Spade or Philip Marlowe—is more the result of a large store of common sense, an excellent memory for faces, and an acquaintance with most of the important members of the criminal world.

Even his childlike enjoyment of the simple things—

Scene from Octavus Roy Cohen's 1922 story "Common Stock" illustrated by Ernest Fuhr in Saturday Evening Post.
(Library of Congress)

especially all things related to eating—precludes his membership among Symons's "Superman" detectives. The crude Hanvey can often prove embarrassing to his more refined companions. In "Common Stock," for example, Gerald Corwin, whose "every cultured gesture" marks him "unmistakably a gentleman," is appalled by Hanvey's habit of "sitting by the hour toying with his [gold] toothpick." When someone mentions that "the weapon might better be concealed," Hanvey is honestly surprised that anyone would want to hide "absolutely the swellest toothpick in captivity." Then, too, his table manners are less than desirable, since "eatin' ain't no art with me. It's a pleasure."

THE CRIMSON ALIBI

The Crimson Alibi (1919), the first novel in the David Carroll series, contains—although the suspects all seem to be wronged innocents, who, in the best tradition of mystery fiction, would be more than justified in killing the unpopular and unscrupulous Joshua Quincy—a backbone of corrupt, highly placed citizens and tough-minded investigators that would later be fleshed out in the American subgenres. Quincy's lawyer, the eminent Thaddeus Standish, though less than fully involved in his client's less savory schemes, nevertheless knew of them—though not "in an official capacity." The police, though considered honest public servants, delight in grilling suspects and using snitches.

The murder, too, foreshadows those of later fiction. Neither mysterious poisons nor other exotic manners of dealing death are employed: Quincy is felled by a silver dagger, his own possession, which has been wiped clean of fingerprints.

LOVE HAS NO ALIBI

Particularly in his later works, Cohen could define a character or create an atmosphere with a few sure strokes; little time is wasted on extraneous details. In *Love Has No Alibi* (1946), for example, one of the least likely murder suspects, Dr. Arthur Maybank, is a mousy little man, rejected even by the army, who has "scraped and struggled and sweated and slaved" to survive; his sparse hair and slumped, skinny shoulders belong to a man who has never had "even the hope of having something." When accused of murder, he is "bewildered," like a man in a trance or "a shock victim." The club where most of the action of the novel takes place has a cabaret in which the dancers are "young and beautifully proportioned and . . . lovely unless, or until, you [happen] to look at their eyes, which [are] hard and wise and blank"—a proper setting for a group of citizens who almost all are hiding shady pasts.

Cohen's crime fiction is an odd cross between the pure-puzzle and the more character-oriented genres. Cohen rigorously followed the fair-play rule of giving his reader all the information necessary to solve the case; all that remains necessary is the kaleidoscopic twist—a clue placed in its proper context—for the case to be solved. *A Bullet for My Love* (1950) hinges on a married couple's special way of telling time, mentioned early in the story, for its solution, while "Common Stock" seems to be a straightforward account of a failed job, until Hanvey reveals that he has been hired to carry the all-important proxy instead of merely acting as guard to the ostensible messenger, Gerald Corwin.

Nevertheless, some psychological development has its place. The denouement of *Love Has No Alibi* focuses on the step-by-step manner in which an ordinary citizen begins a series of murders, almost by accident, while "Pink Bait" tells the story of Tommy Braden's "perfect" con based on the ordinary person's desire to name-drop. A nice touch to the latter work is that Cohen tells it entirely from the con artist's point of view. In addition, even though Jim Hanvey foils Tommy's scheme, the detective's sense of justice allows him to watch over his foe's interests as well as his client's—he warns Tommy that it is dangerous to cash a bad check written by his "victims."

In his later work, Cohen released the reins on his tendency toward sentimentality. Increasingly, his relatively tough-minded police and private investigators gave way to "the slick glamour" of bumbling but good-hearted all-American heroes who unexpectedly manage to solve the crime; noble, innocent heroines; fallen women with hearts of gold; dyed-in-the-wool villains, who are not necessarily the murderers; and polite police officers. As Boucher notes, Cohen wrote about "a set of characters with too much money, too much charm and too much beauty," making them likable and telling "their story at . . . a smooth, fast tempo with . . . lightly amusing dialogue."

DANGEROUS LADY

Throughout most of his career, perhaps as a result of his journalistic and later dramatic experience, Cohen wrote crisply and clearly. Little time is wasted on extraneous details; he is sparing of words, and those he uses he uses to great effect. Unlike *The Crimson Alibi*, which occasionally becomes mired in descriptions, the "glamour" novels have almost no descriptive passages. Details are either implied or given in conversation. In *Dangerous Lady* (1946), for example, the oddities of a relationship between an heiress and a fortune hunter are related not by an omniscient narrator but by the torch singer who loves "the louse": "All of a sudden he slapped her. Smacko! Twice. And hard. She took it. Then she walked around the car and climbed in . . . and they drove off."

Although Cohen was not a major innovator in the detective genre, his extensive canon provided considerable entertainment to legions of mystery readers, and his minor variations on an established formula proved durable, appearing later in the hard-boiled subgenre. Jim Hanvey proved to be a popular and unforgettable figure; in addition to his printed adventures, he appeared in a film, *Jim Hanvey, Detective* (1937), and in a radio play, *The Townsend Murder Mystery* (1933). Although much of Cohen's work is now nearly impossible to find, it deserves its place in the annals of detective and mystery fiction.

Ginia Henderson

PRINCIPAL MYSTERY AND DETECTIVE FICTION
　DAVID CARROLL SERIES: *The Crimson Alibi*, 1919; *Gray Dusk*, 1920; *Six Seconds of Darkness*, 1921; *Midnight*, 1922
　JIM HANVEY SERIES: *Jim Hanvey, Detective*, 1923; *The May Day Mystery*, 1929; *The Backstage Mystery*, 1930 (also known as *Curtain at Eight*); *Star of Earth*, 1932; *The Townsend Murder Mystery*, 1933; *Scrambled Yeggs*, 1934
　MAX GOLD SERIES: *Danger in Paradise*, 1944; *Love Has No Alibi*, 1946; *Don't Ever Love Me*, 1947
　LIEUTENANT MARTY WALSH SERIES: *More Beautiful than Murder*, 1948; *My Love Wears Black*, 1948; *A Bullet for My Love*, 1950
　NONSERIES NOVELS: *The Other Woman*, 1917

(with J. U. Giesy); *The Iron Chalice*, 1925; *The Outer Gate*, 1927; *Child of Evil*, 1936; *I Love You Again*, 1937 (also known as *There's Always Time to Die*); *East of Broadway*, 1938; *Strange Honeymoon*, 1939; *Romance in Crimson*, 1940 (also known as *Murder in Season*); *Lady in Armor*, 1941; *Sound of Revelry*, 1943; *Romance in the First Degree*, 1944; *Dangerous Lady*, 1946; *Lost Lady*, 1951; *The Corpse That Walked*, 1951; *Love Can Be Dangerous*, 1955 (also known as *The Intruder*)

OTHER SHORT FICTION: *Detours*, 1927; *Cameos*, 1931

OTHER MAJOR WORKS

NOVELS: *Come Seven*, 1920; *Sunclouds*, 1924; *The Other Tomorrow*, 1927; *Spring Tide*, 1928; *The Light Shines Through*, 1928; *The Valley of Olympus*, 1929; *Epic Peters, Pullman Porter*, 1930; *Lilies of the Alley*, 1931; *Scarlet Woman*, 1934; *Transient Lady*, 1934; *Back to Nature*, 1935; *With Benefit of Clergy*, 1935; *Kid Tinsel*, 1941; *Borrasca*, 1953

SHORT FICTION: *Polished Ebony*, 1919; *Highly Colored*, 1921; *Assorted Chocolates*, 1922; *Dark Days and Black Knights*, 1923; *Bigger and Blacker*, 1925; *Black and Blue*, 1926; *Florian Slappey Goes Abroad*, 1928; *Carbon Copies*, 1932; *Florian Slappey*, 1938

PLAYS: *The Crimson Alibi*, pr. 1919; *Come Seven*, pr. 1920; *Shadows*, pr. 1920; *The Scourge*, pr. 1920; *Every Saturday Night*, pr. 1921; *The Melancholy Dame*, pr. 1927; *Alias Mrs. Roberts*, pr. 1928

RADIO PLAYS: *The Townsend Murder Mystery*, 1933; The *Amos 'n' Andy* series, 1945-1946

BIBLIOGRAPHY

Bailey, Frankie Y. *Out of the Woodpile: Black Characters in Crime and Detective Fiction*. New York: Greenwood, 1991. This discussion of how African American characters were handled in crime fiction contains some discussion of Cohen's work.

Barfield, Ray. *Listening to Radio, 1920-1950*. Westport, Conn.: Praeger, 1996. Barfield describes old-time radio, including the *Amos 'n' Andy* series.

Beidler, Philip D. "Introduction: Alabama Flowering I." In *Many Voices, Many Rooms: A New Anthology of Alabama Writers*, edited by Philip D. Beidler. Tuscaloosa: University of Alabama Press, 1998. Cohen is one of four Alabama writers compared in this essay, which precedes his "The Fatted Half."

Panek, LeRoy Lad. *The Origins of the American Detective Story*. Jefferson, N.C.: McFarland, 2006. Study of the beginnings and establishment of American detective-fiction conventions, focusing especially on the replacement of the police by the private detective and the place of forensic science in the genre. Provides a context for understanding Cohen.

Priestman, Martin, ed. *The Cambridge Companion to Crime Fiction*. New York: Cambridge University Press, 2003. Chapter on black crime fiction provides a contrast to Cohen's early works and provides perspective on Cohen.

Van Dover, J. K., and John F. Jebb. *Isn't Justice Always Unfair? The Detective in Southern Literature*. Bowling Green, Ohio: Bowling Green State University Popular Press, 1996. Critical examination of the tradition of Southern detective fiction. Sheds light on the context in which Cohen wrote.

G. D. H. COLE and MARGARET COLE

MARGARET COLE
Born: Cambridge, England; May 6, 1893
Died: Goring-on-Thames, Oxfordshire, England; May 7, 1980

G. D. H. COLE
Born: Cambridge, England; September 25, 1889
Died: London, England; January 14, 1959
Types of plot: Police procedural; amateur sleuth

PRINCIPAL SERIES

Superintendent Henry Wilson, 1923-1942
Everard Blatchington, 1926-1935
Dr. Benjamin Tancred, 1935-1936
Mrs. Elizabeth Warrender, 1938-1941

PRINCIPAL SERIES CHARACTER

SUPERINTENDENT HENRY WILSON of Scotland Yard is neither flamboyant nor eccentric. He is a perfect example of the typical English senior police officer of the interwar period. He is competent, thorough, and respected by his colleagues.

CONTRIBUTION

G. D. H. Cole and Margaret Cole contributed little that had an immediate impact on the mystery and detective genre. Although their thirty-odd full-length novels and several collections of short stories are well written, they are, on the surface, very conventional and often predictable. The writing of mysteries was for the Coles an avocation, an escape from a very active involvement in the academic, political, and economic life of Great Britain between the two world wars.

The Coles shared the task of writing, and while one might be responsible for the completion of a particular story, the other never failed to make suggestions or actual contributions to the narrative. The assumption on the part of some critics that their fiction contains few references to their political and economic thought betrays a superficial treatment of their work. Among the most prominent and outspoken socialist thinkers in modern England, the Coles infused their fictional works with ideas, experiences, and bias that give each novel or short story a special significance. Through their polished and often amusing prose, the mystery story becomes an unconscious vehicle for the dissemination of socialist dogma.

BIOGRAPHY

Although he was born in Cambridge, England, late in 1889, George Douglas Howard Cole spent most of his life in Oxford, first as a student and later as a professor. It was during his undergraduate years that Cole developed his passion for socialism. First as a member of the Fabian Society and then as a worker in the Independent Labour Party, he began to make a name for himself among the radical elements in Great Britain in the years before World War I. It was while he was a member of the Fabian Research Department that he met Margaret Isabel Postgate, to whom he was married in 1918.

Born Margaret Isabel Postgate, Margaret Cole was also a native of Cambridge and took her degree at Cambridge University and served as classical mistress at St. Paul's Girls' School in London between 1914 and 1916. Like her husband, Margaret Cole was very interested in adult education, and for a quarter of a century she helped combat illiteracy. Although the Coles became permanent residents of Oxford in 1925, when G. D. H. Cole became a fellow of University College and university reader in economics, they kept a residence in London and remained actively involved in the political life of the capital. Three children did not deter either Cole from pursuing a career, remaining involved in socialist circles, and publishing a remarkable number of books and pamphlets.

During his years at Oxford, G. D. H. Cole distinguished himself as a leading economist, and he gathered around him a group of students and teachers who still remain very active in the political and economic life of Great Britain. G. D. H. Cole died in 1959 after a long illness. Awarded the Order of the British Empire in 1965 and made a dame of the British Empire in 1970, Margaret Cole survived her husband by twenty-one years, dying in a nursing home at Goring-on-Thames (near Oxford) in 1980.

ANALYSIS

G. D. H. Cole's career as a writer of mystery and detective fiction began in 1923 as a cure for the boredom that attended a long recuperation from a mild case of pneumonia. Detective stories were the rage among members of the British intelligentsia in the years between the two world wars, and Cole, who was an avid reader of mystery stories, proposed to try his hand at writing one. Spurred by his wife's contention that he would not finish it, Cole quickly completed *The Brooklyn Murders* (1923). It marked the first appearance of Superintendent Henry Wilson, and it was the only work to which Cole ever willingly made substantial revisions at the request of a publisher. The original draft supposedly contained too many murders.

Already well established as an author of numerous works in the areas of economics and politics, Cole had no difficulty finding a publisher for his first novel. The plot is a simple one, and to a student of detection the murders of the two nephews of Sir Vernon Brooklyn, who are also his heirs, are easily solved. What is important in this work is the examination of greed as a motive for crime. Again and again the Coles would explore this weakness of a capitalist society and its malevolent influence on the human character.

THE DEATH OF A MILLIONAIRE

A second novel, *The Death of a Millionaire* (1925), marked the beginning of the partnership between Cole and his wife. More radical than her husband, and often more intense in her espousal of socialist economic principles, Margaret Cole nevertheless possessed a finely honed sense of humor that somewhat softened her criticism of capitalism in the mysteries she would coauthor.

Corruption in the world of business formed the theme of this second novel, and it is particularly interesting because the reader is given the socialist view of the sordid world of finance with a touch of satire. This lesson in leftist economic theory in no way detracts from the story. The element of humor continued to be an important part of the mysteries written by the

Coles. Many of their characters exhibit that charm and wit so often associated with the British upper classes. The repartee of the gentleman's club and the college senior common room is often echoed in the remarks of the men and women who people their books. With their second mystery the Coles began to experiment with techniques for developing memorable characters using a minimum of words. Over the years they were able to create a host of major and minor actors in their mystery novels who were genuinely alive to their readers.

THE BLATCHINGTON TANGLE

This talent for creating memorable portraits with a minimum of words is ably demonstrated in *The Blatchington Tangle* (1926) when Henry Wilson, the professional police officer, encounters Everard Blatchington, the amateur sleuth. Among the protagonists in this mystery is a rather obnoxious American who immediately becomes a suspect when the body of a crooked financier is found in Lord Blatchington's library. Although G. D. H. Cole may not be accurately described as anti-American, he did have suspicions about the economic policies of the United States in the years after World War I. This attitude hardened into open hostility during and following World War II. His American suspect seems to combine in his personality every unpleasant characteristic associated with his fellow countrymen.

GREEK TRAGEDY

It is interesting to contrast this almost pathological distrust of capitalism in all of its forms with the apologetic tone assumed by the Coles with respect to communism. In *Greek Tragedy* (1939), they offered their readers a glowing endorsement of the Left. In a workers' paradise there might be no Blatchington rubies to tempt a criminal to commit murder.

THE MURDER AT CROME HOUSE

With the publication of *The Murder at Crome House* (1927), the Coles seemed to settle down to the writing of detective fiction that would appeal to an ever-growing audience, instead of using the mystery novel as a device for pleading the cause of socialism. Drawing on their varied experiences, they also began to experiment with various techniques of detection and literary devices that render their novels among the most intellectually stimulating in the genre. The locales of the Coles' mysteries written between 1927 and 1943 are as diverse as the crimes they sought to unravel. *The Murder at Crome House* and *Double Blackmail* (1939) are set in country houses and combine romance with amateur detection. This pleasant mixture is made all the more palatable by a generous portion of humor.

SCANDAL AT SCHOOL

The Coles often used laughter both to lighten the varied tragedies that formed the core of their novels and to give depth to the characters they created with such care. *Scandal at School* (1935) contains an air of authenticity born of a long association with the academic world. G. D. H. Cole was first and foremost a teacher, and it is for his brilliant performance as a lecturer that he is most fondly remembered. Margaret Cole also was no stranger to the classroom. Using the innocence of childhood, they construct a gruesome crime that almost baffles Blatchington. Throughout the mystery, the antics of the students and the responses of their teachers and the other adults add the touch of humor that is so necessary to relieve the tension.

POISON IN THE GARDEN SUBURB

From time to time the Coles explored problems that required a depth of knowledge beyond their areas of expertise. With the thoroughness of first-class scholars they mastered a number of fields and then used their ability to produce remarkable mysteries. In 1929, a year before Dorothy L. Sayers published her classic mystery, *Strong Poison*, the Coles won critical acclaim for their latest addition to Superintendent Wilson's adventures, *Poison in the Garden Suburb*. The knowledge of toxicology displayed by the Coles was truly remarkable—indicative of the care they took while writing their books. While exploring a new subject of endeavor, the Coles did not neglect the exploration of characters: *Poison in the Garden Suburb* contains the memorable portrait of Miss Lydia Redford.

The writing of mystery and detective fiction had begun as an avocation, but by 1930 it had come to absorb an increasing amount of the Coles' time and creative energies. The mysteries that appeared over the next five years were well received by the public and the critics. Having achieved popular success, they were able to experiment with new techniques, literary devices, and characters.

BURGLARS IN BUCKS

In *Burglars in Bucks* (1930), the Coles presented their readers with chronological evidence as it would appear to the investigator, in this case Superintendent Wilson. One by one, letters, telegrams, bits of conversations, and other clues are presented in a confusing way. Thus the reader becomes an amateur sleuth, as bewildered as the professional detective.

END OF AN ANCIENT MARINER

The critics found *End of an Ancient Mariner* (1933) somewhat unnerving because the villain is revealed rather early in the story and then the authors proceed to disclose the reasons for his actions. This is a novel of crime and retribution, a psychological mystery and not a mere whodunit. Unfortunately, in places it is rather carelessly written, probably because the Coles were at that time less concerned with polished fiction than with the realities of the Great Depression. It is interesting to note that the least successful of their mysteries were written and published in those years in which the Coles devoted their prime energies to economics and politics for a scholarly audience. In the midst of a world financial crisis, they explored the theme of the corruption of capitalism in their fiction. *Big Business Murder* (1935) is filled with the technical language of finance made simple for the average reader. Satire is employed to unmask the crooks who dominated the world of business. To the informed reader—the audience for whom the Coles preferred to write—it was a very disturbing book.

DR. TANCRED BEGINS AND LAST WILL AND TESTAMENT

Dr. Tancred Begins: Or, The Pendexter Saga, First Canto (1935) introduced a new and very clever sleuth who was featured again the following year in *Last Will and Testament: Or, The Pendexter Saga, Second (and Last) Canto* (1936). Already masters of character analysis, the Coles used their skill to create a wonderful Cornish setting in which Dr. Tancred might solve his mysteries.

Superintendent Wilson, who began his career as a rather two-dimensional character, gained depth and a certain professional dignity in mysteries such as

Corpse in Canonicals (1930); *Death in the Quarry* (1934), in which he is reunited with Everard Blatchington; *The Brothers Sackville* (1937); *Off with Her Head!* (1938); and *Double Blackmail*. In all these tales, the plots are developed with a literary style only rarely marred by a flippancy that some readers might find irritating. The mysteries are usually well planned, always studious in tone, and at times almost poetic in their descriptions of people and places. In some mysteries, such as *Dead Man's Watch* (1931), the characters and their delineation become more important than the story itself.

MURDER AT THE MUNITION WORKS AND KNIFE IN THE DARK

Two of the Coles' final works, *Murder at the Munition Works* (1940) and *Knife in the Dark* (1942), deal with labor, politics, and social problems. The former book is particularly worthy of mention because of the wealth of detail devoted to labor relations. In a Great Britain besieged by fascism, it became a text for popular consumption on the economic theories of the British Left. The Coles' last published mystery novel, *Toper's End* (1942), appeared just as the tide of battle was turning in favor of the Allies. Another mystery, half completed at the time, was never finished, as the Coles turned their energies to helping reshape postwar England. Although his extreme views on many subjects denied G. D. H. Cole a place in the Labour Party government of Clement Attlee, he continued to publish his ideas both in print and from the podium until his death. Margaret Cole carried on her husband's work until her own failing health forced her to retire. It is regrettable that their witty and entertaining works are all but forgotten, relics of a time when crime and its detection was a genteel obsession.

Clifton W. Potter, Jr.

PRINCIPAL MYSTERY AND DETECTIVE FICTION

SUPERINTENDENT HENRY WILSON SERIES: *The Brooklyn Murders*, 1923; *The Death of a Millionaire*, 1925; *Superintendent Wilson's Holiday*, 1928; *The Man from the River*, 1928; *Poison in the Garden Suburb*, 1929; *Corpse in Canonicals*, 1930 (also known as *Corpse in the Constable's Garden*); *Dead Man's Watch*, 1931; *The Great Southern Mystery*, 1931 (also known as *The Walking Corpse*); *End of an Ancient Mariner*, 1933; *Death in the Quarry*, 1934; *Big Business Murder*, 1935; *The Brothers Sackville*, 1937; *The Missing Aunt*, 1938; *Off with Her Head!*, 1938; *Double Blackmail*, 1939; *Greek Tragedy*, 1939; *Counterpoint Murder*, 1940; *Murder at the Munition Works*, 1940; *Wilson and Some Others*, 1940; *Toper's End*, 1942

EVERARD BLATCHINGTON SERIES: *The Blatchington Tangle*, 1926; *Scandal at School*, 1935 (also known as *The Sleeping Death*)

DR. BENJAMIN TANCRED SERIES: *Dr. Tancred Begins: Or, The Pendexter Saga, First Canto*, 1935; *Last Will and Testament: Or, The Pendexter Saga, Second (and Last) Canto*, 1936

MRS. ELIZABETH WARRENDER SERIES: *Mrs. Warrender's Profession*, 1939; *Knife in the Dark*, 1942

NONSERIES NOVELS: *The Murder at Crome House*, 1927; *Burglars in Bucks*, 1930 (also known as *The Berkshire Mystery*); *The Floating Admiral*, 1931 (with others); *Death of a Star*, 1932; *The Affair at Aliquid*, 1933; *Murder in Four Parts*, 1934; *Disgrace to the College*, 1937

OTHER SHORT FICTION: *A Lesson in Crime, and Other Stories*, 1933; *Death in the Tankard*, 1943; *Strychnine Tonic and A Dose of Cyanide*, 1943; *Birthday Gifts, and Other Stories*, 1946

OTHER MAJOR WORKS

NONFICTION: *Rents, Rings, and Houses*, 1923; *The Intelligent Man's Guide Through World Chaos*, 1932 (also known as *A Guide Through World Chaos*); *A Guide to Modern Politics*, 1934; *The Condition of Britain*, 1937

EDITED TEXTS: *The Bolo Book*, 1921; *The Life and Adventures of Peter Porcupine, with Other Records of His Early Career in England and America*, 1927 (by William Cobbett); *The Ormond Poets*, 1927-1928; *Rural Rides in Southern, Western, and Eastern Counties of England, Together with Tours in Scotland and the Northern and Midland Counties of England and Letters from Ireland*, 1930 (by Cobbett); *The Opinions of William Cobbett*, 1944

OTHER MAJOR WORKS (BY G. D. H. COLE)

POETRY: *The Record*, 1912; *New Beginnings and The Record*, 1914; *The Crooked World*, 1933

NONFICTION: 1913-1920 • *The Greater Unionism*, 1913 (with William Mellor); *The World of Labour: A Discussion of the Present and Future of Trade Unionism*, 1913 (revised 1915); *Labour in War Time*, 1915; *Trade Unionism in War Time*, 1915? (with William Mellor); *Self-Government in Industry*, 1917 (revised 1920); *Some Problems of Urban and Rural Industry*, 1917 (with others); *The British Labour Movement: A Syllabus for Study Circles*, 1917 (revised 1922); *The Principles of Socialism*, 1917; *Trade Unionism on the Railways: Its History and Problems*, 1917 (with R. Page Arnot); *An Introduction to Trade Unionism*, 1918 (revised 1929; also known as *Organised Labour*); *Labour in the Commonwealth: A Book for the Younger Generation*, 1918; *The Meaning of Industrial Freedom*, 1918 (with William Mellor); *The Payment of Wages: A Study in Payment by Results Under the Wage-System*, 1918 (revised 1928); *Workers' Control in Industry*, 1919; *Chaos and Order in Industry*, 1920; *Democracy in Industry*, 1920; *Guild Socialism Re-stated*, 1920; *Guild Socialism*, 1920; *Social Theory*, 1920 (revised 1921)

1921-1930 • *Guild Socialism: A Plan for Economic Democracy*, 1921; *The Future of Local Government*, 1921; *Unemployment and Industrial Maintenance*, 1921; *English Economic History*, 1922?; *British Trade Unionism: Problems and Policy*, 1923; *Labour in the Coal-Mining Industry 1914-1921*, 1923; *Out of Work: An Introduction to the Study of Unemployment*, 1923; *Trade Unionism and Munitions*, 1923; *Unemployment*, 1923; *Workshop Organisation*, 1923; *The Life of William Cobbett*, 1924 (revised 1947); *The Place of the Workers' Educational Association in Working Class Education*, 1924?; *A Short History of the British Working Class Movement*, 1925-1927 (revised 1937, 1948); *Robert Owen*, 1925 (also known as *The Life of Robert Owen*); *William Cobbett*, 1925; *Industrial Policy for Socialists*, 1926; *A Select List of Books on Economic and Social History*, 1927 (with H. L. Beales); *The Economic System*, 1927; *What to Read on English Economic History*,

1928; *Politics and Literature*, 1929; *The Next Ten Years of British Social and Economic Policy*, 1929; *Gold, Credit, and Unemployment: Four Essays for Laymen*, 1930

1931-1940 • *The Crisis: What It Is, How It Arose, What to Do*, 1931 (with Ernest Bevin); *Unemployment Problems in 1931*, 1931 (with others); *How Capitalism Works*, 1931; *The Bank of England*, 1932; *Banks and Credit*, 1932; *British Trade and Industry, Past and Future*, 1932; *Economic Tracts for the Times*, 1932; *Modern Theories and Forms of Industrial Organisation*, 1932; *Scope and Method in Social and Political Theory*, 1932; *Some Essentials of Socialist Propaganda*, 1932; *The Essentials of Socialisation*, 1932; *The Gold Standard*, 1932; *Theories and Forms of Political Organisation*, 1932; *War Debts and Reparations: What They Are, Why They Must Be Cancelled*, 1932 (with Richard Seymour Postgate); *What to Read on Economic Problems of Today and Tomorrow*, 1932; *A Plan for Britain*, 1933; *Saving and Spending: Or, The Economics of "Economy,"* 1933; *Socialism in Pictures and Figures*, 1933 (with J. F. Horrabin); *The Intelligent Man's Guide to Europe Today*, 1933 (with Margaret Cole); *The Need for a Socialist Programme*, 1933 (with Dick Mitchison); *What Is This Socialism? Letters to a Young Inquirer*, 1933; *Planning International Trade*, 1934; *Some Relations Between Political and Economic Theory*, 1934; *Studies in World Economics*, 1934; *What Marx Really Meant*, 1934; *A Study-Guide to Socialist Policy*, 1934?; *Marxism*, 1935 (with others); *Principles of Economic Planning*, 1935 (also known as *Economic Planning*); *The Simple Case for Socialism*, 1935; *Fifty Propositions About Money and Production*, 1936; *Practical Economics: Or, Studies in Economic Planning*, 1937; *The People's Front*, 1937; *What Is Ahead of Us?*, 1937 (with others); *Étude du statut de la production et du rôle du capital*, 1938 (with Thomas Nixon Carver and Carl Brinkmann); *Economic Prospects: 1938 and After*, 1938; *Living Wages: The Case for a New Minimum Wage Act*, 1938; *Persons and Periods: Studies*, 1938; *Socialism in Evolution*, 1938; *The Common People 1746-1938*, 1938 (revised 1946; with Richard Seymour Postgate; also known as *The British Common People*); *The Machinery of Socialist*

Planning, 1938; *British Trade-Unionism Today: A Survey, with the Collaboration of Thirty Trade Union Leaders and Other Experts*, 1939 (revised as *An Introduction to Trade Unionism*, 1953); *Plan for Democratic Britain*, 1939; *War Aims*, 1939

1941-1950 • *A Letter to an Industrial Manager*, 1941; *British Working Class Politics 1834-1914*, 1941; *Chartist Portraits*, 1941; *Europe, Russia, and the Future*, 1941; *James Keir Hardie*, 1941; *The War on the Home Front*, 1941; *A Memorandum on the Reorganization of Local Government in England*, 1942; *Beveridge Explained: What the Beveridge Report on Social Security Means*, 1942; *Great Britain in the Post-War World*, 1942; *The Fabian Society, Past and Present*, 1942 (revised 1952); *Victory or Vested Interest?*, 1942; *Building Societies and the Housing Problem*, 1943; *Fabian Socialism*, 1943; *John Burns*, 1943; *Monetary Systems and Theories*, 1943; *Richard Carlile, 1790-1843*, 1943; *The Means to Full Employment*, 1943; *When the Fighting Stops*, 1943; *A Century of Co-operation*, 1944; *How to Obtain Full Employment*, 1944; *Money: Its Present and Future*, 1944 (revised 1947, 1954; also known as *Money, Trade, and Investment*); *The British Working-Class Movement: An Outline and Study Guide*, 1944 (revised 1949); *The Planning of World Trade*, 1944; *Building and Planning*, 1945; *Reparations and the Future of German Industry*, 1945; *The Co-ops and Labour*, 1945; *Welfare and Peace*, 1945 (with John Boyd Orr); *Labour's Foreign Policy*, 1946; *Banks and Credit*, 1946?; *A Guide to the Elements of Socialism*, 1947; *Local and Regional Government*, 1947; *Samuel Butler and "The Way of All Flesh,"* 1947; *The Intelligent Man's Guide to the Post-War World*, 1947; *The Rochdale Principles: Their History and Application*, 1947; *A History of the Labour Party from 1914*, 1948; *British Social Services*, 1948; *Europe and the Problem of Democracy*, 1948; *The Meaning of Marxism*, 1948; *The National Coal Board: Its Tasks, Its Organisation, and Its Prospects*, 1948; *Why Nationalise Steel?*, 1948; *Consultation or Joint Management? A Contribution to the Discussion of Industrial Democracy*, 1949 (with J. M. Chalmers and Ian Mikardo); *Facts for Socialists*, 1949; *Labour's Second Term*, 1949; *World in Transition: A Guide to the Shifting Political and Economic Forces of Our Time*, 1949; *Essays in Social Theory*, 1950; *Socialist Economics*, 1950

1951-1960 • *British Labour Movement: Retrospect and Prospect*, 1951; *The British Co-operative Movement in a Socialist Society*, 1951; *Weakness Through Strength: The Economics of Re-armament*, 1951; *Introduction to Economic History, 1750-1950*, 1952; *Samuel Butler*, 1952 (revised 1961); *The Development of Socialism During the Past Fifty Years*, 1952; *A History of Socialist Thought*, 1953-1960; *Attempts at General Union: A Study in British Trade Union History 1818-1834*, 1953; *Is This Socialism?*, 1954; *Studies in Class Structure*, 1955; *The Post-War Condition of Britain*, 1956; *What Is Wrong with Trade Unions?*, 1956; *World Socialism Restated*, 1956 (revised 1957); *The Case for Industrial Partnership*, 1957; *William Morris as a Socialist*, 1960; *National Government and Inflation: Six Little Talks on Politics*, n.d

EDITED TEXTS: *Oxford Poetry 1910-13*, 1913 (with G. P. Dennis and Sherard Vines); *Oxford Poetry 1914*, 1914 (with Vines); *Oxford Poetry 1915*, 1915 (with T. W. Earp); *The Library of Social Studies*, 1920-1921; *What Everybody Wants to Know About Money: A Planned Outline of Monetary Problems by Nine Economists from Oxford*, 1933; *Workers' Control and Self-Government in Industry*, 1933 (with William Mellor); *Stories in Verse, Stories in Prose, Shorter Poems, Lectures, and Essays*, 1934 (by William Morris); *Studies in Capital and Investment*, 1935; *Letters to Edward Thornton Written in the Years 1797 to 1800*, 1937 (by Cobbett); *The Rights of Man*, 1937 (by Thomas Paine); *The Essential Samuel Butler*, 1950; *A Report in the UNESCO La Brévière Seminar on Workers' Education*, 1953 (with André Philip); *British Working Class Movements, Selected Documents 1789-1875*, 1965 (with A. W. Filson)

TRANSLATIONS: *The Social Contract and Discourses*, 1913 (by Jean-Jacques Rousseau); *Planned Socialism*, 1935 (by Henri de Man)

OTHER MAJOR WORKS (BY MARGARET COLE)

POETRY: *Bits of Things*, 1914 (with others); *Poems*, 1918

CHILDREN'S LITERATURE: *A Story of Santa Claus for Little People*, 1920

NONFICTION: 1921-1940 • *The Control of Indus-try*, 1921; *An Introduction to World History for Classes and Study Circles*, 1923; *Local Government for Beginners*, 1927; *A Book List of Local Govern-ment*, 1933; *The New Economic Revolution*, 1937; *Books and the People*, 1938; *Marriage, Past and Present*, 1938; *Women of Today*, 1938

1941-1950 • *Wartime Billeting*, 1941; *A Letter to a Student*, 1942; *Education for Democracy*, 1942; *Beatrice Webb*, 1945; *The General Election, 1945, and After*, 1945; *The Rate for the Job*, 1946; *The So-cial Services and the Webb Tradition*, 1946; *Makers of the Labour Movement*, 1948; *Growing Up into Revo-lution*, 1949; *Miners and the Board*, 1949

1951-1971 • *Robert Owen of New Lanark*, 1953; *What Is a Comprehensive School? The London Plan in Practice*, 1953; *Beatrice and Sidney Webb*, 1955; *Plan for Industrial Pensions*, 1956; *Servant of the Country*, 1956; *The Story of Fabian Socialism*, 1961; *Robert Owen: Industrialist, Reformer, Visionary*, 1971 (with others); *The Life of G. D. H. Cole*, 1971

EDITED TEXTS: *Twelve Studies in Soviet Russia*, 1933; *The Road to Success: Twenty Essays on the Choice of a Career for Women*, 1936; *Democratic Sweden: A Volume of Studies Prepared by Members of the New Fabian Research Bureau*, 1938 (with Charles Smith); *Evacuation Survey: A Report to the Fabian Society*, 1940 (with Richard Padley); *Our So-viet Ally*, 1943; *Our Partnership*, 1948 (by Beatrice Webb; with Barbara Drake); *The Webbs and Their Work*, 1949; *Beatrice Webb: Diaries 1912-1924 and 1924-1932*, 1952-1956

BIBLIOGRAPHY

Barzun, Jacques, and Wendell Hertig Taylor. *A Cata-logue of Crime*. Rev. ed. New York: Harper & Row, 1989. Massive, nearly one-thousand-page critical bibliography of mystery, detective, and spy stories. Provides background for understanding the Coles' work. Includes an index.

_____. Preface to *The Murder at Crome House*. New York: Garland, 1976. Analysis of the Coles' relationship, collaboration, and writing style.

Cole, Margaret. *The Life of G. D. H. Cole*. New York: St. Martin's Press, 1971. This biography of G. D. H. Cole by his wife and coauthor provides insight both into her personal life and into the couple's re-lationship.

Ingle, Stephen. *Narratives of British Socialism*. New York: Palgrave Macmillan, 2002. Critical study of those British texts informed by socialism, such as those of the Coles, as well as of texts directly repre-senting socialism in Great Britain.

Roth, Marty. *Foul and Fair Play: Reading Genre in Classic Detective Fiction*. Athens: University of Georgia Press, 1995. A poststructural analysis of the conventions of mystery and detective fiction. Examines 138 short stories and works from the 1840's to the 1960's. Contains only a brief mention of the Coles but helps place them within the mys-tery fiction of the time.

Vernon, Betty D. *Margaret Cole, 1893-1980: A Politi-cal Biography*. Rev. ed. Dover, N.H.: Croom Helm, 1986. Details Cole's political activism, its origins in her experiences, and its consequences for the rest of her life, including her fiction.

MAX ALLAN COLLINS

Born: Muscatine, Iowa; March 3, 1948
Also wrote as Barbara Allan; Peter Brackett; Max
  Collins; Patrick Culhane
Types of plot: Hard-boiled; private investigator; his-
  torical

PRINCIPAL SERIES

Nolan, 1973-
Quarry, 1976-
Mallory, 1983-
Nathan Heller, 1983-
Eliot Ness, 1987-
Disasters, 1999-

PRINCIPAL SERIES CHARACTERS

MALLORY, a former police officer and Vietnam veteran, lives in Port City, Iowa, where he both writes and solves mysteries. Modeled after his creator, Mallory is law abiding and helpful to people in his community, although the books he aspires to write tend to feature hard-boiled characters and plots.

NATHAN HELLER, a native Chicagoan and former police officer, recalls famous people he knew while investigating unsolved crimes. He created the A-1 Detective Agency after leaving the Chicago police force because he was disgusted by corrupt practices with which he had complied, such as lying while testifying in court, to advance professionally. Heller served with the U.S. Marines during World War II.

ELIOT NESS is a fictionalized depiction of the real Ness when he was in his thirties and public safety director in Cleveland, Ohio, combating corrupt police, politicians, and organized crime during the Depression. In short stories and novels, he frequently allies with Heller to solve cases and apprehend criminals.

CONTRIBUTION

Max Allan Collins is an innovative writer whom many critics credit with being the first to write hard-boiled historical detective stories and with shaping the genre for other writers. His most significant protagonist is private investigator Nathan Heller, who appears in works frequently lauded by reviewers. Collins created a female private investigator, Ms. Tree, around the same time Sue Grafton and Sara Paretsky introduced their women detectives. Collins gained popular acclaim when he wrote the *Dick Tracy* detective comic strip. His prominence increased with the release of the film *Road to Perdition* (2002) based on his graphic novel published in 1998. In addition to writing mysteries, Collins has enhanced scholarship of that genre with his nonfictional essays and books.

Collins's peers have recognized his writing with awards. The Private Eye Writers of America (PWA) presented Collins a Shamus Award for outstanding novel for *True Detective* (1983). He received his second Shamus for *Stolen Away* (1991). Many of his other works were also nominated for Shamus awards. In 2006, the PWA honored Collins with its most notable prize, The Eye, recognizing his lifetime contributions to the private investigator genre. The Mystery Writers of America presented Collins an Edgar Allan Poe Award for his critical book, *One Lonely Knight: Mickey Spillane's Mike Hammer* (1984; with James L. Traylor). Reviewers have had mixed opinions of Collins's mysteries. Many critics praise his plotting and action, while others consider his narratives weakened by superfluous details. Some reviewers dislike his occasionally unrealistic, and sometimes demeaning, characterizations of historical characters.

BIOGRAPHY

Max Allan Collins, Jr., was born on March 3, 1948, in Muscatine, Iowa, to Max Allan Collins and Patricia Ann Rushing Collins. His parents encouraged artistic expression. Collins's father worked as a music director for Muscatine High School and Muscatine Community College. When Collins was a toddler, his mother read Chester Gould's *Dick Tracy* comics to him. Later, Collins used his allowance to buy *Dick Tracy* issues. After Collins's mother sent his drawings to Gould, the cartoonist mailed Collins a letter for his eighth birthday, praising his artistry.

Collins read books by Mickey Spillane, Dashiell

Max Allan Collins in 2002. (AP/Wide World Photos)

Hammett, and other detective authors. He began writing fiction while he was in junior high, submitting his work to publishers. At Muscatine High School, Collins acted in plays, ran track, and lettered in football. His senior profile in his high school's *Auroran* yearbook stated that his ambition was to become a professional writer. After graduating in 1966, Collins studied at Muscatine Community College, completing an associate of arts degree in 1968. On June 1, 1968, he married Barbara Jane Mull. Their son Nathan was born in 1982.

Collins was a *Muscatine Journal* reporter from 1968 through 1970. He enrolled in creative writing workshops at the University of Iowa, receiving a bachelor of arts degree in 1970. He was accepted to that university's graduate writers' workshop and earned a master of fine arts degree in 1972. From 1971 through 1977, Collins taught at Muscatine Community College. He attended Boucheron conventions, meeting PWA founder Robert Randisi, who became a supportive colleague. In 1977, when Gould retired from teaching, Collins submitted his successful proposal, "Dick Tracy Meets Angeltop," to write *Dick Tracy*. A contract dispute ended Collins's employment in 1993.

Collins experienced an epiphany in the 1970's

when he read *The Maltese Falcon* (1929-1930) and noticed its copyright, realizing that private investigators had existed throughout the twentieth century. Fascinated by unsolved crimes and mysteries, he envisioned stories set during the Depression and into the 1960's, featuring private eye Nathan Heller investigating crimes associated with famous events and people. To develop his idea, Collins researched in archives and libraries and interviewed eyewitnesses. His first Heller novel, *True Detective*, appeared in 1983.

Collins began writing screenplays in 1994. In 1998, his graphic novel, *Road to Perdition*, was published, securing international attention for his writing. Publishers hired Collins to write novels based on films and television shows. Collins edited anthologies of Mickey Spillane's short stories and finished Spillane's novels in progress after his death. Collins also co-authored mysteries with his wife. In 1999, Collins contributed a chapter to the serial mystery, *Sixteen Thousand Suspects: A RAGBRAI Mystery*, written by Iowa authors to honor the *Des Moines Register*'s Annual Great Bicycle Ride Across Iowa.

Collins has served on the board of directors for the Mystery Writers of America and PWA and has judged nominations for Shamus and Edgar Awards.

ANALYSIS

Max Allan Collins perceives himself as a storyteller who writes primarily to entertain readers. He shapes his stories to appeal to his audience by incorporating cultural references, jargon, and attitudes. Themes of violence and corruption resonate in Collins's writing. He uses dark humor and irony to establish sinister tones. His stories are often set during the 1930's Depression or wars to intensify ominous themes and suggest characters' jaded, pessimistic outlooks. Characters, both male and female, are prone to narcissism and hedonism, with men frequently displaying misogynistic behavior.

Collins focuses on depicting unsolved twentieth century crimes in the United States, appropriating historical persons and events for his stories' foundations. Because he manipulates history, he prints disclaimers and historical notes to distinguish fact from fiction, emphasizing that his protagonist Nathan Heller presents original, factually sound hypotheses to solve infamous cases. Name dropping in these provocative mysteries, thick with historical casts, is often overwhelming and distracts from the crime solving.

Collins creates unreliable, flawed narrators who are often angry and dishonest and survive on the periphery of society. Truth and memory are constant themes as characters lie, create stories and identities, and withhold or divulge information according to their perceptions, motivations, loyalties, and weaknesses. He frequently casts his characters as being more accurate than standard historical accounts, and Heller reveals that recorded facts are untrue. Collins enjoys surprising his readers with unexpected plot twists and variations on clichés.

Family and home are themes that contrast with horrific images in Collins's works. He presents characters' positive attributes, noting people and places to which they have emotional ties, to reveal their vulnerabilities and humanity, no matter how brutal they are to others. Collins emphasizes father-son relationships. Settings in Iowa and Illinois, places familiar to the author, add a sense of realism to his stories and enhance his strong visual writing style.

TRUE DETECTIVE

In *True Detective*, Collins introduces Nathan Heller living in 1933 Chicago. Describing Heller's story as a memoir, Collins implies that his investigator, using first-person narration, is recalling an incident from his past, and his memory might not be completely accurate. A police officer, Heller refuses to lie while testifying in a murder trial involving police and gangster Frank Nitti, Al Capone's associate. After relinquishing his badge, Heller establishes a detective agency, traveling to Atlanta to meet with imprisoned Capone, who hires him to stop Nitti from killing Chicago mayor Anton Cermak. Returning to the Midwest, Heller interacts with his friends, Eliot Ness and Dutch Reagan (whose comments are humorous because Collins knows Reagan's future election to the U.S. presidency). Heller witnesses Cermak's assassination, which the press believes was intended for visiting President Franklin D. Roosevelt, as has been explained in history texts.

Collins states that he presumes histories of infamous crimes are usually incorrect, so he reveals the truth, supported with research, through Heller's eyes as a witness. This premise continues in his second Heller memoir, *True Crime* (1984), which states that John Dillinger has survived federal agents' attempt to kill him. Collins's innovative concept applies private-eye genre elements with various mystery structures. His short story "The Strawberry Teardrop" pairs Heller and Ness as they identify a serial killer, which inspired *Butcher's Dozen* (1988) and Collins's Ness series.

STOLEN AWAY

In *Stolen Away*, Nathan Heller locates a bootlegger's abducted son in Chicago, resulting in speculation that he can find a kidnapped toddler, Charles Lindbergh, Jr. After traveling to the Lindberghs' Hopewell, New Jersey, estate, Heller meets Lindbergh; his wife, Anne Morrow Lindbergh; and Colonel Schwarzkopf, who is in charge of the investigation. Examining the crime scene, Heller evaluates the evidence, including ransom notes, and interviews the staff. Near Washington, D.C., he encounters Gaston B. Means, who claims he knows where the Lindbergh child is located, and Heller assumes Means is a con man. Heller flies with Lindbergh, searching for a boat that the ransom notes state the boy is aboard; their searches are unsuccessful. Heller leaves, disgusted by how the Lindberghs permit Means to manipulate them.

Following the case in newspapers, Heller learns that a child's body, recovered near Hopewell, has been identified by Lindbergh as that of his child. While attending accused kidnapper Bruno Hauptmann's trial, Heller realizes that the man did not abduct the Lindbergh child. He develops a theory that the Lindberghs' son is living on an Illinois farm and travels there. He meets the farmers' adopted boy before violence erupts and assassins attack, wounding Heller. Decades later, a middle-aged man named Harlan Jensen visits Heller, and they discuss the possibility that he is the kidnapped Lindbergh toddler. Having constructed a detailed account, Collins explains why his alternate ending is plausible. Themes of hope, despair, and deceit reinforce Collins's depiction of Heller's investigations, which convinced many reviewers and readers that they were actually reading a nonfictional account in what is often considered Collins's strongest novel.

ROAD TO PERDITION

Family, loss, loyalty, and betrayal are the primary themes in Collins's best-known crime novel, *Road to Perdition*, which explores the mysterious and deadly world of gangsters from their viewpoint. In 1930, Michael O'Sullivan, Jr.'s innocence is shattered when he observes his father killing a group of men. Michael learns that his father is a hit man for the Irish crime boss John Looney in the Tri-Cities stretching across the Mississippi River into Iowa and Illinois. Because of family allegiances, Michael O'Sullivan, Sr., is loyal to Looney, who calls him the Archangel of Death as he performs any hits Looney orders. O'Sullivan intensely loves his wife and two sons and had kept his profession secret until he was observed by his son. John Looney's son Connor kills Michael's mother and younger brother Peter, mistaking him for Michael, whom John had ordered silenced.

Michael and his father flee, heading for safety with relatives in Perdition, Kansas, because they know they are targeted for death in the Tri-Cities. During their travels, which take them first east through Illinois, Michael watches his father kill enemies to avenge his family, then confess his sins to priests. Michael is devastated when he kills a man to save his father's life and is confused about his religious obligations both to honor his father and not to kill. Michael arrives in Perdition only to lose his father to a hit man. He seeks a priest to perform last rites, absolving his father of his crimes. Confession strengthens Michael, who becomes a priest, wanting to tend souls, not destroy them. However, Collins's later novel, *Road to Paradise* (2005), depicts a middle-aged Michael O'Sullivan, Jr., who is reluctantly involved in violent Mafia activity and longs for a normal life with his wife and daughter.

THE LONDON BLITZ MURDERS

Notable authors of classic detective novels become sleuths in Collins's Disasters series. In *The London Blitz Murders* (2000), set in February, 1942, Londoners fear both the Blackout Ripper and German bombing raids. During the Blitz, several women are slain and mutilated. Detective Edward Greeno of Scotland Yard investigates, summoning forensic expert Sir Bernard Spilsbury to examine the bodies. Novelist Agatha Christie Mallowan works in a hospital pharmacy while her second husband is stationed in North Africa. Mallowan, the name she prefers, competently handles her duties, writing in the evenings and awaiting a play based on her writing to be staged in London.

Admiring Sir Spilsbury, who also works at the hospital, Mallowan accompanies him to murder scenes, which intrigue the novelist. She recognizes one of the victims, Nita Ward, as an actress who had auditioned for her play. Mallowan provides names of theater people who might divulge information about Ward. She alerts detectives to clues they have overlooked. As evidence accumulates, Mallowan considers who the most likely suspects are and discovers proof, which results in the murderer's capture.

Collins's disaster mysteries are less hard-boiled than his Heller novels. With a style reminiscent of Christie's cozy mysteries, this book does not fully convey the tension and stress that wartime Londoners constantly experienced. Some reviewers praised Collins's appropriation of Mallowan as a sleuth, while other critics thought her presence at crime scenes was unrealistic and doubted that she would have contributed directly to solving such horrific crimes.

Elizabeth D. Schafer

PRINCIPAL MYSTERY AND DETECTIVE FICTION

NOLAN SERIES: *Blood Money*, 1973; *Bait Money*, 1973; *Hard Cash*, 1981; *Fly Paper*, 1981; *Hush Money*, 1981; *Scratch Fever*, 1982; *Spree*, 1987; *Mourn the Living*, 1999

QUARRY SERIES: *The Dealer*, 1976; *The Broker*, 1976; *The Broker's Wife*, 1976; *The Slasher*, 1977; *Primary Target*, 1987; *The Last Quarry*, 2006

MALLORY SERIES: *The Baby Blue Rip-Off*, 1983; *No Cure for Death*, 1983; *Kill Your Darlings*, 1984; *A Shroud for Aquarius*, 1985; *Nice Weekend for a Murder*, 1986

NATHAN HELLER SERIES: *True Detective*, 1983; *True Crime*, 1984; *The Million-Dollar Wound*, 1986; *Neon Mirage*, 1988; *Stolen Away*, 1991; *Dying in the Postwar World*, 1991; *Carnal Hours*, 1994; *Blood and Thunder*, 1995; *Damned in Paradise*, 1996; *Flying Blind*, 1998; *Majic Man*, 1999; *Kisses of Death*, 2001; *Angel in Black*, 2001; *Chicago Confidential*, 2002

ELIOT NESS SERIES: *The Dark City*, 1987; *Butcher's Dozen*, 1988; *Bullet Proof*, 1989; *Murder by the Numbers*, 1993

DISASTERS SERIES: *The Titanic Murders*, 1999; *The Hindenburg Murders*, 2000; *The Pearl Harbor Murders*, 2001; *The Lusitania Murders*, 2002; *The London Blitz Murders*, 2004; *The War of the Worlds Murder*, 2005

NONSERIES NOVELS: *Midnight Haul*, 1986; *Ms. Tree*, 1988 (illustrated by Terry Beatty); *Road to Perdition*, 1998 (illustrated by Richard Piers Rayner); *Road to Purgatory*, 2004; *Road to Paradise*, 2005; *Antiques Roadkill*, 2006 (as Allan); *Black Hats*, 2007 (as Culhane); *A Killing in Comics*, 2007; *Antiques Maul*, 2007 (as Allan)

OTHER MAJOR WORKS

NOVELS: *Mommy*, 1997; *Mommy's Day*, 1998; *Regeneration*, 1999 (with Barbara Collins); *Bombshell*, 2004 (with Collins)

SHORT FICTION: *Blue Christmas, and Other Holiday Homicides*, 2001; *Murder—His and Hers*, 2001 (with Barbara Collins)

PLAY: *Eliot Ness: An Untouchable Life*, pr. 2005

SCREENPLAYS: *Mommy*, 1995; *Mommy's Day*, 1997; *Mike Hammer's Mickey Spillane*, 1999

NONFICTION: *Jim Thompson: The Killers Inside Him*, 1983 (with Ed Gorman); *One Lonely Knight: Mickey Spillane's Mike Hammer*, 1984 (with James L. Traylor); *The Best of Crime and Detective TV*, 1988 (with John Javna); *The Mystery Scene Movie Guide: A Personal Filmography of Modern Crime Pictures*, 1998; *The History of Mystery*, 2001

BIBLIOGRAPHY

Breen, Jon. "Murdering History: How the Past Became Fair Game for Detective Stories." *The Weekly Standard*, January 3, 2005, pp. 31-34. Discusses Collins's historical mysteries, evaluating the Disasters series books and noting merits and flaws. Contemplates standards for creating historical mysteries and writers' obligations to history and readers.

Crouch, Bill, Jr., ed. *Dick Tracy: America's Most Famous Detective*. Secaucus, N.J.: Citadel Press, 1987. Chapter profiles Collins and his contributions to *Dick Tracy*, providing biographical details that show how that comic detective influenced Collins's historical detective writing.

Hoffman, Carl. "Return to the Primal Noir: Two Modern Authors on the Black Dahlia." *Journal of American Culture* 26, no. 3 (September, 2003): 385-394. Compares Collins's *Angel in Black* with James Ellroy's *The Black Dahlia*, noting strengths and weaknesses in their appropriation of that notorious crime to construct mysteries.

Pronzini, Bill, and Marcia Muller, eds. *1001 Midnights: The Aficionado's Guide to Mystery and Detective Fiction*. New York: Arbor House, 1986. In this work, John Lutz discusses literary elements of *True Detective*. Includes Collins's essays examining books by James M. Cain, Richard Stark, Jim Thompson, William March, and several other authors.

Randisi, Robert J. Interview of Max Allan Collins. *The Armchair Detective* 11, no. 3 (July, 1978): 300-304. Collins describes his writing techniques for his Mallory mysteries and early adventure series and how detective writers influenced his style.

MICHAEL COLLINS
Dennis Lynds

Born: St. Louis, Missouri; January 15, 1924
Died: San Francisco, California; August 19, 2005
Also wrote as William Arden; Nick Carter; John
    Crowe; Carl Dekker; John Douglas; Maxwell
    Grant; Mark Sadler
Type of plot: Private investigator

PRINCIPAL SERIES

The Shadow, 1964-1967
Dan Fortune, 1967-1995
Kane Jackson, 1968-1973
Paul Shaw, 1970-1986
Buena Costa County, 1972-1979
Nick Carter, 1974-1976

PRINCIPAL SERIES CHARACTER

DAN FORTUNE is a one-armed private investigator
of Polish ancestry who resides in the Chelsea district
of New York City and plies his investigative trade primarily among the district's lowly inhabitants. Intelligent and introspective, he is a philosopher of the slums
who intuits solutions and relates to human weaknesses. He is concerned not only with the solutions to
crimes but also with the values that guide and measure
a person's life. Later in the series, he moves to Santa
Barbara, California.

CONTRIBUTION

Michael Collins is the pseudonym under which
Dennis Lynds wrote a hard-boiled detective series and
juvenile mysteries, among other works. Lynds used
various other pen names to write many other mysteries
and novels. The novels of the Dan Fortune series are
probably Collins's most original works. The narrator-
protagonist of these novels is often compared to the
hard-boiled detectives of Dashiell Hammett, Raymond Chandler, and Ross Macdonald. However, although Dan Fortune is a maverick, he lacks the violent, brutal approach to his work characteristic of the
hard-boiled detective. Essentially nonaggressive, even
passive at times, he is marked by his compassion and

vulnerability. Fortune is a more rounded and credible
character than most detectives in this genre.

Strongly competing with the protagonist for primary importance in the early Fortune novels is the setting, the Chelsea district on New York's East Side.
Collins gave the reader a realistic view of this area, its
residents, and the conditions there, which contribute to
the many crimes. The result is a sociological study of
and commentary on the living conditions that shape
the characters, who engage in violence and commit
crimes. So pervasive is the sociological emphasis that
critics have termed his later novels sociodramas. Collins moved Fortune from Chelsea to Santa Barbara in
his fourteenth novel, but his protagonist's character remained the same, and the California landscape played
an important part in the later novels.

Although teeming with characters, the Fortune series novels contain few stereotypes. Collins created individual portraits that are often extremely complex.
The plots are also more complicated than in more orthodox detective fiction and are largely free of coincidences and contrivances. In keeping with the realistic
characters, setting, and plots, the novels focus on the
violence and brutality that stem in large part from the
characters' backgrounds, which Collins described in
detail. Employing a gradual buildup, Collins increased
the intensity of action until the story reached a cathar-
tic climax. Told in a lucid style, the highly original
plots hold interest without destroying credibility.

A member of various writers' guilds, Collins
served as president of the Private Eye Writers of
America in 1985. Among the awards he received are
the Edgar Allan Poe Award for the best first mystery
novel, *Act of Fear* (1967); the Mystery Writers of
America's Special Award for the short story "Success
of a Mission" (1968); a special commendation from
the Arbeitsgemeinschaft Kriminalliteratur for his total
contribution to mystery fiction (1981); a nomination
from the Private Eye Writers of America for best short
story (1984); and guest of honor at the eighth Festival
du Roman et du Film Policiers, Reims, France (1986).

BIOGRAPHY

Michael Collins was born Dennis Lynds in St. Louis, Missouri, on January 15, 1924. His parents were Archibald John Douglas Lynds, a revolutionary politician who had become an actor, and Gertrude (Hyem) Lynds. The family moved to New York, where Collins attended Brooklyn Technical High School and Cooper Union. He then enrolled in Texas Agricultural and Mechanical College at College Station in 1943. From 1943 to 1946, he was in the United States Army Infantry, serving in the European theater of operations. He was awarded the Purple Heart, the Bronze Star, and three battle stars. Following his military service, he returned to the state of New York for the rest of his education, receiving his bachelor's degree in chemistry from Hofstra University in 1949 and his master's degree in journalism from Syracuse University in 1951.

Collins was married three times: to Doris Flood, 1949-1956; Sheila McErlean, 1961-1985; and Gayle Hallenbeck Stone, 1986. With McErlean, he had two daughters, Katherine and Deirdre. Collins worked at many jobs; he was an actor, farmworker, chemist, executive, and teacher. His primary nonliterary employment, however, was as editor of various chemistry trade journals. Although he claimed that he quit his editorial job and became a full-time writer in 1960, he occasionally returned to editing scientific journals. Collins had a highly productive career in various literary genres. He gained major recognition as a writer of detective fiction with such successful novels as *Act of Fear*, which introduced the character Dan Fortune. *A Dark Power* (1968), which he wrote as William Arden, brought forth the series character Kane Jackson and utilized Collins's interest in business and industry, but the novels about industrial espionage were not commercially successful.

Having lived most of his early life in New York, Collins moved to California. There he found what appeared to be an ideal location in which to work. The direct result was his Buena Costa County mysteries, written as John Crowe. Collins did not, however, desert his New York background. Dan Fortune, as well as Paul Shaw in the mysteries written as Mark Sadler, continued to work out of New York headquarters, although Fortune later moved to Santa Barbara, California, where the last of the series novels take place.

Collins died in August of 2005 at the age of eighty-one. He had been ill for some time and died in San Francisco while en route to visit his hospitalized daughter.

ANALYSIS

Dennis Lynds once said of "Michael Collins" that he

> is more than a pen name; he is my alter ego—part of me that isn't the same man who writes my other books. I live far from New York now, but Collins will never leave that complex city-world where everything changes and yet never changes. When I decided to write about Dan Fortune, his city and his people, I knew I needed Michael Collins—the perpetual New Yorker no matter where he is.

Michael Collins and his creation, Dan Fortune, are associated with the Chelsea district on the East Side of New York City. Collins presents a microcosm heavily burdened with crime and poverty. The cast of characters in each novel is large and complex, with virtually all characters playing significant roles. People of numerous nationalities mingle, and multiple ethnic groups struggle to form a cohesive society. Highly varied occupations must fit into the human puzzle: police, priests, prostitutes, smugglers, merchants, racketeers, gangsters, show girls, addicts, gamblers, professional people, and crime lords. Collins presents the communality of the members of Chelsea society as being greater than their differences; the people of Chelsea share ambitions, needs, fears, and weaknesses.

Along with a few continuing characters, each of the Dan Fortune mysteries offers its own memorable cast. For example, in *Freak* (1983), much of the action centers on a four-member band of criminals with extensive records. Jasper "J. J." Murdoch, the leader of the gang, had been mauled and castrated by a bear when young and therefore cannot have sexual relations with women. This caused him to develop a perverted antisocial nature and turn to smashing things and committing brutal killings. Second in command is a large black man with the well-earned name of Dog; the remaining two members of the group are the American Indian Charley and Flaco Sanchez.

As psychological studies, the Fortune novels explore questions pertaining to the evil and violent actions of people. Because few of the characters are stereotyped, virtually all have some saving graces; despite social and economic differences, most characters also have a dark side and the potential for violence and brutality. Collins rips the facades off normal citizens to reveal the violence hidden beneath and the propensity to commit crime. His typical characters wrestle with their fates: The weakest succumb to evil and crime, and the strongest fight against it, yet destiny can destroy any of them. The revelation of true character comes at a moment of crisis; the inner person builds up over an extended period of time and finally explodes into overt action. Although the result is frequently brutal and violent, Collins still saw himself as an optimist; as he once explained, "I write about the darkness in man because I believe it doesn't have to be dark, and that makes me an optimist."

Although Collins populates his novels primarily with the criminal element, he gives the works needed contrast and balance by introducing various socially acceptable characters. His ability to weave the divergent elements into a literary whole may well be his greatest strength as a novelist. Skillful handling of interrelationships among the characters is demonstrated in *Blue Death* (1975), in which Franklin Weaver of International Metals and Refining, an executive, is driven by his business concerns to become involved in four deaths. In this mystery, the plot moves far below the corporate level to include such people as a belly dancer and her husband, as well as other executives and scientists. The settings also shift—from cheap hotels and lowly bars to luxurious office suites and penthouses.

As a protagonist in detective fiction, Dan Fortune is both conventional and unconventional. He must serve as a master investigator who gathers, retains, and fits together the often seemingly disparate pieces relating to a crime. Average in size and appearance and dressed in an old blue duffle coat and a black beret, Fortune patrols the Chelsea district, where he has his office-apartment in a loft. His one distinctive physical feature is his missing left arm. Because of this handicap, dating back to his boyhood, and because he seldom carries his old "cannon," Fortune poses little physical threat to his opponents. However, he has learned to compensate, to use what abilities he does possess. His limited fighting skills consist of cunning, speed, good legs (he is not ashamed to run if conditions favor it), and a quick wit. He will act when necessary; he simply does not seek out or relish violence. The lost arm actually works to his advantage in some ways; for example, it humanizes him in the eyes of others. Also, while the loss tends to alienate him, it drives him to assert his selfhood. Collins indirectly, but effectively, makes the reader aware that the world is filled with disabled people and that virtually all are worse off than Fortune, especially the motley population of Chelsea.

Fortune's inner strength sets him apart from his fellow private investigators. Among his many ennobling traits is his great compassion for others—criminals as well as their victims—especially the downtrodden. As a very sensitive person, even "something of a sentimentalist," he has to guard against becoming too emotionally involved with his clients. Also, as the pseudophilosopher of the slums, he has to guard against becoming too "preachy"; he often makes pithy comments on various aspects of life.

Essentially a passive man, Fortune seems to be sought out by crime. *Minnesota Strip* (1987) offers a typical start to one of his cases. A young woman, seeking his aid in finding her boyfriend and a young Eurasian woman, explains how she chose him from the telephone book: "Your name sounded like good luck: Dan Fortune. Your address sounded cheap. I didn't know about the arm." He accepts the mission and, because of his compassion, charges a much lower rate than usual. Like this case, which becomes a study of prostitution, drug trafficking, white slavery, arms smuggling, and terrorism and involves at least ten violent deaths, all of Fortune's cases tend to burgeon. Despite his reluctance, he is drawn into complicated patterns of crime and violence. In attempting to solve his cases, Fortune does not try to manipulate lives—only to understand them as well as his own. He has a driving need to gain answers to basic human questions and dilemmas, and the role of private investigator gives him the license to inquire. His findings are often presented to his readers in the form of a miniature lecture or sermon.

Fortune has great fluidity of movement among the various social and economic classes—a decided advantage for a private investigator. He has good relationships with the police, especially with Captains Gazzo and Pearce in New York and Sergeant Gus Chavalas in Santa Barbara, and even has a long-lasting, if somewhat ambiguous, relationship with Andy Pappas, a crime lord. His strongest ties, however, are to the poor; he recognizes their shared characteristics as well as their individual needs. A lonely figure, he rides (more often walks) like a knight through the mire and muck of the Chelsea district. He is essentially without armor, made vulnerable by his passion and sacrifice for truth. He not only "gets dirty" in his investigation of the slime found in Chelsea, but also is shot, beaten, drugged, held prisoner, bombarded by insults, and injured in various other ways. Also, there are few women waiting to comfort him; he has only occasional sexual relationships, frequently with women as alienated as he. Nevertheless, he is always determined to fulfill his mission and to complete his quest, even at the risk of his own life.

Throughout his many exploits, the character of Fortune undergoes few changes. Middle-aged when he first appears in *Act of Fear*, he ages very little in the following novels. He does increase his daily fee and expenses, but he is sometimes too modest to insist on them. His personal relationships undergo some modification; for example, his friend on the police force, Captain Gazzo, is gunned down on the East Side in *The Nightrunners* (1978) and replaced by Captain Pearce at Homicide Central, and his bartender-friend, Joe Harris, ceases to appear in the works. Fortune also loses his girlfriend, Marty Adair, to the West Coast and marriage. She is replaced by Kay Michaels, who runs a model agency. Eventually, Fortune moves to a virtually secluded life bearing strong resemblance to that of many other detectives.

Although Collins chooses to place primary emphasis on characterization, he does not shortchange the reader on action. His plots are highly original, while still retaining much of the formula of detective novels. Although complex, his plots are logical and essentially free of melodrama. The motivating act is often seemingly insignificant: A man loses his lease or some-

one's friend breaks an engagement. The complication that follows is the strength of Collins's narrative. Early in the narrative, Collins mixes action scenes with scenes of quiet philosophical discussions. Each work eventually shifts into sudden and violent action. This violent action is usually not committed by Fortune, as he seldom moves to such a state; however, he is frequently its target. The building complication rapidly exposes the weaknesses and obsessions of characters, leading to a multitude of crimes, including a generous number of murders. The story line moves in various directions, acquires complementing subplots, and depends heavily on complex interrelationships among characters and events. The result is to draw Fortune deeper into the web of violence and death.

A typical Collins plot is found in *Minnesota Strip*, in which Fortune is hired by a young woman to find a missing Eurasian woman and the client's boyfriend. Early in the novel it is discovered that the Eurasian woman has been brutally murdered and that the boyfriend has become a self-appointed vigilante seeking freedom and justice in the world. Fortune's investigation takes him from the chaos of the inner city to the cleanliness and orderliness of the suburbs, from the Minnesota Strip to the California Gold Coast, and from brothels to executive suites. He encounters such characters as an Irish Italian who would like to be an American Indian because the Indians have tribes to which they belong and a supposedly benevolent man who is helping Vietnamese escape to the United States but is concerned only with his own profits. There are hangings, stabbings, shootings, and mutilations.

Collins's novels usually move to a last climactic scene, marked by a bloodbath, in which the struggle for order and justice culminates. When the elements finally fall into place, Fortune experiences a revelation. All that remains is the explanation of the solution. This conclusion is more realistic than in most detective works. However, if a reader demands the usual fare of a clear and decisive judgment and action—a resolution that sorts out all elements and categorizes them, with the detective punishing and rewarding justly—then Collins's works may not satisfy. His world is not this simple; the characters and actions are consistently multifaceted and often intentionally ambiguous, and the usual resolution leaves the reader knowing that greed is not abated, drugs are not eliminated, and, given the right set of circumstances, violence leading to murder is a future certainty.

Although Collins's plots are engrossing and entertaining and often deal with significant topics in a realistic manner, the primary value of his novels is found in the highly individualized characters he creates, the sociological studies he offers, and, to a more limited degree, the philosophical statements he makes.

ACT OF FEAR

Act of Fear well illustrates the typical setting, plot, characters, and investigatory methods found in the Dan Fortune novels. Early in the narrative, Fortune explains, "It's not the facts, the simple events, that tell a story. It's the background, the people and what they have inside, the scenery a man lives with, the shadows all around him he never knew were there." Chelsea furnishes this background as well as the cast of characters and the motivation for the story. Although the residents of Chelsea are destined to live out their lives there, most of them do not have an American Dream but, instead, live with their personal nightmares, which are often bred by poverty.

In *Act of Fear*, three seemingly separate crimes are committed: A young, inexperienced police officer is mugged in broad daylight, and all of his possessions are taken, including his summons book; a teenage boy hires Fortune to find his friend, who has been missing for four days; and a chorus girl has been killed. Armed with few clues—primarily a losing stub on a slow horse at Monmouth Park and a charm in the shape of a red Ferrari—Fortune sets out to find the boy and, in the process, to discover the relationship among the three crimes. His investigation takes him from Chelsea to Florida, gets him pursued and beaten by criminals, brings him up against a code of silence, exposes him to several deaths, and occasionally leads him to Marty Adair for the solace her love can give. Further, the investigation brings Fortune in contact with a young female addict living in a tenement, an alcoholic who instructs mechanics, a crime lord and his henchmen, a secret lover turned killer, a woman who works at a travel bureau, and an old garage man. He also encounters a young boy who is willing to sacrifice his best

friend because a girl rejected him, parents who are more worried about themselves than their children, and another young boy who shows promise of escaping the slums. As the detective moves among these people, he lectures his audience on such matters as family obligations, love and marriage, operations of the underworld, the American Dream, the rules of slum life, misplaced loyalty, and the need for self-survival. These many and varied activities are all in a book's work for Dan Fortune, a slightly soiled knight who never quits. Even when he discovers the solution to the crimes, however, neither he nor his audience is fully satisfied with the resolution. Victory for him is always qualified.

RED ROSA

In *Red Rosa* (1988), Lenny Gruenfeld hires Fortune to investigate the attempted murder of her grandmother, Rosa "Red Rosa" Gruenfeld, a leftist political activist with connections to the Communist Party. The murder takes place in Chelsea, but the action leads Fortune to North Paterson, New Jersey, where the local police resent Fortune's investigation. Before the novel ends, the Black Liberation Front, the Communist Party, the Federal Bureau of Investigation, and the Mafia with their ties to local politicians are all involved. As in other Fortune novels, Collins provides histories for many of his characters, especially for Rosa, who was married to Flaco and faked his death with the help of local police and who reappears later in the novel. Despite warnings (from the police and in the form of a brick through a window) and attacks, Fortune persists, even while further attempts are made on Rosa's life. Typically, one crime leads to another, in this case the murder of Johnny Agnew, but although Fortune discovers that Rosa's shooting was accidental and that later attempts on her life were made by her son, Agnew's killer is not caught until the end of the novel. In a Collins twist, it is the Mafia, not the police, who "get" the villain, F. X. Keene—they shoot him. In the course of the novel, Fortune unravels motives, discovers the collusion between Keene and the North Paterson police to frame a black militant for a murder, and decides, with the help of the visiting Kay Michaels, that he is ready for California, his destination at the end of the book.

THE IRISHMAN'S HORSE

In *The Irishman's Horse* (1991), Forune, now living in California, takes on the job of finding Paul Valenzuela, an idealistic diplomat serving in Guatemala; his wife has not heard from him. It is a typical Fortune assignment, one that quickly mushrooms into murder and political corruption. As he investigates the murder of a drug dealer, he is aided by Sergeant Chavalas and is harassed by government agents, who encourage Valenzuela's wife to trust the government, although several government officials are working with Guatemalan drug lords to promote American policy. The Irishman of the title is Tyrone Earl, a drug dealer who helps Fortune escape from danger and later takes him and Paul to Guatemala, where he tells them about the complicity between drug dealers and the government. After Earl gives Paul the information, Paul and Fortune return to California, where Paul and his wife are killed in a car explosion before he can reveal the incriminating evidence to the appropriate government agents. Meanwhile, Earl and his minions are attacked and killed by government troops. The person "behind the scenes" is Martin Dobson, a former elected official and successful entrepreneur who has power without any accountability. Educated at public expense, Dobson has ironically become an Ayn Rand follower and a staunch conservative. In the novel, Collins provides his readers with a sympathetic treatment of the poor and the repressed, both in Guatemala and in the United States. Reading the histories, including Fortune's own, provides readers with the motivations and values of the poor. In this novel, however, the crimes committed by the political "haves" do pay, and the poor are punished and unsuccessful. It is one of the bleakest of the Fortune novels.

CASSANDRA IN RED

Cassandra in Red (1992) begins with the murder of Cassandra "Iron Cassie" Reilly, a homeless political activist in Santa Barbara. The novel deals not only with the plight of the homeless but also with American xenophobia. The police who harass the homeless and the wealthy who want to take the country back from "the bums and foreigners and liberals" create a climate that leads to violence. Fortune is hired by Al Benton, the "Marx of city hall" and the "guru of the gutter."

Initially Jerry Kohner, Cassie's boyfriend, is the suspect, but he kills himself and his family members. As Fortune probes further, he begins to suspect the Latino gangs, the Westside Rockers and the Hondos, but they are also innocent. Collins supplies his readers with individual histories that explain the motivations of Jerry and the Latino kids. In the course of the investigation Fortune is attacked and almost killed—he is saved once by Kay (one of her few appearances in the novel) and once by Super Barrio, a ludicrously costumed figure who is a kind of Latino Superman. Fortune's attention is then devoted to the Seven, a group of students at the Western Service Institute who fancy themselves patriotic militarists devoted to maintaining the purity of the United States. Fortune's investigation leads to the deaths of the school principal and one of the students. This novel, one of Collins's most political, explains how the power and the fear of losing that power cause the most extreme of the "comfortable voting majority" to resort to violence. At the end of the novel Fortune does not see "any bombs bursting, any rockets glaring"; he just sees "stars and the blackness." The novel is an indictment of the far-right.

THE CADILLAC COWBOY

The protagonist of *The Cadillac Cowboy* (1995), also set in California, is Langford "Ford" Morgan, a forty-six-year-old former agent of the Central Intelligence Agency in retirement in Costa Rica. His former wife calls Ford back to California to help her son Johnny prove that he is innocent of the charge of attempted murder of his father, Ralph Baliol. Ford soon finds himself involved in murder and corporate shenanigans. Part of the reason for Ford's return is his notion of "unfinished business," and he resumes sexual relations with his former wife for a while and ignores Lareina Alvaro, a wealthy and beautiful Costa Rican actress. He then becomes enamored of Barbara Allison Schoenhausen, who finally tells him that his "love" is just an "illusion." At the end of the novel Barbara has teamed with Roy Shepherd, the "Cadillac cowboy," a hired killer for Ralph Baliol. Because Baliol had killed his business partner Fletcher Comrie, Ford, who is a witness to Barbara killing Baliol, walks away from the murder, allowing Barbara and Shepherd to get away. Later he sees Lareina again, but their relationship is over. She decides to return to Costa Rica, and he decides to buy the Northern California company Baliol and Comrie had owned and robbed. At the end of the novel Ford realizes there is no security and that his life story is unimportant. Justice will be served not by him but by the authorities.

Max L. Autrey
Updated by Thomas L. Erskine

PRINCIPAL MYSTERY AND DETECTIVE FICTION

THE SHADOW SERIES (AS GRANT): *The Shadow Strikes*, 1964; *Cry Shadow*, 1965; *Shadow Beware*, 1965; *The Shadow's Revenge*, 1965; *Mark of the Shadow*, 1966; *Shadow—Go Mad!*, 1966; *The Night of the Shadow*, 1966; *The Shadow—Destination: Moon*, 1967

DAN FORTUNE SERIES: *Act of Fear*, 1967; *The Brass Rainbow*, 1969; *Night of the Toads*, 1970; *Walk a Black Wind*, 1971; *Shadow of a Tiger*, 1972; *The Silent Scream*, 1973; *Blue Death*, 1975; *The Blood-Red Dream*, 1976; *The Nightrunners*, 1978; *The Slasher*, 1980; *Freak*, 1983; *Minnesota Strip*, 1987; *Red Rosa*, 1988; *Castrato*, 1989; *Chasing Eights*, 1990; *The Irishman's Horse*, 1991; *Cassandra in Red*, 1992; *Resurrection*, 1992; *The Cadillac Cowboy*, 1995

KANE JACKSON SERIES (AS ARDEN): *A Dark Power*, 1968; *Deal in Violence*, 1969; *The Goliath Scheme*, 1971; *Die to a Distant Drum*, 1972 (also known as *Murder Underground*); *Deadly Legacy*, 1973

PAUL SHAW SERIES (AS SADLER): *The Falling Man*, 1970; *Here to Die*, 1971; *Mirror Image*, 1972; *Circle of Fire*, 1973; *Touch of Death*, 1981; *Deadly Innocents*, 1986

BUENA COSTA COUNTY SERIES (AS CROWE): *A Touch of Darkness*, 1972; *Another Way to Die*, 1972; *Bloodwater*, 1974; *Crooked Shadows*, 1975; *When They Kill Your Wife*, 1977; *Close to Death*, 1979

NICK CARTER KILLMASTER SERIES (AS CARTER): *The N3 Conspiracy*, 1974; *The Green Wolf Connection*, 1976; *Triple Cross*, 1976

NONSERIES NOVELS: *Combat Soldier*, 1962 (as Lynds); *Uptown, Downtown*, 1963 (as Lynds); *Lukan War*, 1969; *The Planets of Death*, 1970; *Woman in Marble*, 1973 (as Dekker); *Charlie Chan Returns*, 1974 (as Lynds); *Charlie Chan in the Temple of the Golden Horde*, 2003; *S.W.A.T.—Crossfire*, 1975 (as Lynds)

SHORT FICTION: *Why Girls Ride Sidesaddle*, 1980 (as Lynds); *Crime, Punishment, and Resurrection: Dan Fortune Thrillers*, 1992; *Talking to the World*, 1995 (as Lynds); *Spies and Thieves, Cops and Killers, Etc.*, 2002; *Fortune's World: Stories*, 2000; *Slot-Machine Kelly: The Collected Private Eye Cases of the "One-Armed Bandit,"* 2005

OTHER MAJOR WORKS

CHILDREN'S LITERATURE (AS ARDEN): *The Mystery of the Moaning Cave*, 1968; *The Mystery of the Laughing Shadow*, 1969; *The Secret of the Crooked Cat*, 1970; *The Mystery of the Shrinking House*, 1972; *The Mystery of the Blue Condor*, 1973; *The Secret of Phantom Lake*, 1973; *The Mystery of the Dead Man's Riddle*, 1974; *The Mystery of the Dancing Devil*, 1976; *The Mystery of the Headless Horse*, 1977; *The Mystery of the Deadly Double*, 1978; *The Secret of Shark Reef*, 1979; *The Mystery of the Purple Pirate*, 1982; *The Mystery of the Smashing Glass*, 1984; *The Secret of Wrecker's Rock*, 1986; *Hot Wheels*, 1989

BIBLIOGRAPHY

Ashley, Mike. *The Mammoth Encyclopedia of Modern Crime Fiction*. New York: Graf and Graf, 2001. Discusses the plot structure of Collins's novels, describing them as resembling "pyramids." Notes that Gayle Stone, Collins's third wife, was also a writer and collaborated with Collins on two novels.

Baker, Robert A., and Michael T. Nietzel. *Private Eyes: One Hundred and One Knights*. Bowling Green, Ohio: Bowling Green State University Popular Press, 1985. Contains a brief biography of Collins, as well as a synopsis with an analysis of both the Dan Fortune novels through *Freak* and the Mark Sadler novels through *Touch of Death*. The authors see Fortune as the sociological private eye who succeeded the "naturalistic Spade," the "romantic Marlowe," and the "psychological Archer."

Carpenter, Richard. "Michael Collins." In *Twentieth-Century Crime and Mystery Writers*, edited by John M. Reilly. 2d ed. New York: St. Martin's

Press, 1985. Cites the complex plots and the inde-terminate and ambiguous endings. Discusses Collins's quest to know, placing him in a tradition of existentialist heroes.

Conquest, John. *Trouble Is Their Business: Private Eyes in Fiction, Film, and Television*. New York: Garland, 1990. Focuses on the Dan Fortune character, especially his "wound," and notes that Fortune brings "compassion, ambiguity, philosophy, intuition, and complexity" to the private eye persona.

De Andrea, William L. *Encyclopedia Mysteriosa*. New York: Prentice Hall, 1994. Notes that Lynd's choice of the name "Michael Collins" was made because of his interest in Michael Collins, the Irish revolutionist, and praises Collins for his melding of a political point of view with a solid plot.

Geherin, David. *The American Private Eye: The Image in Fiction*. New York: Ungar, 1985. In "The Compassionate Eye," Geherin discusses the first eleven Dan Fortune novels, focusing on the symbolic use of Fortune's missing arm, the novel as sociodrama, the quest for justice, the New York setting of the novels, and the lack of humor and sex in the novels.

WILKIE COLLINS

Born: London, England; January 8, 1824
Died: London, England; September 23, 1889
Type of plot: Amateur sleuth

CONTRIBUTION

Wilkie Collins is the father of modern English mystery fiction. In his own time, his tales were called "sensation stories." He was the first to broaden the genre to the proportions of a novel and to choose familiar settings with ordinary people who behave rationally, and he was also the first to insist on scientific exactitude and rigorously accurate detail.

Collins was one of the most popular authors of his day, reaching a wider circle of readers in England and the United States than any author except Charles Dickens. Many of his books were translated for a highly appreciative French public. Although Collins claimed that he wrote for the common man, in his heyday critics classed him with Dickens, William Makepeace Thackeray, George Eliot, and Charlotte Brontë.

Now only two of Collins's twenty-two novels are considered masterpieces: *The Woman in White* (1860) and *The Moonstone* (1868). They have been highly praised by such discriminating critics as Thomas Hardy, Walter de la Mare, T. S. Eliot, and Dorothy L. Sayers (who felt so much indebted to Collins that she embarked on a biography of him, a project that E. R. Gregory completed after Sayers's death). It is safe to say that without Wilkie Collins, the modern English detective story could never have achieved its present level.

BIOGRAPHY

William Wilkie Collins was the son of a successful painter, William Collins, and a cultured mother. With his parents and his younger brother, Charles, he spent his twelfth and thirteenth years on the Continent, mostly in Italy, looking at buildings and paintings with his father and becoming proficient in French and Italian.

Back in England, Collins was sent to a private school, where the prefect made him tell stories at night under threat of a cat-o'-nine-tails. He left school at seventeen and preferred being apprenticed to a firm of tea importers to continuing his education at Oxford or Cambridge. At work, he wrote stories instead of bills of lading and requested frequent long holidays, which he usually spent in France enjoying himself and running up debts. In 1846, he left the tea business and entered Lincoln's Inn, becoming a barrister in due time. He never practiced law, but this training enabled him to write knowledgeably about legal matters.

After the death of his father, Collins lived with his mother, who often entertained members of the Pre-Raphaelite group of artists and writers; these became his chief friends.

Wilkie Collins. (Library of Congress)

When Collins was twenty-seven, he met Charles Dickens. Their subsequent friendship led to Collins's involvement in amateur theatricals and to his writing of plays, as well as to the publication of many of his stories in *All the Year Round* and *Household Words* (whose staff he joined in 1856).

At the age of thirty-five, Collins fell in love with Caroline Graves, who became the model for *The Woman in White*. They lived more or less openly together until Caroline married someone else. Collins then formed a liaison with Martha Rudd, with whom he had three children. Caroline returned to Collins's side, however, for the last twenty years of his life.

During these last years, Collins was plagued by ill health. He frequently used opium, which was at that time a household remedy. Because of his illness—or because of the opium—the quality of his writing de-

clined. He did not, however, seem aware of this fact, and his readers continued to be enthusiastic.

ANALYSIS

Wilkie Collins was responsible for turning the early nineteenth century "sensation story" of mystery and imagination into the detective novel. In his own sensation story, *Basil: A Story of Modern Life* (1852), it is possible to see the characteristics that were to mark his famous mystery novels; in fact, everything is there except the detective. There is the righteous young man who falls deeply in love with a beautiful girl who proves to be utterly unworthy of him—not because she is a tradesman's daughter (and this was a surprising innovation) but because of her sexual immorality; there is the young man's adoring sister, his stern father, and the memory of a devoted mother; there is an inscrutable, irredeemable villain, this one named Mannion, a man who has vowed vengeance against the righteous young man because the latter's father had condemned his father to be hanged.

There are scenes of life in mansions and in cottages and vivid descriptions of nature. Here, the vivid pictures are of the coast of Cornwall and surely show the influence of Collins's father, the painter. There is a detailed manuscript, like the later diaries, and lengthy letters from various characters. Finally, there is the happy ending with the villain dead, the mystery exposed, and all the good people living happily ever after. All these elements, with Collins's marvelous skill at narrative construction, were carried over into the detective novels, where the amateur detective was added.

THE WOMAN IN WHITE

The detective in *The Woman in White* is Walter Hartright. His name is significant: His heart is in the right place. He meets the beautiful Laura, for whom he would soon be glad to sacrifice his life, when he comes to Limmeridge House, the Fairlie estate, as drawing master for her and her half sister, Marian Halcombe. The sensible sister, who worships Laura, soon surmises that Laura returns his love. Because her sister is about to be married to Sir Percival Glyde, in accordance with her dead father's last wishes, Marian persuades Hartright to depart.

Before he leaves, Hartright tells Marian about an

encounter with a woman in white that had taken place on the eve of his departure from London. While walking alone across the heath after midnight, he had met a young woman, dressed entirely in white, who asked for his help in getting to London. The young lady supplied no information about herself except that she wished to see Limmeridge House again and that she was devoted to the memory of Mrs. Fairlie. After reaching the outskirts of London and gallantly putting her into a cab, Hartright was startled by the arrival of a chaise containing two men. One of them told a police officer that they were trying to catch a woman in white who had escaped from his asylum.

Marian is intrigued by Hartright's story and discovers in one of her mother's old letters a reference to a child named Anne Catherick who had promised to dress thenceforth only in white and who strongly resembled Laura.

When Laura receives an anonymous letter warning her against her future husband, Hartright begins his detective work. By chance, he finds Anne Catherick, whom he at once recognizes as the woman in white whom he had met at night on the heath. Now she is wiping Mrs. Fairlie's gravestone with her handkerchief. He makes her admit that she had written the warning letter, and he deduces that it was Sir Percival who had caused her to be shut up in the asylum. The next day, the detective leaves Limmeridge House, presumably forever.

After about ten months, Walter Hartright, having narrowly escaped death three times, returns to England and learns of Lady Glyde's death. The fact that the three narrow escapes are mentioned in as many lines shows how much Collins resisted including violence in his books. A good third of the book, then, is given over to events that take place during the detective's absence.

Hartright decides to seek comfort at the tomb of Laura—where, to his utter surprise, he encounters Marian Halcombe and Laura herself. He arranges for the two women to live with him as his sisters in a humble London lodging while he sets about proving that it is Anne Catherick, not Laura, who is buried beside Mrs. Fairlie. This is where his detective work really begins—about two-thirds of the way through the book. From this point onward, his efforts are directed toward restoring Laura to her inheritance. Extensive and clever investigations bring about a happy ending. Clearly, the emphasis is still on mystery rather than detection.

THE MOONSTONE

In *The Moonstone*, the amateur detective Franklin Blake, like Hartright, arrives on the scene at the beginning of the book and falls in love with the heroine, in this case Rachel Verinder. He brings with him a fateful gem, which disappears a few nights later, after a dinner party celebrating Rachel's birthday. A superintendent of police and a Sergeant Cuff, neither of whom would be out of place in a twentieth century detective tale, make no progress in their investigations and are inexplicably dismissed. Rachel rebuffs Blake, and he goes abroad to try to forget her. Eventually, the death of his father brings him back to England, where Rachel steadfastly declines to see him. He discovers that she has been mortally offended by the assistance that he provided to the police after the theft. He cannot understand this and resolves to unravel the mystery himself.

Only the last third of the book is reserved for his detective efforts. Finally he is able to prove to Rachel that he did indeed, as she believed, steal the moonstone, but that he was at the time in a trance induced by an overdose of laudanum. He is also able to prove who had actually taken the jewel from him in his sleep. Again, love triumphs and the real criminal is punished. Once more, the amateur detective's role is relatively small, but it is crucial to the resolution of the mystery.

Collins held very definite theories on the art of storytelling. He declared that to make the reader accept the marvelous, the author must give accurate and precise descriptions from everyday life, including the most prosaic details. Only thus could he hope to fix the interest of the reader on things beyond personal experience and to excite suspense. Collins's gift of observation permitted him to describe minutely and realistically the backgrounds of his characters; his father's social position as a famous painter enabled him to write with confidence about life in big country houses, while his stint at Lincoln's Inn and his habit of collecting police reports provided him with a knowledge of life among the less privileged sections of the London population.

In his preface to *Basil*, Collins points out that since he is writing for people of his own time and about people of his own time, he cannot expect even the slightest error to pass unnoticed. He is irrevocably committed to realism. Later, Collins assured his readers that the legal points of *The Woman in White* were checked by "a solicitor of great experience" and that the medical issues in *Heart and Science* (1883) were vouched for by "an eminent London surgeon."

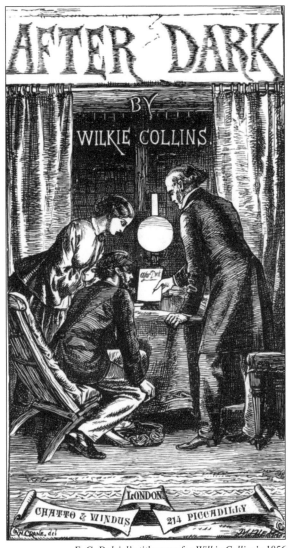

E. G. Dalziel's title page for Wilkie Collins's 1856 collection of stories, After Dark.

Collins reserves the right, however, to ask his readers to take some extraordinary events on faith. These are the events that will capture their imagination and induce them to continue the story. This formula, which had been advanced by Pierre Corneille in the seventeenth century in France and was adopted by Charles Dickens, worked so well that *Harper's Monthly* was restored to popularity by installments of *Armadale* (1866). The first edition of *The Woman in White* sold out in one day in London, and six subsequent editions appeared within six months. It was read, says one biographer, by paperboys and bishops.

Collins's way of telling a story was unique. He usually had each important character write down his own version of the facts, sticking strictly to what he knew from personal observation or from speeches he had overheard. This system resulted in a variation on the epistolary novel, which had been popular in the eighteenth century but had not been used before in mystery stories. In *The Woman in White*, the narrators are Walter Hartright, the drawing teacher; Vincent Gilmore, a solicitor; Marian Halcombe, whose diary is reproduced; Frederick Fairlie, owner of Limmeridge House, where a large part of the action takes place; Eliza Michelson, housekeeper at Blackwater Park, where the villain, Fosco, is introduced; Hester Pinhurn, an illiterate servant of Fosco whose testimony is written for her; and a doctor who reports on the supposed Lady Glyde's death. Nearly all these people provide their testimony at great length and in the language of educated persons; there is very little differentiation of style.

In each narration the reader picks up a clue to the solution of the incredibly complicated and ingenious plot, which contains all the trappings of a modern English detective story: large country estates with lonely pavilions, altered church registers, sleeping draughts, abductions, secret messages, intercepted letters, and an insane asylum. Eventually, all the ends are neatly tied up with the help of several incredible coincidences. For example, Hartright, on a four-day business trip to Paris, happens, on his way to visit the Cathedral of Notre Dame, to see the body of Fosco exposed in the window of the morgue. The tale is so gripping, however, that the enthralled reader takes these unlikely events in stride.

Numerous critics, including Thomas Hardy, have said that Collins is good on plot but weak on characterization. On the whole, this criticism seems just, for the same types recur in novel after novel. Nevertheless, Collins was capable of creating extraordinarily vivid characters; even the servants are real people with real emotions—a departure from most Victorian literature. It is true that his personages are either angels or devils, but they are real. Fosco, for example, is a short, round foreign man, unfailingly polite, fond of his canaries and pet mice, who has cowed his wife into utter subservience, who dominates his host, who is cool and clever and absolutely unscrupulous.

In *The Moonstone* there is another unforgettable full-length portrait: that of Drusilla Clack. This is a caricature that reminds one of Dickens's Mrs. Jellyby in *Bleak House*, a novel written fifteen years earlier (1852-1853). Miss Clack is a conceited, self-righteous single woman, a dedicated worker in the Mothers'-Small-Clothes-Conversion-Society and the British-Ladies'-Servants-Sunday-Sweetheart-Supervision-Society. She is insatiably curious about the lives of others and picks up information and gossip while scattering tracts in any home to which she can gain entry.

Although opinions may vary on Collins's portrayal of character, there is unanimity in praising him as a storyteller. The public of his time was wildly enthusiastic. Installments of his stories were eagerly awaited when they appeared in serial form in a wide variety of English and North American periodicals; any magazine that carried his short stories was in great demand. Probably the best known of these short stories is "A Terribly Strange Bed," originally printed in *After Dark* (1856). It has all the suspense and horror that Sir Arthur Conan Doyle and Edgar Allan Poe later succeeded in creating in their tales. No wonder audiences in England and across the Atlantic in 1873-1874 flocked to hear Collins read his stories.

All the acclaim that Collins received from the public may have contributed to the decline in quality of his later work. After about 1870, he seemed determined to prove that he was more than an entertainer: He began writing didactic books. *Man and Wife* (1870) deals with the injustice of the marriage laws of Scotland; *The New Magdalen* (1873) examined efforts to redeem

fallen women; *Heart and Science* treated the question of vivisection. He had always tried to prove that all forms of vice are self-destructive; he had always made sure that virtue was rewarded; he had often excited sympathy for physical disabilities, for example, with the hearing impaired in *Hide and Seek* (1854) and the visually disabled girl in *Poor Miss Finch: A Novel* (1872). His stepped-up efforts to make the world a better place, however, diminished the literary quality of his stories. The general public did not perceive this until well after the turn of the century, but the enthusiasm of critics diminished during the last twenty years of Collins's life.

Despite the weaknesses of the later novels, Collins's high place in literary history is assured by *The Woman in White* and *The Moonstone*. J. I. M. Stewart, in his introduction to the 1966 Penguin edition of the latter, sums up thus: "No English novel shows a structure and proportions, or contrives a narrative tempo, better adapted to its end: that of lending variety and amplitude to a story the mainspring of which has to be a sustained interest in the elucidation of a single mysterious event."

Dorothy B. Aspinwall

PRINCIPAL MYSTERY AND DETECTIVE FICTION

NOVELS: *Basil: A Story of Modern Life*, 1852; *Hide and Seek*, 1854; *The Dead Secret*, 1857; *The Woman in White*, 1860; *No Name*, 1862; *Armadale*, 1866; *The Moonstone*, 1868; *Man and Wife*, 1870; *Poor Miss Finch: A Novel*, 1872; *The New Magdalen*, 1873; *The Law and the Lady*, 1875; *The Two Destinies: A Romance*, 1876; *My Lady's Money*, 1878; *The Haunted Hotel: A Mystery of Modern Venice*, 1879; *A Rogue's Life*, 1879; *The Fallen Leaves*, 1879; *Jezebel's Daughter*, 1880; *The Black Robe*, 1881; *Heart and Science*, 1883; *I Say No*, 1884; *The Evil Genius: A Dramatic Story*, 1886; *The Guilty River*, 1886; *The Legacy of Cain*, 1889; *Blind Love*, 1890 (completed by Walter Besant)

SHORT FICTION: *Mr. Wray's Cash-Box: Or, The Mask and the Mystery*, 1852; *After Dark*, 1856; *The Lazy Tour of Two Idle Apprentices*, 1857 (with Charles Dickens); *The Queen of Hearts*, 1859; *The Frozen Deep*, 1866; *Miss or Mrs.? and Other Stories*,

1873; *The Frozen Deep, and Other Stories*, 1874; *Alicia Warlock: A Mystery, and Other Stories*, 1875; *The Guilty River*, 1886; *Little Novels*, 1887; *The Yellow Tiger, and Other Tales*, 1924

OTHER MAJOR WORKS

NOVEL: *Antonina: Or, The Fall of Rome*, 1850

SHORT FICTION: *The Seven Poor Travellers*, 1854; *The Wreck of the Golden Mary*, 1856

PLAYS: *The Lighthouse*, pr. 1855; *The Red Vial*, pr. 1858; *No Thoroughfare*, pr., pb. 1867 (with Charles Dickens); *The Woman in White*, pr., pb. 1871 (adaptation of his novel); *Man and Wife*, pr. 1873 (adaptation of his novel); *The New Magdalen*, pr., pb. 1873 (adaptation of his novel); *The Moonstone*, pr., pb. 1877 (adaptation of his novel)

NONFICTION: *Memoirs of the Life of William Collins, R. A.*, 1848 (2 volumes); *Rambles Beyond Railways*, 1851; *The Letters of Wilkie Collins*, 1999 (William Baker and William M. Clarke, editors); *The Public Face of Wilkie Collins: The Collected Letters*, 2005 (4 volumes; William Baker, editor)

MISCELLANEOUS: *My Miscellanies*, 1863; *The Works of Wilkie Collins*, 1900, 1970 (30 volumes)

BIBLIOGRAPHY

Bachman, Maria K., and Don Richard Cox, eds. *Reality's Dark Light: The Sensational Wilkie Collins*. Knoxville: University of Tennessee Press, 2003. Collection of essays on Collins by leading scholars locating detective fiction at the intersection between realism and sensationalism. Bibliographic references and index.

Collins, Wilkie. *The Letters of Wilkie Collins*. New York: St. Martin's Press, 1999. Collected correspondence between Collins and his friends, family, and business colleagues.

Gasson, Andrew. *Wilkie Collins: An Illustrated Guide*. New York: Oxford University Press, 1998. A well-illustrated, alphabetical guide to characters, titles, and terms in Collins's works. Includes a chronology, the Collins family tree, maps, and a bibliography.

Nayder, Lillian. *Wilkie Collins*. New York: Twayne, 1997. A good introductory study of the author. Includes biographical information and literary criticism.

Peters, Catherine. *The King of Inventors: A Life of Wilkie Collins*. Princeton, N.J.: Princeton University Press, 1991. A comprehensive biography, with detailed notes and bibliography.

Pykett, Lyn, ed. *Wilkie Collins*. New York: St. Martin's Press, 1998. An excellent place for the beginning student to start. Includes bibliographical references and an index.

Salatto, Eleanor. *Gothic Returns in Collins, Dickens, Zola, and Hitchcock*. New York: Palgrave Macmillan, 2006. Analysis of the nineteenth century employment of the gothic in fiction, as well as its twentieth century reincarnation in Alfred Hitchcock's cinema. Includes discussion of Collins's work. Bibliographic references and index.

Smith, Nelson, and R. C. Terry, eds. *Wilkie Collins to the Forefront: Some Reassessments*. New York: AMS Press, 1995. Compilations of essays seeking to reevaluate Collins's place within the literary canon and within the history of detective fiction.

Thoms, Peter. *The Windings of the Labyrinth: Quest and Structure in the Major Novels of Wilkie Collins*. Athens: Ohio University Press, 1992. Delves into the function of mazelike structures in Collins's narratives and their mirroring of spiritual or intellectual labyrinths within the stories.

SUSAN CONANT

Born: Merrimack Valley, Massachusetts; May 20, 1946

Types of plot: Amateur sleuth; cozy

PRINCIPAL SERIES

Dog Lover's, 1990-
Cat Lover's, 2005-
Gourmet Girl, 2006-

PRINCIPAL SERIES CHARACTERS

HOLLY WINTER is a dog trainer and journalist in her thirties who writes for *Dog's Life* and lives with her Alaskan malamutes, Rowdy and Kimi, in Cambridge, Massachusetts. She promotes humanitarian treatment of animals and encourages responsible dog ownership and obedience training. Exhibiting many of the traits she admires in dogs, Winter is a loyal friend and nurtures her relationships. A good daughter, she tolerates the interest of her widower father, Buck, in wolf hybrids and strives to honor the dog handler legacy of her deceased mother, Marissa. Crimes confront Winter as she interacts with dog owners and eccentric Cambridge residents.

FELICITY PRIDE is a middle-aged retired kindergarten teacher who is the author of the Prissy LaChatte cat mysteries but lacks experience with felines until she adopts a murdered man's pets. She lacks Winter's sincerity and naïveté. Jaded regarding her profession, Pride jealously resents rival authors whose cat mystery series sell more copies than her books and discourages novice writers whom she perceives as lacking talent. Pride lives in a luxurious house in Newton Park, Massachusetts, that she inherited from her uncle and endures her difficult mother's and neighbors' demands while trying to solve mysteries immediately affecting her.

CHLOE CARTER is a social work graduate student in her twenties who attends a Boston college near her Brighton, Massachusetts, apartment only to fulfill stipulations in her uncle's will so that she may receive his money. Unenthused by her classes and an internship at a help line, narcissistic Carter constantly repaints her apartment and seeks satisfying romance, stylish clothing, and delicious food, meanwhile bumbling into criminal situations. She is immature compared with Winter and Pride but shares their impulsive nature, which often results in her revealing clues and culprits.

CONTRIBUTION

Susan Conant published her first dog mystery, *A New Leash on Life*, in 1990, a year before authors Sue Henry and Mary Willis Walker published crime novels depicting female dog training sleuths and working dogs. Although some critics identify Conant as initiating the dog mystery genre, she and her writing peers had prior literary canine-related mystery inspirations, including Sherlock Holmes. In 1983 Barbara Moore wrote *The Doberman Wore Black*, which featured a veterinarian sleuth assisted by a dog. Nonetheless, Conant established herself as a leading author in that subgenre.

Scholars have generally ignored Conant's contributions to the mystery genre. Although some critics have found fault with Conant's writing style, particularly her plotting and development of mystery elements, others have praised her dialogue, depictions of settings, and characterizations, which became more complex and admirable as her writing matured. Her fan base assured Conant of consistent commercial success, and she continued to produce new dog mysteries annually. In 2005, Conant's reputation as an author who delivered satisfying stories to readers interested in dog mysteries resulted in her introducing a series for cat enthusiasts. Her success also enabled her to pursue writing mysteries with her daughter, addressing a lifestyle and cultural interests unlike those readers experienced in her animal-themed novels.

Conant has striven to introduce readers to the dog world and educate them regarding topics and issues that might otherwise be unfamiliar to them. The Dog Writers' Association of America has rewarded Conant's works with its Maxwell Award several times.

BIOGRAPHY

Susan Jane Conant was born on May 20, 1946, in the Merrimack Valley, Massachusetts, to Eugene A. Conant and Dorothy Morrison Conant. At the time of her birth, Susan's father served as president of Anderson-Wills Incorporated, a business selling automobiles in Lawrence, Massachusetts, where her mother's family lived. A resident of nearby Methuen, Massachusetts, her mother had previously worked as a secretary for Anderson-Wills. Susan's paternal grandfather had worked as a high school principal in Maine. Susan grew up in the Merrimack Valley, spending part of her childhood in Haverhill, Massachusetts. Her father trained pointers and encouraged his daughter's interest in dogs.

In 1964, Susan Conant moved to the Boston area, enrolling at Radcliffe College, where she studied anthropology and social relations. She received a bachelor's degree summa cum laude in June, 1968. Also in 1968, Conant wed Carter Conrad Umbarger, who received his doctorate in psychology from Brandeis University the following year.

Conant moved to Philadelphia, where she was employed as a kindergarten teacher for public schools during 1969. During that year and the next, she served as a group therapist for the Child Study Center of Philadelphia. Conant relocated with her husband to Newton, Massachusetts, and he established a clinical psychology practice in nearby Cambridge. They have one daughter, Jessica.

In 1973, Conant began studies focusing on human development at Harvard University's Graduate School of Education. During 1974 and 1975, she served as a research assistant for the University of Houston. Conant completed a master's degree in education at Harvard in June, 1975. She then enrolled in a doctoral education program at Harvard. Her primary research studied preschool children with language disabilities.

From 1976 to 1978, Conant worked as a teaching assistant for Harvard's Graduate School of Education and as a Harvard Extension School grader. She then was a research associate at the Research Institute for Educational Problems in Cambridge during 1978. Conant received an doctorate in education from Harvard in 1978.

During the next decade, Conant pursued a career as a special education researcher. In the fall of 1986, Conant experienced chronic fevers, aches, and a fluctuating white blood cell count and suffered abnormal fatigue. Conant acquired an Alaskan malamute puppy, which stayed with her during her extended illness. Conant was frustrated when her illness persisted and doctors could not determine what was wrong. Gradually, her symptoms stopped and she recovered. Conant interviewed other people suffering chronic fatigue and wrote a nonfictional book about their experiences.

Conant had enjoyed reading Nancy Drew and other mysteries as a child. While she was sick, she enjoyed mysteries by her favorite authors, including Margery Allingham, and considered writing mysteries. While attending weekly dog training classes in 1988, Conant began writing mysteries when she envisioned a plot involving a trainer disappearing during an obedience exercise. Conant submitted her manuscript to a publisher, who presented her a contract for a dog mystery series.

In addition to novels, Conant wrote articles and reviews for dog magazines, contributing to the opinion column "Point of View" in *Pure-bred Dogs/American Kennel Gazette*. She edited *Pawprints*, the New England Dog Training Club's newsletter. Conant belongs to both the New England Dog Training Club and Charles River Dog Training Club and competes in matches to earn obedience titles with her dogs. She helped establish Alaskan Malamute Rescue of New England and became the Massachusetts coordinator of the Alaskan Malamute Protection League in 1988.

Conant has served on the board of directors of the New England chapter of the Mystery Writers of America and belongs to Sisters in Crime, the Dog Writers' Association of America, and the Cat Writers' Association.

ANALYSIS

Susan Conant's style is reminiscent of that found in popular mystery fiction featuring strong female protagonists, such as the series of Marcia Muller and Sue Grafton, which were popular during the 1980's, when Conant was first inspired to write mysteries. In her character-driven mysteries, Conant presents her stories through the first-person narrative of Holly Winter, whose perceptions of people and situations she encounters are sometimes unreliable and distorted by her emotional reactions. Winter's point of view is the narrative device in all of Conant's dog mysteries. Her voice gains maturity as she survives various attacks and seeks justice for mistreated dogs and people.

Conant's literary strength is her use of humor, particularly her characterizations of eccentric and pretentious people. Winter recognizes the flaws of her Cambridge, Massachusetts, environment, wittily commenting about Ivy League culture and the abundance of psychologists. Conant's professional background as a language educator enables her to present dialogue well.

Conant's depiction of places immerses readers in her settings. Her expertise and insights regarding dogs can be considered both a strength and a weakness. At times, the details are welcome, but sometimes they seem intrusive and overwhelming. Conant admits that she has an interest in teaching readers about proper dog ownership and care. Through her characters, she stresses themes of animal welfare and humanitarian treatment, warning readers of abuses at puppy mills and animal research laboratories.

Conant's experiences as a psychologist's wife and longtime resident of Cambridge provides authenticity while sometimes presenting information that eludes readers unfamiliar with those subjects. Usually, such incidental descriptions and revelations are not essential for resolution of Conant's mysteries and do not serve as red herrings. Conant's mysteries are sometimes predictable and have weak conclusions. Villains' motivations occasionally seem unbelievable and not substantial enough for the individuals to resort to committing crimes or murders. Narrative pacing is frequently slowed by too many unnecessary details and introspection, particularly involving psychological disorders and treatments.

Conant's characterizations of dogs are often more vividly portrayed and developed than those of humans. Her canine characters exhibit authentic dog behavior, while some of her people are caricatures. Through her characters, Conant emphasizes themes of service and loyalty as well as of disobedience and stubbornness. In particular, her canine characters underscore her overall themes of companionship and devotion. Conant's presentations of exploited, abused, and neglected characters, both human and animal, stress her themes of mercy, tolerance, and the possibilities of redemption, reconciliation, and forgiveness.

A NEW LEASH ON DEATH

Conant introduces Holly Winter in her first mystery, *A New Leash on Death*, which foreshadows many of the situations and relationships that are important to Winter in later books in the series. By revealing Winter's reactions to crises, Conant establishes Winter's independent personality and commitment to dogs. Readers learn that the dog trainer is resourceful and determined to protect animals from negligent owners and that she will seek assistance when necessary to achieve her aim.

In *A New Leash on Death*, Dr. Frank Stanton is choked to death with his leash while training Rowdy, an Alaskan malamute. Winter taps her father, Buck, and specific dog breeders for information and contacts while researching a tattoo number to discover the background of Rowdy, who Stanton claimed he owned.

Holly's vulnerabilities are revealed when she reminisces about her mother and wishes she were as talented with dogs as her mother, a dog trainer, had been. Her manipulative side is also shown in her negotiations with her neighbor, Kevin Dennehy, a police officer who has inside information regarding crimes. Knowing he is romantically interested in her, Winter allows Dennehy to keep beer and meat at her house because his strictly religious mother forbids him to have these items in the home they share. Although she convinces Dennehy to divulge secrets, Winter rarely reciprocates and discourages an intimate relationship. Instead, she pursues a romance with her veterinarian, Steve Delaney. Winter also confides in Rita, a therapist who rents an apartment in Winter's three-story house.

Conant reveals the socioeconomic diversity of dog enthusiasts, which enables her to create a broad cast of potential culprits. Greed and pride are emphasized as motives. Winter realizes her resilience and courage when confronted by the killer, who tries to choke her. That ordeal, with Rowdy by her side, establishes the foundation for their future teamwork.

SCRATCH THE SURFACE

Conant's tone in *Scratch the Surface* (2005), the first novel in her cat mystery series, is often sarcastic and cynical. Protagonist Felicity Pride's experiences as an author of cat mysteries are far from ideal. Few fans show up at her book signings, a Russian publisher is selling her book illegally, and her rival Isabelle Hotchkiss has better sales. Pride's problems intensify when Quinlan Coates, a professor, is found dead in her vestibule. A cat waits beside him. Although Pride is a cat mystery writer, she knows nothing about cats. She initially views the cat and murder as an opportunity for publicity that might advance her career but is disappointed by the meager, and often inaccurate, coverage of the case.

Pride makes fumbling efforts to care for both of Coates's cats and solve the mystery of why he was murdered, although such efforts are not natural for someone with her seemingly rigid, selfish, aloof personality, which alienates many of her neighbors and peers. Pride becomes attached to the cats while trying to determine their identity and generously assisting detective Dave Valentine, whom she desires romantically, as she learns more about the cats and their owner's secrets.

Although Conant includes brief chapters revealing the two cats' perspectives, she does not give them human qualities or have them speak. Through Pride, she reveals details of the mystery-writing profession, expressing some dissatisfaction with the process through Pride's thoughts. Pride is not the animal lover that Winter is, but she does develop into a caring person capable of being kind to both people and animals, enhancing her public image as a cat mystery writer.

GAITS OF HEAVEN

In *Gaits of Heaven* (2006), Conant exposes her broad knowledge of psychology, psychiatry, and pharmacology as Winter deals with a couple, Ted and Eumie Green, who refuse to control their Aussie huskapoo Dolfo when they attend a class at her training club. Ted and Eumie ask Winter to help them but ignore her traditional training advice. After Eumie dies from what is assumed to be an overdose but might be murder, Winter permits Eumie's overweight daughter Caprice, who is a Harvard classmate of Winter's cousin Leah, to stay in her home. She soon realizes

that the Green family has extensive problems involving Caprice's father, Monty; her stepfather, Ted; and her stepbrother Wyeth.

Feeling empathy for Dolfo and Caprice, Winter intercedes, putting herself at risk to protect the vulnerable dog and girl. Conant's narrative bogs down as she introduces the characters' countless therapists and other medical professionals. The plot becomes too convoluted, introducing subplots such as mysterious squirrel poisonings and Winter dealing with her husband's former wife, Anita Fairley, who attacks Winter and her dogs.

STEAMED

Because Conant collaborated with her daughter, Jessica Conant-Park, to write *Steamed* (2006), her style is not as apparent as in her animal mysteries. Conant primarily plotted the mystery, which seems formulaic, relying on her daughter to provide information about young-adult culture in the early twenty-first century. The most obvious difference is that dogs are not a major component of the life of the protagonist, Chloe Carter. Instead, she is consumed with gourmet food and how her peers perceive her, looking for acceptance based on her clothes and other superficial factors. She studies only to retain her inheritance, which finances her lifestyle.

Intent on finding a boyfriend, Carter signs up with a dating Web site with the username GourmetGirl. Her blind date with DinnerDude, the obnoxious Eric Rafferty, is disrupted when he is murdered in a restaurant bathroom. Carter passively permits Rafferty's parents to believe she was engaged to their son but pursues a handsome chef, Josh Driscoll, at the reception after Rafferty's funeral. Carter continues her relationship with Driscoll although his knife is revealed to be the murder weapon. Like Winter, Carter unearths lies, suspects her love interest, and cultivates a close relationship with a female friend, but her revelations result more from coincidences and impulsiveness than reasoned action.

Elizabeth D. Schafer

PRINCIPAL MYSTERY AND DETECTIVE FICTION

DOG LOVER'S SERIES: *A New Leash on Death*, 1990; *Dead and Doggone*, 1990; *A Bite of Death*,

1991; *Paws Before Dying*, 1991; *Gone to the Dogs*, 1992; *Bloodlines*, 1992; *Ruffly Speaking*, 1994; *Black Ribbon*, 1995; *Stud Rites*, 1996; *Animal Appetite*, 1997; *The Barker Street Regulars*, 1998; *Evil Breeding*, 1999; *Creature Discomforts*, 2000; *The Wicked Flea*, 2002; *The Dogfather*, 2003; *Bride and Groom*, 2004; *Gaits of Heaven*, 2006; *All Shots*, 2007

CAT LOVER'S SERIES: *Scratch the Surface*, 2005
GOURMET GIRL SERIES (WITH JESSICA CONANT-PARK): *Steamed*, 2006; *Simmer Down*, 2007

OTHER MAJOR WORKS

NONFICTION: *Teaching Language-Disabled Children: A Communication Games Intervention*, 1983 (with Milton Budoff and Barbara Hecht); *Living with Chronic Fatigue*, 1990

BIBLIOGRAPHY

Beegan, Daniel. "Her Life's Work: Going to the Dogs, Books Feature Canines, People in Their Lives." *St. Louis Post-Dispatch*, June 6, 1994, p. 3E. An Associated Press feature profile based on an interview with Conant, which provides biographical information and addresses her goal to educate people regarding dogs through her mysteries.

Conant, Susan. "Mysterious Presence." *Radcliffe Quarterly* 83, no. 4 (Spring, 1998): 11. Conant compares her research and fiction writing, emphasizing the pleasure of being an academic turned novelist, and discusses her difficult relationship with her mother.

Dale, Steve. "Cover to Cover with Mystery Writer Susan Conant." *Dog World* 90, no. 5 (May, 2005): 24-25. Includes personal details about Conant based on conversations with her and her friends and reveals some of her inspirations for her characters and settings.

Heising, Willetta L. *Detecting Women: A Reader's Guide and Checklist for Mystery Series Written by Women*. 3d ed. Dearborn, Mich.: Purple Moon Press, 2000. Lists include Conant's books with a brief biography, placing her in context with other dog writers.

Klein, Kathleen Gregory, ed. *Great Women Mystery Writers: Classic to Contemporary*. Westport, Conn.: Greenwood Press, 1994. Brief sketch of Conant concluding with literary criticism of her early novels.

MICHAEL CONNELLY

Born: Philadelphia, Pennsylvania; July 21, 1956
Types of plot: Police procedural; hard-boiled

PRINCIPAL SERIES

Hieronymus "Harry" Bosch, 1992-

PRINCIPAL SERIES CHARACTER

HIERONYMUS "HARRY" BOSCH, named for the fifteenth century Dutch painter of sins and earthly degradation, is a Los Angeles Police Department homicide detective constantly in trouble with the department bureaucracy for his inability to take orders and his "cowboy" attitude toward murder investigations. Orphaned at eleven when his mother was murdered by an unknown assailant, he sees his mission in life as the pursuit of criminals. His obsession with his cases causes him to solve them in his own way, ignoring the consequences. He is twice divorced, drinks heavily, has few friends, and manages to alienate nearly everyone with whom he comes into contact, including a series of partners on the force, nearly all of whom grudgingly respect his police skills. His experience in the Vietnam War as a "tunnel rat," trained to enter Vietcong tunnels and crawl along in total darkness to find and eliminate the enemy, left indelible marks on his psyche. Images of groping in the dark and searching for the light dominate Bosch's interior mental landscape.

CONTRIBUTION

In many ways, Michael Connelly's novels featuring Hieronymus "Harry" Bosch fit neatly into the convention of hard-boiled detective fiction; however, the novels also display the author's complex plotting skills and his insights into the psychological makeup of both the criminal and the detective. Many of his characters (criminals and sometimes those on the side of the law) are best categorized as "monsters," social or psychological deviants capable of committing horrific crimes of torture and mutilation: the Dollmaker, the Poet, the Follower, and the Eidolon. For Connelly, often the psyches of these characters and that of Bosch are more interesting than the actual solution of the crime. Connelly views almost all pathological actions to be the result of social and familial forces; the born killer seems not to exist in his world. His protagonists must heed philosopher Friedrich Nietzsche's warning, loosely paraphrased by a character in *Lost Light* (2003) as "whoever is out there fighting the monsters . . . should make damn sure they don't become monsters themselves."

Connelly won an Edgar Award for best first novel for *The Black Echo* (1992); Anthony awards for *The Poet* (1996), *Blood Work* (1998), and *City of Bones* (2002); a Nero Award for *The Poet*; Barry awards for *Trunk Music* (1997) and *City of Bones*; and a Shamus Award for *The Lincoln Lawyer* (2005). He was twice elected president of the Mystery Writers of America (2003 and 2004), the only writer ever to be accorded this honor.

BIOGRAPHY

Michael Joseph Connelly was born in Philadelphia on July 21, 1956, and spent the first eleven years of his life there. His mother's extensive library, especially the works of Agatha Christie and Arthur Conan Doyle, opened the world of the mystery story to him. His family moved to Fort Lauderdale, Florida, and he spent the rest of his formative years in that state, eventually attending the University of Florida and graduating with a degree in journalism. At the university, he was introduced to the works of Raymond Chandler by one of his mentors, novelist Harry Crews. Connelly knew from that moment he wanted to be a novelist, but unlike many reporters-turned-crime-novelists, he thought that crime-beat reporting would be the best apprenticeship to the world of crime fiction and majored in journalism with an eye toward future fiction writing. His first jobs after graduation were as a beat reporter in Fort Lauderdale and Daytona Beach. In 1985 he covered the crash of Delta Flight 191, interviewing the survivors, most of whom were from the Fort Lauderdale area. A subsequent magazine article based on this coverage was nominated for a Pulitzer Prize, and soon after he was hired by the *Los Angeles Times* as a crime reporter.

Connelly published his first novel, *The Black Echo*, which introduced Harry Bosch, in 1992, basing it on a murder that occurred the day after he arrived in Los Angeles. After that came *The Black Ice* (1993), *The Concrete Blonde* (1994), and one of the central novels in the Bosch series, *The Last Coyote* (1995), the first book he completed after leaving reporting to write novels full time. Originally intended as the final installment in the series, *The Last Coyote* concerns Bosch's attempt to find his mother's murderer and

Michael Connelly. (Courtesy, Allen & Unwin)

solve the case long relegated to the cold case files by the Los Angeles Police Department. Connelly's next novel, *The Poet*, introduces Federal Bureau of Investigation agent Rachel Walling in the pursuit of a serial murderer who preyed on children. After Connelly became a father, he said that he probably could not or would not write about such a character again.

By Connelly's own admission, the Bosch character was too interesting for him to drop, and in 1997 he returned to Bosch in *Trunk Music*. He has continued to write both Bosch series and nonseries novels, and he published a collection of his earlier journalism, *Crime Beat: A Decade of Covering Cops and Killers* (2006). Connelly and his family moved to Florida in 2002. In that year Clint Eastwood produced, directed, and starred in a film based on the novel *Blood Work*, which famously changed the ending and the identity of the murderer. The publication of *The Lincoln Lawyer* in 2005 introduced a new protagonist for Connelly, cynical lawyer Mickey Haller, who the author planned to use in future novels. In 2006 two events marked watersheds in Connelly's career: the serialization of a new Bosch novella, *The Overlook* (published in book form in 2007), in *The New York Times*, and his selection as one of the five mystery authors to host a personally chosen installment of Court TV's true-crime series *Murder by the Book* (began 2006).

ANALYSIS

Michael Connelly's supreme creation is the haunted and tormented Los Angeles Police Department detective Hieronymus "Harry" Bosch. Through the character of Bosch, Connelly is able to portray much of the loneliness and despair of living in a violent, decadent, and surrealistic Los Angeles that is in many ways a modern embodiment of the Dutch painter Hieronymus Bosch's painting *The Garden of Earthly Delights*.

Much of the corruption Bosch finds in his investigations is in the actual institutions: the Los Angeles Police Department, the press, and the film industry. It seems that the only way Connelly can expose this corruption is with an insider who is also a loner and a renegade: Hence the character of Harry Bosch. Many of those in the police bureaucracy are corrupt—guilty of

cover-ups, shoddy investigations, and outright criminal behavior. The mentality seems to be to seek political gain rather than honesty or justice, and this is especially grating to a detective like Bosch.

One of the most common themes in Connelly's writing is the warning issued by Nietzsche: "He who fights against monsters should see to it that he does not become a monster in the process. And when you stare persistently into an abyss, the abyss also stares into you." Dealing with society's monsters, Connelly seems to say, places one in great danger of becoming a monster. This is evident in Bosch, who, though not a monster, is an emotional train wreck. He has one goal in life—to catch criminals—and everything else in his life is subsumed by this. Bosch has lived much of his life believing his mother's murder would never be solved, and when he solves it in *The Last Coyote*, the double trauma of knowing the details of his mother's murder and the fact that it was related to high-powered political cover-ups causes Bosch to seriously consider retirement. He stares at the monsters, and he fears that he may become one, or already has.

Connelly is justly praised for his complex plots, surprise endings, and the clarity and power of his style, honed at his reporter's desk. The amount of research he does is well known. Each of his novels has the ring of gritty truth, derived both from his own years of experience as a crime-beat reporter and from additional research into forensics, technology, autopsies, weapons, jazz performers, or whatever else is required by his plots. Plot details, even the most minute, are meticulously accurate and give an unusually heightened sense of reality. Especially noteworthy is Connelly's Los Angeles: Many authors set their crime stories on the streets of Los Angeles, but Connelly's detail—street names, highways, buildings, architectural types, neighborhood characteristics, and the archaeology of the La Brea Tar Pits—is unusual in its comprehensiveness and accuracy.

THE LAST COYOTE

The Last Coyote, originally intended to be Harry Bosch's swan song, has become one of Connelly's most critically acclaimed novels. After throwing his commanding officer through a plate-glass window, Bosch is placed on extended leave and required to take anger-management classes before he is reinstated. With spare time on his hands, he resurrects a cold case from thirty years before that the Los Angeles Police Department had never solved: the murder of prostitute Marjorie Lowe, Bosch's mother. In the course of tracking down the killer, Bosch again and again sees a lone coyote in the woods surrounding his house—a rare sighting, Bosch thinks, because civilization has all but driven out these creatures. It is no stretch to assume that Bosch himself is the last of a breed.

Paralleling Bosch's investigations is a subplot involving the psychiatrist assigned to his case. Through this plot device the reader is given a deep look into Bosch's troubled mind. Bosch is angry, rebellious, and resentful of authority. He reveals his stern, almost self-righteous moral code in the first session: "Everybody counts or nobody counts." This is the code, the religion, that Bosch lives by, and he is unyielding in its observance.

CHASING THE DIME

Chasing the Dime (2002) was sparked by an actual incident in Connelly's life: He was issued a phone number that had belonged to a woman who had disappeared. Though not a Bosch series novel and not received as well critically as some of Connelly's other novels (ironically because the plot turns on an almost Hitchcockian device thought to be improbable—the wrong phone number), *Chasing the Dime* is important in Connelly's works because it reinforces many of the major themes of the Bosch novels, particularly the effects of obsessiveness in the face of a mystery. In the novel, Henry Pierce, a chemist and chief executive officer of his own startup company, is about to become a multimillionaire as soon as certain patents are granted and funding is acquired, but his whole life—business, professional, personal, and romantic—is derailed by an obsession to discover what happened to the woman, a prostitute, who previously had his phone number and is now missing. Betrayed by friends and business partners and framed for murder, Pierce becomes adrift in a world of evil that he only slowly begins to understand. He solves the mystery and absolves himself of the murder charge but in the process is nearly killed by a severe beating and loses his fiancé (whom he incorrectly suspects of being in on the plot to destroy him),

his best friends, and the financial backing for his business. Nearly everything Pierce once believed is turned upside-down, and he knows he will live with deep suspicions for the rest of this life.

LOST LIGHT

Lost Light (2003) was Connelly's first Bosch novel written after the terrorist attacks on the World Trade Center. As such, it shows Connelly's increasing interest in the social and political issues of the day, though the focus remains strongly on the psyche of Bosch. It is also the only Bosch novel written in the first person (although the Bosch segments of *The Narrows*, 2004, are also written in first person), allowing the reader an insight into the mind of Bosch not possible with more objective third-person approaches.

Fed up with the Los Angeles Police Department bureaucracy at the end of *City of Bones* (2002), Bosch retires. At the beginning of *Lost Light*, Bosch is a freelance private detective, free of the department but also stripped of the status and security that a gun and badge afford. He chooses to concentrate on cold cases, the ones that got away while he was on the force, and starts with the case of Angella Benton, an apparent innocent bystander in a botched robbery on a motion picture set that resulted in the deaths of a number of bystanders and participants. Bosch is haunted by the placement of her hands in the crime scene photos, innocent and almost prayerlike. He resolves to find her killer and in the process uncovers more bureaucratic corruption and cover-ups in the Los Angeles Police Department, the treachery of friends and colleagues, the depths of venality in the film industry, and the almost unlimited power granted to law enforcement and intelligence agencies by the Homeland Security Act, power that begs to be abused.

In a rare moment of joy and happiness, Bosch discovers at the end of *Lost Light* that his first wife had given birth to a daughter whose existence has been kept from him, and Bosch feels for perhaps the first time in his life a sense of salvation, of pure happiness. In true Connelly fashion, however, all this happiness is crushed even before the opening of the next Bosch novel, *The Narrows*.

H. Eric Branscomb

PRINCIPAL MYSTERY AND DETECTIVE FICTION

HIERONYMUS "HARRY" BOSCH SERIES: *The Black Echo*, 1992; *The Black Ice*, 1993; *The Concrete Blonde*, 1994; *The Last Coyote*, 1995; *Trunk Music*, 1997; *Angels Flight*, 1999; *A Darkness More than Night*, 2001; *City of Bones*, 2002; *Lost Light*, 2003; *The Narrows*, 2004; *The Closers*, 2005; *Echo Park*, 2006; *The Overlook*, 2007

NONSERIES NOVELS: *The Poet*, 1996; *Blood Work*, 1998; *Void Moon*, 2000; *Chasing the Dime*, 2002; *The Lincoln Lawyer*, 2005

OTHER MAJOR WORKS

NONFICTION: *Crime Beat: A Decade of Covering Cops and Killers*, 2006

EDITED TEXTS: *The Best American Mystery Stories 2003*, 2003; *Murder in Vegas: New Crime Tales of Gambling and Desperation*, 2005

BIBLIOGRAPHY

Anderson, Patrick. *The Triumph of the Thriller: How Cops, Crooks, and Cannibals Captured Popular Fiction*. New York: Random House, 2007. Contains a chapter on Connelly that details his life and his works, including the Harry Bosch novels. Discusses *The Black Echo*, *The Last Coyote*, *A Darkness More than Night*, and *City of Bones*, among others.

Bertens, Hans, and Theo D'haen. *Contemporary American Crime Fiction*. New York: Palgrave, 2001. Discusses Connelly extensively in the introduction and devotes a chapter to "Los Angeles Police Department: Ellroy's and Connelly's Police Procedurals."

Fine, David M. *Imagining Los Angeles: A City in Fiction*. Reno: University of Nevada Press, 2004. Sees *The Concrete Blonde* and *The Last Coyote* in the tradition of the "murdered, mutilated or disfigured woman" following the Black Dahlia murder and the works of James Ellroy.

Gregoriou, Christiana. "Criminally Minded: The Stylistics of Justification in Contemporary American Crime Fiction." *Style* 37, no. 2 (Summer, 2003): 144-159. Uses an analysis of style and narrative point of view to argue that the monstrous character of the Eidolon in *The Poet* is a product of his environment, not his birth.

Kreyling, Michael. *The Novels of Ross Macdonald*. Columbia: University of South Carolina Press, 2005. Briefly discusses Harry Bosch as a direct descendant of Ross Macdonald's protagonist Lew Archer but notes that the "world of Harry Bosch is far more lethal than Archer's."

Oates, Joyce Carol. *Uncensored: Views and (Re)views*. New York: HarperPerennial, 2006. Devotes a chapter titled "L.A. Noir" to *A Darkness More than Night*, noting that Bosch is a "flawed, deeply troubled and isolated man."

JOHN CONNOLLY

Born: Dublin, Ireland; May 31, 1968
Also wrote as Laura Froom
Types of plot: Horror; private investigator; thriller

PRINCIPAL SERIES

Charlie Parker, 1999-

PRINCIPAL SERIES CHARACTER

CHARLIE PARKER is a former New York City police detective with a tormented past: the loss of his wife and daughter to a serial killer. Handsome, brooding, and em-pathetic, he is driven to help the vulnerable at whatever cost. There is a dark side—indeed, eschatologically dark—to him, which is impossible for him to ignore. He is a fallen angel, driven to atone for his sin against God by fighting the other fallen angels who prey on humanity.

CONTRIBUTION

John Connolly's first novel, *Every Dead Thing* (1999), brought him nearly equal amounts of praise and condemnation. Critics agreed that the tale is dark, terrifying, thrilling, and disturbing, not only because of its gruesome violence but also because of the hero's single-minded quest for retribution. Some critics extolled Connolly's lyrical prose style and the intensity of the story's drama. Others found the violence simply repellent and the themes irremediably grim. The *Los Angeles Times* reviewer deftly characterized Connolly's literary impact in remarking that the novel "holds the reader fast in a comfortless stranglehold."

Connolly's subsequent novels delve ever more into the supernatural to prepare readers for the psychotic killers and macabre violence of the plots. These novels are as much horror fiction as mysteries. The supernatural elements, however, rather than providing escapism, allow Connolly to examine the pathology and psychology of violent crime. British critic Mark Timlin wrote that as Charlie Parker's character evolves through the novels, Connolly demonstrates the possibility of moral choice and the necessity of action in the face of evil. In this regard, Connolly likes to quote the eighteenth century English political philosopher Edmund Burke, who observed that evil triumphs when good people stand by and do nothing to stop it. It is this thematic approach, critics agree, that makes Connolly's fiction more than simply thrilling entertainment. Connolly is also recognized for the meticulous research behind his settings and behind his use of esoteric supernatural lore.

BIOGRAPHY

John Connolly was born in Dublin on May 31, 1968, and raised in the city's Realto section, a rough neighborhood plagued by drugs. His father was a rent collector and his mother a schoolteacher with an interest in writing. At her urging, he read avidly from an early age. He claimed to an interviewer that he began to write a year after he began reading and that a teacher encouraged him by paying him for each Tarzan story that he wrote. Connolly completed secondary school at the age of seventeen and took a job in the accounting department of a local government office. For three years he largely forgot about writing. At last, bored with the job, he quit and entered Dublin's Trinity College, majoring in English. Among the subjects he studied was American crime fiction. It was his first introduction to authors who came to influence his own

fiction, among them Ross Macdonald, James Lee Burke, and Ed McBain. During one summer, Connolly went to Delaware to work as a waiter. However, he did not like the location and on a whim took a bus to Maine, which entranced him. He returned to Maine during subsequent summer holidays, working there and exploring the state. After taking his bachelor's degree, Connolly earned a master's degree in journalism from Dublin City University.

Following graduation, Connolly worked as a freelance writer for *The Irish Times*, the nation's leading daily newspaper. He specialized in feature stories, particularly about education, but he found the writing formulaic and frustrating. To escape from the grind of journalism, he began writing his first novel, *Every Dead Thing*. Before he finished the manuscript, he mailed out sample chapters to seventy publishers. All turned him down. However, one editor wrote a favorable comment on the rejection slip and encouraged Connolly to finish the work.

Connolly left freelancing and moved to Maine for a year, working as a waiter while he revised the manuscript. He resubmitted the novel, which was accepted and in 1999 brought him the largest advance on royalties for any Irish writer up to that time. The novel was nominated for the Bram Stoker Award for best first novel by the Horror Writers Association and for the Berry Award for the best British crime novel by *Deadly Pleasures* magazine, and it won the 2000 Shamus Award for best first private eye novel from the Private Eye Writers of America, making Connolly the first non-American author to receive the honor. *The White Road* (2002) won the 2003 Barry Award, and several other novels and short stories received award nominations, notably *The Book of Lost Things* (2006), which was nominated for the 2007 Irish Novel of the Year.

Connolly is a dedicated reader and music collector. For his fifth Charlie Parker novel, *The Black Angel* (2005), he included a compact disc, *Voices from the Dark*, whose music selections are to help set the mood for each chapter. Long a resident of Dublin, Connolly has frequently revisited Maine, where many of his stories take place.

ANALYSIS

Reviewers compared John Connolly's novels to those of Stephen King and Thomas Harris in his use of the supernatural and his emphasis on deranged killers. However, in Connolly's treatment, it is history, personal and collective, that receives the primary emphasis. History influences and often overwhelms his characters. History not only contributes to present thought and attitudes but also intrudes in a more tangible manner: Connolly's hero Charlie Parker must deal with the actual, if shadowy, appearances of the dead and the presence of diabolical "black angels" who have fallen from heaven and maim, torture, and kill humans to spite God. In *The White Road* Connolly writes that people, by their actions in this life, make their own hell in which to exist in the afterlife. Conversely, doing a good deed can atone for some past evil. Most important is Connolly's conception of evil itself: the absence of empathy. That is, people commit evil when they treat others merely as objects.

From this moral metaphysics come Connolly's three main themes: compassion, atonement, and salvation. Although these may sound like religious goals, for Parker they have a practical importance and numinous consequences that Connolly does not connect to any faith or organization. (Connolly's research draws freely from Christian, Judaic, animistic, and Manichean beliefs.) *Every Dead Thing* opens with Parker drinking away his frustrations with life and work as a New York City homicide detective while his wife and daughter are being tortured and murdered at home. He discovers the bodies and initially is the prime suspect. This personal history haunts him through the novel as he frees himself from suspicion and then sets off on a quest to track down the murderer, a sadist known as the Traveler. In later novels, family history likewise presses on him: For example, his father, also a New York City police officer, killed a woman and child under mysterious circumstances before taking his own life. Moreover, there is a darkness to each generation of his family that he has inherited. Through *The Killing Kind* (2001) and *The White Road*, it becomes clear that an unimaginably greater history plagues him: He is himself a fallen angel, a status made explicit in *The Black Angel*. He is among twenty former angels doomed to roam among humans, trapped in human form forever unless their bodies are destroyed by violence, in which case they are reborn into a new body.

Nineteen of these angels hunt and kill people, for various reasons, and from their number come the most villainous of Connolly's antagonists, such as Kittim, Reverend Faulkner, and Brightwell. Alone among the black angels, Parker feels compassion for the vulnerable and victimized. The compassion derives from his private and family history; an additional motivation, beginning in *The Black Angel*, is his desire to atone for his original sin against God. He therefore fights the bad angels, an unremitting moral war that has lasted, Connolly intimates, through many incarnations. The novels give little indication that Parker's crusade will win him personal forgiveness from God. Salvation, Connolly hints, is the active pursuit of justice rather than a reward for a good life.

Parker's life cannot be described as good in any conventional moral or religious sense. Working as a private investigator, he is loyal and ethical to clients and friends but frequently ignores all else—laws, customs, judicial procedures, and common morality. In pursuit of a culprit, he regularly kills, both in self-defense and to ensure that villains do not escape. Connolly's novels place little faith in the judicial system or police, assuming that red tape and corruption cripples these institutions in the face of evil. Moreover, Parker's helpers are frequently as criminal and violent as are his nemeses. These include an array of Mafiosi and former convicts, but the most outstanding are Louis and Angel, a biracial gay couple who regularly rescue Parker from dangerous situations by unstinting use of powerful firearms.

Louis and Angel act as foils to Parker in two ways. First, they provide most of the rare comic relief in the novels as they joke with each other and sometimes with Parker, who is otherwise grim, brooding, contrary, and haunted by macabre visions. Second, they have the only stable love relationship in the series. After Parker loses his wife and daughter, he is slow to find another love interest. When he falls in love with another woman, he has difficulty committing himself to her because of fear for her safety and his long ab-

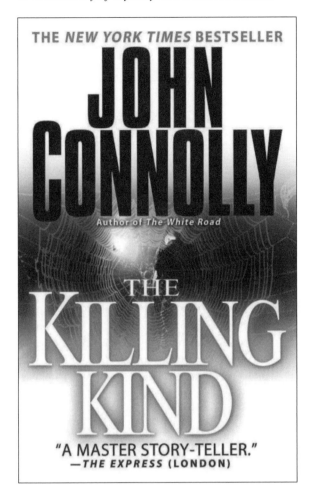

sences during investigations. She becomes pregnant and gives birth to a daughter, and they live together, but Parker's crusades constantly disrupt his family life, and their long-term prospects look doubtful at the end of *The Black Angel*.

Evil expresses itself through grotesque terror in the Connolly novels. Horrible deformities of the human body, mutilation, artworks of human bone and flesh, deadly spiders, subterranean passages, and visitations of the dead are the means of menacing the helpless among the characters and of creating suspense for readers. The extent and superhuman power of the evil that Parker faces impels him to act as his enemies act, with cunning, obsessive perseverance, and violence. Indeed, in Connolly's novels the distinction between justice and vengeance is vanishingly thin, even when he acts on behalf of the innocent and helpless.

THE KILLING KIND

In *The Killing Kind*, Parker is hired to investigate the mysterious suicide of a former girlfriend, Grace Peltier. Before she was discovered dead on a lonely Maine road, Peltier had been researching her master's thesis topic: a fundamentalist sect known as the Aroostook Baptists, who all disappeared in the early 1960's. Parker reluctantly investigates, eventually with help of his friends Louis and Angel, after a mass grave in northern Maine is accidentally uncovered. The grave contains the members of the long-missing sect, or most of them. Parker encounters a murky television evangelist organization that is a front for antiabortion, antihomosexual, anti-Semitic militants. Among its reptilian members is Mr. Pudd, whose uses poisonous spiders to kill those who he considers sinners. Another is a state police officer who has killed Peltier for taking a handmade book, bound in human skin, that implicates the organization in many murders. The book turn out to have been made by Reverend Faulkner, once the leader of the Aroostook Baptists and responsible for their deaths. Before Parker finally kills Pudd and captures Faulkner, Angel is tortured by Faulkner, and Parker meets a series of creepy characters, including the Gollum, an assassin sent by a militant Jewish group to stop Faulkner. Prominent among the themes is the destructive effect of extremist religion and the lingering hold of past atrocities on the living.

THE WHITE ROAD

In *The White Road*, Parker is asked by an old acquaintance to help protect Atys Jones, a young black man, from being killed by white vigilantes. Jones is accused of raping and murdering the daughter of a leading white family in South Carolina. He is innocent but doomed, for the woman's death is linked to a long series of tragedies involving the families of the young man and the woman, going back to the times when the young man's ancestors were slaves owned by the white family. Moreover, Parker's friend, the defense lawyer, has an agenda of his own. He secretly uses Parker to deflect those seeking to kill him because of the gang rape and murder of Jones's mother and aunt twenty years earlier, an event in which the lawyer participated. As Parker tries to shield Jones and unravels the tangled history behind the various rape-murders, he comes across another fallen angel, Kittim, who works for the dead girl's brother and entertains himself by slowing torturing to death those who threaten to expose the family's history. Parker barely escapes that fate, with the help of Louis and Angel (who have already conducted a murderous vigilante campaign of their own on elderly members of a long-ago lynch mob). In the end, nearly everyone is left dead, including Jones and the lawyer. The Old South's history of mob justice, lynching, white supremacists, and simmering racial conflict figures prominently. However, there is a second plot: The Reverend Faulkner of *The Killing Kind* is still alive and manipulates his way out of jail on bond. Faulkner vows to kill Parker and his pregnant girlfriend, Rachel. In the end Parker, Louis, and Angel shoot him dead in a joint volley.

THE BLACK ANGEL

In *The Black Angel*, Parker is enlisted to find a missing young woman, a relation of Louis. The attempt leads him deep into the supernatural. Already haunted by the apparitions of his dead wife and daughter, he discovers that those behind the woman's disappearance and hideous murder are black angels, one of whom steals his victims' souls. He is Brightwell, an immensely obese but agile man. Brightwell is in turn the lieutenant of the chief black angel on Earth. The plot involves their search for the chief angel's twin, captured and immured long ago by Cistercian monks. Catholic medieval history, grotesque artworks, and demonology all eventually lead Parker to the chief angel, who, in a deft stroke of black humor, turns out to be a dealer of antiquities. As in previous novels, many people die as Parker investigates and as, in turn, he becomes the black angels' prey, for they want to punish him for defying them, not only in his present life but also in past lives. The climax sees Parker killing Brightwell (who promises to be reborn and track him down) and trapping the chief angel. This success, however, leads to personal failure. Parker's girlfriend, Rachel, leaves him, taking their infant daughter with her because of attempts on their lives by Brightwell and his agents.

Roger Smith

PRINCIPAL MYSTERY AND DETECTIVE FICTION

CHARLIE PARKER SERIES: *Every Dead Thing*, 1999; *Dark Hollow*, 2000; *The Killing Kind*, 2001; *The White Road*, 2002; *Every Dead Thing/Dark Hollow*, 2003 (omnibus); *The Black Angel*, 2005; *The Unquiet*, 2007

NONSERIES NOVELS: *Bad Men*, 2003; *The Book of Lost Things*, 2006

OTHER MAJOR WORKS

SHORT FICTION: *Nocturnes*, 2004

NONFICTION: *Married to a Stranger: A True Story of Murder and the Multi-Million Dollar Mail-Order Bride Business*, 2006 (with Gaylen Ross)

BIBLIOGRAPHY

Connolly, John. John Connolly. http://www.john connollybooks.com. Connolly's Web site, which includes a newsletter, biography, texts of interviews, and information about his fiction.

Horsley, Lee. *The Noir Thriller*. New York: Palgrave, 2000. Horsley analyzes noir fiction starting with Joseph Conrad, focusing on the theme of hidden evil in normal life, which is important to the Charley Parker novels, though the novels are not addressed directly.

Karim, Ali. "On the Road to Redemption with John Connolly." *January Magazine* (April, 2003). http://www.januarymagazine.com. An extensive article and interview with Connolly that dwells on his background, writing habits, and literary interests.

Nolan, Yvonne. "An Irishman in Darkest Maine." *Publishers Weekly* 249 (September, 2002): 45. Nolan comments on Connolly's use of Maine as a setting for his novels, his views on the appeal of violent crime in fiction, and how he writes.

Schwartz, Richard B. *Nice and Noir: Contemporary Crime Fiction*. Columbia: University of Missouri Press, 2002. Schwartz discusses the mythology and mentality informing noir fiction. The fourth chapter, "Avenging Angel," presents an insightful introduction to themes appearing in the Charlie Parker novels, which are not discussed directly.

THOMAS H. COOK

Born: Fort Payne, Alabama; September 19, 1947
Types of plot: Thriller; police procedural; psychological

PRINCIPAL SERIES

Frank Clemons, 1988-

PRINCIPAL SERIES CHARACTER

FRANK CLEMONS is an Atlanta homicide detective whose wife left him shortly after the suicide of their teenage daughter. Clemons is the son of a minister, and his alcoholism threatens to destroy what is left of his life. In the course of the series, he moves to New York City, primarily out of a sense of loyalty to his girlfriend, the sister of the first victim whose murder he solves. His girlfriend eventually ends up leaving him, and in an effort to occupy his mind, Clemons offers his services as a private investigator, working out of a basement office on Forty-ninth Street. Described as a tall, slender man, Clemons finds that his troubles have aged him, giving him the stooped shoulders of a much older man.

CONTRIBUTION

Thomas H. Cook has elevated the police procedural from a marginalized subgenre of detective fiction to a more popularly acceptable genre of popular literature—the psychological novel. The archetypal Cook hero is an isolated loner with just enough human feelings left to respond to the needs of other individuals. The hero is almost destroyed by his empathy, yet he finds eventual redemption in his sacrifices. Cook pays a great deal of attention to detail, especially in his depiction of the process of suppressed memory recollection. This careful use of the psychological method shows Cook's desire to transcend the boundaries of thriller and true-crime writing. Cook has written only a few novels in the Frank Clemons series, preferring nonseries novels so that he may experiment with and examine a variety of narrators and their individual voices and traumatic life experiences. He has also delved into other genres: He wrote the novelization of the science-fiction television series *Taken* (2002) and mainstream fiction such as *Elena* (1986) and *Moon over Manhattan* (2004), a comic novel he wrote with television interviewer Larry King. Cook's abilities as a writer have been rewarded with growing respect from the mystery reading public and have led to his being presented with the Mystery Writers of America's Edgar Award for best novel for *The Chatham School Affair* (1996).

BIOGRAPHY

Thomas H. Cook was born on September 19, 1947, in Fort Payne, Alabama, the son of Virgil Richard Cook and Myrick Harper Cook. He started writing at an early age and claims that his first novel was based on his experiences with Heiman Zeidman, a Jewish immigrant from Poland who was one of only a handful of Jewish residents in Cook's small, southern town. Zeidman, a close friend of the family, treated the young Cook as a grandson, taking him to films and even on his first trip to New York City. Cook received degrees in English and philosophy from Georgia State College in 1969 and graduate degrees in American history from Hunter College, City University of New York (1972) and Columbia University (1976). He married Susan Terner, who wrote for radio, on March 17, 1978, and has one child, Justine Ariel.

As a student Cook worked in jobs ranging from advertising executive for U.S. Industrial Chemicals to secretary for the Association for Help of Retarded Adults. He also taught English and history at DeKalb Community College in Clarkson, Georgia, for three years before making the difficult decision to become a full-time writer. Also from 1978 to1982, Cook served as contributing editor and book reviewer and editor of *Atlanta* magazine, where his critical abilities, his writing, and his first short stories earned praise. He also wrote a number of feature articles on midcentury America, notably the deterioration of the pop-culture movement; essays on modern southern fiction; and articles about the changes in Atlanta neighborhoods and the gentrification of some of the old neighborhoods, especially the Grant Park area, which would figure as the site of a murder in one of his novels. In addition to his mystery and detective novels, he has written several books of true crime and has contributed reviews and short fiction to a variety of popular publications including *The New York Times Review of Books*.

ANALYSIS

Although Thomas H. Cook has produced several books in the Frank Clemons series, most of his novels are psychological mysteries without recurring characters. The investigators in these psychological novels are isolated, tortured individuals haunted by their own bad luck and their personal tragedies. Nevertheless, they find themselves compelled to help solve some of the more grisly murders in modern crime fiction. Cook's protagonists typically find themselves prisoners of their own pasts. His victims are often young and rich, but the wealth that makes their lives easy cannot shield them from bloody fates. Elements of faith and sacrifice are hallmarks of his fiction, as are his realistic portrayals of violent death. He is drawn to crimes known for their ability to shock—not only in fiction, but in his true-crime books, such as *A Father's Story* (1994), ghostwritten for Lionel Dahmer, father of serial killer Jeffrey Dahmer.

BLOOD INNOCENTS

Blood Innocents (1980) begins in the Central Park Children's Zoo, a place of frolic, fun, and innocence. This morning, however, a horrendous scene meets the eyes of bystanders. Two of the deer donated to the zoo by a wealthy entrepreneur have been stabbed to death—one deer has been stabbed fifty-seven times and the other killed with a single slash. As if this were not horrible enough, the scene has been repeated in Greenwich Village, where two women are found dead—one stabbed fifty-seven times and the other with a single slash across her neck. New Yorkers fear that a crazed killer is loose.

Meanwhile, John Reardon, a New York City police officer born into a family of officers, has nothing left but his job. His wife is dead after a prolonged illness, and he is alienated from his adult son. His bosses see his skill and dedication to his work and assign him to work exclusively on the deer slaying. When the

women are discovered murdered in Greenwich Village, Reardon is assigned to that case as well. Although he has doubts about the guilt of the initial suspect, Reardon finds himself under pressure to arrest someone and bring the case to trial. Big-city politicians decide that the cases are not connected, enraging Reardon and encouraging him to initiate his own private investigation. He is personally dedicated to finding the truth though the pressure to drop his inquiry becomes intense. Reardon, like many of Cook's heroes, has only his stubbornness and devotion to his duty to drive him on to the inevitable conclusion. Like the victims, Reardon experiences his own destruction, but in his case, it leads to his redemption and his acceptance of the consequences of his former life.

SACRIFICIAL GROUND

In *Sacrificial Ground* (1988), the first volume of the Frank Clemons series, Cook's protagonist is a homicide detective in Atlanta whose beautiful teenage daughter has committed suicide and whose wife left him soon after their daughter's death. Clemons, who is slipping into alcoholism, is called to work on a particularly puzzling murder case. The dead teenager, Angelique Devereaux, found at her autopsy to be pregnant, has apparently been living a double life. She was fabulously wealthy—living in a mansion with her sister Karen, an artist—and at the same time "slumming" in the Grant Park area art galleries and carrying on with an unknown lover. Her school friends know little about her and nothing about her activities, and Clemons begins to compare her murder to the death of his own daughter. If this rich, privileged teenager had secrets, he wonders if there might have been secrets that his own daughter had kept from him. Clemons follows Angelique's trail through her last few days of life, finally arriving at a staggering truth. Like all of Cook's novels, the ending comes quickly and is surprisingly intense. The reader cannot help but sympathize with Clemons and his own private devils as he unravels the details of the case.

FLESH AND BLOOD

Cook's second Frank Clemons novel, *Flesh and Blood* (1989), finds the former Atlanta homicide detective living in the grittier north—New York City. Now a private investigator, Clemons lives a comfortable life on the Upper East Side, but he finds himself falling out of love with his girlfriend, the older sister of the murdered teenager in *Sacrificial Blood*. As a private eye, he finds himself less inclined to work for the wealthier people of the city and more drawn toward the needs of Manhattan's poor. That is one reason why he accepts the case of Hannah Karlsberg even though it offers little in the way of financial reward. Hannah, an elderly woman, has been brutally murdered in her apartment. Clemons is hired by her employer, a fashion designer, to locate Hannah's next of kin so that her body can be released and buried.

Clemons finds, however, that Hannah's life and her past present some mysteries, reminiscent of the secrets surrounding Angelique's life in *Sacrificial Blood*. Where had Hannah come from? Who had she encountered? What had she done or had done to her? There are too many questions and too few answers. In search of the truth, Clemons begins his investigation with the fashion industry itself. From the sweatshops of the Lower East Side, where Hannah in her youth was a striker representing the infant American Garment Workers' Union and protesting the inhuman conditions borne by many young women working in the factories, to a small village in Colombia, and finally back to Brooklyn, Clemons's investigation uncovers cruelty and inhumanity that arouse in him a sense of isolation and feelings of betrayal. Cook's knowledge of history and the beginnings of the labor movement in the United States allow him to create this story that leads to a gripping climax.

NIGHT SECRETS

In *Night Secrets* (1990), the third book in the series, Frank Clemons still lives in Manhattan and is still fighting the personal demons that drove him to leave the South. To make a living and to keep himself busy, he has taken on two cases: In the first, he is following a philandering rich wife when she visits men other than her husband; in the second, he is trying to find clues in the murder of an old Gypsy woman. He finds out what he can about Gypsies from his friend Farouk, whose mother was a Gypsy. Although someone has confessed to the murder—a young woman of dubious sanity—Clemons finds himself in a quandary. The young lady who has confessed belongs to an obscure

Gypsy cult that carries out rituals based on a child supposedly born to Christ and Mary Magdalene and has questionable reasons for her confession based on her personal sense of guilt. Clemons is sure the young woman is innocent and tries to clear her but finds her to be obstinate in her desire to be a martyr. Cook's descriptions of New York's big-city atmosphere, alive twenty-four hours a day, complete with homeless people and all-night diners, makes Clemon's profound loneliness real to the reader as he solves both cases.

INSTRUMENTS OF NIGHT

With *Instruments of Night* (1998), Cook departs from detective fiction to introduce a different kind of narrator—someone more creative than deductive and sharing Cook's own choice of career. Paul Graves is a mystery writer who draws on his own tragic past to write his fiction. Graves has been summoned to Riverwood, an artists' community in the Hudson River Valley, for the purpose of creating fiction out of fact. He is asked to write a story that will answer the many questions about the murder of Faye Harrison, the teenage daughter who lived on the estate more than fifty years ago. Graves is not sure he can solve the mystery—he is a fiction writer by trade, not a detective. However, Faye's mother, now elderly and near death, wants some sort of closure to the tragedy of her daughter's fate.

EVIDENCE OF BLOOD

In *Evidence of Blood* (1991), Jackson Kinley, like Paul Graves, is a crime-fiction writer. Coming home after a number of years, Kinley finds a true-crime mystery in his own hometown, Sequoyah, Georgia. The death of Kinley's friend, Sheriff Ray Tindall, leaves many loose ends for the family and friends of the sheriff. What was he investigating when he died? Why had he reopened the case of convicted murderer Charles Overton—and then just as abruptly closed it? As Kinley delves into the facts regarding the murder of teenager Ellie Dinker more than forty years ago, he is faced with even more questions. Why was Ellie's body never found, and what was the truth about the only piece of evidence, the bloody dress? His search for answers leads to a web of corruption and lies—and finally into a deadly secret hidden for more than forty years.

Julia M. Meyers

PRINCIPAL MYSTERY AND DETECTIVE FICTION

FRANK CLEMONS SERIES: *Sacrificial Ground*, 1988; *Flesh and Blood*, 1989; *Night Secrets*, 1990

NONSERIES NOVELS: *Blood Innocents*, 1980; *Tabernacle*, 1983; *Streets of Fire*, 1989; *The City When It Rains*, 1991; *Evidence of Blood*, 1991; *Mortal Memory*, 1993; *Breakheart Hill*, 1995; *The Chatham School Affair*, 1996; *Instruments of Night*, 1998; *Places in the Dark*, 2000; *Interrogation*, 2002; *Peril*, 2004; *Into the Web*, 2004; *Red Leaves*, 2005; *The Cloud of Unknowing*, 2007

OTHER MAJOR WORKS

NOVELS: *The Orchids*, 1982; *Elena*, 1986; *Moon over Manhattan*, 2002 (with Larry King); *Taken*, 2002

PLAY: *American Song*, pr. 2000

NONFICTION: *Early Graves: A Shocking True Crime Story of the Youngest Woman Ever Sentenced to Death Row*, 1990; *Blood Echoes: The True Story of an Infamous Mass Murder and Its Aftermath*, 1992; *A Father's Story*, 1994 (ghostwritten for Lionel Dahmer)

EDITED TEXTS: *Best American Crime Writing*, 2002 (with Otto Penzler); *Best American Crime Writing*, 2003 (with Penzler); *Best American Crime Writing*, 2004 (with Penzler)

BIBLIOGRAPHY

Dahlin, Robert. "Thomas H. Cook: Stretching the Mystery Envelope." *Publishers Weekly* 245, no. 42 (October, 1998): 43. Short profile on Thomas Cook that relates some of the true-life incidents that inspire his writing in general as well as *Breakheart Hill* in particular. It also gives the reader a better sense of Cook's motivations for writing.

Donnelly, Barry. "Cook's Tour." *The Armchair Detective* 30, no. 3 (1997): 294-298. This extended discussion of Cook's writings from *Blood Innocents* to *The Chatham School Affair* attempts to put the author's writing in the context of psychological thrillers and detective fiction of the twentieth century. Includes extensive quotations from correspondence with Cook.

Graham, Keith. "Ex-Atlantan Delves into True-Crime Fiction." *The Atlanta Journal/The Atlanta Constitution*, December 23, 1990, p. N2. Brief profile of Cook that examines his fictional writing and his first true-crime book, *Early Graves*.

Lee, Michael. "The South Rises Again and Again." *The Barnstable Patriot* (October, 2003). This brief article describes how Cook is representative of a new breed of southern writer in step with modern life. Much of Cook's fiction is based in his home state of Georgia and has southern themes as its primary focus.

Shankman, Sarah. Introduction to *A Confederacy of Crime*. New York: Signet, 2001. The purpose of this collection of short stories was to compile a selection of the best unpublished mysteries describing life in the Deep South. Besides Cook, authors include Jeffrey Deaver, Steven Womack, and Julie Smith.

PATRICIA CORNWELL

Born: Miami, Florida; June 9, 1956
Also wrote as Patricia D. Cornwell; Patricia Daniels
　Cornwell
Types of plot: Hard-boiled; police procedural; psychological

PRINCIPAL SERIES

Kay Scarpetta, 1990-
Andy Brazil, 1997-

PRINCIPAL SERIES CHARACTERS

DR. KAY SCARPETTA is Virginia's chief medical examiner. She is a striking blonde woman who is such a brilliant and famous forensic pathologist/detective that she becomes the obsession of several psychopathic serial killers. She enjoys gardening and cooking the northern Italian dishes of her ethnic heritage. She is "Auntie Kay" to Lucy Farinelli, the only child of her sister Dorothy, who frequently leaves her daughter in Scarpetta's care. As Lucy grows from a ten-year-old to a Federal Bureau of Investigation (FBI) agent and finally the founder of her own private investigating firm, Scarpetta also branches out. She becomes an FBI consultant, colludes with Interpol, and relocates to Florida to become a private forensic consultant.

ANDY BRAZIL is a recent college graduate, reporter, and volunteer police officer in Charlotte, North Carolina. At the request of his editor, he patrols with Deputy Chief Virginia West. His energy and impetuousness anger West and Chief Judy Hammer, yet endear him to them. His unorthodox methods help him crack seemingly impossible cases.

CONTRIBUTION

Patricia Cornwell's first work of detective fiction, *Postmortem* (1990), is the only novel to win five prestigious awards in the same year: the Edgar Award from the Mystery Writers of America, the John Creasey Award from the Crime Writers' Association, the Anthony Award sponsored by Bouchercon, World Mystery Convention, and the Macavity Award from Mystery Readers International, all for best debut crime

novel, and the French Prix du Roman d'Aventure. The book stood out because of its protagonist as well as its approach of using forensics to solve a crime. Dr. Kay Scarpetta is a tough yet vulnerable female medical examiner. In 1999, the character of Scarpetta won the Sherlock Award for the best fictional detective created by an American author. Although Scarpetta comes into contact with suspects more often and more closely than real-life medical examiners actually do, crimes are solved in Scarpetta's mind and on her autopsy table. As she examines the victims' bodies, she gathers clues to help identify the killers. This approach was noteworthy because of Cornwell's precise descriptions of actual forensic methods, descriptions that unfold with textbook accuracy and length, before such approaches were popularized by television crime dramas such as *CSI*, which began in 2000. Her fourth Scarpetta mystery, *Cruel and Unusual* (1993), won the Golden Dagger Award of the Crime Writers' Association.

BIOGRAPHY

Patricia Cornwell was born Patricia Daniels on June 9, 1956. Her father, Sam Daniels, was a lawyer, and her mother, Marilyn Zenner Daniels, was a secretary. The family lived in Miami until Cornwell was five years old, when Sam Daniels left the family. Cornwell's mother took her and her two brothers to Montreat, North Carolina. Several years later, Marilyn Daniels began a series of hospitalizations for depression, and she entrusted her children to evangelist Billy Graham and his wife, Ruth, who placed them with a family recently returned from missionary work in Africa.

Cornwell attended King College in Tennessee and transferred to Davidson College in Charlotte, North Carolina, on a tennis scholarship that she later gave up. She graduated in 1979 with a bachelor's degree in English. She began a two-year stint as a reporter for the *Charlotte Observer*. She found her niche as a crime reporter, and the North Carolina Press Association honored her with an award for her investigative reporting series on prostitution. In 1980 she married Charles

Patricia Cornwell (right) with actor Bernadette Peters (left) and First Lady Hillary Rodham Clinton in December, 1999, when all three women were given Police Athletic League women-of-the-year awards. (AP/Wide World Photos)

Cornwell, an English professor seventeen years older than she. In 1981, Charles Cornwell left Davidson College to pursue a divinity degree at Union Theological Seminary. Cornwell accompanied her husband and worked with him to expand a newspaper article that she had written about Ruth Graham into a book published in 1983 as *A Time for Remembering: The Story of Ruth Bell Graham*. The book won the Gold Medallion Book Award for biography sponsored by the Evangelical Christian Publishers Association.

In 1984, Cornwell began writing her first novel about a detective named Joe Constable. Although she had been a crime reporter, she had not experienced crime investigation from the viewpoint of the police. She consulted Dr. Marcella Fierro, a Richmond, Virginia, medical examiner, who hired Cornwell first as a part-time scribe to record autopsies and later as a full-

time computer analyst, a position she held for approximately six years. Cornwell also worked as a volunteer police officer in Richmond and spent three years with homicide detectives on the 4:00 P.M. to midnight shift. Two more novels about Constable followed, and editors repeatedly rejected all three. Finally, Cornwell asked for advice from Sara Ann Fried, an editor with Mysterious Press who had written encouraging rejection letters. She suggested that Cornwell dump her male detective and focus on Dr. Kay Scarpetta, originally a secondary character.

Cornwell's breakthrough came in the summer of 1987 when a series of killings gripped Richmond. One victim was a female physician. In a 1991 interview with Joanne Tangorra of *Publishers Weekly*, Cornwell denied studying the killings but described them as a springboard for thinking about how Scarpetta might cope with a similar situation. In 1988, Cornwell met *Miami Herald* journalist Edna Buchanan, herself a mystery writer, who suggested an agent for Cornwell's newly completed draft. Scribner's bought *Postmortem* for a six-thousand-dollar advance, and the book was published in 1990, the same year that Cornwell and her husband divorced.

Over the next ten years, Cornwell published eleven Scarpetta novels, two mysteries featuring Andy Brazil, a revision of the Graham biography, a children's book, and *Scarpetta's Winter Table*. Her novels soared to the top of the best-seller lists and were translated into twenty-two languages. She is reported to be one of the highest paid mystery writers and commands an advance of several million dollars per book.

Cornwell has used her earnings to fund her interests and research as well as to donate to charitable causes. Research for her 2002 case study, *Portrait of a Killer: Jack the Ripper—Case Closed*, included collecting artifacts and running DNA and forensic tests to prove her theory that painter Walter Sickert was in fact Jack the Ripper. Cornwell later donated her collection of Sickert paintings to Harvard University. She endowed a writing scholarship to Davidson College's Creative Writing Program. In 2006, after her two English bulldogs were treated at Cornell University's Veterinary Hospital, she donated one million dollars to establish the Patricia Cornwell Intensive Care Unit for Companion Animals at the College of Veterinary Medicine. She also helped found the Virginia Institute of Forensic Science and Medicine, serving as chair of the board, and she funded scholarships to the University of Tennessee's National Forensics Academy.

ANALYSIS

Patricia Cornwell's Dr. Kay Scarpetta and Andy Brazil series feature female detectives in new roles: Scarpetta, a medical examiner, and Virginia West and Judy Hammer, police chiefs. The Scarpetta series also broke new ground with its use of forensic technology, much of which Cornwell later used to investigate the series of murders attributed to Jack the Ripper in her true-crime book. The Scarpetta series is the most scrutinized and has attracted praise and censure for the elements that boosted it to the top of the best-seller lists: its narrative technique and its characters.

As the Scarpetta series grew, critics termed the dominance of forensic detail both gripping and formulaic, and the protagonist both compelling and one-dimensional. In a 1991 *Publishers Weekly* interview, Cornwell stated that she was no longer as "infatuated" with forensics and "more interested in the psychological and spiritual nuances of Scarpetta's life." The early volumes in the series are written in the first person from the point of view of Scarpetta. The relentlessly technical and scrupulously precise descriptions of her forensic work function as organizational and moral forces trying to contain the amoral chaos let loose on society by psychopathic and sociopathic killers. They also underscore the less-than-scrupulous nature of the institutions that support these procedures. At times, the crime being investigated takes a back seat to jockeying for position in the institutions dedicated to solving crimes. Scarpetta is a highly educated professional who must fight to keep her position because she is a woman in a male-dominated profession. In later volumes in the series, Cornwell's narrative experiments with multiple points of view help draw back the curtain even further on the people and institutions that seek to maintain the norm. This behind-the-scenes look at what is sometimes a less than single-minded search for truth and justice counterbalances what some critics point out as implausibilities in the plot.

The Andy Brazil series, although not as critically well received, offers a counterpoint. Brazil is an earnest, if blundering, rookie volunteer police officer whose athleticism, stamina, and intellect rival a superhero's. In each volume, solving the killings is second to the routine of the local newspaper, police precinct, government, and underworld. In the debut volume, *Hornet's Nest* (1996), Brazil pops open the trunk of the patrol car instead of activating the siren. On traffic duty he halts a hearse; the coffin slides out and Brazil runs after it. Brazil's enthusiasm influences Chief Judy Hammer and Deputy Chief Virginia West to brush up on their community policing skills, yet he irritates them as he publishes details of the serial killings as well as a profile on West. The trio's personal and professional tensions reveal their altruism and their colleagues' selfishness.

Scarpetta is and is not a typical fictional detective.

She is determined to restore order, yet she is no lone wolf or superhero. She needs her cohorts, even if they are flawed. Scarpetta, her headstrong niece Lucy, and her rough but shrewd colleague, police detective Pete Marino, have messy personal lives. Marriages end in divorce, and love affairs come and go, sometimes violently: Benton Wesley, FBI profiler and Scarpetta's married lover, fakes his own death in *Point of Origin* (1998). Their judgment in all matters is not unerring, but Scarpetta, Lucy, and Marino depend on one another. Each member of the trio contributes information that helps solve the mystery or catch the perpetrator. In *Postmortem*, Marino has been watching Scarpetta's house on a hunch that she may be the next target, and he shoots the murderer before Scarpetta is harmed. In this way, they are as true to type as the more one-dimensional Brazil characters: Their jobs preclude the normal lifestyle that they seek to protect. A *Kirkus Reviews* description of the Scarpetta book *Black Notice* (1999) noted that the "brilliantly paced adventure" complemented the characters that continue to "become more and more themselves."

POSTMORTEM

Postmortem, Cornwell's breakthrough novel, established her protagonist and her technique, and presented two challenges for further works in the series: how to make Scarpetta a more complex character and how to refocus the use of forensic technology. In the novel, a series of killings hit home for Richmond medical examiner Kay Scarpetta when a female physician is murdered. Cornwell uses first-person narration to reveal as much about Scarpetta and her colleagues as she does about the murders. However, Scarpetta appears as absorbed in herself as she is in solving the case: comments about her former husband, her preference for travel by train rather than by airplane, her memory of a nun at her parochial school, and other tidbits are essentially non sequiturs. Because the conversation between Scarpetta and FBI profiler Benton Wesley is so technical, her description of his Florsheim shoes is the best clue to his personality. In contrast, her interaction with Lucy, balanced between technical and emotional topics, reveals her love for her niece as well as Lucy's headstrong personality. Finally, Scarpetta becomes the focus of the killer, who,

in this volume, is a complete unknown. An obsession with Scarpetta is a constant for many of the villains in this series, and several of the villains appear in more than one volume.

BLOW FLY

Beginning with *Blow Fly* (2003), Cornwell started experimenting with narrative techniques such as third-person omniscient narration, which moves the story along from multiple viewpoints, including the killer's. Because *Blow Fly* is the twelfth Scarpetta mystery, readers have had many previous volumes from which to gather details about the main characters' pasts and relationships. The new narrative technique allows the reader to get into each character's head without sacrificing a complex, fast-moving plot. Scarpetta has relocated to Florida. Lucy has grown up and opened her own firm in New York. Marino is retired and discontent. When each of them receives a letter from a nemesis on death row, Jean-Baptiste Chandonne, they reunite. Although the chapters from Chandonne's point of view seem over the top, the chapters written from each of the trio's points of view help probe their motivations as well as the flaws that make them complex characters.

PREDATOR

Predator (2005) is the fourteenth volume in the Scarpetta series. The narrative still switches between viewpoints, but the focus of the plot is on the fine line between good and evil. In this story, Benton Wesley conducts a psychological study of a serial killer. The goal of the study, whose acronym is PREDATOR, is to create the ultimate profile of a predatorial killer. However, as Scarpetta shrewdly suspects, the predator in this story, Hog (Hand of God), confounds all expectations. The villain is neither a man nor a bad-to-the-bone psychopath like the Chandonne twins of previous volumes but a victim of evil herself. The novel ends with Scarpetta and Wesley sifting through decomposing bodies in the hope of finding the truth about who, a decade earlier, had tortured and abused the then twelve-year-old Helen Quincy so severely as to trigger multiple personalities, one of whom is a killer. Cornwell stretches the conventions of the genre. Her characters have developed to the point that they need a more nebulous universe to inhabit. Scarpetta still pursues truth and justice, but right and wrong have become much more difficult to define, and she finds herself defending in some way what in earlier volumes would have been indefensible.

Cecile Mazzucco-Than

PRINCIPAL MYSTERY AND DETECTIVE FICTION

DR. KAY SCARPETTA SERIES: *Postmortem*, 1990; *Body of Evidence*, 1991; *All That Remains*, 1992; *Cruel and Unusual*, 1993; *The Body Farm*, 1994; *From Potter's Field*, 1995; *Cause of Death*, 1996; *Unnatural Exposure*, 1997; *Point of Origin*, 1998; *Black Notice*, 1999; *Potter's Field*, 2000; *The Last Precinct*, 2000; *Origin*, 2002; *Blow Fly*, 2003; *Trace*, 2004; *Predator*, 2005; *Book of the Dead*, 2006

ANDY BRAZIL SERIES: *Hornet's Nest*, 1996; *Southern Cross*, 1998; *Isle of Dogs*, 2001

OTHER MAJOR WORKS

NOVEL: *At Risk*, 2006

CHILDREN'S LITERATURE: *Life's Little Fable*, 1999

NONFICTION: *A Time for Remembering: The Story of Ruth Bell Graham*, 1983; *An Uncommon Friend: The Authorized Biography of Ruth Bell Graham*, 1983; *Ruth, A Portrait: The Story of Ruth Bell Graham*, 1997; *Scarpetta's Winter Table*, 1998; *Food to Die For: Secrets from Kay Scarpetta's Kitchen*, 2001 (with Marlene Brown); *Portrait of a Killer: Jack the Ripper—Case Closed*, 2002

BIBLIOGRAPHY

Beahm, George. *The Unofficial Patricia Cornwell Companion*. New York: St. Martin's Minotaur, 2002. Detailed look at Cornwell's life and each of her books. Useful for excerpts of book reviews of each title and a glossary of terms, characters, and places mentioned in each book.

Cornwell, Patricia. Patricia Cornwell: The Official Website. http://www.patriciacornwell.com. Author's official Web site contains information about Cornwell's life and works.

_____. "Patricia D. Cornwell: Life Imitates Art in the Career of Mystery/Thriller Author." Interview by J. Tangorra and S. Steinberg. *Publishers Weekly* 238, no. 9 (February 15, 1991): 71-73. The first published interview with Cornwell. Discusses her life and how she came to write and publish *Postmortem*.

Dubose, Martha Hailey, with Margaret Caldwell Thomas. *Women of Mystery: The Lives and Works of Notable Women Crime Novelists*. New York: St. Martin's Minotaur, 2000. Biographies of various authors with an overview and analysis of their works. Essay on Cornwell notes her colorful personal life, which involves lawsuits and spectacular incidents of publicity.

Herbert, Rosemary. *The Fatal Art of Entertainment: Interviews with Mystery Writers*. New York: G. K. Hall, 1994. In the interview with Cornwell, she states that she never read mysteries and when she started to write, she just intended to write a novel, but found violence inescapable.

Lucas, Rose. "Anxiety and Its Antidotes: Patricia Cornwell and the Forensic Body." *Literature Interpretation Theory* 15, no. 2 (April/June, 2004): 207-222. Literary criticism that focuses on how Cornwell conforms to and deviates from the conventions of the hard-boiled detective story via her use of the victims' bodies as objects of murder and evidence.

Passero, Kathy. "Stranger than Fiction: The True Life Drama of Patricia Cornwell." *Biography* 2, no. 5 (May, 1998): 66-71. Discussion of highly publicized incidents in Cornwell's life. Includes a chart of the number of weeks each of the first eight Scarpetta novels was on *The New York Times* bestseller list.

Reynolds, Moira Davison. *Women Authors of Detective Series: Twenty-one American and British Authors, 1900-2000*. Jefferson, N.C.: McFarland, 2001. Examines the life and work of major female mystery writers, including Cornwell.

COLIN COTTERILL

Born: London, England; October 2, 1952
Types of plot: Amateur sleuth; historical

PRINCIPAL SERIES

Dr. Siri Paiboun, 2004-

PRINCIPAL SERIES CHARACTERS

DR. SIRI PAIBOUN is a seventy-two-year-old Paris-trained Laotian physician who served nearly forty years beside his wife—a rabid revolutionary—as field surgeon to the communist Pathet Lao before they took control of Laos in the mid-1970's. Reluctantly appointed the country's only coroner in late 1975, the widowed Dr. Siri works in Vientiane, from an ill-equipped morgue in a hospital. Cynical, a fan of Georges Simenon's detective Maigret, Siri is white-haired and stooped, with bushy white eyebrows and emerald-green eyes. The son of a Hmong shaman and the reembodiment of Yeh Ming, a shaman who lived a thousand years before, Siri is a lapsed Buddhist and often dreams of the dead, gaining insight into their personalities and an inkling of how they died.

CHUNDEE "DTUI" CHANTAVONGHEUAN is a trained nurse who serves as Siri's assistant in the morgue. Plain-faced and solidly built, she is the only adult survivor of eleven children and lives with her mother, who suffers from cirrhosis. Dtui is intelligent, kind, and resourceful, with a wicked sense of humor, and a fan of comic books. She has aspirations of furthering her education to become a certified pathologist.

MR. GEUNG is a morgue technician who works with Siri and Dtui. A friendly, hard worker with a cheerful manner, Geung was born with Down syndrome, which limits his learning abilities; however, he possesses an almost photographic memory. He is usually the first to arrive at the morgue each working day.

CIVILAI, two days older than Siri (thus jocularly called "Ai," older brother) and the doctor's best friend, is a member of the ruling politburo. Brilliant, eccentric, scrawny, and bald, he wears large glasses that give him an inquisitive appearance. Civilai shares lunch with Siri daily on the banks of the Mekong River, act-

ing as a sounding board for the doctor's theories, and he often assists his friend in his dealings with the government.

INSPECTOR PHOSY is a member of the National Police Force, and an ally of Dr. Siri. A handsome, slender man in his forties who has the ability to procure items in short supply—such as alcoholic beverages that he shares with Siri as they discuss cases—Phosy tools about Vientiane on a lilac-colored Vespa.

CONTRIBUTION

Colin Cotterill, a career educator in underserved regions of the world and a strong children's advocate, began writing genre fiction early in the twenty-first century. He has drawn considerable attention in short order. His main literary contribution consists of the creation of a unique protagonist operating during a specific—and intriguing—historical time frame, within a colorful, largely unfamiliar cultural environment.

Cotterill knows his territory well, having lived and worked for years among the ordinary folk of Australia, Thailand, Japan, and Laos. A landlocked country, Laos is sandwiched between Vietnam, Cambodia, Thailand, and China. Its capital is Vientiane, situated on the Mekong River along the border of Thailand. The country, the city, and the era—the mid-1970's, after the Pathet Lao, backed by the Soviet Union and North Vietnam, forced King Savang Vatthama to abdicate—are all brought to life by Cotterill's straightforward, ironic, readable prose.

The author paints a geographic, social, and historical backdrop against which a fascinating cast of characters, led by wise man and wise guy Dr. Siri Paiboun, are put into motion. The actors, like breathing humans from any place or time, are prey to all life's foibles, like lust, greed, jealousy, and revenge. They gripe about the weather and the inflation rate. They make errors of judgment and leap to conclusions. Their speech, like that of real people, is peppered with profanity and slang, and they prove by example that despite differences in place, time, and heritage, people are all alike in some ways.

Cotterill's series novels have picked up momentum, both critically and commercially, since *The Coroner's Lunch* debuted to acclaim in 2004. In 2007, following its translation into French, the novel won an award for Best European Crime Novel given by the French National Railways, entitling the author to a year's free rides on French trains. Cotterill's follow-up, *Thirty-three Teeth* (2005), won the Dilys Award as a booksellers' favorite.

BIOGRAPHY

Colin Cotterill was born October 2, 1952, in London and grew up near Wimbledon, where he was an avid reader of comic books, material that inspired his own love of illustration. He attended Berkshire College, earning a teacher-training diploma in 1975, and afterward embarked on a career as a teacher, teaching instructor, and curriculum developer that led him to various parts of the world. He was a physical education instructor in Israel before moving to Australia, where from he taught grades four through six at Corpus Christi in Glenroy, Victoria. In Perth, Western Australia, Cotterill worked with refugees from Vietnam, Cambodia, Laos, and Burma as a teacher with the Migrant Education Department (1978-1979), an experience that spurred his further interest in Southeast Asia. After receiving a graduate diploma at Sydney University, Cotterill worked in New South Wales as an adult migrant educator (1980-1982) and as a materials developer (1985-1986). Between stints, he taught (1982-1983) at Tokai University, Kanagawa, Japan.

From 1986 to 1988, Cotterill served as teacher and curriculum developer at Chiang Mai University in Thailand. For the next two years, working in the television department of Open University in Nonthaburi, Thailand, he was writer, producer, editor, and actor in a nationally broadcast, English-language teaching program in the form of a situation comedy series, *English by Accident*.

Between 1990 and 1994, under the auspices of the United Nations Educational, Scientific, and Cultural Organization, Cotterill served as a teacher trainer and curriculum developer for the Ministry of Education at Dong Dok University and Dakse Teachers' College in Vientiane, People's Democratic Republic of Laos. He returned to Thailand, where from 1995 to 1997 he wrote curricula at Prince of Songkla University in Phuket and became project director for Child-Watch, an organization formed for the protection of sexually abused and exploited children. Cotterill served as a teacher-trainer and materials developer at refugee camps on the Thai-Burmese border, then received a certificate in community welfare from the Sydney Institute of Technology in Australia.

After serving another year with Child-Watch—during which time Cotterill wrote articles and drew cartoons for local publications, and produced a novel and two nonfictional books about child protection, published in English in Thailand—he became involved with ECPAT International (End Child Prostitution, Child Pornography and Trafficking of Children for Sexual Purposes). For two years he acted as training coordinator for the organization in Bangkok.

In 2002, Cotterill settled in northern Thailand, where he works as a writer, cartoonist, and occasional graduate teacher at Chiang Mai University. Following the publication of another Thai-published novel, *Evil in the Land Without: From England to Burma, a Monster Seeks Revenge* (2003), Cotterill released his first internationally distributed novel, *The Coroner's Lunch*, which introduced the mystery series character Dr. Siri Paiboun. The series continued with *Thirty-three Teeth*, which won the Dilys Award; *Disco for the Departed* (2006); and *Anarchy and Old Dogs* (2007). He contributed a Dr. Siri short story to *Damn Near Dead: An Anthology of Geezer Noir* (2006) and also published a comic novel, *Pool and Its Role in Asian Communism* (2005), available only in Thailand. Cotterill was married in 2006.

ANALYSIS

Colin Cotterill's major protagonist, Dr. Siri Paiboun, represents the conjunction of several qualities unusual in mystery and detective fiction. At seventy-two years of age, Siri is more elderly than typical sleuths (Agatha Christie's Miss Marple is a notable exception). The doctor is also a communist of long standing, albeit chronically lackadaisical about adhering strictly to the tenets of socialism. Though other communist detectives exist, including Russians such as Martin Cruz Smith's Arkady Renko and Stuart M. Kaminsky's Inspector Porfiry Rostnikov, Laotian communist sleuths are scarce.

Siri, a Paris-trained physician and longtime field surgeon during successive communist movements, is pressed into service as a coroner despite his advanced age and lack of specialized training. Although he just wants to retire, he is appointed coroner for the entire country, a key official position fraught with political and social consequences. Siri, ever curious, makes the best of a bad situation that features antiquated instruments, eager but meager help from a pair of assistants, a nonexistent budget, and uncooperative bureaucrats. The son of a Hmong shaman and the embodiment of Yeh Ming, an ancient shaman, Siri struggles to understand his own seemingly supernatural powers—he constantly dreams of dead people and gains subtle clues about their demise. He meanwhile has to cope with local superstition and custom, Buddhist beliefs, and atheistic communist thought when traveling to view corpses in the far-flung corners of Laos. His day job is dissecting cadavers brought to the morgue of a hospital in Vientiane, a city of only 150,000, diminished in population because many people fled to neighboring Thailand before the communist takeover.

The milieu of Cotterill's Dr. Siri novels is already intriguing for its ethnic and geographic diversity, its indigenous beliefs and customs, its colorful garb and exotic foodstuffs, and its ancient monuments and temples. Elephants, tigers, bears, extravagant flowers, and gaudy butterflies can be seen in the mountains and jungles and along Mekong riverbanks. The immediate political climate lends a further layer of interest. Each of Cotterill's series novels, beginning with *The Coroner's Lunch*, is set during a time of upheaval in a region of widespread unrest. The Pathet Lao movement that culminated in the forced abdication of the Laotian king mostly escaped notice in the West, grown weary of Southeast Asia after skirmishes in Indochina turned into the full-scale conflict of the Vietnam War. The situation provides opportunities for clashes among various factions: primitive tribes, Communist true believers, bureaucrats and paper-pushers, peasants, Buddhist monks, and ordinary Laotians of every stripe.

Siri—grown cynical but not overly crusty from hav-

ing seen much in his years—moves restlessly among the throng. He has a forceful, direct personality and often must swim against the flow of a rigidly structured society to make waves. Siri is blessed with a subtle, sarcastic wit (his zingers often go right over the heads of his superiors), an insatiable curiosity, an occult connection to mysterious spiritual forces, an intuitive nature, and superior deductive abilities. A cadre of regulars assists him in the pursuit of truth—practical Dtui, cheerful Mr. Geung, efficient Phosy, and his brilliant, witty boyhood chum Civilai—each of whom brings particular skills and lends a distinct personality to the mix.

Realistic dialogue and dark humor are two final indispensable ingredients to the popularity of Cotterill's series. The author has a talent for description and is particularly skilled at matching speech to character in such a way that attributions are seldom necessary: A reader always knows who is speaking. Siri's witty, anarchistic observations, Dtui's sarcastic remarks, and Civilai's grousing comments are echoed in the novel's pun-filled chapter headings, which add to the fun (chapters in *Thirty-three Teeth*, for example, are titled "Tomb Sweet Tomb," "A Day at the Maul," and "Das Capital Royal"). A continuing humorous theme is the sweltering Laotian countryside. This standard exchange, apparently the native manner of greeting, recurs so many times in so many different places between so many different characters that the reader begins to anticipate it:

> "Hot, isn't it?"
> "Damned hot."

Those terse words serve to explain much about Laos and its people: the preoccupation with weather, the natural friendliness of citizens, the fatalistic acceptance of the unchangeable, and the conformity to long tradition. They also underscore the multiple appeals of Cotterill's mystery fiction.

THE CORONER'S LUNCH

The Coroner's Lunch, the first novel in the Dr. Siri Paiboun series, introduces Dr. Siri, the feisty elderly coroner with almost supernatural powers of deduction, thanks to his allegedly being the reincarnation of Yeh Ming, a powerful Hmong shaman. As is typical throughout the series, Siri is presented with a variety of diverse cases to resolve to the satisfaction of a

sets in motion a cast of well-drawn characters with individual mannerisms and speech patterns that bring them to vibrant life. The novel skillfully incorporates colorful Laotian culture, history, and geography while capturing the atmosphere of a volatile era.

THIRTY-THREE TEETH

Thirty-three Teeth, the second novel in the series (the title refers to the legend that Buddha, like Dr. Siri, was alleged to have an extra tooth, a sign of great power) witnesses the hero involved in a number of diverse cases. The coroner enlists the aid of his usual allies—Dtui, Gueng, Phosy, and Civilai—to reconstruct the events surrounding and the causes behind a series of mysterious deaths: two men found together beside a crushed bicycle, a pair of women clawed to death by either an escaped bear or a marauding tiger, and a pair of charred corpses found in Luang Prabang, apparently shot before burning.

Jack Ewing

PRINCIPAL MYSTERY AND DETECTIVE FICTION

DR. SIRI PAIBOUN SERIES: *The Coroner's Lunch*, 2004; *Thirty-three Teeth*, 2005; *Disco for the Departed*, 2006; *Anarchy and Old Dogs*, 2007

OTHER MAJOR WORKS

NOVELS: *Evil in the Land Without: From England to Burma, a Monster Seeks Revenge*, 2003; *Pool and Its Role in Asian Communism*, 2005

BIBLIOGRAPHY

Cotterill, Colin. Colin Cotterill. http://www.colincotterill .com. The author's Web site, featuring Cotterill's cartoons and demonstrating his peculiar sense of humor under sections labeled "The Writing Chappy," "The Cartoon Chappy," and "The Normal, Having a Life Chappy," with links to further information about his life and work, including his diary. Illustrated.

Kirkus Reviews. Review of *The Coroner's Lunch*, by Colin Cotterill. 72, no. 16 (August 15, 2004): 779. The reviewer terms the novel "an embarrassment of riches" for its unique sleuth, political satire, and droll comedy.

Klett, Rex E. "Mystery: The Noir Detectives." Review of *The Coroner's Lunch*, by Colin Cotterill. *Li-*

mistrustful, paranoiac government in transition from kingdom to communist bureaucracy, despite the fact that he has had no training in pathology and is provided with few supplies and inadequate tools to do a proper job. In the initial novel in the series, Siri must work to unravel the truth behind the accidental death of a fisherman, the appearance of three bodies that rise from the Mekong River after being dropped into the water with Chinese bombs tied around their ankles, the sudden demise of the wife of a high-ranking official, and the apparent suicide of the man's mistress. Siri must also cope with efforts from different sources to prevent his work: bodies that are removed from the morgue's freezer, autopsy notes gone missing, sabotage, assassination attempts, and administrative roadblocks.

A fascinating glimpse into a little-known society during events largely ignored in the West following the fiasco of the Vietnam War, *The Coroner's Lunch brary Journal* 129, no. 20 (December, 2004): 94-95. A brief, favorable review, among reviews of eight other works by contemporary noir writers, which cites as strengths the engaging protagonist, the humor, and the alien setting.

Sennett, Frank. Review of *Anarchy and Old Dogs*, by Colin Cotterill. *Booklist* 103, no. 17 (May 1, 2007): 20-21. Siri's investigation involves a possible plot to overthrow the communist government in this work, which the reviewer described as the most thoughtful in the series as it addresses issues concerning the newly formed communist government.

Stasio, Marilyn. "Crime: Immaterial Witness." Review of *The Coroner's Lunch*, by Colin Cotterill. *The New York Times Book Review*, December 26, 2004, 22. A highly favorable review of *The Coroner's Lunch*, called a "wonderfully fresh and exotic mystery."

GEORGE HARMON COXE

Born: Olean, New York; April 23, 1901
Died: Old Lyme, Connecticut; January 30, 1984
Types of plot: Amateur sleuth; inverted; police procedural; private investigator; psychological

PRINCIPAL SERIES

Jack "Flashgun" Casey, 1934-1964
Kent Murdoch, 1935-1973

PRINCIPAL SERIES CHARACTERS

JACK "FLASHGUN" CASEY, a photographer for the Boston *Globe*, later joins the Boston *Express*. Casey weighs in at 215 pounds and stands six feet, two inches tall. A hard-drinking, quick-tempered, but thoroughly professional newspaperman, Casey has a profound contempt for phonies and an energetic and persistent loyalty for a friend in trouble.

KENT MURDOCH, the picture chief for the Boston *Courier-Herald*, is about thirty years old when he first appears; throughout the series, he never goes beyond the age of forty. Darkly handsome, cultured, and sophisticated, he is primarily a cerebral detective, although by no means of the Sherlock Holmes/C. Auguste Dupin school. Murdock handles himself well in a fight, but he fights only as a last resort.

CONTRIBUTION

The crime novels of George Harmon Coxe offer a marked departure from the hard-boiled school of Dashiell Hammett and Raymond Chandler. Although the action is brisk and the dialogue crisp, Coxe's stories are never sensationally violent, tending more toward carefully constructed plots that follow a more workmanlike approach to criminal detection. There is a decided emphasis on clearly developed characterization and a meticulous depiction of physical setting. It was Coxe who introduced into detective fiction the newspaper photographer as amateur sleuth, a refreshing variation on the familiar former-cop-turned-private-eye pattern.

BIOGRAPHY

George Harmon Coxe was born on April 23, 1901, in Olean, New York, the son of George H. Coxe and Harriet C. Coxe. After attending public schools in Olean and the Free Academy in nearby Elmira, Coxe spent the academic year of 1919-1920 at Purdue University in West Lafayette, Indiana. The following year, he attended Cornell University in Ithaca, New York. Coxe left Cornell without finishing and drifted into a variety of odd jobs, including work in a lumber camp and later on an automobile assembly line. During this period he also wrote two stories, which he sold to *Detective Story Magazine*.

Moving west in 1922, Coxe became a journalist for the Santa Monica *Outlook* and later joined the Los Angeles *Express*. Moving back to New York, Coxe worked for the Utica *Observer-Dispatch*, the New

York *Commercial and Financial Chronicle*, and the Elmira *Star-Gazette*. In 1927, Coxe left newspaper work and wrote and sold advertising for Barta Press, an agency in Cambridge, Massachusetts. In 1929, he married Elizabeth Fowler.

In 1932 Coxe gave up advertising and became a full-time writer, turning out crime and detective stories for *Black Mask* and other pulp magazines. From 1932 until the publication of his first crime novel in 1935, he published more than fifty detective stories. From 1935 to 1976, he published sixty-three crime novels, twenty-one of them featuring the exploits of photographer Kent Murdock. From 1936 to 1938 (and briefly in 1944-1945), Coxe worked in Hollywood as a screenwriter. He shared screen credit for *Arsène Lupin Returns* (1938) and for *The Hidden Eye* (1946), for which he had written the original story.

During World War II, Coxe wrote scripts for a radio series, *The Commandos*, and an audition script for *Casey, Crime Photographer*, a radio drama based on the Flashgun Casey stories. In 1945, he served as a special war correspondent in the Pacific theater. After the war, Coxe expanded his interests, writing stories on subjects other than detective fiction for more sophisticated magazines such as *Collier's* and *The Saturday Evening Post*. In 1952, Coxe was elected president of the Mystery Writers of America, and in 1964 he received the organization's Grand Masters Award. Largely inactive after the late 1970's, he died on January 30, 1984.

ANALYSIS

George Harmon Coxe's brief career as a newspaperman proved a determining factor in the style and structure of his detective fiction. Avoiding the more scientific, logical approach of the Arthur Conan Doyle school, Coxe concentrated on the development of characterization, personality, and human fallibility. His victims generally die in conventional ways: They are shot, stabbed, or occasionally, as in *Eye Witness* (1950), bludgeoned to death. A cast of characters is assembled; they are then tracked and observed by the detective hero. The plot proceeds like a journalism primer, raising and gradually answering a series of who, what, when, where, why, and how questions.

"RETURN ENGAGEMENT"

Coxe had been publishing detective stories for more than two years when he sold the first Flashgun Casey story, "Return Engagement," to *Black Mask* in the spring of 1934. The idea of a news photographer as a detective hero was a genuine innovation in the crime-fiction market, then largely the province of sleuthing lawyers, reporters, and private investigators. It came directly from Coxe's personal experience. From his own days as a reporter, he knew that "while the reporter with his pad and pencil could describe a warehouse . . . fire from a safe distance," it was the photographer who accompanied him who "had to edge far closer to get a negative that would merit reproduction." For Coxe, it was a case of giving the photographer his due.

The other fictional creation for which Coxe is known is Kent Murdock. Both Murdock and Casey are Boston newspaper photographers, but it was Casey who brought Coxe a strong following from the time of his debut in *Black Mask*. Closer to the hard-boiled school of Hammett and Chandler than is Murdock, Casey is frequently isolated by self-induced conflict, having antagonized editors, police, and the criminal element. For all of his rough edges, however, Casey is a highly appealing character, both compassionate and sentimental. Like Murdock, he is a combat veteran, having served as an American Expeditionary Force sergeant in France in 1918. Both Casey and Murdock are for the most part uncynical and, when the question arises, patriotic. Although wartime combat seems a *sine qua non*, Coxe's emphasis lies in developing his two most memorable creations, shaping interesting, clearly delineated characters, rather than in portraying action and violence.

MURDER WITH PICTURES

Kent Murdock first appeared in the 1935 novel *Murder with Pictures* and is what Coxe himself has termed a "smoothed-up version" of Jack Casey—the Boston photographer polished and reshaped for an expanded audience. Coxe's reasons for the reshaping were more practical than they were literary. He believed that Murdock, "not unlike Casey in many ways . . . but better dressed and better mannered," would be "more appropriate for a book."

Ironically, Casey has been the more enduring of the two. Although only six novels were written about him, Casey appeared in dozens of short stories as well as a radio series and two feature films: *Women Are Trouble* (1936) and *Here's Flash Casey* (1937). One of the reasons many readers may have identified with Casey is that unlike most fictional detectives, he ages over the years. At his inception he is about thirty-two. By the time he appears in *Deadly Image* (1964), his hair is graying and he has put on weight. By Coxe's own reckoning, Casey in the final book is about forty-five, but his wit and perception remain as sharp as ever.

For a time, Coxe apparently entertained the possibility of a Mr. and Mrs. Kent Murdock as a detective team, perhaps along the lines of Hammett's Nick and Nora Charles. Joyce Murdock, bright, independent, and self-reliant, appears in *Mrs. Murdock Takes a Case* (1941), but she evidently proved to be more dominant a personality than Murdock, or Coxe for that matter, could endure. By the time *The Jade Venus* (1945) was published, Joyce Murdock has been dropped by the author, a similar fate having befallen Hestor, Murdock's estranged first wife, who appeared in *Murder with Pictures* at the beginning of the Murdock series.

Coxe developed other series, although none of them was quite as popular as the Murdock/Casey ventures: Paul Standish, medical examiner; Sam Crombie, a stolid but persistent investigator; Max Hale, a somewhat reluctant detective; and Jack Fenner, Murdock's fearless but good-natured sidekick. Fenner is a private eye who appears in *Four Frightened Women* (1939) and *The Charred Witness* (1942). He is featured in three of the last five of Coxe's novels, most notably in *Fenner* (1971), in which he takes center stage.

Approximately half of the novels Coxe wrote are not series novels; nevertheless, they are characteristically well structured, if somewhat predictable. Often the non-series books are set in exotic locales. Sixteen novels alone are set in the Caribbean, most notably *Murder in Havana* (1943), *One Minute Past Eight* (1957), and *Woman with a Gun* (1972).

BLACK MASK MAGAZINE

Coxe's development as a writer of mystery and detective fiction gained its greatest impetus from his connection with *Black Mask* magazine, an association that began early in 1934. Coxe had been writing for pulp magazines for several years, and he had produced more than thirty short stories for publications such as *Top Notch*, *Complete Stories*, and *Detective Fiction Weekly*; it was not until his association with Joseph Thompson Shaw, who edited *Black Mask* from 1926 to 1936, however, that he further developed and enhanced the lean, economical style and the rigorous, stoic image of the central character that would become primary characteristics of his novels. Coxe was one of the writers whom Shaw was particularly proud of recruiting, along with Frederick Nebel, Paul Cain, and Lester Dent. Yet among Shaw's more notable prizes in his stable of writers were Dashiell Hammett, Raymond Chandler, and Erle Stanley Gardner. Hammett in particular was the example Shaw held up to Coxe and other *Black Mask* writers, specifically requesting them to study the economy of his prose. Coxe's style was thus developed through the process of imitation, an imitation of the better aspects of the prevailing pulp standard. Through this observation of his colleagues' work, Coxe perfected the ability to write a distinctively American prose, developing an acute sense of the rhythm and idiom of the urban American vernacular.

What distinguishes Coxe from the others, however, is the delineation of his hero. The heroes in the plots of the stories and novels of his *Black Mask* colleagues often went Hammett one better, having a hero who not only accepted but also exulted in violence. Each beating and shooting of a "hood" gave clear satisfaction because it was done in support of what was "good."

The world of *Black Mask* crime and detection was essentially nihilistic, a place where people could exert no real control over their existence. Stoicism and violence were often depicted as the only alternatives in a life that seemed to offer little of significance beyond the passing of time. Coxe's protagonists made their way in this world, and although formidable and ready for action, they also seemed to subscribe to a code of unwritten but civilized behavior and values—the code of a gentleman. Clearly, Coxe's heroes owe something to such rugged but refined and polished crime fighters as Richard Harding Davis's Van Bibber and the heroes of the adventure novels of John Buchan.

THE BIG GAMBLE

The hero of a Coxe novel, while considerably less hard-boiled than the typical tough guy found in the work of his contemporaries, possesses all the more admirable requisites of the pulp-fiction hero of the day: chivalry, personal loyalty, and unremitting physical courage. Violence is generally a defensive reaction, a secondary rather than primary solution to a problem, always limited to what is necessary—and no more. Consider the following example, from *The Big Gamble* (1958), which is typical of the way in which a Coxe protagonist (in this case, Murdock) handles himself in a tight spot. Having discovered a man searching his apartment, Murdock apprehends him. As Murdock escorts him to the door, the man, whose name is Herrick, pulls a punch

> that would have floored Murdock if he hadn't been warned by the look he had seen. It was not a clever move because it was a roundhouse punch that started too far back and took too much time. Murdock pulled his chin back. The fist missed by two inches, the force of the blow pulling the big man off balance, and leaving his shoulders and head partly turned. Before he could recover, Murdock stepped in and slammed the side of the gun against the side of Herrick's head, not savagely but with authority.

Herrick leaves peacefully, having been restrained "not savagely but with authority," a phrase that sums up the standard method of operation for a Coxe protagonist in a desperate situation.

Some critics have found Coxe's work anachronistic, viewing the novels of the 1950's through the 1970's as artifacts of the 1930's. For many of Coxe's followers, however, that fidelity to the pace and structure of an earlier time is part of the author's appeal, and his loyal readers are familiar and comfortable with the pattern. His novels are always reliable entertainment: fast-paced, sharply detailed, cleverly plotted, consistently plausible. They are, in the final analysis, detective stories told in a style that is formal yet deceptively simple. Coxe's readers know what to expect, and he rarely disappoints them.

Richard Keenan

PRINCIPAL MYSTERY AND DETECTIVE FICTION

JACK "FLASHGUN" CASEY SERIES: *Silent Are the Dead*, 1942; *Murder for Two*, 1943; *Flash Casey, Detective*, 1946; *Error of Judgment*, 1961 (also known as *One Murder Too Many*); *The Man Who Died Too Soon*, 1962; *Deadly Image*, 1964

KENT MURDOCK SERIES: *Murder with Pictures*, 1935; *The Barotique Mystery*, 1936 (also known as *Murdock's Acid Test*); *The Camera Clue*, 1937; *The Glass Triangle*, 1940; *Mrs. Murdock Takes a Case*, 1941; *The Jade Venus*, 1945; *The Fifth Key*, 1947; *The Hollow Needle*, 1948; *Lady Killer*, 1949; *Eye Witness*, 1950; *The Widow Had a Gun*, 1951; *The Crimson Clue*, 1953; *Focus on Murder*, 1954; *Murder on Their Minds*, 1957; *The Big Gamble*, 1958; *The Last Commandment*, 1960; *The Hidden Key*, 1963; *The Reluctant Heiress*, 1965; *An Easy Way to Go*, 1969

MAX HALE SERIES: *Murder for the Asking*, 1939; *The Lady Is Afraid*, 1940

SAM CROMBIE SERIES: *The Frightened Fiancée*, 1950; *The Impetuous Mistress*, 1958

JACK FENNER SERIES: *No Place for Murder*, 1975; *Four Frightened Women*, 1939 (also known as *The Frightened Woman*); *The Charred Witness*, 1942; *Fenner*, 1971

NONSERIES NOVELS: 1941-1950 • *No Time to Kill*, 1941; *Assignment in Guiana*, 1942; *Alias the Dead*, 1943; *Murder in Havana*, 1943; *The Groom Lay Dead*, 1944; *Woman at Bay*, 1945; *Dangerous Legacy*, 1946; *Fashioned for Murder*, 1947; *Venturous Lady*, 1948; *Inland Passage*, 1949

1951-1960 • *The Man Who Died Twice*, 1951; *Never Bet Your Life*, 1952; *Uninvited Guest*, 1953; *Death at the Isthmus*, 1954; *Top Assignment*, 1955; *Man on a Rope*, 1956; *Suddenly a Widow*, 1956; *One Minute Past Eight*, 1957; *Slack Tide*, 1959; *One Way Out*, 1960

1961-1974 • *Moment of Violence*, 1961; *Mission of Fear*, 1962; *One Hour to Kill*, 1963; *With Intent to Kill*, 1965; *The Ring of Truth*, 1966; *The Candid Imposter*, 1968; *Double Identity*, 1970; *Woman with a Gun*, 1972; *The Silent Witness*, 1973; *The Inside Man*, 1974

OTHER MAJOR WORKS

RADIO PLAYS: *Casey, Crime Photographer*, 1943-1952; *The Commandos* 1943-1950, 1954-1955 (radio series based on his fiction)

SCREENPLAYS: *Arsène Lupin Returns*, 1938 (with James Kevin McGuinness and Howard Emmett Rogers); *The Hidden Eye*, 1945 (with Harry Ruskin)

BIBLIOGRAPHY

Cox, J. Randolph. "Mystery Master: A Survey and Appreciation of the Fiction of George Harmon Coxe." *The Armchair Detective* 6 (October, 1972-May, 1973): 63-74, 160-162, 232-241. Serialized overview of Coxe's writings paying homage to the skill and importance of the author.

Haining, Peter. *The Classic Era of American Pulp Magazines*. Chicago: Chicago Review Press, 2000.
Discusses Coxe's work in the pulps and the role of pulp fiction in American culture.

Knight, Stephen Thomas. *Crime Fiction, 1800-2000: Detection, Death, Diversity*. New York: Palgrave Macmillan, 2004. Broad overview of the important trends and developments in two centuries of detective fiction. Emphasizes the trend toward diversity in the characterization of detectives in later fiction, which helps readers understand Coxe's decision to make his detectives newspaper photographers.

Margolies, Edward. *Which Way Did He Go? The Private Eye in Dashiell Hammett, Raymond Chandler, Chester Himes, and Ross Macdonald*. New York: Holmes and Meier, 1982. This study of the major hard-boiled detective writers mentions Coxe briefly and provides a background from which to understand Coxe.

ROBERT CRAIS

Born: Independence, Louisiana; June 20, 1953
Also wrote as Elvis Cole; Jerry Gret Samouche
Types of plot: Hard-boiled; private investigator; police procedural

PRINCIPAL SERIES

Elvis Cole and Joe Pike, 1987-
Carol Starkey, 2000-

PRINCIPAL SERIES CHARACTERS

ELVIS COLE is a wisecracking, straight-talking West Hollywood private investigator in his thirties said to resemble Kevin Costner, Moe Howard, and Errol Flynn. A Vietnam War veteran with Ranger training and a former security guard, he lives with a cantankerous cat and has a fondness for loud Hawaiian shirts, cooking, classic rock, Disney memorabilia, and his 1966 yellow Corvette. His physical and mental prowess (he is unafraid of violent confrontation) is honed by his practice of the Eastern arts of hatha yoga and tai chi.

JOE PIKE is Cole's muscle and his closest friend, an enigmatic presence and a victim of childhood abuse. Formerly a Force Reconnaissance Marine in Vietnam and a Los Angeles police officer with an inscrutable quietness and a compelling code of integrity, Pike is now a mercenary with an extensive résumé in paramilitary covert operations. A vegetarian who never smiles, Pike listens to the Doors and always wears massive pilot sunglasses. He is tattooed with red arrows along his deltoids to signify his credo: Never Back Up. He shadows with predatory skills and kills without hesitation

CAROL STARKEY is a tough, street-hardened detective in the Los Angeles Police Department Criminal Conspiracy section whose assignment is bomb squad investigations. Currently under the care of therapists, she is haunted by the death of her partner and lover at an explosion site at which she herself was horrifically scarred—indeed, she thinks of herself as a sort of Frankenstein, put back together and returned from the dead. She wrestles with vivid and violent nightmares and copes through a self-destructive regimen of junk food, prescription ulcer medicine, and gin.

CONTRIBUTION

Before Robert Crais turned to detective fiction in the late 1980's, he had for more than a decade enjoyed a lucrative career as one of network television's premiere scriptwriters, developing scripts for top-rated crime shows, most prominently *L.A. Law* (1986-1994), *Hill Street Blues* (1981-1987), *Baretta* (1975-1978), *Cagney and Lacey* (1982-1988), and *Miami Vice* (1984-1989). That long and successful association helped shape the elements of Crais's signature narratives: snappy dialogue, hip characters, fast-paced storytelling, ingenious plot twists, and sustained momentum toward a dramatic shoot-out/showdown. In addition, Crais's long background in the Hollywood environment gives his prose a postmodern edge as he alludes to a wide range of classic films, television, and popular music. From Ernest Hemingway, Crais mastered a prose line that is economic and clean of ornamentation, and from John Steinbeck, he adopted a dark vision of a morally bankrupt universe in which nobility, trust, and compassion are rare.

However, it was Crais's love of the hard-boiled detective fiction of Raymond Chandler and Dashiell Hammett that influenced the creation of Elvis Cole, who solves crimes as much with relentless investigation and hard evidence as with intuitive perceptions and a sixth sense about character. A solitary moral agent in an otherwise seamy and mercenary universe, Cole sees himself as the protector of the vulnerable, particularly imperiled women and lost children. Unlike Chandler and Hammett, Crais renders modern Los Angeles, despite its criminal excesses, with keen compassion, respecting its diversity, its energy, its hard neon beauty, its cheesy glitz, and its unrelenting cool.

BIOGRAPHY

Robert Kyle Crais grew up near Baton Rouge, Louisiana, in a blue-collar family made up largely of Gulf Coast oil refinery engineers and beat police officers. An avid reader as a child, he purchased at the age of fifteen a used copy of Raymond Chandler's *The Little Sister* (1949), in which a distraught woman from Kansas approaches Philip Marlowe to help find her brother. The hard-edged prose style entranced the young Crais, and he decided that he would be a writer.

While supporting himself through a series of menial jobs and attempting college, he produced homemade comic books, amateur films, and even short fiction, for which he received scores of rejection letters. Crais decided he needed to head West to achieve whatever writing success he could. In 1976, he arrived in Hollywood and found work almost immediately writing for television—ironic as he did not own a television at the time and learned scriptwriting by watching department store televisions and studying sample scripts. Eventually he worked on landmark law-and-order series, including *Baretta*, *Cagney and Lacey*, and *Hill Street Blue*s; a script developed for the latter was nominated for an Emmy.

Given his childhood dream of being a novelist, Crais grew uncomfortable with the collaborative dynamic of television production. It was the sudden death of his father in 1985 that ultimately convinced Crais to try novel writing. His mother, long dependent on his father, was suddenly left vulnerable, a complex dilemma that Crais would treat fictionally in his first novel, *The Monkey's Raincoat* (1987), which introduced private investigator Elvis Cole, who helps a distraught wife in her thirties find her husband and son who disappeared after her husband, an out-of-work Hollywood agent, got involved with loan sharks and drug kingpins. The novel—an homage to classic Chandler (Cole speaks in a pitch-perfect hard-boiled first person) and part of the renaissance in noir fiction initiated by Ross Macdonald and Robert B. Parker—found immediate success, unusual in that it was published in paperback without major fanfare. It was recognized with numerous best first mystery novel nominations and won the Macavity Award. Over the next ten years, Crais produced six new Cole titles, dissecting the decadent lifestyles of the entertainment industry, the corruption and moral indifference of the police department, the unrelenting pressure of gang violence and organized crime, and the mayhem of street drug trafficking and the skin trade.

With each title, Crais earned more success, becoming something of a celebrity himself. There was some criticism of his formulaic plots and his preference for action over character—both reminiscent of series television—as well as his disinclination to probe the interior life of his central characters. Despite the presumed intimacy of first-person narration, Elvis Cole remained an inaccessible character known more for quirky habits and smart-alecky banter. It was the publication of *L.A. Requiem* (1999) that changed that perception. This groundbreaking work marked a new maturity. It was far more sophisticated in its structure, having multiple points of view, and explored for the first time not only the interior psychology of Elvis Cole but also the long and troubling background of Cole's sidekick Joe Pike, who until this novel had been a shadowy, if eccentric presence.

In *Demolition Angel* (2000), Crais introduced a new series centering on Carol Starkey, a bomb squad detective/technician. That permitted Crais to examine a classic premise of noir fiction—the sudden intrusion of violence—and the complex psychology of lives spent on the edge, anticipating death, brutal and messy, as part of every working day. In a later title, Crais brought Elvis Cole and Carol Starkey together in *The Forgotten Man* (2005), involving an investigation of the homicide of an unidentified indigent in a run-down hotel, who claimed shortly before he died that he was Cole's estranged father. Crais has written nonseries novels, most prominently *Hostage* (2001), a taut psychological thriller (later a major film) about a hostage negotiator whose family is taken hostage during a standoff involving the family of a bookkeeper for a mob boss. Crais continues to develop Elvis Cole, and unlike other long-running serials that succumb to parody or improbabilities, the plots and the character development have become more intricate, and Elvis Cole, who began the series as a kind of Peter Pan figure, has emerged as a nuanced and psychologically compelling adult.

ANALYSIS

Early in the Elvis Cole series, Robert Crais's dedication to the craft and vision of classic hard-boiled detective-fiction writers is apparent. Cole maintains a private code of integrity and genuine compassion within a Southern California rank with corruption, deceit, violence, and greed. For all his edgy swagger, his hip cynicism, and his violent cunning, Cole espouses a romantic code that values friendship, particularly to

his enigmatic partner Joe Pike, and duty as a kind of moral authenticity maintained against a universe of cutthroat mercenaries and unrelieved pretense. Like the classic hard-boiled detectives, Cole finds his greatest calling—and his deepest professional reward—in rescuing beautiful damsels in distress and lost or kidnapped children. Cole has little interest in puzzling out the psychology of the criminal mind and a crime's motives and rationales but rather accepts as a given that fallible people—Crais's preferred adjective is "lost"—are capable of committing evil. World-weary, Cole refuses to concede. The associations that Crais makes between Cole and childhood, through references to Peter Pan and characters from familiar children's books, cartoon classics, and Disney films, suggest that Cole's unshakeable faith in fundamental values stems from a childlike faith in the ability to triumph over a world of corrupt adults. As the series developed, Crais has allowed Cole to evolve from a hip outsider with an engaging cynicism to a complex character who comes to accept as emotionally necessary the fragile bond to significant others, not only Joe Pike but also to a Louisiana lawyer and part-time television personality named Lucy Chenier, who joined the series in *Voodoo River* (1995).

In the Carol Starkey series, Crais investigates the darkest implications of Cole's problematic moral vision. If Cole, amid a chaotic world busy with crime, is cool, calm, and together (as suggested by his Eastern rituals), Starkey is fragmented, troubled, and coming apart. She is not a private investigator. As a police officer, she must exist within the harrowing reality of mayhem. As a bomb squad detective, she is involved in disarming devices and therefore plunged into criminal activity. She is constantly aware of crime and its consequences because of the scars that she bears, the ghastly cross-stitching on her body that is the result of her own brush with death. Her considerable struggles with private demons—most notably her troubling dreams, her alcohol abuse, and her testy aloofness—suggest a kind of anti-Cole. Whereas with Cole, the truth, finally revealed, heals, with Starkey, the truth hurts, the very message left at a bombing site by the serial bomber in *Demolition Angel*.

THE MONKEY'S RAINCOAT

In the first book of the series, *The Monkey's Raincoat*, Elvis Cole helps Ellen Lang track down her missing son and husband, a hapless talent agent who has become involved in a vast underworld of drug running to help continue his Hollywood lifestyle. The private investigator is first defined to readers through the title of the work itself. Inspired by a haiku by Matsuo Bashō ("Winter downpour / Even the monkey/ needs a raincoat"), it suggests Cole's function as a protector, both to Ellen and to her young son. First Ellen's son, Perry, then Ellen herself are kidnapped as part of a negotiation for two missing kilograms of prime cocaine. As Cole investigates, he affirms a classic theme of noir fiction: how strikingly ordinary people can get involved in nefarious actions and tangled in criminal activity. However, the far larger moral narrative here is the gradual evolution of Ellen out of dependency and midlife confusion into confidence and self-assertion; she will be the one to shoot the syndicate boss who threatens her son. This moral evolution is guided by Cole, who along the way becomes her lover. In the end, after Cole and Joe Pike stage a sophisticated paramilitary raid on the drug lord's compound to rescue Ellen, she uncovers a difficult truth about her dead husband—how desperately he had tried to protect his son from the drug runners—that completes her moral maturation.

L.A. REQUIEM

By positioning the shadowy Joe Pike at the center of *L.A. Requiem*, Crais virtually reinvented the Elvis Cole series at the point where, after a half dozen titles, its formula was starting to wear. Pike asks Cole to help him find a missing woman, a powerful Latino community leader's daughter, who is subsequently found shot dead along a jogging path. As the dead woman's past romantic ties to Pike surface, Crais departs from the restricting structural device of first person to explore not only Pike's difficult childhood but also his brief stint as an officer with the Los Angeles Police Department twelve years earlier. Pike had been suspected of killing his partner during the arrest of a pedophile when his partner threatened the child molester with vigilante-style punishment. When the missing woman's death is linked to a series of killings and a witness places Pike at the scene, the police, who still hold a grudge against Pike, are quite willing to pin the killings on him. Cole, who drops his characteristic flip humor in this case, must examine the value of friendship and the cost of betrayal and reacquaint himself with the necessary element of sacrifice in any relationship and the difficult trick of trust. Without sacrificing the hard edge of a detective thriller, the narrative expands the genre's scope by investigating the damage done by secrets and ultimately how criminal investigations, even the most diligent, lead to resolution but seldom to understanding.

DEMOLITION ANGEL

Published on the heels of the critical success of *L.A. Requiem*, *Demolition Angel* continued that novel's exploration of the implosive nature of the past, the dark power of secrets, and the difficult act of self-forgiveness. Ironically, given the on-the-spot nature of Carol Starkey's detective duties defusing live bombs, she is lost in the past, haunted by her lover's death nearly three years earlier. That struggle—to make peace with her own history and to accept her scarred self—is the centerpiece narrative. A disgruntled bomb squad detective tries to rig an explosive to kill another detective, who is sleeping with his wife, by mimicking the modus operandi (MO) of a serial bomber who, as it turns out, takes umbrage in having his work amateurishly copied. The real bomber, a monomaniac who yearns to be listed among the Federal Bureau of Investigation's (FBI's) Most Wanted, comes to Los Angeles to set things right. However, for Starkey, the investigation into the serial bomber (she comes to communicate with him through an Internet chat room in chilling exchanges that recall Hannibal Lechter and Clarice Starling) is as much an investigation into herself and her past via her growing interest in a rogue FBI agent, Pell, whose sight had been permanently damaged by one of the serial bomber's earliest devices and who now vows revenge. In the end, a violent confrontation with the bomber costs Pell his sight entirely; dependent and vulnerable, he accepts Starkey's invitation to move in with her. The closing scene is not the typical procedural resolution: Starkey and Pell make love in the dark, and the blind Pell quietly tells Starkey, "You're beautiful." It is a complicated, psychologically compelling resolution that

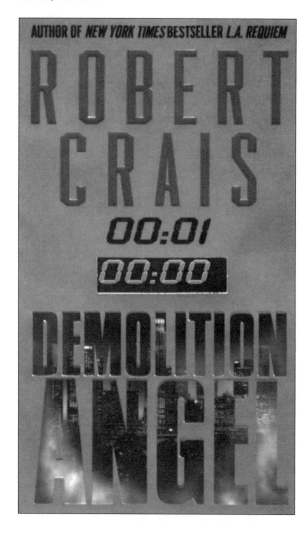

marks Crais as a novelist interested in the subtle evolution of character rather than as a former television scriptwriter interested in the flashy spectacle of action.

Joseph Dewey

PRINCIPAL MYSTERY AND DETECTIVE FICTION

ELVIS COLE/JOE PIKE SERIES: *The Monkey's Raincoat*, 1987; *Stalking the Angel*, 1989; *Lullaby Town*, 1992; *Free Fall*, 1993; *Voodoo River*, 1995; *Sunset Express*, 1996; *Indigo Slam*, 1997; *L.A. Requiem*, 1999; *The Forgotten Man*, 2005; *The Watchman*, 2007

CAROL STARKEY SERIES: *Demolition Angel*, 2000; *The Last Detective*, 2003

NONSERIES NOVELS: *Hostage*, 2001; *The Two-Minute Rule*, 2006

OTHER MAJOR WORKS

TELEPLAYS: *In Self Defense*, 1987; *Cross of Fire*, 1989

BIBLIOGRAPHY

Anderson, Patrick. *The Triumph of the Thriller: How Cops, Crooks, and Cannibals Captured Popular Fiction*. New York: Random House, 2007. Contains a short biography of Crais, with analysis of his *The Last Detective* and *The Monkey's Raincoat*.

Crais, Robert. RobertCrais.com. http://www.robert crais.com. Extensive Web site maintained by the author that provides reviews, synopses, biographical information, and contact numbers.

Jones, Louise. "From Cop TV to Mystery Maestro." *Publishers Weekly* 250, no. 10 (March 10, 2003): 49. Examines Crais's evolution as a mystery writer and discusses *The Last Detective*.

Marling, William. *Hard-boiled Fiction*. Case Western Reserve University. http://www.cwru.edu/artsci/ engl/marling/hardboiled/. A valuable resource, maintained by William Marling, a professor at Case Western Reserve University, of the hard-boiled detective genre with analyses of modern expressions.

Panck, LeRoy Lad. "Robert Crais." In *New Hard-Boiled Writers, 1970s-1990s*. Bowling Green, Ohio: Bowling Green State University Popular Press, 2000. Important overview of the early Cole titles with helpful genre context.

Philips, Gene D. *Creatures of Darkness: Raymond Chandler, Detective Fiction, and Film Noir*. Lexington: University of Kentucky Press, 2000. Accessible and thorough review of the author Crais cites as his major influence.

JOHN CREASEY

Born: Southfields, Surrey, England; September 17, 1908

Died: Bodenham, Salisbury, England; June 9, 1973

Also wrote as Gordon Ashe; M. E. Cooke; Margaret Cooke; Henry St. John Cooper; Norman Deane; Elise Fecamps; Robert Caine Frazer; Patrick Gill; Michael Halliday; Charles Hogarth; Brian Hope; Colin Hughes; Kyle Hunt; Abel Mann; Peter Manton; J. J. Marric; James Marsden; Richard Martin; Anthony Morton; Ken Ranger; William K. Reilly; Tex Riley; Jeremy York

Types of plot: Amateur sleuth; espionage; police procedural; thriller

PRINCIPAL SERIES

Department Z, 1933-1953
Baron John Mannering, 1937-1979
Sexton Blake, 1937-1943
The Toff, 1938-1978
Patrick Dawlish, 1939-1977
Bruce Murdoch, 1939-1972
Roger West, 1942-1978
Dr. Palfrey, 1942-1973
Liberator, 1943-1945
Martin and Richard Fane, 1951-1953
Commander George Gideon, 1955-1976
Mark Kilby, 1959-1960
Dr. Emmanuel Cellini, 1965-1976

PRINCIPAL SERIES CHARACTERS

BARON JOHN MANNERING, an art dealer, is married to Lorna Mannering, a painter. Wealthy and polished, he moves easily among the highest levels of society, but he is kind and considerate toward the humble people who sometimes consult him because they know that they can trust him, whether for an honest valuation of a painting or for help in a perilous situation.

THE HONOURABLE RICHARD "THE TOFF" ROLLISON, a wealthy man-about-town who divides his time between Mayfair and London's East End. Tall, handsome, and polished, he is tough enough to intimidate the most vicious criminal; yet when his investigations carry him into the East End, he is often defended by those whom he has charitably helped in the past.

PATRICK DAWLISH, a British detective as famous as Sherlock Holmes, who operates first as deputy assistant commissioner for crime at Scotland Yard and later independently as an unofficial investigator in cooperation with the Yard. Dawlish is a huge, polite man, handsome despite a once-broken nose, which reminds the reader that he is capable of sudden and decisive action. He is devoted to his wife, Felicity.

ROGER WEST, an inspector at Scotland Yard, nicknamed "Handsome," is a large, powerful man who has two passions, his work and his family. The demands of his job have put great stress on his relationship with his wife, Janet, and at one time a divorce seems inevitable. As the series progresses, however, Janet comes to accept the situation, partly, no doubt, because their two sons, Martin and Richard, seem to thrive despite their father's unpredictable absences and his too-predictable exhaustion when he is at home.

DR. STANISLAUS ALEXANDER "SAP" PALFREY, a specialist in pulmonary diseases, is a pale, round-shouldered, scholarly-looking man with a weak chin, whose real strength is not immediately apparent. He is actually the brilliant and decisive head of Z5, a secret international organization designed to defeat the forces that threaten the peace of the world. In the grimmest situations, he is almost godlike in his serenity; generally he has contingency plans, but always he has faith in the rightness of his cause.

COMMANDER GEORGE GIDEON of Scotland Yard's Criminal Investigation Department (CID) is the hero of John Creasey's most admired series. Gideon is a dogged crime fighter who is often impatient with the politically motivated demands of his superiors. Although Gideon and his wife, Kate, have six children, she cannot forget the loss of a seventh, a loss she blames on Gideon's devotion to duty, which kept him away from her at a crucial time. Gideon's sensitivity is revealed by his understanding of her feelings, his thoughtfulness, and his unfailing interest in family concerns, no matter how pressured he may be.

CONTRIBUTION

John Creasey is notable as the most prolific writer of mystery stories in the history of the genre. Changing from pen name to pen name and from sleuth to sleuth, Creasey mass-produced as many as two novels a week. At his death, he was credited with more than 550 crime novels, which had sold sixty million copies in twenty-six languages. Despite his great commercial success, Creasey was not highly ranked by critics, who pointed out that no matter how clever his plot outlines might be, his characters too often were pasteboard creations rather than psychologically interesting human beings, his situations geared to fast action rather than to the development of atmosphere that characterizes the best mystery novels. Sensitive to such criticisms, in some of his novels Creasey took time for fuller development of character; the Gideon series, written under the pseudonym J. J. Marric, ranks with the best of the genre.

BIOGRAPHY

John Creasey was born on September 17, 1908, in Southfields, Surrey, England, the seventh of nine children of Joseph Creasey, a coachmaker, and Ruth Creasey. The family was poor, and life was difficult, made more difficult for John by a bout with polio that delayed his learning to walk until he was six. John's first encouragement in a writing career came when he was ten; impressed by a composition, a schoolmaster assured John that he could be a professional writer. Then began a long, discouraging period of fourteen years when only Creasey himself had hopes for his future. His family found his dreams laughable; after he left school at fourteen, he was fired by one employer after another, often for neglecting his work in order to write. He later commented that he collected 743 rejection slips during this time.

At last, after nine of Creasey's novels had been turned down by publishers, his tenth was accepted. It was *Seven Times Seven* (1932), and it was a mystery. Its acceptance vindicated Creasey's faith in himself, and he soon decided to depend on writing for his sole income. Clearly he could not support himself on the mystery writer's traditional two books a year. Therefore he decided to work on a number of books at once, concealing his identity under various pseudonyms; during the rest of his life, Creasey continued to produce mysteries, as well as other books, at a feverish pace.

Creasey's method of producing novels brought him popularity and wealth. He bought a forty-two-room manor in England and a Rolls-Royce. When he wished, he traveled, often to the United States, sometimes to other parts of the world. He was also deeply involved in politics, twice running unsuccessfully for Parliament, the second time representing a party that he had founded. Furthermore, he devoted much of his time to refugee work and famine relief.

Meanwhile, Creasey was periodically getting married and divorced. His marriage to Margaret Elizabeth Cooke lasted four years and produced a son; his second marriage, to Evelyn Jean Fudge, lasted twenty-nine years; during that time, two more children were born. There was a brief third marriage to Jeanne Williams, followed by a final marriage to Diana Hamilton Farrell a month before his death.

Although the critics were lukewarm about the quality of many of Creasey's works, his colleagues elected him chairman of the Crime Writers' Association, which he had founded, and of the Mystery Writers of America. In 1946, he was made a member of the Order of the British Empire. Later he was honored twice by the Mystery Writers of America, in 1962 for *Gideon's Fire* (1961) and in 1969 with the Grand Master Award for his contributions to the genre of the mystery novel.

On June 9, 1973, Creasey died of congestive heart failure in Bodenham, Salisbury, England. At the time of his death, he had a backlog of books waiting to be published. The final new work by Creasey did not appear until 1979.

ANALYSIS

It was John Creasey's phenomenal production that led many critics to accuse him of running a mystery-novel factory, of sacrificing quality to quantity. Early in his career, Creasey admitted to turning out two books a week, with a break for cricket in midweek. Later, in response to criticism, Creasey slowed down and took more pains with revision and with character development. Even in this later period, however, Creasey averaged one book a month.

In Creasey's 1935 story "Murder of a Tramp," Richard "the Toff" Rollison combats evil Asian criminals.

The fact that the Roger West and the Gideon mysteries can hold their own with books by writers who were less prolific than he may be explained by Creasey's driving will and by his superb powers of organization. In an interview published in *The New York Times* (June 10, 1973), Creasey was asked why, having attained wealth and success, he continued driving himself to write six thousand words a day. In his reply, Creasey referred to the years of rejection, when neither his family nor the publishers to whom he submitted his works expected him to turn out salable work. Evidently a few successes were not enough for Creasey; each new sale negated that long neglect and validated his faith in his own ability.

Creasey is not unique among writers, however, in having the will to succeed. His productivity is also explained by the system that he devised, a system that he explained in various interviews. He began where all writers begin, with a rough draft, which he turned out in seven to ten days of steady effort. Then, like most writers, he put the draft aside so that he could later

judge it with the eyes of a critic rather than a creator. It was at this point that Creasey differed from most other writers. While the draft of one book was cooling, he began another, and then another, and another. At any one time, he would have as many as fifteen books in process. Eventually, he hired professional readers to study his drafts, suggesting weaknesses in plotting, characterization, or style.

Creasey himself did not return to the first draft until at least six months had passed. By the time he had completed several revisions and pronounced the book ready for publication, it would have been a year since he began to write that particular book. Thus, it is unfair to accuse Creasey of simply dashing off his mysteries, at least in the last twenty-five or thirty years of his life. Instead, he mastered the art of juggling several aspects of the creative process at one time, thinking out one plot, developing another, and revising a third and a fourth, while most writers would have been pursuing a single idea.

Creasey is unusual in that one cannot trace his development by examining his books in chronological order. There are two reasons for this critical difficulty. One is that he frequently revised his books after they had initially been published, improving the style, updating details, even changing names of sleuths. Thus, it is difficult to fit many novels into a time frame. There is, however, an even greater problem. At one and the same time, Creasey would be dashing off a novel with a fast-moving plot and fairly simple characters (such as those of the Toff series) and one of the much-admired Gideon books, which depend on psychological complexity and the juggling of multiple plots, or perhaps one of the suspenseful, slowly developing Inspector Roger West books. Therefore it is as if Creasey were several different writers at the same time, as his pseudonyms suggest; if anyone but Creasey were involved, one would find it difficult to believe that one person could bring out in a single year books that seem to reflect such different stages of artistic development.

Perhaps because his productivity was so amazing, perhaps because he himself was obsessed with it, Creasey's comments about his art generally deal with his system of composition. An intensely practical man, he considered the mystery novel an art form but was impatient with what he saw as attempts to make the art itself mysterious. Responsive to criticism, as well as to sales figures, Creasey was willing to change and to improve to please his public. Not only did he take more pains with his writing after his early books, though commercially successful, were classified as mediocre by the critics, but he also developed a character, Inspector Roger West, specifically to suit the tastes of an American public that until 1952 had not shown an interest in Creasey's work. With *Inspector West Cries Wolf* (1950; published as *The Creepers* in the United States), Creasey captured the American market, and his Inspector West novels continue to be the Creasey books most frequently encountered in American bookstores.

INSPECTOR WEST CRIES WOLF

Inspector West Cries Wolf, the first book by Creasey to be published in the United States, illustrates many of the qualities of his best work. The style is generally simple. For example, the murder of an informer is described briefly: "The man behind Squinty raised his right arm; the flash of his knife showed in the headlamps' beams. The knife fell. Even above the roar of the engine, Roger fancied that he heard Squinty scream." Yet Creasey's finest books have more than fast action. Inspector Roger West is a sensitive and troubled human being, whose marital difficulties are intensified by his profession. When he penetrates a character's mind, Creasey adjusts his rhythms accordingly: "Roger thought: I'm hitting a new low; but although he admitted that to himself, he felt inwardly cold, frozen, the whisky hadn't warmed him." By the end of this thoughtful passage, Roger has become convinced that his comfortable, loving relationship with his wife has vanished forever.

In handling setting, too, Creasey can adjust to his subject. He handles London settings exceptionally well, whether he is describing one of the Toff's favorite East End haunts or the seedy Rose and Crown, where Creasey lingers long enough to create the atmosphere, the reek of stale beer, the air blue with smoke. Similarly, when he sends West to the country house Morden Lodge, Creasey dwells on the contrast between the overgrown, neglected approach to the lodge and the crystal chandelier and red-carpeted stairway

inside it. Not only is Creasey slowing down enough to describe his scene, but he also is suggesting the difference between exterior and interior, a distinction that applies inversely to the characters at the lodge, who at first appear attractive but finally are shown to be as ugly as evil.

Even in his least fleshed-out novels, Creasey's situations are interesting, and his best works have fine plots. In *Inspector West Cries Wolf*, silent burglars are terrorizing London; Creasey's novel twist is the fact that all the gang members have the mark of a wolf on their palms. The police are frustrated by the fact that none of those captured will talk, clearly because they are more afraid of their leader, Lobo, than of the law.

In all Creasey's novels, the problem is stated almost immediately, and soon some elements of suspense are introduced, generally threats to a seemingly helpless person, to someone with whom the protagonist is closely involved, or perhaps to the protagonist himself. *Inspector West Cries Wolf* begins with a telephone call to West, who has barely fallen asleep, demanding that he return to duty because of Lobo's gang. It is obvious that Roger's wife, Janet, is frightened, and even though the fact that she has been threatened is not revealed for several chapters, her very real terror increases the suspense. In the second chapter of the book, a man and his wife are brutally murdered by a member of the wolf-gang, and their young son escapes only by accident. Now the danger of death is no longer theoretical. In the third chapter, West visits the scene of the crime and talks to the young orphan. The hunt is on, and with the peril to West's informers, to his family, and to himself mounting chapter by chapter, the story proceeds. By now, if his reader has the power of imagination, Creasey has captured him.

All Creasey's protagonists are brave and intelligent. Roger West is particularly appealing, however, because in a profession that might tend to harden a man, he continues to be sensitive. Sometimes that sensitivity is an advantage to him, as when he speaks to the young boy whose parents have just been murdered by one of Lobo's men; at other times, it causes him difficulty, as when he understands too well Janet's unhappiness and yet has no choice but to leave her to be protected and amused by his friend Mark Lessing while West pursues his quarry. Because he is sensitive, West is aware not only of Janet's wayward impulses but also of his own, and when Janet's jealousy of Margaret Paterson is inflamed, West must admit to himself that Janet's suspicions have some validity. It is the complexity of Roger West as a character, the fact that his intelligence is used not only to capture criminals but also to analyze his own motives, that places this series so far above some of the other Creasey mysteries.

It has been pointed out that except for those involved in crime, Creasey's characters are generally kindly and decent. In this novel, Janet West honestly wants her relationship with Roger to recover; she displays the same courage in dealing with their subtle problems as she does in facing her kidnappers. Bill Sloan, who finds himself pub-crawling with the mysterious and seductive Margaret, never contemplates being unfaithful to his absent wife. Creasey's noncriminal characters live up to his expectations of them; thus, by the end of *Inspector West Cries Wolf*, compassionate neighbors have offered a home to the orphaned boy.

It is significant that at the end of a Creasey novel there is both an unmasking and punishment of the criminals—as is expected in a mystery—and a reconciliation among all the sympathetic characters. Creasey's faith in human nature is evident in the happy ending for the orphan. It is similarly evident in the restoration of the friendship between Roger and Mark and in the reestablishment of harmony and understanding in the Wests' marriage. Thus in *Inspector West Cries Wolf*, as in all Creasey's books, evil is defeated and goodness triumphs. What marks the difference between a Roger West book and one of Creasey's less inspired works is the seeming lack of haste. However rapidly Creasey may have turned out even his finest mysteries, in the West books at least he developed the atmosphere by paying due attention to detail and brought his characters to life by tracing the patterns of their thoughts and feelings. When to his usual imaginative plot Creasey added these qualities, he produced mystery novels that rank with the best.

Rosemary M. Canfield Reisman

PRINCIPAL MYSTERY AND DETECTIVE FICTION

DEPARTMENT Z SERIES: 1933-1940 • *Redhead*, 1933; *The Death Miser*, 1933; *First Came a Murder*, 1934 (revised 1969); *Death Round the Corner*, 1935 (revised 1971); *The Mark of the Crescent*, 1935 (revised 1970); *The Terror Trap*, 1936 (revised 1970); *Thunder in Europe*, 1936 (revised 1970); *Carriers of Death*, 1937 (revised 1968); *Days of Danger*, 1937 (revised 1970); *Death Stands By*, 1938 (revised 1966); *Menace!*, 1938 (revised 1972); *Murder Must Wait*, 1939 (revised 1969); *Panic!*, 1939; *Death by Night*, 1940 (revised 1971); *The Island of Peril*, 1940 (revised 1970)

1941-1957 • *Go Away Death*, 1941; *Sabotage*, 1941 (revised 1972); *Prepare for Action*, 1942 (revised 1966); *The Day of Disaster*, 1942; *No Darker Crime*, 1943; *Dangerous Quest*, 1944 (revised 1965); *Dark Peril*, 1944 (revised 1969); *The Peril Ahead*, 1946 (revised 1969); *The League of Dark Men*, 1947 (revised 1965); *The Department of Death*, 1949; *The Enemy Within*, 1950; *Dead or Alive*, 1951; *A Kind of Prisoner*, 1954; *The Black Spiders*, 1957

BARON JOHN MANNERING SERIES (AS MORTON): 1937-1940 • *Meet the Baron*, 1937 (also known as *The Man in the Blue Mask*); *The Baron Returns*, 1937 (also known as *The Return of Blue Mask*); *The Baron Again*, 1938 (also known as *Salute Blue Mask!*); *The Baron at Bay*, 1938 (also known as *Blue Mask at Bay*); *Alias the Baron*, 1939 (also known as *Alias Blue Mask*); *The Baron at Large*, 1939 (also known as *Challenge Blue Mask!*); *Call for the Baron*, 1940 (also known as *Blue Mask Victorious*); *Versus the Baron*, 1940 (also known as *Blue Mask Strikes Again*)

1941-1950 • *The Baron Comes Back*, 1943; *A Case for the Baron*, 1945; *Reward for the Baron*, 1945; *Career for the Baron*, 1946; *The Baron and the Beggar*, 1947; *A Rope for the Baron*, 1948; *Blame the Baron*, 1948; *Books for the Baron*, 1949; *Cry for the Baron*, 1950; *Trap the Baron*, 1950

1951-1960 • *Attack the Baron*, 1951; *Shadow the Baron*, 1951; *Warn the Baron*, 1952; *Danger for the Baron*, 1953; *The Baron Goes East*, 1953; *The Baron in France*, 1953; *Nest-Egg for the Baron*, 1954 (also known as *Deaf, Dumb, and Blonde*); *The Baron Goes*

Fast, 1954; *Help from the Baron*, 1955; *Hide the Baron*, 1956; *Frame the Baron*, 1957 (also known as *The Double Frame*); *Red Eye for the Baron*, 1958 (also known as *Blood Red*); *Black for the Baron*, 1959 (also known as *If Anything Happens to Hester*); *Salute for the Baron*, 1960

1961-1970 • *A Branch for the Baron*, 1961 (also known as *The Baron Branches Out*); *Bad for the Baron*, 1962 (also known as *The Baron and the Stolen Legacy*); *A Sword for the Baron*, 1963 (also known as *The Baron and the Mogul Swords*); *The Baron on Board*, 1964; *The Baron and the Chinese Puzzle*, 1965; *Sport for the Baron*, 1966; *Affair for the Baron*, 1967; *The Baron and the Missing Old Masters*, 1968; *The Baron and the Unfinished Portrait*, 1969; *Last Laugh for the Baron*, 1970

1971-1979 • *The Baron Goes A-Buying*, 1971; *The Baron and the Arrogant Artist*, 1972; *Burgle the Baron*, 1973; *The Baron, King-Maker*, 1975; *Love for the Baron*, 1979

SEXTON BLAKE SERIES: *The Case of the Murdered Financier*, 1937; *The Great Air Swindle*, 1939; *The Man from Fleet Street*, 1940; *The Case of the Mad Inventor*, 1942; *Private Carter's Crime*, 1943

THE HONOURABLE RICHARD "THE TOFF" ROLLISON SERIES: 1938-1940 • *The Toff on the Trail*, 193?; *Introducing the Toff*, 1938 (revised 1954); *The Toff Goes On*, 1939 (revised 1955); *The Toff Steps Out*, 1939 (revised 1955); *Here Comes the Toff!*, 1940; *The Toff Breaks In*, 1940 (revised 1955)

1941-1950 • *Salute the Toff*, 1941; *The Toff Proceeds*, 1941; *The Toff Goes to Market*, 1942; *The Toff Is Back*, 1942; *Accuse the Toff*, 1943; *The Toff Among Millions*, 1943 (revised 1964); *The Toff and the Curate*, 1944 (also known as *The Toff and the Deadly Parson*); *The Toff and the Great Illusion*, 1944; *Feathers for the Toff*, 1945 (revised 1964); *The Toff and the Lady*, 1946; *The Toff on Ice*, 1946 (also known as *Poison for the Toff*); *Hammer the Toff*, 1947; *The Toff and Old Harry*, 1948 (revised 1964); *The Toff in Town*, 1948 (revised 1977); *The Toff Takes Shares*, 1948; *The Toff on Board*, 1949 (revised 1973); *Fool the Toff*, 1950; *Kill the Toff*, 1950

1951-1960 • *A Knife for the Toff*, 1951; *The Toff Goes Gay*, 1951 (also known as *A Mask for the Toff*);

Hunt the Toff, 1952; *Call the Toff*, 1953; *Murder out of the Past and Under-Cover Man*, 1953; *The Toff Down Under*, 1953 (also known as *Break the Toff*); *The Toff at Butlin's*, 1954; *The Toff at the Fair*, 1954; *A Six for the Toff*, 1955 (also known as *A Score for the Toff*); *The Toff and the Deep Blue Sea*, 1955; *Make-Up for the Toff*, 1956 (also known as *Kiss the Toff*); *The Toff in New York*, 1956; *Model for the Toff*, 1957; *The Toff on Fire*, 1957; *The Toff and the Stolen Tresses*, 1958; *The Toff on the Farm*, 1958 (also known as *Terror for the Toff*); *Double for the Toff*, 1959; *The Toff and the Runaway Bride*, 1959; *A Rocket for the Toff*, 1960; *The Toff and the Kidnapped Child*, 1960

1961-1970 • *Follow the Toff*, 1961; *The Toff and the Teds*, 1961 (also known as *The Toff and the Toughs*); *A Doll for the Toff*, 1963; *Leave It to the Toff*, 1963; *The Toff and the Spider*, 1965; *The Toff in Wax*, 1966; *A Bundle for the Toff*, 1967; *Stars for the Toff*, 1968; *The Toff and the Golden Boy*, 1969; *The Toff and the Fallen Angels*, 1970

1971-1978 • *Vote for the Toff*, 1971; *The Toff and the Trip-Trip-Triplets*, 1972; *The Toff and the Terrified Taxman*, 1973; *The Toff and the Sleepy Cowboy*, 1974; *The Toff and the Crooked Copper*, 1977; *The Toff and the Dead Man's Finger*, 1978

PATRICK DAWLISH SERIES (AS ASHE): 1939-1950 • *Death on Demand*, 1939; *The Speaker*, 1939 (also known as *The Croaker*); *Secret Murder*, 1940; *Terror by Day*, 1940; *Who Was the Jester?*, 1940; *'Ware Danger!*, 1941; *Death in High Places*, 1942; *Murder Most Foul*, 1942 (revised 1973); *There Goes Death*, 1942 (revised 1973); *Death in Flames*, 1943; *Two Men Missing*, 1943 (revised 1971); *Rogues Rampant*, 1944 (revised 1973); *Death on the Move*, 1945; *Invitation to Adventure*, 1945; *Here Is Danger!*, 1946; *Give Me Murder*, 1947; *Murder Too Late*, 1947; *Dark Mystery*, 1948; *Engagement with Death*, 1948; *A Puzzle in Pearls*, 1949 (revised 1971); *Kill or Be Killed*, 1949; *Murder with Mushrooms*, 1950 (revised 1971)

1951-1960 • *Death in Diamonds*, 1951; *Missing or Dead?*, 1951; *Death in a Hurry*, 1952; *Sleepy Death*, 1953; *The Long Search*, 1953 (also known as *Drop Dead*); *Death in the Trees*, 1954; *Double for Death*, 1954; *The Kidnapped Child*, 1955 (also known as *The Snatch*); *Day of Fear*, 1956; *Wait for Death*, 1957;

Come Home to Death, 1958 (also known as *The Pack of Lies*); *Elope to Death*, 1959; *Don't Let Him Kill*, 1960 (also known as *The Man Who Laughed at Murder*); *The Crime Haters*, 1960; *The Dark Circle*, 1960

1961-1970 • *Rogues' Ransom*, 1961; *Death from Below*, 1963; *A Promise of Diamonds*, 1964; *The Big Call*, 1964; *A Taste of Treasure*, 1966; *A Clutch of Coppers*, 1967; *A Shadow of Death*, 1968; *A Scream of Murder*, 1969; *A Nest of Traitors*, 1970

1971-1976 • *A Rabble of Rebels*, 1971; *A Life for a Death*, 1973; *A Herald of Doom*, 1974; *A Blast of Trumpets*, 1975; *A Plague of Demons*, 1976

BRUCE MURDOCK SERIES (AS DEANE): *Dangerous Journey*, 1939; *Secret Errand*, 1939; *The Withered Man*, 1940; *Unknown Mission*, 1940 (revised 1972); *I Am the Withered Man*, 1941 (revised 1972); *Where Is the Withered Man?*, 1943 (revised 1972)

ROGER WEST SERIES: 1942-1950 • *Inspector West Takes Charge*, 1942 (revised 1963); *Inspector West Leaves Town*, 1943 (also known as *Go Away to Murder*); *Inspector West at Home*, 1944; *Inspector West Regrets—*, 1945 (revised 1965); *Holiday for Inspector West*, 1946; *Battle for Inspector West*, 1948; *Triumph for Inspector West*, 1948 (also known as *The Case Against Paul Raeburn*); *Inspector West Kicks Off*, 1949 (also known as *Sport for Inspector West*); *Inspector West Alone*, 1950; *Inspector West Cries Wolf*, 1950 (also known as *The Creepers*)

1951-1960 • *A Case for Inspector West*, 1951 (also known as *The Figure in the Dusk*); *Puzzle for Inspector West*, 1951 (also known as *The Dissemblers*); *Inspector West at Bay*, 1952 (also known as *The Blind Spot* and *The Case of the Acid Throwers*); *A Gun for Inspector West*, 1953 (also known as *Give a Man a Gun*); *Send Inspector West*, 1953 (also known as *Send Superintendent West*); *A Beauty for Inspector West*, 1954 (also known as *The Beauty Queen Killer* and *So Young, So Cold, So Fair*); *Inspector West Makes Haste*, 1955 (also known as *The Gelingnise Gang*, *Night of the Watchman*, and *Murder Makes Haste*); *Two for Inspector West*, 1955 (also known as *Murder: One, Two, Three* and *Murder Tips the Scales*); *A Prince for Inspector West*, 1956 (also known as *Death of an Assassin*); *Parcels for Inspector West*, 1956 (also known as *Death of a Postman*); *Accident for Inspector West*, 1957 (also known as *Hit and Run*); *Find Inspector West*, 1957 (also known as *The Trouble at Saxby's* and *Doorway to Death*); *Murder, London—New York*, 1958; *Strike for Death*, 1958 (also known as *The Killing Strike*); *Death of a Racehorse*, 1959; *The Case of the Innocent Victims*, 1959; *Murder on the Line*, 1960

1961-1970 • *Death in Cold Print*, 1961; *The Scene of the Crime*, 1961; *Policeman's Dread*, 1962; *Hang the Little Man*, 1963; *Look Three Ways at Murder*, 1964; *Murder, London—Australia*, 1965; *Murder, London—South Africa*, 1966; *The Executioners*, 1967; *So Young to Burn*, 1968; *Murder, London—Miami*, 1969; *A Part for a Policeman*, 1970

1971-1978 • *Alibi*, 1971; *A Splinter of Glass*, 1972; *The Theft of Magna Carta*, 1973; *The Extortioners*, 1974; *The Thunder-Maker*, 1976; *A Sharp Rise in Crime*, 1978

DR. PALFREY SERIES: 1942-1950 • *Traitors' Doom*, 1942; *The Legion of the Lost*, 1943 (revised 1974); *The Valley of Fear*, 1943 (also known as *The Perilous Country*); *Death in the Rising Sun*, 1945 (revised 1970); *The Hounds of Vengeance*, 1945 (revised 1969); *Shadow of Doom*, 1946 (revised 1970); *The House of the Bears*, 1946 (revised 1962); *Dark Harvest*, 1947 (revised 1962); *Sons of Satan*, 1948; *The Wings of Peace*, 1948; *The Dawn of Darkness*, 1949; *The League of Light*, 1949; *The Man Who Shook the World*, 1950

1951-1960 • *The Prophet of Fire*, 1951; *The Children of Hate*, 1952 (also known as *The Children of Despair*; revised as *The Killers of Innocence*, 1971); *The Touch of Death*, 1954; *The Mists of Fear*, 1955; *The Flood*, 1956; *The Plague of Silence*, 1958; *The Drought*, 1959 (also known as *Dry Spell*)

1961-1973 • *Terror: The Return of Dr. Palfrey*, 1962; *The Depths*, 1963; *The Sleep!*, 1964; *The Inferno*, 1965; *The Famine*, 1967; *The Blight*, 1968; *The Oasis*, 1969; *The Smog*, 1970; *The Unbegotten*, 1971; *The Insulators*, 1972; *The Voiceless Ones*, 1973

THE LIBERATOR SERIES (AS DEANE): *Return to Adventure*, 1943 (revised 1974); *Gateway to Escape*, 1944; *Come Home to Crime*, 1945 (revised 1974)

SUPERINTENDENT FOLLY SERIES (AS YORK): *Find the Body*, 1945 (revised 1967); *Murder Came*

Late, 1946 (revised 1969); *Close the Door on Murder*, 1948 (revised 1973)

MARTIN AND RICHARD FANE SERIES (AS HALLIDAY): *Take a Body*, 1951 (revised 1964); *Lame Dog Murder*, 1952; *Murder in the Stars*, 1953; *Murder on the Run*, 1953

COMMANDER GEORGE GIDEON SERIES: 1955-1960 • *Gideon's Day*, 1955 (as Marric; also known as *Gideon of Scotland*); *Gideon's Week*, 1956 (as Marric; also known as *Seven Days to Death*); *Gideon's Night*, 1957 (as Marric); *Gideon's Month*, 1958 (as Marric); *Gideon's Staff*, 1959 (as Marric); *Gideon's Risk*, 1960 (as Marric)

1961-1970 • *Gideon's Fire*, 1961 (as Marric); *Gideon's March*, 1962 (as Marric); *Gideon's Ride*, 1963 (as Marric); *Gideon's Lot*, 1964 (as Marric); *Gideon's Vote*, 1964 (as Marric); *Gideon's Badge*, 1966 (as Marric); *Gideon's Wrath*, 1967 (as Marric); *Gideon's River*, 1968 (as Marric); *Gideon's Power*, 1969 (as Marric); *Gideon's Sport*, 1970 (as Marric)

1971-1976 • *Gideon's Art*, 1971; *Gideon's Men*, 1972; *Gideon's Press*, 1973; *Gideon's Fog*, 1974; *Gideon's Drive*, 1976

MARK KILBY SERIES (AS FRAZER): *Mark Kilby Solves a Murder*, 1959 (also known as *R.I.S.C.* and *The Timid Tycoon*); *Mark Kilby and the Miami Mob*, 1960; *Mark Kilby and the Secret Syndicate*, 1960; *The Hollywood Hoax*, 1961; *Mark Kilby Stands Alone*, 1962 (also known as *Mark Kilby and the Manhattan Murders*); *Mark Kilby Takes a Risk*, 1962

DR. EMMANUEL CELLINI SERIES (AS HALLIDAY; AS HUNT IN UNITED STATES): *Cunning as a Fox*, 1965; *Wicked as the Devil*, 1966; *Sly as a Serpent*, 1967; *Cruel as a Cat*, 1968; *Too Good to Be True*, 1969; *A Period of Evil*, 1970; *As Lonely as the Damned*, 1971; *As Empty as Hate*, 1972; *As Merry as Hell*, 1973; *This Man Did I Kill?*, 1974; *The Man Who Was Not Himself*, 1976

NONSERIES NOVELS: *The Dark Shadow*, 1930's; *The House of Ferrars*, 1930's; *Seven Times Seven*, 1932; *Men, Maids, and Murder*, 1933 (revised 1973); *Four Motives for Murder*, 1938 (as Hope); *Triple Murder*, 1940 (as Hughes); *Mr. Quentin Investigates*, 1943 (as Morton); *Introducing Mr. Brandon*, 1944 (as Morton); *Murder on Largo Island*, 1944 (as Hogarth;

with Ian Bowen); *Keys to Crime*, 1947 (as Martin); *Vote for Murder*, 1948 (as Martin); *The Man Who Stayed Alive*, 1955 (as Ashe); *No Need to Die*, 1956 (as Ashe; also known as *You've Bet Your Life*); *Kill Once, Kill Twice*, 1956 (as Hunt); *Kill a Wicked Man*, 1957 (as Hunt); *Kill My Love*, 1958 (as Hunt); *The Mountain of the Blind*, 1960; *To Kill a Killer*, 1960 (as Hunt); *The Foothills of Fear*, 1961; *Danger Woman*, 1966 (as Mann); *The Masters of Bow Street*, 1972; *The Whirlwind*, 1979

NONSERIES NOVELS (AS M. E. COOKE): *Fire of Death*, 1934; *Number One's Last Crime*, 1935; *The Black Heart*, 1935; *The Casino Mystery*, 1935; *The Crime Gang*, 1935; *The Death Drive*, 1935; *The Stolen Formula Mystery*, 1935; *The Big Radium Mystery*, 1936; *The Day of Terror*, 1936; *The Dummy Robberies*, 1936; *The Hypnotic Demon*, 1936; *The Moat Farm Mystery*, 1936; *The Secret Formula*, 1936; *The Successful Alibi*, 1936; *The Hadfield Mystery*, 1937; *The Moving Eye*, 1937; *The Raven*, 1937; *For Her Sister's Sake*, 1938; *The Mountain Terror*, 1938; *The Verrall Street Affair*, 1940

NONSERIES NOVELS (AS HALLIDAY): 1937-1950 • *Four Find Danger*, 1937; *Three for Adventure*, 1937; *Two Meet Trouble*, 1938; *Heir to Murder*, 1940; *Murder Comes Home*, 1940; *Murder by the Way*, 1941; *Who Saw Him Die?*, 1941; *Foul Play Suspected*, 1942; *Who Died at the Grange?*, 1942; *Five to Kill*, 1943; *Murder at King's Kitchen*, 1943; *No Crime More Cruel*, 1944; *Who Said Murder?*, 1944; *Crime with Many Voices*, 1945; *Murder Makes Murder*, 1946; *Lend a Hand to Murder*, 1947; *Mystery Motive*, 1947; *First a Murder*, 1948; *No End to Danger*, 1948; *The Dying Witnesses*, 1949; *Who Killed Rebecca?*, 1949; *Dine with Murder*, 1950; *Murder Week-End*, 1950

1951-1960 • *Quarrel with Murder*, 1951 (revised 1975); *Death out of Darkness*, 1953; *Death in the Spanish Sun*, 1954; *Out of the Shadows*, 1954; *Cat and Mouse*, 1955 (also known as *Hilda, Take Heed*); *Murder at End House*, 1955; *Death of a Stranger*, 1957 (also known as *Come Here and Die*); *Runaway*, 1957; *Murder Assured*, 1958; *Missing from Home*, 1959 (also known as *Missing*); *Thicker than Water*, 1959; *How Many to Kill?*, 1960 (also known as *The Girl with the Leopard-Skin Bag*)

1961-1969 • *The Edge of Terror,* 1961; *The Man I Killed,* 1961; *The Quiet Fear,* 1961; *Hate to Kill,* 1962; *The Guilt of Innocence,* 1964; *Go Ahead with Murder,* 1969 (also known as *Two for the Money*)

NONSERIES NOVELS (AS MANTON): *Murder Manor,* 1937; *Stand By for Danger,* 1937; *The Greyvale School Mystery,* 1937; *The Circle of Justice,* 1938; *Three Days' Terror,* 1938; *Death Looks On,* 1939; *Murder in the Highlands,* 1939; *The Crime Syndicate,* 1939; *The Midget Marvel,* 1940; *Policeman's Triumph,* 1948; *Thief in the Night,* 1950; *No Escape from Murder,* 1953; *The Charity Murders,* 1954; *The Crooked Killer,* 1954

NONSERIES NOVELS (AS YORK): *By Persons Unknown,* 1941; *Murder Unseen,* 1943; *No Alibi,* 1943; *Murder in the Family,* 1944; *Yesterday's Murder,* 1945; *Wilful Murder,* 1946; *Let's Kill Uncle Lionel,* 1947 (revised 1973); *Run Away to Murder,* 1947; *The Gallows Are Waiting,* 1949; *Death to My Killer,* 1950; *Sentence of Death,* 1950; *Voyage with Murder,* 1952; *Safari with Fear,* 1953; *So Soon to Die,* 1955; *Seeds of Murder,* 1956; *Sight of Death,* 1956; *My Brother's Killer,* 1958; *Hide and Kill,* 1959; *To Kill or to Die,* 1960

NONSERIES NOVELS (AS DEANE): *Play for Murder,* 1947 (revised 1975); *The Silent House,* 1947 (revised 1973); *Intent to Murder,* 1948 (revised 1975); *Why Murder?,* 1948 (revised 1975); *No Hurry to Kill,* 1950 (revised 1973); *The Man I Didn't Kill,* 1950 (revised 1973); *Double for Murder,* 1951 (revised 1973); *Golden Death,* 1952; *Look at Murder,* 1952; *Murder Ahead,* 1953; *Incense of Death,* 1954

OTHER MAJOR WORKS

NOVELS: *Love of Hate,* 1936 (as Fecamps); *Chains of Love,* 1937 (as Cooper); *Love's Pilgrimage,* 1937 (as Cooper); *Love's Triumph,* 1937 (as Fecamps); *True Love,* 1937 (as Fecamps); *One-Shot Marriott,* 1938 (as Ranger); *The Greater Desire,* 1938 (as Cooper); *The Tangled Legacy,* 1938 (as Cooper); *Love's Ordeal,* 1939 (as Cooper); *Roaring Guns,* 1939 (as Ranger); *The Lost Lover,* 1940 (as Cooper); *Adrian and Jonathan,* 1954 (as Martin)

NOVELS (AS MARGARET COOKE): *For Love's Sake,* 1934; *False Love or True,* 1937; *Troubled Journey,* 1937; *A Mannequin's Romance,* 1938; *Fate's*

Playthings, 1938; *Love Calls Twice,* 1938; *The Road to Happiness,* 1938; *Web of Destiny,* 1938; *Whose Lover?,* 1938; *Crossroads of Love,* 1939; *Love Comes Back,* 1939; *Love Triumphant,* 1939; *The Turn of Fate,* 1939; *Love's Journey,* 1940

NOVELS (AS RILEY): *Gun-Smoke Range,* 1938; *Two-Gun Girl,* 1938; *Gunshot Mesa,* 1939; *Masked Riders,* 1940; *Rustler's Range,* 1940; *The Shootin' Sheriff,* 1940; *Death Canyon,* 1941; *Guns on the Range,* 1942; *Range Justice,* 1943; *Outlaw Hollow,* 1944; *Hidden Range,* 1946; *Forgotten Range,* 1947; *Trigger Justice,* 1948; *Lynch Hollow,* 1949

NOVELS (AS WILLIAM K. REILLY): *Range War,* 1939; *Two Gun Texan,* 1939; *Gun Feud,* 1940; *Stolen Range,* 1940; *Outlaw's Vengeance,* 1941; *War on Lazy-K,* 1941; *Guns over Blue Lake,* 1942; *Rivers of Dry Gulch,* 1943; *Long John Rides the Range,* 1944; *Miracle Range,* 1945; *The Secrets of the Range,* 1946; *Outlaw Guns,* 1949; *Range Vengeance,* 1953

PLAYS: *Gideon's Fear,* pr. 1960; *Strike for Death,* pr. 1960; *The Toff,* pb. 1963; *Hear Nothing, Say All,* pr. 1964

CHILDREN'S LITERATURE: 1930's • *Dazzle and the Red Bomber; John Brand, Fugitive; Our Glorious Term; The Captain of the Fifth; The Fear of Felix Corde; The Night of Dread*

1935-1940 • *Ned Cartwright—Middleweight Champion,* 1935 (as Marsden); *The Men Who Died Laughing,* 1935; *Blazing the Air Trail,* 1936; *The Jungle Flight Mystery,* 1936; *The Killer Squad,* 1936; *The Mystery 'Plane,* 1936; *Murder by Magic,* 1937; *The Air Marauders,* 1937; *The Black Biplane,* 1937; *The Fighting Footballers,* 1937 (as Gill); *The Laughing Lightweight,* 1937 (as Gill); *The Mysterious Mr. Rocco,* 1937; *The Mystery Flight,* 1937; *The S.O.S. Flight,* 1937; *The Secret Aeroplane Mystery,* 1937; *The Treasure Flight,* 1937; *Mystery at Manby House,* 1938; *The Double Motive,* 1938; *The Doublecross of Death,* 1938; *The Fighting Flyers,* 1938; *The Flying Stowaways,* 1938; *The Miracle 'Plane,* 1938; *The Missing Hoard,* 1938; *Dixon Hawke, Secret Agent,* 1939; *Documents of Death,* 1939; *Mottled Death,* 1939; *Peril by Air,* 1939; *The Battle for the Cup,* 1939 (as Gill); *The Blue Flyer,* 1939; *The Fighting Tramp,* 1939 (as Gill); *The Flying Turk,* 1939; *The Hidden Hoard,* 1939; *The*

Jumper, 1939; *The Monarch of the Skies*, 1939; *The Mystery of Blackmoor Prison*, 1939; *The Mystery of the Centre-Forward*, 1939 (as Gill); *The Sacred Eye*, 1939; *The Ship of Death*, 1939; *The Ten-Thousand-Dollar Trophy Race*, 1939 (as Gill); *Dazzle—Air Ace No. 1*, 1940; *Five Missing Men*, 1940; *The Poison Gas Robberies*, 1940; *The Secret Super-Charger*, 1940 (as Gill)

1941-1947 • *Log of a Merchant Airman*, 1943 (with John H. Lock); *The Cinema Crimes*, 1945; *The Missing Monoplane*, 1947

NONFICTION: *Heroes of the Air: A Tribute to the Courage, Sacrifice, and Skill of the Men of the R.A.F.*, 1943; *The Printers' Devil: An Account of the History and Objects of the Printers' Pension, Almshouse, and Orphan Asylum Corporation*, 1943; *Man in Danger*, 1949; *Round Table: The First Twenty-five Years of the Round Table Movement*, 1953; *Round the World in 465 Days*, 1953 (with Jean Creasey); *Let's Look at America*, 1956 (with others); *They Didn't Mean to Kill: The Real Story of Road Accidents*, 1960; *African Holiday*, 1963; *Optimists in Africa*, 1963 (with others); *Good, God, and Man: An Outline of the Philosophy of Selfism*, 1967; *Evolution to Democracy*, 1969

EDITED TEXTS: *Action Stations! An Account of the H.M.S. Dorsetshire and Her Earlier Namesakes*, 1942; *The First Mystery Bedside Book*, 1960; *The Second Mystery Bedside Book*, 1961; *The Third Mystery Bedside Book*, 1962; *The Fourth Mystery Bedside Book*, 1963; *Crimes Across the Sea: The Nineteenth Annual Anthology of the Mystery Writers of America*, 1964; *The Fifth Mystery Bedside Book*, 1964; *The Sixth Mystery Bedside Book*, 1965

BIBLIOGRAPHY

Bird, Tom. "John Creasey Remembered." *Short Stories Magazine* 1 (July, 1981): 9-12. Tribute to Creasey emphasizing his short fiction and its influence on the mystery and detective genre.

Harvey, Deryk. "The Best of John Creasey." *The Armchair Detective* 7 (November, 1973): 42-43. Checklist selecting the very best examples of Creasey's work from throughout his prolific career.

Roth, Marty. *Foul and Fair Play: Reading Genre in Classic Detective Fiction*. Athens: University of Georgia Press, 1995. A post-structuralist analysis of the conventions of mystery and detective fiction. Examines 138 short stories and works from the 1840's to the 1960's. Briefly mentions Creasey and helps the reader place him in the broader context of the genre.

Rzepka, Charles J. *Detective Fiction*. Malden, Mass.: Polity, 2005. Overview of detective fiction written in English, placing Creasey's many works in context. Bibliographic references and index.

Scaggs, John. *Crime Fiction*. New York: Routledge, 2005. Contains an essay on hard-boiled fiction that mentions Creasey and provides background for understanding the writer.

EDMUND CRISPIN
Robert Bruce Montgomery

Born: Chesham Bois, Buckinghamshire, England; October 2, 1921
Died: Devon, England; September 15, 1978
Also wrote as Bruce Montgomery
Types of plot: Amateur sleuth; cozy

PRINCIPAL SERIES
Gervase Fen, 1944-1977

PRINCIPAL SERIES CHARACTER

GERVASE FEN, a professor of English language and literature at Oxford University and an infallible amateur sleuth. He is a brilliant, eccentric Oxford don whose powers of deductive reasoning are matched by his wit, impatience, and exceedingly high opinion of himself. By turns childish, charming, irrepressible, and easily bored, Fen is married and a father, although his family plays almost no part in the series.

CONTRIBUTION

Edmund Crispin's Gervase Fen mysteries are among the wittiest and most literate entries in the genre. Carrying on in the tradition of Dorothy L. Sayers and Agatha Christie, Crispin's novels fall into that category of British murder mystery in which an amateur sleuth correctly ferrets out the killer from a small group of suspects, baffling the police with his deductive powers. The hallmarks of Crispin's style are its humor and its playful artifice; he is a writer less concerned with realism than with imaginatively entertaining his readers, and his books are well written, wickedly amusing, and laced with erudite literary references, courtesy of Professor Fen, who sees murder as a grand intellectual diversion. Although psychological motivations figure importantly in his plots, Crispin's stories are not so much explorations of human nature as cleverly constructed jigsaw puzzles, full of unexpected twists and farfetched conclusions.

BIOGRAPHY

Edmund Crispin is the pen name of Robert Bruce Montgomery. Crispin was born in Chesham Bois, Buckinghamshire, England, on October 2, 1921, the fourth child and only son of Robert Ernest Montgomery, a onetime secretary to the High Commissioner for India, and Marion Blackwood (née Jarvie) Montgomery. Reared in the country, Crispin attended the Merchant Taylors' School in Moor Park and went on to study modern languages at St. John's College, at Oxford University. Early interests in both music and writing flourished while Crispin was at Oxford, and he participated in all aspects of the university's musical life, eventually becoming the organist and choirmaster for St. John's College.

It was also at Oxford that Crispin first turned his hand to detective fiction, writing the first of his Gervase Fen novels, *The Case of the Gilded Fly* (1944), while still an undergraduate. After earning his degree in 1943, Crispin taught school for several years before becoming a full-time writer and composer. The success of his Gervase Fen series, which includes nine novels and two collections of short stories, led to Crispin's appointment as the crime-fiction reviewer for the London *Sunday Times*, a position he held for several years.

As a composer, Crispin's works (published under the name Bruce Montgomery) include songs, choral pieces, and a number of film scores, the best known of which are those he wrote for several of the popular "Carry On" comedies. Indeed, for the last two-and-a-half decades of his life, Crispin worked primarily as a composer, editor, and critic; there was a twenty-five year gap between the publication of *The Long Divorce* (1951) and the final Fen novel, *The Glimpses of the Moon* (1977). Crispin spent those years living quietly in Devon, where he died in 1978.

ANALYSIS

The novels and short stories of Edmund Crispin are part of a long tradition of mystery writing that has most often been associated with British detective fiction. It is a style of mystery referred to by Dilys Winn in *Murder Ink: The Mystery Reader's Companion* (1977) as the "cozy"—a reference to the eccentric characters, quaint settings, and somehow genteel crimes that constitute its world. Far removed from the tough, streetwise tone of the hard-boiled genre or the detailed, often violent realism of the police procedural, these mysteries are entertaining intellectual puzzles meant to be read on rainy nights with a cup of tea at one's side.

Crispin's Gervase Fen series is a leading example of the style. His plots, which unfold in such locations as small English villages, film studios, and Oxford University, feature an impossibly self-assured amateur detective who is able to piece together the details of the crime, outsmart the police, and capture the culprit, usually after a chase dominated by elements of farce and slapstick. The mysteries themselves are in the classic mold, centering on a murder—or two or three—committed within the confines of a closed setting or group. Fen's task is inevitably to single out the proper perpetrator from a gathering of suspects, all of whom have motives and not one of whom has a convincing alibi.

The appeal of this format is the opportunity it provides for the reader to solve the crime along with the detective; a convention of the genre in which Crispin—with Fen—delights. A recurring scene throughout the series depicts Fen arriving at a solution to the case well before his companions and announcing this fact with undisguised glee; a self-congratulatory stance intended to twit not only his fellow characters but the reader as well. Crispin prides himself on following the rules of fair play, presenting his readers with all the information necessary for them to arrive at Fen's solution; that the reader is rarely able to do so is a testament to the skill with which Crispin has buried the nuggets of information on which the solution will turn.

BURIED FOR PLEASURE

For Crispin, the conventions of the mystery genre are primarily a springboard to his real aim: entertaining his readers with a combination of wit and imagination. *Buried for Pleasure* (1948) features a character who is himself a mystery writer, and he is first discovered by Fen in a field, acting out a scene he is planning for one of his books. His explanation—"One's plots are necessarily *improbable* . . . but I believe in making sure that they are not *impossible*"—captures the essence of Crispin's approach to storytelling. "Farfetched" and "contrived" are words that might easily be applied to several of his solutions, were they not so expertly constructed and charmingly told. One always senses in a Crispin novel that the author is gently spoofing the genre itself, abiding by its conventions yet refusing to take them seriously.

THE CASE OF THE GILDED FLY AND HOLY DISORDERS

This attitude is seen most clearly in the books' frequent self-referential jokes, a device that begins early in the series with Fen proclaiming in *The Case of the Gilded Fly*, " . . . I'm the only literary critic turned detective in the whole of fiction." It is a pronouncement that at first startles and then delights the reader when it becomes clear that Fen is indeed referring to himself as a fictional character; this remarkable degree of self-knowledge is called into play throughout the series. *Holy Disorders* (1945) finds Fen dubbing a particular type of knot the "Hook, Line and Sinker" because, as he explains, the reader has to swallow it, while a later book describes Fen lost in thought, inventing titles for Crispin. This playful schism between character and creator is occasionally reinforced by footnotes from Crispin himself, elaborating on or taking issue with a com-

ment from Fen. Crispin's willingness to shatter his readers' suspension of disbelief denotes both confidence in his skills as a writer and an engaging notion that, for their author, these stories are an elaborate game, a lark—exactly as Fen's murder cases are for him.

GERVASE FEN

The source of much of the humor and high spirits in Crispin's work is Gervase Fen himself. Drawing on the time-honored idea of British university dons as brilliant eccentrics, Crispin has fashioned his hero in their image. Fen is indeed brilliant and decidedly eccentric, given to odd hobbies and interests as well as sudden shifts in mood that can find him gloomy and petulant one moment and bursting with manic energy the next. Described as tall and lean with a blithely cheerful manner, blue eyes, and brown hair that stands out on his head in unruly spikes, he is impatient and easily bored, shamelessly immodest, and yet capable of acts of great kindness and goodwill. His wife, Dolly, figures peripherally in the earlier books of the series, and the pair enjoy a happy marriage, although their relationship is never developed. Fen seems to spend most of his time in his private rooms at the university.

Fen's two abiding passions are literature and detection, but his restless intelligence propels him enthusiastically down a variety of paths, pursuing momentary interests that he picks up and discards like a child in a room full of toys. In *Holy Disorders*, he has developed a fascination with insects, which he drops, by the time of *Buried for Pleasure*, in favor of running for Parliament. *Love Lies Bleeding* (1948) finds him embarking on a project that brings an impish symmetry to the series' self-reflexive streak: He is writing a detective novel. (Set improbably in the Catskill Mountains, it begins, naturally, "on a dark and stormy" night.) First and foremost, however, Fen is an avid sleuth whose pleasure in his own accomplishments easily equals their brilliance. Interviewed in *Swan Song* (1947) for an article on great detectives, he declares, "The era of my greatest success . . . may be said, roughly speaking, to extend from the time when I first became interested in detection to the present moment. . . ."

HUMOR AND MYSTERY

It could be argued that Crispin's books are as much comic novels as they are mysteries; certainly they owe as much to Evelyn Waugh and H. L. Mencken (two of Crispin's favorite writers) as they do to Dorothy L. Sayers or Michael Innes, with whom he has often been compared. The sheer verbal wit of the books is extraordinary, present in both the dialogue and the descriptive passages, and the parade of comic figures and incidents ranges from an aging don named Wilkes, who stumbles through several of the stories, leaving chaos in his wake, to the black humor of *The Glimpses of the Moon*, in which a severed head finds its way into a number of unlikely places. Frantic chase scenes abound in the stories' conclusions, with Fen leading the way in his beloved rattletrap jalopy, Lily Christine.

Crispin's humor also extends to the animal kingdom. *Love Lies Bleeding* features Mr. Merrythought, a senile bloodhound given to sporadic fits of rage; *The Long Divorce* offers Lavendar the cat, stalker of invisible Martians; and *Buried for Pleasure* boasts a pig with the instincts of a homing pigeon. It is in *The Glimpses of the Moon*, however, that Crispin's four-legged creations reach full flower with a whippet, a tomcat, a tortoise, and a sleepwalking horse. Otherwordly creatures also make an appearance; *Buried for Pleasure* details Fen's encounter with a lively poltergeist. Clearly, Crispin's purpose throughout his books is to amuse his readers as thoroughly as he baffles them, and in this goal he succeeds admirably.

Despite the air of frivolity that characterizes his work, however, Crispin's humor also takes the form of social satire, and many of his novels offer witty, expertly sketched portraits of a particular community or profession. Oxford—a setting Crispin knew well—figures often in the series, with its pubs, peculiar dons, and eager undergraduates portrayed most affectionately. Indeed, Crispin has given the city a chief constable who is well suited to its academic environment: Sir Richard Freeman, who cares as deeply about literature as Fen does about crime. Three of the books are set in the behind-the-scenes world of the performing arts—the theater (*The Case of the Gilded Fly*), the opera (*Swan Song*), and motion pictures (*Frequent Hearses*, 1950)—with all the egos, petty jealousies, and artistic

temperaments that those settings imply. *The Long Divorce* takes place in a small English village where spite, class distinctions, and violence lurk beneath a seemingly peaceful exterior, while *Holy Disorders* examines that most benign of settings, a church, and finds it plagued by the same human flaws that exist in the secular world. *The Glimpses of the Moon* takes on everything from television commercials to modern fiction, and *Love Lies Bleeding* offers a look at a private boys' school in which greed leads to murder, and befuddled masters greet every parent with "Your boy is doing splendidly. I have great hopes for him." Crispin's sharpest satirical portrait, however, is found in *Buried for Pleasure*, in which Fen runs for Parliament, loses interest in the election, publicly ridicules the voters, and ends up winning their support.

THE MOVING TOYSHOP

Crispin's mysteries are as well written as they are witty. Indeed, his extensive vocabulary led writer Catherine Aird to comment in an essay on his work that his books are best read with a dictionary by one's side. A strong grounding in English literature is also of use, as Crispin is among the most literate of mystery writers. Fen, as do many of the characters, quotes liberally from classic works ranging from William Shakespeare to Lewis Carroll, and the majority of the books' titles are literary references. *The Moving Toyshop* (1946) finds Fen playing a game he calls "Unreadable Books" (his choices include James Joyce's *Ulysses*, 1922, and Laurence Sterne's *Tristram Shandy*, 1759), and two of the novels make use of literary conceits: *Love Lies Bleeding*, in which Crispin posits the existence of a lost Shakespearean play, and *The Long Divorce*, which borrows elements from Charles Dickens's unfinished novel, *The Mystery of Edwin Drood* (1870).

That Crispin's writing is so eminently readable is one of the great joys of the Gervase Fen series. Admirers of darker themes and a leaner prose style may quibble with his approach and perhaps opt for the far grittier world of the hard-boiled novels of Dashiell Hammett or Raymond Chandler, but connoisseurs of imaginative plotting, effortless wit, and an elegantly turned phrase will continue to rank Crispin among the most delectable of mystery writers.

Janet E. Lorenz

PRINCIPAL MYSTERY AND DETECTIVE FICTION

GERVASE FEN SERIES: *The Case of the Gilded Fly*, 1944 (also known as *Obsequies at Oxford*); *Holy Disorders*, 1945; *The Moving Toyshop*, 1946; *Swan Song*, 1947 (also known as *Dead and Dumb*); *Buried for Pleasure*, 1948; *Love Lies Bleeding*, 1948; *Frequent Hearses*, 1950 (also known as *Sudden Vengeance*); *The Long Divorce*, 1951 (also known as *A Noose for Her*); *Beware of the Trains: Sixteen Stories*, 1953; *The Glimpses of the Moon*, 1977; *Fen Country: Twenty-six Stories*, 1979

OTHER MAJOR WORKS

SCREENPLAY (AS BRUCE MONTGOMERY): *Raising the Wind*, 1961

EDITED TEXTS: *Best SF: Science Fiction Stories*, 1955-1970; *Best Detective Stories*, 1959-1964; *Best Tales of Terror*, 1962-1965; *The Stars and Under: A Selection of Science Fiction*, 1968; *Best Murder Stories 2*, 1973; *Outwards from Earth: A Selection of Science Fiction*, 1974

BIBLIOGRAPHY

Aird, Catherine. "Gervase Fen and the Teacake School." In *Murder Ink: The Mystery Reader's Companion*, edited by Dilys Winn. New York: Workman, 1977. An analysis of Crispin's most famous character and the British literary tradition in which he fits.

DeMarr, Mary Jean. "Edmund Crispin." In *Twelve Englishmen of Mystery*, edited by Earl F. Bargainnier. Bowling Green, Ohio: Bowling Green University Popular Press, 1984. Critical overview of Crispin's life and work discussing his distinctive contributions to the history of the British detective novel.

"Edmund Crispin." In *Modern Mystery Writers*, edited and with an introduction by Harold Bloom. New York: Chelsea House, 1995. Critical, scholarly essay on Crispin, his cultural significance and ideological investments.

Nover, Peter, ed. *The Great Good Place? A Collection of Essays on American and British College Mystery Novels*. New York: P. Lang, 1999. Compilation of essays focused on crime fiction set at college campuses or feature academic characters. Provides context for the character of Gervase Fen.

Routley, Erik. *The Puritan Pleasures of the Detective Story: A Personal Monograph*. London: Gollancz, 1972. Idiosyncratic but useful discussion of crime fiction in terms of nominally puritanical ideology. Sheds light on Crispin's work.

Sarjeant, William A. S. "Edmund Crispin: A Memorial and Appreciation." *The Poisoned Pen* 3 (May/June, 1980): 3-10. Homage to Crispin provides a brief survey of his work and its significance.

FREEMAN WILLS CROFTS

Born: Dublin, Ireland; June 1, 1879
Died: Worthing, Sussex, England; April 11, 1957
Types of plot: Police procedural; inverted; thriller

PRINCIPAL SERIES

Inspector (later Superintendent) Joseph French, 1925-1957

PRINCIPAL SERIES CHARACTER

INSPECTOR JOSEPH FRENCH of Scotland Yard, is comfortably middle-aged, stoutish, slightly below average height, clean-shaven, with alert but kindly blue eyes, happily married, an amateur gardener, a dapper dresser, and polite. French ages little in the series and resents cases that prevent his spending weekends at home. He believes in "reconstructing his cases from the point of view of time" (*Mystery on Southampton Water*, 1934), and he says about his promotions, a "rise in position means a corresponding increase in loneliness."

CONTRIBUTION

Freeman Wills Crofts's twenty-eight novels featuring Inspector Joseph French are generally under the control of a third-person narrator, who allows the reader to share completely the actions and the thinking of the characters. Opting for the Wilkie Collins-Émile Gaboriau school of detective fiction as opposed to the C. Auguste Dupin-Sherlock Holmes super-sleuth school so popular before World War I, Crofts's trademarks are meticulous planning by the criminal and the even more meticulous "alibi busting" by Inspector French. Crofts's language is simple and straightforward, and his style is natural and unforced. He helped shape the subgenre that is known today as the psychological thriller.

The reader is informed from the outset of everything that French sees, does, and knows, and accompanies him step-by-step as French unravels the mystery. Some find Crofts's method tedious, but fellow writers such as Agatha Christie and Raymond Chandler have written warmly and admiringly of his craft. His appeal is to those who wish to be intellectually stimulated, not those seeking pure entertainment. His popularity in England and throughout Europe has been strong, but he has been less successful in the United States, where tastes run more toward the hard-boiled detective and urban violence. Crofts's finely crafted plots seem to come naturally to a mind trained in mathematics and engineering.

BIOGRAPHY

Freeman Wills Crofts was born June 1, 1879, in Dublin, the son of a British army doctor who died during foreign service while his son was still a child. His widowed mother later married Archdeacon Harding of the Church of Ireland, and Crofts was reared in the Harding home. He attended Methodist and Campbell colleges in Belfast and, at seventeen, began his engineering studies under his uncle, Berkeley D. Wise, then chief engineer of the Belfast and Northern Counties Railway. In 1899, Crofts was appointed junior assistant engineer for the construction of an extension of the Donegal Railway. In 1900, he was named district engineer at Coleraine for the Belfast and Northern Counties Railway and, ten years later, chief assistant engineer at Belfast for the same line. In 1912, he married Mary Bellas Canning, daughter of the manager of a local bank.

During a long illness and recovery in 1919, Crofts began to write to amuse himself. The result was *The Cask*, published in London by Collins in 1920, a novel generally hailed as a masterpiece of pure detection. He continued to publish almost yearly until 1929, when another serious illness forced him to choose between engineering and writing. He elected to continue writing; after he resigned his position with the railway, he and Mary moved near London, where he lived most of the rest of his life. In 1939, he was elected to the Royal Society of Arts. He died April 11, 1957, at the age of seventy-seven. Crofts's other interests included gardening, carpentry, and music, as both an organist and a conductor. These interests are reflected by the characters in his novels. The personal traits most obvious in the novels, and especially in Inspector French, are those of a mind trained in mathematics and engineering methodically applying perseverance and logic to solving a problem or a murder.

ANALYSIS

The horrors of World War I effectively put a stop to most entertaining writing in Europe. The super-sleuth antics of the Sherlock Holmes school lost much of their appeal as the last vestiges of the gaslight era of Victoria and Edward died in the technological advances demanded by war. A new breed of hero was in the making, led in part by John Buchan's short novels for the boys in the trenches. Buchan's novels featured a generally realistic Richard Hannay, who engaged in sophisticated battles of wit with his opponents.

THE CASK

Freeman Wills Crofts's first novel, *The Cask*, begun during his illness in 1919 and published in 1920, reflects the change then under way. The novel features the steady, systematic, and realistic police work that culminated in the creation of Inspector Joseph French in Crofts's fifth novel. The influence of Émile Gaboriau's Monsieur Lecoq—his painstaking reconstruction of the crime and the criminal's movements through his analysis of footprints in the snow, scraps of material, the time necessary to move from one place to another—is apparent in Crofts's early work. H. Douglas Thomson, in his *Master of Mystery* (1931), says of Lecoq, "Here is Inspector French's prototype."

INSPECTOR FRENCH'S GREATEST CASE

Inspector French first appeared in the presumptuously titled *Inspector French's Greatest Case* in 1925. Using bits and pieces from such diverse forerunners as Monsieur Dupin, Sherlock Holmes, Monsieur Lecoq, and Wilkie Collins's Sergeant Cuff, Crofts created one of the most memorable characters in detective fiction. Like his predecessors, French carefully and methodically investigates everything, considers everything, notes everything, catalogs everything. Nothing escapes his attention and consideration. As French himself tells the reader, "The evidence is cumulative," and the reconstruction of the crime, like the railway timetables with which Crofts was so familiar, falls neatly into place as each bit of information is slotted into its appropriate niche.

Crofts's method of building a novel, police procedural or inverted, is relatively simple. Through the impersonal guidance of the unnamed, third-person narrator, the reader is kept informed of the action and of what is going on in the minds of both the criminal and the detective. The narrator lays out before the reader the actions and the thoughts of both. The excitement comes from the sustained attention to detail as the criminal attempts to cover his trail and as Inspector French re-creates the time-and-space sequence of the crime. French measures distances, times how quickly one can row a boat across a particular body of water, clocks how long it would take for a man the size of the suspect to climb out a window, cross a tract of land, scale a wall, and commit the crime. With Crofts, the nineteenth century Holmesian sleuth gives way to the sometimes plodding, always methodical, hardworking, routine investigator of the *roman policier.* Crofts's influence on such detective-fiction writers as A. E. Fielding (Dorothy Fielding), Charles Barry, A. W. Marchmont, and J. S. Fletcher, among others, has been remarked by most historians of the genre. Peter Falk's television investigator, Columbo, is directly descended from Inspector French.

Some critics consider as a flaw in Crofts's work his dependence on the ability of French to remain the patient, kindly, thorough reader of clues and time passage. It is probably true that after twenty-eight novels, Crofts's imagination had worn a little thin, partly as a result of his disinclination to create characters that go much beyond simulacra of types. His criminals are, however, finely drawn, within limits, and are usually well-placed individuals facing financial ruin or suffering from that ancient pair of human flaws, greed and lust. They turn to crime, usually murder, to alleviate their particular problem, plotting and scheming carefully to eliminate what each considers the potential of error. On the surface and to the average speculator, the crime is perfect because it is not obvious, but to Inspector Joseph French something simply does not quite fit, and he begins to test for flaws—and he finds them. His method is simple. He questions everybody and everything; he rereads his notes constantly, looking for what he must have overlooked earlier; and he times and measures and conjectures, and finally finds

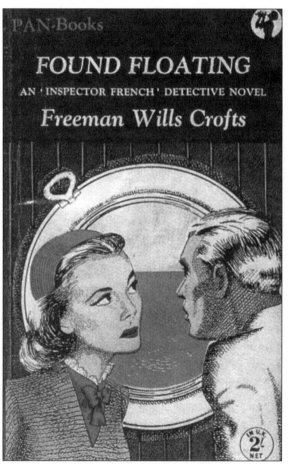

*Paperback reprint of Freeman Wills Crofts's 1937
novel* Found Floating.

what he is looking for. The murderer then pays the ultimate penalty.

THE 12:30 FROM CROYDON

The 12:30 from Croydon (1934) is a fine example of Crofts's inverted detective story and of Inspector French's technique. Charles Swinburn owns a motor manufacturing plant that is in financial trouble, as a result of both the conditions of the time and antiquated machinery. His uncle, Andrew Crowther, who began the plant and made it into a successful business, is retired and in ill health. Crowther sees Swinburn's difficulties as the result of laziness and a refusal to work hard and reminds him of this attitude whenever they meet. Peter Morley, Crowther's son-in-law, is also experiencing difficulties with his business, farming, and Crowther's attitude toward him is much the same. The novel opens with the death of Crowther on a flight to Paris, a death the authorities in Paris do not consider to be of natural causes. The autopsy shows potassium cyanide sufficient to cause death, and the police are notified.

Crofts then takes the reader back in time and outlines the series of events that led to Swinburn's decision to murder his uncle, after Crowther refused to lend him more than a thousand pounds to save the business. Swinburn needs five thousand, at least, to buy new machinery to make the business competitive. Swinburn considers introducing a poisoned pill into Crowther's bottle of Salter's Anti-Indigestion Pills, knowing that eventually Crowther will take that pill and die. Swinburn is aware that he and Elsie, Crowther's daughter and Morley's wife, are the principal beneficiaries to Crowther's estate, and he decides to put his plan into action.

Swinburn also contemplates a future without Una Mellor, the somewhat indifferent lady with whom he is in love—a future that would certainly end should he go bankrupt. Swinburn then takes the valuable paintings his father left him and pawns them in London, acquiring enough cash to get the needed machinery. Using another's name, he purchases an ounce of potassium cyanide on the pretense of wanting to destroy a wasps' nest and buys a bottle of Salter's Anti-Indigestion Pills and experiments until he is able to fill a pill with the poison and put it back together so that it

looks like the other pills. At another dinner engagement with his uncle, as Crowther is preparing to take his usual pill, Swinburn "accidentally" spills a glass of wine and in the confusion slips the deadly pill in among the others. He then takes a cruise to provide an alibi. Later, on a plane trip, Crowther takes the pill and dies.

John Weatherup, Crowther's valet and companion, casually reminds Swinburn of the wine spilling and notes that he had observed the exchange of pills. He mentions money and tells Swinburn that he has written down what he has seen, giving the information in a sealed envelope to Peter Morley, to be opened should something happen to him. It is blackmail, but more urgently it is a direct threat to Swinburn's life, his hopes for the success of the plant, and for a future with Una Mellor. He begins to plan another murder, and the reader accompanies him as he lures Weatherup to the boathouse, kills him, weighs him down and drops him into the lake, and then reenters the house to look for the letter. Although things now appear to be looking up for Swinburn, Inspector French is making visits and asking questions of everyone associated with Swinburn and with Crowther's household. A final visit by French is to Swinburn, which results in the arrest of Swinburn for the murders of Andrew Crowther and John Weatherup.

The trial of Swinburn is short. The prosecution and the defense arguments are given, and evidence of which Swinburn cannot imagine the source is introduced. The scene is calmly and straightforwardly played, while Swinburn mentally and silently feels the horror of what is to happen. He is convicted, his appeal is dismissed, and he is hanged. A few weeks later, Inspector French and the defense attorney team meet for dinner, and French carefully outlines the means by which he trapped and convicted Swinburn. The reader learns how he located the chemist who sold Swinburn the poison, how he traced the lead pipe used to weigh down the body of Weatherup to a plumber who had done work for Swinburn, how he matched up the sawed ends of the pipe to Swinburn's saw, how he came to realize that the key that had been returned to Morley's study on the night of Weatherup's death could have been returned only by someone who knew the house, and how the evidence accumulated to the point that every indicator pointed to Swinburn. It was then that French arrested Swinburn and gave the evidence he had gathered to the prosecution.

MYSTERY ON SOUTHAMPTON WATER

A similar story, but with a more surprising ending, is *Mystery on Southampton Water*. A rivalry between two concrete manufacturers, Brand and King, leads to the accidental death of a nightwatchman. Brand and King fake an auto accident to conceal the death, but Inspector French discovers that the carburetor was smashed so that the car would burn. He also finds the stone used to smash the carburetor. Later, the officials at Chayle, the rival manufacturer, come to Brand, King, and their boss James Tasker with a proposal to franchise them with the new concrete formula in return for 75 percent of their profits. King, on the night the watchman died, had stolen the formula and some cash, which he had placed in the car with the murdered man. The Chayle people do not know this, but King decides to eliminate potential problems by rigging with a bomb the motor boat in which the three executives are traveling. It explodes, but Noel Samson, Chayle's chief engineer, survives. French reenters the scene and analyzes the watchman's death, the faked automobile accident, the boat accident, and the two companies. He has the remains of the boat raised by divers and discovers how the bomb was triggered. He times the trip and concludes that if the three men had not made a detour to visit a sister of one of the men, the craft would have exploded at such a point that no recovery would have been possible and no survival probable.

French has an "inspiration" and times how long it would take for two men to leave King's laboratory, row across the water, climb the wall of Chayle's plant, kill the watchman, burglarize the office, take the body away, and stage the accident. He finds a gramophone and a recording that consists of a dialogue between King and Tasker (Tasker had to memorize his lines) to suggest that King was in his office, when in fact he was rigging the boat for destruction. French times this adventure as well, and finds that it corresponds with the length of the recording. A different dimension of French is now made clear to readers of this book: his ability to interpret people for who they are and for

what they may be hiding. The surprise occurs when Tasker is revealed as the mastermind behind King's actions. Brand is the innocent dupe. Tasker and King are convicted, and Brand leaves for other environments. French returns to London and his wife, home, and garden.

Crofts was an innovator, a good storyteller, and a first-rate craftsman in his chosen literary field. Although most of his Inspector French novels were published in the United States, many of those under the Dodd-Mead Red Badge Books imprint, he was never as much of a force for American readers as he was for British and Continental readers. His books enjoyed steady if not spectacular sales and were translated into nearly all the European languages. Crofts played a significant part in the development of the psychological thriller. His body of work includes splendid examples of the police procedural and inverted subgenres. Finally, Crofts introduced his readers to Inspector (later Superintendent) Joseph French, a very fine literary invention indeed.

William H. Holland, Jr.

PRINCIPAL MYSTERY AND DETECTIVE FICTION

INSPECTOR JOSEPH FRENCH SERIES: 1925-1930 • *Inspector French's Greatest Case*, 1925; *Inspector French and the Cheyne Mystery*, 1926 (also known as *The Cheyne Mystery*); *Inspector French and the Starvel Tragedy*, 1927 (also known as *The Starvel Hollow Tragedy*); *The Sea Mystery*, 1928; *The Box Office Murders*, 1929 (also known as *The Purple Sickle Murders*); *Sir John Magill's Last Journey*, 1930

1931-1940 • *Mystery in the Channel*, 1931 (also known as *Mystery in the English Channel*); *Death on the Way*, 1932 (also known as *Double Death*); *Sudden Death*, 1932; *The Hog's Back Mystery*, 1933 (also known as *The Strange Case of Dr. Earle*); *Mystery on Southampton Water*, 1934 (also known as *Crime on the Solent*); *The 12:30 from Croydon*, 1934 (also known as *Wilful and Premeditated*); *Crime at Guildford*, 1935 (also known as *The Crime at Nornes*); *Man Overboard!*, 1936 (also known as *Cold-Blooded Murder*); *The Loss of the "Jane Vosper,"* 1936; *Found Floating*, 1937; *Antidote to Venom*, 1938; *The End of Andrew Harrison*, 1938 (also known as *The Futile*

Alibi); *Fatal Venture*, 1939 (also known as *Tragedy in the Hollow*); *Golden Ashes*, 1940

1941-1957 • *James Tarrant, Adventurer*, 1941 (also known as *Circumstantial Evidence*); *The Losing Game*, 1941; *Fear Comes to Chalfont*, 1942; *The Affair at Little Wokeham*, 1943 (also known as *Double Tragedy*); *Enemy Unseen*, 1945; *Death of a Train*, 1946; *Silence for the Murderer*, 1948; *Dark Journey*, 1951 (also known as *French Strikes Oil*); *Anything to Declare*, 1957

NONSERIES NOVELS: *The Cask*, 1920; *The Ponson Case*, 1921; *The Pit-Prop Syndicate*, 1922; *The Groote Park Murder*, 1923 (with others); *The Floating Admiral*, 1931 (with others); *Double Death*, 1932 (with others); *Six Against the Yard*, 1936 (with others; also known as *Six Against Scotland Yard*)

OTHER SHORT FICTION: *The Hunt Ball Murder*, 1943; *Mr. Sefton, Murderer*, 1944; *Murderers Make Mistakes*, 1947; *Many a Slip*, 1955; *The Mystery of the Sleeping Car Express, and Other Stories*, 1956

OTHER MAJOR WORKS

RADIO PLAYS: *The Nine-Fifty Up Express*, 1942; *Chief Inspector's Cases*, 1943; *Mr. Pemberton's Commission*, 1952; *East Wind*, 1953; *The Greuze*, 1953

CHILDREN'S LITERATURE: *Young Robin Brand, Detective*, 1947

NONFICTION: *Bann and Lough Neagh Drainage*, 1930; *The Four Gospels in One Story*, 1949

BIBLIOGRAPHY

Craig, Patricia, and Mary Cadogan. Introduction to *Inspector French's Greatest Case*, by Freeman Wills Crofts. London: Hogarth, 1985. Survey of Crofts's career and the character of Inspector French, occasioned by the re-issue of the inspector's first adventure.

Haycraft, Howard, ed. *The Art of the Mystery Story: A Collection of Critical Essays*. Reprint. New York: Carroll & Graf, 1983. Massive compendium of essays exploring all aspects of the mystery writer's craft. Provides context for understanding Crofts.

Roth, Marty. *Foul and Fair Play: Reading Genre in Classic Detective Fiction*. Athens: University of Georgia Press, 1995. A post-structural analysis of the conventions of mystery and detective fiction. Examines 138 short stories and works from the 1840's to the 1960's. Makes only minimal reference to Crofts, but helps readers establish Crofts's place among the writers of classic mysteries.

Routley, Erik. *The Puritan Pleasures of the Detective Story: A Personal Monograph*. London: Gollancz, 1972. Idiosyncratic but useful discussion of crime fiction in terms of nominally puritanical ideology. Sheds light on Crofts's work.

Steinbrunner, Chris, and Otto Penzler, eds. *Encyclopedia of Mystery and Detection*. Rev. ed. New York: McGraw-Hill, 1988. Discusses Croft's contribution to the development of the psychological thriller genre.

DEBORAH CROMBIE
Deborah Lynn Darden

Born: Dallas, Texas; June 5, 1952
Types of plot: Police procedural; cozy

PRINCIPAL SERIES
Duncan Kincaid and Gemma James, 1993-

PRINCIPAL SERIES CHARACTERS
DUNCAN KINCAID is a Scotland Yard detective superintendent from a privileged background. At the beginning of the series, he is a divorced man who is trying to lose himself in his job.

GEMMA JAMES, initially a Scotland Yard sergeant in the series, is the single mother of Toby James. A disparity in social rank between Gemma and Duncan complicates their working relationship. However, despite their differences, the pair begin a romance, which is interrupted sporadically by career and personal issues.

CONTRIBUTION
Deborah Crombie's first book, *A Share in Death* (1983), introduced Scotland Yard detectives Duncan Kincaid and Gemma James and was an immediate success. Crombie's special talent is to create convincing English whodunits despite having been born and educated in Texas. In this Crombie resembles Martha Grimes, but her novels are more wide-ranging than those of Grimes. They are heavily atmospheric with evocative detail that contributes to the experience of the reading. Crombie's idiosyncratic mode of writing is something a little darker than the typical cozy, but she does tend to follow the traditions established by Agatha Christie, Ngaio Marsh, Margery Allingham, and Dorothy L. Sayers. She tends to follow the Christie technique of providing a parade of suspects at the end of a novel and surprising the reader by the final conclusion. However, her characters are far more layered and realistic than Christie's. Crombie has updated the traditions of the Golden Age female mystery novelists and provided believable, likeable new characters. Moreover, the buildup of suspense in the Crombie novels is unmatched.

Like many detective series novels, Crombie's books provide an extended narrative of the relationship between the two main characters, and Crombie adds depth to these characterizations by filling in more background with each book. There are many minor characters who appear and disappear in the series, but the main characters grow. The novels are police procedurals only in the broadest sense; the emphasis is on intuitive discovery. Crombie's strengths include a persuasive British location, appealing series characters, and psychological realism. She is often compared with Elizabeth George as well as Grimes, but Crombie has a stronger emphasis on setting, and her settings are more dynamically involved with the characters and their actions.

Crombie received Agatha and Macavity Award nominations in 1993 for her first novel, *A Share in Death*, and *Dreaming of the Bones* (1997) won the

Deborah Crombie. (Library of Congress)

Macavity Award, was named *New York Times* Notable Book of the Year, and was nominated for numerous awards. Her novels have been published in England, Italy, Japan, Norway, the Netherlands, France, the Czech Republic, and Germany.

BIOGRAPHY

Deborah Crombie was born Deborah Lynn Darden in 1952 in Dallas. She spent a good deal of her childhood reading, began writing poetry in junior high school, and was soon a committed writer. After sporadic experiments with higher education, she graduated from Austin College in Sherman, Texas, in 1977 with a major in biology—she then wished to be a field biologist or ornithologist. For her graduation present, her parents took her to England, and she says:

> that must have been the true turning point in my life. On the bus from Gatwick to London . . . I sat with my nose pressed to the window and tears running down my face. I had the most tremendous sense of homecoming, of belonging, that I still feel whenever I set foot on British soil.

This trip with her parents sparked a repeat trip by herself, and a lifelong love affair with the British Isles.

Crombie's first marriage to Peter Crombie, a Scot, did not survive the publication of her first book. In 1994 she married Rick Wilson. Crombie for a time lived in the United Kingdom, where her stories are set. It was after a visit to Yorkshire that she began her Emma James-Duncan Kincaid series. Crombie eventually settled in Dallas, later noting that if she were to live in England, she would be divided emotionally and that her novels might not be as intense emotionally, as they would lack the element of longing for England. According to M. K. Graff, Crombie "agrees with her role model P. D. James that setting drives her characters, dictating their actions and behavior." Crombie immerses herself in the settings of her novels to present them as vividly as possible.

After publishing her first novel, Crombie became a full-time writer. Previously she worked in newspaper advertising and also for a family business.

ANALYSIS

The interaction between Deborah Crombie's two main characters helps illustrate some British truths about class and money. As the relationship between Gemma James and Duncan Kincaid grows, they each learn something about the class system to which they belong, and so does the reader. The characters' interactions with others provide subtle messages concerning authority and power, including how they affect others. The varied settings provide ample opportunity to present a study of British social values.

Crombie's first books are more completely police procedurals, with clear explanations of the various stages of the investigation from discovery of the body to finding the culprit. She describes autopsies and investigation techniques convincingly. Some of the books end with explorations of various possible perpetrators before zeroing in on the always surprising culprit. A lot of the atmosphere of the books comes from the interaction between the two investigators.

Some of the later books are moody, overcast, even gothic. *A Finer End* (2001), for example, contains undeniable supernatural elements that play a significant part in the story, while in other books, the supernatural may be marginally present as a possibility. In *A Finer End*, the supernatural grows out of the environment, which makes it seem more natural. It may remind the reader of the notion of rememory in Toni Morrison's *Beloved* (1987), in which places are believed to carry images or traces of traumatic events that have occurred there. The notion of the effect of a place and its history on the present action is behind the apparently supernatural deviations from the norm in *A Finer End*. Vivid descriptions of natural scenes and of architecture in this book and others underscore the action and help explain it.

Major themes in Crombie's work include the relationships between parents and children: how strong these bonds are and what they cause people to do and the terrible grief of losing a child. She also writes about the problems inherent in romantic relationships between people from different social backgrounds. Other important concerns are the effect of place on inhabitants, providing opportunities and obstacles, and the causes and effects of betrayal and how it damages that primary necessity, trust. Over and over in the novels, Crombie deals with the issue of trust, not only between Gemma and Duncan but also between other characters.

MOURN NOT YOUR DEAD

The 1996 novel *Mourn Not Your Dead* recounts the bludgeoning death of an unpopular police official, Division Commander Alastair Gilbert, who was widely known for his cruelty. Some missing jewelry suggests the killer may be a burglar who has been operating in the area, but other circumstances suggest a more complicated motive. The fragile-appearing widow and the daughter of the victim are mysterious women whose actions cannot be read. The scene shifts back and forth from Gilbert's village to London as Duncan and Gemma investigate all the tormented links between Gilbert and others—almost any of which could have resulted in a murder. However, the conclusion is a genuine surprise.

This novel continues the romance between Gemma and Duncan, who had tentatively begun a relationship in the previous novel, *Leave the Grass Green* (1995). They must put their relationship aside in favor of the investigation, but they learn something about themselves from the outcome. This novel is straightforward and direct, with detailed representations of minor characters.

DREAMING OF THE BONES

Dreaming of the Bones (1997) is an award-winning novel that has been discussed in academic circles for its use of biography as part of the plot. In this work, the lives of Gemma and Duncan are complicated by the re-emergence of Duncan's former wife, Dr. Victoria "Vic" McClellan, who is writing a biography of poet Lydia Brooke, who apparently committed suicide five years earlier. However, it seems unlikely to Vic that Lydia's death was a suicide, because everything looked good for the poet at the time. Duncan reluctantly agrees to investigate and soon finds evidence that Vic may be right. The investigation has disastrous results, though, including a murder—someone does not wish the inquiry to continue. Through a close examination of Lydia's life and a long-lost poem, Gemma discovers the secret that will lead to the resolution of the case.

This novel is the favorite in the James-Kincaid series for many readers, as it is plausible, romantic, and well written. Those not fans of detective stories like it

also, as it is a fine novel, in part about biography, that can be categorized with books like A. S. Byatt's *Possession* (1990) and Alison Lurie's *The Truth About Lorin Jones* (1998). The novel also exhibits a distinct and unusual form of feminism, which has caught the eye of feminist scholars.

A FINER END

A Finer End begins with the unusual experiences of Duncan's cousin Jack Montfort, who suddenly finds himself writing in Latin and wonders what is happening to him. He is in Glastonbury, the legendary burial place of King Arthur and Guinevere; it is also the location of an old abbey where long ago, tragic events that ended the monks' peaceful worship took place.

Jack calls Duncan, who reluctantly agrees to visit Glastonbury. There Duncan and Gemma find a complex situation involving both history and the present, current and ancient violence. The two have to find a solution that will both end the present violence and right a situation that has been wrong for centuries. The quest to do these things brings them into dangerous situations.

The novel is dominated by the gloomy abbey and the frightening Tor, which pulls people toward it even as they are repelled by it. This novel is well researched; the spookiness is stronger for being founded in fact. The tone of this novel is a departure for Crombie, but the unusual atmosphere makes the book well worth reading.

IN A DARK HOUSE

In a Dark House (2004) is one of the best of the James-Kincaid mysteries, having a complex and yet believable plot, a frightening atmosphere, and plenty of accurate police-procedural techniques to keep the reader informed. As the novel begins, a fire is being set by an arsonist; this fire results in a corpse. The fire takes place next to a home for battered women, and soon Duncan must interview the young female resident who reported seeing something the day of the fire, as well as others staying at the home. Gemma, meanwhile, is investigating the disappearance of a woman whose housemate is a friend of vicar Winifred Catesby. There is another mystery: a child who has been abducted, perhaps by a parent. The mysteries prove to be related, of course, and the threads of story come together in an explosive conclusion.

Duncan's personal life is also in crisis—he is threatened with loss of custody of his son Kit. His relationship with Gemma is uneasy, and the makeshift family they have created seems likely to pull apart. The bond between parents and children and its demands is the underlying theme of this novel, both in the mystery and in the ongoing story of the two detectives. Perhaps more than any other novel in the series, this story focuses on the intense bond between parents and children and the internal and external dangers to it.

Janet McCann

PRINCIPAL MYSTERY AND DETECTIVE FICTION
DUNCAN KINCAID AND GEMMA JAMES SERIES: *A Share in Death*, 1993; *All Shall Be Well*, 1994; *Leave the Grave Green*, 1995; *Mourn Not Your Dead*, 1996; *Dreaming of the Bones*, 1997; *Kissed a Sad Goodbye*, 1999; *A Finer End*, 2001; *And Justice There Is None*, 2002; *Now You May Weep*, 2003; *In a Dark House*, 2004; *Water like a Stone*, 2007

NONSERIES NOVEL: *The Sunken Sailor*, 2004 (with others)

BIBLIOGRAPHY
Bunsdale, Mitzi M. *Gumshoes: A Dictionary of Fictional Detectives*. Westport, Conn.: Greenwood Press, 2006. A thick, well-researched book with articles on the detectives of crime fiction, including Duncan Kincaid. Includes lists of mystery awards and other useful information.

Dingus, Anne. "Briterature." *Texas Monthly* 25, no. 11 (November, 1997): 26. A profile of Crombie that looks at her life, her writing, and *Dreaming of the Bones*.

Dubose, Martha Hailey, with Margaret Caldwell Thomas. *Women of Mystery: The Lives and Works of Notable Women Crime Novelists*. New York: St. Martin's Minotaur, 2000. Contains a brief entry on her life and works.

Graff, M. K. "Deborah Crombie: The Yellow Rose of Mystery." *Mystery Scene* 87 (2004): 18-19. A discussion of the James-Kincaid mystery series, with some biographical information about Crombie.

Hansson, Heidi. "Biography Matters." *Orbis Litterarum: International Review of Literary Studies* 58, no. 5 (1994): 353-370. This essay describes how women's novels use biographies and discusses Crombie's *Dreaming of the Bones* and other novels.

Lindsay, Elizabeth Blakesley, ed. *Great Women Mystery Writers*. 2d ed. Westport, Conn.: Greenwood Press, 2007. Contains an essay discussing Crombie's work and her life and their interactions.

AMANDA CROSS
Carolyn Gold Heilbrun

Born: East Orange, New Jersey; January 13, 1926
Died: New York, New York; October 9, 2003
Types of plot: Amateur sleuth; cozy

PRINCIPAL SERIES
Kate Fansler, 1964-2002

PRINCIPAL SERIES CHARACTERS
KATE FANSLER is a professor of English at a New York City university. She is married, at the end of the third novel in the series, to her longtime friend from the district attorney's office, Reed Amhearst. An academic and a feminist as witty as she is principled, she is a friend of those with imagination and character and an enemy of unthinking conventionality.

CONTRIBUTION
Amanda Cross set out, with the invention of Kate Fansler, to reanimate a venerable but then neglected tradition within detective fiction: that of elegant arm-

chair detection. Learning her lessons from the masters of the old school—Dorothy L. Sayers, Josephine Tey, Ngaio Marsh, and Agatha Christie—Cross infused her whodunits with a healthy moral awareness. She chose the academic milieu, particularly well suited for the testing of ethical positions and social responsibilities, a place where personal and political rivalries can be intense but where murder itself is still a shock. Here, too, the detective can be appreciated as an individual of exceptional sensibility and imaginative power; in this world, in fact, the detective can be a woman.

Through Cross's creation of Kate Fansler, a professor-sleuth, the art of literate conversation at last gained credence in the American detective novel. Through her, too, Cross worked out a dynamic balance between irony and earnestness, between romance and realism, and strove to create out of the detective-story conventions something more.

BIOGRAPHY

Amanda Cross was the pseudonym and persona of Carolyn Gold Heilbrun, who was born on January 13, 1926, in East Orange, New Jersey. She attended Wellesley College, where she was elected to Phi Beta Kappa; she was graduated in 1947, having married James Heilbrun in 1945. She was the mother of Emily, Margaret, and Robert.

Cross's academic life was a full one, starred with accomplishments and recognition. She received both a master's degree and a doctoral degree from Columbia University, in 1951 and 1959 respectively. Her teaching career began at Brooklyn College in 1959; the next year, she moved back to Columbia, where she moved up the academic rungs from instructor to full professor by 1972. Finally, Columbia gave her a chair, making her Avalon Foundation professor in the humanities. She served as visiting professor in numerous places (not unlike the peripatetic Kate Fansler), and she held four honorary degrees. Cross served as president of the Modern Language Association in 1984 and, over the years, received a Guggenheim Fellowship, a Rockefeller Fellowship, and a fellowship from the National Endowment for the Humanities.

It was in 1963 that Cross began to create the kind of detective fiction she enjoyed but could no longer find in the bookstores. Beginning in 1964 she published fourteen Kate Fansler mysteries that, running counter to the prevailing hard-boiled school, secured for her a substantial readership as well as honors. Her awards included a Mystery Writers of America Scroll for *In the Last Analysis* (1964) and the Nero Wolfe Award for Mystery Fiction for *Death in a Tenured Position* (1981). Cross died in New York in 2003.

ANALYSIS

From the beginning, Amanda Cross knew what she wanted to do with her detective. She wrote that Kate Fansler "sprang from [her] brain" as a champion of the decencies, of intelligent conversation, and of a literary legacy that challenges those who know it to be worthy inheritors. Kate was also conceived as a combatant of "reaction, stereotyped sex roles, and convention that arises from the fear of change."

A certain Noël Cowardesque conversational flair is a hallmark of the Cross mystery. This prologue from *In the Last Analysis* illustrates the connection between the sparkling wit and the probing intelligence that make Kate a stimulating teacher, a successful detective, and a good friend:

> "I didn't say I objected to Freud," Kate said. "I said I objected to what Joyce called freudful errors—all those nonsensical conclusions leaped to by people with no reticence and less mind."
>
> "If you're going to hold psychiatry responsible for sadistic parlor games, I see no point in continuing the discussion," Emanuel answered. But they would continue the discussion nonetheless; it had gone on for years, and showed no sign of exhausting itself.

A conversation that goes on for years is just what Cross had in mind: provocative conversation about modern dilemmas and timeless issues, into which, now and then, Death intrudes.

Kate Fansler's conversations ring with allusions, analogies, and epigrams. The first page alone of the first novel makes mention of T. S. Eliot, Julius Caesar, William Butler Yeats, Johann Sebastian Bach, Edna St. Vincent Millay, and Jane Austen. These scholarly references are more than surface ornamentation, it should be said; to this erudite detective, the word-hoard of Western civilization suggests both theme and imaginative method. There is a particular figure, for example, looming behind the mystery of who killed Kate's student on her psychiatrist's couch: Sigmund Freud himself.

POETIC JUSTICE

In *The James Joyce Murder* (1967), it is the Irish literary genius who serves as the intellectual model, and the poet W. H. Auden is the sleuth's guiding spirit in the third novel, *Poetic Justice* (1970). Frustrated by the blind waste of the campus revolts, Kate thinks a line of Auden's: " . . . unready to die, but already at the stage when one starts to dislike the young." She later recovers her tolerance of the young; in later novels she even succeeds in appreciating them, and she matures in other ways as well. That success, her continued

growth as a character, the reader is made to sense, is in large part attributable to such influences as that of Auden, who, for his pursuit of frivolity balanced by earnestness, she calls "the best balancer of all."

Auden's influence reaches beyond the events of one novel, actually, and into the broader considerations of theory. It was Auden, after all, who laid down with such left-handed ease the consummate protocol for Aristotelian detective plotting in "The Guilty Vicarage." Dorothy L. Sayers, whom Kate quotes frequently, edited the perceptive survey *The Omnibus of Crime* (1928-1934) and wrote "Aristotle on Detective Fiction," an entertaining and imaginative look at the detective story's qualifications as genuine art. These two serve as Cross's authorities on matters of form.

Particularly in her early novels, Cross adheres rather closely to the formal requirements and conventional elements of the classic detective story. Her stories begin in peaceful settings or retreats, such as Kate's office, a pastoral campus, or the edenic Berkshires; this is the stage Auden calls False Innocence. Quite soon ironic shadows develop. (The campus is so quiet, for example, because students have captured the administration building.) Then a murder is discovered. Kate finds herself in a predicament because she knows and feels some commitment to the victim, the suspect, or both, and she stays because her sense of decency impels her.

After noting numerous clues and considering various apparently innocent suspects (and engaging in fascinating conversations), Kate, assisted by Reed and sometimes by her own version of the Baker Street Irregulars, tests the evidence, makes her deductions, and reaches a solution. The story ends with an arrest, a confession, or some final illumination and a return to a peaceful state. In Auden's terms, the Real Guilt has been located and True Innocence achieved.

Though her plotting is solid, plotting is not Cross's principal concern. Like any mystery author worth her salt, Cross wants to challenge the conventions and transcend the formula. She is greatly interested in change, growth, and innovation, and she is deeply concerned about resistance to change, stagnation, and suspicion of the new. In one novel Kate calls this kind of poor thinking confusing morality with convention. Kate seems invariably to take the unconventional position—defending psychiatry, supporting young Vietnam draft resisters, advocating feminism—but in reality she, too, is subject to the conventions through which all human beings see and understand their lives, and she, too, is challenged to change. In effect, with each new novel Cross tests her hypothesis that when conventions (literary or social) no longer promote genuine morality or serve a civilizing purpose, they should be modified.

By insisting on the primacy of character—that is, of personal integrity—Cross bends one of the cardinal rules of the detective genre. Sayers herself, following Aristotle, wrote that there can be a detective story without character, but there can be no story without plot. Without neglecting plot, Cross makes character the solution to the crime of *In the Last Analysis*. It is Kate's belief in the intrinsic nature of her friend Emanuel—something that the police investigators cannot know and cannot consider—and her willingness to trust Nicola's dream that lead her to the distant witness who eventually remembers the physical evidence without which the police cannot work. Similarly, the discussions of Freudian analysis and of dreams in that same novel make the point that intuitive and associative thinking can be as productive as deductive logic, and thereby broaden what have been the conventional expectations of ratiocinative tales.

THE THEBAN MYSTERIES AND
THE QUESTION OF MAX

Cross continued to reshape the formal elements of the whodunit with each subsequent novel. In her fourth, *The Theban Mysteries* (1971), she extends the usually brief preamble and predicament segments and withholds the usually numerous suspects so that the crisis in faith between the generations displaces yet illuminates the lesser crisis of the dead parent. The model of ratiocination here is Kate's *Antigone* seminar, a beautifully crafted conversation of a special kind that illustrates the art of deciding what is worth examining. In her next novel, *The Question of Max* (1976), Cross achieved what some consider her greatest success in blending experimentation and tradition: She identifies the murderer from the beginning, the better to focus attention on that individual's character, social conditioning, and misogynist motives.

NO WORD FROM WINIFRED

As she has gone about reshaping the detective story to suit her moral vision, feminism has remained foremost among the positions Cross champions. Kate herself represents the achieving woman in a once all-male domain, and there are distinctive portraits of other academic women: Grace Knowles, "the greatest living medieval scholar"; Miss Tyringham, headmistress of the Theban and "a genius at her job"; Janet Mandlebaum, the first woman on the English faculty at Harvard University; and Patrice Umphelby, "a professor, widely known and widely loved." In *No Word from Winifred* (1986), the central figure of mystery is not an academic but a woman whose distinction lies in knowing what she wants. No Cross novel better illustrates the zest and the discernment that she brings to the investigation of what it means to be an exceptional woman in the late twentieth century.

As the novel opens, Larry Fansler is complaining to his law partner about the risks they will be running by inviting his strong-minded sister Kate to the annual associates party. At the novel's close a year later, this same curmudgeon of a brother is relieved to reflect that "her being there didn't make the slightest difference," expressing the paternalistically mellow sentiment that "a man ought to see his kid sister once in a while." Within this masculine frame of reference exists a most thoroughly feminist mystery quest. Unknown to her unimaginative eldest brother, Kate has, in fact, made a significant difference in the lives of the women and men who help her piece together the puzzle of the missing woman; one of those men is Larry's law partner, Toby Van Dyne.

As usual, allusions enrich the detection process, beginning with Leighton's suspicion that something very wrong has happened at the law office and her desire to play Watson to her aunt Kate's Holmes. Charlotte Lucas is the first clue: Leighton knows her as a very nice coworker; Kate recognizes the name of a character of Jane Austen; the knowing reader is allowed the special pleasure of seeing in this name a reference to a stiflingly conventional approach to marriage.

When Kate needs help, she turns to professionals in both literary and investigatory fields, treating the detective Mr. Fothingale to a British high tea and playing the attentive neophyte in the headquarters of the Modern Language Association in order to take a sleuthing shortcut. In her dual role of professor and detective Kate rings changes on the conventional detective puzzle. By drawing attention to the nature of the story and people's tendency to live by stories, Cross demonstrates that the detective formula can be transformed into an instrument of imaginative expression. Moreover, in *No Word from Winifred* she discriminates between conventional stories and living stories.

This is a feminist book that transcends the stereotypical. Both the women and the men whom Kate encounters along the trail of clues are believable individuals, as recognizable as Geoffrey Chaucer's pilgrims must have been to literate Londoners at the close of the fourteenth century—typical in some ways, atypical in others. Kate is introduced to Winifred's story, what there is of it at first, by Charlie, that is, Charlotte Lucas (who is keeping her relationship with Toby Van Dyne secret). As the biographer of the Oxford novelist Charlotte Stanton, Charlie had escorted Winifred, Stanton's honorary niece, from her rural retreat in the United States to England, where Winifred disappeared.

The "evidence" Charlie brings to Kate consists of Winifred's journal and Charlie's own letters to Toby written during the trip to England. This is the beginning of a chain of communication—much of it written—from woman to sympathetic woman that organizes and gives meaning to the entire narrative, enabling Kate at last to piece together Winifred's surprising story, a classic mystery of identity, unknown parentage, and a love triangle. Of particular stylistic merit are the journal entries, in which an entirely new and compelling voice evokes the missing woman's presence. There is an appealing description of a childhood summer in Oxford and of the pleasure of dressing as a boy.

The motif of the quest is conventionally associated with male adventure stories (in which the female characters may be damsels in distress, tempting witches, or repulsive hags). *No Word from Winifred* reverses this pattern: The men have problems and the women are on quests. First, there is Winifred, whose quest for the

precious time and the quiet place to write is detailed in her journal. Then comes Charlie, who has been tenacious in pursuing her desire to write the biography of Stanton. As a detective Kate is in quest of a solution, and as a connoisseur of character she is committed to preserving Winifred's. Finally, Leighton, who has been casting about for a real occupation and who first brought the puzzle to Kate's attention, decides to set out for the fabled Orient, to meet the paragon of womanhood face to face—and then, Leighton says, perhaps to write a book about the experience.

THE PLAYERS COME AGAIN

Later Fansler novels continued in the same vein of challenging what is "accepted," specifically focusing on feminism and the role of women in modern society. *The Players Come Again* (1990) investigates human interactions, relationships, genealogy, and the influence of Greek myths on the way Western civilization views men and women. Kate's exploration into Gabrielle Foxx, the wife of respected author Emmanuel Foxx, begins the novel. Emmanuel wrote his groundbreaking work *Ariadne* in 1927, a novel extraordinary primarily in that it was written with a female protagonist from a feminine point of view. As Kate uncovers layers of truth she explores Gabrielle's "counter novel," written in a speculative manner that questions the gender roles perpetuated by the ancient myths surrounding Araidne, Theseus, and the Minotaur. A complex story that relies heavily on letters, diaries, photographs, and records for a solution, *The Players Come Again* successfully intertwines plots within plots without losing the edge necessary in a modern mystery.

THE PUZZLED HEART

The Puzzled Heart (1998) returns to a simpler style, a more straightforward mystery in which Kate's husband is kidnapped by a group of nameless individuals who insist she write an article retracting her views on feminism for publication in newspapers, magazines, and journals. Kate, joined by a Saint Bernard puppy named Bancroft, enlists the help of friends to track down Reed and solve a subsequent murder. Kate returns to more of an active academic setting for this novel, investigating colleagues, observing departmental politics, and interacting with students and faculty in pursuit of answers. Although still addressing concerns regarding modern issues (feminism, racism) this novel lacks the complexity of earlier works and relies heavily on action as opposed to research, although the intellectual dialogue continues to amuse fans. After Emma Wentworth, an acquaintance of Reed, offers a quote from a notebook, she says, "I keep those sentences around to quote, because they sum up neatly the bottom line for those on the far right."

"William Bennet, Allan Bloom, and Jesse Helms, in short," Kate said. "Well, yes, as far as their ideas go, if one can accuse Jesse Helms of having anything describable as an idea."

HONEST DOUBT

Fansler's novel *Honest Doubt* (2000) actually casts Kate in the role of mentor to a new investigator, Estelle "Woody" Woodhaven. Woody, a former New York defense attorney turned private eye, is in her mid-thirties, rides a motorcycle, and possesses a portly figure. Although Kate plays only a supporting role, her guiding influence leads Woody through the hallowed ivory towers of stereotypical university life so prevalent in earlier Fansler tales. The victim is an arrogant chauvinist who also happens to be a Tennyson scholar at Clifton College, providing the literary slant Cross favors and seamlessly integrating it into a potential motive for murder.

Cross's characters are, for the most part, gentle people. Further, they are intelligent people, and their stories, under the scrutiny of a lady professor detective, become stories of romance, perhaps, or stories of psychological realism, often ironic and frequently comic, but just as tellingly angry, just as readily compassionate. In using detective fiction as a forum for addressing prevalent issues of today, Cross offers a distinctive weaving of modern academia, feminism, and mystery unique to the genre. Through Kate Fansler, her frivolous air and her sincere heart and her literary mind, the American detective story achieves charm, spirit, and intellectualism.

Rebecca R. Butler
Updated by Fiona Kelleghan and Mickey Rubenstien

PRINCIPAL MYSTERY AND DETECTIVE FICTION

KATE FANSLER SERIES: *In the Last Analysis*, 1964; *The James Joyce Murder*, 1967; *Poetic Justice*, 1970; *The Theban Mysteries*, 1971; *The Question of Max*, 1976; *Death in a Tenured Position*, 1981 (also known as *A Death in the Faculty*); *Sweet Death, Kind Death*, 1984; *No Word from Winifred*, 1986; *A Trap for Fools*, 1989; *The Players Come Again*, 1990; *An Imperfect Spy*, 1995; *The Puzzled Heart*, 1998; *Honest Doubt*, 2000; *The Edge of Doom*, 2002

OTHER MAJOR WORKS

SHORT FICTION: *The Collected Stories*, 1997

NONFICTION (AS HEILBRUN): *The Garnett Family*, 1961; *Christopher Isherwood*, 1970; *Toward a Recognition of Androgyny: Aspects of Male and Female in Literature*, 1973 (also known as *Towards Androgyny*); *Reinventing Womanhood*, 1979; *Writing a Woman's Life*, 1988; *Hamlet's Mother and Other Women*, 1990; *The Education of a Woman: A Life of Gloria Steinem*, 1995; *The Last Gift of Time: Life Beyond Sixty*, 1997; *Women's Lives: The View from the Threshold*, 1999; *When Men Were the Only Models We Had: My Teachers Barzun, Fadiman, and Trilling*, 2001

EDITED TEXTS (AS HEILBRUN): *Gender and Culture* series, 1974-2002 (with Nancy Miller); *Lady Ottoline's Album*, 1976; *The Representation of Women in Fiction*, 1983 (with Margaret R. Higonnet)

BIBLIOGRAPHY

Boken, Julia G. *Carolyn G. Heilbrun*. New York: Twayne, 1996. Focuses on Heilbrun's mysteries written as Amanda Cross, with secondary attention paid to her academic work written under her own name.

Coale, Samuel Chase. *The Mystery of Mysteries: Cultural Differences and Designs*. Bowling Green, Ohio: Bowling Green University Popular Press, 2000. A study of the mysteries of Amanda Cross, Tony Hillerman, James Lee Burke, and Walter Mosely, showing how these writers use the mystery genre to introduce the concerns of minorities into fiction.

Klein, Kathleen Gregory, ed. *Great Women Mystery Writers: Classic to Contemporary*. Westport, Conn.: Greenwood Press, 1994. Contains an essay examining the life and works of Cross.

Kress, Susan. *Carolyn G. Heilbrun: Feminist in a Tenured Position*. Charlottesville: University Press of Virginia, 1997. One of the few studies that looks comprehensively at Heilbrun's oeuvre, as both feminist literary scholar and mystery writer.

Lindsay, Elizabeth Blakesley, ed. "Amanda Cross." In *Great Women Mystery Writers*. 2d ed. Westport, Conn.: Greenwood Press, 2007. Contains biographical information and analysis of the author's works.

Malmgren, Carl D. *Anatomy of Murder: Mystery, Detective, and Crime Fiction*. Bowling Green, Ohio: Bowling Green State University Popular Press, 2001. Malmgren discusses Cross's *A Trap for Fools* alongside many other entries in the mystery and detective genre. Bibliographic references and index.

Reynolds, Moira Davison. *Women Authors of Detective Series: Twenty-One American and British Authors, 1900-2000*. Jefferson, N.C.: McFarland, 2001. Examines the life and work of major female mystery writers, including Cross.

Weigman, Robyn. "What Ails Feminist Criticism? A Second Opinion." *Critical Inquiry* 25, no. 2 (1999): 362-379. Uses the Amanda Cross story "Murder Without a Text" (1991) as a case study in the tensions between two generations of feminists.

JAMES CRUMLEY

Born: Three Rivers, Texas; October 12, 1939
Types of plot: Hard-boiled; private investigator

PRINCIPAL SERIES

Milo Milodragovitch, 1975-
C. W. Sughrue, 1978-

PRINCIPAL SERIES CHARACTERS

MILTON "MILO" MILODRAGOVITCH is a sometimes private eye, sometimes security worker in Meriwether, Montana. A Korean War veteran, a former deputy sheriff, and the son of a former drunken scion of the town who eventually committed suicide, Milo is counting the days until his fifty-third birthday, when he will inherit the family fortune. A heavy drinker and cocaine abuser in the early novels, Milo often identifies with the very members of society he was once paid to police.

C. W. "SONNY" SUGHRUE, a native of Texas, is a part-time private eye and part-time repo man and bartender based in Meriwether, Montana. A Vietnam War veteran, Sughrue is a more controlled, physically capable, and confident investigator than Milo. *Bordersnakes* (1996) uses both characters as narrators; earlier novels had hinted that the two characters had once been partners in a private-eye firm.

CONTRIBUTION

Compared with the output of many mystery-fiction authors, James Crumley's publications have been limited. Since the publication of his first novel, *One to Count Cadence*, in 1969, he has produced only two or three novels per decade. However, Crumley has had an immense impact on the genre of detective fiction.

Perhaps partly because Crumley's first novel was a mainstream book about the military, his detective novels have been afforded the critical respect and reception more typically associated with literary fiction. During the 1980's Random House printed his books in the Vintage Contemporaries line, dedicated to showcasing rising literary talents like Richard Ford, who later won a Pulitzer Prize, and short-story writer Raymond Carver. As a result, Crumley developed a serious readership beyond the ranks of mystery aficionados. Furthermore, his mystery novels managed to both update and subvert the genre parameters within which they were operating. His detectives abused drugs and were respectful to women but also libidinous; the increased level of violence, and occasionally the absurdity of its abundance, in his books reflected a new take on the genre.

BIOGRAPHY

James Crumley was born in 1939 in Three Rivers, Texas, and was raised in south Texas, largely in the town of Santa Cruz. He attended the Georgia Institute of Technology on a Navy Reserve Officer Training Corps scholarship; however, in 1958 he dropped out of college and served a three-year tour in the United States Army. Like his character C. W. Sughrue, Crumley was reluctant to submit to military discipline and often found himself in conflict with his commanding officers. After his Army discharge, he attended Texas College of Arts and Industries on a football scholarship; despite taking time off occasionally to work, he graduated with a bachelor's degree in history in 1964. He then pursued a master of fine arts in creative writing in the writing program at the University of Iowa, where he worked with novelists such as Richard Yates and R. V. Cassell. His thesis was eventually published as *One to Count Cadence*, his first novel.

Crumley became a professor at the University of Montana in Missoula. However, when *One to Count Cadence* was well received, he left and held a series of writing professorships. From 1969 to 1984 he worked briefly for the University of Arkansas at Fayetteville; Colorado State University; Reed College in Portland, Oregon; Carnegie-Mellon; and the University of Texas at El Paso.

Crumley made the move to detective fiction after his friend, the poet and novelist Richard Hugo, loaned him several novels by hard-boiled detective novelist Raymond Chandler. Taken with Chandler's ability to create a memorable character in brief strokes and his character Philip Marlowe's adherence to a code of integrity, Crumley crafted his own detective novel, *The Wrong Case* (1975).

In 1975, Crumley married Judith Anne Ramsey. After divorcing her, he married Bronwyn Pughe in 1979, whom he later divorced. He has five children. He moved to Montana in the mid-1980's, but his wanderlust appears in his novels; a number of them (*The Last Good Kiss*, 1978; *The Mexican Tree Duck*, 1993;

and *Bordersnakes*) send his characters on road trips about the West.

In the mid-1980's Crumley began to spend less time in academic settings and worked as a full-time writer, not only producing magazine pieces but also venturing into film. He wrote a screen adaptation of his novel *Dancing Bear* (1983) and a screenplay called *The Pigeon Shoot* (1987), which was released as a limited edition publication. He worked on screenplays for the science-fiction comic book film *Judge Dredd* (1995) and wrote a screen adaptation of James Ellroy's novel *The Big Nowhere* (1988). In 2006 a film was made from the screenplay he wrote with Rob Sullivan, *The Far Side of Jericho*.

ANALYSIS

James Crumley did not begin his career as a detective novelist. However, many of the elements that define his detective novels are present in his first novel, *One to Count Cadence*: elevated violence, a countercultural perspective, and rebellious characters who refuse to conform to the mainstream. Crumley's main inspiration and primary literary antecedent, as Crumley often states, is Raymond Chandler. Like Chandler, Crumley is a high stylist, who always writes in the first person and relishes the well-turned phrase, particularly apt description, and judicious use of original similes. Just as Chandler's Philip Marlowe is a lone private investigator who works outside the official channels of law enforcement, Crumley's Milo and Sughrue are characters at odds with the authorities, whether they are corrupt police departments or government agencies. Like Marlowe, Sughrue and Milo make up in persistence, endurance, and toughness what they lack in Sherlock Holmesian levels of intellect.

As great as Crumley's debt is to Chandler, however, the plots of his novels follow directions that may have been unimaginable to Chandler. Members of the generation of baby boomers who came of age in the 1960's, Milo and Sughrue are familiar with the counterculture and its politics, with drug users and dealers, the sexual revolution, gay rights, and feminism. Crumley's detectives are more familiar with the down-and-out people in their society than they are with the respectable elements. Their friends are drunks, drug dealers, burned-out veterans, and bartenders. Both detectives drink too much and are willing to snort both cocaine and methamphetamine. Crumley's detectives rarely find themselves at odds with everyday criminals. In the latter novels, particularly, Sughrue and Milo tend to engage in conflicts with corrupt senators, billionaires, corporations, and upper echelon Federal Bureau of Investigation (FBI) and Drug Enforcement Agency (DEA) agents.

The private-eye characters, the first-person, wise-cracking narrative, the pacing, and the violence in Crumley's novels clearly place them within the hard-boiled category of detective fiction. However, violence in Crumley's novels—particularly the latter ones—tends to be simultaneously more extreme and more complicated than in earlier hard-boiled novels. In *Dancing Bear*, Milo shoots more men during the climactic showdown than Philip Marlowe does in his entire series; on the other hand, the violent death of a friend and drunk in *The Wrong Case* sends Milo on an alcohol and cocaine bender that almost kills him.

Crumley's novels also differ from those of other hard-boiled detective writers because they are not essentially urban tales. Although parts of the novels are set in the small town of Meriwether, Montana, and other small cities, the narratives are largely set in the open West, from Montana in the north to Texas in the south. Crumley's detectives do not lose tails by dodging in and out of taxis or subway cars but by following National Forest Service maps onto logging roads. The corruption of humankind and civilization is made even starker when juxtaposed with the mountain forests of *Dancing Bear* and the desert Southwest of *The Mexican Tree Duck* and *Bordersnakes*.

THE WRONG CASE

The Wrong Case, Crumley's first detective novel, introduces Milton "Milo" Milodragovitch. The great-grandson of a Russian Cossack émigré to the old west, Milo is a thirty-nine-year-old private investigator, a Korean War veteran (having enlisted at the age of sixteen), and a former corrupt deputy sheriff whose business has dried up because of the relaxing of Montana divorce laws. Milo's father, while wealthy, had become a drunk and a philanderer in the years before his suicide; Milo's mother (also an alcoholic and, eventu-

ally, also a suicide) placed the family fortune into a trust that Milo will not inherit until he turns fifty-three. Milo's life is further complicated in that his oldest friend, Jamison, is also his oldest enemy; after serving in the Korean War together, Jamison became a police officer with Milo and went on to become a detective lieutenant. Jamison even married Milo's former wife and is raising Milo's son.

The Wrong Case clearly reveals Chandler's influence: Helen Duffy's request that Milo locate her missing younger brother is reminiscent of Chandler's *The Little Sister* (1949), and the brother is similar to a minor character in *The Long Goodbye* (1953). Milo, however, is no Philip Marlowe. Whereas Marlowe is a character almost without a past, Milo is weighed down by the past everywhere he turns: his dead father's clothes, donated to thrift stores, appear on homeless men and drunks.

The case turns out to be one that is wrong in every way. The missing brother is an aggressive homosexual junkie with a fetish for cowboy clothing. Everything Milo thinks he knows about Helen Duffy is wrong, and their budding romance quickly falls apart. Even the inadvertent villain of the story turns out to be a local bar owner with ties to organized crime who hopes he can sell enough drugs to become important. The only lesson that Milo can learn from the chaos is that the two main things a man has to learn to do are to survive and to forgive.

THE LAST GOOD KISS

The Last Good Kiss is Crumley's first novel with C. W. (for Chauncey Wayne) "Sonny" Sughrue. Sughrue is a former Army sergeant who committed a war crime while in Vietnam. After a month in the bush without sleep, he dropped a grenade into a hideaway hole in a village and killed the hidden women and children of a Vietnamese family. To avoid prosecution, he worked for the Defense Intelligence Agency in San Francisco, infiltrating hippie culture. However, he came to identify with the hippies more than with his superiors. Sughrue is a more formidable detective than Milo and more in control of his emotions and actions. While perhaps harboring even fewer illusions than Milo, he is in some ways more of a romantic.

Like *The Wrong Case*, *The Last Good Kiss* owes a

large debt to Chandler. Just as Chandler's *The Long Goodbye* is about Marlowe being hired to protect a drunken and suicidal writer, *The Last Good Kiss* begins with Sughrue being hired to locate poet and famous novelist Abraham Trahearne, a World War II veteran and alcoholic who has gone on a drinking binge. The novel departs from *The Long Goodbye*'s plot, however, when Sughrue is asked by an aging bar owner to locate her runaway daughter, Betty Sue Flowers. With Trahearne in tow, Sughrue begins searching for Betty Sue and soon runs afoul of a mob-connected pornography ring.

Widely regarded as Crumley's best novel, *The Last Good Kiss* brings together many of the author's trademark themes and qualities. The plot goes through several dizzying changes of direction; the dialogue is understated and clipped; Sughrue rebels instinctively against authority, whether it is in the form of law enforcement or social class; minor characters have depth and personality (as well as surprises to reveal); loyalties and alliances shift; and the violence is swift, bleak, rendered in bloody and exquisite detail, and has surprising ramifications for the characters. Like Milo, the novel ends with Sughrue having nowhere to find peace except in his own ability to survive and endure.

DANCING BEAR

Published five years after *The Last Good Kiss*, *Dancing Bear* features Milo. The intervening eight years have not been kind to Milo. His practice has failed, and he is employed as a security worker for an older veteran who helps out hard-luck cases. Milo is hired by an elderly woman, a former lover of his dead father, ostensibly to discover the identities of young lovers she has watched from her porch. Again, the plot darts in directions not anticipated by the reader, and before long, Milo's life is in danger when he discovers that a gigantic corporation, with both underworld and corrupt government connections, is illegally disposing of toxic waste.

Milo's persona as the "antidetective" is revealed again when he is followed while tailing a subject of his investigation, and as a result his subject is killed. Also, he understands too late what seems clear throughout— that he has been set up by his employer. The end sequence of the novel is patterned somewhat after the

rescue sequence in *The Last Good Kiss*. Milo and his confederate burst into a conference, armed and loaded, but hoping that the meeting will not end in bloodshed. Someone reaches for a gun and mayhem ensues. Although this confrontation in *Dancing Bear* is, like the one in *The Last Good Kiss*, tightly written, exciting, and vicious, it does create the formula for the novels to come.

LATER NOVELS

Ten years separate *The Mexican Tree Duck* from *Dancing Bear*. In *The Mexican Tree Duck*, Sughrue seems in some ways to bear a resemblance to a more dangerous incarnation of Milo, with his constant use of cocaine and amphetamine as well as alcohol, than he does the laconic and determined narrator of *The Last Good Kiss*. In *The Mexican Tree Duck*, Sughrue—now as out of work as Milo—is hired to find a drug-dealing biker's mother, who turns out to be the wife of a senator and drug lord. Sughrue gathers together a disparate crowd of Vietnam War veterans to lead assaults on drug cabals dealing in cocaine. Multiple encounters with incompetent and corrupt DEA and FBI agents are counterbalanced with gunfights fueled by automatic weapons. Crumley's *Bordersnakes* picks up on the hints dropped in earlier novels by reuniting former partners Sughrue and Milo. Like *The Mexican Tree Duck*, the novel quickly dissolves into a tangled plot punctuated by episodes of bloody and horrific violence. *The Final Country* (2001) follows the mode of the earlier novels as Milo is betrayed by the woman with whom he falls in love, the climax coming in a hail of gunfire. *The Right Madness* (2005) finds Sughrue betrayed by his employer as he ferrets out a trail of corruption.

Scott D. Yarbrough

PRINCIPAL MYSTERY AND DETECTIVE FICTION

MILTON "MILO" MILODRAGOVITCH SERIES: *The Wrong Case*, 1975; *Dancing Bear*, 1983; *The Final Country*, 2001

C. W. "SONNY" SUGHRUE SERIES: *The Last Good Kiss*, 1978; *The Mexican Tree Duck*, 1993; *The Right Madness*, 2005

MILO AND SUGHRUE SERIES: *Bordersnakes*, 1996

OTHER MAJOR WORKS

NOVELS: *One to Count Cadence*, 1969

SHORT FICTION: *Whores*, 1988; *The Muddy Ford, and Other Things*, 1991

SCREENPLAYS: *The Pigeon Shoot*, 1987; *The Far Side of Jericho*, 2006 (with Rob Sullivan)

BIBLIOGRAPHY

Anderson, Patrick. *The Triumph of the Thriller: How Cops, Crooks, and Cannibals Captured Popular Fiction*. New York: Random House, 2007. Contains a discussion of Crumley's *The Last Good Kiss* that notes the writer's lyrical prose and outlaw attitude.

Crumley, James. "Noir by Northwest: Fictional Madness, Greed and Violence Are Alive and Kicking—Mysteriously, so Is Literary Tough Guy James Crumley." Interview by Ed Murrieta. *The News Tribune*, August 21, 2005, p. E01. Examines Crumley's history and how his personal life interacts with his literary creations.

Kaczmarek, Lynn. "James Crumley: Poet of the Night." *Mystery News* (August/September, 2001). An interview and commentary about Crumley as a writer poised between detective fiction and literary fiction.

Newlin, Keith. "C. W. Sughrue's Whiskey Visions." *Modern Fiction Studies* (Autumn, 1983): 545-555. A discussion of alcohol and drug abuse in Crumley's early fiction.

Scaggs, John. "Sex, Drugs, and Divided Identities: The Detective Fiction of James Crumley." *European Journal of American Culture* 22, no. 3 (2003): 205-214. Considers both the influence of Western novels and films on Crumley's works as well as how Crumley's detectives go through a process of identification with their suspects.

Silet, Charles L. P. "James Crumley." In *Talking Murder: Interviews with Twenty Mystery Writers*. New York: W. W. Norton, 1999. Contains an interview with Crumley by Silet, who has published interviews in *Mystery Scene* and *Armchair Detective*.

E. V. CUNNINGHAM

Howard Fast

Born: New York, New York; November 11, 1914
Died: Old Greenwich, Connecticut; March 12, 2003
Also wrote as Walter Ericson; Howard Fast
Types of plot: Police procedural; inverted; amateur sleuth; espionage; private investigator

PRINCIPAL SERIES

Harvey Krim, 1964-1984
Larry Cohen and John Comaday, 1965-1966
Masao Masuto, 1967-2000

PRINCIPAL SERIES CHARACTERS

HARVEY KRIM, a thirty-five-year-old insurance investigator, is cynical about love, human motives, and insurance companies. Accused of being nasty, unreliable, and unprincipled, he himself cultivates that image. A man who does not like loose ends, who works with police only when it is to his advantage to do so, and who is willing to temper deduction with hunches and to manipulate evidence in a good cause, he easily sees through shams and feels alienated at times. Nevertheless, he is still able to care about certain people.

LARRY COHEN, a district attorney in New York City, is one part of a background team in two comic mysteries. A sharp young criminal lawyer with a nose for the truth, no matter how unlikely, he is nevertheless a dupe for a sharp mind.

JOHN COMADAY, a New York City police commissioner, is the second part of the team. Although a political animal, tough with underlings but smooth with superiors, he is always susceptible to a pretty face.

MASAO MASUTO, a lean, six-foot-tall Nisei attached to the Beverly Hills Police Department, is a Zen Buddhist; his meditative philosophy provides the

Howard Fast (E. V. Cunningham) testifying before a U.S. Senate subcommittee in 1953. (AP/Wide World Photos)

calm, the self-assurance, and the introspective insights that mark his detection. He is married to a Japanese American woman. Masuto speaks Spanish and empathizes with the common worker. He is sometimes cruelly taunted about his Nisei heritage and must learn to deal with the acid tongues of Southern Californians.

CONTRIBUTION

E. V. Cunningham is the pseudonym used by Howard Fast for his mystery fiction. Notable for his prolific output (two or more books a year), he brought a social conscience to the detective genre, with works that expose the pitfalls of power and wealth and the virtues of the simple life. Cunningham was praised for his lifelike characters and action-packed narratives, but it was his commitment to liberal and humanitarian

values that truly distinguished his work. His novels are characterized by a sympathetic treatment of women: They are portrayed as courageous, witty, and in some ways superior to men in intuition, reason, and values, empathizing with cultural outcasts, understanding of the pressures that sometimes force decent men to conform, and disdainful of prejudice, hypocrisy, and abuse of power. His Nisei detective allowed him to explore the values of Zen philosophy while facing the materialism and inhumanity of the rich. In sum, Cunningham combined political statement with enjoyable entertainment.

BIOGRAPHY

E. V. Cunningham was born Howard Melvin Fast in New York City on November 11, 1914, the son of

Barney Fast and Ida Miller Fast. Educated at George Washington High School and the National Academy of Design in New York, he later worked at odd jobs and was a page at the New York Public Library while working on his first novel. In 1933, he received the Bread Loaf Writers' Conference Award. On June 6, 1937, he married Bette Cohen; they had two children, Rachel and Jonathan. From 1942 to 1943, Cunningham served overseas with the Office of War Information. In 1944, while with an Army film project, he became a war correspondent; in 1945, he became a foreign correspondent for *Esquire* and *Coronet*.

Cunningham had a long career as prolific writer, lecturer, and political activist. His early novels, written as Fast, focused primarily on the Revolutionary War, and *The Last Frontier* (1941) received particular praise as a taut and moving story of the abuse and extermination of three hundred Cheyenne. These provocative works tried to humanize history and historical figures, from George Washington to Thomas Paine, admitting their weaknesses and demonstrating the processes that led them to greatness.

In 1943, Cunningham's antifascist feeling, which had led him to work in a hospital for wounded Spanish Republicans during the Spanish Civil War, led him to the communist cause; during this period, he created one-dimensional, doctrinaire works with capitalist villains and proletarian heroes. He continued to write historical fiction, but more and more with a Marxist slant. In 1947, he was imprisoned for contempt, having refused to give the House Committee on Un-American Activities information about the supporters of the Spanish hospital. While serving his term, he wrote *Spartacus* (as Fast; 1951), a controversial treatment of the great slave revolt of 71 B.C.E., which won for him numerous prizes.

Cunningham later founded the World Peace Movement, and, between 1950 and 1955, he served as a member of the World Peace Council. In 1952, he campaigned for Congress on the American Labor Party ticket. Unable to find a publisher, in 1952 he founded the Blue Heron Press in New York to publish his own materials. By 1957, however, tired of communist pressures to change his works and disenchanted with the Communist Party, he wrote *The Naked God: The Writer and the Communist Party* (as Fast), clearly and completely recanting.

Until the 1980's, Cunningham turned out about one book per year: historical fiction, science fiction, and thrillers. These works vary considerably in quality, but they all try to teach, usually focusing on compassion and humanism rather than doctrine. As a consequence, he received the National Association of Independent Schools Award in 1962. Always an idealist, Cunningham believed that books "open a thousand doors, they shape lives and answer questions, they widen horizons, they offer hope for the heart and food for the soul"; thus, a writer has an obligation to portray the truth. He died in New York in 2003.

ANALYSIS

E. V. Cunningham built a series of novels around extraordinary women in a striking variation on the detective genre. Sometimes the leading woman is the criminal; occasionally, she is the co-investigator, the instigator, or the inspiration of the crime. Cunningham's women may not be stunningly beautiful, but they possess an intelligence, a resourcefulness, and an honesty that makes them attractive in every sense. They may have to deal with husbands or lovers who underestimate their spirit and their capabilities, but once caught up in sometimes bizarre situations, they show pluck, courage, and wit. A typical Cunningham woman is wisecracking, tough, and honest Shirley: soft and vulnerable, at times as hard as nails, able to cope with tough cops, death threats, and complex difficulties, bright and funny, and, for the men around her, exasperating. So, too, is Sylvia, a woman of strength and beauty who began life as an abused child but who, through sheer guts and determination, fought her way into polite society, teaching herself languages, reading voraciously, and lying all the way. These women move in a comic world, with the comedy resulting from their perception of male pretensions; they are willing to play the game, to build on men's illusions, delusions, and limitations to achieve their own ends.

PENELOPE

In *Penelope* (1965), a charming socialite, independently wealthy and bored with her banker husband's arrogant complacency, takes to theft. She plays Robin Hood to the local parish and associated charities and charms the police commissioner and district attorney, while providing the police with clue after clue to implicate herself. Ironically, their preconceptions prevent their accepting the truth even when they are confronted with irrefutable evidence.

Another character, Margie, is an innocent mistaken for a thief and then for an oil-rich countess; as a result, she is kidnapped twice and threatened with torture and murder, but somehow she remains unflappable, her whole adventure comic and resolvable.

Others, such as Phyllis, Lydia, Alice, and Helen, move in a more somber world, with loss of family, friends, and lives a real possibility. Phyllis finds her mother brutally beaten to death; Lydia sees her father pushed to suicide, her inheritance stolen, and her own life threatened; Alice's child is kidnapped and terrorized; and Helen must confront sexual sadists. Yet amid such horrors, these women remain quick-witted and humane. Alice, for example, finds her family torn apart when she is caught up in a devilish conspiracy that results in a violent midnight rendezvous, all because a stranger clung to her husband for a second in a subway station. Sally, on the other hand, told that she has only a few months to live, hires a professional gunman to end it all quickly; when she learns that the original diagnosis was wrong, however, she is ready to fight for life and a chance at love.

Masao Masuto series

Cunningham's tribute to women continues in his Masao Masuto series. Masuto's wife, Kati, participates in consciousness-raising sessions and occasionally chides her husband for his insensitivity to her and the family. Even Masuto's belief that most detectives underestimate women and as a result miss evidence relevant to a case grants women an equality that is often missing from detective fiction. *Samantha* (1967) focuses on a young woman's calculated and bloody revenge after she is raped by half a dozen young men on a Hollywood set, while *The Case of the Poisoned Eclairs* (1979) takes a hard look at some of the uglier costs of wealth.

Cunningham always includes people who are tinged with prejudice but convinced that they have none. He is particularly disturbed by anti-Jewish sentiments, having earlier written a semifictional biography of a Polish-Jewish financier who helped in the American Revolution, as well as a history of the Jews. The hero of *The Wabash Factor* (1986) is a Jewish police officer with an instinct for foul play, while Masuto's partner is Jewish and must fight against a Nazi mentality, even in Southern California. In *The Case of the Russian Diplomat* (1978), Arab and German terrorists kidnap and terrorize Masuto's daughter, assassinate a diplomat, and plan an explosion that will take hundreds of innocent lives, all to undermine the Jewish Defense League. In other works, the terrors of the Holocaust continue to affect modern events. Former Nazis, brutal, intolerant, and twisted, dominate the landscape. The villain in *Lydia* (1964) is a suave German actor, one of Adolf Hitler's close associates, who blackmails his fellow Nazis living in the United States. He has no qualms about eliminating all who stand in his way.

An antifascist viewpoint

Furthermore, Cunningham's strongly antifascist sentiments come across in his mysteries. The Federal Bureau of Investigation uses strong-arm tactics, intimidation, and authority to break the rules and manipulate events, and untouchable entrepreneurs and the unimaginably wealthy prove to be frauds, thieves, and murderers. Income-tax evasion leads to multiple murders, which city police are quick to cover up, and politicians engage in white-collar crime and sometimes even drug smuggling. In *Millie* (1973), a general and a senator head a heroin-smuggling operation. In *The Case of the Sliding Pool* (1981), powerful financial forces act to prevent an investigation, and speculators in big industry play games with people's lives and break the rules with impunity. In *The Case of the Murdered Mackenzie* (1984), the Central Intelligence Agency turns civilized Beverly Hills into a jungle, fixing evidence, condoning double murder, and even trying to eliminate nosy local investigators to protect a double agent.

Phyllis

In *Phyllis* (1962), when an American and a Soviet nuclear scientist disappear and leave warnings of atom bombs set to go off if an antinuclear peace pact is not signed immediately, a world-weary police officer and a lonely female physicist are tortured and abused by their own people because they claim, but cannot prove, that the bombs do not exist. Ironically, the alienated Americans have more in common with the Soviet scientist than with their closest American associates. Running through Cunningham's canon is a consistent thread of moralism and sentimentality, though his politics change slightly over the years and some of his mysteries celebrate precisely those capitalist and intellectual types whom he identified as the oppressors in earlier works.

THE WABASH FACTOR AND
THE WINSTON AFFAIR

A related concern is that of conspiracy: Octopus-like secret committees arrange "accidents" to eliminate the best and the brightest—those devoted to peace and humanity. In *The Assassin Who Gave Up His Gun* (1969), such a group is totally committed, carefully calculating, and ultimately indestructible, while in *The Wabash Factor* the method used (causing a stroke with a medical prescription) seems almost certainly unprovable. The latter book uses the mystery genre as an excuse to attack American support of Central American regimes that depend on drugs and death squads for power; it argues that, by turning a blind eye to such horrors, the American government opens the way for drugs and death squads to become a reality in the United States. Cunningham is also interested in the law being used to railroad a cause or a victim; he focuses on this in both *Helen* (1966) and *The Winston Affair* (1959). The latter centers on the court-martial of an American soldier who is accused of killing a British one; the defense counsel is under pressure to let his client hang in the interests of Anglo-American relations. Cunningham throughout his works suggests the world's weaknesses and wrongs through a selected individual crisis.

THE ASSASSIN WHO GAVE UP HIS GUN

Cunningham's heroes are often disillusioned, wary, and alienated. They have seen too much of the lunacies of life, of war, of injustice; they have responded to the horrors, and they have reached a point in life where they are without hope. It is then that they are plunged into a situation that challenges and puzzles them and

demands that they reevaluate their lives. Often this reevaluation is initiated or accelerated by an unexpected but ego-shaking contact with a woman, a woman of competence, intelligence, and conscience. Ironically, before any sort of personal understanding and permanent attachment can be developed, Cunningham's heroes must deal with political ambition, intrigue, and death. The cold, methodical professional killer in *The Assassin Who Gave Up His Gun*, for example, is a rational man whose response to irrationality is to lose himself in his job and do it efficiently. Acting for a secret international political group determined to undermine any major peace movement, he lives on the knife's edge; although recognizing that he himself may be hurt in his turn, after facing a Buddhist's calm acceptance of death, he begins to question his acts. Later, when his assigned victim is a woman to whom he immediately responds, he must play the game to the end, maneuvering to save her though it means his own death.

HELEN AND MILLIE

In *Helen*, a corruptible lawyer, assigned to defend a prostitute who is clearly guilty of the cold-blooded murder of a state supreme court judge (who is also the number-two man in the state's mafia syndicate), finds that he must deal with questions of good and evil. In *Millie*, a successful public relations man responsible for the "images" of senators and rock stars must face the emptiness of his marriage and his profession in a deadly battle for self-respect. Ultimately in Cunningham's works, awareness is not enough; action, even self-destructive action, must result if a person is to be free in heart and mind.

THE CASE OF THE ONE-PENNY ORANGE

Cunningham's detective Masuto has already found his niche, his values, his human contact; now he must try to live accordingly. Masuto's method combines Buddhist meditation with Holmesian ratiocination. Observation is a part of Masuto's religion and of his way of life, and the close observation that allows him to see beauty in the ugly also allows him to see the ugly and mundane behind the facades that surround him. Intuitive leaps of both reason and imagination result, and his colleagues and superiors are left trying to figure out what produced these conclusions, which further investigation, physical evidence, and testimony confirm. For example, *The Case of the One-Penny Orange* (1977) begins as a routine investigation of a local burglary, but it leads to a murdered stamp dealer and a missing SS commander. Masuto links these seemingly unconnected events with a stamp worth half a million dollars and a revenge ritual originating in the bitterness of the Holocaust.

THE CASE OF THE RUSSIAN DIPLOMAT

The Case of the Russian Diplomat, in turn, begins with the apparent drowning of a nude fat man—reported to the police by a hotel hooker—but the nature of the scene leads Masuto to an East German spy, Arab terrorists, and a plot to assassinate some Soviet agronomists. While the federal investigators are still trying to cover up a Russian diplomat's unseemly demise, Masuto is uncovering the actual plot. He does so step-by-step, beginning with marks on the dead man's nose that suggest glasses and gray metal fillings that suggest foreign dental work and proceeding to the incongruity of the death—which to him suggests chloral hydrate. Parts of the puzzle float around in his mind for days, then come together in a pattern that could explain all.

THE CASE OF THE SLIDING POOL AND THE CASE OF THE KIDNAPPED ANGEL

The Case of the Sliding Pool is unique in that identifying the body (a long-buried skeleton) will in effect identify the murderer, while the solution to *The Case of the Kidnapped Angel* (1982) hinges on a sex-change operation and an old-fashioned revenge plot. In Masuto's eyes, crime encapsulates the general illness of humankind. As a Buddhist, he is involved with humankind, but he must constantly battle his own hatred while struggling with people who are an affront to humanity.

Despite Cunningham's sympathy with the proletariat, his dialogue is most credible when it is spoken by the educated. When he attempts slang, heavy accents, or the diction of gangsters, street people, and the down-and-out, rhythms ring so false that some critics have accused Cunningham of having a tin ear. Occasionally, his characters will elaborate on a metaphor that sums up their lives or situation, but in the main, the writing is straightforward and unadorned. It is with

the exchange of wisecracks or cynicisms in his comic mysteries that he feels most comfortable.

Basically, Cunningham disapproves of anyone or anything that tries to reduce humankind to a class, an ideology, a nonentity. He values above all else struggle, self-awareness, love and affection, family, privacy, and humanitarian values. His attack on funeral homes in *The Case of the Murdered Mackenzie* is typical of his sensibilities: He disapproves of any group that tries to force people into mechanical categories or that denies genuine emotion. His style is simple and direct; for him the message outweighs all else.

Gina Macdonald

PRINCIPAL MYSTERY AND DETECTIVE FICTION
HARVEY KRIM SERIES: *Lydia*, 1964; *Cynthia*, 1968
LARRY COHEN AND JOHN COMADAY SERIES: *Penelope*, 1965; *Margie*, 1966
MASAO MASUTO SERIES: *Samantha*, 1967 (also known as *The Case of the Angry Actress*); *The Case of the One-Penny Orange*, 1977; *The Case of the Russian Diplomat*, 1978; *The Case of the Poisoned Eclairs*, 1979; *The Case of the Sliding Pool*, 1981; *The Case of the Kidnapped Angel*, 1982; *The Case of the Murdered Mackenzie*, 1984
NONSERIES NOVELS: *Fallen Angel*, 1952 (as Ericson; also known as *The Darkness Within* and *Mirage*, as Fast); *The Winston Affair*, 1959 (as Fast); *Sylvia*, 1960; *Phyllis*, 1962; *Alice*, 1963; *Shirley*, 1964; *Helen*, 1966; *Sally*, 1967; *The Assassin Who Gave Up His Gun*, 1969; *Millie*, 1973; *The Wabash Factor*, 1986

OTHER MAJOR WORKS
NOVELS (AS FAST): 1933-1940 • *Two Valleys*, 1933; *Strange Yesterday*, 1934; *Place in the City*, 1937; *Conceived in Liberty*, 1939

1941-1950 • *The Last Frontier*, 1941; *The Tall Hunter*, 1942; *The Unvanquished*, 1942; *Citizen Tom Paine*, 1943; *Freedom Road*, 1944; *The American: A Middle Western Legend*, 1946; *Clarkton*, 1947; *The Children*, 1947; *My Glorious Brothers*, 1948; *The Proud and the Free*, 1950

1951-1960 • *Spartacus*, 1951; *Silas Timberman*, 1954; *The Story of Lola Gregg*, 1956; *Moses, Prince of Egypt*, 1958; *The Golden River*, 1960

1961-1970 • *April Morning*, 1961; *Power*, 1962; *Agrippa's Daughter*, 1964; *Torquemada*, 1966; *The Hunter and the Trap*, 1967; *The General Zapped an Angel*, 1970

1971-1980 • *The Crossing*, 1971; *The Hessian*, 1972; *Second Generation*, 1978; *The Immigrants*, 1978; *The Establishment*, 1979

1981-1987 • *The Legacy*, 1981; *Max*, 1982; *The Outsider*, 1984; *The Immigrant's Daughter*, 1985; *The Dinner Party*, 1987

SHORT FICTION (AS FAST): *Patrick Henry and the Frigate's Keel, and Other Stories of a Young Nation*, 1945; *Departures, and Other Stories*, 1949; *The Last Supper, and Other Stories*, 1955; *The Edge of Tomorrow*, 1961; *A Touch of Infinity*, 1973; *Time and the Riddle: Thirty-one Zen Stories*, 1975

PLAYS (AS FAST): *The Hammer*, pr. 1950; *Thirty Pieces of Silver*, pb. 1950; *George Washington and the Water Witch*, pb. 1956; *The Crossing*, pr. 1962

SCREENPLAYS (AS FAST): *The Hill*, 1964; *The Hessian*, 1971

TELEPLAYS (AS FAST): *What's a Nice Girl Like You . . . ?*, 1971; *Twenty-one Hours at Munich*, 1976 (with Edward Hume)

POETRY (AS FAST): *Never to Forget the Battle of the Warsaw Ghetto*, 1946 (with William Gropper)

CHILDREN'S LITERATURE (AS FAST): *The Romance of a People*, 1941; *Tony and the Wonderful Door*, 1952 (also known as *The Magic Door*)

NONFICTION (AS FAST): *Haym Solomon, Son of Liberty*, 1941; *Lord Baden-Powell of the Boy Scouts*, 1941; *Goethals and the Panama Canal*, 1942; *The Picture-Book History of the Jews*, 1942; *The Incredible Tito*, 1944; *Intellectuals in the Fight for Peace*, 1949; *Literature and Reality*, 1950; *Tito and His People*, 1950; *Peekskill, U.S.A.: A Personal Experience*, 1951; *Spain and Peace*, 1952; *The Passion of Sacco and Vanzetti: A New England Legend*, 1953; *The Naked God: The Writer and the Communist Party*, 1957; *The Howard Fast Reader*, 1960; *The Jews: Story of a People*, 1968; *The Art of Zen Meditation*, 1977

EDITED TEXTS (AS FAST): *The Selected Works of Tom Paine*, 1946; *The Best Short Stories of Theodore Dreiser*, 1947

BIBLIOGRAPHY

Browne, Ray. "E. V. Cunningham: The Case of the Poisoned Society." In *Heroes and Humanities: Detective Fiction and Culture*. Bowling Green, Ohio: Bowling Green State University Popular Press, 1986. Cunningham is discussed in the context of a study of humanist ideology in American, Canadian, and Australian detective fiction.

Deloux, Jean-Pierre, ed. "Howard Fast." *Polar* 125 (October 15, 1982): 163-185. Survey of the author's works, his life, and his politics.

Fast, Howard. *Being Red*. Boston: Houghton Mifflin, 1990. Cunningham's autobiographical reflections on the difficulties of being a communist writer in the United States.

Macdonald, Andrew. *Howard Fast: A Critical Companion*. Westport, Conn.: Greenwood Press, 1996. Detailed critical inquiry into Cunningham's life and work. Bibliographic references and index.

McLellan, Dennis. "Howard Fast, Eighty-eight: Novels Included *Spartacus*." *Los Angeles Times*, March 14, 2003, p. B13. Obituary of Cunningham deals with his life and works. Notes his use of Cunningham pseudonym while blacklisted.

Meyer, Herschel D. *History and Conscience: The Case of Howard Fast*. New York, Anvil-Atlas, 1958. Brief but focused study of Cunningham's representation of morality and conscience.

Pepper, Andrew. *The Contemporary American Crime Novel: Race, Ethnicity, Gender, Class*. Edinburgh: Edinburgh University Press, 2000. Examination of the representation and importance of various categories of identity in mainstream American crime fiction. Particularly useful for analyzing Cunningham's women and his Japanese sleuth.

D

CARROLL JOHN DALY

Born: Yonkers, New York; September 14, 1889
Died: Los Angeles, California; January 16, 1958
Also wrote as John D. Carroll
Types of plot: Hard-boiled; private investigator

PRINCIPAL SERIES

    Race Williams, 1923-1955
    Vee Brown, 1933-1936
    Satan Hall, 1935-1951

PRINCIPAL SERIES CHARACTER

    RACE WILLIAMS, a hard-boiled private investigator, first appeared in the June 1, 1923, issue of *Black Mask*. A tough-talking, no-nonsense thirty-year-old, Williams makes his living hunting down criminals for his clients. His credo: "I ain't afraid of nothing providing there's enough jack in it." He also asserts, "My ethics are my own."

CONTRIBUTION

    Usually credited with creating the hard-boiled detective, Carroll John Daly began his writing career in 1922, and between that year and his death he published more than a dozen novels and 250 short stories. Daly was a pathfinder whose writing skills were unpolished but whose sense of audience in the 1920's and early 1930's was unerring. Race Williams, the protagonist in eight novels and a number of the short stories, became the prototype out of which Dashiell Hammett's Sam Spade, Raymond Chandler's Philip Marlowe, Ross Macdonald's Lew Archer, and Mickey Spillane's Mike Hammer developed. Not a gifted writer, Daly focused on providing his readers with violent physical action and uncomplicated plots. Race Williams uses his handguns and his fists in a direct assault on evildoers. He is always his own man. The novels and tales are heavily laden with racial and sexual stereotyping; their popularity in the decades before World War II attests that Daly understood the popular mind.

BIOGRAPHY

    Carroll John Daly was born in Yonkers, New York, on September 14, 1889. The son of Joseph F. Daly and Mary Brennan Daly, he was educated at Yonkers High School and, subsequently, at De La Salle Institute and the American Academy of Dramatic Arts in New York. Daly was married in 1913. Abandoning pursuit of a career on the stage, he became a projectionist and then the owner and operator of theaters in Yonkers and Averne, New York, and Atlantic City and Asbury Park, New Jersey.

    Daly's writing career was launched in October, 1922, with the publication in *Black Mask* of a tale entitled "Dolly." He followed that success with another story for *Black Mask*, "Roarin' Jack," published in December under the pseudonym John D. Carroll. Now a published author, Daly moved his wife and their only child, John Russell Daly, to White Plains, New York, where the family lived until he retired in 1953. A man of many idiosyncrasies, Daly is alleged to have never left home during winter and to have insisted on a highly organized household. His success as a writer and his income from theaters he owned or operated allowed him to live comfortably, though not luxuriously.

    In 1953, Daly and his wife moved to Montrose, California, a suburb of Los Angeles. Their son, John, had found employment as a screen actor and occasional performer on television on the West Coast. Made an honorary member of a writers' club in Santa Monica, Daly lived in a modest apartment and continued writing for a few more years, publishing his last story in mid-1955. His health failing, he and his wife moved to Coachella, a desert area. Daly spent the last three years of his life in and out of hospitals; he died on January 16, 1958, in the Los Angeles County General Hospital.

ANALYSIS

The novels and tales of Carroll John Daly reveal a world constantly beset by a variety of criminals bent on shaping their surroundings to fit their desires for money and the power that it brings. For the most part, Daly's characters are not well developed and represent a very traditional view of the way in which the seven deadly sins corrupt humankind. Yet Daly was able to create in the fictional detectives Race Williams, Vee Brown, and Satan Hall men who were often as avaricious as the criminals they faced and as willing to go beyond the pale of law in bringing their prey to earth.

Race Williams first appeared in the story "Knights of the Open Palm" in *Black Mask* in June, 1923. He is described as being five feet, eleven and one-half inches tall, having black eyes and dark brown hair, and weighing 183 pounds. The reader is thus made aware of the fact that Williams is a physically powerful man to whom fear is probably a stranger. For some time before Daly's work appeared in *Black Mask*, the magazine had been accepting detective stories and Western fiction; the detective stories, however, were usually of the "amateur sleuth" variety, and the Westerns conformed to the conventions that had characterized dime novels for several decades. What made Williams, the forerunner of Sam Spade and the Continental Op, different was that he was not an agency detective or an arm of the police authority. His fists and his gun were for hire, and he was generally not very particular about the character of his employer. He acted according to a simple code: Never kill anybody who does not deserve it.

THE SNARL OF THE BEAST

With Williams as a first-person narrator and characterized by sequential plotting, Daly's stories quickly became a fixture in *Black Mask* in the 1920's and early 1930's. Daly's second novel—and the first to feature Race Williams—was *The Snarl of the Beast* (1927). In it, Williams's help is sought by the police in their attempt to capture a fiendish criminal known as the Beast. This master, who seems impervious to bullets, stalks the streets of the city, and the police are power-

The November, 1947, British edition of Thrilling Detective *featured a retitled version of one of John Carroll Daly's Race Williams stories.*

less to stop him. Williams agrees to hunt down the Beast if he is allowed to collect the reward money. Already a popular figure with readers of *Black Mask*, Williams attracted an even wider audience to Daly's fiction, and Daly went on to produce seven more Race Williams novels.

The appeal of the two-fisted, often two-gun, tough-talking hero is not difficult to fathom. In the United States, the hard-riding, straight-shooting Western hero had been well established by the 1920's. Appearing on the frontier in an age of lawlessness, the Western hero had come to represent truth, justice, and fair play. These "riders of the plains" were more than a match for a variety of evildoers bent on poisoning the well of a fledgling nation. Yet with the passing of the nineteenth century and the disillusionment arising from the ashes of World War I, American audiences seemed less and less interested in the romances of the American West. Even though the 1920's has been romanticized as the Jazz Age, the fact is that the vast majority of Americans were struggling to make ends meet and dreaming of the day "their ships would come in." Fair play, hard work, and honesty had not made them rich or famous. Although they certainly had freedom to do as they pleased, many felt powerless to change the conditions of their existence. Given this growing disenchantment with the American Dream, then, there certainly must have been a yearning to be able to control one's destiny, to exercise power, to be an individual unfettered by rules. Daly's conception of Race Williams provided his readers with a vicarious means of fulfilling that desire.

In story after story, novel after novel, Williams confronts a wide array of malefactors: petty thieves, corrupt politicians, gangland bosses, sinister foreigners, conniving women, and master criminals bent on taking over the nation or the world. Yet no matter what the magnitude of the threat these criminals pose, Williams is their master. He litters the urban streets with their corpses, and he is well paid for his efforts. When Raymond Chandler created Philip Marlowe in the 1930's, he made him a kind of knight-errant who sallied forth into the mean streets to do battle with evil. Williams, although he was the crude prototype from which detectives such as Marlowe developed, is not a crusader. His allegiance is to himself; he does not labor for king and country. Daly's hero, then, whether he is called Race Williams, Vee (short for Vivian) Brown, or Satan Hall, is a man who has power, who has control, who can to some extent shape his world.

The genesis of Daly's hard-boiled private investigator can be traced to "The False Burton Combs," a story that he published in the December, 1922, issue of *Black Mask*. The unnamed first-person narrator of this tale describes himself at the outset:

> I ain't a crook; just a gentleman adventurer and make my living working against the law breakers. Not that I work with the police—no, not me. I'm no knight-errant, either. It just came to me that the simplest people in the world are crooks. They are so set on their own plans to fleece others that they never imagine that they are the simplest sort to do.

Classifying himself as a kind of "fellow in the center—not a crook and not a policeman," this nameless adventurer expresses his willingness to help anybody if the price is right. The protagonist of "The False Burton Combs" is an Eastern version of the bounty hunter figure of the nineteenth century American West. A nameless, faceless, ruthless individual less concerned with the guilt or innocence of an individual than with the price society had placed on his head, the bounty hunter of the frontier was replaced in the twentieth century by the hard-boiled private investigator.

Magazines such as *Black Mask* built their readership by providing stories heavy on action but light on characterization. When "Knights of the Open Palm" appeared in the June, 1923, issue of *Black Mask*, perceptive readers must have recognized in the character of Race Williams (who first appears in that story) the nameless adventurer of "The False Burton Combs." In this story, Williams takes on the Ku Klux Klan, but his motive is not predicated on moral superiority. The Klan is involved in graft and corruption, but its activities with respect to minority groups are of no particular concern to Williams. "I'm just a halfway house between the law and crime," he states, but "I never bumped off a guy who didn't need it." Like many fictional private investigators, Williams often gives grudging respect to some of his adversaries, particularly those who display the same kind of toughness and machismo that he does.

MURDER FROM THE EAST

On occasion, Williams shows gentler emotions. He is very much taken with a beautiful female underworld figure nicknamed the Flame, who first appears in *The Tag Murders* (1930). In *Murder from the East* (1935) Williams involves himself in a case because a twelve-year-old girl has been kidnapped. These flashes of passion and compassion represent Daly's attempts to give Williams some depth of character, but it is the protagonists' belief in rigid justice that dominates all Daly's detective fiction. Cunning and guile are weapons of the weak; Williams uses fists and bullets, emerging sometimes bloody but always victorious.

THE THIRD MURDERER

The Third Murderer (1931) pits Williams against the three Gorgon brothers, powerful gangsters. Williams, as first-person narrator, alludes to Nathaniel

Hawthorne's use of the Gorgon myth in a short story. Here, as occasionally elsewhere, Daly gives the reader a picture of Williams as a man with some formal education. Also in this novel, Williams continues his relationship with the Flame, offering a brief psychological description of her:

> Certainly, if she was built to do great wrong, she might just as well be built to do great good. You see, the dual personality doesn't fit in with my practical nature. I always sort of look on it as synonymous with "two-faced." That is that it's an outward change, and doesn't really take place in the individual—but only in the mind of some one who knows the individual. In plain words, there were times when I thought The Flame was all bad, and the good—that youthful, innocent sparkle—was put on to fool others. But fair is fair. There were times also when I felt that The Flame was really all good, and the hard, cruel face—that went with the woman of the night— was put on to hide the real good in her.

The give and take between these two lovers in *The Third Murderer* eventually results in a scene mirroring the confrontation between Brigid O'Shaughnessy and Sam Spade near the end of Hammett's *The Maltese Falcon* (1929-1930). Yet, unlike Hammett, Daly has Williams let the Flame go, even after telling her, "I've got to turn you in. It isn't you I'm going to live with. It isn't your eyes I'm going to look into the rest of my life. It's myself I've got to live with. It's myself I've got to face in the glass each morning."

Daly's plotlines were not particularly clever nor was he skilled at creating dialogue that had the flavor of genuine human discourse. Still, he had a good sense of pace and moved the narrative along briskly. For the most part, his characters were essentially two-dimensional figures who, by the 1930's, were familiar to a generation quickly growing accustomed to the "cops and robbers" versions of good and evil emanating from Hollywood.

Although the literary reputations of Hammett and Chandler place them in the front rank of writers of detective fiction, a modern reader should understand that it was the work of Carroll John Daly that whetted the popular audience's appetite for the hard-boiled detective.

Dale H. Ross

PRINCIPAL MYSTERY AND DETECTIVE FICTION

RACE WILLIAMS SERIES: *The Snarl of the Beast*, 1927; *The Hidden Hand*, 1929; *The Tag Murders*, 1930; *Tainted Power*, 1931; *The Third Murderer*, 1931; *The Amateur Murderer*, 1933; *Murder from the East*, 1935; *Better Corpses*, 1940

VEE BROWN SERIES: *Murder Won't Wait*, 1933; *Emperor of Evil*, 1936

SATAN HALL SERIES: *Death's Juggler*, 1935 (also known as *The Mystery of the Smoking Gun*); *Ready to Burn*, 1951

NONSERIES NOVELS: *The White Circle*, 1926; *Two-Gun Gerta*, 1926 (with C. C. Waddell); *The Man in the Shadows*, 1928; *Mr. Strang*, 1936; *The Legion of the Living Dead*, 1947; *Murder at Our House*, 1950

BIBLIOGRAPHY

Anderson, George Parker, and Julie B. Anderson, eds. *American Hard-Boiled Crime Writers*. Detroit: Gale Group, 2000. Daly is one of about thirty authors covered in this survey of the genre.

Barson, Michael S. "'There's No Sex in Crime': The Two-Fisted Homilies of Race Williams." *Clues: A Journal of Detection* 2 (Fall/Winter, 1981): 103-112. Examines the character of Race Williams created by Daly.

Geherin, David. "Birth of a Hero." In *The American Private Eye: The Image in Fiction*. New York: F. Ungar, 1985. Credits Daly with the creation of the hard-boiled detective figure.

Haining, Peter. *The Classic Era of American Pulp Magazines*. Chicago: Chicago Review Press, 2000. Looks at Daly's contribution to the pulps and the relationship of pulp fiction to its more respectable literary cousins.

Horsley, Lee. *The Noir Thriller*. New York: Palgrave, 2001. Scholarly, theoretically informed study of the thriller genre. Includes readings of Daly's *The Snarl of the Beast* and *The Adventures of Satan Hall*.

Moore, Lewis D. *Cracking the Hard-Boiled Detective: A Critical History from the 1920's to the Present*. Jefferson, N.C.: McFarland, 2006. Detailed study of hard-boiled detective fiction tracing its origins and subsequent evolution. Contains a discussion of Daly. Bibliographic references and index.

ELIZABETH DALY

Born: New York, New York; October 15, 1878
Died: Roslyn, New York; September 2, 1967
Types of plot: Amateur sleuth; cozy

PRINCIPAL SERIES

Henry Gamadge, 1940-1954

PRINCIPAL SERIES CHARACTER

HENRY GAMADGE, an author and consultant on old books, manuscripts, autographs, and inks, lives in the fashionable Murray Hill district of New York. Young and unmarried when he first appears, Gamadge marries in the course of the series and has a son. Because of his reputation as a writer on the subjects of literary and criminal detection, Gamadge is frequently called on to solve mysteries that have baffled professional investigators.

CONTRIBUTION

Elizabeth Daly's sixteen novels featuring Henry Gamadge, a New York gentleman of independent means whose interest in mysteries associated with old books and manuscripts frequently leads him into mysteries associated with crimes, follow the tradition established in Great Britain during the Golden Age of detective fiction. Working in the vein of Wilkie Collins, Arthur Conan Doyle, Dorothy L. Sayers, and Agatha Christie (who once named Daly as her favorite American author), Daly superimposed on the geography of New York and New England the upper-class settings of these writers' novels. Although Gamadge is American, his language and his social habits are British, to the point that individuals use "torches" instead of flashlights and cars "hoot" rather than honk. Despite these anomalies and sometimes awkward dialogue when working-class individuals are involved, Daly's books are, for the most part, carefully crafted, reflecting her conviction that detective fiction is a high form of literary art.

BIOGRAPHY

Elizabeth Daly was born in New York City on October 15, 1878, the daughter of Joseph Francis Daly, a

justice of the Supreme Court of New York County, and Emma Barker Daly. She was the niece of Augustin Daly, a famous playwright and producer of the 1890's.

Daly was educated at Miss Baldwin's School, Bryn Mawr College, and Columbia University. She received a bachelor of arts from Bryn Mawr in 1901 and a master of arts from Columbia in 1902. In 1902, she returned to Bryn Mawr College, where she was a reader in English and a tutor in French and English until 1906. She also coached and produced amateur plays and pageants.

At the age of sixteen, Daly had experimented with light verse and prose, some of which was published. Her primary interest during most of her life, however, was in amateur theatricals. From an early age, Daly had shown a fondness for games and puzzles, and this fondness resulted in a lifelong interest in detective fiction. She was particularly fond of the works of Wilkie Collins.

In the late 1930's, Daly attempted to write detective stories. It was not until 1940, when she was sixty-two, however, that her first novel, *Unexpected Night*, was published. Fifteen more novels featuring the amateur sleuth Henry Gamadge and one novel of manners, *The Street Has Changed* (1941), followed during the next twelve years. Daly died in St. Francis Hospital, on Long Island, on September 2, 1967.

ANALYSIS

After a false start in 1894, Elizabeth Daly began her career as a writer of detective fiction with the publication, in 1940, of *Unexpected Night*. Set in Maine, *Unexpected Night* introduces Henry Gamadge, a New York socialite and bibliophile who dabbles in criminal investigation. Fifteen Gamadge adventures followed, resulting in a series of novels that provide nostalgic glimpses of a vanishing era while chilling the reader's blood with literate stories of sophisticated wickedness.

Daly's interest in writing detective stories may be traced to her fondness for puzzles and games and to an early appreciation for the works of Wilkie Collins. She was not particularly concerned with the theory of detective fiction. Having devoted the previous thirty or so years of her life to reading, travel, and the production of amateur plays, Daly began to write because she found detective stories fascinating. Like her fictional creation, Henry Gamadge, who repeatedly becomes involved in criminal investigations simply because he loves a mystery and has no job to distract him, Daly wrote because she loved puzzles, enjoyed writing, and had the leisure to indulge herself. As a writer, her only objective appears to have been to baffle and entertain the reader with an ingeniously conceived and well-presented mystery.

Each of the sixteen Gamadge novels is a literate and ingenious exercise in logic that uses an assortment of stock characters as set pieces around which a mystery can be developed. The principal character, Henry Gamadge, is a kind of English gentleman disguised as one of New York's aristocracy. Slightly resembling Dorothy L. Sayers's Peter Wimsey—and sometimes displaying a sophistication even greater than Wimsey's—Gamadge is, nevertheless, not a stereotypical dashing and attractive drawing room detective hero. Daly herself characterized him as "the semi-bookish type, but not pretentious . . . not good-looking, but eye-catching. He represents everything in a man eager to battle the forces of evil."

Despite Daly's characterization, the average reader will find Gamadge too sophisticated to be a convincing representative of a man eager to stand up against evil. After a careful search of the series, the reader may come to the conclusion that Gamadge's involvement with criminal investigations, like Daly's involvement with detective fiction, reflects his enjoyment of puzzles more than any moral passion.

UNEXPECTED NIGHT

Even though Daly had a rather lofty concept of Gamadge, she was careful to balance her descriptions, avoiding the creation of a kind of otherworldly superhero. Although his powers of detection are extraordinary, Gamadge is not perfect, as Daly makes clear in her initial, and typical, description of him in *Unexpected Night*:

> Mr. Henry Gamadge . . . wore clothes of excellent material and cut; but he contrived, by sitting and walking in a careless and lopsided manner, to look presentable

in nothing. He screwed his grey tweeds out of shape before he had worn them a week, he screwed his mouth to one side when he smiled, and he screwed his eyes up when he pondered. His eyes were greyish green, his features blunt, and his hair mouse-coloured. People as a rule considered him a well-mannered, restful kind of young man; but if somebody happened to say something unusually outrageous or inane, he was wont to gaze on the speaker in a wondering and somewhat disconcerting manner.

Because Gamadge is independently wealthy, he has the leisure to pursue his interest in old books and manuscripts and has established a reputation as an authority not only on the papers, inks, and handwriting of old books and manuscripts but also on the mysteries associated with them. It is his expertise in handwriting and ink that gets Gamadge involved in his first case, and his success in solving this and subsequent mysteries ensures that he will be drawn repeatedly, often unwillingly, into mysteries associated with the sordid world of crime.

In addition to Gamadge, Daly's stock characters include Gamadge's wife, Clara, and their son; his assistant, Harold Bantz; his cat, Mickey; and his aging manservant—along with a number of other characters who accumulate as the series develops. The development of these characters, whose individual characteristics are firmly established from their first introduction, is secondary to Daly's primary objective, which is to provide clues to the puzzle facing Gamadge so that during his sometimes lengthy concluding explanation, Daly, through Gamadge, can in effect say to the dubious readers that they have had all the clues.

The style of these stories is literate without being patronizing or bookish. Nevertheless, Daly's writing is somewhat flawed by her inability to develop an ear for the speech of individuals outside her and Gamadge's social and cultural circles and by her insistence on using British spellings and terminology. Workmen with whom Gamadge comes in contact use the same kind of language Gamadge uses but drop their *g*'s ("goin'," "comin'") and interrupt long, articulate explanations with the wrong tense or convoluted syntax. "Color" becomes "colour," and cars, equipped with "lamps" instead of headlights, "hoot" rather than honk.

There are other, more serious flaws, one of which might be said to stem from what is, in itself, one of Daly's virtues as a writer. Daly was a careful crafter who took each manuscript through four revisions. She had the plot firmly in mind before beginning the writing, but once the actual writing began, by her account, "all kinds of things" turned up to influence the final outcome. This creative openmindedness is one of Daly's virtues. Because she did not slavishly follow her preconceived plot, Daly was able not only to avoid the production of a series of formula-written clones of preceding Gamadge tales but to bring a certain freshness to each as well. Although for the most part this is a virtue with Daly, it can, and often does, result in a kind of literary clutter because of Daly's reluctance to discard elements once they have been introduced. Characters, for example, have a way of staying on for the next novel. Gamadge rescues Clara Dawson, then marries her, eventually adding a dog and then a son to the Gamadge household. The household increases steadily as clients or individuals indirectly involved with clients are added to Gamadge's staff. This tendency to save everything and everybody, as some people save string, often arrests the plot's development, making heavy going for the reader.

ARROW POINTING NOWHERE

Another characteristic that weakens Daly's stories is her tendency to be too clever, so that the credulity of the reader is strained by Gamadge's ultimate explanation. In *Arrow Pointing Nowhere* (1944), for example, wadded-up notes picked up by a postal carrier eventually reach Gamadge. The logic of this device is explained by Gamadge at the novel's conclusion:

> Clara's face wore a slight frown. "Henry," she said, "when Mrs. Grove threw that first paper ball out of the window she didn't know a thing about you. The Fenways didn't expect you to call, they can't have talked about you much."
>
> "No, my angel, they can't."
>
> "Then how could she know that you'd understand her message, and somehow get into the house? How did she know you'd care?"
>
> Gamadge smiled at her. "Blake Fenway said he had my books. Perhaps she'd read them."
>
> "They wouldn't tell her all that!"

> "Something of an author is supposed to get in his books, though. Perhaps mine told her that I always answer my letters."

After Gamadge decides to accept the case, other crumpled notes turn up, two of which are railroad timetables marked with arrows. The first points to the Rockville station on the Hudson River, indicating that the person who marked the timetable (whom Gamadge cannot identify but refers to as his client) wants Gamadge to visit Rockville. Later, a second timetable is marked with an arrow pointing away from the Rockville station (arrow pointing nowhere), and Gamadge knows that his client is urging him to get someone at Rockville away from there. In this instance, Gamadge's remarkable ability to decipher the most obscure of clues is exceeded only by the perceptiveness of his unknown client, who understands that Gamadge has accepted the case when he appears on the scene carrying a book called *Men Working*. Other Daly works exhibit this same kind of excessive cleverness, provoking one reviewer to grumble, after reading *The Wrong Way Down* (1946), that although Gamadge was a nice change from the hard-as-nails characters featured in most detective fiction, his solution did put considerable strain on the reader's credulity.

It cannot be denied that the strain is often there, but for those who are not inclined to demand plausibility, the works of Daly offer tantalizing puzzles in an engaging form.

Chandice M. Johnson, Jr.

PRINCIPAL MYSTERY AND DETECTIVE FICTION

HENRY GAMADGE SERIES: *Unexpected Night*, 1940; *Deadly Nightshade*, 1940; *Murders in Volume Two*, 1941; *The House Without the Door*, 1942; *Evidence of Things Seen*, 1943; *Nothing Can Rescue Me*, 1943; *Arrow Pointing Nowhere*, 1944 (also known as *Murder Listens In*); *The Book of the Dead*, 1944; *Any Shape or Form*, 1945; *Somewhere in the House*, 1946; *The Wrong Way Down*, 1946 (also known as *Shroud for a Lady*); *Night Walk*, 1947; *The Book of the Lion*, 1948; *And Dangerous to Know*, 1949; *Death and Letters*, 1950; *The Book of the Crime*, 1951

OTHER MAJOR WORK

NOVEL: *The Street Has Changed*, 1941

BIBLIOGRAPHY

Barzun, Jacques, and Wendell Hertig Taylor. *A Catalogue of Crime.* Rev. ed. New York: Harper & Row, 1989. Massive, nearly one-thousand-page critical bibliography of mystery, detective, and spy stories. Provides context for understanding Daly. Includes an index.

Dubose, Martha Hailey, with Margaret Caldwell Thomas. *Women of Mystery: The Lives and Works of Notable Women Crime Novelists.* New York: St. Martin's Minotaur, 2000. Although Daly is only mentioned, the Golden Age female writers of which she is a part are discussed at length.

Huang, Jim, ed. *They Died in Vain: Overlooked, Underappreciated, and Forgotten Mystery Novels.* Carmel, Ind.: Crum Creek Press, 2002. Daly is among the authors discussed in this book about mystery novels that never found the audience they deserved.

Klein, Kathleen Gregory, ed. *Great Women Mystery Writers: Classic to Contemporary.* Westport, Conn.: Greenwood Press, 1994. Contains a biocritical essay on Daly.

Rowland, Susan. *From Agatha Christie to Ruth Rendell: British Women Writers in Detective and Crime Fiction.* New York: Palgrave, 2001. Although Daly is not discussed in this work, it describes the work of Agatha Christie, who admired Daly's writings.

Waldron, Ann. "The Golden Years of Elizabeth Daly." *Armchair Detective* 7 (November, 1973): 25-28. Mystery writer Ann Waldron looks at the best writings of the creator of the Henry Gamadge series.

LIONEL DAVIDSON

Born: Hull, Yorkshire, England; March 31, 1922
Also wrote as David Line
Types of plot: Thriller; historical; police procedural

CONTRIBUTION

Lionel Davidson's novels are well-crafted thrillers that vary in setting, point of view, and theme. Davidson skillfully depicts scenes in London, Israel, Germany, and Prague, capturing the idiosyncratic speech in each country. His heroes, often cranky bachelors, enjoy drink and women. Although Davidson may coolly poke fun at his heroes and their adventures, some of his novels also consider historical themes and social issues and are suspenseful and humorous. In *The Chelsea Murders* (1978), he treats the genre of the murder mystery itself with irony. In all of his novels, there is an engaging intellectual component.

BIOGRAPHY

On March 31, 1922, Lionel Davidson was born in Hull, Yorkshire. His father was from Poland and his mother from Russia. When he was two years old, his father died. Four years later, the family relocated to London. When he was fourteen, Davidson had to leave school to seek employment, beginning as an office boy for a shipping firm; he soon found a similar position at *The Spectator*. When he was fifteen, his first story appeared in that magazine. Later, he wrote for a Fleet Street agency. During World War II, Davidson joined the Royal Navy. Afterward, he became a freelance journalist in Europe. Davidson married Fay Jacobs in 1949.

The publication of Davidson's first novel, *The Night of Wenceslas* (1960), was delayed for some time because of a strike. Not knowing of the delay and believing that the book was a failure, he began *The Rose of Tibet*, which appeared in 1962. Both books proved to be highly successful. *The Night of Wenceslas* was recognized as both the most promising first novel in 1960, receiving the Author's Club Silver Quill Award, and the best crime novel of the year, winning the Crime Writers' Association's Gold Dagger Award. Davidson's work was likened to that of Graham Greene and Kingsley Amis.

In 1965 Davidson published his first book for adolescents, *Soldier and Me*, under the pseudonym David Line. A year after its American publication, it appeared in England as *Run for Your Life*. His next novel, *A Long Way to Shiloh* (1966), published in the United States as *The Menorah Men*, was written partly in response to his travels in Israel. The novel, a best seller for months, received the Crime Writers' Association's Gold Dagger Award for best crime novel of the year.

Two years later, Davidson published another novel, *Making Good Again* (1968), a low-key thriller, which deals with anti-Semitism and the Holocaust. Soon after he completed the novel, Davidson and his family moved to Israel, which was the setting of two later novels, *Smith's Gazelle* (1971) and *The Sun Chemist* (1976). *Smith's Gazelle*, lyrical and allegorical, was awarded Israel's President's Prize for Literature. In the early 1970's, Davidson wrote a second book for adolescents, *Mike and Me* (1974).

After living in Israel for ten years, Davidson returned once again to England. *The Chelsea Murders*, a bloodcurdling mystery, was set in Chelsea, London. It received the Gold Dagger Award for best crime novel of the year in 1978 and was soon followed by *Under Plum Lake* (1980), a fanciful children's allegory. Davidson spent several years revising this short novel. In 1985, he completed another novel for adolescents, *Screaming High*. In 2001, he was awarded the Crime Writers' Association's Cartier Diamond Dagger award for life achievement.

ANALYSIS

Lionel Davidson's fiction is characterized by its wit and ingenuity. The main characters of his thrillers and mystery novels quickly enter a world of circumstance that tests their mental and physical prowess. Many of the novels are propelled forward by, first, the perplexing mysteries and, second, the protagonists' subsequent action-packed flight from danger. Davidson gracefully fuses an intellectually engaging mystery—which often involves some form of scholarship—with sparkling action. Davidson's interest in scholarship is also suggested by the fact that his novels are well researched. Finally, humor and irony add another dimension to much of his fiction.

THE NIGHT OF WENCESLAS

The Night of Wenceslas, written from the viewpoint of a self-centered, spoiled young Englishman, Nicholas Whistler, plots his journey to a vividly described Prague and his subsequent flight from the communist secret police. Through a complicated set of circumstances, Whistler is tricked by a man into unwittingly passing or almost passing state secrets. After sleeping with a giant Czech woman with "twin luscious bombs" and being pursued by the Czech police, he manages to enter the British embassy dressed as a milk delivery person.

A LONG WAY TO SHILOH

A Long Way to Shiloh is also written in the first person; the main character, Caspar Laing, who likes to drink, has an affair with a young Yemenite woman who is engaged to someone else. Soon after he meets Shoshana, Laing thinks to himself, "Hadn't this girl been demonstrating some rather over-matey solidarity with me of late?" Thus Davidson conveys the young Englishman's carefree attitude through his tone and diction.

The novel also has an engaging plot. Set in modern Israel, it considers the nation's preoccupation with its ancient history. Laing is a renowned young scholar employed by an Israeli archaeologist to help locate an ancient menorah—to which a scroll fragment alludes—before the Jordanians find it. After following numerous faulty leads and barely escaping death at the hands of Arabs, Laing concludes that the menorah is likely to be buried in the middle of a construction site for a vast hotel. Because he fails to prevail over the developer, Laing cannot continue the search. Ironically, a council of rabbis concludes that a library should be constructed in the hotel in the exact area in question. Much of the novel is devoted to Laing's efforts to decipher the fragment and interpret its meaning. Because he cannot pursue his final lead, the novel thereby ends somewhat inconclusively.

THE ROSE OF TIBET

The Rose of Tibet is even more indefinite. By placing the main story within a framing plot, Davidson cleverly renders it suspect. Two stories are presented, one involving high adventure in Tibet and the other—one that is quite rarefied—recounting the story of an editor's effort to get in touch with an author. Charles Houston, an Englishman, has supposedly written an account of his search for his brother in Tibet, his journey through the Himalayas, his affair with a priestess, his own deification by the people, and his flight from the approaching Chinese army. Because the editor is unable to contact Houston (who has been the subject of several newspaper articles), Davidson's reader is confronted with the possibility that an elderly Latin teacher—who passed the manuscript to the editor—actually wrote the narrative himself. It may not have been, as he claims, material that was dictated to him by Houston.

The novel opens with a prologue in which Davidson himself appears as an editor of a publishing company. It closes with the editor's failure to resolve the mystery of Houston's whereabouts and thus the identity of the manuscript's author. Between the opening and ending lie pages of thrilling adventure through the Himalayas. In concise prose, somewhat like Ernest Hemingway's, Davidson describes the inexperienced Houston's fight for survival. At one point, "he tried to eat wood and leaves. He boiled them to make a soup. The soup was bitter . . . and it merely made him vomit. He had to stop quickly, for he could not afford to waste what he had already eaten."

THE SUN CHEMIST

A scholar's work preparing an edition of a famous man's letters is the modus operandi of *The Sun Chemist*; Davidson weaves a story around his protagonist's research on Chaim Weizmann's letters. While Igor Druyanov, a historian, is editing a volume of Israel's founder's letters, his assistant is attacked. In addition, Druyanov soon finds that several scientific notebooks mentioned in the letters are missing. These contain the formula for a fermentation process that converts sweet potatoes into high-octane fuel. Finally, Druyanov's knowledge of the past places him in the direct line of danger in the present, and he is almost killed by another scientist, who attempts to drown him.

As in the novels mentioned previously, Davidson combines physical adventure and intellectual intrigue. Although *The Sun Chemist* does not end in Davidson's typical ambiguity, it is not without his characteristic wit. Ironically, the main clue of the novel is tied to a humorous circumstance. A significant passage in the memoirs was muddied because Weizmann's transcriptionist misunderstood him when he dictated without his false teeth. Davidson's well-researched plot, his humor, and his skillful characterization brought the novel almost universal praise.

THE CHELSEA MURDERS

The Chelsea Murders, a highly ingenious detective story, also received mostly favorable reviews. A group of murders takes place in Chelsea, London, the home of such famous writers as Oscar Wilde, Algernon

LIONEL DAVIDSON

Winner of the
GOLDEN DAGGER AWARD

THE CHELSEA MURDERS

A psychopathic killer is prowling
the streets of London
'Breathtakingly brilliant' — *Spectator*

Charles Swinburne, Leigh Hunt, W. S. Gilbert, and Hilaire Belloc; each victim has the initials of one of these authors. In addition, the murderer tantalizes the police with literary quotations. Most reviewers of the novel commented on Davidson's inventiveness and character portrayal. Nevertheless, some responded negatively to its conclusion and the inclusion of unresolved leads. An insightful reviewer in *The Times Literary Supplement* observed that the novel both "acknowledges and flouts the convention of [its] genre."

MAKING GOOD AGAIN

Making Good Again also reveals Davidson's perspective on mystery and adventure fiction. The central mystery and resultant action skillfully weave a fabric rich in thematic texture. The complex attitudes of postwar Germany toward Jews are presented within the context of a fast-paced plot. Once again, Davidson successfully fuses the concrete and the abstract.

As in so many of Davidson's novels, the main character—James Raison, an English attorney—drinks heavily and has an affair. Nevertheless, through third-person narration, several other characters are fleshed out, including Heinz Haffner, a German lawyer, and another attorney, Yonah Grunwald, who is a concentration-camp survivor. Davidson considers anti-Semitism and its various manifestations along with the meaning of German reparation.

The lawyers hope to discover the fate of Helmut Bamberger—a wealthy German Jew—to determine the status of his fortune, which seems to have been placed in a numbered Swiss bank account. They assume at first that he was one of the millions of Jews who perished in the Holocaust, but later they decide that he is still alive. Raison, a calm Englishman, represents Bamberger's daughter. Haffner, who represents the German government, wishes only to resolve the case. Grunwald, who lives in Israel, hopes to use the estate for charitable purposes. Raison, Grunwald, and an Israeli attorney eventually go to a small German town on the Czechoslovakian border hoping to find news of Bamberger. In a hideous scene in the Bavarian forest, the lawyers are doped and Grunwald is attacked; the old man barely survives.

The novel also addresses more subtle expressions of anti-Semitism. Although Haffner does not consider himself racist and his legal tasks involve providing reparations, he believes that Germany's Jews who survived the Holocaust did so because they were devious. In addition, he detests his daughter's Jewish boyfriend. At the end of the novel, he finally confronts some of his prejudices. Although Davidson treats the German attorney with biting irony—Haffner is both impotent and compulsive—Davidson also presents some profound questions concerning the Holocaust. For example, Haffner believes that "there's no honor anymore. After all, obedience is a part of honor, isn't it—loyalty? But what's one to be obedient or loyal to? Such things happened here." Echoing some of the issues raised by Karl Eichmann's trial and Hannah Arendt's book on it, *Eichmann in Jerusalem: A Report on the Banality of Evil* (1964), Haffner wonders, "how can you prosecute people for crimes under the law that weren't then crimes under the law?"

Although *Making Good Again* explores the philosophical and social issues raised by the Holocaust, it also includes comic relief. Haffner's sister, Magda, who was married to a Nazi and is now widowed, recalls the Nazi period with great nostalgia. A woman of vast appetites, she tries desperately to seduce Raison. Although he keeps her at bay, he tolerates her advances because from her he may learn Bamberger's fate. Finally, to protect himself, when Magda leaves a second-story bedroom to go down a ladder to the kitchen, Raison closes the trapdoor behind her. The half-drunk Magda smashes her head against it as she ascends the ladder. When she recovers several hours later, she still calls for the Englishman: "I know you're there. . . . Süsser, what's the sense in you being there and me here? . . . I want to be with someone." Despite her pleas, Raison continues to hide in the loft; she violently cleans the house. Ironically, the sex-crazed woman knows more about Bamberger and his money than does anyone else. Her revelations to Raison about her husband's takeover of a bank put the lawyers onto a path that may lead to the solution of the mystery of Bamberger's estate. Thus, a scene that seems to function merely as comic relief turns out to be essential to the plot.

Irony has a central role in *Making Good Again*. The lawyers act against their better judgment and play right into the hands of a former Nazi. In the chapter "The Son of Man and Other Sons," Grunwald attempts to drape a cloth over a crucifix in his hotel room so he may pray without its presence; as he does so, the cross falls and breaks. Thus, Grunwald unintentionally breaks the symbol for Christianity—the professed religion of the Nazis. Later, while he is attempting to produce some good from evil by claiming Bamberger's fortune, he is again the victim of violent anti-Semitism.

Davidson's mysteries and thrillers to varying degrees conform to the conventional treatment of these genres. In Davidson's fiction, however, mystery and its myriad uncertainties symbolize the human experience, which is in his view rife with ambiguity.

Kathy Rugoff

PRINCIPAL MYSTERY AND DETECTIVE FICTION

NOVELS: *The Night of Wenceslas*, 1960; *The Rose of Tibet*, 1962; *A Long Way to Shiloh*, 1966 (also known as *The Menorah Men*); *Making Good Again*, 1968; *The Sun Chemist*, 1976; *The Chelsea Murders*, 1978 (also known as *Murder Games*); *Kolymsky Heights*, 1994

OTHER MAJOR WORKS

NOVEL: *Smith's Gazelle*, 1971

CHILDREN'S LITERATURE: *Run for Your Life*, 1966 (as Line; also known as *Soldier and Me*, 1965); *Mike and Me*, 1974 (as Line); *Under Plum Lake*, 1980; *Screaming High*, 1985 (as Line)

BIBLIOGRAPHY

Davidson, Lionel. "A Sudden Smile." In *Julian Symons Remembered: Tributes from Friends*, collected by Jack Walsdorf and Kathleen Symons. Council Bluffs, Iowa: Yellow Barn Press, 1996. Davidson's homage to his fellow mystery writer reveals his own investments in the craft of fiction.

James, Michael. "A Writer After a Good Hiding: Lionel Davidson." *The Times*, March 12, 1994. Describes Davidson's background and notes his successful *The Night of Wenceslas* as bringing gritty new realism to the thriller. His sixteen-year absence from writing ended with the publication of *Kolymsky Heights*. Davidson said he started two other books during his hiatus but abandoned them because he felt they were not good enough.

Priestman, Martin, ed. *The Cambridge Companion to Crime Fiction*. New York: Cambridge University Press, 2003. Critical study consisting of fifteen overview essays devoted to specific genres or periods within crime fiction. Contains a chapter on thrillers, which sheds light on Davidson's work. Bibliographic references and index.

Scaggs, John. *Crime Fiction*. New York: Routledge, 2005. Contains chapters on police procedurals and crime thrillers, which help place Davidson's work in context.

L. P. DAVIES

Born: Crewe, Cheshire, England; October 20, 1914
Also wrote as Leo Berne; Robert Blake; Richard Bridgeman; Morgan Evans; Ian Jefferson; Lawrence Peters; Thomas Phillips; G. K. Thomas; Leslie Vardre; Rowland Welch
Types of plot: Psychological; thriller

CONTRIBUTION

L. P. Davies' fascination with science (and pseudoscience), psychology, psychic phenomena, and the supernatural has resulted in a series of crime and mystery novels that he calls "psychic fiction." The majority of these novels reflect this fascination and feature plots in which the principal character is experiencing some form of identity crisis or mental disorientation as a result of an operation, an accident, or the surreptitious administration of drugs. In developing these plots, Davies frequently introduces elements of science, pseudoscience, or the supernatural. As a result, his novels have sometimes been placed in the category of science fiction rather than crime and mystery. Davies' novels belong in the latter category, however, because like their more traditional counterparts, their solutions depend on the use of the processes of logical deduction. It is this ability to flavor crime and mystery stories with elements of science fiction that constitutes Davies' principal contribution to the literature.

BIOGRAPHY

Leslie Purnell Davies was born on October 20, 1914, in Crew, Cheshire, England, the son of Arthur Davies and Annie Sutton Davies. From 1930 to 1939, Davies worked as a dispensing pharmacist in Crewes. Educated at Manchester College of Science and Technology, University of Manchester, he qualified as an optometrist in 1939 (fellow, British Optical Society). On November 13, 1940, he married Winifred Tench.

During World War II, Davies was in the British army, serving with the Medical Corps in France and with the Eighth Army in North Africa and Italy. He achieved the rank of staff sergeant. Following the war, he spent two years as a freelance artist in Rome before returning to England. From 1946 to 1956, he was postmaster at West Heath, Birmingham. In 1956, he moved to Deganwy, North Wales, where he established a private practice in optometry and operated a gift shop. In 1975, he moved to the Canary Islands, Spain.

The author of more than 250 short stories published under at least ten pseudonyms, Davies used his own name when he published his first crime novel, *The Paper Dolls* (1964). It is a practice that he continued with each succeeding novel he published in the United States.

ANALYSIS

L. P. Davies began his career as a writer in 1964 with the publication of *The Paper Dolls*, a novel rejected by four publishers because it did not fit into any of their categories. The Davies novels that followed *The Paper Dolls* and that Davies calls "psychic fiction" are just as difficult to categorize but could be described as crime and mystery thrillers with science-fiction overtones. These science-fiction overtones are a result of Davies' fascination with science, psychic phenomena, the supernatural, and the workings of the human mind.

There are times when the overtones appear to be the dominant theme. Nevertheless, Davies' novels can be categorized as crime and mystery thrillers because, like other works in the same category, they conclude with down-to-earth solutions that reveal that events that seemed to border on the supernatural have, after all, completely logical explanations. Davies' characters, who often battle forces that appear to combine traditional black magic with twenty-first century technology, use their minds to resolve their problems, arriving at their conclusions by the familiar process of putting clues together and, through logical deduction, weaving them into solutions that are as rational and as satisfyingly plausible as any offered by Peter Wimsey, Father Brown, or Sherlock Holmes.

WHAT DID I DO TOMORROW?

One of Davies' strengths as a writer lies in his ability to bring about these conclusions. In *What Did I Do Tomorrow?* (1972), for example, a very confused young man continues to function rationally, assembling and analyzing clues as any professional sleuth might do, even though he is convinced that someone has transported him five years into the future. His problem is finally explained in terms of psychiatric practices that are relatively well established in fiction and television drama, if not in the real world. Similarly, in *The White Room* (1969), Davies uses an accepted tenet of folk psychology—that the dummy can take over the ventriloquist or the role the actor—to explain what has been happening to a man who believes that someone is manipulating his mind to force him to commit a murder.

THE ARTIFICIAL MAN

Davies followed *The Paper Dolls* with a second novel, *Man out of Nowhere* (1965), but it was not until his third novel, *The Artificial Man* (1965), that he began to write stories involving individuals who are uncertain of their identities. In the novels that followed *The Artificial Man*, Davies returned repeatedly to plots in which the principal character has experienced some form of mental disorientation or depersonalization as the result of an accident, brain surgery, hypnotism, a cunningly devised deception, or the clandestine administration of drugs.

THE SHADOW BEFORE

Davies' preoccupation with characters who are experiencing a disorientation or identity crisis has been described as an obsession, but although it is true that he does work the theme for all it is worth, the careful reader will discover that Davies has something of importance to say about human freedom and moral responsibility. Davies hints at this conviction in words given to a Dr. Cowley, in *The Shadow Before* (1970).

Lester Dunn, the principal character, has had an operation to remove a small brain tumor. During surgery, he has a dream, which seems to be more than a dream. Deeply disturbed, he confronts one of the doctors who performed the surgery, asking questions about such things as "extrasensory perception and precognition." The doctor responds by discussing dreams in general, then concludes his discussion:

> Now it could well be that under the deeper sleep artificially induced by anaesthesia the subconscious selects items, . . . producing a dream that [is a] logical, understandable sequence of happenings. And I see no reason why that sequence shouldn't be projected into the future. But obviously the future of what *could* be, not what *is* to be. And there is a world of difference between the two. It is as if the subconscious were saying to itself: "Because this is how things were yesterday and today, this is how I think they could work out tomorrow." But that dream tomorrow is certainly not inevitable. We are all free agents, even though we are at the mercy of our natural inclinations.

In story after story, the principal characters find themselves in a world turned upside down, victims of some kind of mysterious psychic disturbance. Davies' heroes do not accept this situation, nor do they seek excuses for what is happening or for what they are doing. Instead, they begin a mighty struggle to reorient themselves and to set the world rightside up again. Consistently, each one succeeds, in spite of drugs, deception, and all kinds of diabolical scientific machinations. This pattern suggests that the stories Davies claimed were written only to entertain have a deeper message, namely that each individual is a free agent who has the power to make moral choices and who is morally responsible for the choices made.

STRANGER TO TOWN

Even though he is described as being obsessively concerned with disoriented characters, Davies is not absolutely predictable. He is capable of adding an un-

expected twist to the end of his stories or, as in the case of *Stranger to Town* (1969), of exploiting the notion that he is predictable. The charm of *Stranger to Town*, one of Davies' best stories, could be attributed in part to his skill in creating in the mind of the reader an assumption that this story is simply a variation on a very familiar theme.

Stranger to Town opens with a characteristic Davies scene: A man discovers himself in a strangely familiar place and is at a loss to explain even to himself why he is there. There are people whose names he knows, and there are things he knows that even the local citizens do not know. A widow is confronted with bits of conversation only she and her dead husband could have known. The widow, who belongs to a church that believes in the return of the dead, appears convinced that her husband has come back in the body of this stranger. Eventually, the widow, the townspeople, and the reader discover that things are not as they seem, and that there is a very logical explanation for the supposedly supernatural events accompanying the stranger's arrival in town.

Davies' skill in creating the illusion that something supernatural is involved is demonstrated dramatically in *Stranger to Town*. It is so skillfully done, in fact, that the casual reader, on discovering that he or she has been fooled along with the widow and the citizens of the town, will at first assume that Davies has not "played fair" in spite of his claims to the contrary. What Davies actually does is to suggest interior monologue in the opening pages so that the reader has the impression that it is the stranger's mind that is being exposed. What the casual reader assumes to be interior monologue is, in fact, a description of the stranger's actions from the point of view of the one witnessing them.

THE LAND OF LEYS

Although in general Davies' writing is fast paced and exciting, his habit of returning repeatedly to the identity crisis-disorientation theme can result in writing that labors and plods. *The White Room* and *Assignment Abacus* (1975) both try the reader's patience with plots that move forward one-half step, then return a full step or more as the heroes, on the verge of making major breakthroughs, become disoriented by yet another in what seems to be an interminable sequence of druggings. Plodding through this kind of plot development, the reader is likely to believe that continuing is not worth the effort. Unfortunately, this same feeling can come at the beginning of the book to a reader having previous experience with Davies. *The Land of Leys* (1979), for example, begins with an amnesia victim regaining consciousness only to discover that all clues to his identity have been removed by a person or persons unknown. Discovering this familiar situation in chapter 1, the reader may simply decide that enough is enough.

Although understandable, such an attitude is unfortunate, for it prevents the reader from discovering the variety beneath the surface similarities of plot and characterization. Bringing a distinctive approach to the mystery and detective genre, Davies has produced a series of novels that feature well-told stories while providing the reader with tantalizing excursions into the mysteries of science, science fiction, and the unknown.

Chandice M. Johnson, Jr.

PRINCIPAL MYSTERY AND DETECTIVE FICTION

NOVELS: *The Paper Dolls*, 1964; *Man out of Nowhere*, 1965 (also known as *Who Is Louis Pinder?*); *The Artificial Man*, 1965; *The Lampton Dreamers*, 1966; *The Reluctant Medium*, 1967 (also known as *Tell It to the Dead*); *Twilight Journey*, 1967; *A Grave Matter*, 1968 (also known as *The Nameless Ones*); *Stranger to Town*, 1969; *The White Room*, 1969; *The Shadow Before*, 1970; *Give Me Back Myself*, 1971; *What Did I Do Tomorrow?*, 1972; *Assignment Abacus*, 1975; *Possession*, 1976; *The Land of Leys*, 1979; *Morning Walk*, 1983

OTHER MAJOR WORKS

NOVELS: *Psychogeist*, 1966; *Twilight Journey*, 1967; *The Alien*, 1968; *Dimension A*, 1969; *Genesis Two*, 1969; *Adventure Holidays Ltd.*, 1970

BIBLIOGRAPHY

Joshi, S. T. *The Evolution of the Weird Tale.* New York: Hippocampus, 2004. This work concentrates on supernatural and horror fiction such as that written by H. P. Lovecraft. Contains an essay on Davies and his work.

The New York Times Book Review. Review of *Give Me Back Myself*, by L. P. Davies. 77 (January 23, 1972): 28. Contemporary review of one of Davies' mystery novels, evaluating it for both popular and specialist audiences.

Royle, Nicholas. *The Uncanny.* New York: Routledge, 2003. Extended psychoanalytic study of the representation of supernatural events in literature. Provides perspective on Davies' works. Bibliographic references and index.

Wilson, Neil. *Shadows in the Attic: A Guide to British Supernatural Fiction, 1820-1950.* Boston Spa, West Yorkshire, England: British Library, 2000. This study of Davies' immediate and Victorian precursors helps elucidate both his influences and his innovations. Bibliographic references and index.